MOON HANDBOOKS®

TAHOE

COURTESY OF NORTHSTAR-AT-TAHOE

Northstar-at-Tahoe

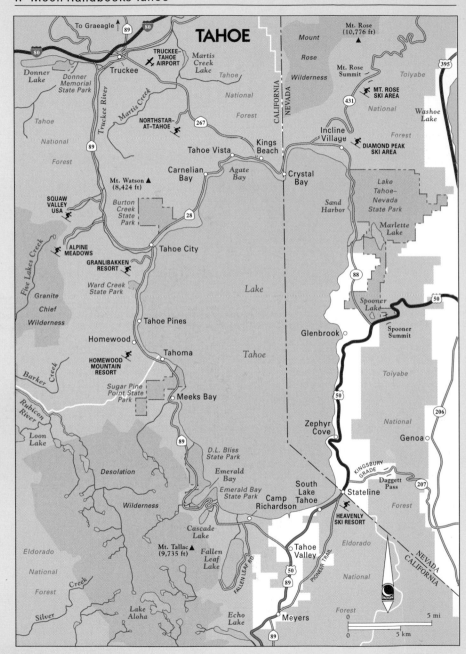

TAHOE

To Graeagle

Mt. Rose
(10,776 ft)

Mount

Rose

Wilderness

Mt. Rose
Summit

Toiyabe

Washoe
Lake

MT. ROSE
SKI AREA

National

TRUCKEE-
TAHOE
AIRPORT

Martis
Creek
Lake

Tahoe

Truckee

Donner
Lake

Donner
Memorial
State Park

National

Forest

NORTHSTAR-
AT-TAHOE

Forest

Incline
Village

DIAMOND PEAK
SKI AREA

Tahoe

National

Forest

Tahoe Vista

Kings
Beach

Carnelian
Bay

Agate
Bay

Crystal
Bay

Mt. Watson ▲
(8,424 ft)

Burton
Creek
State
Park

Sand
Harbor

Lake
Tahoe–
Nevada
State Park

SQUAW
VALLEY
USA

Marlette
Lake

ALPINE
MEADOWS

Tahoe City

GRANLIBAKKEN
RESORT

Ward Creek
State Park

Lake

Spooner
Lake

Granite

Chief

Wilderness

Tahoe Pines

Glenbrook

Spooner
Summit

Homewood

Tahoma

Tahoe

Toiyabe

HOMEWOOD
MOUNTAIN
RESORT

Barker

Creek

Sugar Pine
Point State
Park

Meeks Bay

Rubicon
River

National

Loon
Lake

Zephyr
Cove

Genoa

D.L. Bliss
State Park

Desolation

Emerald
Bay

KINGSBURY GRADE

Eldorado

Emerald Bay
State Park

Camp
Richardson

South
Lake
Tahoe

Stateline

Daggett
Pass

Wilderness

National

Forest

HEAVENLY
SKI RESORT

NEVADA
CALIFORNIA

Eldorado

Mt. Tallac ▲
(9,735 ft)

Fallen
Leaf
Lake

Cascade
Lake

Tahoe
Valley

National

PIONEER TRAIL

FALLEN LEAF RD

National

Forest

Creek

Silver

Lake
Aloha

Echo
Lake

Meyers

Forest

0   5 mi

0   5 km

CALIFORNIA

NEVADA

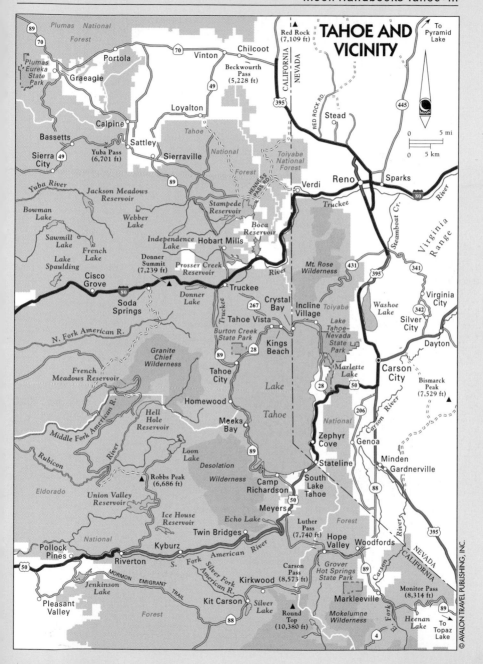

TAHOE AND VICINITY

winter on the lake at the Thunderbird Lodge

MOON HANDBOOKS®

TAHOE

SECOND EDITION

KEN CASTLE

AVALON
TRAVEL

Moon Handbooks Tahoe
Second Edition

Ken Castle

Published by
Avalon Travel Publishing
1400 65th St., Suite 250
Emeryville, CA 94608 USA

Printing History
1st edition—2000
2nd edition—February 2003
5 4 3 2 1

Please send all comments, corrections,
additions, amendments, and critiques to:

Moon Handbooks Tahoe
AVALON TRAVEL PUBLISHING
1400 65th St., Suite 250
Emeryville, CA 94608 USA
email: atpfeedback@avalonpub.com
www.moon.com

ISBN: 1-56691-491-4
ISSN: 1542-5975

Editor: Rebecca K. Browning
Series Manager: Kevin McLain
Copy Editor: Karen Gaynor Bleske
Graphics Coordinator: Susan Mira Snyder
Production Coordinator: Jacob Goolkasian
Cover Designer: Kari Gim
Interior Designers: Amber Pirker, Alvaro Villanueva, Kelly Pendragon
Map Editor: Olivia Solís
Cartographers: Mike Morgenfeld, Kat Kalamaras, Sheryle Veverka
Proofreader: Julie Leigh
Indexers: Karen Gaynor Bleske, Rebecca K. Browning, Beth Polzin

Front cover photo: © Larry Prosor

Distributed by Publishers Group West

Printed in U.S.A. by Malloy Lithography Inc.

Although every effort was made to ensure that the information was correct at the time of going to
press, the author and publisher do not assume and hereby disclaim any liability to any party for any
loss or damage caused by errors, omissions, or any potential travel disruption due to labor or financial difficulty, whether such errors or omissions result from negligence, accident, or any other cause.

ABOUT THE AUTHOR
Ken Castle

Ken Castle can rightfully say that he's seen the highs and lows of Lake Tahoe — from its 10,000-foot peaks to 1,000 feet below the surface in the world's 10th deepest lake. His vantage point underwater, part of a manned submarine expedition in 1979, might very well have been his last perspective of the place he's called his second home for three decades. Fortunately, he survived a close call and has continued to enjoy his ongoing relationship with Tahoe.

The problem occurred when he and Dr. Charles Goldman, an expert on lakes from the University of California at Davis, were in a three-man mini-sub the size of a walk-in closet. They were co-leaders of a research project that was jointly sponsored by the university and the San Jose Mercury News, where Castle was outdoor editor at the time. While exploring an underwater canyon off Rubicon Point, with sheer granite faces, the craft became wedged in a cave-like depression, and there were anxious minutes as the pilot struggled to break free. After several abortive maneuvers, in which the sub banged against one rock wall after another, the vessel finally escaped and returned to a tender ship on the surface.

The effort yielded new scientific information about the long-term "health" of the lake, garnered a national award for community service journalism, and was featured in *National Geographic* magazine.

After that experience, the fresh mountain air of Tahoe acquired new meaning for Castle, who resolved to make the most of his "second chance" by authoring a definitive guide to the region. During his 35-year career as writer, photographer, and editor for San Francisco Bay Area newspapers and national magazines, he's looked into a lot more nooks and crannies at Tahoe than the ones underwater. Starting as a professional print media journalist in his college days, Castle launched and edited specialized outdoor recreation sections for three newspapers, including the *San Francisco Chronicle*.

His work also has been published in *Ski* magazine, where he is contributing editor, and in *Outside, Condé Nast Traveler, Four Seasons, Cowboys & Indians, Hemispheres,* and *Travel-Holiday.* An adventurer at heart, Castle has traveled on six continents, from the jungles of the Amazon to the snowy peaks of the Swiss Alps.

Castle is currently president of International Recreation Resources, a travel- and recreation-oriented marketing and consulting firm based in Burlingame, California. He and his understanding wife, Kathy, regularly enjoy a multitude of sports, including skiing, golf, fishing, scubadiving, river rafting, and hiking.

*For my wife, Kathy, our four-legged "girls" —
Sierra and Snickers, our extended family, and all
of our nieces and nephews, who represent the next
generations of Tahoe fans.*

Contents

INTRODUCTION

INTRODUCTION **3**

THE LAKE 3
  A Bit of History, a Bit of Overview; Growing Concern; Under the Surface

SPECIAL TOPICS

Lake Tahoe Facts and Figures ....*5*   *Flora and Fauna of the Lake Tahoe Basin* *6*

SIGHTS AND EVENTS **11**

LAKE TAHOE AND VICINITY 11
  Truckee/Donner; Squaw Valley; Tahoe City/West Shore; Kings Beach/Tahoe
  Vista/Carnelian Bay; Incline Village/Crystal Bay; South Lake Tahoe;
  Stateline/Zephyr Cove; Kirkwood/Hope Valley/Markleeville; Feather River
  Country/Lakes Basin
RENO/CARSON VALLEY 38
ANNUAL EVENTS 56
  January; March; April; May; June; July; August; September; October; November;
  December

SPECIAL TOPICS

Hollywood Loves Tahoe .... *18*   *Fourth of July Celebrations* *61*
Lake Tahoe's Resort Legacy *30*

TAHOE WITH CHILDREN **67**

SUMMER AND DAY CAMPS 68
  Truckee/Donner; Squaw Valley; Tahoe City/West Shore; Incline Village/Crystal
  Bay; Feather River Country/Lakes Basin; Reno/Carson Valley
CLIMBING AND ROPES COURSES 72
  Truckee/Donner; Squaw Valley; Kirkwood/Hope Valley/Markleeville
FISHING PONDS 73
  South Lake Tahoe; Reno/Carson Valley
NATURE CENTERS AND ZOOS 74
  South Lake Tahoe; Reno/Carson Valley
STARGAZING TOURS 75
THEME PARKS AND AMUSEMENT CENTERS 76
  Incline Village/Crystal Bay; South Lake Tahoe; Reno/Carson Valley

MINIATURE GOLF 79
Kings Beach/Tahoe Vista/Carnelian Bay; South Lake Tahoe; Feather River
Country/Lakes Basin; Reno/Carson Valley

SKATING AND SKATEBOARDING 79
South Lake Tahoe; Reno/Carson Valley

WEDDING SITES AND SERVICES 81

HOTELS AND MOTELS 84
Squaw Valley; Incline Village/Crystal Bay; South Lake Tahoe

RESORTS, INNS, AND RETREATS 88
Truckee/Donner; Squaw Valley; Tahoe City/West Shore; Kings Beach/Tahoe
Vista/Carnelian Bay; Incline Village/Crystal Bay; South Lake Tahoe; Carson
Valley/Genoa; Kirkwood/Hope Valley/Markleeville; Feather River Country/Lakes
Basin

HISTORIC SITES AND STATE PARKS 94
Tahoe City/West Shore; Incline Village/Crystal Bay; South Lake Tahoe; Carson
Valley/Virginia City

GOLF COURSES AND COUNTRY CLUBS 97
North Shore; South Lake Tahoe; Feather River Country/Lakes Basin; Carson
Valley/Genoa

PADDLEWHEEL STEAMERS AND CRUISE BOATS 99
North Shore; South Shore

RESTAURANTS 101
Tahoe City/West Shore; Kings Beach/Tahoe Vista/Carnelian Bay; Incline
Village/Crystal Bay; South Lake Tahoe

PRIVATE CHAPELS AND SERVICES 103
Tahoe City/West Shore; Incline Village/Crystal Bay; South Lake Tahoe

CHURCHES 105
Squaw Valley; Incline Village/Crystal Bay; South Lake Tahoe; Kirkwood/Hope
Valley/Markleeville; Carson Valley/Genoa

SPECIAL TOPICS
Obtaining a Marriage License 82   *Wedding Information Sources* 106

SUMMER RECREATION

ON, IN, AND AROUND THE WATER 110

BOAT CRUISES 113
Tahoe City/West Shore; Incline Village/Crystal Bay; South Shore;
Stateline/Zephyr Cove

PUBLIC LAUNCH RAMPS 121
Tahoe City; Kings Beach; Sand Harbor; Zephyr Cove; South Shore

PRIVATE MARINAS 122
Tahoe City/West Shore; Kings Beach/Tahoe Vista/Carnelian Bay; South Shore;
Stateline/Zephyr Cove; Marinas at Nearby Lakes

RENTAL BOATS, JET SKIS, AND WATER-SKIING LESSONS 125
North Shore; South Shore

KAYAKING AND CANOEING 129
Kings Beach/Carnelian Bay; South Lake Tahoe; Do-It-Yourself Float Trips on the
Truckee River

WHITE-WATER RAFTING AND RIVER KAYAKING 131
Truckee River (Lower); East Fork, Carson River; South and Middle Forks,
American River

SCUBA DIVING 136
South Lake Tahoe; Reno/Carson Valley

BEACHES 138
Truckee/Donner; Tahoe City/West Shore; Kings Beach/Tahoe Vista/Carnelian
Bay; Incline Village/Crystal Bay; South Shore; Stateline/Zephyr Cove

FISHING WATERS AND GUIDES **149**
Tackle Suppliers

LAKES, RESERVOIRS, RIVERS, AND STREAMS 153

CHARTER BOATS AND GUIDES 177
Donner, Davis, and Other Truckee-Area Lakes; Tahoe City/West Shore; Kings
Beach/Tahoe Vista/Carnelian Bay; South Shore; Stateline/Zephyr Cove; Caples
and Alpine County Lakes; Pyramid Lake, Nevada

FLY-FISHING GUIDES AND SCHOOLS 185
Truckee/Donner; South Shore; Kirkwood/Hope Valley/Markleeville; Feather
River Country/Lakes Basin; Reno/Carson Valley

SPECIAL TOPICS

Fishing Licenses .... *150*   *How to Catch a Mackinaw* *156*
Additional Information Sources .... *152*   *Other High-Country Fishing Lakes* *175*

ON THE TRAIL **190**
Wilderness Areas, Trails, and Permits; Major Trails

HIKING TRAILS 199
Truckee/Donner; Tahoe City/West Shore; Incline Village/Mt. Rose; South Lake
Tahoe; Stateline/Zephyr Cove; Kirkwood/Hope Valley/Markleeville; Highway
50/West of South Lake Tahoe; Feather River Country/Lakes Basin; Peak
Experiences; Guided Hikes

NATURE TRAILS 223
Truckee/Donner; Tahoe City/West Shore; Kings Beach/Tahoe Vista/Carnelian
Bay; Incline Village/Crystal Bay; South Lake Tahoe; Stateline/Zephyr Cove;
Kirkwood/Hope Valley/Markleeville; Feather River Country/Lakes Basin;

Reno/Carson Valley
HORSEBACK RIDING EXCURSIONS **230**
Truckee/Donner; Squaw Valley; Tahoe City; Incline Village/Mt. Rose; City of
South Lake Tahoe; Stateline/Zephyr Cove; Kirkwood/Hope Valley/Markleeville;
Feather River Country/Lakes Basin; Reno/Carson Valley

SPECIAL TOPIC

Backcountry Hiking Tips *193*

BIKE TRAILS AND PARKS 240

Bike Rental and Retail Shops; Bike Tours

PAVED BIKE TRAILS 245
Tahoe City/West Shore; Incline Village/Crystal Bay; South Lake Tahoe/Stateline;
Reno/Carson Valley

MOUNTAIN BIKE PARKS 250
Truckee/Donner; Kings Beach/Tahoe Vista/Carnelian Bay; Kirkwood/Hope
Valley/Markleeville

MOUNTAIN BIKE TRAILS 253
Truckee/Donner; Tahoe City/West Shore; Kings Beach/Tahoe Vista/Carnelian
Bay; Incline Village/Crystal Bay; South Lake Tahoe; Stateline/Zephyr Cove;
Kirkwood/Hope Valley/Markleeville; Feather River Country/Lakes Basin

SPECIAL TOPIC

Tips for Mountain-Biking Safety *254*

GOLF AND TENNIS 262

ON THE COURSES 262
Truckee/Donner; Squaw Valley; Tahoe City/West Shore; Kings Beach/Tahoe
Vista/Carnelian Bay; Incline Village/Crystal Bay; South Lake Tahoe; Feather
River Country/Lakes Basin; Reno; Carson City/Carson Valley

ON THE COURTS 284
North Shore; South Shore; West Shore; Truckee/Donner

OTHER SUMMER ACTIVITIES 287

HOT-AIR BALLOON RIDES 288
Truckee/Donner; South Lake Tahoe

GLIDER RIDES 290
Truckee/Donner; Reno/Carson Valley

SCENIC AIRPLANE AND HELICOPTER FLIGHTS 291
South Lake Tahoe; Reno/Carson Valley

HANG GLIDING AND PARAGLIDING 292
Reno/Carson Valley

PARASAILING 292
  Tahoe City/West Shore; South Shore
OUTDOOR AND INDOOR CLIMBING 293
  Truckee/Donner; Squaw Valley; Tahoe City/West Shore; Kirkwood/Hope
  Valley/Markleeville; Reno/Carson Valley
OFF-HIGHWAY VEHICLES (OHVS) 297
  OHV Tours; OHV Trails

SPECIAL TOPIC
Paintball *296*

PICNIC AREAS, HOT SPRINGS, AND SPAS 299
PICNICKING 299
  Truckee/Donner; South Lake Tahoe; Kirkwood/Hope Valley/Markleeville;
  Reno/Carson City
HOT SPRINGS 301
  Truckee/Donner; Kirkwood/Hope Valley/Markleeville; Reno; Carson
  City/Carson Valley
SPAS 304
  Squaw Valley; Incline Village/Crystal Bay; South Lake Tahoe; Feather River
  Country/Lakes Basin; Reno

WINTER RECREATION

ALPINE SKIING 310
ALPINE RESORTS 314
  Truckee/Donner; Squaw Valley; Tahoe City/West Shore; Incline Village/Mt.
  Rose; South Lake Tahoe; Kirkwood/Hope Valley/Markleeville

SPECIAL TOPIC
Ski, Weather, and Road Information Sources *312*

CROSS-COUNTRY SKIING 335
CROSS-COUNTRY SKI RESORTS 338
  Truckee/Donner; Squaw Valley; Tahoe City/West Shore; City of South Lake
  Tahoe; Stateline/Zephyr Cove; Kirkwood/Hope Valley/Markleeville
PUBLIC CROSS-COUNTRY SKI AREAS AND PARKS 348
  Truckee/Donner; Tahoe City/West Shore; City of South Lake Tahoe; Highway 50
  (West of South Lake Tahoe); Kirkwood/Hope Valley/Markleeville; Feather River
  Country/Lakes Basin

WILDERNESS CROSS-COUNTRY TRAILS **351**
Truckee/Donner; Tahoe City/West Shore; Incline Village/Mt. Rose; South Lake
Tahoe; Kirkwood/Hope Valley/Markleeville; Feather River Country/Lakes Basin

OTHER WINTER RECREATION **358**

SNOW-PLAY AREAS: SLEDDING AND TUBING 359
Truckee/Donner Summit; Squaw Valley; Tahoe City/West Shore; Kings
Beach/Tahoe Vista/Carnelian Bay; Incline Village/Mt. Rose; South Lake Tahoe;
Lakes Basin/Feather River Country
ICE SKATING 363
SNOWSHOEING 364
SLEIGH RIDES 365
Dogsled Rides
SNOWMOBILING 366
Truckee/Donner; Tahoe City/West Shore; Kings Beach/Tahoe Vista/Carnelian
Bay; South Lake Tahoe/Stateline; Snowmobile Trails in National Forests

SPECIAL TOPIC
Sno-Park Areas and Permits *361*

ACCOMMODATIONS

TAHOE AND VICINITY ACCOMMODATIONS **376**

MOTELS, SMALL LODGES, AND COTTAGES 381
Truckee/Donner; Tahoe City/West Shore; Kings Beach/Tahoe Vista/Carnelian
Bay; South Lake Tahoe; Kirkwood/Hope Valley/Markleeville; Feather River
Country/Lakes Basin
HOTELS AND CASINOS 396
Squaw Valley; Incline Village/Crystal Bay; South Shore/Stateline
SMALL HOTELS AND CONDOS 405
Truckee/Donner; Squaw Valley; Tahoe City/West Shore; Kings Beach/Tahoe
Vista/Carnelian Bay; Incline Village/Crystal Bay; South Lake Tahoe/Stateline;
Kirkwood; Feather River Country/Lakes Basin; Carson Valley
BED-AND-BREAKFASTS AND COUNTRY INNS 421
Truckee/Donner; Squaw Valley; Tahoe City/West Shore; Kings Beach/Tahoe
Vista/Carnelian Bay; South Lake Tahoe/Stateline; Highway 50 (West of South
Lake Tahoe); Feather River Country/Lakes Basin
PROPERTY MANAGEMENT AND RENTAL AGENCIES 439
Lake Tahoe (All Areas); Truckee/Donner; Squaw Valley/Alpine Meadows; Tahoe
City/Tahoe Vista/Carnelian Bay; Incline Village/Crystal Bay; South Lake
Tahoe/Stateline; Feather River Country/Lakes Basin

SPECIAL TOPICS

Major Reservation Services 378
Key to Tahoe Hotel/Motel Room Rates 382
Key to Tahoe Resort Rates 397
Key to Tahoe Bed-and-Breakfast Rates 421
Tahoe's Famous Rent-a-Mansion 440

MOUNTAIN RESORTS AND LODGES **445**

Truckee/Donner; Tahoe City/West Shore; South Shore/Stateline; Kirkwood/Hope Valley/Markleeville; Lakes Basin/Feather River Country

RENO/CARSON VALLEY ACCOMMODATIONS **461**

HOTELS **463**
Reno/Sparks

MOTELS **474**
Reno/Sparks; Carson City/Dayton; Carson Valley

BED-AND-BREAKFASTS AND COUNTRY INNS **482**
Reno/Sparks; Carson City/Dayton; Virginia City; Carson Valley

SPECIAL TOPIC

Key to Reno Hotel Room Rates 463

CAMPGROUNDS **488**

Truckee/Donner; Jackson Meadows Reservoir Camps; Lake Tahoe; Kirkwood/Hope Valley/Markleeville; Crystal Basin/Highway 50; Lakes Basin/Feather River Country; Reno/Carson Valley; Snow and Winter Camping

DINING AND NIGHTLIFE

TAHOE DINING AND NIGHTLIFE **532**

FOOD AND DRINK **532**
Truckee/Donner/Soda Springs; Squaw Valley; Tahoe City/West Shore; Kings Beach/Tahoe Vista/Carnelian Bay; Incline Village/Crystal Bay; Stateline/Kingsbury/Zephyr Cove (Nevada); South Lake Tahoe/Camp Richardson (California); Kirkwood/Hope Valley/Markleeville; Feather River Country/ Lakes Basin

NIGHTLIFE **585**
North Shore; South Shore

SPECIAL TOPIC

Key to Tahoe Dining Prices 533

RENO AREA DINING AND NIGHTLIFE 590

FOOD AND DRINK 591
Reno/Sparks; Carson City/Dayton; Virginia City; Carson
Valley/Minden/Gardnerville; Genoa

NIGHTLIFE 608
Reno/Sparks; Hotels/Casinos; Carson City/Dayton; Carson Valley/Minden;
Events Centers; Comedy Clubs; Nightclubs, Bars, and Restaurants

SPECIAL TOPIC

Key to Reno Dining Prices *591*

BASICS

TRANSPORTATION 616
Airports; Railway; Airport Bus and Van Shuttles; Public Transportation Lake
Tahoe Area; Public Transportation Reno Area; Ski Shuttles; Limousines and Tour
Services; Rental Cars; Taxis

INFORMATION AND SERVICES 622
Road Conditions; Weather Conditions; Transportation Agencies; Bureaus and
Chambers of Commerce; City and Municipal Parks and Recreation Agencies;
State Parks; Bureau of Land Management; PG&E Recreational Facilities; Fish
and Game/Wildlife Agencies; U.S. Forest Service; Foreign Language Assistance;
Historical Societies; Native American Organizations; Environmental Agencies and
Organizations; Newspapers

SPECIAL TOPIC

Additional Information Sources *623*

RESOURCES 627

SUGGESTED READING 628
INTERNET RESOURCES 630
ACCOMMODATIONS INDEX 633
RESTAURANT INDEX 638
GENERAL INDEX 642

Keeping Current

We are committed to making *Moon Handbooks Tahoe* the most accurate, thorough, and enjoyable guide to the Lake Tahoe, Reno, and Carson Valley areas. We have taken extreme care to provide our diverse readership with up-to-date information. With any guidebook, however, the change of seasons usually means the change of the fees listed herein. If you have a specific need or concern, or are operating on a budget, it's a good idea to call the business ahead of time.

We always welcome comments and suggestions from our readers. If you feel inspired to write, please address correspondence to:

Ken Castle
Moon Handbooks Tahoe
Avalon Travel Publishing
1400 65th Street, Suite 250
Emeryville, CA 94608 USA
email: atpfeedback@avalonpub.com

Maps

Tahoe ii

Tahoe and Vicinity iii

INTRODUCTION

Tahoe and Vicinity Points
of Interest 12
Tahoe and Vicinity Points
of Interest (detail) 13
Reno/Carson Valley Points
of Interest 39
Reno/Sparks Area 41
Virginia City 48
Carson City 53

SUMMER RECREATION

Boat Cruises and Marinas 111
Beaches 139
Fishing Waters 154
Tahoe Rim Trail 195
Hiking Trails 200

Nature Trails 224
Horseback Riding Excursions 231
Bike Trails and Parks 241
Golf Courses 263

WINTER RECREATION

Alpine Ski Resorts 311
Cross-Country Skiing 336

ACCOMMODATIONS

Campground Overview Map 491
Truckee/Donner Campgrounds 493
Tahoe Campgrounds 502
Kirkwood/Hope Valley/Markleeville
Campgrounds 509
Crystal Basin Campgrounds 514
Lakes Basin/Feather River
Campgrounds 520
Reno/Carson Valley Campgrounds ... 525

MAP SYMBOLS

≡ Divided Highway	◉ State Capital	⊀ ⤧ Airport/Airfield
= Primary Road	○ City/Town	▲ Mountain
— Secondary Road	★ Point of Interest	)(Mountain Pass
	• Accommodation	⚡ Ski Resort
------ Unpaved Road	▼ Restaurant/Bar	▪ Other Location

Introduction

Introduction

The Lake

A BIT OF HISTORY, A BIT OF OVERVIEW

Explorer John C. Frémont first saw Lake Tahoe in 1844 from the top of Red Lake Peak, which is south of the basin at what is now Carson Pass. He named it Lake Bonpland after a botanist, but then changed it to Mountain Lake. Subsequently it was named Lake Bigler, for a California governor, but the U.S. Department of the Interior didn't care for that name either, and commissioned Dr. Henry Degroot, a journalist, to come up with a new one. Degroot suggested "tahoe," an Indian word meaning "big water." Decades passed before the name finally stuck, thanks to action in 1945 by the California state legislature.

In the 1860s, Tahoe was the center of a lively commerce that involved the silver mines in Virginia City, where the Comstock Lode was discovered in 1859, and the Central Pacific Railroad, which was pushing over the Sierra toward the town of Truckee. Sixty miles north of Tahoe, gold mines were flourishing at places such as Johnsville, now part of the Plumas-Eureka State Park. To supply wood to the mines, the new boomtowns, and the railroad, an extensive logging empire was established on the east shore of the lake, from Incline Village to Glenbrook. The loggers clear-cut the entire shoreline, leaving scars that would last for decades, until both the mines and the demand for timber petered out in the late 1870s and early 1880s. By then, the only business that showed promise was tourism, and thus began a rush to build resorts.

It is interesting to note that nearly every community around Tahoe owes its existence today to a resort or hotel. During the late 19th and early 20th centuries, travelers from San Francisco would take one train to Truckee, and from there board a second train that rode on a narrow-gauge track to Tahoe City. When they got to the lake, they would have their choice of fabulous resorts such as Tahoe Tavern at Tahoe City, Brockway Springs Hotel near Crystal Bay, the Tallac House on the West Shore, and the Glenbrook

pier at Sugar Pine Point State Park

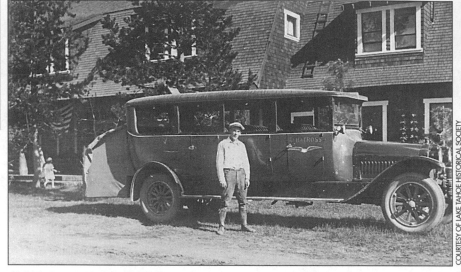

COURTESY OF LAKE TAHOE HISTORICAL SOCIETY

Globin's Resort, touring vehicle

Inn on the East Shore. Of course, without roads the only way to reach the distant resorts was by passenger ferry, and a network of steamships developed to service the lake. A typical day outing for guests of these lavish hotels was to circumnavigate the lake, stopping at various landings to enjoy refreshments and see the sights.

None of the historic, turn-of-the-century inns has survived to modern times. Most were destroyed by fire, a problem that constantly bedeviled Virginia City and Truckee, where firefighting methods were primitive at best. The only resort that made it to the 1960s was Tahoe Tavern, and it was demolished for environmental and commercial reasons. The Tavern was an opulent hotel, often compared to the Ahwahnee in Yosemite, that didn't seem to have any savior during the condominium-building craze. Had it been standing today, it would likely be booked 100 percent of the year. Only now, after so much of the lake's history has vanished, is

The lake is one of the great marvels of our time, one that offers a lifetime of pure joy. It is, as Mark Twain wrote, "surely the fairest picture the whole earth affords."

there a move to preserve what's left and to promote the classic Old Tahoe look.

The lake is a constant swirl of controversy, a fact of life that escapes most visitors who come here to enjoy its natural wonders. Two-thirds of Tahoe is in California, with one-third in Nevada. There are five counties with jurisdiction in the basin, four U.S. Forest Service management units, two state fish and game agencies, and a myriad of cities, towns, and regional agencies. The bistate Tahoe Regional Planning Agency (TRPA), whose mission is to balance growth with the environment, is constantly under fire either by development interests or conservation groups. Everyone has a different idea of what Tahoe's future ought to be, and there is a provincialism that always seems to stand in the way of collective action.

There is no denying that unregulated growth in the late 1950s and 1960s, a lot of it stimulated by the arrival of the 1960 Winter

LAKE TAHOE FACTS AND FIGURES

- Lake Tahoe is 200 miles northeast of San Francisco, California, and 58 miles southwest of Reno, Nevada, in the Sierra Nevada range.

- The North American continent's largest alpine lake, Tahoe stretches 22 miles long and 12 miles wide and covers a surface area of 191.6 square miles. It has 72 miles of shoreline.

- Two-thirds of the lake is in the state of California, and one-third lies in the state of Nevada.

- The lake's average surface is 6,226.95 feet above sea level and the natural rim is 6,223 feet above sea level, making it the highest lake of its size in the United States.

- Mount Tallac at 9,735 feet is the highest peak rising from the shoreline. The highest point in the Tahoe Basin is Freel Peak at 10,881 feet.

- Lake Tahoe is the third-deepest lake in North America and 10th-deepest in the world (Lake Baikal in Russia is the deepest, at more than 4,600 feet). Tahoe's deepest point is 1,657 feet, near Crystal Bay, and its average depth is 989 feet.

- The estimated 39.75 trillion gallons of water contained in the lake is 99.9 percent pure, with visibility to 75 feet below the surface.

- If completely drained, the lake would cover a flat area the size of California to a depth of 14 inches and would take more than 700 years to refill.

- Lake Tahoe is, geologically, a "young lake," having been formed 10,000–11,000 years ago.

- Glaciers are responsible for carving out the broad, U-shaped valleys that hold Emerald Bay, Fallen Leaf Lake, and Cascade Lake.

- Sixty-three streams flow into Lake Tahoe, but only one, the Truckee River, flows out—past Reno and into Pyramid Lake.

- Lake Tahoe loses much of its water to evaporation. If the water that evaporates from the lake every 24 hours could be recovered, it would supply the daily requirements of a city the size of Los Angeles.

- Although the summer's heat can warm the upper 12 feet to a comfortable 68°F, Lake Tahoe never freezes over in the winter. This is because of the constant 39°F maintained at depths below 700 feet, largely because of the constant movement and volume of water.

- The sun shines at Lake Tahoe approximately 274 days a year. Shorts and T-shirts are typical summer-day attire, but jackets and sweaters are advised during the cooler evenings. Weather in the Sierra can be unpredictable. Snowfall, for example, has been recorded in every month and averages 420 inches a year.

Olympics in Squaw Valley and the development of gaming on the South Shore, added an urban blight that still remains around much of the lake. Freshwater marshes were dredged or filled for waterfront homes, thereby interrupting the natural cleansing process of the lake. Traffic has become a major problem, in the way of both congestion and air pollution. The city of South Lake Tahoe is in the middle of a $236-million redevelopment plan that is razing dozens of tacky motels and replacing them with quality resorts, hotels, inns, and open space. Many of the condominium developments, which were cheaply built to cash in on America's craving for inexpensive "second homes," still mar otherwise beautiful forests at both the north and south ends of the lake. Fortunately,

a new breed of entrepreneur is acquiring worn-out lodges and turning them into elegant cottages and bed-and-breakfasts, especially on the North and West Shores.

Despite human tinkering with the landscape, Tahoe endures with an undiminished grandeur. Nothing can taint the first impressions of flying over Lake Tahoe and seeing this giant pool of indigo blue water cradled between mountain ranges. Nothing can detract from the experience of entering Emerald Bay and finding yourself surrounded by cathedrals of granite. And nothing compares to the sense of awe that comes from scrambling up the trails of Desolation Wilderness to visit pristine alpine lakes and revel in the pure glory of nature. If Tahoe had not been carved up into so many fiefdoms, it would unquestionably qualify as a national park.

After making hundreds of visits over the course of 30-plus years, and after traveling around the world many times to exotic destinations, I find that the magic and allure of Lake Tahoe is still as strong as the day I first saw it. The lake is one of the great marvels of our time, one that offers a lifetime of pure joy. It is, as Mark Twain wrote, "surely the fairest picture the whole earth affords."

GROWING CONCERN

As Lake Tahoe entered the new millennium, more than $1 billion worth of resort-related projects was under way, representing a new era that will complete the area's standing as a world-class destination. Tahoe is redefining itself on a scale that has not been seen in perhaps a century, and it is doing so in a way that celebrates its historic architectural heritage. With what is to come in the next few years, Tahoe will be in a league with

FLORA AND FAUNA OF THE LAKE TAHOE BASIN

Trees
alder
aspen
incense cedar
Jeffrey pine
lodgepole pine
ponderosa pine
sierra juniper
sugar pine
white fir
willow

Wildflowers
white
California corn lily
common yarrow
cow parsnip
mariposa lily
ranger buttons

blue/purple
dwarf alpine aster
lupine
meadow penstemon

yellow
buttercup
mountain mule ears
sulphur flowers

pink/red
columbine
Indian paintbrush
shooting star
snow plant
thistle

Mammals
black bear
coyote
Douglas squirrel or chikaree
golden-mantled ground squirrel
mule deer
pine martin
yellow-bellied marmot

Birds
American robin
bald eagle
California gull
Canada goose
dark-eyed junco
hairy woodpecker
mallard
mountain chickadee
red-tailed hawk
Steller's jay
Western tanager
yellow-headed blackbird

Colorado and Utah as a premier alpine resort region, matching those places with panache and sophistication. Indeed, one can already argue that no other place in North America has as much under one deep, blue sky or above one deep, blue lake.

But while the lake is undergoing cosmetic surgery from one end to the other, scientists are urgently searching for ways to ensure that Tahoe's cobalt-blue clarity is preserved for the next millennium. And that is surely the most difficult task. The basin is a complex ecosystem that has been affected ed not only by man but also by nature. It is relatively easy to prohibit watercraft with two-stroke engines, or to ban the use of a fuel additive such as MTBE—two anti-pollution measures that were recently enacted. But it is much harder to locate and control the sources of nutrients that enter the water from soil erosion in the surrounding drainages, or from airborne pollutants that blow in from outside of the basin. Too many nitrates and phosphates can cloud the lake's crystalline transparency, especially since Tahoe is a closed system that retains most of what goes into it. The lake is not on life support yet, but it certainly requires intensive care.

Fortunately, aesthetics and environment are now high priorities among those who hold the future of the lake in their hands. Undisturbed areas are largely off limits from building, a result of moratoriums imposed by the two-state Tahoe Regional Planning Agency (TRPA). Those projects that are going forward represent, in most cases, rehabilitation of sites that were blighted by aging, ramshackle buildings, or by pothole-filled parking lots. Apart from replacing the excesses of the last century, substantial programs are underway to restore and enhance wetlands and protect fisheries and wildlife. One of the largest projects, recently announced by the California Tahoe Conservancy, would begin the long-awaited restoration of the Upper Truckee River marshes at Tahoe Keys in South Lake Tahoe.

For vacationers, the born-again Tahoe will be a vibrant and exciting place. In 2002, projects that had been in the planning stages for a decade or more finally materialized. The most significant are two new alpine villages—one at Squaw Valley, site of the 1960 Winter Olympics, and one at Heavenly, Resort next to Stateline at South Shore. Initial phases of the four-season Village at

the Tallac Hotel's casino, circa 1906

Squaw Valley are now open, with condominiums and a handful of restaurants and shops. That project was undertaken by Canada's Intrawest, which is best known as the owner of the giant Whistler/Blackcomb ski complex in British Columbia. Heavenly Resort now has a dramataic new base area for its gondola with the opening of two Marriott interval-ownership hotels. These, along with ground-floor restaurants and boutiques, form of the nucleus of the Heavenly Village. Concurrent with all of this activity, there were two bombshell acquisitions. One was the purchase of Heavenly by Colorado resort titan Vail, which immediately announced it would spend $40 million over a five-year period to upgrade the ski area. Another was the sale of the 740-room Harveys Resort Casino, the largest hotel at the lake, to its traditional archrival across the street, Harrah's. Both sales generated new optimism about advancing other major South Shore projects, one of them a convention center on the California side of Stateline.

In addition to these blockbusters, the Mountain Village at Kirkwood, southwest of South Lake Tahoe, has continued to open new condominium projects and add other amenities, such as an ice-skating rink. And Northstar-at-Tahoe near Truckee, in a joint venture with Colorado-based East West Partners, is moving along with plans to overhaul and expand its village, adding more condominiums, shops and restaurants. East West is also developing two golf/residential communities in Truckee, and other developers are eyeing nearby Martis Valley for yet more golf and second home projects.

These developments will give Tahoe new attractions and distinctive, upscale communities with a strong sense of place. By centralizing the lodging, restaurants, shopping and recreation into pedestrian-friendly villages, the region hopes to reduce the traffic congestion and pollution

Although very little is left of the lakeside lodges that lured the rich and famous in the early 1900s, architects and designers are incorporating the rustic Old Tahoe look into almost everything that is built these days. The style employs smooth river rock for fireplaces and facades, and heavy log timbers to support cathedral ceilings.

that is an all-too-familiar byproduct of peak-season crowds.

While the ski industry is often the engine that drives Tahoe's construction, a number of hotel and lodging properties also are involved in revitalizing the lake's tourism infrastructure. Buildings that have been around since the late 1960s and '70s are getting a complete facelift. The Hyatt Regency Lake Tahoe at Incline Village, on the Nevada side of the lake, has completed an interior remodel and is moving ahead with plans to add new rooms and a new facade. At Squaw Valley, the Squaw Valley Lodge opened a new, 40-unit wing. On the South Shore, Embassy Suites, which changed ownership in 2001, finished a room remodel of its own. At this writing, rumors were flying that other major hotel brands, among them Ritz-Carlton (which is owned by Marriott), and Hilton were eyeing sites at Tahoe. Among the "hot" locations is the new Highway 267 interchange with I-80 in Truckee.

The energy and dollars that are pouring into the lake from large corporations have not gone unnoticed by the small businesses and public agencies that ring the 72-mile shoreline. Motor inns, lakeside resorts and marinas are being spruced up, and a handful of elegant new bed-and-breakfast inns, such as the luxurious Black Bear Inn at South Shore, have appeared. One big addition is the installation of mileposts, starting at Tahoe City, that provide travelers with specific reference points and highlights.

What most of these projects have in common is the desire to embrace Tahoe's golden era of resorts at the turn of the last century. Although very little is left of the lakeside lodges that lured the rich and famous in the early 1900s, architects and designers are incorporating the rustic Old Tahoe look into almost everything that is built these days. The style employs smooth river rock for fireplaces and facades, and heavy log timbers to support cathedral ceilings.

It is fair to say that the bland, cheaply built condominiums and motels of the last 30 years are going the way of the dinosaur, albeit gradually. The city of South Lake Tahoe is leading the charge with a redevelopment plan that has removed tacky, run-down motels along Highway 50 and replaced them with quality lodges, retail centers and open space. And various transit entities, from casino vans to public buses, are being pooled under one GPS-coordinated system that encourages people to park their cars and take alternative transportation.

Still, there is no coordinated public transit around Tahoe. One attempt at a summer bus, called the Lake-Lapper, was scrapped because of insufficient ridership. Someone who wants to circle the lake must take a car, a boat or a chartered bus or van. Adequate public transit covers most of the North Shore and South Shore, but connections between the two are few and far between. Even a plan for an around-the-lake bicycle trail is proceeding at a snail's pace—owing to the challenging topography, property acquisition problems, and the diverse priorities of an assortment of government agencies.

UNDER THE SURFACE

In the years since the first edition of this book appeared, scientists have unlocked some of the mysteries of Lake Tahoe, the world's 10th-deepest lake. One of the most compelling bodies of research was recently provided by the U.S. Geological Survey, which completed an ambitious mapping of the lake's floor. The USGS used a technology known as "multibeam bathymetry" to create never-before-seen, high-resolution 3-D digital images of the lake and its environs. These colorful, shaded-relief images—like something from a Martian landscape—provide a spectacular new perspective for anyone who is curious about the geology of the lake. You can view them on the Internet at the USGS website at http://walrus.wr.usgs.gov/pacmaps/.

Some of this research will be invaluable to scientists and conservationists who are studying the ecology of the lake and ways to protect it. As Tahoe's popularity has swelled to more than 20 million user-days a year, surpassing the visitation at Yosemite National Park, the lake is facing challenges from several sources. Water transparency has diminished by 30 percent since 1967, though casual observers would be hard-pressed to notice. Phosphorus and nitrogen that enter the lake from storm runoff and erosion have caused a bloom of green algae, reducing the clarity from 100 feet to 70 feet in just three decades.

With most lakes, these nutrients are washed away by the ebb and flow of water. Tahoe, however, is virtually a closed system; it has 63 streams that drain into it but only one outlet, the Truckee River. Scientists calculate that with the size and depth of the lake—a basin filled with 39 trillion gallons of water—it takes one drop 700 years to escape, and two to three decades for phosphorus and nitrogen to be scrubbed from the system.

Looking for Trouble

For more than 40 years, the man most responsible for monitoring the health of Tahoe has been Dr. Charles Goldman, a limnologist (lake specialist) with the University of California at Davis. In 1979, I had the honor of co-leading an underwater exploration of the lake with Goldman, a project that was financed by the *San Jose Mercury News,* the newspaper I worked for at the time. We rented a three-person minisub out of Houston, Texas, where it had been used to inspect and repair oil pipelines in the Gulf of Mexico. The tubular vessel looked like something from the movie *The Abyss,* with a Plexiglas bubble, floodlights, and a big mechanical arm.

Over the course of a week, we towed the sub behind the university's 37-foot aluminum research vessel, the *John Le Conte,* from one end of the lake to the other. On spawning beds off the South Shore, we saw giant Mackinaw trout surely larger than the fishing record of 37.5 pounds. We went down 1,000 feet to look at pinnacles in Crystal Bay, where the lake reaches its deepest level. And we explored an underwater Grand Canyon off Rubicon Point, a sheer granite dropoff that is pockmarked with crevices and ledges. At one point, more than 300 feet below the surface, the sub got stuck in a cave while we were watching crayfish grazing on moss. The bulkheads sweated, and so did we, until the pilot managed to free the vessel.

Today, those exploits seem like crude science. Now Goldman uses a remotely operated vehicle (ROV) with a video camera to inspect the deeper regions of the lake. Tethered to the *John Le Conte,* this little R2D2-style device can dive to 500 feet. (Other researchers have conducted similar underwater surveys, and these have yielded dramatic videos of the sunken steamer *S.S. Tahoe,* tree trunks from ancient forests that grew when water levels receded, and peculiar subsurface "mounts" that rise up from the lake floor. As this edition went to press, yet another major exploration project was being planned.)

Goldman and his colleague, Dr. John E. Reuter, are realizing a lifelong dream: the establishment of the Lake Tahoe Center for Environmental Research. They have acquired an old fish hatchery on the North Shore and plan to upgrade it with modern laboratories and an education center. And they'll use 30 acres of adjoining property volunteered by the California Tahoe Conservancy to study wetlands restoration and stream enhancement, among other projects. While some federal grants have been made to help underwrite this new center, and there has been support from the prestigious League to Save Lake Tahoe and the National Science Foundation, more contributions are needed. (For information, you can contact the Tahoe Research Group at the Division of Environmental Studies, University of California, Davis, CA 95616; 916/752-3938; website: trg.ucdavis.edu.)

Preserving Lake Tahoe is now a top priority for everyone who is involved with the lake. Thankfully, people of good will are making things happen, and they have created a model for the rest of the nation. If everyone contributes to the solutions, the future of this magnificent place will be assured for generations to come.

Sights and Events

Lake Tahoe and Vicinity

When you examine a map of Lake Tahoe's 72-mile perimeter, you begin to realize the amount of time you'd need to fully explore this mountain wonderland. And when you factor in neighboring attractions—such as the vintage logging and railroad town of Truckee—you'll want to plan on a couple of days, at least, to hit all the highlights. The Tahoe basin is a delightful collection of historic mansions, museums, aerial trams, and parks, and every community along the shoreline has its unique charms. Some of them are not obvious, or not well marked. Listed here are not only the must-sees for first-time visitors but also some lesser-known points of interest for returning Tahoe regulars. (Items are keyed to the Tahoe Points of Interest map.)

TRUCKEE/DONNER
Western SkiSport Museum
(see map on page 12, site 1)
On the Donner Summit at Boreal Ski Resort (I-80 at the Castle Peak exit, eight miles west of Truckee), this fascinating museum chronicles the history of skiing from the late 1850s to modern times. It follows the development of alpine jumping at Granlibakken Resort, the arrival of Sugar Bowl and the ski train in the

view of South Shore from Emerald Bay Highway

© KEN CASTLE

SIGHTS AND EVENTS

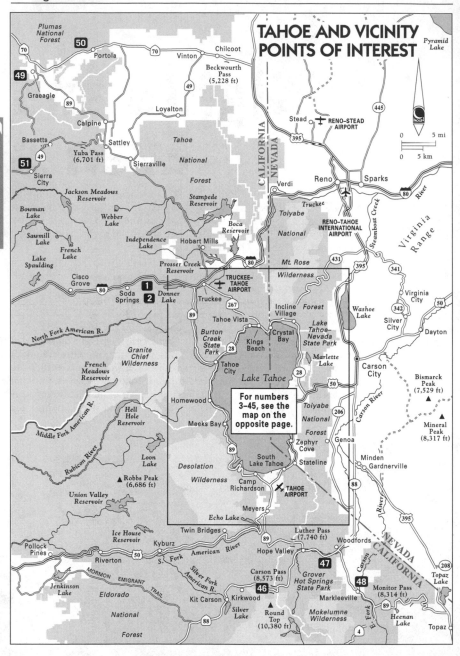

TAHOE AND VICINITY POINTS OF INTEREST

For numbers 3–45, see the map on the opposite page.

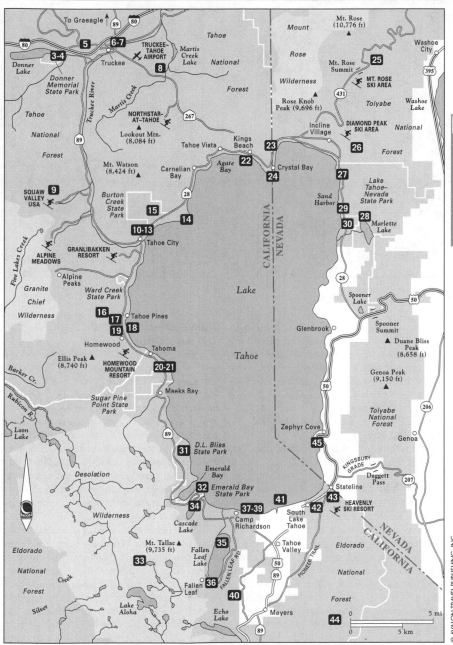

SIGHTS AND EVENTS

downtown Truckee

1940s, and the 1960 Winter Olympics at Squaw Valley. There's a pair of eight-foot-long wooden skis used by "Snowshoe" Thompson, the famous Norwegian mountaineer who hauled mail over the Sierra from the mid-1850s to the mid-1870s. Old ski movies run continuously in the theater.

Hours: Open Sat. and Sun. 10 A.M.–4 P.M.

Admission: Free.

Contact: Auburn Ski Club, P.O. Box 729, Soda Springs, CA 95728; 530/426-3313.

Old Highway 40 Scenic Overlook on Donner Pass (see map on page 12, site 2)

You can reach this great panorama of Donner Lake in one of two ways, by turning off at the Norden/Soda Springs exit of Old Highway 40 and driving beyond Sugar Bowl ski resort until you reach the designated turnoff, or driving up Donner Pass Road at the western end of Donner Lake. If the old bridge at the summit looks familiar, you may have seen it in the movie *True Lies,* starring Arnold Schwarzenegger. Some of the "European" winter scenes were shot here.

Donner Memorial State Park
(see map on page 13, site 3)

Thirteen miles north of Lake Tahoe and just west of Truckee, this 353-acre park features the Emigrant Trail Museum, which is dedicated to the memory of the ill-fated Donner Party, and offers access to sprawling Donner Lake. The lake, called "the Gem of the Sierra," is three miles long, three-quarters of a mile wide, and 200 feet deep. The park, at nearly 6,000 feet, is forested with lodgepole pine, Jeffrey pine, and white fir trees. It has steep granite cliffs and huge boulders, denoting the upheavals of the Earth's crust and the glacier action that scoured the landscape thousands of years ago.

The park has an excellent picnic and day-use area, with shallow swimming inlets and coarse sand beaches. While there is no boat ramp (a private ramp is available on the northwest corner of the lake), visitors can launch cartoppers, inflatables, and sailboards from the beach. Both powerboats and sailboats are allowed on this elongated lake, which can be quite windy in the afternoon. Other amenities include a large campground (open late May–early September) with

© KEN CASTLE

SIGHTS AND EVENTS

154 sites, 2.5 miles of hiking or cross-country skiing trails, 78 picnic sites, and a lakeside interpretive trail that has 18 panels discussing the area's natural and human history. You'll find the park off I-80, at the Truckee–Donner Lake exit.
Admission: Parking is $2 per car. Admission to the museum is $1 for adults 17 and older, free for youth and children 16 and under.
Contact: Donner Memorial State Park; 530/582-7892.

Emigrant Trail Museum and Pioneer Monument (see map on page 13, site 4)

One of the profound tragedies of the westward migration of settlers in the 1840s is remembered at this excellent museum at Donner Memorial State Park in Truckee. Lured by tales of unlimited opportunity in California, George Donner and his brother Jacob (both farmers in Illinois) organized a wagon train of several families and, in April 1846, set out for the promised land. In Wyoming, the Donner Party heeded bad advice and took what they thought was a shortcut, which proved to be a fatal mistake.

The treacherous secondary route over the Wasatch Mountains and across the waterless Great Salt Lake Desert sapped their resources and put the group three weeks behind those who kept to the main trail. When they reached the base of Donner Pass in October, they were halted by early snowstorms and forced to construct emergency shelters at what is now known as Donner Lake. Hampered by the most brutal winter in recorded history and by a lack of food, nearly half of the group perished. Those who survived did so largely by eating the flesh of their dead companions. The fate of the Donner Party prompted a search for a new route over the Sierra Nevada, resulting in the creation of the Mormon-Emigrant Trail south of Lake Tahoe.

The museum, opened in 1962, offers a memorable 30-minute film that reconstructs the ordeal, and has several exhibits on the logging and railroad history of Truckee. A monument outside stands on a stone pedestal that is 22 feet high— the depth of the snow that trapped the settlers. (Another relevant location, the site where the Donner family camped, is the Donner Histori-

cal Site, three miles north of I-80 on Highway 89.) Self-guided nature trails, a large campground, and a beachfront picnic area are included in the park.
Hours: Daily 10 A.M.–5 P.M.
Admission: Adults, $2; children ages 6–12, $1. The day-use fee for the park is $2 per car.
Contact: Donner Memorial State Park, 12593 Donner Pass Rd., Donner, CA 96161; 530/582-7892.

Sierra Nevada Children's Museum (see map on page 13, site 5)

Established in 1992 by volunteers, this unique museum in Truckee offers hands-on educational exhibits that run the gamut of art, science and technology, health, social development, and ecology. Rotating exhibitions feature themes such as "Jungle Impressions," "Dinosaurs in Truckee," "A Night in the Forest" (in which children use flashlights to find animals), and "The Truckee Model Railroad."
Hours: Open Wed.–Sat. 10 A.M.–5 P.M. Open Mon. and Tues. for groups with reservation.
Admission: $3 per person for the museum, $1 for the play structure.
Contact: Sierra Nevada Children's Museum, 11400 Donner Pass Rd., Truckee, CA 96160; 530/587-KIDS.

Truckee (see map on page 13, site 6)

Every vice known to man (and woman) has been practiced at one time or another in this once rollicking railroad and lumber town. Truckee was filled with rowdy saloons, gambling halls, and bawdy houses in the late 1800s and had more kick than a miner's mule. The town is named after a friendly Paiute Indian who helped guide the first party of white settlers through the region in 1844. Its population rose quickly when the Central Pacific Railroad arrived in 1868, as part of the Transcontinental Railroad. This development created two major industries—logging and ice-harvesting—and attracted a resident Chinese population that reportedly numbered as high as 10,000, second in size only to that of San Francisco's Chinatown. But the hardworking Chinese, who threatened to monopolize the profitable logging business, were driven out of town in 1886 by jealous white vigilante groups.

Truckee's fortunes declined after the 1920s, and growth was stagnant until the 1960 Winter Olympics at Squaw Valley fostered northern Tahoe's economic rebirth as a ski resort destination. Today, Truckee is booming again. The town incorporated in 1993, combining the communities of old Truckee, Tahoe Donner, and Donner Lake. Burned-out city refugees looking for greener pastures have pushed the population to 10,000 and attracted new businesses.

Through all of this, however, Truckee has preserved the gritty character of its old section. Nearly 100 of its 300 downtown structures were built before the turn of the last century. Most of the historic buildings are concentrated along **Commercial Row,** where visitors can stroll along the wooden walkways and enjoy a slice of the Old West. While this section of town has become gentrified (with gourmet restaurants and stores catering to travelers), there are rustic places as well. Among these spots are the **Southern Pacific Railroad Depot,** which houses a visitors' center, an interesting gallery of old photographs, and a working station for freight and Amtrak passenger trains. Other intriguing places include the **Bar of America,** whose walls are adorned with pictures of famous outlaws and gunslingers; and **Cabona's** clothing store, which always seems to have the latest in country chic. The **Truckee Hotel,** an institution on Bridge Street since 1873, has been restored to its former Victorian elegance and is a marvelous place to stay if you don't mind the trains tooting their way through town. Jibboom Street, once notorious as Truckee's famous red-light district, has an old two-story jailhouse that is now a museum.

Also worth checking out are the **Squeeze In,** a tiny breakfast house with creative omelets;

Every vice known to man (and woman) has been practiced at one time or another in this once rollicking railroad and lumber town. Truckee was filled with rowdy saloons, gambling halls, and bawdy houses in the late 1800s and had more kick than a miner's mule.

Earthsong, whose basement is stocked with a variety of aromatic spices and coffees; **Bob Roberts Jewelers,** with Western silver and gold pieces and crystal geodes; **Truckee Books,** with a variety of local lore; and **Richardson House,** a historic bed-and-breakfast above Commercial Row. The century-old **Masonic Building,** destroyed by an explosion in 1993, was rebuilt and now houses a restaurant, **Dragonfly,** which has a second-floor balcony dining area. The Capitol building, built in 1870 and the second oldest structure in town, once housed a saloon and dance hall and, later, Piper's Opera Company. Among the notables associated with Truckee is the great silent-screen comedian Charlie Chaplin, who filmed *The Gold Rush* and other movies in the area. Truckee is a convenient stop along I-80 and is 20 minutes north of Lake Tahoe. **Contact:** Truckee Donner Visitors Center; 530/587-2757 or 800/548-8388.

Old Truckee Jail Museum
(see map on page 13, site 7)

Built in 1875 and closed in 1964, this was the longest operating jail in California. The two-story building, behind Commercial Row, holds four cells, two on the ground floor and two on the second floor; the upstairs area was reserved for women and juvenile prisoners. Apart from the steel-lined cells with iron bars, there's a historical photo display, ice-harvesting and logging paraphernalia, skiing memorabilia, some Chinese artifacts, and a few Native American baskets. The museum is operated by the Truckee-Donner Historical Society.

Hours: Open Sat. and Sun. 11 A.M.–4 P.M. end of May–early Sept., with special group tours by reservation.

Admission: Free.

Contact: Old Truckee Jail Museum, 10142 Jibboom St.; Truckee Donner Historical Society; 530/582-0893.

Martis Creek Lake Recreation Area
(see map on page 13, site 8)

A wildlife refuge, a campground, and catch-and-release fishing are the attractions of this lake, where powerboats are prohibited. It's on Highway 267, south of the Truckee-Tahoe Airport.

Contact: U.S. Army Corps of Engineers; 530/639-2342.

SQUAW VALLEY

Squaw Valley USA
(see map on page 13, site 9)

The site of the 1960 Winter Olympics has become one of the world's great ski destinations, although not much is left to remind anyone of the Games. Still, owner Alexander Cushing has created a unique year-round attraction—a goosebump ride on a cable car that soars 2,000 feet above the valley to his High Camp Bath and Tennis Club, at 8,200 feet. If you don't mind the thin air at elevation 8,200 feet, you can iceskate, swim in an artificial rock lagoon, hike on a variety of trails (the favorite one is to Shirley Lake), and even play tennis. Just don't think of chasing a lost ball over the sheer rock face next to the courts. Instead, count your blessings and have a tall one at Alexander's, the restaurant and bar complex adjacent to the club. There's also a small Olympic Museum inside the lodge. The swim lagoon is quite elaborate, and includes a heated outdoor spa with a temperature of 102°F, a poolside café, a barbecue and an outdoor bar. There are also deck chairs and umbrellas for lounging around the pool, along with spacious men's and women's changing rooms that include showers, lockers, towels and extra swim suits for sale if you forget yours.

Even if high places bother you, you can always plant your feet firmly on the ground (or rather, in a marsh) on the 18-hole golf course at the Resort at Squaw Creek, one of Tahoe's most lavish resorts with 405 rooms. Also, you can ride horseback to the top of a ridge to view Lake Tahoe. Another popular outing is to rent a bike and pedal on the designated bike trails and lanes through the Valley some 6.5 miles to Tahoe City, a route that parallels the scenic Truckee River

most of the way. After all of that activity, you might be ready for one of the boutique spa treatments at the Resort at Squaw Creek's new spa, where the killer treatment is something called the Tahoe Hot Rocks. Finally, to cap off your day, you can pause to enjoy a meal, snack or beverage at the new Village at Squaw Valley, which opened with its first buildings in 2002. On the ground level, below some 300 deluxe condominiums, are several restaurants and shops, and during summer weekends you can enjoy music, art and other cultural events in the new plaza. The hottest people-watching place is Balboa's, a trendy, San Francisco-style restaurant-and-bar complex with outdoor tables.

The Christy Inn—former home of Squaw Valley's late founder, Wayne Poulsen—is another famous structure in the area. It houses Graham's, a gourmet restaurant, and a small inn. Wayne and his wife, Sandy, two longtime residents of the valley, produced their share of talented Olympic skiing contenders. Another family, the McKinneys, contributed Olympic skier Tamara McKinney and the late Steve McKinney, who

Squaw Valley Cable Car over Squaw Valley Lodge

© KEN CASTLE

SIGHTS AND EVENTS

HOLLYWOOD LOVES TAHOE

For nearly 100 years, since the invention of the motion picture, film studios and directors have found stunning backdrops at Lake Tahoe for their productions. Many items of memorabilia, including movie posters, are on display at the Gatekeeper's Cabin Museum in Tahoe City, thanks to the efforts of the North Lake Tahoe Historical Society, which has chronicled Tinseltown's various efforts in the region.

In 1994, I personally watched one of the most expensive and spectacular shoots ever done at Tahoe—the filming of the blockbuster action flick *True Lies*, starring Arnold Schwarzenegger and Jamie Lee Curtis.

During the winter, a second-unit production crew commandeered much of the Boreal Ski Area on I-80, leasing a large section of the parking lot and constructing the facade of a fortresslike European chalet on the summit of the ski slopes. This set and a section of Old Highway 40 near the Sugar Bowl Ski Area figured prominently in the opening sequence of the movie, which involves secret agent Schwarzenegger making a daring escape from the heavily guarded mansion over snow-covered terrain.

Night after night for several weeks, the crew shot chase scenes with snowmobiles and skiers and had planned to film the crash landing of a helicopter, which was to be one of the more spectacular stunts of the movie. But the scene was ultimately canceled. Whether this was because of budget constraints, logistical challenges, or emotional issues is not known. But the loss of several Hollywood notables (including the deaths of actor Vic Morrow and a child during the filming of John Landis's *The Twilight Zone*) in several well-publicized helicopter disasters may have had an impact.

Another notable film made at Tahoe was *The Bodyguard*, with Kevin Costner and Whitney Houston. Segments were shot during the winter at Fallen Leaf Lake and several scenes used the home of a prominent surgeon there. Also, scenes from *The Godfather II*, starring Al Pacino, were shot in and around the Kaiser Estate on the West Shore in 1974.

Other recent productions included 1994's *Cobb* with Tommy Lee Jones (as mercurial baseball slugger Ty Cobb), 1988's *Things Change* with Don Ameche, 1983's *Survivors* with Robin Williams and Walter Matthau, 1987's *Surrender* with Michael Caine and Sally Field, and 1987's *Assassination* with Charles Bronson and Jill Ireland.

The Historical Society also has charted these films as part of Tahoe's movie lore:

- *The American President* with Michael Douglas (1990s).

- *Hot Dog—The Movie* (late 1970s).

- *40 Pounds of Trouble* with Tony Curtis (1963).

- *Wild Is the Wind* with Anthony Quinn and Anna Magnani.

- *Johnny Dark* with Tony Curtis (1954).

- *A Place in the Sun* with Elizabeth Taylor and Montgomery Clift (1951).

- *The Country Beyond* with Gary Cooper (1938).

- *And So They Were Married* with Melvin Douglas and Mary Astor (1936).

- *Rose Marie* with Jennette MacDonald, Nelson Eddy, and James Stewart (1935).

- *Call of the Wild* with Clark Gable and Loretta Young (1934).

- *Lightning* with Will Rogers (1931).

- *Confessions of a College Co-Ed* with Bing Crosby and Sylvia Sidney (1931).

- *The Storm* with Lupe Velez and William Boyd (1930).

- *Betrayal* with Gary Cooper (1929).

- *The Gold Rush* with Charles Chaplin (1925, silent).

- *Our Hospitality, The Navigator,* and *The Frozen North* with Buster Keaton (1923 and 1924, silent).

- *Snow Stuff* (1916, silent).

set a world speed-skiing record. Squaw Valley is an eclectic community of corporate entrepreneurs, upscale second-home owners, and an assortment of daredevils, mountaineers, and adventurers. West of Highway 89 and south of Truckee, Squaw Valley boasts several excellent restaurants, overnight lodges, and dramatic views of Granite Chief, the area's highest peak at 9,050 feet.

Hours: In summer (late June–Sept. 1), the cable car operates daily from 9:40 A.M.–9 P.M. Operation depends on weather—high winds can close it—so call ahead. Swim lagoon and spa are open 11 A.M.–7 P.M. and the ice rink is open 11 A.M.–9 P.M. from late June until Sept. 1. Alexander's Café is open daily for lunch and dinner until 9 P.M.

Admission: Combination cable car ride and activity packages vary widely by type of activity and time of day. But basic cable car rides during the day are $17 for adults, $14 for seniors, $5 for children 4–12, and free for three and under.

Contact: Squaw Valley USA; 530/583-6955 or 530/583-6985; website: www.squaw.com.

TAHOE CITY/WEST SHORE

Watson Cabin Museum
(see map on page 13, site 10)

Built in 1909 by Robert Montgomery Wilson, this honeymoon cottage with original furnishings is the oldest structure standing in Tahoe City. It also houses the city's first indoor private bathroom. Volunteer docents dress up as turn-of-the-century Tahoe residents during tours conducted by the North Lake Tahoe Historical Society. It's on North Lake Boulevard (Highway 28), on the lake side of the road.

Hours: Daily noon–4 P.M., June 1–Labor Day, and noon–4 P.M., Labor Day–Oct. 1, closed Tuesday.

Admission: $2 donation requested for adults, $1.50 for juniors and seniors, free for children 12 and under.

Contact: Watson Cabin Museum, 560 N. Lake Blvd., Tahoe City, CA 96145; 530/583-8717. North Lake Tahoe Historical Society; 530/583-8717.

SIGHTS AND EVENTS

© KEN CASTLE

Marion Steinbach Basket Museum

Gatekeeper's Cabin and Marion Steinbach Indian Basket Museum

(see map on page 13, site 11)

One of Tahoe's best collections of historic lore, including memorabilia from the passenger steamship SS *Tahoe* and the posh Tahoe Tavern Resort, are on display in this reconstructed log cabin (the original was destroyed by fire in 1978). New displays include scale models of four famous vessels—*The Tahoe, The Nevada, The Governor Stanford,* and *The Marian B.* From 1910 to 1968, the Tahoe City cabin was inhabited by federal employees from the Bureau of Reclamation, who manually controlled water releases from Lake Tahoe into the Truckee River by manipulating 17 gates in a dam. Water from the lake is routinely diverted to the city of Reno and Pyramid Lake, but with the advent of computer technology the gatekeeper's position was eliminated. Now, historic archives on North Tahoe are displayed here, as well as interesting photographs, old newspapers, and exhibits of the lake's bygone days.

Recently, a 2,400-square-foot wing adjoining the cabin was opened to showcase a world-class collection of Native American baskets. More than 1,000 baskets from local tribes—as well as from Southwestern, Northwestern, Alaskan, and Plains Indians—are displayed, along with 100 dolls. This now-permanent collection (from the estate of the late Marion Steinbach) was donated to the North Lake Tahoe Historical Society, which raised more than $400,000 in two years to build the addition.

The basket museum has its own research library, and the original building contains the Ellen Attardi Library, which holds Tahoe memorabilia, including photographs, newspaper accounts, oral histories and transcriptions, court ledgers, and other artifacts relating to Lake Tahoe's history. Some of the more remarkable items include author/naturalist John Muir's most famous letters, inscriptions, and manuscripts. The museums are at William B. Layton Park between Fanny Bridge and the Truckee River Bank, and there's room outside for picnicking next to the shoreline.

Hours: Daily 11 A.M.–5 P.M. June 15–Labor Day, and Wed.–Sun. May 1–June 15 and Labor Day–Oct. 1. Closed Mon. and Tues. and in winter.

Admission: $2 donation requested for adults, $1.50 for juniors and seniors, and free for children 12 and under.

Contact: North Lake Tahoe Historical Society, 130 W. Lake Blvd., Tahoe City, CA 96145; 530/583-1762.

William B. Layton State Park

(see map on page 13, site 12)

This park houses the Gatekeeper's Cabin and Marion Steinbach Indian Basket Museum, but it has just been expanded to provide new pedestrian access to the lake, although the shoreline is largely cobble. It also has paved bike trails, restrooms, interpretive panels, and new landscaping. The park adjoins Tahoe's outlet to the Truckee River, where the dam that releases water downstream attracts sightseers hoping to catch a glimpse of large trout. To provide the additional land, the California Department of Parks and Recreation ordered the demolition of two longtime hang-outs—The Bridge Tender Café and Izzy's, a burger joint, both of which were on state property. The Café moved to new quarters across the street, but Izzy's is no more. The expanded park creates a junction for three paved bike trails—one heading south along the West Shore, one going north along the Truckee River to Squaw Valley, and one going east through Tahoe City to Dollar Point. New walking/cycling paths also link the park to Tahoe City's Commons Beach, a vast white-sand and lawn-covered recreation area that has picnic tables and a playground. Parking is limited, mostly intended for the Museum and Cabin. But across Highway 89 is a much larger public parking and staging area, the preferred location for cyclists, river rafters and sightseers.

Admission: No charge to use the park.

Contact: California Department of Parks and Recreation, Sierra District, Tahoma, CA; 530/525-7232.

Fanny Bridge

(see map on page 13, site 13)

It's not hard to figure out how this bridge at the

junction of Highways 89 and 28 in Tahoe City got its name. Most summers, when the lake is spilling into the Truckee River, sightseers peer over the bridge to see and feed—but not fish for—large rainbow trout in the waters below. There are several restaurants and bicycle and raft concessions next to the bridge.

Dollar Point
(see map on page 13, site 14)
Named after San Francisco shipping tycoon Robert S. Dollar, this promontory—three miles northeast of Tahoe City—offers both public and private beaches, several condominium developments, and the lake's headquarters for the U.S. Coast Guard (one mile east in Lake Forest, California). The area was once considered as a site for the Lick Observatory, but ultimately the telescope was built 200 miles west on Mt. Hamilton in the San Francisco Bay Area. Dollar Point, originally named Chinquapin by the Washoe Indians, still contains the old Wychwood Estate. Wychwood consists of a cluster of small chalets and a main house built in 1916 by Mrs. Lora Josephine Knight of St. Louis, the same woman who later constructed the splendid Vikingsholm Castle at Emerald Bay. Currently, the property is part of the Chinquapin condominium complex, and use of facilities is restricted to guests and owners.

Burton Creek State Park
(see map on page 13, site 15)
Lake Tahoe's second largest state park (at 2,036 acres) is largely undeveloped, except for about six miles of dirt roads, and is best accessed by hiking, mountain biking, and cross-country skiing. The park is adjacent to the Tahoe State Recreation Area, on the north side of Highway 28 in Tahoe City. Burton Creek (which bisects the park from its northeast corner to the southeast corner) meanders past Antone Meadows Natural Preserve and Burton Creek Natural Preserve, where black bears and other wildlife have been seen. The area is a scenic mix of meadows, forest, and riparian habitat. In winter, Lakeview Cross-Country grooms trails throughout the park.
Admission: Free.

Contact: Burton Creek State Park; 530/525-7982.

Blackwood Canyon
(see map on page 13, site 16)
Found off Highway 89 at Kaspian on the West Shore of Lake Tahoe, this paved road winds 7.5 miles to a high ridge overlooking the lake. It becomes a dirt road at that point, and intersects the Pacific Crest Trail at Barker Pass. A short hike on the well-marked trail provides inspiring views of Desolation Wilderness to the west and Lake Tahoe to the east.
Contact: Lake Tahoe Basin Management Unit; 530/573-2600.

Eagle Rock (see map on page 13, site 17)
This enormous rock formation along Highway 89, one mile north of Homewood, is the neck of an eroded basalt volcano. Some people believe it was named after the bald eagles that once nested there.
Contact: U.S. Forest Service Visitor Center; 530/573-2600.

Fleur du Lac (Kaiser Estate)
(see map on page 13, site 18)
You can't see much of this exclusive gated residential estate from Highway 89, but several tour boats, especially from different points on the lake, regularly cruise past the lakeside entrance. The property, built in 1937 by industrialist Henry J. Kaiser, was used in the acclaimed movie *The Godfather, Part II*, starring Al Pacino. Some of the structures were removed after the film was completed, but the rock boathouse and the yacht club remain. Twenty-two exclusive condominiums, many of them used by corporations for executive retreats, are here. No public access is allowed. It's at 4000 W. Lake Blvd. in Homewood, on the West Shore.

Tahoe Maritime Museum
(see map on page 13, site 19)
Originally founded in 1987, the Tahoe Maritime Museum opened at Sugar Pine Point State Park, near the Ehrman Mansion, in July, 2000, with a small exhibit. But with the recent acquisition of

the old Homeside Motel in Homewood, the organization has moved its operations here, and plans to build a larger and more permanent facility in the future. There are exhibits here now, and it's easy to find the museum since it is located next to the Homewood Mountain Resort parking lot. The volunteer supporters are looking to house a collection that represents the best boats, engines and artifacts in the world, with a setting that allows for an interactive, educational experience. Current exhibits focus on Tahoe's nautical history, from the early steamers that plied the waters in the late 1800s and early 1900s, to the high-speed hydroplane racers that ripped through the waters during the 1950s and 1960s. Within the current collection are two important vessels: a 1925 Belle Isle Bearcat runabout called *Cherokee,* and a mid-1920s-era racing boat that originally was christened *Cigarette IV* but eventually was renamed *Mercury.* The first boat was owned by the Ehrman family's daughter, Esther, who raced it in the annual Lake Tahoe Power Boat Club regattas. Though having several owners, the vessel has never left the lake. The second craft was the pride and joy of prominent summer resident Stanley Dollar Jr. (Dollar Point is named after him), who won the 1938 Lake Championship Free-For-All that was held in July at the famous (and long-gone) Tahoe Tavern resort. The Mercury has a bullet-shaped duraluminum hull and ran on a Curtis engine. Also on regular display are several pulling boats and miscellaneous small craft that belonged to the Ehrmans, including a 26-foot rowing shell once used daily by Charles Ehrman, and a square-transomed Old Town Canoe. A galvanized, hand-riveted fishing boat, one of over 50 rowing hulls that were built by local boatman Ernie Pomin, is on view outside the North Boathouse. In November of 2000, workers recovered from the lake a sunken, 25-foot launch, the *Shanghai,* that was built in the 1890s. Used for lake excursions and later for towing, the vessel was found in 300 feet of water offshore from Homewood. It was graciously donated to the museum by Edna and Sarah Obexer.

Hours: Open Fridays, Saturdays, Sundays and holidays from June through Labor Day Weekend in September. Call or consult the website for hours.

Admission: Free, but donations are welcome.

Contact: Tahoe Maritime Museum, 5205 West Lake Blvd., Homewood, P.O. Box 181, Carnelian Bay, CA 96140, 530/583-5028; website: www.tahoemaritimemuseum.org.

Ehrman Mansion
(see map on page 13, site 20)

Built at the turn of the last century, this Queen Anne-style Victorian in Sugar Pine Point State Park represents the opulent post-mining period, when wealthy businessmen constructed elegant summer homes at Lake Tahoe. The three-story rock and wood estate, completed by West Coast financier Isaias W. Hellman in 1902, was designed by well-known architect Walter Danforth Bliss.

Hellman, who later became president of Wells Fargo Nevada National Bank, called his 11,703-square-foot summer retreat "Pine Lodge." It had all the latest comforts, including electricity supplied by a wood-burning steam generator in an adjacent tank house. Hellman even had tons of topsoil brought in to create a beautifully manicured but steeply sloping grass lawn, which today provides visitors with magnificent picnic grounds. A long pier that still extends from the shoreline enabled guests to come and go from Tahoe's passenger steamers. A cadre of butlers, maids, cooks, and groundskeepers constantly tended to the estate and its guests. After Hellman's death in 1920, the home was operated by his daughter, Florence Ehrman, and later by her daughter, Esther Lazard. In 1965, the mansion and nearly 2,000 acres in the General Creek watershed were acquired by the California State Park System.

Visitors who tour the mansion will see the spacious living and dining rooms with their oak floors, polished wood ceilings, and elegant fireplaces. The dining table, 30 feet long and eight feet wide, could accommodate 30 guests at one sitting. On the second floor, circular master bedrooms anchor the north and south ends; six guest bedrooms and eight bathrooms are in between these chambers. Much of the original furniture was auctioned off in 1965, but the volunteer

Tahoe Sierra State Parks Foundation has redecorated the estate with period pieces. On August 14—the state park's Living History Day—park guides and volunteers dress in period clothing and re-create the feel of the place in its heyday. Sugar Pine Point State Park is on Highway 89, one mile north of Meeks Bay. It also has a small beach, a trail system, and a large campground.

Hours: Free tours are held every hour 11 A.M.– 4 P.M. daily, July–early September.

Admission: The day-use fee for parking is $2 per car.

Contact: Ehrman Mansion; 530/525-7982.

Sugar Pine Point State Park
(see map on page 13, site 21)

This 2,011-acre park, named for the majestic sugar pine trees that used to be common on the West Shore of Lake Tahoe, sits on a forested promontory 10 miles south of Tahoe City on Highway 89. Major highlights include the elegant Ehrman Mansion (see number 28); a 19th-century log cabin; a nature center with bird and animal exhibits; and the General Creek watershed, which creates a natural entryway into the 62,469-acre Desolation Wilderness. In the developed area of the park east of the highway, day visitors can see the mansion, the cabin, the Tahoe Maritime Museum, and the Edwin L. Z'Berg Natural Preserve, all of which border 1.75 miles of Tahoe shoreline. The cabin was built in 1860 by former Indian fighter and trapper General William Phipps, who is believed to be the first permanent settler of record on the lake's West Shore, although the presence of grinding rocks and bedrock mortars indicates that Washoe Indians inhabited the area for generations before his arrival.

An attractive small swimming beach and a vast manicured lawn shaded by tall trees offer excellent picnicking opportunities. And if you continue northward along the shoreline, there are delightful—and virtually unused—white sand beaches. The park is also a staging area for cyclists riding the paved West Shore Bike Path, which begins here and extends north to Tahoe City. Near the east-side parking lot is the nature center, housed in the old water tower and gen-

erating plant once used by the Ehrman Mansion. Some 11 miles of hiking trails wind through the park, including the Dolder Nature Trail, which follows the lakeshore and passes the world's highest (in elevation) working lighthouse. In the summer of 2002, the east side of the park underwent a major restoration, with a new entry road, a kiosk with restrooms, a new parking area, and a new connection to the disabled-access paved lakefront trail from the parking area. Plans were also underway to create two interpretive displays of Lake Tahoe history—one outdoors and another inside the Old Carriage House

On the west side of the highway, the General Creek Trail is a 6.5-mile loop with an optional side trip to Lily Pond. Lost Lake, a spectacular alpine jewel, is accessible via a 15-mile round-trip and requires some cross-country trekking by seasoned hikers. In winter, the park offers 20-plus kilometers of marked cross-country ski trails. A local West Shore citizens group is campaigning to restore the cross-country ski trails that were used in the 1960 Winter Olympics for the Nordic and Biathlon events. The start/finish line was in Tahoma and many of the 50 kilometers of trails extended into what is now state land. If the group achieves its objective, there will be a new Olympic Trails Park between Sugar Pine and Homewood, with many newly restored trails for winter and summer recreationists. Among the existing amenities here is General Creek Campground, which has 175 sites and is open year-round. Interpretive programs are conducted by ranger-naturalists throughout the year.

Admission: $2 parking fee per car.

Contact: Sugar Pine Point State Park; 530/525-7982.

KINGS BEACH/TAHOE VISTA/CARNELIAN BAY

Tahoe Tessie's Lake Tahoe Monster Museum (see map on page 13, site 22)

Some call it hokey, others say it's mysterious, but the occasional sighting of a long-necked prehistoric creature in Lake Tahoe has spawned a local folklore and a line of cutesy souvenirs. This place— created by local entrepreneur Bob McCormick, who trademarked the name "Tessie"—is a souvenir store with a room in the back devoted to news clippings of Tessie sightings as well as reports on other unusual phenomena. The kids will probably love it, especially when they see the green stuffed monster toys and T-shirts.

Hours: 10 A.M.–6 P.M. daily, June–September.
Admission: Free.
Contact: 8612 N. Lake Blvd., Kings Beach, CA 96143; 530/546-8774.

INCLINE VILLAGE/CRYSTAL BAY

Stateline Fire Lookout
(see map on page 13, site 23)
Poorly marked and generally overlooked by most visitors, this facility, which straddles the California/Nevada border and has long figured in a boundary dispute between the two states, is without a doubt the best high-elevation vantage point on the North Shore. At 7,017 feet, it offers spectacular vistas of Crystal Bay and Brockway Beaches, as well as the entire Tahoe basin and its watershed. There's an excellent self-guided interpretive trail with detailed signposts explaining the human and natural history of the area, as

well as several strategically placed picnic tables. One drawback is that bothersome clouds of gnats and midges occasionally descend upon the area along the paved walkways.

If you plan to reach the lookout, don't expect to find signs. At Crystal Bay in Nevada, turn up Reservoir Road between the Tahoe Biltmore Lodge and Casino and the old Tahoe Mariner Casino, turn right at the firehouse, and continue up the hill until you reach a point where a steeper U.S. Forest Service road doubles back to the left above you. Follow this road for one-quarter mile, beyond the green metal gate, to the parking lot. If the gate is closed, park and walk the distance.
Admission: Free.
Contact: Lake Tahoe Basin Management Unit; 530/573-2600.

Cal-Neva Resort
(see map on page 13, site 24)
Once owned by singer Frank Sinatra, this historic casino straddles the California/Nevada border on the North Shore of Tahoe. The Indian Room on the California side houses an excellent Washoe Indian historical display.

© KEN CASTLE

view of Incline Village homes

Contact: Cal-Neva Resort, 2 Stateline Rd./P.O. Box 368, Crystal Bay, NV 89402; 775/832-4000 or 800/CAL-NEVA (800/225-6382).

Mt. Rose (see map on page 13, site 25)

Drive up Highway 431, also known as Mt. Rose Highway, from Incline Village to find wonderful vistas of Lake Tahoe. Designated turnouts on this sometimes winding road provide ample viewing and photography opportunities. At Mt. Rose Ski Area (elevation 8,933 feet) there's a hiking trail to the summit, which reaches 10,776 feet and requires a strenuous 12-mile round-trip trek. **Contact:** Toiyabe National Forest, Carson Ranger District; 775/882-2766.

Ponderosa Ranch
(see map on page 13, site 26)

Anyone who grew up watching *Bonanza,* the most popular Western series in television history, will enjoy a nostalgic visit to the Cartwright Ranch to commune with the ghosts of Ben, Hoss, Adam, and Little Joe. This open-air museum and theme park offers guided tours of the original ranch house, set where the 1960s series and two recent made-for-television movies were filmed.

Situated on a hill above Incline Village, the ranch features a complete Western town comprised of the Silver Dollar Saloon, the Ponderosa Museum, several stores, and an extensive collection of authentic wagons and automobiles. You won't see live horses or cattle, but there are free pony rides for the kids and a handful of animals at a petting zoo. The morning haywagon breakfast ride (the wagons are pulled by a tractor) offers a meal of flapjacks and bacon on a hill overlooking Lake Tahoe. There's no gourmet restaurant at the ranch, but you can order a Hossburger in Hop Sing's Kitchen. An authentic 19th-century church is popular for weddings, and both the saloon and the barbecue area can be booked for large groups. Ponderosa Ranch isn't exactly Knott's Berry Farm in scope or activities, but you never know where or when a gunfight will break out. On Highway 28 in Incline Village. **Hours:** Daily 9:30 A.M.–6 P.M. May–October.

rocky shoreline near Incline Village

© KEN CASTLE

Admission: Adults, $11.50; children 5–11, $6.50; tots four and under, free.
Contact: Ponderosa Ranch, 100 Ponderosa Rd., Incline Village, NV 89451; 775/831-0691; website: www.ponderosaranch.com.

Memorial Point
(see map on page 13, site 27)

This vista point and interpretive center offers a good panorama of Lake Tahoe, along with displays of natural and human history. It is on a promontory on Highway 28, 1.5 miles south of Incline Village. Facilities here include a parking lot for 20 cars, restrooms, observation platforms and trails that descend to the lakeshore. Don't bring your bathing suit, because there is no beach. **Contact:** Lake Tahoe-Nevada State Park; 775/831-0494.

Lake Tahoe-Nevada State Park
(see map on page 13, site 28)

The largest park in the Tahoe basin encompasses five management areas along the East Shore, stretching from Cave Rock on U.S. 50 near Zephyr Cove to Sand Harbor on Highway 28 near Incline Village. The heaviest use is at Sand Harbor and Spooner Lake. Spooner has become popular with hikers, anglers (catch-and-release fishing only), picnickers, mountain bikers, and cross-country skiers. In summer, several trails originate here, including side routes to the Tahoe Rim Trail, a trail around the lake; the North Canyon Road to Marlette Lake; and the famous Flume Trail, with a breathtaking single-track cycling path notched into the cliffs above Lake Tahoe. The Marlette/Hobart Backcountry Areas, which are accessible at Spooner Summit on U.S. 50, contain 13,000 acres of forest, including three primitive hike-in campsites with fire pits and pit toilets.

Of the other sections in the park, Cave Rock—seven miles north of Stateline—offers one of Tahoe's most dependable public boat-launching ramps (accessible even during drought years when the lake level is low), a small beach with a fine view, a comfort station, and six picnic tables. Once a sacred place for Washoe Indians who used the waters as a burial ground, the rock is three miles south of Glenbrook. U.S. 50 follows a tunnel through this huge formation, the neck of an ancient volcano. Farther up the road on Highway 28, Memorial Point (one mile north of Sand Harbor) is a paved parking area with a scenic vista and trails to a rocky shore. Hidden Beach, two miles north of Sand Harbor, has limited parking, but it's a great spot for sunbathing, swimming, and boating.

Admission: At Spooner, parking is $5 per car, and there is a fee of $2 per bike for more than four bikes on a vehicle. At Cave Rock, fees are $5 per car, $10 for boat-launching (with a car), and $2 for a 15-minute "photo stop." There is no fee for parking at Memorial Point and Hidden Beach.

Contact: Lake Tahoe-Nevada State Park; 775/831-0494; Cave Rock; 775/588-7975.

Sand Harbor (see map on page 13, site 29)

With its crystalline beauty and polished circular rock formations, this mile of white-sand beaches, Jeffrey pines, and protected coves is a real stand-out. Set in 14,000-acre Lake Tahoe-Nevada State Park (which also includes Spooner Lake and the famous Flume Trail for mountain bikes), Sand Harbor is arguably the most picturesque piece of public real estate on the lake. Fine white sand and gently sloping contours create vivid turquoise hues in the shallows, giving the area a distinctly South Pacific flavor, although the water is quite cold. Photographers, sunbathers, and boaters frequent the rocky shoreline both north and south of here. In August, Sand Harbor is the site of an annual Shakespeare festival. Recently, Incline Village patrons of the festival, after a years-long fundraising campaign, completed a permanent outdoor stage with state-of-the-art sound and light systems and dressing rooms, along with a new food concession building. Also at the park are a boat-launching area, picnic grounds, paved walkways, restrooms and a snack bar. Because of Sand Harbor's popularity, the small parking lot is often filled between 11 A.M. and 3 P.M. on weekends.

Admission: $6 per car for parking and $12 for boat launching in summer. Off-season (October 1–April 30) parking rate is $3.

Contact: Lake Tahoe-Nevada State Park; 775/831-0494; website information at: www.state.nv.us/stparks.

Thunderbird Lodge (George Whittell Estate)
(see map on page 13, site 30)

Listed on the National Register of Historic Places, this massive, 16,500-square-foot stone mansion sits on the shoreline of a beautiful cove just south of Sand Harbor, on the Nevada side of Lake Tahoe. It is the nearest thing that Tahoe has to William Randolph Hearst's quirky and extravagant San Simeon castle in Southern California, though it is on a much smaller scale. The Thunderbird was built by George Whittell, an eccentric multimillionaire from San Francisco, between 1938 and 1941. It is a medieval-style, three-story French château that has 140 acres of prime lake frontage and more than a mile of shoreline. Intensely private, Whittell had peculiar tastes and, apparently, a siege mentality. He kept wild animals such as lions, tigers and a baby elephant on the property, and he installed an extensive security system to discourage curiosity-seekers. He also dug a 600-foot-long secret tunnel, some 30 feet underground, to connect a cavernous boathouse to the main building. Other lavish amenities include a manmade three-story waterfall, a lighthouse, several guest chalets and additional stone structures.

Whittell died in 1969, and the estate was acquired by equally eccentric mutual fund tycoon Jack Dreyfuss, who sold it for $50 million to the Del Webb Corporation in 1996. After more than three years of intricate negotiations involving the U.S. Forest Service, the University of Nevada at Reno and Del Webb, the property was conveyed to the government in 1999 as part of the most expensive land swap in Forest Service history. In exchange for 3,300 acres near Las Vegas (valued at $40 million), the agency got 134 acres of the estate. A nonprofit organization called the Thunderbird Lodge Preservation Society got the mansion and the six acres that it sits on, and has been upgrading the furnishings and creating interpretive displays. Regular tours were started in 2002, with reservations required and available through the Incline Village Crystal Bay Visitors and Convention Bureau. Docent-led tours, restricted to 15 people at one time, last for an hour. Visitors will see most sections of the estate, including the maids' quarters, old kitchen, the infamous Card House (where major carousing occurred), the underground tunnel (with its lion cage), and the Boat House. During some months, the famous *Thunderbird* yacht that was built for Whittell in 1940 may be berthed in the Boat House. The one-of-a-kind yacht, a John Hacker wooden boat with dual aircraft engines, is 55 feet long. Apart from public tours, the lodge also is available for special functions such as weddings and corporate meetings. These are enhanced by the Lighthouse Room, a 2,400-square-foot multipurpose room that has a floor-to-ceiling wall of glass overlooking the lake. Here, guests might easily be distracted by the compelling views of rock islets, the boulder-strewn shoreline and the snow-capped Sierra peaks. As this edition went to press, plans were also underway for several lake excursion boats to visit the Lodge, using the small cove and beach to unload passengers.

Hours: 9 A.M.–3 P.M. on Wed. and Thurs. May 1–Oct. 31 for public tours (by reservation only.) Group tours by arrangement are available on a limited basis Nov.–April.

Admission: $22 for adults and teens, $12 for children under 12.

Contact: Thunderbird Lodge Preservation Society; 775/832-8750, or, to book tours, the Visitors Bureau at 800/GO-TAHOE; website for the lodge: www.thunderbirdlodge.org.

SOUTH LAKE TAHOE

D. L. Bliss State Park
(see map on page 13, site 31)

Named after a pioneering lumberman, railroad owner, and banker, 1,237-acre D. L. Bliss State Park offers one of Tahoe's most scenic beaches, a spectacular overlook at Rubicon Point, and the amazing Balancing Rock. Bliss is a day hiker's paradise. A short walk along the Rubicon Trail from Calawee Cove Beach will take you to Rubicon Point, from which you can peer more than 100 feet into the clear depths of Lake Tahoe. If you follow the ridgetop trail south and west along Emerald Bay, you'll reach Vikingsholm Castle at adjoining Emerald Bay State Park. The trail continues around the bay and up an embankment to Eagle Point, a distance of about seven miles one-way.

Shorter hikes can be made to an old lighthouse (three-quarters of a mile one way) and to Balancing Rock (half a mile one way). The rock, a phenomenon at Tahoe since the time of the first settlers, weighs 130 tons and rests precariously on a narrow granite pedestal. Eventually, continued erosion around the waist of the rocks will cause the boulder to fall.

D. L. Bliss State Park, nine miles north of South Lake Tahoe on Highway 89, encompasses 3.5 miles of shoreline and boasts spectacular Calawee Cove Beach—a protected cove with a sandy area flanked by boulders and forested bluffs—and Lester Beach, a long, flat white-sand beach. The park also has one of Tahoe's best campgrounds with 168 campsites, 15 picnic sites, and four miles of trails.

Admission: $2 per car. Only 25 parking permits are sold each day, and they are usually gone by 10 A.M.

Contact: D. L. Bliss State Park; 530/525-7277.

Emerald Bay State Park
(see map on page 13, site 32)

This 593-acre state park on the southwest shore of Lake Tahoe contains three major attractions: Emerald Bay, Eagle Falls, and Vikingsholm Castle.

Emerald Bay: This is Tahoe's most-photographed natural wonder, a glacier-carved blue and turquoise bay surrounded by granite peaks, which is spectacular any time of the day or year. The blue-green bay is three miles long and one mile wide, with a narrow entrance from the east. Motorists can find several excellent high vantage points along Highway 89, or take one of a half dozen tour-boat excursions that circumnavigate the bay.

Within Emerald Bay is Fannette Island, the only island in the lake. Rising 150 feet above the water, this rocky island (believed to be a remnant of the glacial action that created the bay) is crowned by a crumbling stone structure called the Tea House. The founder of the sprawling Vikingsholm estate, at the head of Emerald Bay, built this house in 1928. Using a motorboat to reach the island, residents and guests once enjoyed afternoon refreshments at a large oak table in the center of a 16-square-foot room. Today, only the shell of the building, which unfortunately has been vandalized over the years, remains.

The island is available for day-use activities between 6 A.M. and 9 P.M., but camping, picnicking, and pets are prohibited. February 1–June 15, Fannette is closed to protect nesting Canada geese, which number as many as 100 in some years. In 1969, Emerald Bay was designated a National Natural Landmark by the U.S. Department of the Interior. The park includes a campground with 100 sites and a boat camp with 20 sites.

Eagle Falls: Eagle Falls is a series of three successive waterfalls that pour into Emerald Bay. The lower falls are in the state park, while the upper falls are on U.S. Forest Service land across the road. You can hike (very carefully—the rocks are slippery) to the foot of the lower falls

Emerald Bay

or begin at the Eagle Falls Trailhead on the west side of Highway 89. Visitors will find the best view of the other falls, the largest of which is over 75 feet high, from a footbridge that crosses Eagle Creek. A brisk uphill hike to Eagle Lake, a beautiful natural impoundment accessible from a marked trail, takes you a mile from the parking lot. Beyond the lake, the trail enters Desolation Wilderness. On weekends, the lot and most of the roadside spaces fill rapidly, so it's best to go early in the morning or late in the afternoon.

Vikingsholm Castle: Getting to this unique mansion requires a hike down a steep, one-mile paved trail that drops 500 feet in elevation. But it's worth the effort, because visitors will see one of the finest examples of Scandinavian architecture in the Western Hemisphere.

Vikingsholm was built in 1928 and 1929 by Mrs. Lora Josephine Knight, who spared no expense in creating a replica of an eleventh-century Viking castle. The granite foundation and stonework, turrets, and high-pitched roofs—some of them covered by sod—were constructed out of materials found at the lake. An army of 200 workers completed the 38-room mansion in just one summer, using old-fashioned techniques such as hand-hewing huge timbers and forging hinges and latches. Some sections of the home contain no nails, pegs, or spikes. During the construction, Mrs. Knight prowled the cities of Norway, Finland, Sweden, and Denmark for 18th- and 19th-century antique furniture; what she couldn't buy she had duplicated, as precisely as possible, from drawings of museum pieces. Recently, park workers have been doing repairs and upgrades at the building. Tours (offered every 30 minutes in summer) allow visitors to see two ornately carved dragon beams, paintings on ceilings and walls, and six fireplaces of Scandinavian design.

Hours: Daily 10 A.M.–4 P.M. mid-June–Labor Day.

Admission: Adults and teens 16 and over, $1; teens and children 15 and under, free.

Contact: D. L. Bliss State Park; 530/525-9529, or Eagle Point Campground; 530/541-3030 (summer only).

Mt. Tallac (see map on page 13, site 33)

Found west of Fallen Leaf Lake, this is one of Tahoe's dominant mountains, rising to 9,735 feet in elevation. There's a trail to the summit, but it's an arduous all-day hike.

Cascade Lake
(see map on page 13, site 34)

Mostly in private ownership, this lake and adjoining Cascade Falls can be seen from Highway 89 or from a short Forest Service path at the Bayview Trailhead. Naturalist John Muir and author Mark Twain are among the notables who visited this spot, and the lake was a popular film location in the 1930s for movies such as *Lightnin'*, with Will Rogers, and *Rose Marie* with Jeanette MacDonald and Nelson Eddy.

Fallen Leaf Lake
(see map on page 13, site 35)

The second largest alpine lake in the basin was named after a Delaware Indian chief who was a guide for Colonel Jack "Cock-Eye" Johnson during a series of Tahoe-Sierra explorations in the late 1840s and 1850s. At the head of this three-mile-long lake is a lodge and a group of cabins known as the Stanford Camp. Faculty members and graduates of Stanford University have occupied the area since the early 1900s and continue to use it as a summer retreat and conference center. Other than the marina, there is limited public access to the lake, which is surrounded by private homes. One of them was used in the Kevin Costner/Whitney Houston movie *The Bodyguard*. On Fallen Leaf Road off Highway 89, north of Camp Richardson.

Contact: Lake Tahoe Basin Management Unit; 530/573-2600; Fallen Leaf Campground; 530/573-2674.

Glen Alpine Springs Resort
(see map on page 13, site 36)

This is the last remaining historic resort at Lake Tahoe, out of dozens of famous resorts that sprang up between the 1880s and the 1940s. It stands today, largely frozen in time from the 1920s, because it is well off the beaten path and because several of its buildings were made of

LAKE TAHOE'S RESORT LEGACY

"No grander scenery! No better climate! No more beautiful place!" screamed the colorful fold-out brochure.

It's the summer of 1906, and you've been through an exhausting two days of travel from San Francisco to "The Tallac," one of South Lake Tahoe's fabled resorts.

Your journey began in Oakland with an overnight rail trip through the Sierra Nevada to the town of Truckee. The next morning, you transferred to a narrow-gauge train that chugged along the banks of the Truckee River, past beaver dams and wading fishermen. At Tahoe City, the locomotive backed its cars along Tavern Pier, a remarkable railroad trestle extending one-eighth of a mile from shore. You and the other passengers disembarked and quickly boarded the steamer S.S. *Tahoe*, which was waiting in a slip next to the pier.

This luxuriously-appointed vessel, 169 feet long, had a gleaming white hull, brass fittings, and rich mahogany cabins. She was twice the length of most steamships on Tahoe, earning her the nickname of "Queen of the Lake." As soon as the baggage was loaded, the captain fired up her twin steam engines and headed south along the West Shore, cutting through mirror-smooth waters at a furious 18 knots an hour—so fast that men held on to their derbies and ladies clutched their bonnets.

Before you knew it, the S.S. *Tahoe* had arrived at its destination, and you immediately understood why everyone from New York to San Francisco raved about this place. Even a casual observer would have no trouble believing that the Tallac Hotel, in its own right, was on a par with the Waldorf-Astoria and the Palace. Named after a 9,785-foot peak just west of here, the resort was actually a self-contained community, with its largest and most opulent buildings fronting the lake.

Originally built in the mid-1870s by Ephraim "Yank" Clement and operated as Yank's Hotel, it became The Tallac when Virginia City mining mogul Elias "Lucky" Baldwin bought the property in 1881. Over the next 25 years he made the hotel the talk of high society, sparing no effort to bring modern conveniences to the mountains. And he charged the highest lodging tariffs of the day, up to $21 a week for a double room and $1 per day extra for a private bath. More than 250 people could stay at one time.

stone walls and tin roofs, making them impervious to the fires that destroyed so many classic lakefront hotels. Tucked away on mountain slopes west of Camp Richardson, Glen Alpine Springs was reopened to the public for the first time in the summer of 1999, through a joint effort between the U.S. Forest Service and a nonprofit foundation called Historic Preservation of Glen Alpine Springs. There are several notable points about this resort. It was developed in the 1880s around a mineral springs that gushed carbonated water, which still flows today. Nathan Gilmore, an entrepreneur, discovered the springs in 1863 and soon made a fortune bottling the water and selling it to health-conscious San Franciscans. Over the following years, the resort evolved from a few tent cabins to a large hotel complex with fine dining and an attentive staff. In the 1920s, noted architect Bernard Maybeck, who designed the Palace of Fine Arts in San Francisco, added his creative touch to Glen Alpine, resulting in several unique stone buildings. One of these, a former recreation hall, now contains a fledgling museum, which is open during the summer when it is occupied by docents. Among the most dramatic buildings is the restaurant and kitchen, an octagonal structure on a hill. The resort closed for World War II and never reopened, but it has survived nicely through the decades, and many artifacts from its heyday are being collected for the museum. To get here, drive up Fallen Leaf Lake Road, past the marina and general store, to the paved parking lot for the Glen Alpine trailhead of Desolation Wilderness. Put on good boots and hike for one mile on an uneven trail of mostly creek bed cobblestone. Bring insect repellent for the mosquitoes that sometimes inhabit the marshy area around Lilly Lake, as well

"In those days, families might spend two or three months at The Tallac," said Linda Cole, historian for the U.S. Forest Service. One of the biggest draws, she said, was a billiard parlor for women, something that was a novelty in such a male-dominated society. When they weren't busy shooting pool, the blue-blooded ladies would stroll along the promenade three times a day, changing their wardrobe at least that many times to display their latest Parisian and New York plumage. People came to see and be seen and, said Cole, to "get away from the hustle of city life and just do nothing."

Cole is director of the Tallac Historic Site, a 150-acre complex of 28 homes, cabins, and other structures adjoining Camp Richardson on Highway 89, just north of the South Lake Tahoe "Y" intersection with Highway 50. Tallac is one of the lake's most interesting attractions, not only because it preserves important history from the "Era of Opulence" but also because it serves as a vibrant center for local artists and musicians who are members of the Tahoe Tallac Association.

Although nothing is left of the hotel except the foundation of the casino kitchen, there is an excellent museum inside the restored home of "Lucky" Baldwin, where visitors can see photographs and memorabilia from the resort. Occasionally, open house tours are conducted of the nearby Pope Estate, which was built in 1894 and later bought as a summer retreat by the George Pope family of San Francisco.

Under the auspices of the Tahoe Heritage Foundation, volunteers have been meticulously restoring the Pope residence as well as other buildings. Recently, they completed work on the Pope Estate Boathouse, reconstructing an interior—complete with an old wooden vessel—that can be viewed through a window from the outside. Also, they converted a second and larger boathouse into a small performing arts center, known as Valhalla Boathouse Theater. During the annual Great Gatsby Festival in summer, when participants dress up in period costumes and arrive in vintage automobiles, the entire grounds come alive. (Information on events, tours, and museum hours can be obtained by calling 530/541-5227.)

While Tallac Hotel was the largest and the most extravagant resort at South Lake Tahoe, it had company. Clearly, its counterpart on the North Shore was Tahoe Tavern, an impressive, four-story resort that was virtually a self-contained community.

continued on next page

---

as drinking water for your hike. It's a moderately steep uphill walk to the resort, but the buildings are right next to the trail. For access to the museum, it's best to call in advance. Docents are on the premises during the summer, mid-June–mid-September, 10:30 A.M.–3:30 P.M., when hikers can visit a small interpretive center. Tours of the grounds are conducted Saturday and Sunday at 1 P.M., and sometimes on an impromptu basis during the week. museum. 1030 to 330 interpretive center, 1 P.M. sat and Sunday for tours of grounds; museum after one-mile hike; bring lunch and snack.
Hours: Interpretive center open daily 10:30 A.M.–3:30 P.M., mid-June–mid-September. Docents lead tours of the grounds at 1 P.M. on Sat. and Sun., and sometimes on an impromptu basis midweek.
Contact: Historical Preservation of Glen Alpine Springs, 530/573-2405, or Lake Tahoe Historical Society Museum (summer only), 530/541-5458.

Lake Tahoe Visitor Center
(see map on page 13, site 37)
Operated by the U.S. Forest Service, this is the best place for information on recreation in the national forests, including backcountry permits and maps for Desolation Wilderness. Beyond that, the major attraction is the Stream Profile Chamber, an underground cutaway view of Taylor Creek that allows you to see migrating kokanee salmon. The best time to view the kokanee is late summer–early fall. It's on Highway 89 north of Camp Richardson in South Lake Tahoe.
Admission: Free.
Contact: Lake Tahoe Basin Management Unit; 530/573-2600.

LAKE TAHOE'S RESORT LEGACY (cont'd)

Built in 1901, this internationally famous hostelry, with shingled and gabled exteriors, grew over a period of 25 years, reaching its zenith in the 1920s and 1930s. Just south of Tahoe City, on the West Shore, the resort featured manicured lawns and gardens and had access to virtually any outdoor pursuit—from skiing and sleigh rides to golf and fishing.

Among the hotel's notable attractions was its lengthy pier, which doubled as a rail station for trains from Truckee (with a trestle on the wooden platform) and as an embarkation point for lake cruises on elegant motor launches. Talk about convenience! Arriving passengers could leapfrog from one means of transportation to the other.

Sadly, the hotel no longer exists. After a long period of decline and disrepair, what was left of this palatial resort was demolished in the 1960s, making way for a hot new residential concept called—you guessed it—the "condominium."

Resorts flourished elsewhere at Tahoe during the lake's early history as a tourist destination. On the east shore, Glenbrook was a thriving community of no fewer than four hotels, most of them built between the 1860s and the 1880s after a sawmill was established to supply lumber for Virginia City and its booming silver mines. Glenbrook also served as a stagecoach stop on the route between California and Nevada, and it was considered a cool oasis for mining moguls and other high-powered businessmen to escape the summer heat of Carson Valley.

By 1900 both the mining and timber industries were in decline, and Glenbrook became primarily a leisure destination. Three of the hotels were physically merged to become one resort, which operated until 1976. Guests enjoyed a relaxing vacation, plus the bonus of a nine-hole golf course—still in existence today—that was nestled in the trees. Since the resort was part of a 3,300-acre ranch, the proprietors offered horseback riding and occasionally staged rodeos, drawing buckaroos from both states. Other pastimes included fishing on the lake and lazing on a sandy beach.

While the highbrows flocked to Tallac and Glenbrook, vacationers of average means supported a thriving lodge and resort business at the south end of the lake, at what is now Stateline and the city of South Lake Tahoe. Long before high-rise casinos and condominiums appeared on the landscape, there were rustic lodges and motor inns with names such as the Bijou, Lakeside, and Al Tahoe. Today those places are gone, but the names are still used to reference certain districts of the community, and to designate streets, parks, and other landmarks.

Are any of Tahoe's early-20th-century resorts still standing?

Why did Lake Tahoe's early resorts fade from the scene? "The problem was that they were summer hotels and not built to withstand the winters," said Dr. Lyndall Landauer, past president of the Lake Tahoe Historical Society, author of a historical retrospective of Tahoe, and frequent lecturer on the area's history. "Before the ski resort industry developed, no one stayed here in winter. For one thing, Highway 50 wasn't regularly plowed between Twin Bridges and Meyers until 1947. And by the time skiing became a popular activity, most of these old hotels couldn't afford to make the heating and water system upgrades that would allow them to stay in business."

While new resorts have sprung up to fill the year-round demands of today's vacationers, those early lodges that flourished between the Gay '90s and the Roaring '20s gave the lake a colorful legacy and helped establish Tahoe as one of the world's great mountain destinations.

Notes: For information on tours and hours of operation for the Tallac Historic Site and Glen Alpine Resort, visitors can contact the Tallac Museum at 530/541-5227. Also, they can visit the Lake Tahoe Historical Society Museum, 3058 Lake Tahoe Blvd. (Hwy. 50), next to the South Lake Tahoe Chamber of Commerce. Hours of operation vary by season. For information call 530/541-5458. Recommended reading for history buffs include Dr. Landauer's book, *The Mountain Sea, A History of Lake Tahoe* (Flying Cloud Press), and the elaborate twin-volume pictorial work *The Saga of Lake Tahoe,* by E. B. Scott (Sierra-Tahoe Publishing Company). Both are available at Tahoe-area bookstores and museums.

Tallac Historic Site
(see map on page 13, site 38)
Three of Tahoe's grand old homes, one of them an excellent museum celebrating the "Era of Opulence," are at this 150-acre South Lake Tahoe site managed by the U.S. Forest Service. Though it is well off Highway 89 and sequestered in tall pine trees, the site, which is listed on the National Register of Historic Places, has become not only an important historic landmark at the lake but also the focal point of Tahoe's burgeoning arts and music community. As an added bonus, it adjoins some of South Tahoe's finest white-sand beaches.

Tallac was the location of a palatial resort built in 1880 by Elias J. "Lucky" Baldwin, a California entrepreneur who catered to the nouveaux riches from San Francisco, Sacramento, and Virginia City. The resort featured two lavish hotels, a massive casino (boasting 500 electric lights), and several accessory buildings; it accommodated more than 250 well-heeled guests with a spacious ballroom, a string orchestra, croquet, tennis, steamer rides, and strolls along a promenade. Seven years after Baldwin's death in 1909, his daughter Anita, bowing to the influx of automobiles and the construction of other elaborate estates around the lake, dismantled the resort. But three large summer estates and 33 other structures remain, including the following:

Baldwin Estate: This hand-hewn log home, built in 1921, contains the Tallac Museum, which has exhibits on local Washoe Indian culture, the significance of the Baldwin family in California history, photographs of the hotel and casino, and a presentation room for a 15-minute slide show. The site was historically used by Native Americans, who migrated each summer from the Carson Valley to the area stretching from Taylor Creek to Camp Richardson. Admission to the museum is free, and there is a small bookstore inside. The museum is open daily (except Monday) 10 A.M.–4 P.M., mid-June–Labor Day, with a reduced schedule through October 1.

Pope Estate: Celebrating its 100th anniversary in 1994, this estate is dominated by an elegant main house, which is in the process of being restored. It offers a commanding view of Lake Tahoe from its living room windows. The estate, built in 1894, was purchased by the George Pope family of San Francisco in 1923 and became whimsically known as the "Vatican Lodge." As a summer retreat, the home was a great place to entertain the rich and famous, from author John Steinbeck to silent-screen star Rudolph Valentino. Several adjacent cottages contained maids' and workers' quarters, laundry facilities, and children's play areas. Although visitors can stroll through the estate and look inside the cottages, guided tours of the main house—offered on Tuesday, Friday, and Saturday at 1 P.M. and 2:30 P.M.—are by reservation only. A small fee is charged for admission.

Heller Estate: Known as Valhalla, this 1923 estate built by Walter Heller borders Camp Richardson and is the community events center for the historic site. The nonprofit Tahoe Tallac Association holds a variety of jazz, bluegrass, and classical music concerts on the grounds here late June–early September, and there are periodic arts-and-crafts exhibits as well. The small cabins north of the estate house regular summer attractions including a cultural arts store, a photo arts gallery, fiber arts and folk crafts exhibits, a fine art gallery, and a variety of children's workshops. The biggest event is the annual Great Gatsby Festival in mid-August, when association members dress in period costumes, serve gourmet food, and display antique cars.

Valhalla Boathouse Theatre: Recently restored and converted into a waterfront theater, this boathouse—one of six that formerly graced the estate—is open for music concerts and other community functions. It is jointly managed by the U.S. Forest Service and the Tahoe Tallac Association. For program information, contact the Association at 530/542-4166.

Pope Estate Boathouse: Another recent restoration contains an interesting historic display—a 40-foot commercial motor cruiser that was built in 1921 for Walter Scott Hobart. Named Quic-Chadkidn (meaning "Quit your kidding"), this slow but stable vessel towed the famous ferryboat SS *Tahoe* to her scuttling point along the east shore of the lake in 1940. Visitors can peer through windows of the boathouse to see the

SIGHTS AND EVENTS

vessel and various old-fashioned tools and marine equipment.

Hours: Weekends 11 A.M.–3 P.M. Memorial Day–mid-June, and daily 11 A.M.–3 P.M. mid-June–Labor Day.

Admission: Parking is free.

Contact: Tallac Historic Site; 530/541-5227; Lake Tahoe Basin Management Unit; 530/573-2600; website: www.r5.fs.fed.us/ltbmu.

Camp Richardson
(see map on page 13, site 39)

This enclave of buildings, set in heavy forest north of South Lake Tahoe on Highway 89, has been a resort since the early 1920s. The land is owned by the U.S. Forest Service, but the cabins, lodge, and recreation amenities are run by private concessions. Amenities include hiking and biking trails, beaches, boat rentals, kayaking, water-skiing, sailing cruises, a campground, riding stables, cross-country skiing, and the Beacon Restaurant.

Contact: Richardson's Resort; 530/541-1801; website: www.camprichardson.com.

Angora Lakes and Lookout
(see map on page 13, site 40)

An obscure road in South Lake Tahoe leads to a scenic fire lookout and two alpine lakes, one of which has a swimming beach, a rowboat rental concession, and a small overnight lodge. To get here, turn south on Fallen Leaf Road from Highway 89. Drive about two miles, then take a left. Turn right, after the first half mile, onto a dirt road labeled "1214." Continue two miles to Angora Fire Lookout (elevation 7,290 feet) for a breathtaking view. A parking lot and a trail to Angora Lakes Resort are farther up the road. The lot fills up fast on weekends.

Contact: Lake Tahoe Basin Management Unit; 530/573-2600.

Tahoe Keys Resort
(see map on page 13, site 41)

This 750-acre private waterfront community in South Lake Tahoe encompasses 11 miles of inland waterways with access to Lake Tahoe. Before the complex was built, the land was part of the Truckee Marsh, where the Upper Truckee River flows into Lake Tahoe. The Tahoe Keys offer Tahoe's largest inland marina, as well as a plethora of condominiums, palatial waterfront villas, and private homes. There's a restaurant and launch ramp at the marina. It's at the end of Tahoe Keys Boulevard off of U.S. 50 in South Lake Tahoe.

Contact: Tahoe Keys Resort; 530/544-5397.

Lake Tahoe Historical Society Museum (see map on page 13, site 42)

This small museum covers the development of Lake Tahoe, including the Lake Valley Railroad and the famous passenger steamers. Other displays include Native American arrowheads and dolls, a collection of ranch tools, several pairs of old skis, and a 140-year-old pipe organ. A video titled *Lake Tahoe: 1915–1930* features clips of films made in the area. Behind the museum is a tollhouse from 1859 and a log cabin built in the 1930s. The museum is next to the South Lake Tahoe Chamber of Commerce.

Hours: From mid-June to Labor Day, Tues.–Sat., 11 A.M.–5 P.M.; also, Fri. and Sat. in early June and late September, 11 A.M.–4 P.M.

Admission: Adults and teens, $2; children 5–12, $1; free for under 5.

Contact: Lake Tahoe Historical Society Museum, 3058 Lake Tahoe Blvd., South Lake Tahoe, CA; 530/541-5458.

Heavenly Resort Gondola
(see map on page 13, site 43)

How's the view from the top? Just hop on Heavenly's new gondola for a quick lift some 3,000 feet above the lake, where you can fully appreciate the grandeur of Tahoe and its snowcapped mountains. The gondola ascends 2.4 miles in 17 minutes, travelling through forest and over boulder-strewn ridges. The 14,000-square-foot observation platform, a unique structure that encircles a large rock outcropping, is at the midway station, and you must disembark on the way up in order to enjoy the view (there is no unloading station on the downhill side at this writing). The top terminal is somewhat anticlimactic, since it's in a small depression and doesn't have a view of the lake. It does, however, have access to three hiking trails, which vary 1.6–4 miles long and offer picturesque views of the lake. You'll need to wear sturdy hiking boots—not sandals or sneakers—to negotiate these trails, and take plenty of water and sun-screen. At the observation deck, the facilities include a snack bar, restrooms, souvenir kiosk and picnic tables. You can hang out here for the view of Stateline's high-rise casinos and the city of South Lake Tahoe. The best time to arrive is just before sunset, when the light is magical and the paddle-wheel cruiseboats chug back and forth to Emerald Bay. For return visits, the best deal is to buy a day pass, which allows for unlimited use. Between the two new Marriott hotels near Stateline, within walking distance of casinos and other lodging, the gondola is open year-around except for spring and fall maintenance periods, and except during high winds. (Note: As of 2002, the vintage Heavenly tram to Monument Peak, at the California entrance, is no longer open for public sightseeing, only for special events.)

Hours: 10 A.M.–sunset Mon.–Fri., 9 A.M.–sunset Sat. and Sunday.

Admission (gondola): Adults and teens 14 and over, $20; children ages 6–13, $12; children five and under, free. A full-day sightseeing ticket is priced at $25 for adults and $17 for children 6–13.

Contact: Heavenly Resort; 775/586-7000; website: www.skiheavenly.com.

Freel Peak (see map on page 13, site 44)

At 10,881 feet, this is the tallest peak around Lake Tahoe. It is south of Heavenly Ski Resort in the Carson Range and can be seen from many points in the basin.

STATELINE/ZEPHYR COVE

Zephyr Cove (see map on page 13, site 45)

Developed as a resort in the early 1900s, this protected and scenic cove on the east shore of Lake Tahoe in Nevada is owned by the U.S. Forest Service but is operated privately under a special-use permit. The constant beehive of activity here results largely from the berthing of

the *M.S. Dixie II,* a large stern-wheel sightseeing vessel modelled after vintage Mississippi riverboats, and the *Woodwind II,* a 54-foot-long catamaran sailing vessel. Apart from the main beach area, the Forest Service recently acquired land to the north that includes a decaying mansion formerly owned by the Dreyfuss estate. There are plans to allow a private concessionaire to rehabilitate the 11,000-square-foot home, perhaps as a restaurant or conference center. While the estate is not open to the public at this writing, the grounds and the waterfront, including a soft sandy beach, have unrestricted access. You can reach Zephyr North by walking from the main parking area, or by parking off Highway 50 near the fire station and crossing the road (be careful!). Other amenities at Zephyr Cove include a beach, a recently modernized campground, rustic cabins, riding stables, picnic areas, large pier, lodge with restaurant, beachside café and bar, souvenir shop, water-sports rentals and tours, snowmobile tours, and a marina.

Admission: The day-use fee for parking is $6 at the main beach and pier.

Contact: Zephyr Cove Resort; 775/588-6644.

KIRKWOOD/HOPE VALLEY/MARKLEEVILLE

Carson Pass (see map on page 12, site 46)

About 20 miles southwest of South Lake Tahoe, this famous pass on Highway 88 features a plaque commemorating the discovery of Lake Tahoe in 1844 by explorer John C. Frémont, who saw part of the lake when he climbed the top of Red Lake Peak (elevation 10,061 feet). A few years later, scout Kit Carson forged the Mormon-Emigrant Trail (the main east/west route from Utah to California) near this pass. From a marked turnoff here, visitors can see Red Lake, Hope Valley, and the Carson Valley below. There's a U.S. Forest Service visitors center just west of this point.

Grover Hot Springs State Park
(see map on page 12, site 47)

Need to relieve aching muscles or tired feet?

Skiers and hikers have made Grover Hot Springs a favorite retreat for years, but almost everyone enjoys the therapeutic value of this natural mineral springs. At the end of Hot Springs Road off Highway 4/89, about 3.5 miles west of Markleeville and a 45-minute drive from South Lake Tahoe, the park features two concrete pools fed by runoff from six springs.

The water issues from the ground at 148°F but is cooled to 102–104° for the hot pool, while the other pool remains cool. Unlike most mineral springs, there is very little sulphur in the water, and the main ingredient is sodium carbonate. The hot pool is open daily year-round (usually until 9 P.M.) except for the Christmas, New Year's, and Thanksgiving holidays and occasional cleaning days.

Beyond the springs, the 519-acre park offers excellent hiking trails. At 5,900 feet, the meadows of Hot Springs Valley are surrounded by mountains rising abruptly on three sides. Hawkins Peak, at 10,023 feet, is three miles northwest of the valley, and Markleeville Peak, 9,417 feet, is four miles southwest. Hikers can take the Burnside Trail to Burnside Lake, which rises more than 2,000 feet in less than four miles, or make a short walk to a small waterfall. One of the Sierra's finest campgrounds, with 76 sites, is a quarter mile from the springs, and there are 25 picnic sites nearby.

Admission: Fees for the pools are $2 for adults and $1 for youths and children 17 and under. Parking (for hikers) is $2 per car year-around, except for the hot springs, where parking is free.

Contact: Grover Hot Springs State Park; 530/694-2248 (office) or 530/694-2249 (mineral pool).

Alpine County Museum
(see map on page 12, site 48)
South of Lake Tahoe in Markleeville, this complex, which is operated by the Historical Society of Alpine County, includes a one-room schoolhouse built in 1882 and an old log jail from the mid-1800s. The interior of the school, restored in 1968, is adorned with original artwork by former students. The jail is believed to be the only one of its kind, with two hand-riveted iron cells, heavy iron-bar doors, vertical log walls, and a log foundation. Farming, mining, and lumbering tools and artifacts are presently housed in the jail. Nearby, a museum contains exhibits that explore the county's history, including an old country store and a blacksmith shop, Washoe basketry, toys and dolls, rocks and gems, old bottles, and a collection of scenic paintings by local artist Walt Monroe.

Hours: Open Thurs.–Mon. 11 A.M.–4 P.M. end of May–October.

Admission: $2 donation per person.

Contact: Alpine County Historical Complex, P.O. Box 517, Markleeville, CA 96120; 530/694-2317; website: www.alpinecounty.com.

FEATHER RIVER COUNTRY/LAKES BASIN
Plumas Eureka State Park
(see map on page 12, site 49)
When a group of nine miners discovered gold on the east side of Eureka Peak in 1851 ("Eureka! I've found it!"), they touched off a massive development that led to some 62 miles of shafts being dug in this forested region an hour's drive north of Truckee. Before the boom ended in 1943, several mining companies had extracted $25 million worth of gold. They used three water- and steam-powered stamp mills. The most famous of these mills, called the Mohawk, had 60 stamps; each stamp could crush 2.5 tons of ore each day. The largest operators were the Sierra Buttes Mining Company, a British firm, and the Jamison Mine. Around this extensive mining district, the towns of Jamison City, Johnsville, and Eureka Mills sprang up. Today, most of this once-rich mining empire is contained within the 2,000-acre state park, which adjoins the golfing mecca of Graeagle to the east and the fabulous Lakes Basin area to the south.

The focal point of the park is the museum, which was originally constructed as a miner's bunkhouse. Here, displays chart the history of the mines and showcase the diverse flora and fauna of the area. Outside and across the street stands the

Mohawk Stamp Mill, a stable, a mine office, and a blacksmith shop, all of which are maintained in a "near-restored" condition. In the summer months, tours of the buildings and blacksmithing demonstrations are conducted by park staff and docents, who re-create the era once a month by dressing up in 1890s clothing. Historians believe that the gravity-powered tramway that brought ore down from the mountain was used for recreation in winter, and thus may have been California's first ski lift. Today, the small Plumas Eureka Ski Bowl operates on the site.

The mining complex is reason enough to visit Plumas Eureka State Park, but visitors can also take advantage of a wealth of recreation, including a well-designed forested campground offering 67 sites (with free hot showers); five picnic sites; 8.6 miles of hiking trails; two lakes; and 3.5 miles of fishing along Jamison Creek. Moreover, hikers and backpackers can use the park as a staging area for extended trips into the Lakes Basin or climb to the 7,447-foot summit of Eureka Peak, an elevation gain of 1,500 feet. The park is off Highway 89, five miles west of Graeagle on County Road A-14 to Johnsville.

Admission: $2 per car for day use; a donation is requested for the museum.

Contact: Plumas Eureka State Park; 530/836-2380.

Portola Railroad Museum
(see map on page 12, site 50)
Anyone who has ever loved trains, even model trains, will feel more than a twinge of excitement when visiting this 35-acre open-air museum 45 minutes north of Truckee in the quaint hamlet of Portola. The opportunity to operate a diesel locomotive for one hour, on a 2.5-mile loop track with your own private instructor, is the big draw. If you can't play engineer (you'll need to schedule that kind of thing well in advance), you and the kids can climb on and through many of the 36 locomotives and 95 freight and passenger cars on the grounds and in the 220-foot shop building. Some of the largest and rarest diesel engines in the world are on display, and several are undergoing restoration. While this place is consid-

erably less developed (and less formal) than other rail museums, it has a vibrancy that is simply compelling. To reach the museum, drive north of Truckee on Highway 89 to the Sattley turnoff. Follow this road to Highway 70, then turn west toward Portola.

Hours: Daily 10 A.M.–5 P.M. (March–Oct.); train rides on weekends 11 A.M.–4 P.M. (late May–early Sept.), weather permitting).

Admission: Suggested donation of $5 per person. Operating a diesel locomotive for one hour with an instructor costs $195, and operating vintage diesel switchers or road switchers costs $95.

Contact: Feather River Rail Society, P.O. Box 608, Portola, CA 96122; 530/832-4532 (reservations and information for Run the Locomotive Program) or 530/832-4131 (museum), website: www.wplives.com.

Kentucky Mine Museum
(see map on page 12, site 51)
Northwest of Truckee on Highway 49, this museum offers displays of mining history in Sierra County and has an outdoor amphitheater that hosts occasional concerts during the summer. Exhibits trace the history of the Kentucky Consolidated Gold Mining Company, formed in 1853, and also showcase the lives of loggers, Native Americans, mill workers and miners. The mine had a 10-stamp mill in 1888 and was operated until 1953, although hobbyists used it almost exclusively in later years. One mile east of Sierra City on Highway 49 in Sierra County Park.

Hours: Open Wed.–Sun. 10 A.M.–5 P.M. end of May–early September. Tours are held at 11 A.M. and 2 P.M.

Admission: Museum: suggested donation of $1 per person. Tours: $5, including museum admission. For a program of performances, contact the phone numbers below or check out the website.

Contact: Sierra County Historical Society; 530/862-1310 or the Sierra County Chamber of Commerce 800/200-4949; website: www.sierracounty.org.

Reno/Carson Valley

Lake Tahoe has much to offer in the way of natural beauty and high-alpine attractions. But the cities and towns on the eastern slopes of the Sierra Nevada are destinations in their own right, boasting historical sites, high-desert scenery, silver mines, hot springs, and big-city comforts. From the growing nest of high-rise casino/hotels in Reno to the Old West town of Virginia City, plenty of attractions await those who venture forth from the Lake Tahoe area on day trips or for extended stays. Sites are keyed to the Reno Points of Interest map.

Pyramid Lake
(see map on page 39, site 1)
There is beauty in desolation, and this weird, shimmering lake in the middle of the desert 32 miles north of Sparks has a compelling allure that is uniquely its own. Named after the pointed tufa mounds on the east shore, Pyramid Lake extends for some 25 miles within the Pyramid Lake Paiute Indian Reservation. It is the last remnant of a prehistoric inland sea called Lake Lahontan, which once covered much of Nevada and Utah. Cradled among burnished pink and gold mountains, the lake has many moods, all of them interesting. Afternoons can bring tempestuous winds and dancing dust devils, yet mornings and evenings are often hauntingly still. From various high vantage points, the lake has an eerie, photogenic quality, more like a matte painting than reality.

Pyramid has been popular with anglers since the turn of the century. Despite its relatively shallow and alkaline depths (300 feet), it is home to the giant Lahontan cutthroat trout; the world record of this species, a 41-pounder, was caught here by a Paiute Indian in 1925. There's a new marina to service boaters, as well as charter boats and fishing guides (a reservation fishing license is required). The lake has two fish hatcheries, Numana and David Dunn, both operated by the tribe and part of a program to restore the endangered Lahontan fish population. The hatch-

eries, with net-covered holding pens, are open to the public Monday–Friday 9 A.M.–3 P.M.

Another facility, the Marble Bluff Dam Pyramid Lake Fishway, operated by the U.S. Fish and Wildlife Service, is one mile north of tribal council headquarters in Nixon on State Route 447. It has a fishway designed to allow the migration of the endangered cui-ui sucker and the threatened Lahontan trout from the lake to spawning areas in the Truckee River. Visitors can observe fish runs during March, April, and May, as well as the sorting of the cui-ui and trout. The fishway and fish-handling building are open Monday–Friday, and there is no admission charge for tours but you must make reservations. For information, call 775/265-2425 or 775/574-0187.

Pyramid also encompasses the Anaho Island National Wildlife Refuge, home to one of the largest white pelican nesting colonies in North America as well as cormorant, great blue heron, and seagull nesting colonies. Although it is closed to public access, the island can be viewed from boats. For casual visitors, the lake has sandy beaches and wading areas, some with hot springs bubbling up under the cool water.

The lake is 32 miles north of Sparks on Highway 445. The road passes a historical marker that describes a Paiute Indian ambush of a white volunteer army led by Major William Ormsby in 1860. The conflict began after Native Americans raided a trading post 25 miles east of Carson City, reportedly in retaliation for the kidnapping and rape of two young Indian women. In an ill-advised show of bravado, Ormsby led a ragtag army of 105 settlers into a canyon along the Truckee River, where they were attacked and slaughtered. A few weeks later, the Presidio in San Francisco sent a force of Army regulars, who defeated the Indians after a three-hour battle. In 1879, President Ulysses S. Grant set aside 475,000 acres for the reservation.

Contact: Pyramid Lake Tribal Council, P.O. Box 256, Nixon, NV 89424; 775/476-1155 (ranger station) or 775/574-1000 (tribal offices).

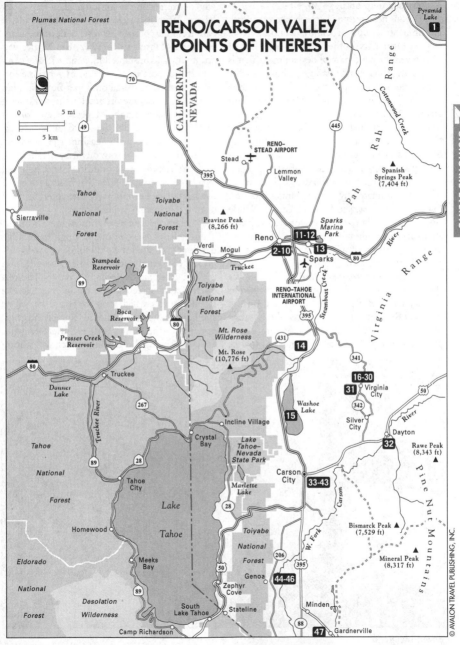

RENO/CARSON VALLEY POINTS OF INTEREST

SIGHTS AND EVENTS

© AVALON TRAVEL PUBLISHING, INC.

Reno (see map on page 39, site 2)

The famous neon arch that stretches across North Virginia Street and proclaims Reno as "The Biggest Little City in the World" seems out of date, given the rapid pace of development that is revitalizing the central casino and business district. Reno is no longer a little city, but a fledgling metropolis. Motorists approaching Reno from any direction see a growing skyline of high-rise hotels, distinguished by two giant white globes that house a theater in the National Bowling Stadium and a light-and-sound show in the Silver Legacy Resort Casino. Hotels are springing up and sprucing up on both sides of The Strip, which is dominated by casino giants Eldorado, Harrah's, the Legacy and Circus Circus. While side streets still have seedy liquor stores, pawn shops and aging motels, these are gradually disappearing as part of a massive, city-sponsored redevelopment effort.

Among the last vestiges of the "old" Reno was the classy Mapes Hotel, which was demolished in January 2000. Built in 1947 and listed on the National Register of Historic Places, the 12-story Mapes once drew Frank Sinatra, Sammy Davis Jr., Dean Martin, Liberace and other luminaries who performed in the stunning, glass-walled Sky Room. With its brick and terracotta facade, it was the last art deco-style hotel built in the United States. Closed since 1982, the Mapes was crumbling and unstable and, despite strong community support to save it, no buyer came forward. It was dynamited on Super Bowl Sunday, and the first casino resort hotel in the world went out with a bang. But the Mapes was not alone. It joined the less notable Harolds Club and Nevada Club—small, grimy casinos that were acquired and promptly torn down by neighboring Harrah's Reno. Those buildings were replaced by a large, landscaped plaza that hosts a variety of live music, food events and other entertainment during the warm weather months.

Much of the new development focuses on the Truckee River, which flows through town. One developer acquired the old Holiday Hotel Casino and converted it into an upscale hotel/casino and spa called Siena. Recently, Century Theaters opened a 12-screen movie complex called the Regal Theaters, which is on Sierra and 1st Streets and borders the river. Other redevelopment components in the same block include a two-tier concourse along the Truckee, which will feature

downtown Reno

outdoor dining and specialty stores. And the city of Reno continues to study how it can develop other entertainment attractions such as historical museums, an aquarium, boutiques, and new restaurants in the downtown area.

With new housing subdivisions, shopping malls and golf courses springing up around the city's perimeter, this growth is certainly a stimulus for revitalizing the central business district. It will take more time to complete the transition, but in a few short years Reno has made giant strides in polishing up its image. The 1995 opening of the Silver Legacy, which created a giant, interconnected gaming, shopping and dining complex with the adjoining Eldorado and Circus Circus hotels, was perhaps the biggest step in that direction. Now The Strip has become a mecca for families and upscale convention-goers, all attracted to Reno's reasonable hotel prices, fine restaurants and scenic mountain vistas. Is Reno about to hit the big-time as a major travel destination? You can bet on it.

Contact: Reno-Sparks Convention and Visitors Authority, P.O. Box 837, Reno, NV 89504-0837; 800/FOR-RENO (800/367-7366); website www.playreno.com.

SIGHTS AND EVENTS

Fleischmann Planetarium
(see map on page 39, site 3)

Also known as "the Space Place," the University of Nevada planetarium features rotating exhibits and presentations that run the gamut from dinosaurs to black holes and planetary volcanoes to international hot air balloon expeditions. There's an admission-free astronomy museum, and every Friday night the public is given free access to the observatory, where they can peer into a 12-inch telescope. The newly remodeled theater dome has six-channel digital sound and features star shows and laser displays. Fleischmann Planetarium is 1.5 miles north of the Reno Arch on the University of Nevada campus.

Hours: Open Fri. and Sat. 9:30 A.M.–10 P.M., Sun.–Thurs. 9 A.M.–8:30 P.M. Closed on holidays.

Admission: Ages 13 to 59, $7; children 12 and under and seniors over 60, $5. Children under age six are not admitted in the theater for evening shows.

Contact: Fleischmann Planetarium, 1650 N. Virginia St. in Reno; 775/784-4811 (for a recording of show times), 775/784-4812 (reservations).

Liberty Belle Slot Machine Collection
(see map on page 39, site 4)

Do slot machines and prime rib go together? They do at the Liberty Belle Saloon and Restaurant, which is not only a popular dining establishment but a living museum of gaming history. The owner's grandfather, Charles Fey, invented the first slot machine, dubbed the Liberty Bell, in 1898. The forerunner of today's three-reel slot machine, it was followed in 1901 by a five-card draw poker machine and in 1929 by the silver dollar machine. Fey's creations, along with those of others, surround the dining room and bar. If you visit during off-hours, you may have a chance to see the rest of the collection in a room upstairs. Some of the early slots dispensed cigarettes, candy, and other items before plain ol' money became the standard. Marshall Fey, one of Charles' grandsons and co-owner of the restaurant, has authored a definitive history called *Slot Machines,* and autographed copies of this lavish coffee-table book are available at the bar for $30.

Hours: Weekdays 11 A.M.–10 P.M. and weekends 4 P.M.–11 P.M.

Contact: The Liberty Belle Saloon and Restaurant, 4250 S. Virginia St. in Reno; 775/825-1776.

Mackay School of Mines
(see map on page 39, site 5)

Named after John Mackay, a Virginia City mining baron, this exhibit at the University of Nevada features mining paraphernalia, minerals, fossils, and silver from the Mackay household.

Hours: Open Mon.–Fri. 8 A.M.–5 P.M.

Admission: Free.

Contact: Mackay School of Mines, 1650 N. Virginia St. in Reno; 775/784-6987.

National Automobile Museum
(see map on page 39, site 6)

Detroit has nothing on Reno when it comes to celebrating the automobile. Close to the casino district downtown, the National Automobile Museum is not only the city's premier museum attraction, it's also one of the finest car collections in the entire country. Displays of more than 200 classic, vintage, and special interest vehicles are couched in theme "galleries," including four period street scenes that range from the turn of the century to the present.

After starting your tour with a 22-minute, high-tech multimedia theater presentation that features a moving conveyor belt of real cars, you step through a marvelously detailed service station to reach the classic machines of the 1930s and 1940s. Among the highlights of the museum are Elvis Presley's 1973 Cadillac Eldorado, the 1949 Mercury that actor James Dean drove in the movie *Rebel Without a Cause,* Al Jolson's classic 1933 Cadillac V-16, and the 1907 Thomas Flyer, the only car to win an around-the-world race. The Changing Exhibits Gallery might include such treats as a rare 1930 Ruxton—a front-wheel-drive sedan that was one of only 500 cars produced—or a 1939 Bugatti Type 57C, one of a line of famous racing machines.

The museum was built in 1989, primarily to save some of the more than 1,400 cars collected by the late casino mogul Bill Harrah. When

Holiday Inn bought Harrah's casinos, the new owners began dismantling the collection, selling 1,000 pieces before a group of local businessmen stepped in to establish the museum. It houses a café and a gift shop, and guided tours are given on weekends. Most visitors use the Acousti-guide audio tour system, which allows you to tour at your own pace as a narrator describes each exhibit.

Hours: Daily 9:30 A.M.–5:30 P.M. and Sun. 10 A.M.–4 P.M.

Admission: Adults, $7.50; seniors 62 and older, $6.50; children 6–18, $2.50; children five and under, free. Adopt-a-car memberships are available.

Contact: National Automobile Museum, 10 Lake St. in Reno; 775/333-9300.

National Bowling Stadium
(see map on page 39, site 7)

Reno's biggest attraction is no longer gaming or automobiles; it's the world's largest and most technologically advanced bowling center. Opened in February 1995, this massive six-story building in the heart of downtown Reno consumes an entire square block. Its tiered roofline sports a giant silver dome that houses a circular theater showing films on special events and attractions in the Reno and Lake Tahoe areas.

Eighty championship lanes fill a cavernous tournament room with 44-foot-high ceilings (the grand opening featured indoor fireworks!). The video scoring system is 450 feet long, and there's a 16-square-foot video wall that can display instant replays and sponsors' messages between games. Screens over each pair of lanes measure 8 feet high by 11 feet wide and can be joined to create a continuous image from one end of the stadium to the other. The computerized video BowlerVision scoring system also allows for arcade games such as "Strike Bingo" and "Crap Shoot." The center, named "Bowling Center of the Decade" by Bowlers Journal International, was featured in the offbeat 1996 film comedy *Kingpin,* starring Woody Harrelson, Bill Murray, and Randy Quaid.

Built by the Reno-Sparks Convention and Visitors Authority at a cost of $45 million, the bowling center hosts major pro and amateur tournaments, which fill up most of the schedule. Seats are available for 1,200 spectators, media and VIPs. Also inside the stadium is the Lane 81 Pro Shop, which has its own bowling lane so that shoppers can try before they buy. On the fifth floor is a four-story screen theater that has six-channel surround sound and a changing program of documentary features. A recent addition, in late 1999, is Kicks, a diner and dance club that celebrates the ageless rock n' roll of one-time chart-buster Paul Revere and the Raiders. Kicks is open for lunch and dinner, then converts to a dance club with DJ music later in the evening. Completing the amenities at the stadium are staging rooms, lockers, a visitor center, and a three-level parking garage.

Admission: There is usually no fee to watch tournaments; however, some tournaments may charge admission by special arrangement with the stadium.

Contact: National Bowling Stadium, 300 N. Center St. in Reno; 775/334-2600.

Nevada Historical Society Museum
(see map on page 39, site 8)

Nevada's oldest museum and research library has permanent and changing exhibits that vividly chronicle the state's long, rich history, from the early days of Native Americans to the casinos of the 20th century. Next to Fleischmann Planetarium and the University of Nevada, the museum features scenes that celebrate the lives of famous people like Jedediah Smith, the first American explorer to enter what is now Nevada; newspaperman and author Mark Twain; and Bugsy Siegel, the man most credited with developing the gaming industry in Nevada. There's an exhibit of priceless baskets fashioned by the renowned Washoe Indian basket weaver Dat So La Lee. The research library houses books, maps, microfilm documents, and more than 350,000 photographs relating to the history of Nevada and the Great Basin.

Hours: Museum, Mon.–Sat. 10 A.M.–5 P.M. Library, Tues.–Sat. noon–4 P.M. Closed Sun. and holidays.

Admission: $2 for adults, free for youths 17 and under.

Contact: Nevada Historical Society Museum, 1650 N. Virginia St., Reno, NV; 775/688-1190, website: www.clan.lib.nv.us.

Nevada Museum of Art
(see map on page 39, site 9)

Modern art, pop art, photography, and Native American art of the 19th and 20th centuries are featured at this new museum, which houses the E. L. Wiegand Gallery. Well-known traveling exhibitions stop here for six-week stays throughout the year. Permanent exhibits include Native American baskets, sculpture, paintings, drawings, and decorative pieces. Collections by noted artists such as Maynard Dixon, Stuart Davis, Michael Heizer, Wayne Thiebaud, Chris Unterseher, Robert Cole Caples, and others are also owned by the museum. Educational programs and a gift shop are available.

Hours: Noon–6 P.M. daily except Monday.

Admission: Adults, $5; seniors 55 and older and students 13 to 17, $3; children 6–12, $1; and children five and under, free.

Contact: Nevada Museum of Art, 160 W. Liberty St., Reno, NV; 775/329-3333.

The Wilbur D. May Center
(see map on page 39, site 10)

A must-see for any visitor to Reno, this museum makes an especially great destination for families. It combines exhibits on the life of a famous adventurer with an arboretum and botanical garden containing native plants from the Great Basin. Wilbur May was born in 1898 with a malformed leg and later vowed to let no disability hamper his life. He became a successful businessman who founded the May Department Stores, as well as a pilot, a musical composer, an African big-game hunter, the owner of a 2,600-acre ranch, and Reno's most generous philanthropist. The museum gallery reflects his 40 trips around the world and his penchant for collecting, including rare Tang Dynasty pottery, Eskimo scrimshaw, Egyptian scarabs, Greek icons, Italian amulets predating the birth of Christ, and even a shrunken human head from South America.

The 10,000-square-foot museum, designed to resemble May's home, features four large rooms, including a big-game hunting trophy room with numerous African animal species, a ranch room with a collection of Western paraphernalia, and a living room with a television that shows a film on May's career. Another wing of the museum contains the beautiful arboretum, a peaceful place with lush greenery, waterfalls, rock gardens, and native songbirds. Displays are changed quarterly with plants that reflect the seasons, and sometimes include exotic species from around the world. Outdoors is the Great Basin Adventure, designed for children ages 2–12, which features a petting zoo, pony rides, an old-fashioned log flume ride, a mine replica with shaft slides and gold panning, a wetland habitat for nature walks, and a few miscellaneous dinosaur replicas (one-third the actual size). The museum is at Rancho San Rafael Park on the hills north of downtown Reno.

Hours: Museum: Mon.–Sat. 10 A.M.–5 P.M. and Sun. noon–5 P.M. Arboretum and park: daily 8 A.M.–sundown year-round.

Admission: Adults, $4.50, seniors and children ages 4–12, $3.50, and for kids three and under, $2.50. Seasonal exhibit admission prices vary; call for current program. Admission to the arboretum is free, though donations are welcome.

Contact: The Wilbur D. May Center, 1502 Washington St. in Reno; 775/785-5961 or 775/785-4319; website: www.maycenter.com.

Sparks Heritage Foundation Museum
(see map on page 39, site 11)

A short drive from downtown Reno into neighboring Sparks brings you to this museum, which features railroad memorabilia (including a collection of lanterns) and celebrates small-town America at the turn of the century. The collection includes milk separators, family quilts, vintage clothing and toys, photographs, farm implements, various law enforcement patches, and railroad and mining artifacts dating back to the early 1900s, when Sparks was a newborn railroad town.

Hours: Open Tues.–Fri., 11 A.M.–4 P.M.; Sat.–Sun., 1 P.M.–4 P.M.

Admission: Free but donations gladly accepted.
Contact: Sparks Heritage Foundation Museum, Victorian Square, 820 Victorian Ave. in Sparks; 775/355-1144.

Victorian Square
(see map on page 39, site 12)

Sparks' turn-of-the last-century-themed collection of restaurants, shops, and entertainment venues is growing by leaps and bounds, with many new developments and special events. One of the largest is the recent opening of a 14-screen Century Theater complex, with an attractive art deco façade, by the Syufy group. Two major parking complexes, a boutique shopping center, and more restaurants are on the drawing board for this six-square-block area. July–September, the Hometowne Farmer's Market holds forth every Thursday evening with fresh produce, cooking demonstrations, fresh baked breads, and live music. Victorian Square also is a major venue for Hot August Nights, the 1950s-style car extravaganza that takes over the Reno area in early August. The newly enlarged John Ascuaga's Nugget casino/hotel adjoins Victorian Square.
Contact: Sparks Community Chamber of Commerce; 775/358-1976.

Sparks Marina Park
(see map on page 39, site 13)

Created by accident in 1997 when winter flooding from the nearby Truckee River spilled over into an empty gravel pit and rapidly filled it to overflowing, this water-oriented park shows how you can take a negative and turn it into something positive. Operated by the Parks and Recreation Department of the city of Sparks, this 100-acre facility, originally opened in 1999, features a lake that covers 77 surface acres. It also has a two-mile lighted cycling and pedestrian path around the shoreline, two swimming beaches with lifeguards in summer, two sand volleyball courts, numerous picnic tables and gazebos, an acre-sized dog-run area with grass and water access, a large playground, fishing piers and fish-cleaning station, restrooms and showers, large parking lot, scuba-diving facilities (but the lake is quite murky), and bike/boat rental concessions.

The lake is stocked regularly with trophy-sized rainbow and German brown trout, along with black bass, and you can hook them (catch-and-release is encouraged) from shore or from a small boat or canoe. No fuel-powered engines are allowed on the lake, although electric motors are permitted. At this writing, all boats must be hand-launched. Other restrictions include no open fires or charcoal barbecues, although portable gas barbecues are permissible, and no dogs on the beaches. Natural springs recharge the lake with two million to three million gallons of fresh, cold water each day, keeping the deepest areas (approximately 120 feet) brisk with temperatures in the 40s. (To prevent the lake from overflowing, excess water is pumped into the Truckee River, about a half-mile away.) During the warmest days of the summer, however, the shallow areas near the beaches heat to higher than 70°F, quite comfortable for swimming. Amazingly, the lake water is remarkably clean—cleaner, in fact, than some parts of Lake Tahoe, which is one of the purist lakes in the nation. Plans for future amenities include a boathouse and an amphitheater. Right now, the Parks Department offers free Sunday evening concerts in mid-summer. As an attraction for scuba divers, the city in 2001 sunk an old F-4 fighter jet in 50 feet of water. Apart from the public access areas of the lake, a developer from Balboa Island, California, is building a vast residential and retail community on the privately-owned east shore. This complex is expected to offer a casino, waterfront dining, and shopping. Upscale homes and condominiums are being built on the water's edge and along a newly-dug canal that meanders through the residential area. To reach the city park, head east from downtown Reno on I-80 to McCarran Boulevard, then north on McCarran, then east (right) on either Nichols or Lincoln.
Hours: 6 A.M.–10 P.M. daily, year-around. Lifeguard hours for swimming beaches are 10 A.M.–6 P.M. daily in summer and on weekends in May and September. No swimming is allowed during winter and early spring.
Admission: No fee for day use. However, groups can rent gazebo areas at rates ranging from $30 for up to 50 people to $120 for over 150.

Contact: City of Sparks Parks and Recreation Department, P.O. Box 857, Sparks, NV 89432; 775/353-2376.

Bowers Mansion
(see map on page 39, site 14)
Built in 1864 by one of the early Comstock mining entrepreneurs, this historic two-story granite stone mansion is in Washoe County, 20 miles south of Reno and 10 miles north of Carson City. The building is a fine example of the extravagance that Sandy and Eilley Bowers lavished on their home from the riches they extracted from Virginia City mines. After her husband died at a young age and his fortune eventually dwindled, Eilley Bowers moved back to Virginia City and lived out the remainder of her life as a fortune-teller. Over the years, the home had several owners and, unfortunately, much of the original furniture was sold. But the county has faithfully restored the building and found suitable period pieces as replacements.

Guided tours are offered daily from the visitors center (behind the mansion) from Memorial Day to Labor Day and on weekends only during spring and fall. The park next door includes amenities such as swimming pools, a snack bar, a volleyball court, a children's playground, horseshoe pits, and picnic and barbecue facilities.

Hours: Mansion, daily 11 A.M.–4:30 P.M. (closed 1 P.M.–1:30 P.M.) Memorial Day–Labor Day and on weekends only May 1–Memorial Day weekend and Labor Day–Oct., with 11 half-hour tours offered each day; closed Nov.–April. Park, daily 8 A.M.–9 P.M. in summer and 8 A.M.–5 P.M. in winter.

Admission: Adults, $4; seniors and children 16 and under, $3.

Contact: Bowers Mansion Regional Park, 4005 U.S. 395 in the Washoe Valley; 775/849-0201 or 775/849-1825 (ranger's office).

> *Virginia City is often called "the liveliest ghost town in the West." The National Historic Landmark, in a desolate canyon southeast of Reno, was the birthplace of the Comstock silver bonanza of 1859, which fueled the economies of San Francisco, northern Nevada, Lake Tahoe, and even the Union during the Civil War.*

Washoe Lake State Park
(see map on page 39, site 15)
This large park between Reno and Carson City offers a variety of recreation, including camping, boating, fishing, hiking, mountain biking, and horseback riding trails. The main entrance is on East Lake Boulevard, three miles east of U.S. 395.

Admission: $3 per car for day use, $5 for boat launching, $11 for camping and $13 for camping/boat launching combination.

Contact: Washoe Lake State Park; 775/687-4319.

Virginia City
(see map on page 39, site 16)
Often called "the liveliest ghost town in the West," this National Historic Landmark in a desolate canyon southeast of Reno was the birthplace of the Comstock silver bonanza of 1859, which fueled the economies of San Francisco, northern Nevada, Lake Tahoe, and even the Union during the Civil War. Once occupied by 30,000 people, Virginia City yielded over $400 million worth of silver and gold ore before a series of fires and the demise of the mines reduced it to a hamlet of a few hundred.

Many historic buildings, including the ornate mansions of the silver barons and several unique museums, are interspersed with saloons, jewelry stores, T-shirt and souvenir shops, old-fashioned casinos, and food concessions. One of the newest attractions is Piper's Opera House, which was recently reopened and now offers plays and musical performances throughout the year. There's an operating vintage steam train, called the Virginia and Truckee Railroad, that takes passengers on a short run through the hills. And there's an underground mine tour that allows visitors to get a taste of what the miners experienced. Perhaps the best chronicle of life here is the windswept cemetery, where the epitaphs tell of lives filled with hardship and heartbreak. If you want to get a good overview of the history and layout of the town, consider hopping on the Virginia City Trolley for a 2.5-mile, 20-minute narrated tour, at nominal cost. You can make arrangements through Virginia City Tours at 775/786-0866. Also, you can tour on a horse-drawn carriage with a surrey, through Happy Hoofers Carriage Tours. Prices $15 per adult or $45 for three adults. Call 775/847-0975 or 775/847-0311.

The town's biggest and most popular event of the year is the annual Virginia City International Camel Races in mid-September. Virginia City is 23 miles (35 minutes) from downtown Reno, via U.S. 395 south to Highway 341.

Contact: Virginia City Chamber of Commerce; 775/847-0311 (information center in a railroad car downtown); the Virginia City Convention and Tourism Authority; 775/847-7500; website: www.virginiacity-nv.org; or the Reno-Sparks Convention and Visitors Authority; 800/367-7366; website: www.playreno.com.

The Castle Mansion
(see map on page 39, site 17)
Once referred to as "the house of silver door-knobs," this grand, château-style Victorian mansion was built in 1868 by Robert Graves, a superintendent of the Empire Mine. The architectural style is based on a castle in Normandy. Sitting majestically on a hill high above the business district of Virginia City, the magnificent white home features richly appointed rooms, crystal chandeliers, Carrara marble fireplaces, steel engravings dating from 1852, and Italian hanging stairways. What's unusual is that unlike other historic homes, this one has all of its original furnishings. One of the best tours at Virginia City.

Hours: Daily 11 A.M.–5 P.M. Memorial Day–early October.

Admission: Adults, $5; children 12 to 18, $4; free for 11 and under.

Contact: The Castle, 70 S. B St. in Virginia City; 775/847-0275.

Chollar Mine
(see map on page 39, site 18)
This facility offers a half-hour walking tour of a real underground mine that produced more than $18 million in gold ore. You can try your hand at gold panning during the summer; it's taught by an experienced panner, with gold guaranteed.

downtown Virginia City

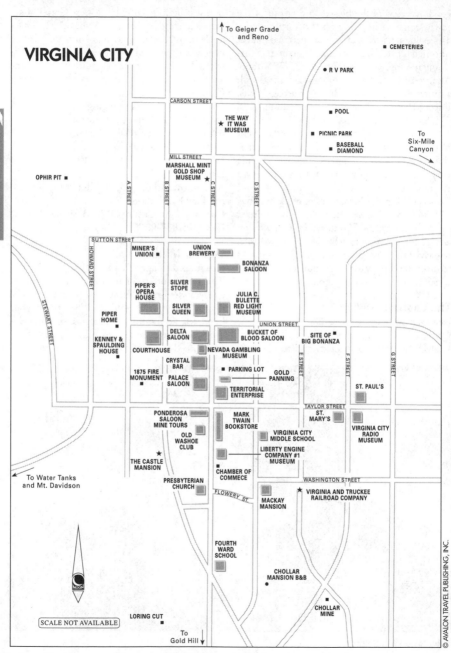

VIRGINIA CITY

To Geiger Grade
and Reno

CEMETERIES

R V PARK

CARSON STREET

THE WAY
★ IT WAS
MUSEUM

POOL

PICNIC PARK

BASEBALL
DIAMOND

To
Six-Mile
Canyon

MILL STREET

MARSHALL MINT
GOLD SHOP ★
MUSEUM

OPHIR PIT ■

A STREET

B STREET

C STREET

D STREET

SUTTON STREET

HOWARD STREET

MINER'S
UNION ■

UNION
BREWERY

BONANZA
SALOON

PIPER'S
OPERA
HOUSE

SILVER
STOPE

SILVER
QUEEN

JULIA C.
BULETTE
RED LIGHT
MUSEUM

STEWART STREET

PIPER
HOME ■

KENNEY &
SPAULDING
HOUSE ■

DELTA
SALOON

BUCKET OF
BLOOD SALOON

UNION STREET

SITE OF ■
BIG BONANZA

E STREET

F STREET

G STREET

COURTHOUSE

CRYSTAL
BAR

NEVADA GAMBLING
MUSEUM

1875 FIRE
MONUMENT ■

PALACE
SALOON

■ PARKING LOT

GOLD
PANNING

TERRITORIAL
ENTERPRISE

ST. PAUL'S

PONDEROSA
SALOON
MINE TOURS

OLD
WASHOE
CLUB

MARK
TWAIN
BOOKSTORE

TAYLOR STREET
ST.
MARY'S

VIRGINIA CITY
RADIO
MUSEUM

★
THE CASTLE
MANSION

VIRGINIA CITY
MIDDLE SCHOOL

LIBERTY ENGINE
COMPANY #1
MUSEUM

To Water Tanks
and Mt. Davidson

PRESBYTERIAN
CHURCH

CHAMBER OF
COMMECE

FLOWERY ST.

WASHINGTON STREET

★ VIRGINIA AND TRUCKEE
RAILROAD COMPANY

MACKAY
MANSION

FOURTH
WARD
SCHOOL

CHOLLAR
MANSION B&B ●

MooN

SCALE NOT AVAILABLE

LORING CUT
■

To
Gold Hill ↓

CHOLLAR
MINE

© AVALON TRAVEL PUBLISHING, INC.

Hours: Daily noon–5 P.M. in summer, 1 P.M.–4 P.M. in spring and fall.
Admission: Adults, $5; children 4–14, $2; children under four, free. Gold panning, offered in summer only, is $5 per pan.
Contact: Chollar Mine, S. F St. at D St. in Virginia City; 775/847-0155.

Comstock Firemen's Museum
(see map on page 39, site 19)
Inside this small museum are several historic fire engines, which always seemed to be in use, judging from the checkered history of Virginia City and its frequent encounters with fire.
Hours: Daily 10 A.M.–5 P.M. May–October.
Admission: Free; although donations are welcome
Contact: Liberty Engine Company Number 1, 125 S. C St. in Virginia City; 775/847-0717.

Fourth Ward School
(see map on page 39, site 20)
Walk right in and have a seat at one of the old-fashioned desks. Maybe the schoolmarm will show up, maybe not. The school was built in 1876 to accommodate 1,025 students, and it boasted all the latest comforts, including modern heating, water piped to all floors, and outside bathrooms. The four-story building housed 16 classrooms with high ceilings and large windows, two study halls, a gymnasium, and a vocational training area. Students from grade school through high school were educated here, and the school continued operating until 1936. Today the school houses rotating exhibits on Nevada's history, including occasional displays of Native American artifacts.
Hours: Daily 10 A.M.–5 P.M. mid-May–October.
Admission: Free, but donations are accepted.
Contact: Fourth Ward School, S. C St. at Hwy. 431 in Virginia City; 775/847-0975.

Mackay Mansion
(see map on page 39, site 21)
Built in 1860, this elegant mansion is the oldest home on the Comstock. It was once the office of the Gould and Curry Mining Company, and the mansion's first resident was George Hearst, father of newspaper baron William Randolph Hearst. The property contains the original mine office, a vault, ore samples, and records. An interesting footnote in history is that the building managed to escape the Great Fire of 1875, which destroyed 90 percent of the city, and ultimately became the home of John W. Mackay, the "Bonanza King" and "Boss of the Comstock," who, with a net worth of $100 million, was the richest man in town. The museum features Comstock mining artifacts, Civil War collectibles, Victorian furnishings, and a well-manicured garden. It is a popular spot for weddings and special group functions.
Contact: The Mackay Mansion, 129 S. D St. in Virginia City. As this edition went to press, the Mansion had changed ownership, and its hours and functions were undetermined. For up-to-date information, contact the Virginia City and Gold Hill Chamber of Commerce; 775/847-0311.

Marshall Mint Gold Shop and Museum (see map on page 39, site 22)
Housed in the historic Assay Office, the museum features gold nuggets, gem crystals, and collectible coins.
Hours: Daily 10 A.M.–5 P.M.
Admission: Free.
Contact: Marshall Mint Gold Shop Museum, 96 N. C St. in Virginia City; 775/847-0777 or 800/321-6374.

Ponderosa Mine Tour and Saloon
(see map on page 39, site 23)
Here is where most visitors come to sample the life of a miner in the 1870s. Guided tours, which are held frequently, provide a glimpse of what used to be more than 700 miles of underground shafts. Guides describe the tools and the mining processes used to extract silver, and point out tunnels, crosscuts, drifts, stopes, raises, winzes, and shafts.
Hours: Daily 10 A.M.–6 P.M. from Memorial Day to Labor Day and 11 A.M.–4:30 P.M. the rest of the year.
Admission: Adults, $4; children 12 and under, $1.50.
Contact: Ponderosa Saloon, corner of C and Taylor Sts. in Virginia City; 775/847-0757.

SIGHTS AND EVENTS

Nevada Gambling Museum
(see map on page 39, site 24)

Want to know how the cardsharps did it, and continue to do it? Here you can see cheating devices, guns, and knives—all the basic tools of the trade. The exhibits cover 150 years of gaming, with more than 100 antique slot machines from the 1800s and 1900s. Inside you'll find the requisite souvenir/gift shop.

Hours: Daily 10 A.M.–6 P.M. June–Aug. and 10 A.M.–5 P.M. Sept.–May.

Admission: $2 for 12 and over, free for under 12.

Contact: Nevada Gambling Museum, 20 S. C St., Virginia City, NV; 775/847-9022.

Julia C. Bullette Red Light Museum
(see map on page 39, site 25)

Did you think that all of those miners spent their free time gambling and drinking? Not exactly. They also went looking for ladies of the night. This quirky museum of vintage erotica and antique medical equipment generally reflects on the life of Julia Bullette, a "soiled" dove of the 1860s. The museum and local book stores also carry her life story. There's a restaurant here as part of the complex.

Hours: 7 A.M.–9 P.M. daily, year-round, though closing times often vary in the low season.

Admission: Adults, $1.

Contact: Bullette Red Light Museum, 5 S. C St. in Virginia City; 775/847-9394.

Piper's Opera House
(see map on page 39, site 26)

The first opera house built in Nevada (the two original buildings were destroyed by fire) was recently acquired from the Piper family by a non-profit foundation that has begun restoration of the building and has reopened it to the public. Since reopening in 2000, the organization has launched an ambitious schedule of live performances, including Shakespearean plays, big band concerts, dance ensembles and comedy acts. The 350-seat theater is festooned with pictures, posters and artifacts of the notables who performed there over the years, including humorist and author Mark Twain. (Among those who make appearances these days is actor Hal Holbrook, whose

one-man imitation of Twain has been a major success around the country.) Shows are held throughout the year, and the schedule and nature of performances vary. When you visit the building, note some of its remarkable features, including the tongue-and-groove maplewood dance floor, which was installed without nails and is supported by railroad car springs. The building is at the corner of B and Union Streets.

Hours: Daily noon–4 P.M. May–mid-October. Contact the theater for a calendar of events, or check out this website: www.virginiacity-nv.org /Calendars/Pipers/pipers.html.

Admission: Free during daytime hours except during performances. Admission for evening and matinee shows varies, but usually runs $8–15 per person.

Contact: Piper's Opera House Programs, Drawer J, Virginia City, NV 89440; 775/847-0433.

Territorial Enterprise
(see map on page 39, site 27)

It's easy to miss this fascinating museum, simply because it's housed in the basement of a fairly mundane T-shirt shop. But inside you'll discover the actual newspaper office of Mark Twain, along with his desk and the paper's printing facility. The best souvenir is a reproduction of the October 27, 1873, edition, describing a devastating fire that leveled most of the business district. Next to the headline, "Virginia City in Ruins," a column reads in part:

> *A breath of hell melted the main portion of town to ruins. Our eyes are still dazed by the lurid glare; our ears are still ringing with the chaos of sounds of a great city passing away on the whirlwind of a storm.*

Ah, what prose.

Hours: Daily 10 A.M.–5 P.M.

Admission: $1 per person.

Contact: Territorial Enterprise, 63 N. C St. in Virginia City; 775/847-0525.

Virginia and Truckee Railroad Company (see map on page 39, site 28)

Gunslingers may be waiting around any bend

of the tracks. Maybe they'll board the train and ask for "donations." This is a short but enjoyable ride from Virginia City through Tunnel 4 to Gold Hill, with views of the high desert mountains and mining operations along the way. An authentic steam locomotive pulls open cars and a caboose that are more than 70 years old. All 30-minute round-trip rides are narrated by the conductor. Special excursion and party rates are available. The station is on F Street, south of Washington Street.

Hours: Daily 10:30 A.M.–5:45 P.M. May–October.

Admission: Adults, $6; children, $3, under five, free. An all-day pass costs $12.

Contact: Virginia and Truckee Railroad Company; 775/847-0380.

Virginia City Radio Museum
(see map on page 39, site 29)

This recent addition to the town's historical offerings is in the lower level of a Victorian home. The collection contains more than 100 radios, accessories, tubes, vintage music recordings, and phonographs dating from 1915 to 1950, including cowboy movie star Hoot Gibson's 500-pound radio phonograph.

Hours: Daily 10 A.M.–5:30 P.M. during the summer.

Admission: Adults, $2.50; children, $1.50.

Contact: Virginia City Radio Museum, 109 S. F St., Virginia City; 775/847-9047.

The Way It Was Museum
(see map on page 39, site 30)

Every visitor should stop here first to get an orientation on Virginia City and its history. On the north end of town, the museum features a continuous video presentation on the Comstock Lode, Piper's Opera House, and the life and times of Mark Twain. There's a scale model of the hundreds of miles of underground mine workings that lay beneath Virginia City. Also here are early maps of the Comstock, the original Sutro Tunnel mule-train mine cars, a mineral collection, period costumed dolls, a fully equipped blacksmith's shop, a collection of early medicines in bottles and tins, and a large photo gallery of historic prints.

SIGHTS AND EVENTS

© KEN CASTLE

Piper's Opera House

Hours: Open Mon.–Fri. 10 A.M.–5 P.M., and Sat. and Sun. 10 A.M.–5:30 P.M.
Admission: Adults, $3; children 11 and under, free when accompanied by an adult.
Contact: The Way It Was Museum, 66 N. C St. in Virginia City; 775/847-0766.

Gold Hill Hotel
(see map on page 39, site 31)
Just south of Virginia City, down a winding road, is this vintage hotel, which was built in 1859. Now functioning as an upscale inn and restaurant, the hotel has period furnishings, a quaint saloon, and an excellent book store. There are historic lectures on Tuesday night, and a dinner theater Wednesday and Thursday.
Hours: Open daily year-around.
Contact: Gold Hill Hotel, 1540 Main St., Virginia City; 775/847-0111.

Dayton State Park
(see map on page 39, site 32)
Situated beside the Carson River on U.S. 50, 12 miles east of Carson City, this park includes nature trails, the historic Rock Point Mill Site, and picnic and barbecue facilities. You can camp overnight, on a first-come, first-served basis, or spend the day fishing and swimming.
Admission: $2 for entrance and day-use, $12 for camping.
Contact: Dayton State Park; 775/687-5678.

Carson City (see map on page 39, site 33)
Nevada's only territorial and state capital is not named after the famous scout Christopher "Kit" Carson. Still, his name was attached to so many places by his friend, explorer John C. Frémont, that the town, named after the Carson River, indirectly pays homage to him. Founded in 1858, Carson City owes its development as a lively center of commerce and industry to the Comstock mines and the Tahoe lumber companies that flanked the town to the east and west. As silver and gold poured out of Virginia City, Gold Hill, and Silver City, mills were built on the Carson River to process the ore. This activity led to the construction of the Virginia and Truckee Railroad, which connected the mines with the reduction mills. The U.S. Mint in Carson City was completed in 1869 under pressure from mine owners who wanted to save on the cost of shipping the ore to San Francisco.

With so many fortunes being made in the region, a vast residential district of stunning homes grew up on the west side of town. This district is the largest of its kind in Nevada, and today it forms the basis for walking tours. Ornate and fabulous houses dating from the early 1860s can be seen along the side streets, especially on Mountain, West Robinson, Division, and West King Streets. These peaceful, tree-lined avenues create a marked contrast to traffic-congested Carson Street (U.S. 395).

Travelers should make a point of seeing the Governor's Mansion (circa 1909), the Bliss Mansion (circa 1879), the Yerington House (circa 1863), and the Roberts House (circa 1859). Maps available at the Carson City Convention and Visitors Bureau describe these and 55 other historic sites in town, including museums and state government buildings. Today, Carson City is still thriving as a burgeoning bedroom community for Reno, 30 miles to the north, and Lake Tahoe, 14 miles to the west. New housing subdivisions and shopping centers are popping up everywhere.
Contact: Carson City Convention and Visitors Bureau, 1900 S. Carson St., Ste. 200, Carson City, NV 89701; 775/687-7410 or 800/NEVADA-1 (800/638-2321); website: www.carson-city.org.

Brewery Arts Center
(see map on page 39, site 34)
What is now becoming a significant arts complex on the west side of Carson City includes the former Carson Brewing Company and, more recently, the former St. Teresa of Avila Catholic Church, which has been converted into a performance hall. The center has rotating exhibits, concerts by name artists, workshops, and arts and crafts classes. Situated within a redevelopment district in an historic group of buildings, the

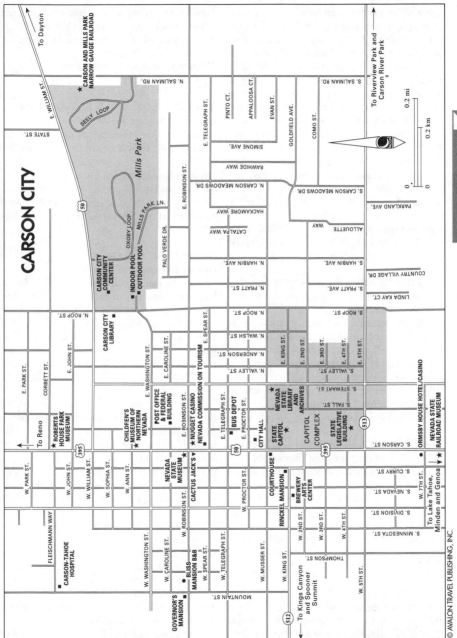

CARSON CITY

To Dayton

CARSON AND MILLS PARK
NARROW GAUGE RAILROAD

E. WILLIAM ST.

STATE ST.

SEELY LOOP

Mills Park

N. SALIMAN RD.

OXBOY LOOP

MILLS PARK LN.

CARSON CITY
COMMUNITY
CENTER

INDOOR POOL
OUTDOOR POOL

PALO VERDE DR.

E. ROBINSON ST.

E. TELEGRAPH ST.

PINTO CT.

APPALOOSA CT.

EVAN ST.

SIMONE AVE.

RAWHIDE WAY

N. CARSON MEADOWS DR.

S. CARSON MEADOWS DR.

GOLDFIELD AVE.

COMO ST.

S. SALIMAN RD.

To Riverview Park and
Carson River Park

0.2 mi

0.2 km

0

HACKAMORE WAY

CATALPA WAY

ALLOUETTE WAY

PARKLAND AVE.

N. HARBIN AVE.

S. HARBIN AVE.

COUNTRY VILLAGE DR.

LINDA KAY CT.

N. PRATT ST.

S. PRATT AVE.

N. ROOP ST.

S. ROOP ST.

N. WALSH ST.

N. ANDERSON ST.

N. VALLEY ST.

S. VALLEY ST.

E. KING ST.

E. 2ND ST.

E. 3RD ST.

E. 4TH ST.

E. 5TH ST.

N. ROOP ST.

CARSON CITY
LIBRARY

E. CAROLINE ST.

E. WASHINGTON ST.

E. SPEAR ST.

CORBETT ST.

E. PARK ST.

E. JOHN ST.

E. ROBINSON ST.

CHILDREN'S
MUSEUM OF
NORTHERN
NEVADA

POST OFFICE
& FEDERAL
BUILDING

NUGGET CASINO

NEVADA COMMISSION ON TOURISM

E. TELEGRAPH ST.

E. PROCTOR ST.

BUS DEPOT

S. STEWART ST.

S. FALL ST.

CITY HALL

STATE
CAPITOL

NEVADA
STATE
LIBRARY
AND
ARCHIVES

CAPITOL
COMPLEX

STATE
LEGISLATIVE
BUILDING

S. CARSON ST.

ORMSBY HOUSE HOTEL/CASINO

NEVADA STATE
RAILROAD MUSEUM

To Reno

ROBERTS
HOUSE PARK
MUSEUM

W. PARK ST.

W. JOHN ST.

W. WILLIAM ST.

W. SOPHIA ST.

W. ANN ST.

NEVADA
STATE
MUSEUM

CACTUS JACK'S

W. ROBINSON ST.

W. PROCTOR ST.

COURTHOUSE

RINCKEL MANSION

BREWERY
ARTS
CENTER

W. 2ND ST.

W. 3RD ST.

W. 4TH ST.

THOMPSON ST.

S. DIVISION ST.

S. NEVADA ST.

S. CURRY ST.

W. 7TH ST.

S. 7TH ST.

To Lake Tahoe,
Minden and Genoa

CARSON-TAHOE
HOSPITAL

FLEISCHMANN WAY

W. WASHINGTON ST.

W. CAROLINE ST.

BLISS
MANSION B&B

W. SPEAR ST.

W. TELEGRAPH ST.

W. MUSSER ST.

W. KING ST.

GOVERNOR'S
MANSION

MOUNTAIN ST.

S. MINNESOTA ST.

W. 5TH ST.

To Kings Canyon
and Spooner
Summit

STATE ST.

N. ROOP ST.

50

395

395

513

512

Brewery Center's organizers hope to create an arts campus by combining two city blocks. The future complex would include an outdoor amphitheater with a covered stage, public arts plaza with walkways, art exhibition space, and additional parking. Right now the center includes a 100-seat black box theater, the King Street Gallery and Artisans' Store, the BAC Stage Kids resident theater company, art classes for children and adults, and a yearly schedule of more than 130 events. Most of the musical performances are held inside the former church, which is an impressive space with brilliant acoustics. For a schedule, check the website or contact the Center office.

Hours: Weekdays 9 A.M.–5 P.M.; the gallery is open Mon.–Sat. 10 A.M.–4 P.M.

Contact: Brewery Arts Center, 449 W. King St. at Division St. in Carson City; 775/883-1976; website: www.breweryarts.org.

Carson and Mills Park Narrow Gauge Railroad (see map on page 39, site 35)

Visitors to Mills Park can ride behind a narrow-gauge, oil-fired steam locomotive and see two- and four-axle switch engines and a rail bus.

Hours: Open Wed.–Sun. 11 A.M.–5 P.M. (weather permitting) from Memorial Day to Labor Day.

Admission: General, $1.50; children two and under are free when accompanied by an adult.

Contact: Carson City Railroad Association; 775/887-2523.

The Children's Museum of Northern Nevada (see map on page 39, site 36)

This museum features interactive family exhibits on the humanities, fine arts, and science.

Hours: Open Tues.–Sun., 10 A.M.–430 P.M.

Admission: Adults, $5; children ages 14 and under, $3; children two and under, free.

Contact: The Children's Museum of Northern Nevada, 813 N. Carson St. Carson City, NV; 775/884-2226.

Governor's Mansion

(see map on page 39, site 37)

Built in 1908, this Colonial-style mansion can be toured only once a year on Nevada Day, October 31.

Admission: Tours are free but arrangements must be made. Open house is held during Nevada Day, a state holiday that is celebrated on the last Saturday of October.

Contact: Governor's Mansion, 606 N. Mountain St., Carson City, NV; 775/882-2333.

Nevada State Library and Archives

(see map on page 39, site 38)

A library, archives, historic preservation offices, and rotating exhibits are contained within this building.

Hours: Open Mon.–Fri. 8 A.M.–5 P.M.

Admission: Free.

Contact: Nevada State Library and Archives, 100 Stewart St., Carson City, NV; 775/684-3360.

Nevada State Museum

(see map on page 39, site 39)

One of the finest museums on the West Coast houses a number of unique exhibits, including America's largest complete skeleton of an Imperial mammoth, found in Nevada's Black Rock Desert; an amazingly realistic replica of an 1870s gold mine; and a reconstructed Western ghost town. The museum itself once held a branch of the U.S. Mint, and coins were minted here from 1870 to 1893.

Today the museum showcases, beautifully and thoroughly, Nevada's natural and human history from prehistoric times (represented by a "walk-through" of the Devonian Sea) to the Lost City Indian pueblos of the Great Basin and the wildlife of Nevada. There's an exhibit on Washoe Indian basket weaver Dat So La Lee, whose works are regarded as among the finest in the world. Also here are extensive collections of cowboy gear, firearms, arrowheads, buttons, bottles, and gaming memorabilia.

Hours: Daily 8:30 A.M.–4:30 P.M. in fall and winter, 8 A.M. and 5 P.M. in spring and summer; the bookstore and gift shop are open daily 9:30 A.M.–4:30 P.M.

Admission: Adults, $3; seniors 55 and older, $2.50; youths 17 and under, free.

Contact: Nevada State Museum, 600 N. Carson St., Carson City, NV; 775/687-4810.

Nevada State Railroad Museum
(see map on page 39, site 40)

Att the south end of town, this museum houses more than 25 pieces of railroad equipment from Nevada's past, most of them from the Virginia and Truckee Railroad, the richest and most famous short line of the 19th century. The railroad buffs who serve as volunteer guides offer enthusiastic tours of the main building, which has steam locomotives, restored coaches, and freight cars. But if you can get them to take you into the storage warehouses behind the museum, you'll find the majority of rolling stock in varying stages of decay, waiting for the funds needed to restore them. During the summer season through September, visitors can ride the museum's nearly 70-year-old railbus on a short circular track. Rail enthusiasts in the area have mounted a campaign to restore the rail line between Virginia City and Carson City, allowing vintage trains to serve these historic communities once again. The museum includes a bookstore and gift shop.

Hours: Open daily 8:30 A.M.–4:30 P.M.
Admission: Adults, $2; children and youths under 18, free.
Contact: Nevada State Railroad Museum, on U.S. 395 at 2180 S. Carson St., Carson City, NV; 775/687-6953.

Roberts House Park and Museum
(see map on page 39, site 41)

Tours of the recently remodeled Roberts House, the oldest Victorian home in Carson City, are available. Victorian-style weddings can even be arranged.

Hours: Open Fri.–Sun., 1 P.M.–3 P.M., or call for a tour.
Fee: $3 per person.
Contact: Roberts House Museum, Roberts House Park, 1207 Carson St., Carson City, NV775/887-2174.

Nevada State Capitol
(see map on page 39, site 42)

Carson City's most prominent landmark, bearing a silver-colored cupola, is this building which was completed in 1871. There are changing historic exhibits and state governors' portraits. Corner of Musser and Carson Streets.

Hours: Open Mon.–Fri., 8 A.M.–5 P.M.
Admission: Free.
Contact: Nevada State Capitol; 775/687-4810.

Stewart Indian Museum
(see map on page 39, site 43)

The museum is primarily a collection of photographs, with a store selling Native American crafts. But plans call for this to be the site of a major Native American cultural complex. Once housed here was the Stewart Indian Boarding School, which was closed by the U.S. Bureau of Indian Affairs in 1980. The big annual event is the Father's Day Pow Wow and Arts and Crafts Festival, usually held in June.

Hours: Daily 9 A.M.–5 P.M.
Admission: Free.
Contact: Stewart Indian Museum, 5366 Snyder Ave. in Carson City; 775/882-6929.

Genoa (see map on page 39, site 44)

Dating from an 1851 post established by Mormon traders, this is Nevada's first permanent settlement. It's on the Mormon-Emigrant Trail on the eastern slope of the Sierra Nevada and was a resting place where settlers stopped before tackling the rugged high country en route to California's goldfields. The town was the seat of Carson County, Utah Territory, from 1855 until the creation of Nevada Territory in 1861. It was an important station for the Pony Express and stagecoaches. Today there are several interesting spots worth visiting in the small town's historic district. Outside of Genoa, new subdivisions are flourishing, and the Golf Club at Genoa Lakes has brought considerable business to the area. One popular stop is David Walley's Resort, Hot Springs and Spa, which is open to the public and offers a series of refreshing outdoor pools of various temperatures. Genoa is 12 miles south of Carson City off U.S. 395.

Genoa Courthouse Museum
(see map on page 39, site 45)

The original Douglas County courthouse features rotating and permanent exhibits.

Hours: Daily 10 A.M.–4:30 P.M. May–mid-October.

Admission: Free, but donations are welcome.

Contact: Genoa Courthouse Museum, Main and 5th Sts., 775/782-4325.

Mormon Station Historic State Monument (see map on page 39, site 46)

This is the site of Nevada's first town, which was founded by Mormon settlers in the 1850s. It features a restored stockade and trading post, 19th-century artifacts, and other historic displays.

Hours: Daily 9 A.M.–5 P.M. May–October.

Admission: Free, but donations are welcome. Fee for group tours.

Contact: Mormon Station Historic State Monument, 2295 Main St. in Genoa; 775/782-2590.

Carson Valley Museum and Cultural Center (see map on page 39, site 47)

In downtown Gardnerville, this new museum showcases local natural history, agriculture and Native American exhibits, particularly those involving the Washoe Tribe, which spent the winters in Carson Valley. The cultural center also housed the town's school from 1916 to 1985.

Hours: 10 A.M.–4:30 P.M. daily.

Admission: Free, but donations are welcome.

Contact: Carson Valley Museum and Cultural Center, 1477 Hwy. 395, Gardnerville, NV; 775/782-2555.

Annual Events

History, geography, and just plain cabin fever contribute to the diversity of special events that are held throughout Lake Tahoe, Reno, and the Carson Valley each year. The basin specializes in events such as mountain bike tours, vintage boat shows, ski competitions, dogsled races, and winter carnivals. Reno has a flare for highly visual and dramatic crowd-pleasers, including the Great Reno Balloon Race, the National Championship Air Races, and a celebration of the 1950s hot-rod lifestyle known as Hot August Nights—the city's biggest blowout. And the Carson Valley, with its long tradition of silver mining, railroading, and lumbering, stages events centered around historic places and people, among them the famous author and newspaperman Mark Twain. Virginia City, where the Comstock Lode silver mine propelled a desolate high-desert valley into a cradle of riches, does almost anything to get attention: Its signature event, the International Camel Races, takes place each September.

Visitors planning a trip to any of these areas during major events should book accommodations early. Hot August Nights, which lures the crowds with more than 3,000 cars from the 1950s and 1960s, sells out virtually every room in Reno eight months in advance. Lodging, however, can often be found in neighboring Lake Tahoe and Carson City.

Apart from the marquee events mentioned above, there are less flamboyant but equally charming local festivals that exemplify the lifestyle and culture of the region. Lake Tahoe has a burgeoning arts community that continues to offer quality events such as jazz, bluegrass, and classical music concerts, art displays, and food and wine tastings. Native American tribes, particularly the Washoe and Paiute, hold powwows in Carson City and Lake Tahoe, and visitors are welcome to learn more about their traditions and handicrafts. The Father's Day Pow Wow, with its many arts and crafts vendors, takes place each June at the Stewart Indian Museum in Carson City and is one of the biggest such gatherings.

What follows is a list of the area's annual events. If you plan on attending any of them, it is important to verify dates and locations by calling the contact numbers provided, as scheduling changes are frequently made.

JANUARY

Feather River Country/Lakes Basin

Residents of Plumas County dress in historic costumes to commemorate one of the oldest

American sites for skiing, dating back to the 1860s, for the **Historic Skiing Revival Series.** Anyone over the age of 18 can try to ski on 12- to 14-foot-long skis. A series of three races is held, beginning in late January and continuing through March at Gold Mountain ski area (formerly Plumas Eureka Ski Bowl) in the historic town of Johnsville, California.

Contact: Plumas County Visitors Bureau; 530/283-6345 or 800/326-2247.

MARCH

Lake Tahoe

North Lake Tahoe and Truckee pull out all the stops for the **Snowfest Winter Carnival,** a 10-day extravaganza of winter events that includes a parade, ice carving, ski and snowboard races, live comedy and music, the legendary Polar Bear Swim, a torchlight ski parade and fireworks, a dress-up-your-dog contest, a children's costume contest, a crafts fair, food events, and many humorous spectator activities. The entire North Shore, including a dozen-plus alpine and cross-country ski areas and several communities, participates in more than 125 events. Opening day is the Friday before the first Sunday in March.

Contact: Snowfest Winter Carnival; 530/581-1283; website: www.snowfest.com.

For Nordic skiers who are in good shape, the challenging 18-kilometer **Echo Summit to Kirkwood Cross-Country Race** spans two drainages and a mountain pass, from Echo Summit on U.S. 50 to the Kirkwood Cross-Country Center on Highway 88. It takes place mid-March.

Contact: Kirkwood Cross-Country Center; 209/258-7248.

The **Great Ski Race** is a challenging 30-kilometer cross-country race, held the first Sunday in March. It runs from Tahoe Cross Country in Tahoe City to the Cottonwood Restaurant in the Hilltop Lodge at Truckee. Considered the largest cross-country ski event in the West, with more than 800 participants each year, it raises funds for the Tahoe Nordic Search and Rescue Team.

Contact: Tahoe Cross Country; 530/583-5475.

Feather River Country/Lakes Basin

A series of races held earlier in the year culminates in the **Historic Longboard Skiing Revival Series,** a world championship event for skiers using longboards—those 14- to 16-foot-long pioneer—style skis. It's held in Johnsville, California.

Contact: Plumas County Visitors Bureau; 530/283-6345 or 800/326-2247.

Reno/Carson Valley

For its **St. Patrick's Day Celebration,** Fitzgerald's casino hotel in downtown Reno becomes the center of traditional Irish merrymaking with food, live music, an arts and crafts fair, and a ceilidh (the party to end all parties).

Contact: Fitzgerald's; 775/785-3300 or 800/648-5022.

To celebrate the arrival of the spring equinox, Native American tribes assemble for the **Spring Awakening Pow Wow,** including dancing, singing and drumming on the grounds of the Stewart Indian School in Carson City, Nevada. The event also features various arts and crafts.

Contact: Stewart Indian School; 775/882-6929.

APRIL

Lake Tahoe

Boarding for Breast Cancer is Tahoe's most celebrated one-day snowboarding event, and it draws large crowds of riders and young people in general at Sierra-at-Tahoe resort in South Lake Tahoe. There are pro events with half-pipe and big air competitions, but the highlight is usually a music festival that features top-name entertainment such as the Foo Fighters, Beastie Boys, Luscious Jackson and Royal Crown Revue. The festival's purpose is to raise awareness about breast cancer prevention.

Contact: Sierra-at-Tahoe; 530/659-7453.

The **Lake Tahoe Pioneering in Film Festival** is a new South Shore function that attracts celebrities, industry insiders, and film aficionados for a celebration of moviemaking in general. The three-day event includes premiers of new films and screenings of old ones, as well as parties and VIP receptions. Venues include the Valhalla

Grand Hall and Boathouse at the Tallac Historic Site and several of the major Stateline casino hotels. Co-sponsored by the American Film Institute. Usually held in early April.
Contact: 530/577-7770 or check out this website: www.tahoefilms.org.

Reno/Carson Valley

Some of the best jazz bands and groups from schools throughout the West, along with professional musicians, perform at the **Reno International Jazz Festival,** which is considered one of the top competitions around. At the University of Nevada, Reno.
Contact: 775/784-4542.

He-man antics such as black powder, candle, and cannon shoots draw huge crowds to the **Eagle Valley Muzzle Loaders Spring Rendezvous,** an encampment southwest of Carson City along Canyon Road. The event is usually held in late April.
Contact: 775/884-4542.

MAY

Lake Tahoe

For the **Highway 50 Wagon Train,** hundreds of people dressed in period garb ride horses, authentic covered wagons, and buggies along the original route of the Pony Express, retracing the trail from Zephyr Cove, Nevada, to Old Hangtown (Placerville) in California. The mile-long train becomes a major parade as it rolls through South Lake Tahoe, usually during the second week of June. Two days of events—including gunfights, Civil War reenactments, performing fiddlers, clogging demonstrations, square dancing, and barbecues—are held at Round Hill Center in Nevada and at the Campground by the Lake in South Lake Tahoe.
Contact: Highway 50 Association; 530/644-3761.

Feather River Country/Lakes Basin

The **Mohawk Valley Spring Arts and Crafts Fair** is held in downtown Graeagle, California.
Contact: Plumas County Visitors Bureau; 530/283-6345 or 800/326-2247.

Reno/Carson Valley

Bean-counters and bean-eaters have a gastronomic field day at this annual **Cinco de Mayo Chili Cook-Off and Parade,** in the historic mining town of Virginia City, Nevada.
Contact: Virginia City Chamber of Commerce; 775/847-0311.

The Peppermill Hotel/Casino in south Reno comes alive with Hispanic and Latin music, dance, food, arts and crafts in the annual **Cinco de Mayo** festival, on the north parking lot.
Contact: 775/827-5995.

Usually held on the last weekend in May, the **Kit Carson Trail—Wild West Tour** is a walk through historic homes on the Kit Carson Trail in Carson City. Meet interesting characters in traditional 1800s garb. This is a one-day event that runs 10 A.M.–3 P.M., starting at Telegraph Square.
Contact: 775/687-7410 or 800/NEVADA-1 (800/638-2321), Carson City Convention and Visitors Bureau.

Comstock Historic Preservation Week, in the onetime silver-mining boomtown of Virginia City, Nevada, includes a Victorian house and garden tour and a walking tour of historic sites related to Mark Twain, who was a reporter for the *Territorial Enterprise* during the heyday of the Comstock Lode. Events include a costume ball, history lectures, plays, entertainment, a parade, and tours of vintage homes.
Contact: Virginia City Chamber of Commerce; 775/847-0975.

Booths, music, and food are parts of the annual street celebration **Spring Arts and Crafts Festival,** in downtown Minden, Nevada, south of Carson City. Usually held the last weekend of the month.
Contact: 800/727-7677.

JUNE

Lake Tahoe

More than 1,000 participants are drawn to **America's Most Beautiful Bike Ride,** the only time of the year when cyclists can circle the 72-mile perimeter of Lake Tahoe on road bikes under controlled conditions. The route follows U.S.

50 and circumnavigates the lake on a clockwise basis on Highways 89 and 28. You can make your trip shorter with a Half Ride Fun tour, which involves taking a boat cruise across the lake from Stateline at South Shore. Or you can extend the tour to a Century by doing and out-and-back side trip to Truckee. The ride is usually held in early June.

Contact: Bike the West; 775/588-9658 or 800/565-2704; website: www.bikethewest.com.

Pilots and aviation enthusiasts gather at the Truckee Tahoe Airport for the **Truckee Tahoe Airport AirAffair,** where festivities include aircraft displays, classic sports cars, gliders, hot air balloons, model airplanes, aircraft collectibles, food, dancing and live music. This general aviation airport is just south of downtown Truckee.

Contact: 530/587-4540.

The **Valhalla Renaissance Festival,** usually held on two successive weekends, celebrates 16th-century Europe and includes jousting knights on horseback, archery contests, magicians, country dancers, belly dancers, jugglers, artisans, musicians and one-act plays on three stages. Events invite attendees to try archery, the javelin throw or the tomato toss. There are also food and refreshments booths. Some proceeds benefit the Tahoe Tallac Association, which is restoring famous turn-of-the-century estates at the Tallac Historic Site. Although the event has been held at Historic Camp Richardson Resort in South Lake Tahoe, organizers at this writing were looking for a larger site.

Contact: Historic Camp Richardson Resort; 530/542-4166.

Ultradistance runners trek through snow, ice, and broiling granite canyons for the **Western States 100-Mile Endurance Run,** a test of high-elevation endurance from Squaw Valley to Foresthill in Auburn.

Contact: Race director; 916/638-1161 or 530/583-6985.

Every Thursday June–September, the vendors at the all-day open-air **Farmer's Market** offer fresh produce, flower arrangements, pastries, and regional food specialties. You'll find it at the top of Dollar Hill in Tahoe City.

Contact: Placer County Visitor Information Center; 530/887-2111.

Feather River Country/Lakes Basin

Volunteers dress up in period clothing and operate several facilities, including a blacksmith shop, for **Living History Day** at Plumas Eureka State Park in the vintage mining town of Johnsville in eastern Plumas County.

Contact: Plumas Eureka State Park; 530/836-2380.

Reno/Carson Valley

One of the West's largest and richest rodeos, the **Reno Rodeo** draws thousands of spectators to the Reno Livestock Events Center. The festivities, held in mid-June, include a parade through downtown Reno with a celebrity grand marshal, as well as country music concerts.

Contact: Reno Rodeo Association; 775/329-3877 of 775/688-5751.

On Thursday evening 4 P.M.–9 P.M., mid-June–late August, Victorian Square in Sparks (the city next to Reno) is transformed into the open **Sparks Hometowne Farmer's Market,** with more than 80 vendors offering fresh picked produce, specialty foods and breads. Activities include cooking demonstrations, a children's play area, and music from local bands.

Contact: City of Sparks; 775/353-2291.

On Friday evenings throughout the summer, downtown Reno hosts the **Rolling on the River Concert Series,** running from 5:30 P.M.–8:30 P.M. This consists of a variety of ongoing music concerts.

Contact: 775/324-4440, Ext. 1222.

The **Carson City Rendezvous** is a re-creation of an 1800s mountain man encampment, complete with a Native American village. You'll find live music, dancing, arts and crafts, a gunfighters' show, camel rides, petting zoo, food booths and live country and western music at Mills Park in Carson City, Nevada. This three-day event is usually held on the second weekend in June.

Contact: Carson City Convention and Visitors Bureau; 775/687-7410 or 800/NEVADA-1 (800/638-2321).

Participants of the **Carson City Garden Tour** can walk through some of Carson City's most beautiful gardens. Presented by Nevada Landmark Society and Redevelopment.

Contact: 775/882-1805 or Carson City Convention and Visitors Bureau; 800/NEVADA-1 (800/638-2321).

The **Father's Day Pow Wow** is a major three-day gathering of more than 35 Native American tribes features dancing and other cultural events. Food stands, a parade, and arts and crafts exhibits fill the grounds of the Stewart Indian School, at 5366 Snyder Ave. just east of downtown Carson City, Nevada.

Contact: Stewart Indian School; 775/882-6929.

Sponsored by the Carson Valley Historical Society, the two-day weekend **Snowshoe Thompson Festival** commemorates the famous Norwegian mail carrier of the mid- to late 1800s. Mormon Station State Park in historic Genoa, Nevada's oldest town, hosts a craft fair, cultural displays and demonstrations, entertainment, an antique faire, children's games and ethnic food. Usually held in late June.

Contact: 775/265-6097 or 775/265-7074.

JULY

Lake Tahoe

The six-day **American Century Celebrity Golf Championship,** usually beginning the first week of July, attracts top entertainment and sports stars such as Dan Marino, John Elway, Steve Young, Michael Jordan, Smokey Robinson, Randy Quaid, and some 70 others for the three-day stroke-play competition. Players with accredited U.S. Golf Association handicaps of 10 or less may compete in the tournament, which is televised live on national networks. The public can buy gallery tickets for all days of the event at the gate. It's held in Stateline, Nevada, at Edgewood Tahoe Golf Course, rated one of America's top courses.

Contact: Lake Tahoe Visitors Authority; 530/544-5050 or 800/AT-TAHOE (800/288-2463).

The **Valhalla Arts and Music Festival** is a summerlong series of concerts featuring major jazz, bluegrass, New Age, folk, Latin, and classi-cal artists. The series begins in July and lasts through early October at the Tallac Historic Site, 3.5 miles north of South Lake Tahoe on Highway 89. The weeknight and weekend concerts, along with arts and crafts festivals, are sponsored by the nonprofit Tahoe Tallac Association, which raises funds for the restoration of the historic estates. Concerts are held in the Valhalla Boathouse Theatre, a 200-seat structure built in the 1890s, or in the nearby Valhalla Grand Hall.

Contact: Tahoe Tallac Association, P.O. Box 19273, South Lake Tahoe, CA 96151; 530/541-4975 (summer) or 530/542-4166 (winter).

The annual **California Trail Days** offers living history demonstrations at Donner Memorial State Park in Truckee.

Contact: 530/633-9404.

Local historical figures are depicted in the annual **Lake Tahoe Chautauqua Festival,** which is held at Sand Harbor in Incline Village.

Contact: 800/GO-TAHOE (800/468-2463).

Truckee Regional Park in the town of Truckee is the site of the **Cannibal Cruise Car Show and Fair,** a combination car show, dance, and rally. Includes barbecue, rock n' roll party, games, street fair, and other events. Sponsored by the Truckee Optimists Club.

Contact: 530/582-9062.

The difficult **Death Ride** road bike ride, known as Alpine County's "Tour of the California Alps," starts at Markleeville. Riders cover 16,000 feet in elevation gains, 129 miles, and five mountain passes.

Contact: Alpine County Chamber of Commerce; 530/694-1756; websites: www.deathride .com or www.alpinecounty.com.

For the **Lake Tahoe Shakespeare Festival** (an event known to many as "Bard on the Beach"), noted troupes perform a series of Shakespearean plays in a natural outdoor amphitheater, outfitted with stage and props, at Sand Harbor, Lake Tahoe-Nevada State Beach. You can bring your own short beach chair or rent one, and food and drink are available during the evening performances. Performances are held late July–end of August. New, state-of-the-art stage and sound/light system and new dining service have been implemented recently.

FOURTH OF JULY CELEBRATIONS

LAKE TAHOE

Donner Lake, Truckee
A big parade through downtown Truckee precedes the fireworks show. Contact Truckee-Donner Chamber of Commerce; 530/587-2757.

High Camp at Squaw Valley
Contact Squaw Valley USA; 530/583-6985.

Tahoe City Commons Beach
Contact 530/583-3494.

Kings Beach State Recreation Area
The celebration is often held before or after July 4. Contact North Tahoe Public Utility District; 530/546-3270.

Incline Village, Nevada
Contact Incline Village and Crystal Bay Visitor's Bureau; 800/GO-TAHOE (800/468-2463).

South Shore
Of the various fireworks displays in and around Lake Tahoe, this is the most extravagant. Pyrotechnics burst with dazzling colors over the water in front of the Stateline casinos, and the summer's largest audience gathers for the show. The best vantage point is on one of the various cruise boats such as the *Tahoe Queen*, the *M.S. Dixie II*, or the *Woodwind I* or *II*, which allow passengers to view the fireworks from the lake. A large flotilla of private boats anchors offshore from Lakeside Marina, and thousands of spectators line the beaches. Contact Lake Tahoe Visitors Authority; 530/544-5050 or 800/AT-TAHOE (800/288-2463); website: www.virtualtahoe.com.

FEATHER RIVER COUNTRY/LAKES BASIN

Mohawk Valley
Fireworks are the highlight of a three- to four-day Independence Celebration at Graeagle in eastern Plumas County. Other activities include a parade, picnic, garage sale, and band concerts. Contact Plumas County Visitors Bureau; 530/283-6345 or 800/326-2247.

RENO/CARSON VALLEY

Reno
The Skyfire celebration includes entertainment and a spectacular pyrotechnics display at Rancho San Rafael Park. Contact 775/332-3333.

Carson City
The fireworks display is part of a five-day carnival called 4th of July Cavalcade of Spectaculars, which is held at Mills Park. Contact Carson City Convention and Visitors Bureau; 775/687-7410 or 800/NEVADA-1 (800/638-2321).

Virginia City, Nevada
Contact Virginia City Chamber of Commerce; 775/847-0311.

The beach is on Highway 28 just south of Incline Village.

Contact: Promoter: 800/74-SHOWS (800/747-4697) or Incline Village/Crystal Bay Visitors and Convention Bureau; 800/GO-TAHOE (800/468-2463); website: www.laketahoeshakespeare.com.

The **Lake Tahoe Summer Music Festival** is a series of outdoor concerts—among the most ambitious at Lake Tahoe—running July–August at various sites on the North Shore, including Topol Pavilion at Homewood, Granlibakken Resort, Squaw Valley, Sand Harbor, and Tahoe Donner. The eclectic musical styles span the gamut of classical, folk, operatic, Broadway, and jazz.

Contact: Lake Tahoe Summer Music Festival, P.O. Box 62, Tahoe City, CA 96145; 530/583-3101.

The **Rage'n @ the Ranch Mountain Bike Race** is a series of mountain bike races held at Donner Ski Ranch on Donner Summit west of Truckee. There are cross-country and dual slalom competitions.

Contact: 530/426-3635.

Nautical themes are prominent in the annual **Living History Day** presented by the Tahoe Maritime Museum at Sugar Pine Point State Park on the West Shore.

Contact: 530/525-WAKE (530/525-9253).

The famous **Tevis Cup Western States Trail Ride** is a 100-mile horseback endurance ride that travels the same route as the footrace in June, from Squaw Valley to Auburn.

Contact: Western States Association; 530/823-7282.

The new Village at Squaw Valley is the site of the **Squaw Valley Art and Wine Festival,** which includes fine artwork, crafts, wine bars, brewery tastings, music and theater performances.

Contact: Squaw Valley USA; 530/583-6985; website: www.squaw.com.

Reno/Carson Valley

The prestigious downtown Reno hotel fills its outdoor Special Event Plaza (corner of 4th and Virginia Streets) with two days of live music, food and microbrews for the **Great Eldorado BBQ, Brews and Blues Festival.**

Contact: Eldorado Hotel; 775/348-9264 or 800/648-5966.

Wingfield Park in downtown Reno celebrates the local Basque heritage with the annual **Reno Basque Festival,** which includes traditional food, dancing, a Basque Mass, barbecue, children's games and grownup's games such as weight carrying and wood chopping.

Contact: 775/787-3039.

Held in Carson City during the last week in July, the **Silver Dollar Car Classic** showcases cars and trucks with celebrations of rock n' roll music, parades, a poker run, a show and shine, and dance parties. Events are free and are held at Mills Park at the Pony Express Pavilion. There's a Friday night street dance that is usually held at 3rd and Carson Streets.

Contact: Carson City Convention and Visitors Bureau; 775/687-7410 or 800/NEVADA-1 (800/638-2321); website: www.carson-city.org.

On several **"Steam Up" Weekends** in the summer, the Nevada State Railroad Museum, in Carson City, provides opportunities for visitors to hop aboard one of the historic trains and take a 20-minute, one-mile ride. The tour is narrated by a conductor who spins anecdotes and historic information on the Virginia and Truckee Railroad. The museum is open daily.

Contact: Nevada State Railroad Museum; 775/687-6953.

The old-fashioned **The Way It Was Rodeo,** in Virginia City, Nevada, features riding, roping, and dogging contests. It's usually held in late July.

Contact: Virginia City Chamber of Commerce; 775/847-0311.

Uptown Downtown Artown is the Reno Summer Arts Festival, featuring more than 150 performances and exhibits in dozens of locations city-wide. Highlights include touring Broadway musicals, jazz concerts, ballet by the river, chautauqua outdoor theater, film festival and art workshops for kids. Events are held each week throughout July.

Contact: 775/322-1538 or check the schedule of events on the website at www.artown.org.

AUGUST

Lake Tahoe

The **Concours d'Elegance Wooden Boat Show** is the largest and longest-running show of antique and classic wooden boats in the country. More than 125 vessels, including many "woodies" dating back to the early 1900s, are on display, usually at the Sierra Boat Company in Carnelian Bay on the North Shore of Lake Tahoe. The event is generally held in early August as part of Tahoe Wooden Boat Week. Proceeds benefit the Tahoe Maritime Museum.
Contact: Tahoe Yacht Club; 530/581-4700; website: www.tahoeeyc.com.

Powerful swimmers race across the 2.7-mile length of Donner Lake in the **Donner Lake Swim.** First held in 1979, this sanctioned annual event is the oldest open-water competition of its kind. All competitors must be registered with United States Masters Swimming.
Contact: Pacific Masters Swimming; 530/582-1214.

The Tallac Historic Site, a complex of vintage mansions on the southwest shore of Lake Tahoe, comes alive with the sights and sounds of the Roaring '20s for the **Great Gatsby Festival.** Highlights include vintage car displays, strolling musicians, an old-time fashion show, picnics, an Ice Cream Social and Craft Fair, a dance and many participants in period clothing. Many events take place at the historic Pope Estate, an early 1900s mansion. Tallac is on Highway 89 just north of Historic Camp Richardson Resort in South Lake Tahoe.
Contact: Tallac Historic Site; 800/632-5859 or 530/544-3029; website: tahoe.com/gatsby.

The **Lake Tahoe Airfest** brings aerobatics and aerial demonstrations to the South Lake Tahoe Airport, usually during the last weekend of August. Events include dancing, singing, karate exhibitions and rides for children. Between aerial performances, visitors can wander among the static displays in the Piper hangar, which houses vintage military and civilian aircraft as well as a hot air balloon. Parking is limited, but shuttle service is available from many areas in South Lake Tahoe.
Contact: 530/541-0480.

The **Truckee Championship Rodeo** is two days of bucking broncos, bull riding, steer wrestling, calf riding, and other events held at McIver Arena, on Highway 267 in Truckee. The weekend rodeo, usually held in mid-August, is preceded by a week of activities that include a fashion show, hayrides, a tack auction, a beard and mustache contest, country-and-western karaoke, and celebrity team penning.
Contact: 530/582-9852.

Feather River Country/Lakes Basin

The outdoor **Graeagle Fall Festival** is an arts and crafts festival held at the Community Square in Graeagle in eastern Plumas County.
Contact: Promoter; 707/937-3773.

Festivities for **Portola Railroad Days** center around the large open-air Portola Railroad Museum, with operating diesel engines, in downtown Portola.
Contact: Portola Railroad Museum; 530/832-5444.

Reno/Carson Valley

One of the largest events in the entire region, **Hot August Nights** is a four-day blowout of car mania celebrating the hot rods, music, and lifestyle of the 1950s and 1960s. Nightly cruising on Virginia Street (the Strip), in downtown Reno, is combined with free live music, concerts by name acts (such as the Beach Boys and Smokey Robinson), a car auction, a massive automotive flea market, show 'n' shine car shows held in parking lots everywhere, and rallies too numerous to mention. Reno hotels sell out as much as a year in advance, so plan ahead. Several events are also held at Lake Tahoe. It all happens the first week of August.
Contact: Hot August Nights; 775/356-1956 or the Reno-Sparks Convention and Visitors Authority at 800/FOR-RENO (800/367-7366); website: www.hotaugustnights.net.

The **Nevada State Fair,** held at the Reno Livestock Events Center, includes livestock exhibits and events, entertainment, rides, and midway games.
Contact: Nevada State Fair; 775/688-5767.

The weeklong **Reno-Tahoe Open** golf tournament, started in 1999, draws top-ranked

SIGHTS AND EVENTS

professional golfers for a nationally televised tournament at the private Montreux Golf and Country Club, on the Mt. Rose Highway southwest of downtown Reno. This is a great opportunity to walk one of the most scenic courses in the region as it meanders along the eastern slopes of the Sierra through pine forest and palatial homes. The course was designed by Jack Nicklaus. Local resorts, hotels and other attractions have booths at the club, and nighttime events are held in the city. Name and underwriting sponsor of the event may vary.

Contact: 775/322-3900 or the Reno-Sparks Convention and Visitors Authority at 800/FOR-RENO (800/367-7366).

SEPTEMBER

Lake Tahoe

Highlights of the three-day **South Lake Tahoe's Labor Day Celebration** include the Great Lake Tahoe Sternwheeler Race, the largest Labor Day fireworks display west of the Mississippi, and a fishing derby. The sternwheeler race, involving the *Tahoe Queen* and the *M.S. Dixie,* covers a six-mile course and can be seen from South Shore beaches, from a flotilla of boats that follow along, or from the decks of either vessel (tickets are limited and go fast). The fishing derby is held at Camp Richardson Resort Marina. Other events include arts and crafts fairs, picnics, ski and snowboard tent sales, and live outdoor entertainment.

Information: Lake Tahoe Visitors Authority; 530/544-5050 or 800/AT-TAHOE (800/288-2463); website: www.virtualtahoe.com.

The historic district of Truckee, Commercial Row, comes alive for two-day **Truckee Railroad Days,** which includes a parade, the National Handcar Races, a chili cook-off, displays and train memorabilia vendors.

Contact: 530/546-1221.

The five-day **Tahoe International Film Festival** provides a venue for independent films and filmmakers from around the world. Various North Shore locations include the Cal-Neva Resort, PlumpJack Squaw Valley Inn, and other locations. More than 50 independent films are chosen for screening, and they include feature films, animation, shorts and documentaries. Some showings are world premiers. Associated events include a black tie party, filmmaker celebration, children's programs, panel discussions, workshops and closing night party.

Contact: 530/583-FEST (530/583-3378); website: www.tahoefilmfestival.org.

Feather River Country/Lakes Basin

More than 50 sellers of antiques display their wares at the **Antique Fair** on Labor Day weekend at Graeagle in eastern Plumas County.

Contact: Plumas County Chamber of Commerce; 530/832-5444.

Reno/Carson Valley

Rib cookers compete for prizes and whip up plenty of samples for sale at **The Best in the West Nugget Rib Cook-Off.** Also featured are nightly entertainment and an arts and crafts fair. At Victorian Square and John Ascuaga's Nugget in downtown Sparks, Nevada.

Contact: John Ascuaga's Nugget; 775/356-3300 or 800/843-2427. Also, check out the hotel's website at www.janugget.com.

Auto fans head to Virginia City, Nevada, for the **Ferrari Club of America Hill Climb,** an event that includes a parade and car show, along with timed races up the 7.4-mile truck route from Silver City to Virginia City. Ferraris and Shelby Cobras participate, and there is a viewing stand for spectators. Held the last weekend of September or the first weekend of October.

Contact: Virginia City Chamber of Commerce; 775/847-0311.

The Great Reno Balloon Race is one of Reno's most colorful spectacles of the year, and it is totally free to the public. The nation's top 140 balloonists make a mass ascent from Rancho San Rafael Park in balloons of all sizes and many weird shapes. There is a Dawn Patrol for super-early risers, and the rest of the balloons take off at first light. Food booths and displays are set up on the field north of town. This event is held the second weekend of September.

Contact: Event promoter; 775/826-1181; website: www.renoballoon.com.

Hundreds of planes soar into the high-desert skies for the **National Championship Air Races,** world's longest-running air race, which includes pylon racing, aerobatics, skywriting, skydiving, and other events during the third week of September at Reno-Stead Airport.
Contact: Reno-Sparks Convention and Visitors Authority; 800/FOR-RENO (800/367-7366); Reno Air Races; 775/972-6663.

Nevada's oldest town hosts the **Genoa Candy Dance,** an annual arts and crafts fair, which features more than 300 booths, food vendors, and a dinner and dance Saturday evening. At Mormon Station and the Genoa Town Park, usually the third weekend of September.
Contact: 775/782-8141 or 775/782-TOWN (775/782-8696).

Steam engines are cranked up for rides and other festivities over for the **Nevada State Railroad Museum Steam Up,** Labor Day weekend at the Nevada State Railroad Museum in Carson City.
Contact: Nevada State Railroad Museum; 775/687-6953.

The **100-Mile Endurance Race** is an equestrian endurance ride held over two days and including two laps out and back from the desert, beginning at Virginia City, Nevada.
Contact: 775/847-0523.

Owners of Harley-Davidsons and custom tour bikes gear up for the four-day **Street Vibrations,** which roars through Reno. Crafts, parades, ride-in shows, poker runs, and nightly entertainment are among the festivities.
Contact: Road Shows; 775/329-7469.

People with nothing better to do race camels around an arena in the **Virginia City International Camel Races.** Some of them also race water buffalo and ostriches. Other humorous events, a parade, and general quirkiness take place in Virginia City, Nevada, on the second weekend in September.
Contact: 775/3297469 or 775/847-7500.

OCTOBER
Lake Tahoe
The **Autumn Food and Wine Festival** is a great way to sample the award-winning recipes of North Shore restaurants, along with accompanying wines. More than 50 of Tahoe's finest restaurants and West Coast wineries offer bites and sips at the Resort at Squaw Creek in Squaw Valley.
Contact: 800/824-6348; website: www.mytahoevacation.com.

The annual **Donner Party Hike** seeks to retrace—with a less drastic outcome, of course—the ill-fated route of the Donner Party of the 1840s, half of whom perished during an early winter.
Contact: 530/587-2757 or Donner Memorial State Park; 530/587-8808.

The **Kokanee Salmon Festival,** in early October, is held in conjunction with the annual spawning run of landlocked salmon up Taylor Creek in South Lake Tahoe. Two days of family activities include the Kokanee Kookoff, educational programs, art displays, nature walks, a children's fishing booth, and tours of the Lake Tahoe Visitor Center's Stream Profile Chamber, an underground viewing area with windows below water level.
Contact: 530/573-2674.

Runners race through 26.3 miles of spectacular scenery during the mid-October **Lake Tahoe Marathon Week.** The run starts in Tahoe City on the North Shore and finishes at Pope Beach on the South Shore. Other race options include a half-marathon, 5K run and a Kids Fun Run.
Contact: 530/544-7095; website: www.laketahoemarathon.com.

Reno/Carson Valley
The **Celtic New Year Celebration** is billed as the biggest pipe band competition on the West Coast. Held at the Reno Livestock Events Center, this event features Celtic dancing, entertainment, food booths and crafts.
Contact: 775/332-3336; website: www.RenoCeltic.org.

A Columbus Day parade, Italian food booths, entertainment, grape stomping, and a spaghetti tournament are the highlights of the **Great Italian Festival,** held in early October at the Eldorado Hotel Casino in downtown Reno, Nevada.
Contact: Eldorado Hotel Casino; 775/786-5700 or 800/777-5325.

Apparitions from bygone days come back to haunt the old Carson City homes visited on the **Kit Carson Trail "Ghost Walk."** Volunteers dress up in ghostly apparel to regale visitors with their tales, usually in late October. The tour meets at the Nevada State Museum. **Contact:** Carson City Convention and Visitors Bureau; 775/687-7410 or 800/NEVADA-1.

Nevada joined the Union as a state on Halloween in 1864, but recently its observance was changed so that it doesn't compete with ghosts and goblins. Now held for four days in advance of Halloween, the **Nevada Day Celebration** is a Carson City fête includes a parade, live music, a rock-drilling contest, a music and art show, a beard contest, and a fancy ball at the Governor's Mansion. Wear your finest 1860s period clothing. The parade is the largest held in Nevada. All of downtown Carson City is closed off to traffic to accommodate booths and merriment. **Contact:** 775/687-7410 or 800/NEVDA-1.

Nothing to sniff at, the **World Championship Outhouse Races,** otherwise known as "Power to the Potties," pits teams who put wheels on outhouses and make a run through downtown Virginia City on C Street. Other activities include the Toilet Paper Plunge and the Corncob Toss. Held in early October. **Contact:** Virginia City Chamber of Commerce; 775/847-0311.

NOVEMBER
Lake Tahoe
The Tallac Historic Site at South Lake Tahoe comes alive with holiday crafters, artists, boutiques, carolers, holiday treats and characters from author Chales Dickens during the **Holiday Faire Victorian Style.** **Contact:** Tallac Historic Site; 530/542-4166.

Some bebop and cool notes emanate from the Hyatt Regency in Incline Village and other North Shore venues during the annual **North Shore Jazz Festival.** **Contact:** 800/553-3288.

Reno/Carson Valley
Held the day after Thanksgiving in Virginia City, **Christmas on the Comstock** features fireworks, a candlelight parade, and a Christmas tree lighting ceremony at the end of town. **Contact:** Virginia City Chamber of Commerce; 775/847-0311.

Reno's River Holiday and Festival of the Trees includes caroling, hot cider, storytelling, tree lighting, food, and entertainment along the Raymond I. Smith Truckee River Walk in downtown Reno the day after Thanksgiving. **Contact:** Event promoter; 775/334-2414 or 775/334-2262

DECEMBER
Lake Tahoe
Squaw Valley ski instructors light up the night for the **Christmas Eve Torchlight Parade** down the slopes. **Contact:** Squaw Valley USA; 530/583-6955; website: www.squaw.com.

Reno/Carson Valley
Some of Carson City's most elegant old homes are gussied up in holiday decorations and opened to the public for the **Victorian Home Christmas Tour.** **Contact:** 775/882-1805.

Usually held on the first Saturday of December, the gala **Hometowne Christmas,** at Victorian Square in Sparks, Nevada, features a parade, holiday music, a crafts fair, and a spectacular tree-lighting ceremony in the evening. It's sponsored by the city of Sparks. **Contact:** Sparks Redevelopment Agency; 775/353-2291.

The highlight of the **Silver and Snowflake Festival of Lights,** usually held during the first weekend of December in Carson City, Nevada, is the ceremonial lighting of the big tree in front of the state capitol, the oldest tree in the town. Caroling, live music, sleigh rides, and other merriment are among the festivities. **Contact:** Carson City Convention and Visitors Bureau; 775/885-0411.

Tahoe with Children

In the Lake Tahoe and Reno areas, there's lots of stuff to keep kids busy. Options range from excellent summer and day camps to those electronic junior slot machines known as video arcades. Happily, keeping small fry happy doesn't have to cost much. For example, you can tour a trout hatchery for free. If your goal is to enhance your child's education, by all means visit one or more of the excellent museums in Lake Tahoe, Reno, Virginia City, and Carson City. In particular, the railroad museums (there are three in the region) are usually a hit. So is the Ponderosa Ranch, with its Western town, petting zoo, and movie sets. Also, consider the nature centers and self-guided walks at state parks and U.S. Forest Service visitor centers (see the summer recreation chapter).

When all else fails, or if the Great Outdoors is pelting you with too much liquid sunshine or copious white flakes, you can certainly turn to the indoor theme parks, and Reno has a corner on the market for those. The new Silver Legacy casino/hotel, Reno's answer to Las Vegas, is guaranteed to keep everyone wide-eyed. And the Boomtown Hotel Casino, with its indoor miniature golf and a thrilling motion theater, is a youngster's paradise. And keep in mind that if you feel like climbing the walls, or if you've reached the end of your rope, you and your offspring can reconnect at a climbing wall or a challenging ropes course, of which several are offered in the Tahoe basin.

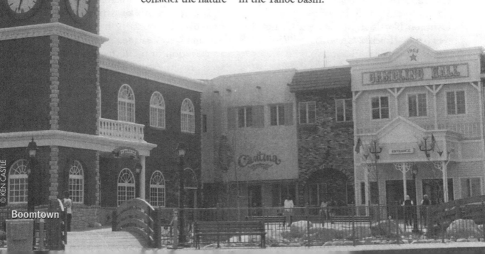

© KEN CASTLE

Boomtown

Summer and Day Camps

TRUCKEE/DONNER

Tahoe Donner Equestrian Center

Tahoe's most complete riding facility offers permanent riding arenas and skilled instructors. It's in the Tahoe Donner residential resort community above Truckee, and the instructors are first-rate. Five-day horsemanship camps, held June–August, teach Western and English riding styles for beginner–advanced levels. Book early, because the courses fill rapidly. Closed during winter (beginning at the end of September).

Fees: Call for pricing.

Policies: Reservations are required.

Contact: Tahoe Donner Equestrian Center, 151509 Northwoods Blvd., Truckee, CA 96161; 530/587-9470; website: www.tahoedonner.com.

Minors' Camp at Northstar

This is a licensed child-care center that offers a day camp for children ages 2–10. Full- and half-day programs include lunch, and activities might include pony rides, art, science, water play, singing, and junior ropes courses. Open to overnight and day guests.

Fees: $33 for morning session (9 A.M.–1 P.M.), $55 for all-day session (9 A.M.–5 P.M.).

Policies: Reservations are recommended, and all children must be toilet-trained. Bring bathing suit, rubber-soled shoes for hiking, change of clothes, sweatshirt, and towel.

Contact: Northstar-at-Tahoe, P.O. Box 129 (Hwy. 267), Truckee, CA 96160; 530/562-2278; website: www.skinorthstar.com.

SQUAW VALLEY

Mountain Buddy's Club

The Resort at Squaw Creek is a lavish hotel at Squaw Valley that has earned high marks for its supervised children's and teen programs, which are available to guests throughout the year. There's an array of organized events including arts and crafts, games, sports, cooking classes, and science experiments. Winter activities range from sledding and ice skating to building snow forts and going on scavenger hunts. In the summer, nature hikes and supervised swim play are on the roster. Separate programs are scheduled for teens and kids age 4–12 (children must be toilet-trained). Baby-sitting is available for children three and younger. At the Resort Activity Center on the second floor.

Hours: All-day sessions go 9 A.M.–5 P.M.; half days run 9 A.M.–noon. (1:30 P.M. with lunch) and 1 P.M.–5 P.M. There's also an evening program that allows parents to have the night out.

Fees: Full days for $90 (lunch included), half days for $45, and evenings ranging $45–65.

Policies: Reservations must be made 24 hours in advance. A cancellation notice of four hours is required.

Contact: The Resort at Squaw Creek, 400 Squaw Creek Rd., Squaw Valley, CA 96146; 530/581-6624; website: www.squawcreek.com.

Tahoe Extreme Soccer Camp

Former professional soccer player JoJo Saunders and his wife, Christine, have been running weeklong youth soccer camps at Squaw Valley since 1993. Young people ages 7–18 participate in daily World Cup tournament play under the supervision of a hand-picked staff of European and Brazilian pro players and coaches. The staff-to-player ratio is one to five, and there is a mix of nationalities with kids from over 22 countries, including Russia, Taiwan and New Zealand. Since Squaw Valley is at an elevation of 6,200 feet, the kids practice soccer for just six hours a day and then choose up to two more activities from a long list that includes mountain biking, water-skiing, hot air ballooning, parasailing, golf, horseback riding, and other pursuits included in the Tahoe Extreme Sports Camp listed below. The Saunders operate both programs. Kids sleep dorm-style in the Children's World (winter sports) center, with separate dorms for boys and girls and 24-hour supervision.

Policies: Parental approval is mandatory for each activity.

Fees: $1,195 per week, with an advance deposit required. Includes six hours of daily soccer coaching, two other recreation activities, all meals, lodging, and transportation from Reno-Tahoe International Airport.

Contact: Tahoe Extreme Soccer Camp, P.O. Box 3297, Olympic Valley, CA 96161; 530/550-0778 or 800/PRO-CAMP (800/776-2267); email: sqwasocr@nbn.com; website: www. 800procamp.com.

Tahoe Extreme Sports Camp

For kids and teens who just can't seem to work off all of their youthful energies, this program is a Mulligan stew of summer camps with so many outdoor activities available that your offspring will never be bored. Operating at Squaw Valley USA since 1997, the one-week sessions are available to kids of all athletic abilities and skill levels ages 8–18. They can choose up to five activities per day, including paintball, ropes course, glider flights, hot air balloon rides, water-skiing, go-kart racing, river rafting, in-line skating, golf, mountain biking, indoor rock climbing, horseback riding, ice skating, swimming, tennis, bungee-jumping, and parasailing. The kids stay dorm-style in the Squaw Valley Children's World center (normally used for winter kids' programs), with boys and girls in separate dorms and with 24-hour, in-room supervision. The camper-to-staff ratio is four to one. Sessions run mid-June–mid-August.

For kids and teens who just can't seem to work off all of their youthful energies, the Tahoe Extreme Sports Camp program is a Mulligan stew of summer camps with so many outdoor activities available that your offspring will never be bored.

Fees: $1,495 per week, including up to five activities (some are at extra cost) per day, all meals, lodging, and transportation from Reno-Tahoe International Airport in Reno.

Policies: Parental permission is mandatory for each activity.

Contact: Tahoe Extreme Sports Camp, P.O. Box 3297, Olympic Valley, CA 96161; 530/550-0778 or 800/PRO-CAMP (800/776-2267); email: sqwasocr@nbn.com; website: www .800procamp.com.

TAHOE CITY/WEST SHORE

Nike Lake Tahoe Tennis Camp

If you want your physically talented son or daughter to swat balls like Venus Williams or Andre Agassi, this tennis camp at Granlibakken Resort is the place to start. Held every year, this seven-day, six-night tennis camp is for young people ages 9–18. It includes meals, housing, instruction, video analysis, and a personal skills evaluation. Special off-court activities include swimming, beach games, river rafting, ice skating at Squaw Valley, volleyball, bingo, ice cream/movie/pizza nights, miniature golf, arcade games, casino night, a graduation ceremony, and even a dance. The camp runs from June to August at Granlibakken Resort, 625 Granlibakken Rd., Tahoe City, CA.

Fees: Resident rate is $795, extended day rate (8:30 A.M.–9 P.M.) is $495. Check the website for schedule.

Contact: U.S. Sports Development, 919 Sir Francis Drake Blvd., Kentfield, CA 94904; 415/459-0459 or 800/NIKE-CAMP (800/645-3226); website: www.esportscamps.com.

Ropes Course at Granlibakken

This four-seasons resort offers a variety of activities and sports camps for kids, as well as corporate team-building sessions for adults. An impressive ropes course has a series of both low- and high-element challenges using poles, cables, and native pine trees. Activities are designed to increase personal self-confidence and mutual respect within a group, as well as improve communication, problem-solving, and productivity. Certified trainers guide you and your team through the course, providing a safe and secure environment for all. At this writing, the management of the program was in transition.

Hours: Call for times of operation.

Fees: Prices vary depending on group size and

program. Ask about the discount rates available for large groups and nonprofit organizations.

Contact: Granlibakken Resort, P.O. Box 6329, Tahoe City, CA 96145; 530/583-4242 or 800/543-3221; website: www.granlibakken.com.

Tahoe City Parks and Recreation Day Camps

The Tahoe City Public Utilities District (PUD) sponsors a variety of day camps for children, among which the most popular is Camp Skylandia, at Skylandia Park at Lake Forest in Tahoe City. This area provides acres of forest, a beach, a pier and plenty of room for nature exploration. Activities include large group games, arts and crafts, weekly field trips, beach time and various special events. Campers are grouped according to school grade levels, and the camps are appropriate for kids in grades 1–5. Sessions are held daily, Monday–Friday, 9 A.M.–3:30 P.M., mid-June–mid-August. Another program, called the After Camp Club, kicks in from 3:30 P.M.–5:30 P.M.–extend activities to a full day.

Fees: These range $30–100.

Contact: Tahoe City Public Utility District, Parks and Recreation Department, 221 Fairway Dr., P.O. Box 33, Tahoe City, CA 96145; 530/583-3796 or 530/583-1475.

INCLINE VILLAGE/CRYSTAL BAY

Camp Hyatt

Taking care of families with children is a specialty of the Hyatt Regency Lake Tahoe, and there are always supervised programs available in both summer and winter. For hotel guests, Camp Hyatt has activities such as chaperoned hiking, beach play, crafts, or snow play for youngsters ages 3–12, giving Mom and Dad a chance to whoop it up on their own. (The facility is also a licensed day-care center.) At this writing, because of an extensive remodelling of the hotel, the program was temporarily put on hold until a new facility is built for it. Consult the concierge desk or website for up-to-date information.

Contact: Camp Hyatt, Hyatt Regency, P.O. Box 3239, Incline Village, NV 89450-3239; 775/832-1234 or 800/553-3288; website: www.hyattlaketahoe.com.

South Lake Tahoe Ice Arena and Recreation Complex

The city of South Lake Tahoe offers a variety of inexpensive Parks and Recreation Department activities for children, which are open to nonresidents as well as residents. In 2002, a long-awaited new indoor ice-skating arena opened next to the city's campground, and this is the first year-around facility of its type at South Shore. Other city programs include Youth Summer Day Hikes, which are designed to introduce your child to practical outdoor skills while having fun, swimming at a large aquatics complex, skateboarding, volleyball, horseshoes, nine-hole golf, and disc golf, with most facilities either at the recreation center or at Bijou Community Park.

Hours: The ice skating arena offers sessions five days a week (except for Tues. and Thurs.) 1 P.M.–5 P.M. and 7 P.M.–9 P.M., year-around.

Fees: Ice skating arena: nonresident fees are $7.50 for adults, $6.50 for youth 6–17, and $2 for skate rentals.

Contact: City of South Lake Tahoe Parks and Recreation Department, 1180 Rufus Allen Blvd., South Lake Tahoe, CA 96150; 530/542-6056 (administration), 530/542-6262 (ice arena), 530/542-6097 (Bijou Municipal Golf Course), or 530/542-6055 (parks, swimming complex, and general recreation programs).

Kids Camp

Need to get rid of the wee ones for a night on the town? Look to Kids Camp, the only nighttime supervised children's program in South Shore. Established by Mark Heidt in 1991, it operates out of Harveys at Stateline but is open to the general public as well as to hotel guests. The evening "camp" is for boys and girls ages 6–13, who are treated to fun activities such as movie trips, bowling, ice skating, swimming, and excursions to the Harveys game arcade.

Hours: The session runs 6 P.M.–10 P.M. and meets at Harveys concierge desk. Open year-round.

Fees: $75 per child for daytime (9 A.M.–4 P.M.),

$45 per child for nighttime, including meal and activities, with additional hours available upon request.

Policies: Reservations are required.

Contact: Kids Camp, P.O. Box 2238, Stateline, NV 89449; 775/588-0752 or Harveys Concierge at 775/588-2411; website: www.tahoekids.com.

Tallac Historic Site Living History for Kids

Enormously popular, these programs give a taste of what life and culture were like in the 1920s. This is not a day camp (though it could easily become one), but a collection of five interactive adventures that are held on weekday afternoons, Monday–Friday, in the months of July and August. Each program has a different topic, and each gives children hands-on experience in the ways of their grandparents and great-grandparents. Volunteers from the Tahoe Heritage Foundation, which performs restoration work on the Tallac Historic Site in South Lake Tahoe, dress up in period clothing and lead groups of children in various activities lasting from one hour to 90 minutes. Programs include "Washoe Ways" (games and activities that celebrate Tahoe's Native American tribes); "Kitchen Kids" (1920s cooking experiences that include making marshmallows, baking cupcakes, and making and canning applesauce); "When Grandma Was a Kid" (fun games including learning to walk on stilts); "Boat Buddies" (children see some of Tahoe's nautical history and race miniature steam-powered boats); and "Children's Garden Party" (youngsters come dressed in party clothes and make hats, eat cookies and drink lemonade—just as well-to-do children did in the 1920s). Venues include the Pope Estate, which is a restored mansion; the Pope Boathouse, which contains an old wooden Tahoe cruiser; and the Baldwin Estate gardens. The Tallac Historic Site is next to Camp Richardson on Highway 89 two miles north of the South Tahoe "Y" intersection with Highway 50.

Hours: Programs begin at 1 P.M. each day, Mon.–Fri., in July and August.

Policies: Parents may take grownup tours or spend time in the museum while their kids are in a program. All sessions are by reservation, and phone requests must be accompanied by a credit card payment. Recommended ages are 6–12, except for the Kitchen Kids program, which is 8–12.

Fees: $5 to $7.50 per child for most programs.

Contact: Tahoe Heritage Foundation, P.O. Box 8586, South Lake Tahoe, CA 96158; 530/541-5227; website: www.tahoeheritage.org.

FEATHER RIVER COUNTRY/LAKES BASIN

Shaffer's High Sierra Camp

For young people aged 10–16, this is a residential summer camp in Tahoe National Forest that offers a myriad of outdoor activities, including hiking, biking, rafting, canoeing, swimming, nature education and other, largely noncompetitive programs. The camp is 30 minutes north of Truckee on Highway 49, near the spectacular Lakes Basin Recreation Area and the dramatic Sierra Buttes. The site is on the North Fork of the Yuba River at 6,200 feet elevation, and there are more than 70 lakes and miles of hiking trails nearby. Campers can choose their preferred activities for five activity periods. Sessions are one week or two weeks and run mid-July–late August.

Policies: Registration is on a first-come, first-served basis, and requires a deposit. Pickups can be arranged at the Reno-Tahoe International Airport in Reno.

Fees: Tuition ranges $850–1,695, and some activities such as river rafting and equestrian programs are at additional cost.

Contact: Shaffer's High Sierra Camp, 248 San Marin Dr., Novato, CA 94945; 800/516-3513; website: www.highsierracamp.com.

Walton's Grizzly Lodge

This is a unique facility at the headwaters of the Feather River near Portola in Plumas County, about a 45-minute drive north of Truckee or an hour north of Reno. Set at a 5,000-foot elevation (above the smog and poison oak), Walton's Grizzly Lodge has been a

TAHOE WITH CHILDREN

family-operated summer camp for boys and girls, ages 7–14, for many years. The campground is nestled among 50 acres of ponderosa pine and features a private lake. Dormitories, complete with indoor showers and restrooms, accommodate children by age group. Activities include campouts, hiking, swimming in a creek, fishing, horseback riding, archery, volleyball, softball, soccer, Ping-Pong, trampolining, in-line skating, wrestling, gymnastics, tennis, golf, and challenge courses. Adding to the fun are campfire entertainment, theme dances, games, computers, and arts and crafts. Camp sessions are two weeks long from the end of June until the end of August. The camp meets flights from around the world at the Reno-Tahoe International Airport. A free video is available on request.

Fees: $1,050 for one week to $2,100 for two weeks.

Contact: Walton's Grizzly Lodge, P.O. Box 519, Portola, CA 96122; 530/832-4834 or winter at 510 W. Main St., Grass Valley, CA 95945; 530/274-9577; website: www.grizzlylodge.com.

RENO/CARSON VALLEY

Galena Creek County Park Campfire Programs

On Mt. Rose Highway in Washoe County, these Friday night offerings can include ranger-led slide shows and talks (covering such topics as bats, bears, and owls), astronomy sessions, storytelling, and, occasionally, bluegrass music. Bring a lawn chair, a blanket, and marshmallows. On some Saturdays, another program is geared to youths ages 12 and older. Call ahead to check on the weekend's schedule, or write to the park at the address below for a brochure. From Incline Village at Lake Tahoe, take the Mt. Rose Highway toward Reno and look for the park on the east side of the summit. Take the north entrance to Galena Creek County Park.

Hours: Starts around 8 P.M. on Fri., July–September.

Fees: None.

Contact: Galena Creek County Park, 18350 Mt. Rose Hwy., Reno, NV 89511; 775/849-2511.

Climbing and Ropes Courses

TRUCKEE/DONNER

Northstar Adventure Park

Active kids with seemingly limitless energy will find plenty of things to challenge them at this resort adventure center, which offers a ropes course and a 25-foot-high, granitelike, multifaced outdoor climbing wall, both of which are behind Northstar Village.

Hours: Climbing wall: Wed.–Sun., 10 A.M.–6 P.M.; Challenge Ropes Course: Thurs.–Sat. 1 P.M.–5 P.M. and on Sun. 10 A.M.–2 P.M.; Junior Ropes Course: Wed.–Sun., 10 A.M.–5 P.M. (ages four and above). Map and Compass Course (orienteering): Wed.–Sun. by appointment.

Fees: Climbing wall: $11 an hour, $20 for an all-day pass. Challenge Ropes Course (games and exercises with ropes, cables, and tall fir trees): children (minimum age 10) and adults, $43 per person; discounts for more than two people are available. Junior ropes course for kids ages 4–13 (parent assist is required): $13. Map and Compass Course: introductory, $15 (including lesson, map, compass, and vest rental) and $10 for under age 17 (including single lift ride, map, and compass rental). Shoe rentals are optional. Corporate team building sessions are available.

Contact: Adventure Associates, 1030 Merced St., Berkeley, CA 94707; 530/562-2285 in summer or 510/525-9391 other times; websites: www.skinorthstar.com/summer or www.adventureassoc.com.

The Sports Exchange

This is a used sports equipment store that features two indoor climbing rooms designed for top roping and bouldering. The Sports Exchange sells used equipment on consignment and houses a new café.

Hours: Daily noon–8 P.M. and in summer, 10 A.M.–8 P.M.

Fees: A day pass costs $10 and includes rental climbing shoes; without shoes it's $7. Family rates and monthly passes are available.

Policies: Children under 10 must be accompanied by an adult.

Contact: The Sports Exchange, 10095 W. River St., Truckee, CA 96161; 530/582-4510.

SQUAW VALLEY
Headwall Climbing Walls
At the Cable Car tram building of the Squaw Valley USA ski resort, these unique climbing walls feature 25 easy-to-difficult routes, both indoors on a 30-foot-high course and outdoors on a 45-foot-high course. It's a challenging workout (at 6,200 feet!) for kids and adults. Harnesses and ropes are required and are supplied to participants.

Hours: Daily 10 A.M.–8 P.M. year-around, though hours may vary during spring and fall.

Fees: $12 per session, as long as you want. Climbing shoe rental costs $4.

Contact: Squaw Valley Cafe, 1960 Squaw Valley Rd., Squaw Valley, CA 96146; 530/583-7673; website: www.squaw.com.

KIRKWOOD/HOPE VALLEY/MARKLEEVILLE
Kirkwood Climbing Wall
This 30-foot outdoor wall has a straight surface, an incline, and an overhang and will keep kids challenged as long as their muscles can hold out. The wall is in the new Kirkwood Village and is supervised, but a parent must be present for any child who is 14 or under. The wall is open weekends and holidays 10 A.M.–4 P.M. Kirkwood is on Highway 88 and is a 40-minute drive southwest of the city of South Lake Tahoe.

Hours: 10 A.M.–4 P.M. late June–early Sept., weather permitting.

Fees: $15 for one hour. Rental shoes are extra.

Contact: Kirkwood Mountain Resort, 1501 Kirkwood Meadows Dr., P.O. Box 1, Kirkwood, CA 95646; 209/258-7357; website: www.skikirkwood.com.

Fishing Ponds

SOUTH LAKE TAHOE
Saw Mill Pond
Young anglers can cast a line at this attractive little fishing area just west of the "Y" intersection of U.S. 50 and Highway 89 at the corner of Lake Tahoe Boulevard and Saw Mill Road. You must supply your own bait and equipment. The California Department of Fish and Game stocks the pond with trout in the spring. It's open April–November, weather permitting.

Fees: None.

Contact: Lake Tahoe Basin Management Unit, 870 Emerald Bay Rd., Ste. 1, South Lake Tahoe, CA 96150; 530/573-2600.

Tahoe Trout Farm
If the fish aren't cooperating in Tahoe's many lakes and streams, you might try this place. It offers free admission and use of bait and tackle. Public fishing requires no license, boat, or catch limit. There are two ponds, and you pay only for what you catch. To reach the trout farm, turn south off U.S. 50 at Blue Lake Avenue.

Hours: Open 10 A.M.–7 P.M., from Memorial Day to Labor Day.

Fees: $3–20 per fish, depending on the pond and the weight of your catch. Credit cards are accepted.

Contact: Tahoe Trout Farm, 1023 Blue Lake Ave., South Lake Tahoe, CA 96151; 530/541-1491.

RENO/CARSON VALLEY
Sparks Marina Park
This new and expanding recreation complex in the city of Sparks has a large, manmade lake that

TAHOE WITH CHILDREN

covers 77 acres, averages 60 feet deep and is regularly stocked with rainbow and German brown trout. All you need is a Nevada fishing license (nonresident licenses are available) to try your luck; there is no charge for the fish. The park has cycles and small-craft boats for rent, and also offers picnic areas, covered gazebos, a two-mile walking path around the lake, volleyball courts, a dog running area, and sandy day beaches for swimming or sunning. The marina is at the end of Lincoln off McCarran Boulevard, just north of I-80.

Fees: None for park admission.

Contact: City of Sparks Parks and Recreation Department, 98 Richards Way, Sparks, NV 89432; 775/353-2376.

Nature Centers and Zoos

SOUTH LAKE TAHOE

Lake Tahoe Visitor Center

Free maps, brochures, wilderness permits, interpretive programs, and six self-guided nature trails are available here. One major attraction is the recently remodelled and expanded Stream Profile Chamber, which affords the opportunity to watch cutthroat and rainbow trout, kokanee salmon, and other aquatic life through the windows of an underground viewing chamber. Campfire programs are available in August. You'll find the center on Highway 89, four miles south of the "Y" intersection of U.S. 50 and Highway 89.

Hours: Mid-June–Oct., daily 8 A.M.–5:30 P.M. (weekends only April–mid-June). Interpretive programs are scheduled between 10 A.M. and 8 P.M. June–Labor Day.

Fees: The campfire programs are free.

Contact: Lake Tahoe Basin Management Unit, 870 Emerald Bay Rd., Ste. 1, South Lake Tahoe, CA 96150; 530/573-2674 or 530/573-2600.

RENO/CARSON VALLEY

Animal Ark

This is a nonprofit nature center and wildlife sanctuary, on 38 acres of juniper-covered hills north of downtown Reno, featuring educational information about the predators of North America. Many wildlife species are housed at the center, including the kit fox, mountain lion, bobcat, gray wolf, North American black bear, and a pair of Bengal tigers. Recent expansion has added new animal exhibits that contain native trees and rocks, as well as ponds and glass or covered viewing areas. Educational displays, along with volunteers to assist visitors, are found throughout the park, and animal demonstrations depicting natural behavior also are offered. The area has picnic grounds and is framed by rolling hills and junipers. Take U.S. 395 north to Exit 78, Red Rock Road. Turn right and drive 11.5 miles, then turn right on Deerlodge Road, a gravel route, and go one mile farther.

black bear

BOB RACE

Hours: Daily except Mon., 10 A.M.–4:30 P.M., April 1–Nov. 1. Closed in winter.

Fees: Adults, $6; seniors, $5; children (12 and under), $4; free for two-year-olds and younger.

Contact: Animal Ark, 1265 Deerlodge Rd., P.O. Box 60057, Reno, NV 89506-0057; 775/969-3111; email: mail@animalark.org; website: www.animalark.org.

Sierra Safari Zoo

Families can see more than 200 individual animals representing some 40 species at this nonprofit zoo, which was founded in 1989 by the Sierra Nevada Zoological Society. Nevada's largest zoo, the four-acre compound is north of downtown Reno near Stead. Hands-on experience is emphasized with a one-acre petting area, where people can feed deer, antelope, and other creatures. Baboons, sloths, lions, tigers, wallabies, ostriches, camels, zebras, monkeys, and hyenas are among the residents. Take U.S. 395 to the Red Rock exit in Stead.

Hours: Daily 10 A.M.–5 P.M. April 1–Oct. 31.

Fees: Adults, $5; seniors and children, $4; kids two and under, free. Group rates are available. Monday is free except for group tours.

Contact: Sierra Safari Zoo, 10200 N. Virginia St., Reno, NV 89506; 775/677-1101.

Lahontan National Fish Hatchery

Five miles south of Gardnerville, Nevada, the hatchery features cutthroat and rainbow trout. Free self-guided tours, interpretive exhibits, and brochures help visitors learn more about the life-cycle of the trout. Special guided tours can be arranged by calling ahead.

Hours: Daily 8 A.M.–3 P.M.

Fees: Entrance is free.

Contact: Lahontan National Fish Hatchery, 710 U.S. 395, Gardnerville, NV 89410; 775/265-2425.

Stargazing Tours

Star Safaris

This company, which calls itself America's leading astronomy tour operator, provides nightly stargazing sessions July–October, weather permitting, at two Tahoe-area resorts: Squaw Valley and Kirkwood. Guides use a 30-inch computerized telescope, which is on a prominent, midmountain vantage point. The two-hour programs include visual tours of the solar system, the Milky Way galaxy and beyond, and offer views of star clusters, nebulas, galaxies, and planets. Participants, who can include novices to advanced amateur astronomers, use binoculars, the naked eye, and one of California's largest commercial telescopes. At Squaw Valley, north of Lake Tahoe, sessions are held at High Camp (elevation: 8,200 feet), and guests can arrive early to have dinner at Alexander's Café, which is open until 9 P.M. in the summer. Access by Squaw Valley's Cable Car is required, at extra cost. At Kirkwood, which is 40 minutes south of South Lake Tahoe on Highway 88, the viewing location is at the top of Chair #2. Some advice: Bring very warm clothing including hats or earmuffs, and avoid evenings that have a full moon, which can inhibit viewing. And here's a tip: Consider going during the annual Persiod Meteor Showers, which occur every August and are particularly spectacular from mountaintop viewing areas that are devoid of city lights.

Hours: For Squaw Valley, nightly at 9 P.M., weather permitting, with guests encouraged to arrive by 8:30 P.M. For Kirkwood, sessions are on Sasturdays only.

Fees: For Squaw Valley, $49 for adults, $29 for children 12 and under, with Cable Car tickets (after 5 P.M.) costing an extra $7 for adults and $5 for children. For Kirkwood, call for prices.

Contact: Star Safaris; 800/870-3616, Squaw Valley; 530/583-1742, or Kirkwood; 209/258-7293.

Theme Parks and Amusement Centers

INCLINE VILLAGE/ CRYSTAL BAY

Ponderosa Ranch

Your kids may never have heard of *Bonanza*, but they'll love the assortment of Western-style happenings at the Ponderosa Ranch outdoor theme park, on a hillside above Incline Village. The Cartwright Ranch House is the actual set used in the series (as well as several TV-movie spin-offs). Tours of the park, an entire Old West theme town, and a vast open-air museum of vintage cars and wagons will appeal just as much to adults. Amenities include video arcades, indoor and outdoor shooting galleries, the Mystery Mine, retail shops, a saloon, walking tours, ATV rides, and gunfight shows. Pony rides and a petting zoo are free with admission. Haywagon breakfast rides (wagons pulled by tractors) depart daily 8 A.M.–9:30 A.M. in summer and offer flapjacks and other vittles served on a hill overlooking the lake. Or the wee ones could have a Hossburger for lunch.

Hours: Daily from 9:30 A.M.–5 P.M. (late April–Oct.) and 10 A.M.–4 P.M. in winter (weather permitting). Breakfast haywagon ride, 8 A.M.–9:30 A.M.

Fees: Adults, $11.50; ages 5–11, $6.50; free for four and under. Breakfast rides are additional.

Contact: Ponderosa Ranch, 100 Ponderosa Rd., Incline Village, NV 89451; 775/831-0691; website: www.ponderosaranch.com.

SOUTH LAKE TAHOE

Harrah's Family Fun Center

This is a 12,000-square-foot facility in the lower level of Harrah's Lake Tahoe at Stateline in South Shore features a Play Pal Jungle Gym, a redemption center, virtual reality laser tag, and video games. A new indoor playground has two levels of slides, ball pools, and climbing areas. No supervised child care is available.

Hours: Weekdays 9 A.M.–midnight, and 9 A.M.–1 A.M. on weekends.

Contact: Harrah's Casino Hotel, P.O. Box 8,

Borges Carriage Rides at Stateline, South Shore

Stateline, NV 89449; 775/588-6611 or 800/HARRAHS (800/427-7247); website: www.harrahstahoe.com/FunCenter.html.

Harveys Virtual Forest Arcade

In the lower level of Harveys, this is a vast electronic playland offering the newest technology in video and redemption games, and is a favorite hangout of teens and pre-teens. There are simulated skiing machines, Daytona racing, and motion simulator games. Winners can redeem tickets for prices.

Hours: Open Sun.–Thurs. 10 A.M.–10 P.M., and 10 A.M.–1 A.M. Fri.–Saturday.

Contact: Harveys Resort Casino, P.O. Box 128, Hwy. 50, Stateline, NV 89449; 775/588-2411 or 800/-HARVEYS (800/427-8397); website: www.harveystahoe.com.

Tahoe Amusement Park

This outdoor amusement center, on U.S. 50, features a mini-Ferris wheel, a giant slide, and a merry-go-round. Other amenities include a video arcade, a tilt-a-whirl, Paratrooper, Willy the Whale, a miniature train, a roller coaster, go-carts (including new two-seaters), and electric cars. A snack bar serves up hot dogs, pretzels, and cotton candy.

Hours: Open May–Sept., Sat. and Sun. only in May, 11 A.M.–6 P.M.; from Memorial Day–Labor Day, daily 11 A.M.–7 P.M., closed Monday.

Fees: A Family Book of 40 tickets is $20, single tickets are $.65 apiece.

Contact: Tahoe Amusement Park, 2401 Lake Tahoe Blvd., South Lake Tahoe, CA 96105; 530/541-1300.

RENO/CARSON VALLEY

Boomtown Fun Center

Commanding a prominent location on a hill next to I-80 west of Reno, the casino/fun house hybrid Boomtown Fun Center is a great spot to turn the kids loose. The place is mostly wall-to-wall slot machines and gaming, but the Fun Center is an indoor wing devoted to more than 200 arcade and video games. There's a 1908 antique carousel, an indoor Ferris Wheel, a themed 9-hole miniature golf course, and an iWerks 3-D Dynamic Motion Theater, where the seats move viewers in sync with the action playing out on the screen. The theater, which features four different films, is fairly intense and realistic, even for adults. The Tumbleweed Pizza Cafe, a party room, and a prize redemption center are adjacent to the action. A newly constructed hotel, an RV park, a gas station, and restaurants are also available at Boomtown.

Hours: Daily 10 A.M.–10 P.M. Sun.–Thurs. and 10 A.M.–midnight Fri.–Saturday.

Fees: You can pay for each attraction but the best deal is an all-day pass for unlimited uses (including shows), and this ranges $9–14, depending on the age of the child.

Contact: Boomtown Hotel Casino, I-80 W and Garson Rd./P.O. Box 399, Verdi, NV 89439; 775/345-6000 or 800/648-3790; website: www.boomtowncasinos.com.

Circus Circus Hotel Casino

Entertainment reigns supreme for all ages at the Big Top under the big roof, as jugglers, trapeze artists, wirewalkers, and other daredevils do their stuff to take your mind off that losing streak or to keep the kids occupied while you roll the dice. The Midway features carnival games, a redemption center, a video arcade, a shooting gallery, and free circus acts at regular intervals throughout the afternoon and evening. Restaurants and restrooms are above the Midway.

Hours: Weekdays 10 A.M.–midnight, and 10 A.M.–1 A.M. on weekends. Circus acts are performed daily 11 A.M.–midnight.

Contact: Circus Circus Hotel Casino, 500 N. Sierra St./P.O. Box 5880, Reno, NV 89503; 775/329-0711 or 800/648-5010; website: www.circusreno.com.

Idlewild Playland

This 49-acre complex in Reno features amusement rides including a train, electric cars, a carousel, planes, a roller coaster, baby bumper boats, and a tilt-a-whirl. Kids will also enjoy going for rides on animals. Picnic and party areas, a swimming pool, volleyball courts, and baseball fields are among the other amenities. There's also a skate park across the street. Individual ride tickets and discount ticket books are available.

Hours: Daily 11 A.M.–6 P.M. on weekdays and 10 A.M.–6 P.M. on weekends. Closed during winter until Feb. (weather permitting).

Fees: Parking and admission are free. There's a nominal charge for some rides.

Contact: Idlewild Playland, 1900 Idlewild Dr., Reno, NV 89509; 775/329-6008.

Reno Hilton Fun Quest Center

This is a massive, 40,000-square-foot indoor fun center, and it's not likely that Junior will run out of things to do here. In the lower level of this large Reno hotel, the center has over 200 video arcade and redemption games, interactive laser tag arenas, a six-person space battle video game, bumper cars, a batting cage, and "Tumble Town" (a supervised soft play area for ages 1–8). The Hilton is at the corner of Mill and Glendale.

Hours: Open Sun.–Thurs., 10 A.M.–11 P.M.; Fri. and Sat., 10 A.M.–midnight.

Fees: Major games range $2–6 each.

Contact: Reno Hilton, 2500 E. 2nd St., Reno, NV 89595; 775/789-2FUN (775/789-2386); website: www.funquest.net.

Wild Island

When the mercury starts soaring in the high desert of Reno, as it inevitably does in midsummer, Wild Island is the place to cool off. The 11-acre park, just east of John Ascuaga's Nugget off I-80, has a series of water rides that include speed slides, a wave pool, and a lazy river. The recently added Hurricane Cove, an interactive water play area, has a giant cascading waterfall that spills 650 gallons of water from a bucket on top of a tree house. And in 2000 the park unveiled the Scorpion, a new speed slide with a double tube that is 3.5 stories high. If that's not enough adventure, there are two 18-hole miniature golf courses that use theatrical settings and coordinating soundtracks, with such scenes as a European street, a 41-foot castle, and an old grist mill. A futuristic game arcade called Tut's Tomb and a go-cart raceway with sprint cars (for drivers up to 42 inches tall) and Indy cars (for those over 42 inches) are also available at the park.

Hours: The water park is open 11 A.M.–7 P.M. in summer, until 5 P.M. the rest of the year. Other attractions are open until 11 P.M. on weekdays and midnight on weekends.

Fees: The waterpark is $14.95 for kids under four feet tall, $18.95 for kids over four feet, $4.95 for seniors over 60, and free for children three and under. After 4 P.M., all admissions are $9.50. Golf course, $4.95 for 18 holes and $5.95 for 36 holes. Indy cars are $4.95 for five minutes, sprint cars are $2.75 for five minutes, electric scooters are $3.50 per 15-minute ride, the Frog Hopper is $2 per ride, and Frog City (includes slide complex, Bounce House and Frog Hopper) is $4 all day. Group rates are available.

Contact: Wild Island, 250 Wild Island Ct., Sparks, NV 89434; 775/331-WILD (775/331-9453) (recorded message) or 775/359-2927 (office); website: www.wildisland.com.

Miniature Golf

KINGS BEACH/TAHOE VISTA/CARNELIAN BAY

Well on its way to becoming the largest miniature golf course in Northern California, **Magic Carpet Golf** has two courses, one with 19 holes and another with 28 holes (each has an extra finishing hole at the end). A new third course with 18 holes was under construction as this edition went to press.

Hours: Daily (weather permitting) 10 A.M.–11 P.M. (weekends only in spring and fall). Closed during winter.

Fees: $5.50 for 19 holes; $8 for 28 holes.

Contact: Magic Carpet Golf, 5167 N. Lake Blvd., Carnelian Bay, CA; 530/546-4279.

SOUTH LAKE TAHOE

Recently remodeled, this outdoor **Magic Carpet Golf** location has both a 19-hole course and a 28-hole course.

Hours: Daily 10 A.M.–7 P.M., weather permitting, April–November.

Fees: The fee for 19 holes is $6 per round, and for 28 holes is $8 per day/night.

Contact: Magic Carpet Golf, 2455 Lake Tahoe Blvd., South Lake Tahoe, CA; 530/541-3787.

FEATHER RIVER COUNTRY/LAKES BASIN

Outdoor **Graeagle Miniature Golf and Driving Range** is 50 minutes north of Truckee on Highway 89.

Hours: Daily 10 A.M.–7 P.M. Closed during winter.

Fees: $3–5 for miniature golf and $3–5 for a bucket of balls for the driving range.

Contact: Graeagle Miniature Golf and Driving Range, Hwy. 89, Graeagle, CA; 530/836-2107.

RENO/CARSON VALLEY

This outdoor **Magic Carpet Golf** course has two 19-hole courses and one 28-hole course.

Hours: Daily 10 A.M.–10 P.M.

Fees: The cost is $5.50 for 19 holes, $8 for 28 holes. Party packages are available.

Contact: Magic Carpet Golf, 6925 S. Virginia St., Reno, NV; 775/853-8837.

Skating and Skateboarding

SOUTH LAKE TAHOE

Bijou Skate Park

This is regarded as one of the top five public skate parks in California. It opened at the Bijou Community Center in late 1996 and draws legions of young skaters and skateboarders. The concrete bowls and jumps offer creative transitions, enough to keep youngsters occupied for hours. Managed by the South Lake Tahoe Parks and Recreation Department, the outdoor skate course is in Bijou Community Park on Al Tahoe Boulevard, just south of U.S. 50.

Hours: Open as weather permits.

Fees: There is no fee for use of the park.

Contact: Bijou Skate Park; 530/542-6055.

RENO/CARSON VALLEY

Roller Kingdom

This roller rink is open year-round. It offers a snack bar, rentals, and sales.

Hours: Closed Mon. for private parties. Open Tues., 1 P.M.–4 P.M.; Wed., 5 P.M.–9 P.M.; Thurs., 6:30 P.M.–9 P.M.; Fri., 6 P.M.–8:30 P.M., 8 P.M.–10:30 P.M. and 10 P.M.–midnight; Sat., 10 A.M.–10:30 A.M. (free skating lessons), 10:30 A.M.–1 P.M. (tiny tot session), 1 P.M.–3:30 P.M., 2:30 P.M.–5 P.M. and the same evening sessions as on Fri.; Sun. (family day), 1 P.M.–5 P.M. and 7:30 P.M.–10 P.M. (adult night).

Fees: Skating rink: $5 per session. Skate rentals:

$2, Rollerblades, $4. **Contact:** Roller Kingdom, 515 E. 7th St., Reno, NV; 775/329-3472.

Skate Trak

This facility in Carson City offers year-round skating opportunities. There are morning, afternoon, and evening sessions for adults, children, and families.

Hours: Open Fri., noon–4 P.M., 7 P.M.–9:30 P.M., and 9 P.M.–11:30 P.M.; Sat. noon–2:30 P.M. and 2:30 P.M.–5 P.M. evening, 7 P.M.–10 P.M.; Sun. family session, 1 P.M.–4 P.M.

Fees: Skating sessions: $3.50–4.50. Skate rentals: $1.50 for roller skates and $3 for in-line skates.

Contact: Skate Trak, 3520 U.S. 50 E, Carson City, NV 89701; 775/884-4500 (recording of schedule and hours) or 775/884-1399 (special functions).

Wedding Sites and Services

Something about Lake Tahoe tugs at the heart. Here nature's handiwork has created a place for hopeless romantics, with glacier-carved mountains, pristine bays, and sandy beaches. Tahoe works its magic in many ways: the grandeur of Emerald Bay, the blue waters plied by paddlewheel excursion boats, stunning sunsets from the top of Heavenly's tram or gondola, miles of white sand beaches and rocky shoreline, the twinkle of lights in the evening around the lake. There are towering hotels that overlook more riches than any slot machine could deliver, European restaurants

where you can dine on soft-shell crab as water laps at the piers, and cozy little inns with big fireplaces that invite togetherness. Could there be a more ideal spot for two people to join in matrimony?

Unique in the world among alpine lakes, Tahoe has become a popular destination for couples to say their vows—as well as enjoy a romantic honeymoon. You can take your pick of just about any venue imaginable for a wedding: a historic church, a famous lakeside estate, a rocky overlook at Emerald Bay, an excursion boat, a ski resort, a hotel, a beautiful beach, or any one of more than two dozen wedding chapels that have sprung up in recent years. It can be an elaborate affair for

Silver Lake Chapel

a large group, with dancing and entertainment, or a simple ceremony in a small chapel.

Nevada has always had a reputation as an easy place to obtain a marriage license and a cheap, quick ceremony. South Lake Tahoe, in particular, has catered to this business; production-line weddings are nothing unusual in the summer here. Recent changes that facilitate the issuance of licenses in California have generated even more business. Everybody, it seems, has a chapel, even if it's a converted motel room or a former knick-knack shop in a casino. The chapels range from inauspicious places, with enough highway noise to drown out the pastor, to elaborate venues with artificial lighting and video camera systems. Because of fierce competition among wedding providers, the cost of a basic, no-frills ceremony can be dirt cheap (less than $200). Of course, you can also go soup-to-nuts and hold an elegant, luxurious event that everyone in your party will enjoy.

In recent years, as the wedding industry has grown, so, too, have the demands from consumers. There is now a more upscale, sophisticated environment for those who want it. Wedding planners can customize a ceremony to very exacting (and sometimes quirky) specifications. Outdoor weddings have become nearly as popular as indoor weddings, and there are dozens of lakefront sites with gazebos, lawns, or decks to accommodate vows with a view.

The only restrictions in planning the special day are your imagination and your budget. Using Tahoe and its landscape as an outdoor chapel, you can devise a beautiful ceremony that doesn't have to be expensive. Consider some of the weddings that have been performed here in recent years:

• Hiking to the top of Mt. Tallac, an exhausting climb with an elevation gain of 3,255 feet (to the summit at 9,735 feet). The bride and groom wore hiking boots with their wedding attire, and by the time they reached the top, after six hours on foot, it was amazing that they had any stamina left to say their vows.

OBTAINING A MARRIAGE LICENSE

CALIFORNIA

Confidential Marriage License
No blood test or waiting period is required. Applicants must sign a form stating they are living together as husband and wife. Must be at least 18 years old and bring picture identification. You are required to buy the license (approximately $45) in the county where the ceremony will be performed.

Licenses may be obtained from the following: California wedding chapels; El Dorado County Recorder, Clerk Office, 3368 Lake Tahoe Blvd., Ste. 108, South Lake Tahoe, 530/573-3408; Placer County Clerk-Recorder in Auburn, 530/889-7983; or the Placer County Sheriff's Department, 530/581-6305.

Regular License
Blood tests are not required. Both members of the couple must be at least 18 years old, possess picture identification, and have a witness. Obtain a license from your hometown county courthouse or the El Dorado County Recorder, Clerk Office, 3368 Lake Tahoe Blvd., Ste. 108, South Lake Tahoe; 530/573-3408. License fees vary by county (approximately $50) and can be used anywhere in California.

NEVADA

No blood test or waiting period is required. Both members of the couple must be at least 18 years old and bring picture identification. Those 16–18 years of age can be married with parents or legal guardians either present or by obtaining notarized written consent.

Licenses ($50 fee for the license, $10 more for a certified copy, cash only) can be obtained from the following: Douglas County Clerk in Minden, 775/782-9015; Carson City Clerk, 775/887-2084; Douglas County Administration Building, 175 Hwy. 50 at Kahle Drive in Stateline, 775/586-7290; or Washoe County Justice Court in Incline Village, 775/832-4166.

WEDDINGS

Afterward, the couple ate chocolate éclairs and drank champagne.

• Sailing above Tahoe in a hot air balloon. One couple not only recited their vows 4,000 feet in the air, but wrote a poem after their lofty experience and included it in cards sent out to friends and family.

• A beach ceremony at Sand Harbor, on the Nevada side of the lake, in which the bride made her entrance by walking barefoot through the water across a shallow cove. She and her fiancé were married at the end of a carpeted aisle, and following the ceremony, their families and guests blew bubbles above the newlyweds.

• A winter wedding in which the couple took the Heavenly Ski Resort tram to its mid-mountain terminal, said their vows from the deck of the lodge, and then skied off into the horizon.

A number of celebrities have said "I do" at the lake in years past. Actor Tom Selleck, for example, married his lady love on a quiet and secluded sand beach on the Nevada side. And comedian-actor Robin Williams also chose Tahoe for his wedding. Clearly, the opportunities for a memorable wedding (and a fun-filled honeymoon) beckon from every corner of this alpine paradise. No doubt about it, Tahoe is for lovers.

There are as many wedding possibilities as there are attractions in Lake Tahoe. Outdoor weddings beside the shore or on a mountain overlooking the lake are among the more popular ceremonies. You can tie the knot in a state park, in a national forest, or in one of Tahoe's several historic estates. When considering any of these options, it's best to work through a local wedding coordinator who knows how to deal with the paperwork, especially if you want a ceremony on public lands. Usually, most chapels and some churches will perform offsite ceremonies. The following list includes the major hotels, resorts, churches, theme parks, and chapels that regularly perform weddings. But the possibilities extend far beyond this group. For

You can take your pick of just about any venue imaginable for a wedding: a historic church, a famous lakeside estate, a rocky overlook at Emerald Bay, an excursion boat, a ski resort, a hotel, a beautiful beach, or any one of more than two dozen wedding chapels that have sprung up in recent years.

other ideas, consult the chapters on accommodations (especially bed-and-breakfast inns, most of which promote weddings), resorts, beaches, sights, and restaurants and nightlife.

Prices for Wedding Services

To rent banquet space in hotels, conference centers, restaurants, and historic buildings, figure on spending between $100 and $400 per hour, usually with minimum two-hour rentals required. Price depends on the size of the room and of the wedding party. For outdoor ceremonies on lawns, beaches and piers, plan on between $300 and $500 for a half-hour event. Often there are add-on costs for setup and take-down, and catering is charged separately. For chartered boats on the lake, you can rent banquet space on the large paddlewheelers (while sharing the boat with other passengers), usually for a per-person meal, drink and ride cost. To charter motor and sailing vessels for your exclusive use, the range can vary greatly, $500–2,000 for a two-hour voyage.

Prices from rental chapels are usually quite competitive. They often start at a rock-bottom ("standard" or "basic") rate of $150 for a quick ceremony and go up, depending on how many frills you want. Advertised or unadvertised specials may be offered, especially during slow periods. In general, minister fees range $75–200, photography $75–700, videography $100–250, flowers $75–1,500, catering $25–125 per guest, cakes $50–350, and live music $150–600. Prices are usually open to negotiation for large and elaborate weddings.

In addition to the facilities listed here, Lake Tahoe has a number of independent wedding consultants and coordinators, who can arrange virtually any type of ceremony indoors or outdoors, as well as attend to all of the details including the honeymoon. To find them, check out the websites or contact the visitor information centers listed above.

WEDDINGS

Hotels and Motels

SQUAW VALLEY

PlumpJack Squaw Valley Inn

Several features make this 60-room hotel a unique and convenient place for a wedding any time of the year: It lies at the base of Squaw Valley USA, with its multitude of summer and winter recreational amenities; there are two large indoor banquet areas and one of the best in-house catering departments at Tahoe (thanks to its famous gourmet restaurant); and up to 150 guests (larger than the average wedding party) can stay in the hotel. Couples usually choose to perform their vows outside on a grassy knoll beside the swimming pool. Other close-at-hand venues include the top of the Squaw Valley tram (beware of winds!) and the Queen of the Snows Catholic Church.

PlumpJack has an attractive eclectic interior that might best be described as Shakespearean art deco. The banquet areas are huge—4,500 square feet each—and are on separate floors. The $250 rental fee includes both rooms as well as all setup and breakdown, with one bar, all tables, chairs, and candelabra. There are additional fees for dance floor rental and storage and stage setup. A special bonus: The lucky couple gets to stay in the plush penthouse suite on their wedding night free of charge. An additional plus is that the property does just one wedding per weekend, so there is no rush to be out the door for the next ceremony.

Amenities: Two banquet rooms, each capable of seating 185 people in rounds of eight, and an outside pool deck that can accommodate 150. If you book the reception and catering, rooms are discounted to the wedding party for reservations of 10 or more rooms.

Contact: PlumpJack Squaw Valley Inn, 1920 Squaw Valley Rd./P.O. Box 2407, Olympic Valley, CA 96146; 530/583-1576 or 800/323-7666; website: www.plumpjack.com.

The Resort at Squaw Creek

Rising out of the forest next to the foothills of the Squaw Valley USA ski area, this luxurious hotel offers plenty of atmosphere for weddings: spacious outdoor patios and decks, a top-ranked golf course, award-winning restaurants, and banquet rooms with majestic views of the valley and towering peaks. Beamed ceilings and massive windows impart grandeur and sophistication, and the superb catering and service, offered at a multitude of indoor and outdoor wedding sites, work to create a memorable setting for any ceremony. If money is no object, and you want to impress your guests with gourmet food and sparkling mountain vistas, this is a great place to do it.

Amenities: The resort has a variety of wedding locations, some as bucolic as a wooden bridge over a stream. Receptions include catered two- or three-course meals, wedding cakes, linens, tables, chairs, a dance floor, a bandstand, and a DJ. A wedding planner arranges ministers, florists, photographers, menus, and entertainment, and you can even order ice sculptures. Wedding packages for any time of the year offer ceremonies on-site, and you get a free wedding night suite if you have a reception for at least 100 guests.

Contact: The Resort at Squaw Creek, 400 Squaw Creek Rd./P.O. Box 3333, Olympic Valley, CA 96146; 530/583-6300 or 800/403-4434; website: www.squawcreek.com.

INCLINE VILLAGE/CRYSTAL BAY

Cal-Neva Resort

Perched on a rocky knoll overlooking Crystal Bay, Cal-Neva Resort boasts the most picturesque setting of any major hotel on the lake. Exquisite lake views from the balconies and patio terraces of the hotel provide several idyllic backdrops for a wedding ceremony. Cal-Neva supplies convenient catering services, a relaxation spa, and all the elements needed to ensure a cozy honeymoon. If you're looking to have a grand reception, there's the historic Indian Room with its wood-beamed ceilings and rustic memorabilia, or the famous Frank Sinatra Celebrity Showroom. One popular setting for vows is a gazebo on a large elevated patio, but there are also two indoor chapels to choose from. This hotel has lots of history, some of it spicy, including rumored dalliances between Marilyn Monroe and John F. Kennedy. The property was once owned by Frank Sinatra. Because the hotel straddles the state line, you can have your wedding in either California or Nevada. And here's another service: You can have your wedding broadcast live on the Internet!

Amenities: Three chapels with lake views and ministers are available. They include a gazebo overlooking the lake, with a seating capacity of 400; the Lady of the Lake Chapel, with its churchlike setting and a capacity of 120; and the Lakeview Chapel, with a capacity of 50. The hotel has a full-service wedding department, including florist, wedding boutique, photographer, gown and tux rental, and beauty salon. Honeymoon packages are available.

Contact: Cal-Neva Resort, 2 Stateline Rd./P.O. Box 368, Crystal Bay, NV 89402; 775/832-4000 or 800/225-6382; website: www.calnevaresort.com

Hyatt Regency Lake Tahoe

Nestled among the tall trees at Incline Village, the Hyatt Regency has its own private beach with grand views of Lake Tahoe. The Lakeside Lodge, which is across the street from the main building, is the best location to tie the knot. It's right on the beach, affords wonderful vistas, is next to the Lone Eagle Grille restaurant with its banquet rooms, and has proximity to a new pier. But the main hotel also offers banquet rooms, a ballroom, and large tents that can be set up on the lawn. The Hyatt is close to great restaurants, golf courses, and other points of interest on the North Shore, and the interior recently underwent a major facelift that has given it an Old Tahoe look with beamed ceilings and river-rock trim.

Amenities: Wedding, reception, and honeymoon packages are available. Locations consist of the Lakeside Lodge, with three sections each seating 100 to 120 people; the Donner Room,

which seats 10 to 40; the Pool Deck, which seats 25 to 75; the Water Gardens, which seats 200; the Regency Ballroom, which seats up to 900 in sections of 50 guests; and the outside lawn, which offers special tents and can seat up to 400. The hotel can provide tables and linens, silver plates and crystal glassware, fine china, a dance floor, a bandstand, and a wedding coordinator. Breakfast, lunch, and dinner menus and wine and bar service are also available. Couples must hire their own musicians, pastor, photographer, and florist, and a recommendation list is provided.

Contact: Hyatt Regency Lake Tahoe, 111 Country Club Dr./P.O. Box 3239, Incline Village, NV 89450; 775/832-1234, ext. 4460, or 800/233-1234; website: www.laketahoehyatt.com.

SOUTH LAKE TAHOE

Caesars Tahoe Wedding Chapel

Do you like special effects? If you're a fan of Hollywood movie magic, this may be the place for your nuptials. Clearly the most high-tech of the wedding chapels at Tahoe, this one has a novel feature—an "environmental" ceiling. By pushing a few buttons, the wizards behind the scene can produce any mood or time of day—from dawn to moonlight, or even a combination, if you prefer. The setting is quite ethereal, from the grand white player piano to the marble altar. Video cameras film everything, and the resulting tape has fade-ins, fade-outs, and a moody soundtrack. The chapel is on the ground floor of the hotel, and the location is a little strange; it's next to the hotel's indoor swimming pool. Fortunately the grand foyer is air-conditioned, and there are finishing rooms where brides can attend to those final touches.

Amenities: A chapel, a minister, candles, grand piano music, videography, still photography, and flowers are available. Couples must obtain their own marriage license from Douglas County. The hotel is available for receptions and accommodations. The minimum chapel time is 30 minutes.

Contact: Caesars Tahoe Wedding Chapel, 55 U.S. 50/P.O. Box 6930, Stateline, NV 89449;

WEDDINGS

775/588-4422 or 800/833-4422; website: www.caesarswedding.com.

Fantasy Inn

The lake's most unusual small hotel displays European and Old Tahoe architectural touches and has elaborate theme rooms geared specifically to couples. These include the Romeo and Juliet, Graceland, Rainforest, and Roman suites. A small but elegant and tastefully decorated chapel with video cameras adjoins the inn's lobby, and there's a lawn for outdoor ceremonies and small receptions. The on-site coordinator can arrange weddings here and in other locales around the lake. The theme suites, always popular, make great honeymoon retreats with their oversize tubs for two, oversize beds, and ceiling-mounted televisions. Everything is deluxe and intimate, with no crowds or clanging slot machines to distract newlyweds.

Amenities: Among the services available are indoor and outdoor weddings, a candlelight ceremony, video, flowers, a marriage license and certificate, music, and romantic gifts. Packages include the full service, a honeymoon suite, toasting glasses with champagne, and breakfast in bed.

Contact: Fantasy Inn, 3696 Lake Tahoe Blvd., South Lake Tahoe, CA 96150; 530/541-7275 or 800/624-3837; website: www.fantasy-inn.com.

Forest Inn Suites

This deluxe condominium-hotel has an elegant new wedding chapel with reception rooms, as well as new honeymoon suites with fireplaces and spas. The property, on 5.5 forested acres, has a grand lobby with stonework and beamed ceilings, two heated pools and a health club with steam and sauna.

Amenities: All-inclusive wedding and honeymoon packages are available. Wedding coordinators can also arrange flowers, photography, cake, engraved champagne glasses, embroidered towels, an outdoor ceremony, and limousine or carriage ride.

Contact: Forest Inn Suites, 1 Lake Pkwy., South Lake Tahoe, CA 96150; 530/541-6655 or 800/822-5950; email: Info@ForestInn.com; website: www.forestinn.com/Wedding.htm.

Harveys Wedding Chapel

Here is an attractive chapel that faces the rear parking lot of the casino hotel, a not particularly scenic vista, although a tier of curtains stretches across the lower portion of the 18-foot-high windows so that guests see trees and sky. The interior is well appointed, with a marble altar, a mirrored and concave ceiling, and comfortable upholstered chairs. The chapel is on the third level next to the convention center. As a hotel, Harveys has many excellent features, including spacious and modern rooms with dramatic lake views, good service, and some of the best restaurants in Tahoe.

Amenities: The hotel can provide a pastor, chocolates, champagne, a cake, a reception, video and still photography, and music. Flowers and off-site weddings also are available.

Contact: The Wedding Chapel at Harveys, U.S. 50/P.O. Box 128, Stateline, NV 89449; 775/588-2411 or 800/553-1022; website: www .harveystahoeweddings.com.

Horizon Casino Resort

The hotel has a small, windowless chapel next to the ground-floor arcade, and it is functional if not inspiring. Many of the guest rooms at this hotel, however, have great views of the lake, for the Horizon is situated on the shoreline side of the highway. The hotel recently underwent an extensive remodeling, but the chapel remains basically a square room with simple appointments. However, for both a view and a memorable ceremony, you can always make arrangements for the Presley suite, where the King himself used to stay back when this was the Sahara Tahoe and he would perform here. The large suite, which has a kitchen, a living room, a dining room, an exercise room, and a separate bedroom, makes a perfect honeymoon retreat and has a sweeping, high vista of Lake Tahoe. The chapel seats 50, but ceremonies also can be arranged outdoors on the courtyard or by the lake, as well as on skis or from a horse-drawn sleigh or carriage.

Amenities: The hotel can provide a pastor, music (vocalist, pianist, or prerecorded), video or still photography, champagne, flowers, and candles.

Contact: The Wedding Chapel at the Lake Tahoe

Horizon, U.S. 50/P.O. Box 6833, Lake Tahoe, NV 89449; 775/588-1162 or 800/567-1162; website: www.horizoncasino.com.

Timber Cove Lodge Weddings

As part of the Best Western Timber Cove Lodge, this is a large but moderately priced wedding venue that is on the shoreline of Lake Tahoe and has its own chapel, grassy knolls, a boathouse, a banquet room, a beach and a 1,000-foot pier—longest at the lake. Weddings can be arranged at any of these sites. The Capella del Lago ("Chapel of the Lake") is designed to evoke the flavor of old Italian chapels, and can accommodate up to 40 people. A large lawn fronts the beach and the lake and can seat a large party of up to 200 guests. For a reception, there's a spacious outdoor party tent with a dance floor.

Amenities: Packages can include marriage license, photography, video, flowers, champagne, toasting glasses, and wedding cake. The staff also can arrange live or recorded music, limousine, hair styling and makeup, reception, and accommodations. A nonrefundable deposit is required, and one hour is reserved for each ceremony.

Contact: Timber Cove Lodge Marina Resort, 3411 Lake Tahoe Blvd./P.O. Box 128, South Lake Tahoe, CA 96150; 530/541-6722, ext. 7411; website: www.timbercovetahoe.com/weddingsattimbercove.

The Ridge Tahoe

This lofty and luxurious condominium resort at the top of Kingsbury Grade next to the Nevada side of Heavenly ski area offers sweeping views of Tahoe to the north and of Carson Valley to the east. Rooms are large, open and well-lit by spacious windows with beautiful Sierra vistas.

Amenities: The Valley View Room can accommodate 75 for a wedding, 65 for a reception or 40 for a sit-down banquet. Other venues include the Clubhouse Pool Deck (suitable for 65 for a ceremony) and the Knoll Pool Deck (suitable for 100). Catering services and a portable dance floor for 15 couples are available, as are accommodations in the condominium units. Other facilities include a private chairlift to Heavenly (in winter), indoor and outdoor tennis courts, and a fitness center.

Contact: The Ridge Tahoe, 400 Ridge Club Dr., Kingsbury, NV 89449; 775/588-3553, ext. 4605 website: www.ridge-tahoe.com.

Tahoe Seasons Resort

Across from the original California base of Heavenly ski resort, this secluded, wooded condominium resort hotel offers panoramic views, gourmet cuisine and a romantic honeymoon suite with private spa and fireplace. Facilities can accommodate up to 160 guests for weddings and receptions.

Contact: Four Seasons Resort, 3901 Saddle Rd., South Lake Tahoe, CA 96150; 800/540-4874; website: www.tahoeseasons.com.

WEDDINGS

Resorts, Inns, and Retreats

TRUCKEE/DONNER

Ice Lakes Lodge

Talk about an ideal location for a ceremony! This new lodge on Donner Summit has the look and feel of a Tyrolean Inn, and it sits on the water's edge at Serene Lakes, two beautiful alpine jewels with forested shorelines. The Lodge includes overnight guest rooms, a deck, a lawn with shade trees, a full-service restaurant, cocktail lounge and a huge lobby with sitting area and fireplace. An entire wedding party of 50 or so can stay, play and partake of the ceremony all in one place. Plus the bride and groom can hop into a small dinghy and sail off into the sunset. On Soda Springs Road past the main entrance to Royal Gorge Cross Country Resort. Nearby are hiking and biking trails, along with both downhill and Nordic skiing. One of the lodge's most endearing qualities is the tranquil nature of the location, far away from traffic and crowds. Facilities include outdoor set-up and full catering for receptions.
Contact: Ice Lakes Lodge, 1111 Soda Springs Rd., Soda Springs, CA 95728; 530/426-7660.

Northstar-at-Tahoe

This forested, four-seasons resort a few miles north of Lake Tahoe offers skiing in the winter, and golf, tennis, and cycling trails in summer. Wedding and reception sites can be arranged at any of several indoor and outdoor locations, from the well-appointed golf clubhouse to the ski hill.
Amenities: On-site wedding and lodging facilities are available. Sometimes there are ski/wedding packages that offer two nights' lodging, two-day lift tickets, dinner, champagne and a chocolate basket in the room, and access to Northstar's Recreation Center.
Contact: Northstar-at-Tahoe, Northstar Dr. and Hwy. 267/P.O. Box 2499, Truckee, CA 96160; 530/562-1010 or 800/GO-NORTH (800/466-6784); website: www.skinorthstar.com.

Rainbow Lodge

Charming from top to bottom, this 1920s bed-and-breakfast has a country feel, with stone, wood, and warm interior colors. There's a large dining room, a lobby with a fireplace, and a full bar, along with attractive spots for a ceremony beside the Yuba River.
Amenities: The inn is available for weddings in summer only, June–September. An outdoor garden with a gazebo is behind the lodge and seats 150 people. The indoor wedding site seats 45 guests. A buffet catered by the lodge can be stationed in the dining room, on an outdoor deck, or on a lawn. Rental fees include linens, glassware, setup, and cleaning. The bride and groom must arrange all other services, such as the marriage license, a minister, cake, flowers, photography, and music; a referral list is provided for those services. Lodging accommodations are also available for the wedding party.
Contact: Rainbow Lodge, 50800 Hampshire Rocks Rd./P.O. Box 1100, Soda Springs, CA 95728; 530/426-3871 (reservations) and 530/426-3661 (lodge); website: www.royalgorge.com.

Sugar Bowl

When the lifts close down in summer, the historic, European-style lodge remains open for special functions and meetings, including weddings. This classic Bavarian building has one of the best outdoor decks in the Sierra, as well as a grand dining room and lots of stone and wood accents. There's also a 27-room hotel (with a deluxe suite for honeymooners) that can accommodate up to 85 people. Access is via gondola or road. There are great photo opportunities nearby at the famous Rainbow Bridge on the Donner Summit overlooking Donner Lake.
Amenities: Sites include an outside lawn next to a creek, a large deck overlooking the mountains, and the dining room. The resort can provide a fully catered buffet or sit-down meal in the restaurant or on the lodge deck, with a capacity of up to 500 people. Head chef John Ketter is renowned for his gourmet menus and

imaginative buffets. The staff can perform other planning tasks as well, including selection of a minister, a photographer, flowers, and entertainment. The lodge is available June–October, any day of the week.

Contact: Sugar Bowl, Old Hwy. 40/P.O. Box 5, Norden, CA 95724; 530/426-6724 or 530/426-9000; email: sales@sugarbowl.com; website: www.sugarbowl.com.

SQUAW VALLEY
Christy Inn

Once the home of Wayne and Sandy Poulsen, founders of the Squaw Valley USA ski area, this rustic property includes a rambling guest house and a gourmet restaurant, Graham's. Weddings can be performed in the restaurant or outside on the summer garden area and deck followed by an indoor reception.

Amenities: The indoor seating capacity is 80, and the outdoor capacity is 200.

Contact: Christy Inn, 1604 Christy Ln./P.O. Box 2008, Olympic Valley, CA 96146; 530/583-3451 or 530/583-0454, fax 530/583-2040.

Squaw Valley USA

Now a four-seasons resort, this ski area operates the High Camp Bath and Tennis Club, a complex of restaurants and recreation facilities at elevation 8,200 feet. Weddings can be held here any time of the year, winter or summer, on a spacious patio or deck above sheer granite cliffs, with the distant valley 2,000 feet below. The wedding party and guests arrive on the Squaw Valley Cable Car, which terminates at High Camp.

Amenities: Five indoor seating areas are available, along with outdoor venues for the ceremony. The independent concession that runs High Camp can provide all catering, beverages, and setup and teardown, as well as provide recommendations for the pastor, cake, flowers, and entertainment. Prices vary, depending on the size and wishes of the wedding party.

Contact: High Camp Food and Beverage, P.O. Box 2288, Olympic Valley, CA 96146; 530/583-2555; website: www.squaw.com.

TAHOE CITY/WEST SHORE
Granlibakken Resort

The delightful Granlibakken Resort is tucked away in a cozy and secluded forest setting of 74 acres, yet is close to Tahoe City and many points of interest. Designed as a tennis, ski, and conference resort, the facility has a new Executive Lodge, which works well for wedding parties, since there are 36 units that can sleep 80 people. Another 123 condominium and motel units in the remainder of the complex can handle more than 250 additional guests, so you can bring the entire wedding party. Adjoining the Executive Lodge is a spacious lawn with a beautifully landscaped knoll where couples exchange vows. If you rent that wing, you get access to a small multipurpose room that can accommodate 30 people with a dance floor. Larger parties have a choice of the Mountain Ballroom or Cedar House, as well as some spacious outside decks and patios. Catering is provided on-site by Granlibakken, and there is a staff wedding coordinator available to make all arrangements.

Amenities: 159 rooms, a lawn area with seating for 200, the Mountain Ballroom with seating for 350 (can be divided into three rooms), the Grand Hall for 150, and Cedar House for 75. Mountain and garden decks are also available. Use of the resort catering office is required for all functions, and there is a minimum catering charge. There are surcharges for bartender, dance floor, and additional time if you exceed four hours.

Contact: Granlibakken Resort Sales Department, 625 Granlibakken Rd./P.O. Box 6329, Tahoe City, CA 96145; 530/583-4242 or 800/543-3221; email: granconf@sierra.net; website: www.granlibakken.com.

River Ranch Lodge

Situated next to the Truckee River, this popular overnight lodge and restaurant has a spacious patio that is suitable for outdoor events of up to 150 guests. Or it can accommodate up to 60 guests in a cozy dining area, which has a large stone fireplace. The site of this rustic lodge actually dates back to 1888, when passengers from a

WEDDINGS

narrow gauge train used to stop here on their journey between Truckee and Tahoe City.

Amenities: 19 guest rooms, bar, restaurant, outdoor deck, parking lot, access to bike trails, river rafting concessions, and ski areas.

Contact: River Ranch Lodge, Hwy. 89 and Alpine Meadows Rd., P.O. Box 197, Tahoe City, CA 96145; 530/583-4264 or 800/535-9900; email: info@riverranchlodge.com; website: www.riverranchlodge.com.

Stanford Alpine Chalet

At the base of Alpine Meadows ski area, this large, four-story retreat has a tranquil forest setting, a Great Room with huge cathedral picture windows (suitable for a reception or ceremony), lodging in 14 guest rooms with private baths, spacious balconies with sweeping views of the Sierra peaks, and a heated outdoor swimming pool. The property is ideal for small parties of 25 to 30 people. The Great Room, on the top floor, has high ceilings, a large fireplace, and comfortable overstuffed furniture (which can be removed for a ceremony or dining).

Amenities: There's an on-site manager and staff to assist with arrangements. Other amenities include a volleyball court, basketball half-court and horseshoe pit.

Contact: Stanford Alpine Chalet, 1980 Chalet Rd., Alpine Meadows; P.O. Box 6436, Tahoe City, CA 96145; 530/583-1550, fax 530/583-2082. Information and photos at website: www.northtahoeweddings.com.

Sunnyside Lodge

This elegant lodge, on the wind-protected West Shore of Tahoe, offers inspiring vistas of the lake and has its own restaurant, marina, large deck, and overnight lodge. A minimum of 100 people is required to book a wedding, and the lodge can accommodate up to 250 people. This is a particularly popular venue, and it is reserved for private events six months or more in advance.

Amenities: Special menu selections, personalized parties, overnight accommodations, and other wedding arrangements.

Contact: Sunnyside Lodge, 1850 W. Lake Blvd./P.O. Box 5969, Tahoe City, CA 96145; 530/583-7200 or 800/822-2754; email:sunnysidel @jps.net; website: www.sunnysideresort.com.

KINGS BEACH / TAHOE VISTA / CARNELIAN BAY

North Tahoe Community Conference Center

This private beachfront setting at Kings Beach on the North Shore has a lakefront terrace for the ceremony, a lakeview suite for the reception, and enough deck space to accommodate up to 500 people.

Amenities: On-the-spot marriage license, a minister, catering, beverage service, and a photographer are available.

Contact: North Tahoe Community Conference Center, 8318 N. Lake Blvd., P.O. Box 69, Kings Beach, CA 96143; 530/546-7249; website: www.northlaketahoe.net.

Shore House at Lake Tahoe

This splendid small bed-and-breakfast inn just happens to have a million-dollar view of the lake from a large lawn and adjoining private pier. The Shore House specializes in intimate weddings of from two to 15 people for couples that are guests, and from two to eight people for couples that are not guests, year-round. Proprietor Marty Cohen is an ordained minister and can perform a ceremony on the pier, on the lawn, or in the lakefront dining room. Wedding packages come with a champagne toast. Optional services include appetizers and a cake.

Amenities: Nine guest rooms, dining room, outdoor spaces and in-house minister.

Contact: Shore House at Lake Tahoe, 7170 N. Lake Blvd./P.O. Box 343, Tahoe Vista, CA 96148; 530/546-7270 or 800/207-5160; email: shorehouse@tahoeinn.com; website: www.tahoeinn.com.

INCLINE VILLAGE/CRYSTAL BAY

Diamond Peak Ski Resort

This medium-sized ski resort on the East Shore of the lake offers dramatic vistas, along with indoor and outdoor wedding venues. Small weddings can be accommodated during the winter, but most are held in summer, either at the main lodge or at the mountaintop Snowflake Lodge, which has a new deck and offers a spectacular, close-up vista of Lake Tahoe. The lodge, which is reached by a quad chairlift, can accommodate more than 100 people.

Amenities: The regular day lodge is available throughout the summer on short notice, but the Snowflake Lodge requires arrangements as gear must be transported by lift or 4x4 to the top of the mountain. Rates vary depending on time of year and location of residence (locals get a better deal). Deposits are required, and prices are higher during prime times, with additional charges for other facilities and cleaning. The wedding party must provide all catering, a pastor, a photographer, flowers, and music. The ski area will provide setup and teardown of tables and chairs.

Contact: Diamond Peak Ski Resort, Group Sales Office, 1210 Ski Way, Incline Village, NV 89451; 775/832-1132; website: www.diamondpeak.com.

Tahoe Biltmore Lodge and Casino

This modest-sized casino hotel offers either a wedding chapel or a chapel setting for the nuptials.

And you can throw a giant reception for up to 400 people in the recently remodelled Nevada Room, which has 6,400 square feet of flexible event space. The Biltmore provides free wedding coordination, dinner entrées that range $11–27, and inexpensive room rates for wedding parties that start at $39, based in availability.

Amenities: Large multipurpose room, on-site catering, new dance floor and stage, free-standing brass fireplace, chapel and chapel-like setting, and complete arrangements that include flowers, minister, live music, photography, videography, cake and champagne.

Contact: Tahoe Biltmore Lodge and Casino, P.O. Box 115, Crystal Bay, NV 89420; 775/833-6733 (Group Sales) or 800/245-8667 (room reservations); website: www.tahoebiltmore.com.

SOUTH LAKE TAHOE
Heavenly Resort

The main attractions here are the observation platform accessible from the new gondola near Stateline, with stunning views 3,000 feet above the lake, and the Top of the Tram, which is 2,000 feet above lake level and has a huge deck the

© SHERRY MCMANUS/HEAVENLY SKI RESORT

WEDDINGS

A Heavenly couple enjoys a spectacular sunset from the gondola observation deck at 9,100 feet.

overlooks the basin and Stateline casinos. Advantages of the tram site are its wind-protected location (since it is lower down on the mountain) and its proximity to full catering and restaurant services at the mid-mountain station of Monument Peak. Weddings can be arranged, winter or summer, at several mountain locations, with full catering and banquet facilities available. At the Top of the Tram there's a restaurant, a full bar and seating for up to 150 people indoors or 250 outdoors.

Amenities: Heavenly offers catering services and the tram ride; all other arrangements, including pastor, photographer, flowers, cake, music, limousine, formal wear, and accommodations, must be made by the couple; a referral list is provided. Tram discounts are available for groups.

Contact: Heavenly Ski Resort, P.O. Box 2180, Stateline, NV 89449; 530/542-5153 or 775/586-7000, ext. 6228; website: www.skiheavenly.com.

Strawberry Lodge

Nestled among the Sierra pines along the banks of the American River, this historic, rustic lodge has hosted weddings since 1858. The lodge has marvelous common facilities, including a big lobby with a stone fireplace, a gazebo outside, a large recreation room, and beautiful guest rooms with antique furnishings.

Amenities: Wedding parties have use of the grounds and the main ballroom, a full bar, a restaurant with extensive wine list, a fixed-price buffet menu for 35 or more people, a rehearsal dinner in the lodge's celebrated wine cellar, and 43 hotel rooms. A minister, honeymoon suite, and river house are also available. The bride and groom must arrange decorating, musical entertainment, photography, and the wedding cake. A nonrefundable, one-third deposit is required to reserve the lodge.

Contact: Strawberry Lodge, 17510 U.S. 50, Kyburz, CA 95720; 530/659-7200; website: www.strawberry-lodge.com.

Tallac Vista Conference Center

This is a large, contemporary retreat, formerly a private home, that is situated on 12 acres of land on a South Tahoe mountainside near the California base of Heavenly ski resort. The building's main room is light and open with rustic beams, a cathedral ceiling, skylights, large picture windows, and multilevel decks and verandas. There are panoramic views of the lake and mountains from several vantage points. Facilities include a large reception area, a side room and a loft. Tallac Vista will accommodate up to 75 people. Ceremonies can be held indoors in the main room or outdoors at the Lakeview area. The retreat is operated as a noncommercial venture by the Tahoe Tallac Association and is owned by the California Tahoe Conservancy, a state agency that acquires and manages land to protect the environment. One drawback: Because of insufficient parking at the facility, all guests must park below the site at a designated area and take a private shuttle bus, or arrange for pickups by the bus at their hotels.

Contact: Tahoe Tallac Association; 530/542-4166; email: tta@sierra.net; website: www .valhalla-tallac.com.

CARSON VALLEY/GENOA
David Walley's Resort, Hot Springs and Spa

Owned by Quintus Resorts (which also owns The Ridge Tahoe up the road), this historic hot springs spa on the eastern slopes of the Sierra is being turned into a major resort with luxurious condominiums. Bride and groom can have an upscale wedding here, and unwind afterwards in the mineral springs (many couples end up in hot water soon enough anyway!). The springs are in a tranquil setting, with marshes and quacking ducks on one side and snow-crested mountains on the other. There are six outdoor mineral pools, and surrounding them is DW's Restaurant, which has full wedding and banquet services, and a large gazebo that overlooks the marshes and ponds. Most ceremonies are held in the gazebo, with receptions following in the restaurant, and even large parties with up to 300 people can be accommodated. A new condominium complex adjacent to the hot springs resort features luxurious rooms and suites, some with Jacuzzi tub and shower. The resort is near two major golf courses and restaurants in the historic town of Genoa, and is just 30 minutes away from Stateline at Lake Tahoe (up the Kingsbury Grade).

Amenities: Gazebo and lawn for outdoor ceremonies, restaurant for banquets, 42-unit condominium hotel for overnight guests, natural hot springs pools, recently refurbished bath house, large spa with body wraps and other treatments, two outdoor tennis courts, weight room, freshwater relaxation pool, and deli-style café.

Contact: David Walley's Resort, Hot Springs and Spa, 2001 Foothill Rd. (1.5 miles south of Genoa), Genoa, NV 89411; 775/782-8155 or 800/628-7831, ext. 8123.

KIRKWOOD/HOPE VALLEY/MARKLEEVILLE

Kirkwood

With a new mountain village, this four-seasons resort in the uncrowded Carson Pass area of Highway 88 offers both winter and summer venues, from the mountain to the meadows. The village with its plaza, along with several new condominium buildings, add to the aesthetics. In early to mid summer, wildflowers bloom profusely on the slopes.

Amenities: The resort can supply catering, indoor and outdoor facilities, accommodations in condominiums, restaurants, and a horse-drawn sleigh or wagon. All other services must be supplied by the bride and groom.

Contact: Kirkwood Ski Resort, P.O. Box 1, Kirkwood, CA 95646; 530/258-6000; website: www.skikirkwood.com.

Sorensen's Resort

This rustic and historic resort is set in beautiful Hope Valley, about a 20-minute drive south of Lake Tahoe. If you're looking for a simple, casual ceremony in a woodsy setting, with a cozy log cabin for your wedding night, this is an ideal Tahoe retreat. Weddings can be held near a pond, on a deck, or in the authentic Norway House, and there's a small but excellent café for receptions. Accommodations are quite diverse in the various cabins and structures on the property.

Amenities: Indoor and outdoor sites, catering, flowers, champagne, reception, and log cabin accommodations are available. A nonrefundable consultation fee charged to all wedding parties is due at the time of booking. Fifty percent of food, lodging, and facility fees are required within seven days of booking.

Contact: Sorensen's Resort, 1255 Hwy. 88, Hope Valley, CA 96120; 530/694-2203 or 800/423-9949.

FEATHER RIVER COUNTRY/LAKES BASIN

Gray Eagle Lodge

Situated in the spectacular Lakes Basin area just a few miles south of Graeagle, in Plumas County (north of Truckee), this summer lodge, with its plethora of hiking trails and mountain lakes, is so popular that it's amazing the owners can squeeze in weddings once in a while. When you see the grand lodge building, with its beamed ceilings, stone fireplace and extensive wine bar, it's easy to see why couples fall in love with this place right away. The lodge can arrange wedding ceremonies, banquets, and receptions. And there are several cozy cabins adjoining the main building that can accommodate a medium-sized wedding party. In addition to hiking, you can fish in nearby lakes, horseback ride at two stables, and play golf at six courses.

Amenities: Lodge with restaurant and bar, outdoor meadows, streams and lakes, cabins for overnight accommodations.

Contact: Gray Eagle Lodge, Gold Lake Rd., P.O. Box 38, Graeagle, CA 96103; 530/836-2511 or 800/635-8778; website: www.grayeaglelodge.com.

WEDDINGS

Historic Sites and State Parks

TAHOE CITY/WEST SHORE

Ehrman Mansion, Sugar Pine Point State Park

This elegant mansion, built in 1902, is a living museum and a great place for weddings, though you can't use any of the rooms for an indoor ceremony. Couples have their choice of outdoor venues: the front porch, a nearby gazebo (the favorite), croquet courts, and a large grassy area that slopes down to Lake Tahoe. The spacious lawn, shaded by tall pine trees, is an ideal spot for a reception. There's a dock where the couple can leave (or arrive) by boat. The state park, on the West Shore halfway between Tahoe City and South Lake Tahoe, does not supply much of anything except ground. You are responsible for chairs, catering, and music (no amplifiers, please). During the busy summer season when tours are being given at the mansion, weddings must be held at 5 P.M. or later.

Amenities: Several outdoor sites. Fees are charged according to the size of the wedding party and according to whether both the ceremony and reception are held. Deposits are required. For groups larger than 15, use fees include parking; for smaller groups, there is a per-vehicle parking fee. The site is suitable for up to 150 people. **Contact:** Sugar Pine Point State Park, P.O. Box 266, Tahoma, CA 96142; 530/525-7232.

INCLINE VILLAGE/CRYSTAL BAY

Thunderbird Lodge (George Whittell Estate)

Formerly owned by two reclusive multimillionaires, this historic lakefront estate south of Incline Village has everything a wedding party could ask for: a spectacular site on the rocky shores of Tahoe's scenic Nevada side, a sandy cove, a boathouse where the bride and groom can arrive in grand style, a full-on catering service,

Ehrman Mansion at Sugar Pine Point State Park

© KEN CASTLE

WEDDINGS

extravagant entertainment rooms with vistas on the lake, and wooded grounds and gardens that beckon for photo ops. It might also help that the estate is listed on the National Register of Historic Places. Covering 16,500 square feet, this rambling mansion with its quirky corridors, including an underground tunnel to a boat house, arguably represents to Lake Tahoe what San Simeon castle represents to Southern California. The Thunderbird was built in 1936 by George Whittell, an eccentric San Francisco tycoon who liked to keep wild animals such as lions and tigers. It is a medieval-style, three-story French château that has 140 acres of prime lake frontage and more than a mile of shoreline (see the Lake Tahoe section in the Sights and Events chapter). Today, the Thunderbird Lodge Preservation Society, a nonprofit organization that oversees the estate, offers 5,400 square feet of space for group events such as conferences and weddings.

> *The Thunderbird Lodge was built in 1936 by George Whittell, an eccentric San Francisco tycoon who liked to keep wild animals such as lions and tigers.*

Rooms in the lodge offer ample opportunity for modest to large wedding functions, including receptions. In the new wing, the Lighthouse Room, with 2,400 square feet and floor-to-ceiling picture windows overlooking the lake, can handle up to 120 people. In the original building, The Old Lodge room offers 1,500 square feet with a 100-person capacity. Either can be used for a formal dinner or reception, or for the ceremony itself. Staffers can arrange catering, music, floral arrangements, photographer, and other necessities. In addition to the mansion, the famous 55-foot *Thunderbird* yacht, which was built for Whittell in 1940 and is often berthed in the boat house, can be used for special functions. Everything is upscale, so expect to pay a king's ransom (or a small fortune from your parents) to pull off a wedding here. But without a doubt there is nothing else like this place at Lake Tahoe.

Contact: Thunderbird Lodge Preservation Society, P.O. Box 6812, Incline Village, NV 89450; 775/832-8750; website: www .thunderbirdlodge.org.

Sand Harbor, Lake Tahoe-Nevada State Park

It's easy to understand why this beautiful lake frontage has been the site of many weddings. Spectacular turquoise waters, unusual rock formations that jut from the lake, and sweeping vistas of snow-capped mountains make for a scenic venue. The park recently constructed a wooden boardwalk leading to an elevated overlook called Inspiration Point, where most couples choose to say their vows. Afterward, you can have your reception at the Ramada, a large covered area with picnic tables, electricity, running water, and restrooms. You must supply your own catering service.

Amenities: An indoor/outdoor covered area suitable for 150 guests, a separate parking area for 30 cars, picnic tables, barbecue grills, a fire pit, and a metal food preparation counter and sink. There are fees for renting the Ramada, and additional parking/access fees for each vehicle. Reservations are advised well in advance.

Contact: Lake Tahoe-Nevada State Park, 2005 Hwy. 28, Incline Village, NV 89451; 775/831-0494.

SOUTH LAKE TAHOE
Valhalla Grand Hall

Valhalla, a Norwegian word for "heavenly place," is an apt description for one of the lake's most romantic and stunningly beautiful wedding venues. This large building, with rustic wooden rafters, ornate stonework and hanging lamps, presents a regal setting for wedding parties of up to 125 people. Built in 1923, the structure has a wraparound, lodgepole pine porch that is ideal for cocktails or outdoor dining. It also has hardwood floors, French doors opening onto the porch, a massive 20-foot-tall stone fireplace and walk-in hearth, an indoor second floor balcony, and a large lawn with pine forest and picnic tables that face Lake Tahoe. Wedding ceremonies must be held indoors, but

WEDDINGS

receptions may be held inside or outside. There is a two-hour minimum rental, and the renting party must make all arrangements, including set-up and clean-up. The property is part of the Tallac Historic Site, which consists of several estates and cabins left over from the turn of the century, when the area was dominated by the luxurious Tallac Hotel. Guests can wander through the site and see the other buildings, including the two recently restored boathouses. The lake shoreline is accessible and offers good photographic opportunities, and there is a privately operated beach and large pier next door at Camp Richardson Resort (where the *Woodwind* trimaran is docked). Valhalla is administered by the U.S. Forest Service in cooperation with the nonprofit Tahoe Tallac Association (which also rents the Tallac Vista Conference Center, mentioned above). There is a relatively short season—April 15–November 30—and the hall is in great demand, requiring a year's notice. Only one event per day is allowed. The Hall is three miles north of the South Lake Tahoe "Y" intersection on Highway 89, at the Tallac Historic Site.
Contact: Tahoe Tallac Association; 530/542-4166; email: tta@sierra.net; website: www .valhalla-tallac.com.

Vikingsholm Castle, Emerald Bay State Park

This 38-room, Scandinavian-style mansion sits on the most beautiful piece of real estate at Lake Tahoe—the shores of Emerald Bay. Thousands of visitors tour the vintage-1920s home after making a steep hike down from the parking lot on Highway 89. If you want to get married here, you'll have to hike in as well, or arrive by boat. There are no changing rooms. In fact, none of the rooms in the mansion can be used for weddings. However, an outdoor courtyard surrounded by the building is available, along with a small stretch of beach (depending on the water level). It's best to have your ceremony in the morning (before the weekend hordes arrive), in the evening (after they've left), or in the off-season. You'll need to bring everything, including tables, chairs, and food. Most peo-

ple elect to have just the wedding ceremony here, not the reception.
Amenities: An outdoor courtyard and a beach-front area. There's no vehicle access, but there is a limited docking area for boats. Fees are typically not charged for parties of less than 25 people. The maximum party size is 150. As this edition went to press there were no parking fees, but the California Department of Parks and Recreation was considering them.
Contact: Emerald Bay State Park, P.O. Box 266, Tahoma, CA 96142; 530/525-7232.

CARSON VALLEY/VIRGINIA CITY

The Corley Ranch

This historic working ranch off Highway 395 in Gardnerville has a variety of wedding sites, most of them outdoors. You can choose from the gazebo or several arbors for the ceremony, then hold the reception inside an antique barn, where you can have a country western band kick things up a notch. And the guests will never get bored. They can tour the property in a house-drawn wagon and watch cowpokes do their thing. Indoor facilities also include a vintage 1897 "Cook House" that has a full kitchen and can accommodate 40 people. The ranch can arrange for the pastor and for on-site catering from a variety of different services.
Contact: The Corley Ranch, 859 Hwy. 395 S, Gardnerville, NV 89410; 775/265-2760 or 775/265-3045; website: www.corleyranch.com.

Gold Hill Hotel

East of Carson City is this historic hotel—Nevada's oldest—at the foot of the famous Comstock Lode mining town of Virginia City. This complex, now a bed-and-breakfast inn, not only can offer wedding and reception venues, but can house a party of 40 or more in its 19 rooms and cottages. The main building includes an historic lounge and saloon, as well as a gourmet dinner house, Crown Point Restaurant, which seats 75. An outdoor gazebo area can accommodate 120 guests. Most of the rooms include luxurious touches with period antiques. And you can avail yourself of Virginia City's considerable resources, ranging from a horse-drawn buggy with a surrey to an authentic vintage 1800s steam train that operates on a two-mile stretch of track between Virginia City and Gold Hill. Heck, you can even arrange for the bride or groom to be kidnapped by gunslingers. Or stage your own "shotgun" wedding.

Contact: Gold Hill Hotel, Hwy. 342, P.O. Box 710, Virginia City, NV 89440; 775/847-0111; website: www.goldhillhotel.net.

The Mackay Mansion

The onetime silver mining boomtown of Virginia City is home to this popular and noteworthy estate, although the property changed ownership and programs had yet to be developed as this edition went to press. The lovely, authentic Victorian mansion has a grand parlor, an outdoor garden for ceremonies of any size, and a full wedding planning service. It is an idyllic place in an otherwise desolate high-desert canyon. The town and its historic buildings are fascinating, and the mansion, once owned by a silver baron, is elaborate and impressive. The bride can even arrive in a horse-drawn buggy.

Amenities: The mansion offers an indoor wedding facility seating 30, a one-acre outdoor garden seating 500, a band pavilion, a dance floor, flowers, video and still photography, round-trip transportation from Reno (for up to eight people), and carriage rides around Virginia City. A referral list is available for caterers, wedding cakes, entertainment, and Victorian-era vintage clothing. Services are performed by a retired minister or a justice of the peace. The wedding couple must obtain their own marriage license.

Contact: Virginia City Chamber of Commerce, Virginia City, NV 89440; 775/847-0311.

Golf Courses and Country Clubs

NORTH SHORE

The Chateau

On the 9th green of Incline Championship Golf Course, The Chateau offers spectacular mountain scenery and views of Lake Tahoe. The 4,500-square-foot property has high ceilings, rich woodwork, large windows, and two spacious decks. It can accommodate large groups of up to 400 people.

Amenities: Integrated sound system, audio visual equipment, large kitchen, preset dance floor, bar and convenient parking. Available year-round.

Contact: The Golf Courses at Incline Village, 955 Fairway Blvd., Incline Village, NV 89451; 775/832-1240; website: www.ivgid.org.

Old Brockway Golf Course

The restaurant (formerly the The Moose's Tooth Café) in the recently completed log lodge building that serves as the new clubhouse for this historic, nine-hole golf course is available for weddings. The interior has log accents with vaulted pine ceilings, two fireplaces, and patio seating with lake views. The facility can be exclusively booked.

Contact: Old Brockway Golf Course, 400 Brassie Ave., Kings Beach, CA 96143; 530/546-9495.

SOUTH LAKE TAHOE

Edgewood Tahoe

Few places of any kind at Tahoe create such an immediate sense of awe as this splendid country club, which not only has a world-famous golf course that attracts frequent celebrities but also offers a spectacular clubhouse. The building sits on the shoreline of the lake and has soaring cathedral ceilings, giant picture windows, a restaurant and bar, and two large banquet rooms. The South Room can hold 100 people and the North Room can hold 250 people. There's also a large deck that overlooks the lake, and there's an ascending and winding walkway that leads from a large parking lot with a gated entrance. Members of the wedding party can arrive in deluxe carriages offered by Borges Carriage Rides, which operates at Incline.

WEDDINGS

Amenities: Edgewood's kitchen and catering services are upscale and exquisite, and the staff can provide recommendations for bands, DJs, cakes, florists, pastors and photographers. Availability is very limited due to the popularity of Edgewood for meetings and other private functions. The facility is open year-round.

Contact: Edgewood Tahoe Golf Course, Lake Pkwy. (behind Horizon Casino Resort)/P.O. Box 5400, Stateline, NV 89449; 775/588-2787; email: edgewood@edgewood-tahoe.com; website: www.edgewood-tahoe.com.

Lake Tahoe Golf Course

Ceremonies can be held indoors in the dining room or outdoors on an elegant covered patio, with room to accommodate 40 to 80 people. The clubhouse, relatively new, overlooks one of Tahoe's most scenic golf courses. It is on Highway 50 just a few miles west of the "Y" intersection in South Lake Tahoe.

Amenities: Oak dance floor, table setup and arrangement, choice of linen, china and glassware, cleanup, wedding consultation, PA system, CD player for background music, big-screen TV, round tables, head table, and one-hour rehearsal arrangement. Weddings have a 4.5-hour time block. Closed in winter.

Contact: Lake Tahoe Golf Course, 2500 Hwy. 50 W, South Lake Tahoe, CA 96150; 530/577-0788, ext. 4; email: ltgc@weddingstahoe.com.

FEATHER RIVER COUNTRY/LAKES BASIN

Nakoma Resort and Spa

To say that Nakoma is one of a kind is an understatement. This grand lodge with its peaked, tepee-style roof lines offers an architecturally stunning venue for a wedding. An hour's drive north of Truckee in Plumas County, just west of the town of Portola, this new lodge is part of a second-home community that includes a remarkable golf course called The Dragon, which literally snakes its way along a rim high above the Feather River. What makes Nakoma unique is that the structure was originally designed in 1924 by famed American architect Frank Lloyd

Wright, but was not built until late 2000. A separate wedding chapel with window vistas overlooking the golf course and Feather River Canyon adjoins the clubhouse, and is next to a large, well-manicured lawn that also can be used for a reception or ceremony. The gourmet restaurant includes banquet rooms and an elegant cocktail lounge. And if the bride or groom has a case of nerves, there's the Ritual Day Spa where a massage will ease muscle tension and anxiety. Finally, any of four new luxury villas, each with spectacular views, can be used for the start of the honeymoon.

Contact: Nakoma Resort and Spa, 348 Bear Run, Clio, CA; 530/832-6304 or 800/418-0880; website: www.nakomaresort.com.

CARSON VALLEY/GENOA
The Golf Club at Genoa Lakes

Nestled against the eastern Sierra slopes in the lush Carson Valley, with views of wetlands and snow-capped peaks, this lush and popular golf course has a large and impressive new clubhouse. A banquet pavilion, part of a new restaurant called Antoci's Supper Club, is the main venue for receptions and special occasions. The course is just a 30-minute drive over Kingsbury Grade from Stateline and South Lake Tahoe, and is near Nevada's oldest town.

Amenities: Restaurant, bar and catering services.

Contact: The Golf Club at Genoa Lakes, 1 Genoa Lakes Dr./P.O. Box 350, Genoa, NV 89411; 775/782-6645, ext. 249; website: www.genoalakes.com.

Sierra Nevada Golf Ranch

This scenic golf course, nestled against the eastern slopes of the Sierra just 30 minutes over Kingsbury Grade from South Lake Tahoe, offers an impressive, 20,000-square-foot stone and wood clubhouse that looks like a hunting lodge. There's a reason for that; it used to be the site of the Little Mondeux Ranch and Gun Club. The clubhouse is decorated top to bottom with unique Western and golf motifs, and the lounge features a massive stone fireplace, leather saddles, bar stools and overstuffed chairs. There are views of the Sierra foothills and of Carson Valley, and the course looks out over babbling brooks and cascading waterfalls.

Amenities: Two elegantly designed and versatile banquet rooms. The Mountain View Room seats 100 and the Nevada Room seats up to 200. One of the exceptional and unique locations is the top of the course's buried cart barn, which can be tented to accommodate up to 300 guests. The club can perform all catering and assist in other wedding party arrangements.

Contact: Sierra Nevada Golf Ranch, 2901 Jacks Valley Rd., P.O. Box 316, Genoa, NV 89411-0316; 775/782-7700.

Paddlewheel Steamers and Cruise Boats

NORTH SHORE

Tahoe Gal

This small but roomy excursion boat, a replica of a paddlewheel steamer, is based in Tahoe City at the Lighthouse Shopping Center. It offers a spacious top deck and an enclosed cabin that can handle up to 150 passengers. There's also the private Commodore Salon, which is available during regular cruises only and can seat up to 25 people. The boat normally sails along the West Shore of the lake, and on some departures visits Emerald Bay. The *Tahoe Gal* operates daily during the summer and is available for charters any time of the year.

Amenities: The vessel has a full bar, a galley for lunch and dinner, and catering facilities. The ship's captain can perform the wedding ceremony, and staff members can assist with other arrangements including flowers, video and still photography, a limousine, and lodging. Local pickup can be provided for charters.

Contact: North Tahoe Cruises, 850 N. Lake Blvd./P.O. Box 7913, Tahoe City, CA 96145; 530/583-0141 or 800/218-2464; website: www.tahoegal.com.

SOUTH SHORE

M.S. Dixie II

Lake Tahoe's newest paddlewheel cruise boat sails daily out of Zephyr Cove on the Nevada side of the lake. Weddings can be conducted with a pastor of the couple's choice on the top observation deck before departure. Ceremonies may be held during any one of three cruise itineraries: the sunset dinner-dance (Sunday–Friday), the champagne brunch, or the historic Glenbrook breakfast. The ship's captain does not perform ceremonies.

Amenities: The *Dixie* can supply food and beverages, including champagne, along with a keyboardist or acoustic guitar player for the ceremony. The wedding party is obliged to arrange everything else, including the cake, flowers, and photography. There are no facilities to accommodate gifts.

Contact: Zephyr Cove Resort, P.O. Box 1667, Zephyr Cove, NV 89448; 775/588-3508 or 888/MSDIXIE (888/673-4943); website: www.tahoedixie2.com.

The Party Boat

This 52-foot luxury yacht, which operates on a charter basis out of Tahoe Keys Marina, can handle a wedding party of up to 49 people. The boat features a spacious indoor cabin, an upper deck, a flying bridge, conference cabins, and two bathrooms.

Amenities: Chairs are available, but the wedding party must provide all other services, including pastor, food, drinks, photography, and flowers. Scenic cruises to Emerald Bay and other points on Lake Tahoe are available on request. The boat is available year-round, weather permitting.

Contact: Tahoe Keys Marina, 2435 Venice Dr. E, Ste. 100, South Lake Tahoe, CA 96150; 530/542-2111 or 888/542-2111; website: www.tahoesports.com.

Tahoe Para-Dice II

Sailing out of Tahoe Keys Marina at South Lake Tahoe, this is the grand belle of the lake. If money

WEDDINGS

is no object, the *Para-dice II* is the royal way to have a wedding on Tahoe. This sleek, new vessel is a modern, luxurious 80-foot motor yacht with a flying bridge, a huge enclosed first deck, an enclosed second deck with executive-style lounge, and a hosted bar. It can accommodate up to 149 passengers, and its home port puts it within 30 minutes of Emerald Bay. The cabins can be customized with tables, chairs, tablecloths, silverware, and china, and the charter company can arrange all or part of your wedding. The boat is ideal for moderate to large wedding parties, because it can be fully chartered, offering a private, exclusive affair.

Amenities: The lower deck, normally set up with tables and chairs, can be used for both the ceremony and dancing. There are large picture windows and a full bar. Live entertainment is available. There is a charter fee, and catering is extra. A deposit is required to reserve a date.
Contact: Lake Tahoe Cruises, P.O. Box 14292, South Lake Tahoe, CA 96151; 530/541-3364 or 800/23-TAHOE (800/238-2463); website: www.laketahoecruises.com.

Tahoe Queen

Recently refurbished, this vessel is a Mississippi River-style paddle wheel cruiser with several decks and private areas appropriate for weddings. The boat, which operates year-round from Ski Run Marina in South Lake Tahoe, has a glass bottom and seats up to 500 passengers. It also has a full kitchen and a huge dining facility, an area for private parties, and a regular dance band that plays during dinner cruises. When weather permits, weddings are conducted in the open on the third-level observation deck, with park benches used for theater-style seating. Otherwise, vows are exchanged in the second-deck oak room near the stern of the boat, overlooking the paddle wheels. You can also book a vocalist to furnish an appropriate love song or two. Full dinner service is available (at one of two seatings), and the band usually cranks up for dancing and entertainment in the second-deck cocktail lounge.
Amenities: Wedding parties may choose a day-time cruise to Emerald Bay, which lasts just over two hours, or a dinner cruise with live music, which lasts 3.5 hours. Services include a wedding coordinator (at extra charge), a singer, band or DJ, champagne, a wedding cake, photography, video, and flowers. A deposit is due at the time of booking (refundable with 30 days' notice), with the balance due two weeks before the wedding date.
Contact: Lake Tahoe Cruises, P.O. Box 14292, South Lake Tahoe, CA 96151; 530/541-3364 or 800/23-TAHOE (800/238-2463); website: www.laketahoecruises.com.

Woodwind Sailing Cruises

Two luxurious sailing vessels—one operating out of Zephyr Cove in Nevada and another operating out of Camp Richardson in California—provide various options for wedding parties. The newest and largest is the *Woodwind II,* a 55-foot custom Shaw catamaran that berths at Zephyr Cove Resort and can carry up to 50 people. There's plenty of space to roam on this vessel. On the *Woodwind I,* a 41-foot custom Brown trimaran, there's just enough room in the cockpit for a memorable ceremony. Just ask country singer Reba McIntire, who chartered the boat for her wedding a few years ago. A popular tradition on Lake Tahoe since 1975, the *Woodwind I* sails several times a day out of Camp Richardson, at the southwest side of Tahoe, April 1–October 31. A ceremony typically takes 90 minutes and is conducted under full sail.
Amenities: The Woodwind cruises can provide the minister, photographer, videographer, flowers, champagne, and informal catering with trays of hors d'oeuvres from Zephyr Cove Resort. Weddings must be booked months in advance, and couples must supply their own wedding license (from Nevada or California). Either formal or casual attire is suitable, and guests can either stand or sit on the deck as well as in the cockpit.
Contact: Woodwind Sailing Cruises, P.O. Box 1375, Zephyr Cove, NV 89448; 775/588-3000 or 888/867-6394; website: www.sailwoodwind.com.

Restaurants

TAHOE CITY/WEST SHORE

Chambers Landing

Not only is this prestigious West Shore establishment regarded as among Tahoe's top gourmet restaurants, it's also one of the best wedding venues around. Operated by renowned chef Graham Rock, the restaurant offers a full catering service, and is right on the lake. Ceremonies can be held on the beach or on a secluded lawn with gazebo. Afterward the wedding party can gather and sip champagne at the old boathouse on the landing. Receptions are usually held in the restaurant, though options include the pool patio or the lawn. Open end of May–late October.

Amenities: This facility can handle both small and large weddings (up to 300 people) and has wedding consultants who can arrange rehearsal dinners, the ceremony, a customized reception, and lakeside lodging in 15 nearby luxury town houses for members of the wedding party.

Contact: Chambers Landing, 6300 Chambers Lodge Rd. (off Hwy. 89), Tahoma, CA 96142; 530/525-7262.

Forest Inn and Black Bear Tavern

Built in 1933, this is a classic Old Tahoe restaurant, with peeled logs, cathedral ceilings and stone fireplaces. It is a special, romantic place for dinner, and with its outdoor patios it creates a wonderful venue among the pines and nearby creek.

Amenities: Catering, outdoor wedding venue, indoor reception venue, restaurant and bar.

Contact: Forest Inn and Black Bear Tavern, 2255 W. Lake Blvd./P.O. Box 8311, Tahoe City, CA 96145; 530/583-8626, fax 530/581-3555.

Sierra Vista

This century-old historic building with its impressive river-rock fireplace and spectacular views of the lake offers four dining areas that can be used for indoor and outdoor receptions, rehearsal dinners and ceremonies. There is access from the Tahoe City Marina, so the wedding party can arrive by boat, yacht, or even sea plane. Facilities can accommodate 40–300 people.

Amenities: Restaurant, bar, deck and marina.

Contact: Sierra Vista, 700 N. Lake Blvd., Tahoe City, CA 96145; 530/583-0233; website: www.sierravistatahoe.com.

Wolfdale's

This established and highly regarded restaurant has a lakefront setting for a rehearsal dinner, garden wedding, or reception. Chef/owner, known for award-winning cuisine, will design a customized menu.

Amenities: Restaurant, bar, deck, and garden.

Contact: Wolfdale's, 640 N. Lake Blvd./P.O. Box 875, Tahoe City, CA 96145; 530/583-5700, fax 530/583-1583; website: www.wolfdales.com.

KINGS BEACH/TAHOE VISTA/CARNELIAN BAY

Gar Woods Grill and Pier

With its shoreline location and long guest pier, this North Shore restaurant is a popular site for weddings, especially for couples who want to roar off into the sunset on a boat. Ceremonies can be held on the beach, the pier, the deck, or inside the restaurant. The facility can accommodate groups of 20–150 in the upstairs private dining rooms. Each room has an Old Tahoe feeling with hand-crafted hickory chairs and photos of old Gar Wood racing boats hanging from knotty-pine walls. Floor-to-ceiling windows offer spectacular vistas of the lake.

Amenities: The restaurant is available for catered receptions, either during regular mealtimes or at other times.

Contact: Gar Woods Grill and Pier, 5000 N. Lake Blvd./P.O. Box 1133, Carnelian Bay, CA 96140; 530/546-3366 or 800/298-2463; website: www.garwoods.com.

WEDDINGS

INCLINE VILLAGE/CRYSTAL BAY

Big Water Grille

A stunning mountaintop location near the Diamond Peak ski area provides this restaurant with what is arguably the most magnificent view from any restaurant at North Shore. As an excellent gourmet dinner house, the grill has achieved quite a buzz among locals and visitors alike for its eclectic menu of Asian and Hawaiian dishes. Through the large picture windows and deck, you can get panoramic views of Crystal Bay and the surrounding peaks of Tahoe. Interiors reflect the Old Tahoe style of architecture with beamed ceilings, local artwork, and native-rock fireplace.

Amenities: Restaurant and lounge to handle groups of from two to 150.

Contact: Big Water Grille, 341 Ski Way, Incline Village, NV 89451; 775/833-0606, fax 775/833-0627; website: www.bigwatergrill.com.

SOUTH LAKE TAHOE

Riva Grill

At the new Marina Village on the lake at the intersection of Ski Run Boulevard and Highway 50, this new, two-story restaurant has a large banquet area on the second floor, though the room is cut in half by a glass-enclosed foyer. Each section has vaulted ceilings with mahogany beams, skylights and floor-to-ceiling windows that look out over the lake. There's also a large deck, and the restaurant sits on the waterfront facing the home port of the *Tahoe Queen* paddlewheel excursion boat (which is also available for receptions and has live music and a dance floor). The restau-

rant combines contemporary design with the nostalgic ambience of Tahoe's wooden boating era—and is the companion of Gar Woods Grill on the North Shore.

Amenities: Restaurant, deck, banquet/reception area and catering, capable of accommodating 25 to 200 people for dining and dancing. The facility is not available on weekends July 1–September 10.

Contact: Riva Grill, 900 Ski Run Blvd., South Lake Tahoe, CA 96150; 530/542-2600, fax 530/542-3366; email: riva@sierra.net; website: www.rivagrill.com.

Tep's Villa Roma

It looks fairly nondescript from the outside—an Italian restaurant that has been popular with locals for more than 20 years. Inside, however, is one of the largest and newest banquet facilities at Lake Tahoe, along with an attractively appointed wedding chapel that can seat up to 125 guests. Private reception rooms for dining and dancing can accommodate groups of from 20 to 200.

Amenities: Chapel with bride's dressing room, music and pedestal floral arrangments. Restaurant with bar and banquet rooms. Extensive catering menu with Italian dishes. Package weddings and other related needs, from cake to photos to flowers, can be arranged by an in-house wedding coordinator. There is no surcharge for banquet rooms.

Contact: Tep's Villa Roma, 3450 Lake Tahoe Blvd., South Lake Tahoe, CA 96150; 530/541-8227 or 800/490-3066; email: info@tepsvillaroma.com; website: www.tepsvillaroma.com.

Private Chapels and Services

TAHOE CITY/WEST SHORE

A Chapel at Lake Tahoe

Adjacent to the Truckee River, this rustic Tahoe-style chapel features open beam ceilings, track lighting, fresh greenery, and a cream-colored interior. The building was recently renovated.

Amenities: The riverside wedding chapel seats two to 36 people, and off-site group seating is available for up to 400 people. California confidential licenses are issued with no blood tests or waiting period. The minister is always on-site. Professional consultation and planning services include arranging for the minister, the ceremony, the marriage license, music, flowers, catering, photography, videography, a limousine, and lodging. The chapel can plan events around the lake (including wedding ceremonies on the snow or on the lake). The chapel fee includes recorded music, dressing rooms for the bride and groom, and coordinator services. The reception room and deck are available for rent by the hour. There is a nonrefundable deposit to reserve a date, with a one-week advance reservation recommended.

Contact: A Chapel at Lake Tahoe, 3080 N. Lake Blvd., Tahoe City, CA 96145; 530/581-2757 or 800/581-2758.; website: www.chapelatlaketahoe.com.

INCLINE VILLAGE/CRYSTAL BAY

Dream-Maker Wedding Chapel

This chapel specializes in lakeside and panoramic lakeview, mountaintop weddings. One of the more famous (and quiet) ceremonies held here was that of actor Tom Selleck. The chapel is open daily, except Thanksgiving and Christmas Day.

Amenities: The main chapel, at 907 Tahoe Blvd., seats 42. The smaller chapel is next to the Marriage License Bureau at the Center Point Building, 865 Tahoe Blvd., Ste. 104. Facilities include the chapel, a bridal dressing room, a minister, a hostess, a witness, and recorded music

for one hour. Out-of-chapel wedding packages include indoor or outdoor ceremonies with panoramic views. Advance payment in full is required to reserve a date. Other services include a DJ, photography, videography, a cake, catering, flowers, wedding accessories, romantic gifts, formal wear, gowns, accessories, a limousine, and accommodations.

Contact: Dream-Maker Wedding Chapel, 865 Tahoe Blvd./P.O. Box 6395, Incline Village, NV 89451; 775/831-6419 or 800/252-3732; website: www.wedtahoe.com.

SOUTH LAKE TAHOE

Alpine Meadow Wedding Chapel

This small chapel offers a candlelight service, background music, optional flowers, and a non-denominational minister. Receptions can be held in a garden setting and can accommodate 30–200 guests.

Amenities: Chapel, garden area, catering, flowers, and consulting.

Contact: Alpine Meadow Wedding Chapel, 3025 Hwy. 50, South Lake Tahoe, CA 96150; 530/577-0438 or 800/824-6376; website: www.getmarried.com.

Chapel of the Bells

The chapel, operating since 1979, has a convenient location near major hotels and the many attractions of South Lake Tahoe.

Amenities: The chapel seats 25. An outdoor gazebo and garden seats 40 and stands 100. Cost includes the license, which can be issued the same day, and clerical fee. Other services include photography, videography, flowers, a cake, a reception, accessories, and accommodations.

Contact: Chapel of the Bells, 2700 Lake Tahoe Blvd. (U.S. 50), P.O. Box 18410, South Lake Tahoe, CA 96151; 530/544-1112 or 800/247-4333; website: www.weddingslaketahoe.com.

Chapel of the Pines

A variety of indoor and outdoor venues throughout

WEDDINGS

Tahoe and the Carson Valley can be used for weddings arranged through this chapel.

Amenities: Indoor venues include the *M.S. Dixie II,* Genoa Community Church, a local chapel, and a hotel or private home where you are staying (no charge). Outdoor venues range in price $15–600 and include Logan Shoals Vista Point, Spooner Lake Meadow, a beach site, a 90-minute cruise on a 42-foot trimaran, on horseback, Eagle Falls at Emerald Bay, on a ski slope, tram, or sleigh. Other services include photography, videography, flowers, live music, catering, a cake, personal services, formal wear, and lodging. A deposit of half the total wedding cost is required to set the date; 48-hour cancellation notice is required.

Contact: Chapel of the Pines, P.O. Box 1519, Stateline, NV 89448; 775/588-2821 or 800/426-2858; website: www.chapelofthepines.com.

Cloud 9 Chapel and Suites

This facility offers two chapels, one with a formal, church-like setting and pews that seat 50 people, and another, less formal chapel with a pink floral interior that seats 30 guests. A reception hall, which holds up to 75 people, can also be rented. Cloud 9 is in the same complex as the Value Inn motel. This operation offers several wedding packages, oriented to the budget-minded, and can combine ceremony and reception with stays in the motel, which has a honeymoon suite. Off-site weddings also can be arranged.

Amenities: California and Nevada marriage licenses may be issued on the premises with no blood tests or waiting period. Other services include photography, flowers, off-site wedding locations, wedding consultations, receptions, and honeymoon suites.

Contact: Cloud 9 Chapel, 2659 U.S. 50/P.O. Box 13884, South Lake Tahoe, CA 96151; 530/544-1411 or 800/545-0611; website: www.cloud9-wedding-inn.com.

LakeFront Wedding Chapel

Rising from the ashes after a devastating fire destroyed the building in which this chapel was housed, the "new" LakeFront Wedding Chapel is arguably the most complete and visually at-

tractive venue on the lake at South Shore. Rebuilt from the ground up with weddings in mind, the born-again chapel actually has three sites for ceremonies. The new Outdoor Garden Terrace features evergreens and flowers and is right at the water's edge. This area can accommodate up to 125 guests for the ceremony or reception. The large indoor LakeFront Wedding Chapel, housing a similar number of guests, is decorated with cheerful light earth tones and pastels, and is enhanced by candlelight, flowers, and panoramic views of the lake and surrounding mountains. And the new Lake-View Room, which accommodates 40 to 60 people depending on the function, has an intimate setting with original artwork and bronze accents, all highlighted by large picture windows with views of the lake.

Amenities: The chapel can arrange receptions with cake and champagne, cold or hot buffets, barbecues, and full dinners served tableside. Arrangements also can be made for honeymoon lodging, photography, videography, live music, and candles. A variety of prepriced packages are available.

Contact: LakeFront Wedding Chapel, 3351 Lake Tahoe Blvd., South Lake Tahoe, CA 96150; 530/544-6119 or 888/WED-TAHO (933-8246); website: www.lakefrontwedding.com.

Love's Lake Tahoe Wedding Services

Although the prominent Love's Wedding Chapel at the bottom of Kingsbury Grade on Highway 50 was demolished in early 2002 after 33 years of weddings, the former operator, well-known South Tahoe clergyman Reverend Ron Darby, still conducts weddings at various locations around South Shore. These include Round Hill Beach and Horizon Chapel in Nevada, and Timber Cove Lodge in California. Darby can also do the planning for ceremonies, including arrangements for photography, videography, flowers, reception facilities, formal attire, limousines, and accommodations. The couple must supply the marriage license.

Contact: Love's Lake Tahoe Wedding Services, P.O. Box 2308, Stateline, NV 89449; 775/588-8007 or 800/MARRY-US (800/627-7987).

Mountain Lake Weddings and A Country Chapel

This 1930s ranch house has been converted to a romantic country chapel, with a beautiful, award-winning garden that includes pines, aspens, climbing vines and flowers. There's also an outdoor gazebo with a cobblestone pathway and lawn seating area. The chapel has handcrafted alder seating, tiffany chandeliers and a fireplace.

Amenities: A reception area seats up to 400 people. A California nonblood test marriage license is offered with the notary fee waived. In addition to weddings performed here, the coordinators have organized ceremonies at Heavenly's Top of the Tram, the Tallac Historic Site and Valhalla Estate, in a hot air balloon, in a horse-drawn sleigh, on skis and snowmobiles, and on a 52-foot yacht. Coordination services include photography, videography, cake, flowers, live musical performers, catering, decorator, limousine, and minister. A nonrefundable deposit is required for all reservations. No refunds are given for cancellations of fewer than 21 days.

Contact: Mountain Lakes Weddings and A Country Chapel, 3135 Lake Tahoe Blvd., South Lake Tahoe, CA 96150; 530/544-4896 or 800/896-4656; website: www.mountainlakeweddings.com.

Churches

SQUAW VALLEY

Queen of the Snows Catholic Church

Built for the 1960 Winter Olympics at Squaw Valley, this large church hosts both Catholic and non-Catholic weddings. The interior is made of blond wood, and international flags hang down from the side walls. A large window behind the altar faces eastward for a dramatic view of Squaw Peak and the Squaw Valley tram. Catholics may ask the local priest to perform the ceremony; otherwise, couples must supply their own pastor. No weddings are permitted December–Easter. The church is on Squaw Valley Road, across from the Squaw Valley Stables.

Amenities: The church seats up to 360 people. It's recommended that you book at least six months in advance.

Contact: Corpus Christi Catholic Church (a separate facility), P.O. Box 1878, Tahoe City, CA 96145; 530/583-4409.

INCLINE VILLAGE/CRYSTAL BAY

Ponderosa Ranch Chapel

Among its various wedding venues, this Western theme park at Incline Village has an authentic 1870 country church that seats 125 people and is available May–October. The ranch includes sets used for the filming of television's most popular Western, *Bonanza,* during the 1960s and early 1970s. There's a large saloon/dance hall with complete catering available, an outdoor picnic area with rustic tables, and a hilltop barbecue site. Also on the premises is a photographer who can capture the moment in old-fashioned tintype photos. The wedding service is performed by the Church of the Ponderosa minister.

Amenities: Ponderosa provides a variety of services, including flowers, champagne, a horse and buggy, photography, an antique limousine, a cake, catering, and reception areas. Tablecloths, napkins, and plates are not supplied for outdoor receptions. Reservations are required.

Contact: Ponderosa Ranch, 100 Ponderosa Ranch Rd., Incline Village, NV 89451; 775/831-0691; website: www.ponderosaranch.com.

SOUTH LAKE TAHOE

St. John's in the Wilderness Episcopal Church

Without a doubt, this is Lake Tahoe's single most inspiring church for a wedding. An old stone building right on the East Shore of the lake, St. John's has a pulpit backed by a window that offers an incredible view of the basin and the snow-covered mountains. For noncongregational weddings, either the bride or the groom must be

WEDDINGS

WEDDING INFORMATION SOURCES

There are several Lake Tahoe and Reno area wedding associations and websites that you can consult for a variety of services. Here are the major ones:

GENERAL (LAKE TAHOE)

Weddings at Tahoe
This website is a treasure trove of listings and links for wedding services on all sides of the lake. See it at www.weddingstahoe.com.

NORTH LAKE TAHOE

North Lake Tahoe Wedding and Honeymoon Association
Publishes a comprehensive wedding services guide with more than 100 members listed. Contact: P.O. Box 7998, Tahoe City, CA 96145; 530/581-1810 or 800/358-5683; website: www.northtahoeweddings.com. Also check out wedding information from the North Lake Tahoe Resort Association at this website: www.tahoefun.org.

Truckee Donner Chamber of Commerce
Call for brochures and other information at 530/587-2757 or click on Wedding and Event Services on the organization's website at www.truckee.com.

Lake Tahoe Incline Village and Crystal Bay Visitors Bureau
Provides information on wedding services along the northeast side of Lake Tahoe in Nevada. Contact: 775/832-1606 or 800/GO-TAHOE (800/468-2463); website: www.gotahoe.com.

SOUTH LAKE TAHOE

South Lake Tahoe Wedding and Honeymoon Association
Publishes a wedding guide for the South Lake Tahoe area. Contact: 800/AT-TAHOE (800/288-2463) or consult the website: www.TahoeWeddings.org.

Lake Tahoe Visitors Authority
This South Tahoe information source offers links to many wedding providers, chapels, and providers on its website: www.virtualtahoe.com/Weddings.

Tahoe Douglas Chamber of Commerce and Visitors Center
You can get information on wedding sites and services along the southeast side of Lake Tahoe in Nevada by calling 775/588-4591 or by clicking on the Weddings box at website: www.tahoechamber.org.

RENO/CARSON CITY/CARSON VALLEY

Reno-Sparks Convention and Visitors Authority
A list of wedding chapels and services in the Reno/Sparks area and the Nevada side of Lake Tahoe can be obtained by calling 800/FOR-RENO (800/367-7366). Or consult the website: www.renolaketahoe.com.

Carson City Convention and Visitors Bureau
Information on wedding venues in and near the state capital can be obtained by calling 800/NEVADA-1 (800/638-2321) or visiting the bureau's website: www.carson-city.org.

Carson Valley Chamber of Commerce and Visitors Authority
Not to be confused with Carson City above, this office represents the communities of Genoa, Gardnerville, Minden, and Topaz Lake, all of which are south of Carson City. Contact: 775/782-8144 or 800/727-7677; website: www.carsonvalleynv.org.

Episcopalian, and even then considerable negotiating and preparation is entailed (count on at least one year for reserving a date).

Amenities: The church seats 240 people. Marriage classes are free with any local Episcopal priest. Catering on-site is available.

Contact: St. John's in the Wilderness Episcopal Church, 1776 U.S. 50/P.O. Box 236, Glenbrook, NV 89413; 530/542-1127 or 775/882-8460.

Tahoe Community Church

You can have personalized Christian weddings at this church, or in-house wedding coordinators can arrange locations at any of several sites around South Shore in California or Nevada. You can write your own vows and go over the ceremony in advance with a pastor.

Amenities: The church can seat up to 100 people, and there is ample parking. Four ordained ministers are associated with the church.

Contact: Tahoe Community Church, 145 Daggett Ln., P.O. Box 6598, Lake Tahoe, NV 89449; 775/588-5860, fax 775/588-3827; website: members.aol.com/tahoecomch/weddings.html.

KIRKWOOD/HOPE VALLEY/MARKLEEVILLE

Silver Lake Chapel

This small church, situated near the shore of Silver Lake in the Carson Pass area, has a large picture window that faces the water and Thunder Mountain, a unique pulpit made from a hollowed-out tree, and antique benches seating approximately 100 people. There's no electricity in the chapel, which was built by local volunteers, although a generator is available.

The church is open July 4–Labor Day and is on Highway 88 at Plasse's Resort, southwest of South Lake Tahoe.

Amenities: The wedding ceremony must be performed by licensed clergy. No beverages of any kind may be served in the chapel, decorations may not be hung with nails or tacks, furniture may not be moved, no receptions are permitted in or around the chapel, and only dripless candles may be used.

Contact: Norma Cuneo (for information and reservations), 245 Boarman St., Jackson, CA 95642; 209/223-0464.

CARSON VALLEY/GENOA

Genoa Community Church

Built in 1859 in Nevada's first town, this is one of the state's oldest churches and is among the most delightful wedding sites in the region. Just 30 minutes from South Lake Tahoe, the church—an old-fashioned white clapboard building with a steeple and a bell—is in a quiet, tree-shaded area with views of grazing cattle, mountains, and the small historic community of Genoa. The church seats 75 people (wooden pews seat 50 and chairs, 25), is open to outside ministers, and has a fully operating antique organ. Two-hour rentals for weddings are available seven days a week. There's an elegant bed-and-breakfast inn with a bridal suite next door.

Amenities: The town does not arrange for the services of a minister, photographer, florist, or caterer but will provide names of local sources. Reservations are required.

Contact: Genoa Community Church, P.O. Box 14, Genoa, NV 89411; 775/782-8696 or 775/782-2518.

WEDDINGS

Summer
Recreation

On, In, and Around the Water

You can drive, hike, skate, or cycle around Lake Tahoe, but it's hard to beat seeing it from out on the water. Probably every type of known watercraft is put to use here, from polished, old-fashioned "woodies" to sleek fiberglass speedboats. It's a diverse fleet that sets out from Tahoe's marinas in the summer: large tour vessels, Hobie Cats, luxury motor cruisers, old woodies, personal watercraft, fishing boats, rowboats, rubber rafts, paddle craft, parasailing boats, sailing yachts, and water-ski boats. If it floats, you'll probably see it on the lake.

Boating on Tahoe provides a wonderful perspective, allowing you to see elegant estates close up, revel in the ambience of Emerald Bay and its granite peaks, view the skyline of high-rise casino/hotels, and explore rocky coves and white-sand beaches along the 72-mile shoreline. And the only way to see Fleur du Lac—a stone mansion featured in Francis Ford Coppola's movie *The Godfather, Part II*—is by boat. While the gated compound is closed to visitors from the highway, it is quite approachable from the water and is a primary point of interest for commercial sightseeing cruises. So, too, is George Whittell's regal Thunderbird Lodge, a French-style château in a cove south of Sand Harbor on the east shore. The lake is not only the lifeblood of

© KEN CASTLE

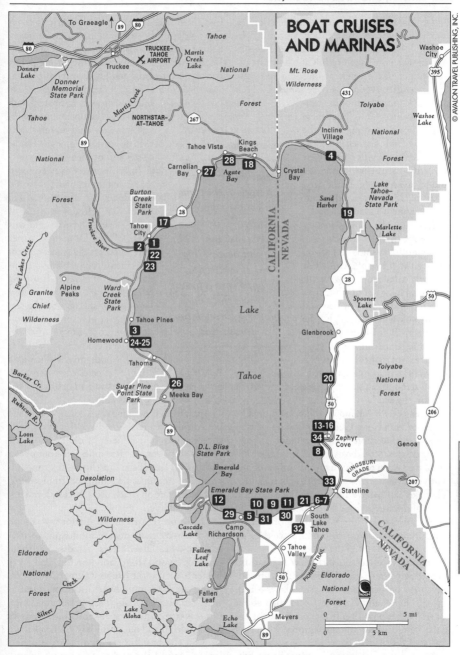

BOAT CRUISES AND MARINAS

© AVALON TRAVEL PUBLISHING, INC.

ON THE WATER

Tahoe residents but also the prime attraction for four million visitors a year. To appreciate the richness of Tahoe's nautical heritage, plan a trip in August when the Tahoe Yacht Club holds its annual Concours d'Elegance, a three-day showcase of handcrafted wooden vessels, some of which date back to the turn of the century. Watching 60 to 70 of these elegant boats motoring along the shoreline from Carnelian Bay to Homewood is a visual feast. Certainly the social elite, celebrities, and business tycoons of the early 1900s made the most of their stay at this alpine wonderland.

Tahoe is a lake of many moods. In the morning, it can be calm and tranquil, so smooth that you can see the ripple of a damselfly. By early afternoon, however, it can be a raging sea of whitecaps, whipped into a frenzy by powerful winds blowing through the mountains. The lake never freezes in winter, but it stays cold year-round except in the shallows. Not surprisingly, wetsuits are a prerequisite for anyone who water-skis, sails a dinghy, kayaks, swims, or dives in the lake.

Water safety is paramount. All boats should be equipped with Coast Guard–approved flotation vests, a ship-to-shore radio or phone, and signaling devices. Small boats should avoid the middle of the lake in the afternoon and early evening, when the winds are most likely to kick up a fuss. The lake can behave like a small ocean, with rollers and waves posing hazards to the unwary. In general, sticking to the West Shore or the leeward side affords some protection, since the East Shore gets the brunt of the winds.

Starting in October 2001, new regulations were enacted to restrict the types of marine engines used on Tahoe and three sister lakes—Fallen Leaf, Echo, and Cascade. Concerned about air and water pollution from conventional engines, the bi-state Tahoe Regional Planning Agency (TRPA) mandated that all two-stroke, carbureted and fuel-injected engines be prohib-

> *Tahoe is a lake of many moods. In the morning, it can be calm and tranquil, so smooth that you can see the ripple of a damselfly. By early afternoon, however, it can be a raging sea of whitecaps, whipped into a frenzy by powerful winds blowing through the mountains.*

ited from lake waters. The regulations cover most older outboards used for water-ski boats, fishing boats, personal watercraft, and sailboats. Boaters who get caught with the wrong power package can be cited and fined, and patrols canvass the lake for violators during the peak of the season. For visiting boaters with outboards, the options are to invest in a new engine, rent boats with approved engines at Tahoe, or stay out of the water.

Initially, there was concern that stringent regulations would shut down use of personalized watercraft. However, most of these operators have bought new fleets of Sea-Doos and other water scooters that meet current and future government standards. So the wake-jumping buckaroos are still alive and kicking. For specifics on the regulations, contact TRPA headquarters at 775/558-4547 or consult the agency's website under "Consumer's Guide to Boating at Lake Tahoe" at ceres.ca.gov/trpa/. A good general-interest website on boating at the lake is www.boattahoe.com.)

Apart from the engine crackdown, TRPA also passed rules that established a 600-foot no-wake zone around the perimeter of the lake. All watercraft must travel at five miles per hour or less within 600 feet of the shoreline. This zone was created to minimize noise impacts from motorized watercraft on beach users, hikers, kayakers, fish and wildlife.

Once you get past the regulations, you soon discover why residents are so anxious to protect the lake. This boaters' paradise has small rocky coves and white sand beaches, and every boater has a favorite hangout. Emerald Bay, offering the lake's only boat-in campground as well as its only island, is probably the top choice. On a warm summer weekend, hundreds of boats swirl in and out of the bay. Some of them stop on the beach for a picnic, while others linger around the rocks of Fannette Island, where a crumbling stone teahouse that is part of Vikingsholm Castle (now a state park) offers a reminder of bygone extravagance. Sand Harbor, at Incline Village, has its charms, including a rocky promontory and pristine public beaches. At the south end of the lake, a labyrinth of waterways snakes through Tahoe Keys, a man-made waterfront residential community. Zephyr Cove and Camp Richardson, on opposite shores close to South Lake Tahoe, offer a myriad of family recreation activities and fine beaches. And boaters can tie up for a gourmet lunch or dinner at places such as Chambers Landing, Homewood, Sunnyside, Carnelian Bay, and Tahoe City, where waterfront restaurants are plentiful. Slips and mooring buoys can sometimes be in short supply, however, and you may have to wait for a spot.

Don't have a boat? No problem. You can rent or charter just about anything, from a 52-foot motor yacht to a small runabout. No matter how you choose to explore the lake, being on the water is pure bliss.

Boat Cruises

No introduction to Lake Tahoe and its history would be complete without taking a cruise. Sightseeing voyages operate year-round—even in winter—although there is a larger selection spring–fall. Excursion boats consist of motor yachts, sailing vessels, and Tahoe's trademark paddle wheelers, replicas of vintage Mississippi riverboats.

The paddle wheelers get the lion's share of attention and represent the most popular outing for visitors. Both the *Tahoe Queen* and the *M.S. Dixie II*, berthed at South Shore marinas, can carry more than 500 passengers each. They offer narrated, two-hour cruises to Emerald Bay, serve lunch and dinner (sometimes breakfast), feature live entertainment in the evenings, and are virtually impervious to strong winds. The *Queen* and the *Dixie* are longtime competitors, but now there's a third "wheel"— the *Tahoe Gal*, which inaugurated cruises from the North Shore in the summer of 1994. However, the *Gal* is much smaller, has side wheels instead of stern wheels, and makes most of its runs along the West Shore. Apart from these high-profile vessels, other, more contemporary options exist for exploring the lake. There are two elegant sailing vessels, several luxury motor yachts, and a couple of fishing cruisers that double as sightseeing boats.

All vessels listed are keyed to the Boat Cruises and Marinas map.

TAHOE CITY/WEST SHORE

Tahoe Gal (see map on page 111, site 1)
Sure, she looks diminutive and hokey, but she's a lot of fun. Launched in May of 1994, the 70-foot-long, 149-passenger side-wheel boat is reminiscent of the famed Mississippi riverboats, and it came from—you guessed it— La Crosse, Wisconsin. Whereas the big paddle wheelers berthed at the South Shore are impressive, the *Tahoe Gal* is, well, kind of cute. There's a large air-conditioned salon with a full galley and bar on the lower deck, and room for tables and chairs on the top deck, behind the bridge. This vessel offers two-hour cruises along the West Shore and three-hour cruises to Emerald Bay. The main points of interest are the resorts, lakeside homes, and Fleur du Lac (Kaiser Estate), a mansion that you may have seen in the film *The Godfather, Part II*. Optional tableside lunch is served, depending on the cruise and the time of year. Lunches are quite tasty and creative, and the staff is enthusiastic. Tours are narrated.
Services: Shoreline, Emerald Bay, and dinner cruises are offered. Apart from scheduled trips, the *Tahoe Gal* can accommodate special functions such as weddings and catered corporate meetings; the vessel's salon can seat 25 people. It operates June–November from Lighthouse Marina, at Lighthouse Mall in Tahoe City.
Essentials: Shoreline cruises are $19 for adults and $8 for children 12 and under. The Emerald

ON THE WATER

Bay cruise is $24 for adults and $12 for children 12 and under. A Happy Hour cruise, offered six days a week (excluding Sunday), is $10 per adult and $7 for children. Dinner cruises (all meals are extra) are $20 for adults, $10 for children, and Sunday dinner cruises are $27 for adults, $14 for children. Lunch, at extra cost, is available on all Emerald Bay cruises and dinner, also extra, is available for shoreline and jazz cruises. Reservations are suggested.

Contact: North Tahoe Cruises, P.O. Box 7913, Tahoe City, CA 95730; 530/583-0141 or 800/218-2464; website: www.tahoegal.com.

Avalanche (see map on page 111, site 2)

Skippered sailing cruises that tour the North Shore are made aboard this 35-foot sailboat, which takes small groups of up to six people. The vessel leaves daily from Tahoe City Marina, and guests can be hands-on or just sit back and enjoy the cruise.

Services: Two-hour afternoon cruises depart daily and include cold beverages. Romantic, two-hour sunset cruises depart daily except Wednesday, and include refreshments and appetizers. Also available are half-day charters along the West Shore, full-day charters to Emerald Bay to visit Fannette Island and Vikingsholm Castle, and private sailing charters.

Essentials: Afternoon cruise, $40 per person; sunset cruise, $50 per person; half-day cruise, $500 charter; and full-day Emerald Bay cruise, $800 charter.

Contact: Tahoe Sailing Charters, Tahoe City Marina, 700 N. Lake Blvd., Tahoe City, CA 96145; 530/583-6200; website: www.tahoesail.com.

Kingfish (see map on page 111, site 3)

The *Kingfish*, a 43-foot vessel built in 1985, is outfitted for fishing, but it also offers 2.5-hour narrated cruises to Emerald Bay, generally in the afternoon. The boat operates out of Homewood, from the pier next to the West Shore Cafe. It travels along the shoreline, passing Sugar Pine Point, Fleur du Lac, the Ehrman Mansion, Rubicon Point, and Emerald Bay. Don't expect a lot of frills; passengers are encouraged to bring a small ice chest and picnic basket for goodies.

Services: Tours, gourmet dinners, birthday cruises, and wedding cruises are available year-round.

Essentials: For Emerald Bay tours, cruises are $22 for adults, $20 for seniors 65 and over, $15 for children 6–12, and free for kids five and under. All guests should bring their own food. The boat departs from 5110 W. Lake Blvd. in Homewood.

Contact: *Kingfish* Guide Service, P.O. Box 5955, Tahoe City, CA 95730; 530/525-5360; website: www.kingfishtahoe.com.

INCLINE VILLAGE/CRYSTAL BAY

Sierra Cloud (see map on page 111, site 4)

This 55-foot-long sailing catamaran, recently bought by Tahoe boating mogul Bob Hassett, operates from the pier of the Hyatt Regency Lake Tahoe at Incline Village. Custom-built by manufacturer Larry Pollock, the vessel has a beam of 300 feet, providing ample room for up to 49 passengers. Cruises, mostly in the afternoon, are along the east shore of the lake and to the historic Thunderbird Lodge, a château owned by a reclusive multimillionaire who kept wild animals such as lions on the property. At this writing, a cruise and visit to the lodge was offered once a week, on Sunday morning, leaving at 8 A.M. and 9 A.M. Don't expect wind or real sailing at that time of day; just enjoy the tranquil, sometimes mirror-smooth waters and the mega-million-dollar estates along the Incline shore. At Thunderbird, passengers are offloaded onto a small, sandy cove, and docents from the Thunderbird Lodge Preservation Society take over for a one-hour tour of the mansion. Among the highlights: a 600-foot underground tunnel that leads to a large boathouse, which sometimes houses a vintage, 55-foot-long motor yacht.

Essentials: Regular cruises are $40 per adult, $20 for children 12 and under; Sunday Thunderbird lodge cruise/tour is $60 for adults, $40 for children. Charter rates are $1,500 for two hours.

Contact: Action Watersports, c/o Hyatt Regency Lake Tahoe, Incline Village, NV; 775/831-4386; website: www.action-watersports.com/sailing.htm.

SOUTH SHORE

Paradise (see map on page 111, site 5)

Berthed at Tahoe Keys Marina, this sleek, 81-foot pleasure cruiser, the largest yacht of its type on the lake, was launched in 1998 for charters. Recently acquired by Lake Tahoe Cruises (the company that owns the *M.S. Dixie II* and runs Zephyr Cove Resort), the *Paradise* is part of a fleet that includes the *Tahoe Queen* and the *Tahoe Princess*. This vessel is the epitome of pampered luxury. It has a fully enclosed lower salon with large picture windows, full-service bar, tables, chairs and a custom sectional sofa. The upper deck has tables and chairs and a built-in lounge with overstuffed leather couches and chairs behind the captain's helm. There are open deck areas fore and aft on the lower deck and aft on the upper deck. The vessel can accommodate banquets (buffet and table service) as well as live entertainment and dancing.

Services: Available year-round for weddings, floating executive conferences, and private charters. Accommodates up to 149 passengers.

Essentials: The charter rate for one hour is $800 before 3 P.M., $1000 after 3 P.M.

Contact: Lake Tahoe Cruises, 900 Ski Run Blvd., South Lake Tahoe, CA 96150; 530/541-3364 or 800/238-2463; website: www.laketahoecruises.com.

Tahoe Princess (see map on page 111, site 6)

More like a floating atrium than a cruise boat, this 70-foot pontoon vessel was launched in 1992, initially as a shuttle barge to cope with a drought that lowered the lake level and made several marinas difficult to enter. But the once dowdy *Princess* has been gussied up with new carpeting, new windows, new restrooms, and a new coat of paint. Now she is one of the most popular vessels on the lake for large wedding parties. The big advantage is that she has only one spacious deck, enabling a group to stay together throughout a cruise. Though she is moored elsewhere, the boat boards at Ski Run Marina Village. This is a slow boat, so don't expect fast runs to any point on the lake.

Services: Charters only, with an emphasis on weddings. Buffet dining (there is no galley) and entertainment can be arranged.

Essentials: Charter rates are $600 per hour.

Contact: Lake Tahoe Cruises, 900 Ski Run Blvd., South Lake Tahoe, CA 96150;

© KEN CASTLE

Tahoe Queen paddlewheel boat

ON THE WATER

530/541-3364 or 800/238-2463; website: www
.laketahoecruises.com.

✕ Tahoe Queen (see map on page 111, site 7)
Departing from Ski Run Marina Village in South
Lake Tahoe, this authentic Mississippi paddle
wheeler is 144 feet long and can carry 500 passengers. The vessel has daily two-hour tours of
Emerald Bay (variable in winter) and, in summer,
nightly dinner-dance cruises. Recently the boat
and its sister vessels were acquired by Aramark
Corporation (which owns the *M.S. Dixie II* and
runs Zephyr Cove Resort) from Hornblower
Cruises, so it's best to call or check the web site for
current schedules and cruises.

Apart from its sightseeing cruises, the *Queen* also
has been used as a ski shuttle in winter between
the south and north shores of the lake, although
as this edition went to press the program was
undergoing substantial change. Typically, ski
cruises are sold as complete packages with ground
transportation, all-day lift ticket and après ski
party (or optional three-course dinner) featuring live music on the return voyage.

The *Queen* was manufactured in 1982 in La
Crosse, Wisconsin (not by the company that
built the *M.S. Dixie II*). The interior is luxurious
and elaborate, with oak and brass accents
throughout. The vessel derives all of its thrust
from its paddle wheels, making it entirely authentic. During the evening cruises, a popular
local band plays music for dancing, and dinner
entrées usually include a choice of fresh seafood,
steak, chicken or vegetarian. Lunch offerings
vary, with selections including everything from
burgers to salmon.

Services: Daily, year-round departures to Emerald Bay, with a nightly sunset dinner-dance cruise
(3 hours) in summer, and on Saturdays only in
winter. Call for information on ski shuttles between the north and south shores. The *Queen*
has a glass-bottomed viewing area, a full bar, a
dance floor, and a restaurant. Special arrangements can be made for weddings, anniversaries,
and groups.

Essentials: The two-hour early afternoon Emerald
Bay cruise is $23 for adults, $20 for seniors, and $8
for children ages 4-12. (Children on the 10 A.M.

cruise are half-price, and for other cruises there's a
family package that is $50 for two adults and two
children.) Dinner-dance cruises, offered on Fridays and Saturdays only, are $52 for adults, $49 for
seniors and $28 for children (not including tax,
gratuity or beverages). Midweek dinner cruises,
Sunday through Thursday, cost $41 for adults,
$38 for seniors, and $18 for children. Daily summer Heritage Tours, which cost $23 for adults,
$20 for seniors and $8 for children, go to Emerald
Bay and include a video, "A Walk in the Sky,"
about famous architects who have done work in
Tahoe. Complimentary bus service to Marina Village is available from Stateline and other points in
South Lake Tahoe. Major credit cards are accepted. Reservations are required for dinner cruises
and the ski shuttle.

Contact: Lake Tahoe Cruises, 900 Ski Run
Boulevard, South Lake Tahoe, CA 96150,
530/541-3364 or 800/238-2463; website:
www.laketahoecruises.com.

Tahoe Star (see map on page 111, site 8)
As the private yacht of gaming legend William
Harrah, this 54-foot-long luxury motor cruiser
has hosted famous celebrities such as Sammy
Davis Jr., Frank Sinatra, Bill Cosby, Liza Minel-
li, Robin Williams, David Letterman, Natalie
Cole, Steve Martin, and Jay Leno. Available for
both charter and scheduled cruises, the *Star* can
carry up to 36 guests in comfort. The boat has a
heated main salon, teak trimming, large viewing windows, wraparound upholstered seating, a
fully stocked bar, state-of-the-art stereo system, a
spacious stern deck, and a fly bridge. Custom-
built by the acclaimed Huckins Yacht Corporation of Florida, the vessel is fitted with twin
turbocharged V-8 diesel engines and easily cruises up to 30 knots, making it one of the fastest
yachts of its size on the lake.

Services: Emerald Bay cruise, historic East Shore
cruise to Glenbrook Bay with its celebrity homes,
sunset cocktail cruise and private charters. Weather permitting, the *Star* operates April 1–October 31 out of Roundhill Pines Marina, on the
Nevada side of the lake.

Essentials: Emerald Bay and East Shore cruises
cost $24 for adults, $12 for children 12 and

under. Private charters by the hour and longer are available. Call for cruise times and reservations.

Contact: Harrah's Lake Tahoe, *Tahoe Star* Charters, P.O. Box 8, Stateline, NV 89449-0008, tel.775/588-1554; website: www.tahoestar.com.

Tahoe Thunder
(see map on page 111, site 9)
This is a sleek 33-footer that is Tahoe's fastest Coast Guard–inspected speedboat. With 800 horsepower, this open-deck, catamaran-hull vessel literally flashes across the water, making the trip from Timber Cove Marina to Emerald Bay in as little as six minutes. Custom-built for owner Bob Hassett by Commercial Watersports of Lake Havasu, Arizona, the all-fiberglass vessel has two 502-cubic-inch engines and can cruise at 60 knots. The *Thunder* carries 12 passengers, and will take both adults and children, though infants are not recommended. This is the roller coaster ride of Tahoe, and if you don't like speed and the rumble of loud engines, this will not be your cup of tea. Bring a jacket, and hold on to your hat.

Services: One-hour trips between Timber Cove and Emerald Bay, offered daily May–October. Also available for charters, and the company will make private pickups anywhere on the lake.

Essentials: $35 for adults, $20 for children under 12, for hourlong cruises. Private charters, $400 per hour, with a minimum of one hour. Docked at Timber Cove Resort and Marina in South Lake Tahoe.

Contact: *Tahoe Thunder,* 3411 Lake Tahoe Blvd., P.O. Box 9653, South Lake Tahoe, CA 96158;530/544-2942; website: www.action-watersports.com.

The Party Boat
(see map on page 111, site 10)
This 52-foot Harbor Master, which runs out of the Tahoe Keys Marina, is specifically for chartered groups and does not run regular tours. It can accommodate 49 passengers in complete comfort. Amenities include a flying bridge, two bathrooms, conference cabins, indoor and outdoor areas, a bar, a kitchen, and a salon.

Services: The boat is available for weddings,

family reunions, parties, club events, fundraisers, and corporate meetings. It can be booked for scenic cruises to Emerald Bay and other parts of Lake Tahoe.

Essentials: Two-hour (the minimum) charters are $1100, three hours are $1,550, and four hours are $2,000, which includes captain and crew. You can bring your own food and beverage or arrange catering through the company.

Contact: Tahoe Sports, Tahoe Keys Marina, 2435 Venice Dr. E, South Lake Tahoe, CA 96150; 888/542-2111 or 530/542-2111; website: www.tahoesports.com.

Windsong (see map on page 111, site 11)
In the summer of 2000, boating impresario Bob Hassett introduced his latest acquisition, a 65-foot MacGregor sailboat that is now the largest excursion sailing vessel on the lake. The *Windsong,* a cutter-design, fiberglass monohull that was built in 1992, has seen service in Maui, Hawaii, and in Washington state. Operating out of Timber Cove Marina, the vessel can carry up to 24 people, and there is plenty of deck space to stretch out and enjoy a true sailing experience. With brisk afternoon winds, the single-masted boat will scoot along at 15 knots, and passengers with sailing skills can take the helm or help trim the sails. The boat carries a two-person crew, including the skipper. While the best vantage point is on deck, there's a huge cabin with plenty of seating if weather prompts you to go below. As a backup, the *Windsong* has a 200-horsepower turbo diesel engine for fast motoring. Cruises are made in the open part of the lake, depending on prevailing winds. Afternoon usually is the best time.

Services: Two-hour voyages from Timber Cove Marina. Snacks and soft drinks are served on board.

Essentials: Adults, $35, children, $20 under 12. Charters also available.

Contact: *Windsong,* 3411 Lake Tahoe Blvd., P.O. Box 9653, South Lake Tahoe, CA 96158;530/544-2942; website: www.action-watersports.com.

Woodwind I (see map on page 111, site 12)
There are two *Woodwinds,* one a trimaran and the

© KEN CASTLE

Woodwind I sailing catamaran

other a catamaran. The *Woodwind I* offers cruises out of Historic Camp Richardson Resort on the West Shore and the *Woodwind II,* the largest vessel, sails out of Zephyr Cove Marina on the East Shore. Whichever vessel you choose, you'll have a distinctive experience. The first *Woodwind* is an elegant 41-footer that has been a Lake Tahoe tradition since 1975. If you time your voyage for the afternoon, you'll almost certainly see her sails unfurled and feel the power of the winds pushing her through the waters. While sightseeing powerboats offer mere cruises, the *Woodwind* provides an exhilarating experience, ideal for those with a yen for adventure. The three-hull design affords great stability under sail, and the spacious cockpit and wide decks leave plenty of room to stretch out and enjoy the ride. Features include glass-bottomed windows, a heated, enclosed cabin, and a bathroom. Guests need not have sailing experience (the crew handles all of the rigging), and no special clothing or shoes are required. The *Woodwind* cruises along the West Shore to historic Emerald Bay, where you'll get views of Mt. Tallac and Desola-

tion Wilderness. As might be expected, the craft is enormously popular and is booked well in advance. The capacity on board is 30, and the vessel sails four to six times daily.

Services: Ninety-minute cruises begin daily in late morning April 15–October 15. The schedule varies depending on the time of year. Sunset champagne cruises generally leave at 7 P.M. The vessel is available for weddings (averaging 100 per year), private charters, birthday parties, and company outings.

Essentials: Regular cruises are $24 for adults, $22 for seniors, and $10 for children 3–12; children two and under go for free. Sunset cruises are $30 for adults. Charters run $600–900 for two hours. Major credit cards accepted. Reservations are recommended.

Contact: Woodwind Sailing Cruises, Camp Richardson; 530/542-2212; website: www.sailwoodwind.com.

STATELINE/ZEPHYR COVE

M.S. *Dixie II* (see map on page 111, site 13)

Lake Tahoe's newest and largest cruise boat was launched at Zephyr Cove, Nevada, in May of 1994. A successor to the smaller M.S. *Dixie,* which operated on the lake for 22 years, the new paddlewheel vessel was built in La Crosse, Wisconsin, and was transported in several sections to Lake Tahoe. It is 151 feet long, has three enclosed decks, and can carry 550 people and accommodate 200 for dinner. During 3.5-hour dinner-dance cruises, there are two seatings; while one group dines, the other group drinks and dances to live music in the upper deck lounge. The best open-air views are from the hurricane deck, next to the pilothouse.

For dinner, there's a choice of charbroiled New York steak, broiled Alaskan halibut, or honey Dijon chicken breast, accompanied by Caesar salad, dessert, and unlimited California wine. Daytime departures offer optional drinks, snacks, sandwiches, and hot appetizers. The *Dixie* leaves for cruises of Emerald Bay every day on a year-round basis, with more departures scheduled in summer. Those who want to have a peek directly at the netherworld of Tahoe can check out the

M

ON THE WATER

glass-bottomed viewing window, but there's usually not much to see.

Services: Champagne brunch cruise, Glenbrook breakfast cruise, Emerald Bay shoreline cruise, Emerald Bay dinner cruise, sunset dinner-dance cruise, weddings, charters, a smoke-free dining room, and free shuttles between Stateline casino/hotels and Zephyr Cove (four miles away).

Essentials: Champagne brunch and breakfast cruises are $29 for adults, $10 for children 3–11; children two and under are free. Emerald Bay sightseeing cruises are $24 for adults and $7 for children. Emerald Bay sightseeing/dinner cruises (two hours long, only in summer) are $39 for adults, $17 for children (with dinner). The sunset dinner-dance cruise (3.5 hours) is $49 for adults and $29 for children. There are discounts for senior citizens. Traveler's checks and major credit cards are accepted. Reservations are recommended.

Contact: *M.S. Dixie II,* c/o Zephyr Cove Resort, P.O. Box 12309, Zephyr Cove, NV 89448; 775/588-3508; website: www.tahoedixie2.com.

Sailing Ventures
(see map on page 111, site 14)

Up to six people can sail off into the afternoon winds or into the sunset on one of several sailboats from this company, which operates out of Tahoe Keys Marina at South Lake Tahoe. Owner Mike Tolda, who has more than 20 years of sailing experience at Tahoe, offers skippered charters on 25- to 30-foot Catalinas.

Services: Variety of sailing lessons, from two-hour introductions to skippering a bareboat charter. There's also a sailing club for frequent boaters.

Essentials: Lessons range from $150 per person for two hours. Charters begin at $375 for two hours, with skipper, depending on type of boat selected. Maximum of six passengers. Call for lesson packages and club membership information.

Contact: Sailing Ventures, P.O. Box 11760, Zephyr Cove, NV 89448; 530/542-1691 or 877/542-1691; website: www.sailtahoe.com.

© KEN CASTLE

M.S. *Dixie II* paddlewheel boat

The Tahoe (see map on page 111, site 15)

Yachtsman Steve Dunham, who owns the *Wood-wind* sailboats, recently restored this classic wooden motor cruiser, which is the oldest excursion boat on the lake. Designed by famed naval architect William Garden in 1950, *The Tahoe* was built for E. B. Scott, author of the two-volume history of the lake called *The Saga of Lake Tahoe*. Originally certified for 25 passengers, *The Tahoe* made sightseeing cruises between Tahoe City's palatial Tahoe Tavern Resort (now gone) and Emerald Bay for 15 years. The boat had been out of commission since 1969, sitting in a berth at the North Shore. With the cooperation of Pat Began of the Sierra Boat Company, Dunham gutted the boat, replaced its old 750-horsepower engine with a 500-horsepower electronic fuel-injected Ford V-8, refinished its mahogany hull, installed new upholstery, overhauled the bar and relaunched the 40-footer in 1999. It is available during the warm weather months for charters.

Services: *The Tahoe* can be rented for small group charters and, although it can seat 20, it is most comfortable for eight to 12 people. It operates out of Zephyr Cove Marina at the South Shore.

Essentials: Available on an hourly basis, with a two-hour minimum. Catering can also be arranged. Call for prices.

Contact: Tahoe Classic Boat Cruises, P.O. Box 1375, Zephyr Cove, NV 89448; 775/588-1855; website: www.tahoecruises.com.

Woodwind II (see map on page 111, site 16)

In 1997, as a companion to South Shore's *Woodwind I,* owner Stephen Dunham launched *Woodwind II,* a larger, more spacious catamaran-style motor sailer measuring 54 feet long and 30 feet wide, with a 50-person capacity. This boat, which cruises along the Nevada shoreline, has more interior cabin space with a full bar and food service, a glass bottom, private cabins, two bathrooms, and spacious seating inside and outside.

Services: Ninety-minute cruises begin daily in late morning April 15–October 15. The schedule varies depending on the time of year. Sunset champagne cruises generally leave at 7 P.M. Both vessels are available for weddings (averaging 100 per year), private charters, birthday parties, and company outings.

Essentials: Regular cruises are $24 for adults, $22 for seniors, and $10 for children 3–12; children two and under go for free. Sunset champagne cruises are $30 for adults. Charters run $1,000 to $1,500 for just under two hours. Major credit cards are accepted. Reservations are recommended.

Contact: Zephyr Cove Resort, P.O. Box 1375, Zephyr Cove, NV 89448; 888/867-6394 or 775/588-3000; website: www.sailwoodwind.com.

Public Launch Ramps

All properties listed are keyed to the Boat Cruises and Marinas map.

TAHOE CITY
Lake Forest, Tahoe City
(see map on page 111, site 17)
Operated by the Tahoe City Public Utility District, this facility offers a boat ramp and fishing. In 2002, the ramp was upgraded, parking was added, and an L-shaped pier was installed. There is no fee for launching but there is a $10 parking charge. It's off Highway 28 north of Tahoe City, near the Coast Guard Station, and is open 24 hours a day.
Contact: Tahoe City Public Utility District, P.O. Box 33, Tahoe City, CA 96145; 530/583-5544.

KINGS BEACH
Kings Beach, Tahoe Vista
(see map on page 111, site 18)
A boat ramp, sailboat and nonpowered craft rentals, restrooms, and fishing are available. Launching is free, but there's a parking fee at Kings Beach State Recreation Area. At the bottom of Coon Street in Kings Beach, California, the facility is open 24 hours a day.
Contact: North Tahoe Public Utility District, P.O. Box 33, Tahoe Vista, CA 96148; 530/546-7248.

SAND HARBOR
Sand Harbor, Lake Tahoe-Nevada State Park (see map on page 111, site 19)
A boat ramp, restrooms, fishing areas, and a telephone are available. The round-trip launch fee is $12. Self-launch at your own risk. In 1999, the park added docks and rebuilt the wave suppressors. Off Highway 28, two miles south of Incline Village, Nevada. Sand Harbor is open daily 8 A.M.–7 P.M.
Contact: Lake Tahoe-Nevada State Park, P.O. Box 8867, Incline Village, NV 89452; 775/831-0494 or 775/885-4384.

© KEN CASTLE

Zephyr Cove

ON THE WATER

ZEPHYR COVE

Cave Rock (see map on page 111, site 20)

Dredging work that was performed here several years ago has allowed this public boat ramp, operated by Nevada State Parks, to offer the most consistent public self-launch on the lake. The ramp will accommodate boats up to 30 feet in length, and the launch fee is $12. Day-use parking only is $6. Restrooms, fishing areas, and a telephone are provided. On U.S. 50 at Lake Tahoe-Nevada State Park north of Zephyr Cove, Nevada, it's open 24 hours a day.
Contact: Lake Tahoe-Nevada State Park, P.O. Box 8867, Incline Village, NV 89452; 775/588-7975.

SOUTH SHORE

El Dorado Beach
(see map on page 111, site 21)

Facilities include a boat ramp, a picnic site with benches and barbecue grills, a beach, a swimming area, a children's playground, powered and nonpowered boat rentals, restrooms, telephones, and limited parking. Boat launching is $13 for nonresidents, $10 for residents Open 24 hours a day, it's at U.S. 50 and Lakeview Avenue in South Lake Tahoe, California. Note: During drier than normal years, when the lake level drops (as it did in the summer of 2002), this ramp may be closed.
Contact: South Lake Tahoe Parks and Recreation Department; 530/542-6056.

Private Marinas

All properties listed are keyed to the Boat Cruises and Marinas map.

TAHOE CITY/WEST SHORE

Tahoe City Marina
(see map on page 111, site 22)

Powerboat rentals, sailing and powerboat charters, seaplane rides, parasailing, moorings (slips and buoys), a 25-foot hoist, food, gas, supplies and repairs are available. Travel lift and forklift launching only, with costs at $40 each way, or $75 round-trip, for boats up to 24 feet long. Tahoe City Marina has the following companies operating there: North Tahoe Woody Tours, Tahoe Sailing Charters, Lake Tahoe Aqua Sports, and Commodore Seaplanes. Open daily 8 A.M.–6 P.M.
Contact: Tahoe City Marina, 700 N. Lake Blvd., Tahoe City, CA 96145; 530/583-1039.

Sunnyside Marina
(see map on page 111, site 23)

Moorings (buoys), food, gas, repairs and waterskiing lessons (High Sierra Water Ski School) are available. Launching is by forklift only, and is $50 each way, by appointment, for boats up to 25 feet long. Open daily 8 A.M.–6 P.M., late May–early September.

Contact: Sunnyside Marina, 1850 W. Lake Blvd., Tahoe City, CA 96145; 530/583-7201 (boat repairs), 530/583-7417 (rentals).

Homewood High and Dry Marina
(see map on page 111, site 24)

A forklift or elevator for launching, powered and nonpowered rentals, moorings (buoys), food, restrooms, fishing, gas, supplies, repairs, and year-round dry-rack storage are available. The launch operation is open May–September. Forklift launching costs $35 each way for boats up to 21 feet long, $45 for boats measuring 22 feet and over. On Highway 89, it's open daily 8 A.M.–5 P.M. (7 A.M.–6 P.M. in July and August).
Contact: Homewood High and Dry Marina, 5190 W. Lake Blvd., Homewood, CA 96141; 530/525-5966.

Obexer's (see map on page 111, site 25)

Moorings (slips and buoys), a deepwater ramp, a launching trailer for deep draft sailboats, a travel lift and forklift, food, gas, supplies, and repairs are available. The launching fee is $15 for same-day round-trip (self-launching only), $10 each way if on different days. Obexer's is open daily, 7 A.M.–8 P.M.

ON THE WATER

Contact: Obexer's, 5355 W. Lake Blvd. (Hwy. 89)/P.O. Box 186, Homewood, CA 96141; 530/525-7962; website: www.obexersboat.com.

Meeks Bay Marina
(see map on page 111, site 26)
On Highway 89, 10 miles south of Tahoe City, this 110-slip marina has a boat ramp, fishing, moorings (slips), food, gas, and supplies. The launching fee is $25 round-trip and $15 one-way. Managed by the Washoe Tribe of Nevada and California, Meeks Bay has been spruced up substantially, with a completely renovated marina and new docks. Rentals include powerboats, kayaks, canoes and water toys, and the marina is managed by Action Watersports. There's an adjacent campground with 28 sites and a resort with 21 lodging units. It's open Memorial Day–October, daily 8 A.M.–8 P.M.
Contact: Meeks Bay Resort, P.O. Box 787, Tahoma, CA 96142; 530/525-5588; website: www.action-watersports.com.

KINGS BEACH/TAHOE VISTA/ CARNELIAN BAY
Sierra Boat Company
(see map on page 111, site 27)
Moorings (buoys), gas, supplies, repairs, and fishing are available. Boats weighing up to 10,000 pounds can be launched. Fees for hoist launching powerboats are $40 each way for fewer than 21 feet, $45 for over that. For sailboats, it's $5.50 per foot. Open daily 8 A.M.–5 P.M.
Contact: Sierra Boat Company, 5146 N. Lake Blvd. (Hwy. 28)/P.O. Box 69, Carnelian Bay, CA 96140; 530/546-2551.

North Tahoe Marina
(see map on page 111, site 28)
Facilities include powered craft rentals, moorings (slips and buoys), and a snack bar, the Sunsets on the Lake restaurant, gas, supplies, repairs, and a fishing charter center. There is no boat launching available to the public. Open daily 8 A.M.–6 P.M.

Contact: North Tahoe Marina, 7360 N. Lake Blvd., Tahoe Vista, CA 96148; 530/546-8248 or 800/58-MARINA (800/586-2746).

SOUTH SHORE
Historic Camp Richardson Marina
(see map on page 111, site 29)
On Highway 89, two miles north of the "Y" intersection near South Lake Tahoe, Camp Richardson Marina has a large pier (the longest floating pier on the lake), a boat ramp, powered and nonpowered rentals, a water-ski school, kayak rentals, parasailing rides, sailing excursions, Emerald Bay rafting tours, fishing charters, moorings (buoys), snacks, gas, a marine supply store, and boat repair facilities. The self-launching fee is $25 per boat. Parking costs $5 on weekends, but is waived if you spend $20 or more on services. It's open 7 A.M.–7 P.M. daily.
Contact: Camp Richardson Marina; 530/542-6570; website: www.camprichardson.com.

Ski Run Marina Village
(see map on page 111, site 30)
Powered, nonpowered, and sailboat rentals, fishing charters, Hornblower Cruises, parasailing, personal watercraft, beach area with water toys, moorings (buoys), food, gas, supplies, and repairs are offered at this marina, off U.S. 50 on Ski Run Boulevard in South Lake Tahoe. Adjacent to a lakeside shopping and dining complex that includes the Riva Grill. The launching and pump-out facilities are not available to the public. The hours are 7 A.M.–7 P.M. daily.
Contact: Ski Run Marina Village, 900 Ski Run Blvd., South Lake Tahoe, CA 96150; 530/544-0200; website: www.tahoesports.com.

Tahoe Keys Marina
(see map on page 111, site 31)
The marina offers a boat ramp, powered and sail rentals, moorings (slips), food, restrooms, fishing, gas, supplies, and repairs. Launching is $25

ON THE WATER

round-trip (a forklift and travel lift are available), and this is the most consistently dependable boat-launching site at South Shore when the lake level falls during dry years. Off U.S. 50 in South Lake Tahoe, the marina is open 8 A.M.–6 P.M. daily.
Contact: Tahoe Keys Marina, 2435 Venice Dr., South Lake Tahoe, CA 96150; 530/541-2155.

Timber Cove Marina

(see map on page 111, site 32)
Lift launching costs $25 round-trip, although at this writing the facility was closed because of successive dry years that have dropped water levels in the lake. Aside from powered, non-powered, and sail rentals, the marina offers moorings (buoys), food, gas, supplies, repairs, high-speed powerboat excursions, large sailing yacht excursions, and fishing charters. It's open 8 A.M.–6 P.M. daily.
Contact: Timber Cove Marina, 3411 Lake Tahoe Blvd., South Lake Tahoe, CA 96150; 530/544-2942.

Lakeside Marina

(see map on page 111, site 33)
A boat ramp, powered and nonpowered boat rentals, moorings (slips and buoys), gas, supplies, and repairs are available at this marina, off U.S. 50 at the end of Park Avenue in South Lake Tahoe. The launching fee is $20 round-trip, and the facility is open 8 A.M.–7 P.M. daily, April–October.
Contact: Lakeside Marina, 4041 Lakeshore Blvd., South Lake Tahoe, CA 96150; 530/541-6626.

STATELINE/ZEPHYR COVE

Zephyr Cove Marina

(see map on page 111, site 34)
Off U.S. 50 in Zephyr Cove, this marina offers powered, nonpowered, and sail rentals, moorings (buoys), food, restrooms, a telephone, campsites, fishing, gas, supplies, and cruises. No launching is available. Parking costs $6. Zephyr Cove Marina is open 8 A.M.–6 P.M. daily.
Contact: Zephyr Cove Resort, P.O. Box 830, Zephyr Cove, NV 89448; 775/588-3833.

© KEN CASTLE

Lakeside Marina at South Lake Tahoe

MARINAS AT NEARBY LAKES

Several other lakes in the area have marinas and boat ramps as well (unmapped).

Donner Lake

Rentals at **Donner Lake Marina** include powered fishing boats, personal watercraft, pontoon boats, ski boats, kayaks, canoes and fishing equipment. Boats are available at two locations—Donner Lake Village Resort and at Donner Memorial State Park. Reservations are advised. All major credit cards are accepted. The marina is open 9 A.M.–5 P.M. daily. (A public boat ramp operated by the town of Truckee is available nearby with launching at $7 per boat for California residents, $10 for nonresidents, plus additional parking fees.)
Contact: Donner Lake Village Resort, 15695 Donner Pass Rd., Truckee, CA 96161; 530/582-5112 (marina) or 530/587-6081; website: www.truckeesports.com.

Echo Lake

Off U.S. 50 south of Meyers, **Echo Chalet** marina offers a boat ramp, rental skiffs with outboards, a grocery store and deli, nine cabins for overnight stays, marine supplies, and water taxi service to a pier adjacent to the Pacific Crest Trail at the end of Upper Echo Lake. Launch rates are $10 for trailerable boats, $6 for car tops. The water taxi costs $7 per person, $3 for dogs, each way. Hours of operation are 8 A.M.–6 P.M. Sunday–Friday and 7 A.M.–6 P.M. on Saturday, late May–early September (the access road is closed in winter).

Contact: Echo Chalet, 900 Echo Lake Rd., Twin Bridges, CA 95735; 530/659-7207.

Fallen Leaf Lake

Facilities at **Fallen Leaf Marina** include a boat ramp, powered and nonpowered rentals, a deli, and a store. Launch fees range $10–25, depending on size of boat. Operating late May–September, the marina is open daily, 8 A.M.–7 P.M. in summer, 9 A.M.–5 P.M. at other times.

Contact: Fallen Leaf Marina, 400 Fallen Leaf Rd., South Lake Tahoe, CA 96150; 530/541-3366 or 530/541-6330.

Pyramid Lake

At **Pyramid Lake Marina** you'll find a boat ramp, restrooms, a campground, outboard-powered fishing boat rentals (14- and 16-footers), and fishing charters. The launch fee is $6 per day, and tribal permits must be obtained from the Pyramid Lake Indian Reservation. Thirty miles north of Reno on Highway 445 in Pyramid Lake, Nevada, it's open 7 A.M.–6 P.M. daily.

Contact: Pyramid Lake Fisheries, Star Route, Sutcliffe, NV 89510; 775/476-1156.

Topaz Lake

Topaz Landing, just off U.S. 395, 18 miles south of Gardnerville, Nevada, on the state line, Topaz Lake has a boat ramp, restrooms, buoys and slips, private and public campgrounds with waterfront RV sites, boat rentals (powered fishing skiffs), a bar, and a general store with fishing tackle and groceries. Gas, fishing licenses, and lodging can be obtained nearby at Topaz Lodge and Casino. Launching fees are $5 round-trip. The marina is open January 1–September 30, 7:30 A.M.–7 P.M. daily.

Contact: Topaz Landing, 3505 Topaz Ln., Gardnerville, NV 89410; 775/266-3550.

Rental Boats, Jet Skis, and Water-Skiing Lessons

Virtually everything that floats is available for rent at the various marinas and beachfront concessions around Lake Tahoe. Personal watercraft (Jet Skis), water-ski boats, small fishing skiffs, pontoon boats, sailboats, and fast runabouts are among the many offerings. There are also less serious watercraft such as paddleboats, canoes, ocean kayaks, and big-tired water cycles. Several water-ski schools operate on the lake during summer.

Prices for rentals can vary depending on time of year, time of day, and size of craft. In general they run about as follows:

Personal watercraft (Sea-Doos and Polaris): $100–120 per hour.

Water-ski boats, runabouts, and motorized pontoon boats: $90–175 per hour, less if you rent for at least three hours with an outfitter that

will give you the fourth hour free. Some rentals include the price of fuel, while others do not.

Water-skiing lessons: $90–125 per hour, including all equipment, instruction, and tows.

Water-ski tows: $100–120 per hour.

Fishing skiffs: $40–50 per hour for 14- or 15-foot aluminium or fibreglass boats with small outboard motors (5–10 horsepower range).

Hobie Cats and small day-sailers: $35–45 per hour, with discounts of 25 to 30 percent for each additional hour.

Sailboats (20 feet and longer): $60–plus.

Kayaks and canoes: $20–30 per hour; some daily rates available.

Pedalboats (or paddleboats), Aqua Cycles, Toobies, and other water toys: $20–35 per hour.

Parasailing: $45–60 per ride.

NORTH SHORE

Action Watersports of Tahoe

This facility is on a private beach owned by the Incline Village General Improvement District and is used by guests of the Hyatt Regency Lake Tahoe, local residents, and vacation renters in Incline. It offers rental powerboats, Polaris personal watercraft, the *Sierra Cloud* sailing yacht, and water-skiing lessons and equipment. The company now operates from a recently built, 350-foot pier that is in front of the Hyatt's Lone Eagle Grille restaurant.

Contact: Action Watersports of Tahoe, 967 Lakeshore Blvd., Incline Village, NV 89451; 775/831-4386.

Goldcrest Water Ski School

At Kings Beach since 1983, this company specializes in water-ski lessons for youngsters, offering tips on slalom and tricks, with full rentals including kneeboards and wakeboards.

Contact: Goldcrest Water Ski School, 8194 N. Lake Blvd., Kings Beach, CA 96145; 530/546-7412.

High Sierra Water Ski School

With two locations on the North Shore, this complete ski school (a U.S. Coast Guard–licensed, AWSA-certified facility, with everything included) offers personal watercraft rentals; powerboat charters, tours, and rides; Ski Nautique powerboat rentals (by the hour or the day); sailing lessons, rentals, and charters; a pro shop; sales; and equipment rentals and repairs. The school has been operating at the lake for more than 20 years. Major credit cards are accepted.

Contact: Sunnyside Marina, 1850 W. Lake Blvd., Tahoe City, CA 96145, 530/583-7417; or Homewood High and Dry Marina, 5190 W. Lake Blvd., Homewood, CA 96141, 530/525-1214; website: www.highsierrawaterskiing.com.

North Tahoe Marina

North Tahoe Marina, which is at Highways 267 and 28, offers powerboats (18 to 21 feet long, from runabouts to water-ski boats), rental gear (skis, inner tubes, wetsuits, wakeboards, a pro shop, picnic facilities, and the Sunsets on the Lake restaurant.

© KEN CASTLE

boating and personal watercraft riding on the lake

Contact: North Tahoe Marina, 7360 N. Lake Blvd., Tahoe Vista, CA 96145; 800/58-MARINA (800/586-2746) or 530/546-4889.

Tahoe City Marina

This operation has a rental fleet of 20- to 22-foot Four Winns and SeaSwirl powerboats. Lake Tahoe Parasailing also operates out of the marina. This full-service facility offers guest docks, a newly remodelled boathouse building with a 3,000-square-foot clubhouse overlooking the lake, fuel, and a chandlery, and is next to two malls, Tahoe Boatworks Mall and Marina Mall, which have several shops and three restaurants.
Contact: Tahoe City Marina, 700 N. Lake Blvd., Tahoe City, CA 96145; 530/583-1039; website: www.tahoecitymarina.com.

Tahoe Water Adventures

This facility features 19- and 23-foot powerboats, three-person Sea-Doos, water-ski boat rentals, canoes, kayaks, a restaurant (Lakehouse Pizza), and a full bar. It's open daily in summer dawn–dusk. Checks and major credit cards are accepted.
Contact: Tahoe Water Adventures, 120 Grove St., Tahoe City, CA 96145; 530/583-3225.

Todd Kelly's Water Ski School

Former Olympic skier Todd Kelly, who last competed in the 1994 Games in Norway, is now doing much of his skiing on the water, offering lessons for first-timers to advanced water-skiers. His main area of operation is along the protected West Shore, mainly out of Homewood. He can meet clients at Obexer's Marina, Chamber's Landing, and other locations. Kelly has been teaching the sport for more than 15 years. The school is open May–September.
Contact: Todd Kelly's Water Ski School, P.O. Box 211, Homewood, CA 96141; 530/525-6839; website: www.tkwss.com.

SOUTH SHORE

Action Watersports of Tahoe

The South Shore concession of this company is at a prime shoreline site at Timber Cove Marina next to Timber Cove Lodge. It offers powerboats (from runabouts to water-ski boats), sailboats (Hobie Cats and day-sailers), personal watercraft, pedal boats, Aqua Cycles, Sunkats (electric-powered floating lounge chairs), several pontoon boats, parasailing rides, and kayaks. Visa and MasterCard are accepted.
Contact: Action Watersports of Tahoe, 3411 U.S. 50, South Lake Tahoe, CA 96150; 530/541-7245; website: www.action-watersports.com.

Camp Richardson Marina

The marina offers Four Winns powerboats, personal watercraft, 20-foot pontoon boats with outboards, two-person open-cockpit ocean kayaks, and two-passenger paddleboats. The marina is open daily May 15–October 15. Reservations are accepted.
Contact: Camp Richardson Marina, 1900 Jameson Beach Rd., Camp Richardson, South Lake Tahoe, CA 96158; 530/542-6570; website: www.action-watersports.com.

H2O Sports

This operation is north of Stateline in Zephyr Cove at Roundhill Pines Beach, one of the more attractive beaches on the South Shore. Personal watercraft, water-ski lessons, parasailing, two-person open-cockpit ocean kayaks, and pedal-powered sea cycles are available. The marina also has a water-ski school operated by Don Borges.
Contact: H20 Sports, 350 U.S. Hwy. 50, P.O. Box 311, Stateline, NV 89449; 775/588-4155. Also: Don Borges Water Skiing; 530/541-1351; website: www.rhpbeach.com.

Lakeside Marina

This is the closest full-service marina to the popular Stateline area of South Shore—just a five-minute

ON THE WATER

walk north of Harveys Resort Casino. It rents personal watercraft, pontoon party boats, and high-performance runabouts and ski boats.
Contact: Lakeside Marina, 4041 Lakeshore Blvd., South Lake Tahoe, CA 96150; 530/541-6626.

Lake Tahoe Water Ski School

In business since 1989, owners Scott and Heather Longoria offer water-skiing lessons with a large staff of AWSA-certified instructors, charter tows, wakeboards, kneeboards, and wetsuit and equipment rentals. They use up to three Ski Nautique and Master-Craft competition ski boats. Reservations are recommended. At Camp Richardson Marina, the school is open Memorial Day to Labor Day.
Contact: Lake Tahoe Water Ski School, P.O. Box 5298, Stateline, NV 96157; 530/544-7747.

Lakeview Sports

Lakeview Sports operates a small concession at El Dorado Beach, next to U.S. 50 and just west of Stateline. Offerings include Fun Island rafts, kayaks, canoes, water cycles and personal watercraft (which are launched next to the public boat ramp at El Dorado City Park). Rentals can be made at the beach; to reserve, contact the shop.
Contact: Lakeview Sports, 3131 U.S. 50, South Lake Tahoe, CA 96150; 530/544-0183. Paddleboats are $20 for a half hour; $25 an hour; personal water craft $75 for half hour, $100 hour.

Ski Run Boat Company

This company, at Ski Run Marina Village, has 18- to 20-foot Four Winns water-ski boats and runabouts, 18- to 23-foot pontoon boats, 15-foot aluminium fishing skiffs, personal watercraft (Sea Doo's), parasailing rides, water toys, water-ski package with wetsuits, kayaks and Coleman three-person canoes.
Contact: Ski Run Marina, 900 Ski Run Blvd., South Lake Tahoe, CA 96150; 530/544-0200; website: www.tahoesports.com.

Tahoe Keys Boat Rental

Offering rentals (full, half day and sunset), sales, repairs, personal watercraft, fishing charter boat, patio boats, sailboats (up to 25 feet long), and powerboats (18 to 25 feet long), this facility is at the Tahoe Keys Marina, off U.S. 50 and Tahoe Keys Boulevard. It's open daily 7 A.M.–8:30 P.M. May–October, weather permitting. Major credit cards are accepted.
Contact: Tahoe Keys Boat and Yacht Rentals, 2435 Venice Dr. E, Ste. 91, South Lake Tahoe, CA 96150; 530/544-8888 or 888/542-2111; website: www.tahoesports.com.

Zephyr Cove Resort Marina

This large-scale operation, four miles north of Stateline, offers speedboats, fishing boats, water-ski boats, personal watercraft rentals (half hour to full day; one- to three-rider models, with full instruction, wet suit, and life vest included) and parasailing (dry launch and land from boat, 500 feet above lake, any age or dress). Reservations are accepted, as are major credit cards.
Contact: Zephyr Cove Resort Marina, 760 U.S. Hwy. 50/P.O. Box 830, Zephyr Cove, NV 89448; 775/588-3833 or 775/588-3530; website: www.tahoedixie2.com.

Kayaking and Canoeing

Paddle sports, from kayaking to river rafting, are high on the list of alternative summer excursions, simply because they are readily accessible and offer magnificent scenery. Several companies provide half-day or full-day outings in sturdy touring kayaks along the North Shore and West Shore of the lake, and others offer the thrill of rafting on California's best white-water rivers.

Getting up close and personal with Lake Tahoe means getting down to the water—way down. During calm mornings, you can take guided kayak tours, usually in large ocean kayaks, around the perimeter of the lake. This is a great way to see the shoreline, its magnificent homes, and its multitude of parks and beaches. Generally, you can bring your lunch or snacks and stop at a scenic spot to enjoy the beauty of the lake. Two-hole kayaks are often available for couples. Tours with lessons depart from several locations, from Camp Richardson to the North Shore. Those who have established reasonable proficiency can rent watercraft on their own. Just beware of afternoon winds. Nothing is tougher than paddling against waves and gales.

KINGS BEACH/CARNELIAN BAY

Tahoe Paddle and Oar

Operating from Carnelian Bay and Kings Beach on the North Shore, owner Phil Segal runs a sizable enterprise with more than 70 touring kayaks and canoes for rent. He can handle large groups of up to 40 people. Using Perception, Ocean and Seward sea kayaks, paddlers can take guided tours along spectacular rocky coves and beaches. Put-ins are at Segal's center next to the Kayak Café in Carnelian Bay, on Highway 28 between Gar Woods restaurant and Sierra Boat Company, and at the North Tahoe Beach Center in Kings Beach. From either place you can paddle a route that proceeds around Brockway Point to Crystal Bay and through the "boulder fields" to Buck's Beach—a pristine "locals" hangout when the lake level is low. The tours last 2.5 hours and go about five miles. The Kayak Café, open year-round, has a large kayak selection and a convenient car-launching ramp to the water. Fresh bagels, pastries, coffee, and sandwiches are available through lunchtime. At Kings Beach, Segal operates a retail store.

Hours: From 10 A.M. daily (in summer). The Kayak Café opens at 6 A.M. daily.

Fees: $70 per person (two-person minimum) for the Crystal Bay tour, $90 per person (four-person minimum) for the Sand Harbor Tour, which also goes alongside the historic Thunderbird Lodge at Incline Village. Kayak rentals start at $15 per hour (two-hour minimum), and canoes are $20 per hour. There are also daily rates.

Contact: Tahoe Paddle and Oar, P.O. Box 7212, Tahoe City, CA 96145; 530/546-3535. The retail and tour operations are at 8299 N. Lake Blvd. (Hwy. 28), Kings Beach, CA 96143. The rental operation is next to the Kayak Café at 5155 N. Lake Blvd in Carnelian Bay; website: www.tahoepaddle.com.

SOUTH LAKE TAHOE

Kayak Tahoe

Steve, Mike, and Susan Lannoy have been running this unique paddling operation since 1989, and they are headquartered at Timber Cove Marina in South Lake Tahoe. The large pier and gentle, protected waters in front of a public white sand beach are excellent for novices to practice kayak maneuvers, and the touring kayaks are beamy and stable. By far, the most popular tour is in spectacular Emerald Bay, with guests meeting guides and kayaks right in the bay. The launch site is on a beach that is accessible via a quarter-mile hike down an embankment at Eagle Point State Park, below the public campground there. Tours explore the bay, Vikingsholm Castle and, with smaller groups, Fannette Island. On longer trips, you can paddle to the Emerald Bay Boat-In Camp for lunch or hiking, or travel outside of the bay north toward D.,L. Bliss State Park or south toward Camp Richardson, depending on winds. There's a choice of two tours, one lasting 3.5 hours, the other, 5.5 hours. For strong and experienced kayakers, you can arrange trips from Timber Cove to the East Shore, along Cave Rock, Nevada Beach and Zephyr Cove, again depending on prevailing winds. The company offers a variety of lessons, sunset and moonlight tours, and river kayaking to see wildlife on the Upper Truckee River.

Hours: Daily 9 A.M.–5:30 P.M., May 27–Oct. 2.

Fees: $60–75 per person for guided Emerald Bay Tours, which leave at 9 A.M. Rentals are $14–28 per hour or $50–70 for the day for touring kayaks. Choice of single- or double-hole kayaks.

Contact: Kayak Tahoe, Box 550399, South Lake Tahoe, CA 96155; 530/544-2011; email: contactus@kayaktahoe.com; website: www.kayaktahoe.com.

DO-IT-YOURSELF FLOAT TRIPS ON THE TRUCKEE RIVER

Several winters of plentiful snowfall have resulted in strong spring runoff and have raised water levels at Lake Tahoe to near-record highs, thus providing summerlong water releases from the outlet dam at Tahoe City into the Truckee River. These releases have revived a long-dormant industry—do-it-yourself raft trips—and on hot summer days it seems as if everyone in town is on the river. This is generally a Huck Finn–style, leisurely float along 4.5 miles of mostly flat water, with a few riffles here and there, from the "Y" intersection of Highways 89 and 28 at Tahoe City to a cove next to the River Ranch Resort. You definitely want to take out here because from this point on the river is a raging torrent of dangerous rapids. The Placer County Sheriff's office mon-

itors the river daily, and if the flow is too swift deputies will close it to all rafting. When the river is tranquil, hundreds of people, including families with children, make the trip each day, and many of them stop for impromptu picnics on sandbars or refreshing swims in shallow eddies. There are garbage cans and portable toilets along the way, but please respect private property next to the river. Also keep in mind that it is possible to capsize if you aren't paying attention, and there are a few deep spots, so this experience is not recommended for nonswimmers or toddlers. Depending on the flow, the trip takes 1.5 to three hours. Two commercial rafting companies that rent rafts have a well-organized system of rentals and return shuttles, though on busy weekends the crowds and jockeying for parking space can make the whole thing somewhat chaotic. It's best to take public transportation to the "Y." (Note: Truckee River Raft Rentals has a 300-car paved parking lot across from River Ranch, with bathrooms and showers, where its customers can park and catch the shuttle bus to the put-in. Otherwise, parking in Tahoe City is extremely limited.)

Hours: From 8:30 A.M.–6 P.M. daily, with the last departure required by 3:30 P.M.

Fees: Both companies offer essentially the same services at the same prices: raft, life jackets, paddles, and bus ride back to Tahoe City, for $30 for adults, $25 for children 6–12, and $2 per child five and under. Discounts may be available for early morning and late-afternoon trips.

Contact: Mountain Air Sports/Truckee River Rafting, 55 W. Lake Blvd. in Tahoe City; 530/583-7238 or 888/584-7238. Also, Truckee River Raft Rentals, 185 River Rd./P.O. Box 1799, Tahoe City, CA 96145; 530/584-0123.

White-Water Rafting and River Kayaking

There's nothing like cold mountain water to take the edge off a hot summer day. Happily, visitors to Lake Tahoe can partake of Northern California's favorite ritual for cooling off: smashing through frothy rapids while screaming in devilish delight. Some of California's best white-water river trips are easily accessible from Tahoe, and a few guide services offer hotel pickup, shuttle to the river, and return on the same day. The rafting season usually begins in April, with the first runoff from melting snow, but most participants prefer to wait until warmer days in mid- to late summer. No matter what time of the season you go, wearing a full wet suit is a good idea, and generally the guides will provide them. They'll also tell you what to do if the boat flips over (a rare but possible occurrence), if it gets wrapped on a rock, or if another boat starts a water fight with bailing buckets. River rats frequently have their choice of experiences—paddleboats that require five or six folks to stroke in unison, or oar boats that invite passengers to sit back and relax while the guide does all the work. One of the delights of a full-day trip is enjoying a catered lunch on the banks of the river, and most rafting companies excel in their gourmet repasts. What follows is a brief rundown on the main rivers within reach of Lake Tahoe.

Commercial rafting began on the **Truckee River, Lower Section,** east of Truckee, in the summer of 1996, after two years of strong spring runoff created a viable white-water experience. A handful of outfitters have permits to run a 5.5-mile portion of the river between Boca Bridge and Floriston, roughly paralleling I-80. This rafting run is quite a discovery; it contains scenic canyons and good fishing waters. It also has more than its share of debris, a result of years of discards that include old cars, the wreckage of a small airplane, railroad paraphernalia, and construction rebar that occasionally pokes out of the water.

The outfitters give it a Class III+ rating (moderately difficult), but my experience with the river is that more technical skill is necessary than the rating would imply. It's easy to become lulled into a false sense of security because the first part of the run is fairly benign, with a few decent but not too challenging rapids. However, the last section is like being in a pinball machine, bouncing from boulder to boulder, and there's a hairball drop called Bronco that probably should rate as a Class IV+, and if you don't hold on tight you could get pitched overboard. I recommend that children and those without previous white-water experience portage this rapid, and fortunately there's a convenient spot to make an exit. It's a short walk across a railroad bridge to the final takeout point, and from above you can watch the hardcore river cowboys try their luck at taming Bronco. Like many rivers, varying water levels can change this river dramatically, requiring adjustments in the approaches. There are two other runs on the lower Truckee: one from Floriston to Verdi (just inside the Nevada state line) that is eight miles long and contains several Class II+ rapids and required portages; and another from Verdi to downtown Reno that is nine miles long and is a tame Class II, making it suitable for just about anyone, including families.

At present, outfitters run paddleboats (be prepared to paddle hard) on the upper stretches, though if you feel more comfortable with an oar boat (the guide does all of the work), ask if one is available. One major benefit from the presence of commercial rafting on the lower Truckee is that the guides are committed to an ongoing refuse cleanup campaign, which will greatly improve the aesthetics of the canyon.

Close to South Lake Tahoe, **Carson River, East Fork** is a mellow to moderate rafting experience under normal runoff, with most rapids rated Class II or III. But the season is short—usually mid-April to late June—because there are no dams to control the flows. The most popular run is 19.5 miles long; it begins three miles south of Markleeville on Highway 89 at Hangman's Bridge (where vigilantes lynched an alleged murderer in 1874) and ends in Nevada five miles south of Gardnerville. While some tours can do

ON THE WATER

the river in a day, most involve two days with an overnight campout on public lands.

There are many notable features to recommend a trip on the East Fork, among them the transition from alpine terrain with pine trees (at 5,500 feet) to high desert bluffs with chaparral. The scenery is spectacular and constantly changing, and the river is a good introduction to white water. Sidewinder Rapid, rated Class III, is probably the most difficult rapid. A highlight of the trip is a stop at East Carson Hot Springs, about halfway down the run, where you can soak in a natural pool that averages 104°F. Just before the takeout above Ruhenstroth Dam (which has a dangerous 30-foot waterfall), you'll float through a spectacular gorge that is lined by rock formations called "The Crags."

Walker River, West Fork is an ass-kicking, seasonal river for very experienced river rats only. The 12- to 14-mile run from Sonora Bridge to Walker is sprinkled with challenging Class IV and V rapids, and if you take a paddle option it's a constant push. The West Walker, paralleling U.S. 395 in California, plunges 100 feet per mile—a significant gradient—and while there are no big drops, there are hundreds of nonstop waves and holes, with the signature rapid called White Mile. The river is usually runnable starting in June and can last through the end of July, depending on the runoff, which pours from drainages in Yosemite. Terrain is mostly open, high desert. Because of the very cold water, wearing a wet suit is a necessity. Because this is a Class V river, few outfitters run it, and you'll probably need to have at least a small group before being able to book it.

One of the nation's most popular white-water rivers, the **American River, South Fork** is a 1.5-hour drive from Lake Tahoe. With its headwaters in Desolation Wilderness, the South Fork offers rich gold mining history, waters that range from placid to pulverizing, and a panoramic canyon filled with rollicking "haystacks." The full run of 20.5 miles is normally done in two days, but outfitters also cover two stretches in single-day trips. The first, from Chili Bar to Lotus, is about 11 miles long and contains two Class III+ rapids: Meatgrinder, a long rock garden with a sub-

merged boulder at the end, and Troublemaker, a maze of boulders and strong rapids. The second stretch, from Lotus to Salmon Falls Bridge at Folsom Lake, is nine miles long and includes hair-raisers such as Satan's Cesspool, a Class III+ rapid with two precipitous drops, as well as a large rock where a peanut gallery of spectators usually gathers to watch the action.

There are several advantages in running the American River: a low elevation (less than 1,000 feet at the highest put-in), consistently hot temperatures in summer, and good, developed campgrounds along the route. Some outfitters have permanent midpoint stations with hot showers, picnic grounds, and bathrooms, along with shaded campsites. One drawback is that weekends can see 2,000 or more river rats in one day, with a succession of buses disgorging mobs of people. At Coloma, rafters pass one of California's most famous historic sites—the place where James Marshall discovered gold at John Sutter's mill in 1848, triggering the '49er Gold Rush. Those who have time after their river excursion might wish to explore the vintage towns of Placerville or Auburn, where historic districts with boutiques and antiques beckon shoppers.

The **American River, Middle Fork** is grueling, exciting, and a hell of a long day (10 hours) on a river, but for advanced rafting aficionados it's one of the best "secrets" of the Sierra. With its headwaters rising from the Sierra west of Squaw Valley, the Middle Fork drew dozens of mining towns along its banks in the 1800s. Even today, the river gives up respectable amounts of gold and is actively dredged.

River rats like the Middle Fork because it has scenic canyons and much more of a wilderness feeling than the other area rivers. There are powerful Class IV and V rapids along the 25-mile run, as well as a mandatory portage at Ruck-a-Chucky Falls. Those who sign up for this trip should be in good physical condition, because paddlers will have to negotiate tortuous sections, such as the infamous Tunnel Chute rapid, a man-made diversion slot blasted out of the rock by gold miners. Boats go through one by one, or sometimes not at all, depending on the hydraulics. The put-in is about 23 miles east of

Auburn, and the takeout is near the confluence of the Middle Fork and North Fork of the American, though some companies do shorter runs. The Middle Fork, with its flows controlled by dams, is runnable May–September, and its elevation of 1,100 feet assures warm to hot temperatures on most summer days.

Customs and Prices

River running companies usually offer several rivers, though they may specialize in one or two. Rates vary from river to river, and also depend on whether meals are provided. Midweek prices tend to be 10 percent to 15 percent lower than weekend prices. Also, there are frequently discounts for groups and for youths 16 and under. Personal flotation vests are provided to all clients, and some outfitters offer helmets as well. You'll need to wear old sneakers that can get wet, wet (river) sandals, or neoprene dive booties. Here are the price ranges for tours:

• **Truckee River, Lower:** $65–75 for half-day trips, $95–120 for full-day trips with lunch.

• **Carson River, East Fork:** $70–80 for half-day trips, $90–125 for full-day trips with lunch.

• **West Fork, Walker River:** $100–125 for a full-day trip with lunch.

• **South Fork, American River:** $65–100 for half-day trips, $95–125 for full-day trips with lunch.

• **Middle Fork, American River:** $120–150 for full-day trips with lunch.

Note: Two-day trips on most rivers run $225–275 per person, and include all meals. On the South Fork of the American River, many outfitters have tents and rental sleeping bags, as well as their own private campgrounds. On others, you'll need to bring your own overnight gear.

TRUCKEE RIVER (LOWER)

I.R.I.E. Rafting Company/Truckee Whitewater Adventures

This partnership specializes in environmental education and low-impact camping on its river trips. All guides have backgrounds in local natural history and will take time to explain things to clients. The company, operating since 1994

(though its owners have many more years of experience in the industry), runs the Lower Truckee, the East Fork of the Carson and the North and Middle Forks of the American. Polices vary per river on the minimum allowable age for children. On all overnight tours, available on the East Carson and Middle Fork American, guides prepare creative organic meals. Trips include gear such as wetsuits, life vests and helmets. Different-sized rafts are used depending on water levels

Contact: I.R.I.E., P.O. Box 26, Floriston, CA 96111; 530/587-1184, email: irie@cwo.com; website: www.irierafting.com.

Tahoe Whitewater Tours

Choose from three guided day rafting trips: the South Fork of the American River, East Fork of the Carson River, or the lower Truckee River (the white-water stretch). Owner Mike Miltner shuttles from a meeting point near Alpine Meadows. On the lower Truckee, he offers half-day trips in rafts on the stretch from Boca to Floriston and full-day trips in inflatable kayaks from Verdi to Reno. For the South Fork of the American, Miltner provides round-trip transportation Lake Tahoe. Reservations are required.

Contact: Tahoe Whitewater Tours, P.O. Box 7466, Tahoe City, CA 96145; 530/581-2441 or 775/787-5000 800/442-7238; website: www.gowhitewater.com.

Tributary Whitewater Tours

Outfitters Lorraine and Dan Buckley, in business since 1978, run the lower Truckee and East Fork Carson Rivers, as well as the South and Middle Forks of the American. Inflatable, self-bailing kayaks are an option on the Carson. Group transportation from Lake Tahoe is available. Age restrictions for children depend on each river, but range 4–16. The season is June–September.

Contact: Tributary Whitewater Tours, 20480 Woodbury Dr., Grass Valley, CA 95949; 530/346-6812 or 800/672-3846; email: rafting@whitewatertours.com; website: www.whitewatertours.com.

EAST FORK, CARSON RIVER

American River Recreation

This company offers one- and two-day trips on the East Fork of the Carson during the short spring runoff season. All trips make a stop at the natural springs where river rats can soak in the mineral pools. The company also runs the South Fork of the American River, where it has a riverfront base camp that has hot showers, flush toilets, a volleyball area, horseshoe pit, and amphitheater. Among the promotions are special family trips that offer a 50 percent discount for children.

Contact: American River Recreation, P.O. Box 465, Lotus, CA 95651; 530/622-6802 or 800/333-7238; email: info@arrafting.com; website: www.arrafting.com.

Current Adventures Kayak School and Trips

This is a professional kayak school that offers private or group lessons for all levels, with a raft-along option for nonpaddlers. Two-day, overnight trips on the East Fork of the Carson River are scheduled late April–late June. This river is considered a good first-time overnight experience for class II+ paddlers and above. Guides prepare all meals, and participants can soak in the mineral hot springs that is about midway down the 21-mile stretch of river. Shuttles are available to the put-in.

Contact: Current Adventures, P.O. Box 828, Lotus, CA 95651; 888/4-KAYAKING (888/452-9254) or 530/642-9755; website: www.kayaking.com.

Sunshine Rafting Adventures

Owner Jim Foust has been running the East Fork of the Carson since 1982, and he does both the upper stretch, which is 7.3 miles long, and the so-called "main" stretch, which is 20 miles long, offering one- or two-day outings. Inflatable, self-bailing kayaks are an option for the main stretch. Groups meet at the Carson River Resort, near Hangman's Bridge outside of Markleeville. Wetsuit rentals are available.

Contact: Sunshine River Adventures, P.O. Box 1445, Oakdale, CA 95361; 209/ 848-4800 or 800/829-7238; website: www.sonnet.com/sunraft.

River and Rock Adventures

Longtime river guides Scott and Melanie Cleland, along with partner Curtis Gray, recently acquired the river rafting operation of Access to Adventure in 2001. They run the East Fork of the Carson, along with the three forks of the American. On the Carson, guests have the option of using one- or two-person inflatable, self-bailing Star and Hyside kayaks. On the South Fork of the American, there is a choice of runs: Chili Bar, The Gorge, or both, and there is a campground in Coloma for overnight trips. The season is May–October (but only through June to early July for the Carson).

Contact: River and Rock Adventures, 4430 Las Encinitas Dr., Fair Oaks, CA 95628; 916/955-7625 or 866/748-7625; website: www.riverandrockadventures.com.

Tahoe Whitewater Tours

See listing under Truckee River, page 133.

Tributary Whitewater Tours

See listing under Truckee River, page 133.

SOUTH AND MIDDLE FORKS, AMERICAN RIVER

All-Outdoors Adventure Trips

In business for more than 35 years, outfitter Greg Amstrong is one of the original pioneers on the South Fork of the American River. From April to October, he offers half-day, one-day, and two-day trips on the South Fork. He also runs the North and Middle Forks. No shuttle service is available. Children must be at least eight years old.

Contact: All-Outdoors Adventure Trips, 1250 Pine St., Ste. 103, Walnut Creek, CA 94596; 925/932-8993 or 800/247-2387; email: rivers@aorafting.com; website: www.aorafting.com.

American River Recreation

See Carson River, above.

Beyond Limits Adventures

Half-day, one-day, and two-day guided rafting trips on the South and Middle Forks of the American River are available. Overnight excursions include four meals and camping at the company's resort (camping gear can be rented), which has its own outdoor beer garden with microbrews on tap. One- and two-day trips include equipment and shuttle. At its River Park Resort in Coloma, an affiliate company, California Canoe and Kayak, conducts one- and two-day kayaking classes on the river. Beyond Limits owner Mike Doyle has been in business since 1979. Trips run daily April–October. Reservations are required, though last-minute trips are possible if space permits.

Contact: Beyond Limits Adventures, P.O. Box 215, Riverbank, CA 95367; 209/869-6060 or 800/234-RAFT (800/234-7238); email: bla@rivertrip.com; website: www.rivertrip.com and for California Canoe and Kayak, www.calkayak.com.

CBOC Whitewater Rafting Adventures

Guided rafting trips on the South Fork American River—either half day, full day, or two days—are available April–September. The outfitter also runs the Middle Fork.

Contact: CBOC Whitewater Rafting Adventures, P.O. Box 554, Coloma, CA 95613; 530/621-1236 or 800/356-2262; website: www.cbocwhitewater.com.

Earthtrek Expeditions

Operating since 1976, this company offers guided rafting trips on all three forks of the American River April–October. On the South Fork, half-day, full-day, and two-day trips are available, with a minimum age of eight. On the Middle and North Forks, full-day and overnight wilderness trips are offered, with a minimum age of 14. Bus transportation from the Lake Tahoe area can be arranged for groups at extra cost.

Contact: Earthtrek Expeditions, P.O. Box 1010, Lotus, CA 95651; 530/642-1900 or 800/229-8735; email: trek@inforum.net; website: www.earthtrekexpeditions.com.

I.R.I.E/Truckee Whitewater Adventures

See Carson River, previous page.

Mariah Adventure Connection

This company offers one- and two-day trips on both the South and Middle Forks of the American River April–September. The one-day trips involve either the Chili Bar to Lotus section or the Lotus to Folsom Lake section ("The Gorge"), depending on the day of the week. On request, the company can arrange to do both stretches in one day. Mariah also runs the North Fork. The company has its own campground at Lotus, complete with hot showers, flush toilets, and a hot tub.

Contact: Mariah Adventure Connection, P.O. Box 475, Coloma, CA 95613; 530/626-7385 or 800/556-6060; email: getwet@raftcalifornia.com; website: www.raftcalifornia.com.

OARS

This established company (circa 1970) operates on the South and Middle Forks of the American River. For the South Fork, half-day, one-day, or two-day trips are available; for the Middle Fork, one-day or two-day trips are offered. Equipment, life jackets, guides, and transportation are included. Any size group is acceptable. Children must be at least seven years old to ride the South Fork. Reservations are required, with a minimum 24-hour notice.

Contact: OARS, P.O. Box 67, Angels Camp, CA 95222; 209/736-4677 or 800/346-6277; email: reservations@oars.com; website: www.oars.com.

Tahoe Whitewater Tours

See Truckee River, above.

Tributary Whitewater Tours

See Truckee River, above.

Whitewater Connection

This company has grown from a tiny three-boat, one-river operation to one of California's largest white-water outfitters. It was the first major river company to convert entirely to self-bailing rafts, and all boats and life jackets are custom-designed.

ON THE WATER

The centerpiece of all overnight trips is a 40-acre private base camp on the banks of the South Fork of the American River. The camp features hot showers and flush toilets, and an irrigation system keeps the camp green and lush throughout the hot summer months. Meals are gourmet affairs, starting with shrimp cocktails and hors d'oeuvres, followed by a main course of steak, lobster, and chicken, complete with wines from local foothill wineries. For two-day trips, camping gear is available for rent. In a season that lasts April–September, trips are run on the South Fork American River. Choose from half-day, full-day, and two-day trips. Next-day reservations are available.

Contact: Whitewater Connection, 7237 Hwy. 49/P.O. Box 270, Coloma, CA 95613-0270; 530/622-6446 or 800/336-7238; website: www.whitewaterconnection.com.

Whitewater Excitement

Norm Schoenhoff, operating since 1979, runs the three forks of the American River with guided half-day, full-day, and two-day rafting trips. The company operates a campground at Coloma on the South Fork American River, and recently it constructed a 1,400-square-foot "hang out"

area with a shaded deck, an espresso bar, and a shaved ice cart. The season is April–September.

Contact: Whitewater Excitement, P.O. Box 5992, Auburn, CA 95604; 530/888-6515 or 800/750-2386; website: www.whitewaterexcitement.com.

Whitewater Voyages

Bill McGinnis is one of the pioneers of whitewater rafting, and his San Francisco Bay Area company offers a myriad of trips with an emphasis on creature comforts. On the South Fork of the American, his walk-in overnight campground, called River Park, provides skilled chefs, happy-hour beverages and hors d'oeuvres, lavish meals, a sandy beach for swimming, a volleyball area, and running water with warm showers and flush toilets. Half-day, full-day, and two-day guided rafting trips are run on the South Fork April–October. The minimum age is seven. The company also offers a five-day summer camp for youngsters ages 12–17 at its facility in Coloma. Tent and wet suit rentals are available.

Contact: Whitewater Voyages, 5225 San Pablo Dam Rd., El Sobrante, CA 94803; 510/222-5994 or 800/488-7238; website: www.whitewatervoyages.com.

Scuba Diving

The incredible clarity of the water at Lake Tahoe makes it especially attractive for diving. Underwater visibility (100 feet or more) approaches the kind of "vis" that warm-water divers experience in the tropics, and it's possible to see unique underwater rock formations, fish, and, occasionally, the wreckage of an old boat. However, divers should be aware that the risks of high-elevation diving exceed those at sea level. Special diving depth tables are needed to determine safe, no-decompression times, and in general the times are considerably less than in the ocean. Because of the cold temperatures of the lake, full wet suits are required all summer, and dry suits are required in winter. If you intend to dive in Tahoe, go with an experienced local diving guide and watch out for the frequent boat traffic on the surface. Popular diving locations include

Sand Harbor on the Nevada side, Carnelian Bay on the North Shore, Sunnyside near Tahoe City, and Emerald Bay on the West Shore, where the California Department of Parks and Recreation has established a protected underwater preserve (no collecting!). Here it is possible to view two sunken barges, one of which has a surface buoy attached to it for use by dive boats.

The closest thing to a wall dive is the steep drop-off at Rubicon Point, which is accessible from the beach at D. L. Bliss State Park, and plunges more than 1,000 feet below the surface. The easiest dive, in terms of logistics, is Sand Harbor, which has a nice beach and offers the lure of turquoise waters that lap against unique boulder piles and attract schools of large Mackinaw trout. Off Baldwin Beach, on the West Shore, is a submerged ancient forest that is a tricky dive for two reasons: it requires a long swim from shore and there's the possibility of snagging equipment on branches. Other diving waters in the region include Donner and Fallen Leaf Lakes, near Tahoe, which are attractive because it's possible to find (and legally retrieve) historic debris such as old bottles, wagon wheels, pieces of porcelain, and other artifacts. Following is a list of local dive shops:

SOUTH LAKE TAHOE

SunSports

Neal Melton has been running Lake Tahoe's only dive shop since 1986. He has a staff of four PADI instructors/divemasters, and they specialize in high-altitude diving. The shop, on Highway 50 close to Marina Village, offers classes, gear rental and diving in Tahoe. Also rents kayaks in the summer.

Fees: Courses range $125–395. Call for information on dive tours.

Contact: SunSports, 3564 Lake Tahoe Blvd., South Lake Tahoe, CA 96150; 530/541-6000; email: sunsport@cwia.com; website: www.sunsports-tahoe.com.

RENO/CARSON VALLEY

Sierra Diving Center

Operating since the mid-1970s, this Reno store offers a full range of scuba instruction and gear rental, with dives at Lake Tahoe, Donner Lake, Fallen Leaf Lake and Sparks Marina Park. At Lake Tahoe, diving is from shore, at places such as Sunnyside, Sand Harbor (Diver's Cove), D. L. Bliss State Park, and Carnelian Bay. Visiting divers are welcome and can rent all necessary equipment. Dive tours include orientation for high-elevation diving with discussion of dive tables. One to three dives can be made per tour. Instruction involves high-altitude diving techniques.

Hours: Weekdays 9 A.M.–6 P.M., 9 A.M.–9:30 P.M. Wed., and 10 A.M.–5 P.M. Saturday.

The incredible clarity of the water at Lake Tahoe makes it especially attractive for diving. Underwater visibility (100 feet or more) approaches the kind of "vis" that warm-water divers experience in the tropics, and it's possible to see unique underwater rock formations, fish, and, occasionally, the wreckage of an old boat.

Fees: $50 per shore dive. Rental gear over and above a tank is extra.

Contact: Sierra Diving Center, 104 E. Grove St., Reno, NV 89502; 775/825-2147, website: www.sierradive.com.

Strictly Scuba

Owner John Sawyer has been operating this store since 1992, and he frequently gets requests from visiting divers for tours at Lake Tahoe. With a 21-foot deep-v powerboat, Sawyer can take up to four divers on excursions to Emerald Bay, Rubicon Wall, Cave Rock, Sand Harbor and Crystal Bay. A typical two-tank dive outing includes a stop at the Wall and a shallow dive on the shipwrecks in Emerald Bay. Night dives are available at Cave Rock. Snacks and drinks are served on the boat. He also offers a one-day PADI high-altitude diving course that includes classroom instruction and two dives at the lake. Full PADI certification courses and Nitrox (enriched oxygen) diving also are available.

Hours: Open Mon.–Sat. 8 A.M.–6 P.M.

Fees: $40 per person for a shore dive; $40 for complete rental package (tank, BC, belt, wet suit, regulator, mask, fins, and snorkel); high-altitude diving course, $95.

Contact: Strictly Scuba, 2384 S. Curry St. #1, Carson City, NV 89703; 775/884-DIVE (775/884-3483), website: www.divetahoe.com.

Tropical Penguin Scuba and Water Sports

This Reno-based store can take divers to Sand Harbor, Emerald Bay, and Rubicon Wall, with shore dives, depending on location. This company also runs the dive operation at Sparks Marina Park, where it also offers guided dives on a sunken F-4 fighter jet. Offers orientation dives in Fallen Leaf, Tahoe, Donner and other lakes, accompanied by a PADI-certified instructor. Good source of information for local alpine diving sites. The shop offers PADI open-water certification as well as altitude diving courses. A complete rental gear package is available, including choice of wetsuits or dry suits (need to be certified for dry suits).

Fees: Certification courses are about $250. Call for prices on orientation dives.

Contact: Tropical Penguins Scuba and Water Sports, 180 W. Peckham, Ste. 1160, Reno, NV 89509; 775/828-3483; website: www .tropicalpenguinscuba.com.

Beaches

You don't have to get *in* the water to enjoy it. Even if Lake Tahoe didn't bask in the splendor of snowcapped Sierra peaks or boast the greatest concentration of ski resorts in North America, it would still be famous for its beaches. No other alpine lake in the country is blessed with the kind of white sand beaches that rim much of Tahoe's 72-mile shoreline. Some of these beaches extend for miles, offering a dazzling combination of aquamarine waters, bays, coves, rocky points, and forest.

The amount of sandy beach varies with the water elevation in the lake. During drier-than-normal winters, the lake level can recede and expose hundreds of acres of new beach. That has been the case in recent years, after back-to-back dry years and low lake levels. As water is released from Tahoe into the lower Truckee River through a dam at Tahoe City, the water level drops over the summer and reaches its lowest point in September and October, before winter storms arrive. This can be the best time to enjoy Tahoe's beaches, because that's also when they're the least crowded.

Each major city and community around the lake has its own beaches. There are also numerous private beaches at resorts and town house developments. Although the lake is cold all year in its deeper areas, the shallows can be brisk but comfortable, especially on warm days. What is particularly captivating is the clarity of the water everywhere. Mirroring the sand and rocks below, the lake shifts colors, from a bright turquoise close to the surface to a rich, deep blue as the shelf gradually disappears into the depths. The hues are striking from the high vantage points along the West and East Shores, and the effect reminds more than one visitor of a tropical island paradise.

More than 30 developed public beaches offer a multitude of recreational opportunities, from simple sunbathing to kayaking, Jet Skiing and parasailing. Each beach has its own personality and attracts its own following. There are beaches suited to families with small children, who can play on paddleboats, dinghies, and other water toys while their parents enjoy a much-deserved rest. Some beaches primarily draw teenagers, who thrive on loud music, volleyball, and mutual admiration. And there are beaches that have become popular with the clothing-optional set.

Some of the best beaches offer an insight to Lake Tahoe's heady social history, with magnificent mansions nestled in the trees just above the white sand. Emerald Bay, Baldwin Beach, and Sugar Pine Point State Park all have venerable estates that are open to the public, as well as fine swimming beaches. Also, there's a bit of culture at Sand Harbor on the East Shore, where a Shakespeare festival hits the boards each summer. Nothing goes better together than the Bard and the beach. To beach or not to beach? That is the question. Or is it?

All beaches listed are keyed to the Beaches map.

TRUCKEE/DONNER
West End Beach
(see map on page 139, site 1)
This large, family-oriented beach on the west end of Donner Lake gets its share of users since it's fairly visible from I-80 above. There are scenic views of the surrounding peaks, and the beach is an active place for sailboaters and windsurfers, who enjoy the strong afternoon winds that kick

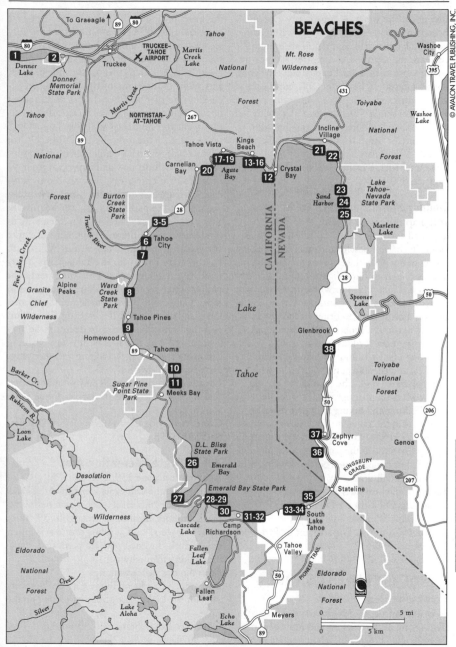

BEACHES

ON THE WATER

up out on the water. A large grassy area and a boat ramp are close by. Boating, water-skiing, volleyball, basketball, and tennis are among the recreational options. Amenities include restrooms, picnic facilities, fire pits, barbecue grills, concession stands, horseshoes, playgrounds, and a swimming area. No pets are allowed.

Fees: Admission is $3 for adults, $2 for youth and children 2–17, and free for two and under.

Location: At the end of Donner Pass Road in Truckee, California.

Contact: Truckee Donner Parks and Recreation District; 530/582-7720.

Donner Memorial State Park

(see map on page 139, site 2)

Donner Lake—the "other" big lake near Tahoe—boasts its share of beach hangouts. The southeast corner of the park, close to the campground, has a series of narrow but delightful sunning beaches and a shallow lagoon where the water gets pleasantly warm during summer days. This lagoon is a great place to bring a canoe or an inflatable raft, and is probably the warmest natural swimming area for kids in the region. Waterskiers, windsurfers, and Jet Skiers all share the beaches, and there's a concession stand with additional water toys. The picnic/day-use area is just west of the campground, shaded by pine trees. Fishing and hiking are other recreational options, and the Emigrant Trail Museum, which traces the journey of the ill-fated Donner Party, is open year-round at the park. Pets are allowed in the park but not on posted beach areas, and must be leashed at all times.

Fees: The day-use fee is $2 per car.

Location: Off I-80 on Donner Pass Road in Truckee, California.

Contact: California Department of Parks and Recreation; 530/582-7894.

TAHOE CITY/WEST SHORE

Commons Beach

(see map on page 139, site 3)

This is one of the loveliest and most beautifully landscaped beaches in Tahoe, and it's right in the heart of Tahoe City, although it drops off from the side of Highway 28 and is not easily seen by passing motorists. Once you descend the stairs, however, you are met with a panorama of green lawn, children's play areas, sandy beaches, and picturesque views of the West Shore, including the pier at Tahoe Tavern and moored boats bobbing gently in the water. As this edition went to press, the California Tahoe Conservancy and the Tahoe City Public Utility District had begun a $4 million renovation program that includes new and larger playgrounds, new group picnic areas, new restrooms with changing areas, new landscaping, new walkways and bike paths, and a lower boardwalk along Highway 28. These improvements are in tandem with the State Department of Parks and Recreation's project to expand William B. Layton State Park, near the Tahoe City "Y" by removing two commercial buildings and providing better access to the shore. The goal is to make Commons Beach a focal point of Tahoe City, and to that end the existing fire station eventually may be moved to open up the area even more. The beach is within easy walking distance of restaurants, lodging and shopping. No pets are allowed.

Location: Off Highway 28 on Commons Beach Road, next to the fire station in Tahoe City, California.

Contact: Tahoe City Public Utility District; 530/583-3796.

Tahoe State Recreation Area

(see map on page 139, site 4)

Managed by the California Department of Parks and recreation, this small beach—with restrooms, picnic facilities, fire pits, barbecue grills, 39 campsites, showers, and a playground—is open dawn–dusk. Leashed pets are permitted. Parking is along the highway.

Fees: No charge for walking.

Location: Just east of Tahoe City on Highway 28, past the Lighthouse Shopping Center on the right.

Contact: Tahoe State Recreation Area; 530/583-3074.

Lake Forest Beach
(see map on page 139, site 5)

A picnic/barbecue area, restrooms, a pier, and bicycling/hiking trails are provided at this beach, which attracts lots of swimmers. No pets are allowed.

Location: At Lake Forest Road and Highway 28, one mile east of Tahoe City, California.

Contact: Tahoe City Public Utility District; 530/583-3796.

Kilner Park (see map on page 139, site 6)

This small park offers 300 feet of beach, tennis courts, volleyball and cycling trails.

Location: On Highway 89 and Ward Avenue, south of the Tahoe City "Y" intersection with Highway 28, in Tahoe City, California.

Contact: Tahoe City Public Utility District; 530/583-3796.

William Kent Campground
(see map on page 139, site 7)

This rocky beach with room for sunbathing has campsites, restrooms, picnic tables, fire pits, and barbecue grills.

Location: Off Highway 89, south of Tahoe City, California.

Contact: U.S. Forest Service; 530/583-5544 or 530/573-2674.

Kaspian Recreation Area
(see map on page 139, site 8)

Covered with cobblestones and coarse rocks, this beach has restrooms, lakeside picnic tables, fire pits, barbecue grills, campsites (across the highway), shore fishing, and access to Blackwood Canyon, a good spot for hiking, mountain biking, four-wheeling, and in-line skating.

Location: Off Highway 89, south of Sunnyside Lodge in Tahoe City, California.

Contact: U.S. Forest Service; 530/583-3642 or 530/573-2674.

Chambers Beach
(see map on page 139, site 9)

At Chambers Landing on the West Shore, this is a small and not particularly inspiring public beach situated next to one of the more exclusive town house enclaves on the lake, complete with a private dock and the famous Chambers Landing restaurant. This is a peculiar arrangement,

© KEN CASTLE

beach at Sugar Pine Point State Park

ON THE WATER

with a private beach reserved for owners and their guests right next to the public beach. Parking is available in the lot only for owners and those dining at the restaurant; everyone else must park along Highway 89 and walk in. A picnic area and restrooms are provided. No pets are allowed on the beach.

Location: Near McKinney-Rubicon Springs Road off Highway 89, in Tahoma, California.

Contact: Tahoe City Public Utility District; 530/583-3796.

Sugar Pine Point State Park
(see map on page 139, site 10)
Sugar Pine Point State Park, the largest of Lake Tahoe's California parks at 2,000 acres, is divided into two sections by Highway 89. The smaller east side has the stately Ehrman Mansion and a huge grassy area that is shaded by pine trees and slopes gently down to the shoreline. This is one of the finest picnic areas on the lake, though it's less well known because it is set off from the road. There's a free pier and a mostly rocky shoreline, but a small beach is sometimes available for swimming and sunning. Amenities include restrooms, showers, picnic facilities, fire pits, and barbecue grills. The park is laced with cycling trails and connects with the West Shore Bike Path. Other nearby recreational opportunities include hiking, tennis, and swimming. No pets are allowed.

Fees: There is a $2 per vehicle parking fee.

Location: Off Highway 89, 10 miles south of Tahoe City, California.

Contact: California Department of Parks and Recreation; 530/525-7982.

Meeks Bay Beach
(see map on page 139, site 11)
There are two beaches here, one run by the U.S. Forest Service, another by Meeks Bay Resort and Marina. Ensconced in a scenic, wind-protected cove on the West Shore south of Sugar Pine Point State Park, the public beach is small but visually appealing. Parking is in a pine-shaded lot, just steps away from the small, level stretch of white sand. This is an excellent location to launch a kayak or rubber dinghy to paddle along the shore-

line. The resort beach next door has an array of water toys for rent and is especially popular among families with young children. Both beaches are close to Highway 89, so expect some noise from the traffic. Facilities include restrooms, picnic areas, fire pits, barbecue grills, and a small boat launch (at the resort). No pets are allowed.

Fees: For Meeks Bay Resort, the day use is $7 per car; for the Forest Service side, it's $5.

Location: About 10 miles south of Tahoe City, California.

Contact: Meeks Bay Resort and Marina, $7 per car; 530/525-6946; U.S. Forest Service; 530/573-2674.

KINGS BEACH/TAHOE VISTA/CARNELIAN BAY
Buck's Beach (Speedboat Beach)
(see map on page 139, site 12)
This is a now-you-see-it, now-you-don't type of beach, depending entirely on how wet (or dry) the winters are and how high (or low) the lake level is. At this writing, low levels have once again exposed an area that was completely inundated in 1996. It is a special hideaway for local beachgoers. When the area is available, it is a relatively small but scenic spot that has a protected sandy beach, a bouldered promontory jutting into the water, and a series of rocky islets. The beach, which was hidden behind a few blocks of houses just west of the Cal-Neva Resort at Crystal Bay Point, was a favorite destination of kayakers and canoeists, many of whom would land here from nearby Kings Beach. Parking is very limited—on the street only—and access is via a narrow path and stairway that lead between private homes to the shoreline.

Location: At the end of Speedboat Road at Crystal Bay, California.

Contact: North Tahoe Public Utility District; 530/546-4212.

Coon Street Picnic Area
(see map on page 139, site 13)
The long, wide beach has restrooms, picnic facilities, fire pits, barbecue grills, and playgrounds.

Location: At Coon Street and Brockway Vista Avenue in Kings Beach, California.
Contact: North Tahoe Public Utility District; 530/546-4212.

Kings Beach State Recreation Area
(see map on page 139, site 14)

Usually crowded and very visible from Highway 28, this sandy beach is a hangout for the younger set, primarily because it has so many water sports and water toy concessions (including Jet Skis, kayaks, paddleboats, and rowboats) and because there's an area for impromptu beach volleyball games, swimming, sunbathing, and the attendant preening. The relatively flat beach extends for nearly 3,000 feet alongside the community of Kings Beach, affording access to shops and restaurants. There's a seven-acre day-use park, a playground, a boat launch, restrooms, and a picnic/barbecue area. Powerboats are prohibited.
Fees: Parking costs $5.
Location: On North Lake Boulevard, west of Deer Street, in Kings Beach, California.
Contact: North Tahoe Public Utility District; 530/546-4212.

Secline Beach
(see map on page 139, site 15)

You'll find picnic facilities at this 300-foot beach. Leashed pets are permitted.
Location: Off Highway 267 at the end of Secline Street in Kings Beach, California.
Contact: North Tahoe Public Utility District; 530/546-4212.

North Tahoe Beach Center
(see map on page 139, site 16)

Earmarked for future improvements, this 550-foot-long beach has restrooms, picnic facilities, volleyball courts, fire pits, and barbecue grills.
Location: At the intersection of Highway 28 and Highway 267 in Kings Beach, California.
Contact: North Tahoe Public Utility District; 530/546-4212.

Agatam Beach
(see map on page 139, site 17)

This 300-foot beach has restrooms, picnic tables, fire pits, barbecue grills, and a lawn area. Leashed pets are permitted. As this edition went to press, this and two other beaches—Moondunes and Sandy—were being combined to form one large beach at Tahoe Vista.
Location: At Highway 28 and Agatam Street in Tahoe Vista, California.
Contact: North Tahoe Public Utility District; 530/546-4212.

Moondunes Beach
(see map on page 139, site 18)

Restrooms, fire pits, and barbecue grills are available at this small, 600-foot beach, where people come to sunbathe and swim. Shallow, sandy bottom is ideal for wading. Leashed pets are permitted. This beach is now merged with Agatam and Sandy beaches.
Location: At Highway 28 and National Avenue near Pino Grande in Tahoe Vista, California.
Contact: North Tahoe Public Utility District; 530/546-4212.

Tahoe Vista Recreation Area
(see map on page 139, site 19)

Among the offerings at this beach are a picnic/barbecue area, restrooms, a turf area, and a boat ramp. Recently, the ramp was widened and lengthened substantially, and there is a new floating dock. Leashed pets are permitted.
Fees: $5 for parking.
Location: At National Avenue and North Lake Boulevard in Tahoe Vista, California.
Contact: North Tahoe Public Utility District; 530/546-4212.

Carnelian Bay Lake Access/Patton Landing (see map on page 139, site 20)

Great things have happened here. The California Tahoe Conservancy, a public agency, recently acquired nearly 1,000 feet of beach, including what was formerly known as Patton Beach, for general access. There are two beaches here, separated by the Sierra Boat Company. Facilities at each include public restrooms, public parking, picnic tables and fire pits. These are rocky beaches with no sand. The east beach has a 22-space lot, while the west beach shares

ON THE WATER

the Gar Woods Grill parking lot. The east beach, where Patton Landing is, has a car-top boat launching area suitable for kayaks, canoes and rafts. No launching of motorized vessels is permitted. Also, a food concession, Kayak Café, serves coffee and pastries for breakfast and deli sandwiches for lunch. The concessionaire maintains that beach.

Location: Off Highway 28, between Onyx Street and Gar Woods Grill and Pier in Carnelian Bay, California.

Contact: Kayak Café, 530/546-9337.

INCLINE VILLAGE/CRYSTAL BAY

Burnt Cedar Beach
(see map on page 139, site 21)

This beautifully maintained private beach and the adjacent grassy picnic grounds are available only to residents and guests staying at condominiums and homes in Incline Village. The quality and cleanliness of the facilities, including the Olympic-sized swimming pool, are compelling reasons for vacationing at Incline. If you rent a condo, be sure to ask for beach passes from the owner. Amenities include restrooms, picnic facilities, fire pits, a barbecue grill, playgrounds, a pool, and a large lawn.

Location: On Lakeshore Drive in Incline Village, Nevada.

Contact: Incline Village General Improvement District (IVGID), 775/832-1310.

Incline Beach
(see map on page 139, site 22)

Across from the Hyatt Regency in Incline Village, this private beach is smaller than nearby Burnt Cedar Beach and is also off-limits to nonresidents. Amenities include restrooms, picnic facilities, fire pits, barbecue grills, playgrounds, a boat launch, and a grassy area. If you are staying at the Hyatt, you can avail yourself of various watercraft rentals, ranging from paddle boats to motor boats, that are offered by a concessionaire.

Location: On Lakeshore Drive in Incline Village, Nevada.

Contact: Incline Village General Improvement District; 775/832-1310.

Sand Harbor, Lake Tahoe-Nevada State Park (see map on page 139, site 23)

With its wonderfully transparent waters, unique smooth rock formations, and protected coves, this is arguably Tahoe's finest and most spectacular white sand beach—and there is still a lot of it left despite the recent high water levels. Like something out of the South Pacific, the offshore colors are striking, varying from turquoise to indigo with the depth of the water.

The beach is one mile long, bordering the south and west sides of Sand Point, a small, slightly elevated peninsula off Highway 28. The combination of granite boulders and Jeffrey pines adds to its distinctive appearance, and there are shallow coves for swimming as well as for launching boats. Of course, the views of snowcapped peaks across the lake add to the ambience.

Beachgoers will enjoy swimming, picnicking, playing volleyball, or just hanging out on the sand. Other assets include the annual Shakespeare at Sand Harbor Festival, a series of plays performed by visiting theater companies in a sandy outdoor amphitheater. Performances are held several evenings each week. There's a large parking lot off the highway, as well as restrooms, covered picnic facilities, paved walkways allowing wheelchair access, barbecue grills, a boat launch, lifeguards, nature trails, and a visitor center. No pets are allowed (except at the boat launch).

Fees: $6 per vehicle for day use, with an extra $6 for boat launching.

Location: On Highway 89, four miles south of Incline Village in Nevada.

Contact: Lake Tahoe-Nevada State Park; 775/831-0494.

Chimney Beach
(see map on page 139, site 24)

Sandwiched among the scenic rock gardens of the East Shore, this small sand beach south of Sand Harbor is a favorite among locals—perhaps because it is on what many regard as the most attractive shoreline of Tahoe. Features include plenty of sand, turquoise water that looks like something from the Caribbean, smooth boulders that poke out of the lake, and spectacular vistas of snowcapped peaks. Getting to the site requires a quarter-mile walk from either of two parking lots on Highway 28, with steep grades at the beginning. The beach is named after a large chimney—a remnant of a caretaker's cabin that once served the nearby Whittell Estate, known as the Thunderbird Lodge. As this edition went to press, that grand estate was in the process of being opened to the public. Restrooms, fire pits, and barbecue grills are provided at the beach. Users are advised not to park on the road. Dogs are permitted, but glass containers are prohibited.

Location: On Highway 28 south of Sand Harbor.

Contact: U.S. Forest Service; 775/355-5302 or 775/882-2766.

Secret Harbor/Paradise Beach
(see map on page 139, site 25)

This undeveloped beach area is popular with nudists. Restrooms and parking are available. Dogs are permitted.

Location: South of Sand Harbor off Highway 28 in Nevada.

Contact: U.S. Forest Service Visitor Center; 530/573-2674.

SOUTH SHORE

Lester Beach, D. L. Bliss State Park
(see map on page 139, site 26)

Blissful? You bet. In 1,237-acre D. L. Bliss State Park, the spectacular, 3.5-mile-long Lester Beach on the West Shore has just about everything: flat sandy areas, rocky points, secluded coves, and an elevated, forested shoreline where one of Tahoe's most scenic hiking trails originates. There are shallows warm enough for swimming, and plenty of areas for picnicking and water sports, including kayaking. Motor and sail yachts frequently anchor in a small cove here, and tall pine trees line the hill above the beach. The area is adjacent to a large campground, but the beach is nearly two miles off Highway 89. Restrooms, picnic facilities, fire pits, and barbecue grills are available. The five-mile Emerald Bay Trail begins at the south end of Lester Beach, and a trail to Rubicon Point starts at the north end. The views from here, especially in the late afternoon, are truly inspiring. No pets are allowed. Open May–October, weather permitting.

Fees: $2 per vehicle for day use.

ON THE WATER

© KEN CASTLE

private beach (available to many hotel guests) at Lakeside Beach

Location: About 11 miles south of Homewood off Highway 89 in Tahoma, California.
Contact: California Department of Parks and Recreation; 530/525-7277.

Emerald Bay Beach
(see map on page 139, site 27)
Would you walk a mile for a spectacular beach? This one will test your stamina, especially going back uphill for an elevation gain of 500 feet. But it is so romantic and idyllic it's worth the sweat—if the water level is low enough. It fronts the famous Vikingsholm Castle, a replica of a Scandinavian castle. Beachgoers are surrounded on three sides by steep-walled mountains; little Fannette Island, the only island in the lake, is a short distance offshore. The beach is quite popular with motorboaters and users of other watercraft, and the bay itself—the most photographed place in Tahoe—is a constant beehive of activity. When the water is calm, particularly in the morning, this is a wonderful spot to bob lazily in a rubber dinghy. Restrooms, picnic facilities, a one-mile hiking trail, and a pier are available. No pets are allowed. Vikingsholm Castle tours are scheduled every half hour daily 10 A.M.–4 P.M. late June–early September (weekends only during the rest of June and September).
Fees: Use of the beach is free.
Location: At the base of Emerald Bay State Park, on Highway 89, eight miles north of South Lake Tahoe, California.
Contact: California Department of Parks and Recreation; 530/525-7277.

Baldwin Beach
(see map on page 139, site 28)
This relatively narrow stretch of white-sand beach is backed by the meandering Tallac Historic Site, a series of shaded lakefront mansions tucked into stands of stately pine trees. Tallac frequently hosts fairs, art shows, and music festivals, a plus for beachgoers in search of a little culture. Sloping trails and stairways lead from Tallac to the shoreline. There's a public parking area, but you'll have to walk a bit to reach the beach. Restrooms, picnic facilities, fire pits, and barbecue grills are available. Nearby is the Lake Tahoe Visitor Center, offering several nature walks and the Stream Profile Chamber. No dogs are allowed.
Fees: There is a $3 per-vehicle parking fee.
Location: On Highway 89, four miles north of the "Y" intersection in South Lake Tahoe, California.
Contact: U.S. Forest Service Visitor Center; 530/573-2674.

Kiva Beach **(see map on page 139, site 29)**
This is an attractive beach with views of South Lake Tahoe and Stateline. Facilities include restrooms, picnic tables, barbecue grills, and swimming areas. Leashed dogs are permitted.
Location: Off Highway 89, 2.5 miles north of the "Y" intersection in South Lake Tahoe, California.
Contact: U.S. Forest Service Visitor Center; 530/573-2674.

Jameson Beach
(see map on page 139, site 30)
Next to Richardson's Resort, this privately managed beach on Forest Service land is usually Action City. It has a swimming lagoon, a cornucopia of watercraft rentals, a water trampoline, parasailing rides, a water-ski school, cruise boats, and kayak tours. There are also picnic tables, barbecue grills, and a marina complex. Live music, from jazz to rock, emanates from the patio of the Beacon Restaurant, a popular beachfront bistro, offering hip vibrations while you tan. There are places to get in a game of beach volleyball, and the Tallac Historic Site and Baldwin Beach are within a short walk.

The view from Jameson Beach to the north includes striking West Shore peaks and the vibrant blue surface of the lake. Bike rentals and a paved bike trail are at the entrance of the resort, and many people cycle to the beach. That is certainly the easiest access, as parking in a small beachside lot is extremely limited, and most motorists must park along Jameson Beach Road. No pets are allowed.
Fees: $5 for parking for nonguests, no charge for use of the beach.
Location: 2.5 miles north of the "Y" intersection in South Lake Tahoe, California.

Contact: Camp Richardson's Resort; 530/541-1801.

Pope Beach (see map on page 139, site 31)

Inspiring views of South Lake Tahoe, the Tahoe Keys, and Heavenly Ski Resort await at Pope Beach, a lazy, languid kind of place near the point where the Upper Truckee River empties into the lake. There's plenty of room to accommodate the large crowds that flock here. Facilities include restrooms, picnic areas, fire pits, and barbecue grills, and swimming is available. The parking lot fills up fast on weekends. No dogs are allowed.

Fees: There is $3 per day vehicle parking fee.

Location: Off Highway 89, two miles north of the "Y" intersection in South Lake Tahoe, California.

Contact: U.S. Forest Service Visitor Center; 530/573-2674.

Cove East Beach

(see map on page 139, site 32)

This sandy beach, owned by the California Tahoe Conservancy, is not well marked and is not developed. But it has a great location next to the channel that connects the lake to Tahoe Keys Marina, which is on the west side, and the Upper Truckee River marsh, which borders it on the southeast side. In 2001, the Conservancy acquired major wetland areas here and was in the planning stages for a restoration that will result in more habitat for wildlife. Possible future amenities may include a self-guided nature trail or a small nature interpretive center. Apart from watching the boats come and go at the marina, you can do a little birding here. The marsh, which will be expanded to 23 acres, is habitat for Canada geese, ducks and even raptors such as osprey and bald eagles. Note: Some construction may be present.

Location: From Highway 50, turn north on Tahoe Keys Boulevard, then right on Venice Drive until you reach the end of the road at the marina. Park on the street (not in the marina lot), and look for a path that leads to the beach.

Contact: Tahoe Conservancy; 530/542-5580. (Note: the Conservancy does not maintain a public information service since it usually does not manage recreational facilities.)

Regan Beach

(see map on page 139, site 33)

You'll find restrooms, picnic facilities, playgrounds, volleyball nets, swimming access, a grassy field, and food stands at this beach. No alcohol, dogs, or fires are permitted.

Location: West of U.S. 50 at Lakeview and Sacramento Streets in South Lake Tahoe, California.

Contact: South Lake Tahoe Parks and Recreation Department; 530/542-6055.

El Dorado Beach

(see map on page 139, site 34)

Restrooms, picnic facilities, fire pits, barbecue grills, and a boat launch are available when the lake level permits. No lifeguards are on duty. Pets are not allowed. There are no fees except for boat launching, which is $13.

Location: The beach is between Rufus Allen Boulevard and Lakeview in South Lake Tahoe, California.

Contact: South Lake Tahoe Parks and Recreation Department; 530/542-6055.

Connolly Beach

(see map on page 139, site 35)

No lifeguards are on duty at this beach, which offers restrooms and picnic facilities. A boat launch is available at the nearby Timber Cove Lodge resort. There are no fees.

Location: Off U.S. 50 across from Johnson Boulevard and behind Timber Cove Lodge in South Lake Tahoe, California.

Contact: South Lake Tahoe Parks and Recreation Department; 530/542-6055.

STATELINE/ZEPHYR COVE

Nevada Beach

(see map on page 139, site 36)

This is the closest quality beach to Stateline, and it is just far enough off the beaten path to offer relief from the traffic along busy U.S. 50. At the end of Elk Point Road on the east side of Lake Tahoe,

ON THE WATER

the beach is adjacent to a large and popular campground. It has a series of rolling dunes, formed by the strong afternoon winds that blow on this side of the lake. The best time to come is morning to early afternoon. Restrooms, picnic facilities, fire pits, barbecue grills, and a boat-in area (at south end) are available. No dogs are permitted.

Fees: There is a $3 per day vehicle parking fee.

Location: Off U.S. 50 on Elk Point Road near Round Hill, Nevada.

Contact: U.S. Forest Service Visitor Center; 530/573-2674.

Zephyr Cove Beach
(see map on page 139, site 37)

Nestled in beautiful Zephyr Cove—so named because of the strong afternoon zephyr winds noted by early pioneers—this scenic 1.5-mile-long beach offers a myriad of water sports. Zephyr Cove is home to the *M.S. Dixie II* paddlewheel cruiseboat and the *Woodwind II* sailing catamaran. A campground and a resort with cabins are adjacent to the beach, and two restaurants are on-site. If you're too lazy to get up and fetch a margarita and nachos, relax—a cocktail waitress from the bar and grill will be along shortly to take your order. Recreationists will find opportunities for volleyball as well as other beach sports such as parasailing, paddleboats, ski boats, Jet Skis, and fishing charters. Amenities include restrooms, picnic facilities, fire pits, and barbecue grills. Pets are allowed on the resort grounds but not on the beach.

Fees: $6 per vehicle for parking.

Location: Off U.S. 50 at Zephyr Cove, Nevada.

Contact: Zephyr Cove Resort; 775/588-6644.

Cave Rock, Lake Tahoe-Nevada State Park **(see map on page 139, site 38)**

People come to the beach at Cave Rock to fish, swim, and water-ski. There's a picnic/barbecue area, restrooms, and a boat ramp.

Fees: $6 per vehicle for day use, $6 more for boat launching.

Location: Off U.S. 50, seven miles north of Stateline, Nevada.

Contact: Lake Tahoe-Nevada State Park; 775/831-0494.

Zephyr Cove Beach

© KEN CASTLE

ON THE WATER

Fishing Waters and Guides

Imagine a six-pound Mackinaw trout peeling out line like a runaway fire truck. Or a five-pound Lahontan cutthroat trout dancing on the surface of a mirror-smooth lake. The fish that inhabit the waters of Lake Tahoe and its surrounding lakes and streams are feisty and strong, and they represent worthy adversaries for freshwater anglers. The entire region is a mighty fish trap, drawing thousands of anglers a year from every corner of the globe. Whether you tease these fish with a worm and a flasher, a damselfly nymph, or a big Rapala, you'll find that the sheer variety of trout (nine species by one count) creates an amazing year-round fishery. Add to these some prized kokanee and chinook salmon, a smattering of black bass, perch, and mountain whitefish, and you've got quite a stew.

After wetting a line, more than a few believers have left this region feeling that it may be the single best freshwater fishing destination in the lower 48 states. Consider a few salient points:

• Within a 75-mile radius of Lake Tahoe are more than 450 lakes, reservoirs, rivers, and streams.

• Most of the popular trout species sought by anglers exist here—lake trout (Mackinaw), rainbows, German brown trout, golden trout, cutthroat trout, and brook trout. There are also several hybrids, as well as the feisty kokanee salmon and recent arrivals such as chinook

enjoying the quiet of fishing in the Tahoe area

FISHING

salmon. You can find largemouth and small-mouth bass and catfish as well.

• Though hundreds of lakes exist in the high country, with many of them stocked regularly by various public agencies, fishing pressure is amazingly light. Of those who trek into Desolation Wilderness, for example, 15–20 percent fish, and of those only 5–10 percent go there strictly to fish. This means that a lot of big, smug fish are swimming around in alpine lakes with scarcely a tease from humans.

• While high-elevation fisheries elsewhere in the country shut down for winter, Tahoe and many of its neighboring waters offer year-round access. You can fish for Mackinaw any time of the year in Tahoe, Fallen Leaf, and Donner Lakes. Most rivers and streams in Nevada, on the eastern slopes of the Sierra, are legally fishable all year. Furthermore, the high desert lakes east of Tahoe, particularly Pyramid and Topaz, can offer great action in mild, shirtsleeve temperatures, even in January.

• Wild trout, the most coveted prize of fly-fishers, exist in several lakes where "zero kill" regulations are in force, thus giving casters multiple opportunities to land trophy-sized fish. Among these waters are Martis Creek Lake and Spooner Lake. There are also minimum size requirements that encourage the development of larger fish in designated stretches of the Truckee River, the East Fork of the Carson River, and the North Fork of the Yuba River. The majority of these are within an hour's drive from most points around Lake Tahoe or Reno.

• There's more than quantity and diversity in the Tahoe fisheries. If you consider big fish to be a measure of an area's worth, you'll find lunkers in Tahoe (the record Mackinaw was 37.5 pounds, and the record kokanee was four pounds, 13 ounces), Donner Lake (which once held a state record for brown trout), Lake Davis (large rainbows up to nine pounds), Red Lake (trophy-sized brook trout up to 18 inches), and Pyramid Lake (Lahontan cutthroat trout up to 10 pounds).

Virtually every fishing technique known to humanity is employed in the quest for these fish. At Tahoe and Donner, you can troll deep with long, lead-core line or with monofilament on downriggers; you can jig with live minnows and lures,

FISHING LICENSES

Always obtain copies of the latest fishing regulations and amendments from sporting goods and fishing tackle dealers.

California
Licenses are required for anyone 16 and older. As of 2002, a one-year, resident license is $30.45; a non-resident license is $81.65. A two-day license for either residents or nonresidents costs $11.05. Anglers who fish Lake Tahoe or Topaz Lake can use either a California or Nevada license to fish from boat or shore.

Note: All anglers must display their licenses by wearing them while fishing.

Nevada
Licenses are required for anyone 12 and older. As of 2002, a one-year resident license is $21 for those 16–64, and $5 for ages 12–15 and for seniors 65 years of age or older with five years of continuous Nevada residency. A one-day resident permit is $7, with $2 for each consecutive day. Nonresident licenses are $51 for those 16 and older and $9 for ages 12–15. A nonresident one-day fishing permit is $12, with $4 for each consecutive day. All anglers who take or possess trout must also buy a Nevada Trout Stamp for an additional $5.

Note: The second Saturday in June of each year is a free fishing day, when anyone may fish without a license. Anglers who fish Lake Tahoe or Topaz Lake can use either a Nevada or California license from boat or shore. Anglers who fish the Truckee and East Carson Rivers on both sides of the state line must have licenses from both states.

A Nevada fishing license is not required for fishing Pyramid Lake, which is on the Paiute Indian Reservation.

drift with minnows, or top-line with plugs. On the surrounding lakes and reservoirs, you can use the standards for trout: spinners, spoons, salmon eggs, worms, and Power Bait. Fly-fishers can run the gamut of patterns, from dry flies on the high alpine lakes to nymphs in the rivers. Nymphing, in fact, is a highly practiced art form in rivers such as the Truckee and the East Fork of the Carson, and in lakes such as Martis Creek and Davis.

If you're fishing a body of water for the first time, you'll learn its idiosyncrasies much faster by hiring a guide, or by enrolling in one of the local fly-fishing schools. More than 50 guides provide half-day, full-day, or multiday fishing excursions in the Tahoe/Reno area. Tahoe alone accounts for the lion's share of outfitters, with some two dozen offering boat trips. And there are a dozen fly-fishing guides and instructors who can show you the techniques of casting, wading, reading the water, and learning the local entomology. Guides' fees depend on the type of fishing. On Tahoe, some of the larger partyboats that can fish a half-dozen or more anglers tend to be the least expensive, starting at around $55 for three hours of fishing. Half-day excursions (five hours) run $75–90 per person, with full-day rates averaging $120–130 per person, including all gear. Guided flyfishing trips usually range from $175 for a half-day to $250 for a full day, sometimes with gear and waders provided. Two-day clinics for beginning to advanced anglers run $200–250 per person per day, often with lunch included.

Once you've learned successful angling methods from a professional, you'll have a much better chance of catching fish on your own. Nothing beats the benefit of years of experience, and it's an investment worth making if you plan to continue your forays for fish around Tahoe. Also, to supplement your knowledge with the latest fishing conditions, contact the tackle shops and outfitters listed in this chapter.

Fishing pressure is amazingly light. Of those who trek into Desolation Wilderness, for example, 15–20 percent fish, and of those only 5–10 percent go there strictly to fish. This means that a lot of big, smug fish are swimming around in alpine lakes with scarcely a tease from humans.

One point to keep in mind is that fishing regulations and license fees vary between California and Nevada. However, in areas of shared jurisdictions, such as Lake Tahoe and Topaz Lake, both of which straddle the state line, California and Nevada fishing agencies have moved to eliminate confusion by agreeing to honor licenses from either state.

The major areas of difference exist on the Truckee River and the East Fork of the Carson River. California sets specific seasons for its jurisdiction on these waterways, but Nevada allows year-round fishing on its sections, which are in lower elevations.

Be aware of license requirements. While a license issued by either state is good for Tahoe and Topaz, if you fish just one small stretch of the Truckee River that crosses the state line, you'll need licenses from both states. And there are even more vagaries. At Pyramid Lake, which is in Nevada, anglers need to buy a permit from the Paiute Indian Reservation. This is available from fishing guides or local stores on the reservation. Check the regulations wherever you intend to fish, because seasons, limits, access, and the best fishing methods are always subject to change.

TACKLE SUPPLIERS
Truckee/Donner

Hooks and Books, contacted through Thy Rod and Staff Flyfishing, P.O. Box 10038, Truckee, CA 96162; 530/587-7333; email: cyberfly@cyberfly.com, is a mail-order service carrying more than 500 fly-fishing books and videos, as well as hard-to-get Tiemco and Daiichi hooks and fly-tying tools.

Longs Drugs, Sporting Goods Department, 11411 Deerfield Dr., Truckee, CA 96162; 530/587-5772, a large chain store, stocks fishing tackle and sporting goods, and also sells fishing licenses.

M

FISHING

ADDITIONAL INFORMATION SOURCES

Alpine County Chamber of Commerce: Call for the latest in fishing and tips or pick up a complete fishing packet; P.O. Box 265, Markleeville, CA 96120; 530/694-2475; website: www.alpinecounty.com.

California Department of Fish and Game (Headquarters): 3211 S St., Sacramento, CA 95816; 916/227-2244; website: www.dfg.ca.gov.

California Department of Fish and Game (Region 2 Office): 1701 Nimbus Rd., Rancho Cordova, CA 95670; 916/358-2900.

Nevada Division of Wildlife: P.O. Box 10678, Reno, NV 89520; 775/688-1500; website: www.state.nv.us/cnr/nvwildlife.

Plumas County Visitors Bureau: Knowledgeable about the Feather River, Lake Davis, and Lakes Basin areas; 91 Church St., Quincy, CA 95971; 530/283-6345 or 800/326-2247; website: www.plumas.ca.us.

Mountain Hardware and Sports, 11320 Donner Pass Rd., Truckee, CA 96161; 530/587-4844, is a favorite among fishing guides and anglers, who uniformly insist that the fishing department here has the best and largest selection of flies in the region. You can also buy fishing licenses, tackle, boat and RV supplies, float tubes, waders, camping supplies and rafts.

Truckee River Outfitters and Fly Shop, 10200 Donner Pass Rd., Truckee, CA 96161; 530/582-0900, stocks a variety of flies and fly tackle only.

Tahoe City/West Shore

Chuck's Bait and Tackle, 8692 N. Lake Blvd., P.O. Box 2116, Kings Beach, CA 96143; 530/546-8425.

Homewood Hardware, 5405 W. Lake Blvd., Homewood, CA 96141; 530/525-6367, is an all-purpose hardware store that also carries a full line of fishing supplies.

Mother Nature's, 551 N. Lake Blvd., Tahoe City, CA 96145; 530/581-4278, is upstairs in an art/furnishings boutique and is an Orvis-authorized dealer offering rods, reels, flies, books and information on casting clinics.

Swigard's True Value Hardware, 200 N. Lake Blvd., Tahoe City, CA 96145; 530/583-3738, carries a full line of fishing equipment and supplies.

South Shore

Payless Drug Store, 1020 Al Tahoe Blvd., South Lake Tahoe, CA 96150; 530/541-2434, carries fishing, biking, camping, and tennis equipment, saucers, and sportswear.

The Sportsman, 2556 Lake Tahoe Blvd., South Lake Tahoe, CA 96150; 530/542-3474, is co-owned by Jack Martin and Rick Muller, veteran guides widely regarded as among the most knowledgeable anglers in the basin. They offer rentals, sales, equipment, and accessories for backpacking, camping, fishing (licenses are available), and alpine skiing.

Tahoe Fly Fishing Outfitters, 3433 Lake Tahoe Blvd., South Lake Tahoe, CA 96150; 530/541-8208, carries fly-fishing equipment and licenses.

Kirkwood/Hope Valley/Markleeville

Woodfords Station, 290 Pony Express Rd., Woodfords, CA 96120; 530/694-2930, is a general store, market, and café where you can obtain fishing gear and licenses, camping gear, ice, food to go, beer, wine, and tourist information. Open 7 A.M.–6 P.M.

Feather River Country/Lakes Basin

Blairsden Mercantile and Hardware, 282 Bonta St., Blairsden, CA 96103; 530/836-2589, is where to come for tackle and fishing information for the Feather River and the Lakes Basin areas.

Grizzly Country Store, 7552 Lake Davis Rd., Portola, CA 96122; 530/832-0270, carries tackle and dispenses information on fishing conditions at Lake Davis.

Reno/Carson Valley

Angler's Edge, 1420 "A" Hwy. 395, Gardnerville, NV 89410; 775/782-4734, in Gardnerville near the Carson and Walker rivers and Topaz Lake, specializes in fly-fishing gear.

The Gilly Fishing Store, 1111 N. Rock Blvd., Sparks, NV 89431; 775/358-6113, offers a full array of fishing tackle (full line for fly, bass, and trout), rod building, reel repair, a complete line of classes, and licenses.

Mark-Fore and Strike Sporting Goods, 490 Kietzke Ln., Reno, NV 89502; 775/322-9559, carries equipment for fishing (tackle, bait, fly-fishing), camping (tents, stoves, sleeping bags), boating (mercury outboards), water-skiing, and backpacking. There's also a 24-hour fishing hotline at 775/786-FISH (775/786-3474).

Reno Fly Shop, Independence Square, 294 E. Moana Ln. #14, Reno, NV 89502; 775/825-FISH (775/825-3474) is a full-service fly shop, which has fly-tying and rod building service, you'll find equipment, stream-fishing lessons, Nevada/California licensed guide service (full and half day), cold-weather clothing and accessories, and specialized equipment for fishing Pyramid Lake.

Rick's Discount Fishing, 2166 Victorian Ave. (formerly B St.), Sparks, NV 89431; 775/356-6614, has fishing tackle, custom spoons, spinners, lake trolls, and a mail-order service.

Lakes, Reservoirs, Rivers, and Streams

The following is a list of major fishing waters in the Lake Tahoe area (all public facilities are keyed to the Fishing Waters map). In most cases, the season for trout is open year-round, and the general limit is five of any species or combination, including Mackinaw. But there are exceptions. One is Lake Tahoe, where the fish limit is five but only two can be Mackinaw. For eastern brook trout, California anglers can take 15 if at least 10 are less than eight inches total length, or five if they are over eight inches.

LAKE TAHOE (see map on page 154, site 1)

Fishing Lake Tahoe for the first time can seem like a daunting task at best. There's a lot of water in a lake that is 22 miles long, 12 miles wide, and 1,645 feet deep. Without a boat, chances of success are close to zilch, and even with a boat your odds are slim unless you have the requisite electronic fish-finding gear. Statistics have shown that an unguided angler typically fishes for 10 hours before getting a Mackinaw. The best strategy for new arrivals is to go out with a guide and learn the ropes. So many factors affect the success rate that someone with years of experience can shorten your learning curve tremendously. Tahoe has between 20 and 25 guides, with boats ranging from spartan to decadent, and you can always find a charter if the weather is decent.

What you discover is that while there are certain places that tend to attract fish (usually not the deepest points in the lake), nothing is predictable. A Mackinaw trout, the largest species, can be one heck of a monster. The record mack, caught in 1974 by guide Robert Aronsen, weighed in at 37 pounds, six ounces, but biologists believe there are lake trout here that exceed 50 pounds. When you consider the fact that an average-sized Mackinaw caught by anglers is about seven years old, it's possible that these fish might live 40 or more years. During late summer and fall, kokanee salmon can add to your creel, and rainbow are possible at any time with surface trolling. Brown trout, once a major species, have been on a severe decline as a result of an extended drought that dried up spawning streams and seriously impacted the fishery. The Nevada Division of Wildlife annually stocks about 40,000 catchable rainbows in the lake. Mackinaw and kokanee are planted sporadically, but most are sustained by natural reproduction.

The game fish feed on minnows, chubs, and tiny freshwater shrimp, among other food sources. (Anglers have a rare chance to observe just exactly how they feed by visiting the Taylor Creek Stream Profile Chamber at the Lake Tahoe Visitor Center, operated by the U.S. Forest Service near Camp Richardson on the West Shore.)

FISHING

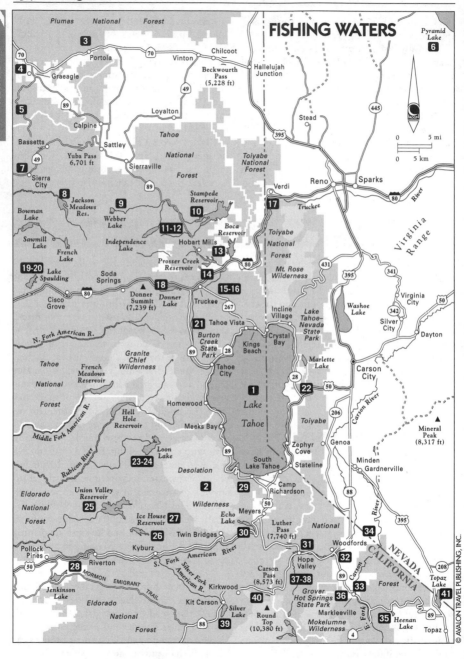

FISHING WATERS

Because Tahoe never freezes over, you can fish the lake all year, if you go prepared with warm clothes and a boat heater. Often the best fishing is during the winter months, when you may catch your limit of Mackinaw (two) within an hour of leaving the dock. (In total, your limit cannot exceed five game fish.)

Special Restrictions at Lake Tahoe: You can fish at Tahoe with either a valid California or Nevada fishing license. On the California side of the lake, fishing is prohibited in tributary streams (to protect spawning trout) and within 300 feet of the mouth of these streams October 1–June 30. On the Nevada side, closed areas are within a 200-yard radius of the mouths of Third, Incline, and Wood Creeks; within a 500-yard radius of the Sand Harbor Boat Ramp; and within the boat-launch area inside the jetty at the Cave Rock Boat Ramp. Only specific minnows and suckers caught from Lake Tahoe can be used as bait. However, the limit at Tahoe—five fish per day, including no more than two Mackinaw—is the same for both sides of the lake.

DESOLATION WILDERNESS
LAKES (see map on page 154, site 2)

This area is a vast mountain kingdom of granite lakes and free-flowing streams on the west side of Lake Tahoe. While Desolation is acknowledged as the most popular wilderness in the region, and quotas are set for overnight camping, only a small percentage of these backcountry travellers seem inclined to wet a line. Surveys have shown that just about 5 percent of all visitors enter Desolation with the primary purpose of fishing, though 15 to 20 percent fish the region as an incidental activity. Still, it's estimated that as many as 40,000 people enjoy fishing there.

Recently, the California Department of Fish and Game has put its aerial trout-stocking program on hold while it finalizes results of a joint survey with the U.S. Fish and Wildlife Service over the continuing depletion of mountain yellow-legged frogs, which are threatened with extinction. Formerly, the DFG dropped fingerling trout from airplanes in some 100 lakes at Desolation. But evidence that the trout devour the frogs means that stocking is not likely to be resumed any time soon, except in very limited circumstances. Another issue, also raised by the Forest Service, was whether stocking the lakes is compatible with wilderness values, especially with planes diving into box canyons to drop their loads. In response, the DFG points out that passenger planes headed to and from Reno and Tahoe airports fly over Desolation on a daily basis, with private aircraft often passing through at relatively low altitudes.

Despite the cessation of aerial plants, the news for anglers heading into Desolation is not exactly, well, desolate. Lakes with brook trout, for instance, are in good shape because those fish naturally reproduce. In fact, some lakes are overloaded with brookies, and the lack of fishing pressure is leading to stunted growth. For those lakes that contain trophy brook trout and attract more anglers, the DFG may consider restocking once every five years or so. "We're not just going willy-nilly into these lakes anymore," says DFG Associate Biologist Stafford Lehr. "There will be a pragmatic approach based on the best data that we have." One study of 5,000 alpine lakes in California has concluded that between 65 percent and 85 percent of them will have some level of self-sustaining fish, even without stocking. Hardy species also include the coveted Golden trout, which manage just fine in the streams and lakes where they currently exist. "There aren't that many people fishing the high country any more, but the ones who do will find a diverse angling experience," says Lehr. Also, lakes and reservoirs on the perimeter of Desolation—such as those in Crystal Basin west of the wilderness—will continue to have managed fisheries of regularly planted rainbows, browns and other species.

So, by all means take your fishing rod into Desolation. Plan your trip just after the thaw in early summer or in fall, when the fish are feeding. If go in early summer, be aware that mosquitoes are prolific and hungry, and you'll need to smother yourself with repellent. The grassy, wooded lakes that offer such a great food source for fish tend to have large populations of insects. If this doesn't sound appealing, head for higher ground at the

HOW TO CATCH A MACKINAW

METHODS

Long Lining

The old-timers, some of them dyed-in-the-wool traditionalists, swear by deep trolling with Rapalas or Rebels behind lead-core or metal line. When fish are 300 feet deep—not unusual for midsummer—this can mean putting out 1,200 feet of line. Cranking in that kind of yardage is tedious and tiring, and you hardly feel the fish fight, anyway. But it may be just the ticket for those who like to sit back, sip a margarita, and watch the scenery go by.

Drifting

Although it is not consistently productive, drifting or "mooching" with live minnows and light monofilament line of six- to eight-pound test, with a medium sinker, is perhaps the most interesting and challenging way to entice the Mighty Mack. You drag the sinker along the bottom, with the minnow swimming a few feet above it. Strikes are almost imperceptible; often they consist of one or two slight twitches, so it's necessary to keep a consistent and careful eye on your rod tip. When you get a bite, your immediate impulse is to set the hook. Don't do it, or you've lost a fish. Open the bale and let the fish take out as much as 100 feet of

line, for what may seem like an eternity. If a Mackinaw detects any resistance while he's mouthing the bait, he'll spit it out. Once he bites, you've got a great fight on your hands. In general, drifting works best in the spring, at places such as Emerald Bay.

Downrigging

A good trolling compromise to the long-line system is using a downrigger. Most of the charter boat skippers are equipped with both downriggers and outriggers, so they can troll at varying depths with different lures. With a downrigger, you can use medium-weight monofilament or wire line (12-pound test or greater), a medium-weight rod, a salmon-type quick-release, and lures or live bait. When a fish strikes, you'll need to set the hook immediately; once you've got him, there's no extra weight between you and Mighty Mack. Another advantage of downriggers is that, when used with electronic fish-finders, you can adjust for depth and be on the fish with more precision. Still, it's a rather boring style of fishing; you won't have much to do until a fish hits.

Jigging

This is the nouveau style of fishing at Lake Tahoe,

rockbound, granite lakes. Look for inlets that can host spawners, and lakes that have populations of forage fish such as redsided shiners. These should provide good angling opportunities.

Day hikers have a disadvantage when it comes to fishing these high lakes, especially in midsummer. Unless you get started very early, the bite may well be a bust by midday. You can improve your odds, however, with a float tube or raft. When trout go deep during the heat of the day, follow them with night crawlers, Power Bait, or salmon eggs. Use a sinker on light line, bounce or drift it on the bottom, and float the bait about four feet above it. As for flies, try black woolly worms with a flash of purple, and a local pattern called the Antron Caterpillar, used with sinking line. The value of floating cannot be overstated; if the shore is too brushy or wooded for casting, this may be

your only viable option. When I go backpacking with someone, I take a two-person raft, and we've never been skunked at any high-mountain lake.

Those who fish Desolation regularly have their favorite fishing holes. Here are the ones that seem to be on every list of those in the know:

Cathedral Lake

It's not particularly attractive, it has its share of bugs, and it's on the heavily traveled route to Mt. Tallac. Still, this circular lake with a big rockfall is the easiest to reach for the prized golden trout. With its relatively small surface and protected location, there is rarely any wind to stir a ripple, so these fish are wary and skittish. Still, the alternative for catching a golden is to hike up some miserable, talus-covered, off-trail slope.

although it definitely has its critics. The standard setup for jigging is a medium-weight rod with a level-wind reel, medium-weight line, and a minnow on a treble hook with a four-ounce (or larger) Bomber jig. Varying the depth, you work the rod constantly with light jerks. The idea is to make a Mackinaw mad enough to attack your bait. Unfortunately, he might just swipe at it with his body, and you could end up foul-hooking him in the side. If he swallows the hook, it will be tough extracting a barbed treble hook in time to release the fish without killing him. (Unless you're using a single barbless hook and you keep the fish in water while removing the hook, the chances of the fish surviving after release are slim.) Jigging has also been practiced with large chrome bars, though this method is less popular. Fish are particularly susceptible to jigging during the spawning months of early fall. Some guides swear by this as the most productive method; others simply swear at it.

RELEASING A MACKINAW

Fishery biologists who have seen some of the man-handling that goes on with attempts to release Mackinaw are appalled. Some anglers yank the fish into the boat, let it gasp for a minute or longer in the air, grab it by the gills, puncture its air-inflated bladder with a nail, and then dump it overboard as it bleeds. Even if the fish disappears into the depths, the chance of survival with this method is slim to none.

Because Mackinaw are brought up from great depths, often more than 200 feet, the bladder inflates, causing the fish to swell up like a balloon. Before the fish can be returned, you must gently deflate it, being very careful not to touch the sensitive gills. A hypodermic needle (especially a large one) works fine, because it doesn't leave a permanent puncture wound. Also, advise biologists, the longer you leave a fish out of water, the less chance it will have to survive. If you plan to release the fish, especially in the summer, keep it in the net overboard while you remove the hook (preferably with needle-nose pliers) and deflate the bladder, or place the fish in a live well or container of water while you work on it.

Decide in advance of going on a charter boat if you intend to keep your fish, and advise the skipper. There's no point in wasting fish if you don't have a place to store your catch until it is time to eat it.

Gilmore Lake

Off the Glen Alpine Trailhead (near Fallen Leaf Lake), this lake has seen the Eagle Lake strain of rainbows, German browns, and Mackinaw. It's easy to reach on a day hike, and consequently gets its share of people.

Granite Lake

From the Bayview Trailhead, this attractive lake is just a mile away, but the steep terrain you have to traverse to reach it puts off many people. Because of the short distance and hiking time, this is probably the best shot you've got for a morning or evening rise. It's a good place for brook trout, the main species here.

Heather Lake

Also accessible from the Glen Alpine Trailhead, this lake is spectacular, with granite walls and rock islands. In the past, it has produced some of the biggest brown trout in the region. But there's no guarantee anymore now that fish plants have been halted. You can look for browns swimming near the surface from the trail that follows a ledge high above the water on the north side. Obviously, the fish know what you've just realized—that you'll never reach them. They achieve their size from a food source of shiners and chub, and tend to ignore lures or baits.

Middle Velma Lake

Although you can hike there and back within a day (a long trek), the best way to fish the spunky rainbows here is to backpack in and camp overnight. Of the lakes accessible from the Eagle Falls Trailhead, this is usually the top producer. Although hikers abound, fishing pressure is light.

FISHING

LAKE DAVIS (see map on page 154, site 3)

As a haven for big rainbow trout—we're talking the 10- to 12-pound variety that resemble steelhead and have pink flesh—Davis has become the undisputed champion of northern Sierra lakes. In addition to Eagle Lake trout, there are resident German browns that can reach up to eight pounds and largemouth bass exceeding seven pounds. Their girth can be attributed to substantial weed cover and an ample food supply of golden shiners. The lake, with 32 miles of shoreline on 4,000 acres, offers not only good trolling in relatively shallow water (average depth: 21 feet) for lure anglers, but is a paradise for fly-fishers using waders, float tubes, or prams and casting to the offshore weed beds. Fishing is best in early spring and late fall, when the bite may last all day, but becomes lethargic in high summer, when the most productive times are early morning or around sunset.

Unfortunately, Davis has become a persistent problem for Fish and Game managers because of an intrusive alien known as the pike. This voracious fish appeared in 1994, apparently from an illegal introduction, and resulted in an undesirable pike population. Pike consistently pose threats to fish in other California waterways, particularly the Sacramento River Delta. Pike are dominant competitors that can drive out other, more desirable fish species. In 1997 the lake was subsequently "treated" (i.e., all fish species poisoned with a chemical known as rotenone) and then replanted with Eagle Lake catchables and subcatchables. Since the lake is full of nutrients and is very resilient, the trout soon bounced back. But in 1999, so did the pike, posing a continuing dilemma for Fish and Game. More recent efforts by the department have involved detonating explosives in the lake, in shallow coves where the pike spawn. Using this and other methods, including gill-netting, purse seining, and electric shock, biologists are hoping they can to keep the pike contained and restricted in number. Despite some misconceptions among out-of-town anglers, the control efforts have not had a negative impact on trout fishing. In 2002, as part of its mitigation strategy, the DFG planted 50,000 catchable, half-pound rainbow trout, which have a better chance than fingerlings of surviving predation. And when trout are killed during any pike eradication effort, the DFG replaces them on the order of two to one. In any case, trout fishing continues to be good to superb, even after relatively dry winters, and Davis continues to be a top draw for anglers. (By the way, if you should happen to catch a pike, regulations require you to kill it and pass it along to the DFG. Either of the two stores mentioned below will be glad to take the carcass off your hands.) The lake has free public boat ramps, a concession with rental boats, and several U.S. Forest Service campgrounds.

Fish: Eagle Lake strain of rainbow trout, brown trout, largemouth bass, and catfish.

Tackle and bait: Worms, Power Bait, Rapalas, Dick Nites, crank baits, spinners, worm-and-flasher combos, and flies such as damselfly, callibaetis, and midge larva patterns.

Limit: Five for trout, five for bass, and no limit for catfish.

Season: Year-round.

Elevation: 5,775 feet.

Location: On Grizzly Peak Road or Lake Davis Road, 20 minutes north of Portola and 45 minutes north of Truckee. Take the Sattley turnoff from Highway 89.

Contact: Grizzly Country Store at Lake Davis; 530/832-0270, website: www.grizzlystore.com; or Dollard's Sierra Market in Portola; 530/832-5251.

FEATHER RIVER, MIDDLE FORK
(see map on page 154, site 4)

This is a stunningly beautiful river that has easy access points at Blairsden, and as such gets a fair amount of fishing pressure at concentrated areas. Early in the season, May–mid-June, spin casters can take some decent-sized rainbows near the bridges. Fly-fishers have their favorite spots, which often require hiking some distance or negotiating unmarked four-wheel-drive roads. The La Porte Road off Highway 70 usually has the best access. Wade and cast to the downstream riffles and pocket waters; along some stretches, you'll be able to cast 45 to 50 feet. The fish in this river are robust and deep-bodied; they reach up to two pounds, in the 12- to 16-inch range, and there are naturally reproducing rainbows and a few browns. Fall is visually the most spectacular time of year for the Feather because of its bright yellow and red foliage, but trout will be skittish from the lower water. You won't get more than one cast per fish.

Fish: Rainbow and brown trout.

Tackle and bait: Panther Martins, worms or grasshoppers, and flies such as stonefly and caddis patterns.

Limit: Five.

Season: Last Saturday in April–November 15.

Location: Fed by Frenchman and Davis Lakes in Plumas County, this river parallels Highway 70 from Sloat to the junction with Highway 89 at Blairsden. From there it flows to Clio, then returns to parallel Highway 70 through Portola to Beckwourth.

Contact: The Sportsmen's Den in Quincy; 530/283-2733. Plumas County Visitors Bureau; 530/283-6345 or 800/326-2247.

GOLD LAKE (see map on page 154, site 5)

The largest lake in the water-studded Lakes Basin northwest of Tahoe is Gold Lake. It is best fished by trolling with Rapalas, Rebels, worm-and-flasher combinations, spinners, and spoons off a shelf on the southwest end, or around a series of rock islands on the east end. There's a public boat landing just off the main road. This attractive region has several excellent lodges, most of which are booked a year in advance.

Fish: Mackinaw, brown, rainbow, and brook trout.

Tackle and bait: Spinners, crank baits, and worms.

Limit: Five, any combination.

Season: Year-round, but the lake is snowbound in winter.

Elevation: 6,620 feet.

Location: On Gold Lake Road off Highway 89, seven miles west of the town of Graeagle and a one-hour drive north of Truckee.

Contact: Gold Lake Lodge; 530/836-2350.

PYRAMID LAKE
(see map on page 154, site 6)

Like a mirage shimmering in the high desert north of Reno, Pyramid Lake is a weirdly beautiful expanse of blue. Named after a pyramid-shaped tufa mound, this large, relatively shallow lake (300 feet deep) hosts some monster cutthroat trout. As the last vestige of prehistoric Lake Lahontan, a massive inland sea that once (a long, long, long time ago) covered most of Nevada and the Great Basin, the lake is owned and managed by the Pyramid Lake Paiute Indians, and all anglers must buy a special fishing permit from the tribe (available at the marina and at stores on the reservation).

The lake depends on flows from the Truckee River for its survival, and the cutthroat trout fishery has had a checkered history, a result of overfishing, cross-breeding with undesirable species, and loss of stream spawning habitat from river tributaries that were dammed up. In recent years, however, the lake has been in reasonable shape, although new threats of drought continue to pose problems with the water level. Two hatcheries at the lake release hundreds of thousands of cutthroat into Pyramid each year. The lake has always had a reputation for huge trout—the world record, in fact, was caught in 1925 by a Paiute who landed a 41-pounder (on display at the Nevada State Museum in Carson City). Today, 8- to 10-pound fish are not uncommon. Anglers can fish the lake by motorboat or from shore; typically trollers have the edge in the early and late season, and shore anglers have the edge in between. Fish can be at any part of the lake, but fly anglers prefer The Nets and the mouth of the river, and boats prefer places such as Pelican Point, Warrior's Point, Hell's Kitchen and Anderson Bay.

Something that is unique to Pyramid is the sight of dozens of fly anglers standing on mostly submerged stepladders in the shallows near the net pens used by the hatcheries. They may cast for two to three hours before landing a fish. The best times for shore anglers are in late fall and early spring, when the water is cooler and fish are closer to the surface. Some caveats: The

NEVADA COMMISSION ON TOURISM

Pyramid Lake

dry heat can cause rapid dehydration (even in winter, when temperatures can be in the 70s), and the lake is infamous for its raging afternoon winds and sudden thunderstorms, which can be very dangerous for boaters. The shoreline has sandy beaches, and there's a new marina, a launch ramp ($6 per boat), and a campground with full facilities.

Fish: Lahontan cutthroat trout. An endangered, suckerlike fish called the cui-ui is protected and must be released.

Tackle and bait: Artificial lures only. FlatFish, Kwikfish, Krocodile spoons, Apex, and Torpedoes in different colors (chartreuse, green, and fluorescent orange seem to work best); and flies including size four to eight black, brown, white, olive, and purple woolly worms.

Limit: Two per day, only one of which may be over 24 inches. The second fish may be 16 to 19 inches, or you may catch two fish that are 16 to 19 inches.

Season: October 1–June 30.

Special restrictions: Release all fish less than 16 inches and between 19 to 24 inches in length. You must buy a Paiute Tribe permit, at $6 for one day and $32 for the season; a state license is not required. Nontribe members cannot use live bait.

Elevation: 3,500 feet.

Location: In Nevada, 32 miles northeast of Reno on Highway 445.

Contact: Pyramid Lake Store, 29555 Pyramid Lake Rd., Sutcliffe, NV; 775/476-0555; or Pyramid Lake Tribal Council, P.O. Box 256, Nixon, NV 89424; 775/574-1000.

YUBA RIVER, NORTH FORK
(see map on page 154, site 7)

You may have to rub shoulders with gold miners using dredges, but this is a scenic and generally underfished river, bordered by good Forest Service campgrounds and unique Gold Country towns. When the insects are working and the hatch is on, you can expect 20-fish days. The majority are small native rainbows, 10 to 14 inches. There are a few browns, but they are hard to come by. The real joy of fishing here is the beauty of the canyon. Plan on doing a lot of hiking to work the North Fork effectively, and don't even think of wading it until flows are below 1,000 cubic feet per second.

Fish: Rainbow and brown trout.

Tackle and bait: From the western boundary of Sierra City to the confluence with Ladies Canyon Creek, only artificial lures with barbless hooks may be used. Outside of this area, there are no gear restrictions. For flies, try elkhair caddis, beadhead hare's ear, blue-winged olives, and stonefly nymphs.

Limit: Two trout with a minimum size of 10 inches in the restricted area; five in unrestricted areas.

Season: Last Saturday in April–November 15.

Location: In Sierra County, the river parallels Highway 49, northwest of Truckee (off Highway 89) through the towns of Sierra City and Downieville.

Contact: C and R Guide Service, Grass Valley; 530/477-0780; website: www.wildtrout.com.

JACKSON MEADOWS AND MILTON RESERVOIRS
(see map on page 154, site 8)

These lakes, connected by the Middle Fork of the Yuba River and just a short distance from each other, offer great variety for both bait-and-lure anglers and fly-fishers. Jackson Meadows, with a large population of redsided shiners, yields respectable rainbows in the 12- to 14-inch range, of which an estimated 65 percent are caught by boat trollers. Milton has the capacity to kick out trophy-sized brown trout (up to 14 pounds) and is a favorite for fly-fishers. It is a diversion structure for water from Jackson Meadows, and as such has a rich food source with weeds, insects, and reintroduced crayfish. The 30-acre lake, 27 feet deep, is excellent for float tubing. Wading anglers should look out for a deep hole that was used for habitat improvement in the lake bottom.

Fish: Rainbow and brown trout.

Tackle and bait: Worms, salmon eggs, and small spinners for Jackson Meadows. Artificial lures with barbless hooks only for Milton.

Limit: Five in Jackson Meadows with no size limit; two in Milton, with a maximum size limit of 12 inches total length.

Season: For Jackson Meadows, year-round, but it is snowbound in winter. Milton is open the last Saturday in April–November 15.

Elevation: 6,100 feet.

Location: On Highway 89 and Henness Pass Road, 33 miles northwest of Truckee.

Contact: Mountain Hardware and Sports, 113200 Donner Pass Rd., Truckee; 530/587-4844.

LITTLE TRUCKEE RIVER
(see map on page 154, site 9)

The upper section of the Little Truckee River, set among scenic valleys and high meadows, has a checkered pattern of ownership (Webber Lake, with the headwaters of the river, is entirely private, for example). It's important to check current maps and contact the U.S. Forest Service for the best public access points other than from the highway. This stretch of river supports both native and planted rainbow trout. The section between Stampede and Boca Reservoirs has naturally reproducing brown trout, as well as "spillover" rainbows from Stampede Reservoir; it has benefited from habitat improvements and regulated water flows. The best access for this area is from Boca-Stampede Road at the Hirschdale exit of I-80.

Fish: Rainbow and brown trout.

Tackle and bait: For the section below Webber Lake, try lures such as Panther Martins and Rooster Tails or flies such as caddis and woolly buggers. In all sections of the Little Truckee, try hare's ears for nymphs or dry flies such as Parachute Adams, size 14–18, or Light Paradun.

Limit: Two in the section from Stampede Reservoir Dam downstream to Boca Reservoir. Maximum size limit is 14 inches total length. Only artificial lures with barbless hooks may be used.

Season: Last Saturday in April–November 15.

Location: There are two sections of this river. The first originates at Webber Lake and flows eastward 16 miles to Stampede Reservoir; it is accessible mainly from Highway 89 north of Truckee. The second section is sandwiched

FISHING

between Stampede and Boca Reservoirs, north of I-80 and east of Truckee.

Contact: Mountain Hardware and Sports, 113200 Donner Pass Rd., Truckee; 530/587-4844.

STAMPEDE RESERVOIR
(see map on page 154, site 10)

Of the reservoirs north of Truckee, this is by far the most popular among anglers. Despite its diverse trout population, the lake has seen its hottest action for kokanee. The productiveness of the fishery is constantly threatened by a substantial annual drawdown to supply the downstream water needs of Pyramid Lake in Nevada—primarily to support a threatened species of sucker fish called the cui-ui. In 1994, for example, Stampede was lowered to about one-third of its normal capacity. The lake, which under normal conditions encompasses 3,400 acres with 24 miles of shoreline, is operated by the U.S. Fish and Wildlife Service.

For shore anglers, the best strategy is to fish the weedy flats around the inlet streams. Trollers should fish along the bottom for Mackinaw and browns, and mid-depth for rainbows and kokanee. Electronic fish locators are highly advisable for finding schools of kokanee. The best time for salmon is early in the spring when the fish are close to the surface. They go deep in summer, around 90 feet, then return to the top in fall, but by then their discoloration makes them less palatable. Fish average 12 to 14 inches. In the past, big rainbows up to seven pounds and browns up to 21 pounds have been caught, but lunkers such as these are not as common as they once were. Boaters should beware of the ferocious afternoon winds. The lake is also used by Jet Skiers and water-skiers. The Forest Service has good campgrounds at three locations around the lake.

Fish: Rainbow, Mackinaw, brook, and brown trout, along with kokanee salmon and mountain whitefish.

Tackle and bait: Worms, salmon eggs, Power Bait, small spinners, attractor blades, and wedding rings with a piece of white corn, and flies such as woolly buggers, nymphs, and midges.

Limit: Five.

Season: Year-round.

Elevation: 5,949 feet.

Location: Approximately eight miles north of I-80 on Stampede Meadow Road at the Hirschdale exit, which is six miles east of Truckee. The lake is just north of Boca Reservoir.

Contact: Longs Drugs, Sporting Goods Department, P.O. Box 8085, Truckee, CA 96162; 530/587-5772.

INDEPENDENCE LAKE
(see map on page 154, site 11)

Independence is one of the best lakes in the region for healthy populations of naturally reproducing fish. It contains the last remaining pool of genetically pure Lahontan cutthroat trout, which were isolated here when downstream reservoirs were built. The lake is virtually surrounded by private land, mostly controlled by the Sierra Pacific Power Company, which serves northern Nevada. The only access is from one corner of the upper end, where anglers can walk in for shore fishing. Unfortunately, the lake is large and really requires the use of a boat to have much success; it is not particularly easy to fish from a float tube or a raft. Most anglers seek out the kokanee, which are not large, averaging about 10 inches. It is illegal to fish any tributaries or within 300 feet of the mouths of tributaries to Independence Lake.

Fish: Brown, Lahontan cutthroat, and brook trout, and kokanee salmon.

Tackle and bait: Spinners, spoons, and flies. Only artificial lures with barbless hooks may be used.

Limit: Zero kill on cutthroat trout (catch-and-release only); five for other species, except for an additional 10 brookies under eight inches.

Season: Year-round, but the lake is snowbound in winter.

Elevation: 6,949 feet.

Location: Off Jackson Meadows Road from Highway 89, north of Truckee.

Contact: Mountain Hardware and Sports, 113200 Donner Pass Rd., Truckee; 530/587-4844.

SAGEHEN CREEK
(see map on page 154, site 12)

There is relatively easy access to Sagehen, and you've got a pretty good shot at catching small brown and rainbow trout in a very small meadow stream. With tight banks and trees down to the water's edge, this creek will put your casting accuracy to the test. Successful anglers may have to crawl on their knees upstream and make precise presentations to reach these extremely spooky fish.

Fish: Brown, rainbow, and brook trout.

Tackle and bait: Artificial lures with barbless hooks from the Highway 89 bridge upstream to the gauging station at the east boundary of Sagehen Creek Station. The stream is closed upstream from approximately one-eighth of a mile above the station at a point where the stream splits into two sections. Use attractors and suggestive patterns such as yellow Humpies, Royal Wulffs, hare's ear, and pheasant tail in sizes 14 to 18.

Limit: Catch-and-release only in the wild trout section.

Season: Last Saturday in April–November 15.

Location: This creek crosses Highway 89, about two miles north of the Hobart Mills exit north of Truckee.

Contact: Thy Rod and Staff Flyfishing; 530/587-7333.

BOCA RESERVOIR
(see map on page 154, site 13)

This lake, covering nearly 1,000 acres, suffered heavily during the recent prolonged drought, when, in 1994, it dwindled to 11 percent of its normal size. Trolling in the many arms and coves is the best way to take fish here, using worm-and-flasher setups or minnow-type lures. Because of a major drawdown in recent years, call ahead to make sure boat ramps are accessible. Forest Service campgrounds are available at three locations.

Fish: Rainbow and brown trout and kokanee salmon.

Tackle and bait: Worms, eggs, Power Bait, small spinners, and flies such as woolly buggers and midges.

Limit: Five trout.

Season: Year-round.

Elevation: 5,700 feet.

Location: Head east of Truckee on I-80, take the Hirschdale exit, and continue a short distance north to the lake.

Contact: Longs Drugs, Sporting Goods Department, P.O. Box 8085, Truckee, CA 96162; 530/587-5772.

PROSSER CREEK RESERVOIR
(see map on page 154, site 14)

Rainbows and naturally reproducing brown trout head up the main fare at this open, windswept reservoir covering 740 acres amid rolling hills. Years ago, the Department of Fish and Game planted brook and cutthroat trout, but these have not become major species. Trolling is best along the shoreline close to willows and weeds, in the various arms of the lake. Boats are restricted to 10 miles per hour, so there are no water-skiers to encroach on anglers. The Forest Service maintains three campgrounds, none of which is aesthetically pleasing. There's also a public boat ramp. Note: The water level declines radically in the fall months.

Fish: Rainbow and brown trout.

Tackle and bait: Worms, salmon eggs, small spinners, Power Bait, worm-and-flasher combinations, and flies such as nymphs, midges, and black woolly buggers.

Limit: Five.

Season: Year-round.

Elevation: 5,711 feet.

Location: From I-80 at Truckee, head north on Highway 89 for approximately 2.5 miles, then go east on good dirt and paved roads.

Contact: Longs Drugs, Sporting Goods Department, P.O. Box 8085, Truckee, CA 96162; 530/587-5772.

TRUCKEE RIVER, MIDDLE SECTION—CALIFORNIA
(see map on page 154, site 15)

The Truckee River is not easy to fish at any point, but it's especially difficult here. It has pocket water, riffles, pools, and fast water. Footing is tricky, and accurate casting and wading are critical. The fish average 9–12 inches, with the occasional larger trout of 18–20 inches in the wild trout section. Because of the somewhat confusing and varied restrictions, anglers need to pay close attention to Department of Fish and Game regulations. There is considerable fishing pressure here as the Truckee flows through shallow canyons, then enters a deep-cut gorge between I-80 and the Southern Pacific Railroad tracks. For fly anglers, early in the season is best for presenting patterns such as stonefly initiations, beadhead hare's ear (size 14), and various sculpin imitations (sizes 2–6)—sculpin are the predominant forage fish here. Later in the season, late June–early August, dry fly-fishing is better at dusk, with elkhair caddis imitations, in sizes 14 to 16, and soft hackles (partridge and green, grouse and peacock) in sizes 12 to 18. At this writing, the U.S. Fish and Wildlife Service was attempting to reintroduce Lahontan cutthroat trout into the lower reaches of the river. Several rafting companies conduct white-water trips down the Truckee, so expect some river traffic.

Fish: Rainbow and brown trout. Native wild trout exist from Trout Creek to Gray Creek in California.

Tackle and bait: Legal restrictions vary depending on location. From Trout Creek below Truckee to Glenshire Bridge, only artificial lures with barbless hooks are allowed; from Glenshire Bridge to Boca Bridge, only artificial flies with barbless hooks are allowed. Beyond this bridge to the Nevada state line, any type of gear may be used.

Limit: Two from Boca Bridge to the confluence of Gray Creek with no size restriction. Two also from Trout Creek to Glenshire Bridge and from 100 yards upstream of the I-80 bridge at Union Mills downstream to Boca Bridge, with the additional requirement that the minimum size is 15 inches.

Season: Last Saturday in April–November 15.

Location: There are several distinct sections of this river, which flows east of Truckee to the Nevada state line.

Contact: Mountain Hardware and Sports, 113200 Donner Pass Rd., Truckee; 530/587-4844.

MARTIS CREEK LAKE
(see map on page 154, site 16)

This is California's first "wild trout" lake, with naturally reproducing Lahontan cutthroat trout. It is also one of the best fly-fishing reservoirs in the Tahoe area for big fish as well as a popular place for neophyte fly casters, because of its easy access and wide-open shoreline. Eagle Lake-strain trout (they have large bodies and small heads) have done well since they were introduced in the early 1990s; sizes are increasing, with 20-inchers occasionally caught. Brown trout are not faring as well, and with a diminishing forage base, they may be on their way out. Also, the cutthroat trout have almost completely disappeared. This 80-acre lake, administered by the U.S. Army Corps of Engineers, is suited for float tubes, canoes, and rowboats, which can be launched easily from the open shoreline; no motors are allowed on boats. A good campground is nestled in pine trees adjacent to the lake.

Fish: Lahontan cutthroat, Eagle Lake-strain rainbow, and German brown trout.

Tackle and bait: Only artificial lures with barbless hooks may be used, including spinners and size 12 to 16 flies such as blood midge emergers, damselfly, caddis, and callibaetis.

Limit: Zero. Catch-and-release only.

Season: Last Saturday in April–November 15.

Elevation: 6,300 feet.

Location: Six miles southeast of Truckee. From King's Beach head north on Highway 267, then turn right and drive half a mile east on a maintained dirt road to the lake.

Contact: Mountain Hardware and Sports, 113200 Donner Pass Rd., Truckee; 530/587-4844.

TRUCKEE RIVER, LOWER SECTION—NEVADA
(see map on page 154, site 17)

Except for one restricted area, it's basically open season for the section of the Truckee River which flows through the downtown casino district. If the jackpots aren't hitting in the clubs, down-and-outers can always try their luck at angling. On most of the river (consult Nevada Division of Wildlife regulations for specifics), you can fish any hour of the day or night, except within 1,000 feet downstream of Derby Dam, which is closed to fishing. Try spinners, spoons, salmon eggs, worms, flies—anything you've got. Who knows? Maybe your luck will change.

Fish: Rainbow, brown, and cutthroat trout.

Tackle and bait: There are two sections of the river, with varying regulations. The portion from the I-80 bridge upstream from Crystal Peak Park to the California state line requires artificial lures

© KEN CASTLE

fly-fishing on the Truckee River

with single barbless hooks. Below the bridge, there are no gear restrictions.

Limit: Above the I-80 bridge, two trout and 10 mountain whitefish with a minimum size for trout of 14 inches. Below the I-80 bridge, five trout, 10 mountain whitefish, and 15 warmwater game fish, of which not more than five may be black bass.

Season: Year-round.

Location: From the Nevada state line through downtown Reno and points east.

Contact: Reno Fly Shop, 294 E. Moana Ln. #14, Reno; 775/825-3474.

DONNER LAKE
(see map on page 154, site 18)

Close to the main highway, this elongated lake with over seven miles of shoreline gets plenty of fishing pressure, and rainbow trout are easily caught throughout the season. As with Lake Tahoe, hiring a guide is the best approach for newcomers, as unguided anglers will find it tough to fish for Mackinaw and kokanee, which are among the prizes here. Anglers must fish deep for Mackinaw (80 feet or more), and the best months to bag lake trout are in the spring and fall. Otherwise, early morning top-lining for rainbows and kokanee can be productive. There was once a significant population of brown trout (setting a state record some years back), but that fishery has declined recently. Rainbow trollers generally congregate at the south side of the lake, and Mackinaw trollers and jiggers hover in China Cove. The beehive of water-skiers and Jet Skiers does not make life pleasant for boat anglers. Look out for afternoon winds in summer.

Fish: Mackinaw, rainbow, and brown trout, and kokanee salmon.

Tackle and bait: Worms, salmon eggs, small spinners, Power Bait, FlatFish, Rapalas, Rebels, and jigs such as minnow/Bomber combinations. Note: Only minnows caught in Donner Lake may be used.

Limit: Five.

Season: Year-round.

Elevation: 5,970 feet.

Location: Take Donner Pass Road off I-80 at Truckee; follow it to the lake.

Contact: Mountain Hardware and Sports, 113200 Donner Pass Rd., Truckee; 530/587-4844.

LAKE SPAULDING
(see map on page 154, site 19)

You thought there was no place to catch chinook salmon in the Tahoe area? Guess again. Thanks to an ambitious program started by the California Department of Fish and Game in November 1994, Spaulding has become a hot Sierra fishing hole for respectable-sized salmon in the 24- to 26-inch range. Right now, it's the closest lake to Tahoe that is stocked with the species. This historic new fishery was a cooperative effort of Kokanee Unlimited, PG&E (which owns the lake), and the Department of Fish and Game. The salmon can thrive thanks to the forage population of Japanese pond smelt and good creeks that provide spawning habitat.

Fish: Chinook salmon and Mackinaw and brown trout.

Tackle and bait: Rapalas, Rebels, Spaulding smelt, Bomber combinations, jigs, worm-and-flasher combinations, Apex lures, and Power Bait. No live bait is allowed.

Limit: Five trout or salmon.

Season: Year-round, but the reservoir may be snowbound in winter.

Elevation: 5,014 feet.

Location: Twenty-eight miles west of Truckee at the Highway 20 exit from I-80 near Yuba Gap.

Contact: California Department of Fish and Game, 10457 New Town Rd., Nevada City, CA 95929; 530/265-0805.

FULLER LAKE
(see map on page 154, site 20)

An attractive little reservoir close to giant Lake Spaulding, Fuller Lake offers a pine-studded shoreline, scenic mountain vistas, a delightful picnic area, and plenty of spunky rainbow trout. Also, large brown trout are found in the lake, and many are taken early and late in the season at the inlet of Bowman Tunnel. A small outboard, rowboat, canoe, or float tube all work well for fishing Fuller Lake, but shore anglers can have success as well. There's a small, unimproved boat-launching area. The beauty of the lake, its easy access, and the relative lack of crowds make for an excellent family fishing spot.

Fish: Rainbow and brown trout.

Tackle and bait: Night crawlers, spinners and spoons, woolly worms, and dry flies for morning and evening rises.

Limit: Five.

Season: Year-round.

Elevation: 5,600 feet.

Location: Off Highway 20 on Bowman Lake Road, about a 50-minute drive west of Truckee, via I-80.

Contact: California Department of Fish and Game, 1701 Nimbus Rd., Rancho Cordova, CA 95670; 530/355-0978.

TRUCKEE RIVER, UPPER SECTION OF THE MAIN
(see map on page 154, site 21)

Wet winters and record water releases from Lake Tahoe have kept this 14-mile stretch of the Truckee a vibrant fishery. Because of riverfront Forest Service campgrounds and easy access from busy Highway 89, the area receives substantial fishing pressure, although anglers who fish here should be aware that much of the river frontage is private property. If you fish upstream from the Alpine Meadows Road, you'll have mostly slow water, with big pools fed by riffles where large brown trout can lurk. Then, fed by a series of seven streams, the river picks up speed, and, during normal runoff years, roars past River Ranch Lodge and can be very hazardous. Even where you feel comfortable wading, be sure to wear felt-bottomed shoes and use a wading staff to pick your way through the algae-covered rocks.

In July and August, the river is heavily used for commercial rafting and tubing from Tahoe City to River Ranch, so your best strategy at that time is to fish before dusk. If dry flies aren't working on showing fish, use emerging patterns, such as soft hackles (partridge and orange, for example), or cripple patterns when trout are seemingly surface feeding. Normally, the best times to fish the Truckee are late June–early August, and again in late September through the end of the season. There is no fishing allowed for 1,000 feet below the Lake Tahoe outlet dam.

Fish: Rainbow and brown trout and mountain whitefish.

Tackle and bait: Panther Martins, worms, salmon eggs, flies such as yellow Humpies, elkhair caddis, and nymphs such as beadhead green rock worms or sparkle pupae, pheasant tail, and hare's ear.

Limit: Five.

Season: Last Saturday in April–November 15.

Special restrictions: No fishing from Fanny Bridge at Lake Tahoe to 1,000 feet downstream.

Location: Between Truckee and Tahoe City, running parallel to Highway 89.

Contact: Mountain Hardware and Sports, 113200 Donner Pass Rd., Truckee; 530/587-4844.

SPOONER LAKE
(see map on page 154, site 22)

In the fall of 1996, Nevada State Parks drained Spooner to replace an outlet structure, and the Nevada Division of Wildlife is now managing it as a diverse fishery with mainly cutthroat trout, with some rainbows and browns thrown in for good measure. The browns are planted with the intent of having them devour the pesky and persistent population of undesirable tui chub, which survived even after the lake draw-down. This forested lake continues to be a favorite stillwater fishery for fly-fishers. One reason is that no motors are allowed on the lake.

Fish: Cutthroat, rainbow and brown trout.

Tackle and bait: Check with the Nevada Division of Wildlife, since this lake is in transition: 775/688-1500.

Limit: Zero kill; catch-and-release only.

Season: Year-round, but the lake is frozen in winter.

Elevation: 6,981 feet.

Location: In Nevada at Lake Tahoe-Nevada State Park, on Highway 28 near U.S. 50, 11 miles northeast of South Lake Tahoe.

Contact: Tahoe Fly Fishing Outfitters, 3433 Lake Tahoe Blvd., South Lake Tahoe, CA 96150; 530/541-8208; email: info@tahoeflyfishing.com; website: www.tahoeflyfishing.com.

LOON LAKE
(see map on page 154, site 23)

This large reservoir produces decent-sized rainbows, averaging 11 inches but occasionally reaching 16 to 18 inches, and browns averaging 14 inches but occasionally reaching 20 inches. Biologists believe there is natural brown trout reproduction from the streams. There's a large forage fish population of golden shiners, Lahontan redsides, tui chubs, and California roach. The best approach is trolling next to the dams and in the upper coves. For rainbows, you seldom need a downrigger; try early morning surface trolling. For browns, try a downrigger with a Rapala or FlatFish. A public boat ramp and several Forest Service campgrounds are on both the south and north shores. You get spectacular views of the gray, granite peaks of Rockbound Pass in Desolation Wilderness to the east.

Fish: Rainbow and brown trout.

Tackle and bait: FlatFish, Rapalas, Needlefish, Kastmasters, night crawlers, and spoons in red, chartreuse, and fluorescent orange.

Limit: Five.

Season: Year-round.

Elevation: 6,500 feet.

Location: On Ice House Road, in the Crystal Basin Recreation Area, 35 miles off U.S. 50.

Contact: Wild Sports, 9396 Greenback Ln. in Orangevale; 916/989-8310.

GERLE CREEK RESERVOIR
(see map on page 154, site 24)

This small, rock- and pine-rimmed lake, where motorboats are prohibited, is great for anglers with rafts, canoes, or float tubes. Brown trout naturally reproduce here, and they can get up to 18 inches. Adult browns three to five years old enter Gerle Creek in October to spawn. The lake has been made more attractive to the fish through habitat improvements from Cal Trout and REI, the major retail outdoor equipment store. Anglers can try the early morning and afternoon rises on the tree-shaded west side and on the south side near the dam. There's a rocky island that is popular with swimmers, and a concrete fishing pier that is accessible to anglers in wheelchairs. A Forest Service campground is next to the lake. The creek itself can provide better fishing than the reservoir, with five-pounders.

Fish: Brown trout.

Tackle and bait: Spinners and spoons, such as Panther Martins, Kastmasters, and Mepps; worms and Power Bait; and flies.

Limit: Five.

Season: Year-round for the reservoir; the last Saturday in April–November 15 for Gerle Creek.

Elevation: 5,231 feet.

Location: In the Crystal Basin area at the end of Ice House Road, about 30 miles north of U.S. 50.

Contact: Ice House Resort; 530/293-3321. Wild Sports, 9396 Greenback Ln. in Orangevale (east of Sacramento), 916/989-8310.

UNION VALLEY RESERVOIR
(see map on page 154, site 25)

Dedicated local anglers who fish the Crystal Basin lakes rate this fishery the best of the bunch, primarily for rainbow trout and kokanee. The average size for kokanee runs 13 to 17 inches, and the best time to catch them is late summer or early fall near the creek inlets. Mackinaw up to 16 pounds have been caught, but they are generally on the smaller side; using downriggers or deeplining at 100 feet is necessary to bag them. The macks seem to prefer waters that are one-third to one-half the distance from the bottom. Good trolling waters are off the peninsula that has the Fashoda Tent and Sunset Campgrounds, or off Yellowjacket Campground on the north side. Rainbow trolling is excellent in the small forks by the powerhouses. You'll find public boat ramps at Yellowjacket and West Point, but Yellowjacket is the easiest to reach. Good Forest Service camp-

grounds are plentiful, and supplies are available nearby at Ice House Resort.

Fish: Rainbow, Mackinaw, and brown trout, kokanee salmon, and smallmouth bass.

Tackle and bait: Flashers with wedding rings, Needlefish, Rapalas, and Rebels.

Limit: Five.

Season: Year-round.

Elevation: 4,900 feet.

Location: In the Crystal Basin Recreation Area, 18 miles north of U.S. 50 on Ice House Road, between South Lake Tahoe and Placerville.

Contact: Wild Sports, 9396 Greenback Ln. in Orangevale; 916/989-8310.

ICE HOUSE RESERVOIR
(see map on page 154, site 26)

In the Crystal Basin Recreation Area, this elongated, 680-acre lake is one of the best around for catching decent-sized German brown trout, with fish averaging in the 12- to 14-inch range as well as the occasional monster. In 1993, a 10-pound brown was reported. Kokanee were stocked here in the early 1980s, but they have not become a significant fishery. Trolling with a variety of spinners and spoons, and with worm-and-flasher combinations, is the best bet. Fish near the creeks, where baitfish congregate, and along the sandy beaches. A fine U.S. Forest Service campground with tree-shaded sites and a public boat ramp are on the west end.

Fish: Eagle Lake rainbow, brown, and brook trout.

Tackle and bait: Rapalas, Needlefish, Krocodiles, FlatFish, Rebels, and minnow imitations; downrigger with J-plugs; Power Bait and night crawlers.

Limit: Five.

Season: Year-round, but the reservoir is snowbound in winter.

Elevation: 5,500 feet.

Location: On Ice House Road, east of Placerville and 12 miles north of U.S. 50.

Contact: Ice House Resort; 530/293-3321. Wild Sports, 9396 Greenback Ln. in Orangevale (east of Sacramento), 916/989-8310.

WRIGHTS AND DARK LAKES
(see map on page 154, site 27)

Wrights is one of the more attractive natural lakes in the Crystal Basin area and is a popular entry point for hiking and backpacking in Desolation Wilderness. It is heavily used by campers as well and has a number of summer cabins around the shoreline. The fishing is spotty at best, since the water tends to be warm and is a beehive of swimmers, canoes, and sailing dinghies (no motors are allowed). The best place to fish is in the upper (eastern) end, near a large creek inlet with thick growths of willows; this is also the deepest area.

Much smaller Dark Lake, less than a half mile away, is a beautiful spot for float-tubing, especially during the evening rise, and it gets its share of fly-fishers. Dark has rainbows and a few browns that were planted in the early 1990s. The habitat includes lots of aquatic growth and cover at both lakes, which are rimmed with thick forest. The best times to fish are just after the thaw, in early summer and in the fall. Forest Service campsites are in high demand at Wrights, and they are among the most difficult to reserve. Even if the fish aren't biting, the dramatic granite peaks are awe-inspiring. You can try fishing the Desolation Wilderness lakes on day hikes from Wrights (be sure to get a wilderness permit). It's also a short drive to the Crystal Basin reservoirs.

Fish: Rainbow and brown trout.

Tackle and bait: Power Bait, salmon eggs, small spinners and spoons, night crawlers, and flies such as damselflies, midges, Muddler Minnows, leeches, and elkhair caddis.

Limit: Five.

Season: Year-round, but the lakes are icebound in winter.

Elevation: 7,000 feet.

Location: Eight miles north of U.S. 50 via Wrights Lake Road, which is about 35 miles east of South Lake Tahoe.

Contact: Wild Sports, 9396 Greenback Ln. in Orangevale; 916/989-8310.

JENKINSON LAKE
(see map on page 154, site 28)

A Mackinaw fishery that's better than Lake Tahoe? Hard to believe, but many anglers swear that it's true. Heavy stocking by the California Department of Fish and Game, a relatively low elevation, numerous pockets and holes, and prolific Japanese pond smelt have created an incredible fishery for almost every species in the lake. The average Mackinaw runs three to six pounds—compared to two to five pounds in Tahoe. Brown trout are also big producers, especially in spring and fall, with three- to six-pounders pulled in monthly, and 9- to 10-pounders on occasion. Rainbows typically run 12 to 18 inches, and most are caught on Power Bait.

Motorboats are permitted on the lake, and the preferred tactic is trolling on the bottom along the shoreline with downriggers for Mackinaws and browns. The best fly-fishing is in the upper arm, and the best trolling is behind the peninsula of the second dam and in the narrows near Hazel Creek Campground. Even shore anglers do well, especially from the two dams and in the upper arms, with lures such as Kastmasters. Two boat ramps are owned by the Eldorado Irrigation District (with a fee for launching), and there are 182 well-maintained public campsites along the lake.

Fish: Mackinaw, rainbow, and brown trout, and smallmouth bass and bluegill.

Tackle and bait: Blue Rapalas, chartreuse Power Bait, Needlefish, salmon eggs, Rooster Tails (yellow and orange), and night crawlers with flashers. Flies such as ant and mosquito patterns also work.

Limit: Five.

Season: Year-round.

Elevation: 3,478 feet.

Location: Five miles south of Pollock Pines on Sly Park Road off U.S. 50, a 45-minute drive west of South Lake Tahoe.

Contact: Sly Park Resort; 530/644-1113.

FISHING

FALLEN LEAF LAKE
(see map on page 154, site 29)

The amazing thing about Fallen Leaf Lake is that it is close to the Tahoe resorts but gets very little fishing pressure. That's too bad, since this is a decent place to catch kokanee salmon and Mackinaw. Fallen Leaf, in fact, is managed as a kokanee fishery, although it has limited numbers of rainbow and brown trout and abundant numbers of smaller Mackinaw trout (one to three pounds). Early morning trolling is the best fishing method, using Imperial Magics, Al Wilson blades, and lead-core line. Begin with four or five colors early in the year, then drop to 8–10 colors by fall. The kokanee bite usually begins in late July and runs through September. For Mackinaw, try drift-fishing with minnows.

One problem with this large lake is the limited access for boats, consisting of a pay ramp at Fallen Leaf Marina. Most of the surrounding land (except for a U.S. Forest Service campground on the south end) is privately controlled, with several exclusive summer homes (including one featured in the movie *The Bodyguard*) and a summer retreat owned by the Stanford Alumni Association. Fallen Leaf empties into Taylor Creek, which is the single most important spawning habitat for kokanee on Lake Tahoe.

Fish: Kokanee salmon and rainbow, brown, and Mackinaw trout.
Tackle and bait: Live minnows (but only those caught from Fallen Leaf), worms-and-flashers, spinners, and Rapalas.
Season: Year-round, but the road is snowbound in winter.
Limit: Five.
Elevation: 6,400 feet.
Location: Off Highway 89 on Fallen Leaf Road, near Camp Richardson, about five miles north of the "Y" intersection at South Lake Tahoe.
Contact: The Sportsman in South Lake Tahoe; 530/542-3474. Fallen Leaf Marina; 530/544-0787.

ECHO LAKES
(see map on page 154, site 30)

Rainbow and cutthroat trout averaging 12 inches (but occasionally up to 14 inches) are the most productive in these beautiful lakes, which are framed by granite peaks and provide an entry point to Desolation Wilderness. Neither brook trout nor kokanee are planted here, so they are apparently spawning on their own. Biologists surmise that brookies are migrating from upstream lakes in Desolation, and they tend to congregate in Upper Echo Lake. Kokanee are relatively small and are caught mainly in spring.

The two lakes are connected by a narrow channel, and summer homes line the shorelines. Upper Echo Lake is smaller and easier to fish from outboards or canoes, while Lower Echo Lake is large, exposed, and subject to powerful afternoon winds. There's a marina with a boat ramp, a general store, and cabins at Lower Echo Lake, and a water taxi that makes regular runs to Upper Echo Lake and the trailhead leading into Desolation Wilderness. Parking can be very difficult in the summer. No water-skiing is allowed.

Fish: Rainbow, brook, and cutthroat trout, and kokanee salmon.
Tackle and bait: Spinners, spoons, and worm-and-flasher combinations trolled from boats. The lakes are not generally considered to be productive for fly-fishing.
Limit: Five, plus 10 brookies under eight inches.
Season: Year-round, but the lakes are icebound in winter.
Elevation: 7,414 feet.
Location: Just north of U.S. 50 at Echo Summit, via Echo Lakes Road, the lake is a 20-minute drive from South Lake Tahoe.
Contact: Echo Chalet; 530/659-7207.

CARSON RIVER, WEST FORK
(see map on page 154, site 31)

Though typically not as productive as the East Fork of the Carson River, the West Fork of the Carson has some scenic waters in Hope Valley, and its tributaries near Blue Lakes often have brook trout as well as other species. In recent years, the U.S. Fish and Wildlife Service has begun experimenting with plantings of Lahontan cutthroat trout, which seem to be taking. The river downstream from Sorensen's Resort is generally accessible off of Highway 88.

Fish: Rainbow, cutthroat, and brown trout.
Tackle and bait: For spin anglers, small (about one-sixteenth of an ounce) Panther Martins and Rooster Tails work well. For fly anglers, try woolly buggers and White Millers, depending on the time of day.
Limit: Five.
Season: Last Saturday in April–November 15.
Location: Flowing from the headwaters in the Blue Lakes region eastward through Hope Valley (near the Highway 88/89 junction south of South Lake Tahoe), paralleling much of Highway 88 in California.
Contact: Woodfords Station in Woodfords; 530/694-2930, or Horse Feathers Fly Fishing School at Sorensen's Resort; 530/694-2203.

INDIAN CREEK RESERVOIR
(see map on page 154, site 32)

This is one of the best lakes in the region for fly-fishing and float tubing for large trout. Although it used to be a catch-basin for wastewater from South Lake Tahoe, the 160-acre reservoir is now supplied with freshwater from spring runoff and the West Fork of the Carson River. While the best chance of landing big fish is by belly boat, raft, or canoe, shore anglers also have success near the two dams. There's a small but attractive public campground on the lake with 29 campsites run by the Bureau of Land Management, complete with hot showers; camping is available on a first-come, first-served basis.

Fish: Rainbow, brook, Kamloops, and Lahontan cutthroat trout.
Tackle and bait: Green or gold Panther Martins, pink or orange Power Bait, salmon eggs, Super Dupers, and large garden worms. Flies include size-10 black woolly worms, black leeches, green matukas, silver Hiltons, Muddler Minnows, and Antron Caterpillars, a local pattern. Try Adams or mosquito patterns in the evening.

Limit: Five, plus 10 brookies under eight inches.
Season: Year-round.
Elevation: 5,600 feet.
Location: Four miles off Highway 4/89 on Diamond Valley Road between Woodfords and Markleeville, south of the Highway 88 junction.
Contact: Grover's Corner in Markleeville; 530/694-2562.

CARSON RIVER, EAST FORK— CALIFORNIA
(see map on page 154, site 33)

Here is one of the best rivers in the region for catching a native trout, or perhaps a trophy brown weighing over five pounds. It's the only free-flowing river left on the eastern flanks of the Sierra, so without dams the native trout have abundant spawning habitat. Fly-fishers will find quality but not quantity if they make short, 30-foot casts upstream. Later in the season, if the water is clear, unbroken, and shallow, fish get spooky and are best approached with blind casts—definitely a challenge. In September and October, try small flies such as a Griffith Gnat or a black or gray midge, in sizes 20–26. For spin-casting anglers, plenty of catchable rainbows are available upstream from Hangman's Bridge, an area that is much easier to reach from Highway 4 and has lots of riffles and pockets.

Two tributaries, Silver and Wolf Creeks, get little pressure but can offer paydirt for those with the patience to work them. On Silver Creek, fly-fishers can try a beadhead hare's ear, a black ant, or a green inchworm pattern with a black head. On Wolf Creek, try any orange thorax flyfished underneath deeply cut banks. Early in the season, be careful wading during a high runoff. By mid- to late summer you should be able to wade and walk most of the East Carson on the California side. Because of back-to-back wet winters, the rainbows in these waters have been increasing in size.

Fish: Rainbow, cutthroat, and brown trout, and mountain whitefish.
Tackle and bait: Only artificial lures with barbless hooks may be used in the wild trout section; other tackle and bait, including salmon eggs and

FISHING

night crawlers, are allowed above there. Panther Martins and Rooster Tails work well for spin casters. In warm months, nymphs such as hare's ear and woolly buggers work well for fly anglers, and in cooler months (early in the season) dry flies such as White Wulff, elkhair caddis with a yellow body, Royal Wulff, and White Millers yield bites.

Limit: Catch-and-release only is allowed on the section from Hangman's Bridge downstream to the Nevada state line (nine miles). Upstream from Hangman's Bridge, the limit is five.

Season: Last Saturday in April–November 15.

Special restrictions: Fishing is closed year-round upstream from Carson Falls and in the tributaries here.

Location: From Markleeville, drive nine miles north on Highway 89. Turn right onto Highway 4 and continue 2.5 miles to the access on the left side of the road.

Contact: Carson River Resort in Markleeville; 530/694-2229, website: www.carsonriverresort.com, or Horse Feathers Fly Fishing School at Sorensen's Resort in Hope Valley; 530/694-2203 or 800/423-9949.

CARSON RIVER, EAST FORK—
NEVADA (see map on page 154, site 34)

This section of the river sees consistent fishing pressure, primarily from residents in the Gardnerville area. There are some steep, cut banks that are difficult to negotiate, but you'll generally get more and warmer water than the California side, and the fishery is managed for large brown trout.

Fish: Rainbow, brown, and brook trout.

Tackle and bait: Same as for the California side (see number 33). When the river warms up in the Carson Valley, spin casters may find better luck with black and gold or black and silver Rapalas. Also, Nevada allows the use of live bait, including Tahoe suckers, mountain suckers, speckled dace, fathead minnows, and mosquitofish. Buy only from dealers authorized to sell live bait in the Carson River basin.

Limit: Five.

Season: Year-round.

Location: From Markleeville, drive approximately nine miles north on Highway 89 and 18 miles north on Highway 88. Turn right onto U.S. 395 and drive 9.5 miles through the towns of Minden and Gardnerville. Continue 2.5 miles past the last stoplight. Follow the right-hand turn lane into a wide dirt parking area where there is river access.

Contact: Angler's Edge in Gardnerville; 750/782-4734.

HEENAN LAKE
(see map on page 154, site 35)

Originally built in 1929 to store irrigation water for Nevada pasturelands, this premier, 130-acre trophy trout lake has been an important source of cutthroat brood stock for the California Department of Fish and Game since the 1940s. Historically, as many as two million eggs were taken annually from the lake to supply other California lakes, but in recent years that number has dropped to about 500,000. In 1994, a massive green algae bloom that resulted from six years of drought caused a major fish kill, and the lake was closed to fishing. The combination of a drop in water level from 31 feet to 10 feet and the subsequent oxygen depletion from the algae resulted in the loss of more than 1,200 trophy-sized cutthroats, which normally can live up to 10 years.

However, wet winters subsequently broke the drought and restored water levels, so the fishery is bouncing back and the DFG has resumed its limited two-month catch-and-release fishing season. Now, for anglers who want the chance to tangle with big fish—averaging 20 inches in length and not infrequently reaching 27 inches—Heenan is the hot spot. Float tubes and small boats with electric motors are the approved—and preferred—methods of taking them. Be patient; this is not fast and furious action. Use flies with sinking lines, or troll with lures. Owned by the State of California, the lake is part of the larger Heenan Lake Wildlife Refuge, which covers

1,652 acres of prime habitat that attracts, among other creatures, bald eagles. All tributaries to Heenan Lake are closed to fishing year-round.

Fish: Lahontan cutthroat trout.

Tackle and bait: Only artificial lures with barbless hooks may be used.

Limit: Zero. Catch-and-release only.

Season: Friday, Saturday, and Sunday only from the Friday before Labor Day through the last Sunday in October.

Elevation: 7,000 feet.

Location: In Alpine County off Highway 89 east of Markleeville.

Contact: Alpine County Chamber of Commerce; 530/694-2475; email: alpinecounty@ alpinecounty.com; website: www.alpinecounty.com.

PLEASANT VALLEY CREEK
(see map on page 154, site 36)

Now entirely under private ownership and management, this clear, spring-fed stream is a spawning area and tributary to the East Fork of the Carson River. As such it has big brood stock, including naturally reproducing brown trout. Local fishing guide Jim Crouse manages this stream, allowing five anglers per day, at a permit fee of $80 per person, and requiring catch-and-release fishing. This is a good spot for early season fishing if the East Carson is too high.

Fish: Rainbow, brown, and cutthroat trout.

Tackle and bait: Only artificial lures with barbless hooks may be used. Try a small caddis green rock worm early in the season, a Muddler Minnow, or a gray grasshopper pattern. Also try black ant, hare's ear, elkhair caddis, and White Miller, in sizes 14 and 16.

Limit: Two.

Season: Last Saturday in April–November 15.

Location: In eastern Alpine County south of South Lake Tahoe. About 1.5 miles south of Markleeville on Highway 4/89, turn west on Hot Springs Road, toward Grover Hot Springs. From there take a left onto Pleasant Valley Road. Proceed through a residential area to the top of a hill where a dirt road begins and takes you downhill to Pleasant Valley. You'll need to have

the special private fishing permit before entering the property.

Contact: Pleasant Valley Fly Fishing Preserve, c/o Jim Crouse, P.O. Box 10465, South Lake Tahoe, CA 96158; 530/542-0759; website: www.worldwidefishing.com/b487.htm. Permits may also be obtained on a space-available basis from the Carson River Resort in Markleeville; 530/694-2229.

RED LAKE (see map on page 154, site 37)

Want to catch trophy-sized brook trout? This is the place. Fed by several springs and Red Lake Creek, this 85-acre lake in the shadow of Carson Pass, next to Highway 88, has become the brook trout capital of the region. The Department of Fish and Game owns all of the water rights as well as surrounding lands, so the agency offers good protection for the fishery. There are no motor restrictions. Boaters will get best results working the upper end of the lake near the inlet and along the south shoreline, where there is a submerged shelf—it is the deepest place in the lake and is heavily favored by the trout. A free public launch ramp with limited parking is on the northeast end of the lake, near the dam.

Fish: Brook, cutthroat, and rainbow trout.

Tackle and bait: Power Bait, worms, Rooster Tails, Prince nymphs, woolly buggers, and leeches.

Limit: Five, including brookies. This is a special exception to the general state limit of 10 brookies under eight inches.

Season: Year-round.

Elevation: 8,002 feet.

Location: On Highway 88 east of Carson Pass and west of the junction with Highway 89.

Contact: Tahoe Fly Fishing Outfitters, 3433 Lake Tahoe Blvd., South Lake Tahoe, CA 96150; 530/541-8208; website: www.tahoeflyfishing.com.

BLUE LAKES
(see map on page 154, site 38)

For the solo (unguided) angler, the two Blue Lakes

provide perhaps the best chance of bagging trout in the entire Tahoe region, since they are heavily planted here by the California Department of Fish and Game. The best methods are trolling in small boats or casting from float tubes. For shore anglers, fishing from the dams at Upper Blue Lake can be productive. Upper Blue Lake, at 344 acres, has a large population of cutthroat trout as well as rainbows, and also has the most stable water level of the lakes in the area. Some beaver ponds near Lost Lakes, just above Upper Blue, are full of 12- to 14-inch brook trout.

The Blue Lakes region has 16 lakes, about three-fourths of them accessible by vehicle (mainly four-wheel drive). For fly-fishers, early season fishing at Wet Meadows, Granite, Tamarack, and Summit Lakes is worthwhile. For the evening rise, a White Miller is particularly effective. Golden trout can be caught at Raymond Lake, but the tiring, three-hour hike on slippery shale and steep switchbacks usually puts off most anglers. There are good PG&E campgrounds at both Blue Lakes.

For the solo (unguided) angler, the two Blue Lakes provide perhaps the best chance of bagging trout in the entire Tahoe region, since they are heavily planted here by the California Department of Fish and Game.

Fish: Rainbow, brook, and cutthroat trout.

Tackle and bait: Worms, Power Bait, Ford Fenders, Super Dupers, Kastmasters, Rooster Tails, Panther Martins, and flies such as elkhair caddis, Adams, woolly worms with Flashabou, White Miller, and a local pattern called the Antron Caterpillar.

Limit: Five trout, plus 10 brookies under eight inches.

Season: Year-round, but the road is snowbound in winter.

Elevation: 8,000 feet.

Location: On Blue Lakes Road, approximately 12 miles south of Highway 88, and west of the junction of Highway 89. The first six miles of the road are paved, but the rest is on generally adequate but occasionally bumpy dirt and gravel—OK for two-wheel drives.

Contact: The Sportsman in South Lake Tahoe; 530/542-3474.

SILVER LAKE
(see map on page 154, site 39)

Surrounded by resorts and cabins and next to Highway 88, Silver Lake gets heavy fishing pressure. The lake contains some big browns, going five to eight pounds, as well as lunker rainbows, going to five pounds. A few years ago, the Department of Fish and Game planted some Mackinaw trout, but these apparently did not flourish. Trollers should fish 10 to 25 feet deep along the shoreline and around a large rock island. There are powerboat rentals at Kay's Silver Lake Resort, where you'll also find a launch ramp. Fly-fishers will find the best action from float tubes in the fall, and earlier in the season along the Silver Fork of the American River, just across the highway. Area accommodations include Kit Carson Lodge and Kirkwood Ski Resort, and there are several good campgrounds nearby. Dramatic peaks frame the lake, which is rimmed by granite and forest, and the historic Mormon-Emigrant Trail runs on the ridge to the east. There are excellent restaurants at both Plasse's and Kit Carson Lodge.

Fish: Rainbow and brown trout.

Tackle and bait: Worms, salmon eggs, small spinners, Power Bait, worm-and-flasher combinations, Panther Martins, and flies such as mayflies and mosquito midges.

Limit: Five.

Season: Year-round, but the lake is snowbound in winter.

Elevation: 7,260 feet.

Location: On Highway 88, 40 miles southwest of South Lake Tahoe.

Contact: Kay's Silver Lake Resort; 209/258-8598. Plasse's Resort; 209/258-8814.

CAPLES LAKE
(see map on page 154, site 40)

Here's a marvelous Mulligan stew of trout. Take your pick—just about every kind lives in man-

OTHER HIGH-COUNTRY FISHING LAKES

Apart from Desolation Wilderness, there are several other good fishing lakes within an hour's drive of Lake Tahoe.

Fourth of July Lake
This lake in Mokelumne Wilderness is accessible from the Woods Lake Trailhead off Highway 88 at Carson Pass. The trail to get here is steep and has some tricky sections, but it can be done on a day hike. There are good populations of self-sustaining, but somewhat stunted, brook trout.

Star Lake
This lake is near the section of the Tahoe Rim Trail that traverses the South Tahoe peaks. It's about a six-mile hike from the Big Meadow Trailhead on Highway 89, 5.5 miles south of U.S. 50. The lake has a burgeoning population of brook trout, and fishing for this small, spunky fish is often quite good.

Grouse Lake area
This area lies north of I-80 and Lake Spaulding in Tahoe National Forest. Motorized vehicles are prohibited, making the lakes accessible only by foot or by bicycle. Vehicles, mainly four-wheel drives, can be driven to Grouse Ridge Lookout or to Meadow Lake. Trailheads are off Bowman Road or at Summit City on a dirt road off paved Jackson Meadows Road northeast of Truckee. Among lakes with good reports are Baltimore (large brookies up to 17 inches), Milk (brookies to 10 inches and rainbows to 13 inches), Glacier (golden trout), and Big Downey (some trophy rainbows; bring your float tube).

Big Bend/Kingvale area
The lakes in this area are accessible on trails south of I-80. Good catch reports come from Natalie (10- to 12-inch cutthroat trout), Upper Loch Leven (a lively brook trout fishery), and Salmon (a good population of brookies, with some 14–16 inchers).

---

made Caples Lake, including rainbows averaging 10 to 14 inches. The beauty of the 600-acre lake is that you don't have to be up at the crack of dawn to catch fish. Caples Resort guide Bruno Huff starts at around 9 A.M. and catches fish all day. Shore anglers do fair, but trollers with small powerboats do better. Trolling just off the north, east, and south shorelines with spinners and spoons is effective; worms or Power Bait with flashers also work well. If you seek the big lake trout, you'll have to go deeper with downriggers or jigs.

Caples is a popular ice-fishing lake in winter, but check on ice conditions with the resort before venturing out. It's too large and too deep for fly-fishing, and winds can be a problem in the afternoon. However, Caples is quite scenic, surrounded by spectacular volcanic peaks. The single resort here has boat rentals (there's a 5 mph speed limit on the lake), a launch ramp, and tackle, along with an excellent restaurant. A Forest Service campground is across the highway, and there are some great undesignated boat-in camping spots along the eastern arm of the lake.

Fish: Rainbow, brown, brook, and Mackinaw trout.

Tackle and bait: Rapalas, Rebels, FlatFish, Torpedoes, Triple Teasers, Canadian Wonders, feathered crappie jigs, salmon eggs, Power Bait, and worms.

Limit: Five, plus 10 brookies under eight inches.

Season: Year-round, but the lake freezes over in winter.

Elevation: 7,800 feet.

Location: On Highway 88, four miles west of the Carson Pass, southwest of South Lake Tahoe.

Contact: Caples Lake Resort; 209/258-8888.

TOPAZ LAKE
(see map on page 154, site 41)

Big rainbows and browns make this high-desert lake, surrounded by rolling hills, sagebrush, and sandy shoreline, especially popular. Lake records are set almost annually, and anglers have pulled in 12-pound brown trout and 10-pound rainbows during the past decade. The average size of rainbows caught is around 1.5 pounds. Trout move all over the lake, which is 1,800 acres in size and is used for agricultural irrigation. One of the top spots is The Rock on the east side near Douglas County Recreation Area, where shore fishing can be productive. Plenty of services are at the lake, including a marina with powerboat rentals, an RV park, a county campground, a restaurant, and a casino. There are two boat ramps available, one at Topaz Marina, the other in the county park.

Fish: Eagle Lake-strain rainbow trout, brown trout, tiger trout (a hybrid of brown and brook trout), black bass, and mountain whitefish.

Tackle and bait: Chartreuse Power Bait; night crawlers; black, gold, or silver and gold Rapalas; Needlefish; worm-and-flasher rigs; white Rooster Tails; Panther Martins; and chrome Krocodiles.

Limit: Five trout, 10 mountain whitefish, and 15 warmwater game fish, of which no more than five may be black bass.

Season: January 1–September 30.

Special restrictions: The area within a 100-yard radius of Topaz Marina is closed to fishing.

Elevation: 5,000 feet.

Location: Straddling the California/Nevada state line on U.S. 395, 18 miles south of Gardnerville and about an hour's drive from South Lake Tahoe.

Contact: Topaz Marina; 775/266-3550.

PRIVATE LAKES

East Peak Lake

This privately owned high-elevation lake (8,000 feet) at Heavenly ski resort is used for snowmaking during the winter. But in summer it is open for small groups of guided fly-fishers, as long as no major on-mountain construction projects are under way. Anglers get a quality fishing experience with an opportunity to hook 16- to 28-inch rainbow trout, which are planted here on an annual basis. Guides and trips to East Peak are arranged exclusively by Tahoe Fly Fishing Outfitters, which has a store in South Lake Tahoe. The number of anglers is limited, and all fishing is catch-and-release with single barbless hooks. The outfitter can supply the necessary gear, including float tubes and

tackle. East Peak is on the Nevada side of the mountain, with lifts and day lodges nearby, but anglers can be shuttled there (on a dirt road) at no extra charge.

Fees: Half-day fishing is $200 for one angler, $275 for two, and $350 for three; full day, with lunch included, is $300 for one angler, $400 for two, and $500 for three. Equipment rentals are $15 for rod and reel and $20 for float tubes and fins. Season and day passes for the lake are available.

Contact: Tahoe Fly Fishing Outfitters, P.O. Box 1224, South Lake Tahoe, CA 96156; 530/541-8208; website: www.tahoeflyfishing.com.

Sawmill Lake

This is a secluded 10-acre reservoir at Northstar-at-Tahoe resort. It is stocked with trophy-sized rainbow trout, but is reserved for catch-and-release flyfishing only. Main methods are float tubing and shoreline stalking. Access is limited to four rods at a time and reservations are strongly recommended. While you can reserve a fishing day by phone, it must be confirmed by pre-payment. Equipment is available at extra cost and there is a guide on-site daily to provide helpful hints.

Fees: $100 for a full day, $65 for a half-day, and $150–275 for half-day to full-day guiding and instruction. All equipment is provided except leaders and flies.

Contact: Sawmill Lake Flyfishing, c/o Northstar-at-Tahoe, P.O. Box 129, Truckee, CA 96160; 530/582-5393; website: www.northstarattahoe.com.

Tahoe Trout Farm

Geared mainly toward families with children, the trout farm charges no admission and provides free use of bait and tackle. You pay only for what you catch. It is open to the public, with no license or boat required and no catch limit. Hours are 10 A.M.–7 P.M. daily, from Memorial Day to Labor Day.

Contact: Tahoe Trout Farm, 1023 Blue Lake Ave./P.O. Box 13118, South Lake Tahoe, CA 96151; 530/541-1491.

Charter Boats and Guides

Rates are fairly consistent among the charter operations at both Lake Tahoe and Donner Lake. The standard four- to five-hour trips run $75–90 per person. Longer trips run $90–130 per person. Special evening or afternoon rates are often available, and there are frequently discounts for children, seniors and nonfishing passengers.

DONNER, DAVIS, AND OTHER TRUCKEE-AREA LAKES

Big Daddy's Guide Service

Guide Bryan Roccucci is the "Big Daddy," and he's a specialist on light tackle fishing for trophy trout and kokanee salmon. His prime haunts include Lake Davis and Gold Lake, and he uses a new 23-foot Boulton Powerboat to chase the big ones. The vessel, powered by a MerCruiser inboard, has plenty of room for four anglers, and features a full stand-up canvass top with side and back curtains, along with a heater for foul weather. Roccucci is set up with the latest in state-of-the-art fish finding electronics and downriggers. There's a two-person minimum for guided all-day trips, which run seven hours. Clients must bring their own lunches and liquids.
Contact: Big Daddy's Guide Service, P.O. Box 557, Quincy, CA 95971; 530/283-4103; website: www.bigdaddyfishing.com.

Dillard Guided Fishing

Using a 23-foot Chris Craft with a Chevrolet 350 I/O engine, guide Ed Dillard can scoot around Davis Lake in fine fashion. He trolls with light tackle, fishes bait, or even fly-casts, depending on the desires of his clients. Dillard specializes in family outings and has special rates for children. Although guiding just since 1999, he's lived in the area and fished its waters for nearly 30 years. Dillard can supply rods and tackle, but guests should bring lunches and ice chests for any fish they keep. The boat can accommodate up to three anglers, and it has a canvas top for hot or inclement weather.

Contact: Dillard Guided Fishing, P.O. Box 96, Beckwourth, CA 96129; 530/832-4919; website: www.dillardfishing.homestead.com.

Sierra Anglers

Over the years, many guides have given up on Donner Lake. While it has yielded record brown trout and respectable Mackinaws, it can be a tough lake to fish, especially in the summer. But Keith Kerrigan includes Donner in his buffet of North Lake Tahoe–area lakes. And if Donner isn't cooperating, no problem; he'll trailer his 21-foot Eagle powerboat to Stampede Reservoir, Lake Davis, or even Eagle Lake. Kerrigan fishes both lures and flies, depending on the body of water and conditions. For success at Donner, he recommends hitting the fish very early in the morning or in the evening just before sunset, when there's often a two-hour window of opportunity. Spring and Fall are the best times of the year. In May, Kerrigan switches to the kokanee runs at Stampede, and in mid-summer he goes for rainbows at Davis when the damselfly hatch is in full swing. In October, he's on the prowl for the big Eagle Lake trout. While customers always have the say-so on where they want to fish, "I try to direct them to the best fishing at that time." Kerrigan's policy is a bold one: "No fish, no pay." He provides all gear for both tackle and fly-fishing, as well as float tubes, waders and fins, for up to four anglers per trip. For Mackinaw fishing on Donner, he has soft, custom rods that provide maximum play, and for kokanee, he's converted some Fisher fly rods to bait set-ups and trolls his own homemade bugs and spinners with downriggers. Another twist: Kerrigan posts snapshots of his clients' latest and greatest catches on his website.
Contact: Sierra Anglers, P.O. Box 4127, Truckee, CA 96160; 530/582-5689; website: www.sierraanglers.net.

Tight Lines Guide Service

Rick and Tresa Kennedy of Grass Valley, Calif., specialize in ultralight trolling and fly-fishing for trophy trout and landlocked kokanee salmon.

They are multifaceted fishing fanatics, judging from the array of impressive hardware and gear that they provide. Northern reservoirs, including Donner, Boca near Truckee and Davis near Portola, are among their top destinations. They troll for trout with downriggers and sideplaners, with both conventional and spinning tackle. Their custom-designed 22-foot Jetcraft is equipped with Bottomline electronics, sideplaners and a mast. Clients fish with high-quality G. Loomis rods and Shimano Calcutta reels. For new anglers, there's a combo trip that offers fly-fishing at dawn followed by trolling with tackle later in the day (a mix that fly-fishing purists would avoid like the plague). The Kennedys clean and ice all fish that you choose to keep.

Fees: $100 per person for Boca Reservoir, with a $200 minimum boat charge; anglers 15 years and under are $65. On Lake Davis, it's $125 per person, with a $250 minimum boat charge.

Contact: Tight Lines Guide Service, 664-A Freeman Ln. #251, Grass Valley, CA 95949-9630; 530/273-1986; website: www.fishtightlines.com.

TAHOE CITY/WEST SHORE

Kingfish Guide Service

Operating out of Homewood Marina on the West Shore of Lake Tahoe, Larry Schuelke run the 43-foot *Kingfish,* one of the largest fishing vessels on the lake. Amenities include heaters, fish-finding electronics, radar, Calstar rods, Penn reels, outriggers, and downriggers. Although the boat can hold up to 40 people, Schuelke fishes a maximum of 10, with a minimum of two. Hisr prime method is trolling with steel line and downriggers equipped with 20-pound test monofilament, using live bait. He fishes year-round in waters between Emerald Bay and Stateline Point off the Cal-Neva Resort. On lighter loads, he will jig and drift. Fishing is strictly for Mackinaw. He also runs 2.5-hour tours of Emerald Bay in summer. The boat departs from 5165 W. Lake Blvd. in Homewood. All guests should bring their own food. The boat departs from 5165 W. Lake Blvd. in Homewood.

Contact: *Kingfish* Guide Service, P.O. Box 5955, Tahoe City, CA 96145; 530/525-5360, 800/622-

5462, or 775/742-2472 (cellular boat phone); website: www.kingfishtahoe.com.

Mac-A-Tac

Skipper/owner Kevin Roach, who has more than 15 years of experience fishing Lake Tahoe, leaves out of Sunnyside Marina on the West Shore. His 28-foot Bayliner is equipped with a Chevrolet 350 inboard engine, a cabin, heaters, and a toilet, and can accommodate up to six anglers. Roach's preferred fishing method is trolling for Mackinaw trout with downriggers 140 to 220 feet deep, and mainly Sabre and Fenwick Ugly Sticks graphite rods with Penn level-wind reels and Fenwick braided 30-pound line. In spring, he fishes shallower with six-pound test line, but on downriggers with sensitive clips. Roach prefers big artificial lures such as Rapalas, but he occasionally fishes with minnows. He runs two trips a day year-round, morning and afternoon, and sticks to waters off the West and North Shores. All gear and tackle is provided. Licenses are available on board.

Contact: Mac-A-Tac, P.O. Box 433, Tahoe City, CA 96145; 530/546-2500 or 775/831-4449.

Mickey's Big Mack Charters

Mickey Daniels, who is considered one of the top Mackinaw fishermen in Lake Tahoe, has two well-equipped vessels—the 32-foot *Big Mack,* which can carry 8–10 people, and the 43-foot *Big Mack II,* which can carry 10–12 people. Both boats have V-8 inboard engines, large cabins and heaters, heads, and plenty of deck space for roaming. Daniels is based at the Sierra Boat Company in Carnelian Bay and sticks to the North Shore waters between Tahoe City and Stateline Point, trolling in 180 to 220 feet of water with both wire line and downriggers set up with light line and tackle. He uses custom-made Seeker rods with Penn reels for long-lining, and steelhead rods with Abu-Garcia reels for downriggers. Standard rigs include minnows with dodgers, Silver Horde, and Apex lures. Fishing on the boat is by the lottery system, which means that when your number is called you work the fish; the rest of the time you can drink, sleep, or sightsee. In the fall, Daniels top-lines for rainbows, which are usually incidental to the Mackinaw fishing. He fishes year-round, including winter, which is the best time to catch big fish, and he'll do both morning and afternoon runs. All gear is provided, but bring snacks, liquids, and a fishing license (a one-day license is available on board).

Contact: Mickey's Big Mack Charters, P.O. Box 488, Carnelian Bay, CA 96140; 530/546-4444 or 800/877-1462.

Reel Deal Sport Fishing

Pete Henderson started Reel Deal in 1996, and he's got a fleet of three comfortable fishing and cruising boats operating out of Tahoe City Marina. The vessels consist of a 28.5-foot Bayliner, a 25.5-foot Skipjack, and a 24-foot Sea-Ray, any of which can accommodate up to six anglers. He'll troll with long wire lines with flashers and minnows or, if the bite is strong, he'll use light steelhead rods with 6-pound monofilament, and downriggers. Departures are made throughout the day, so if you don't want to get up before dawn, then consider the early evening bite. Prime fishing grounds are Kings Beach on the North Shore and along much of the West Shore. Skippers clean and bag your fish, if you wish. Henderson, who also owns the Java Stop, a coffeehouse in Tahoe City, brings some of his fresh brew on board, along with snacks. He fishes year-round.

Contact: Reel Deal Sport Fishing, P.O. Box 7724, Tahoe City, CA 96145; 530/581-0924.

Reel Magic Sportfishing

Skipper Steve Beals has an attractive motto: "No fish, no pay." He challenges anglers not to catch fish, if they can help it. Beals fishes for Mackinaw trout and rainbows April–mid-October on his 26-foot Sea Ray, which comes complete with a flying bridge, heaters, fish-finders, and a cabin with flush toilets. He prefers trolling with monofilament and lead-core line, with some downrigging and outrigging, and deep-lining with steel line. In the spring, he fishes for rainbow trout in 30 to 40 feet of water, and for Mackinaw in the 120- to 150-foot range. Beals uses Fenwick and custom rods, Daiwa reels, and a variety of plugs. The vessel departs from the Tahoe City Marina in the morning, usually 5 A.M.–11 A.M., but Beals will do occasional afternoon trips by request, from 3 P.M. until dark. The maximum number of anglers is six, but he prefers to take three.

Beals will fish for a minimum of six hours. All gear is provided, but clients should bring their own food and beverages.

Contact: Reel Magic Sportfishing, P.O. Box 10104, Truckee, CA 96162; 530/587-6027 or 530/277-6027 (boat phone).

KINGS BEACH/TAHOE VISTA/CARNELIAN BAY

Pyramid-Tahoe Fishing Charters
(See listing under Pyramid Lake, page 184.)

SOUTH SHORE

Blue Ribbon Fishing Charters

Skipper John Hinson, who has been fishing Lake Tahoe since 1969, is a light tackle specialist. He makes daily runs for Mackinaw trout and kokanee salmon from the Tahoe Keys Marina, fishing year-round, primarily along the South Shore; trips depart in the morning and last approximately five hours. Hinson uses an open Lund skiff with an outboard motor, and has a trolling motor and electric downriggers. He carries limited parties of no more than four passengers. Your catch is cleaned, filleted, and bagged. Open and private charters are accepted. One-day fishing licenses are available. Rods, tackle, bait, and beverages are included.

Contact: Blue Ribbon Fishing Charters, 1262 Pine Valley Rd., South Lake Tahoe, CA 96150; 530/541-8801 or 530/573-0400; website: www.tahoedigital.com/blueribbon.

Dennis' Eagle Point Sport Fishing

At Tahoe Keys Marina at South Lake Tahoe, skipper Dennis Mitchell fishes for Mackinaw and kokanee, using a variety of methods that include trolling, light-tackle jigging, and drifting with minnows. His new 26-foot Sea Swirl cabin cruiser can take two to six anglers for five hours, leaving both mornings and afternoons. Mitchell will fish any part of the California side of the lake, depending on where fish are holding, but is most productive jigging. He's set up with new electronic fish finders and carries custom trolling rods with level-wind Ambassador reels and Fenwick light spinning rods equipped with six-pound test monofilament for drifting. Mitchell has fished the lake since 1971. He fishes year-round, and in summer he does two trips a day, one leaving before sunrise, the other after 12 P.M. Mitchell concentrates on kokanee salmon in late July and August, but will combine kokanee and Mackinaw on the same trip if clients desire. Mitchell supplies all bait and equipment, coffee and sodas. He'll also clean or fillet your catch.

Contact: Dennis' Eagle Point Sport Fishing, P.O. Box 9536, South Lake Tahoe, CA 96151; 530/577-6834 or 530/957-6169 (boat).

First Strike Sportfishing

Chris Ziegler, a U.S. Coast Guard–licensed captain, has more than 10 years of fishing experience on Lake Tahoe. Using Tahoe Keys Marina at South Lake Tahoe as his base, he operates a sleek, 24-foot Lund motor cruiser with a heated sports cabin. Ziegler can carry six passengers but prefers to fish four. He seeks out Mackinaw by jigging with light tackle and drift-fishing, and goes for the rainbows and browns by top-lining on the surface. His primary fishing grounds are along the west shore (California side) of the lake. Fishing trips can be arranged for either the morning or late afternoon, and all charters include bait, tackle, free coffee, snacks, and other refreshments. Your catch will be cleaned and sacked.

Fees: $80 per person for five-hour charters, $95 for seven-hour charters (including lunch).

Contact: First Strike Sportfishing, P.O. Box 13107, South Lake Tahoe, CA 96151; 530/577-5065; website: www.sportfishingtahoe.com.

Four Reel Sportfishing

Using a new, custom-built 32-foot Farallon motorcruiser, guide Neil Cohn offers fishing in comfort, with a heated cabin, private head, refrigerator, modern fish-finding electronics, Cannon downriggers, outriggers, and Shimano/Penn fishing rods and reels. All gear is provided. Cohn, who has fished the lake for a dozen years, top-lines, jigs and even drifts with live bait, for Mackinaw, German brown trout, rainbows and kokanee salmon. Charters run year-around, and a continental breakfast is available for the early risers. With a boat this size, there's room for family and friends, up to six people. Operates from Tahoe Keys Marina, making morning and afternoon runs of four to five hours each.

Contact: Four Reel Sportfishing, South Lake Tahoe, CA 96150; 530/543-1353 or 530/721-0436; website: www.fourreelsportfishing.com.

Hernandez Guide Service

A veteran guide, on Lake Tahoe since 1973, skipper Bruce Hernandez specializes in jigging, which he prefers over trolling because of its more interactive nature. His trips depart from Tahoe Keys Marina in South Lake Tahoe once a day in the morning on his 25-foot Tiara Pursuit cruiser, which is equipped with a Chevy 350 inboard/outboard engine, a trolling motor, a cabin, fish-finders, and a variety of tackle. He uses Fenwick 6.5-foot rods with Ambassador level-wind reels, 14-pound test Spider Wire, and Bomber jigs with minnows. He uses downriggers for Mackinaw, and trolls and jigs for kokanee. Hernandez fishes mostly the West and North Shores of the lake, although he moves to the South Shore in October. Occasionally he drifts for rainbow and brown trout, working the shoreline and the drop-offs to 70 feet. He'll take up to six anglers but he prefers to take four. Hernandez operates April–November. He provides all bait and tackle, coffee, soda, or beer.

Contact: Hernandez Guide Service, P.O. Box 11689, Tahoe Paradise, CA 96155; 530/577-2246.

Mile High Fishing Charters

Born and raised at Lake Tahoe, Joby Cefalu is another recent addition to the burgeoning ranks of local fishing guides, having started his charter service in 1999. He'll take four anglers in his new, 22-foot Bayliner Trophy, which is fully equipped with the latest electronics, an enclosed cockpit, cabin, and head. Cefalu sticks to three

FISHING

fishing methods—top-lining, jigging, and trolling or drifting with downriggers. Although he is based out of the Tahoe Keys Marina, he will pick up anglers from any part of the lake. And when you walk on board in the morning, you won't be getting cold doughnuts; you'll be treated to piping hot homemade breakfast burritos—just the ticket for getting your engines warmed up. Cefalu provides all tackle, using Ugly Stick rods and Abu-Garcia reels. He runs morning, afternoon and evening charters, and fish are cleaned and bagged.

Contact: Mile High Fishing Charters, P.O. Box 17028, South Lake Tahoe, CA 96151; 530/541-5312 or 866/552-FISH; website: www.fishtahoe.com.

Rick Muller's Sport Fishing

The jig is up, or rather down, with skipper Rick Muller, who has made jigging his passion, recently producing an instructional video on jigging techniques in Tahoe. Muller, one of the self-styled "new breed" of angler and co-owner of the Sportsman outdoor equipment store in South Lake Tahoe, zips from one end of the lake to the other in his speedy 24-foot Bayliner Trophy and boasts a 90 percent limit success rate for Mackinaw trout. He also fishes for kokanee salmon. Moving frequently to find fish is his modus operandi. "It's nothing for me to put 60 miles a day on the boat," he says. Muller jigs with a minnow and four-ounce Bomber setup, usually in 100 to 200 feet of water. He's got the latest in electronic fish-finding gear and has made something of an art out of locating fish. He uses 6.5-foot rods with limber tips, level-wind reels, and 13- to 17-pound test monofilament line. Muller, who works out of the Sportsman shop in South Lake Tahoe, leaves seven days a week from Tahoe Keys Marina and can take four to six anglers.

Contact: Rick Muller's Sport Fishing, P.O. Box 8773, South Lake Tahoe, CA 96158; 530/544-4358 or 530/542-3474 (The Sportsman).

Don Sheetz Guide Service

Trolling and jigging are the main pursuits of veteran guide Don Sheetz, who has been fishing the lake since 1968. He runs a 22-foot Starcraft with a Chevy V-6 Vortex motor and is equipped with a cuddy cabin, live well, bait tank, Porta-Potty, ice box, electronic fish-finder, electric downriggers, and an array of fishing tackle. Sheetz leaves from the Tahoe Keys Marina and operates April–October, taking up to six anglers. He trolls about three-quarters of the time with various lures and blades, using Walker downriggers and steel line, and jigs the rest of the time with the standard minnow-and-Bomber setup. His custom-built rods use 6-pound line on Abu-Garcia reels. He makes one five-hour run per morning and covers waters from Edgewood Tahoe Golf Course in the south to Sugar Pine Point State Park on the West Shore, working both Mackinaw and, when the bite is on, kokanee salmon. Trips include fishing gear, tackle, bait, sweet rolls, coffee, and soda, and cleaning and sacking your catch.

Contact: Don Sheetz Guide Service, P.O. Box 13631, South Lake Tahoe, CA 96151; 530/541-5566 or 877/270-0742; website: www.tahoefishingguides.com.

Tahoe Angler Sportfishing

Guide Tim Hennessy, a master light tackle specialist, practices what he preaches. His recent catch of a 29-pound Mackinaw, the largest that Tahoe has given up since the mid-1980s (the record is 37 pounds-plus), puts him in an elite group of anglers. Hey, just to hear him tell the tale is worth the trip on his boat. Any doubts? If so, then you can go directly to his website where there is a photo of the beaming Hennessy holding his trophy lake trout. Of course, he's got a worthy vessel to do battle with the wily Macks—a 27-foot Farallon sport fishing boat that has modern fish-finding electronics, a spacious heated cabin, a large deck and all necessary tackle. Operating from South Lake Tahoe, Hennessy runs trips for two to six anglers year-round, and cleans and sacks your fish. Both morning and sunset charters are available.

Contact: Tahoe Angler Sportfishing, 1012 Industrial Ave., South Lake Tahoe, CA 96150; 530/542-2019; website: www.tahoeangler.com.

Tahoe Sportfishing

With six boats, ranging from 26 feet to 45 feet, captain John Schearer has the largest fishing charter operation at Lake Tahoe. Originally formed in 1953, the company is headquartered at Ski Run Marina (now Marina Village) in South Lake Tahoe, but also has a satellite operation at Zephyr Cove Resort on the Nevada side of the lake. Schearer caters to corporate groups, families, and casino guests from Stateline, and runs more than 1,600 trips per year. His Mackinaw vessels include a 34-foot Sportfisher with twin diesel engines, two 31-foot Island Hoppers, a 26-foot Offshore Fisherman, and a 26-foot Farallon Sportfisherman. All have cabins and heaters and can take from three to 12 anglers. Queen of the fleet, and the largest fishing boat on the lake, is a 45-foot Delta called the *Prophet*, a saltwater-style party boat typical of San Francisco salmon vessels. It has a caverous heated cabin and can take up to 35 passengers, though most Tahoe anglers would not care to fish with a crowd that size. The vessel is often used by school and university groups as a kind of floating lab for environmental studies, as well as by scuba divers for chartered trips. The 34-footer, the *Dory-L*, is a luxurious motor yacht with a spacious cabin, a flying bridge, and a large deck, and it's used mostly for family groups. All of the boats and their skippers offer a combination of fishing techniques for Mackinaw, including slow trolling, jigging, and drifting with live minnows. Boats also surface-troll for rainbow and brown trout. The larger vessels are equipped with both downriggers and outriggers and a selection of custom-made, 7.5-foot medium-light rods set up with salmon-sinker release systems. Trips include fishing gear, tackle, bait, sweet rolls, coffee, beer, and soda, and cleaning and sacking your catch. Guides can also arrange to have your fish delivered to selected Lake Tahoe restaurants for lunch or dinner. During the trout season, Schearer can arrange guided fly-fishing trips on local streams and lakes. Company offices are at 900 Ski Run Blvd. in South Lake Tahoe, next to the *Tahoe Queen* paddle wheeler, and at Zephyr Cove Marina north of Stateline.

Contact: Tahoe Sportfishing, 900 Ski Run Blvd., South Lake Tahoe, CA 96150; 530/696-7797 or 800/696-7797; Zephyr Cove at 775/586-9338; website: www.tahoesportfishing.com.

Tahoe Trophy Trout

Skipper Gene St. Denis operates what he calls "A Year-Round VIP Guide Service." He launches his 19.5-foot Alumaweld Boat from El Dorado ramp in South Lake Tahoe, and from there fishes for Mackinaw, rainbows, browns and kokanee, using topline techniques during winter and Scotty downriggers in summer. In fact, in winter, when most people are on the ski slopes or warming up the slot machines in the casinos, St. Denis is at his best. In 1998 he landed 98 brown trout, and during the first six months of 1999 he landed 22 Mackinaw that were over 10 pounds. He gets around quite well in his new boat, which is powered by a four-stroke 90 hp Honda outboard. The vessel has a full canopy with sides and back, new fish finding electronics, VHF marine radio, Scotty downriggers, and an assortment of rods, reels and tackle. The boat can carry one to four passengers, and St. Denis offers half-day to full-day charters.

Contact: Tahoe Trophy Trout, P.O. Box 17440, South Lake Tahoe, CA 96151; 530/544-6552 or 530/318-1497 (cell phone).

Tahoe Topliners

He may be one of the new kids on the block when it comes to running a guide service, but Mike Nielsen, in his 20s, has been fishing Tahoe for a decade and has enough youthful enthusiasm to float a battleship. As the fishing operator at Historic Camp Richardson Resort on the South Shore, Nielsen specializes in light tackle trolling for rainbows and browns—which are not exactly the easiest fish to catch in Tahoe. Using downriggers and 10-pound test monofilament—no lead-core lines—and a variety of artificial lures and live bait, he'll go anywhere on the lake in his zippy, 23-foot Starcraft Islander. If the bite slows on surface fishing, he'll do vertical jigging for Mackinaw, using minnows and lures. When the kokanee salmon are biting, he'll go after them, as well. In 1999, his debut year on the lake, Nielsen and his clients landed 22 fish that weighed between 10 and 21 pounds (including a

10.5-pound rainbow), which is not too shabby for a rookie guide. Nielsen supplies all terminal tackle, including rods and reels, along with coffee and donuts in the morning and snacks and drinks in the early evening. In summer, he'll do morning trips, departing between 5 A.M. and 6 A.M., and evening trips, leaving between 4 P.M. and 6 P.M. and returning by dark. Another bonus: He'll clean and bag your catch.

Contact: Tahoe Topliners, P.O. Box 410, South Lake Tahoe, CA 96156; 530/544-1526; website information at: www.tahoefishingguide.com.

STATELINE/ZEPHYR COVE

Avid Fisherman

This fishing service on Lake Tahoe was organized by Rob Janetti, whose family has lived in the area for a half-century and who has personally fished the lake for more than 35 years. Janetti sticks to the east shore on the Nevada side, from Sand Harbor in the north to Round Hill in the south. These waters are typically the best for topline trolling for rainbow and brown trout. He'll also fish for kokanee salmon when they're running, as well as the Tahoe mainstay—Mackinaw trout. His charter boat is a 25-foot Crestliner that is equipped with Furano Electronics, VHF radio, GPS, live fish wells for catch-and-release, a barbecue, and a head. He provides all bait and tackle, and uses Garcia graphite rods, Ambassadeur reels, and Scotty downriggers. Janetti prefers to fish with no more than four anglers but can carry up to six passengers, and children are always welcome. For his five- to six-hour trips, he'll provide a small lunch, snacks, and drinks. Janetti usually leaves from the public boat-launching area at Cave Rock, just north of Zephyr Cove in Nevada and a short drive from the Stateline casinos.

Fees: $75 per person.

Contact: Avid Fisherman, P.O. Box 11448, Zephyr Cove, NV 89448; 775/588-7675; website: www.avidfisherman.net.

O'Malley's Fishing Charters

Never on Sunday, says Leonard O'Malley, who'll not fish on the Sabbath, thank you. (Some-

body's got to pray for those big Macks to bite!) But on the other six days of the week, he scours the lake for Mackinaw, rainbow trout, and kokanee, using his late-model 22-foot Radoncraft, which is equipped with a walk-around cuddy cabin, an inboard/outboard engine, a trolling motor, and downriggers. He'll try almost anything to catch fish—except wire line. He trolls, jigs, and drifts but finds his best success with downriggers. O'Malley operates out of a pier near Zephyr Cove and spends most of his time working the Nevada shoreline and the waters off South Lake Tahoe. His favorite setup is a Shakespeare 8.5-foot Ugly Stick with an Abu-Garcia 6500 level-wind reel, but he also has a few light spinning rods with eight-pound test line for drifting with minnows. O'Malley's season generally runs March–November, and he'll take up to six anglers but prefers no more than four people for his five-hour morning charters. Rates include all gear and refreshments; cleaning and bagging your catch is provided. Clients meet at Zephyr Cove and are shuttled to the boat, one mile away.

Contact: O'Malley's Fishing Charters, P.O. Box 10598, Zephyr Cove, NV 89448; 775/588-4102.

Tahoe Sportfishing

(See listing, under City of South Lake Tahoe)

This large operation offers fishing out of Zephyr Cove Resort in Nevada.

CAPLES AND ALPINE COUNTY LAKES

Bruce "Bruno" Huff

The King of Caples, Bruno Huff is one of the premier trout-fishing guides in the area, a personable man with a knack for fishing and a zest for cooking. He's a chef at the Caples Lake Resort, which has achieved quite a reputation for its fine gourmet dining, but in between his stints in the kitchen he's out there fishing six days a week. His energy and sense of humor are reason enough to book him as a guide, but his fishing prowess is almost legendary. In 1995, he and his clients boated 1,187 trout and released 80 percent of them (at the request of his customers). Huff's main waters are Caples and the other lakes along Highway 88, including Silver, Bear River, Red, and Blue. He also fishes Topaz Lake and the East and West Forks of the Carson River. In winter, conditions permitting, he'll ice-fish in Caples for rainbow and Mackinaw trout, using the standard Swedish pimple along with feathered, crappie-style jigs. The rest of the time he trolls with lures such as FlatFish, Rapalas, Triple Teasers, Canadian Wonders, Torpedoes, and a variety of spoons. On the rivers, he fishes with a combination of flies and tackle. Huff uses Fenwick and Charlie Thomas rods and Shakespeare and Abu-Garcia level-wind reels. His boat is a 17-foot Boston Whaler equipped with both a 50-horsepower Mercury outboard and a 15-horsepower Johnson troller. All gear is provided. Bring your own snacks and beverages.

Contact: Bruno Huff, P.O. Box 263, Markleeville, CA 96120; 530/694-2145.

PYRAMID LAKE, NEVADA
Cutthroat Charters

George Molino owns Pyramid Lake Store, which is where most visiting anglers go to pay homage to the ingenuity of tackle producers and to seek wisdom in their quest to conquer the mighty cutthroat trout. If anybody knows how to coax a reluctant trout to the hook, it's Molino, who has been guiding on this massive lake for 10 years. He knows the best fishing spots, and he's got an arsenal of homemade lures and flies that he's tested on the battlefield. He's also got a brand new, custom-rigged, 26-foot Boulton vessel that has every bell and whistle one might need for Pyramid, including Cannon downriggers for trolling, Bottom Line depth-finders for spotting fish, and sufficient awning to cover up from the harsh desert sun. Molino, a member of the Paiute Tribe that owns and manages the lake, takes four to six anglers on four-hour, half-day trips, generally leaving at 7 A.M. and noon. He fishes Pelican Point, Warrior's Point and a few special places, using Apex lures, spoons and occasionally, Flatfish. If fish are in the shallows—usually in March and April when they are spawning—he'll also do guided fly-fishing trips for two to four anglers, and his store can provide waders for shore angling. Ask him about a killer pattern that looks like a beetle and is made from floating Neoprene, a bit of flashing material and a number 12 hook. The season runs October 1–June 30, and Molino leaves from the marina at Sutcliffe. Note: A Tribal permit is an additional $6 per day and is required, though a Nevada state fishing license is not required. You can obtain permits, along with snacks, sandwiches and drinks, at Pyramid Lake Store.

Contact: Cutthroat Charters, 29555 Pyramid Hwy., Sutcliffe, NV 89510; 775/476-0555..

Fly-Fishing Guides and Schools

Suddenly, Truckee has become the fly-fishing capital of Northern California, with an explosion in the number of guides and charter services. Some stay for a season and then move on; the ones listed here were in business when this edition went to press. Those guides who have the most experience have been operating in the region for several years. Typically, they have advanced to a stage in which they are creating their own fly patterns and are working the area's streams and still waters with a high rate of success and proficiency. One thing that all guides promote is teaching the first-time or novice fly fisher, which comprises the largest share of their clientele.

Fees range $170–200 for half-day trips, and $180–275 for full-day trips with lunch. Quotes are usually based on either one angler or two, so the best deal involves taking a friend or significant other. Many guides also give fly-fishing clinics that cover casting techniques, entomology, knots, flies and reading the water. These range $185–250 per person per day, and usually last for two days. If you want to rent gear and go on your own, local fly and fishing shops offer combo packages that include waders, rod and reel, and sometimes float tubes, for $30–40 per day.

TRUCKEE/DONNER

California School of Flyfishing

Ralph and Lisa Cutter, husband-and-wife instructors, have achieved a great reputation for their fly-fishing school in Truckee, which they've operated since 1981. Lisa, one of a handful of certified female fly-fishing guides, punches out 100-foot casts with great dexterity. The Cutters' classes run May–mid-November, with both stillwater and fast-water experience, at venues that usually include the Truckee River and Martis Creek Lake. Introductory two-day courses with one to three anglers include textbook, all gear, and deli lunch each day, and cost $489. Classroom sessions are done at the Cutters' home in Truckee. Another two-day course for intermediates, called "The

Complete Flyfisher," fishes both freestone and stillwater and runs $489 per person, including deli lunch. Anglers are urged to bring their own gear. Ralph, a firefighter in Incline Village, and Lisa do most of the teaching, assisted by other instructors. The couple uses a variety of rods, including Loomis, Fenwick, Sage, and Scott. In 2000, the Cutters achieved a major milestone: They were inducted into the Fly Fishing Hall of Fame in Montana. Ralph is the author of *Sierra Trout Guide,* a comprehensive coffee-table-sized book that is the definitive work on California's coldwater fisheries. The Cutters do not offer guided trips in the Tahoe region.

Contact: California School of Flyfishing, P.O. Box 8212, Truckee, CA 96162; 530/587-7005 or 800/58-TROUT (800/588-7688); website: www.flyline.com.

Four Seasons Fly Fishing

Brian Slusser has lived at Lake Tahoe since 1993. During the winter he's a Professional Ski Patroller, but when spring arrives he's out on the mountain streams and lakes to tease the trout. Slusser fishes the lower Truckee River, the Little Truckee River, and Boca and Prosser reservoirs. People who are new to fly-fishing, including women and children, are his favorite clients. He'll do fly casting clinics for one or two days, as well as four-day immersion sessions with lessons and on-the-water experience. Slusser favors dry flies with green drake, caddis, and stonefly patterns. He'll take up to up to four anglers, providing all gear, including float tubes for the lakes, and a selection of flies. Full-day trips include a box lunch.

Contact: Four Seasons Fly Fishing, P.O. Box 5122, Tahoe City, CA 96145; 530/550-9780.

Johnson Tackle and Guide Service

How about mountain biking and fly-fishing together? Guide Randy Johnson offers this option in the Bowman Lake region of Tahoe National Forest, which is northwest of Truckee above Lake Spaulding. As a guide in the area since 1978, he

cycles to a half dozen backcountry lakes on Forest Service roads, with rides no longer than 90 minutes. And he's a veritable supply house of gear—with carbon-frame bikes, float tubes, custom flies, custom fishing rods by Spirit Rod Works (a local company), and other tackle. Johnson's other prime spots are the Truckee River, from the catch-and-release section beginning at Trout Creek to the Nevada state line; Lake Davis in Plumas National Forest north of Truckee; and the Truckee trio of Boca, Stampede, and Prosser Creek Reservoirs and their tributaries. He customizes all trips to a client's skill level, and focuses on novices. He will even take newcomers—including youngsters 12 and older—on the Truckee River for personalized instruction on casting, reading the water, and stream entomology. On the river, he generally uses subsurface nymphs such as free-floating caddis larva. Short-line indicator nymphing is the main fishing method. At Lake Davis, Johnson fishes the offshore weed beds for big Eagle Lake trout (averaging 16 to 22 inches), using damselfly patterns and other stillwater techniques. All fishing is catch-and-release. The season is April–mid-November. He'll supply all gear, including rods, flies and waders, at no extra charge, and also provides sodas and lunch.
Contact: Johnson Tackle and Guide Service, P.O. Box 26, Tahoma, CA 96142; 530/525-6575; website: www.flyfishingtahoe.com.

Riffleworks

Tim O'Connor, a professional ski instructor for 20 years, has a knack for teaching people the finer points of outdoor sports—and flyfishing is his warm-weather passion. A native of Pennsylvania and a guide in Vermont for six years, O'Connor has been fishing in the Tahoe region since 1989. He specializes in taking anglers to the smaller creeks and tributaries near Truckee and in other parts of the Tahoe National Forest. His favorites are the Little Truckee River, Sagehen Creek, Donner Creek, Martis Creek "and a few places that I won't mention." He tends to shy away from the lower reaches of the Truckee River because of its difficulty for all but the most experienced fly fishers. He prefers beginning fly fishers, who comprise about 40

percent of his clientele. To get them started, he offers two-day casting clinics, with 20 hours of instruction, on local waters. In addition to the smaller streams, O'Connor runs float fishing trips on the Middle Fork of the Feather River and float tube fishing on Milton Lake, both of which are about an hour's drive from Truckee. Trips can be for five hours to a full day. Riffleworks can handle groups of up to a dozen people, and has enough gear, including waders and wading shoes, to outfit all of them. He brings sandwiches and sodas for half-day trips and a hearty lunch for the full-day outings.
Contact: Riffleworks, 12277 Sierra Dr. E, Truckee, CA 96161; 530/582-8660.

John Roberts

A resident of Truckee, Roberts guides fly anglers in his back yard—mostly the lower Truckee River, considered one of the best, and at the same time, one of the most challenging flyfishing streams in America. He specializes in taking beginners, and draws much of his clientele from the major North Shore hotels. Roberts says he enjoys showing neophytes the skills of casting, reading the water, and understanding the entomology of the river. He provides all necessary gear, including waders, and will take up to two anglers at a time.
Contact: John Roberts, 10570 Rosa Court, Truckee, CA 96161; 530/582-8548; website: www.fishtheleader.com.

Thy Rod and Staff Flyfishing

Veteran guide Frank Pisciotta, who has fished in California for more than 35 years, guides on the trophy trout waters of the Truckee River from Trout Creek, east of town, downstream to Floriston; Martis Creek Lake; Milton Reservoir below Jackson Meadows Reservoir; and the North Fork of the Yuba River. Lake Tahoe's only Orvis-endorsed guide, Pisciotta requires catch-and-release fishing and the use of barbless hooks, regardless of regulations. All skill levels are welcome, and he will guide/instruct to the specific desires of the client. He can supply Orvis rods and reels, leaders, tippets, and flies for no extra charge, as well as a light lunch, snacks and bev-

erages. Trips are wading and float-tubing, with float tubes provided if needed. Additionally, Pisciotta runs The Reel School of Fly Fishing, offering two-day basic skills clinics as well as special clinics for women only, float-tube and pontoon boat fishing on stillwaters, and intermediate casters. All instruction is "on stream."
Contact: Thy Rod and Staff Flyfishing, P.O. Box 10038, Truckee, CA 96162; 530/587-7333; website: www.cyberfly.com.

Truckee River Outfitters and Fly Shop
This is a seasonal business that is operated as a Tahoe satellite of the well-respected Reno Fly Shop (see below). It offers trips from a half-dozen guides, and also sells a variety of flies and other fly-fishing tackle. These guides fish the lower Truckee River, Little Truckee, Martis Lake, Milton Lake and Prosser Reservoir. The store is open 9 A.M.–6 P.M. daily, April–October.
Contact: Truckee River Outfitters and Fly Shop, 10200 Donner Pass Rd., Truckee, CA 96161; 530/582-0900; website: www.renoflyshop.com.

SOUTH SHORE
Alpine Fly Fishing
A veteran with more than 30 years of experience, Jim Crouse provides lessons and guided trips in the prime waters of Alpine County south of Tahoe, including the East and West Forks of the Carson River, Wolf Creek, and Silver Creek (both tributaries of the Carson River's East Fork), and, occasionally, Indian Creek Reservoir. Recently he became director of the Pleasant Valley Fly Fishing Preserve near Markleeville, which is open to small groups of anglers on a daily permit/fee basis. Crouse fishes for native rainbows in the upper reaches of the East Fork of the Carson River, as well as the catch-and-release section on the lower river from Hangman's Bridge to the Nevada border. His territory ranges from Hope Valley to Markleeville, between Highways 88 and 4. Crouse uses caddis and mayfly patterns when hatches are on, but most of the time fishing is subsurface with flies such as woolly buggers. "I try to get away with the biggest and strongest patterns that I can, and go small only when I

have to," he says. He has some specialty flies that he ties and provides to his clients. Crouse also fishes Lost Lake, Granite Lake, Tamarack Lake, and other waters in the Blue Lakes region. Crouse will plan morning or evening trips or a combination; he prefers weekday outings. Included are transportation from South Lake Tahoe, rod and reel, flies, and beverages. In addition to guided trips, Crouse offers private fly-tying lessons.
Contact: Alpine Fly Fishing, P.O. Box 10465, South Lake Tahoe, CA 96158; 530/542-0759; website: www.worldwidefishing.com/california/b487/.

Trout Creek Flies and Guiding
South Shore fly-fishing aficionado Geoff Beer, who has developed many local fly patterns, offers a complete guide service, including introductory fly-fishing classes, advanced dry fly and nymphing classes, and private lake and stream fishing. A well-known conservationist with over 20 years of experience fishing local waters, Beer will take anglers to the east and west forks of the Carson River, Indian Creek Reservoir, the Truckee River, and the east and west forks of the Walker River. The big attraction, of course, is that you will be able to field-test his custom fly patterns first-hand.
Contact: Trout Creek Flies, P.O. Box 11528, Zephyr Cove, NV 89448; 530/541-1589; website: www.tahoedigital.com/troutcreek.

Tahoe Fly Fishing Outfitters
A dozen fishing guides, including Victor Babbitt, the owner of the store, can offer fly-fishing excursions to streams and alpine lakes in both California and Nevada, as well as guided trips on Lake Tahoe. Waters include the East and West Forks of the Carson River, the East and West Forks of the Walker River, the Upper and Lower Truckee River, Pleasant Valley Creek, Taylor Creek, Trout Creek, Spooner Lake, Heenan Lake, Caples Lake, Raymond Lake, Topaz Lake, Hinkson Slough, Round Lake, Dardanelles Lake, and Desolation Wilderness. The store, which opened in 1994, carries a full supply of flies and other tackle, including rental gear such as waders, fins, float tubes, and rod/reel combinations.

FISHING

Contact: Tahoe Fly Fishing Outfitters, P.O. Box 1224, South Lake Tahoe, CA 96156; 530/541-8208.

KIRKWOOD/HOPE VALLEY/MARKLEEVILLE

Horse Feathers Fly Fishing School

Instructor Judy Warren has owned this school since 1970 and has based it out of scenic Sorensen's Resort in Alpine County since 1983. Her specialty is teaching novice anglers, particularly women and children, in a congenial, nonintimidating environment. Using the streams of Hope Valley, she provides quality, custom-made equipment, to all clients and teaches them the basics, such as casting, reading water, knot-tying, streamside entomology, and selecting flies. She is active in the organization California Trout and is the author of Angling Alpine, a field guide to the rivers, streams, and 60 lakes of the county. Warren is also associated with Little Antelope Pack Station, which offers guided trips into Carson-Iceberg Wilderness on horseback.

Contact: Horse Feathers Fly Fishing School, Sorensen's Resort, Hwy. 88, Hope Valley, CA 96120; 530/694-2399.

FEATHER RIVER COUNTRY/ LAKES BASIN

Baiocchi's Plumas-Sierra Troutfitters

Fly-fishing guides are not exactly prolific in the small communities of Plumas County north of Truckee, but Jon Baiocchi has staked his claim to the lightly fished Middle Fork of the Feather River, the wild trout waters of Yellow Creek, and the born-again Lake Davis. Baiocchi uses a 14-foot aluminum boat for Davis—good for approaching the shallows where he prefers to stalk fish—and a pontoon boat for floating the Feather. He fishes a 15-mile stretch of the river from Clio downstream. Baiocchi will take fly fishers of all ability levels, and specializes in beginners. He also holds one- and two-day casting clinics in the millpond behind his house in Graeagle, in case neophytes prefer to learn proper techniques on still water before hitting a stream. Baiocchi can take two anglers at a time, and will provide rods, tackle, float tubes, flies, liquids and lunch.

Fees: $200 per day for one person, or $250 for two people. Casting clinics are $125 per person per day.

Contact: Baiocchi's Plumas-Sierra Troutfitters, P.O. Box 1035, Graeagle, CA 96103; 530/836-1115.

C&R Guide Service

Ralph Wood, who spent his apprentice years in New Hampshire learning fly-fishing on small freestone brooks and streams, brings his ample talents to the Sierra Nevada. A well-known fishing guide and fly-tying expert who lectures extensively, Wood fishes the North Fork of the Yuba River (among the few guides to do so), the Middle Fork of the Feather River, and the lower stretch of the Truckee. Anglers looking to escape the well-beaten waters of the Truckee might well consider an outing on the Yuba below the quaint town of Sierra City, which is one of the most picturesque mountain hamlets in the state. Here, the river has native rainbows and browns up to 20 inches in length, and special Fish and Game regulations require the use of barbless artificial lures with single hooks, a minimum-sized fish of 10 inches, and a limit of two. Sierra City, by the way, is a great place to stay with its quaint resorts, bed-and-breakfast inns, and proximity to the spectacular Sierra Buttes and Lakes Basin Recreation Area. On full day packages, Wood supplies a light lunch. He also furnishes all necessary flies, leaders and tippets. Fly fishers with at least moderate experience will probably best appreciate his services and knowledge.

Fees: $125 for a half day, $200 for a full day, and $50 more for a second angler.

Contact: C&R Guide Service, 619 Kate Hayes St., #3, Grass Valley, CA 95945; 530/477-0780; website: www.wildtrout.com.

Flyfish with Don

Don Rotsma teaches high school physics and chemistry in Reno most of the year, but when fishing season rolls around, he's hard at play in his main stamping grounds at Lake Davis, where he lives. With more than 30 years of experience, Rotsma offers both flyfishing courses, such as an introduction to Stillwater, and guided trips. He frequents other waters in the area, as well, including Martis and Milton lakes. For Davis and other lakes, he uses a 17-foot bass boats with swivel chairs, but often unloads anglers to wade or tube in selected areas. Clients should bring their own gear. Classes cover local entomology and fly selection, casting, equipment, wading, tubing and boating strategies.

Fees: $125 for a half day, $165 for a full day, and $25–35 more, respectively, for a second angler. Overnight trips, with two days and one evening of fishing, are $300 per angler, including lunches, dinner, snacks and drinks. Overnight camping and room accommodations are extra and by request.

Contact: Don Rotsma, 86 Pinehaven Ln., Lake Davis (Portola) CA 96122; 530/832-4047; website: www.flyfishwithdon.com.

Stillwater Guide Services

Reno flyfishing guide Chris Wharton, who has fished local stillwaters for more than 15 years, offers personalized service. His goal is to impart clients with the knowledge and skills to hook more and larger trout, and he specializes in reservoirs such as Davis Lake, Jackson Meadow Lake and Milton Lake, along with Martis Creek Reservoir. Clients will learn how to read water and locate spots where fish hold. At Davis, Wharton homes in on the major hatches of damselflies and blood midges. He uses float tubes, wading and casting from shore as his prime methods of stalking trout.

Fees: $195 per day for one person, $225 for two; half-day is $135 for one, $165 for two. Half-day beginners introduction to Stillwater fishing is $150, and covers casting, equipment, fly selection, use of a float tube, and three hours of flyfishing. Two-day overnight trips are $395 per person, $495 for two, and include meals and beverages (accommodations on your own.) All full-day trips include hot barbecue lunch and beverages. Float tubes and waders can be supplied if needed.

Contact: Stillwater Guide Services, Reno, NV; 775/747-0312 or 888/867-2127; website: www.out4trout.com.

RENO/CARSON VALLEY

Reno Fly Shop

One of a handful of fly-fishing shops in northern Nevada, the Reno Fly Shop, owned by Dave Stanley, has about a half-dozen guides who book their outings exclusively through the shop. They fish the Truckee River in both California and Nevada, the Little Truckee River, both forks of the Walker River, and Martis Creek, Davis, Heenan, Frenchman, and Milton Lakes. The shop is also a good source of information for fishing Pyramid Lake. If you like variety, you can book a half-and-half combo—morning on Martis Creek Lake and evening on the Little Truckee River. The Nevada section of the Truckee is legally fishable year-round (and is generally below the snowline in winter).

The Orvis-endorsed shop also conducts regular fly-tying clinics, two-day dry-land casting seminars in Reno and Truckee, clinics on nymphing and dry fly-fishing, women-only sessions, and, once a year, clinics for youngsters 10 and older. A full selection of local fly patterns is available at the shop, where clients meet. All fishing is strictly catch-and-release. The season runs year-round, depending on the body of water. Clients are encouraged to bring their own gear, but gear is available at no charge. Hours are 10 A.M.–6 P.M. Monday–Thursday and 8 A.M.–6 P.M. Friday, Saturday, and Sunday.

The shop offers a one-day introduction to fly-fishing clinic, as well as one-day on-stream clinics on nymphing, stillwater fishing and dry fly-fishing.

Contact: Reno Fly Shop, 294 E. Moana Ln. #14, Reno, NV 89502; 775/825-FISH (775/825-3474) or 775/827-0600; email: renoflyshop@powernet.net; website: www.renoflyshop.com.

On the Trail

Sooner or later, almost everyone who comes to Lake Tahoe has the urge to explore the natural wonders that surround the basin. There are several options for anyone wanting to hoof it: high-country hiking, nature trails, or *literally* hoofing it—on horseback.

Hiking in the high country takes you to flowering meadows and indigo alpine lakes, granite peaks and volcanic buttes, verdant fir forests and towering waterfalls. Perhaps nowhere in the West, with the exception of Yosemite, is there such geologic diversity and inspirational scenery. Surely, for anyone who travels the globe, there is little comparison to the hypnotic beauty of Emerald Bay. Scramble to the top of one of Tahoe's 10,000-foot peaks and the whole of creation seems to unfold below: the Sierra in its rugged majesty, with the arid valleys of Carson and Washoe snuggling up to the eastern slopes. If you head out on Tahoe's trails, be prepared for considerable elevation gain on some routes, where your heart and lungs will get a workout. But you can also enjoy a rewarding hike with only modest effort on routes that skirt the basin's shoreline or begin at high-altitude trailheads reachable by car or sightseeing tram.

With few exceptions, the majority of trails are on public lands, usually those that the U.S. Forest Service manages. These are the five forest jurisdictions in the region:
• Lake Tahoe Basin Management Unit, which encompasses the Tahoe rim and the drainages that face the lake.
• Eldorado National Forest, which includes U.S. 50 west of South Lake Tahoe, Crystal Basin Recreation Area to the west of South Lake

kids enjoying Tahoe on horseback

Tahoe, and Highway 88 from Silver Lake to Carson Pass.

• Plumas National Forest, which contains the Lakes Basin and Feather River drainage near the resort community of Graeagle and northwest of Truckee and I-80.

• Tahoe National Forest, which embraces much of the North Shore between Tahoe City and Truckee, part of the crest above the West Shore, Donner Pass, the Sierra Buttes, Highway 89 north of Truckee, and most of the Lakes Basin.

• Toiyabe National Forest, which covers Mt. Rose, Spooner Summit, and the Carson Range on the East Shore, and most of the high country on Highway 88 from its junction with Highway 89 east toward Markleeville and Gardnerville.

Apart from federal lands, both California and Nevada have trail systems in their state parks. In California, these include D. L. Bliss, Sugar Pine Point, Donner Memorial, Emerald Bay, Burton Creek (undeveloped), Washoe Lake, Lake Valley State Recreation Area, Tahoe State Recreation Area, Plumas Eureka, and Grover Hot Springs. In Nevada, the 14,000-acre Lake Tahoe-Nevada State Park is the largest in the region; it embraces Sand Harbor, Spooner Lake, and Cave Rock. Also, a profusion of county, city, and public utility (PG&E) recreation areas offer trails. Throughout the region, trails can cross private lands, and hikers should respect any No Trespassing signs they may encounter.

WILDERNESS AREAS, TRAILS, AND PERMITS

Within the national forests bordering Tahoe are four official wilderness areas: Desolation, Granite Chief, Mt. Rose, and Mokelumne. A wilderness designation means that access is restricted to hiking and horseback riding, and no mechanized vehicles—such as mountain bikes, four-wheel-drive vehicles, and hang gliders—are allowed. Although trails are generally maintained, hiking in wilderness can be a raw, challenging experience. When you venture into one, be prepared for anything, from high-water stream crossings to sudden storms to forest fires.

Desolation Wilderness

The most popular hiking/backpacking destination in the region, Desolation Wilderness has 63,475 acres of subalpine forests, granite peaks, and glacially formed valleys. There are 130 reasons why so many people come here, all of them lakes—fabulous, deep-blue gems scattered across a rocky landscape. Elevations range from 6,500 feet to over 10,000 feet, and sometimes passes and saddles may be snowbound well into midsummer. Alpine timber and flora abound along most of the access routes but thin considerably at the higher elevations. You can enter Desolation from the west out of Crystal Basin Recreation Area (the least crowded alternative), from the east out of Lake Tahoe, or from the south at Echo Lakes on the Pacific Crest Trail. The heaviest use occurs at the Eagle Falls, Fallen Leaf, Echo, and Wrights Trailheads.

As might be expected, Desolation has the most stringent regulations. Backcountry campers, for instance, must obtain permits by reservation or by personally visiting a Forest Service office. From the Friday before Memorial Day to September 30, there is a quota of 564 overnight users per day (cut from 700 just a few years ago), with specific numbers of permits varying from one entry point to the other, although a single permit may be issued for up to 12 people. Half of the quota permits can be reserved up to 90 days in advance, by phone or in person, and half are issued on the actual day of entry on a first-come, first-served basis. The permit must specify a particular date of entry and a particular trailhead. (There are 45 "zones" that can be accessed from any of 15 trailheads; for a list of them, call or write to the appropriate Forest Service offices.) Thus far, day hikers have not been subject to restrictions. However, you must register at the trailheads for your free wilderness permit (one per party is OK) and carry a copy. Permit boxes are stationed at most trailheads; those without self-registration (mainly on the west entry points) require a visit to the nearest Forest Service office. Another major restriction in Desolation, which deters a number of backcountry campers, is the unconditional ban on open campfires; only portable gas stoves are allowed.

Fees: $5 per party (or per permit) to reserve an overnight access to Desolation Wilderness; date changes are an extra $5. Also, backcountry camping fees are required, at $5 per person for one night, or $10 per person for two or more nights up to 14 days (nonrefundable). The cost of a single permit will not exceed $100. Children 12 and under are free. You can also buy a $20 per person Annual Camping Pass, which is valid until December 31 of each year. Day hikers who enter the Wilderness from the Lake Tahoe side at Eagle Falls are required to pay a $3 parking fee. This is waived for overnight permit holders, but you must obtain a parking pass to be exempt.

Contact: You can write, fax, or call in your reservation for a permit for your first-night stay in any zone. Call 530/644-6048 (and have a credit card ready), fax a written request to 530/295-5624, or mail a request to the U.S. Forest Service, Eldorado National Forest, 3070 Camino Heights Dr., Camino, CA 95709. The Forest Service will not mail permits; you must pick them up in person at one of the designated offices. For west side entries to Desolation, you can pick up your permit at the Camino office, which is five miles east of Placerville on Highway 50, and is open daily 8 A.M.–5 P.M. From the east side (Lake Tahoe side), you can pick up your permit at the Lake Tahoe Visitor Center (near Camp Richardson), two blocks north of the "Y" (Highway 50/89 junction) in South Lake Tahoe on Hwy. 89; 530/573-2694, or at the office of the Lake Tahoe Basin Management Unit (next door at the Tallac Historic Site), 870 Emerald Bay Rd., Ste. 1, South Lake Tahoe, CA 96150; 530/573-2694; website: www.r5.fs.fed.us/ltbmu.

> *The most popular hiking/backpacking destination in the region, Desolation Wilderness has 63,475 acres of subalpine forests, granite peaks, and glacially formed valleys. There are 130 reasons why so many people come here, all of them lakes—fabulous, deep-blue gems scattered across a rocky landscape. Elevations range from 6,500 feet to over 10,000 feet, and sometimes passes and saddles may be snowbound well into midsummer.*

Granite Chief Wilderness

On the West Shore of Lake Tahoe, the 25,700-acre Granite Chief Wilderness borders the back of the Alpine Meadows and Squaw Valley ski areas, then extends southward toward Twin Peaks and Barker Pass. It includes several streams and the headwaters of the American River, and the terrain varies from granite cliffs to glaciated valleys. The southern section is forested with mixed conifer, red fir, and lodgepole pine at higher elevations, with deciduous and evergreen woodlands farther down. This wilderness isn't as crowded as Desolation (with the exception of the Five Lakes basin, a high-traffic area) and doesn't require a wilderness permit. However, campfire permits are required.

Contact: Tahoe National Forest, Hwy. 49 and Coyote St., Nevada City, CA 95959; 530/265-4531; website: www.r5.fs.fed.us/tahoe/.

Mokelumne Wilderness

Between Highways 88 and 4 south of South Lake Tahoe, Mokelumne Wilderness is the largest wilderness in the area, with 100,600 acres of remote backcountry, cut through by sections of the famous Mormon-Emigrant Trail. The elevation ranges from 4,000 feet near Salt Springs Reservoir to over 10,000 feet at Round Top. There are many small lakes in the valleys north of Mokelumne Peak, and vistas of the deep and rugged Mokelumne River Canyon. Wilderness permits are required May 25–September 15 for overnight users only. Campfires are allowed in many areas with a permit. However, campfires are not allowed at the following lakes: Frog, Winnemucca, Round Top, Fourth of July, and Emigrant, which are the most heavily used destinations in the wilderness. Dogs must be on leashes.

BACKCOUNTRY HIKING TIPS

Travelers into the wildlands of the Tahoe Sierra should always go prepared. Here are some things to keep in mind:

• Bring a compass, a Forest Service map, and a U.S. Geological Survey topographic map for the specific trail you're taking. Trust no map entirely. Contact the appropriate jurisdiction to find out the latest trail conditions, since slides, runoff, overgrowth, and other natural factors can alter routes from year to year.

• Wear sturdy hiking boots, not sneakers or sandals. Many of the trails have sharp granite scree, which can cut into thin-soled shoes.

• Wear thick hiking socks and use talcum or other drying powders liberally, and bring fresh socks to change midway through an all-day hike. Carry bandages or moleskin to treat emerging blisters before they become a problem.

• Carry a day pack. My preference is a large fanny pack, such as the type produced by Mark Pack of Oakland, with twin water bottles connected to the pack with cloth fasteners. This is more comfortable than a shoulder pack, which can dig in under your arms and impede blood circulation.

• No matter how gorgeous the weather may seem, it can change rapidly. Tahoe is known for its afternoon thundershowers, which can occur at any time of the summer, but particularly in June and July. This situation makes it absolutely imperative for you to bring raingear. Failing to do so can subject you to the risk of hypothermia, a potentially life-threatening situation. Lightweight raingear, such as fold-up ponchos and two-piece suits, will do the job.

• Carry a flashlight and matches—just in case you underestimate the time it takes to finish your hike and end up in the dark, trying to descend a rocky stairway.

• Bring extra layers of clothes. Temperatures can change radically between 6,000 feet and 9,000 feet, especially if you're climbing a peak. A sweater or sweatshirt and a windbreaker are minimal requirements.

• Don't be stingy with water. On full-day hikes, bring three water bottles (I prefer something with electrolytes such as Gatorade), or bring some water plus a water-purifying device such as a Katadyn filter. Although most hikes visit lakes or cross streams, some are on arid routes where you can't depend on finding an alternate water source.

• Be extremely careful when fording streams. During early summer, they can be dangerously high. Even in midsummer, the morning flows may be fordable while the afternoon flows can become high and treacherous. When crossing streams, you may wish to bring a pair of water slippers to protect your feet. Also, carry a hiking staff for stability.

• Do not bury or leave trash anywhere along the trail. Pack it out with you.

• In addition to a picnic lunch (one of the real treats of hiking), pack plenty of high-energy snacks such as gorp, hard candies, and nuts. Take more than you think you'll need.

• Bring a wide-brimmed hat, sunglasses, sunscreen, and lip balm. In summer, the sun can be ferocious, especially when reflected from hot granite rock.

• Bring a small first-aid kit to treat cuts and scrapes. You won't need to worry about poison oak in Tahoe—it doesn't grow above 5,000 feet.

• Always fill out the wilderness permit, when required, and let someone know when and where you're going and when you expect to return.

• Keep your dog on a leash. You may think that it's great to let Fido run free, but he could be a nuisance to other hikers or to wildlife. Most public lands that allow dogs require them to be leashed.

Contact: Eldorado National Forest, Eldorado Information Center, 3070 Camino Heights Dr., Camino, CA 95709; 530/644-6048; website: www.r5.fs.fed.us/eldorado/.

Mt. Rose Wilderness

Northeast of Lake Tahoe above Incline Village on the west side of the Mt. Rose Highway (Highway 431), the 28,000-acre Mt. Rose Wilderness offers outstanding views of Tahoe and the Great Basin areas above Reno in Nevada. This is mostly steep, arid land with mixed conifer and red fir forests, ranging from 6,000 feet to 10,000 feet, and there are very few lakes. Mountain meadows, however, offer a profusion of wildflowers. There is access at four trails, and all except the trail to Mt. Rose receive light use. Part of the reason for this is that the U.S. Forest Service, as of this edition, had not produced a detailed map, and no trail maps are available. Also, there are trails that originate outside of the wilderness and go into it, such as one from Galena Creek County Park. No wilderness permits are required at present, but overnight users must obtain a campfire permit, and portable stoves are encouraged.

Contact: Toiyabe National Forest, Carson Ranger District, 1536 S. Carson St., Carson City, NV 89701; 775/882-2766; website: www.fs.fed.us/htnf/.

MAJOR TRAILS

Pacific Crest National Scenic Trail

Many of the day hikes and extended backcountry trips in the Lake Tahoe basin involve this famous trail (PCT), which, in its entirety, stretches 2,638 miles from Mexico to Canada. The concept of a hiking and horseback trail spanning the West Coast had been around since the 1920s, but it wasn't until passage of the National Trails System Act in 1968 that the PCT began to take shape. Under the direction of the U.S. Forest Service, trail construction was completed in May 1990. The PCT is for humans and horses only, and all mechanized vehicles, including mountain bikes, are prohibited. The route crosses 19 major canyons, reaches 900 lakes, and climbs 57 major mountain passes as it winds through 24 national forests, seven national parks, and various other public lands.

The trail enters all five forest jurisdictions in the Tahoe region, from Plumas National Forest in the north to Eldorado National Forest in the south. The largest segment is in Tahoe National Forest, where it extends for 97 miles. The majority of day hikers who enter Desolation Wilderness encounter the trail from most of the major access points on the eastern side. The PCT is easily recognizable by the uniform, triangular trail markers and its wide, well-maintained routes.

Near Lake Tahoe, access points are at the following trailheads: Highway 49 east of the Sierra Buttes, Norden at I-80, Barker Pass at the end of Blackwood Canyon Road on the South Shore, Echo Lake and Little Norway on U.S. 50, and Carson Pass on Highway 88. Perhaps the most impressive segment of the trail in this region bisects Desolation Wilderness, where it is the main north/south artery.

A permit isn't required for travel on the PCT as such, but you must obtain one to pass through wilderness and other special areas, as well as for use of portable stoves or for building campfires in the backcountry. Permits are free and can be acquired from any Forest Service office in the region. One advantage for PCT users is that if you start on the trail in Desolation Wilderness, you aren't subject to the area's quota system. However, it's advisable for all users planning multiday trips on the PCT to check with Forest Service offices along their route for any special restrictions. For example, campfires are not allowed in any portion of Desolation Wilderness, but they are allowed in Mokelumne Wilderness and in Tahoe National Forest.

Contact: For permit information, contact any of the U.S. Forest Service offices in the preceding wilderness area listings.

Mormon-Emigrant Trail

Hikers in the Carson Pass and Mokelumne Wilderness areas along Highway 88 have the opportunity to retrace parts of the pioneer Mormon-Emigrant Trail, carved through the Sierra in 1848. The impetus for the route began when the United

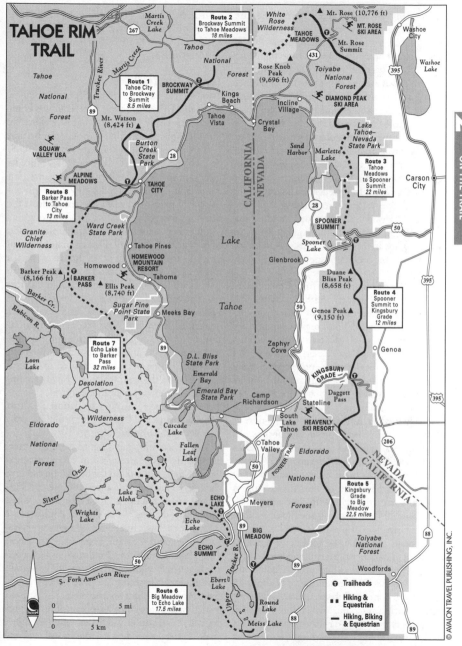

TAHOE RIM TRAIL

© AVALON TRAVEL PUBLISHING, INC.

States Army asked Brigham Young and the Church of Latter-Day Saints (Mormons) to recruit 500 men to fight for California in the Mexican-American War. By the time the Mormon battalion arrived in San Diego, however, the conflict was over. So they turned to the task of finding an alternative trans-Sierra route to the difficult Truckee Route, which crossed the Truckee River more than two dozen times. Starting just east of Coloma, where gold was discovered at Sutter's sawmill in 1848, the Mormons followed a ridge south of Silver Lake, descended to Twin Lakes (now known as Caples Lake), climbed over Carson Pass, and followed the Carson River through Hope Valley on a course that is now south of Highway 88. When they reached the Carson Valley, they joined the Truckee Route to Salt Lake City. In the ensuing years, thousands of settlers and gold-seekers pushed their way west on this trail.

Today the trail is accessible from Caples Lake, the Kirkwood ski resort, and Silver Lake. The most spectacular portion, one of the truly undiscovered outings in the Tahoe region, can be traveled by foot or horseback from a trailhead just behind the stables at Plasse's Resort on the west end of Silver Lake. From here, hike on steep and dusty switchbacks through canopied forest until you ascend to an open ridge. There you connect with the Mormon-Emigrant Trail—now a wide road occasionally used by motorized dirt bikes—next to the site of an old general store and supply post. At this point, head northeast past Scout Carson Lake and massive Thimble Peak (elevation 9,870 feet). Along the spine of this ridge are splendid views of two drainages, Silver Lake on the left and Summit City Canyon on the right, with contrasting geology. Thimble Peak is surrounded with reddish volcanic formations, while the canyon has massive granite peaks and a plunging gorge more typical of the Sierra. The trail drops into Sunrise Bowl at Kirkwood, then follows a dirt road to Caples Lake on Highway 88, for a total distance of about 15 miles. If you don't mind the equestrian and biking traffic, which isn't too intrusive, this route makes for a great two- or three-day backpacking outing. You'll have to arrange your own shuttle, however. No permits are required.

Contact: Eldorado Information Center (top of Carson Pass on Hwy. 88); 530/644-6048; Kirkwood; 209/258-6000; Caples Resort; 209/258-8888.

Tahoe Rim Trail

A milestone was reached in September 2001, when the 165-mile Tahoe Rim Trail was completed after nearly 18 years of volunteer efforts by the nonprofit Tahoe Rim Trail Association and various government agencies, mainly the U.S. Forest Service and Nevada State Parks. Since its inception in 1984, the Rim Trail Organization has been funded through donations and assisted by several public agencies. The trail follows the ridgeline around Lake Tahoe, passes through six counties in two states, and incorporates a portion of the Pacific Crest Trail. Dedication of the trail capped a major effort to finish the last leg of it, a section extending northwest from Mt. Rose in Nevada to the base of Martis Peak in California. Though the trail is complete, ongoing maintenance is still a necessity, and this takes continued donations. The volunteer organization offers various sponsorship opportunities, solicits members and holds events throughout the year. It also produces detailed maps and brochures on the trail, which are highly recommended for anyone planning a trip.

Contact: Tahoe Rim Trail Association, P.O. Box 4647, Stateline, NV 89449; 775/588-0686; website: www.tahoerimtrail.org.

The Tahoe Rim Trail is signed with light-blue, triangular "TRT" markers and can be accessed at eight trailheads around the basin. You can hike them in segments, using a new commercial shuttle system, or you can arrange your own shuttle. Portions of the trail can be done as day hikes (see references below), but some segments are more easily negotiated as overnight trips, since distances range from 12 miles to 32 miles one-way. Camping is generally allowed anywhere along the trail, except along the section in Lake Tahoe-Nevada State Park on the East Shore, where it is restricted to designated campsites. Also, campfires are prohibited in Desolation Wilderness (and sometimes in other areas depending on conditions), and any overnight camping there requires a permit (see

Desolation Wilderness, above, for details). For day hiking, permits can be obtained at registration boxes at the trailheads or from the Forest Service's Lake Tahoe Visitor Center near the Tallac Historic Site on Highway 89 north of South Lake Tahoe. For information on the new shuttle service, which debuted in 2002 and has selected dates during the summer, contact the Rim Trail Association. Also, there is an ongoing service from Spooner Day Lodge to the Mt. Rose trailhead, on even days of the month (costing $15). For information, contact Spooner Lake Outdoor Company at 775/887-8844; website: www.spoonerlake.com.

Following is a brief, clockwise description of each TRT trailhead:

• **Tahoe City to Brockway Summit:** 18.5 miles of trail meander through aspens and conifers and provide views of Lake Tahoe, Martis Valley, Truckee River Canyon, and Mt. Watson (elevation: 8,424), the dominant peak on the North Shore. The trail passes through interesting geologic formations, including a cinder cone and lava flows, which are remnants of ancient volcanoes. Hikers can stop at Watson Lake, 12 miles east of Tahoe City, for a rest, a picnic lunch, or an overnight camping spot. Most of the trail is a narrow, two-foot-wide path, with a 10 percent grade, though some areas are steeper and rockier. Parking for the Tahoe City North Trailhead is across from the Community Center on Fairway Drive, .1 mile north of Highway 89 on the west end of town.

• **Brockway Summit to Tahoe Meadows:** 18 miles of trail start from Highway 267 (between Truckee and Kings Beach). Terrain includes dense forest, open meadows of mule ears, and more ancient volcanoes. You can take a spur path up the flanks of Martis Peak, where there is an abandoned fire lookout, and enjoy views of Truckee, distant Donner Summit, Lake Tahoe, the Sierra Crest and the Carson Range. On the Nevada side, the trail proceeds through the Mt. Rose Wilderness and is mostly on open ridges with ongoing views of Tahoe. Closer to the Mt. Rose Highway 431/, you can see views of Mt. Rose (9,698 feet) and the Carson Valley below. Parking for the trailhead is on a large dirt parking area a

half mile south of Brockway Summit on the east side of the highway, and paved pullout parking on the west side.

• **Tahoe Meadows to Spooner Summit:** 22 miles of Nevada trail wind through large granite peaks of the Carson Range. Side trails connect to the famous Flume Trail, Lake Tahoe's famous and most heavily-used mountain bike path. Near the trailhead, there's a 1.3-mile wheelchair-accessible Tahoe Meadows Interpretive trail, which is a half mile west of the Mt. Rose summit on Highway 431. Views of Lake Tahoe, and of the surrounding peaks, are some of the best of the entire Tahoe Rim Trail. You can make a side trip to the top of Marlette Peak (elevation: 8,780 feet) for truly panoramic views. A good overnight camping spot is at Marlette Peak Campground, which is 13 miles south of Highway 431 and nine miles north of Spooner Summit. Also, consider exploring a spur trail to Christopher's Loop below Herlan Peak, where you are rewarded with a bird's-eye view of Sand Harbor and Incline Village. The Tahoe Meadows trailhead, on Highway 431 one mile west of the summit on the south side of the road, has vault toilets and a paved parking lot.

• **Spooner Summit to Kingsbury Grade:** 12 miles of scenic trail that switchbacks among huge trunks of ancient firs and large exposed granite outcroppings, with ridge-top views of Lake Tahoe to the west and Washoe Valley to the east. There's a long traverse across the volcanic sides of South Camp Peak, six miles from the Spooner Trailhead (elevation: 8,866 feet), and there are stunning views from the top of Genoa Peak (elevation: 9,150 feet). The trailhead location is on the south side of Highway 50 at the U.S. Forest Service Picnic and Day-Use area, next to a large dirt parking lot.

• **Kingsbury Grade to Big Meadow:** 22.5 miles of trail pass through an often windy stretch of the Carson Range, with the possibility of snowdrifts, mud and mosquitoes lasting into July. There is lots of water here, with creeks and sunny meadows, which are often carpeted with brilliantly colored wildflowers. Views encompass Hope Valley to the south, Lake Tahoe to the north, and Hell Hole Canyon. Most of the route maintains a 10 percent or less grade, and is clearly marked with the light blue triangular TRT signs. A good overnight spot is hemlock-ringed Star Lake, which is 8.5 miles from Kingsbury and is surrounded by three of the highest peaks in the Tahoe basin, including Freel Peak (elevation: 10,881 feet) and Jobs Sister (elevation: 10,823 feet). The route heads through Monument Pass (five miles from Kingsbury) and the upper reaches of Heavenly Ski Resort. The Kingsbury trailhead is at the parking lot of the Heavenly Stagecoach base area. To get here, turn south on Tramway Drive at the summit of Highway 207 (Kingsbury Grade), about three miles east of the Highway 207/Highway 50 intersection at Stateline, Nevada. Look for the TRT trail sign at the south end of the parking lot.

• **Big Meadow to Echo Lake:** 17.5 miles of trail passes through the less-visited Meiss Country, which offers beautiful alpine lakes, vast meadows of wildflowers, and spectacular granite peaks. Long gentle traverses through rolling landscape typify most of the route, though there are some occasional ascents and descents. Early in the season, standing water can make for muddy paths and pesky mosquitoes, so come prepared. At Meiss Meadow, the TRT connects with the Pacific Crest Trail. Among the standout points of interest are Round Lake, 2.8 miles from the trailhead under steep volcanic peaks, and Showers Lake, which is cradled in a granite basin 6.8 miles in and is a good camping spot. Other views are of the Upper Truckee River Basin. The trail reaches Echo Summit (elevation: 7,380 feet) before continuing on to stunning Echo Lake, a half mile west of there. The trailhead at Big Meadow is on Highway 89 about five miles south of U.S. 50 and Meyers. Parking is on the north side of the highway, but the trail marker is on the south side.

• **Echo Lake to Barker Pass:** 32 miles of trail on this route, which is on the Pacific Crest Trail, is the longest and most rugged segment of the TRT. It goes smack through Desolation Wilderness (be sure to have your overnight permit from the Forest Service!) and offers some magnificent views of rock-rimmed valleys, lakes and ponds. In the summer months, you can take a water taxi from the marina at Lower Echo Lake (this is also a good place to indulge in ice cream and pick up any last-minute provisions) to the far end of Upper Echo Lake, a distance of 2.5 miles. There, the trail winds uphill and has increasingly stunning views behind you. Clearly, the most dramatic vista—arguably in the entire Tahoe area—is of vast Lake Aloha (elevation: 8,160 feet) which is a labyrinth of small granite ponds that make for excellent swimming on a hot day. The peaks that frame this elongated body of water include Pyramid (elevation: 9,983 feet), Mt. Price (elevation: 9,975 feete) and Jacks Peak (elevation: 9,856 feet). When you continue northward, you'll negotiate Dicks Pass (elevation: 9,210 feet), the highest pass in Desolation Wilderness. Along the way, you'll see several gorgeous alpine lakes, such as rock-rimmed Heather, Fontanillis and the three Velma lakes, all of which make great camp sites. The trailhead starts at the dam below Echo Chalet, and there is a paved parking lot near here at Lower Echo Lake. The lake is about one mile from the turnoff at Highway 50.

• **Barker Pass to Tahoe City:** 13 miles of trail provide glorious views of granite canyons, and include a 100-foot waterfall at the head of Ward Canyon, near the Sherwood Forest (backside) of Alpine Meadows ski resort. Five miles north of Barker Pass, the trail climbs moderately along a ridge to Twin Peaks, affording excellent views of Granite Chief Wilderness to the west and Lake Tahoe to the east. As it descends toward Tahoe City, the trail goes through Page Meadows, a great spot for wildflowers but another ambush point by voracious mosquitoes in early to mid summer. Carry repellent and face netting during these times. The Barker Pass trailhead is on Blackwood Canyon Road, off Highway 89 at the Kaspian Campground, which is four miles south of Tahoe City. The trail and roadside parking are 7.5 miles west of the highway, up a moderately steep but paved road. (Note: You can also access this segment of the trail from Ward Canyon Road, two miles from the junction of Highway 89 and Pineland Drive. Parking is limited to the roadside.) If you're doing a shuttle, you can park the second vehicle at the Truckee River Access and Recreation Parking Lot on Highway 89, an eighth of a mile south of the junction of Highway 89 and Highway 28.

Hiking Trails

TRUCKEE/DONNER

Loch Leven Lakes Trail
(see map on page 200, site 1)

Some wondrously beautiful small alpine lakes, with waters often warm enough for swimming, are in store for the hiker who ascends this hot, dusty trail. The trailhead itself is not well marked, but it's relatively easy to find next to the parking area. The trail works its way upward on a moderately steep grade to the southwest, climbing a rocky shelf as it rises to a vista point that overlooks busy I-80. Once across the Southern Pacific Railroad tracks, it switchbacks through cool and majestic fir forest. At the summit, it opens up into granite outcrops once again, then descends down a plateau to Lower Loch Leven. Considering the effort required to get here, it's tempting to jump into this first lake, which has accessible shoreline and smooth rock slopes for swimming and sunning. The lake is small and elongated, and you can easily swim laps across it. Those who continue on, however, will find even more picturesque scenery at Middle and High Loch Leven, both within 1.3 miles. The route climbs and descends small ridges and offers views of valleys, high alpine meadows, and glaciated mountain terrain. Good fishing and lakeside camping are available at all three lakes, though the trail is heavily used and you may have to share this spot with others.

Difficulty: Moderately strenuous.
Distance (one way): 2.2 to 3.5 miles.
Time (one way): Two to three hours.
Elevation (low/high): 5,680 feet to 6,800 feet.
Location: The trailhead is about 18 miles west of Truckee. From I-80 eastbound, take the Big Bend exit; from I-80 westbound, take the Rainbow Road exit. The trailhead begins one-quarter mile east of the Big Bend Visitor Center. A small parking area and restrooms are across the road from the trailhead.
Contact: Tahoe National Forest, Nevada City Ranger District; 530/288-3231.

Summit Lake Trail
(see map on page 200, site 2)

For the first mile, this hike follows the Pacific Crest Access Trail (Trail 15E18) east and then follows the PCT for one mile north, passing through a tunnel under I-80. Shortly after the underpass, the intersection with the Summit Lake Trail (Trail 15E09) is clearly marked. The trail climbs moderately and crosses two small creeks, which are separated by a low, glaciated granite ridge. Beyond the second creek, the trail arcs through a meadow that teems with colorful wildflowers from spring through late summer. Head past the junction with the Warren Lake Trail, keeping to the right, and continue out to the edge of an open, descending ridge. Enter a wooded area for the brief hike to the south corner of Summit Lake. Several campsites are available, and there is fishing for brook and rainbow trout.

Difficulty: Easy.
Distance (one way): Two miles.
Time (one way): One hour.
Elevation (low/high): 7,200 feet to 7,400 feet.
Location: From I-80 at Donner Summit, west of Truckee, take the Castle Peak Area/Boreal Ridge Road exit, which is immediately west of the highway's Donner Summit roadside rest area. (Unattended parking at the rest area is not permitted.) On the south side of the highway, look for a sign identifying the trailhead, and go east for .4 miles. The trailhead provides access to the Pacific Crest Trail and four other destinations, of which Summit Lake is one of the most popular.
Contact: Tahoe National Forest, Truckee Ranger District; 530/587-3558.

Hole in the Ground Trail
(see map on page 200, site 3)

Beginning at the Donner Summit section of Highway 80 across from Boreal ski area (west of Truckee), this relatively new trail climbs to the top of Andesite Ridge and affords access to attractive Sand Ridge Lake, a high-elevation basin that makes an ideal lunch spot. Because the trail is

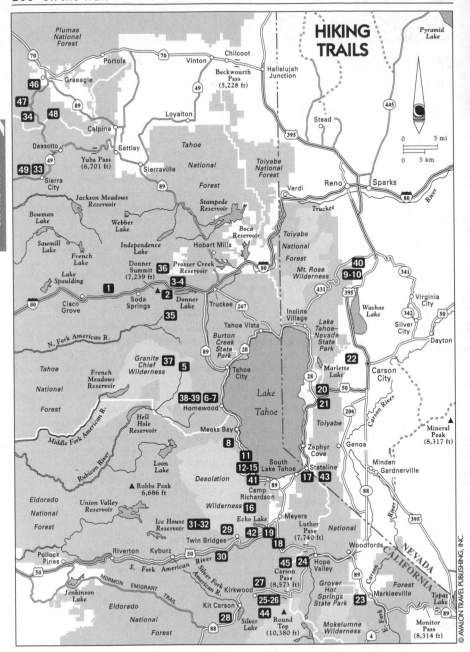

HIKING
TRAILS

also open to cycling, you may encounter mountain bikers along the way and at the lake. Andesite Ridge has some lofty perspectives of Donner Summit, and from there the trail descends through old growth red fir forest and crosses Castle Creek. It intersects with the Pacific Crest Trail (PCT), which provides an alternative loop return to Castle Valley and is also (by law) free of cyclists. The lake is reached via a short spur trail from Hole in the Ground Trail.

Difficulty: Moderately strenuous.

Distance (one way): 7.8 miles.

Time (one way): Four to five hours.

Elevation (low/high): 7,200 feet to 8,000 feet.

Location: Take I-80 west of Truckee to the Castle Peak exit. Head north on Castle Peak road for 1.5 miles. High clearance vehicles (i.e. SUVs) are recommended on this road. The trail starts on the left (west) side. As an alternative (and if you don't have an SUV), start at the Lower Lola Montez Lake Trailhead. This can be reached by taking the Soda Springs exit off I-80, and, on the north side of the freeway, following the paved road east past the fire station for .3 mile. The trail starts on the north side of the road. Because Hole in the Ground Trail is new, it may not be shown on all maps.

Contact: Tahoe National Forest, Truckee Ranger Station; 530/587-3558.

Commemorative Emigrant Trail
(see map on page 200, site 4)

This relatively new trail, not shown on many maps, parallels the routes taken by the emigrants in the mid-1800s and is just a few miles north of Truckee. It has very little elevation gain, but it does have good views of Prosser Reservoir and distant Mt. Rose. While the original pioneer trail has been largely obliterated by roads and reservoirs, hikers can gain some perspective on what settlers might have experienced in the eastern Sierra foothills before ascending much steeper mountains ahead of them. Starting at the Alder Creek Road trailhead, the route crosses the creek several times and heads through pine forest before reaching Highway 89. It then passes through the Donner Camps Picnic Area, on the east side of the road, where there is an in-terpretive trail describing the tragedy of the Donner Party in the mid 1800s. (If you like, you can start your hike at this point, where there is off-highway parking, picnic tables and toilets.) For several miles beyond, you walk on a raised gravel path that winds through wetlands, and good wildlife-viewing opportunities exist along the way. The trail carries you over several dirt roads before you reach Prosser Reservoir. At one section, you must choose between two options for crossing Prosser Creek. You can ford the creek if the water level is low enough; or you can play it safe and use the Highway 89 bridge (recommended). Overall, this is a good early season hike because of its modest elevation. With generally sparse tree cover and mostly open terrain, the trail can get hot and dusty during the peak of summer. If you elect to go in early summer, be sure to pack insect repellant for the wetlands and be cautious of midday high water levels in the streams.

Difficulty: Moderate.

Distance (one way): 15 miles.

Time (one way): Six to seven hours.

Elevation (low/high): 6,000 to 6,200 feet.

Location: From I-80, take Highway 89 north (at Truckee) approximately 2.3 miles to County Road 780 (Alder Creek Trail Road). Turn left (west) on 780 and proceed for three miles. The trail starts on the south side of road 780 across from road 780-12. As one alternative, you can simply drive north on Highway 89 to the Donner Camps Picnic Area (watch for it on the right side of the road) and begin there. As another alternative, you can access it near Stampede Reservoir. In this case, drive seven miles east of Truckee on I-80, take the Hirschdale exit, and cross under the freeway on County Road No. 894 (Stampede Road). Follow this road for nine miles, past the Sierra/Nevada County line (at which point the road becomes road 270) to the intersection of Dog Valley Road (County Road 261). Turn left (west) and proceed for 2.5 miles to the end of the pavement. The trail begins on the west side of Road 261 past the end of the pavement.

Contact: Tahoe National Forest, Truckee Ranger Station; 530/587-3558.

TAHOE CITY/WEST SHORE

Five Lakes Trail

(see map on page 200, site 5)

This popular, well-beaten trail gets heavy use, so much so that the Forest Service has issued severe restrictions on camping within 600 feet of the small lakes, none of which are individually numbered or named. The trail originates in a residential area and immediately starts a steep ascent along a series of forested switchbacks. Once above the trees, the trail follows the contour of a spectacular rocky canyon, and there are breathtaking views of the Alpine Meadows Ski Area and of sheer, striated granite walls. Just after the trail enters Granite Chief Wilderness, it changes to dirt and duff through a canopy of pines. At a junction, there's a quarter-mile spur to the lakes, of which only one is immediately evident. Scouting cross-country (a topographic map is helpful), you can soon reach the other lakes, which are small but attractive. Camping is prohibited near the shorelines; still, these lakes get pounded by waves of anglers, picnickers, and resident dog-walkers. So impacted is the area that in 1992 the U.S. Forest Service removed 65 campsites and fire rings for revegetation. Those who want a longer hike, and are able to arrange a shuttle, can continue for another 2.5 miles to Squaw Valley USA.

Difficulty: Moderately strenuous.

Distance (one way): 2.5 miles.

Time (one way): 1.5 to two hours.

Elevation (low/high): 6,040 feet to 6,920 feet.

Location: From Tahoe City, travel four miles north on Highway 89 to Alpine Meadows Road. Turn west and drive 1.5 miles to the trailhead on the right. Parking is along the side of the road only.

Contact: Tahoe National Forest, Truckee Ranger District; 530/587-3558.

Barker Pass to Twin Peaks on the Pacific Crest Trail

(see map on page 200, site 6)

Although this route doesn't reach any lakes, the high elevation, easy access, and lofty views of both Lake Tahoe and its major Sierra peaks make it a first-rate hike, most of which is well within the ability of families with children. The beauty of this West Shore outing is that the lion's share of the elevation gain, from Lake Tahoe to Barker Pass, is accomplished by driving. This part of the famous Pacific Crest Trail heads north from the pass, traveling along the backbone of a ridge that has wonderful vistas on both sides—one of the Tahoe basin, the other of Granite Chief Wilderness. You don't need to go the full five miles to Twin Peaks to appreciate the views; in fact, going half the distance will do. The first vista is at a ridge one mile north of Barker Peak, which has a sweeping view of Tahoe. The next one is about one mile farther, up some switchbacks to an area of crested knolls at 8,434 feet. The PCT itself does not climb to the top of Twin Peaks. The easiest access to the summit is on a spur route about .2 miles up the trail, where it begins a gentle descent. These peaks are remnants of an ancient volcano, dated at 5–10 million years old. From the top, enjoy lofty views of Tahoe's dominant mountains, including Tinkers Knob, Mt. Rose, Freel Peak, Mt. Tallac, Dicks Peak, and Pyramid Peak. This can be a hot, dusty hike, so take plenty of water.

Difficulty: Easy to moderate.

Distance (one way): Five miles.

Time (one way): 2.5 to three hours.

Elevation (low/high): 7,640 feet to 8,880 feet.

Location: Drive 4.2 miles south on Highway 89 from Tahoe City to Blackwood Canyon Road. Turn right at the Kaspian picnic area and go 7.1 miles on a paved, winding road to one-third of a mile beyond where the pavement ends and becomes dirt and gravel. The Barker Pass Trailhead is quite obvious on the right, and is usually packed with cars. There are no restrooms at this trailhead, but there are some at the Ellis Peak Trailhead one-third of a mile back up the road. Note: Always phone the Forest Service to see if the road is open. The winter of 1996 washed out a bridge and the road was closed for most of the year.

Contact: Tahoe National Forest, Truckee Ranger District; 530/587-3558.

Ellis Peak Trail

(see map on page 200, site 7)

This hike combines the chance to ascend a walkable mountain, Ellis Peak, with the opportunity to enjoy a picnic at tranquil Ellis Lake. The trailhead, which begins 1,800 feet above Lake Tahoe, is easy to reach. At the outset, the trail ascends along several switchbacks in deep forest until it reaches the ridge at 8,270 feet. Follow the ridge for 1.5 miles as the trail passes through sections of open forest and meadows rich with wildflowers in spring, along with vistas of Lake Tahoe. When the trail intersects a dirt road, take the right fork for 100 yards until you reach another road branching off to the east. Follow that spur for .3 miles to Knee Ridge (elevation 8,520 feet); from there, it is a short distance to Ellis Peak. This lofty perch affords striking views of Tahoe to the east and Granite Chief Wilderness and Hellhole Reservoir to the west. After your climb, retrace your steps to the first intersection. To reach Ellis Lake, continue on the left fork of the road for 0.2 miles. This small lake makes a relaxing spot for lunch.

Difficulty: Moderate.

Distance (one way): 2.5 miles.

Time (one way): 1.75 to two hours.

Elevation (low/high): 7,800 feet to 8,740 feet.

Location: At Barker Pass. Drive 4.2 miles south of Tahoe City on Highway 89 to the Kaspian picnic area. Turn right on Blackwood Canyon Road and go 7.1 miles west until the pavement ends at the summit. The Ellis Peak Trailhead is on the south side of the road, where it becomes dirt and gravel. There is limited parking here, and the trail gets heavy use. Be sure to check with the Forest Service to make sure that the road is open.

Contact: Tahoe National Forest, Truckee Ranger District; 530/587-3558.

Meeks Bay Trail

(see map on page 200, site 8)

Most day hikers will choose the first lake in this lovely string of six alpine pearls, simply because of the effort and time required to reach the others. The entire route, connecting with a trail to the three Velma Lakes, is a popular three- to four-day backpacking jaunt. From the trailhead, the first 1.3 miles is over a level dirt road. Then the marked trail ascends gradually (no switchbacks) through moderate forest over dirt and duff, with few vistas. It parallels Meeks Creek, passes a small spring, and skirts several meadows, which are lush with wildflowers in early to midsummer. The trail becomes sandy as it climbs the eastern slopes of a canyon, and the vegetation thins a bit before you arrive at Lake Genevieve. This greenish, shallow lake, towered over by Peak 9054, is bordered by pines and has gentle, sloping contours that accommodate wading and swimming. Though quite attractive, Genevieve has its share of insects, so bring your bug repellent. The trail, which is part of the unofficial Tahoe-Yosemite Trail, continues to the left, reaching the other lakes via a series of switchbacks leading another 1,000 feet to Phipps Pass.

Difficulty: Moderate.

Distance (one way): 4.5 miles to Lake Genevieve, five miles to Crag Lake, 5.7 miles to Hidden Lake, 5.9 miles to Shadow Lake, 6.3 miles to Stony Ridge, and 8.0 miles to Rubicon Lake.

Time (one way): Three to six hours, depending on the destination.

Elevation (low/high): 6,240 feet to 8,880 feet.

Location: From Tahoe City or South Lake Tahoe, take Highway 89 about 12 miles to Meeks Bay Resort. Parking is across the highway from the resort at a small dirt parking lot, and it fills rapidly on summer weekends. A wilderness permit is required and may be obtained from the U.S. Forest Service.

Contact: Lake Tahoe Basin Management Unit; 530/573-2600.

INCLINE VILLAGE/MT. ROSE

Mt. Rose Trail

(see map on page 200, site 9)

In winter, alpine skiers can take chairlifts almost to the summit of Mt. Rose (elevation 10,778 feet) for dramatic vistas of Reno, the Washoe Valley, and Lake Tahoe. In summer, it takes considerable effort to do this on foot, but it's well worth it—if you've got the stamina and

ON THE TRAIL

lung power. From the trailhead, follow a dirt road for an easy three miles through mostly lodgepole pine forest mixed with areas of sagebrush and mule ears. In late spring and early summer, a vibrant meadow at the midpoint is awash with color from lupine, paintbrush, and larkspur wildflowers. The last two miles, from the base of Mt. Rose, follow steep switchbacks, sometimes on slippery rock, to the ridgeline. At the top, there's a logbook where hardy souls can inscribe their names. Because of the not infrequent high winds that can rake this peak in afternoons, come with extra clothing to keep warm. By all means, bring a picnic lunch to enjoy the panorama from the highest walkable mountain in the Tahoe basin. If you're trying to decide whether to scale this peak or Mt. Tallac on the West Shore, consider this: The elevation gain is 1,255 feet less for Mt. Rose.

Difficulty: Strenuous.

Distance (one way): Six miles.

Time (one way): 3.5 to four hours.

Elevation (low/high): 8,800 feet to 10,776 feet.

Location: Take the Mt. Rose Highway (Highway 431) 7.5 miles north of Incline Village. Park at the trailhead, one mile south of the summit. There's limited parking, but the Mt. Rose Campground (several hundred yards above the trailhead) provides additional space.

Contact: Toiyabe National Forest, Carson Ranger District; 775/882-2766.

Ophir Creek Trail
(see map on page 200, site 10)

The Ophir Creek Trail connects the pristine Tahoe Meadows, on the southwest side of Mt. Rose, to the eastern, high-desert slopes of the Sierra next to a 200-acre county park. Its chief attractions are the wildflowers that blossom in the meadows in early to midsummer, views of Mt. Rose (elevation 10,778 feet), and a panorama of the Washoe Valley and Washoe Lake. The topography changes abruptly from dense forest to rugged, open rock canyons. Along the trail are three small lakes—Upper and Lower Price and Rock—that are shallow, marshy, and not really worth the effort it takes to reach them.

From the trailhead, follow the wide dirt road through moderate forest past Tahoe Meadows (you may encounter some mountain bikers). After about 1.5 miles, the trail narrows, climbs a ridge, and then begins a long, steep descent through thinning forest and down an open, brushy canyon next to a huge rockfall. This side of the mountain is hot, dusty, and desolate, but the trail parallels the creek and meanders through an unmarked boulder field. Finally, it enters a canopy of forest once again and provides distant vistas of the Washoe Valley and busy U.S. 395. A left fork drops sharply for one-quarter mile to Upper Price Lake, but this side trip is one you can ignore. There is no hospitable shoreline here and the bottom is muddy, with extensive algae and weed growth on the lake's surface. Both Upper and Lower Price Lakes were severely damaged when part of Slide Mountain slid into them in 1983.

If you continue on past the junction, you can catch glimpses of the lake from the main trail. Along this shaded ledge, you have the option of ending your hike and returning to the Mt. Rose Highway or continuing down a steep, brushy decline to Davis Creek County Park. If you choose to do this, remember that you'll have 3,600 feet of elevation to scale on your way back.

Difficulty: Moderate to strenuous.

Distance (one way): Three miles to Upper Price Lake and six miles to Davis Creek County Park.

Time (one way): 1.5 to two hours for the shortest hike, four to 4.5 hours for the longest hike.

Elevation (high/low): 8,600 feet to 5,300 feet.

Location: About 6.5 miles northeast of Incline Village on the Mt. Rose Highway (Highway 431), look for a dirt turnout on the right and a large sign marking the trailhead. (Note: You can also begin at the opposite end of the trail, at Davis Creek County Park in Washoe Valley. To reach the park, head 17 miles south of Reno on U.S. 395 to the Franktown Road turnoff. Parking is right off U.S. 395 on Franktown Road. Be aware that this is a tough uphill hike.)

Contact: Toiyabe National Forest, Carson Ranger District; 775/882-2766. Davis Creek County Park; 775/849-0684.

SOUTH LAKE TAHOE

Rubicon Trail

(see map on page 200, site 11)

This is the most spectacular half-day hike at Lake Tahoe, and the favorite route for exploring the lake's promontories and rocky coves. The trail seesaws up and down, from rocky bluffs to sandy coves, and there are breathtaking, picturesque views of the lake from different elevations. Two of the best stops are at Rubicon Point, which overlooks the deepest section of Tahoe that adjoins the shoreline, and at the site of an old lighthouse. Sometimes scrambling over giant boulders (be careful!) next to the trail yields even more stunning panoramas, of boats whizzing below, and of the city of South Lake Tahoe in the distance.

Pine forest extends to the edge of the cliffs, and much of the trail is well shaded. Although it is generally wide, there are narrow sections with steep drop-offs, so parents with children need to be cautious (especially at Rubicon Point, where there is a chain-link railing). Boats frequently anchor in the rocky inlets along the trail, and there are a few lovely but narrow sand beaches around Emerald Point. You can pause here to watch paddle-wheelers and motor cruisers enter the mouth of Emerald Bay, or continue into Emerald Bay State Park to Vikingsholm Castle, where tours are given in summer. Recent extensions of the trail across Eagle Creek allow hikers to proceed to the south side of the bay and from there continue on to Eagle Point (about 1.5 miles farther), which is directly opposite Emerald Point. To return to your car, you'll have to double back on the same route.

The Rubicon Trail is so inspiring that you might wish to pack a picnic lunch and a swimsuit, so that you can take your time, enjoy each stop, and savor an entire day.

Difficulty: Moderate.

Distance (one way): 3.1 miles to Emerald Point, 4.4 miles to Vikingsholm Castle.

Time (one way): 2.5 to three hours.

Elevation (low/high): 6,230 feet to 6,580 feet.

Location: At D. L. Bliss State Park on the West Shore. Take Highway 89 north for 10 miles from South Lake Tahoe to the park and drive a wind-ing 2.5 miles on the entrance road to the shoreline beyond the campground. The trail begins at the southernmost end of the parking lot near Calawee Cove Beach. However, parking is extremely limited here and spaces fill up quickly, especially on weekends. An alternative, often available throughout the day, is to park in the spaces next to the Lighthouse Trail, and take this path to the Rubicon Trail. If you do this, walk the spur to Calawee Cove Beach first so that you can hike the entire Rubicon and see its most spectacular overlook, at Rubicon Point. You can always cut off this section on the way back. Throughout the park, there is a $5 fee for day-use parking. Pets are not allowed.

Contact: D. L. Bliss State Park, California Department of Parks and Recreation; 530/525-7277.

Eagle Falls Trail

(see map on page 200, site 12)

One of Tahoe's signature—and most popular—hikes takes you into Desolation Wilderness and visits some of the region's most attractive alpine lakes. Prepare a picnic lunch and allow for a full-day hike, giving you enough time to enjoy each lake.

The first mile of the trail, along an uphill series of rocky stairways, seems almost like a freeway, since it's jammed with people making the short trek to Eagle Lake. There's a bridge across Eagle Creek, and when the runoff is highest it affords a good view looking down on several cataracts of Eagle Falls. Eagle Lake is a circular blue jewel, but it's constantly crowded. Keep going, up the steep trail to the left at the sign for Velma Lakes, and you'll lose the hordes. The trail is a continuous climb along an exposed granite cliff, but you can stop at many points to admire the bird's-eye view of Eagle Lake. Fortunately, the trail soon enters dense woodlands for a cool respite from the sun. After 2.5 miles of switchbacks, it reaches the crest of the hill and a fork to the left for the Bayview Trail, which leads to Granite Lake and Emerald Bay. (If you have two cars, you might consider parking one here and returning on this trail.) Keep to the right for another three-quarters of a mile and take the second fork to the left.

ON THE TRAIL

© KEN CASTLE

hikers along Eagle Lake

Hike on for a half mile, enjoying lofty vistas of Middle Velma Lake to the north, until you reach another ridgeline and a junction with the Pacific Crest Trail. The sign here is somewhat confusing, but the correct route is to Dicks Lake to the right (the left fork goes to Dicks Pass). A short spur takes you to a good camping spot in trees above this nearly circular lake, and a great view of its bouldered shoreline. You can stop here to admire this pristine body of water, or continue on less than a quarter mile to Fontanillis Lake, which is more spectacular.

Fontanillis is a large, elongated lake with several arms and protected granite coves. If you follow the forested trail along its east banks, you'll find a natural swimming hole and good picnic spot at the far end, in a completely sheltered arm with rock islands. This is a wonderful spot to bring an inflatable raft or float tube, and it would not be difficult to spend hours here lounging in the water or sunning on a rock. From the top of the outlet at Fontanillis, you can see Upper Velma Lake below. If you wish, follow the

drainage for a shortcut side trail to this lake, over smooth rocky ledges; Upper Velma is constantly in view. (If you choose to take this route, when you reach the trail on the east shore, turn left to rejoin the path to Middle Velma Lake.) Or continue on the same trail from Fontanillis until it reaches another intersection at Middle Velma Lake. Both of these lakes have their charms. Upper Velma is a grassy, shallow lake with moderate tree cover and a flat granite plateau that forms the eastern shoreline; Middle Velma is deeper, with a pronounced, bouldered shoreline. Both lakes have excellent undesignated campsites, but Middle Velma usually has more people. To complete your long day's loop, follow the signs to the Eagle Falls or Bayview Trailhead.

Difficulty: Strenuous.

Distance (one way): Five miles to Fontanillis Lake.

Time (one way): 3.5 to four hours.

Elevation (low/high): 6,580 feet to 8,500 feet.

Location: Take Highway 89 about eight miles north of South Lake Tahoe to the Eagle Falls picnic area on the left, opposite Emerald Bay. Parking in the paved area is limited to 30 vehicles and is usually full; more parking is available along the road, but it, too, can be crowded. The best advice is to come early in the morning.

Contact: Lake Tahoe Basin Management Unit; 530/573-2600.

Cascade Creek Falls Trail

(see map on page 200, site 13)

This is a short but scenic hike to the top of a 200-foot waterfall, which tumbles into Cascade Lake. Take the left fork from the Bayview Trailhead and follow a wide, well-marked path to the north ridge of Cascade Lake. The trail ascends gradually until it reaches a rocky stairway to the ledge with the falls. The best views of the falls are from this somewhat distant point. Closer to the falls themselves, the path disappears into the rocks, but it's possible to scamper through them and get near the edge of the water. Be careful! Depending on the amount of runoff, wet rocks can be slippery and the footing tricky. Get a good bearing on the route back to the trail, because it is hard to identify. From the ledge above the falls, there's a good view looking east across Cascade Lake and, beyond, to Lake Tahoe.

Difficulty: Easy.

Distance (one way): One mile.

Time (one way): 20 to 30 minutes.

Elevation (low/high): 6,800 feet to 6,910 feet.

Location: From South Lake Tahoe, drive north on Highway 89 to the Bayview Campground, opposite Emerald Bay's Inspiration Point. There's a parking lot next to the trailhead, and wilderness permits are required.

Contact: Lake Tahoe Basin Management Unit; 530/573-2600.

Granite Lake Trail

(see map on page 200, site 14)

This is a short, steep, and dusty hike, but Granite Lake is well worth the effort thanks to its swimming, fishing, and picnicking attractions. At the trailhead, there are two forks; the other one, to the left, leads to Cascade Falls. Instead, follow the signs on the right fork leading to Granite and Dicks Lakes. The trail switchbacks

through dense forest up the side of Maggie's Peak climbing into Desolation Wilderness in a seemingly unrelenting ascent. About midway up, the forest cover begins to thin out and there are striking views of Emerald Bay, Cascade Lake, and Fallen Leaf Lake. When you have finally reached the top, you descend a bit off the trail to the shores of Granite Lake, a lovely spot ringed by granite rock and moderate fir forest. Rocky outcrops make for excellent swimming or casting spots, and the lake has a sizable population of eastern brook trout. You can turn around here for a short day hike or continue on the Bayview Trail until it intersects with the Eagle Falls Trail (see number 15) after 2.7 miles. From this junction, you can easily reach Middle and Upper Velma Lakes, Dicks Lake, and Fontanillis Lake. This route is a slightly longer (one mile) alternative to the Eagle Falls Trail, but it has 330 feet less elevation gain.

Difficulty: Strenuous.

Distance (one way): One mile.

Time (one way): One hour.

Elevation (low/high): 6,910 feet to 7,700 feet.

Location: At Bayview, across from Inspiration Point over Emerald Bay. From South Lake Tahoe, drive 7.5 miles north on Highway 89 to the Bayview Campground, which is on your left across from the Vista parking area. Drive through the campground until you see the trailhead; there is very limited parking in a paved lot here, so you may have to park at Inspiration Point across the highway. A wilderness permit is required for this hike.

Contact: Lake Tahoe Basin Management Unit; 530/573-2600.

Mt. Tallac Trail

(see map on page 200, site 15)

This trail reaches two small alpine lakes—Floating Island and Cathedral—but neither is particularly attractive and both can be swarming with mosquitoes, even in midsummer. The main reason to do this hike is to get a great view of Fallen Leaf Lake, from the backbone of a ridge on its north flank, and of Lake Tahoe, from a rocky knob that is left of the trail just before reaching Cathedral Lake. A number of hikers start up this trail with the intention of going all the way to the summit of Mt. Tallac, but often find the grade a lot more than they expected.

In the 1890s, Floating Island Lake had a natural, grass-covered island of twisted roots and shrubs. It was about 20 feet in diameter, sported a 12-foot-high conifer, and could support the weight of several visitors. It wasn't anchored, so enterprising anglers could paddle it around the lake. The island disappeared sometime after the turn of the century. Cathedral Lake has moderate timber on one side and a huge rockfall on the other. Considering the lakes' lack of aesthetic beauty and the ravenous insects that inhabit them, neither swimming nor picnicking would be high on your list of activities here.

You can turn back at Cathedral for a moderate hike, or, if you've got the stamina—and plenty of water—continue up the steep switchback of Tallac. This is where the going gets tough, big time. Those who reach the top are rewarded with an inspiring, 360-degree view of Tahoe and Fallen Leaf Lake, as well as several peaks and lakes in Desolation Wilderness. Bring a jacket, as it can be cool and windy on the summit. Congratulate yourself in accomplishing an elevation gain of almost 3,300 feet and surviving Tahoe's toughest one-day hike. Note: There's another, somewhat easier route to Tallac via the Glen Alpine Trail (see hike number 20), if you take the fork to Gilmore Lake and continue on past the lake. Still, the last part is steep and rocky.

Difficulty: Moderately to very strenuous.
Distance (one way): 2.5 miles to Cathedral Lake, five miles to the summit of Mt. Tallac.
Time (one way): 1.5 to four hours, depending on the destination.
Elevation (low/high): 6,480 feet to 9,735 feet.
Location: From South Lake Tahoe, drive north on Highway 89 for 3.5 miles. Watch for the Mt. Tallac Trailhead sign directly across from the entrance to Baldwin Beach; turn left down the dirt road and continue to the trailhead parking area. A wilderness permit is required and may be obtained from the U.S. Forest Service.
Contact: Lake Tahoe Basin Management Unit; 530/573-2600.

Glen Alpine Trail
(see map on page 200, site 16)

One of Tahoe's top hikes penetrates the heart of Desolation Valley, reaching three of the most spectacular lakes in the region. Although there are several hiking options from this trailhead, the best route takes you up to Suzie and Heather Lakes and, just beyond, to awesome Lake Aloha, a man-made labyrinth of rock pools that stretches for more than two miles in a vast rock valley. Except for the fact that the route is consistently uphill until you reach Suzie Lake, the trail is well marked and not technically difficult.

It begins near a group of heavily forested summer cabins, passes the historic Glen Alpine Resort (where a museum is now open in summer), and begins a long series of switchbacks and rock stairways over a major ridge before dropping down to Suzie Lake. This elongated body of water with both exposed and forested shoreline, peninsulas, and protected inlets is enchanting. There are a few undesignated camping spots around the perimeter, especially on the west and north sides. Incredible as this lake is, the short, three-quarter-mile hike to Heather Lake is even more so. The trail enters the basin in a narrow cut next to an outlet and rises high above the north shore. The entire lake, except for one brushy area on the same side as the trail, is encased in steep granite walls, with a large rocky island. If you have Polaroid sunglasses, you can look down to the water and see large trout swimming near the surface. Be careful along this section of the trail (especially when hiking with children), since it drops off abruptly.

The trail continues for another mile up a series of switchbacks, with stunning views of Heather, until it intersects with the Pacific Crest Trail. At this point, you can climb to one of several rocky overlooks for a view of magnificent Lake Aloha to the west and the lakes you've just passed to the east. Aloha, artificially dammed, is in the center of Desolation Wilderness. It consists of a myriad of mostly shallow granite pools, framed by Mt. Price (elevation 9,975 feet), Pyramid Peak (9,983 feet), and Jack's Peak (9,856 feet). Although this is not the most spectacular vista of Lake Aloha (a better one is on the east side, off

the Pacific Crest Trail from Echo Lakes), the Glen Alpine Trail is the easiest route to get there.
Difficulty: Moderate to strenuous.
Distance (one way): 5.8 miles.
Time (one way): 3.5 to four hours.
Elevation (low/high): 6,560 feet to 8,120 feet.
Location: From South Lake Tahoe, travel north on Highway 89 (Emerald Bay Road) to Camp Richardson, then turn left on Fallen Leaf Road. Follow this to the western end, drive past the marina, and take a narrow and bumpy asphalt road to the large, paved parking lot. A wilderness permit is required and is available at the trailhead. Restrooms are there, too.
Contact: Lake Tahoe Basin Management Unit; 530/573-2600.

Heavenly Gondola Trails
(see map on page 200, site 17)
Now that the gondola has supplanted the aerial tram as the main summer sightseeing lift at Heavenly Ski Resort, there's a new trail system that affords million-dollar views of Tahoe nearly 3,500 feet above the lake.

It's probably the easiest trailhead in the basin to reach, since hikers can step out of their hotels at Stateline, walk a few hundred yards to the gondola base station, and be at the top terminal in about 15 minutes. But it won't be an inexpensive hike; tickets are $20 for adults, $18 for seniors (65+), and $12 for children (6–12). The best approach is to make a day of it on the mountain, stopping first at the Observation Deck (which can only be accessed one way—from the ascent) and enjoying the views. You can buy a snack there, as well as at the top, but you'll need to bring sufficient liquids for your trek. There are three routes, most of them along Jeep roads, and covering about eight miles. The East Peak Trail meanders through the forest with a slight uphill climb of 400 vertical feet, takes an hour to complete, and affords spectacular views of Tahoe and Carson Valley. A more moderate hike, on the Sky Meadows Trail, accesses fields of wildflowers and requires a 500-foot descent. That's the easy part; the hard part is the uphill climb back to the gondola station. Out and back, allow for 90 minutes. Finally, the East Peak Lake Trail begins

with a gradual uphill climb and continues along a scenic ridgeline for about a mile before descending to East Peak Lake, where you can enjoy a picnic lunch. This trek takes about three hours. The Heavenly hiking trails are open daily during the summer 10 A.M.–6 P.M.
Difficulty: Easy to strenuous.
Distances: 1.6 to over four miles round-trip.
Time: One to three hours, plus 35 minutes for the round-trip gondola ride.
Elevation (low/high): 8,700 feet to 9,600 feet.
Location: At the top of the gondola at Heavenly Ski Resort. Base station is between the two new Marriott hotels at the new Heavenly Village, which is one long block west of the Stateline casinos on U.S. 50.
Contact: Heavenly Ski Resort; 775/586-7000; website: www.skiheavenly.com.

Big Meadows Trail
(see map on page 200, site 18)
This trailhead offers several good, moderate hikes to three scenic alpine lakes: Round, Dardanelles, and Scotts. If you work a shuttle, you can even do a one-way hike past Meiss Lake to Highway 88 and Carson Pass, a distance of about eight miles. Dardanelles and Round Lakes can be combined easily on a single hike, while Scotts is accessible via a separate, easterly spur from Big Meadows. The trail to the first two lakes climbs steeply for one-half mile from the highway through Jeffrey pine and white fir to Big Meadows. After you cross the creek and travel across the meadow, which can be marshy, you enter a dense lodgepole forest. In another 1.5 miles, the trail drops nearly 250 feet along an aspen-covered bank to a junction. Take the left fork, which contours around a wall of fused boulders and lava mudflows. After another short climb up a small hill, the trail arrives at Round Lake, the largest lake in Meiss Country. The brownish-green lake is ideal for swimming or for fishing for cutthroat trout. To reach Dardanelles Lake on the same hike, double back and take the left fork at the trail junction. Follow it one-quarter mile to an unmarked trail on the left that crosses the creek. The trail winds through rolling hills and past willows before crossing two more streams. A short climb up a small hill leads

to the lake, which is surrounded by picturesque granite cliffs on one side and flat granite shelves on the other.

Difficulty: Moderate.

Distance (one way): 2.7 miles to Round Lake, three miles to Scotts Lake, 3.5 miles to Dardanelles Lake.

Time (one way): Two to three hours, depending on the destination.

Elevation (low/high): 7,200 feet to 8,070 feet.

Location: Off Highway 89 about five miles south of U.S. 50, near South Lake Tahoe, in the Meiss (pronounced "mice") Country between Luther and Carson Passes. Park in the Big Meadows lot on the east side of the highway. Follow the trail at the lower end of the lot about 200 yards to the highway; cross cautiously and look for the trail marker.

Contact: Lake Tahoe Basin Management Unit; 530/573-2600.

Echo Lakes Trail
(see map on page 200, site 19)

Catch a water taxi to the best vistas of Desolation Wilderness in what is perhaps South Tahoe's most diverse and interesting day hike. At the Echo Chalet and Marina, you can pick up the lake taxi (it operates continuously between 10 A.M. and 6 P.M. in summer and charges a fee for one-way or round-trip) for a delightful 15-minute cruise across Lower Echo Lake, through a snaking, narrow channel to smaller Upper Echo Lake, and to a dock that connects with a trail offering two options.

The first route is a short, relatively easy hike back to the marina on a well-maintained trail above the summer cabins that surround both lakes. It has marvelous views and makes a terrific outing for families with children, especially if you bring a picnic lunch. The second option is to follow the Pacific Crest Trail 3.4 miles to Lake Aloha, which is a considerable climb over a hot, talus-covered trail that, for nearly one-third of the route, hugs the side of a granite canyon. However, if you elect to take this trail, your efforts will be rewarded. The trail and its four spurs have access to nearly a dozen lakes, some of them reachable after a short jaunt from the main route.

The first fork, at 1.5 miles, goes to Tamarack Lake, a five-minute detour. This is a lovely but windy lake with moderate forest around the shoreline and good campsites for backpackers. If you continue on the trail to Lake Aloha, pause along the way to appreciate the remarkable views of Echo and Tamarack Lakes behind you. Reaching the ridge top after a strenuous climb, the trail levels off through shaded forest, and another fork offers a side trip to Lake of the Woods, a worthwhile detour if you have time. (You probably won't, if you want to make it to Aloha and back to Upper Echo Lake in time to catch the water taxi.)

Other spurs lead to Lucille and Margery, small lakes that you can see from the PCT. Beyond these, a somewhat confusing junction provides two routes to Lake Aloha; both, it turns out, reach the same spot at the south end of this massive lake. If you take the left fork, the water comes into view much sooner. At Aloha, you can continue on the PCT along the eastern shoreline, or take another fork to the left that follows the western shoreline. This trail goes along the top of the stone wall that forms a meandering dam, and is hard to discern in some places. If you follow it up the side of the western slopes, you can reach a rocky overlook that makes this entire effort worthwhile. Sprawling beneath you is a gigantic maze of hundreds of granite islands and ponds that make up Aloha, framed by several imposing peaks. The lake was created when it was dammed to supply water to Sacramento. Despite its artificial nature, this is a truly impressive and amazing panorama—perhaps the most spectacular in the whole of Desolation Wilderness. Bring your camera and plenty of film. If it's a warm day, pick the lake of your choice and enjoy a cool, refreshing dip, then retrace the trail back to Upper Echo Lake. At the dock, there's a telephone to call for the water taxi; carry $.20 for this, and be sure to get back by 6 P.M., or you'll have an additional (but relatively easy) 2.5-mile walk back to the parking lot.

Difficulty: Easy to moderately strenuous.

Distance (one way): From Upper Echo Lake (via water taxi), 1.5 miles to Tamarack and 3.4

miles to Lake Aloha. From Lower Echo Lake to Upper Echo Lake, 2.5 miles.

Time (one way): 1.5 hours for the short hike; 3.5 hours for the long hike.

Elevation (low/high): 7,420 feet to 8,430 feet.

Location: Take U.S. 50 from South Lake Tahoe to Echo Summit and turn onto Johnson Pass Road. Stay left through the residential area and the road will lead you to two parking lots next to Lower Echo Lake. Most likely you'll have to park in the upper lot, the larger of the two. The lower lot is adjacent to Echo Chalet, a complex that includes a store, a marina, and rental cabins, and has limited parking.

Contact: Lake Tahoe Basin Management Unit; 530/573-2600.

STATELINE/ZEPHYR COVE

Tahoe Rim Trail North (Spooner Summit) (see map on page 200, site 20)

This is arguably the most scenic original section of the now-completed 165-mile hiking and equestrian trail that follows the ridge tops of the Tahoe basin. The trail, funded by a volunteer organization, connects preexisting trails (including parts of the Pacific Crest Trail through Desolation Wilderness) with new segments constructed since 1984. The Spooner Lake North route offers options of half-day, full-day, and overnight hikes, with two walk-in campgrounds around midpoint. Some of the best scenery—with bird's-eye views of Spooner Lake and Lake Tahoe to the west and Carson City and the Washoe Valley to the east—can be enjoyed within the first 3.5 miles. There are several inspiring rocky overlooks that make for great picnic spots. Right from the trailhead, the going is mostly uphill, and ranges from exposed ridges to dense forest. For a shorter hike, you can stop at the high points and return, or you can continue down steep switchbacks on a fork to Marlette Lake, a scenic swimming and sunning location, for a full day. Mountain bikes are currently prohibited from these segments of the trail.

Difficulty: Moderate.

Distance (one way): Five miles to Marlette Lake, 13 miles to Tunnel Creek.

Time (one way): Three-plus hours.

Elevation (low/high): 7,000 feet to 8,600 feet.

Location: It's easy to miss, since it is right next to the westbound lanes of U.S. 50, one-half mile east of its junction with Highway 28. There is a small dirt parking pullout (a limited number of cars can be accommodated) and a sign designating the trailhead.

Contact: Lake Tahoe-Nevada State Park, Nevada Parks Division; 775/831-0494.

Tahoe Rim Trail South (Spooner Summit) (see map on page 200, site 21)

This trail winds through aspen and pine forest to a ridgeline that overlooks both Lake Tahoe and the Carson Valley. Short spur trails can take you to a rocky ledge that has a fabulous high-elevation view of Stateline and South Tahoe. By traveling cross-country, you can climb Duane Bliss Peak (elevation 8,658 feet), South Camp Peak (8,866 feet), or Genoa Peak (9,150 feet). Off-highway-vehicle roads that parallel parts of the trail are popular with mountain bikers, and can also be used for loops and access to Kingsbury Grade. If you choose to hike the entire 12 miles one way, you'll need to arrange a shuttle, leaving a car at the small parking area at Kingsbury Grade. This is at the end of Andria Drive (an extension of North Benjamin Drive), about two miles north of Highway 207.

Difficulty: Moderate.

Distance (one way): Two miles to Duane Bliss Peak, three miles to South Camp Peak, four miles to Genoa Peak, and 12 miles to Highway 207 (Kingsbury Grade).

Time (one way): One hour for the shortest route, two hours to Genoa Peak.

Elevation (low/high): 7,000 feet to 9,150 feet.

Location: On the south shoulder of U.S. 50, one-half mile east of the junction with Highway 28, on the Nevada side. Look for the rest stop near the Nevada Department of Transportation building on Spooner Summit. There is more parking available here (as well as restrooms) than across the highway at the North Trailhead.

Contact: Tahoe Rim Trail Fund, 298 Kingsbury Grade/P.O. Box 4647, Stateline, NV 89449; 775/588-0686.

Marlette Lake Trail
(see map on page 200, site 22)
Although this is a scenic outing for hikers, the trail is virtually a freeway of mountain bikes, some of which come screaming downhill from Marlette Lake. Fortunately, the trail is wide, since it is essentially a jeep path most of the way. For the first three miles, there is a gradual ascent (no switchbacks) from Spooner Lake through North Canyon, a picturesque drainage with creeks, aspen groves, pines, and meadows, with wildflowers in abundance during late spring and early summer. Jagged granite peaks on the east side are impressive. There is a short, steep climb to the top of Snow Pass before the trail descends to Marlette Lake. A century ago, this wooded lake, a reservoir, was used as a water source for the silver mining industry in Virginia City, east of the ridge. Water was sent to Incline Village through a flume, and logs were floated through a tunnel to the Washoe Valley and the mines. Hiking to the north end, next to the dam, brings you to the beginning of the Flume Trail to Incline. A short walk on this path affords a stunning view of Lake Tahoe from over 1,500 feet above its surface. Watch out for bike riders! No fishing or swimming is allowed at Marlette, and dogs are permitted only on a leash. There are great picnic spots and sunning rocks at the south end.
Difficulty: Moderate.
Distance (one way): Six miles.
Time (one way): Three to four hours.
Elevation (low/high): 7,000 feet to 8,157 feet.
Location: Begin at Spooner Lake in Lake Tahoe-Nevada State Park, 15 miles north of South Lake Tahoe or 12 miles south of Incline Village at the junction of Highway 28 and U.S. 50, on the Nevada side of the lake. There is a paved parking lot, and a day-use fee is charged. Note: This is the most popular trail in the Tahoe basin for mountain bikers, because it is the main access for the famous Flume Trail. Parking can be impossible on busy weekends.
Contact: Lake Tahoe-Nevada State Park, Nevada Parks Division; 775/831-0494.

KIRKWOOD/HOPE VALLEY/MARKLEEVILLE

Burnside Lake Trail
(see map on page 200, site 23)
Because of the proximity of a campground and frequent visitors to the hot springs, this trail gets heavy use. It's a good day hike, however, and afterward you can soak any tired muscles in the public mineral pool (temperatures hover around 102–104°F; the fee is $4 for adults, $1 for children). The trail travels west along Hot Springs Valley and a small creek. Not far up the trail there is an easy, quarter-mile spur trail to a 40-foot, unnamed waterfall, which is impressive during strong runoff. Beyond this junction, the well-marked trail climbs steadily to Burnside Lake, via switchbacks and straight inclines, through alternating dense forest and open, rocky terrain. In summer, this trail can get very hot, and it's wise to take twice as much water as you think you'll need. Along the way, enjoy vistas of Nevada and, occasionally, sections of Grover Hot Springs State Park. The 10-acre lake is rimmed with trees and rocks, and is a popular swimming and fishing spot. Many hikers bring inflatable rafts and float tubes, as well as picnic lunches.
Difficulty: Moderate to strenuous.
Distance (one way): Five miles.
Time (one way): Three to 3.5 hours.
Elevation (low/high): 5,800 feet to 8,160 feet.
Location: At Grover Hot Springs State Park in California, about a 50-minute drive from South Lake Tahoe. Go west on Hot Springs Road from the town of Markleeville (off Highways 88 and 4). The trailhead is in 4.5 miles on the right side of the road, before you come to Hot Springs Creek. There's also access in the park's camping area, although there is no parking available there.
Contact: Toiyabe National Forest, Carson Ranger District, 775/882-2766; Grover Hot Springs State Park, 530/694-2248.

Highway 88 to Meiss Lake Trail
(see map on page 200, site 24)
With its shallow waters, Meiss is one of the warmest lakes in the Tahoe area, making it ideal for swimming. From the trailhead, follow the

trail up the hillside, which is covered with mule ear and sagebrush, to a saddle. From here, enjoy views of the surrounding peaks before continuing along an old jeep route, where the trail crosses the Upper Truckee River and leads into a large meadow. Follow the path to the right .6 miles down the gentle slopes to Meiss Lake. Fishing here is prohibited.

Difficulty: Moderate.

Distance (one way): Four miles.

Time (one way): Three to 3.5 hours.

Elevation (low/high): 8,320 feet to 8,560 feet.

Location: Take U.S. 50 south from South Lake Tahoe to Highway 89 and turn left. Continue to the intersection of Highways 89 and 88 and turn right on Highway 88. Go one mile past the Carson Pass Sno-Park; turn left on the dirt road and park in the dirt parking area. The trailhead is on the other side of the highway, just across from the parking area.

Contact: Lake Tahoe Basin Management Unit; 530/573-2600.

Woods Lake to Round Top Loop
(see map on page 200, site 25)

One of the best hikes in the Tahoe region, this route encompasses three alpine lakes, a spectacular peak, and marvelous vistas of Mokelumne Wilderness, distant Lake Tahoe, Carson Pass, and Nevada's Carson Valley. The beauty of this hike is that you can make a full loop and constantly see new terrain. At the end of the hike, you can jump into tranquil, idyllic Woods Lake to cool off, or enjoy lunch at the shaded picnic tables beside the shoreline.

Look for the trailhead east of the campground (remember to fill out a wilderness permit) and begin the gradual ascent to Winnemucca Lake. The trail begins in forest but soon emerges onto rolling, hilly meadows, which are alive with wildflowers in early summer. It's an easy 1.25-mile hike to Winnemucca, a large, rock-rimmed lake cradled in an exposed valley below a high mountain. There are a few good campsites here and sunning rocks on the lake's south side, but the area is subject to frequent winds. Continue for one mile up the well-maintained trail to Round Top Lake, enjoying gorgeous views of Winnemucca below.

At the crest of the trail, you'll have a striking vista of Round Top Lake, a shallow, almost circular body of water flanked on the south and

ON THE TRAIL

© KEN CASTLE

A hiker takes a breather at Round Top Lake.

west by the sheer, jagged cliffs of the Sisters peaks. You have a choice at this point: You can take the right fork back to Woods Lake, continue straight to Fourth of July Lake (one mile down a very steep path), or take a challenging 1.5-hour side trip to the summit of Round Top Peak. If you make a run at Round Top, the last third of the way is on steep, wide terrain over loose soil and unconsolidated rock, with extremely tricky footholds. Still, many people of average ability make it to the top (or to the ledge just below the peak), where they are rewarded with incredible views for 50 miles or more in almost every direction. Strong, cold winds can buffet the south side of the peak, so dress accordingly. As difficult as it is scrambling all the way up to the top, it is even more difficult slip-sliding back down—in this venture, a hiking staff can come in handy. At Round Top Lake, follow the trail to Woods Lake, past the Lost Cabin Mine and down a series of moderately steep, forested switchbacks to the campground, enjoying lofty views of the lake as you descend.

Difficulty: Mostly moderate, with the option of a strenuous hike to the peak.
Distance (round-trip): Four miles.
Time (round-trip): Four to five hours.
Elevation (low/high): 8,570 feet to 10,380 feet at the top of Round Top Peak.
Location: From South Lake Tahoe, take Highway 89 south to the dead end at Highway 88, then head west on Highway 88 to the Woods Lake Campground just over the crest of Carson Pass (a total distance of about 20 miles). Turn left on the two-mile paved access road to the campground and look for the nearest available parking at the campground or on the side of the road (the 30 or so spaces at the campground often fill up before 10 A.M.).
Contact: Eldorado National Forest, Eldorado Information Center; 530/644-6048.

Emigrant Lake Trail
(see map on page 200, site 26)
Hikers follow the old route of the Mormon-Emigrant Trail, which pioneers used in the mid-1800s, for 2.5 miles, mostly along the south side of Caples Lake and on the eastern outskirts of

Kirkwood ski resort. The trail then climbs to a junction, where you take the left fork, cross a stream (be careful of the water level in early summer), and continue up a series of forested switchbacks to the lake. The lake is fringed by moderate forest and is surrounded by several high peaks. It receives heavy use in the summer.
Difficulty: Moderate.
Distance (one way): Six miles.
Time (one way): Three to 3.5 hours.
Elevation (low/high): 7,758 feet to 8,600 feet.
Location: The trailhead is at the west end of the dam at Caples Lake on Highway 88, approximately 22 miles southwest of South Lake Tahoe. Limited parking is available west of the dam. A wilderness permit is required and may be obtained from the U.S. Forest Service.
Contact: Eldorado National Forest, Eldorado Information Center; 530/644-6048.

Lake Margaret
(see map on page 200, site 27)
The highly recommended half-day hike to Lake Margaret seems to have it all—meadows alive with wildflowers, mixed aspen and pine forest, a lush and beautiful meandering stream (Caples Creek), awesome peaks, and a mirror-smooth, rock-rimmed lake that offers a few splendid swimming and picnicking spots. The trail is well marked except for two places where it crosses small streams, and then you'll have to look for log bridges and indications of the trail on the opposite side. Also, you'll have to scramble up a short ledge of boulders just before you reach Lake Margaret.

While there isn't much elevation gain or loss, negotiating the trail isn't exactly like taking a casual stroll in the woods, and I found that several families considered it more challenging (and longer) than they had expected. Still, the lake is worth the reward. It's a charming alpine beauty with an elevated granite peninsula that makes for an ideal sunning, picnicking, and swimming spot. Once this is occupied, however, there are only a couple of other good hangouts, but with less favorable access for swimming. The lake is fairly small and gets heavy use from both day hikers and overnight campers. In early to midsummer, sections of the trail that pass through wetlands can be soggy and mosquito-ridden. Late August–September are best for avoiding those problems.

Difficulty: Easy to moderate.

Distance (one way): 2.5 miles.

Time (one way): 1.5 to two hours.

Elevation (low/high): 7,520 feet to 7,740 feet.

Location: Difficult to find and easy to miss, the trailhead is on a side road on the north side of Highway 88 between the Caples Lake spillway trailhead and the Kirkwood Inn. The side road is generally not signed, but is roughly adjacent to a highway horse-crossing sign. If you can't find it, ask at the inn. The side road curves around a corner where you'll see the trailhead; parking is limited, for about 15 to 20 cars.

Contact: Eldorado National Forest, Eldorado Information Center; 530/644-6048.

Shealor Lakes Trail
(see map on page 200, site 28)

For swimming and picnicking, this may be the best hike in the region. Two lakes are visible from the highest point on the hike, but the trail leads to the largest (the other is shallow and choked with weeds). Cradled in a granite depression, the main lake is a swimmer's delight, since its shoreline consists of smooth, gently sloping rock and several shallow, sandy wading areas. Except for the western edge of the lake, flanked by an imposing peak, the shoreline is easily accessible and accommodates several groups of hikers. There also are a couple of good camping sites nestled in the trees. What makes this lake so compelling, apart from its granite shoreline, is that there is room to spread out on the rocky ledges. Moreover, you can hike to a splendid overlook on the northeastern side of the lake and view colorful rock striations in the cliffs and valleys below.

The trail begins under forest canopy, then climbs a rocky, exposed ridge, from which you can see Silver Lake behind you and Shealor Lakes below. Switchbacks descend 500 feet to your destination, and each turn has a spectacular view. Remember that you'll have to ascend every inch of that 500 feet on your way back, but the trail is well marked and graded, and even children have

no trouble with it. This is the perfect place to bring your float tube and picnic lunch, and just hang out for the day. Since the trailhead is tricky to find, usage is not nearly as heavy as at Lake Margaret, another short hike to the east of here (see hike number 28).

Difficulty: Easy.

Distance (one way): 1.5 miles.

Time (one way): 45 minutes to one hour.

Elevation (low/high): 7,200 feet to 7,700 feet.

Location: The trailhead is difficult to find, with no sign on the westbound side of Highway 88 (the sign is on the eastbound side). The trail is off a dirt driveway on the northeast side of the highway approximately one mile west of Kay's Resort at Silver Lake, or a half mile east of Plasse Road. There is parking amid the trees for 8–10 vehicles, and the trail itself is signed.

Contact: Eldorado National Forest, Eldorado Information Center; 530/644-6048.

HIGHWAY 50/WEST OF SOUTH LAKE TAHOE

Horsetail Falls Trail
(see map on page 200, site 29)

A great half-day hike, this route follows Pyramid Creek to Lower Horsetail Falls, so named because of the narrow column at the summit and the wide plume at the bottom. The trailhead has become a popular picnic spot, with its shallow swimming holes and shaded forest. The canyon bearing the falls was carved out by glaciers, the last of which rolled through here more than 10,000 years ago. Several lakes, including Avalanche, Pitt, and Ropi, feed the falls, which are at their strongest in midsummer. The trail parallels the creek much of the way, and follows granite walkways usually marked by "ducks" (rock piles). At the sign designating the boundary of Desolation Wilderness, you can enjoy good distant views of the lower and upper falls, or continue on a rougher and somewhat indistinct trail that peters out entirely once it reaches the rocky bluffs. There are some cold, refreshing ponds along the way, where you can have a picnic or take a dip. Some hikers go all the way to the top, but this is not recommended

ON THE TRAIL

because of the poor footing, steep drop-offs, and unmarked routing. You can get close to the coursing power of the lower falls, if you want to, by inching out along the rocks. If you are bringing children, don't take them beyond the wilderness sign. As you return to the trailhead, enjoy the spectacular views of Lover's Leap, south of the highway, and other peaks of Eldorado National Forest.

Difficulty: Easy to moderate.
Distance (round-trip): 1.5 to two miles.
Time (round-trip): 1.5 to two hours.
Elevation (low/high): 6,110 feet to 6,310 feet.
Location: At the big curve of U.S. 50 at Twin Bridges, about 16 miles east of South Lake Tahoe. The area often is packed with cars, and you may have to park some distance up the road. A wilderness permit is required and may be obtained from the U.S. Forest Service.
Contact: Eldorado National Forest, Eldorado Information Center; 530/644-6048.

Lover's Leap Trail
(see map on page 200, site 30)

Follow this trail through heavy forest to a dramatic high overlook of Pyramid Peak, Turtle Rock, and the drainage of the South Fork of the American River. The gradual climb leads to a large, relatively flat, wide-open rock and grass summit that is about the size of a football field. You can enjoy different vistas from varying parts of the perimeter, including some of the upper slopes of the Sierra-at-Tahoe ski area to the east, Desolation Wilderness to the north, U.S. 50 below, and several attractive surrounding valleys. The sheer walls that drop toward the river are nationally popular with rock climbers. The route to the top is shared with horseback riders, joggers, and mountain bikers.

Difficulty: Moderate.
Distance (one way): 2.5 miles.
Time (one way): 1.5 to two hours.
Elevation (low/high): 5,900 feet to 6,900 feet.
Location: Off U.S. 50, one-quarter mile west of Strawberry (about 35 minutes west of South Lake Tahoe). Turn south at the 42 Mile picnic site, take a right across the bridge following Packsaddle Pass Road, and go one mile to the junction

with Strawberry Canyon Road. Take Strawberry for one-half mile to the trailhead.
Contact: Eldorado National Forest, Eldorado Information Center; 530/644-6048.

Wrights Lake to Smith Lake Trail
(see map on page 200, site 31)

Among the premier hikes in the region, this short but vigorous outing through the "back door" of Desolation Wilderness encompasses four uniquely different but equally spectacular alpine lakes. Wrights Lake has something for almost everyone: one section that is deep and fishable, and another that is warm and shallow, with rock and boulder islands. There's a pine-covered picnic area with tables and barbecues, next to the best swimming access. No outboard motors are allowed, so the lake is great for canoes, rafts, and small sailing dinghies.

The first of two hikes from the trailhead begins at the east end of the lake, next to an inlet. There are two forks beyond here; the left fork leads north around the lake and, not far beyond, the right fork leads to Grouse and Smith Lakes (continuing straight ahead takes you to Twin Lakes). Take the right spur, and follow it across smooth but rising granite slabs, with the trail indicated by "ducks" (rock piles), until it climbs into red fir and lodgepole pine forest. A moderate ascent along a rocky stairway eventually reaches a creek, and the trail crisscrosses the water until it rises abruptly to a shelf. Just over the ridge is the incredibly beautiful and tranquil Grouse Lake, framed by granite walls, moderate tree cover, and a small meadow. Enjoy a rest stop here before continuing a steep half mile to Hemlock Lake, with great vistas of Wrights Lake below. Hemlock, too, is magnificent; the north end has a shallow, sandy shoreline bordered with trees, while the south end has a high, sheer-walled cliff with spectacular striations. This wonderful, wind-protected lake makes an ideal wading, swimming, and floating destination.

The trail continues for about one-third of a mile farther, initially on duff-covered forest trail, then up a steep, bouldered path with sections of slippery talus. There is an open promontory with lush wildflowers (including Indian paintbrush and lupine) and a lofty panorama of Crystal Basin and its reservoirs below. Beyond this point, the trail turns to granite walkways again before reaching Smith Lake. This almost perfectly round, glacial lake has deep waters and is cradled by rockfalls and towering Mt. Price (elevation 9,975 feet), which separates this drainage from Lake Aloha to the east. The southwest corner of the lake has the only patch of level ground here, but there are few trees and no obvious sites for tents. Although it is marvelous to behold, the lake is quite cold, exposed to the winds, and is not hospitable for swimming. The trail ends here, so you'll need to retrace your steps (carefully!) back to Hemlock and Wrights Lakes.

Difficulty: Moderate to moderately strenuous.

Distance (one way): 2.8 miles.

Time (one way): 2.5 to three hours.

Elevation (low/high): 7,000 feet to 8,500 feet.

Location: At Wrights Lake, a 55-minute drive west of South Lake Tahoe. Take U.S. 50 west and turn right on Wrights Lake Road about four miles west of Strawberry. There is a sign for the turnoff, but it's easy to miss the road. It rises steeply for eight miles along switchbacks and on bumpy pavement before reaching the Wrights Lake Campground. At the junction of three roads in the campground, take the right fork and follow it for approximately 1.5 miles past summer cabins to the Twin Lakes and the Grouse Lakes Trailhead. Parking is very limited—accommodating about 15 vehicles—so get here early. Otherwise, you'll have to park back at the campground. A wilderness permit is required at the trailhead.

Contact: Eldorado National Forest, Eldorado Information Center; 530/644-6048.

Wrights Lake to Island Lake Trail
(see map on page 200, site 32)

Of the two hikes from this trailhead into Desolation Wilderness, this is the more heavily traveled. The large lakes—Twin and Island—are popular with backpackers and anglers, and there are many small, unnamed lakes surrounding them. The thing to know about this hike is that it is mostly over crumbling rock or smooth granite, with very little tree cover. Thus the temperatures can be quite hot in summer, and extra water is advised. Families with children enjoy this hike because the outlet from Twin Lakes sends wide ribbons of water over lightly polished granite, creating natural water slides.

The trail meanders up a continuous rocky surface, paralleling a creek that cuts through a deep gorge just below Twin Lakes. All of the lakes are in a glacier-scoured canyon, amid open terrain surrounded by impressive granite walls. Flat, rocky peninsulas jut from the southern and eastern sections of Lower Twin Lake; these make great places for sunning and picnicking. The trail to Island Lake crosses a small dam of logs and rocks at Lower Twin Lake (be careful!) and rises gradually on the north slopes, dipping down to several small ponds and scenic Boomerang Lake. At several points, the route is nearly obscured by overgrown brush and wildflowers—wear long pants or tights to avoid scratches and scruffs. Island Lake, the largest in the area, is aptly named for its handful of small rock islands. The lake's irregular perimeter is mostly elevated, with manageable, but not particularly easy, access to the water's edge. At the head of the canyon, the lake gets its share of wind, and the water is cold. The most impressive elements of these glacial lakes are the rock formations and peaks surrounding them. There are many photogenic vantage points over these lakes and the Crystal Mountains. The trail ends at Island Lake; retrace your steps to the starting point.

Difficulty: Moderate.

Distance (one way): 3.1 miles.

Time (one way): 2.5 to three hours.

Elevation (low/high): 7,000 feet to 8,100 feet.

Location: The trailhead is at the east end of the Wrights Lake Campground, eight miles north of U.S. 50 on Wrights Lake Road, about a 55-minute drive west of South Lake Tahoe. For detailed directions, see the Wrights Lake to Smith Lake Trail, hike number 21. A wilderness permit is required and may be obtained from the U.S. Forest Service.

Contact: Eldorado National Forest, Eldorado Information Center; 530/644-6048.

FEATHER RIVER COUNTRY/LAKES BASIN

Sierra Buttes Lookout via the Tamarack Lakes Trail

(see map on page 200, site 33)

Of all the mountains in the Tahoe region, surely the Sierra Buttes are the most dramatic. Their jagged peaks are reminiscent of the Swiss Alps, and from almost any vantage point they command attention and awe. Thus, hiking to the fire lookout tower at the summit is virtually a pilgrimage for any self-respecting mountain trekker; many people come to this region specifically to scale the Buttes. There are easier routes to the top (one of them is from the Pacific Crest Trail higher up), but this one is regarded as the most scenic, though it's no cakewalk.

From the trailhead, follow the rough gravel road for one-quarter mile until it forks, then head to the right. After a half mile, you reach a sign reading "Sardine Lakes and Sand Pond via Trail." This is the Tamarack Connection Trail. Keep to the right and you will see another sign marked "Sierra Buttes L.O." in 200 yards. The twin Tamarack Lakes (elevation 6,754 feet) are on your left. Continue another half mile to a sign directing you to the left. The trail follows a ridge, above Young America Lake (elevation 7,250 feet), to the lookout. From this wildfire detection station, catch your breath and drink in the views of Mt. Lassen and Mt. Shasta to the north, Mt. Rose to the east, and the many sparkling lakes below.

Difficulty: Strenuous.

Distance (one way): 3.5 miles.

Time (one way): 2.5 to three hours.

Elevation (low/high): 6,220 feet to 8,587 feet.

Location: From Truckee, drive 32 miles north on Highway 89 to Highway 49. Head 16 miles west on Highway 49 to the intersection with Gold Lake Road at Bassett's Station and turn north. Continue for 1.4 miles to Salmon Creek and turn left onto the bridge. Go for about .3 mile and turn right onto Packer Lake Road. Proceed for 2.5 miles and turn left onto Forest Service Road 93 (Packer Saddle Road). Continue for .1 mile. On the left side of the road is a large sign reading "Lower and Upper Tamarack Lakes and Sierra Buttes." The hike begins here; there is ample parking.

Contact: Tahoe National Forest, Downieville Ranger District; 530/288-3231.

Round Lake Loop Trail

(see map on page 200, site 34)

No hike in the entire Tahoe region connects so many lakes with such varying and unique features as this one. It is the most favored day hike in the aptly named Lakes Basin, a region rich in volcanic rock formations, productive fishing waters, unique mountain lodges, and remnants of the Gold Rush. The trail is excellent for family outings, thanks to its relatively modest elevation, minimal ups and downs, and diversity of terrain. By all means, savor this one at a leisurely pace—bring a picnic lunch, a swimsuit, and a fishing rod. The trail touches or overlooks nine lakes, from diminutive ponds to large impoundments.

Traveling clockwise, start your hike in the direction of Round Lake, following a well-maintained trail for 1.7 miles to the lake. Stop here for a while, if you wish, but do continue on to more scenic lakes. Follow a steep, rocky trail for .9 mile to Silver Lake, a beautiful, rock-rimmed body of water that is arguably the most attractive of the group and a compelling spot for a picnic lunch. At Silver, there's a junction, and the left fork (signed for Mt. Elwell) continues for about a half mile to a series of three small ponds known as Helgramite Lakes—a worthy detour. Back on the main trail, which

> *Of all the mountains in the Tahoe region, surely the Sierra Buttes are the most dramatic. Their jagged peaks are reminiscent of the Swiss Alps, and from almost any vantage point they command attention and awe. Thus, hiking to the fire lookout tower at the summit is virtually a pilgrimage for any self-respecting mountain trekker; many people come to this region specifically to scale the Buttes.*

begins a long descent, hike for about one-eighth of a mile until you reach an overlook of magnificent Long Lake, the second largest in the basin, flanked by Mt. Elwell (elevation 7,812 feet). Shortly afterward, you reach another junction; take the right fork, which passes Cub, Little Bear, and Big Bear Lakes (Little Bear and Big Bear offer good swimming and fishing possibilities). Beyond Big Bear, take the right fork of a third junction back to Gold Lake Lodge and the parking area. (To top off a memorable day, consider making dinner reservations well in advance at one of the fabled, old-fashioned lodges in the area such as Gray Eagle, Sardine Lake, or Gold Lake.)

Difficulty: Moderate.

Distance (round-trip): 3.75 miles.

Time (round-trip): Three to four hours.

Elevation (low/high): 6,475 feet to 6,874 feet.

Location: From Truckee, drive 32 miles north on Highway 89 to Highway 49. Head 16 miles west on Highway 49 to the intersection with Gold Lake Road at Bassett's Station, and go right for about five miles to Gold Lake. The trailhead is at the parking lot of Gold Lake Lodge. The driving time from Truckee is around 50 minutes.

Contact: Plumas National Forest, Beckwourth Ranger District; 530/836-2575.

PEAK EXPERIENCES

If you've got good hiking boots and strong legs and are in reasonably good physical condition, consider scaling one or more of Tahoe's walkable mountains. You don't need ropes or pitons to reach the summit of any of these peaks, though you may have to scramble cross-country or climb some rocks on the last section of your hike. But once you reach the top, you'll treasure both the effort and the view. Except where noted, these are all strenuous hikes.

Peaks are keyed to the Hiking Trails map.

Truckee/Donner

Mt. Judah (see map on page 200, site 35)
Now part of the Sugar Bowl ski resort, this peak has great views of Donner Summit, Donner Lake, Truckee, and Anderson and Castle Peaks, as well as the more distant Sierra Buttes. The length of this strenuous hike depends on the trailhead you set off from. For the longer hike, take the Castle Peak Area/Boreal Ridge Road exit, which is immediately west of I-80's Donner Summit roadside rest area. (Unattended vehicles are not allowed in the rest area.) Follow the sign to the Pacific Crest Trail and go .4 mile to the PCT trailhead. You can reduce the distance by 3.5 miles by accessing the PCT off Old Highway 40 at Donner Summit Lake Mary Road. Hikers must travel northeast cross-country from Roller Pass along the crest of Mt. Judah to reach the highest point.

Elevation, distance: 8,243 feet; 2.5 to six miles one way.

Contact: Tahoe National Forest, Truckee Ranger District; 530/587-3558.

(see map on page 200, site 36)
This is the highest peak in Tahoe National Forest, with panoramic views of the Sierra Divide and Donner Pass. It's a strenuous climb to the top, though. To reach the trailhead, take Highway 89 north from Truckee to Forest Service Road 07 (to Jackson Meadows Reservoir). Turn west and drive 1.3 miles, then turn left on Independence Lake Road. Continue south about one-half mile to the junction with Sierra County Road S301. Turn right at the first intersection and continue west for three miles to the trailhead.

Elevation, distance: 9,143 feet; 4.5 miles one way.

Contact: Tahoe National Forest, Sierraville Ranger District; 530/994-3401.

Squaw Valley

Tinkers Knob (see map on page 200, site 37)
From the top of Tinkers Knob, enjoy an impressive 360-degree view of Granite Chief Wilderness, the headwaters of the North Fork of the American River, and Donner Pass. To reach the Granite Chief Trailhead, go south on Highway 89 from Truckee (or north from Tahoe City), turn west on Squaw Valley Road and drive 2.2 miles to the Squaw Valley Fire Station. The trailhead is on the east (right) side of the fire station and is clearly marked. It soon intersects with the Pacific Crest Trail; head north to the Tinkers Knob Saddle.

It's a short climb from here to the top. Be aware that this is a strenuous hike.

Elevation, distance: 8,950 feet; seven miles one way.

Contact: Tahoe National Forest, Truckee Ranger District; 530/587-3558.

Twin Peaks (see map on page 200, site 38)
Sweeping vistas of Lake Tahoe, Mt. Rose, Tinkers Knob, and the Desolation and Granite Chief Wilderness areas are the main attractions of this extremely difficult hike. The access point for this trek is the Granite Chief Trailhead (see Tinkers Knob, above). When the trail intersects with the Pacific Crest Trail, head south to reach Twin Peaks.

Elevation, distance: 8,800 feet; 14.5 miles one way.

Contact: Tahoe National Forest, Truckee Ranger District; 530/587-3558.

Tahoe City/West Shore
Ellis Peak (see map on page 200, site 39)
Ellis provides impressive panoramas of Lake Tahoe to the east and Granite Chief Wilderness and Hellhole Reservoir to the west. This is the least strenuous of the peak hikes. It's near Barker Pass at the end of Blackwood Canyon Road on the West Shore. For a detailed description, see Ellis Peak Trail hike, above.

Elevation, distance: 8,640 feet; 2.5 miles one way.

Contact: Tahoe National Forest, Truckee Ranger District; 530/587-3558.

Incline Village/Mt. Rose
Mt. Rose (see map on page 200, site 40)
The highest peak of the group, Mt. Rose affords views of Reno and the Washoe Valley to the east and Lake Tahoe to the west. It's above Incline Village on the North Shore. For a detailed description, see Mt. Rose Trail hike, above.

Elevation, distance: 10,778 feet; six miles one way.

Contact: Toiyabe National Forest, Carson Ranger District; 775/882-2766.

South Lake Tahoe
Mt. Tallac (see map on page 200, site 41)
Splendid vistas of Emerald Bay, Cascade Lake, Fallen Leaf Lake, and Desolation Wilderness are the reward for climbing to the top of Mt. Tallac, on the West Shore of Lake Tahoe across from Baldwin Beach. For a detailed description of the trail, see hike number 18.

Elevation, distance: 9,735 feet; five miles one way.

Contact: Lake Tahoe Basin Management Unit; 530/573-2600.

Ralston Peak (see map on page 200, site 42)
You get great views of Lake Tahoe and Desolation Wilderness from this lofty perch, including Ralston and Echo Lakes below and Round Top at Carson Pass to the south. The trailhead parking is across from Camp Sacramento on the north side of U.S. 50, about six miles west of Echo Summit. The road on the east end of the parking area leads to the trailhead 200 yards away.

Elevation, distance: 9,235 feet; four miles one way.

Contact: Eldorado National Forest, Eldorado Information Center; 530/644-6048.

Stateline/Zephyr Cove
Genoa Peak (see map on page 200, site 43)
Genoa offers great views of Tahoe and the Carson Valley. To get there, you must hike cross-country from the section of the Tahoe Rim Trail between Spooner Summit on U.S. 50 and Daggett Pass on the Kingsbury Grade on Highway 207. For a detailed description, see Tahoe Rim Trail South hike, above.

Elevation, distance: 9,150 feet; four miles one way.

Contact: Tahoe Rim Trail Fund, 298 Kingsbury Grade/P.O. Box 4647, Stateline, NV 89449; 775/588-0686.

Kirkwood/Hope Valley/Markleeville
Round Top Peak
(see map on page 200, site 44)
This volcanic peak has spectacular panoramas of Carson Pass, Lake Tahoe, the Carson Valley, and Mokelumne Wilderness. It's tough going

on loose soil and scree for the last quarter mile. Bring a hiking staff and be very careful! The trail leaves from Woods Lake, east of Caples Lake. For a detailed description, see Woods Lake to Round Top Loop hike, above.

Elevation, distance: 10,380 feet; four miles one way.

Contact: Eldorado National Forest, Eldorado Information Center; 530/644-6048.

Little Round Top
(see map on page 200, site 45)

From Little Round Top, climbers enjoy panoramic views of Caples Lake, Carson Pass, and surrounding peaks. To reach the trailhead, turn north off Highway 88 at the CalTrans Maintenance Station near Caples Lake. Continue for two miles to Schneider Cow Camp, where parking is available. Follow the four-wheel-drive road for one-half mile to the trailhead. The last part, near the junction of the Pacific Crest Trail, requires a cross-country ascent.

Elevation, distance: 9,500 feet; 2.5 miles one way.

Contact: Eldorado National Forest, Eldorado Information Center; 530/644-6048.

Feather River Country/Lakes Basin
Eureka Peak (see map on page 200, site 46)

In Plumas Eureka State Park, a one-hour drive northwest of Truckee, this strenuous loop trail offers a 360-degree view of the Lakes Basin and, to the north, Mt. Lassen. The trail begins at the west side of Eureka Lake Dam, at the end of the county road from Graeagle to Johnsville.

Elevation, distance: 7,447 feet; a three-mile loop.

Contact: Plumas Eureka State Park; 530/836-2380.

Mt. Elwell (see map on page 200, site 47)

In the Lakes Basin area northwest of Truckee, this strenuous hike offers views of Long Lake, the Lakes Basin, the Sierra Buttes, and, to the distant north, Mt. Lassen. You should allow at least six hours for the complete loop. The trailhead is on the road leading to Gray Eagle Lodge, southwest of Graeagle on the Gold Lake Road.

There's lots of scree on the way up, and the last .7 mile before the summit has an elevation gain of nearly 800 feet. By the time you finish this trek, you'll be ready for a glass of wine and a full-course meal at Gray Eagle Lodge, a great place to rest your feet and rejuvenate.

Elevation, distance: 7,812 feet; 3.8 miles one way.

Contact: Plumas National Forest, Beckwourth Ranger District; 530/284-7126.

Haskell Peak (see map on page 200, site 48)

On a clear day, the spectacular views that you can get on this moderate hike might include the neighboring Sierra Buttes, Mt. Rose, Mt. Lassen, and Mt. Shasta. The trail sees light use, mainly because the trailhead is well off the Gold Lake Road in the Lakes Basin area. The trail climbs moderately for the first mile, then levels off in an open area with a view of Haskell Peak before climbing on rocky steps for the last quarter mile. Besides grand vistas, there are some interesting volcanic rock formations. To reach the trailhead, proceed 3.7 miles north of Bassett's Station on the Gold Lake Road (at the intersection with Highway 49) and turn right at the Haskell Peak Road sign. Then follow Forest Road 09 for 8.4 miles until you reach a sign that says, "Haskell Peak Trail 11E02." Parking is sufficient on both sides of the road.

Elevation, distance: 8,107 feet; 1.5 miles one way.

Contact: Tahoe National Forest, Downieville Ranger District; 530/288-3231.

Sierra Buttes (see map on page 200, site 49)

With a jagged profile reminiscent of the European Alps, this is the most impressive-looking of all the area's mountains. The strenuous hike is 2.5 to 3.5 miles one way, depending on which route you take. A manned fire lookout station is at the top. It's near Highway 49 and the Gold Lake Road.

Elevation, distance: 8,587 feet; 2.5 to 3.5 miles one way.

Contact: Tahoe National Forest, Downieville Ranger District; 530/288-3231.

GUIDED HIKES

If you don't like going it alone, or if you prefer the added benefit of learning about local geology, flora, and fauna from a knowledgeable source, consider signing up for a guided hike. Recently, several resorts and independent companies have begun offering treks at various locations around Tahoe. You'll need to call ahead for specific routes, dates, and fees.

Squaw Valley USA

By riding the cable car to High Camp, you can gain 2,000 feet in elevation and select from several hiking options. The benefit in doing this is to use High Camp as a base. And what a base! Although it's on a plateau at 8,200 feet, High Camp has creature comforts that you'd never expect. You can take a dip in a spacious, rock-rimmed swimming lagoon; enjoy a hot barbecue luncheon at tables around the pool or in Alexander's restaurant in the lodge; or use the clean, modern locker rooms for a shower and a change. There is no place at the lake that pampers hikers like this one does. And don't forget the lofty view of Squaw Valley from any of several large, wooden decks.

This spot is enormously popular with families, and the options extend beyond hiking to activities such as bungee jumping, ice skating, and mountain biking. Among the intermediate treks (you can do them by yourself if you wish) are an hourlong hike to Shirley Lake, which is mostly downhill; a 45-minute hike to Emigrant Peak; and a 90-minute hike to Granite Chief Peak. Guided hikes are usually offered daily (especially on weekends or by arrangement) and may or may not have a fee (the cost of the Cable Car ride is $17 for adults, $5 for children 12 and under). By far the most popular outings (drawing hundreds of people) are the full-moon hikes on one or two days each in July and August. Hikers meet at the cable car at 6:30 P.M.–catch a ride to High Camp. You finish the hike by descending back to the valley, which is bathed in moonlight. Because these hikes are so popular, be sure to call in advance for dates and fees; reservations may be necessary. The ski resort also offers stargazing nights with telescopes and university astronomers.
Contact: Squaw Valley USA; 530/583-6985; website: www.squaw.com.

Sugar Bowl

Several scenic hikes begin at this vintage ski area, which is perched high on the Donner Summit. Guided hikes are periodically available, along with rock climbing instruction from neighboring Alpine Skills International, a well-known mountaineering center on Old Highway 40 east of the Sugar Bowl ski area. At the resort itself, moderate hikes can be made to the summits of Mt. Judah (elevation 8,243 feet) and Mt. Lincoln (8,363 feet), both of which are normally served by ski lifts in the winter. The starting point for both of these treks is the Pacific Crest Trailhead at Donner Summit Lake Mary Road, at elevation 7,088 feet. It's about two miles, one way, to either of the peaks.

If you're looking for something with less of an uphill grade, try the easy trek to Flora and Azalea Lakes (about three miles round-trip), which begins on the north side of Old Highway 40 near the Sugar Bowl Road. All of these hikes offer verdant meadows and midsummer wildflower displays, excellent views of the Donner Summit and its surrounding peaks, and vistas of Donner Lake to the east.
Contact: Sugar Bowl Ski and Sports; 530/587-1369; website: www.sugarbowl.com.

Sorensen's Resort

This rustic resort at the junction of Highways 88 and 89 south of South Lake Tahoe offers several unique guided hikes during the summer, including the area's only hike with llamas, those whimsical but surefooted camelid creatures that hail from South America. Llamas are gentle, well-trained pack animals that can carry up to 90 pounds or so of gear. But for these short afternoon or early evening hikes through Hope Valley, you won't need more than a lunch (provided by Sorensen's Cafe), liquids, and maybe a jacket. Your stuff goes on the back of your own personal llama, which you lead along the trail. Llama trips are by reservation only and cost $45 for adults and $15 for children under 12, and, for nonguests, $10 more for adults and $5 more for children. Sorensen's offers other hikes, as well, notably wildflower walks, birding excursions, and one-day treks along the historic Mormon-Emigrant Trail. The resort uses local botanists, naturalists, and historians to lead these trips and, while outsiders may participate, they are oriented to guests of Sorensen's. The excursions, ranging in price $45–65, are offered late May–end of October. Call for a schedule.

Contact: Sorensen's Resort, 14255 Highway 88, Hope Valley, CA 96120; 530/694-2203 or 800/423-9949; website: www .sorensensresort.com.

Tahoe Trips and Trails

This Tahoe City company offers a variety of guided hikes, mountain biking and multisport tours. Three- and five-day programs are available, with a different hike each day, some on trails known only to locals. Other routes involve taking the cable car to High Camp at Squaw Valley, and from there accessing the Pacific Crest Trail. From the PCT there are views of Tahoe, Shirley Canyon, and Granite Chief and Desolation wilderness areas. On the southwest end of Tahoe, there's a hike into Desolation and an optional trek to the top of Mt. Tallac at 9,735 feet. All hiking programs include overnight stays at unique inns including PlumpJack at Squaw Valley and Mourelatos' Lakeshore Resort in Tahoe Vista. Prices range $700–1,200 per person. Multisport tours combine hiking, mountain biking, horseback riding, river rafting and lake kayaking, with trips costing $735 to $1,295 per person, including all overnight accommodations.

Contact: Tahoe Trips and Trails, P.O. Box 6952, Tahoe City, CA 96145; 800/581-HIKE (800/581-4453) or 530/583-4506. Schedule of trips, pricing and descriptions are available on the website at www.tahoetrips.com.

Nature Trails

Opportunities also abound around Lake Tahoe for those who prefer brief walks to long, demanding hikes. The area features numerous trails around the lake and in the adjoining forestland on which you can enjoy natural history, wildlife photography, and beautiful vistas. Self-guided nature trails—some with signposts, others with maps and markers—offer wonderful learning experiences, especially for youngsters. If you'd like to identify the alpine trees and plants that grow in the Sierra, several of these walks will be informative. The meadows and marshes of public access areas can be rich with wildflowers in early summer, as well as fascinating birdlife such as osprey, bald eagles, herons, cranes, and waterfowl. To see such creatures, plan on visiting these places early in the morning or just before sunset. It's always a good idea to come armed with binoculars, a camera, a water bottle—and a little patience.

Trails are keyed to the Nature Trails map.

TRUCKEE/DONNER

Sierra Discovery Trail

(see map on page 224, site 1)

Created by Pacific Gas and Electric as a community service project, this is one of the newest and most fascinating self-guided nature trails in the region. The one-mile walk takes you through wetlands, forest, and streamside habitats, with interpretive signs and a waterfall along the way. The information kiosk at the parking lot describes the Drum-Spaulding hydroelectric project, which links 31 reservoirs, 12 powerhouses, and 53 miles of river on the western slopes of the Sierra. A boardwalk crosses wetlands to a bridge spanning the Bear River, and from there the loop trail meanders through the forest, with a scenic rest area at the midpoint. Restrooms and a nearby picnic area with tables and barbecues beside the river make for a great family outing. The trail is about 30 miles west of Truckee off I-80, near Lake Spaulding and Fuller Lake. From the freeway, follow Highway 20 for 4.6 miles. Turn

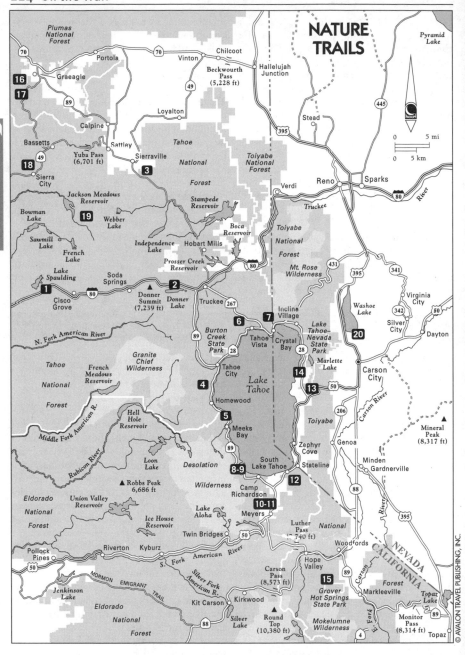

NATURE
TRAILS

© AVALON TRAVEL PUBLISHING, INC.

right on Bowman Lake Road, then go .6 mile to the parking lot.
Contact: PG&E; 916/894-4687.

Donner Memorial State Park
(see map on page 224, site 2)
Two interesting self-guided nature trails originate in this California state park, and they can be combined for a total trip of 2.5 miles. One begins just behind the Emigrant Trail Museum and loops through the forest; it is incorporated into a Junior Ranger program for youngsters. The second departs from the day-use access road and parallels Donner Lake, offering information on the geology, flora and fauna, and human history of the area. This trail meanders mostly through forest, but there are spur trails to the shoreline and beaches, and good picnic sites abound. At this edition went to press, the park has been greatly expanded through the acquisition of a vast new area, called Schallenberger Ridge, and more hiking opportunities are being developed there. Also, local organizations are working on the creation of a Donner Rim Trail, similar in concept to the Tahoe Rim Trail, but most access points are not yet marked or developed. Donner Lake has a warm, protected lagoon that is excellent for swimming. Several times a week throughout the summer months, rangers offer guided hikes ranging in length from two hours to all day; contact the park at the number below for specific schedules and programs. The park is at the Truckee–Donner Lake exit off I-80. The day-use fee is $2 per car.
Contact: Donner Memorial State Park; 530/582-7892.

Cottonwood Creek Botanical Trail
(see map on page 224, site 3)
This half-mile nature trail helps you identify some of the common trees and plants in this mid-alpine region (about 5,400 feet). The trail originates at Cottonwood Campground, just off Highway 89 about 21 miles north of Truckee, and follows Cottonwood Creek, crossing it at two bridges. Get a brochure at the trailhead and proceed to 14 numbered stations to learn about white fir, black cottonwood, Jeffrey pine, Western

juniper, incense cedar, bitterbrush, California wild rose, and other foliage. Many people disregard a quarter-mile spur trail that branches off from the main path close to the trailhead—that's a shame, because it leads to an overlook of the Sierra Valley. You can do the nature trail first, then return to the overlook without retracing much ground.
Contact: Tahoe National Forest, Sierraville Ranger District; 530/994-3401.

TAHOE CITY/WEST SHORE
Page Meadows
(see map on page 224, site 4)
Although there are no designated trails, this large meadow is considered one of the prime places to view wildflowers in early to midsummer. From Highway 89, two miles south of Tahoe City, turn on Pineland Drive. Then turn right on either Forest Service Road 15N60 or Forest Service Road 16N48 to get to the meadow. The area is popular with mountain bikers as well as hikers.
Contact: Lake Tahoe Basin Management Unit; 530/573-2600.

Sugar Pine Point State Park
(see map on page 224, site 5)
Several short to medium walks weave throughout Sugar Pine Point State Park. About 10 miles south of Tahoe City on Highway 89, the park is also home to a nature museum containing several displays, maps, and books, and the Ehrman Mansion.
• **Dolder Trail 3:** For the best views of Lake Tahoe, take the trail that begins near the Ehrman Mansion and leads to the Edwin L. Z'Berg Natural Preserve. The one-mile loop starts high then drops down to follow the lakeshore. Along the way, it passes the world's highest (in elevation) working lighthouse, which is unnamed.
• **General Creek Trail:** This 6.5-mile loop follows the General Creek drainage and enters Forest Service land. An optional side trip goes four miles from the campground to Lily Pond.
Contact: Sugar Pine Point State Park; 530/525-7982.

KINGS BEACH/TAHOE VISTA/CARNELIAN BAY

North Tahoe Regional Park
(see map on page 224, site 6)

In addition to a large day-use area for field sports, tennis, and picnicking, this park offers about six miles of multiuse trails, some with views of Lake Tahoe. Hikers and mountain bikers share the trails, some of which lead to the famous Fibreboard Freeway, a wide dirt road that traces the ridge of the North Shore. The park is off Highway 28 at Tahoe Vista. Turn north on National Avenue and follow signs to the parking lot.

Contact: North Tahoe Public Utility District; 530/546-5043.

INCLINE VILLAGE/CRYSTAL BAY

Stateline Lookout Trail
(see map on page 224, site 7)

Here is one of the best high-elevation vantage points at Lake Tahoe. This half-mile paved loop trail, which begins at a fire lookout 1,000 feet above Crystal Bay on the North Shore, includes detailed markers explaining the natural and human history of the area. From Highway 28, turn north on Reservoir Drive, east of the Tahoe Biltmore Lodge and Casino. Turn right on Lakeview Avenue, then left on Forest Service Road 1601 (by the iron pipe gate). Park in the lot just below the lookout.

Contact: Lake Tahoe Basin Management Unit; 530/573-2600.

SOUTH LAKE TAHOE

D. L. Bliss State Park and Emerald Bay State Park (see map on page 224, site 8)

Several short nature trails exist in these neighboring parks on the West Shore of Lake Tahoe, about nine miles north of South Lake Tahoe on Highway 89. Before heading out on one of the footpaths, stop at the new nature center at the entrance of D. L. Bliss State Park to check out the informative displays. The day-use fee for entering the parks is $2 per car.

• **Balancing Rock Nature Trail:** Pick up a trail guide at the D. L. Bliss office and follow this half-mile path in the northwest section of the park. The brochure has text that corresponds with 19 numbered trail markers to explain the relationship between the soils, plants, and animals found in the park. The highlight of the walk is the Balancing Rock, a 130-ton granite boulder perched precariously on a slender stone base. The rock has been eroding over time and will eventually fall when enough material is lost to break the equilibrium between the two pedestals.

• **Lighthouse Trail:** Another short trail at D. L. Bliss visits the site of an old lighthouse on Rubicon Point, which overlooks one of the deepest areas of Lake Tahoe. From this high vantage point, you can see more than 100 feet into the blue depths.

• **Vikingsholm Trail:** The most famous hike at Emerald Bay State Park follows a steep, one-mile trail from the Harvey West parking lot on Highway 89 down to Vikingsholm Castle, a Scandinavian-style estate constructed in 1928. Currently, park rangers conduct tours through the mansion every half hour 10 A.M.–4 P.M. during summer. The trail drops 500 feet in elevation, so the going is much tougher on the way back. If you want to hike further once you are on the beach, you can go 1.5 miles along a new trail on the south shore to Eagle Point.

Contact: D. L. Bliss and Emerald Bay State Parks; 530/525-7277.

Lake Tahoe Visitor Center
(see map on page 224, site 9)

Four miles north of South Lake Tahoe on Highway 89 is the Lake Tahoe Visitor Center, the focal point of the U.S. Forest Service's Lake Tahoe Basin Management Unit. The Forest Service staffs an information desk here with maps and books, and posts listings of naturalist-led activities. Some short walks depart from the visitor center, and several attractions are nearby.

• **Fallen Leaf Dam Trail:** The 2.5-mile loop begins across the highway from the visitor center and follows Taylor Creek to the dam at Fallen Leaf Lake. A two-mile extension loop to Sawmill

Cove provides more scenic vistas from the North Shore of the lake.

• **Forest Tree Trail:** Take this quarter-mile trail and you'll get a living lesson on the Jeffrey pine, the most dominant tree in the Lake Tahoe basin. Placards along the way trace the tree's life cycle, from germination to decomposition.

• **Lake of the Sky Trail:** Starting just behind the visitor center, this short, easy walk leads past the center's amphitheater to the shore of Lake Tahoe. Interpretive signs along the way discuss the first impressions Lake Tahoe made on notables such as author Mark Twain and naturalist John Muir.

• **Rainbow Trail:** This half-mile walk extends from a forest of Jeffrey pine to a mountain meadow, with a chance to see wildflowers along the way in early and midsummer. It takes you to the Stream Profile Chamber, a wonderful underground viewing chamber on Taylor Creek that allows visitors to observe trout and other aquatic life. In October, bright red kokanee salmon migrate upstream to dig their nests; these, too, can be viewed through the chamber windows.

• **Smokey's Trail:** Especially educational for kids, this easy, one-eighth-mile walk ventures just outside the visitor center. Children who complete the trail and can remember the procedures for building a safe campfire will receive a reward from the Forest Service.

• **Tallac Historic Site Trail:** Walking down this easy, three-quarter-mile footpath is like traveling in a time machine to a bygone era. From the Kiva Beach Picnic Area, stroll along the historic promenade and past the remains of Elias J. "Lucky" Baldwin's Tallac House, the Tallac Casino, and the Tallac Hotel. Then enter the grounds of the Baldwin-McGonagle, Pope, and Valhalla (Heller Estate) summer homes. Before you head out, ask for the Tallac Historic Site brochure at the visitor center.

Contact: Lake Tahoe Visitor Center, 870 Emerald Bay Rd., South Lake Tahoe, CA 96150, 530/573-2674; Lake Tahoe Basin Management Unit, 530/573-2600.

Moraine Trail (see map on page 224, site 10)

This one-mile trail follows the shore of Fallen Leaf Lake on a relatively flat route through a forest. Take Highway 89 north about four miles from South Lake Tahoe to Fallen Leaf Road. Continue for two-thirds of a mile to Fallen Leaf Campground. Drive through the campground and park just before campsite number 75 on the right. Look for the trailhead sign near the parking area. There is no day-use fee.

Contact: Lake Tahoe Basin Management Unit; 530/573-2600.

Angora Lakes Trail
(see map on page 224, site 11)

Two sparkling lakes framed by cliffs await at the end of this half-mile hike, one of the best short walks in the Tahoe region. The elevation gain is just 270 feet. The lakes are popular for swimming and fishing, and a small overnight lodge offers rowboat rentals and a snack shack. From South Lake Tahoe take Highway 89 north about four miles to Fallen Leaf Road and turn left. Turn left again at the first paved road. Continue to Forest Service Road 12N14 (dirt and gravel) then turn right. Continue past the Angora Fire Lookout to the road's end at the parking lot.

Contact: Lake Tahoe Basin Management Unit; 530/573-2600.

Bijou Community Park
(see map on page 224, site 12)

In the heart of South Lake Tahoe is this large city park with several trails that meander through meadows, offering views of Freel Peak and other mountains. The park is at 1021 Al Tahoe Blvd., off U.S. 50.

Contact: South Lake Tahoe Parks and Recreation Department; 530/542-6055.

STATELINE/ZEPHYR COVE
Spooner Lake Trail
(see map on page 224, site 13)

The pleasant 1.75-mile nature walk that circles Spooner Lake is especially scenic in autumn, when the aspen groves concentrated on the south end blaze bright yellow and orange. The adjacent meadows are a riot of wildflowers in the early summer. Throughout the year, except for winter, birdwatching can be excellent, and you might catch a glimpse of an osprey or a migrating bald eagle as you stroll. Bicycles are not allowed on the trail and outboard motors are prohibited on the lake, which guarantees peace and quiet. Swimming is not recommended due to the ubiquitous, though harmless, leech; besides, the shoreline is fairly muddy. Naturalist-rangers offer interpretive programs throughout summer, including wildflower walks. Spooner Lake is in Lake Tahoe-Nevada State Park on Highway 28, one-quarter mile north of the junction with U.S. 50 near South Lake Tahoe. There is parking in a large paved lot as well as in overflow areas, which are often necessary with the large influx of mountain bikers drawn to the park. Day-use fees are $5 per car.

Contact: Lake Tahoe-Nevada State Park; 775/831-0494.

Prey Meadows/Skunk Harbor
(see map on page 224, site 14)

This easy, 1.5-mile walk on the east shore (Nevada side) of the lake off Highway 28 gains just 600 feet in elevation and offers a pleasant stroll through a mixed conifer forest with occasional views of Lake Tahoe. You can see the remains of an old railroad grade, built in the 1870s as part of a system to supply timber to Virginia City. When you reach a fork in the road, you can take the left fork to Prey Meadows, lush with wildflowers in early summer, or the right fork to Skunk Harbor, a small picturesque cove that offers great swimming and sunbathing in the summer.

Contact: Lake Tahoe Basin Management Unit; 530/573-2600.

KIRKWOOD/HOPE VALLEY/MARKLEEVILLE
Grover Hot Springs State Park
(see map on page 224, site 15)

Famed for its hot mineral springs, this California park also offers a short, self-guided loop called the Transition Trail, which has 26 numbered stations that go with a brochure describing the area's natural history. The terrain covered includes glaciers, riparian vegetation, trees, and the large meadow next to the springs. About 1.25 miles in length, the trail begins at the Hot Springs Creek Bridge near the campground and takes about an hour to walk. Another hike, a half-mile walk from the campground on a dirt road, leads to an unnamed waterfall, which cascades about 30 feet. The park is four miles west of Markleeville at the end of Hot Springs Road, off Highway 4 south of its intersection with Highway 88. The day-use fee is $2 per car.

Contact: Grover Hot Springs State Park; 530/694-2248.

FEATHER RIVER COUNTRY/LAKES BASIN
Plumas Eureka State Park
(see map on page 224, site 16)

Four trails, ranging in length from 1.3 to three miles, make this a good family destination. Here, about 60 miles northwest of Truckee, you can explore the site of the famous Jamison gold mine, recounted in the park's museum, or hike to three small lakes and a high peak. Plumas Eureka State Park is west of Graeagle on County Road A14 (to Johnsville), about five miles from its intersection with Highway 89.

• **Eureka Peak Loop:** If you go to the top of the mountain, this is a strenuous, three-mile hike, but you can take an easier, 2.6-mile round-trip to Eureka Lake from the ski hill parking lot.

• **Grass Lake Trail:** From its trailhead at the Upper Jamison Campground, this hike takes you out of the park and into Plumas National Forest, continuing 1.3 miles to Grass Lake. The trail continues on to more interesting and dramatic lakes, including Smith, Wades, Jamison, and Rock.

• **Little Jamison Creek Trail:** On this scenic, 1.5-mile stretch from the museum to the campground, you'll pass through a forest of white fir, Jeffrey pine, and incense cedar, as well as the Jamison Mine complex.

• **Madora Lake Loop:** A delightful, 1.5-mile walk, this forested trail circles a small, lush lake surrounded by reeds and water lilies. The trailhead is next to a parking lot and picnic ground about 2.5 miles east of the museum/park office building via County Road A14.

Contact: Plumas Eureka State Park; 530/836-2380.

Frazier Falls Trail
(see map on page 224, site 17)
This easy walk in the Lakes Basin area leads for half a mile to a scenic fenced overlook of dramatic 100-foot Frazier Falls. The trailhead is at Gold Lake Road about six miles from the Highway 89/Gold Lake Road intersection. The falls make an ideal spot for a great family picnic or to just relax and take in the beautiful surroundings.
Contact: Plumas National Forest, Beckwourth Ranger District; 530/836-2575.

Sand Pond Interpretive Loop Trail
(see map on page 224, site 18)
Near the ruggedly beautiful Sierra Buttes northwest of Truckee, this flat trail extends for three-quarters of a mile from the Sardine Lake Campground to Sand Pond, a favorite swimming hole. At the southeast end of the lake the trail splits. The right fork takes you around Sand Pond, and the left fork is the Sand Pond Interpretive Loop Trail. This trail provides access to a forest/marsh transitional zone and posts information on some of the natural history of the area. Among the wildlife that can be seen is the occasional beaver. Signs along the route also explain the local ecology. To get here, take Highway 89 north from Truckee to Highway 49, then drive west to Gold Lake Road at Bassett's Station. Continue for approximately 1.4 miles, then turn left at the Salmon Creek Bridge. Proceed west toward Sardine Lake for one mile to the Sand Pond Swim Area parking lot.
Contact: Tahoe National Forest, Downieville Ranger District; 530/288-3231.

Woodcamp Creek Interpretive Trail
(see map on page 224, site 19
Want a great outing for the entire family? Head to the Woodcamp Creek Interpretive Trail at Jackson Meadows Reservoir, 33 miles northwest of Truckee. The mile-long trail starts at the Woodcamp Picnic Site, a day-use area next to several campgrounds on the southwest side of the lake, across the dam. You can obtain a leaflet for the self-guided walk at the trailhead. Twenty-six markers explain various types of trees, their life cycles, and the topography along the creek. Take Highway 89 about 17 miles north to Forest Service Road 19N07 (to Jackson Meadows Reservoir) and continue on this paved road for 16 miles until it reaches the campground.
Contact: Tahoe National Forest, Sierraville Ranger District; 530/994-3401.

RENO/CARSON VALLEY
Washoe Lake State Park
(see map on page 224, site 20)
At one time this area just north of Carson City, Nevada, was home to the Washoe Indians, a semi-nomadic people who followed animals and plants with the seasons. They conducted rabbit drives near the lake and used willows and cattails to make baskets. This is prime birdwatching habitat: The park's wetlands and the Scripps Wildlife Management Area to the north provide refuge for many waterfowl. Ducks, coots (mud hens), and pelicans nest near the south end of the lake, and the wet playa areas east of the sand dunes play host to sandhill cranes, great blue herons, and white-faced ibis. The best way to view birds is to stop at the wetlands area, about two miles off the highway, or walk along the beach on the northeast shore of the lake past the dunes.

Visitors can also follow the Deadman's Creek Trail, which originates in the day-use area and travels for one mile across Eastlake Boulevard and 200 feet up to an overlook and a gazebo. To reach the park, take the Lakeview exit from U.S. 395 about one mile north of Carson City and follow Eastlake Boulevard to the park entrance. The day use fee is $3.
Contact: Washoe Lake State Park; 775/687-4319.

Horseback Riding Excursions

Much of Lake Tahoe's history was written by pioneers who braved the Sierra Nevada on horseback, and it seems only fitting that visitors should explore the backcountry the same way. The slap of leather and the clip-clop of hooves have a timeless appeal, but the chief advantage of an equestrian trip is the ability to cover a lot of ground in a short span of time—and with style. Fortunately, many of the trails leading into the wilderness areas around Tahoe accommodate horses as well as hikers.

Hiring a wrangler is the best introduction to the region, though there are ample opportunities to put together your own trip if you own a horse. Guided rides lasting from an hour to several days are available through over a dozen corrals and pack stations scattered around Tahoe, Reno, and the Carson Valley. The diversity of terrain that exists for hikers is there for riders as well. You can take a leisurely jaunt along the Truckee River, a daylong excursion into a wilderness area such as Desolation or Mokelumne, or even a weeklong pack trip that will really give you a chance to clear the cobwebs from your mind.

Horseback riding has long been a tradition in the Sierra Nevada, and it is considered a good family outing. I wouldn't advise taking youngsters under age 10 on long rides, though, unless they are already comfortable with horses. Some operations will take children as young as four on short rides, but the typical minimum age is six or seven. But even though horseback riding is a good family outing, it's not a guaranteed safe venture. Because there's a chance you may fall off your horse, outfitters are emphatic about having you sign a waiver releasing them from any liability. For the most part, the companies listed here have years of experience, but, like any business, they vary in quality. Outfitters range from a makeshift corral that operates in summer only to a year-round facility with boarding stables and riding arenas. While it's difficult to evaluate the quality of an outfitter, you can usually check some of the most obvious signs: cleanliness of the corral or stables; general health and disposition of the animals; and attitude of employees toward their guests. Be leery of any operation that allows or encourages unguided rides. If you have doubts about an outfitter, contact the county animal control office or the nearest U.S. Forest Service ranger station, whichever has regulatory authority.

When booking a trip, ask if your guide is able to share the history and lore of the area. I'm not particularly fond of wranglers who sit in their saddles, mute as a lump of coal, while I'm left to ponder what it is I'm seeing. Horse packing is a profession that certainly is not immune to burnout, especially when wranglers are leading four or five rides a day. But an enthusiastic guide who truly enjoys the high country and interacts with guests always enhances the riding experience.

Of course, the most important relationship is the one between you and your horse. In years of backcountry riding, I've come to accept the fact that all horses are not created equal. They have idiosyncrasies, and they're not reluctant to test a rider. You can expect some kind of quirk from your assigned steed, whether it's squeezing your leg against a tree trunk, traveling under low-hanging branches, or stopping frequently to nibble on foliage. Right off the bat, you need to establish who's in control by showing firmness and resolve.

As with many outdoor pursuits, there is always an element of risk involved. Backcountry trips that offer incredible vistas frequently require negotiating steep, narrow, and rocky trails. The most surefooted animal, one with plenty of experience in the mountains, is the one you want to be on, not some flatland filly that's just been added to the pack string. An educated horse inspires confidence, but it's still a good idea for the rider to help out as much as possible on tough terrain. Move in sync with your horse, leaning forward on the uphill sections and backward on the downhill sections. When encountering other recreationists, such as mountain bikers, off-roaders, or hikers, pull off the trail,

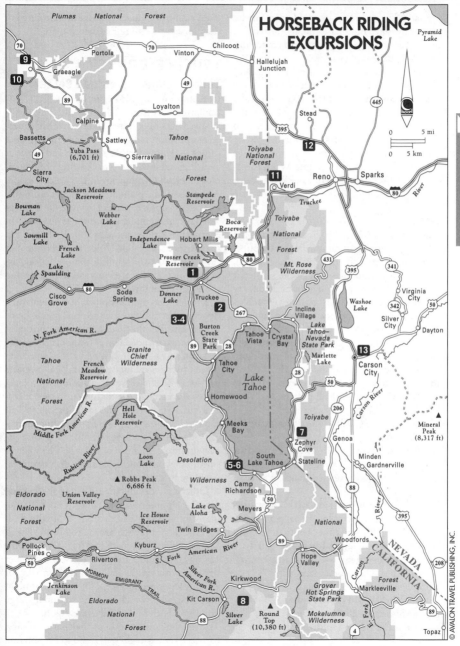

HORSEBACK RIDING EXCURSIONS

stop, and let the traffic pass. Horses can be spooked by different things, from motorized dirt bikes to parasailers, and taking a spill could ruin your whole day—or worse.

Deciding where to go is more than just selecting an outfitter. With a one- or two-hour ride, you can get a spectacular view of Lake Tahoe from one of its surrounding peaks. But the most memorable trips are the overnighters. To see jagged granite massifs and pristine alpine lakes, sign up for a pack horse trip in one of these destinations: Desolation Wilderness, Mokelumne Wilderness, Mt. Rose Wilderness, or the Lakes Basin.

Prices

Some outfitters charge by the hour and some charge by the trip. You can usually get discounted rates for groups and occasionally for children, though most companies charge the same for adults and youngsters. Pricing for backcountry trips are based on a variety of factors, such as how many are in your party, how long you'll be gone, and what you may need in the way of guide services and provisions. Each outfitter will have varying prices, so call ahead for exact rates. On average, expect to pay the following:

One-hour rides: $26–36 per person.

Two-hour rides: $40–50 per person.

Half-day rides: $65–85 per person.

Full-day rides: $90–125 (sometimes including lunch and liquids) per person.

Two-day, overnight ride with campout: $185–270 per person per day (usually including meals), with lower rates for groups of three or more.

Three-day, two-night ride with campout: $450–525 (usually including meals) per person, and generally with a minimum of four people.

Spot trips (wrangler/guide takes you to a campsite and returns by prearrangement): $300–375 per person for a round-trip.

Riding lessons: $50–60 per hour.

Breakfast, lunch and dinner rides: $25–50.

Wagon rides: $15–25 per person.

Pony rides for young children: $6–10 for 30 minutes.

All properties and excursions listed are keyed to the Horseback Riding Excursions map.

TRUCKEE/DONNER

Tahoe Donner Equestrian Center
(see map on page 231, site 1)

Looking for a place to take the kids? This facility specializes in children and is the only equestrian operation at Tahoe to offer summer riding camps for youngsters. The modern and spacious boarding stables house a pack string of 35 horses. Owned and maintained by the Tahoe Donner Association (the planned residential community that occupies a plateau above the town of Truckee), the equestrian center is first-rate in every way. Although the area doesn't have the grandeur of Desolation Wilderness, it does offer ridgeline vistas and a miniforest of quaking aspens, which are covered in vivid foliage during the autumn months.

Shorter rides overlook much of the residential development and traverse the small Tahoe Donner ski area. But the most scenic ride, one that is highly recommended, is a two-hour trip into the lush, green Euer Valley, where a historic ranch owned by descendants of the original pioneers provides a blissful sense of isolation. (By arrangement, you can stay overnight here in one of several rustic cabins in the late Spring or Fall months.) The trail descends from the high northern ridge of Tahoe Donner, following a meandering stream for much of the way. The valley is surrounded by mountains, and riders never feel too close to civilization.

Other day rides follow a ridge trail and provide views of Donner Pass and Summit Lake. Particularly impressive about this facility are the clean corrals, large practice arenas for English and Western riding, well-mannered horses, personable and outgoing guides and instructors, and summer day camps for youth. Trail rides are normally for eight or fewer people except for the Friday-night barbecue rides, which can accommodate large groups on both horses and a haywagon.

Trips: One-hour, two-hour, half-day, full-day, barbecue (Friday night only), and full-moon trail rides on 100 kilometers backing Tahoe National

Forest. All tours are guided. Private rides, pony rides, lessons, horsemanship camps (English and Western, beginning–advanced), and full-service boarding are available. Sunday brunch rides are occasionally offered.

Weddings, birthday parties and other special events can be arranged.

Essentials: There are discounts for children. Closed in winter, after the end of September. Reservations are recommended. To get there, head three miles north of Truckee on Highway 89, turn left on Alder Creek Road, and continue until you reach the center.

Contact: Tahoe Donner Equestrian Center, 15275 Alder Creek Rd., Truckee, CA 96160; 530/587-9470; website: www.tahoedonner.com.

Northstar Stables
(see map on page 231, site 2)

Northstar-at-Tahoe is the area's first true four-seasons resort, and it has a cornucopia of recreational amenities ranging from an excellent ski hill to an 18-hole golf course. In summer, horse-back riders have access to a network of trails north of Mt. Watson (elevation 8,424 feet) and some sweeping if distant views of Lake Tahoe east of Mt. Pluto (elevation 8,617 feet).

The most popular outings are the one-hour rides up Porcupine Hill, where you can get commanding views of Martis Valley. Half-day rides follow wooded trails east of the downhill ski area, to a lookout that embraces the valley and Donner Pass, or to points near Brockway Summit, which affords a commanding vista of Lake Tahoe. Full-day rides, for experienced riders only, reach the crest of the ridgeline, encompassing the Tahoe Rim Trail and points such as Watson Lake. Other destinations include Gray Lake in the new Mt. Rose Wilderness, east of Highway 267 off the Brockway Summit, and Red Rock Desert, 20 miles north of Reno on the west side of Pyramid Lake. This well-established facility, operated by veteran rider Terry Kauffman, has a string of about 25 horses.

Trips: Trail rides are one and two hours in duration. All tours are guided. Longer rides, pony

ON THE TRAIL

COURTESY OF NORTHSTAR-AT-TAHOE

riding horseback at Northstar-at-Tahoe

rides for children, lessons, and boarding are available.

Essentials: Open June–October 8 A.M.–5 P.M. daily. Reservations are recommended. Six miles north of Lake Tahoe at the Northstar Drive exit off Highway 267.

Contact: Northstar Stables, 910 Northstar Dr./P.O. Box 129, Truckee, CA, 96161; 530/562-2480; website: www.northstarattahoe.com.

SQUAW VALLEY
Squaw Valley Stables
(see map on page 231, site 3)

This family-run operation allows you to get picturesque views of Lake Tahoe, Squaw Valley (site of the 1960 Winter Olympics), and several high peaks, depending on the duration of the trip. Most rides take place on the mountain above an 18-hole golf course, which covers much of the meadow, and are geared to beginning and intermediate riders. The half-day ride ascends about 700 feet to Juniper Ridge, with views of the valley, Lake Tahoe, and the posh Resort at Squaw Creek. Shorter rides go partway up the hill. All rides are on private land, and all are guided. The stables have been operated by Eric and Maita Pavel since 1981, but historically date back to the 1930s, when a train that ran from Truckee to Tahoe City would drop off recreationists at Squaw Valley. The Pavels have a string of about 30 horses, mostly quarter horses, plus several Shetland and Welsh ponies.

Trips: One-hour, two-hour, and half-day rides. There are no overnight trips. All tours are guided and leave every half hour. Pony rides, private rides, lessons, and boarding are available.

Essentials: Open daily from 8:30 A.M.–4:30 P.M. from the week before Memorial Day to Labor Day. Closed in winter. Reservations are recommended. Minimum age is seven, and maximum number of riders per tour is seven. At the Squaw Valley exit off Highway 89 between Tahoe City and Truckee.

Contact: Squaw Valley Stables, 1525 Squaw Valley Rd./P.O. Box 2481, Olympic Valley, CA 96146; 530/583-7433; website: www.squaw.com

TAHOE CITY
Alpine Meadows Stables
(see map on page 231, site 4)

Gentle trail horses and personable wranglers are part of this well-run operation. The modest corral isn't the fanciest you'll ever see, but don't let that be a deterrent. The stables are perched on the edge of a spectacular canyon, and even short rides can bring you to some of the best high-elevation vantage points on the North Shore, with views of granite peaks such as the Munchkins and of Alpine Meadows Ski Area. In June and July, a half-day ride to Page Meadows is popular with mountain wildflower aficionados, though you'd better come prepared to slather on plenty of mosquito repellent. This route, mostly on a wide forest road, is also shared with mountain bikers. Overnight trips can be arranged to Granite Chief Wilderness, and there's a new ride to Paradise Lake that originates at a separate staging area on the Donner Summit.

The main stables are easy to reach, just off Highway 89 between Truckee and Tahoe City, and not far from the popular River Ranch Lodge. The operation has been a family-owned business since 1967, and current owner Larry Courtney puts a high emphasis on safety and customer satisfaction. His 18 to 20 horses are carefully selected after they've proven themselves with his guides for two years, and the care they receive certainly shows.

Trips: One-hour, two-hour, and half-day rides. All tours are guided. Pack charters are available.

Essentials: Daily 9 A.M.–6 P.M., May 15–November 1. Three-quarters of a mile off Highway 89 on Alpine Meadows Road between Tahoe City and Truckee.

Contact: Alpine Meadows Stables, 2600 Alpine Meadows Rd., Tahoe City, CA 96145; 530/583-3905.

INCLINE VILLAGE/MT. ROSE
Tin Cup Adventures

See Carson City section, below. Offers rides in the Mt. Rose Wilderness.

CITY OF SOUTH LAKE TAHOE

Cascade Stables
(see map on page 231, site 5)

Not only is this one of the oldest and best-run stables in the region, it's also on the most attractive piece of real estate of any equestrian center in the basin. Well off Highway 89 on the West Shore, just before you ascend to Emerald Bay, Cascade has lakeside frontage that is to die for, with an excellent picnic spot on a sandy beach. Owner Harold "Shrimp" Ebright is the latest member of the Ebright clan to manage the business, which has been going since 1935. He accommodates guests for one- and two-hour rides, mostly on private trails, up to and around Cascade Lake and Cascade Falls, as well as to a meadow overlooking the shore of Lake Tahoe. His backcountry "spot trips"—packing you and your gear into a predetermined site for several days—are among his most popular offerings.

The corral is on the doorstep of Desolation Wilderness, and the recommended trip, leisurely enough for most riders, covers Dicks, Fontanillis, and the three Velma Lakes, with camping stays at Dicks or Middle Velma. Surrounded by jagged peaks and granite canyons, these are among Desolation's most spectacular lakes. But you'll encounter plenty of hikers, anglers, and backpackers on the trail. As another option, Ebright will trailer horses to the popular Meeks Bay Trail, which covers Genevieve, Crag, and Stony Ridge Lakes. Breakfast, taken on a private beach next to Lake Tahoe, usually includes ham and eggs and fried potatoes and onions. Dinner includes steak, fried potatoes and onions, salad, beans, garlic bread, and a dessert of watermelon or pie.

Trips: One-hour, two-hour, breakfast and dinner rides, as well as backcountry pack horse charters. Pack trips do not include meals.

Essentials: Open late June–October, daily 8 A.M.–5 P.M. Reservations are required for breakfast and dinner rides. Off Highway 89 near Cascade Lake and Emerald Bay in South Lake Tahoe.

Contact: Cascade Stables, P.O. Box 7034, South Lake Tahoe, CA 96158; 530/541-2055.

Camp Richardson Corral and Pack Station (see map on page 231, site 6)

One of Tahoe's historic corrals, Camp Richardson has been run by the same family since 1934. Current operator Jill Ross and her grown children, Roberta and Quint Ross, enjoy a good reputation, and their corral is well situated for explorations of lush, wooded West Shore attractions such as Desolation Wilderness, Fallen Leaf Lake, and a couple of hillside overlooks of Lake Tahoe. It's about a 15-minute drive from Stateline, or a few minutes north of the "Y" intersection on Highway 89. If you're staying in town, you can take the Tahoe Trolley to get here. For guests of Camp Richardson Resort, one of the lake's premier family lodges, the stables are just a short walk away.

The one- and two-hour rides travel through meadows or pine forest and offer vistas of Lake Tahoe or Fallen Leaf Lake. The corral usually has a couple of dozen horses available, and the animals are well cared for. The facility itself is spacious, with several buildings and a large parking lot, along with an outdoor picnic area. With a string of 30 horses, this is one of the busiest operations at the lake, so don't expect much personalized attention.

Trips: One-hour, two-hour, and half-day guided trail rides over the Aspen, Meadow, and Fallen Leaf Lake Trails. (Half-day rides take in Floating Island Lake, a heavily wooded backcountry lake that is undistinguished, except as a breeding ground for mosquitoes.) Breakfast rides, evening steak rides (which go to Fallen Leaf Lake), wagon rides, and boarding are available. Winter sleigh rides are available December–March.

Essentials: The minimum age is six (eight on pack trips, younger ages on wagon rides). It's open May–September, daily 8 A.M.–5 P.M. Reservations are necessary. It's on Emerald Bay Road near Fallen Leaf Road.

Contact: Camp Richardson Corral and Pack Station, P.O. Box 8335, South Lake Tahoe, CA 96158; 530/541-3113.

ON THE TRAIL

STATELINE/ZEPHYR COVE

Zephyr Cove Resort Stables
(see map on page 231, site 7)

Just four miles northeast of the Stateline casinos on the Nevada side, this operation, which dates back to the 1930s, offers lofty views of Zephyr Cove and its resident paddle wheeler, the *M.S. Dixie II.* You and your horse will do a lot of climbing along heavily forested trail, ranging from 1,000 feet to 2,500 feet above Tahoe, depending on whether you take a one- or two-hour ride. From the highest point, you can see a big chunk of the lake, including Emerald Bay and most of South Shore. You might also pass by McFall Creek and some other scenic points in Toiyabe National Forest.

Dwight and Louise McGill, who have owned the business since 1986, like to keep groups small, between four and six riders per wrangler. They have a string of 55 horses, and they can run departures every 10 to 15 minutes, so no one has to wait very long. Another unique feature is the addition of a lunch ride, as well as breakfast and dinner rides. All meals are served buffet-style in a picnic area about a 10-minute ride from the stables; for dinner, a more leisurely affair, there are other activities such as horseshoe pitching and dummy roping. Breakfast includes scrambled eggs, fried potatoes, ham, English muffins, and fresh fruit salad. Lunch consists of hamburgers, hot dogs, or barbecue chicken breasts with baked beans and potato salad. Dinner is a hearty meal with steak and chicken, corn on the cob, tossed salad, baked beans, and a fresh-baked dessert such as apple pie or cake. Meal rides are extremely popular, so book well in advance. Another nice feature: You can get here on the free Zephyr Cove shuttle bus from many points in South Lake Tahoe. Parking at the stables is limited, on a dirt hill, but there is additional parking (for a fee) at the Zephyr Cove Resort lot across U.S. 50.

Trips: One-hour, two-hour, breakfast, lunch, and dinner rides. There are no overnight or backcountry trips. All trail rides are guided. Reservations are required for all meal rides and two-hour rides, and recommended for shorter rides.

Essentials: Open daily 9 A.M.–5 P.M. in summer and 10 A.M.–4 P.M. in spring and fall. The stables operate May–November. The minimum age is seven, and the maximum weight is 225 pounds. Four miles north of the Stateline casinos on U.S. 50 at Zephyr Cove Resort.

Contact: Zephyr Cove Resort Stables, P.O. Box 1672, Zephyr Cove, NV 89448; 775/588-5664; website: www.zephyrcovestables.com.

KIRKWOOD/HOPE VALLEY/MARKLEEVILLE

Kirkwood Stables and Lazy K Pack Station (see map on page 231, site 8)

Carson Pass is one of the undiscovered gems of Lake Tahoe, even though it was clearly "discovered" nearly 150 years ago by Kit Carson and became a major route for settlers migrating across the Sierra. Kirkwood is a bustling ski resort in winter, but in summer it becomes a quiet, peaceful gateway to Mokelumne Wilderness and a great escape from the crowds at Tahoe. The stables are operated by Jim and Karen Hagan, who have painstakingly built a network of trails that parallel a series of dramatic bluffs and pinnacles surrounding the resort. The Hagans have a string of 25 horses at their stables next to the Kirkwood Inn on Highway 88.

From Kirkwood, the most popular short ride (75 minutes) is to pristine Caples Creek, an attractive stream that meanders through spectacular rocky terrain. Another ride can be made along the Red Cliffs Trail to Thunder Saddle Bowl in the ski area. Overnight rides can be made from nearby Silver Lake, where the Hagans will trailer horses to a staging area, to Kirkwood. As one of the most scenic equestrian routes in Northern California, this 18-mile journey is on the old Mormon-Emigrant Trail, now a jeep road, and it offers vistas from a ridgeline that overlooks two drainages. On the north side is Thimble Peak (elevation 9,827 feet), a reddish volcanic formation that flanks the Kirkwood ski area on the west and resembles the Utah Badlands. On the south side is Summit City Canyon, a deep drainage with sheer granite walls. From the trail, which is mostly above tree line, you can see both areas simultaneously—an incredible and memorable experience. There are also high views of Silver and Scout Carson Lakes. Camp for this two-day venture is at Summit Meadow Lake, where the Hagans have a summer kitchen set up complete with a wood-burning stove and a Dutch oven. All meals are included, and dinner might range from chicken cordon bleu to stuffed pork chops, with a dessert of fresh berry cobbler.

Four- and five-day mountain horsemanship clinics (bring your own horse or rent one) are offered several times during the season. The Hagans' horses are dependable, surefooted animals, and that's a good thing, too, because there are some steep descents on rough terrain, especially dropping into Sunrise Bowl behind Thimble Peak.

Trips: Guided rides (from one hour to overnight) on private land and within Eldorado National Forest; pack trips to Mokelumne Wilderness and Carson Pass (fishing and swimming are available); spot trips to the place of your choice; rides in a Western-style wagon; and horse-drawn sleigh rides in the winter (though these are no longer in Kirkwood, as of this writing). Campground sites are available at Caples and Silver Lakes (run by PG&E and the U.S. Forest Service) and at Plasse's Resort (private tent or RV sites).

Essentials: Open daily 9 A.M.–5 P.M. June–October. Reservations are recommended. The stable is at Kirkwood Resort off Highway 88.

Contact: Kirkwood Stables and Lazy K Pack Station, P.O. Box 89, Kirkwood, CA 95646; 209/258-7433 (Kirkwood); website: www.kirkwood.com.

FEATHER RIVER COUNTRY/LAKES BASIN
Graeagle Stables
(see map on page 231, site 9)

Recently acquired by longtime Plumas County outfitter Russell Reid, this corral is situated in the heart of Graeagle, on Highway 89, so it's easy to find. While a cursory look might lead someone to conclude that there is little proximity to the backcountry here, au contraire: A trail that begins behind the stables parallels Smith Creek and offers some nice outings into the pine forest and Sierra Nevada foothills. The emphasis here is on short, one-hour to half-day rides. There are also four- to five-day riding camps for children and youths, from ages 8–18. These are morning, half-day instructional camps, customized to ability levels. Also available by arrangement are lunch and dinner rides, as well as rides in a large Conestoga wagon. The pack string consists of about 18 horses, and the facilities include a recently renovated barn and a new riding arena.

Trips: One-hour, two-hour and half-day trips.
Essentials: It's open May–September, daily 9 A.M.–5 P.M. Closed in winter. In Graeagle on Highway 89.
Contact: Graeagle Stables, 1540 Chandler Rd., Quincy, Graeagle, CA 96103; 530/836-0430; website: www.reidhorse.com.

Gold Lake Pack Station and Stables
(see map on page 231, site 10)

You can see a half dozen lakes in a day, or a dozen lakes in two days in this scenic but relatively undiscovered trove of lakes an hour's drive north of Truckee. Outfitter Russell Reid, a horseman for more than 20 years who teaches equestrian courses at Feather River College, is the largest outfitter in the region. At Gold Lake, his stables offer immediate access to this distinctive mountain playground, which straddles Tahoe and Plumas National Forests.

The most popular short ride is the 2.5-hour jaunt on the Round Lake Trail, which affords views of Big Bear, Little Bear, Silver, and Long Lakes. Half-day trips stop for lunch at Round Lake (bring your own food or arrange with the packer). Overnight rides usually add Gold, Wades, Grass, and Jamison Lakes to those listed above. The best campsite is at Wades Lake, a nearly circular alpine gem flanked at one end by a sheer-walled cliff. Three- and four-day deluxe trips, custom tailored to the pace and preferences of clients, with all meals provided, also are popular. Reid runs 25 to 30 head of horses and mules and has a few old-fashioned line tents at his corral that are available to guests for camping the night before their trip.

One unique experience is a ride in a replica of the famous Conestoga "Prairie Schooner" covered wagon, pulled by a team of Belgian horses. These rides, ranging from special dinner rides to wagon treks, are on the Beckwourth Emigrant Trail, off Highway 70 east of Portola. Guests can ride in the wagon or on horseback, and some trips are accompanied by a chuckwagon. These are by reservation.

Trips: Hourly, 2.5-hour, half-day, and full-day guided trail rides, pack trips (overnight, wrangler-guided, and spot trips), wagon rides, and cookouts. Lessons, horsemanship classes, and boarding are available.

Essentials: Special overnight and guided trips are available, as are spot trips for campers and anglers. The minimum age is five. Open May–October, daily 9 A.M.–dusk. Winter wagon and sleigh rides are sometimes offered. Eight miles south of Graeagle on Gold Lake Road, off Highway 89, in the Lakes Basin Recreation Area.

Contact: Gold Lake Pack Station and Stables, 1540 Chandler Rd., Quincy, CA 95971; 530/836-0940 (summer) or 530/283-2014 (off-season); website: www.reidhorse.com.

RENO/CARSON VALLEY

Verdi Trails West
(see map on page 231, site 11)
This former dairy ranch is a complete equestrian center that offers a full plate of activities, from trail rides and haywagon rides to English and Western lessons and equestrian summer camps for kids. There's a picnic area nestled in a grove of quaking aspens adjacent to the Truckee River. The ranch extends over 3,000 aces and includes barns, corrals, pastures, and riding arenas. The rental string consists of 25 horses.

The center operates seven days a week, year-round, and if there's enough snow on the ground, they'll run sleigh rides. Trails, generally on private land, range over rolling, open foothills northwest of the ranch, with gradual climbs above the little community of Verdi. Among the more popular riding destinations is Dog Valley. The center

is just off I-80 at Exit 2 near Boomtown, the casino/theme park that is a major road stop, and is a 15-minute drive from downtown Reno.

Trips: One-hour to all-day trail rides, other rides by arrangement; haywagon rides and, in winter, sleigh rides. Corporate picnics and weddings also can be arranged, along with private family parties, barbecues, and picnics.

Essentials: Verdi Trails specializes in summer camps for kids. Individual riding lessons also are available. All rides and activities require reservation. No children under 6. Open daily from 9:30 A.M.–5 P.M., year-round.

Contact: Verdi Trails West, 175 Trelease Ln., P.O. Box 972, Verdi, NV 89439; 775/345-7600 or 888/345-7603; website: www.verditrailsranch.com.

High Sierra Stables
(see map on page 231, site 12)
You can enjoy lofty, panoramic views of the high-desert that surrounds Reno during a 90-minute trail ride at this facility, which is operated by Kathleen Kelly from her home 10 minutes north of town off Highway 395. Rides, suitable for ages seven and up, rise up from Golden Valley on gradual trails that climb 1,000 feet through sagebrush and juniper. The stunning views from a ridge top at about 5,700 feet elevation include Peavine Mountain, Red Rock, Hungry Valley, Antelope Valley, and Silver Lake in Lemmon Valley. In spring, wildflowers can be abundant and plentiful. You can also catch glimpses of the Reno skyline and of Sparks, the city's neighbor. A string of 15 to 25 horses, ranging from Arabians to thoroughbreds, are well-mannered and child-friendly. All ability levels are accommodated (there are small Morgan horses for children), and five-day riding camps are offered for youngsters.

Trips: One hour, 90 minutes, two hours, three hours and half-day. Guides accompany all outings. Special rides, by arrangement, can be made for experienced riders. Also, summer dinner rides can be arranged. Rides continue through winter, since the area receives very little snow.

Essentials: Open 9 A.M.–5 P.M. seven days a week, year-round. Facilities and services include riding lessons, dinner rides, full moon rides, a horse camp and private rides for experienced riders. All rides are by appointment only. To get here, drive north on Highway 395 and exit at Golden Valley Road, south of Stead.

Contact: High Sierra Stables, 3105 Indian Ln., Reno, NV 89506; 775/972-1345.

Tin Cup Adventures
(see map on page 231, site 13)

You know it's going to be a different kind of ride when co-owner Mike Tristram (that's a she) explains that she and Dennis (a he) call their trips "adventures," not rides, that their idea of backcountry cooking is stir-fry in a wok, and that intelligent campfire discussions should focus on truly practical things—such as how to talk to a coyote. This husband-and-wife team, who admit they are refugees from the newspaper business (ah, that explains everything!), have been running trips for more than five years in the recently designated Mt. Rose Wilderness. This region is replete with stunning meadows and mountain wildflowers, aspen thickets, and picturesque views of Mt. Rose (elevation 10,778 feet), along with other peaks of Toiyabe National Forest. The wilderness extends from the Lake Tahoe side of the crest, along Mt. Rose Highway, to the Carson Valley side. It is not exactly brimming with lakes, but there are creeks, springs, and ponds that enhance the lushness of the area, particularly in early summer.

Using both mules and horses, the Tristrams take groups of up to eight people on one-day rides (four to six hours) to Thomas Creek, where a buffet lunch is served beside the creek or in Timothy Meadows near Painted Rock. Another excursion, for experienced riders only, goes to Gray Lake and a high point overlooking Lake Tahoe. Campouts in the wilderness include everything except sleeping bags. The couple also offer year-round rides (weather permitting) in Eldorado Canyon southeast of Dayton, as well as in the surrounding Pine Nut Mountains and the Virginia Mountains around Virginia City. For a unique experience, they will take as many as 30 riders (most of whom supply their own horses) on a moonlight trek across a dry lake bed in the Black Rock Desert northeast of Reno. This overnight outing takes place once a year in mid-August and is one of the more popular rides.

Trips: All-day to five-day tours are offered. Customized outings include extended camping adventures (overnight trips of any duration), hiking excursions, and drop camps (you hike or ride to your own camp; they pack in your gear, leave you there, and return to pack out your gear at a later date). The Black Rock Moonlight Ride is a special overnight trip to the Black Rock Desert (100 miles northeast of Reno) scheduled once a year in mid-August. The final destination is the Black Rock Hot Spring on the Lassen-Applegate Trail (reservations for this trip are required by August 1).

Essentials: Youths and children 15 years of age or younger are charged less when accompanied by a parent or legally responsible adult. Group rates are available. Customized adventures, including drop camps for hiking and extended camping trips, can be arranged. Reservations are required on one-day adventures (minimum of three days notice) and overnight trips (minimum of 10 days notice). Open year-round, weather permitting.

Contact: Tin Cup Adventures, 220 Wayne Rd., Carson City, NV 89704; 775/849-0570; website: www.bigtackstore.com/tincup.

Bike Trails and Parks

On any given summer day, it seems as if half the visitors in Lake Tahoe are pedaling and puffing. With paved cycling trails bordering much of the lake, and with some of the country's most captivating mountain bike routes, Tahoe has become a cycler's paradise. Perhaps the signature trail in the basin, and among the world's most dramatic, is the Flume Trail, a single-track route notched into the side of plunging cliffs on the eastern shoreline high above the lake. If you traveled no other path in the entire region except for the Flume, you will have experienced one of the all-time great cycling treks.

But there is a cornucopia of delightful two-wheel outings throughout the basin and, as the region develops a collective approach to signage and trail management, Tahoe could well become the alpine cycling center of the

biking along the Truckee River Bike Trail

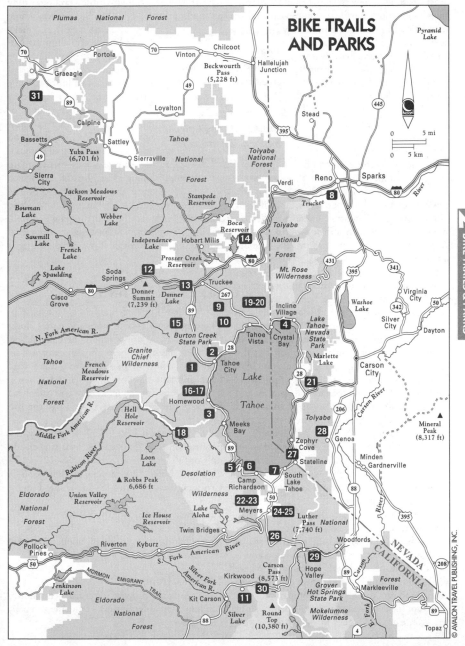

BIKE TRAILS & PARKS

© AVALON TRAVEL PUBLISHING, INC.

West Coast. Even now, the number and variety of trails is substantial, and they accommodate a range of abilities, from easygoing sightseers with children to hardcore pedalers with Camelback water slings. Some local visionaries would like to see a paved trail circling all 72 miles of the lake (so far there are 22 miles), and that may well happen sometime in the future. But so far, public agencies have shied away from the cost and commitment of notching out trails along some of the narrow, winding stretches of Highways 89 and 28. For now, cyclists who elect to go with the flow of automobile traffic in areas where there are no marked bike lanes do so at their own risk. Happily, several public agencies around the lake are adding new paved trails and lanes, so the prospects are growing for two-wheeled access.

> *Some local visionaries would like to see a paved trail circling all 72 miles of the lake (so far there are 22 miles), and that may well happen sometime in the future.*

As for venturing into the backcountry, there are hundreds of miles of Forest Service roads and trails throughout the region. Unfortunately, trail markers are scarce, many maps are outdated, and it's easy to get lost. Even local riders spend a lot of time in trial-and-error scouting to sort out the maze of forks and logging roads, some of which lead to dead ends. Realizing Tahoe's potential for cycling, the various recreational agencies and user groups are discussing plans to inventory and mark the trail systems. Until then, mountain biking is best approached with a high degree of caution and planning. Before setting out, even on the established routes described here, check out trail conditions thoroughly with the appropriate governmental jurisdictions and experienced riders, such as employees at a local bike shop. Trail configurations can change from year to year, depending on the harshness of the winter and on logging activity, and old maps may not be reliable. Whenever you head into the high country, always leave word with someone on where you're going and when you expect to return. It's also a good idea to ride with a companion.

Except for the paved trails on the perimeter of the lake, everything goes up—way up. If you haven't done much high-altitude cycling, riding at an elevation of 6,000 to 9,000 feet, where most of the trails exist, can make you feel like you're climbing Mt. Everest with lead boots. There are steep uphill ascents, roller-coaster descents, and a lot of variable terrain. While Lake Tahoe offers some truly rewarding vistas for mountain bikers, there are few easy or entry-level rides. A good way to ease into the trail system is to visit one of Tahoe's mountain biking parks, the oldest of which are at the Northstar and Squaw Valley ski areas and North Tahoe Regional Park. Recently, Kirkwood joined the pack, as well. Taking lifts makes it easier to cover the elevation, and riding downhill is not as exhausting as climbing uphill.

BIKE RENTAL AND RETAIL SHOPS

There are plenty of bike shops and rental kiosks scattered around the perimeter of Lake Tahoe, and the majority of them offer an extensive selection of mountain bikes, children's bikes, road bikes, and tandems.

Rental rates vary so make sure you call ahead for exact prices. Generally, you'll pay the following:

Adult mountain bikes: $30–40 per day, depending on features (such as front suspension only or full suspension). Hourly, $8–12.
Children's bikes: $20–28 per day. Hourly, $6–9.
Cruisers (basic bikes): $18–28 per day. Hourly, $5–8.
Tandems: $38–45. Hourly, $9–14.
Kids Trailers: $28–34 per day. Hourly, $6–8.
Note: Half-day rates are usually about 25 percent less than full-day rates.

Truckee/Donner

Back Country Bicycles: You can rent mountain bikes, kid's bikes, trailers, tandems and baby joggers here.

Contact: Back Country at either of two locations—Truckee, 11429 Donner Pass Rd., 530/582-0909, or Tahoe City, 255 N. Lake Blvd., next to the Naughty Dawg; 530/581-5861; website: www.thebackcountry.net.

Paco's Truckee Bike and Ski: One of the most respected shops in the region, Paco's rents and services bikes and has a large selection of parts. **Contact:** Paco's Truckee Bike and Ski, 11200 Donner Pass Rd. in Truckee; 530/587-5561; website: www.pacosbikeandski.com.

Tahoe City/West Shore

Olympic Bike Shop: The longest established specialty bike shop (since 1973) in the North Tahoe area offers sales, service, rentals, and demos. **Contact:** Olympic Bike Shop, 620 N. Lake Blvd., Tahoe City; 530/581-2500; website: us.worldpages.com.

Porter's Ski and Sport: Two of the four branches of Porter's Ski and Sport rent touring bikes for the paved trails and carry a variety of accessories. **Contact:** Porters Ski and Sport, Tahoe City, 501 N. Lake Blvd., 530/583-2314, and 885 Tahoe Blvd., Incline Village, NV; 775/831-3500.

Tahoe Bike and Ski: Rents mountain bikes and sells parts and accessories in the Kings Beach area. **Contact:** Tahoe Bike and Ski, 8499 N. Lake Blvd., Kings Beach, CA; 530/546-7437.

Tahoe Gear: You'll find sales, service, and rentals at this shop on the West Shore Bike Path. **Contact:** Tahoe Gear, 5095 W. Lake Blvd. in Homewood; 530/525-5233.

Truckee River Raft Company: This outfit, which rents the popular inflatables for floating the Truckee River, also rents mountain bikes next to Fanny Bridge at the Tahoe City "Y" intersection of Highways 28 and 89.

Contact: Truckee River Raft Company, Fanny Bridge, Tahoe City; 530/583-0123.

West Side Sports: This shop rents and repairs mountain bikes, and is on the popular West Shore Bike Path. **Contact:** West Side Sports, 5395 W. Lake Blvd. (Hwy. 89), Homewood; 530/525-0310.

Incline Village/Crystal Bay

Village Ski Loft/Village Bicycles: Poised at the end of the East Shore's famous Flume Trail, this shop offers mountain bike rentals, service, and information on trail conditions. **Contact:** Village Ski Loft/Village Bicycles, 800 Tahoe Blvd., Incline Village, NV; 775/831-3537; website: www.villageskiloft.com.

South Lake Tahoe/Stateline

Anderson's Bicycle Rental: A large selection of mountain bikes, children's bikes, trailers, and tandems is offered at Anderson's, next to the Pope-Baldwin Bike Path just north of the "Y" intersection on Highway 89 in South Lake Tahoe. **Contact:** Anderson's Bicycle Rental, 645 Emerald Bay Rd. in South Lake Tahoe; 530/541-0500.

Camp Richardson Resort: This sports shop, on Highway 89 two miles north of the "Y" intersection, offers rentals of mountain bikes, tandems and beach cruisers. **Contact:** Camp Richardson Resort; 530/542-6584; website: www.camprichardson.com.

Lakeview Sports: Rentals include mountain bikes, tandems, kids bikes, and beach cruisers. Sales, service, and repairs are also available. At the head of the bike trail on Lake Tahoe. **Contact:** Lakeview Sports, 3131 U.S. 50 in South Lake Tahoe; 530/544-0183; website: www.tahoesports.com.

Sierra Ski and Cycle Works: Rentals, sales, demos, and repairs are offered, along with maps and trail information.

BIKE TRAILS & PARKS

Contact: Sierra Ski and Cycle Works, 3430 U.S. 50 in South Lake Tahoe; 530/541-7505; website: www.sierraskiandcycleworks.com.

Shoreline Bike Shop: This longtime rental and retail store carries mountain bikes, kid's bikes, kid's trailers and maps of the Shoreline Mountain Bike Trail that begins nearby.
Contact: Shoreline Bike Shop, 259 Kingsbury Grade, Stateline, NV; 775/588-8777; website: www.shorelinesnowboards.com.

South Shore Bike Shop: The mountain bike and BMX specialists at South Shore Bike Shop offer rentals, repairs, and sales.
Contact: South Shore Bike Shop, 1132 Ski Run Blvd. in South Lake Tahoe; 530/541-1549.

Tahoe Bike Shop: Rentals, parts, and accessories are available at Tahoe Bike Shop, which has been serving Lake Tahoe for more than 30 years. On Highway 50 at Tahoe Keys Boulevard, close to bike routes.
Contact: Tahoe Bike Shop, 2277 Lake Tahoe Blvd. in South Lake Tahoe; 530/544-8060.

Tahoe Fly Fishing Outfitters: Mountain bike rentals and extensive tackle are available here (yes, you can do both on one ride!).
Contact: Tahoe Fly Fishing Outfitters, 3433 Lake Tahoe Blvd. in South Lake Tahoe; 530/541-8208; website: www.tahoeflyfishing.com.

Tahoe Sports: This large South Tahoe sporting goods store rents mountain bikes at both of its locations.
Contact: Tahoe Sports, Crescent V Shopping Center (near Stateline) at the intersection of Highway 50 and Pioneer Trail, and at the South Y Center (intersection of Highways 50 and 89), both in South Lake Tahoe.

Village Mountain Surf and Sports: Free trail maps are given to those who rent mountain bikes here. The shop offers sales, service, and apparel.
Contact: The Village Mountain Surf and Sports, 3552 Lake Tahoe Blvd. (U.S. 50) in South Lake Tahoe; 530/541-2726 or 530/541-4444.

BIKE TOURS
AAA Sierra Adventures
This Reno-based company offers a variety of tours in the Reno/Tahoe area, arranging for rental gear as well. Among the more popular outings near Reno is a descent from Peavine Summit, a 4,000-vertical-foot rollercoaster ride from an elevation of 8,300 feet, over winding single track and mixed terrain. The company provides shuttle service to the top, along with maps, information and support, and can also book round-trip tours from its Reno base camp. Cost is $95 per person (with six per tour), with mountain bike rentals extra. Shuttles only run $25 per person, with a minimum of five people. Rentals are from $9 per hour, or from $19 per day. Other mountain bike tours are available for pre-booked dates and include guide service, maps, water bottles, road repair service, historical information, trail food, water and luxury shuttle service.
Contact: AAA Sierra Adventures, 2204 Dickerson Rd., Reno, NV; 775/323-8928 or 866/323-8928; website: www.wildsierra.com.

Bike the West
Curtis Fong, a longtime cycling and skiing impresario and local broadcast personality, organizes what is clearly the road biking event of the year at Tahoe, called America's Most Beautiful Bike Ride. This is a 72-mile ride around the perimeter of Tahoe, with an optional out-and-back side trip to Truckee that turns this into an official century ride. It is traditionally held on the first Sunday of June. The start/finish line is at Stateline, Nevada, and the tour (this is not a race) moves clockwise around the lake. The toughest part of the route is on the west side, on Highway 89, which has steep grades and blind curves, especially near Emerald Bay. And, of course, riders must share the narrow road with cars. You can do a half-ride, however, and bypass this section by taking your bike on a chartered cruise of the *Tahoe Queen* paddlewheel steamer from South Lake Tahoe to Tahoe City. You will have a leisurely cruise of about two hours, enjoy a continental breakfast, and then ride from the North Shore around the much easier east side of the lake. The

event is well-organized, and the roads are signed to alert motorists. Registration usually includes a t-shirt, food, goody bag and entertainment. The turnout hovers around 2,000 riders. In mid-September, Fong also offers what he calls OAT-BRAN (One Awesome Tour Bike Ride Across Nevada), which begins at Tahoe and follows I-50—nicknamed "America's Loneliest Highway"—for 420 miles to the Utah border. The five-day trip has rest stops every 20 miles, and has the option of camping or staying in hotels or motels along the way. There are several minimountain ranges to cross, with a total of 17,000 vertical feet. Participants return in vans.

Contact: Bike the West, P.O. Box 5123, Lake Tahoe, NV 89449; 775/588-9658 or 800/565-2704; email: tgft@bikethewest.com. Prices, schedules, descriptions and reservation forms can be accessed on the Internet at www.bikethewest.com.

Cyclepaths Mountain Bike Adventures

This bike shop offers tours for all ability levels, as well as rentals, sales, and service. Tours include vehicle shuttle and support, half-day to weekend excursions, a kids camp, self-guided trips, and professional instruction.

Contact: Cyclepaths Mountain Bike Adventures, 1785 W. Lake Blvd. in Tahoe Park; 530/581-1171; website: www.cyclepaths.com.

Tahoe Athletic Adventurez

One- and two-week wilderness camping sessions include mountain biking, from basics to advanced riding, with scenic and technical rides in the Tahoe area. The programs, which also involve white-water rafting, rock climbing, horseback riding, and day hikes, are aimed at young people ages 10 to 16, and run mid-June–late August. Also offers corporate team-building for adults, and special events. For a list of sessions, contact the company at the address below or check out the website.

Contact: Tahoe Athletic Adventurez, P.O. Box 5443, Tahoe City, CA 96145; 530/426-0102; website: www.tahoeadventurez.com.

Tahoe Trips and Trails

This local tour company offers three levels of guided rides, from easy to strenuous. Tours are upscale and range from weekend getaways to five-day adventures. They include meals and lodging, but not equipment. Cycling can be combined with other activities such as hiking and rafting. Prices range $395–995 per person.

Contact: Tahoe Trips and Trails, P.O. Box 6952, Tahoe City, CA 96145; 530/583-4506 or 800/581-HIKE (800/581-4453); website: www.tahoetrips.com.

Paved Bike Trails

Of Lake Tahoe's 72-mile shoreline, 22 miles have designated bike paths that parallel the highways. Most of them are on the West and South Shores, and they are in five unconnected segments. Although it's possible to ride on the road, doing so is not advised. There are steep hills, hairpin turns, and narrow shoulders, and cyclists must share the road with retirees driving motor homes, 18-year-olds with souped-up four-wheel-drive vehicles and raging hormones, and gamblers who have lost their last buck and imbibed too many free cocktails. Does this sound like a winning combination? Not exactly. Until more paved bike trails are constructed, the best

advice is to stay off the main roads. They are too congested and too dangerous. Herewith is a rundown of the bike paths and a few side trips in Lake Tahoe and Reno.

Trails listed are keyed to the Bike Trails and Parks map.

TAHOE CITY/WEST SHORE

Truckee River Recreation Trail
(see map on page 241, site 1)
This gentle but scenic paved trail borders the meandering river and Highway 89 for six miles, from Tahoe City to the Squaw Valley turnoff.

You can continue to the new Village at Squaw Valley on roadside lanes and dedicated bike trails for another two miles. In normal to high-water years, float tubers, rafters, and fly-fishers can be seen along the river, and River Ranch, a resort and restaurant at Alpine Meadows Road, is a great hangout for lunch or people-watching on the spacious outdoor patio that overlooks the river. Another great hangout is the new Balboa Café at Squaw Valley, where there is outside seating, a plaza with occasional entertainment, and places to lock your bike. One thing to be aware of is that this trail is also used by in-line skaters and runners.

The longest and most scenic paved bike trail in the basin winds along the wooded West Shore … along the way there are stunning vistas of the lake and some good beaches.

Distance: six miles to Squaw Valley turnoff, or eight miles to the Village at Squaw Valley.

Difficulty: Easy.

Location: The trail parallels the Truckee River and Highway 89 in North Tahoe.

Trailheads, parking: The trailhead is at a large parking lot one-half mile south of Tahoe City on Highway 89. Three trails set off from here, including the West Shore Bike Path. Another option is to park at Squaw Valley and make a round-trip from there.

Dollar Point Trail

(see map on page 241, site 2)
Though short, this trail has several good places to stop along the way, including Lake Tahoe-Nevada State Park, Burton Creek State Park, and Lake Forest Beach. You can enjoy a picnic on the beach, or drop into any of several restaurants. There are some pleasing vistas of aspens, pines, and, in early summer, wildflowers. You can use this paved trail as a feeder route to the network of dirt mountain bike trails that originate at the Lakeview Cross-Country Ski Area, which is in a residential part of

© KEN CASTLE

the Truckee River Recreational Trail

town just one-half mile north of Highway 28. Look for the sign that designates the ski area.

Distance: 2.5 miles one way.

Difficulty: Easy to moderate, with a half-mile climb to Dollar Hill.

Location: The trail parallels Highway 28 from Tahoe City east along the North Tahoe shoreline.

Trailheads, parking: The trailhead is at Lake Tahoe-Nevada State Park, east of Tahoe City on Highway 28. Parking is available.

West Shore Bike Path
(see map on page 241, site 3)

The longest and most scenic paved bike trail in the basin winds along the wooded West Shore from Tahoe City to Sugar Pine Point State Park, with only a few minor ups and downs. Along the way there are stunning vistas of the lake, some good beaches, and several small towns including Tahoma and Homewood. Picnic tables and rest stops are scattered along the route, so you can pack a lunch, or if you wish, eat at any of several popular restaurants. This is a great family outing, with one caveat—parts of the trail consist of bike lanes along busy Highway 89, and the trail crosses the road at several points. Dismount from your bike and cross with care! Other parts of the trail pass through residential areas just west of the highway. While the main section of trail stretches between Tahoe City and Sugar Pine Park, there are two connecting trails that branch north and east of Tahoe City, creating interesting side trip options for lengthening your casual ride to an all-day outing, if you wish.

Distance: Nine miles one way.

Difficulty: Easy to moderate.

Location: Along Highway 89 from Tahoe City on the north to Sugar Pine Point State Park on the south.

Trailheads, parking: If you're staying in Tahoe City or along West Shore Boulevard (Highway 89), the path and starting point are just outside your door. Otherwise, park your vehicle at one of these places:

• General Creek Campground, Sugar Pine Point State Park: One mile south of Tahoma on High-

way 89, the campground offers ample parking for a $5 day-use fee.

• Ehrman Mansion, Sugar Pine Point State Park: East of Highway 89, in another section of the park, is an even better option—parking at the historic Ehrman Mansion, which has large, grassy, tree-shaded grounds with a pier and considerable shoreline access. This is an idyllic spot for a picnic or a rest after your ride. One suggestion: Get here early, because parking is limited. During summer, you can take a guided tour of the fully furnished mansion, one of Tahoe's grand old estates. By parking at Sugar Pine, you can cycle to Tahoe City, pausing, if you wish, at the beachfront marinas at Homewood, Chambers Landing, and Sunnyside, all of which offer excellent and upscale lakeside restaurants. Other popular cycling stops include Black Bear Tavern and Norfolk Woods Inn.

• Truckee River Recreation Trail and Public Access: You'll find a large parking lot one-half mile south of Tahoe City on Highway 89, with several picnic tables and vault toilets next to the river. From here, you can go in one of three directions—south to Sugar Pine, north to Squaw Valley, or east to Dollar Point. You can do out-and-back rides on any of these trails, or combine them. Pedal round-trip on all three trails for a total distance of 30 miles.

• Kaspian Campground: This public campground, managed by the U.S. Forest Service, is at the intersection of Highway 89 and Blackwood Canyon Road, four miles south of Tahoe City, and includes parking, restrooms with flush toilets, and special bicycle campsites. There are three options from here as well: north, south, or west. You can follow the bike trail along the lake, or, if you're ambitious (and very much in shape), head up Blackwood Canyon Road. If you elect to do the latter, be prepared for a long, gradual uphill grade for four miles or so, then a steep switchback for another three miles. The views are spectacular from the summit of Barker Pass. You can stop at the Pacific Crest Trail, just beyond where the pavement ends. You'll find a trailhead jammed with cars and four-wheel-drive vehicles. If you haven't had enough exercise at this point, consider locking your bike and hiking for a bit on the trail to enjoy the vistas of the Sierra and Lake Tahoe. Or rest and then coast back down the way you came. Traffic is not heavy on this road, but it's wise to be cautious on switchbacks and curves.

INCLINE VILLAGE/CRYSTAL BAY

Incline Village/Lakeshore Drive Bike Path (see map on page 241, site 4)

Known to Incline Villagers as "the Joggers' Trail," this wooded, paved path is maintained by Washoe County. It starts at Gateway Park on Highway 28, passes close to the shore of Lake Tahoe's Crystal Bay, accesses two beaches that are reserved for Incline Village residents and guests, offers views of many million-dollar-plus homes and gated estates, and ends at the Hyatt Regency.

Distance: 2.5 miles one way.
Difficulty: Easy.
Location: In Incline Village on the North Shore of Lake Tahoe.
Trailheads, parking: Parking is available at Gateway Park on Highway 28.

SOUTH LAKE TAHOE/STATELINE

Fallen Leaf Lake Paved Roads
(see map on page 241, site 5)

Rising gradually, this route follows residential roads to the intersection with Angora Ridge Road (dirt and gravel), then goes downhill until it reaches Fallen Leaf Road. You can continue north to Highway 89 and the beaches around Camp Richardson, then merge with the bike lane to go back to the "Y" intersection near your starting point. If you have a mountain bike, consider a side trip to Angora Lakes (about three miles one way), where there's a log bike rack to lock your bike at the parking area, a short trail to the lakes, and a lodge with a snack stand and a rowboat concession. This is also a favorite swimming spot. Other side trips can be made down Fallen Leaf Road to Glen Alpine Falls or Fallen Leaf Lake Dam. Bicy-

clists may ride free of charge onto the fee beaches. Bicycles are not allowed in Desolation Wilderness, on the self-guided trails around the Forest Service visitor center, in Taylor Creek Marsh, or on dirt paths within the Tallac Historic Site. Use caution on the narrow roads and trails around Fallen Leaf Lake.

Distance: 3.5 miles one way.
Difficulty: Moderate.
Location: In South Lake Tahoe.
Trailheads, parking: Begin at intersection of Lake Tahoe Boulevard and Tahoe Mountain Road, west of the "Y" intersection of U.S 50 and Highway 89. To follow the route in the opposite direction, park at Camp Richardson.

Pope-Baldwin Bike Path
(see map on page 241, site 6)

This nearly level cycling path leads past two of South Lake Tahoe's most spectacular beaches and a trio of famous old estates. It begins at Highway 89, north of the "Y" junction with U.S. 50, in the area where four lanes narrow to two. There are bicycle rental outfits all along this road; you'll even find family four-wheel cycling wagons at Camp Richardson. Picnic spots await at Pope and Baldwin Beaches and at Fallen Leaf Campground. Probably the best public parking spot is at the Tallac Historic Site, a series of lakefront homes once inhabited by the rich and famous. There's a museum with free admission and, on certain days, a tour of the Pope Estate. Art and music festivals are regularly held here during the summer. Tallac is situated in pine trees, behind Baldwin Beach, and you would be hard-pressed to find a more inspirational place on the South Shore. You can picnic here, or have a great repast at the Beacon Restaurant at Camp Richardson, which has outdoor dining on a large patio on the beach and, frequently, live music (everything from jazz to rock to country and folk) that keeps the place hopping.

Distance: 3.4 miles one way.
Difficulty: Easy.
Location: On the southwest side of the lake on Highway 89, just one-half mile north of the "Y" intersection with U.S. 50.

Trailheads, parking: Parking is available at Camp Richardson and at the Tallac Historic Site.

South Lake Tahoe Bike Path
(see map on page 241, site 7)
This increasingly popular paved bike path connects to other bike trails and lanes throughout the city of South Lake Tahoe and into Nevada. One recently completed section, the mile-long Linear Park Bike Trail, allows cyclists to pedal from Stateline to the new Marina Village complex at Ski Run Boulevard, all on paved trail. From there, cyclists can follow a combination of paved trail, designated bike lanes and signed routes west to the "Y" intersection of Highways 50 and 89. One route allows cycling north to Camp Richardson, on and off Highway 89 to the Pope-Baldwin Bike Path. Along the South Tahoe routes, there are views of Tahoe Meadows, Trout Creek, the Upper Truckee River and Truckee Marsh.

Distance: 6.5 miles one way.
Difficulty: Easy.
Location: You can start at Camp Richardson and cycle to Stateline one-way (taking the trolley one-way), at Stateline behind the Shell Station, at Marina Village near Embassy Vacation Resort, or at El Dorado Beach and Picnic Area on U.S. 50, in the city of South Lake Tahoe.
Trailheads, parking: Parking is available at the beach and picnic area, Camp Richardson, Stateline and Marina Village.

RENO/CARSON VALLEY
Reno Bike Trails
(see map on page 241, site 8)
Like the Lake Tahoe bike paths, Reno's trails also border bodies of water. Some of the city's most scenic routes include:

• **Truckee River Trail** At 6.5 miles, the Truckee River Trail is Reno-Sparks' longest path. It begins at Broadhead Park, near Wells Avenue and Kuenzli Lane, and continues along the river, ending near the Vista Boulevard offramp on I-80.

• **Idlewild Route:** This path also follows the Truckee River. Considerably shorter at 3.3 miles, the route begins at Riverside and 1st Streets and continues through Idlewild Park to Caughlin Ranch.

• **Virginia Lake:** While not a true bike path, this ride does afford a scenic and easy one-mile loop. Picnic tables, barbecue grills, and restrooms are on-site.

• **Bowers Mansion to Franktown:** This is a scenic, sparsely traveled country road. The four-mile stretch starts at Bowers Mansion, a turn-of-the-century home, then makes a right turn on Franktown Road and winds through farmland, meadows, stands of towering pine trees, and large estates. Bowers Mansion is approximately 15 miles south of Reno.

Mountain Bike Parks

Mountain bike parks offer unique cycling advantages, and the Lake Tahoe area has three of them: the downhill ski resorts of Northstar-at-Tahoe and Kirkwood, and North Tahoe Regional Park in Tahoe Vista. At the ski areas, the obvious attraction is being able to take a chairlift to the top of a slope, then ride downhill—which saves on the grunting and groaning. The network of service roads and trails that crisscross most ski areas makes for an excellent trail system, and the chances of getting lost are considerably less than on unmarked forest roads. Also, there's a bike shop around to make repairs, as well as snack bars and restaurants that serve munchies.

Parks listed are keyed to the Bike Trails and Parks map.

TRUCKEE/DONNER
Northstar-at-Tahoe
(see map on page 241, site 9)
At this all-seasons resort six miles south of Truckee, two chairlifts serve an elaborate trail system, which offers everything from easy meadow jaunts to an all-day ride that takes you to a mountain lake. There are roads and single-track trails, and some are tricky to negotiate, especially with unconsolidated rock and sand. The resort has over 100 miles of trails, and one of them connects with the North Shore's most popular mountain route—the Fibreboard Freeway, which goes to Brockway Summit on the east and Tahoe City on the north. Unlike the labyrinth of trails that covers the high terrain of North Tahoe, the Northstar routes are well marked. There is no charge for using the trails—only for riding the lifts. If you're ambitious and don't mind a lot of climbing (about 1,500 feet worth), you can start cycling from Northstar Village. But if you're of average ability, do yourself a favor and take the lifts. All cyclists are required to wear helmets. Here are some of the routes at Northstar:

Watson Lake Loop: Taken at a leisurely pace, this makes a good half-day trek (a round-trip of 9.2 miles) for intermediate cyclists, especially if

© KEN CASTLE

Bikes rule at the area's several bike parks.

you combine a picnic lunch with a stop at Watson Lake. Take the Echo and Lookout lifts at Northstar to Route 507, at elevation 7,800 feet. Follow that for three-tenths of a mile to Route 500, then ride on this fairly level road for 1.6 miles with a gradual climb to Route 100. It's two-tenths of a mile farther to Route 114, and then seven-tenths of a mile on that to Watson Lake. There are nice views of Lake Tahoe all along the trail. Watson Lake is set in a meadow with some sunning rocks, but because of the cold water temperature and muddy bottom, it's not a good place for swimming. The lake gets heavy use in summer from cyclists and some off-road-vehicle enthusiasts. To return to Northstar, retrace your path to Route 100, the Fibreboard Freeway. It's a gradual downhill all the way for 1.75 miles to Sawmill Flat, where there's a caboose used as a warming hut for cross-country skiers during winter. From there, it's about two

COURTESY OF NORTHSTAR-AT-TAHOE

BIKE TRAILS & PARKS

biking on top of Northstar-at-Tahoe

miles back to Northstar Village on the Big Springs Trail or Village Run.

Sawmill Flat Loop: This makes a good beginner or family trip, since it is relatively short (three miles round-trip), has a view of Northstar Reservoir and surrounding mountains, and has an elevation gain of just 200 feet. From the top of the Echo Lift, take Route 501 to Route 500, and follow that until you reach the caboose. Between here and the reservoir is an open meadow with good places for a picnic. To return, follow the same route back, and at the top of Echo Lift take the Big Springs Trail back to Northstar Village, enjoying views of Martis Valley on the way down. An alternate return is the Village Run, but this is steeper and rockier.

Tahoe City (one way): This 12-mile ride (buy a one-ride lift ticket) follows the same trail as the Watson Lake Loop, but joins new Route 115 (the continuation of the Fibreboard Freeway) to Tahoe City, a distance of 7.6 miles from Mt. Watson. The road is well graded, wide, and unmarked. Park a second car at Tahoe City (one good spot is near the high school), or return the same way to the trails that lead back to Northstar Village (a long round-trip of about 25 miles). If you do this route, allow for a full day and about seven hours of riding. You can stop for lunch at one of the restaurants in Tahoe City.

Amenities: Two chairlifts modified to carry bicycles; Northsport in Northstar Village, which offers rentals and repairs; a mountain bike school; a day lodge with restrooms and a telephone; and Northstar Village restaurants.

Fees: All-day ride ticket, $29 for adults; single ride, $17; child (12 and under), $17 for an all-day ticket, $12 for a single ride. Full-day rentals of full-suspension cross-country mountain bikes are $40 for adults, $27 for juniors and $17 for children. Half-day (afternoon) rentals are $29 for adults, $20 for juniors and $10 for children. Bike rentals are based on size, not age, and include use of a helmet and gloves.

Contact: Northstar-at-Tahoe; 530/562-1010. Northsport Shop; 530/562-2268; website: www.northstarattahoe.com.

KINGS BEACH/TAHOE VISTA/CARNELIAN BAY

North Tahoe Regional Park
(see map on page 241, site 10)
Set well off of Highway 28 at Tahoe Vista (just west of the junction with Highway 267 at Kings Beach), this major recreation area has both gentle and advanced terrain and a system of trails that connects with other North Tahoe mountain biking routes including the Fibreboard Freeway. There's also a mile-long paved trail that begins in the parking lot and goes through a wooded area of tall trees to Pinedrop Street and out to Highway 267. To access the park, go north on National Avenue from Highway 28 until it reaches the recreation complex, which includes restrooms and a parking lot (a fee is charged).

Amenities: A mountain bike racetrack, picnic areas, a softball field, a playground, a Parcourse, nature and hiking trails, restrooms, and sledding hills.

Fees: There's a $3 parking fee per car. Admission to the park is free.

Contact: North Tahoe Public Utility District; 530/546-5043; website: www.northlaketahoe.net.

KIRKWOOD/HOPE VALLEY/MARKLEEVILLE

Kirkwood Resort
(see map on page 241, site 11)
This high-elevation ski resort on Highway 88 south of Lake Tahoe runs two chairlifts for mountain biking on weekends in the summer. The area is great for summer rides for three reasons: It usually offers a vivid display of wildflowers; it is surrounded by spectacular volcanic peaks; and the historic Mormon-Emigrant Trail winds through much of the resort. The Snowkirk 1 and Caples 2 lifts provide access to trails of varying ability levels, with six miles of dirt road and seven miles of single-track. Among the more impressive routes are those through Emigrant Valley along Red Cliffs, and those that reach into Devil's Corral, the large open meadow at the base of Thunder Saddle. This meadow can be a riot of color during the wildflower blooms, which often persist later in the summer than at other areas closer to Lake Tahoe. The Caples 2 chairlift brings you to the top of a prominent ridge that has sweeping views of Caples Lake to the east and Kirkwood Meadows and the new Kirkwood Village below. From this point you have a choice of riding downhill on a service road, intended for intermediate riders, or on one of several single-track plunges that should be attempted only by expert riders. To reach Kirkwood from South Lake Tahoe, take Highway 89 south and Highway 88 west to Kirkwood, about a 45-minute drive. The park is open 10 A.M.– 4 P.M. weekends and holidays, late June–mid-September.

Amenities: Two chairlifts, 17 trails, bike rentals, restaurants, a grocery store, and condominium rentals. Lift ticket, trail map, rentals, and accessories can be obtained at the Kirkwood Sports and Adventure Center in the Village Plaza.

Fees: Full-day lift ticket, $16 for adults, $13 for children 12 and under. Bike rentals range $15–40 per day. You can buy a season pass that includes unlimited access.

Contact: Kirkwood Sports and Adventure Center; 209/258-7240; for general information, including overnight lodging, contact Kirkwood Resort; 209/258-6000; website: www.kirkwood.com.

Mountain Bike Trails

Beyond the developed mountain biking parks is a vast labyrinth of dirt trails and roads, some of which change course annually depending on logging activities, damage from snowmelt, and restrictions from government agencies. Because virtually no published map is up to date, it's imperative to check with local bike shops, the U.S. Forest Service visitor centers, and state and regional recreation agencies for the latest information. Also, many of the trails are shared by other users such as hikers, horseback riders, and off-roaders, so observe common trail courtesy by slowing down on blind curves and yielding to uphill traffic. Always carry plenty of water, snacks, and insect repellent—the latter for marshy areas that are sometimes rife with mosquitoes.

Trails listed are keyed to the Bike Trails and Parks map.

TRUCKEE/DONNER
Lower Lola Montez Trail
(see map on page 241, site 12)

Since much of the trail is over Toll Mountain Estates, a private gated community, cyclists are requested to stay on the trail and observe the property rights of the landowners. From the trailhead, follow the trail north for one-quarter mile to a marked dirt road. Turn right and continue to the lower Castle Creek crossing. (The creekbed is lined with wire meshing—use caution in crossing to avoid flat tires.) The single-track trail begins again one-quarter mile after the creek crossing and then climbs steeply for another quarter mile. Turn right where it ties in with the road again. For the next quarter mile, the road ascends gently. At the end of the road, which is also the beginning of the Motor Vehicle Restricted Area, the trail leads to an open meadow. From there, it's a quarter mile to Lower Lola Montez Lake, a popular camping and swimming spot. The trail is well marked throughout, and receives heavy use by hikers, especially on the weekends. Remember to be considerate and controlled during your descent.

Distance: Three miles one way.
Difficulty: Moderate, over single-track trail and dirt road.
Elevation (low/high): 6,640 feet to 7,200 feet.
Location: From I-80 west of Truckee, take the Soda Springs exit on the north side of the freeway. Follow the paved road east for three-tenths of a mile to the parking area.
Contact: Tahoe National Forest, Truckee Ranger District; 530/587-3558.

Coldstream Canyon Trail
(see map on page 241, site 13)

After parking, head up the dirt road for a tenth of a mile, then take the right fork. Follow this short, steep, paved section—it very soon becomes a dirt road again. Veer right, staying on the main road that runs along the right side of two large ponds and continue the gradual climb up the valley. (Some of the valley is private property, so please stay on the road and respect the landowner's rights.) When you come to the 180-degree bend in the railroad, cross the tracks and continue on the road. Stay left at the next two forks. After crossing the creek, you will begin a short, steep climb that intersects a newly built logging road. Continue the gradual climb that follows the South Fork of Cold Creek. At the end of the logging road, a single-track trail, once an old jeep road, begins to climb the last few miles to the saddle below Tinkers Knob. Portions of the climb are steep and technical. You will cross the creek two more times; if you look carefully along the west bank of the creek, you can see the old flume used to transport logs off the mountain by the early loggers.

Once at the saddle below Tinkers Knob, you will be rewarded with a breathtaking view of the Deep Creek drainage to the south. The saddle is an excellent spot to stash your bike, grab your lunch, and hike the short, steep trail to the top of Tinkers Knob (elevation 8,950 feet). Descend the same way you rode up. Watch for horses on the single-track section of the ride and cars after the 180-degree bend in the railroad. Note: The

BIKE TRAILS & PARKS

TIPS FOR MOUNTAIN-BIKING SAFETY

Whenever you cycle off-road, consider the following guidelines:

• Always wear a helmet (even on paved trails) and carry a first-aid kit. Knee pads aren't a bad idea, either. It's easy to hit a rut and take a dive.
• Carry more water than you think you'll need. With the high elevations (6,000–9,000 feet) and warm summer temperatures, you'll need it. Don't embark on an all-day trip without a minimum of three water bottles (preferably pint-size) per person. As a backup, you might carry a water filter/purifier such as Katydyn, which filters Giardia, a microorganism that is becoming more frequent in wilderness lakes and streams.
• Carry a repair kit for patching flat tires and making other adjustments. Know how to fix gears, reinstall a chain, and repair brakes.
• Carry a flashlight, extra food, matches, and warm clothes. You may think that you'll be back before dark, but don't count on it. If your bike breaks down beyond your ability to repair it, or if you sustain an injury, you might need to spend a night outdoors.

• Take as many maps as you can lay your hands on, but always update your information by checking with a local bike shop or with the appropriate offices of the U.S. Forest Service. (If the seasonal aide isn't familiar with your particular route, ask to speak with a recreation supervisor.) Carry a U.S. Geological Survey topographic map, a Forest Service map, and perhaps one of the privately produced maps available locally. And don't forget your compass. Even with all of this material, there's the problem of inadequate signage, construction activity, vandalism, and, sometimes, official indifference. If you come across a trail fork that should have a sign but doesn't, you can do everyone a favor by reporting it to the local Forest Service office. With so many off-the-beaten-path roads and trails to maintain each year, and with diminishing budgets and staffs, each forest can use all the help it can get.
• If you're renting a bike—and there are plenty of places to do so—check the policy of the rental agreement to make sure that it covers off-road cycling.

Pacific Crest Trail is just beyond the saddle. Remember, bikes are not permitted on the PCT.

Distance: 20 miles round-trip.

Difficulty: Strenuous, on dirt road and single-track trail.

Elevation (low/high): 6,000 feet to 8,600 feet.

Location: Take I-80 to the first Truckee exit, Donner Pass Road. Turn south off Donner Pass Road just east of Donner Memorial State Park onto Coldstream Road (unmarked). Follow the road for four-tenths of a mile. Park where the pavement ends.

Contact: Tahoe National Forest, Truckee Ranger District; 530/587-3558.

Verdi Peak from Boca Rest Campground
(see map on page 241, site 14)
You'll follow the Verdi Peak Road (Forest Service

Road 972) for the majority of the gradual climb on this ride. At the junction of Forest Service Roads 72 and 72-28, turn right onto Forest Service Road 72-28. This is the home stretch—it's approximately three more miles up to the peak and fire lookout. Descend back to the junction of Forest Service Roads 72-28 and 72. Either turn left here and retrace your ascent back to the Boca Rest Campground or turn right on Forest Service Road 72 and descend to Henness Pass Road. Turn left on Henness Pass Road and descend to the junction with the paved Stampede Road, where you will turn left. The last leg of your ride is on Stampede, heading back to the campground.

Distance: 28 miles round-trip via Forest Service Road 72 starting from the Boca Rest Campground.

Difficulty: Strenuous, mostly due to the distance.

Elevation (low/high): 5,600 feet to 8,400 feet.
Location: Take I-80 east from Truckee to the Hirschdale exit and turn left. Cross the bridge and the railroad tracks and continue to the Boca Rest Campground. Look for the Forest Service sign indicating that Verdi Peak is 14 miles ahead; the sign is across the street from the campground. Begin the ride here.
Contact: Tahoe National Forest, Truckee Ranger District; 530/587-3558.

TAHOE CITY/WEST SHORE

Pole Creek Area
(see map on page 241, site 15)
There are many mountain biking options in the Pole Creek and Silver Peak area. To get to the spectacular scenery below the ridgeline and the head of the drainage, follow Forest Service Road 8, which climbs gradually. You will come to a sign for Upper Pole Creek; turn left here and continue climbing. You will experience forested areas, beautiful meadows, and awesome mountain peaks. With a good topo map, you can find Silver Peak (south of the head of the Pole Creek drainage) and easily bike to the summit in an hour. As always, use caution descending the well-graded lower portion of Forest Service Road 8.
Distance: Three to 10 miles one way.
Difficulty: Easy to moderate.
Elevation (low/high): 6,000 feet to 8,100 feet.
Location: From Truckee, take Highway 89 south for approximately seven miles, then watch the right side of the road for the parking area where Forest Service Road 8 begins. Park here.
Contact: Tahoe National Forest, Truckee Ranger District; 530/587-3558.

Ellis Peak and Ellis Lake
(see map on page 241, site 16)
This motorcycle/biking/hiking trail is very steep going until you reach the ridge. But the grind is worthwhile thanks to the view from the ridge; the stretch where the trail becomes ridable again is breathtaking. Follow the ridge for 1.5 miles, riding through beautiful flower-filled meadows and later through sections of open forests. The trail soon intersects Forest Service Road 14N40. To reach Ellis Lake, follow the road to the left for two miles. To reach Ellis Peak, follow the road to the right. Approximately 100 yards down the road, another marked dirt road will veer off to the east (left). Follow that road for three-tenths of a mile. Stash your bike and hike the last steps to Ellis Peak (elevation 8,640 feet). The view of Tahoe to the east, Granite Chief Wilderness and Hellhole Reservoir to the west, and Desolation Wilderness to the south is breathtaking.
Distance: Four miles one way.
Difficulty: Difficult, due to steepness over singletrack trail and dirt road.
Elevation (low/high): 7,800 feet to 8,640 feet.
Location: From I-80 in Truckee, take Highway 89 south to Tahoe City. Continue south on Highway 89 for another 4.2 miles to the Kaspian picnic area. Drive or ride west on Blackwood Canyon Road on the seven-mile climb to Barker Pass. The Ellis Peak Trailhead is on the south side of the road, where the pavement ends on the summit.
Contact: Lake Tahoe Basin Management Unit; 530/573-2600.

Ward Canyon to Stanford Rock to Twin Peaks (see map on page 241, site 17)
Cross over Ward Creek and start the long ascent to Stanford Rock. The trail to Twin Peaks is down and to the left of Stanford Rock. Stay on the ridgeline until you get to the saddle before starting up the side of Twin Peaks. As you climb, look for the turn that drops down back into Ward Canyon (you will take this trail back down). The trails may be a little hard to spot, but there are cliffs on all sides, so it is hard to wander off. The view from Twin Peaks is spectacular. After your rest, go back to the trail you saw that takes you down and to the left. Do not start climbing up toward the rock; you should head downhill for approximately two miles of steep switchbacks to the side of Ward Creek and then back to the pavement.
Distance: Nine miles one way.
Difficulty: Moderate to strenuous; at times you may need to carry your bike.
Elevation (low/high): 5,900 feet to 7,199 feet.

Location: Take Pineland Drive off Highway 89 and follow it to Twin Peaks Road; turn left. This road turns into Ward Creek Boulevard. After one mile, there is a rock erosion system on your right, and a dirt turnout on your left, with a sign below that reads "Stanford Rock, four miles."

Contact: North Lake Tahoe Resort Association; 530/583-3494.

McKinney-Rubicon Trail
(see map on page 241, site 18)

A world-class off-highway-vehicle road, McKinney-Rubicon offers a variety of biking opportunities from loop rides to difficult peak climbs. This bumpy road traverses numerous areas of river rock and is used frequently by all-terrain vehicles, motorized dirt bikes, and four-wheel-drive vehicles, which can make it quite dusty. For a great but challenging loop, arrange a shuttle and park the second car at Blackwood Canyon. From the McKinney-Rubicon Trailhead, ride 1.9 miles and head northwest on the Buck Lake Trail. Continue about 1.5 miles to the Ellis Peak Trail. Follow the Ellis Peak Trail northwest through Barker Pass to Blackwood Canyon. Warning: Roads beyond the McKinney-Rubicon Springs Road to Barker Pass have few or no signs.

Distance: Six to 18.5 miles one way.

Difficulty: Moderate to strenuous.

Elevation (low/high): 6,400 feet to 7,200 feet.

Location: From Highway 89 north of Tahoma, turn west onto McKinney-Rubicon Springs Road. Drive one-quarter mile and turn left on Bellevue. Continue one-quarter mile and turn right on McKinney Road. Bear left onto McKinney-Rubicon Springs Road and continue to a one-lane dirt road and park one-quarter to three-quarters of a mile along the road (there are wide turnouts). To arrange a car shuttle, continue about five miles on Highway 89 to the Ellis Peak Trailhead in Blackwood Canyon.

Contact: Lake Tahoe Basin Management Unit; 530/573-2600.

KINGS BEACH/TAHOE VISTA/CARNELIAN BAY

Brockway Summit to Martis Peak
(see map on page 241, site 19)

From the top of Brockway Summit on Highway 267, between Truckee and Kings Beach, this ride is a steady climb on a good dirt road with a panoramic 360-degree view from the summit of an old fire lookout. Follow the main road, which is marked with orange diamonds. This road is used in wintertime for snowmobiling and cross-country skiing, and the markers are often high up in the trees. Use here is heavy.

Distance: Eight miles round-trip.

Difficulty: Moderate, on dirt road.

Elevation (low/high): 7,000 feet to 8,650 feet.

Location: Take Highway 267 south from Truckee and turn left one-half mile south of Brockway Summit on a dirt road. Park here.

Contact: Tahoe National Forest, Truckee Ranger District; 530/587-3558.

Brockway Summit to Glenshire
(see map on page 241, site 20)

Follow the main dirt road and take the third left. Soon after this left, you will start an eight-mile descent beside a creek, then into Klondike Meadow, continuing along another creek, West Juniper. Stay straight along this road and don't turn at any intersections. When you find yourself on the pavement (Glenshire Road), make your first left. This road will bring you to downtown Truckee in approximately five miles. Commercial Row offers an abundance of restaurants, bike shops, and great shopping.

Distance: 10 miles one way.

Difficulty: Easy to moderate on good dirt roads.

Elevation (low/high): 7,120 feet to 8,660 feet.

Location: Take Highway 267 north from Kings Beach just past the crest of Brockway Summit to the dirt access road on the right. (Heading from Truckee, the dirt access road is just before the summit on the left.)

Contact: North Lake Tahoe Resort Association; 530/583-3494.

INCLINE VILLAGE/CRYSTAL BAY

Marlette Lake/Flume Trail
(see map on page 241, site 21)

Not just another mountain bike ride, the Flume is THE ride at Lake Tahoe. If you have only one day for an off-road cycling trip, if you are in decent physical shape, and if you are neither a beginner nor afraid of heights (such as, say, a narrow path with a sheer drop-off of 1,500 feet), the experience is truly magnificent. This is definitely not a family ride, and children should not be on the trail. It's tough even for adults, since there's a long uphill climb to Marlette Lake, and you may have to walk your bike for a good part of the way. Also, there are some tricky spots just below the Marlette Lake Dam, where the Flume actually begins, and erosion has begun to eat away into some sections of the trail. Finally, unless you've got a lot of stamina to do the round-trip (not recommended for most riders), you'll want to hop on the new shuttle that meets at the bottom of Tunnel Ranch Road and returns both you and your bike to Spooner Lake. Operated by concessionaire Max Jones, the shuttle—consisting of a van and bike trailer—runs seven days a week 1 P.M.–6 P.M. every hour on the hour, and the one-way fee is $10 per person. (Jones also offers bike rentals and demos at rates of $8–14.50 per hour, along with accessories, repairs and food at the Spooner Lake day lodge.)

Historically, the trail was part of an old water flume line that once carried timber from Lake Tahoe to the silver mines in Virginia City. Long abandoned, it was "rediscovered" a few years ago by local resident Max Jones, an avid mountain biker who also operates the Spooner Lake cross-country ski area. Jones cleared debris from much of the trail and, in a few short years, it has become the single most popular mountain bike route in the basin, drawing hundreds of riders a day on summer weekends.

The trail begins east of the picnic area near Spooner Lake. Turn left on the dirt road that heads toward the meadow and follow a sandy road for five miles to Marlette Lake (a scenic

© ANN MARIE BROWN

challenging stretch of single-track in Tahoe National Forest

place to stop, rest, and have lunch). Turn left across the dam, where a sign announces the actual start of the Flume Trail. After negotiating a few technical spots down sandy embankments, you reach the ledge and its awesome view of Lake Tahoe. From here, the single track follows a narrow ridge at 7,700 feet—fully 1,500 feet above Lake Tahoe. You may encounter hikers and a few bass-ackward cyclists coming UP the trail (the fools!). Continue along this route until you reach Tunnel Creek Road, which in turn emerges on a street at Ponderosa Ranch. If you are super ambitious, you can make a loop by turning right and riding to the top of the ridge. You will reach Twin Lakes in one-half mile. Seven-tenths of a mile past the lake sign, turn right or continue to the next main road and turn right. Turn right again on Forest Service Road 504, climb the ridge, and where the road forks, continue straight to Marlette Lake. From there, it is back to Spooner (and sliding down some sandy, squirrelly turns). The worst alternative is returning to Spooner by riding on Highway 28, a very dangerous route considering the traffic and narrow to nonexistent shoulders.

Distance: Five miles to Marlette Lake and 12 miles to Incline Village, one way.

Difficulty: Strenuous; not for beginners or anyone afraid of heights.

Elevation (low/high): 7,000 feet to 8,300 feet.

Location: Take Highway 28 to the Spooner Lake parking lot in Lake Tahoe-Nevada State Park. A parking fee ($5 per vehicle) is charged, and there is strict enforcement on parking in designated areas. If you take a second car to arrange a shuttle, limited parking is available at Tunnel Creek Road by Ponderosa Ranch at Incline Village.

Contact: Lake Tahoe-Nevada State Park, Sand Harbor; 775/831-0494, or Spooner Lake; 775/831-0494; for information on shuttles, consult this website: www.theflumetrail.com.

SOUTH LAKE TAHOE

Angora Ridge
(see map on page 241, site 22)
Enjoy a moderate ride that ends with spectacular

views of Fallen Leaf Lake and Mt. Tallac. Ride along Fallen Leaf Road, take the first left, continue one-half mile, and turn right on Angora Ridge Road (Forest Service Road 12N14). You can park or lock your bike at a trailhead to Angora Lakes and continue by foot. There's a lodge, cabins, and good swimming opportunities.

Distance: Two miles to Angora Lookout and four miles to Angora Lakes, one way.

Difficulty: Moderate.

Elevation (low/high): 6,360 feet to 7,440 feet.

Location: From South Lake Tahoe, drive two miles north of Highway 89. Turn left on Fallen Leaf Road. Park past Fallen Leaf Campground on the right.

Contact: Lake Tahoe Basin Management Unit; 530/573-2600.

Twin Peaks (see map on page 241, site 23)
Take this short, steep ride to the top of a mountain peak for great views of Lake Tahoe. A shorter one-mile loop may be made on the trail as well. It is open for public use 9 A.M.–7 P.M. daily. Caution: This is a very popular off-highway-vehicle area.

Distance: A one- to two-mile loop.

Difficulty: Moderate to strenuous.

Elevation (low/high): 6,400 feet to 7,010 feet.

Location: Off Lake Tahoe Boulevard approximately two miles from the junction of U.S. 50 and Highway 89. Turn left on Sawmill Road.

Contact: Lake Tahoe Basin Management Unit; 530/573-2600.

Mr. Toad's Wild Ride
(see map on page 241, site 24)
A technical ride for the experienced mountain biker, this trail drops from 9,000 feet to 6,800 feet in three miles. Take the Tahoe Rim Trail from the Big Meadows parking lot 2.5 miles to Tucker Flat. Turn left and follow the drainage of Saxon Creek. In two miles, the trail forks again. The right fork leads to Oneidas Street off of the Pioneer Trail. The left fork leads to Highway 89, south of the Highway 89/U.S. 50 junction. Watch for hikers and equestrian riders on the trail and pass with caution and courtesy.

Distance: Three miles one way.
Difficulty: Strenuous.
Elevation (low/high): 6,800 feet to 9,000 feet.
Location: Take Highway 89 five miles south from Meyers to the Big Meadows parking lot for the Tahoe Rim Trail.
Contact: Lake Tahoe Basin Management Unit; 530/573-2600.

Tahoe Rim Trail
(see map on page 241, site 25)

To experience breathtaking scenery with exceptional views of Lake Tahoe, take the Tahoe Rim Trail past Freel Peak, the highest peak in the basin, at an elevation of 10,881 feet. A longer trip is possible by arranging a car shuttle and parking one car at Heavenly Ski Resort's Stagecoach parking lot. The trailhead begins one-eighth of a mile up Stagecoach Run. Note: Mountain bikes are not allowed on the trail from Armstrong Pass toward Fountain Place, or the trail heading east toward High Meadows, which is private property. Policies on the Rim Trail are subject to change, so check first before embarking on a ride.
Distance: 18 miles one way.
Difficulty: Moderate to strenuous.
Elevation (low/high): 7,280 feet to 9,600 feet.
Location: From Meyers, drive 5.5 miles south on Highway 89 to the Big Meadows parking lot. The trail starts at the north end of the parking area.
Contact: Lake Tahoe Basin Management Unit; 530/573-2600.

Meiss Trail (see map on page 241, site 26)

Rising abruptly from Highway 89 for the first half mile, this trail levels off as it reaches Big Meadows. Trails leading to Round, Scotts, and Dardanelles Lakes provide access into Meiss Country with views of aspen-covered hills from lodgepole-cloaked forests. Note: This trail eventually intersects the Pacific Crest Trail, where mountain bikes are not allowed.
Distance: Five miles one way.
Difficulty: Moderate to strenuous.
Elevation (low/high): 7,280 feet to 8,400 feet.
Location: Take Highway 89 five miles south

from Meyers to the Big Meadows parking lot. Follow the trail at the southern end of the parking lot; it leads across the highway to the trailhead.
Contact: Lake Tahoe Basin Management Unit; 530/573-2600.

STATELINE/ZEPHYR COVE
Shoreline-Nevada Beach Trail
(see map on page 241, site 27)

This is an easy ride—with a few short hills—that gives occasional cyclists a nice mix of inland forest and spectacular beachfront views of Tahoe on the Nevada side of South Shore. Credit for promoting this route goes to Bob Daly, owner of Shoreline Bike Rentals on Kingsbury Grade, who cobbled together parts of a county-owned paved bike path with dirt trails that extend through Nevada Beach (you can see a map on his website at www.shorelinesnowboards.com). The result is a scenic 6.5-mile loop that begins and ends at Kahle Community Park, takes about an hour to negotiate at a leisurely pace, and is suitable for the entire family. If you like, you can stop at the midpoint for a deli sandwich or a burrito at the newly reconstructed Round Hill Shopping Center, or grab some food for a picnic at the beach and make it a two-hour or longer trip. One of the highlights is a little-known scenic rest area that is on the paved portion, in wooded terrain, about one-third of the way into the ride. There are great views from here, and this also is an excellent venue for a picnic.
Distance: 6.5 miles round-trip.
Difficulty: Easy, with a few moderate grades.
Elevation: 6,000 feet to 6,200 feet (mostly at lake level).
Location: From U.S. 50 at South Lake Tahoe, take Kingsbury Grade (Highway 207) east about an eighth of a mile to Kahle Community Park, watching for a driveway on the left side of the road that enters the parking lot. Park here or, if you rent a bike, you can park at Shoreline Bike Rentals across the road. Then ride up Kingsbury Grade to Pine Ridge Street. Turn left (just past the Century 21 office) and continue

through a residential area until you reach the end of the street at a cul-de-sac. The paved trail begins there. Follow it to Kingsbury Middle School, making sure to pass the school on the uphill (i.e. western) side on Lake Village Drive until that street ends and the path resumes. Continue along the path through forest to the busy intersection of Elks Point Road and Highway 50. Cross the highway and ride along Elks Point to the entrance of Nevada Beach. Proceed to the Forest Service campground. Take the dirt trail that begins between campsites 20 and 21 and continue through a fairly flat meadow, from which there are access points to the shoreline and beach if you choose to stop. This trail loops back to Highway 50 and an intersection with Kahle Drive. Cross the highway again and follow Kahle Drive back to Kahle Community Park.

Contact: Shoreline Bike Rentals, 259 Kingsbury Grade, Stateline, NV; 775/588-8777; email: shorline@sierra.net; website: www.shorelinesnowboards.com.

Genoa Peak
(see map on page 241, site 28)
Enjoy a moderate ride along a ridgeline with scenic views of the Lake Tahoe Basin to the west and Carson Valley to the east. Several spurs off the main road access peaks, with Genoa Peak the highest (elevation 9,150 feet). An excellent 10-mile loop off the main ridge is possible. Note: Mountain bikes are not allowed on the Tahoe Rim Trail, from Highway 207 to Spooner Summit. Take Genoa Peak Road (Forest Service Road 14N32) instead. A longer trip is possible if you can arrange a car shuttle. Park the second vehicle off of U.S. 50 behind the Nevada Department of Transportation Station (NDOT), one-quarter mile south of the Highway 28 and U.S. 50 junction.
Distance: Eight to 12 miles one way.
Difficulty: Moderate.
Elevation (low/high): 7,720 feet to 8,680 feet.
Location: From U.S. 50 at South Lake Tahoe, take Kingsbury Grade (Highway 207) east for 2.5 miles and turn left on North Benjamin Road, which turns into Andria Drive in one-

half mile. Continue to the end of the pavement and park.
Contact: Lake Tahoe Basin Management Unit; 530/573-2600.

KIRKWOOD/HOPE VALLEY/MARKLEEVILLE
Blue Lakes Road to Red Lake
(see map on page 241, site 29)
From Highway 88 in Hope Valley, follow the Blue Lakes Road south through Faith Valley and then into Charity Valley. There the county road turns to dirt and rises in elevation, eventually cresting at the Blue Lakes. From here, follow Forestdale Creek Road (Forest Service Road 013) north to Red Lake and Highway 88. This heavily traveled, off-highway-vehicle trail leads to several scenic alpine lakes and undesignated campsites. Along the way, riders enjoy spectacular high vistas of Sierra peaks. You'll experience steep descents and rough four-wheel-drive terrain for about two miles from the Blue Lakes, but then the road levels out and is well graded through moderate forest before reaching Red Lake. You can return the way you came or take Highway 88 back to Hope Valley (use caution along the highway) for a 21-mile loop. Note: The gravel and dirt road from Hope Valley to Blue Lakes is heavily traveled by RVs and four-wheel-drive vehicles on weekends.
Distance: Four miles one way, eight miles roundtrip, or a 21-mile loop.
Difficulty: Moderate to strenuous.
Elevation (low/high): 8,050 feet to 8,200 feet.
Location: The ride starts at Highway 88 in Hope Valley.
Contact: Toiyabe National Forest, Carson Ranger District; 775/882-2766.

Caples Lake to Strawberry
(see map on page 241, site 30)
This is a lodge-to-lodge tour, from Caples (where you can rent mountain bikes) on Highway 88 to Strawberry on U.S. 50. It's advisable to arrange a shuttle here (allow 90 minutes for this), parking a second car at Strawberry. Considering the

elevation drop of over 3,000 feet, there's a long and steep downhill from the top of a ridge beyond Schneider Cow Camp. The entire route is on a jeep trail, and since you start at 7,797 feet, you gain just 800 feet before starting your long descent. Views of Caples Lake, Thimble Peak, Round Top, and Little Round Top mountains are spectacular along the four-mile stretch of road from the maintenance station to the top of the ridge. The eight-mile Strawberry Canyon Jeep Trail has some fairly steep sections, so be careful on the descent. Be sure to take your topo map and carry lots of water; the rocky areas can get quite hot. Once you reach Strawberry Lodge, you can relax, have an ice cream cone, or eat lunch at the restaurant.

Distance: 12 miles one way.

Difficulty: Strenuous.

Elevation (low/high): 5,500 feet to 8,600 feet.

Location: From Highway 88 at Caples Lake, turn off at the Caples CalTrans Maintenance Station, and look for the jeep road to Schneider Cow Camp where this route begins. This area is also used for the Kirkwood Cross-Country Center during the winter months, and the route is skied in the famous Echo Summit to Kirkwood Race each year in March.

Contact: Caples Lake Resort; 209/258-8888.

FEATHER RIVER COUNTRY/LAKES BASIN

Mills Peak Lookout Ride

(see map on page 241, site 31)

To reach the Mills Peak Lookout, travel 1.5 miles on County Road 721, then turn north on County Road 822 and continue 4.5 miles. The lookout offers vistas of eastern Plumas County. Forest Service lookout personnel may be on duty during the summer months. The easy, 0.4-mile Red Fir Nature Trail, which has interpretive signs, can be accessed off County Road 822, but you'll have to park your bike and walk if you want to explore. (Note: Gray Eagle, Gold Lake, and Elwell Lakes Lodges are situated along the Gold Lake Road.)

Distance: Six miles one way.

Difficulty: Moderate to strenuous, on gravel, rock, graded, and dirt roads.

Elevation (low/high): 6,500 feet to 7,340 feet.

Location: From Highway 89 near Graeagle, take the Gold Lake Road (County Road 519) to the junction with Mills Peak Road (County Roads 721/822). Or from Highway 49, take the Gold Lake Road approximately eight miles north to the junction with Mills Peak Road. Park across from this intersection at the turnout.

Contact: Plumas National Forest, Beckwourth Ranger District; 530/836-2575.

Golf and Tennis

On the Courses

Golf is not just a casual diversion in the Tahoe-Reno area; it is a passion. Some of the top courses in the country, and some of the oldest in California and Nevada, are within a 50-mile radius of Lake Tahoe. The region now has over 40 courses, with all but six of them open for public play. Amazingly, one-third of these courses came into existence since the mid-1990s as developers scrambled to meet the demand for tee times. Many of these new tracks are tied to residential projects, particularly along the eastern slopes of the Sierra from Reno to the south end of Carson Valley. In August of 1999, the first

annual PGA Reno-Tahoe Open was held at the private Montreux Golf and Country Club in the western foothills of Reno, and the nationally televised tournament drew yet more attention to the area's golfing wonders. In 1999, Lahonton, a private course in an exclusive new residential community, opened in the foothills south of Truckee. As this edition went to press, new golf communities were under construction, in pre-construction or in proposal form in Truckee, Reno, and Genoa, south of Carson City. East West Partners, a Colorado company, was moving ahead with two golf and second-home projects in Truckee, on either side of I-80. The first, close to the new interchange of Highway 267 and I-80, is Old Greenstone. South of downtown Truckee, in Martis Valley, no fewer than three

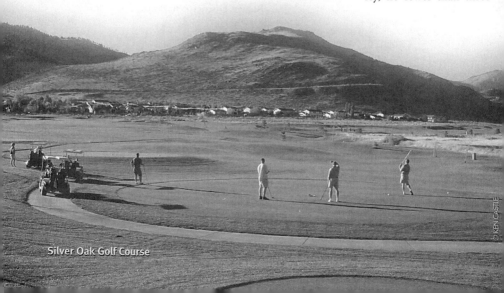

Silver Oak Golf Course

© KEN CASTLE

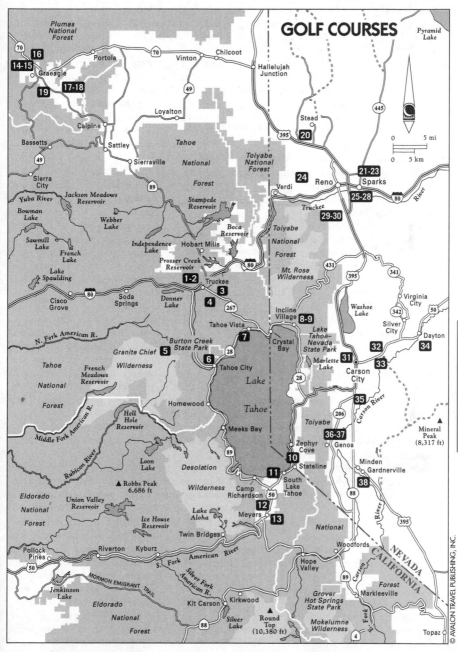

GOLF COURSES

GOLF AND TENNIS

golf/residential projects are proposed for this area, although controversy swirls over anything that would impact such a large tract of open space. In Reno, Sommersett Development Company is creating an 18-hole Tom Kite-designed course and a nine-hole short course, but both may end up being private. As the housing components sell out, courses are being removed from public play. For example, in early 2002, Arrow Creek Golf Club, on the eastern Sierra north of the Mt. Rose Highway, privatised the second of its two courses. Overall, greens fees continue to increase year after year, but you can often get discounted rounds by buying a golf-and-lodging package, now offered by several tour operators, hotels and some local visitors bureaus. Also, fees are substantially lower during the so-called shoulder periods, usually in spring and fall, and hit rock-bottom in winter at the Reno-Carson Valley courses, many of which are open year-round. Of course, if you don't mind playing late in the afternoon, twilight fees are in effect at most courses.

What makes a golf vacation here so attractive is the diversity of terrain. You can play a hilly, forested course at Lake Tahoe on one day and a links-style, high-desert course the next day. Expect to encounter plenty of wildlife, including deer, marmots, coyotes, and waterfowl on the fairways and in the out-of-bounds areas, some of which are sensitive and protected wetlands. The top designers in the sport—Arnold Palmer, Jack Nicklaus, Robert Trent Jones Sr. and Jr., Peter Jacobsen, Johnny Miller, and Robert Muir Graves, among others—have left their trademarks at these courses, so there is plenty of challenge for any player. Proximity is another advantage; from Reno or Tahoe, you can drive to most of these places within an hour.

As might be expected, it's tough to get tee times at the premier mountain courses because their season is short and demand is high. These

> *What makes a golf vacation here so attractive is the diversity of terrain. You can play a hilly, forested course at Lake Tahoe on one day and a links-style, high-desert course the next day. Expect to encounter plenty of wildlife, including deer, marmots, coyotes, and waterfowl.*

include Edgewood in South Lake Tahoe, Incline Championship, Tahoe Donner, Whitehawk, Plumas Pines, Graeagle Meadows, Northstar-at-Tahoe and the Resort at Squaw Creek. You can extend the season to year-round by playing the Reno and Carson Valley courses, which are closed only by occasional snowfall. If you're having trouble getting tee times, consider these excellent but less well known courses: Genoa Lakes, Dayton Valley, Lake Tahoe, Sierra Nevada Golf Ranch, Incline Executive, Red Hawk, Washoe, Wildcreek, Sunridge and Silver Oak. By all means, try to play at Lakeridge in Reno, which many golfers consider to be the city's most spectacular public course. For high-handicap players, there is mild terrain at Sierra Sage, Empire Ranch, Rosewood Lakes, Carson Valley, Eagle Valley, and Graeagle Meadows. And the best-kept golf secrets in the entire region are Tahoe's secluded nine-holers, especially Old Brockway, which has numerous elevation changes and can test all of your skills. (Glenbrook, one of the world's greatest nine-hole courses, regrettably went private in 1998 after well-heeled local property owners bought it to keep the public out of their gated community. Now this gorgeous, forested course sees very little use except in July and August.)

Keep in mind a few things when you're playing these courses. In summer, afternoon thundershowers are not uncommon in both the mountain and high-desert areas. When lightning is flashing close by, the last thing you want in your hands is a big, fat 9-iron. The better part of valor is to retreat to the clubhouse and wait until the storm blows over (which it often does within an hour), or just quit for the day. Another frequent environmental factor is afternoon wind—especially at the Reno and Carson Valley courses, where most players prefer morning tee times. Also, with so many of these courses bordering nature preserves, respect the signs asking you to stay out of the wetlands. Such habitats are crucial to the local wildlife, which, after all, contribute to the enjoyment of playing golf here. Finally, spikeless golf shoes are now a requirement just about everywhere in the region.

Properties listed are keyed to the Golf Courses map.

TRUCKEE/DONNER

Tahoe Donner Golf Course
(see map on page 263, site 1)

Above Truckee on a plateau that encompasses a vast residential/resort development, this picturesque and meticulously groomed course is difficult to play, and equally difficult to secure tee times at, since residents get most of the prime spots during the short season. This course has six par 5s and eight par 4s, but even big boomers will have to use finesse to avoid landing in creeks or in the heavily forested out-of-bounds areas. Although the scorecard rates the second hole as the number one handicap, the course strategy booklet (available for a few extra dollars at the pro shop) gives that distinction to the first, a 450-yard, par 5 "warm-up" that sets the tone for the rest of your round. The hole is long and straightaway, and the narrow corridor offers little forgiveness for a hook or slice. Your drive is apt to land on an uphill slope, and you'll need a 3-iron or 7-wood for a long second shot to a two-level green that will challenge your putting skills. The 18th (421 yards, par 4) is one of the most spectacular finishing holes in the Sierra. It requires a strong downhill drive of 210 to 230 yards, then a carefully negotiated long second shot that must sail over a watery labyrinth of streams and ponds to reach a large green. On the second, third, and fourth holes, you have to dodge some large trees in the fairway, which can block even solidly hit balls.

Stats: Designed by Bill Williams; 18 holes, 6,917 yards, and 72 par.

Amenities: Driving range, putting green, cart rentals, pro shop, restaurant, bar, and snack bar.

Fees: Including mandatory cart, $100 with cart.

Hours: 7 A.M.–dusk, mid-May–mid-October.

Contact: Tahoe Donner Golf Course, 12850 Northwoods Blvd., Truckee, CA 96161; 530/587-9440; website: www.tahoedonner.com.

Coyote Moon Golf Course
(see map on page 263, site 2)

The theme of this 18-hole public course, which opened in the summer of 2000, is "a walk in the woods." Just south of the Tahoe Donner Golf Course and just above Donner Pass Road on Northwoods Boulevard, Coyote Moon uses forested terrain and some huge rock outcroppings for its elongated layout. But there are surprisingly generous fairways, so you don't feel as if you're playing in hallways. Water hazards consist of three man-made lakes and Trout Creek, which come into play on seven holes. Initially the developers—the same company that operates Plumas Pines—intended to make the course part of a planned residential community. But now it is exclusively a golf course, with no need to worry about slicing into somebody's picture window. The signature hole is the 13th, a long par 3 across the creek with a 100-foot elevation drop. The pin is 227 yards from the back tees, and there is a generous green and landing area that is surrounded by snowcapped mountains. Another memorable hole is the 12th, a short par 5 that plays slightly uphill into an incredible rock canyon, with bunkers bordering the rocks. One of the most challenging holes is the 17th, a 470-yard par 4 that tees off across the creek and parallels it to the green. Another difficult hole is the first, a hard dogleg left that requires a precise iron shot off the tee to the landing zone. Overshooting puts you in the trees while undershooting forces you to make an obstructed angling shot over foliage and the creek. The 256-acre course, which acquired a permanent clubhouse in 2001 and is now managed by East West Resorts of Colorado, provides obstacles for low handicappers and escape routes for high handicappers.

Stats: Designed by Brad Bell; 18 holes, 7177 yards, and 72 par.

Amenities: Clubhouse with full restaurant and pro shop, large putting green and chipping area, and cart rentals (carts are required).

Fees: $85–125.

Hours: Dawn–dusk, May–October.
Contact: Coyote Moon Golf Course, 10685 Northwoods, Truckee, CA 96161; 530/587-0886; website: www.coyotemoongolfcourse.com.

Ponderosa Golf Course
(see map on page 263, site 3)
One mile south of Truckee, this nine-hole course is well maintained and mostly level, with few surprises. Wide fairways are forgiving, there are no fairway water hazards, and the course is easily walkable. There are two par 5s, five par 4s, and two par 3s. The toughest hole is the 507-yard ninth, a par 5 that has a dogleg on the right, Highway 267 on the left, and a well-bunkered green. The greatest elevation change is the third (145 yards, par 3), which requires a steep uphill tee shot across a road to the green. Homes and pine trees parallel the first four holes. At Highway 267 and Reynolds Way in Truckee.
Stats: Nine holes, 3,018 yards, and 36 par.
Amenities: Putting green, power and pull cart rentals, club rentals, pro shop, lessons, club repair, and snack bar.
Fees: $23–32.
Hours: 7 A.M.–7 P.M., May–October.
Contact: Ponderosa Golf Course, 10040 Reynolds Way, Truckee, CA 96160; 530/587-3501.

Northstar-at-Tahoe Golf Course
(see map on page 263, site 4)
Now here's a course with a Jekyll and Hyde personality: the front nine has friendly, wide-open fairways overlooking the Martis Valley, while the back nine has a devilish layout that requires players to slash through an obstacle course of dense forest, barrancas, and water hazards. Drivers in front, irons in back, plenty of extra balls in your bag—and you have the basic strategy. But the 14th (489 yards, par 5) sneaks up on you like Jack the Ripper. Consider a 5-iron off the tee, and gauge your second shot carefully (maybe another 5-iron); there's a small uphill rise that slopes off toward a blind green. Lurking here is a barranca, and it's better to lay up in front of it than to risk a lost ball. Scout the distance before your second stroke, and use a wedge for your third shot to

the small green, taking care to avoid a deep bunker on the left. The 17th (359 yards, par 4) and the 18th (552 yards, par 5) will also give you fits; they require threading the needle between stands of pine and aspen, and the 17th veers left across a creek. Water comes into play on 14 holes, so plan on dunking a few if you're a high handicapper. At Northstar-at-Tahoe, off Highway 267 on Basque Drive.
Stats: Designed by Robert Muir Graves; 18 holes, 6,897 yards, and 72 par.
Amenities: Driving range, putting green, cart rentals, club rentals, pro shop, bar, restaurant, and snack bar.
Fees: $75.
Hours: 7:30 A.M.–dark, May–October.
Contact: Northstar-at-Tahoe Golf Course, P.O. Box 129, Truckee, CA 96160; 530/562-2490; website: www.skinorthstar.com.

SQUAW VALLEY
The Resort at Squaw Creek
(see map on page 263, site 5)
"The course that Titleist built" is how locals describe this mean-spirited, links-style track, which has a penchant for swallowing balls. Most of the back nine resembles a waterfowl sanctuary, with elevated wooden cart paths crisscrossing the wetlands. A wayward ball off the tee will sink in the ooze like a rock in quicksand, and about the eighth time this happens you'll be ready to break your driver in half. The front nine presents some tight, narrow fairways notched into the hillside and sandwiched between rows of mature pines. You may wonder how on Earth anyone managed to build a golf course here. Actually, the course was designed on about two-thirds of the normal land area. The number one handicap is the eighth, a par 4, 338-yard hole that requires an iron off the tee and pinpoint accuracy on the second shot to reach a speck of a green or become lost in the marsh. By the time you get to the last holes, it's likely that the wind will be kicking up through the meadow and you'll be too distraught to appreciate the sweeping vistas of Squaw Valley's imposing peaks. The 429-yard 17th (a par 4) often throws a fierce headwind

your way and makes it tough to use a driver without risking the wrath of the Marsh Monster. Your second stroke must carry a creek to a diminutive green surrounded by bunkers. Arguably this course, built in 1992, is the most difficult in the Sierra. It will test the resolve of seasoned players.

Stats: Designed by Robert Trent Jones Jr.; 18 holes, 6,931 yards, and 71 par.

Amenities: Driving range, putting green, chipping greens, beverage cart, cart rentals, pro shop, bar, five restaurants, 403-room hotel, spa, swimming pools, and conference center.

Fees: $85–115, including mandatory cart rental.

Hours: 8 A.M.–dark, June–October.

Contact: The Resort at Squaw Creek, 40 Squaw Creek Rd., Olympic Valley, CA 96146; 530/581-6637; website: www.squawcreek.com.

TAHOE CITY/WEST SHORE
Tahoe City Golf Course
(see map on page 263, site 6)
In the heart of Tahoe City, this nine-hole course is the oldest at Lake Tahoe (circa 1917), beating Brockway by seven years. Like Brockway, it was a staple of Sinatra, Hope, and Crosby. Except for holes four and five, the course is basically flat and wide open, but has some scenic views of the lake, which is directly across the street. There are four par 4s, four par 3s, and one par 5. The 419-yard third, a par 4, has an out-of-bounds that consists of retail businesses on the left and a well-bunkered green. However, the fifth (294 yards, par 4) is the trickiest, with a slight dogleg right, a water hazard on the right, and a sunken green with a narrow slot through tall pines.

Stats: Designed by May Webb Dunn; nine holes, 2,570 yards, and 33 par.

Amenities: Driving range, putting green, and pro shop.

Fees: $33 for nine holes, $55 for 18 walking (July–August), extra for cart.

Hours: Dawn–dusk, April–November.

Contact: Tahoe City Golf Course, 251 N. Lake Blvd., Tahoe City, CA 96145; 530/583-1516; email: tcgc@tcgc.com.

KINGS BEACH/TAHOE VISTA/CARNELIAN BAY
Old Brockway Golf Course
(see map on page 263, site 7)
It would be a mistake to dismiss this as a lightweight nine-holer, but that's what many passersby think when they see the first two holes, which are relatively flat and somewhat nondescript when viewed from Highway 267 or North Lake Boulevard. Ah, but there's pure gold in the rest of the course, and plenty of challenge with narrow fairways, varying terrain elevations, and woodlands. Not only that, but Old Brockway has a colorful history. In 1934, this was the site of the first Bing Crosby Open, long before it became a PGA-sanctioned event. The course was built in 1924, and has retained its original form. From its inception, it was intended as an amenity to the Brockway Hotel, a luxurious resort that was destroyed by fire. Hollywood's famous Rat Pack—Dean Martin, Frank Sinatra, et al—used to play here regularly, and holes one, two, three, eight, and nine are together known as "The Loop" or "Whiskey Run," commemorating Martin's drinking habits on the course. There's a story that another famous golfer, Bob Hope, while teeing off on the second hole, inadvertently hit a deer, causing the ball to ricochet to about 10 feet from the pin—reportedly his best shot in Tahoe. Although most of the course is invisible from the highway, it has an interesting layout, with five par 4s, two par 3s, and two par 5s. Because several holes parallel homes or highway, slices and hooks will get you into trouble fast. The number one handicap hole is the seventh, a long (553-yard) par 5 that slopes uphill and has a wide ditch fronting an elevated and bunkered green. On the short, 195-yard third hole, you tee off on top of a high rock garden through a narrow slot between homes and forest, to a lower green. Recent improvements include a 6,700-square-foot clubhouse and restaurant, the addition of electric carts, new greens and bunkers on holes 1 and 2, and a redesign of hole 9 to accommodate an expansion of the nearby Safeway supermarket. Old Brockway has been certified as an Audubon Society

Sanctuary, the only 9-holer west of the Mississipi to receive that designation.

Stats: Designed by John Dunn; nine holes, 3,400 yards, and 36 par.

Amenities: Driving range, putting green, cart rentals, pro shop, and restaurant.

Fees: $38 for nine holes, $65 for 18 holes walking (high season), with cart extra.

Hours: 6:30 A.M.–dark, April–November.

Contact: Old Brockway Golf Club, 7900 N. Lake Blvd., Kings Beach, CA 96143; 530/546-9909; website: www.oldbrockway.com.

INCLINE VILLAGE/CRYSTAL BAY

The Mountain Course at Incline Village (see map on page 263, site 8)

Carved into a lushly forested hillside above Incline Village's prestigious Championship Course, this track is not only spectacularly scenic but is also a sterling challenge for your short game. Forget about woods; there are 14 par 3s, no par 5s, and the longest hole (the 18th) is 399 yards. You'll get plenty of practice with your short irons and wedges, and plenty of exercise, too, since the course seesaws up and down the mountain. Perhaps the most interesting hole is the 122-yard 15th, a par 3 that has a high, elevated tee requiring an 8- or 9-iron to carry a stream to a lower green bordered by three bunkers. Short gets you in the stream and long gets you in the woods. The 17th (125 yards, par 3) is almost the reverse; you tee off to an elevated green. Narrow fairways, dense out-of-bounds, and water hazards on the majority of the holes necessitate more than a few extra balls in your bag. This course has been rated as one of the top five executive courses in the United States. It is also one of the easier courses in Tahoe for securing a tee time. The course is on Golfer's Pass Road off Mt. Rose Highway (Highway 431).

Stats: Designed by Robert Trent Jones Jr.; 18 holes, 3,513 yards, and 58 par.

Amenities: Putting green, cart rentals, pro shop, bar, and snack bar.

Fees: Including mandatory carts, $50.

Hours: 6:30 A.M.–7 P.M., mid-May–early October.

Contact: The Mountain Course at Incline Village, 690 Wilson Way, Incline Village, NV 89451; 888/236-8725 or 775/832-1150; website: www.golfincline.com.

The Championship Course at Incline Village (see map on page 263, site 9)

This premier course combines the scenic beauty of green hills, aspen and pine forest, and lofty panoramas of Lake Tahoe. Set in the uncrowded "banana belt" of the lake's most upscale community (and surrounded by million-dollar-plus estates), the Championship Course is extremely popular. A diverse layout with frequent elevation changes offers four par 5s, 10 par 4s, and four par 3s. Creeks and ponds provide water hazards, some of them blind, on eight holes of the front nine and four holes of the back nine. The number one handicap hole is the par 5 fourth, a double dogleg left that is 619 yards and bordered by out-of-bounds along the length of the hole. But for a lot of players the 18th (411 yards, par 4) is more difficult. The tee shot must carry two creeks and be straight down a tight fairway lined with houses. There's a dogleg left, and if you don't get an accurate drive to a narrow landing you'll have a tough second shot. In any case, you'll have to cope with a well-bunkered and elevated green that slopes away from you. The signature hole is the 16th (406 yards, par 4), with its dramatic view over Lake Tahoe and snow-capped Sierra peaks.

Stats: Designed by Robert Trent Jones Sr.; 18 holes, 6,915 yards, and 72 par.

Amenities: Driving range, putting green, cart rentals, pro shop, bar, restaurant, and snack bar.

Fees: Including mandatory carts, $115.

Hours: 6 A.M.–7 P.M., early May–mid-October.

Contact: Incline Championship Course, 955 Fairway Blvd., Incline Village, NV 89451; 888/236-8725 or 775/832-1146; website: www.golfincline.com.

SOUTH LAKE TAHOE

Edgewood Tahoe Golf Course (see map on page 263, site 10)

The grande dame of Sierra courses, Edgewood boasts lakeside frontage and an elegant, palatial clubhouse that contains a gourmet restaurant and enough banquet rooms to host a myriad of social functions, weddings, and conferences. This is the site of the Lake Tahoe Celebrity Golf Championship, a major televised event held each July. But perhaps its greatest distinction is having the only two holes—the signature 17th (207 yards, an easy par 3) and the finishing 18th (574 yards, par 5)—right on the shore of Tahoe. It's easy to be swept up by the scenic lake vistas and the carefully manicured fairways and greens, but you'd better pay attention if you're going to avoid bogeys. Try for a fade off the tee on the tough, 462-yard ninth, a par 4 with a narrow fairway, a dogleg right, out-of-bounds to the left, and trees to the right. The 10th (431 yards, par 4) has a lake that eats into most of the fairway and guards the green along with four bunkers. On the 15th (372 yards, par 4), an uphill tee shot that slopes to a hidden fairway requires a look-see through a periscope, but is less difficult than it seems. And on the 16th, an island of a green is surrounded by bunkers, virtually assuring you of practice with your sand wedge. On most of the holes, the greens are designed to make Silly Putty out of frustrated putters. Note: Edgewood is the most popular course on the lake, and the most difficult for getting tee times.

Stats: Designed by George Fazio; 18 holes, 7,491 yards, and 72 par.

Amenities: Driving range, putting green, cart rentals, pro shop, bar, restaurant, banquet rooms, and snack bars.

Fees: Including cart rental, $200 daily.

Hours: 7 A.M.–3 P.M., May–October.

Contact: Edgewood Tahoe Golf Course, 180 Lake Pkwy./P.O. Box 5400, Stateline, NV 89449; 888/881-8659 or 775/588-3566; website: www.edgewood-tahoe.com.

Bijou Golf Course
(see map on page 263, site 11)
Built in 1920, this scenic nine-holer, which is in Bijou Meadows just off U.S. 50 near the center of South Lake Tahoe, is a respectable track for players of all abilities. Operated by the city, the course takes no reservations, but is one of the easiest to get on in the Tahoe Basin. There are

five par 4s and four par 3s, and Bijou Creek provides water hazards on five holes until mid-summer. Pine trees line many of the holes, and there are vistas of Freel Peak and Heavenly Ski Resort. The number one handicap hole is the 346-yard sixth, a par 4, which has a demanding first shot that must carry a creekbed and meadow. The ideal landing is 220 yards off the tee, providing the best approach to a very small green. The eighth (215 yards, par 3), plays straightaway to an equally diminutive green surrounded on three sides by the creekbed; overhit, and you're in the ditch. Recently, the ninth hole was shortened about 30 yards, to a 165-yard par 3. In general, greens are small and have lots of tricky undulations.

Stats: Nine holes, 2,031 yards, and 32 par.

Amenities: Driving range, putting green, cart rentals, pro shop, and snack bar.

Fees: $15 for nine holes walking.

Hours: 7:30 A.M.–6:30 P.M., April–October.

Contact: Bijou Golf Course, 3464 Fairway (at Johnson Blvd.); write to 1180 Rufus Allen Blvd., South Lake Tahoe, CA 96150; 530/542-6097.

Lake Tahoe Golf Course
(see map on page 263, site 12)
Owned by the California Department of Parks and Recreation, this course is one of Tahoe's sleepers. It is frequently easier to get tee times here than on the lake's premier tracks, and it has a modern and spacious new clubhouse. But the course is not exactly a breeze; there are potential water hazards on 16 holes, including sections of the Upper Truckee River, although there are enough straightaway fairways to make up for double bogeys. The number one handicap hole is the 13th, a sticky, 447-yard par 4 that requires a long and straight drive into the wind to a narrow landing that has a hidden pond on the right and bunkers on the left. Your second shot requires a fairway wood or long iron to a small green with bunkers in front, though most players will settle for laying up short of the green and hoping for a precise chip shot and putt. Of the other holes, the ninth (589 yards, par 5) has three water hazards—a lake, a creek, and a pond—and the 10th (427 yards, par 4) demands an accurate drive

GOLF AND TENNIS

that must carry two water hazards and avoid wooded out-of-bounds to the right, with a second shot to a narrow green that slopes from back to front. This course has great diversity, including scenic riparian habitat with pines and aspens, and a huge rocky bluff behind the 10th that is unique in the region.

Stats: 18 holes, 6,707 yards, and 71 par.

Amenities: Driving range, putting green, cart rentals, pro shop, bar, and snack bar.

Fees: $70 with cart, $48 walking, seven days a week.

Hours: 6 A.M.–8 P.M., April–October.

Contact: Lake Tahoe Golf Course, 2500 Emerald Bay Rd. (U.S. 50), South Lake Tahoe, CA 96150; 530/577-0788.

Tahoe Paradise Golf Course
(see map on page 263, site 13)

Built in 1960, this course was the first 18-holer in South Lake Tahoe, and it's a challenge for anyone who doesn't hit straight off the tee. "Like playing golf in your hallway" is the way one starter describes this tight track of narrow fairways through pine thickets, although what's visible from U.S. 50 looks anything but difficult. There are 12 par 4s and six par 3s, and two of the holes have water hazards. The top handicap hole is the 18th (377 yards, par 4), which requires a tee shot through a gap no wider than 50 yards, down to a large landing area and a green that is bunkered on the right. The 14th (295 yards, par 4) is also downhill, with a dogleg right that offers a skimpy landing area and a green that slopes from back to front. As a rule, hitting behind most of the holes means "bye-bye ball." The signature hole is the 5th (110 yards, par 3), which has a pond in front and a view of Mt. Tallac and the surrounding peaks. In general, the course has modest facilities and fair maintenance, but with its short yardage, it seems like an executive course.

Stats: 18 holes, 4,028 yards, and 66 par.

Amenities: Driving range, putting green, cart rentals, pro shop, and snack bar.

Fees: $50 with cart, $35 walking.

Hours: 7 A.M.–7 P.M., April–November.

Director of golf: Dawn Beeman.

Contact: Tahoe Paradise Golf Course, 3021 U.S. 50, South Lake Tahoe, CA 96150; 530/577-2121; website: www.tahoeparadisegolf.com.

FEATHER RIVER COUNTRY/LAKES BASIN

Plumas Pines Country Club
(see map on page 263, site 14)

Beautifully designed, exquisitely manicured, and spectacularly scenic, this course, set in a lush valley framed by rugged Sierra peaks, provides a memorable experience for any player. It demands a high level of skill, with tight, pine-framed fairways and frequent water hazards. There are blind doglegs, heavily bunkered greens, and houses paralleling many of the holes, putting a premium on accuracy. Expect to lose more than your normal quota of balls. The course has four par 5s, 10 par 4s, and four par 3s, with three tee boxes per hole. Duck ponds, lakes, or streams come into play on 11 holes, and you'll have to carry the water on seven of them, either with tee or fairway shots.

The number one handicap hole, and the signature of the course, is the ninth (395 yards, par 4); this has a dramatic view across a small lake toward the clubhouse, which sits on a high hill overlooking the course. Your tee shot on Hot Dog Hill must carry the lake and stay left of a deep rough that is in a direct line to the green. Dense foliage on the left is played as a lateral hazard, and there's a slight dogleg right to an elevated green, with a sharp falloff behind the hole. Other difficult holes include the second (419 yards, par 4), a dogleg left with a narrow neck fairway and a lateral water hazard left; the fourth (484 yards, par 5), which has a slot of a fairway, a completely guarded green on a dogleg right, the Feather River on the left, and homes on the right, and is called "Double Trouble"; and the 18th (539 yards, par 5), which has a double dogleg and out-of-bounds on the left, a lateral hazard on the right, and an uphill approach to a two-tiered green. The course brochure says that some of these holes are known to make grown men cry, so keep your towel handy. The best advice is to play Plumas Pines with someone who's already been through a nervous breakdown.

Stats: Designed by Homer Flynt; 18 holes, 6,504 yards, and 72 par.

Amenities: Driving range, pro shop, accommodations, restaurant, snack bar, and bar.

Fees: Including cart, $55 on weekdays, $70 on weekends.

Hours: Dawn–dusk, May–October.

Contact: Plumas Pines Country Club, 402 Poplar Valley Rd./P.O. Box 746, Blairsden, CA 96103; 530/836-1420; website: www.graeagle .com/plumaspines.

Feather River Park Resort
(see map on page 263, site 15)

Set along the Middle Fork of the Feather River on Highways 70 and 89, this nine-holer is part of a large but low-key resort complex that has rustic cabins and various recreational amenities near the central business district of Graeagle. The flat, open course is pleasantly framed by scattered pine trees, and even the two par 5s, at 433 yards and 439 yards, can be reached in two shots. There is nothing intimidating here, the pace of play is unhurried, and the course is popular with retirees and youngsters.

Stats: Nine holes, 2,582 yards, and 35 par.

Amenities: Pro shop, bar, accommodations, and Sunday brunch.

Fees: $16–18.

Hours: 8 A.M.–dusk, April–October.

Contact: Feather River Park Resort, P.O. Box 37, Blairsden, CA 96103; 530/836-2328.

Feather River Inn Golf Course
(see map on page 263, site 16)

Built in 1915 by the Feather River Inn, this is the most challenging of the two nine-holers in Graeagle and offers a good warm-up for playing nearby Plumas Pines (see course 14). There are tight, tree-lined fairways on mostly level terrain, and the course has seven par 4s and two par 3s. The second hole (411 yards, par 4) is the number one handicap. The finishing hole, surrounded by the resort and with an uphill green, is one of the most scenic anywhere. The inn, a grand old lodge built in the tradition of the Ahwanee Hotel in Yosemite (but still in need of some renovation), offers accommodations and other recreational amenities. The course is at the junction of Highways 70 and 89.

Stats: Nine holes, 2,744 yards, and 34 par.

Amenities: Equipment rentals and sales, pro shop, bar, snack bar, conference facility, accommodations, and Sunday brunch.

Fees: $18.

Hours: 7 A.M.–dusk, April–November.

Contact: Feather River Inn Golf Course, 65899 Hwy. 70/P.O. Box 67, Blairsden, CA 96103; 530/836-2722; website: www.yol.com/web/ featherriverinn/index.html.

Graeagle Meadows Golf Course
(see map on page 263, site 17)

This is a mostly flat but scenic course in the golfing mecca of Graeagle, California, a one-hour drive north of Truckee. It's not as technical as neighboring Plumas Pines Country Club (see course number 14), and not nearly as difficult either (there are just two tee boxes per hole). But some elevated tees, water hazards, and strategically located pine trees can make life interesting for players. The layout has the standard four par 5s, 10 par 4s, and four par 3s, but every hole has a name, and the number-one handicap hole—"Eagle's Roost" (413 yards, par 4)—has a sharp dogleg right and a bunkered green. But some might argue that "Feather's Edge," the seventh (543 yards, par 5), is the trickiest because it tees off across the Middle Fork of the Feather River, although it's pretty much a straightaway shot to the green from there. The 16th (161 yards, par 3) has a giant pine blocking the middle of the green, which definitely puts some stress on your tee shot. The well-maintained course is in vogue with retirees, who give it a relaxed, unhurried pace.

Stats: Designed by Ellis Van Gorder; 18 holes, 6,688 yards, and 72 par.

Amenities: Driving range, pro shop, bar, restaurant, and snack bar.

Fees: $45–60 with cart.

Hours: Dawn–dusk daily, mid-March–October.

Contact: Graeagle Meadows Golf Course, 18 Hwy. 89, Graeagle, CA 96103; 530/836-2323; website: www.playgraeagle.com.

GOLF AND TENNIS

The Dragon at Gold Mountain
(see map on page 263, site 18)

Opened in summer of 2000, this spectacular semiprivate course is in the rolling hills of Plumas County between Graeagle and Portola, about an hour's drive north of Truckee. It is part of a 1,280-acre, 427-homesite residential community that has year-round recreational amenities, including a ski hill. The course offers stunning views of the Mohawk Valley, distant Eureka Peak, and the awesome Feather River Canyon. Its serpentine layout through the hills and plateaus above the river resulted in the name, but this Dragon generally looks fiercer than it is. Tee-boxes are tucked into narrow slots between the trees, but the holes usually open up into wide fairways. Still, there are many ways for The Dragon to put a bite in your game. One hole, the fourth, a short par 4 (324 yards from the back tee), overlooks the river and borders a 200-foot cliff that might as well be a black hole for balls. Because of bunkers on the

right, your drive must be solidly hit and aimed close to the drop-off in order to have a clear second shot at a shallow green that is set on a precipice. Other challenging holes are the sixth, a long par 4 (471 yards) that breaks to the left, and the eighth, a par 3 (215 yards) that requires your tee shot to carry a lake. Dramatic vistas beckon at every point on this course, starting with the par 5 first that has a downhill tee shot and a lofty panorama of the peaks and valleys surrounding Gold Mountain. County Road A-15 divides the championship course, with seven holes on the north side next to the river canyon and 11 holes on the south side snuggling against the hills. Homes surround the course but do not intrude on fairways, and the scattered trees, some of them 500-year-old cedars, provide considerable open space. There are eight lakes and some seasonal creeks for water hazards. Each hole has four tee boxes, so there's usually relief from the toughest routes. Some unique features of The Dragon include a spacious clubhouse,

Nakoma Lodge at The Dragon Golf Course

called Nakoma, that came from a 1923 design by famed architect Frank Lloyd Wright. In its short existence, Nakoma has already become the talk of the golf world. It resembles a cross between Native American tepees and Asian pagodas, with towering steeples and pods of rooms in contrasting shapes. The complex houses fine dining, conference and banquet facilities, four luxury overnight villas, a grill, a pro shop, swimming pool, spa and exercise room. The clubhouse is on a prominent ridge with a commanding panorama of the valley.

Stats: Designed by Nelson and Haworth; 18 holes, 7,175 yards, and 72 par.

Amenities: Clubhouse, pro shop, dining facilities, spa, pool and driving range.

Fees: $120–140.

Hours: Dawn–dusk daily, April–October.

Contact: The Dragon at Gold Mountain, County Rd. A-15/P.O. Box 880, Graeagle, CA 96103; 530/832-0880 or 877/372-4661; website: www.dragongolf.com.

Whitehawk Ranch Golf Course
(see map on page 263, site 19)

Nestled in the pristine Mohawk Valley 45 minutes north of Truckee, this course opened in May 1996 and quickly became one of the Sierra's unique and scenic tracks, one that is certainly in a league with Edgewood at Lake Tahoe. As part of an upscale planned community with an elevation of 4,500 feet, Whitehawk is a study in environmental awareness and aesthetic design. There are four tee boxes for each hole, allowing plenty of options for players of varying abilities. Yardage ranges from 4,645 to 6,920, with a par of 71 for both ends. The course, with three par 5s, 11 par 4s, and four par 3s, encompasses forest and open meadow, with homes bordering holes 4–7. Sulphur Creek meanders through several holes, and there are lakes on others. Apart from water hazards, the tall native grass that borders the fairways, particularly on the back nine, can also swallow up balls.

© KEN CASTLE

Whitehawk Ranch Golf Course

On the demanding 14th (435 yards, par 4), your second shot (try a 6-iron) is along a tight fairway with a lake and an obtrusive tree on the right, and a tricky back pin placement on a green that has an elevated rear deck. On the equally challenging 16th (455 yards, par 4), you'll play into the wind, cross Sulphur Creek with your tee shot, aim for a target bunker at 300 yards (staying clear of trees on the left side), and then play to a heavily bunkered hole that doglegs to the left. Among four signature holes, the fourth is the first that plays into the trees, and the 16th has a grand view of the upper Mohawk Valley and its lush pasturelands. The holes are beautifully manicured, and the vistas are stunning.

Stats: Designed by Dick Bailey; 18 holes, 6,920 yards, and 71 par.

Amenities: Golf shop, snack bar, and driving range.

Fees: $105–125 (high season), including cart and use of practice facilities.

Hours: Dawn–dusk.

Contact: Whitehawk Ranch Golf Course, 1137 Hwy. 89/P.O. Box 170, Clio, CA 96106; 530/836-0394 or 800/332-HAWK (800/332-4295); website: www.golfwhitehawk.com.

RENO

Sierra Sage Golf Course
(see map on page 263, site 20)

With gently rolling hills and wide-open fairways, this links-style, high-desert course off U.S. 395 near Stead Air Field is a modest track that won't win any design awards but will provide high-handicap golfers with an outing that is gentle on the psyche. Fairways are mostly flat and wide, and water hazards on six of the holes won't phase experienced players. There are three par 5s, 11 par 4s, and four par 3s. The toughest hole is the fifth (475 yards, par 4), which tees off over a deep depression and has an uphill lie to a blind, well-bunkered green on a dogleg left. Out-of-bounds is mostly sagebrush, and the surrounding vistas can best be described as arid and desolate. Stead is a workingman's town with various industrial parks and is the site of the annual Reno Air Show.

Stats: 18 holes, 6,623 yards, and 71 par.

Amenities: Driving range, putting green, cart rentals, club rentals, restaurant, and bar.

Fees: $36.

Hours: Daylight to dusk year-round.

Red Hawk Golf Club in Sparks, Nevada

© KEN CASTLE

Contact: Sierra Sage Golf Course, 6355 Silver Lake Blvd., Reno, NV 89506; 775/972-1564.

Red Hawk Golf Club
(see map on page 263, site 21)

An historic ranch in the rolling hills and wetlands of Sparks, Reno's companion city, is the site of this attractive golf complex, which opened in 1997. It's part of a 1,300-acre residential development, called Wingfield Springs, that will include more than 2,000 homes. There are two courses, one public and one private. Public play is allowed on the Springs Course, which is on the former Spanish Springs Ranch, one of many businesses developed in the early 1900s by George Wingfield, a pioneering entrepreneur of banking, gaming, and mining interests who was once referred to as "the owner and operator of Nevada." The other course (The Hills Course) was designed by Hale Irwin and is restricted to members only.

The front nine holes of the Springs Course have four man-made lakes, surrounded by rock retaining walls, that come into play on four holes, and natural wetlands bordering three holes. Most challenging is the ninth, a par 4, 420-yard hole that requires you to carry a corner of the wetlands on your tee shot, then hit a straight second shot to avoid more marshes on the left. The back nine holes have two very large, spring-fed lakes and two man-made lakes, along with more wetlands, but they differ from the front nine. The 17th, a 210-yard par 3, is a bruiser, because the tee is on a narrow spit between two of the lakes and requires your shot to carry diagonally across the water to the green. The back nine, with distant snowcapped mountains of the Sierra reflecting in the lakes, are the most scenic. Among the unique features of Red Hawk (so named because of the prevalence of red-tailed hawks) is the use of state-of-the-art Penn A-4 bentgrass on greens, allowing for fast and consistent surfaces.

Stats: Designed by Robert Trent Jones Jr., 7,127 yards, and 72 par.

Amenities: Learning center/golf school, food and beverage, pro shop, putting green, driving range, Freddie's Roost Sports Bar and Grill, and a 40,000-square-foot 18-hole putting course—the only one in Northern Nevada.

Fees: $60–95, including cart.

Hours: Dawn–dusk daily (with evening hours for the practice range), and at least a 10-month season, Feb.–November.

Contact: Red Hawk Golf Club at Wingfield Springs, 7755 Spanish Springs Rd., Sparks, NV 89436; 775/626-6000. The website has a detailed, hole-by-hole description, at www.wingfieldsprings.com.

D'Andrea Golf Club
(see map on page 263, site 22)

Anything with an Italian theme plays well in Reno, so it should come as no surprise that a golf club borrowing from the style of old Tuscany would come along sooner or later. This course is in a vast "hidden" bedroom community in Sparks. It is seven miles east of downtown Reno, on Vista Boulevard, which meanders through one new residential development after another. Built on a ranch that was settled in the early 1900s by a family from Northern Italy, the course is part of the D'Andrea master-planned golf community; it is snuggled against the foothills of the Pah Rah Range, which forms the eastern flank of Washoe Valley. Easily reached from Highway 80 (one mile off the freeway), the course uses distinctive rock formations and high elevations (holes rise to 450 feet above the valley), so players can get bird's-eye views of the Reno skyline. The entire project, encompassing the course and 2,200 homes, sprawls over 861 acres. But to dispel any notion that golf is just window dressing for upscale housing, developer Jenamar Communities of Granite Bay, Calif., hired renowned course architect Keith Foster, who worked on nationally ranked courses such as Augusta National, Bighorn, Harbour Pointe and Walking Stick. The signature hole at D'Andrea is the par-4, 330-yard 16th, which is on the highest point of the course. This short, tricky hole begins a three-hole stretch playing downhill to the clubhouse, and it offers striking panoramas down the canyon of Sparks and Reno. Golfers who play this hole aggressively might be rewarded with a rare eagle or two-putt birdie, or they might be slapped with double bogies from missed shots that go to the right or beyond the gree. D'Andrea has five par 3 holes, of which the longest, the 12th, is 246 yards from the back tee and plays down from elevated tees, affording yet more scenic vistas. The 18th is a particularly impressive finishing hole. It is a strong par 4 that plays to 475 yards, with tees benched in the hillside well above the fairway, creating a dramatic view of the hole. A large native rock outcropping creates some drama, because the best strategy is to play close to the rocks. The green is set into the hillside naturally, with bunkers guarding the surface.

Stats: Designed by Keith Foster, championship 18-hole course, 6,849 yards, par 71.

Amenities: New clubhouse with restaurant, lounge, pro shop, underground cart storage and elevated views of the valley.

Fees: $85–95.

Hours: Dawn–dusk, year-round.

Contact: D'Andrea Golf Club, 2351 N. D'Andrea Pkwy., Sparks, NV 89434; 775/331-6363; website: www.jenamar.com/D'Andrea/Dandrea.htm.

Wildcreek Golf Course
(see map on page 263, site 23)

Spread out over a wide area in a scenic valley north of town, Wildcreek has both a championship and a nine-hole executive course. The main course has a half dozen holes on hillside terraces, giving players some tricky sidehill lies and a fair amount of pitch. Ten holes have either lakes or lateral water hazards, and there are lots of bunkers and out-of-bounds areas with sagebrush, thus providing plenty of diversity. The course has four par 5s, 10 par 4s, and four par 3s. The number one handicap hole is the fifth (389 yards, par 4), which has an elongated lake on the left that half-circles the small green, and a river and bunkers to the right. The biggest trouble is off the tee, because of a narrow fairway and a tight, intimidating approach to the green. Use a 5-wood or mid- to long-iron off the tee, and a 7- to 9-iron for your second shot. The signature hole, which, at 609 yards, is also the longest, is the par 5 18th. Here you'll have to tee off into a landing area on a plateau that is difficult to see from the tee box. Your second shot

D'Andrea Golf Club in Sparks, Nevada

© KEN CASTLE

will have to play down between two lakes to a fairway that is 50 yards wide, and from there you need a precise shot uphill to a green surrounded by traps. The executive course, with four lakes, is a fair test of your short game; the longest hole is the sixth (220 yards, par 3), featuring several water hazards. Recently, Wildcreek has undergone major renovations including repaving of cart paths, refurbishing of the clubhouse and the addition of global positioning systems for all carts. Wildcreek is one of two courses owned by the Reno-Sparks Convention and Visitors Authority; the other is Northgate (see course number 10).

Stats: Designed by Benz and Phelps. The championship course is 18 holes, 6,932 yards, and 72 par; the executive course is nine holes, 2,840 yards, and 27 par.

Amenities: Driving range, putting greens, chipping greens, club and cart rentals, pro shop, bar, and snack bar.

Fees: $53 including mandatory cart.

Hours: 6:30 A.M.–7 P.M. The championship course is open Feb.–Dec.; the executive course is open year-round.

Contact: Wildcreek Golf Course, 3500 Sullivan Ln., Sparks, NV 89431; 775/673-3100; website: www.golf.renolaketahoe.com.

Northgate Golf Club
(see map on page 263, site 24)
A lot of no-man's land exists between the tees and fairways on this hilly, high-desert course northwest of downtown Reno. It's full of sagebrush, rocks, ravines, and sand. If you're not off the tee here, you'll spend a lot of time chasing balls in rabbit warrens. Because of the clay soil, exposed ridges, prevailing afternoon winds, and hot sun, the fairways can become bulletproof in midsummer. As one of two courses operated by the Reno-Sparks Convention and Visitors Authority—along with Wildcreek—Northgate gets a lot of use. It has four par 5s, 10 par 4s, and four par 3s, and there are four tee boxes on each hole. Plenty of average players will feel like beaten alley cats after spending a few hours searching for balls in the bramble. The top handicap hole is the fifth (410 yards, par 4), a hard dogleg right

with a difficult landing area full of grass bunkers, and a two-tiered green that challenges your putting skill. Miss the green here and you'll be up and down like a yo-yo. But for a lot of players the greatest frustration occurs in the back nine. Among the dillies are the 371-yard, par 4 15th (an uphill tee shot to a blind dogleg right guarded by grass and sand bunkers); the 436-yard, par 4 14th (a drive over sage and dirt to a narrow landing, nasty out-of-bounds on the right, and grass bunkers bordering the fairway); and the 407-yard, par 4 17th (a tee shot over desert and sand bunkers to the left of the landing). Some nice touches at this course include ball cleaners on each cart and ice water at the drinking stations. As with its sister course, Wildcreek, Northgate has added global positioning systems for all carts.

Stats: Designed by Benz and Polette; 18 holes, 6,966 yards, and 72 par.

Amenities: Driving range, putting green, chipping green, cart rentals, club rentals, pro shop, bar, and snack bar.

Fees: $51 including mandatory cart.

Hours: 6:30 A.M.–7:30 P.M., Feb.–December.

Contact: Northgate Golf Club, 1111 Clubhouse Dr., Reno, NV 89523; 775/747-7577; website: www.golf.renolaketahoe.com.

Rosewood Lakes Golf Course
(see map on page 263, site 25)
Situated near the eastern foothills of Reno east of the airport, this city-owned course is challenging but not too intimidating, and is especially popular with women. It is aptly named, since lateral water hazards come into play on all 18 holes. The layout, with four tee boxes, stretches through a labyrinth of wetlands, with cattails and marsh grass dominating the out-of-bounds ground cover. On the fifth and eighth holes, both par 3s, it's necessary to make accurate shots over the wetlands (167 and 160 yards, respectively) from tee boxes on a berm. The seventh (540 yards, par 5) is the number one handicap hole, and requires a straightaway tee shot that stays left of berms on the right. But the 17th (401 yards, par 4) has danger written all over it—a dogleg right with lakes on the left and right, and a difficult approach with a river to the left of an elevated

green. The 15th (547 yards, par 5) is interrupted by a lake in its midsection, requiring a drive that lays up in front of it, and an accurate approach to a well-bunkered green. Except for the last four holes, the fairways are generously wide, and high handicappers get plenty of chances for par. Waterfowl and their natural predator, the coyote, are plentiful on the course, so don't be surprised if Wile E. comes thrashing out of the reeds to present you with an unmarked hazard. The course won the Environmental Steward Award from the Golf Course Superintendent Association of America in 1992 and 1994.

Stats: Designed by Brad Benz; 18 holes, 6,693 yards, and 72 par.

Amenities: Driving range, putting green, cart rentals, restaurant, and snack bar.

Fees: $46 for nonresidents walking.

Hours: 7 A.M.–7 P.M. (until 8 P.M. in the summer) year-round.

Contact: Rosewood Lakes Golf Course, 6800 Pembroke Ln., Reno, NV 89502; 775/857-2892; website: www.cityofreno.com/com_service/golf.

Washoe Golf Course
(see map on page 263, site 26)

Built in 1934 and operated by Washoe County, this is the oldest course in Reno and a favorite of local players. The front nine is relatively flat, while the much less forgiving back nine meanders up the hillside. Tall trees parallel the fairways throughout the course, and there are water hazards on five holes. There are three par 5s, 12 par 4s, and three par 3s. Most difficult is the 12th (475 yards, par 4), which has a dogleg left, an obstructed view from the fairway, and a small green, bunkered on the left, that falls away left to right. Use a driver or long iron off the tee and a long iron or fairway wood for the second shot. Even if you reach the green without mishap, you could lose strokes on putting. The ninth (426 yards, par 4) will give you something to think about as well. It's a straightaway shot into the wind uphill, to a small green with traps on both sides. Washoe is the site of the annual Reno Open, and past luminaries such as Ben Hogan have played here.

Stats: 18 holes, 6,995 yards, and 72 par.

Amenities: Driving range, putting green, cart rentals, and restaurant.

Fees: For nonresidents, $29 walking.

Hours: 7 A.M.–dark year-round.

Contact: Washoe Golf Course, 2601 S. Arlington, Reno, NV 89509; 775/828-6640; website: www.washoegolf.com.

Hilton Bay Aquarange
(see map on page 263, site 27)

If you're staying at the Reno Hilton—or even if you're not—you might as well get some practice on the hotel's four floating greens, in an artificial lake outside. Each green has cups with sensors, and there are different promotional giveaways for hitting cups at various ranges. A hole-in-one could get you an all-expenses-paid vacation.

Amenities: Gift shop.

Fees: $7 for a large bucket of balls, $4 for a medium bucket, $3 for three rental clubs.

Hours: 8 A.M.–midnight on weekends, 9 A.M.–10 P.M. on weekdays, Nov.–April; 7 A.M.–2 A.M., May–October.

Contact: Reno Hilton, 2500 E. 2nd St., Reno, NV 89595; 775/786-6699; website: www.reno-hilton.net/bigfun/index.shtml.

Brookside Reno Municipal Golf Course (see map on page 263, site 28)

This used to be an 18-hole course, but it was eaten away by the Reno-Tahoe International Airport, which owns the land, until only nine flat, mostly straightaway holes remained. But there is some respectable distance, with two par 5s, four par 4s, and three par 3s. The number one handicap is the third (385 yards, par 4), which requires a strong drive and an approach shot to a green that is bunkered on the right and left. However, most players consider the first (540 yards, par 5) to be the most difficult, mainly because of a ditch on the left. There are lakes on three holes, and two of those sandwich a narrow fairway off the tee on the ninth (150 yards, par 3). Brookside, built in 1956, is operated by the city of Reno.

Stats: Nine holes, 2,882 yards, and 35 par.

Amenities: Putting green, cart rentals, club rentals, bar, and snack bar.

Fees: $12 for nine holes walking.
Hours: Daylight to dusk year-round.
Contact: Brookside Reno Municipal Golf Course, 700 S. Rock Blvd., Reno, NV 89502; 775/856-6009; website: www.cityofreno.com/com_service/golf.

Lakeridge Golf Course
(see map on page 263, site 29)

Players flock to this challenging course in the southwest foothills of Reno for one simple reason: the signature 15th hole. You can see pictures of it everywhere—an island green just off the shore of a large, mirror-smooth lake—but the impact doesn't sink in until you're on the highest tee box on a hillside 130 feet above the water with the whole city stretching out in the distance. When the wind is raging, which it does with great regularity, you've got to make careful adjustments to get a par 3 on this 239-yard ego-killer. Frustrated players frequently can be seen spraying Mulligans into the drink. But the 15th is not the highest handicap hole; that distinction belongs to the fourth (599 yards, par 5). This is a dogleg right that demands a tight, well-placed tee shot to a narrow landing at the bend, and a couple of strong fairway shots with a wood or long iron to reach a well-bunkered green. Lakeridge is Reno's premier public course, though the fairways tend to harden and dry by mid- to late summer. The layout undulates through the hills, especially on the back nine, and water comes into play on 12 holes. With rocky outcrops and abrupt elevation changes, there is a Badlands feel to the place. Local wildlife is everywhere, and includes geese as well as large, lumbering marmots called rock chucks.

Stats: Designed by Robert Trent Jones Sr.; 18 holes, 6,717 yards, and 72 par.
Amenities: Driving range, putting green, cart rentals, club rentals, bar, restaurant, and snack bar.
Fees: $78–93, including mandatory cart.
Hours: 6 A.M.–7 P.M., March–December.
Contact: Lakeridge Golf Course, 1200 Razorback Rd., Reno, NV 89509; 775/825-2200; website: www.lakeridgegolf.com.

Wolf Run Golf Club
(see map on page 263, site 30)

This relatively new course is a joint venture between private developers and the University of Nevada at Reno boosters club, which helped provide financing. It is in the southwest corner of Reno on the old Fieldcreek Ranch, which dates back to the 1880s. There isn't much elevation variance at this high desert course, but there is plenty to keep things interesting, including mature trees, rocky terrain, and water from Whites Creek on nine of the 18 holes. Golfers enjoy vistas of the Sierra Nevada to the south and Truckee Meadows and Reno to the north. The course is close to U.S. 395 and is surrounded by the Fieldcreek Estate residential development, though it is not part of that project. The challenge is in playing across Whites Creek and some small canyons. The toughest hole is the second, a 575-yard par 5 that plays uphill slightly and into prevailing breezes. There are well-placed bunkers near the greens and 50 yards out, requiring you to choose your strategy carefully. The sixth, a par 4, demands that you cross the ubiquitous creek not once but twice. A large lake comes into play on the 17th, a par 3 where you must carry the water. Because of the association with UNR, you can expect to see plenty of students (including university teams) and faculty here. Incidentally, the tee boxes are named after the school team (Wolf Pack) with monikers such as Predator, Hunter, Prowler, and Stalker. And if you need to break a tie, there's the special "Wolfpaw" 19th hole.

Stats: Designed by Lou Eiguren and Steve Van Meter with Links Construction; 18 holes, 7,000 yards, and 71 par.
Amenities: The existing ranch house, built in the 1940s, is the centerpiece for the clubhouse, which has a pro shop, bar and grill, locker rooms, and a meeting room. There's also a practice range with target greens and 35 to 40 stations.
Fees: $70–75 with cart and range access.
Hours: Dawn–dusk year-round.
Contact: Wolf Run Golf Club, 1400 Wolf Run Rd., Reno, NV 89511; 775/851-3301.

GOLF AND TENNIS

CARSON CITY/CARSON VALLEY

Silver Oak Golf Course
(see map on page 263, site 31)

Adjacent to U.S. 395 on the north edge of Carson City, this is one of the easiest new courses to find. Aimed at the mid-range and mid-handicap golfer, the beautifully-manicured course, which opened fully in 2001, is surrounded by the first elements of a 1,200-unit housing development and a K-Mart shopping center. At first it seems to be mainly on flat ground, but five holes of the back nine wind interestingly up a ridge through some hills, offering views of the Carson Valley and Carson City to the south. The toughest hole is the 12th, a 510-yard par 5 that has an uphill double dogleg and plays into the wind. The ninth is a 580-yard par 5 that plays downhill, next to a lake, and across a second lake to an island green. There are four or five tee boxes on each hole.

Stats: Designed by Tom Duncan and Sid Solaman; 18 holes, 6,564 yards, par 71.

Amenities: A temporary clubhouse with golf shop and snack bar.

Fees: $40 with cart.

Hours: Daily year-round.

Contact: Silver Oak Golf Course, 1251 Country Club Dr., Carson City, NV 89703; 775/841-7000.

Eagle Valley East Eagle Valley West
(see map on page 263, site 32)

Of the two 18-hole courses here, the East Course is flat, easy, and predictable—a great track for neophytes and casual players. The West Course, however, will eat you alive. It is hilly, narrow, and full of water traps and barrancas. Typical of high-desert, links-style courses, it has plenty of sagebrush, sand, jackrabbits, and afternoon winds. There is a kinship, of sorts, with Northgate in Reno (see course number 10), because the design and terrain are very similar, which is to say, not easy on high handicappers. And there is a bit of distraction from the trap range that thunders incessantly next to holes five and six. There are four par 5s, 10 par 4s, and four par 3s. The number one handicap is the third (567 yards,

par 5), on which you must carry a water hazard off the tee and hit to a sharp dogleg left on the approach to the green. Earning the "You've gotta be kidding" award, however, is the 15th (559 yards, par 5), which has a high ridge at mid-landing (blocking any chance of seeing the green) and a barranca below that; sidecut fairways and a sharp dogleg right complete the nightmare. The sage, rocks, and dry grass in out-of-bounds will steal your ball, if the rabbits don't.

Stats: West Course: Designed by Homer Flynt; 18 holes, 6,851 yards, and 72 par. East Course: 18 holes, 6,658 yards, and 72 par.

Amenities: Lighted driving range, putting green, bar, restaurant, snack bar, and free supervised children's playroom.

Fees: East Course, $22 walking; West Course, $39 with mandatory cart.

Hours: 6:30 A.M.–6 P.M. year-round.

Contact: Eagle Valley East and West, 3999 Centennial Park Dr., Carson City, NV 89706; 775/887-2380; website: www.eaglevalleygolf.com.

Empire Ranch Golf Course
(see map on page 263, site 33)

This public course, which opened in 1997, is on a former cattle ranch and mining area four miles from downtown Carson City, just off U.S. 50 east of its intersection with U.S. 395. It is nestled between high bluffs on 250 acres of mostly open and level terrain adjoining the East Fork of the Carson River. The course includes 46 acres of wetlands and a half dozen lakes, providing plenty of water hazards to swallow mishit balls. Although the course sits in a valley, most of the holes afford picturesque views of the Sierra Nevada mountains. Players can start on any nine for a complete 18 holes, and, apart from having three course options, there is the attraction of some of the lowest green fees in the region. Among the more challenging holes is the seventh on the White Course, a par 4 with 437 yards that requires your tee shot to carry wetlands and your second shot to avoid a large lake snuggling next to the green on the right side. The course is not designed to be nasty (there is always a bailout option for high handicappers), but is a convincing challenge for those who shoot between 80 and 105. A 6,500-square-foot clubhouse sits on a rise overlooking the three courses.

Stats: Designed by Cary Bickler; 27 holes in three 9-hole courses, ranging from 3,325 yards to 3,571 yards, with any of three 18-hole combinations available, each at 72 par.

Amenities: Large driving range (50 to 60 positions), pro shop, clubhouse with sports bar and grill, electric cart and club rentals, and instruction. Full tournament facilities are available. Pull-carts are allowed Monday–Thursday.

Fees: $35–40 for 18 holes.

Hours: Dawn–dusk year-round.

Contact: Empire Ranch Golf Course, 1875 Fairway, Carson City, NV 89701; 775/885-2100; website: www.millard-nv.com.

Dayton Valley Country Club
(see map on page 263, site 34)

This is one of the finest courses in the region, with some of the finest, most beautifully sculpted and manicured tracks anywhere. Eleven miles east of Carson City, in the middle of the high desert (but in what is really a growing residential community), the course is a delight to play, as long as you adhere to one cardinal rule: Get an early morning tee time. By afternoon, the winds can whip through the wide-open course with ferocity. Despite the lack of trees, however, the course has fascinating, technical terrain, with velvety, almost surrealistic fairways, creative use of hillocks, water hazards on 12 holes, and a maze of bunkering. There are four par 5s, 10 par 4s, and four par 3s. The most difficult is the 450-yard ninth, a par 4 that requires you to negotiate three water hazards, find a narrow landing off the tee without hitting into water on the left, and negotiate an approach with water on both sides and in front of the small, elongated green. Anything other than an accurate shot lands you in water or bunkers. The 17th (478 yards, par 4) is a minefield of large bunkers, with a fairway that zigzags between them to a postage-stamp green. There is nothing predictable or mundane about Dayton Valley, one of the true jewels of golf.

Stats: Designed by Arnold Palmer; 18 holes, 7,161 yards, and 72 par.

Amenities: Driving range, sand traps, putting green, cart rentals, club rentals, clubhouse, bar, restaurant, and snack bar.

Fees: $65–85 with cart for morning starts.

Hours: Dawn–dusk year-round.

Contact: Dayton Valley Country Club, 51 Palmer Dr., Dayton, NV 89403; 775/246-PUTT (775/246-7888); website: www.daytonvalley.com.

Sunridge Golf Course
(see map on page 263, site 35)

The entrance to this place, through a nondescript tract housing development on the south edge of Carson City, is less than inviting. But the course, with a whopping 10 man-made lakes (originally designed as holding areas for treated wastewater), is the toughest in Carson Valley, if not in all of Nevada. Shielded from U.S. 395 by a ridge of homes, the course is largely out of sight, literally and figuratively. When it opened in 1998, big dollars were spent on this layout, as evidenced by the tunnels, bridges, and giant lakes. It stretches out north to south in long fingers, sandwiched between hills on the west and a floodplain on the east.

High handicappers will definitely not feel comfortable here, with so many hazards and narrow fairways. There are blind greens on uphill lies, such as the seventh hole, a par 3, 165-yard nightmare that requires you to carry a gully and a bunker to reach an invisible, elevated green. The back nine has four holes—14–17—hugging a hillside. With water, water everywhere, you'll need a bagful of balls, preferably ones that you won't miss when they plop into the drink. There are some lofty views of the Carson Valley from the top of the seventh, and of Sierra peaks from the ninth, but by then you won't be in much of a mood to enjoy them. Masochists will love this place.

Stats: Designed by Tom Duncan and a local committee; 7054 yards, 18 holes, par 72.

Amenities: Clubhouse with pro shop, restaurant, and bar; driving range; and instruction.

Fees: $55–75 with cart.

Hours: Dawn–dusk year-round.

Contact: Sunridge Golf Course, 1000 Long Dr.,

GOLF AND TENNIS

Carson City, NV 89705; 775/267-4448; website: www.sunridgegolfclub.com.

The Golf Club at Genoa Lakes
(see map on page 263, site 36)

Snuggling against the eastern Sierra in Nevada's oldest town, this spectacular course, opened in 1993, has a backdrop of mountain vistas that extends southward for miles, a vast wetlands that attracts geese, ducks, and shorebirds, and a sprinkling of stately cottonwoods. The long, links-style course is situated in a new, gated residential community that borders the Carson River and is a 30-minute drive from South Lake Tahoe. Thirteen holes have water hazards, and the bunkers have a unique design in which the grass tapers sharply over the edges to a flat sand base. The course has four par 5s, 10 par 4s, and four par 3s. There's a strategy in playing this course: Try for a morning tee time to avoid afternoon winds; play from the forward tee boxes (there are four for each hole) if you're an average player; and be off the tee to avoid trouble, which lurks everywhere. If you play from the gold tees, you'll be hitting over water on 12 holes. The number one handicap hole is the 474-yard seventh, a par 4 that plays uphill and into a strong prevailing wind, with a tough approach shot to a green that slopes from front to back. The signature hole is the 13th, a par 5 that is Nevada's longest at 652 yards, and requires concentration to keep from losing balls on the right out-of-bounds. The 18th (449 yards, par 4) has a hard dogleg left and requires carrying a large lake, which continues as a left-side hazard all the way to the green. The course is off U.S. 395 on Jacks Valley Road. A recently opened and luxurious clubhouse offers gourmet Italian meals.

Stats: Designed by Peter Jacobsen; 18 holes, 7,263 yards, and 72 par.

Amenities: Clubhouse, driving range, chipping green, putting green, cart rentals, pro shop, lessons, restaurant, and snack bar.

Fees: $90–100 (high season).

Hours: 6 A.M.–6 P.M.

Contact: The Golf Club at Genoa Lakes, 1 Genoa Lakes Dr./P.O. Box 350, Genoa, NV 89411; 775/782-4653; website: www.genoalakes.com.

Sierra Nevada Golf Ranch
(see map on page 263, site 37)

In 1998, what was once a trap range and hunting club called Little Mondeau was turned into a premier golf course surrounded by mountains, pastures, and valleys on the eastern Sierra. It's in the historic Nevada town of Genoa, on the back side of Kingsbury Grade connecting to the South Shore of Lake Tahoe. This is the tiny community's second course, after The Golf Club at Genoa Lakes (see course number 33), which is a few miles south of here. In making his local debut, designer Johnny Miller (with the help of John Harbottle) joins other big names such as Palmer, Nicklaus and Trent Jones Jr. in the Tahoe-Reno golf scene. The result is one of the most elegant and upscale public courses in the valley, and one that is convenient to golfers staying at Tahoe. Meandering through savanna desert, the front nine holes include five that are west of Jacks Valley Road; these ascend to a point some 300 feet above the valley. The back nine winds down the side of a mountain and through high-desert terrain east of the road. Scenic holes include the 17th, a par 3 that carries across a lake to an island green connected by a peninsula. Water hazards are on just four holes, but there are challenges aplenty, with sage, elevation changes, and prevailing winds, which can be strong in the afternoon. Unique among local courses, this one has a two-million-gallon reservoir above the seventh tee that holds springwater from James Canyon for irrigation. Each hole has five tee boxes, and all carts are equipped with Par View, a global positioning system that provides a layout on each hole, shows bunkers and hazards, has an electronic scorecard, and allows golfers to order lunch or snacks on the ninth and 18th tees. One of the major assets of Sierra Nevada is the palatial clubhouse, which houses a restaurant and bar along with a pro shop.

Stats: Designed by Johnny Miller and John Harbottle; 18 holes, 7,358 yards, and 72 par.

Amenities: A posh clubhouse with a golf shop, bar and grill, and two banquet rooms capable of seating 200 each; a large practice facility that includes a terraced, horseshoe-shaped driving range with target greens; a separate practice tee for golf instruction; and a 13,000-square-foot putting green.

Fees: $70–90 with cart.

Hours: Dawn–dusk year-round.

Contact: Sierra Nevada Golf Ranch, 2901 Jacks Valley Rd./P.O. Box 316, Genoa, NV 89411; 775/782-7700.

Carson Valley Golf Course

(see map on page 263, site 38)

Here's a course that meanders over a wide area, just as the East Fork of the Carson River and its minor tributaries meander through most of the holes. Off U.S. 395, in the southern outskirts of Gardnerville, the course has four par 5s, nine par 4s, and five par 3s. Although mostly on level ground, the presence of the river creates an ongoing water hazard, and there are stately cottonwood trees that frame tight fairways. The top handicap hole is the 460-yard sixth, a par 5 that features, you guessed it, the river; too long of a drive could land in the drink, and even laying up is not much help—the second shot could also end up in water, for the river extends diagonally up to the green and flanks it on the right. Safe haven is only on the narrow approach to the left. The 16th (355 yards, par 4) has a similar configuration, with the river a left-side hazard that leaves only a spit of land for the green. The 11th (260 yards, par 4), seems beguilingly easy: a wide fairway with an easy dogleg left. The problem is that the green is perched on a plateau, which in turn is snuggled against a bluff, and only an accurate wedge shot will keep it from bouncing against the "wall" or rolling off the edge. The 14th (324 yards, par 4) could use a ball with eyes, capable of navigating a phalanx of cottonwoods. In general, this course has a rustic, wilderness feel, with cart paths crossing wooden bridges and following dirt river embankments. An enticement for playing here is that one of the town's better Basque restaurants, the Carson Valley Country Club, is right next door.

Stats: Designed by Red Swift; 18 holes, 7,263 yards, and 71 par.

Amenities: Driving range, putting green, cart rentals, club rentals, pro shop, full bar, on-course beverage cart, and a nearby Basque restaurant.

Fees: $35–40 with cart.

Hours: 7 A.M.–6 P.M. year-round.

Contact: Carson Valley Golf Course, 1027 Riverview Dr., Gardnerville, NV 89410; 775/265-3181; website: www.carsonvalleygolfcourse.com.

On the Courts

If you've got the lungs to play an energetic game at an elevation of 6,300 feet or higher, you'll find tennis courts just about everywhere—at resorts, hotels, public recreation areas, and schools. In the Tahoe area, by far the largest concentration of tennis clubs and courts is on the North Shore. Throughout the basin, there are several highly regarded tennis pros who can fix an iffy backhand or polish up a serve. In Tahoe's thinner air, be sure to use hard, high-elevation balls if you don't want your game to wind up in the stratosphere.

In Tahoe's thinner air, be sure to use hard, high-elevation balls if you don't want your game to wind up in the stratosphere.

NORTH SHORE

Granlibakken Racquet Club

Six courts are available free of charge to guests of this resort. Professional staff, tennis camps, and clinics are offered. Every summer the Nike Lake Tahoe Tennis Camp is held for youngsters ages 9–18. (For information, contact U.S. Sports at 800/645-3226.)

Contact: Granlibakken Racquet Club, Hwy. 89, west of Tahoe City, CA; 530/583-4242; website: www.granlibakken.com.

Incline Village Tennis Complex

Six courts (two lighted), a pro shop, and lessons are available. For nonresidents, fees are $11 per hour ($8 after noon) for play and $45 per hour for lessons. Reservations are necessary.

Contact: Incline Village Tennis Complex, Southwood Blvd. off Hwy. 28, Incline Village, NV; 775/832-1235 or 775/832-1310 (recreation center).

North Tahoe High School

Four lighted courts are available on a first-come, first-served basis. Adult lessons are occasionally offered during the summertime, through the Tahoe City PUD.

Contact: Tahoe City Public Utilities District, Department of Parks and Recreation, 221 Fairway Dr., P.O. Box 33, Tahoe City, CA 96145; 530/583-3796, ext. 18 or 29.

North Tahoe Regional Park

Five lighted tennis courts are available on a first-come, first-served basis. Lessons, including children's and adult clinics, are offered by a local tennis pro. Some drop-in play is available on league nights.

Contact: North Tahoe Regional Park, at Donner Rd. and National Ave. off Hwy. 28 in Tahoe Vista, CA; 530/546-7248.

Resort at Squaw Creek

Two courts at Squaw Valley's largest hotel are available during daylight hours, at $12 per hour. Racket rentals are available at $5 per racket.

Contact: Resort at Squaw Creek, 400 Squaw Creek Rd., Olympic Valley, CA 96146; 530/583-6300 or 800/403-4434; website: www.squawcreek.com.

Tahoe Lake School

Two lighted courts are available on a first-come, first-served basis. Children's lessons for kids seven and older are offered during the summer.

Contact: Tahoe Lake School, 375 Grove St., Tahoe City, CA; 530/583-3796.

Squaw Valley USA

The High Camp Bath and Tennis Club at mid-mountain has six tennis courts at its elevation 8,200 day lodge, and play is free. But you'll have to pay for the Cable Car ride to the top, which is $17 per adult for one round-trip.

Contact: Squaw Valley USA; 530/583-6985.

SOUTH SHORE

George Whittell High School

Two lighted courts are available, but you must make reservations. Fees were not available.

tennis at Northstar-at-Tahoe

The high school is on Warrior Way in Zephyr Cove, Nevada.
Contact: Kahle Community Center; 775/588-0271.

Lakeland Village Beach and Ski Resort

This large condo/resort complex on the lake just west of the Stateline offers two tennis courts for guests only.
Contact: Lakeland Village Beach and Ski Resort, 3535 Lake Tahoe Blvd. in South Lake Tahoe; 530/541-7711.

The Ridge Tahoe

The premier private tennis facility at South Shore is available only to guests of this upscale resort. Removed from the hustle and bustle of Stateline, the Ridge is a favorite retreat for celebrities who play the casino showrooms, and guests have reportedly included comedian Bill Cosby, who happens to be an avowed tennis fan. On a peak 1,600 feet above Lake Tahoe (at an elevation of 7,600 feet), with commanding views of both Nevada and California, this time-share and overnight resort has four tennis courts, including one indoor court (in a tent) and one tournament court. Racquets and balls are available for guests, and tennis pro Kyle Horvath holds free clinics for beginners, children, and advanced intermediates several times a week. He also offers private and semiprivate lessons as well as racket stringing and regripping. (Horvath, a USPTA pro, offers lessons throughout the South Shore area under his company, High Sierra Tennis Management Co., and also can be reached at 530/545-8864).
Fees: Private lessons, $40 per hour; $30 for children; semiprivate lessons (two people), $50 an hour; $40 for children. Three-lesson package for adults is $100.
Contact: The Ridge Tahoe, 1 Ridge Club Dr., Kingsbury, NV; 775/588-3553.

South Tahoe Middle School

Four lighted courts are available on a first-come, first-served basis. Four-week summer tennis lessons for children and teens are offered through the South Lake Tahoe Parks and Recreation Department.

Contact: South Tahoe Middle School, 2940 Lake Tahoe Blvd., South Lake Tahoe, CA; 530/542-6055.

South Tahoe High School

Six unlighted courts are available on a first-come, first-served basis.

Contact: South Tahoe High School, 1735 Lake Tahoe Blvd., South Lake Tahoe, CA; 530/542-6055.

Zephyr Cove Park

Six lighted tennis courts are available on a first-come, first-served basis. Call for fees and policies. Lessons may be offered for youths in the summer. The courts, which are operated by the Douglas County Recreation Department, are at U.S. 50 and Warrior Way in Zephyr Cove, Nevada.

Contact: Kahle Community Center; 775/588-0271.

WEST SHORE

Kilner Park

This facility, operated by the Tahoe City Parks and Recreation Department, offers two lighted courts on a first-come, first-served basis.

Contact: Kilner Park, on W. Shore Blvd. (Hwy. 89) south of Sunnyside, CA; 530/583-3796.

Sugar Pine Point State Park

One court is available on a first-come, first-served basis. Parking fee at the park is $2 per vehicle; no playing fee.

Contact: Sugar Pine Point State Park, off Hwy. 89 between Tahoma and Meeks Bay, CA; 530/525-7982.

TRUCKEE/DONNER

Northstar-at-Tahoe

Use of these 10 courts is free, but they are reserved exclusively for guests and residents. Lessons, however, are open to the public. Two- and five-day tennis camps, taught by Northstar's USTA pro and staff, are available for adults and juniors.

Contact: Northstar-at-Tahoe, on Hwy. 267 between Truckee and Kings Beach, CA; 530/562-1010; website: www.northstarattahoe.com.

Other Summer Activities

If you ever tire of Tahoe's conventional outdoor activities, you won't lack for something unusual to do. Everything is possible, and everything is available. If you aren't nervous about high places, you might consider signing up for a rock climbing course. And if you're looking for more down-to-earth pursuits, there's always a spirited ride on an off-highway-vehicle road in one of the area's forests or Bureau of Land Management Areas.

Few things can make you appreciate the tranquil beauty of Lake Tahoe and its rugged peaks as much as the view from a higher vantage point—a hot air balloon, a glider, a parasail, or an airplane.

Soaring is a popular sport on the east slopes of the Sierra, where the Minden Airport caters to gatherings of gliders each spring and summer. Unique climatic conditions here create waves, which are narrow bands of moving air, as well as thermals, circular vortexes of hot air rising from the high desert. Glider pilots often can sample both conditions in a matter of days, and wave-riders have been known to follow currents for 100 miles or more. From both Minden and Truckee, you can hire pilots to give you a taste of soaring over the ridges and mountains of the Sierra—certainly an unforgettable experience.

Also unforgettable is **hot-air ballooning**, which is celebrated with the annual Great Reno Balloon Race in September. But most times of the year, including winter, if the weather is calm and the skies are clear, you can drift above the Carson and Washoe Valleys, or even above Lake Tahoe itself.

Chartering an **airplane** can get you over the Sierra's backcountry lakes, and the view of Desolation Wilderness, in particular, is mesmerizing. The high alpine jewels are easily visible, and the highlight is giant Lake Aloha, a granite basin of rocky ponds that stretches for miles between dramatic rocky peaks. This is a tour to be done early in the morning, however, before the winds kick up and create more turbulence than you can stomach. Also, consider a gentle flight over the Lake Tahoe shoreline, where you can view palatial waterfront mansions and the aquamarine colors of the lake. Of course, if your budget doesn't include any of these options, you can always take a quick ride on a parasail towed by a boat on the lake.

Hot-Air Balloon Rides

TRUCKEE/DONNER

Mountain High Balloons

Balloonist Ray Shady launches at Prosser Creek Reservoir, east of Truckee, and offers passengers delightful views of the area's man-made lakes, pristine meadows, and lush forestland. He says he skims over the treetops "low enough to pick pinecones" and flies high enough to see Lake Tahoe to the south. He operates two balloons, each with a capacity of four plus pilots. At their option, guests can take the controls of the balloon and learn to fly.

Hours: Flights are scheduled May–Dec., weather permitting. Reservations are recommended.

Fees: $95 for a half hour, $175 for an hour; kids under 10 fly free when accompanied by an adult.

Contact: Mountain High Balloons, 10867 Cheyenne Way, Truckee, CA 96161; 530/587-6922 or 888/GO-ABOVE (888/462-22683).

SOUTH LAKE TAHOE

Balloons over Lake Tahoe

This professional, well-run operation pioneered a unique balloon adventure: landing on and

When the skies are clear and cobalt blue, Balloons over Lake Tahoe is one of the premier excursions at the lake, and one of the best guided outings anywhere. Pilot and crew are cheerful and supportive, and at the end of the hourlong flight, champagne, hot beverages, pastries, fruit, and other snacks are served on the yacht.

taking off from a boat in the middle of Lake Tahoe. The experience is positively breathtaking as you float gently over the lake, getting lofty views of Stateline casinos, Emerald Bay, Tahoe Keys, and the peaks of Desolation Wilderness. One group of passengers ascends from the South Tahoe Airport, flies over the lake, then lands on the bow of a 40-foot catamaran-style powerboat called Vivid Dreams, which was custom-designed to accommodate such a maneuver. A second group of passengers on the boat trades places with the first group, and the balloon takes off over the lake again.

When the skies are clear and cobalt blue, this is one of the premier excursions at the lake, and one of the best guided outings anywhere. Pilot and crew are cheerful and supportive, and at the end of the hourlong flight, champagne, hot beverages, pastries, fruit, and other snacks are served on the yacht. The company is operated by Mark and Dawn Boulet, who are based in Fort Lauderdale, Florida, but spend summers in Tahoe, where they've been operating since 1991. Free shuttle service is provided anywhere in the South Lake Tahoe area.

OTHER ACTIVITIES

© KEN CASTLE

Floating gently and quietly on the breezes, hot-air balloons offer a different aerial perspective on the Tahoe area (one company even combines balloons and boats—landing you on the bow of a catamaran in the middle of the lake).

Policies: Children must be at least seven years of age. The company schedules six to eight passengers per flight.

Hours: Flights depart 6 A.M.–10 A.M. daily in summer. Reservations are required.

Fees: $185 per person. A credit card is required to reserve a flight.

Contact: Balloons over Lake Tahoe, P.O. Box 7797, South Lake Tahoe, CA 96158; 530/544-7008; website: www.balloonsoverlaketahoe.com.

Lake Tahoe Balloons

In 2002, new owners Harley and Tammy Hoy acquired this company and immediately invested in two, brand-new balloons, including a Firefly that can carry 16 people. The unique aspect of a flight over Lake Tahoe is that the balloon uses a 100-foot-long barge, the *Tahoe Flyer*, as both a launching and landing platform. The vessel, a contraption that looks like something from Kevin Costner's *Waterworld* but is Coast Guard-approved, was built by previous owner Bob Allen. It has been gussied up somewhat by the Hoys, who have now created an enclosed area where passengers can wait for their turn to fly—and enjoy a deluxe continental breakfast and hot beverages. Up to 24 people can be accommodated on a morning voyage, with half going on one flight and the remainder on the second. The balloon soars gently over the water, up to about 10,000 feet elevation, and offers spectacular views of South Shore, the Stateline casinos, the surrounding mountains, and scenic Emerald Bay. Guests are picked up from their hotels by a shuttle and taken to Tahoe Keys Marina, where the barge is berthed. The company bases its operation at South Shore during the warm weather months, then moves to Gardnerville in Nevada for the remainder of the year. October–May, flights launch from Lampe City Park and fly over Carson Valley, on the east slopes of the Sierra range. Of course, the end of each flight is capped off by a champagne toast.

Hours: Flights leave daily, depending on weather, May–Oct., with assembly times as early as 5 A.M. During the rest of the year, flights are from Gardnerville at dawn. Reservations are recommended 24 to 72 hours in advance.

Fees: $195 per person for adults, $97.50 for children (7-12) with two paying adults.

Contact: Lake Tahoe Balloons, P.O. Box 19215, South Lake Tahoe, CA 96151; 530/544-1221 or 800/872-9294; website: www.laketahoeballoons.com.

OTHER ACTIVITIES

Glider Rides

TRUCKEE/DONNER

Soar Truckee

Operating since 1980, this is a veritable mecca of gliding at the Truckee-Tahoe Airport. The array of activities includes sightseeing flights, towing (for gliders), rental gliders, lessons, soaring meets, barbecues on a grass lawn, a private campground for visiting fliers (complete with access to hot showers in the office), and a bunk room with TV and VCR. Like to fly? Come and stay for a spell. Not surprisingly, with such diverse facilities, this place gets VIPs from around the world. Sightseeing flights, usually over Truckee and Martis Reservoir, are made in Schweizer 2-33 gliders and last for a half-hour. Manager Mike Johnson's fleet includes two gliders and three Piper Pawnees.

Hours: Daily 9 A.M.–5 P.M., May 1–Oct. 1.
Fees: $115 for the flight; camping for pilots, $5 per night.
Contact: Soar Truckee, 13184 Sailplane Way/P.O. Box 2657, Truckee, CA 96160; 530/587-6702; website: www.soartruckee.com.

RENO/CARSON VALLEY

High Country Soaring

Scenic, narrated, one-passenger rides are offered out of the Minden-Tahoe Airport over Carson Valley and above the Sierra with classic views of Lake Tahoe. The airport is situated at an elevation of 4,700 feet but is next to mountains that rise up to more than 14,000 feet. If you've got an iron stomach, you can ask for the ultimate E-ticket ride—"Top Gun" aerobatics. The company has a fleet of German-made gliders. For pilots, it offers instruction in cross country flying and aerobatics. Facilities include a hangar, lounge with TV, an Internet connection for the latest weather briefings, and a nearby restaurant.

Hours: Year-round 9 A.M.–sunset.
Fees: $100 for a 45-minute trip. Major credit cards accepted.
Contact: High Country Soaring, P.O. Box 70, Minden, NV 89423; 775/782-4944; website: www.highcountrysoaring.

Soar Minden

Established in 1978, this company offers an hourlong glider flight to Lake Tahoe that circles directly over Emerald Bay and Fallen Leaf Lake. Its fleet consists of four twin-passenger Grob sailplanes, one SGS 2-32 three-passenger glider, and Pawnee tow planes. Other flights soar over Carson Valley at elevations high enough to see Lake Tahoe to the west. Winter brings waves, summer brings thermals. Flights depart from Minden-Tahoe Airport, which is about 30 minutes southeast of South Lake Tahoe in the town of Minden. Gift certificates are available, as are soaring lessons for pilots of all levels. The company operates year-round.

Hours: Daily 9 A.M. to when the last person comes down.
Fees: One person, $95–210; two passengers, $160–275; aerobatic rides, $175; and the excursion flight to Lake Tahoe, $210 for one person, $275 for two.
Contact: Soar Minden, 1138 Airport Rd., P.O. Box 1764, Minden, NV 89423; 775/782-7627 or 800/345-7627; website: www.soarminden.com.

Scenic Airplane and Helicopter Flights

SOUTH LAKE TAHOE

Emerald Bay Aviation and Flying Start Aero

This longtime charter and flight instruction center offers tours over Lake Tahoe or Carson Valley and also runs an air taxi service between the San Francisco Bay Area and Lake Tahoe. Using a four-passenger Cessna and a four-passenger Piper Cherokee, pilot John Brown can take up to three people on hourlong flights. By circling around the lake, you can get a bird's-eye view of Emerald Bay, Fallen Leaf Lake, Stateline, Sand Harbor and other major points of interest. Apart from Tahoe, there are routes that will take you over Freel Peak at Heavenly ski resort, Horsetail Falls off Highway 50, Pyramid Peak, and Kirkwood ski resort with its dramatic bluffs. Other flights can be arranged from Minden Airport over Carson City, Virginia City and the east flank of the Sierra range. Flights are made year-round, weather permitting, and winter, with its still air and deep blue skies, often is the best time. Another good time is just before sunset, when any clouds in the sky turn to a dramatic, billowy pink. The company also offers aircraft rentals and lessons, and new pilots can sharpen their skills with high-altitude flying instruction. Emerald also does half-day excursion flights between South Lake Tahoe and Yosemite National Park.

Hours: Daily, 9 A.M.–dark.

Fees: $100 per person per hour, with a minimum of two people. Lessons are $50 for flight and ground instruction, and rentals are $90 per hour, from either the South Lake Tahoe Airport or the Minden Airport.

Contact: Emerald Bay Aviation/Flying Start Aero, 1150 Airport Rd., Minden, NV 89423; 775/783-8359; website: www.flyingstartaero.com.

RENO/CARSON VALLEY

Airborne Expeditions

Hover over Lake Tahoe, cruise above the Reno skyline, or scoot through high desert canyons in this sightseeing heli service, which is operated by Sierra Nevada Helicopters in Reno. The company, started in 1989 by pilot Jon Mayer, has a fleet of late-model Eurocopter A-Star jet helicopters, considered the most ideal for sightseeing flights because they allow for unobstructed, 180-degree panoramic views. The company can also arrange weddings on remote mountain sites that are accessible only by helicopter.

Fees: Offerings include a 20-minute flight over downtown Reno and the surrounding high desert for $99 per person, a 30-minute flight across the top of the Sierra Nevada to Truckee and Lake Tahoe for $149 per person, a 30-minute flight over historic Virginia City and Carson City as well as Lake Tahoe for $149 per person, a 45-minute flight that combines Tahoe and Virginia City/Carson City for $209, and all of the foregoing in one 65-minute flight for $299 per person. Wedding flights range $750–1,500, extra with minister, photographer, flowers and ground transportation.

Contact: Sierra Nevada Helicopters, 1880 Gentry Way (in the Jet West Facility), Reno, NV 89502; 775/825-1100; website: www.sierranevadahelicopters.com.

Biplane Odyssey

In the summer, Reno pilot Peter Foreman takes a leave from his job flying jet airliners and jumps into his Great Lakes biplane, a replica of a 1929 design that was built in 1976, for sightseeing and aerobatic flights over Reno and Lake Tahoe. The plane is a two-hole, open-cockpit affair, à la the Red Baron, so there is room for just one passenger, who sits in the front. Wanna try your hand at flying? Go ahead, take the stick and Foreman will give you instructions through the intercom. If you're up for a few thrills (it helps to be a rollercoaster junkie), he'll run his plane through the hoops—with loops, rolls, inverted flight, Split-S's, and something called Cuban Eights. Keep your seatbelt fastened and don't eat linguica before flying.

Flights range from 7,500 feet to 10,000 feet. Bring warm clothes; Foreman will supply the leather cap and goggles. Flights depart from Reno-Stead Airport north of downtown Reno from April to early October.

Hours: Flights are held in the mornings between 6:30 A.M. and 9 A.M. Make reservations because Foreman is available only half the days of the month.

Fees: $50 for a 20-minute "Barnstormer" around the airfield, $75 for a 30-minute "Acro" flight.

Contact: Biplane Odyssey, 4776 Scenic Hill Circle, Reno, NV 89503; 775/747-1485 or 750/747-1907; website: www.barnstormer1.com.

Hang Gliding and Paragliding

RENO/CARSON VALLEY
Adventure Sports
Operating since 1986, Ray Leonard and Jackie Danskin are outfitter/guides who offer hang gliding and paragliding instruction in and around Carson City. Tandem flights are available.

Hours: Call for a current schedule and appointments.

Fees: Fees range $75–125.

Contact: Adventure Sports, P.O. Box 20066, Carson City, NV 89721; 775/883-7070; website: www.pyramid.net/advspts.

Parasailing

A handful of companies operate parasailing excursions at Lake Tahoe. Harnessed to a parasail, most fliers take off from the stern of a specially designed boat and are towed for 10 to 20 minutes or so around the lake. Flights are generally at around 400 feet above the surface, though some companies offer optional higher trips up to 1,200 feet (at additional cost). Most boats can take four to six passengers, who alternate on the parasail. Age restrictions vary, though children as young as four have been accepted as long as they are accompanied by an adult. Since the upper weight limit is around 280 pounds, tandem flying can combine two adults or an adult and a child. No previous experience is necessary, as the flight is controlled by the captain of the boat. Landings usually are made on the boat but can take place on the water and, in some cases, on the beach. Prices range from $45 for low-altitude rides to $100 for high-altitude rides, with tandem (two-person) rides going for $90–120. It's possible to find discounts for early morning excursions. Rides typically last 8–12 minutes, and observers can often accompany parasailers as boat passengers for about $15 per person. In the summer, companies will operate until sunset as long as there is business and as long as winds do not exceed 20 knots. Here are the major parasailing operations:

TAHOE CITY/WEST SHORE
Lake Tahoe Parasailing
At Tahoe City Marina, this company, now part of Lake Tahoe Aqua Sports, was the first to introduce dry parasailing from a boat and is the oldest parasailing facility on the lake. Offerings consist of daily excursions from sunrise to sunset, May–September. Flights, averaging 10 to 12 minutes, are at about 400 feet altitude, and up to six passengers can be accommodated. The boat is a 30-foot custom-designed Nordic with a wide platform on the stern.

Contact: Lake Tahoe Parasailing, 700 N. Lake Blvd., Tahoe City, CA; 530/583-7245; website: www.laketahoeaquasports.com.

SOUTH SHORE
Action Watersports
This company is behind Timber Cove Lodge in South Lake Tahoe, about 1.5 miles west of the

Stateline casinos. It also operates parasailing from Camp Richardson on the West Shore and from a private beach in front of the Hyatt Regency at Incline Village. The season is May to September.

Contact: Action Watersports, 3411 Lake Tahoe Blvd. (U.S. 50), South Lake Tahoe, CA 96158; 530/541-7245 (Timber Cove), 530/542-6570 (Camp Richardson), or 775/831-4386 (Incline Village); website: www.action-watersports.com.

H2O Sports

This operation is north of Stateline in Zephyr Cove at Roundhill Pines Beach, one of the more attractive beaches on the South Shore.

Contact: H20 Sports, 350 U.S. Hwy. 50, P.O. Box 311, Stateline, NV 89449, 775/588-4155; or Don Borges Water Skiing, 530/541-1351; website: www.rhpbeach.com.

Ski Run Boat Company

Parasailing was introduced in 1996 at this multifaceted water sports operation, one of the largest at South Shore. Flights are available at 400 feet, 800 feet, and 1,200 feet, and there is a discount for customers who sign up before 10 A.M. All operations are on a 28-foot Premium parasail boat with a 10-foot-wide landing platform. It's open May–October.

Contact: Marina Village, 900 Ski Run Blvd., South Lake Tahoe, CA; 530/544-0200; website: www.tahoesports.com.

Zephyr Cove Resort

This company offers flights along the East Shore of the lake out of Zephyr Cove Marina, close to Stateline.

Contact: Zephyr Cove Resort, U.S. 50, Zephyr Cove, NV; 775/588-3833; website: www .tahoedixie2.com.

Outdoor and Indoor Climbing

Lake Tahoe and its environs offer a myriad of climbing opportunities, from spectacular peaks to indoor walls. If you are new to climbing or new to the area, be sure to check with local climbers before heading to a site. If you are looking to take climbing lessons, consider one of the sources below. Note: Unsupervised rock climbing areas for climbers of beginner to advanced levels abound in the Lake Tahoe region. Popular sites include Big Chief (between Tahoe City and Truckee), Cave Rock (advanced climbing at Zephyr Cove, Nevada), the Donner Summit area (more than 400 routes off Old Highway 40 west of Truckee), Eagle Creek Canyon (beginner climbing on a 75-foot wall near Emerald Bay), Lover's Leap (off U.S. 50 near Strawberry), and Twin Crags (a beginner climbing area on Highway 89 north of Tahoe City). For further information regarding trail locations, maps, and supplies, contact the Sierra Mountaineer at 775/856-4824 in Reno or 530/587-2025 in Truckee.

TRUCKEE/DONNER

Alpine Skills International

This is the climbing mecca of the Tahoe region, and, some might argue, of the Sierra Nevada north of Yosemite. Headquartered on Donner Summit, ASI offers instruction, will all equipment, as part of the John Hoffman School of Rock Climbing. One-, two-, and four-day courses are available, from beginner to advanced levels. Clinics include an introduction to rock climbing, the "Next Move" (for intermediates), and "Learning to Lead" (for potential guides), all offered June–September. There are weekend rock climbing courses, a half-day rock anchoring clinic, a one-day session called "Climbing Multi-Pitch," a five-day rock skills course, "Klimbing Kids" for young gym climbers (ages 5–11), and a two- or four-day intermediate to advanced course. In addition to peaks and faces near Donner Pass, ASI takes experienced climbers to other places, such as the popular Lover's Leap, an impressive rocky peak on U.S. 50 west of South Lake Tahoe.

OTHER ACTIVITIES

COURTESY OF NORTHSTAR-AT-TAHOE

the ropes course at Northstar-at-Tahoe

The center is on Old Highway 40 (Donner Pass Road) just above the Sugar Bowl ski area.

Fees: Prices range from $68 for a clinic to $416 for a four-day intensive climbing seminar. Participants must arrange for their own lodging.

Contact: Alpine Skills International, P.O. Box 8, Norden, CA 95724; 530/426-9108, fax 800/916-PEAK (800/916-7325); website: www.alpineskills.com.

High Adventure at Northstar

Adults and kids will find plenty of things to challenge them at this ropes course and 25-foot-high, granitelike, multifaced outdoor climbing wall, which is behind Northstar Village.

Hours: Climbing wall: daily 10 A.M.–6 P.M. Adventure Challenge course: Thurs.–Sun. from 12:30 P.M.–5 P.M. Orienteering course: Wed.–Sun. by appointment. Junior ropes course: Wed.–Sun. 10 A.M.–5 P.M.

Fees: Climbing wall: $11 an hour, $20 for an all-day pass. Adventure Challenge Course (games and exercises with ropes, cables, and tall fir trees): children (minimum age 10) and adults, $43 per person; discounts for more than two people are available. Map and Compass Course: introductory, $15 (including lesson, map, compass, and vest rental); $10 for under age 17 (including single lift ride, map, and compass rental); and free for children seven and under. Shoe rentals are optional. Corporate team building sessions are available. Junior ropes course for kids ages 4–13 (parent assist is required): $13.

Contact: Adventure Associates, 1030 Merced St., Berkeley, CA 94707; 530/562-2285 in summer or 510/525-9391 other times; websites: www.northstarattahoe.com or www.adventureassoc.com.

The Sports Exchange

This used sports equipment store features two indoor climbing rooms designed for top roping and bouldering. The Sports Exchange sells used equipment on consignment and houses a new café.

Hours: Daily 10 A.M.–6 P.M. (summer hours).

Fees: A day pass costs $10 and includes rental climbing shoes; without shoes it's $7. Family rates and monthly passes are available.

Policies: Children under 10 must be accompanied by an adult.

Contact: The Sports Exchange, 10095 W. River St., Truckee, CA 96161; 530/582-4510.

SQUAW VALLEY

Squaw Valley Adventure Center

What began as an indoor operation with the Headwall Climbing Wall, a fixture of the Squaw Valley Cable Car building since 1992, has blossomed into a full-fledged Adventure Center with a ropes course that may be the Taj Mahal of all ropes courses. Nestled among the tall pines of Shirley Canyon, the Challenge Ropes Course looks like something out of a *Mad Max* movie. Built out of steel cable and huge beams, the course is dominated by several 50-foot-high towers with "tree houses," rope extension bridges, and a giant swing. This will test even the most fearless of corporate climbers, and you could say that it is a metaphor for life. Other features include the Mohawk Walk, the Tension Traverse and the Whale Watch. While the course is intended for groups in team-building sessions, individuals can try their skills for a hour or two at a time, with reservation. If high wires and five-story poles make you nervous, there's always that old standby—the Headwall wall. This consists of an indoor, 30-foot-wall, and an outdoor, 45-foot-wall, that together offer 25 routes, for beginner to intermediate climbers. Harnesses and ropes are required and are supplied to participants.

Hours: Daily noon–8 P.M.

Fees: For Challenge Ropes Course, $40 per person for two hours (reservations required); for Headwall Climbing Wall, $12 per session, as long as you want. Climbing shoe rental costs $4.

Contact: Squaw Valley Cafe, 1960 Squaw Valley Rd., Squaw Valley, CA 96146; 530/583-7673. For Squaw Valley Adventure Center, call 530/583-0150; website: www.squaw.com.

TAHOE CITY/WEST SHORE

Ropes Course at Granlibakken Resort

This all-seasons resort offers a variety of programs and sports camps for kids, as well as corporate team-building sessions for adults. There's an impressive ropes course that has a series of both low- and high-element challenges using poles, cables, and native pine trees. Activities are designed to increase personal self- confidence and mutual respect within a group, as well as improve communication, problem-solving, and productivity. Certified trainers guide you and your team through the course, providing a safe and secure environment for all. At this writing, the program, operated as a concession, was undergoing management changes.

What began as an indoor operation with the Headwall Climbing Wall, a fixture of the Squaw Valley Cable Car building since 1992, has blossomed into a full-fledged Adventure Center with a ropes course that may be the Taj Mahal of all ropes courses. Nestled among the tall pines of Shirley Canyon, the Challenge Ropes Course looks like something out of a Mad Max movie.

Hours: Call for schedule.

Fees: Prices vary depending on group size and program. Ask about the discount rates available for large groups and nonprofit organizations.

Contact: Granlibakken Resort, 625 Granlibakken Rd., P.O. Box 6329, Tahoe City, CA 95730; 530/583-4242 or 800/543-3221; website: www.granlibakken.com.

KIRKWOOD/HOPE VALLEY/MARKLEEVILLE

Kirkwood Climbing Wall

This 30-foot wall with a straight surface, an incline and an overhang will keep both adults and kids challenged as long as their muscles can hold out. The wall is in the new Kirkwood Village and is supervised, but a parent must be present for any child who is under 14. The wall is open weekends and holidays 10 A.M.–4 P.M. Also, beginning to intermediate rock climbing lessons are offered by ski mountaineer and guide Doug Robinson. Kirkwood is on Highway 88 and is a 40-minute drive southwest of the city of South Lake Tahoe.

Fees: $15 per hour (shoes included).

Contact: Kirkwood Mountain Resort, 1501 Kirkwood Meadows Dr., P.O. Box 1, Kirkwood, CA 95646; 209/258-7357; for "Moving Over Stone" courses with Doug Robinson, contact 831/684-9465; website: www.kirkwood.com.

RENO/CARSON VALLEY

Rocksport Indoor Climbing Center

This facility, built in 1995, consists of a large room with a multitude of rock and bouldering faces, complete with overhangs. At this writing, expansion plans were under way to provide additional and bouldering surfaces covering up to

12,000 square feet in the space formerly occupied by Sierra Mountaineer, which is no longer in business.

It is northern Nevada's only full-service rock-climbing center, and it has 6,500 square feet of varied top rope, lead climbing and bouldering terrain. Climbs can reach 30 to 35 feet high, and there are more than 40 routes. The center offers supervised climbing for drop-ins, as well as lessons and seminars. There's a bouldering section for climbing without ropes, with a floor of rubber cushioning below. Activities include Team Rocksport for youngsters On Saturday and Sunday there are special sessions for youngsters, 10 A.M.–1 P.M., with staff belayers and discounts on climbing and gear rentals. Lessons for all ages are offered by arrangement, and parents may belay their children if they have experience.

Hours: Weekdays 10 A.M.–10 P.M., 10 A.M.–8 P.M. on Sat., and 10 A.M.–6 P.M. on Sunday.

Fees: $12 for a day pass, $8 for shoes and harness; students are $10. Ladies' Night (Tuesday) costs $8 for a pass, $2 for gear, and $10 for a lesson; Wednesday lessons are $25 for two hours, including gear and day pass; Monday Night Madness offers climbing and all equipment for two people for $20.

Contact: Sierra Mountaineer, 1901 Silverado Blvd., Reno, NV 89512; 775/352-ROPE (775/352-7673); website: www.rocksportnv.com.

Sierra Mountain Guides

If you're looking for someone to show you Tahoe's more impressive peaks and climbing routes, or just to teach you the fundamentals of climbing, this consortium of local guides can fix you up. They offer the entire spectrum of rock climbing, ice climbing, winter mountaineering, and spring backcountry skiing, with permits in Tahoe and Eldorado National Forests. Among the area's classic climbs are those at Lover's Leap on Highway 50 near South Lake Tahoe, and on the crags at Donner Summit west of Truckee. All ability levels, from beginner to advanced, are welcome, and the guides provide all equipment including climbing shoes. A half-dozen guides are in Truckee, Minden, Gardnerville, and Reno.

Fees: Half-day and full-day rates range $120–295 per person, with lower rates applying to higher ratios of students to guide.

Contact: John G. Cleary, Sierra Mountain Guides, P.O. Box 19727, Reno, NV 89511; 775/852-4049; website: www.sierramtnguides.com.

PAINTBALL

At Homewood Mountain Resort, on the West Shore, would-be commandos can splatter themselves silly while chasing each other through the woods of this medium-sized ski area. Using paintballs that are biodegradable and FDA-approved, groups board the Madden triple chairlift at the base and stake out their war zones on the upper mountain in the Paintball Playground. There are two designated playing fields of about two acres each, with scenic vistas of Lake Tahoe. The area rents paintball markers, coveralls, goggles, and gloves, and sells paintballs and CO_2 refills. It's open late June–early Sept., Wed.–Sun., 9 A.M.–3:30 P.M.

Fees: $40 for an all-day lift ticket, field pass, and rental package with 100 paintballs, marker, goggles, and CO_2; $25 for a half day. For those who are self-equipped, the rate is $20 a day and $10 for a half day.

Contact: Homewood Mountain Resort, Highway 89, P.O. Box 165, Homewood, CA 96141; 530/525-2992; website: www.skihomewood.com.

Off-Highway Vehicles (OHVs)

If you've got a few spare tires, a replacement front end, an axle or two, and maybe super-duper shocks, you might be ready for what Tahoe can dish out to man and machine. The national forests and other public lands around the basin are laced with four-wheel-drive and dirt bike roads, often shared with mountain bikers and hikers. Literally hundreds of miles can be explored with four-wheel-drives, and the rewards can include isolated fishing lakes and campsites. If you don't want to batter your own vehicle, however, you can always sign up for a tour. People with bad backs need not apply.

OHV TOURS

Lake Tahoe Adventures

If you've got a strong bladder, you can take guided tours on all-terrain vehicles (four-wheel ATVs), in Jeeps, and in Hummers from the Meeks Bay area (the West Shore of Lake Tahoe) over the famous Rubicon Trail. You can drive an ATV if you have a license, or just sit back in a 4x4 and let a guide do the driving while you do the hanging on. There's also an entirely different trip, one that runs year-round, to the Pine Nut Mountains of Nevada outside of Carson City. This three-hour trip in a four-wheel-drive explores the rugged high desert country near the historic silver mining town of Virginia City. The company has Jeeps, ATVs, and the famous Hummer of Desert Storm fame. All drivers must wear issued helmets.

Fees: Rubicon two-hour scenic Jeep tour, $45 per person (with a two-adult minimum), plus additional hours at $20 per person per hour; children under 12, $20, when accompanied by two adults. Rubicon ATV tours, $49–275 per person of from one to six hours; "Top of the World" Hummer tours with views of Lake Tahoe and Carson Valley, $75 per person (three-adult minimum) for two hours, $35 for children under 12 when accompanied by three adults.

Contact: Lake Tahoe Adventures, P.O. Box 11521, South Lake Tahoe, CA 96155; 530/577-2940; website: www.laketahoeadventure.com.

Northstar ATV Tours

This four-seasons resort south of Truckee offers two-hour All-Terrain-Vehicle tours on its vast ski holdings. Riders follow trails through both wooded and cleared terrain, visiting Sawmill Lake and various high vantage points. Several ridges that have panoramic views of Lake Tahoe to the south and Martis Valley to the north. Helmets, gloves and goggles are provided. Riders must wear long pants, have sturdy shoes, and be at least 16 years old. All ATVs are built to seat the driver only. Tours are limited to five participants and reservations are required. Meeting place is the Guest Services Center in Northstar Village.

Fees: $80 per person.

Contact: Northstar-at-Tahoe, P.O. Box 129, Truckee, CA 96160; 530/562-1330 or 800/GO-NORTH (800/466-6784); website: www.northstarattahoe.com.

Ponderosa Ranch Outback ATV Adventure Tours

This western theme park, patterned after the famous "Bonanza" television series of the 1960s, has traded its four-legged steeds for four-wheel All-Terrain-Vehicles. Two-hour rides that reach up to 8,000 feet in elevation—about 2,000 feet higher than the Ranch—are offered daily during the summer, A.M.–3:30 P.M., and prices include admission to the park. All trips are guided and are limited to licensed drivers age 16 or older. Tours use the old equestrian trails in the Carson Range, and offer spectacular views of Lake Tahoe. Rides follow a loop and never repeat a trail. All vehicles are fully automatic, and basic instruction on their operation is provided in advance of tours, along with safety helmets, goggles and gloves. Breakfast and luncheon rides are available, at extra cost. Reservations for all rides are strongly recommended.

Fees: $85 per person, including free admission to the theme park.

Contact: Ponderosa Ranch, 100 Ponderosa Ranch Rd., Incline Village, NV 89451;

OTHER ACTIVITIES

775/832-RIDE (775/832-7433); website: www.ponderosaranch.com.

OHV TRAILS

The national forests around Lake Tahoe and the Bureau of Land Management areas east and south of Carson City offer a multitude of off-roading possibilities. One of the most famous jeep and dune buggy trails in America—the Rubicon Trail—extends from Georgetown in the Gold Country foothills west of Tahoe to the very shores of the lake, a distance of 22 miles. The narrow passages, rocky climbs, and occasional mud holes make this route very difficult.

National Forests

For a detailed description of off-roading trails in national forests, contact the following:

Tahoe National Forest, Sierraville Ranger District, P.O. Box 95, Hwy. 89, Sierraville, CA 96126; 530/994-3401.

Tahoe National Forest, Truckee Ranger District, P.O. Box 399, Truckee, CA 95734; 530/587-3558.

U.S. Forest Service, Lake Tahoe Basin Management Unit, 870 Emerald Bay Rd., South Lake Tahoe, CA 96150; 530/573-2600.

Bureau of Land Management Areas

Off-roading trails on BLM lands are mostly in Nevada and include the following developed areas:

Sand Mountain: Sand dunes in a vast, 4,795-acre recreation area are 25 miles east of Fallon (which is east of Carson City). Speed is limited to 15 miles per hour around the camp area and 25 miles per hour on all access roads. All off-highway vehicles must use a fluorescent orange whip flag eight feet above ground level.

Contact: Bureau of Land Management, Carson City District, 1535 Hot Springs Rd., Ste. 300, Carson City, NV 89706-0638; 775/885-6000.

Sand Springs: 25 miles east of Fallon, Nevada, this half-mile, self-guided interpretive loop trail winds through the fenced, 40-acre Sand Springs Desert Study Area, where you can learn about the plants and animals of the Great Basin. You'll also see a historic 1860 Pony Express station, which was buried under sand until archaeologists discovered and excavated it in the 1970s.

Contact: Bureau of Land Management, Carson City District, 1535 Hot Springs Rd., Ste. 300, Carson City, NV 89706-0638; 775/885-6000.

Picnic Areas, Hot Springs, and Spas

Picnicking

Lake Tahoe and its surroundings, from the high mountain region to the Carson Valley, beckons to those with a picnic basket, a bottle of chardonnay, some crab salad, and maybe a loaf of sourdough bread. Although picnics have their own intrinsic pleasures, they're usually much more satisfying when they follow an appetite-building activity such as bicycling, fishing, hiking, or boating. A visit to one of the following dedicated picnic areas will allow you to combine an alfresco meal with outdoor sports or a nature or history walk. This list is by no means exhaustive (in fact, it functions more as a supplement to the campgrounds profiled in the accommodations sec-

tion. Virtually every campground around here has some area set aside for independent picnicking—but not all picnic areas offer camping). One thing to keep in mind is that you should avoid leaving scraps for the local wildlife. In fact, when picnicking in high-elevation forest, make a point of keeping food locked tightly in your car (inside a cooler or other container) before and after your meal. Here are my favorite spots to picnic in the Tahoe area:

TRUCKEE/DONNER
Donner Memorial State Park
The pine-shaded picnic/day-use area is just west of the campground in this state park. Boating, fishing, hiking, and water-skiing are among the

© KEN CASTLE

Picnicking at Kaspian, West Shore of Tahoe

recreational options. The Emigrant Trail Museum, which traces the journey of the ill-fated Donner Party, is open year-round at the park.
Fees: Parking is $2 per vehicle.
Location: Off I-80 on Donner Pass Road in Truckee, California.
Contact: California Department of Parks and Recreation; 530/582-7892.

Fuller Lake

This was a small Forest Service campground until the campsites were removed recently. Now it's a day-use picnic area only—and what an idyllic spot it is. Tree-shaded picnic tables and barbecues are right on the water's edge of this tranquil, forested mountain reservoir at an elevation of 5,600 feet. Bring a canoe or a rowboat to explore the lake or try your luck at fishing.
Location: Four miles north of Highway 20 on Bowman Road and 3.5 miles west of the I-80 intersection, about an hour's drive from Truckee.
Contact: U.S. Forest Service Supervisor's Office; 530/265-4531.

Martis Creek Lake Recreation Area

Tree-shaded picnic facilities are next to a campground and favorite catch-and-release fly-fishing waters just outside of Truckee. The area encompasses a 3,000-acre wildlife refuge. Powerboats are prohibited.
Location: Off Highway 267, three miles north of Northstar Drive in North Truckee, California.
Contact: Martis Creek Lake Recreation Area; 530/639-2342.

SOUTH LAKE TAHOE

Bijou Community Park

Picnic/barbecue areas, basketball hoops, horseshoes, jogging trails, grassy fields, a playground, restrooms, volleyball, a concession stand, a gazebo, a nine-hole golf course, and a skateboard area are offered at this large city park in the heart of South Lake Tahoe, south of U.S. 50.
Location: Al Tahoe Boulevard near Johnson Street in South Lake Tahoe, California.

Contact: Bijou Community Park; 530/542-6056.

Spooner Lake

This is a popular starting point for the Flume Trail mountain bike ride, as well as a diverse recreational fishery. Facilities include picnic tables, restrooms, barbecue grills, and hiking and cycling trails. With all the aspen trees here, you'll be treated to an excellent display of fall colors.
Location: At the intersection of Highway 28 and U.S. 50 on the Spooner Summit in Nevada.
Contact: Lake Tahoe-Nevada State Park; 775/831-0494.

KIRKWOOD/HOPE VALLEY/MARKLEEVILLE

Ferguson Point

You'll find this scenic, high-country picnic area on the east shore of Silver Lake near the Kit Carson Lodge. Ten picnic sites, tables, benches, refuse containers, and restrooms are provided, and there's a boat ramp nearby. Fishing, swimming, and water-skiing are available.
Location: In the Eldorado National Forest, west of Carson Pass on Highway 88 in California.
Contact: U.S. Forest Service; 530/386-5164 or 530/644-6048.

Grover Hot Springs State Park

Delightful hot mineral pools make this a worthy spot for a picnic. A pretty, wooded campground with 76 sites is nearby. The park, which is open year-round, also has a swimming pool, a fishing stream, self-guided nature trails, piped water, showers, and restrooms.
Fees: Parking is free.
Location: On Hot Springs Road, three miles west of Highway 89 in Markleeville, California.
Contact: Grover Hot Springs State Park; 530/694-2248.

Woods Lake

Tucked away in Eldorado National Forest is one of the most attractive picnic areas in the high country. It lies beside a small, wooded alpine lake with easy access to excellent hiking trails into Mokelumne Wilderness. Picnic tables, piped water, and barbecues are provided. Parking is limited, and spaces fill fast on weekends.

Location: About 35 miles southwest of South Lake Tahoe and just west of Carson Pass off Highway 88 in California.

Contact: Eldorado National Forest, Amador Ranger District; 209/295-4251.

RENO/CARSON CITY

Bowers Mansion Regional Park

Outside of the historic Bowers Mansion, visitors will find a picnic/barbecue area, a playground, a swimming pool, restrooms, volleyball nets, and horseshoe pits. Tours of the mansion are offered daily. Open 11 A.M.–4:30 P.M.

Fees: Charged only for the use of the swimming pool and tours of the Mansion.

Location: At 4004 U.S. 395 N (next to Davis Creek County Park), south of Reno, NV.

Contact: Bowers Mansion Regional Park; 775/849-1825 or 775/849-0201.

Davis Creek County Park

A picnic/barbecue area, campsites, nature exhibits, restrooms, volleyball nets, and hiking trails are offered at this county park. Cast a line into the creek and you might catch something to toss onto a grill for lunch.

Location: Off U.S. 395 at 25 Davis Creek Road, south of Reno, NV.

Contact: Davis Creek County Park; 775/849-0684.

Washoe Lake State Park

Enjoy swimming, birdwatching, fishing, windsurfing, romping in sand dunes, horseback riding on equestrian trails, and, of course, picnicking. Restrooms, a dump station, a birding area, and a boat ramp are provided at this state park. Leashed pets are permitted.

Fees: The day-use fee is $3.

Location: Off U.S. 395 between Lakeshore and East Lake Boulevards, north of Carson City, Nevada.

Contact: Washoe Lake State Park; 775/687-4319.

Hot Springs

TRUCKEE/DONNER

Sierra Hot Springs

Formerly known as Campbell Hot Springs, this resort and spa have been around in some form for 150 years. It was recently acquired by the New Age Church, which also operates Hardin Hot Springs north of Calistoga, the famous wine country spa community near San Francisco. The springs are just a 30-minute drive north of Truckee, but it's a bit of a challenge to find and traverse the dirt entrance road, which is 1.5 miles east off Highway 49 near its intersection with Highway 89 at Sierraville. Adjoining the Main Lodge are three natural hot mineral pools, which vary in temperature and which contain silica and small amounts of sulphur. The spa amenities include a heated swimming pool; an outdoor pool called the Medicine Bath, which has a sandy bottom and is surrounded by rock tile; and a Hot Pool, which is inside a large geodesic dome. In addition, there are private rooms in the Phoenix Baths, and these also use the warm springwater. Other services include massage, water yoga and various alternative health treatments. No nudity is allowed within view of the road. Well-behaved children are accepted, and there are specific times that youngsters may use the pools. No alcohol is allowed on the property. The resort is on 900 acres of forest and rolling hills.

Fees: $10 for three hours at the springs, or all day until midnight for $15 per person. In addition, at least one member of the party must pay a membership fee ($5 per month as of this writing) to the Church, which enables it to offer the clothing optional policy.

Contact: Sierra Hot Springs, P.O. Box 366, Sierraville, CA 96126; 530/994-3773; website: www.sierrahotsprings.org.

KIRKWOOD/HOPE VALLEY/MARKLEEVILLE

Grover Hot Springs State Park

In an idyllic valley surrounded by mountains, this unique California state park offers both hot and cold outdoor mineral pools with a low sulphur content. Facilities include cramped changing rooms and showers. Summer hours are 9 A.M.–9 P.M. daily; winter hours are 2 P.M.–9 P.M. on weekdays and 9 A.M.–9 P.M. on weekends. Swimsuits are required. **Fees:** $2 for adults 18 and over; $1 for youths.

Location: Four miles west of Highway 89 on Hot Springs Road just outside Markleeville and about a 45-minute drive from South Lake Tahoe.

Contact: Grover Hot Springs State Park; 530/694-2249 (pool information).

RENO

Steamboat Villa Hot Springs Spa

The public is welcome to indulge in the various hot springs baths and therapies at this historic spa, which is operated by the nonprofit New Age Church of Being. Reportedly it was newspaperman and novelist Mark Twain who coined the name by exclaiming, on one of his many forays from Virginia City, "Behold, a steamboat in the desert!" While the first spa was developed during the city's mining era in the mid- to late 1800s, it was Dr. Edna Carver who formalized a therapeutic spa regimen in 1909. In recent years, the building has been completely renovated, inside and out, though it still retains a charming, inviting ambience. Steamboat Villa is the oldest known site in the world of continuous hot springs activity that produces surface mineral deposits, primarily sulfates but also including the rare borax. The most common geothermal features on the site are fumeroles, or steam vents,

The public is welcome to indulge in the various hot springs baths and therapies at this historic Steamboat Villa Hot Springs Spa, which is operated by the nonprofit New Age Church of Being. Reportedly it was newspaperman and novelist Mark Twain who coined the name by exclaiming, on one of his many forays from Virginia City, "Behold, a steamboat in the desert!"

which vary in size from "peepholes" to "blowholes." When the water reaches the surface, it's at a scalding temperature of 200–220°F, but it is cooled for use in the indoor and outdoor baths. Private rooms with tiled single tubs, floors and walls are used for indoor baths, with the water drained, disinfected and replenished for each use. There's a freshwater shower in each tub room. The outdoor tub, which can accommodate five people, is in the back of the spa building and overlooks lawn and Steamboat Creek. The tub is flow-through, so fresh mineral water is constantly replenishing the tub. Bathing suits are required for this tub. Also on the premises are a public steam room powered by geothermal mineral water, a therapeutic massage service with a variety of therapies, and a gift shop. Therapies include Japanese, Swedish, sports, aromatherapy and acupressure massages as well as body wrap, mud body mask, salt glow, and healing stones. The hot springs is 12 miles south of Reno (two miles beyond the Mt. Rose Highway turnoff) and is reached by turning east on Rhodes Road.

Fees: Drop-in charge for nonmembers is $14, which provides use of a private tub for 45 minutes. Massages range $35–97, with other therapies $30–85. Packages that combine various options for a full day at the spa range $120–198 per person. Reservations are required at least 24 hours in advance for all visits.

Contact: Steamboat Villa Hot Springs Spa, 16010 S. Virginia St., P.O. Box 18106, Reno, NV 89511; 775/853-6600; website: www .steamboatsprings.org.

CARSON CITY/CARSON VALLEY

Carson Hot Springs Resort

Originally discovered in 1849, during the height of the Gold Rush, this private hot

David Walley's Resort, Hot Springs and Spa

springs spa, in a considerably less scenic venue than other spas in the area, offers private indoor baths, an outdoor pool and patio, and an adjoining bar. The natural mineral water flows from the ground at 121°F, and is lowered by air spray and evaporative cooling when pools are drained and filled each day. The outdoor swimming pool temperature is kept at 98°F in the summer and 102°F in the winter, although individual room temperatures can be controlled as desired, from 95 to 110 degrees. Bathing suits are required in the swimming pool, but are optional in the private rooms. Other amenities on the site include massage therapy, a restaurant and bar, parking lot, an inexpensive motel, efficiency rooms (apartments), and a new and remodelled bed-and-breakfast inn, which is housed in an 1860 building that was originally used as a lodge. This has two rooms and comes with a home-cooked breakfast in

the morning. Open 7 A.M.–11 P.M. daily, except Christmas.

Fees: The cost for the outdoor pools is $10 for adults and youths over 12, $8 for seniors over 55 and children 12 and under. Private indoor hot tubs ("mini spa rooms") with the same mineral water cost $15 for adults and $10 for seniors, with a time limit of two hours. Users must be at least 18 years old. Massages are $45–80, depending on length.

Contact: Carson Hot Springs Resort, 500 Hot Springs Rd., Carson City, NV; 775/885-8844; website: www.carsonhotspringsresort.com.

David Walley's Resort, Hot Springs and Spa

This clean and modern outdoor hot springs resort in the town of Genoa, south of Carson City, was originally built by David and Harriet Walley over a century ago. It had a luxury hotel featuring gourmet dining, and it was adjacent to the Pony Express route and the Mormon-Emigrant Trail. Upscale visitors throughout the years have included President Ulysses S. Grant, author Mark Twain, and actors Clark Gable and Ida Lupino. Twelve miles from South Lake Tahoe via the Kingsbury Grade, the resort has several outdoor pools kept at varying temperatures, as well as one large pool for swimming. Recently acquired by Quintus Resorts, which is selling interval ownerships at the property, the facility now has a full luxury spa. Services include therapeutic body massage using aromatic oils, salt glow body scrub, seaweed algae body treatment, Moor mud treatment, body hydration therapy, and nine types of facials. Amenities consist of a luxurious, 42-room condominium hotel with standard and premium suites, two cabins, a restaurant, snack and juice bar, changing rooms and showers, and fitness center. Open daily 7 A.M.–10 P.M. No children under 12 are allowed in hot pools—only in the freshwater relaxation pool, which is heated to 85°F.

Fees: $20 per person for all-day use of hot springs, relaxation pool, weight room and lockers. Spa treatments range $45–100, and there are packages that combine treatments. Reservations are advised for therapies, but not needed for soaking in the outdoor mineral pools. At 2001 Foothill Rd., Genoa, NV; 1.5 miles south of the historic town of Genoa and 30 minutes southeast of Stateline at Lake Tahoe.

Contact: David Walley's Resort, Hot Springs and Spa; 775/782-8155 or 800/628-7831; website: www.davidwalleys.com.

Spas

Recently, there's been a boom in new spas throughout the Tahoe and Reno areas, primarily at hotels that are reallocating space to accommodate the latest wave of New Age therapies. And people are responding, because a relaxing massage or body wrap is a great way to top off a day of skiing, golfing, mountain biking, or hiking. Among the menu of new therapies, by far the most popular is the hot stone massage, which was originally developed in Arizona but has caught on in a big way throughout the United States. This massage, lasting 45–80 minutes, involves smooth river-type stones that are heated and coated with oil, then gently placed on various sensitive areas such as the back of the neck, forehead, legs, back, and palms of the hands. In some versions of this therapy, cold stones are alternated with hot ones. Other popular therapies are Shiatsu and Swedish massage, aromatherapy, detoxifying body wraps using seaweed or mud from the Dead Sea, fruit-scented and herbal exfoliations, hydro water therapy, and deep pore cleansing facials. At many spas, you can also get manicures, pedicures and hair styling. Spas are heavily booked during the peak periods in summer and winter, and it's best to make reservations several days or even weeks in advance.

Prices run the gamut, sometimes for similar therapies, and depend on the respective property. You can save money by purchasing an all-inclusive lodging/spa getaway, which comes with a selection of therapies. Also, combining several treatments into a full day of pampering typically brings a substantial discount, and sometimes there are deals for couples, as well. For a la carte items, here are the price ranges:

• Massages: $45–140, depending on style of massage and duration. Regular Swedish or sports massage are at the lower end of the price range, with hot stones at the upper end.
• Body wraps: $45–90, with mud and seaweed wraps the most expensive.
• Hydrotherapy bath treatments: $60–80.
• Facials: $65–125, depending on duration and process.
• Manicures and pedicures: $35–80, depending on duration and type.

Note: The spas that are listed here are in hotels or associated with resorts. However, there are more than 70 independent spas and therapy purveyors throughout the region. One word of caution: If you go walking through the Yellow Pages under the "Massage" listings, keep in mind that "massage" is a code word for bordello. Houses of prostitution, called "ranches," are legal in many parts of Nevada, with a number of them east of Carson City near Fallon and east of Reno beyond Washoe County.

SQUAW VALLEY

The Resort at Squaw Creek Health and Fitness Center and Spa

This major hotel/resort opened a new, 10,000-square-foot spa in mid-2000 as part of a major expansion. As the largest spa at North Lake Tahoe, the new center has a rustic alpine feeling with stone and wood accents. There are eight massage rooms that offer a variety of new services including something called the Tahoe Hot Stone Massage. What's that, you ask? Various sizes of basalt stones are heated to a comfortable temperature and then applied to the body in a rhythmical massage technique—sort of a "rolling stones" method. And, they promise, you WILL get satisfaction. Two body treatment rooms have custom facials, body wraps, body masks, hydrotherapy and rejuvenating scrubs. Massage treatments include acupressure, Shiatsu, deep tissue, meditative, sports and aromatherapy. The new facility also includes a larger fitness area with exercise machines, a beauty salon, bigger reception area, fresh juice bar, lounge for relaxing before and after treatments, and a 4,000-square-foot expansion of the Sun Plaza Deck, an area for outside dining that overlooks the Squaw Valley meadow. Near this are outdoor hot tubs and a large swimming pool. By the way, while you're de-stressing, your kids can work off their own anxieties in a newly enlarged video game room that is next to the fitness center.

The hot stone massage, lasting 45–80 minutes, involves smooth river-type stones that are heated and coated with oil, then gently placed on various sensitive areas such as the back of the neck, forehead, legs, back, and palms of the hands.

Contact: The Resort at Squaw Creek, 400 Squaw Creek Rd., Olympic Valley, CA 96146; 530/583-6300 or 800/403-4434; website: www.squawcreek.com.

INCLINE VILLAGE/CRYSTAL BAY

Euro Spa at Cal-Neva Resort

Cal-Neva Resort's in-house spa features massage therapy, body and skin care treatments, scalp massage, hydrotherapy, herbal wraps, manicures, pedicures, a fitness facility, lockers, a Jacuzzi, steam/sauna rooms, and a relaxation lounge. Robes, slippers, towels, and hair dryers are provided. It's open daily 9 A.M.–9 P.M.; appointments are required.

Contact: Cal-Neva Resort, 2 Stateline Rd./P.O. Box 368, Crystal Bay, NV 89402; 775/832-4000 or 800/CAL-NEVA (800/225-6382); website: www.calnevaresort.com.

The Spa at Hyatt Regency Lake Tahoe

Talk about a facial—the venerable Hyatt at Incline Village was undergoing a $60 million makeover as this edition went to press, and most spa and exercise services have been moved to temporary quarters until a new and much larger facility (15,000 square feet) is completed. Therapies consist of Swedish relaxation massage, aromatherapy massage, sea botanical body wrap, honeysuckle body scrub, European facial, glycolic peel, and deluxe foot treatment. But expect much more in the new spa and fitness center. Exercise equipment is available for stretching, toning and aerobics. The spa operates 8 A.M.–8 P.M., and the fitness center operates 6 A.M.–10 P.M.

Contact: Hyatt Regency Lake Tahoe, Country Club Dr. at Lakeshore Dr., Incline Village, NV 89451; 775/832-1234 or 888/899-5024; website: www.laketahoehyatt.com.

SOUTH LAKE TAHOE

Cho-Cho Salon at Caesars

In the Health Spa of Caesars Tahoe hotel and casino, this place offers a complete beauty service for men and women with something called "European thalassotherapy." This involves body polishing and scrubbing, a seaweed bath, a massage, and a thermal wrap. The seaweed bath contains a formula of 90 percent microburst seaweed at a temperature of 96–100°F. Open 9 A.M.–7 P.M. daily; appointments are recommended.

Contact: Caesars Tahoe, 55 U.S. 50/P.O. Box 5800, Stateline, NV 89449; 775/588-4243; website: www.caesars.com/tahoe/.

Elements—The Spa at Tahoe Lakeshore Lodge

This new spa, at a recently refurbished beach-side lodge, offers a variety of treatments and massages that are based on the holistic medicine of Ayurveda and on Native American healing techniques. They include several styles of massage therapies; salt glow and exfoliation scrubs; native clay, enzymatic sea mud and herbal scrubs; body wraps; facials; and hydrotherapy baths. The lodge includes luxury rooms and condominiums. Spa hours are 9 A.M.–7 P.M., and reservations are subject to availability. Minimum age requirement is 16.

Contact: Tahoe Lakeshore Lodge and Spa, 930 Bal Bijou Rd., South Lake Tahoe, CA 96150; 530/541-2180; website: www.tahoe-lakeshorelodge.com.

Harveys Health Club and Spa

This large fitness and spa facility is inside of Harveys Casino Resort. Apart from an extensive exercise area with machines, you can relax at Michelle's Body Essentials, a day spa that offers a variety of treatments. These include seaweed and herbal wraps, soothing stones massage, aromatherapy massage, body polishing, facials and Swedish body massage. Hours of operation are 9 A.M.–9 P.M. daily, including holidays. The fitness center, free to hotel guests, is open 6 A.M.–10 P.M. daily.

Contact: Michelle's at Harveys, Hwy. 50 at Stateline, NV 89449; 775/588-2411 ext. 2943; website: www.tahoespa.com.

The Spa at Harrah's Lake Tahoe

This major hotel at Stateline offers a complex of health, spa and beauty services. Within the health club, which has exercise machines, the spa has a menu that isn't quite as exotic or extensive as other resort spas in the region, but it includes basic massage, deep tissue massage, and a half-dozen aromatherapy massages. There's also a large indoor, glass-domed swimming pool. Hours of operation: 6 A.M.–8 P.M. daily.

Contact: Harrah's Lake Tahoe, P.O. Box 8, Stateline, NV 89449; 775/588-6611 or 800/427-7247; website: www.harrahstahoe.com.

FEATHER RIVER COUNTRY/LAKES BASIN

Spa Rituals at Nakoma Resort and Spa

This large recreational community, centered around The Dragon golf course north of Truckee, offers a full-service spa inside its spectacular Frank Lloyd Wright-designed clubhouse, called Nakoma. The name is from a Chippewa Indian reference to the daughter of the Goddess of the Moon. You'll feel like a god or goddess yourself after a few hours in the spa, which is in the lower level of the lodge building below the restaurant, cocktail lounge and pro shop. The menu of therapies is extensive, and includes aromatherapy baths, sea algae wrap, organic Moor mud body wrap, Balinese spice body mask, Jamu Asian massage, stone therapy massage, reflexology, sports/deep tissue massage, golfer's therapeutic massage, German Krauter Bad ("herbal bath") hydrotherapy bath, antioxidant facial, and a variety of manicures and pedicures. Also, personal trainers conduct fitness and wellness programs, including yoga, water aerobics, and Tai-Chi. Spa hours are 9 A.M.–7 P.M. for massages, 10 A.M.–6 P.M. for cosmetology. There's also a large selection of spa products for sale. It's 50 miles north of Truckee via Highway 89 north to County Road A-15.

Contact: Nakoma Resort and Spa, P.O. Box 1070, Graeagle, CA 96103; 530/832-5352 or 877/418-0880; website: www.nakomaresort.com.

RENO

Chonnes Salon and Spa at John Ascuaga's Nugget

Some of the more contemporary spa treatments—including those oh-so-popular hot stones—are available at this casino hotel spa. Among the offerings: Dead Sea salt glow, mud wrap, herbal body wrap, hot stone massage (using smooth basalt stones), and Swedish massage. The Nugget is somewhat famous for its huge and attractively-designed indoor pool, which has a retractable skylight. Open: 9 A.M.–6 P.M., pool and health club, 6 A.M.–10 P.M.

Contact: John Ascuaga's Nugget, 1100 Nugget Ave., Sparks, NV 89431; 775/356-3300 or 800/648-1177; website: www.janugget.com.

The Health Spa at Atlantis

On the third floor above the casino, this hotel spa at the Atlantis Casino Resort, next to the Reno Convention Center, offers lovely indoor and out-door rooftop swimming pools (one with a waterfall), and a variety of spa services, including six different types of massages, among them a "Treatment of the Month" special. Also, there's a variety of facials. The fitness center is open 6 A.M.–10 P.M., and the spa treatments are available 8 A.M.–8 P.M. daily.

Contact: Atlantis Casino Resort, 3800 S. Virginia St., Reno, NV 89502; 775/954-4135 or 800/723-6500; website: www.atlantiscasinoresort.com.

Peppermill Salon and Spa

South Reno's other major hotel casino has an in-house spa with wellness and deep tissue massages, European and deep pore cleansing facials, herbal exfoliation, specialty masks and nail salon. Other amenities include a year-around waterfall pool, Jacuzzi, hair styling, health club with strength training equipment, and dry sauna. The spa is open 8 A.M.–10 P.M., the health club 5 A.M.–10 P.M.

Contact: Peppermill Hotel Casino, 2707 S. Virginia St., Reno, NV 89502; 775/826-2121 or 800/282-2444; website: www.Peppermill-Reno.com.

© KEN CASTLE

the hot stone massage at Resort and Spa Nakoma

Siena Hotel Spa Casino

The newest casino hotel in downtown Reno has the look of an executive hotel and the feel of a leisure resort. With its Tuscan-styled architecture and pleasant interior appointments, this property clearly espouses the good life for its guests. A large spa that is adjacent to a rooftop swimming pool offers plenty of opportunity for relaxing. And everything—including the spa gift shop—is upscale. Siena treatments include six different massages, nine body treatments and scrubs, four hydrotherapy and balneotherapy treatments, six aromatherapy salt baths, and six European facials. Aromatherapy, using different essences to sooth the body and other senses, is the underlying technique here. Of the various body scrubs, there's one called Siena Desert Scrub, which consists of crushed walnuts and oatmeal blended with essential oils and applied with an ayate cactus cloth to soften the skin. That might make you hungry for dinner, and Siena obliges with a well-regarded restaurant that overlooks the Truckee River. Open daily, 9 A.M.–9 P.M.

Contact: Siena Hotel Spa Casino, 1 S. Lake St., P.O. Box 3340, Reno, NV 89505; 775/337-6260 or 877/743-6233; website: www.sienareno.com.

Silver Legacy Health Spa, Pool, and Barbary Salon

This downtown casino hotel offers a complete line of exercise equipment and full massage therapy in an elegant setting on the fourth floor, adjacent to the swimming pool. You must be a guest of the Silver Legacy, Eldorado or Circus Circus to gain entry. Services include Swedish and sports massage, whirlpool baths, steam rooms, saunas, outdoor swimming pool and sun deck, strength training and cardiovascular equipment, and the Barbary Salon for hair styling, facials, manicures and pedicures. Spa guests must be 18 or older. Robes and sandals, along with free fruit juices and coffee, are provided. Open 6 A.M.–9 P.M. daily.

Contact: Silver Legacy Resort Casino, 407 N. Virginia St., Reno, NV 89501; 775/325-7051 or 800/687-7733; website: www.silverlegacyreno.com.

The Spa at Harrah's Reno

This major hotel on the Strip offers a complex of health, spa and beauty services. Within the health club, which has exercise machines, the spa has a menu that isn't quite as exotic or extensive as other resort spas in the region, but it includes basic massage, deep tissue massage, and a half-dozen aromatherapy massages. Hours of operation: 6 A.M.–8 P.M. daily.

Contact: Harrah's Reno, 219 N. Center St., Reno, NV 89501; 775/786-3232 or 800/427-7247; website: www.harrahsreno.com.

Winter Recreation

Alpine Skiing

No mountain region in North America can offer the profusion of ski resorts and lifts that encircle Lake Tahoe, and nowhere in the world will skiers find as much variety within an hour's drive of wherever they're staying. When you add up the chairlifts, gondolas, and trams—more than 135 at last count—it's hard to find a comparable destination. No fewer than 16 resorts, some of them of international caliber, grace the snowy peaks of this region. And when it comes to après-ski life, Tahoe is all aces, thanks to the proximity of major casinos and their year-round roster of big-name acts and Broadway-style entertainment. Tahoe wins the aesthetics award as well, with a huge

lake that never freezes in winter and million-dollar views from every corner of the basin. Not surprisingly, Lake Tahoe has become popular with skiers from Europe and Japan, as well as from all over the United States.

Tahoe historically gets more snow than the Rocky Mountains. Typically, Sierra snow has a higher moisture content than that of the Rockies, and more of it falls at one time than almost anywhere else in the interior of the United States (the only exceptions are Snowbird and Alta in Utah). Two- to four-foot dumps are not uncommon, and these create an excellent base for skiing. But the white stuff does not fall uniformly

skiing at Heavenly

COURTESY OF HEAVENLY SKI RESORT

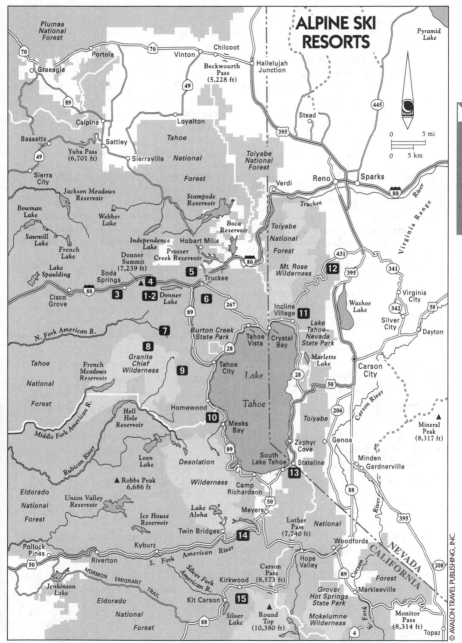

ALPINE SKI RESORTS

ALPINE SKIING

around the basin. Ski areas closest to the water, such as Heavenly and Diamond Peak, tend to experience warmer climates, which can affect the storm track. But both resorts have more than compensated for these conditions by installing extensive snowmaking systems. Few will argue that the true snowbelt is Donner Summit, often described as the snowiest place in America (with an average of 500-plus inches a year).

Storms rake the peaks of the summit with a fury, and areas such as Sugar Bowl, Donner Ski Ranch, and Boreal reap the benefits. Weather-predicting is no easy task in the Sierra, and it's possible to have a blizzard sitting on Donner Summit while the South Shore is clear and dry. The lake and its environs are a collection of microclimates, so there's always varying snow depths and conditions. During storms, strong winds can shut down the highest peaks and ridges, or clouds can create dense whiteouts. Happily, there's always a port in the storm—lower-elevation resorts tucked in the forest that offer protected skiing.

Soon, there will be more than ample snow and spectacular scenery to attract skiers. Three

SKI, WEATHER, AND ROAD INFORMATION SOURCES

Ski Reports
The following services provide recorded telephone reports on Lake Tahoe ski conditions:

California State Automobile Association Ski Report Hot Line: 415/864-6440.

City Line, a service of the *San Francisco Chronicle,* has specific ski reports, updated daily by Tahoe ski areas and the National Weather Service. Call 415/512-5000 and enter one of the following numbers:

• Alpine Meadows Ski Area, 6411
• Boreal Ski Resort/Soda Springs, 6413
• Diamond Peak Ski Resort, 6426
• Donner Ski Ranch, 6415
• Heavenly Ski Resort, 6416
• Kirkwood, 6419
• Mount Rose, 6421
• Northstar-at-Tahoe, 6423
• Sierra-at-Tahoe, 6424
• Squaw Valley, 6427
• Sugar Bowl, 6429
• Tahoe Donner, 6429

Weather Reports
For weather reports updated daily by the National Weather Service, call the *San Francisco Chronicle's* City Line at 415/512-5000 and enter 3140 for weather conditions in the Sierra.

Websites
Several websites offer up-to-date information, in-cluding same-time photo images from strategically placed weather cams. Some ski areas have websites that show current ski and weather conditions (see listings for each resort in this chapter). In addition to these, you might look in on the following:

• North Lake Tahoe Resort Association:
  www.tahoefun.org
• Lake Tahoe Visitors Authority (South Lake Tahoe): www.virtualtahoe.com
• Reno-Sparks Convention and Visitors Authority: renolaketahoe.com
• Ski Lake Tahoe: skilaketahoe.com
  (association of six major resorts)
• Lake Tahoe News Network: www.tahoe.com
  (includes weather forecasts and local news compiled by newspapers in the Tahoe area)
• *Ski* and *Skiing* magazines: www.skinet.com
• AMI News: www.aminews.com
  (resort and recreation site)
• Resort Cam Sneak Peek:
  www.rsn.com/cams/tahoe
  (includes live weather cam view of Lake Tahoe)
• Lake Tahoe Weather:
  www.yaws.com/tahoe/tweathr.shtml

Road Conditions
Call 530/445-1534 or 800/427-7623 for updated highway conditions in California, and 775/793-1313 for Nevada.

completely new alpine villages have opened, and a fourth is in pre-construction phases. At Kirkwood, a new mountain village with a plaza opened for the winter of 1999–2000, giving this high-elevation resort more lodging, dining and shopping options. More buildings have been added since then, along with a new ice-skating rink and swimming center. At South Lake Tahoe, Heavenly's new base area next to the Highway 50 gondola kicked off the 2002–03 winter with the opening of two Marriott hotels—the Grand Residence Club and the Timber Lodge—that form the anchors for a pedestrian village. Ground-level tenants include new restaurants and shops, and more are on the way. This provides many more options for skiers who stay in and around Stateline, where most of the hotels are. At Squaw Valley, Intrawest, the company that owns Whistler in Canada, opened the first phase of the Village at Squaw Valley in early 2002, with new condominiums, restaurants and shops across from the Cable Car building, and much more to come over the next few years. Finally, Northstar-at-Tahoe and East West Partners of Colorado are moving ahead with plans to remove much of the old village and replace it with a substantially larger one.

First-time visitors to Lake Tahoe find it difficult to grasp the distances around the basin. From one end of the lake to the other, it's 22 miles—easily a 45- to 60-minute drive. There is good public transportation within South Tahoe and most of the North Shore, but not much linking them. On weekends, the narrow two-lane roads and resort parking lots can be jammed, and it's best to take buses and shuttles where they are available. Skiers staying at the South Tahoe hotels and motels have the best network of transportation—a luxury coach

When you add up the chairlifts, gondolas, and trams—more than 135 at last count—it's hard to find a comparable destination. No fewer than 16 resorts, some of them of international caliber, grace the snowy peaks of this region. And when it comes to après-ski life, Tahoe is all aces, thanks to the proximity of major casinos and their year-round roster of big-name acts and Broadway-style entertainment. Tahoe wins the aesthetics award as well.

that runs between Stateline and Reno-Tahoe International Airport 16 times a day, and frequent free or low-cost shuttles to Heavenly, Sierra-at-Tahoe, and Kirkwood. There's also a daily shuttle to the Squaw Valley (reservations are required) and high-speed ferryboat service by Lake Tahoe Cruises from South Lake Tahoe to the North Shore. Also on the North Shore, the Tahoe Area Regional Transit system (TART) and ski area buses serve most of the region, with pickup points at numerous locations. From Reno, daily buses serve major North Shore resorts, and the savings in staying in a less pricey room may justify that expense.

For the greatest mobility, you may want to get a rental car. Having your own wheels also helps when dining out, shopping, or sightseeing, especially on the North Shore. But be aware that driving can be hazardous on icy roads, and chains or four-wheel-drive vehicles may be required during snowstorms. Sometime, perhaps in the not-so-distant future, Tahoe will have a regional transportation system that will help eliminate the traffic jams, pollution, and hassles of winter driving.

There are three tiers of ski resorts in the region: the big names (Squaw Valley, Heavenly, Alpine, and Kirkwood); the big areas with less fame but no less enjoyable terrain (Sierra-at-Tahoe, Northstar-at-Tahoe, Sugar Bowl, Diamond Peak, Mt. Rose, and Homewood); and finally the self-proclaimed "family" resorts with less daunting slopes (Boreal, Donner Ski Ranch, Granlibakken, Soda Springs, and Tahoe Donner). For beginners and lower intermediates, the smaller resorts provide less intimidating environments as well as individualized attention.

For intermediates, some of the best slopes and base amenities are at the middle group of ski areas. The beauty of spending a ski week in Tahoe is the opportunity to sample several resorts, and various packages, such as one offered by the North Lake Tahoe Resort Association, include a discounted interchangeable lift ticket that is valid at multiple locations.

Variety is really the hallmark of Lake Tahoe skiing. There is every type of terrain imaginable, from open bowls to intimate forests. Because of slope configurations and the complexity of Sierra mountains, runs tend to be narrower than in the Rockies, and there are more traverses and access trails. But grooming is practiced with near fanaticism, and ski areas know how to make the most of their snow cover and conditions. The couloirs, gullies, and chutes are welcomed by snowboarders, who have more natural half-pipes in Tahoe than anyplace else in the country.

One of the great pleasures of skiing at Lake Tahoe is that when the lifts close, the action doesn't stop. Fine restaurants, nightclubs, casino showrooms, and 24-hour gaming can entertain even the most hopeless insomniac. And if you just want to relax, there's always a spa or hot springs close by.

Unless otherwise indicated, the fees listed in this chapter are based on the 2002–03 ski season. Prices are subject to change.

Alpine Resorts

TRUCKEE/DONNER

Sugar Bowl (see map on page 311, site 1)
Built in 1939, this resort has retained its Old World charm while undergoing a major facelift in recent years. Recent additions include a terrific new mountain, Judah, which opened in the winter of 1994–95. This peak, sporting four quad chairs, more than 20 mostly intermediate runs, and a separate base lodge, is one of the finest terrain additions in the Lake Tahoe area. It provides quite a modern contrast to the original base area, which is accessible only by gondola or chairlift and has an aristocratic, Tyrolean ambience. It's no coincidence that the inspiration for its design, along with the first ski school director (the noted Hanness Schroll), was Austrian.

Sugar Bowl was once the playground of the rich and famous, among them Walt Disney, who was an early investor, actor Errol Flynn, and many of the social and business leaders of San Francisco (who still own it). The Sugar Bowl Lodge, in a rambling, wood-frame building, offers 28 rooms (almost always booked throughout the season) and one of the best gourmet restaurants in the region. Access to the base area used to be exclusively by the Magic Carpet gondola (the first gondola built in the United States) from the parking lot, but now with a second base area

at Mt. Judah, skiers can drive directly to the slopes. Receiving an average of 500 inches of snow per year, Sugar Bowl has a reputation as the snowiest ski resort in Tahoe—smack in the middle of the Donner Summit—allowing for early and late season skiing on natural snow. In the winter of 1999–2000, Sugar Bowl replaced its oldest ski lift—Disney, which was the first chairlift built in Northern California—with a new high-speed quad. And in 2001, the ski area replaced the old Mt. Lincoln Chair with a new express quad.

Sugar Bowl has four mountain faces, dominated by Mt. Lincoln (elevation 8,383 feet) and Mt. Disney (7,953 feet). Most of the runs from these peaks are advanced to expert, and there are some narrow chutes and gullies that create natural half-pipes for snowboarders, who are much in evidence. Most of the intermediate runs are on the west side of Disney, the east side of Lincoln, and much of Mt. Judah. Judah has become popular with cruising skiers due to its tree-lined runs and scenic vistas of Donner Pass and Castle Peak.

Lifts: One access gondola, one access double chair, seven quad chairs (four of them high-speed), two double chairs and two surface lifts.
Vertical descent: 1,500 feet.
Terrain: 1,500 acres, 84 runs (longest, three miles). Base elevation: 6,883 feet; summit: 8,383

feet. Beginner, 17 percent; intermediate, 45 percent; advanced, 38 percent. Snowmaking covers 300 acres.

Lift ticket prices: Adults (22–59), $54; young adults (13–21). $42; children (6–12), $13 (five and under, free); seniors (60–69), $30 (70 and over, free). Half-day rates (12:30 P.M.–4 P.M.), adults, $40. The ski area will issue a credit voucher for an early departure, before 12:30 P.M., worth $16 toward the purchase of another all-day adult ticket.

Strategy for skiing the mountain: Parking is limited at the Magic Carpet base but is more readily available at the new Mt. Judah slopeside parking lot. If you are staying in Truckee, you can take a shuttle bus up the back side of Old Highway 40, past Donner Lake, to the Judah base area. Warm up on Christmas Tree Ridge (where most of the beginner and lower intermediate runs are), then tackle Disney, Lincoln, and Judah. Crow's Nest off Mt. Disney has some of the least crowded intermediate runs, with best snow conditions before midday. Lincoln and Judah have good north-facing runs that hold powder well into the afternoon. If you want to avoid lines at the gondola by day's end, either leave early or park at Judah.

Best beginner runs: Pioneer Trail, Pine Marten and Sleigh Ride.

Best intermediate runs: Trailblazer, Sunset Boulevard, Coldstream, Crowley's Run (formerly Lake View) and Upper and Lower MacTavish.

Best expert runs: Bacon's Gully, Silver Belt and Sugar Bowl. Hard-core double-diamond runs include The Palisades and Fuller's Folly.

Restaurants/bars: Cafeteria, café, mid-mountain café, outdoor barbecues, hotel dining room, three bars.

Equipment rental: Standard and high-performance/demo packages (skis, boots, poles) and snowboards are available.

Instruction: Group lessons, $70 for adults and $60 for young adults including two hours of instruction and all-mountain lift ticket. Private lessons, $70 per hour ($20 for each additional person).

Transportation: A free daily shuttle runs hourly from Truckee.

Day care: Licensed program for ages 3–6, all-day or half-day.

Snowboarding: A terrain park off the Easy Rider run on Mt. Judah has natural hits, swales, and bowls. A man-made halfpipe is at the bottom of the Mt. Lincoln Chair, and many areas of the mountain provide natural half-pipes.

Special programs/camps: Discounted first-timers package, junior racing program, masters race training and advanced skier development. Kids 6–12 can participate in an all-day Summit Adventure Camp, which includes lunch and all-day lesson.

Major events of the season: New Year's Eve Party and Fireworks and Tiki Cup (luau on the snow in April).

Other services: A 28-room hotel, fine-dining restaurant, ski shops, rental shops, child-care center and lockers at The Village base area, plus the new Main Lodge at the Mt. Judah base area with ticketing, rental/retail shop, Mountain Sports Learning Center, cafeteria and bar. In 2001, the Main Lodge was expanded to accommodate another 200 people.

Location: On Old Highway 40 off I-80 at the Soda Springs/Norden exit, 10 miles west of Truckee.

Contact: Sugar Bowl, P.O. Box 5, Norden, CA 95724; 530/426-9000, Snowphone (snow conditions) 530/426-1111; website: www.sugar-bowl.com.

Donner Ski Ranch
(see map on page 311, site 2)

The most affordable adult lift ticket in the Truckee/Tahoe area combined with the dependable natural snowfall on Donner Summit make this one of the great ski values of the region. It's a low-key place—with fixed-grip chairlifts and a rustic day lodge—but that's fine with Donner's loyal clientele. And there are 400 acres of terrain out there, although not much is immediately visible from the entrance. An inspiring view of Donner Lake to the east is found off the top of Chair 1, but the majority of cruisin' stuff is on the back side, a tranquil valley full of lovely, gladed ski runs. There are no flats to pole over, and while most of the runs are around one-half mile in length, lift lines are short and there is amazing variety. The ski area allows snowboarding without restriction.

Lifts: One triple, five doubles.

Vertical descent: 750 feet.

Terrain: 460 acres, 45 runs (longest, 1.2 miles). Base elevation: 7,031 feet; summit: 7,781 feet. Beginner, 25 percent; intermediate, 50 percent; advanced, 25 percent. Snowmaking coverage on 15 percent of the terrain.

Lift ticket prices: Weekends and holidays: Adults, $20; children, $10; seniors, $5. Midweek, nonholiday: Adults, $10; children, $10; seniors, $5.

Strategy for skiing the mountain: Don't let the steep face under Chair 1 scare you; first warm up on the South Trail, then take the scenic North Trail for the eagle's view of Donner Lake and surroundings from Mt. King (elevation 7,851 feet) and gradually work your way to the back side, skiing chairs 3, 2, and 5, in that order. If morning conditions are icy, head immediately to Chair 5, which faces south and softens first. Most intermediate skiers prefer Chair 3 for its sense of seclusion and idyllic, forested environment.

Best beginner run: BJ's Road.

Best intermediate run: Lyla's.

Best expert run: The Face.

Restaurants/bars: Old Highway 40 Restaurant/Bar, a cafeteria (breakfast, lunch, dinner, snacks), Ranch Bar.

Equipment rental: Standard and high-performance/demo packages (skis, boots, poles) and snowboards are available.

Instruction: Group lessons for adults and children, $14. Private lessons, $40.

Transportation: None.

Day care: None.

Snowboarding: Unlimited mountain access.

Special programs/camps: Mountain Sports School for age six and older, $30 for skiing and $40 for snowboarding; adults, $45 for skiing and $49 for snowboarding. Prices include rentals, lesson and unrestricted lift ticket.

Other services: Ski shop (accessories, souvenirs, ski and snowboard maintenance and repairs), lockers, and condos.

Location: Ten miles west of Truckee at Donner Summit. From I-80, take the Soda Springs/Norden exit.

Contact: Donner Ski Ranch, P.O. Box 66, Norden, CA 95724; 530/426-3635; website: www.donnerskiranch.com.

Soda Springs

(see map on page 311, site 3)

One of the first ski areas in the Tahoe region, Soda Springs is operated by the same management staff as at neighboring Boreal. Both resorts (along with Alpine Meadows, Mt. Bachelor, Oregon, and Park City, Utah) belong to the Powdr Corporation of Salt Lake City. Soda Springs, which is open daily through Easter, is on Donner Summit, just a quick exit off I-80. It's a good venue for beginners, or for intermediates looking to get in a half-day of skiing. The vertical is almost the same as at Boreal. All intermediate to advanced runs are off the Crystal triple chair, and all beginner runs are off the Lion's Head double. The area also has lift-served inner tubing (two surface tows that hook on to the tubes and pull riders up the mountain); a new snowshoeing area with trails and rentals; and a sledding hill for sleds and saucers.

Lifts: One triple midway stop, one double.

Vertical descent: 652 feet.

Terrain: 200 acres, 16 runs (longest, one mile). Base elevation: 6,700 feet; summit: 7,352 feet. Beginner, 30 percent; intermediate, 50 percent; advanced, 20 percent. Snowmaking coverage on 30 acres.

Lift ticket prices: Tickets are $22 for adults (over 18), $16 for youth (ages 8–17) and $10 for children (under 7). A two-hour tubing ticket is $14.

Strategy for skiing the mountain: You don't need one—this is the best place for uncrowded skiing on busy or holiday weekends.

Best beginner run: Sunshine.

Best intermediate run: Meadow.

Best expert run: Mad Dog.

Restaurants/bars: Cafeteria (breakfast, lunch, dinner).

Equipment rental: Standard and performance ski and snowboard packages; snowshoes; sleds and saucers.

Instruction: Beginning ski or snowboard packages include equipment rental, 90-minute group lesson, and lift ticket for $50. An intermediate to advanced group lesson for 90 minutes is $28. Private one-on-one lesson with children (ages four and up) or parent and child is $32, including child's all-day lift ticket, rental equipment and one hour private ski or snowboard lesson.

Transportation: None.

Day care: None.

Snowboarding: Facilities include a terrain park and Kids X Park.

Special programs/camps: Racing program for high schools and clubs.

Major events of the season: Announced each year.

Other services: Lockers, ski check and a retail ski/board shop.

Location: One mile off I-80 on Highway 40 at the Soda Springs/Norden exit, 13 miles west of Truckee.

Contact: Soda Springs, P.O. Box 39, Truckee, CA 96160; 530/426-3666, lodging reservations 530/426-1012; website:www.skisodasprings.com.

Boreal Ski Resort
(see map on page 311, site 4)

There isn't much elevation here, and what you see from the freeway is mainly what you get: short, fall-line runs from the ridge. But what you don't see is the back side, where many skiers have made pleasant discoveries. Boreal's assets consist of quick access from the highway, a snowmaking system that usually enables it to claim the earliest opening date (around mid-October), high elevation, consistent snowfall, and popularity with snowboarders and beginning skiers. The resort is spread out lengthwise, with most of the tree-lined runs at opposite ends. Several short but steep runs are in the drainage between the Accelerator and 49er chairlifts. The large day lodge is well positioned for nonskiing parents to watch the progress of their children on easy slopes off the Gunnar's and Claim Jumper lifts. Vans Terrain Park, with jumps and obstacles for snowboarders, is off the 49er Chairlift, and the resort, an early proponent of the sport, offers a myriad of boarding programs. This and other terrain gardens are open to both snowboarders and skiers. When you're not busy skiing, check out the ski museum next to the parking lot; it contains fascinating memorabilia and photographs of skiing's long history at Lake Tahoe. By the way, the food here is good and reasonably priced, and includes conveniences such as a salad bar.

Lifts: Two quads (one high-speed detachable), three triples, four doubles.

Vertical descent: 500 feet.

Terrain: 380 acres, 41 runs (longest, one mile). Base elevation: 7,200 feet; summit: 7,700 feet. Beginner, 30 percent; intermediate, 55 percent; advanced, 15 percent. Snowmaking coverage on 200 acres.

Lift ticket prices: Adult all-day is $35, valid every day 9 A.M.–9 P.M. (includes night skiing); children (5–12) and seniors (60–69), $10; adult night (valid 3:30 P.M.–9 P.M.), $20; children (5-12), $10; and seniors, $14. Note: A shared one-day ticket is available for parents.

Strategy for skiing the mountain: If you're not on a learning curve, stay away from the slopes fronting the day lodge, which are filled with novice skiers and snowboarders. Less crowded spots are at opposite ends of the area and on the back side. Take the Accelerator Quad lift to the top and work your way to one of these areas. You'll find few skiers on the Cedar Ridge and Lost Dutchman triples. If snowpack is ample (or if conditions are a little icy), try the Quicksilver Quad on the back side.

Best beginner run: Sunset Boulevard, which is also the longest run at Boreal (one mile) and its most scenic, winding down from the top of the ridge.

Best intermediate run: Central Pacific.

Best expert run: Waterfall, on the front side of the mountain.

Restaurants/bars: A cafeteria (breakfast, lunch, dinner), Sundeck BBQ, and a bar overlooking the mountain.

Equipment rental: Standard and high-performance ski packages and snowboard packages are available 9 A.M.–9 P.M.

Instruction: 13/4-hour group lessons, $28. Learn-to-ski and snowboard packages (lesson, lifts, and gear), $54 for adults and $48 for children 8–12. Kids Club (ages 4–10) has a ski and snowboard school, with all-day sessions (including lunch) costing $70 and half-day sessions, $55. One-hour private lessons are $62.

Transportation: None.

Day care: No licensed day care, but there is a nonsupervised Infant Care Area with couches, toys, changing tables, windows and a porch.

Snowboarding: Vans Terrain Park and the gentler Family Terrain Zone, for beginning snowboarders and skiers. Facilities include half-pipe, snow-skate park and nighttime terrain park.

Major events of the season: Numerous snowboard events.

Other services: Boreal Motel, slopeside lodging with 35 rooms; lockers; and a ski and snowboard retail shop.

Location: Ten miles west of Truckee at Donner Summit. From I-80, take the Boreal/Castle Peak exit.

Contact: Boreal Mountain Resort, P.O. Box 39, Truckee, CA 96160; 530/426-3666 or 530/426-1012 (lodging); website: www.rideboreal.com.

Tahoe Donner
(see map on page 311, site 5)
This is a small resort with one large, open ski bowl and two chairlifts, in the Tahoe Donner residential resort community above Truckee. Since it is primarily a learn-to-ski area, there isn't much for strong intermediates or advanced skiers. The terrain has scant tree cover and not much variation. Still, beginners will find lots of economical lift-and-lesson deals.

Lifts: One quad chair, one double, one surface lift.

Vertical descent: 600 feet.

Terrain: 120 acres, 13 runs (longest, one mile). Base elevation: 6,750 feet; summit: 7,350 feet. Beginner, 40 percent; intermediate, 60 percent. No snowmaking.

Lift ticket prices: Adults, $26; children (7–12) and seniors (55–69), $12. Seniors 70 and over and children six and under accompanied by an adult ski free.

Strategy for skiing the mountain: This is a good, uncrowded area for families with small children. The layout is obvious and easy.

Best beginner run: Mile Trail.

Best intermediate run: Race Course.

Best expert run: Skip's Plunge (the only expert run).

Restaurants/bars: Cafe, and a restaurant at the clubhouse.

Equipment rental: Standard packages (skis, boots, poles) are available.

Instruction: 90-minute group lessons for adults and children seven and older, $26. Private lessons (one hour), $55.

Transportation: 800/CAL-TRANS (800/225-8726) or the Truckee-Donner Chamber of Commerce, 530/587-2757.

Day care: None.

Snowboarding: There are several rail-slides.

Special programs/camps: First-time ski lesson package includes 90-minute group lesson, ski and boot rental, and all-day lift ticket for the Snowbird beginner chair only, $40 for adults, $35 for children 7–12. First-time snowboard package, with same components, is $55 for adults, $50 for children 7–12. Snowflakes children's ski school (ages 3–6) includes a 30-minute lesson for $42.

Other services: Retail ski shop, short lockers, tall lockers, and rental shop with shaped skis, telemark skis, and step-in snowboards.

Location: Five miles up Northwoods Boulevard from Donner Pass Road, or take Aldercreek Road to Northwoods, also five miles. From eastbound I-80, take the first exit in Truckee, which is Donner Pass Road.

Contact: Tahoe Donner, 11509 Northwoods Blvd., Truckee, CA 96161; 530/587-9444; website: www.tahoedonner.com.

Northstar-at-Tahoe
(see map on page 311, site 6)
A complete year-round resort, Northstar is one of Tahoe's most popular intermediate mountains, with meticulously groomed runs in an intimate, secluded forest environment. Its well-designed layout has ego-building lower intermediate and beginner runs on the front side,

and advanced intermediate and expert runs on the back side, and recently opened expert terrain on a new mountain face—Lookout Mountain. This was the first ski area in Tahoe with a "village," and was one of the few ski-in, ski-out overnight lodging complexes.

Most skiing begins a third of the way up the mountain, at a day lodge that is reached via gondola or chairlift. Beginner runs are concentrated on the lower mountain, with a long, flat road back to the village. The majority of expert runs off the front face of Mt. Pluto (elevation 8,610 feet) are short and steep, while those on the back are longer and more varied. Steep, expert runs on Lookout Mountain can be accessed via the newly installed Lookout Mountain high-speed quad. Cruising terrain is the mainstay on the front side, with scenic runs off West Ridge providing views of the Martis Valley and Truckee. The back side consists of long, fall-line runs on advanced intermediate terrain (even though the trails are marked black diamonds) and tree skiing in fresh powder. For the real hairball stuff, Lookout Mountain is the ticket; it offers steep mogul runs, tree-skiing and ungroomed powder (along with a few groomed runs, as well).

Because of its wind-protected location and dense forest, Northstar is one of the best foul-weather ski venues in North Tahoe. The main day lodge offers typical skier's fare, but the mountaintop Summit Deck and Grill provides gourmet Southwestern cuisine (including the finest salsa in Tahoe). And with the recent addition of 200 more indoor seats, skiers can now take a break here even during inclement weather. You'll find good restaurants in the village (try Timbercreek for dinner and Pedro's Pizza for lunch or dinner). Among Northstar's attributes are one of the country's best instructional programs for youngsters. For techno-weenies, the ski area pioneered Vertical Plus, an electronic lift pass that calculates vertical feet skied.

Lifts: Six-passenger high-speed gondola, five express quads, two triples, two doubles, two Magic Carpets, two surface lifts.

Vertical descent: 2,280 feet.

Terrain: 2,420 acres, 63 runs (longest, 2.9 miles). Base elevation: 6,330 feet; summit: 8,610 feet. Beginner, 25 percent; intermediate, 50 percent; advanced, 25 percent. Snowmaking coverage on 50 percent of runs (200 acres) served by eight lifts. 220 acres of off-piste terrain on the backside of Mt. Pluto for advanced to experts only.

Lift ticket prices: Adults (ages 23 to 59), $57; young adults (13 to 22), $47; children (5–12), $19 (under 5, free); seniors (60 to 69), $33; seniors (70 and over), $10. Adult/young adult afternoon lift ticket (after 12:30 P.M.), $45/$41; child afternoon, $16.

Strategy for skiing the mountain: With long lines forming at the gondola and access chair at the village, weekend skiers should go early or late in the day. Intermediates should stay clear of the congested mid-mountain area around Main Street, filled with beginners and converging skiers. The best skiing is on the back side early in the morning, before the crowds arrive. Trails on the east side, including Logger's Loop, Sunshine, and Sidewinder, seem to get the least use most times of the day. Because of Northstar's popularity, the parking lots can fill quickly and lift sales are halted when the mountain reaches capacity on weekends and holidays. If you're not staying there, go early and have breakfast.

Best beginner run: Village.

Best intermediate runs: Isolated and uncrowded Logger's Loop on the front side, West Ridge/Iron Horse (advanced intermediate) on the back side.

Best expert run: Any of the five runs on Lookout Mountain.

Restaurants/bars: In the village: Timbercreek (fine dining with steaks, poultry, seafood), Pedro's Pizza and Village Food Company (gourmet deli items, espresso). On the mountain: The Lodge at Big Springs (breakfast, lunch, barbecue and weekend dinners), Summit Deck and Grille (mountaintop restaurant with both indoor and outdoor seating).

Equipment rental: Standard and high-performance/demo packages (skis, boots, poles) and snowboards are available at mid-mountain and in the Village.

ALPINE SKIING

Instruction: Free lessons daily for advanced intermediate and above, ages 13-plus. Adult First Time Package (skiing or snowboarding) with one hour, 45-minute group lesson, $69. Starkids (ages 5–12), full-day program with lunch, $84. Private lessons offered for adults and children.

Transportation: Free daily ski-area shuttle service is available (December–March) between Northstar, Tahoe Vista, Kings Beach, Incline Village, and Truckee. Call 530/562-2257 for the Northstar schedule. Northstar's ski shuttle connects to TART public buses for skiers from the West Shore and Tahoe City.

Day care: At Minors' Camp, for toilet-trained children ages 2–6. Reservations recommended, at 530/562-2278.

Snowboarding: Allowed throughout the resort. Widest variety of terrain and the biggest halfpipe is at Snowbomb.com Terrain Park, off the Pioneer Chair. For riders, there's an on-mountain hangout at the Snowbomb.com Park, with snacks, music, and videos.

Special programs/camps: Vertical Plus frequent skier/rider program that offers electronic ticketing, members' only lift lines and discounts, interchangeable with sister resort Sierra-at-Tahoe. Polaris Park, an evening adventure park at mid-mountain, featuring boarding, tubing, snowtoys, skiing and entertainment for the entire family, open Friday, Saturday, and holiday evenings.

Other services: Village Mall: general store, ski/snowboard rental shop, repair shop, souvenir/gift store, gas station, recreation center (outdoor spas, saunas, exercise/arcade room); overnight ski storage; ski and basket check; mountain photos; sleigh rides; cross-country trails, snowmobile tours, and transport gondola.

Location: Off Highway 267, six miles south of Truckee.

Contact: Northstar-at-Tahoe, P.O. Box 129, Truckee, CA 96160; 530/562-1010, Snowphone 530/562-1330, reservations: 800/GO-NORTH (800/466-6784); website: www.northstarattahoe.com.

SQUAW VALLEY
Squaw Valley USA
(see map on page 311, site 7)

Spread out over six impressive peaks, this former Winter Olympics site is one of the world's top ski areas, with a reputation based on hairball runs and a profusion of Olympic-caliber skiers. This is the most insistently European-style layout in Tahoe, with the majority of the runs above tree line in vast, naked bowls. There is a plethora of nooks and crannies to challenge skiers with nerves (and legs) of steel: cornices, steep faces, endless mogul fields, and couloirs. Steep peaks rise abruptly from the valley floor, and an ascent in the tram over the sheer wall and jagged rocks of Broken Arrow (elevation 8,020 feet) is a thrill unto itself. Squaw has some new and impressive lifts, including a Funitel (gondola-type lift) and three high-speed six-passenger detachable chairs. And it has the beginnings of what will be a world-class village. During the 2002–03 season, Intrawest, the owner of Whistler in Canada, completed the first phase of a $250 million, 13-acre alpine village at the base of the ski area. And, at this writing, the second phase was nearing completion. Now, Squaw Valley has deluxe new condominiums, new restaurants (try Balboa's across from the Cable Car Building!) and stores, along with plazas and meandering walkways that are reminiscent of European hamlets.

> *Spread out over six impressive peaks, the former Winter Olympics site of Squaw Valley is one of the world's top ski areas, with a reputation based on hairball runs and a profusion of Olympic-caliber skiers. This is the most insistently European-style layout in Tahoe, with the majority of the runs above tree line in vast, naked bowls.*

The resort is divided into three sections: the lower mountain (elevation 6,200 feet); the upper mountain (mid-elevation of 8,200 feet); and Snow King (elevation 7,550 feet), on the east side next to the Resort at Squaw Creek. The most challenging runs are chairlifts that originate at the lower mountain and reach points such as KT-22 (elevation 8,200 feet), so named because Sandy Poulsen, the wife of Wayne Poulsen (who co-founded the ski area with Alex Cushing), required 22 kick turns to get down the first time she skied the peak. The best beginner and lower intermediate skiing is on the upper mountain, though runs there are short by Tahoe standards.

With its dearth of trees and a high exposure, this area is subject to powerful winds and whiteouts during inclement weather, making it easy for skiers to become disoriented. The most protected skiing is off Snow King, which is largely in the trees and has longer intermediate runs. In general, there are frequent terrain changes with bumps, undulations, drops, and gullies throughout the ski area. Intermediate skiers may find that a lot of runs are either too boring or too difficult. Squaw Valley has reasonably priced restaurants and creative food throughout its lift system, and a delightful sit-down restaurant at scenic (and windy) High Camp, which is also the location of an ice skating rink and an outdoor heated pool and Jacuzzi, which open in March during spring skiing.

Lifts: 110-passenger aerial cable car, Funitel/gondola, pulse lift, five quads, three six-pacs, eight triples, eight doubles, three Pony tows, one Magic Carpet.

Vertical descent: 2,850 feet.

Terrain: 4,000 acres, six peaks (longest run, three miles). Base elevation: 6,200 feet; summit: 9,050 feet. Beginner, 25 percent; intermediate, 45 percent; advanced, 30 percent. Snowmaking covers 400 acres.

Lift ticket prices: Adults, $58; teens (13-15) and seniors (65-75), $28; children (12 and under), $5. Night skiing is free with all lift tickets.

Strategy for skiing the mountain: With the new funitel and overall increased uphill lift capacity, there is rarely a wait for the Cable Car, though there are other ways to reach the top. For intermediate and advanced skiers, one tip is to ride the Squaw One Express Chair from the base. This chair unloads close to the Siberia Express and other upper mountain lifts. As for the enclosed conveyances, the Funitel reaches the Gold Coast Lodge, while the Cable Car reaches the High Camp Lodge; both are at 8,200 feet elevation. Another option is to make your warm-up runs off the Red Dog and Squaw Creek chairs, then work your way over to the upper mountain. If you come early and reach the top without a long wait, head immediately for the Shirley Lake and Solitude lifts, which have the most protected snow. By late morning, Siberia Bowl and Emigrant soften and offer good skiing. On weekends the worst congestion is at Gold Coast and Shirley Lake. At the end of the day, downloading on the funitel or cable car may be preferable to skiing the Mountain Run, which is something of a zoo. For advanced and expert skiers, some of the resort's hidden treasures are off these chairs: Olympic Lady, Silverado, and Granite Chief.

Best beginner runs: Riviera, East Broadway (at elevation 8,200 feet).

Best intermediate runs: Shirley Lake, Emigrant, Red Dog.

Best expert runs: Headwall, Cornice II, West Face of KT-22.

Restaurants/bars: On the upper mountain: High Camp Bath and Tennis Club, Alexander's, Poolside Bar and Grill, Terrace Bar and Grill, Oyster Bar. At the base, the Olympic Plaza offers a variety of restaurants, snack stands and bars.

Equipment rental: Standard and high-performance/demo packages (skis, boots, poles), snowboards, telemark gear and helmets are available.

Instruction: Group ski and snowboard lessons, $42. Private lessons, $85 per hour. First-time beginning skier or snowboarder package, $69 (includes rentals, two-hour lesson and beginner lift ticket).

Transportation: Squaw Valley ski shuttles are available from the north, south, and west shores of Lake Tahoe, as well as from Reno. Reservations are required 12 hours in advance, and the longest trip, from the South Shore, takes 90 minutes. call 530/581-7181 for the north and west shores, and 530/542-5930 for South Shore. Also, a free shuttle operates for skiers daily from the Resort at Squaw Creek; call 530/426-3651 or 530/583-6985 for information. Gray Line Tours operates daily ski shuttle service (December–April) from downtown Reno casino/hotels (a 42-mile trip); call 775/331-1147 or 800/822-6009. For information on high-speed ferryboat water shuttle from the South Shore, contact Lake Tahoe Cruises at 530/541-3364 or 800/238-2463.

Day care: Toddler care for children 2–5 years is available at Squaw Kids Children's Center, a 12,000-square-foot center that has a separate drop-off area apart from the day lodge. Rates are $82 per child for a full-day program, and include supervised play and lunch. No infant care is available. Reservations are required, at 530/581-7166.

Snowboarding: Riviera Half-Pipe and All-Terrain Park, open 9 A.M.–9 P.M. daily, and Mainline Terrain Park with a Superpipe, open 9 A.M.–4 P.M. daily.

Special programs/camps: Squaw Kids Children's Center (ages 4–12): $82 (lift, lesson, lunch; rentals are $15 extra). For first-time skiers or snowboarders, the Fun in the Sun Adventure Package (includes ticket, lesson and equipment) is $69. "Just For Women"—a series of three- and five-day clinics taught by women for women—is scheduled throughout the season, with prices ranging $455–585. The ski school also holds special half-day telemark skiing and snowboarding clinics.

Other services: High Camp Bath and Tennis Club: an Olympic-sized ice skating rink, a heated swimming lagoon (spring and summer only), a Jacuzzi spa, a snowtubing zone, tennis courts, a climbing wall, retail shops, half-pipe and terrain parks, snowboard park, several restaurants and bars, lockers and overnight ski check service. In the valley, winter sleigh rides, cross-country skiing, dogsled tours and snowshoeing are available.

Location: Off Highway 89, six miles north of Tahoe City and 12 miles south of Truckee. From I-80, take the Truckee exit.

Contact: Squaw Valley USA, P.O. Box 2007, Olympic Valley, CA 96146; 888/SNOW-3-2-1 (888/766-9321), Snowphone 530/583-6955, central reservations 888/SNOW-3-2-1 (888/766-9321); website: www.squaw.com.

TAHOE CITY/WEST SHORE
Alpine Meadows Ski Area
(see map on page 311, site 8)

This is one of Tahoe's titans. Big bowls, powder chutes, open meadows, and scenic forest create a sizable and marvelously diverse playground for skiers of all abilities. Alpine's reputation for having the longest season in the region, typically

© KEN CASTLE

search and rescue dogs at Alpine Meadows

running until Memorial Day, is based on the huge catch-basin known as Alpine Bowl, which seems to stockpile snow in copious amounts when storms roll across Ward Peak (elevation 8,637 feet). Sherwood, the back bowl, is the most distant section of the resort; it offers sunny, east-facing slopes with open powder fields for intermediates and experts. From the top of the Summit Quad, skiers have a 360-degree panorama of the lake, the surrounding peaks, and Ward Valley, an area slated for future development. Alpine's philosophy is traditional, and the resort resists anything trendy, although it has now fully accepted snowboarding. Purists—the older crowd and the classic, proficient skiers—are the main clientele. The place has a European quality, with its steep slopes and vintage double chairlifts. It's worth noting that winds atop Ward Peak can be fierce during inclement weather.

Lifts: One six-passenger chair, one high-speed quad, four triples, five doubles, and three surface lifts.

Vertical descent: 1,802 feet.

Terrain: 2,100 acres, 100-plus runs (longest, 2.5 miles). Base elevation: 6,835 feet; summit, 8,637 feet. Beginner, 25 percent; intermediate, 40 percent; advanced, 35 percent. Snowmaking coverage on 185 acres.

Lift ticket prices: Adults, $56; teens, $42; children (12 and under), $10; children six and under, $6; seniors (65–69), $30 and 70-plus, $8. No half-day tickets.

Strategy for skiing the mountain: If there's fresh powder, head for Sherwood Bowl first thing to cut new tracks. Follow the sun to Alpine Bowl well before the early afternoon winds kick up. Scott Peak (elevation 8,289 feet) is a nice, protected slope for afternoon skiing, and there's a good view of the lake from the top.

Alpine Meadows Ski Area

© KEN CASTLE

ALPINE SKIING

Best beginner run: Subway.

Best intermediate runs: Kangaroo, Weasel, Lakeview.

Best expert runs: Scott Chute, Waterfall in Wolverine Bowl, Idiot's Delight, Keyhole.

Restaurants/bars: Cafeteria (burgers, salads, ethnic foods), Kealy's Alpine Bar, Treats (espresso, desserts), Chalet (mid-mountain chalet serving soups, sandwiches, desserts), and Compactor Bar (drinks, cocktails, big-screen TV).

Equipment rental: Super sidecut skis, Fatboys, standard and high-performance/demo and telemark packages (skis, boots, poles) are available. Also, there's a snowboard center with a selection of boards and boots.

Instruction: Beginner snowboard and ski packages (two-hour lesson, rental equipment and free use of beginner lifts) are $65. Intermediate and advanced skiing and snowboard packages are $93. Additional afternoon sessions are $20. Group lessons only are $36. Private lessons are $75 per hour, and semiprivates (2–4 people) are $120 per hour. Children's packages for separate groups of ages 4–6 and 7–12 are $85, including full day of instruction, equipment and lift pass.

Transportation: call 530/583-4232 for shuttle schedule. Resort shuttle connects with Tahoe Area Regional Transit (TART) buses at the base of Alpine Meadows Road; call 530/581-8225 for TART schedule. For information on high-speed boat shuttles from South Shore, contact Lake Tahoe Cruises at 530/541-3364 or 800/238-2463.

Day care: None.

Snowboarding: New Superpipe, with 17-foot walls, and Roo's Ride Terrain Park are accessible from Kangaroo Chair. Also, there are large untracked and ungroomed areas called Adventure Zones, which are off-piste destinations such as Estelle Bowl, High Traverse and Promised Land.

Special programs/camps: Women's Wintersports Camps, with multiday programs, ranging $493–538; five-day High Performance Clinic (no beginners), $688; Masters Ski Program for advanced skiers with racing and expert terrain

instruction, $780 to $1,940; two-day Snowboard Camp, $237.

Other services: ski and sports shop, Alpine Repair Shop, lockers, free ski corral, snowboard center, and overnight RV parking.

Location: Off Highway 89, south of Truckee and a few miles north of Tahoe City.

Contact: Alpine Meadows Ski Area, 2600 Alpine Meadows Rd./P.O. Box 5279, Tahoe City, CA 96145; 530/583-4232, Snowphone 530/581-8374, lodging 800/441-4423; website: www.skialpine.com.

Granlibakken Ski Resort
(see map on page 311, site 9)

The oldest ski area in the Lake Tahoe basin—named after a Norwegian word meaning "the hill sheltered by fir trees"—has one small, open hill and two runs geared mainly to beginners. Granlibakken was built in 1927 by Southern Pacific Railroad and the Tahoe Tavern Resort and historically was used as a site for Olympic ski jumpers. For three decades, Olympic tryouts were held here, along with the Junior National Jumping Championships. Famous jumpers who competed at Granlibakken include Roy Mikkelsen (1932 and 1936 Olympics) and Wayne Poulsen, founder of Squaw Valley USA and 1938 California state champion for jumping, downhill, and slalom. The hill was maintained by the Lake Tahoe Ski Club until the late 1950s.

While this is not really much of a ski hill, the resort keeps it open primarily for sentimental reasons, and it operates Friday–Sunday and on holidays. There's a cozy, rustic day lodge offering meals, lessons, and rentals, and next to the ski hill is a popular snowplay area. The surrounding Granlibakken Resort is a full-service conference center with excellent condominium accommodations, meeting rooms, and a restaurant. Granlibakken is the closest skiing destination to Tahoe City.

Lifts: One poma.

Vertical descent: 280 feet.

Terrain: Open slope with two runs. Base elevation: 6,330 feet; summit: 6,610 feet. Beginner, 50 percent; intermediate, 50 percent. No snowmaking.

Lift ticket prices (2001-2002): Adults, $18; children (12 and under), $10; half-day: adults, $12, children, $8.

Off-site lift ticket sales: None.

Restaurants/bars: A snack bar in the warming hut.

Equipment rental: Standard packages (skis or snowboard, boots, poles) are available. Also available are cross-country skis, boots and poles.

Instruction: Group lessons for adults and children (12 and under), $20 for skiing and $25 for snowboarding. Private lessons, $35 per hour for skiing, $40 for snowboarding.

Transportation: A shuttle is available from Reno-Tahoe International Airport for skiers who fly in.

Day care: None.

Snowboarding: Equipment rentals are available, and riders have access to the entire hill.

Special programs/camps: Beginner ski lesson package, $40, and beginner snowboard package, $45 (one-hour lesson, rentals, lift ticket).

Other services: Snowplay area open daily ($4), saucer rentals ($3), and Ski Hut Retail Shop. Lodging packages are available with lift tickets to other North Shore ski areas.

Location: One-half mile south of Tahoe City off Highway 89.

Contact: Granlibakken Ski Resort, 725 Granlibakken Rd./P.O. Box 6329, Tahoe City, CA 96145; 530/581-7533 (ski hill), 530/583-4242 (main desk, resort), or 800/543-3221 (reservations); website: www.granlibakken.com.

Homewood Mountain Resort
(see map on page 311, site 10)

This is the best "hidden" family resort in the region and the closest to the lake—right across the street. From Highway 89 on the West Shore, you can see only a fraction of what is a spacious, medium-sized resort with extraordinary close-up views of the water. Don't be put off by the steep face at the base of the mountain. There are two separate base areas (the second was once a separately owned ski area sharing the same ridge). Both have recently undergone renovation. Between the two mountain faces are 33 intermediate runs and 20 expert runs, providing all the variety any skier could want.

Skiing on the north side is mostly in trees, but the south side offers one large bowl (Quail Face) for experts only. A decent beginner's area, with five lifts, is at the base of the north side, with longer runs on the south side. Homewood installed one of the nation's first quad chairs, though it is not high-speed. Its protected location makes for a great bad-weather skiing venue, but low elevation and proximity to the lake can cause rapid thaws on the bottom runs, especially in spring. The area specializes in low-cost children's programs and midweek two-for-one adult lift deals. It also has one of Tahoe's more active snowboard programs, including lessons for older adults.

Lifts: One quad, two triples, one double, four surface lifts.

Vertical descent: 1,650 feet.

Terrain: 1,260 acres, 56 runs (longest, two miles). Base elevation: 6,230 feet; summit: 7,880 feet. Beginner, 15 percent; intermediate, 50 percent; advanced, 35 percent. Snowmaking coverage on 15 acres.

Lift ticket prices: Adults, $42 weekends; juniors (11 to 18), $27; children 10 and under, free; seniors (62+), $10. Note: Value Days—nonholiday midweek days of Monday–Thursday, are $25 for adults and juniors. If you arrive at the resort by Tahoe Area Regional Transit (TART), you get a $5 discount on each adult daily ticket.

Strategy for skiing the mountain: Park in the less crowded South Lot, or take the TART bus from various North Shore pickup points. The best sun exposure and warm-up runs are off the Quail double chair. Then work your way up the Ellis triple chair and over the ridge to the intermediate's paradise off the Quad. For an easy way back to the base lodge at the end of the day (the alternative is a snaking trail called Lombard Street), you can download on the Madden triple chair and treat yourself to a great view of Lake Tahoe.

Best beginner runs: Rainbow Ridge, Homeward Bound (connecting trails) on the ridge and south side, together offering a single two-mile run.

Best intermediate runs: High Grade, Smooth Cruise on the south side.

Best expert runs: Dutch Treat on the south side, Glory Hole on the north side.

Restaurants/bars: Hofbrau, Hava Java, South Side Lounge, Warming Hut Snack Bar.

Equipment rental: Standard demo packages (skis, boots, poles) and snowboards are available, along with high performance skis.

Instruction: 90-minute lessons for intermediate and above, $30; 90-minute beginner group lessons, $30. Ski Beginner Package, $55 for adults (skiing or snowboarding), $45 for juniors and children. Private lessons are $70.

Transportation: Free ski shuttle service is available between North and South Lodge and downtown Homewood; call 530/525-2992 for schedule information. North and West Shore access is provided by Tahoe Area Regional Transit (TART), with connections to Reno-Tahoe International Airport.

Snowboarding: The Shredwood Forest Terrain Park is to the right of the top terminal of the Quad Chair.

Special programs/camps: Frequent Flyer Program offers $5 off an all-day lift ticket each time a member uses it, and every fifth lift ticket purchased is free. Membership cost is $15. Information: 530/525-2992.

Other services: Repair/sports shops and new snowboard terrain park lockers.

Location: On Highway 89 in Homewood, six miles south of Tahoe City.

Contact: Ski Homewood, 5145 W. Lake Blvd., Homewood, CA 96141; 530/525-2992, Snowphone 530/525-2900, lodging 877/525-SNOW (877/525-7669); website: www.skihomewood.com.

INCLINE VILLAGE/MT. ROSE

Diamond Peak Ski Resort

(see map on page 311, site 11)

Magnificent, close-up views of Lake Tahoe from the scenic east shore, coupled with long intermediate romps from Crystal Ridge and the summit of Diamond Peak (elevation 8,540 feet), provide the chief attractions for this resort. Its growing popularity has resulted in heavily-used base facilities on weekends and holidays. In response to these growing pains, the resort has expanded its food service capacity and also offers a large sun deck and menu at both the Base Lodge and the mid-mountain Snowflake Lodge. The view of Lake Tahoe from this deck is spectacular, and crowds are lighter.

Because of the "banana belt" climate on the sunny east shore of the lake, the resort offers shelter on windy days. It also has an extensive snowmaking system to supplement natural snowfall. The lower mountain, which is the original ski area, contains the majority of lifts and has mostly short, north-facing runs. But two-thirds of the terrain is on the upper mountain, reached by just one chairlift, the Crystal Quad. This area is a totally different environment, with lengthy intermediate trails, expert powder chutes off the ridge, and acres of tree skiing in Solitude Canyon and Golden Eagle Bowl for powder fanatics. West-facing exposure, winds on the exposed ridges, and less snowmaking here often shorten the season for this part of the mountain, but when the snow is right, Diamond Peak is one of the great secrets of Tahoe skiing.

The area is no slouch with statistics—it has the fourth longest vertical at Lake Tahoe. Other pluses include a friendly attitude, better than average food service, and one of the region's best and most affordable programs for children. Among the unique features of the resort are two Launchpads or conveyor belts that load skiers onto the lifts. These enable the lifts to be operated at a faster speed than normal

Lifts: Three quads, three doubles.

Vertical descent: 1,840 feet.

Terrain: 655 acres, 30 runs (longest, 2.5 miles). Base elevation: 6,700 feet; summit: 8,540 feet. Beginner, 18 percent; intermediate, 46 percent; advanced, 36 percent. Snowmaking: 75 percent coverage, including 20 acres of advanced terrain in Solitude Canyon.

Lift ticket prices (2001-2002 season): Adults, $41; youths (13–17), $33; children (6–12) and seniors (60+), $15. Children five and under ski free. A family special, selling for $54, includes all-day adult lift ticket and all-day child lift ticket. Each additional child is $13, adults are $35, and teens are $28 as part of this package. There's also an interchangeable parent pass, allowing two parents to trade off.

Strategy for skiing the mountain: Warm up on Red Fox or Coyote on the lower mountain, then get to the top of Crystal Quad. Intermediate and advanced skiers can ski the upper mountain most of the day. Make it a point to have lunch at Snowflake Lodge for the view of the lake. If winds pick up in mid-afternoon, finish your day on the lower, more protected slopes.

Best beginner run: Lodgepole.

Best intermediate run: Crystal Ridge. It's also the longest and most scenic.

Best expert run: Lightning.

Restaurants/bars: Base Lodge, Snowflake Lodge (large sun deck with barbecue atop Lakeview Lift).

Equipment rental: Standard and high-performance packages (skis, boots, poles) and snowboards are available.

Instruction: One hour, 45-minute group ski or snowboard clinic for adults, $24. First-time beginner ski/snowboard package, $48 (group lesson on super sidecut skis, boots, poles, and beginner lift ticket) or $63 for four hours. First-time beginner snowboard packages, $49 (two-hour lesson, rental gear, and beginner lift ticket). Private ski lessons, from $55 (one-hour morning) to $150 (half-day).

Transportation: Free daily ski-area shuttle service is available throughout Incline Village and Crystal Bay. call 775/832-1177.

Day care: On-site accommodation is available at Diamond Peak for potty-trained children ages 3–6, by arrangement. Call 775/832-1130 for more information. For all other arrangements, call 800/GO-TAHOE (800/468-2463).

Snowboarding: Terrain park on Spillway run.

Special programs/camps: Sierra Scout adventure lessons (ages 7–12), skiing and snowboard, are $74 all day (four hours of instruction, rental gear, lift ticket, lunch, and supervision). Bee Ferrato Child Ski Center (ages 3–6) offers an all-day session for $79 (all-day group lesson, equipment rental and supervised lunch).

Other services: Lockers, ski check service (no basket check), and the Village Ski Loft retail store.

Location: In Incline Village, two miles east of Highway 28 on the Nevada side of Lake Tahoe.

Contact: Diamond Peak Ski Resort, 1210 Ski Way, Incline Village, NV 89451; 775/832-1177, Snowphone 775/831-3211, reservations 800/GO-TAHOE (800/468-2463); website: www.diamondpeak.com.

Mt. Rose (see map on page 311, site 12)

Bring your ski legs. This mountain, which rises to the west of Reno, is the third highest in the Tahoe region (next to Heavenly and Kirkwood). It's not a cruiser's paradise, though intermediates will find enough to keep them occupied. What defines this area are its challenging advanced runs, which require you to keep sharp edges. The resort actually comprises what used to be two separate areas, Mt. Rose and Slide Mountain (now called East Bowl), on opposing flanks of the peak. From the summit you can ski either side, and there are services such as ticket sales, parking, a cafeteria, and restrooms on both sides. But the ski school, rental and retail departments, and most of the food services are on the Mt. Rose side.

Terrain varies from steep, tree-lined runs at Rose to the wide-open Sunrise Bowl at Slide. There's good beginner terrain from the two lower chairlifts at Rose, but none in the East Bowl. On powder days, this area excels, and its high elevation holds snow late into spring. From the summit, there are sweeping views of Reno, the Washoe Valley, and Lake Tahoe. The Mt. Rose day lodge, remodeled several times in recent years, serves quality meals (Mexican food is a specialty) and has one of the most efficient ski/boot rental operations in Tahoe. Management seems responsive to customers, and there is strong repeat business from Reno residents. In recent years, the access road from both the Reno side and the Incline Village side has been greatly improved, to the extent that there are very few road closures by the Nevada Department of Transportation. Snowmaking extends from the base area and its beginner slopes to the summit, covering 50 percent on the main side of the

ALPINE SKIING

ALPINE SKIING

© KEN CASTLE

snowboarding at Mt. Rose

mountain. There are eight food locations, seven in the main lodge, which consist of Lodgepole Café, Higher Grounds, Senor Barasca's (with a great taco and burrito bar!), Timbers, View-B-Que, Pit Stop and The Barge. In East Bowl (the former Slide Mountain), there's the Zephyr Café.

Lifts: One high-speed detachable six-pack, two quads, two triples and one surface lift (Wonder Carpet near Rosebuds Children's Center).

Vertical descent: 1,440 feet.

Terrain: 900 acres, 44 trails (longest, 2.5 miles). Base elevation: 8,260 feet; summit: 9,700 feet. Beginner, 30 percent; intermediate, 30 percent; advanced, 40 percent. Snowmaking coverage on 25 percent of the mountain.

Lift ticket prices: Adults, $45; teens (13–19), $35; children (6–12), $12, seniors (60-69), $23. Children five and under and adults 70 and older ski free midweek and nonholiday periods. Daily specials are available.

Strategy for skiing the mountain: With its northeastern exposure, the East Bowl has the sunniest disposition in the morning, but it's hardly the easiest place for a warm-up run. Still, early in the day is best for skiing the East Bowl; then work your way back to Rose. If the wind picks up, the runs off the Lakeview Chair will be more protected than those from the top of the Northwest Passage Chair.

Best beginner run: Galena on the Rose side.

Best intermediate run: Bruce's in the East Bowl.

Best expert run: Northwest Passage on the Rose side.

Restaurants/bars: Cafeteria (breakfast, lunch), deli/food court, tavern (full bar).

Equipment rental: Standard and high-performance packages (skis, boots, poles) and snowboards are available.

Instruction: First-time packages for both skiing and snowboarding, with 90-minute lessons, are $49 for adults, $25 for children (6–12). Private lessons, $29–39.

Transportation: Sierra Nevada Stage Lines operates two daily ski shuttles from several Reno locations, including John Ascuaga's Nugget, Harrah's Reno, Sands Regency, Reno Hilton, Peppermill, Holiday Inn and Atlantis Casino Resort, December–April. call 775/331-1147 or 800/822-6009.

Day care: None.

Snowboarding: Three terrain parks are on the mountain. Badlands and Doubledown on in the East Bowl next to the Zephyr Chair and Snake Eyes is off West Ramsey's on the main side.

Special programs/camps: First-time skier package: $49, including rental gear, instruction and beginner lift access. The ski area is well-known to locals for its daily specials, which include Two-fer Tuesday (two-for-one lift passes), Student Wednesday (show a student ID and get a ticket for $19), Ladies Day Thursday (full-day lift pass for $19), and Runs 'n Roses (daily family package for two adults and two children), at $96 any day except holidays.

Other services: Sports shop, repair shop, basket check, and outdoor barbecue deck.

Location: On Mt. Rose Highway (Route 431), 12 miles northeast of Incline Village and 22 miles south of Reno.

Contact: Mt. Rose, 22222 Mt. Rose Hwy., Reno, NV 89511; 775/849-0704 or 800/SKI-ROSE (800/754-7673) (outside Nevada), road conditions 775/793-1313, lodging 800/FOR-RENO (800/367-7366), 800/TAHOE-4-U (800/824-6348), or 800/GO-TAHOE (800/468-2463); website: www.skirose.com.

SOUTH LAKE TAHOE

Heavenly Ski Resort
(see map on page 311, site 13)

Newly transformed by the addition of a gondola and a village, Heavenly is the only Western ski area to straddle two states (California and Nevada). It also has the distinction of offering the highest summit elevation (10,040 feet) in the Tahoe region. While the resort is a vast ski complex with bowls, glades, and ridge tops, it is known primarily as an intermediate skier's mountain. Among its many assets is one of the largest snowmaking systems in North America, which guarantees good coverage in lean snow

years. Heavenly has four separate base areas—two in California and two in Nevada—and each has its own ticket windows and services. For skiers who stay in the major hotels and casinos at Stateline, the easiest access is by walking a few hundred yards to the gondola in the new Heavenly Village. The resort is one of only two in the region that has a lift system beginning at lake level, and is the only ski area in the country that is within walking distance of casino gaming and high-powered, showroom entertainment. You can ski, eat and gamble in your ski boots! And plenty of big changes for Heavenly are in the wings. In May of 2002, Vail Resorts bought the resort from American Skiing Company, thus signalling an expansion of its ski area portfolio beyond Colorado. Over a five-year period, Vail hopes to spend upwards of $50 million for improvements and additions.

Despite the fanfare over the gondola, the top terminal, at this writing, does not provide access to beginner terrain. So any group with novices will have to drive or take the bus to the original California base or to the Boulder base in Nevada, where there are ample beginner trails. (This situation may be rectified in the near future, as more runs are opened at the top of the gondola.) Don't be put off by the steep mountain face that you see upon first blush at the California base. This is the famous (or infamous) Gunbarrel run, which is often pockmarked with moguls. If hairball, nail-biting terrain is not to your liking, you can literally rise above it all by going much higher, as most snow sliders do, to reach the cruising stuff at the top. For prime powder, the longest intermediate runs, and the best protection from winds, try the Nevada side. For impressive views of Lake Tahoe, take the gondola and get off at the Observation Deck (you can only do this on the way up right now). As a scenic alternative, enjoy the somewhat lower panorama from Monument Peak Lodge at the Top of the Tram, where you'll find a restaurant, bar, and large deck. On the Nevada side, three modern lodges offer superior facilities and decent, if undistinguished, meals.

Most of the advanced and expert runs are on the upper portion of the Nevada side, in Milky

Way Bowl and Mott and Killebrew Canyons. There are some narrow, congested trails and convergence points, especially on the Ridge Run, and extra care and slower speeds are advised for these areas. Heavenly has very little beginner terrain for the size of the mountain, but it is well utilized by the ski school here. Heavenly's free shuttle bus system to and from area lodging is the most extensive in Tahoe.

Lifts: One gondola, one aerial tram, one high-speed six-passenger chair, five high-speed quads, eight triples, five doubles, six surface lifts and two Magic Carpets.

Vertical descent: 3,500 feet.

Terrain: 4,800 skiable acres, 82 runs (longest, 5.5 miles). Base elevation: 6,540 feet (California side), 7,200 feet (Nevada side); summit: 10,040 feet. Beginner, 20 percent; intermediate, 45 percent; advanced, 35 percent. Snowmaking on 69 percent of cleared trails.

Lift ticket prices (2001-2002): Adults, $57; youth (13 to 18), $47; juniors (6–12) and seniors (65 and over), $29. Children five and under ski free. Half-day, multiday, and group rates are available. Gondola and tram rides alone, $20 for adults and teens, $12 for children and $18 for seniors (65+).

Strategy for skiing the mountain: To newcomers, this can be a somewhat confusing ski area, mainly because of its size and the maze of connecting trails. If you're an intermediate, the gondola is the fastest and most convenient way to reach the midpoint between the California and Nevada sides. From the top of the gondola, you can ski down into either network of lifts and trails, and then download at the end of the day (there is no ski route to the bottom of the gondola). If you need to begin your day at the original California base (for beginners, child care and other services), you can take the free shuttle bus from your hotel or motel and avoid the parking crunch. Intermediates and beginners should forget about skiing the lower California side of the mountain; your options to return include a snaking beginner's trail that isn't worth the effort, downloading on the tram (too long of a wait), or downloading on the Gunbarrel Express Quad. The latter is the best alternative, since it is relatively quick and it has a million-dollar view of Lake Tahoe and Stateline to boot. Reaching the top of the California side is pokey; allow an hour on weekends to ride the three necessary chairlifts. A better way to avoid all of this (until Vail Resorts gets newer and more convenient lifts in place) is to hop on the less frequent shuttle to either of the Nevada bases (Stagecoach or Boulder) and ride just two lifts to the summit. This is what the locals do if they have to ski on a weekend. In general, the skiing is less crowded and snow quality can be better (drier) on the Nevada side.

Best beginner run: Mombo Meadows on the California side.

Best intermediate run: Olympic Downhill on the Nevada side.

a bird's-eye view of Lake Tahoe and the surrounding snow-capped peaks from nearly 3,000 feet above

© SHERRY MCMANUS/HEAVENLY SKI RESORT

Best expert runs: Mott Canyon and Milky Way Bowl on the Nevada side, Gun-barrel on the California side.

Restaurants/bars: Monument Peak Restaurant at the Top of Tram (breakfast, lunch, dinner), Sky Meadows Deck and East Peak Lodge (outdoor barbecues), Slice of Heaven (Italian, pizza), Black Diamond Cantina at Boulder Lodge (Mexican), Observation Deck snack bar, four cafeterias, and four bars. Mountain Caterers is an on-slope picnic experience at secluded off-trail areas with picturesque views and can include cheese, fruit and cracker trays, hot cocoa, wine, choice of entrée, and dessert. To make arrangements, contact the catering department at 775/586-7000, ext. 6228.

Equipment rental: Standard and high-performance/demo packages (skis, boots, poles), including super sidecut skis, and snowboards are available.

Instruction: 90-minute ski instruction clinic, with lift ticket and equipment rental, $89. First-time snowboard lesson, with gear and lift access, $89. Private lessons, $85–360, depending on number of hours.

Transportation: Free shuttle service is available from Heavenly bus stops near most lodging properties, leaving every 20 to 30 minutes (8 A.M.–5:30 P.M. daily). Buses go to all four base facilities, including the new gondola at Heavenly Village.

Day care: Fully licensed child-care center for infants as young as six weeks and children up to six years. Options range from complete indoor daycare to a combination of skiing, snowplay and indoor play. Prices: $75–129 for full-day program. Reservations are required, at 775/586-7000, ext. 6912.

Snowboarding: The entire mountain is open to snowboarders, plus there are two terrain parks (Groove on California and Olympic on Nevada), bordercross on Comet, and a halfpipe on California trail. Several terrain features also are constructed regularly on the mountain, including spines, rolls and flat-tops. Related facilities include the Boardinghouse, a snowboard sales and rental outlet off the mountain.

Special programs/camps: Free do-it-yourself demo program with new shaped skis of your choice, operating out of designated test centers, operating from the Top of the Tram and at East Peak Lodge. Special 8 A.M., pre-opening access to virgin or freshly groomed snow with a 90-minute clinic, which you must buy the night before. Women's ski seminars, three-day programs with video analysis, are held on several dates. The Ski with a Ranger program is an interpretive mountain tour led by U.S. Forest Service rangers who describe the mountain, Lake Tahoe geology, and wildlife; the free tours depart twice daily.

Other services: Two ski demo centers, six on-mountain sports shops, eight off-site sports shops, on-mountain photography, local cable TV live reports, lockers, free ski checks at four locations, and overnight ski storage.

Location: At the end of Ski Run Boulevard, off U.S. 50, in South Lake Tahoe. (Note: closest access from Stateline is on the gondola, but there is no beginner there at this point as there is on the other California side). Also, Boulder Lodge on the Nevada side offers beginner trails.

Contact: Heavenly Ski Resort, P.O. Box 2180, Stateline, NV 89449; 775/586-7000, reservations 800/2-HEAVEN (800/243-2836); website: www.skiheavenly.com.

Sierra-at-Tahoe
(see map on page 311, site 14)

Tahoe's most underrated resort is often overlooked by out-of-towners because of its low profile and modest distance from South Lake Tahoe (25 minutes). Yet this is an amazingly well designed mountain, with exceptional terrain for all ability levels. It features north-facing, fall-line runs, an intimate, forested setting, and an enlightened management that listens to consumers. Sierra-at-Tahoe boasts the region's most extensive beginner terrain, with a 2.5-mile top-to-bottom run (Sugar 'n' Spice) that allows novice skiers maximum access to the mountain. Intermediates have one section of the ski area to themselves, with a series of wide, undulating runs through sylvan forest from the Puma and West Bowl Express quad chairs. The highest peak is Huckleberry Mountain (elevation 8,852 feet), where challenging advanced runs cascade down the front and intermediate and beginner runs fan out from the back. Also from the back side, there are gates that access 600 acres of intermediate and advanced terrain.

On the summit, there's a world-class vista of Lake Tahoe from a large day lodge that houses the Grand View Grill and Lake View Deck. The area has four terrain parks for skiers and snowboarders, a large half-pipe and a superpipe. A four-lane tubing hill, a ski-biking course, and a new snowplay center with rental gear and clothing also are available. Owned by the same company that operates Northstar (near Truckee), Sierra-at-Tahoe offers many special touches in food service and instruction, a joint lift ticket, and the electronic Vertical Plus program, all of which help make this resort an outstanding experience for any type of skier or rider. Beginners are well pampered and have more terrain to ski than at any other Tahoe resort. The only drawback is a cramped base lodge with a rabbit warren of corridors. One thing that everyone raves about is the quality of the ski area's food, which includes locally-produced wines, beers and coffees, along with some of the best appetizers, Mexican platters and breakfasts you'll find at Tahoe ski resorts.

Lifts: Three high-speed quads, one triple, five doubles, and one Magic Carpet surface lift.

Vertical descent: 2,212 feet.

Terrain: 2,000 acres, 46 runs (longest, 2.5 miles). Base elevation: 6,640 feet; summit: 8,852 feet. Beginner, 25 percent; intermediate, 50 percent; advanced, 25 percent. Snowmaking on 27 acres.

Lift ticket prices : Adults, $53; young adult (13 to 22), $43; seniors (60 to 69), $32; children (5–12), $11; super senior (70 and older), $12.

Strategy for skiing the mountain: By all means take the free shuttle buses from South Lake Tahoe. Begin your day on the back side, the sunniest area in the morning. Then ski down the ridgeline to the Nob Hill lift and from there over to the runs off Puma, where the afternoon sun creates a particularly spectacular view of Desolation Wilderness to the north.

Best beginner run: Sugar 'n' Spice.

Best intermediate run: Powder Horn.

Best expert run: Castle.

Restaurants/bars: Cheeseburger in Paradise (remember that Jimmy Buffett song?), The Aspen Café (charbroiled entrées, garlic fries and Mexican), The Sierra Pub (full-service bar with wine, microbrews, and cocktails), The Bake Shop, Rama Java, The Grand View and Grill and Lake View Deck at the summit (barbecue), and West Bowl Express Snacks.

Equipment rental: Standard and high-performance/demo packages (skis, boots, poles), including super sidecut skis, and snowboards are available.

Instruction: First Time Package is $69, including two-hour clinic, rental gear and limited lift ticket, and the Breakthrough package, $32 for the clinic only or $92 with gear and lift ticket. For strong intermediate through expert skiers or riders, there are free lessons with the purchase of a lift ticket. Private clinics are $75 per hour.

Transportation: A free ski shuttle bus stops at multiple locations around the South Shore. Call 530/541-7548 for information.

Day care: Dyno-Tykes, a licensed day-care center (ages 18 months to 5) offers an all-day session for $80. Reservations are recommended for weekends. Includes snowplay, arts and crafts, story time, music, lunch and snacks.

Snowboarding: Unlimited access, plus three terrain parks, a halfpipe and a superpipe.

Special programs/camps: Wild Mountain Ski and Snowboard Camp (ages 4–12), $90 including lesson, lifts, lunch and equipment. Vertical Plus program is a frequent slider/glider and rider membership program with electronic lift access, separate lift line and various discounts. Sliders can redeem their vertical feet for various prizes and food and beverage deals. Large selection of snow toys and ski bikes.

Other services: Tubing center with lift access ($15 for two hours, $30 for all day), groomed three-mile snowshoe loop trail ($15 for snowshoe rental), ski repair, sports shop, lockers, and ski basket check.

Location: Off U.S. 50 at Echo Summit on Sierra-at-Tahoe Road, 12 miles west of South Lake Tahoe.

Contact: Sierra-at-Tahoe, 1111 Sierra-at-Tahoe Rd., Twin Bridges, CA 95735; 530/659-7453,

Snowphone 530/659-7475; website: www
.SierraTahoe.com.

KIRKWOOD/HOPE
VALLEY/MARKLEEVILLE

Kirkwood (see map on page 311, site 15)
With its awesome, serrated peaks, this just might
be the most visually impressive resort in the Tahoe
region. One look from Kirkwood Meadows and
there's no doubt about it: This is a skier's mountain.
Much like Squaw Valley USA, the resort is in a box
canyon, but its topography—ridgelines capped
with pinnacles and bizarre fingers of rock—is vast-
ly different. Kirkwood will be appreciated most by
strong intermediate to super-expert skiers, although the children's center at Timber Creek provides some excellent beginner slopes and unique
terrain parks. From Thimble Peak (elevation 9,876
feet), there are no fewer than 11 double-black-
diamond runs, and they represent a world of hurt
for lesser skiers. In fact, there's a skull-and-cross-
bones sign at the base of the Wagon Wheel Chair
to underscore the point.

Kirkwood unveiled its long-awaited Mountain Village in the winter of 1999, giving the resort a new look and a lively place to hang out.
The buildings include the Mountain Club, a
deluxe condominium hotel, and Snowcrest, a
ski-in/ski-out condominium complex at the base
of Olympic Run and Cornice Chair. With 40
units, the Mountain Club has all of the comforts of a first-class hotel, including spa/gym, ski
check and full concierge service. It is connected
by a heated plaza to The Lodge at Kirkwood, a
19-unit condo complex and the main portal for
the mountain, and it houses a sports shop, boutiques, a coffee house and a deli. For the 2002–03
season, three more condominium projects
opened: Meadowstone, a 32-unit luxury condominium complex; Timber Ridge, a 28-unit town
home complex; and the first units of The Sentinels, another town home project. Also, the resort added an ice-skating rink and a swimming
complex. The Village, part of a 10-year, $250
million plan, is expected to include an outdoor
ice skating rink and additional lodging units over
the coming years.

Kirkwood's got every kind of terrain a ski area
could want—bowls, cornices, saddles, chutes,
glades, and, fortunately, a few flats for beginners.
The resort, with its high base elevation of 7,800
feet, is a favorite with early- and late-season skiers.
Pluses include a variety of lodging (all in condos),
good food service, and high-quality, user-friendly
ski instruction. Negatives include its distance from
South Lake Tahoe (35 minutes by car) and occasional tricky driving over high passes.

Lifts: Two quads, seven triples, one doubles, and
two surface lifts.

Vertical descent: 2,000 feet.

Terrain: 2,300 acres, 65 runs (longest, 2.5 miles).
Base elevation: 7,800 feet; summit: 9,800 feet.
Beginner, 15 percent; intermediate, 50 percent;
advanced, 20 percent, and expert, 15 percent.
Snowmaking covers 55 acres on four runs from
top to bottom.

Lift ticket prices: Adults, $54; junior (13 to
18), $43; children (6–12), $12. Children five
and under, $6. Half-day and multiday rates are
available.

Strategy for skiing the mountain: Make sure
your ski legs are warmed up before tackling anything serious on this mountain. Be aware that
the trail ratings are deceptive; some intermediate-
signed runs would be diamond runs at other resorts, and some diamond-signed runs are readily
negotiable by strong intermediates. Ski the Sunrise Bowl first thing in the morning, followed
by Juniper and Flying Carpet off the Caples Crest
Chair, then work your way over to The Reut
(Chair 11). Once you're warmed up, you might
take a shot at Cornice lift, where advanced intermediates like the brisk, fall-line plunge of Sen-
tinel Bowl. Modest cruising runs are off the
Solitude and Hole 'n Wall chairs.

Best beginner runs: Snowkirk and Graduation.

Best intermediate runs: Devil's Draw, Sunrise
Bowl, Buckboard.

Best expert runs: Eagle Bowl, Thunder Saddle
(double diamond), Olympic.

Restaurants/bars: Red Cliffs Lodge (food court
with Chinese, Mexican, Italian, deli, and grilled
foods), Timber Creek Lodge, Snowshoe Thompson's at Timber Creek (cafeteria, pizza), Bub's
Sports Bar and Grill, Sunrise Grill, Kirkwood

ALPINE SKIING

Inn (home-style dining), Zak's Bar, Off the Wall Bar and Grill (fine dining) in The Lodge at Kirkwood, and Monte Wolfe's Coffee House and Deli in The Mountain Club.

Equipment rental: New super sidecut skis are part of the standard rental inventory, along with high-performance skis and snowboards.

Instruction: Two-hour group ski and snowboard clinics, $40. Learn to ski or snowboard package, $75 (four-hour lesson, gear, and beginner lift). Private lessons, $80 per hour ($45 for each additional person).

Transportation: A daily shuttle from South Shore lodging properties is available seven days a week, with reservations required and a nominal fee charged.

Day care: Mini Mountain Child Care Center, a licensed facility for kids ages 2–6, is available all day for $95, or half-day for $80. The center features professional supervision and daily indoor and outdoor activities.

Snowboarding: There are three terrain parks: a beginner park in the Timber Creek Area, an intermediate/advanced park beneath Chair 5 on Race Course Run, and a Super Park beneath Chair 2 on Flying Carpet. A half-pipe is below Chair 5 on Race Course run. Snowboard rentals have been combined with ski rentals at three facilities, Red Cliffs, Mountain Village and Timber Creek.

Special programs/camps: Special women-only ski workshops include video and lunch on the village plaza and cost $100 with a lift ticket or $50 for those who already have a lift ticket. All Conditions/All Terrain and Adventure Clinics for advanced intermediate through expert skiers are offered throughout the season for between $750 and $950, including lift tickets, two dinners, classroom sessions, video critique, instruction and a logo sweatshirt. Mighty Mountain Children's Ski and Snowboard School (ages 4–12), $90 for all-day programs (lift ticket, lessons, gear, lunch, and supervision) and $75 for half-day program (no lunch).

Other services: Cross-country ski and snowshoe center, sleigh rides, dog-sled rides, lift-accessed tubing hill, family play area, Mountain Club Spa, two specialty ski shops, snowboard center, day-care center, three rental shops, photography services, four conference rooms, real estate offices, medical clinic, general store, post office, eight condo complexes, lockers and ski basket check.

Location: Off Highway 88 at Carson Pass, 30 miles southwest of South Lake Tahoe.

Contact: Kirkwood, P.O. Box 1, Kirkwood, CA 95646; 209/258-6000, Snowphone 877/KIRKWOOD (877/547-5966), reservations 800/967-7500; website: www.kirkwood.com.

Cross-Country Skiing

Just as Lake Tahoe boasts the greatest concentration of downhill ski lifts in North America, so, too, does it offer a bounty of riches for the cross-country skier. The region is justly famous as the home of Royal Gorge, the largest Nordic resort on the continent. But a half-dozen other privately operated cross-country areas, combined with numerous routes on public lands, create an unparalleled opportunity for skinny skiers to find their favorite vistas of the Sierra.

Around the perimeter of Tahoe itself are no fewer than four organized cross-country areas, all of them with spectacular panoramas of the lake from varying elevations. It isn't necessary to be a strong skier or to negotiate arduous trails, either, to be rewarded with such vistas. Cheap skiing (free or for a minimal charge of around $5) is almost everywhere you turn at a number of trails operated by public agencies, such as the U.S. Forest Service and the California and Nevada state parks systems. One compromise in using these trails, however, is to forego the comforts of grooming and machine-set track (with a few notable exceptions). Most of the public trails are on the West Shore of the lake, extending from Tahoe City in the north to South Lake Tahoe,

Royal Gorge Cross-Country Ski Resort

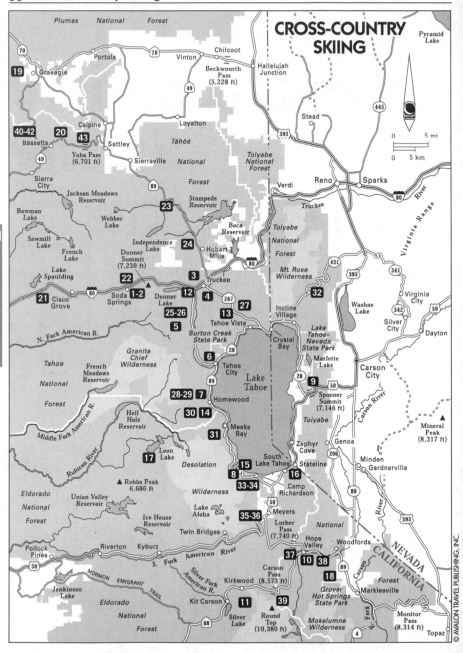

CROSS-COUNTRY SKIING

and are easy to reach from Highway 89. But don't overlook the locally operated community trail systems, especially ones maintained by the North Tahoe Public Utility District and the city of South Lake Tahoe.

There's plenty of excellent skiing outside of the basin as well. Notable venues include Kirkwood to the south, Crystal Basin and Donner Summit to the west, and the Plumas and Lakes Basin areas to the north. Also, between Truckee and the North Shore of the lake are several "hidden" trail systems, less well known routes to destinations such as Martis Peak or along the backbone of mountains framing the North Shore.

Every area has its own unique charm. You can stride or skate in open meadows, explore secluded valleys that seem miles from nowhere but are quite close to civilization, climb to scenic overlooks of frosted peaks and plunging canyons, or follow meandering mountain streams through aspen and pine forest to frozen alpine lakes. Enjoying an outdoor picnic lunch on a huge granite outcropping, with a million-dollar view before you and a warm midday sun above, is one of the great pleasures of backcountry skiing. The more adventurous can even sign up for full-moon tours or overnight snow-camping.

Considering the prodigious amounts of snow that can blanket the Sierra, there are several factors to be aware of. One is that after a storm the usually high moisture content of the snow can create avalanche hazards on many steep slopes. If you're venturing into the high country on trails that are not patrolled, or are cutting your own tracks, contact the local office of the U.S. Forest Service for the latest information on avalanche conditions. Outside of the developed areas, it's not wise to travel alone. Even when skiing with a friend, tell someone where you're going and when you expect to return. More than one skier has been caught in a sudden change of weather and become lost or disoriented. Carry a fanny pack or knapsack with extra food and liquids, and have sufficient layers of clothing to survive lower temperatures.

Enjoying an outdoor picnic lunch on a huge granite outcropping, with a million-dollar view before you and a warm midday sun above, is one of the great pleasures of backcountry skiing. The more adventurous can even sign up for full-moon tours or overnight snow-camping.

Another consideration when taking Forest Service trails is that they are minimally signed, and sometimes lack signs altogether. If you are not familiar with orienteering—using a compass and USGS topo maps—don't venture out on unmarked routes. Wherever you go, be especially careful in crossing streams or skiing on ice-covered lakes; if you are uncertain about your footing, use an alternate route. Remember that snow conditions are constantly changing. Consider also your altitude, your physical conditioning, and the dangers of hypothermia.

Many cross-country areas also offer snowshoe rentals, so even nonskiers now have a chance to explore the backcountry. Snowshoes are noted in the following listings when they are available. **Note:** Except where noted, prices are based on the 2002–03 season and are subject to change.

Schools and Guide Services

Beginners who want to learn proper technique, out-of-practice novices who want to polish their skills up, and anyone interested in guided cross-country excursions can take advantage of a pair of schools and guide services in the Tahoe area.

Alpine Skills International

Operated by the husband-and-wife team of Bela and Mimi Vadasz, ASI is a highly respected mountaineering school on Donner Pass. Headquartered next to Sugar Bowl ski area, it offers two-, three-, and five-day courses in cross-country and telemark skiing, in the backcountry and at neighboring lift-served ski areas. There is no organized trail system; instead, classes use the Pacific Crest Trail, Mt. Judah, and Donner Peak and are rewarded with sweeping vistas of Donner Lake and the Donner Pass area. ASI has a considerable selection of tours

CROSS-COUNTRY SKIING

and clinics, which must be arranged in advance. Some examples: two-day introductory back-country skiing courses, at $218, and three-day telemark and Nordic downhill camps, at $394. Intermediate and advanced courses also are available, including a three-day traverse from Sugar Bowl to Squaw Valley ($368) that involves snow camping and avalanche safety and survival skills. ASI's office and staging area are conveniently near groomed cross-country trail systems at Royal Gorge, Clair Tappaan, and Donner Summit. In 2000, ASI sold its vintage Donner Spitz Hutte and no longer offers overnight lodging and meals, so participants must make their own arrangements.

Location: West of Truckee on Old Highway 40, south of the Soda Springs/Norden exit off I-80. **Contact:** Alpine Skills International, P.O. Box 8, Norden, CA 95724; 530/426-9108; email: asi@alpineskills.com; website: www.alpineskills.com.

Sierra Ski Touring

Veteran backcountry ski guide and author David Beck provides individualized instruction for backcountry skiers, as well as an overnight ski touring program that uses a ski hut in Meiss Meadow, near the summit of Carson Pass off Highway 88. The two-story hut, an old mining cabin built in the 1800s, has a wood-burning stove but no electricity. Up to eight guests who bring their own sleeping bags can stay at the hut, and Beck provides three meals. Dinners might include chicken and dumplings, stir-fry dishes, or spaghetti. To reach the cabin, skiers must negotiate 2.5 miles from Highway 88, carrying in their personal gear. Call for prices for the hut tours, or check the website. Beck also conducts avalanche safety and winter survival courses.

Contact: Sierra Ski Touring, P.O. Box 176, Gardnerville, NV 89410; 775/782-3047; website: www.highsierra.com/sst.

Cross-Country Ski Resorts

All resorts listed are keyed to the Cross-Country Skiing map.

TRUCKEE/DONNER

Royal Gorge Cross-Country Ski Resort (see map on page 336, site 1)

Perched on snowy Donner Summit, this is North America's largest cross-country ski area, and it has just about everything you could want: an immaculate trail system that is revitalized daily with a fleet of snow-grooming machines; an extensive network of warming huts; a backcountry overnight wilderness lodge, unique among U.S. Nordic ski areas, which serves gourmet meals; four surface lifts that form something of a mini downhill ski area served by a large day lodge with a restaurant and sun deck; and rental equipment that is always on the cutting edge of technology.

John Slouber, the owner of Royal Gorge, has created not only the ultimate cross-country resort but one of the great winter resorts of the world. A former downhill racer who was educated in France, Slouber is one of the sport's most persistent innovators, and his standards for client service are the highest in the industry. Apart from the physical layout of the resort, what stands out is the quality of the staff, consisting of amiable and helpful young people from Australia, New Zealand, South Africa, and Europe, who give Royal Gorge a true international flavor.

Guests who stay a week in the Wilderness Lodge are treated to sumptuous French-style buffets for breakfast and lunch, and a full-course dinner with table service and wine. The lodge, an old hunting retreat built in the late 1800s, is not exactly a luxury hotel; there are private bedrooms with double beds or bunks, but toilets are shared and all shower facilities are outside in a separate building. If you can deal with these minor inconveniences, you'll enjoy the meals and the posh, knotty-pine sitting room with its big, overstuffed couches, wood-burning heaters, and vast library of books and games. Recently, the resort added two log cabins, each with fireplace, queen-sized bed, Jacuzzi and private bathroom, next to the lodge. These are quite popular, and their occupants can join lodge guests for all meals and activities. For other deluxe accommodations, you can stay at the 32-room Rainbow Lodge, also owned by Royal Gorge.

The resort has five track systems, and it would take more than a week for most skiers to explore them all. The best beginner terrain is at Lake Van Norden, a wide-open area with a shallow, frozen lake and no substantial elevation changes. Additional low-impact terrain weaves through dense forest from Summit Station (the main day lodge and parking area) to the Wilderness Lodge, but there are few vistas from these trails and some of them parallel a not-very-scenic power line. To see the spectacular sights, you've got to be a strong intermediate skier or better and spend most of a day on the trails. A moderately strenuous but highly recommended intermediate route of 16 kilometers round-trip is to the base of Devil's Peak (elevation 7,704 feet), a jagged, dramatic uplift whose walls rise abruptly from an open meadow. There's a warming hut here from which you can admire the view.

More difficult, with steeper ups and downs, is the track to Point Mariah in the Palisade Peak System. Those who make it (an all-day trip of 22 kilometers round-trip from Summit Station) get a bird's-eye view of the awesome Royal Gorge, which plunges 4,417 feet down sheer granite cliffs to the South Fork of the American River. Over on the Ice Lakes Track System, the adrenaline rush is along an expert trail called Razorback, which follows a narrow ridgeline that overlooks Serene Lakes on the north and a steep drop-off to the south. Several trails connect with the Sugar Bowl ski area at one end of the system and with Rainbow Lodge (12 kilometers from the Wilderness Lodge) at the other end, making it possible to do an inn-to-inn ski tour of several days. If you start at Summit Station Trailhead, the Rainbow Interconnect is 22 kilometers one-way.

Kilometers of track: 330K of groomed, set track on 9,172 acres.

Types of trails: Striding, skating, and telemark skiing on 90 trails (28 beginner, 46 intermediate, and 16 advanced), with elevations ranging from 5,800 feet to 7,538 feet. There are four surface lifts for telemark and downhill skiing on cross-country micro-skis, at a separate downhill area next to the Royal Gorge Summit Station. The

a strider going for speed at the Royal Gorge Cross-Country Ski Resort

longest trail here is the 22-kilometer Rainbow Interconnect Trail.

Trail pass fees: Adults, $26 on weekends, $21.50 on weekdays; youths (ages 13 to 16), $14 on weekends, $12 on weekdays; children 12 and under ski free. Adult afternoon pass: $16.50 to $21. Multiday passes and group rates are available.

Facilities: Two overnight lodges (Wilderness and Rainbow), one day lodge, rentals, a retail shop, ski patrol, ski school, four trailside cafés, and 10 warming huts.

Services: Snowmaking on 15 kilometers of trail, private or group lessons, tours, video clinics, telemark or skating clinics, rentals, sleigh rides, children's snow school, and skiable disability program.

Rental packages: Micro and mid-length skis with boots and bindings, skating skis with bindings, high-performance and demo skis, and high-performance snowshoes are available.

Instruction: Group lessons, $20 per person or $40 including trail pass. Learn-to-ski packages for adults, $49.50, and for children, $29.50 (rentals, group lesson, and trail pass). Private lessons, $30 per hour for one person, $15 per hour for additional people. Pee-Wee Snow School (ages 4–9), $49.50 all day (rentals, trail pass, supervision, lesson, and lunch); morning session (with lunch), $34.50; afternoon session, $24.50.

Transportation: A free shuttle bus runs daily between Rainbow and Summit Station for Rainbow guests and skiers on the Interconnect Trail. On weekends and holidays, there is additional service to Sugar Bowl and Donner Ski Ranch. Limousine service is available to and from Reno-Tahoe International Airport.

Special programs: Skating and telemark clinics are available for $20, or $40 including trail pass. Held throughout the season are specialized clinics for women, seniors, skaters and downhill cross-country skiers. One program allows you to bring your large dog and try ski-joring (having your dog tow you on a harness). Trail pass for the dog is $5. Overnight packages that include trail pass, instruction, meals, lodging, and sleigh ride are available at Wilderness Lodge, starting at $149 per person per day for adults and $90 for children (low season midweek).

Major events of the season: Gold Rush 50K and Silver Rush 30K ski races (March).

Location: Take the Soda Springs/Norden exit off I-80 on Donner Summit. The Van Norden Trailhead is one mile east on Old Highway 40, and the Summit Station is another three-quarters of a mile beyond. Follow well-marked signs.

Contact: Royal Gorge Cross-Country Ski Resort, 9411 Hillside Dr./P.O. Box 1100, Soda Springs, CA 95728; 530/426-3871 or 800/500-3871 (outside Northern California); website: www.royalgorge.com.

Clair Tappaan Lodge
(see map on page 336, site 2)

A modest track system winds through the Donner Pass area behind this Sierra Club lodge and nudges close to the adjacent Donner Ski Ranch alpine ski area. The terrain is mostly scattered forest and wide-open meadow. The snowy summit has some of the most dependable snow cover in the Sierra and is especially ideal for spring.

Kilometers of track: 12K of machine-groomed trails.

Types of trails: Striding trails, a telemark area, and one skating lane, through mixed forest, meadows, and ridges (60 percent beginner, 40 percent intermediate).

Trail pass fees: Free to lodge guests, otherwise $7 per person donation.

Facilities: Two overnight lodges—one main one that is similar to a hostel (it was built in 1935 by volunteers) and another that is nearby and sleeps groups of up to 25 people. In addition, you can arrange for visits to any of four backcountry huts that are throughout the Tahoe area. All are owned by the Sierra Club, but are open to nonmembers as well as members.

Services: At Clair Tappaan, meals are prepared for lodge guests, who must perform one task a day, such as sweeping or washing dishes, and supply their own bedding. At the Hutchinson Lodge, groups must bring their own food but there is a kitchen for meal preparation.

Rental packages: Striding, telemark, and skating skis, bindings, and boots, and snowshoes are available. Packages of skis, boots and poles are $13 for track skis, $9 for kids skis and $16 for metal-edge backcountry touring skis.

Transportation: A free shuttle runs to the Royal Gorge and Norden area, via Sugar Bowl ski area buses.

Special programs: Groups can receive discounts for midweek visits.

Location: West of Truckee on Old Highway 40. Take the Soda Springs/Norden exit off I-80.

Contact: Clair Tappaan Lodge, P.O. Box 36, Norden, CA 95724; 530/426-3632; website: www.sierraclub.org/outings/lodges/tappaan.html.

Tahoe Donner Cross-Country
(see map on page 336, site 3)

Despite the fact that this sizable ski area originates in a populated residential community above Truckee, the trail system allows for a blissful escape from civilization—especially in the isolated and remarkably beautiful Euer Valley, now recognized as a historic area, which is three kilometers north of the lodge. Although the pristine valley is just 100 feet below the plateau that supports the cross-country center, it might as well be another world. In summer the Circle E Ranch, owned by descendants of a pioneer family, uses the lush meadow for grazing cattle, but in winter it becomes a wonderful tour route for beginning and intermediate skiers. Trails parallel the South Fork of Prosser Creek and pass some rustic cabins and barns. The entire valley is surrounded by major peaks, including Castle (elevation 9,103 feet), Red Mountain (7,900 feet), and Prosser Hill (7,171 feet).

A good, easy tour route is Last Roundup, a 7-kilometer loop from the lodge. Once in the valley, you can stay there all day, since a large warming hut, the Euer Valley Cookhouse, provides full food and beverage service on weekends and free, self-service hot tea and springwater on weekdays. But if you can tear yourself away from here, another, larger system of trails called Home Range meanders through aspen groves and scattered pine, and offers a large meadow for beginners in front of the lodge. For the best views, intermediates and experts can climb for six kilometers along Hawk's Peak to the top of

Sunrise Bowl, which sits on Donner Ridge at 7,800 feet (a 1,100-foot elevation gain from the base area). Here you'll find another warming hut, with southwest-facing vistas of Donner Summit and Castle Peak. The ski area is well groomed and managed, with special features like the excellent homemade goodies at the Alder Creek Cafe, a fully stocked equipment rental department, and myriad programs for kids. The Tiny Tracks Snow School is something of a signature for the Nordic center, with its Old West Kiddie Corral and weekend instruction for youngsters ages five to nine in all aspects of ski technique.

Kilometers of track: 105K of machine-groomed track.

Types of trails: Track system with wide skating lanes on 40 trails (30 percent beginner, 40 percent intermediate, and 30 percent advanced). Beginner trails are one-way only.

Trail pass fees: Adults, $19; teens (13 to 17) and seniors (60 to 69), $14; children under 12 and seniors over 70 are free.

Facilities: Three warming huts, one cookhouse, and one day lodge.

Services: Half-day and multiday trail passes, twilight skiing, night skiing, lessons, rental equipment, and the Tiny Tracks Snow School.

Rental packages: Striding and skating skis, demos, and snowshoes are available. Rental packages (skis, boots and poles) run $17 per day.

Instruction: Group learn-to-ski lesson, $40 (trail pass, lesson, and rental).

Transportation: Call for information.

Special programs: Exclusive night skiing is available on Wednesday and Friday evenings, 5 P.M.–7 P.M. The ski area is a participant in North Lake Tahoe Resort Association's Cross-Country Interchangeable Trail Pass.

Location: West of Truckee, take the Donner Memorial State Park exit from I-80. Drive one-half mile east on Donner Pass Road to the bottom of Northwoods Boulevard, then turn left onto Northwoods and follow the signs to the cross-country center, about three miles from the turnoff.

Contact: Tahoe Donner Cross-Country, 11509 Northwoods Blvd., Truckee, CA 96161;

CROSS-COUNTRY SKIING

530/587-9484, Snowphone 530/587-9494; website: www.tahoedonner.com.

Northstar-at-Tahoe Cross-Country, Telemark and Snowshoe Center
(see map on page 336, site 4)

The cross-country area here is integrated with the downhill ski area, and a lot of Nordic skiers feel that the parking, lift access, and crowds are too much of a hassle. That's a shame, since the trail system escapes the alpinists and affords tranquillity and wonderful views of Lake Tahoe and the Martis Valley. There's also a unique warming hut—an old railroad caboose at Sawmill Flat.

The area is divided into three trail systems, all of them beginning at the cross-country day lodge within walking distance of the mid-mountain alpine lodge. You'll have to board the Big Springs Express Gondola or the Echo Triple Chair from Northstar Village to reach this point. From there, you can explore the Big Springs network, mostly beginner and intermediate trails, with great views of Martis Valley. An easy to intermediate outing connects the Holiday and Picnic Trails, about a 4.3-kilometer loop that circles through forest but has several open vista points, some with picnic tables. On the east side of the resort, Sawmill Flat has the greatest variety of trails, as well as the best view of Lake Tahoe, along the Tahoe beginner trail. From the Nordic lodge, this vantage point is about four kilometers, and a lot of skiers choose this for their lunch stop. A good halfway rest point is the caboose, a novel but effective warming hut in an open meadow. Although it's necessary to wade through the parking and lift system with alpine skiers, all three of the trail systems are well away from the lifts and there is no feeling of commingling on the hill. Also, Northstar's variety of on-the-hill accommodations (including condos and a lodge) make access to the trails a matter of simply walking out your door in the morning.

Kilometers of track: 50K of machine-groomed track.

Types of trails: Skating lanes with 38 trails (33 percent beginner, 45 percent intermediate, and 22 percent advanced). Lift access is only via the Big Springs Express Gondola and the Echo Triple

Chair. Snowshoeing is offered on all trails as well as on two wilderness trails.

Trail pass fees: Adults, $26 ages 13 and older; children, $15 (ages 12 and under).

Facilities: Two warming huts and one day lodge.

Services: Rentals, lessons, and both skiing and snowshoeing tours.

Rental packages: Striding, skating, and telemark skis, boots, and bindings are available, at $26 for adults and youths (13+), $15 for kids (5-12). Snowshoes are $21 for adults.

Instruction: Daily lessons in striding, skating, and telemark skiing. Group lessons are $30 for adults (13+) and $15 for children (5-12)

Transportation: Free ski shuttles run from the town of Truckee and all points within Northstar-at-Tahoe.

Major events of the season: The Gourmet Cross-Country Ski Tour (March).

Location: Eight miles south of Truckee at the Northstar-at-Tahoe resort, on Northstar Drive, off Highway 267.

Contact: Northstar-at-Tahoe Cross-Country Center, P.O. Box 129, Truckee, CA 96160; 530/562-2475 or 800/GO-NORTH (800/466-6784/reservations); website: www.skinorthstar.com.

SQUAW VALLEY

The Resort at Squaw Creek Cross-Country Ski Center
(see map on page 336, site 5)

If you're looking for a trail system that is easy on the body, look no further. You won't find much difficult terrain here. Most of the trails, named after Olympic venues such as Cortina and Grenoble, are on the golf course and the adjacent meadow fronting the palatial Resort at Squaw Creek. There are three intermediate trails with modest ups and downs, and two advanced trails that extend up the hill behind the hotel. This is a good area for novice and senior skiers, and the vista of Squaw Valley and its massive peaks provides truly pleasant surroundings.

Kilometers of track: 18K of groomed track.

Types of trails: Striding and skating lanes with 11 trails (60 percent beginner, 25 percent intermediate, and 15 percent advanced). Trails can also be used for snowshoeing.

Trail pass fees: Adults, $13; children, $8; seniors, $6. Half day (skiing after 1 P.M.): $11 for adults, $6 for children, and $5 for seniors.

Facilities: No warming huts; all facilities are at the hotel ski shop.

Services: Twilight skiing, private or group lessons, rentals, and a retail store.

Rental packages: Standard, upgraded recreation and high-performance demo skis, boots, and poles are available, at $15 for adults, $10 for children (6-12). Also, there's a selection of snowshoes, at $15 for adults, $13 for children.

Instruction: Group striding lessons, $25; package, $35 (including complete rental, lesson, trail pass). Private lessons, $40 ($25 for each additional person) plus $10 for rentals. 90-minute skating clinic, by appointment only, $40, or $45 with rentals.

Transportation: Call for information.

Special programs: Snowshoe tours, at $25 per person, including gear and guide. $18 for juniors

Location: At the Resort at Squaw Creek, in Squaw Valley. From Truckee, drive 10 miles south on Highway 89 and turn right into the main Squaw Valley parking lot. Continue one-third of a mile; the Squaw Valley Cross-Country Ski Center is on the left.

Contact: The Resort at Squaw Creek Cross-Country Ski Center, 400 Squaw Creek Rd./P.O. Box 3333, Olympic Valley, CA 96146; 530/583-6300; website: www.squawcreek.com.

TAHOE CITY/WEST SHORE

Tahoe Cross-Country Ski Area
(see map on page 336, site 6)

This is the closest major cross-country center to Tahoe City, and one of the area's hidden jewels. It's also dog-friendly, so by all means bring your faithful companion (but check "dog" hours). Since 1999, the area has been operated under the nonprofit Tahoe Cross-Country Ski Education Association. The board of directors consists entirely of unpaid community volunteers. Kevin and Vallie Murnane, the center's

managers, oversee all of the daily operations. Considering its out-of-sight venue, it is surprisingly large and scenic. The trail network, with both skating and striding lanes, has been here for about 20 years and is well known to the mountain bike set. Most of the trails meander below Mt. Watson (elevation 8,424 feet), one of the highest points on the North Shore. They range from aspen- and pine-fringed avenues to meadows and high ridges, and some of the property includes Burton Creek State Park, part of which is a protected wildlife preserve.

The most scenic trail is Lakeview, which is rated intermediate and has a moderate uphill grade to a short but sweeping view of Lake Tahoe; the lookout point is about four kilometers from the lodge. On the west side of the ski area, Red Trail, another intermediate loop, is a mostly open hill with striking vistas of Mt. Watson. For experts, the Extra Gold Trail, which is used for the annual Great Ski Race between Truckee and Tahoe City, will test your stamina. Track is machine-set by snow groomers on a daily basis. The facility is run in cooperation with the Tahoe City Public Utility District, Department of Parks and Recreation.

Kilometers of track: 65K of machine-set trail with skating lanes and tracks winding through 3,000 acres of national forest.

Types of trails: 17 trails (30 percent beginner, 50 percent intermediate, and 20 percent advanced). Note: Dogs are allowed on eight kilometres of trail all day Monday–Friday, and 3 P.M.–5 P.M. weekends and holidays.

Trail pass fees: Adults, $18; juniors (10-17), $13; senior (60 to 69), $13. Children nine and under who are accompanied by an adult, and seniors 70 and over, ski free. Afternoon trail pass (after 12:30 P.M.): adult, $13; juniors and seniors, $8; and children under 10, free.

Facilities: Two warming huts, one day lodge/café.

Services: Clinics, lessons.

Rental packages: Striding and skating skis, boots, and bindings are available, as are snowshoes.

Instruction: Striding and skating group lessons, $16 (includes lesson and trail pass). Private lessons, $35 per hour.

Transportation: There is no ski shuttle service.

Special programs: Beginner special package is $44 for adults, and includes trail pass, group lesson, and equipment rental.

Major events of the season: The Great Ski Race from Truckee to Tahoe City. This is the biggest race of the year and is held on the first Sunday in March.

Location: 2.5 miles east of downtown Tahoe City, off of Highway 28. The route to get here passes through a residential area above the highway. Look for a small sign on the highway, or for the gas station at Dollar Hill. If you're headed east, turn left at Fabian Way, then right on Village Drive. Go around the corner, turn left at Country Club Drive, and look for the ski area's day lodge on the left.

Contact: Tahoe Cross Country Ski Area, Tahoe City, CA 96145; 530/583-5475; website: www.tahoexc.org.

Granlibakken Resort
(see map on page 336, site 7)
Here is one of Tahoe's great, off-the-beaten-path cross-country ski treks. Granlibakken, a secluded, all-seasons resort of clustered condominiums, has one of Tahoe's original downhill ski areas. From the top of the poma lift you can follow a fire road uphill for one mile to Lookout Point, with its view of Lake Tahoe, and for another two miles to Page Meadows, for a round-trip of six miles. Or you can take a longer route from the ski hut at the downhill area along a path that reaches the fire road farther east, via a short but substantial uphill climb. None of these trails is maintained, and there are no signs at all in Page Meadows.

Kilometers of track: 7.5K, primarily on one trail.

Types of trails: No set track, but the first 1.5 miles are packed with a snow groomer, with the remaining 1.5 miles to Page Meadows ski-set (25 percent beginner, 75 percent intermediate). There is one poma chairlift.

Trail pass fees: None.

Facilities: One warming hut at the ski hill.

Services: None.

Rental packages: Striding and skating skis, boots, and bindings are available.

Instruction: None.

Transportation: There is no ski shuttle.

Special programs: None.

Major events of the season: None.

Location: At the end of Granlibakken Road off Highway 89, one-half mile south of Tahoe City.

Contact: Granlibakken Resort, P.O. Box 6329, Tahoe City, CA 96145; 530/583-4242 or 800/543-3221; website: www.granlibakken.com.

CITY OF SOUTH LAKE TAHOE

Camp Richardson Cross-Country and Snowshoe Center
(see map on page 336, site 8)
New skating lanes and forested striding tracks offer the only organized cross-country skiing that is actually on the shores of Lake Tahoe. In fact, you can ski on a snow-covered beach next to the Beacon Restaurant and Camp Richardson cabins. Trails are set and marked. The main system is behind the Winter Sports Center (across the road from the lodge) and extends to Fallen Leaf Lake with a trail system that offers additional ski routes. You can also ski up to Taylor Creek and take the marked Forest Service trails from there to the east shore of Fallen Leaf Lake. As a new operation, the emphasis of the center is on beginners and families, and the trail system is expected to expand in the coming years.

Kilometers of track: 35K of groomed and skier-packed trails.

Types of trails: Striding area next to the West Shore of Lake Tahoe or through the woods to Fallen Leaf Lake and Taylor Creek (60 percent beginner, 30 percent intermediate, and 10 percent advanced).

Trail pass fees: Adults, $10; children (12 and under) ski free. Half-day, $5.

Facilities: Rental shop across the road from the Camp Richardson main lodge, which stays open all year.

Services: Overnight lodging and rentals, dinner at the Beacon Bar and Grill on the beach.

Rental packages: Skis, boots, bindings, poles, snowshoes (including for kids), and sleds are available.

Instruction: None offered.

Transportation: Buses run from the South Shore and Stateline areas.

Special programs: Monthly full-moon outings along the beach and through the neighboring Tallac Estates, weather permitting.

Major events of the season: None.

Location: At Camp Richardson Resort on Emerald Bay Road (Highway 89), two miles north of the "Y" intersection of Highway 89 and U.S. 50.

Contact: Camp Richardson Cross-Country and Snowshoe Center, Hwy. 89/P.O. Box 9028, South Lake Tahoe, CA 96158; 530/542-6584 or 800/544-1801; website: www.camprichardson.com.

STATELINE/ZEPHYR COVE

Spooner Lake

(see map on page 336, site 9)

Relatively undiscovered Spooner Lake is one of the gems of Lake Tahoe, even though passers-by can see little more than a modest trail system encircling a frozen, snow-covered lake. Ah, but what you see is only a fraction of what you get. For intermediate to expert skiers, this is one of the most spectacular trail systems anywhere. The route to the high-country trails around Snow Pass climbs gradually along a drainage fringed with aspen and pine forest, leading to three challenging routes: Marlette Lake, 9.7 kilometers from the lodge; the Carson Range Trail, a 20-kilometer loop from Marlette Lake with plenty of steep climbs; and the Bear Mountain Loop, 13.2 kilometers from the lodge. All three are expert routes, and they reward you with some of the best vistas of Tahoe, especially Bear Mountain, where a high trail comes close to the lake. The trail to Snow Pass is the same one used by mountain bikers in the summer to reach the famous Flume Trail, which begins just northwest of Marlette Lake. In winter, the Flume Trail is closed, even to skiers. As it happens, Max Jones, the man who made the Flume Trail famous, operates the cross-country area (with Patti McMullan), most of which is in Lake Tahoe-Nevada State

Park. Although strong Nordic skiers thrive on the higher trails, the flat loop around Spooner Lake is a very scenic 4.5-kilometer tour. Most of the trails throughout the 8,000 acres of terrain are buffed daily with a large snow-grooming machine. This is the closest major cross-country area to South Lake Tahoe, 12 miles from the Stateline casinos on the Nevada side of the lake.

Kilometers of track: 90K of machine-groomed track, plus 15K of snowshoe trails.

Types of trails: 21 trails (30 percent beginner, 40 percent intermediate, 30 percent advanced).

Trail pass fees: Adults, $17.50; students (16–22), $9; youths (7–15), $4; seniors over 60, $5; seniors (over 70) and children (six and under) ski free.

Facilities: Two overnight backcountry cabins, two warming huts, one day lodge.

Services: Snack service, lessons, rentals, and shuttle bus service from South Shore and North Shore.

Rental packages: Skis, boots, and bindings and snowshoes and Kinder Sleds are available. Kids six and under get free ski rentals.

Instruction: Including all-day trail pass and performance rentals, $38 for adults, $25 for students (16-22 with ID) and $18 for juniors (9-15).

Transportation: There is shuttle service from South Lake Tahoe and Incline Village daily.

Special programs: An overnight touring program offers stays for up to four people each in two small backcountry log cabins, which can be reached only by skis or snowshoes. These cabins are fully furnished and have kitchens with propane cooking stoves, futons with bedding, wood-heating stoves and drinking water. There are no showers. Rates range from $139 per night midweek to $319 for a two-night stay on weekends.

Location: Just north of the junction of U.S. 50 and Highway 28, at the parking lot for Lake Tahoe-Nevada State Park. Incline Village is 12 miles north.

Contact: Spooner Lake, P.O. Box 981, Carson City, NV 89701; 775/887-8844 or 888/858-8844; website: www.spoonerlake.com.

KIRKWOOD/HOPE VALLEY/MARKLEEVILLE

Hope Valley Cross-Country Ski Center (see map on page 336, site 10)

Hope Valley, in Toiyabe National Forest, is an idyllic place with beautiful frozen lakes and distant vistas of Carson Pass and its prodigious peaks. Operator Steve Lannoy runs a small cross-country program out of historic Sorensen's Resort, where one of the trails (Indian Head) originates. Most skiers, however, will need to drive to one of seven other trailheads. The closest is the Burnside Lake Trail, where a large flat serves as the teaching area and the starting point for a 14-mile round-trip to the lake, which is at the end of a wide Forest Service road. But a less ambitious loop of five or six miles, mostly on machine-set track, can be made on the Sawmill Trail, which branches off from Burnside. Stronger skiers who continue on will get dramatic views from Sweet Vista, overlooking Stevens Peak (elevation 10,061 feet) and Red Lake Peak (10,061 feet) to the west, as well as the drainage for the West Fork of the Carson River.

Other good trails are north on Highway 89, not far from its intersection with Highway 88. There's a good beginner trek on the south side of Grass Lake, with flat but scenic terrain through ponderosa and Jeffrey pine. The best views of Hope Valley are from the Willow Creek Trail, a five-mile, out-and-back, intermediate track branching eastward from Highway 89, and from the Snowshoe Thompson Trail, a meandering six-mile trail from Luther Pass to the highway intersection. The modest Nordic center at Sorensen's has a full-service rental and instruction program. Most of the trails do not have machine-set track, so skiers will have to cut their own after new snow. There are no skating lanes on trails. Trail systems on U.S. Forest Service lands are open to other winter uses, which includes snowmobiling.

Kilometers of track: 96K of marked trails, 10 of which are groomed.

Types of trails: Striding and telemark.

Trail pass fees: Although this is a nonprofit op-

eration, voluntary donations are requested to underwrite the cost of maintaining the trail.

Facilities: One day lodge. There's a special area for kids.

Services: Overnight lodging, a sauna, a café, rentals, lessons, and tours.

Rental packages: Striding and telemark skis, demos, and snowshoes are available, at $15–17.

Instruction: Beginner lessons are $25, with rental equipment, $35. Private lessons are available by appointment.

Transportation: No shuttle services available.

Special programs: Guided wildlife and moonlight tours and backcountry skills seminars.

Major events of the season: Snowshoe Thompson Tour, a family outing with various routes, held in spring in conjunction with Norway's recognition of Snowshoe Thompson.

Location: At Sorensen's Resort, on Highway 88 west of the intersection with Highway 89.

Contact: Sorensen's Resort, 14255 Hwy. 88, Hope Valley, CA 96120; 530/694-2266 or 530/694-2203 (off-season).

Kirkwood Cross-Country Center (see map on page 336, site 11)

A must for any visiting Nordic skier, Kirkwood is one of the largest and best-maintained cross-country resorts in the region, with unique topography that includes lava rock buttes, sloping tiers of granite boulders, and picturesque views of Caples Lake and Little Round Top Mountain. There are three separate trail systems, each with its own attractions, but all of them, except for three trails, are negotiable by intermediates.

Most of the gentle beginners' trails are in Kirkwood Meadows, from the base of the downhill ski area to Highway 88, a distance of five kilometers. This is open, flat terrain bordered by condominiums and houses. Across the road, next to the large cross-country center, a vast, unseen intermediates' mecca drops into a valley and extends through the woods, crossing Caples Creek several times. This area includes a Kiddies' Kilometer, festooned with wooden wildlife figures. It also contains the scenic High Trail, which rises back to the ridgeline for a view of the lower drainage. The system here offers loop trails ranging from 1K to 5K, interesting rock formations, and two of the three expert trails (Agony and Ecstasy), which ascend steep slopes to connect with the upper trail system. That system, called Schneider, can be reached more easily by driving two miles east on Highway 88 and turning north on Schneider Cow Camp Road to a parking lot. From here, there's another large beginner network, on the lower trails, and a labyrinth of intermediate trails that eventually lead to Coyote Pass, the route used for the annual Echo Summit to Kirkwood Cross-Country Race. The most scenic trails are Lower and Upper Outpost, flanked on one side by bizarre lava buttes and on the other by a stunning panorama of Caples Lake and the peaks of Mokelumne Wilderness. Because the intermediate trails are generally above tree line, or are sparsely vegetated, there are almost uninterrupted views. Kirkwood provides meticulously groomed and machine-set trails, as well as an excellent staff of instructors managed by Debbi Waldear, a former Olympic contender who exemplifies the best in the sport. Not surprisingly, the area is a favorite of Tahoe residents.

Kilometers of track: 80K of machine-groomed track.

Types of trails: Skating lane with three interconnected trail systems (20 percent beginner, 60 percent intermediate, and 20 percent advanced).

Trail pass fees: Adults, $20; juniors (13–18), $15; children (7–12), $6; seniors (65 and over), $15; children six and under are free.

Facilities: Four warming huts, day lodge with retail and rental shops, and two separate trailheads and parking areas.

Services: Restaurant/bar, lessons, rentals, and tours.

Rental packages: Top-of-the-line waxless striding, skating, and telemark gear, and snowshoes are available for rent.

Instruction: Beginner's package is $42 for adults, $35 for juniors (13 to 18), and $25 for children (6–12) and includes a full-day trail pass, equipment, and lesson. Skater's package is $45 for adults, $40 for juniors, and $30 for children. Telemark package, for adults only, is $45 and includes rental and lesson at the alpine resort. Private lessons are $40 by arrangement.

Transportation: A shuttle from South Shore lodging properties is available seven days a week, at a nominal round-trip fare.

Special programs: Night walking with snowshoes and headlamps, moonlight skiing, and periodic telemark clinics. Two trails are "dog friendly," but owners are required to bring plastic bags.

Major events of the season: Telemark clinics (January and February) and 14-mile Echo Summit to Kirkwood Tour and Race (March).

Location: On Highway 88 at Kirkwood Meadows, next to Kirkwood Inn.

Contact: Kirkwood Cross-Country Center, Hwy. 88/P.O. Box 1, Kirkwood, CA 95646; 209/258-7248 or 800/967-7500 (reservations); website: www.kirkwood.com.

CROSS-COUNTRY SKIING

Public Cross-Country Ski Areas and Parks

All properties listed are keyed to the Cross-Country Skiing map.

TRUCKEE/DONNER

Donner Memorial State Park
(see map on page 336, site 12)
A flat, marked loop trail follows a campground access road around the southeast shoreline of Donner Lake to Split Rock and returns through the forest. The trail has groomed, machine-set track, but no skating lanes. It sees heavy weekend and moderate weekday use. Note: Free naturalist-led cross-country ski and snowshoe tours are held throughout the winter, and frequently include history discussions about the Donner Party, the pioneer group that met with tragedy in the 1840s. Level of difficulty ranges from beginner to advanced, and tours may range from one to five miles in length. There's usually a full-moon tour, weather permitting, in February; call park headquarters for dates.
Terrain: Beginner; a gentle 2.5-mile loop; elevation 6,000 feet.
Maps: To obtain a USGS topographic map of the area, ask for Truckee.
Location: Southeast of the Donner Lake exit off I-80. Parking is available at the Donner Memorial State Park Museum, at $5 for a Sno-Park Permit.
Contact: California Department of Parks and Recreation, Donner Memorial State Park; 530/582-7892.

TAHOE CITY/WEST SHORE

North Tahoe Regional Park
(see map on page 336, site 13)
This 300-acre regional park, above Tahoe Vista off Highway 28, is one of the bargains of cross-country skiing—if you don't mind the occasional rough edges and intermittent grooming. Parking is available for more than 100 vehicles in a large lot and along the access road, and there are restrooms at the trailhead. The park is managed by a private concessionaire, and there are fees for parking, trail use, snowplay, and sled/saucer rentals. (The park also has two snowmobile tracks with rental snowmobiles available, but these are not allowed on the ski trails.) For nonresidents, use fees (2001-2002 season) were $3 for the trail and $3 for parking. Use fee for the snowplay area was $3, with rentals extra at $5.

Beginner routes afford some of the best views of Lake Tahoe, along the Lake View Trail. Intermediate routes weave through dense forest and can actually be followed to Old Brockway at Kings Beach, next to the junction of Highways 267 and 28. Advanced trails follow a high ridgeline providing additional views of the lake. Most are designed to be loop routes. The trails are patrolled on a part-time basis, and you may encounter some bare spots when you're at lower elevations. Hours of operation are 9 A.M.–5 P.M. on weekends, 10 A.M.–4 P.M. weekdays.
Terrain: Beginner to advanced; 11K of trails; elevation 6,000 feet to 6,600 feet.
Location: From Truckee, take Highway 267 south to Kings Beach at Lake Tahoe. Turn west on Highway 28, then right on National Avenue and follow signs for one mile to the park.
Contact: 530/546-5043 or North Tahoe Parks and Recreation, 530/546-7248.

Sugar Pine Point State Park
(see map on page 336, site 14)
As this edition went to press, this large California state park on Tahoe's heavily wooded West Shore was the focal point of a grassroots citizens' effort to restore the Nordic trail system that was used in the 1960 Winter Olympics and to build a museum or visitor center commemorating that event. Tahoma resident David Antonucci is spearheading the campaign, and a feasibility study completed in early 2000 found that 80 percent of the trails can be recovered. Though Squaw Valley, several miles north, was the site of the alpine skiing events, Tahoma hosted the start and finish of the Nordic and

Biathlon events. Race courses varied in length 5–50 kilometers, and stretched from what is now Sugar Pine Point State Park north to the small community of Homewood. Antonucci has spent a decade locating and mapping that trail network, as well as searching for—and finding—artifacts and landmarks from the Winter Games. Supporters of the recovery plan hope to create an Oympic Trails Park that would keep alive Tahoe's Olympic Nordic heritage. This new park also would provide a year-round recreation area that would be a major attraction on the West Shore. If the group succeeds, this will be a prestigious place for cross-country skiing and will offer a greatly expanded trail system. At present, Sugar Pine, which is open in the winter, encompasses land on both sides of Highway 89 but has a fairly modest trail network. For recreational skiers and snowshoers, the park offers two distinct environments: one along General Creek in the forest near the campground, the other along the shoreline of Lake Tahoe on the grounds of the Ehrman Mansion. The shortest ski route is the 1.1-mile Orange Trail; the longest is the 3.3-mile Red Trail. The easier routes are on the east side of the park. Park rangers groom all four trails on an irregular basis. There's a $2 parking fee for each vehicle. Camping, with toilets but no showers, is available. No snowmobiles are allowed. Note: Free, naturalist-led cross-country ski and snowshoe tours are offered several times during the winter. Ski tours range from two-mile introductory sessions to six-mile intermediate tours, and may include specialized sessions on skating, off-track skiing, and overnight winter camping and survival. A five-mile, full-moon tour along the General Creek drainage is usually held in February; call park headquarters for dates. Sno-Park Permit is needed, at $5.

Terrain: Beginner to intermediate; four marked trails totaling 8.3 miles; elevation 6,400 feet.

Location: One mile south of Tahoma on Highway 89.

Contact: California Department of Parks and Recreation, Sugar Pine Point State Park; 530/525-7232.

CITY OF SOUTH LAKE TAHOE

Tallac Historic Site Trail
(see map on page 336, site 15)

The flat, marked trail here winds through historic estates just above the shore of Lake Tahoe. As you ski you'll enjoy stunning views of Mt. Tallac. Rental equipment is available next door at Camp Richardson. This route can be connected with the Taylor Creek Trail across the highway (see number 41). Snowmobiles are not allowed on the trail.

Terrain: Beginner; a two-mile loop; elevation 6,200 feet.

Location: Parking is three miles north of South Lake Tahoe on Emerald Bay Road (Highway 89), and requires a $5 Sno-Park permit.

Contact: U.S. Forest Service, Lake Tahoe Basin Management Unit; 530/573-2600.

Bijou Community Park
(see map on page 336, site 16)

The only cross-country ski area in the center of South Lake Tahoe, Bijou is operated by the city's parks and recreation department. The groomed trail system meanders through 154 acres of mostly flat meadow, with some hilly wooded areas. There is a skating lane as well as a striding track. A plowed parking lot and restrooms are available. There is no fee for the trails.

Terrain: Beginner to low intermediate; four miles of machine-set track; elevation 6,000 feet.

Location: At the Bijou Community Park recreation complex, which is at the corner of Al Tahoe Boulevard and Johnson Street (off U.S. 50) in South Lake Tahoe.

Contact: South Lake Tahoe Parks and Recreation Department, Bijou Community Park; 530/542-6055.

HIGHWAY 50
(WEST OF SOUTH LAKE TAHOE)
Loon Lake Winter Recreation Area
(see map on page 336, site 17)

This relatively undiscovered trail system sets off from elegant Loon Lake Chalet, a spacious warming hut. Facilities include electric heating, a dining

CROSS-COUNTRY SKIING

area, a small kitchen with a stove and hot water, a propane barbecue, outdoor restrooms, air mattresses, and a loft for overnight use. On winter weekends, the warming hut is open to the public 9 A.M.–3 P.M., and belongings must be stored in the loft on the third floor. A staff ranger is usually on duty for search-and-rescue missions.

Seven defined trails, ranging from one to four kilometers, offer a variety of touring experiences in the Crystal Basin area, with views of steep, granite peaks in Desolation Wilderness to the east. Only one of the trails—South Shore—is unmarked; this extends from Loon Lake Campground along the shoreline. A more challenging route for intermediate to advanced skiers connects the North Star Trail (2.5 miles) to the Telemark Loop (1.5 miles) on the north shore of the lake. Trailheads are signed with trail name, mileage, kilometers, and difficulty. Trails are not groomed, and track setting occurs only on an intermittent basis. The chalet, with a capacity of 20 people, may be rented for up to seven days at a time and is available for $65 per night plus a reservation fee. Also, a security deposit is required when keys are collected at the Eldorado National Forest Camino Information Center.

Terrain: Beginner to advanced; 9.75 miles of ungroomed, marked and unmarked trails; elevation 6,378 feet to 6,700 feet.
Location: From South Lake Tahoe, travel west on U.S. 50 to Riverton (where the highway goes from two to four lanes). Turn right on Ice House Road and continue 30 miles to the lake. This road has some steep and potentially icy grades but is intermittently plowed by the Sacramento Municipal Utility District (SMUD). Call ahead for road conditions. Limited parking is available at the chalet.
Contact: Eldorado National Forest; 530/644-6048 or 800/280-CAMP (800/280-2267).

KIRKWOOD/HOPE VALLEY/MARKLEEVILLE
Grover Hot Springs State Park
(see map on page 336, site 18)
In addition to a relatively flat area for beginning skiers, Grover Meadow, this delightful state park

on the eastern slope of the Sierra Nevada offers a major bonus—a soak in a natural hot springs pool, which is open throughout the winter. The meadow gets only two to five feet of snow on average, but it's quite scenic, surrounded by 10,000-foot peaks. Naturalists with the California Department of Parks and Recreation offer free introductory cross-country ski lessons (bring your own gear) two or three times a season, unless there is insufficient snow, when an alternate location is chosen. This session lasts about three hours. A full-moon ski tour is usually given during February, and off-site tours on the Carson Pass and at Red Lake also are offered for intermediate skiers. Call the park for a schedule of winter activities. Incidentally, winter camping is available at a picnic site for $12, and includes flush toilets but no hot showers. Charge for the hot springs is $2 for adults, $1 for children.
Terrain: Beginner to lower intermediate; a two-mile loop; elevation 5,900 feet.
Location: At the Grover Hot Springs Pool parking lot, south of Highway 89 and four miles west of Markleeville at the end of Hot Springs Road.
Contact: Grover Hot Springs State Park; 530/694-2248.

FEATHER RIVER COUNTRY/LAKES BASIN
Plumas Eureka State Park
(see map on page 336, site 19)
Found in the heart of the Lakes Basin, this California state park offers three ungroomed trails. The longest is the Jamison Canyon Loop Trail, a marked, three-mile beginner route that starts at the state park museum, winds through the campground, crosses two creeks, and returns to the main road. It also accesses more advanced skiing in the canyon and Grass Lake basin. The loop ends at County Road A14, and you'll need to walk a short distance along the road to return to the museum and the parking lot. One section of the trail (along the access road to the campground) has potential avalanche danger. Another trail, around Madora Lake, also begins at County Road A14, and provides an unmaintained trailhead with skiing

along an ungroomed loop trail of 1.5 miles. The third trail, an ungroomed, intermediate route of 1.3 miles, begins at the parking lot of Plumas Eureka Ski Bowl (which was not in operation at this writing) and goes to Eureka Lake. Advanced skiers can continue to the historic Eureka Peak. When the ski area is open, cross-country skiers can buy a single-ride ticket to the top of the hill ending near the lake. Note: Park naturalists offer beginning cross-country ski and snowshoe tours for free five or six times a season (bring your own gear); for dates, contact the park office.

Terrain: Beginner to intermediate; three trails totaling about 5.8 miles; elevation 5,150 feet.

Location: From Graeagle on Highway 89, turn left on County Road A14 and go five miles to the museum and park office.

Contact: California Department of Parks and Recreation, Plumas Eureka State Park; 530/836-2380.

Yuba Pass Sno-Park
(see map on page 336, site 20)

This area is very popular with snowmobilers and skiers, as wheeled vehicles are prohibited on groomed routes. Trails are groomed both north and south of the Sno-Park through the California Off-Highway-Vehicle Program. You'll find an excellent, 4.5-mile (one-way) Nordic trail heading to Bear Trap Meadows; the trailhead is north of the Sno-Park, marked "Snowmobile and Nordic Ski Trailhead." Snowmobiles share the route for one mile, after which cross-country skiers have it to themselves.

Terrain: Beginner to advanced; 100 miles of skiing terrain; elevation 6,700 feet.

Maps: To obtain USGS topographic maps of the area, ask for Haypress Valley, Sattley, and Webber Peak.

Location: From Truckee, follow Highway 89 approximately 25 miles north from its intersection with I-80, heading toward Sierraville. Turn left on Highway 49 and drive another 18 miles toward Bassett's Station. The Sno-Park is six miles east of Bassett's Station on Highway 49. Sno-Park permits are $5 and may be obtained at Bassett's Station.

Contact: Tahoe National Forest, Sierraville Ranger District; 530/994-3401.

Wilderness Cross-Country Trails

The following are unmaintained cross-country trails on national forest lands. Unless otherwise indicated, many should not be attempted by beginners. For trails of any length, you need to be proficient in the use of a map and compass and should plan to start your trek early in the day. Be prepared for any type of weather, including a possible emergency overnight stay, since storms can arise at any time in the Sierra and impair visibility. Bring extra food, liquids, a flashlight, spare clothing, and survival gear for any half-day or all-day trek. Before leaving, notify a responsible person of your whereabouts and, especially, of your return date. Route-finding is an important skill, as storms may drop two feet of new snow and completely obliterate markers, signs, and groomed or ski-cut trails. Be aware of your strengths and limitations. And always inquire with the local U.S. Forest Service ranger or

information station about current conditions. Trails may close at any time due to weather-related problems.

Sites listed are keyed to the Cross-Country Skiing map.

TRUCKEE/DONNER

Big Bend (see map on page 336, site 21)

Big Bend, a dispersed recreation area with no marked trails, is available for all users. While the region is open to motorized vehicles such as snowmobiles, it is mainly used for skiing, snowshoeing, and snow play. The elevation changes approximately 1,000 feet from canyon floor to ridge top, and the south slope of the canyon goes from granite to forested slope and back to granite at the top to the ridge. Users should consult Forest Service maps for road and trail locations and private land designation. Restrooms are available near the trailhead parking lot.

Terrain: Beginner to intermediate with no set trails; the slope is moderately steep, and there are granite boulders and rock outcrops from the trailhead to the South Fork of the Yuba River; elevation 5,700 feet to 7,000 feet.

Maps: To obtain USGS topographic maps of the area, ask for Cisco Grove and Soda Springs.

Location: Parking is available at the Loch Leven Lakes Trailhead parking area. From Truckee, take I-80 about 10 miles west to the Big Bend exit. Turn left onto Hampshire Rocks Road and follow it one-quarter mile to the parking lot.

Contact: Tahoe National Forest, Truckee Ranger District; 530/587-3558.

Peter Grubb Hut/Castle Peak/ Donner Summit
(see map on page 336, site 22)
A marked Nordic ski trail begins at the Castle Peak/Boreal interchange at Donner Summit and follows the summer road approximately one-quarter mile to an intersection. From this intersection, Nordic skiers can take the trail to the north, which continues up Castle Valley and over Castle Pass. From there, an unmarked trail continues on to the Peter Grubb Hut. For experienced skiers, more difficult routes continue on to Castle and Basin Peaks. Make reservations to stay at the Peter Grubb Hut through the Sierra Club at the Clair Tappaan Lodge at Norden; phone 530/426-3632 for details. This is a very popular skiing area. Snowmobiles are prohibited in Castle and Round Valleys.

Terrain: Intermediate to advanced, with a moderate upslope toward the hut and a difficult downhill over Castle Pass; three miles one way; elevation 7,200 feet at the trailhead, 7,800 feet at the hut, and 9,100 feet at Castle Peak.

Maps: To obtain USGS topographic maps of the area, ask for Norden and Soda Springs.

Location: Along the north side of I-80 at the Castle Peak interchange. Sno-Park parking is available along the Boreal frontage road south of the freeway, and a $5 permit is required.

Contact: Tahoe National Forest, Truckee Ranger District; 530/587-3558, backcountry and avalanche information 530/587-2158.

Wheeler Loop
(see map on page 336, site 23)
This marked route follows a county road around the north side of Kyburz Marsh to Kyburz Flat, an open, flat area that offers plenty of skiable terrain and receives moderate use. Access from Highway 89 is on County Road 450. Note: Cross-country skiing south of Kyburz Road February 1–July 15 is discouraged, in order to protect nesting waterfowl in Kyburz Marsh.

Terrain: Beginner; a five-mile loop through a relatively flat area with open timber and marsh; elevation 6,400 feet.

Maps: To obtain USGS topographic maps of the area, ask for Sardine Peak and Sierraville.

Location: Drive 17 miles north of Truckee on Highway 89 to the marked trailhead. If you reach Jackson Meadow Road, you've gone one mile too far. Parking is difficult if the road shoulder has not been plowed.

Contact: Tahoe National Forest, Sierraville Ranger District; 530/994-3401.

Sagehen Summit
(see map on page 336, site 24)
This unmarked route follows a road up a creek bottom, and lateral roads offer many side trips for the adventurous skier. Sagehen Campground (2.5 miles west of Highway 89) makes a good winter camp. The area is also used by snowmobilers; the route crosses a groomed snowmobile trail one-quarter mile in from Highway 89.

Terrain: Intermediate to advanced; there is a gradual incline on the five-mile loop; elevation 6,400 feet.

Maps: To obtain USGS topographic maps of the area, ask for Hobart Mills and Independence Lake.

Location: At Sagehen Summit on the west side of Highway 89, eight miles north of Truckee. There is parking for four to six vehicles when the road is plowed.

Contact: Tahoe National Forest, Truckee Ranger District, 530/587-3558, backcountry and avalanche information 530/587-2158.

Cabin Creek Trail
(see map on page 336, site 25)

A marked route follows old logging roads and the Cabin Creek Road. It's a nice area for downhill practice while cross-country skiing. The trail is becoming popular among skiers and also receives moderate snowmobile use.

Terrain: Intermediate to advanced, with gently rolling slopes on a nine-mile loop; elevation 6,000 feet.

Maps: To obtain a USGS topographic map of the area, ask for Truckee.

Location: From I-80, take Highway 89 south for three miles. Turn right onto Cabin Creek Road and continue one mile west to the unmarked trailhead. There is limited parking near the trailhead when the road is plowed.

Contact: Tahoe National Forest, Truckee Ranger District; 530/587-3558, backcountry and avalanche information 530/587-2158.

Pole Creek Trail System
(see map on page 336, site 26)

These unmarked trails follow Forest Service roads along the Pole Creek and Silver Creek drainages. The area is a popular cross-country skiing destination and is closed to snowmobiling. Some loops offer downhill practice areas.

Terrain: Beginner to very advanced; 11 miles one way; elevation 6,200 feet to 8,400 feet.

Location: Six miles south of Truckee on Highway 89. Some free parking is available on the west side of the road.

Contact: Tahoe National Forest, Truckee Ranger District; 530/587-3558, backcountry and avalanche information 530/587-2158.

Martis Lookout Trail
(see map on page 336, site 27)

The unmarked route follows Martis Lookout Road to Martis Peak, with views of Lake Tahoe, the Sierra crest, and Mt. Rose. This is a very popular area, which can be a problem because there is only limited parking.

Terrain: Advanced; a moderate climb to Martis Peak on an eight-mile loop; elevation 7,200 feet to 8,650 feet.

Maps: To obtain a USGS topographic map of the area, ask for Martis Peak.

Location: One-quarter mile north of Brockway Summit. A limited area adjacent to the highway is plowed for parking.

Contact: Tahoe National Forest, Truckee Ranger District; 530/587-3558.

TAHOE CITY/WEST SHORE
Page Meadows
(see map on page 336, site 28)

Page Meadows is mostly flat and surrounded by a scenic forest. The tricky part is to avoid getting lost since there are no signs or set track. Snowmobiles are not allowed.

Terrain: Beginner to low intermediate; no set trails; elevation 6,400 feet.

Location: From Highway 89, two miles south of Tahoe City, turn right on Fountain Avenue, left on Tahoe Park Heights Drive, right on Big Pine Drive, and left on Silvertip. Park along the street where the snowplowing ends. Parking is extremely limited. Ski down the road to the meadow.

Contact: U.S. Forest Service, Lake Tahoe Basin Management Unit; 530/573-2600.

Blackwood Canyon Road
(see map on page 336, site 29)

This unmarked road winds through Blackwood Canyon. Follow the road to an obvious junction and stay to the right. This path will lead you to a beautiful meadow where snowmobiles are not allowed. For a longer, more strenuous outing, continue upward to Barker Pass, where it meets the Pacific Crest Trail. Some steep uphill climbs must be tackled, but once at the top you are rewarded with views of the canyon and Lake Tahoe. Snowmobiles are allowed on this part of the trail.

Terrain: Intermediate to advanced; 2.5 miles to the meadow, seven miles to Barker Pass; elevation 6,200 feet to 7,680 feet.

Location: Take Highway 89 three miles south of Tahoe City to Blackwood Canyon Road, across from the Kaspian picnic area. Continue to the

Blackwood Canyon Sno-Park next to the highway (a $5 permit is required).
Contact: U.S. Forest Service, Lake Tahoe Basin Management Unit; 530/573-2600.

McKinney-Rubicon Springs Road
(see map on page 336, site 30)
Following the tree-lined road along McKinney Creek, this unmarked trail has a 720-foot elevation gain. The moderate path leads through a forest to two lakes. Snowmobiles are allowed on some parts of the trail.
Terrain: Intermediate; two miles to McKinney Lake, three miles to Lily Lake; elevation 6,400 feet to 7,120 feet.
Location: From Highway 89 south of Homewood, turn west onto McKinney-Rubicon Springs Road and drive a quarter mile. Take the first left onto Bellevue and drive one-quarter mile. Take the second right onto McKinney Road (follow the signs to Miller Lake) and drive another quarter mile. Bear left on McKinney-Rubicon Springs Road. Go straight at the stop sign and park where the snowplowing ends. Parking is limited.
Contact: U.S. Forest Service, Lake Tahoe Basin Management Unit; 530/573-2600.

Meeks Creek
(see map on page 336, site 31)
Follow an old logging road along Meeks Creek for 1.75 miles. You can ski the full loop by crossing the creek and following the road back to Highway 89. For more exercise, try skiing the meadow. Use caution when crossing snow bridges, as they may be weak. Snowmobiles are not allowed.
Terrain: Beginner to intermediate; a 3.5-mile loop; elevation 6,200 feet.
Location: Drive 12 miles south on Highway 89 from Tahoe City. South of Homewood, parking is along the highway one-quarter mile south of the Meeks Bay fire station or one-half mile north of Meeks Bay Campground.
Contact: U.S. Forest Service, Lake Tahoe Basin Management Unit; 530/573-2600.

INCLINE VILLAGE/MT. ROSE
Tahoe Meadows
(see map on page 336, site 32)
Not only is this a great place to try moonlight skiing, but the fairly flat meadow also offers a great place to exercise—and a wonderful view of Mt. Rose. Snowmobiles are allowed.
Terrain: Beginner; gentle terrain with no set trails; elevation 7,000 feet.
Location: From Incline Village, take Highway 28 to Mt. Rose Highway (Highway 431). Just before the summit, where the road levels out, look for a large meadow to the right. Park in the turnout by the meadow.
Contact: Toiyabe National Forest, Carson Ranger District; 775/882-2766.

SOUTH LAKE TAHOE
Angora Road
(see map on page 336, site 33)
Though this trail provides some of the best available views of Lake Tahoe and Fallen Leaf Lake, skiers face steep grades at several points. Some snowmobiles are usually present. There's a lodge with cabins at the lakes, but they are open only during summer. Granite shorelines surround the lakes, which are frozen in winter.
Terrain: Advanced; two miles to Angora Lookout, four miles to Angora Lakes; elevation 7,200 feet to 7,470 feet.
Location: Take Lake Tahoe Boulevard 2.5 miles south of the "Y" intersection in South Lake Tahoe. Turn right on Tahoe Mountain Road and climb to the ridge top. Turn right at the "T" intersection on Glenmore Way. Take an immediate left on Dundee Circle and another left on the next street. Park along the road. Ski or walk down the road and turn left on Forest Service Road 12N14. This road leads to Angora Lookout and up to Angora Lakes.
Contact: U.S. Forest Service, Lake Tahoe Basin Management Unit; 530/573-2600.

Taylor Creek
(see map on page 336, site 34)
Covering a large area, these flat, developed ski

trails are suitable for cross-country enthusiasts of all skill levels. The combined loop traverses open meadows and aspen groves. When you reach the dam and Sawmill Cove there are views of Fallen Leaf Lake. Although the trails are heavily used, they are not congested. Skiers can access them from the Historic Camp Richardson Resort trail system. Snowmobiles are not allowed.

Terrain: Beginner to intermediate; Fallen Leaf Dam Trail (a 2.5-mile loop), Fallen Leaf Campground Trail (a 2.5-mile loop), and Sawmill Trail (a two-mile loop)—you can combine the dam and sawmill trails for a 4.5-mile loop; elevation 6,200 feet.

Location: Take Highway 89 north from South Lake Tahoe approximately 3.5 miles to the Taylor Creek Sno-Park. A $5 Sno-Park permit is required.

Contact: U.S. Forest Service, Lake Tahoe Basin Management Unit; 530/573-2600.

Trout Creek/Fountain Place
(see map on page 336, site 35)
This unmarked trail leads through a meadow and down an unplowed road. Snowmobiles are allowed. Ski two miles along Fountain Place Road to Trout Creek. Advanced skiers may continue on to Fountain Place, approximately four miles.

Terrain: Advanced; six miles one way; elevation 6,400 feet to 7,720 feet.

Location: From Meyers on U.S. 50, turn right on the Pioneer Trail. Continue three-quarters of a mile to Oneidas Street and turn right. Park on Oneidas where the snow plowing stops.

Contact: U.S. Forest Service, Lake Tahoe Basin Management Unit; 530/573-2600.

Echo Lakes (see map on page 336, site 36)
An unmarked, almost flat trail parallels the lakes before climbing in elevation to Desolation Wilderness. If you are planning a trip into the backcountry, be sure to check the avalanche danger level and obtain a wilderness permit. Day-use permits are available at the trailhead; overnight users must register at the U.S. Forest Service office in South Lake Tahoe or at the Eldorado National Forest Camino Information

Center on U.S. 50. Pick up the *Echo Lakes Cross-Country Skiing* brochure from the Forest Service office for additional information. Snowmobiles are not allowed.

Terrain: Intermediate to advanced; 2.5 miles to the northwest corner of Upper Echo Lake, five miles to Lake Margery, and six miles to Lake Aloha; elevation 7,420 feet to 7,470 feet (Echo Lakes only).

Location: Take U.S. 50 to Echo Summit and turn north onto Echo Lakes Road. Park in the Echo Lakes Sno-Park (a $5 Sno-Park permit is required). Overnight parking is allowed for Desolation Wilderness campers. Parking is not allowed on the north side of the road.

Contact: U.S. Forest Service, Lake Tahoe Basin Management Unit; 530/573-2600.

KIRKWOOD/HOPE VALLEY/MARKLEEVILLE

Grass Lake (see map on page 336, site 37)
You can ski over a frozen bog surrounded by aspen groves. Unmarked paths lead to Hope Valley. Grass Lake is also popular for moonlight skiing. Snowmobiles are not allowed.

Terrain: Beginner; three miles on unmarked paths to Hope Valley; elevation 7,000 feet.

Location: Take Highway 89 south from South Lake Tahoe to Luther Pass and park in one of the plowed turnouts.

Contact: U.S. Forest Service, Lake Tahoe Basin Management Unit; 530/573-2600.

Hope Valley
(see map on page 336, site 38)
Aspen and pine trees surround this large, flat meadow. Use caution when crossing streams, as ice or snow bridges are usually weak. Snowmobiles are not allowed on land managed by the California Department of Fish and Game but may venture onto Forest Service lands. Cross-country rental equipment and instruction are available at nearby Sorensen's Resort, just east of the intersection.

Terrain: Beginner to intermediate; the open meadow area has no set trails; elevation 7,000 feet.

Location: Take Highway 89 south from South

Lake Tahoe to Highway 88. Limited parking is available along the road near the Burnside Lake turnoff. Cross the road and ski the meadow northwest of the road.

Contact: California Department of Fish and Game, 530/355-0978; U.S. Forest Service, Lake Tahoe Basin Management Unit, 530/573-2600.

Winnemucca Lake Loop
(see map on page 336, site 39)

Providing a beautiful tour through the Sierra, this trail climbs from Carson Pass to Winnemucca Lake, then descends to Woods Lake east of Caples Lake. From there, it follows the road from Woods Lake to the old highway, which it follows in a gentle grade back up to Carson Pass. Because of its length and steepness, the route is not recommended for beginners, but there are several bowls that offer a great opportunity to try out your telemark turns. The trail is marked with X-C symbols, blue diamonds, and pink flagging. Be aware of the possible avalanche danger along this trail near Round Top Peak.

Terrain: Intermediate to advanced; a six-mile loop; elevation 7,900 feet to 8,650 feet.

Location: At Carson Pass on Highway 88, just west of Hope Valley and the Highway 88/89 junction.

Contact: Eldorado National Forest, Amador Ranger District; 209/295-4251.

FEATHER RIVER COUNTRY/LAKES BASIN

Packer Lake Trail
(see map on page 336, site 40)

The unmarked route follows the Gold Lake Road for about 1.5 miles, then turns left, following the Upper Sardine Lake route. It branches to the north onto Packer Lake Road and continues for four miles to Packer Lake. Along the way, you get scenic views of the Sierra Buttes and Packer Lake. There is moderate use from cross-country skiers and snowmobilers.

Terrain: Beginner to intermediate; a very gradual slope, but the 11-mile round-trip distance is too far for beginners; elevation 5,400 feet to 6,400 feet.

Maps: To obtain USGS topographic maps of the area, ask for Gold Lake, Haypress Valley, and Sierra City.

Location: At the junction of Highway 49 and Gold Lake Road, near Bassett's Station. Limited parking is available.

Contact: Tahoe National Forest, Downieville Ranger District; 530/288-3231.

Upper Sardine Lake
(see map on page 336, site 41)

Skiers get one of the best winter views of both Sardine Lakes and the Sierra Buttes on this very scenic trip. The unmarked route follows Gold Lake Road approximately 1.5 miles, turns left onto Sardine Lake Road, continues one mile to Lower Sardine Lake, then branches to the right and heads around the shore of Lower Sardine Lake for one mile to Upper Sardine Lake. It receives moderate use by cross-country skiers and snowmobilers.

Terrain: Beginner to intermediate; the seven-mile round-trip route rises fairly gradually, but beginners may have trouble with the last half mile; elevation 5,400 feet to 6,000 feet.

Maps: To obtain USGS topographic maps of the area, ask for Haypress Valley and Sierra City.

Location: At the junction of Highway 49 and Gold Lake Road, near Bassett's Station. Limited parking is available.

Contact: Tahoe National Forest, Downieville Ranger District; 530/288-3231.

Gold Lake Road
(see map on page 336, site 42)

From its junction with Highway 49 to Graeagle, the snow-covered Gold Lake Road offers excellent cross-country opportunities for beginning and intermediate enthusiasts as well as providing great views of the Sierra Buttes and the surrounding area. Since it is also a county highway, the slope in any direction is gradual and travel is easy for beginners. Gold Lake Road is groomed through the Off-Highway-Vehicle Program (please use caution when a snow groomer is on the trail) and receives heavy use by snowmobilers and cross-country skiers. Limited parking is available across from Bassett's Station. The Little Truckee Summit-

Yuba Pass Trail can be accessed by following (for approximately 12 miles) the marked snowmobile trail that intersects this trail.

Terrain: Beginner to intermediate; 17 miles one way on an easy, gradual slope; elevation 5,400 feet to 6,400 feet.

Maps: To obtain USGS topographic maps of the area, ask for Clio, Gold Lake, and Haypress Valley.

Location: At the junction of Highway 49 and Gold Lake Road. Limited parking is available at the trailhead parking lot.

Contact: Tahoe National Forest, Downieville Ranger District; 530/288-3231.

Lunch Creek/ Yuba Pass Ski Trail
(see map on page 336, site 43)

This marked ski trail leads north and west from Yuba Pass through Bear Trap Meadows and along Lunch Creek Road. Several hills adjacent to Lunch Creek Road lend themselves to telemark practice. Approximately one mile of the trail overlaps a snowmobile route. By parking one car at Lunch Creek and one at Yuba Pass, skiers can make an excellent loop. The trail receives light to moderate use by skiers and moderate use by snowmobilers in the immediate vicinity of Yuba Pass.

Terrain: Intermediate; a nine-mile loop; elevation from 5,000 feet to 6,700 feet at Yuba Pass.

Maps: To obtain USGS topographic maps of the area, ask for Calpine, Clio, Haypress Valley, and Sattley.

Location: Access to the trail is at Lunch Creek Road, approximately one mile west of Yuba Pass. Limited parking is available at Lunch Creek. Yuba Pass is a Sno-Park area, so a $5 permit is required. Permits can be obtained at the Sierraville Service and Country Store, one-quarter mile south of the Highway 89/49 junction in Sierraville; 530/994-3387.

Contact: Tahoe National Forest, Downieville Ranger District; 530/288-3231.

CROSS-COUNTRY SKIING

Other Winter Recreation

What if you don't ski? Or what if your muscles burned out skiing KT-22 at Squaw Valley USA? There's definitely more than one way to play in the snow at Lake Tahoe. Whether you're taking a break during a ski vacation or looking for activities to entertain young children, the lake affords a wealth of winter recreational alternatives. Snowmobiling tends to be the number one option, and guided tours use hundreds of miles of scenic trails, encompassing several national forests and most sides of Lake Tahoe. Then there are sleigh rides, some of which can include dinner, and dogsled tours, which

are great for kids and couples. Recently, snowshoeing has become popular at several state parks and at most of the cross-country ski areas, and it's possible to take short, easy hikes through frosted meadows and pristine forest or even along snow-covered beaches. For hardy adventurers, there are winter camping, ice climbing, and backcountry skiing. And for those who just want an hour or two of gliding along the ice, Tahoe's outdoor ice skating rinks may fill the bill.

© KEN CASTLE

horse-drawn sleigh

Snow-Play Areas: Sledding and Tubing

It doesn't take much to create a spot for sliding down the snow; usually a modest hill will do. There are plenty of ad hoc snow-play hills throughout Tahoe, and anyone with a saucer, a tube, or a cardboard box can get in on the action. It should be pointed out that while this kind of snow-sliding can be fun and exhilarating for youngsters, it frequently leads to limb, back, hip, and head injuries. Aging adults should not try any of these shenanigans, and kids ought to wear helmets, at the very least, for protection, since rocks and trees don't make very soft landing zones. Here are some of the better-known spots:

TRUCKEE/DONNER SUMMIT

Boreal Mountain Playground and Ski Area

In addition to its ski slopes, Boreal Mountain Playground and Ski Area features a snow-play zone at the west end of its parking lot. Only plastic disks may be used, and the entry fee includes disk rental. It's off I-80 at Donner Pass. Parking is available in front of the Boreal Lodge, but it's often crowded. Boreal's sister resort of Soda Springs, off I-80 west of Boreal at the Norden/Soda Springs exit, is a veritable snow tubers paradise. It features two surface lifts that access several tubing flumes, and also offers sledding and snowshoeing—all on one lift ticket. There is night tubing on Friday, Saturday, and holidays.

Fees: $12 entry fee at Boreal, $14 two-hour tubing ticket at Soda Springs.

Contact: Boreal Ski Resort, 530/426-3666; or Soda Springs 530/426-3901; websites: www.borealski.com and www.skisodasprings.com.

Donner Memorial State Park

The park features a snow-play area but no sled slope. (A Sno-Park permit is available at the park.) No snowmobiles or overnight parking are allowed. The snow-play area is next to the Emigrant Trail Museum. From Highway 80, take the Donner Lake exit and proceed to the park on Donner Pass Road.

tubing is fun for all ages

© SHERRY MCMANUS/HEAVENLY SKI RESORT

Fees: The day-use parking fee is $5 (Sno-Park Permit needed).

Contact: Emigrant Trail Museum; 530/582-7892.

Kingvale Tubing and Sledding Center

This is a long-existing area on I-80 west of Donner Summit, off the Kingvale exit. There is rental equipment available.

Fees: Sledding hill, $10 all day. For tubing, $15 for three hours.

Contact: Kingvale Tubing and Sledding Center; 530/426-1941 or 530/587-7291.

Northstar-at-Tahoe

Northstar-at Tahoe offers snow toys, snow scoots, and other sliding implements at its Polaris Park, which operates into the evening with

WINTER RECREATION

lights, 4 P.M.–9 P.M. Anyone from age five and up may participate. It's south of Truckee off Highway 267.

Fees: These range $8–24.

Contact: Northstar-at-Tahoe; 530/562-1010; website: www .northstarattahoe.com.

Snowflower Sno-Park at Yuba Gap

This is a privately owned membership campground open to the public for winter sports. It includes an 850-foot-long sledding hill, as well as a 4.9-mile cross-country ski trail. A trail pass is $10 per person. Bring your own saucer or sled, or buy one at the general store. Snowflower is one mile off I-80 from the Yuba Gap exit (between Emigrant Gap and Cisco), and has a lodge with food service (open on weekends and holidays

There are plenty of ad hoc snow-play hills throughout Tahoe, and anyone with a saucer, a tube, or a cardboard box can get in on the action.

only) and a trading post with supplies. The park is operated by Thousand Trails.

Fees: Parking requires a California state Sno-Park permit, which is $5 per day and can be obtained at the campground.

Contact: Snowflower Country Store, 41776 Yuba Gap Dr., Emigrant Gap, CA 95715; 530/389-8241.

Tahoe Donner

Tahoe Donner's Snow Play Area at Trout Creek Recreation Center, part of a major residential community above Truckee, offers a large and well-maintained snow play area. Youngsters 12 and under must be accompanied by an adult. The center is on Northwoods Boulevard northwest of downtown Truckee.

Hours: Open weekends and holiday periods from 9:30 A.M.–4 P.M., conditions permitting.

Fees: $4 for ages seven and over, free for six and under and 70 and older. Includes plastic sled or disc.

Contact: Tahoe Donner; 530/587-9437; website: www.tahoedonner.com.

SQUAW VALLEY
Squaw Valley USA

The ski resort has a snow-tubing park at its High Camp mid-mountain day lodge complex, next to the Olympic Ice Pavilion. This facility has a dedicated surface lift that allows sliders to hook on and ride back up to the top. The course is exciting, but not too extreme, and is suitable for all members of the family.

Hours: Daily during winter, depending on snow conditions.

Policies: Restricted to ages four and up, with one person per tube. Tubing space is limited and sessions may sell out. Inquire at the base of the mountain at the Cable Car Ticket booth or at the information booth for status.

Fees: Adults, $7; child, $6. Cost of a lift or tram ticket is additional and is required. Buy tubing tickets at High Camp at the Olympic Ice Pavilion.

tubing

Contact: Squaw Valley USA, 1960 Squaw Valley Rd., Olympic Valley, CA 96146; 530/583-5585; website: www.squaw.com.

TAHOE CITY/WEST SHORE
Blackwood Canyon Sno-Park

Blackwood Canyon is on the west side of Highway 89, three miles south of Tahoe City. There is avalanche danger, so avoid steeper terrain along the north side of Blackwood Canyon. Parking is available, but it's often crowded. A good spot to try is at the intersection of Jackson Meadow Road and Highway 89.

Fees: The day-use parking fee is $5.
Contact: Tahoe National Forest; 530/265-4531.

Granlibakken Resort

South of Tahoe City, Granlibakken Resort and conference center features a snow-play area on a 40-foot hill for saucers only. Amenities include a warming hut with a refreshment stand (snacks are served only on Friday, Saturday, Sunday, and holidays). The hill is open daily 9 A.M.–4 P.M. The resort is off Highway 89 at the end of Granlibakken Road.

Fees: Day use is $4; saucer rentals are $3.
Policies: No inner tubes or toboggans are allowed.
Contact: Granlibakken Resort, P.O. Box 6329, Tahoe City, CA 96145; 530/581-7333 or 530/581-7533; website: www.granlibakken.com.

KINGS BEACH/TAHOE VISTA/CARNELIAN BAY
North Tahoe Regional Park and Winter Play Area

The fully supervised sledding hill here is regularly groomed and has some nice facilities such as heated restrooms, a snack bar with hot food, and a cleared parking lot. There is a daily charge to access the hill, and this includes use of the park's tubes and saucers. A private concessionaire runs the operation, and also offers a double oval track for snowmobile rides. The park is on the North Shore at the top of National Avenue off Highway 28 at Tahoe Vista.

SNO-PARK AREAS AND PERMITS

Snow-cleared parking lots are on main highways (marked by distinctive brown highway signs) in the central Sierra Nevada snow country of California. The season is Nov. 1–May 30 each winter (weather permitting).

Vehicles must have a Sno-Park permit displayed on the dashboard. The parking fee is $5 per day (good at any Sno-Park on the date issued) and $25 for a season permit (good at any Sno-Park during the entire winter season). Cars parked without a valid permit displayed are subject to a citation.

Permits are sold at a variety of sporting goods stores throughout central California, businesses near the Sno-Parks, and all Northern California State Automobile Association offices (for members only). They are also available at Donner Memorial State Park, which is a Sno-Park area. For mail orders, send a check made out to the California Department of Parks and Recreation for $25 (season permit) or $5 for each day permit (specify dates to be used) to: Permit Sales, Sno-Park Program, P.O. Box 942896, Sacramento, CA 94296-0001. Allow two weeks for processing. Call 530/324-1222 for a site map of all Sno-Park locations. You can also check out the website at www.calohv.ca.gov or email: pubinfo@calohv.com.

Fees: There is a $3 day-use fee.
Contact: North Tahoe Regional Park, 6600 Donner Rd., Tahoe Vista, CA 96148; 530/546-5043 or 530/546-4212; email: ntpud@jps.net (attention: Parks); website: www.northlaketahoe.net.

INCLINE VILLAGE/MT. ROSE

There's an unsupervised tubing hill on the driving range next to the château right at **Incline Village.**

Sledding is available at the Washoe County regional **Galena Creek Park,** which is on the east slopes of the Mt. Rose Highway (Highway 431) just below the summit. It is more easily reached from Reno than from Lake Tahoe; 775/849-2511.

WINTER RECREATION

Mt. Rose is an undeveloped area eight miles up from Incline Village on the Mt. Rose Highway (Highway 431). There is no contact phone number. Bring your own equipment or rent locally.

SOUTH LAKE TAHOE

Echo Summit

With an extensive sledding hill and some cross-country skiing terrain, Echo Summit snow-play area has become quite popular. No snowmobiles are allowed. (A Sno-Park permit is available at the lodge.) The area is on the south side of U.S. 50 at Echo Summit.

Fees: The day-use parking fee is $5 (Sno-Park Permit).

Contact: Meyers Shell and Food Mart in Meyers, CA; 530/577-4533.

Hansen's Tube and Saucer Hill

Two banked and maintained runs for tubes and saucers are featured on the hill. All equipment is furnished (no outside equipment is allowed on the hill). There's a snack bar selling hot and cold beverages and food. The hill is open 9 A.M.–5 P.M. daily and 5 P.M.–9 P.M. on selected Fridays and Saturdays, weather permitting. Hansen's is on the corner of Ski Run Boulevard and Needle Peak Road, close to Heavenly Ski Resort. You can park in an area on Needle Peak Road.

Fees: $6 per person per hour, or $12 per person for three hours. Youths under 18 must be accompanied by a parent or guardian. Children two years and younger play for free.

Contact: Hansen's Resort, 1360 Ski Run Blvd./P.O. Box 316, South Lake Tahoe, CA 96156; 530/544-3361; website: www .hansensresort.com.

Sierra-at-Tahoe Snowsports Resort

The resort offers a tubing hill, along with ski-bikes and snow toys, at its ski area, which is 12

kids play at Northstar-at-Tahoe

miles west of South Lake Tahoe off Highway 50. You don't have to drive there if you don't want to; merely hop on one of the resort's free shuttle buses from any of several points in the South Tahoe area. This is a popular family area, and it serves wonderful meals along with locally-produced coffees, wines and beer.

Fees: Prices vary depending on activity.

Contact: Sierra-at-Tahoe, 1111 Sierra-at-Tahoe Rd., Twin Bridges, CA 95735; 530/659-7453; website: www.sierratahoe.com.

Taylor Creek

At Taylor Creek, you'll find a snow-play area, a small sledding hill, and cross-country skiing access to Fallen Leaf Lake. No snowmobiles are allowed. The area is on the west side of Highway 89 near Camp Richardson, one mile west of Echo Summit.

Fees: The day-use parking fee is $5 (Sno-Park Permit).

Contact: South Tahoe Shell; 530/541-2720.

LAKES BASIN/ FEATHER RIVER COUNTRY

Bassett's Station

Bassett's Station, at the intersection of Gold Lake Road and Highway 49 northwest of Truckee, is a popular gathering spot for those who want to play in the snow. Parking is available, but it's often crowded.

Fees: The day-use parking fee is $5 (Sno-Park Permit).

Contact: Tahoe National Forest; 530/265-4531.

Yuba Pass

At Yuba Pass, you'll find a snow-play area, cross-country skiing (north of Highway 49) and groomed snowmobile trails. Parking is available, but often crowded. On the south side of Highway 49 at Yuba Pass.

Fees: There is a $5 day-use parking fee (Sno-Park Permit).

Contact: Tahoe National Forest; 530/265-4531.

Ice Skating

Olympic Ice Pavilion

This Olympic-sized ice skating rink at the High Camp Bath and Tennis Club at the top of Squaw Valley's tram has a grand view of the ski area and its spectacular, rocky peaks. Since it can get pretty windy here, it's best to phone ahead and check conditions before visiting. There are wind enclosures to protect the rink, and on a sunny day skating here is a magnificent experience (though you might get a bit winded from the 8,200-foot altitude). Other amenities at the club include restaurants and bars, retail shops, a heated swimming lagoon, and a spa. Squaw Valley USA is off Highway 89, 12 miles south of Truckee, on Squaw Valley Road.

Hours: A Cheap Skate discount package runs Sun.–Thurs. 4 P.M.–9 P.M. The pavilion is open daily year-round, 11 A.M.–4 P.M.

Fees: Adults, $20; children 12 and under, $10 (including cable car ride, rentals, and two hours of skating).

Contact: Squaw Valley USA, 1960 Squaw Valley Rd., Squaw Valley, CA 96146; 530/581-7246; website: www.squaw.com.

The Resort at Squaw Creek

Squaw Valley has a corner on ice skating arenas, and this magnificent resort, the largest in the valley, has a spacious outdoor rink that is open to the public. Skaters can enjoy fine views of the adjacent meadows, the Squaw Valley ski resort, and the surrounding mountains.

Hours: Sessions are two hours each and run continuously, with a half-hour break, 9 A.M.–5 P.M.

Fees: Adults, $15; youth (6-13), $10; children (1–5), $5. Cost includes skating and rentals. Without rentals, it's $5 per session. Private lessons are available. No group lessons.

Contact: The Resort at Squaw Creek, 400 Squaw

WINTER RECREATION

Creek Rd., Squaw Valley, CA 96146; 530/ 581-6624 or 530/583-6300; website: www .squawcreek.com.

South Lake Tahoe Ice Arena

Eagerly anticipated for two decades, the city of South Lake Tahoe Ice Arena was finally unveiled in mid-2002, and it's clearly one-of-a-kind at Tahoe. The biggest draw is that it is completely enclosed in a 37,000-square foot building, thus offering year-around skating. Further, it's an NHL regulation sized ice rink, so it can easily accommodate ice hockey tournaments. The rink includes a huge rental department, with 600 skates, as well as a concession that serves pizza, soups and nachos. There are also bleachers for spectators, locker rooms, a video arcade, and a pro shop. More than a dozen instructors offer lessons that range from beginning to advanced. The rink is at 1176 Rufus Allen Blvd., near the city campground, which is just off Highway 50.

Hours: Sessions five days a week (except for Tues. and Thurs.) 1 P.M.–5 P.M. and 7 P.M.–9 P.M., year-around.

Fees: $7.50 for nonresident adults, $6.50 for youth 6–17, and $2 for skate rentals.

Contact: City of South Lake Tahoe Parks and Recreation Department, 1180 Rufus Allen Blvd., South Lake Tahoe, CA 96150; 530/542-6262 (ice arena).

Kirkwood Village Ice Rink

As part of its new village expansion, Kirkwood announced plans to open a $1.5 million, 6,000-square-foot ice rink for the 2002–03 winter season. As this edition went to press, details of the operation were still evolving, but the rink, at the edge of the village plaza, is slated for daily operation throughout the winter, including evening hours. Call or check the website for updated information.

Contact: Kirkwood, P.O. Box 1, Kirkwood, CA 95646; 209/258-6000; website: www .kirkwood.com.

Snowshoeing

It takes little skill to immediately enjoy over-the-snow hiking on today's modern snowshoes. Worlds apart from the old-fashioned wooden snowshoes, several companies have introduced lightweight aluminum alloy models that are sleek and easy to use. Many of these are available for rent at winter sports stores and at cross-country ski centers around Lake Tahoe. In fact, most Nordic resorts offer snowshoeing on designated trails. Also, snowshoe tours are frequently offered by rangers in state parks and national forests. In California, Donner Memorial State Park near Truckee, and Sugar Pine Point State Park on the West Shore, and in Nevada, Lake Tahoe-Nevada State Park on the East Shore, occasionally offer guided snowshoe nature walks during the winter. (For the California state parks, tour schedules are listed on this website: www.ceres.ca.gov/sierradsp.) Kirkwood Cross-Country Center, on Highway 89, conducts snowshoe clinics at designated times of the season and rents snowshoes throughout the winter. Here are some favorite snowshoe areas:

Boca-Stampede Reservoir

The reservoir is a level snow-play area for beginners. Drive five miles east of Truckee on I-80 and take the Hirschdale Road exit. Go north half a mile toward the reservoir.

Fees: There is a $5 day-use parking fee (Sno-Park permit).

Contact: Paco's Bike and Ski, Truckee, 530/587-5561; or The Backcountry, Truckee, 530/582-0909.

Donner Memorial State Park

The state park offers flat terrain for beginners. There are no snowshoe rentals available. Take the Donner Pass Road exit from I-80 in Truckee, then head south to the park entrance.

Fees: There is a $5 day-use parking fee (Sno-Park permit).

WINTER RECREATION

Contact: Emigrant Trail Museum; 530/582-7892.

Tahoe Meadows

This is a great beginner's location, with a flat area off the highway (near a hut provided by the Tahoe Rim Trail Association) fanning out into the meadows. It's one-half mile west of the summit from Reno to Incline Village off Highway 431.
Fees: Use of the area is free.
Contact: Alpenglow Sports, Tahoe City, 530/583-6917; or Tahoe Bike and Ski, Kings Beach, 530/546-7437.

Carson Pass Area

In the Carson Pass area, trails fan out on mild to rugged terrain around Hope Valley, along scenic creeks and around frozen lakes. Take Highway 89 south of South Lake Tahoe to Highway 88, and watch for turnouts around the junction.
Fees: There is a $5 day-use parking fee (Sno-Park permit).
Contact: Tahoe Sports, South Lake Tahoe, 530/542-4000; or Hope Valley Outdoor Center in Woodfords (Hwy. 88), 530/694-2266.

Sleigh Rides

Borges Sleigh Rides

Dashing through the snow in the proverbial one-horse open sleigh, the Borges family spins tales of Tahoe while passengers enjoy a pleasant ride through aspens and meadows at a site that is just across the street from Caesars Tahoe. The family has operated the sleigh rides, and more recently carriage rides, at Stateline for over 20 years. Visitors can ride in one of five handmade sleighs, which seat from two to 20 passengers and are pulled by 2,000-pound blond Belgian or rare American-Russian Bashkir Curlies. The 35-minute ride features running commentary from the driver, who might regale passengers with songs, poems, and history. Everyone is snuggled up in warm blankets. Carriage rides are available in summer at three locations: Horizon, Caesars Tahoe, and Embassy Suites. Sleigh and carriage rides can be hired for weddings. The Borges family owns a fleet of 15 horse-drawn vehicles, with sizes that can accommodate from two to 20 passengers. Borges is on private land adjacent to Caesars Tahoe, on U.S. 50 at Stateline, Nevada. Free shuttle service is provided from area hotels and motels.
Hours: Rides are offered daily in winter 10 A.M.—sunset (weather and snow conditions permitting). In summer, rides begin daily at noon.
Fees: Adults, $20, children (12 and under), $10, with discounts for groups of 20 or more.

Contact: Borges Sleigh Rides, P.O. Box 5905, Stateline, NV 89449; 775/588-2953 or 800/726-RIDE (800/726-7433), fax 775/588-7583; email: borges@sierra.net; website: www.sleighride.com.

Camp Richardson Corral

On the West Shore, just a four-mile drive on Highway 89 north of the "Y" intersection in South Lake Tahoe, Camp Richardson Corral offers sleigh rides lasting about 45 minutes, when snow conditions permit. The sleigh holds 12 to 14 people, and rides meander through the forest or along the shoreline of the lake. Reservations are required.
Hours: Rides begin at 11 A.M. and depart every hour on the hour.
Fees: Call for details.
Contact: Camp Richardson Corral, P.O. Box 8335, South Lake Tahoe, CA 96158; 530/541-3113.

Kirkwood Ski Resort

The Meadows are the soul of Kirkwood, a four-seasons resort west of Carson Pass on Highway 88. And taking a horse-drawn sleigh ride across the Meadows is one way to appreciate the rugged beauty of the high peaks that comprise the box canyon surrounding the resort. Kirkwood Stables operates the rides, as well as summer trips. A western-style sleigh

WINTER RECREATION

can carry up to nine adults on a 30-minute outing, and wrangler Jim Hagan supplies warm blankets. The sleigh departs from the main lodge next to the parking lot. Evening rides can be arranged for groups by reservation, and weddings also can be accommodated. The resort is on Highway 88, 30 miles southwest of South Lake Tahoe.

Hours: Sleigh rides start daily at 2:30 P.M., but call ahead to verify times.

Fees: Call for information.

Contact: Kirkwood Ski Resort, P.O. Box 1, Kirkwood, CA 95646; 209/258-7433; website: www.skikirkwood.com.

DOGSLED RIDES
Husky Express

Dotty Dennis is an institution at Lake Tahoe. This diminutive lady with a big voice is a veteran 25-year-plus "musher" who runs the area's only commercial dogsled tours. It's always enjoyable—some would even say romantic—to scoot along on the snow, bundled up in blankets in the sled, behind Dotty's powerful team of huskies. Her trail system is in Hope Valley, one-half hour south of South Lake Tahoe off Highway 88. She schedules trips by reservation (weather and snow permitting), and is heavily involved in an annual series of dogsled races held at Hope Valley. Her sled holds 375 pounds (two adults and one or two small children).

Fees: Adults, $85, small children, $45, for a one-hour ride ($130 minimum per sled). Checks and cash only; credit cards are not accepted.

Contact: Husky Express and Sierra Ski Touring, P.O. Box 176, Gardnerville, NV 89410; 775/782-3047, email: huskyx@nanosecond.com.

Snowmobiling

Sure it's noisy, but snowmobiling is one heck of an adrenaline rush. It's also the fastest way to see some of Lake Tahoe's spectacular backcountry vistas, including dramatic views of the lake itself. There isn't much of a learning curve needed to run a snowmobile, and guides provide instruction before every tour. All you really need to know is how to start the engine (with a pullcord, just like cranking up your lawn mower), how to go (depress the thumb throttle), and how to stop (apply the hand-grip brakes, just like on a bicycle). Then there is strategic "leaning": if one side of the snowmobile starts to sink into soft snow, you and your passenger lean to the other side. Leaning also helps when rounding corners.

One thing to know about snowmobile trails is that they can be full of washboard ruts if they're heavily used or if there is not enough snow to groom them every day. That means that your body will absorb a fair amount of pounding—not terrific if you have a back problem. It's also a good idea not to drink a lot of coffee beforehand or you'll need to make unscheduled stops, which is difficult if you're in a large group.

When you sign up for a snowmobile trip, it isn't necessary to bring anything with you. Some riders wear their own ski clothing, but because of occasional oil spots (or pine tar from trees), you're better off renting a one-piece snowmobile suit, which is a lot warmer anyway, even if it makes you look puffed out like an astronaut on a moon walk. Helmets are mandatory, and you can also rent boots and gloves. If you want to bring a camera, snacks, or drinks, bundle them up in a fanny pack or knapsack and stow it on the rear rack on your snowmobile.

One of the decisions you'll need to make is whether to ride single or tandem. Children (who must be at least six years old) are always assigned to ride with a parent, but two adults will find that sharing a snowmobile is rather uncomfortable—for the second rider. It's more enjoyable if everyone has their own machine, even though it costs more. Teens must be at least 16 years old and have a driver's license before they are allowed to operate solo.

Although snowmobiles are powerful vehicles that can rip through the woods, the guided tours are not races. A lead guide sets the pace, and with larger groups, usually 12 people or more, a chase guide follows in the last machine. Often groups will be divided, with parents and kids in a slow group, and single-rider machines in a faster group. The tours normally last about two hours, and your guide will make frequent stops to explain points of interest, have refreshments, and check on everyone in the group.

Almost every snowmobile outfitter in the Tahoe Basin has a specific territory, and the scenery varies depending on whom you go with. Trips range from short excursions with panoramic vistas of Lake Tahoe to extended all-day trips into the mountainous backcountry north and south of the lake. You can arrange for a picnic lunch, if you wish, and some companies offer overnight rides with stays in local lodges. If the size of the group matters to you (or if you want a more personalized experience), you may wish to schedule a separate ride for your family, book on a weekday rather than a weekend, or go with a smaller outfitter. The large companies can be hectic on busy weekends, when the staff often seems overwhelmed with business and short on patience. If you don't care to drive your own machine, consider taking a more leisurely and comfortable snowcat tour, which is offered by at least two North Lake Tahoe guide services. These track-driven, over-the-snow motor coaches are usually heated and have cushy, padded seating.

Snowmobile tours range $75–130 for two-hour trips. Shorter rides of an hour to 90 minutes run $75–85, with half-hour trips going for $40–50. These rates are for single riders. Tandems (two riders) are generally $20–30 more. I personally don't recommend tandem riding except for children. For a second adult, the ride isn't very comfortable, and the greater weight makes the machine less nimble to drive. If you don't

Almost every snowmobile outfitter in the Tahoe Basin has a specific territory, and the scenery varies depending on whom you go with. Trips range from short excursions with panoramic vistas of Lake Tahoe to extended all-day trips into the mountainous backcountry north and south of the lake. You can arrange for a picnic lunch, if you wish, and some companies offer overnight rides with stays in local lodges.

want to do a backcountry tour, you can find oval track riding at several area golf courses and one regional park, when there is sufficient snow. These rides, generally a half-hour in duration, cost $35–50. Snowcat tours, a relatively recent addition at Tahoe, cost about $125 per hour. Most companies accept credit cards.

TRUCKEE/DONNER
Cold Stream Adventures

These are deluxe snowmobile and snowcat tours that originate near Truckee and use a private road to explore Cold Stream Canyon, which provides vistas of Anderson Peak, Tinkers Knob and Donner Lake. Operator Larry Hahn takes small groups of guests to a wilderness cabin, where they stop for snacks and hot refreshments. The trail is regularly groomed but is a bit more rugged than many routes on public lands. And snowmobile riders occasionally have the chance to drive through ungroomed snow. A two-hour trip generally covers 22 miles. Hahn caters to high-end destination travelers, including celebrities, and his rates are about 40 percent higher than those of other outfitters. He assigns a guide to every four people, and provides helmets for all riders. The trailhead is near Donner Memorial State Park, but all guests assemble at Hahn's office in Truckee. Hahn also offers customized tours of from several hours to a full day for groups of up to 15 people, including lunch at the cabin. He also offers moonlight tours once a month. His fleet consists of 15 snowmobiles and one 12-passenger Thiokol snowcat. The snowcat tour comes with wine and cheese at the cabin, and lasts about three hours.

Hours: Daily, 9 A.M.–5 P.M. during winter, depending on snow conditions.

Policies: Helmets, but not clothing, are provided. Weight limit per snowmobile is 320 pounds,

WINTER RECREATION

and double riders are accepted but drivers must be 16 or older. All trips require reservations.

Contact: Cold Stream Adventures, 11760 Donner Pass Rd. (office), Truckee, CA; mailing address is 8975 Cold Stream Rd., Truckee, CA 96161; 530/582-9090; website: www .coldstreamadventures.com.

Eagle Ridge Snowmobile Outfitters

Operator Dave Ceruti offers a variety of tours on nearly 200 miles of groomed trails that traverse 650 square miles of Tahoe National Forest. His is the only snowmobile company in the region that provides overnight excursions, with stays at unique country inns, most of which you can ride to. From the trailhead at Little Truckee Summit, 14 miles north of Truckee on Highway 89, groups head out on two- and three-hour trips to places such as Webber Lake, Hobart Mills, Treasure Mountain, and Jones Valley. The two-hour tour is one of the most scenic in the region, with stops to see a waterfall, frozen lakes, and a couple of historic sites. Those with previous snowmobiling experience will best enjoy this outing, since there are tight turns, narrow trails,

and steep plunges, all of which make the route more technical than others around Tahoe. There's even an open meadow that serves as an oval where riders can bear down on the throttle.

All-day tours often reach the spectacular Sierra Buttes and Lakes Basin, and riders usually are offered a barbecue along the trail or lunch at historic Bassett's Station on Highway 49. From there, riders proceed along the Gold Lake Road, which is frozen over in winter and makes an excellent, scenic snowmobile route past the jagged buttes. Two-day tours spend a night at Sierra Valley Lodge in Calpine, at High Country Inn in Sierra City (below the buttes), or at Coppin's Meadow Lodge, an exquisitely appointed four-room inn on the Jackson Meadows Road that is completely snowbound in winter and accessible only by snowmobile or skis. Eagle Ridge has a large and modern fleet of Ski-Doo touring machines.

Hours: Daily 9 A.M.–5 P.M.

Policies: Rates include helmets; clothing and boots are available at extra charge. Overnight tours include meals. Major credit cards are accepted.

snowmobiling at Northstar-at-Tahoe

WINTER RECREATION

Contact: Eagle Ridge Snowmobile Outfitters, P.O. Box 1677, Truckee, CA 96160; 530/546-8667 or 775/831-7600; website: truckeesports.com/eagleridge.htm.

Northstar-at-Tahoe

Snowmobile tours are among the optional activities at this large winter resort between Kings Beach and Truckee. Two-hour, 18-mile tours begin near Northstar Village, follow groomed trails on the perimeter of the downhill ski area, and enter the trail system of the cross-country center up to Sawtooth Ridge, which overlooks Martis Valley and the town of Truckee. Two-hour moonlight tours are run to the famous lookout of Mt. Watson, with an elevation gain of about 2,000 feet. The resort offers snowmobiles with heated handlebars. There is no minimum group size for departure. Make reservations through the Northstar Activities Center.

Hours: December–March, day tours leave at 10:30 A.M. and 1:30 P.M. Moonlight tours are offered on selected evenings.

Policies: Fees include helmets. Rental clothing, including gloves and boots, is available for adults and children at extra charge. Major credit cards are accepted. There is a 300-pound weight limit per machine; machine operators must be at least 15 years old (parental consent is needed for riders under 18). Reservations are recommended.

Contact: Northstar-at-Tahoe, P.O. Box 129, Truckee, CA 96160; 530/562-2267; website: www.northstarattahoe.com.

TAHOE CITY/WEST SHORE

TC Sno Mo's

Opposite the Tahoe City Shell station on 205 River Rd. near the "Y" intersection of Highways 28 and 89, this small, personable operation provides regular backcountry tours. The two-hour, 22-mile guided outings reach Mt. Watson for a million-dollar view of Lake Tahoe from 2,000 feet above the shore. From Tahoe City, the trail zigzags up a hillside through aspen and pine forest to the top of a cinder cone. From here, riders have a commanding view of distant Martis Valley, Donner Pass, and Castle Peak to the north. Then the trail follows a forest road along a ridgeline, with spectacular views en route to a rocky knob at Mt. Watson. The panorama of the lake from here is positively inspiring; it is arguably the best overlook of Tahoe, and it allows you to see virtually the entire lake from north to south. Late afternoon is a particularly enchanting time, as the muted sunlight casts a warm glow on the basin. Groups are small, with one guide for every five people; the guides themselves are both knowledgeable and amiable. The equipment consists of Polaris snowmobiles.

Hours: Trips depart two or three times daily, from 9:30 A.M. to 5 P.M.

Policies: All rentals includes a mandatory helmet. Drivers must be at least 16 years of age; youngsters accompanying parents must be at least four years old. Some credit cards are accepted. Reservations are recommended.

Contact: TC Sno Mo's, P.O. Box 1198, Tahoe City, CA 96145; 530/581-3906; website: www.snowmobilelaketahoe.com.

Tahoe City Snowmobiles

This is a track system that is in the heart of Tahoe City on the historic Tahoe City Golf Course. It has several machines, helmets, a children's snow park, a restaurant and a bar, and is within walking distance of several restaurants and lodges.

Hours: 9 A.M.–4 P.M. daily, snow permitting.

Policies: All drivers must have a valid driver's license, and all children must be accompanied by a parent. Rides are charged per half hour.

Contact: Tahoe City Golf Course, 251 N. Lake Blvd. (Hwy. 28 behind Bank of America), Tahoe City, CA 96145; 530/583-1516.

KINGS BEACH/TAHOE VISTA/CARNELIAN BAY

High Sierra Snowmobiling

This is a large oval track on Old Brockway Golf Course, at the intersection of Highways 267 and 28 on the North Shore. It is geared primarily to families with kids who want to take a spin on a snowmobile. Refreshments and food are available at Moose's Tooth Café.

WINTER RECREATION

Hours: Daily 9 A.M.–5:30 P.M.

Policies: You must have a valid driver's license to operate a machine, and all children must be accompanied by a parent.

Contact: Old Brockway Golf Course, 7900 N. Lake Blvd. (intersection of Highways 267 and 28), Kings Beach, CA 96143; 530/546-9909.

Lake Tahoe Snowmobile Tours

This company offers trips to the summit of Mt. Watson, the highest point on the North Shore of Lake Tahoe. A commanding vista of the entire lake from this lofty perch, as well as views of six ski resorts, are just a few of the attractions encountered on these tours. Guests meet at the Lake Tahoe Snowmobile Tours office in front of the Cal-Neva Resort at Crystal Bay, get outfitted, and then drive four miles to the staging area, which is on Highway 267 one mile south of Northstar-at-Tahoe ski resort. The tours roam through national forestland on over 100 miles of machine-groomed trails, climbing to a panoramic vantage point high above the lake. Tours are geared to all ability levels, and equipment consists of a large and modern fleet of Ski-Doo snowmobiles. All machines are equipped with hand warmers, and a complete clothing package of snowsuit, snow boots and helmet is included with each tour at no additional charge, except during holiday periods.

Hours: The Summit Tour (two hours) departs three times daily at 10 A.M., noon, and 2:30 P.M. Open daily from 7:30 A.M.–7:30 P.M., Nov.–mid-April.

Policies: Machine operators must be at least 16 years old and have a valid driver's license; children must be at least five years old and must be accompanied by a parent (at double rider price). Moonlight, private party, and all-day private tours also are available. Reservations are recommended.

Contact: Lake Tahoe Snowmobile Tours, 9980 N. Lake Blvd., Crystal Bay, NV (in front of Cal-Neva Resort); mail inquiries to P.O. Box 18754, South Lake Tahoe, CA 96151; 530/546-4280 or 775/831-4202; website: www.laketahoesnowmobile.com.

North Tahoe Regional Park and Winter Play Area

This public park offers the largest double oval snowmobile track on the lake, and a concessionaire provides rental machines and rides. The park is at the top of National Avenue in Tahoe Vista, just off Highway 28 on the North Shore (west of the junction with Highway 267). One advantage of snowmobiling here is that the park has heated restrooms, a snack bar with hot lunches (chili, hot dogs, etc.), a cleared parking lot, and a supervised sledding hill, so there's something for every member of the family.

Hours: The track is open 9 A.M.–5 P.M. daily.

Policies: Helmets are provided. Drivers must have a driver's license. Major credit cards are accepted. Reservations are recommended.

Contact: North Tahoe Regional Park, 6600 Donner Rd., Tahoe Vista, CA 96148; 530/546-5043 or 530/546-4212; email: ntpud@jps.net (attention: Parks); website: www.northlaketahoe.net.

Snowmobiling Unlimited

In business since 1981, Bob and Cindy Wolff run the oldest snowmobile operation at Lake Tahoe, and their motto is "doing whatever it takes to please the customer." That may explain their high rate of repeat business. Their territory covers 75 square miles of national forestland in North Lake Tahoe, on the trail system that surrounds Mt. Watson. Guided tours begin on the Brockway Summit three miles north of Kings Beach on Highway 267, and are available in shorter increments, such as one to one and a half hours (more suitable for families with young children), as well as the standard two-hour outing and even a three-hour trip. The crowning view, available from the longer rides, is from Mt. Watson, overlooking Lake Tahoe. The Wolffs will organize custom rides for almost any occasion—birthdays, weddings, anniversaries—and they can offer trail riding or off-trail riding. The equipment consists of about 40 machines.

Hours: Daily 7 A.M.–7 P.M., Dec.–April, weather permitting.

Policies: Helmets are provided, and suits, gloves, and boost are available. All trips must be reserved, and there are no specific times for de-

COURTESY OF HEAVENLY SKI RESORT

a snowmobile tour to the top of Tahoe

partures; these are at the convenience of the customer. The weight limit is 300 pounds per machine. Drivers must be at least 16 years old with a driver's license, and youngsters (preferably age four and up) must be able to hang on for at least an hour.

Contact: Snowmobiling Unlimited, Brockway Summit (Hwy. 267), P.O. Box 1591, Tahoe City, CA 96145; 530/583-7192; website: www .snowmobilingunlimited.com.

SOUTH LAKE TAHOE/STATELINE
Tahoe Paradise Golf Course
This is a half-mile groomed track at this 18-hole course, which is on Highway 50 west of the city of South Lake Tahoe. It is open when there is sufficient snow on the ground. Both single and double riders are permitted. The center has other snow activities including a saucer mountain, with saucers provided.

Hours: Daily, snow conditions permitting, during winter months, 9 A.M.–4 P.M.

Policies: All snowmobile drivers must have a driver's license. Ride periods are 30 minutes.

Contact: Lake Tahoe Adventures, 3021 Emerald Bay Rd. (Hwy. 50), Tahoe Paradise, CA 96150; 530/577-2940; website: www .snowmobiletahoe.com.

Lake Tahoe Golf Course
This is a quarter-mile circular track that is on Highway 50 west of the city of South Lake Tahoe. It is open only when there is sufficient snow on the ground.

Hours: Daily, snow conditions permitting, during winter months.

Policies: All snowmobile drivers must have a driver's license. Ride periods are 30 minutes. Reservations are not required.

Contact: Lake Tahoe Snowmobile Circle Track at Lake Tahoe Golf Course, 2500 Hwy. 50, South Lake Tahoe; mail to Lake Tahoe Snowmobile Tours, P.O. Box 18754, South Lake Tahoe, CA 96151; 530/541-4869; website: www.laketahoesnowmobile.com.

WINTER RECREATION

Lake Tahoe Winter Sports Center

This is one of the larger operations at Lake Tahoe, running 50 to 60 Arctic Cats out of a staging area in Hope Valley on Blue Lakes Road, just south of Highway 88. One advantage is that it owns a fleet of buses to pick up clients at their hotels in South Lake Tahoe. Riders are then taken to the rental center on U.S. 50, outfitted with gear and helmets, and shuttled to the trailhead, about a 20-minute drive. The trail explores the scenic Carson Pass area, with vistas of high, snowcapped peaks from an elevation that reaches 9,000 feet. You ride on snow-covered roads, through meadows, through forest, and along ridgelines in Toiyabe National Forest, for a 25-mile round-trip. Tours leave every two hours, starting at 9 A.M., and half- and full-day tours with lunch can be arranged. The Winter Sports Center also operates an oval track at Tahoe Paradise Golf Course, which is nearby.

Hours: Two-hour trips leaving at 11 A.M., 1 P.M., and 3 P.M. An early-bird special leaves at 9 A.M. Open seven days a week, Nov.–May.

Policies: Half- and full-day tours with lunch can be arranged. Helmets are provided on all outings. Rental clothing, including snowsuits, boots, goggles, and gloves, is available at extra cost. Single riders are recommended. There is a maximum of six snowmobiles per guide. You must arrive 45 minutes before bus departure. First passengers must be at least 16 years old; children and second passengers must be able to hold on for two hours. Major credit cards are accepted. Reservations are recommended.

Contact: Lake Tahoe Winter Sports Center, P.O. Box 11436, Tahoe Paradise, CA 96155; 530/577-2940; website: www.taho4fun.com.

Zephyr Cove Snowmobile Center

The largest snowmobile tour service in the region, Zephyr Cove runs over 100 Ski-Doo snowmobiles and has an extensive free shuttle bus system that picks up riders at Stateline hotels. All outfitting is done at Zephyr Cove Resort, four miles from South Lake Tahoe. From there, guests are taken to the trailhead at Spooner Summit on U.S. 50, northeast of Stateline in

Nevada. Weekends can be incredibly busy, so if you're looking for a more personal experience, schedule a tour on a weekday. With so many machines on the trail system at one time, it's frequently necessary to detour on spurs to allow other groups to pass. The route is quite scenic; it includes a high ledge at 9,000 feet with a bird's-eye view of Lake Tahoe and the Stateline casinos, and an overlook of Carson Valley and points east in Nevada. Bring your camera. Trails meander through pine and aspen forest, and the return route to the staging area can be rather steep (depending on snow cover). There's a spot where the group stops for hot chocolate, about midway through the tour. Three two-hour tours are offered daily, and a three-hour "Top of the Top" tour provides single riding over the best available terrain. Moonlight and private tours are available. Families, groups, and first-time riders are welcome. The season runs November–April.

Hours: Daily 9 A.M.–4 P.M., with evening and sunset tours offered, weather and conditions permitting.

Policies: Helmets are free and mandatory for all trips. Clothing rentals, including parkas, gloves, bibs, and boots, are available at extra cost. The combined weight limit for a double is 400 pounds. Machine operators must be at least 15 years old and have written parental consent; all riders are required to sign a risk acknowledgment waiver and leave a damage deposit on a credit card. Children as young as five can ride along. Major credit cards are accepted. Reservations are required.

Contact: Zephyr Cove Snowmobile Center, 760 U.S. 50/P.O. Drawer 830, Zephyr Cove, NV 89448; 775/589-4908; website: www.tahoedixie2.com.

SNOWMOBILE TRAILS IN NATIONAL FORESTS

Most national forestland within the Tahoe Basin is open to snowmobilers, provided there is at least six inches of snow on the ground. Wilderness, roadless areas, and developed ski areas are closed to all motorized vehicles. If you are venturing into the following areas on your own, go prepared with food, water, and survival equipment. Always carry maps and contact the local office of the U.S. Forest Service for the latest trail conditions. Be aware that fresh storms can create avalanche hazards, and the roar of a snowmobile can set off slides. Be sure to obtain a Sno-Park permit for parking in designated California Sno-Park areas.

Truckee/Donner

In Tahoe National Forest, just north of Truckee off Highway 89, the **Little Truckee Summit/Yuba Pass** trail network is the largest in the region for snowmobilers. It extends west of the highway near Prosser Creek Reservoir past privately owned Webber Lake and Jackson Meadows Reservoir to Bassett's Station. From there, it continues along Gold Lake Road to Gold Lake. The routes are used by a commercial snowmobiling outfitter, although they are open to the general public. Trails are also used by cross-country skiers. A detailed map can be obtained from the U.S. Forest Service.

Contact: Tahoe National Forest, Truckee Ranger District, Hwy. 89/P.O. Box 399, Truckee, CA 95734; 530/587-3558.

Tahoe City/West Shore

Blackwood Canyon Sno-Park provides views of Barker Pass, Ellis Peak, and Bear Lake, with unmarked, ungroomed trails featuring big bowls, meadows, and forests winding through Blackwood Canyon. It's a good day trip; most of the route follows a paved road that is snowbound in winter. Avalanche danger exists after storms. This is a popular cross-country ski area as well, so watch for pedestrians. Take Highway 89 three miles south of Tahoe City to Blackwood Canyon Road, across from the Kaspian picnic area. Continue to Blackwood Canyon Sno-Park. A Sno-Park permit is required ($5 day-use fee).

Hours: In winter, Mon.–Fri., 8 A.M.–4:30 P.M.
Contact: U.S. Forest Service, Lake Tahoe Basin Management Unit, 870 Emerald Bay Rd., Ste. 1, South Lake Tahoe, CA 96150; 530/573-2600.

Kings Beach/Tahoe Vista/Carnelian Bay

Brockway Summit's 13 miles of groomed trails lead to Mt. Watson, Watson Lake, and Stumpy Meadows. Along the three- to four-hour ride, you get great views of Lake Tahoe and Martis Meadows. From Kings Beach on Highway 28, take Highway 267 four miles to Brockway Summit. Park along the highway (parking is limited). Several commercial outfitters also operate in this area.

Hours: In winter, Mon.–Fri. 8 A.M.–4:30 P.M.
Contact: U.S. Forest Service, Lake Tahoe Basin Management Unit, 870 Emerald Bay Rd., Ste. 1, South Lake Tahoe, CA 96150; 530/573-2600.

Incline Village/Mt. Rose

Beautiful ungroomed trails in **Tahoe Meadows,** in the shadow of Mt. Rose in Nevada, provide great views of Lake Tahoe for snowmobilers and cross-country skiers. From Incline Village, take Highway 28 to Mt. Rose Highway (Highway 431). Just before the summit where the road levels out, look for a large meadow to the right. Park in the turnout by the meadow (parking is limited).

Hours: In winter, Mon.–Fri., 8 A.M.–4:30 P.M.
Contact: U.S. Forest Service, Lake Tahoe Basin Management Unit, 870 Emerald Bay Rd., Ste. 1, South Lake Tahoe, CA 96150; 530/573-2600.

South Lake Tahoe

Good for a two- to three-hour trip, forested, ungroomed **Hell Hole** provides limited views of Lake Tahoe. After storms, some avalanche potential exists in the Hell Hole area. From U.S. 50 in Meyers, take the Pioneer Trail 1.5 miles to Oneidas Street and turn right. Park where the snowplowing ends. Follow Fountain Place Road three miles to Hell Hole Road and turn right.

Hours: In winter, Mon.–Fri., 8 A.M.–4:30 P.M.
Contact: U.S. Forest Service, Lake Tahoe Basin Management Unit, 870 Emerald Bay Rd., Ste. 1, South Lake Tahoe, CA 96150; 530/573-2600.

At **Spooner Summit,** plenty of groomed trails, enough for at least two to three good hours of riding, lead to panoramic views of Lake Tahoe. Take U.S. 50 to Spooner Summit.

WINTER RECREATION

Parking is available in the large turnout in front of the Spooner rest stop. These trails are used by commercial outfitters, but are also open to the general public.

Hours: In winter, Mon.–Fri., 8 A.M.–4:30 P.M.

Contact: U.S. Forest Service, Lake Tahoe Basin Management Unit, 870 Emerald Bay Rd., Ste. 1, South Lake Tahoe, CA 96150; 530/573-2600.

Kirkwood/Hope Valley/Markleeville

Although used for commercial snowmobiling, the unattached snowmobiler can ride a network of groomed the **Hope Valley/Blue Lakes** ungroomed trails in Toiyabe National Forest from Highway 88 (near the Forest Service's Hope Valley Campground) southward to just west of Ebbetts Pass on Highway 4. Obtain a detailed trail map from the Forest Service.

Contact: Toiyabe National Forest, Carson Ranger District, 1536 S. Carson St., Carson City, NV 89701; 775/882-2766.

Lakes Basin/Feather River Country

Snowmobilers will find an ungroomed trail around **Lake Davis,** starting from a staging area at the lake's southeastern end (Lake Davis Road and Grizzly Road). Access to Lake Davis via Grizzly Road is usually kept plowed and well maintained. An additional three-mile loop trail to the Smith Peak Lookout is on the west side of Lake Davis. Services are available nearby. From Truckee, drive north on Highway 89 to the Sattley turnoff. Heading toward Sattley, drive to Highway 70. Turn left, heading toward Portola, and drive 1.25 miles to the Lake Davis turnoff. Turn right on Grizzly Road and drive five miles to Lake Davis.

Contact: Plumas County Visitors Bureau, 91 Church St./P.O. Box 4120, Quincy, CA 95971; 530/283-6345 or 800/326-2247.

Gold Lake Road winds through the Lakes Basin (connecting Highways 89 and 49) and is snowbound in winter, creating **Lakes Basin Recreation Area.** The road is groomed and marked for snowmobilers and cross-country skiers. There are numerous ungroomed trails branching off the main route, including a route to the Mills Peak Lookout. A staging area at the highway's northern end moves with the snowline, ranging from Mohawk Chapman Road to Gray Eagle Lodge Road. A second staging area with restrooms is at Bassett's Station, at the southern end of Highway 89 at the Highway 49 intersection.

Contact: Plumas County Visitors Bureau, 550 Crescent St./P.O. Box 4120, Quincy, CA 95971; 530/283-6345 or 800/326-2247; website: www.plumas.ca.us.

Accommodations

Tahoe and Vicinity Accommodations

Selecting accommodations at Lake Tahoe is like choosing from a 50-course buffet. Depending on your budget and the season, you can stay in nondescript motels or upscale hotels and condominiums. There are close to 18,000 rooms for rent in the basin, and two-thirds of them are in the south end, where Stateline's high-rise casino/hotels are surrounded by dozens of motels, most of which cater to the gambling crowds. Given the substantial distances between points on the North Shore and the South Shore—

which are an hour apart if you're driving—you should choose your location based on where you intend to spend the most time. The two ends of the lake vary greatly in style and topography, with most of the population concentrated in South Shore. Both areas are undergoing significant changes as new resort-oriented villages begin to take shape.

Truckee Hotel

Recently, many of the older and, frankly, dilapidated 1960s-era motels have been disappearing as South Lake Tahoe redefines its commercial strip along U.S. 50 as part of a major redevelopment. The objective of the plan is to bring in quality hotels, a convention center, a transit center, new shopping areas, and additional open space. The city is certainly well on its way to accomplishing those goals. Over a 10-year period, new hotels have been replacing old ones at a regular clip. Among the early examples were Embassy Suites Resort in 1991, Fantasy Inn in 1992, and Embassy Vacation Resort in 1997. In late 2002, two more properties were added to the mix as Marriott made a splashy debut at Lake Tahoe with simultaneous openings of its Grand Residence Club and the Timber Lodge, both interval-ownership projects. These large condominium-hotels form the core of Heavenly Ski Resort's new village and are on Highway 50 a block west of the Stateline casinos. And more changes are likely now that Harrah's is the new owner of Harveys, its long-time competitor. Plans have been discussed about creating a convention center—something that Tahoe has sorely lacked—and perhaps another hotel, both across the street from the Heavenly Village. Not to be outdone, Kirkwood Mountain Resort, on Highway 88, has unveiled several new condominium complexes, an outdoor ice rink, and a swimming center as part of its evolving four-seasons village.

The winds of change also are blowing across North Lake Tahoe. The Hyatt Regency Lake Tahoe in Incline Village is continuing to reinvent itself, having completed a major interior renovation and now rebuilding the Aspen Terrace. This is a three-story structure at the rear of the hotel that has been demolished and will be replaced by upscale rooms and a new 15,000-square-foot spa. Other plans involve refacing the entire exterior of the main tower to reflect an

Perhaps the most dramatic turnaround is on the West Shore, where the mom-and-pop lodges of the 1950s and 1960s are giving way to new and younger owners; the new owners generally choose to convert their accommodations into boutique inns. Some of the nicest cabins and small lodges are here, nestled in wooded surroundings.

Old Tahoe look, using river rock and exposed beams. Intrawest, the Canadian company that owns Whistler and Blackcomb, opened the first phases of its new Village at Squaw Valley in early 2002, providing a glimpse of what will come over the next several years. Northstar-at-Tahoe, near Truckee, is planning to replace its small village with a much larger one, including new condominiums, restaurants, shops, and an ice-skating rink, all part of a project being conducted by East West Partners of Colorado. In general, the town of Truckee seems headed for major growth in the way of new second-home golf communities, which could double the population in a few short years. Adding to the impetus is the completion of the Highway 267 bypass from I-80 around the downtown, and the possibility that major hoteliers may be interested in building at the new interchange.

Deciding where to stay is, in large part, a factor of what you wish to do. For skiers and gamblers, U.S. 50 at South Shore offers proximity to the casinos, restaurants, and shopping, as well as regular stops for the shuttles that serve the ski resorts. It's easy to step outside of your lodging and catch a bus to Heavenly, Sierra-at-Tahoe, or Kirkwood. The Stateline hotels have such a complete transportation infrastructure that guests arriving at the Reno or Tahoe airports can get along just fine without a car. You can take the Tahoe Casino Express from Reno 14 times a day directly to the front door of any of the "Big Five" properties at Stateline. In winter, the ski buses are frequent and convenient, and in summer the South Tahoe Trolley will take you to beaches, shopping, and restaurants. Public transportation, with the exception of the Tahoe Casino Express, is also available for most of the other accommodations along U.S. 50.

Getting away from the crowds and traffic at South Shore means taking to the back roads and

MAJOR RESERVATION SERVICES

Central Reservations

An umbrella organization that books properties for the entire Lake Tahoe region, North Lake Tahoe Resort Association offers thousands of lodging units, varying from condos and homes to hotel rooms and bed-and-breakfast inns. You can find just about any combination of amenities you want, including private beaches, piers, tennis courts, pools, and recreation rooms. You can also get bookings for rental cars, airlines, and recreational activities. The association maintains an annual calendar of events and a color travel planner. The website offers online booking for some properties, email request forms for others.

Rates: $–$$$$

Contact: Lake Tahoe Central Reservations/North Lake Tahoe Resort Association, 245 N. Lake Blvd./P.O. Box 5459, Tahoe City, CA 96145; 530/583-3494 or 888/434-1262; email: info @tahoefun.org; website: www.tahoefun.org.

Heavenly Tahoe Vacations

Concentrating on the South Shore, this one-stop reservation service is owned and operated by Heavenly ski resort. It offers complete vacation packages with a variety of lodging—including major ho-

tels, condominiums, and motels—and other components such as lift tickets, airfare, car rentals, and other activities.

Rates: $–$$$$

Contact: Heavenly Tahoe Vacations, P.O. Box 2180, Stateline, NV 89449; 775/586-7050 or 800/2-HEAVEN (800/243-2836), fax 775/586-4420; website: www.skiheavenly.com.

Lake Tahoe Incline Village/Crystal Bay Visitors Bureau

This office, in Incline Village on the east shore of the lake, provides lodging information and reservations for the Crystal Bay and Incline Village properties in Nevada. It offers a toll-free telephone service and also operates a website that links to properties with online booking capabilities. It covers hotels, condominiums, homes, and motels.

Rates: $–$$$$

Contact: Lake Tahoe Incline Village/Crystal Bay Visitors Bureau, 969 Tahoe Blvd., Incline Village, NV 89451; 775/832-1606 or 800/GO-TAHOE (800/468-2463); website: www.gotahoe.com.

South Lake Tahoe Reservations

The Lake Tahoe Visitors Authority, headquartered

side streets. For example, on the south side of U.S. 50, next to Heavenly, is the luxurious Tahoe Seasons Resort, and on the north side, next to the lake, is the boaters' paradise of Tahoe Keys, a waterfront complex with many second homes and condominiums for rent. Condos and town houses are widely available throughout the lake area, and there are some truly beautiful residential communities such as Glenbrook on the South Shore and Chinquapin on the North Shore. If you have a family or a group of two or more couples, renting a custom house is an excellent value, and there are property management companies that offer 24-hour service. A little-known fact is that Lake Tahoe has more private homes for rent than any other mountain resort region in the United States. Of course, you'll need to have a car to stay at some of these places, though a few are close to bus and shuttle stops.

Decide what type of environment you prefer— a small motel near the Stateline casinos, a mountain chalet at Squaw Valley, the luxury and service of a resort hotel, or a charming beachfront condominium. In general, accommodations are more plentiful and the price selection is greater on the South Shore. If you're looking for bargains and basics, check out the small motels and lodges near the "Y" intersection of U.S. 50 and Highway 89. For picturesque views of Lake Tahoe, look at condominiums and houses in the mountain residential areas. Some of the most impressive places are in Incline Village on the East Shore, on Kingsbury Grade on the South Shore, around Tahoe City, and above Highway 89 on the West Shore. For seclusion, consider Glenbrook (a gated community) on the South Shore, and Northstar, Alpine Meadows, and Squaw Valley on the North Shore. When you want to be on the water, it's hard to

in South Lake Tahoe, can making booking arrangements for more than 60 South Shore properties, varying from deluxe casino hotels and condominiums to motels and small inns. It also publishes a twice-yearly travel planner for the area.
Rates: $–$$$$
Contact: Lake Tahoe Visitors Authority, 1156 Ski Run Blvd., South Lake Tahoe, CA 96150; 530/544-5050 or 800/AT-TAHOE (800/288-2463); website: www.virtualtahoe.com.

Squaw Valley USA Central Reservations
Operated by Squaw Valley ski resort, this service provides bookings for nearly 50 properties, including hotels, motels, condominiums, and bed-and-breakfast inns, for Squaw Valley, Truckee, North Lake Tahoe, and Reno. The service also can arrange rental cars, airline transportation, lift tickets, ski lessons, child care, and other activities in the area. The website features online reservations request forms.
Rates: $–$$$$
Contact: Squaw Valley Central Reservations, 1960 Squaw Valley Rd., Olympic Valley, CA 96146; 530/583-5585 or 800/403-0206; website: winter.squaw.com.

Tahoe Douglas Chamber and Visitor Center
This office, on the Nevada side of South Shore, offers information and operates a website that provides access to lodging availability through TahoeReservations.Com. It includes areas outside of the lake in Genoa and Carson Valley.
Rates: $–$$$$
Contact: Tahoe Douglas Chamber of Commerce, P.O. Box 7139, Lake Tahoe, NV 89449-4161; 775/588-4591; email: info@tahoechamber.org; website: www.tahoechamber.org.

TahoeReservations.Com
This online service provides secured, real-time bookings and availability for more than 30 major properties in the South Shore area, including casino hotels, motor inns, vacation homes, and condominiums. The service was intending to add North Shore properties as well. If you don't have a specific property in mind, you can check availability throughout the system. There are links to each property for descriptions.
Rates: $–$$$$
Contact: website: www.TahoeReservations.com.

beat the palatial houses and condominiums from Crystal Bay to Incline Village, or the waterfront properties of the Tahoe Keys in South Lake Tahoe.

Along the California side of the North Shore, you'll find a motel strip on Highway 28, but many of these places have charming rustic cabins, cottages, and beachfront rooms. There's been a whirlwind of refurbishment lately, and some of the aging properties have been revitalized. You may have to stop and look closely to find these diamonds in the rough, because the improvements are not always evident from the highway.

Perhaps the most dramatic turnaround is on the West Shore, where the mom-and-pop lodges of the 1950s and 1960s are giving way to new and younger owners; the new owners generally choose to convert their accommodations into boutique inns. Some of the nicest cabins and

small lodges are here, nestled in wooded surroundings. The West Shore has wind-protected shoreline and beaches, access to the best hiking and cycling trails in the region, proximity to major ski resorts, and a selection of fine gourmet restaurants. One drawback is that many of these accommodations front Highway 89, and the traffic in summer can be heavy and noisy. If this bothers you, ask for the room or cabin that is farthest from the road.

The price ranges listed here are merely a guideline. They fluctuate wildly depending on the day and time of year. You'll find the highest rates in July, August, late December, and March, which represent the peak of the summer and winter seasons. Weekends and holidays will usually be more expensive. At the major casino/hotels, special promotions (sweetened with goodies such as meals, shows, and drinks) can often be obtained for the regular cost of the room alone. Midweek bargains, Sunday–Thursday, are especially enticing, often representing discounts of 30–50 percent. Go in April, May, June, October, and November for the best prices.

Lake Tahoe excels in its selection of alternative accommodations, including condominiums and rental homes. Because of the large number of nonresident property owners, there is always a variety of rentals available most any time of the year, including holiday periods when hotels and motels are booked. It's hard to argue the fact that homes represent the best value in accommodations at the lake, and most nearly equal the mountain experience that a lot of people are looking for. Through property management companies and through contact with individual owners, there are easily 1,000 or more rental houses throughout the lake—and at some incredible prices. Think of it this way: You could pay $200 a night for a luxury room at any of the major hotels, or you could pay the same amount for a 3,000-square-foot $600,000 home with three or four bedrooms, a big screen television, a hot tub, a game room, and, quite possibly, a private pier next to the lake. Obviously, with a group of two or three couples, or two families, the cost per person becomes wonderfully affordable. And look at all of that room to roam! It's no wonder that this category of lodging is the fastest growing at the lake.

As a mountain destination, Lake Tahoe has the largest inventory of rental houses in North America, far beyond those of other ski resort areas such as Vail, Whistler, Aspen, Park City, Sun Valley, and Killington. The reason for this is that Lake Tahoe's communities were established long before ski resorts were built, so there's been a bed base here since the late 1800s. And the diversity of homes is amazing. There are

There are easily 1,000 or more rental houses throughout the lake—and at some incredible prices. Think of it this way: You could pay $200 a night for a luxury room at any of the major hotels, or you could pay the same amount for a 3,000-square-foot $600,000 home with three or four bedrooms, a big-screen television, a hot tub, a game room and, quite possibly, a private pier next to the lake.

palatial, lakefront estates where many celebrities stay when they arrive in Tahoe to perform or to simply relax. There are mountain chalets within walking distance of ski lifts. And there are reasonably priced waterfront properties in the Tahoe Keys, a labyrinth of artificial waterways that meander into the lake. I've toured large homes—in one case, two homes joined together—that comfortably sleep 18–20 people in private bedrooms. Some of the best values (and views) are on mountain residential streets above the cities and hamlets of the lake—and away from the highway traffic noise. One area often overlooked by visitors is Donner Lake, which is part of Truckee and routinely offers some unbelievable rental bargains. For example, just by driving through the area, I found a brand-new five-bedroom, three-bath home with a redwood deck, a two-car garage, and a lovely lake view—a property that sleeps 16 people—for the paltry sum of $215 a night or $1,430 a week. While this was being rented directly by the owners (a property management company would add 30 to 50 percent to the cost), it gives you an idea of how far you can stretch your money.

Condominiums are another good value, because there are so many of them. Since thousands of condo units were built during the boom days of the late 1960s to the mid-1970s, a lot of them have a certain cookie-cutter appearance: weathered wood exteriors occasionally spruced up with a paint job; inexpensive, some might say, slapdash, construction that was not the most suitable for long and cold winters; the obligatory sliding glass doors and adjoining wood deck; and—God forbid!—some abysmal holdovers such as rust-colored couches, shag carpeting (extending into bathrooms), putrid green walls, and beds with sagging mattresses.

One look at these places is enough to make you flee to Motel 6. But this is typical of the run-of-the-mill condos around Tahoe, particularly in Tahoe City, Kings Beach, and South Lake Tahoe. Fortunately, however, a lot of owners—at the urging of their property managers—are remodeling with fine upgrades such as tile or wood floors, area rugs, whirlpool bathtubs, new kitchens with granite countertops, and more contemporary furniture. So the rule of thumb is:

don't judge a condo by its exterior. And there are several new and considerably more upscale condo and town house properties, particularly at Incline Village, Glenbrook, Kingsbury (around the Nevada side of Heavenly Ski Resort), and Squaw Valley.

Keep in mind that the list here does not include all properties in the Tahoe area. Be sure to consult other chapters on mountain resorts and lodges and unique inns.

Motels, Small Lodges, and Cottages

TRUCKEE/DONNER

Best Western Truckee Tahoe Inn

Close to the ski and golf resort of Northstar-at-Tahoe and the historic town of Truckee, this property looks much like a typical motel. But on the inside it has many personalized features that give guests extra value for their money. The walls are festooned with photographs from the Truckee Championship Rodeo, which is held at the McIver Arena next door in mid-August. In addition to the standard rooms, there are some well-appointed two-room suites, each room with a television set and a sofa bed in the living room. If you stay in one of these units, you can borrow movie videotapes for free from the library at the front desk. There's also a free continental breakfast in the morning, with rolls, toast, cereal, and juice, in an upstairs dining area. On Highway 267, the inn has quick access to I-80, is about eight miles from Lake Tahoe, and is within a 20-minute drive of the Squaw Valley and Alpine Meadows ski resorts. This is one of the highest-rated Best Western lodges, with a AAA Three-Diamond rating.

Rooms: 100 deluxe rooms and minisuites with phones, televisions, free movies, and a free breakfast buffet.

Amenities: A spa, a Jacuzzi, a pool, a fitness room, continental breakfast, Pizza Hut Express, sports equipment, disposable swimwear, and a conference room.

Rates: $$–$$$.

Contact: Best Western Truckee Tahoe Inn, 11331 Hwy. 267, Truckee, CA 96161; 530/587-4525 or 800/824-6385.

Boreal Inn

Owned by Boreal ski area, which is next door, this small motel has spacious rooms that are just steps from the slopes. Most come with two queen beds, TV, and telephone. Continental breakfast is included in room tariff, and children four and under stay for free. Rooms are comfortable and include both standard and deluxe units.

Policies: No pets are allowed.

Rates: $$–$$$

Contact: Boreal Inn, I-80 at Donner Summit, P.O. Box 39, Truckee, CA 96160; 530/426-1012; email: info@borealski.com; website: www.borealski.com.

Holiday Inn Express

This attractively designed Holiday Inn Express, with woodsy, pine exteriors, opened in 1999. It is close to major ski resorts (Squaw Valley, Sugar Bowl, Alpine Meadows, and Northstar) and close to shops and restaurants in downtown Truckee. Given the rustic mountain treatment, the interior of the lobby has rock floors, and there is a great room with large stone fireplace, television, and tables and chairs for the free continental breakfast. That repast includes a variety of breads, pastries, juices, coffees, and teas. The property also has a large seasonal outdoor swimming pool.

Rooms: 65, varying from one king to two queen beds, and including six minisuites. Guest rooms

TAHOE ACCOMMODATIONS

include a wet bar, refrigerator, coffeemaker, hair dryer, iron and board, cable TV, ceiling fans, and two-line phones with data port. The minisuites include two queen beds and some have natural gas fireplaces. All rooms are nonsmoking and air conditioned.

Amenities: Great room with large fireplace and continental breakfast serving and seating areas; outdoor swimming pool; on-site parking.

Rates: $$–$$$$.

Contact: Holiday Inn Express, 10527 Coldstream Rd., Truckee, CA 96161; 530/582-9999 or 877/TRUCKEE (877/878-2533); website: www.hiexpresstruckee.com.

The Inn at Truckee

Formerly the Super 8 Motel, this 43-unit motor inn was completely renovated in 1998 and was dressed up in the Old Tahoe design elements that are proving so popular with the local hospitality industry. The lobby has the obligatory large river-rock fireplace and a free toast and pastry bar that is open 5 A.M.–11 A.M. daily and serves fresh pastries, a selection of breads, hot beverages, and orange juice. The inn also has a two-story spa and sauna. Many fast-food and traditional restaurants, along with shops, are within walking distance. Close to major ski and golf resorts.

Rooms: 43 appointed with king, queen, or two double beds, phones with free local calls, and televisions.

Amenities: Spa and sauna, 24-hour front desk, morning continental breakfast.

Policies: Children and pets are welcome.

Rates: $$–$$$. Children 15 and under stay free when accompanied by an adult.

Contact: The Inn at Truckee, 11506 Deerfield Dr. (intersection of Highways 80 and 89), Truckee, CA 96161; 530/587-8888 or 888/773-6888; website: www.innattruckee.com.

Loch Leven Lodge

This small, older lodge is on the sunny north shore of Donner Lake, a short distance from downtown Truckee, and is a favorite with fishermen, boaters, and skiers.

Rooms: 8, all with lakefront views, queen beds,

KEY TO TAHOE HOTEL/MOTEL ROOM RATES

$ = economy (less than $50 per room)
$$ = standard ($50–80 per room)
$$$ = deluxe ($81–110)
$$$$ = luxury (over $110)

cable TV, and gourmet coffee. Six units are suites that include bedroom, private bath, living room area, kitchenette, and dinette. There's one lakefront town house that has master bedroom with private bath, bunkroom (sleeps four) with private bath, balcony, living room with queen sofa bed, fireplace, full kitchen including microwave and dishwater, and dining area.

Amenities: 5,000-square-foot redwood deck on the lake, putting green and spa on the deck, and boat moorage.

Rates: $$–$$$$.

Contact: Loch Leven Lodge, 13855 Donner Pass Rd., Truckee, CA 96161; 530/587-3773 or 877/436-6637; website: www.truckee.com /lochleven.

TAHOE CITY/WEST SHORE

Grubstake Lodge

Grubstake is an Old Tahoe-style (i.e., rustic) motel and lodge. Its cottages have televisions, private baths, some kitchens, and some fireplaces.

Amenities: Public phones.

Rates: $.

Contact: Grubstake Lodge, 5335 W. Lake Blvd./P.O. Box 526, Homewood, CA 96141; 530/525-5505.

Homewood Marina Lodge

The cottages and motel rooms here come with kitchens, cooking utensils, fireplaces, and some lake views.

Amenities: A private beach, a large lawn, a café, a bar, and public phones.

Rates: $–$$.

Contact: Homewood Marina Lodge, 5180 W.

Lake Blvd./P.O. Box 526, Homewood, CA 96141; 530/525-6728.

Lake of the Sky Motor Inn

Rooms: 23 completely remodeled guest rooms with phones, televisions, some lake views, and in-room coffee. Free continental breakfast and local calls.
Amenities: A pool (during the summer only), a sauna, and a conference room.
Rates: $–$$$.
Contact: Lake of the Sky Motor Inn, 955 N. Lake Blvd./P.O. Box 227, Tahoe City, CA 96145; 530/583-3305.

Mother Nature's Inn

Here is a truly unique and charming small motel. It directly connects Mother Nature's Wildlife Art—one of Tahoe's best galleries—and Cabin Fever, a delightful boutique with mountain furniture, lamps, knickknacks, and country-style gifts. You can reach the motel rooms through the store, if you wish, but there's a more discreet back door and parking area. Fred and Candi Wickman, who have owned the gallery for several years, acquired and refurbished the motel in 1998 (the building previously housed a restaurant and small inn) and decorated its nine rooms with art reproductions and furniture that complement the gallery. Every room has a wildlife name—such as bear, moose, raccoon, wolf, cougar, and elk—and is furnished with queen or double log beds. All have private bath with shower, air conditioning and heating, small refrigerator, coffeemaker, and cable TV. The inn is in the center of Tahoe City, within easy walking distance of beaches, shops, restaurants, the Truckee River trails, and a nine-hole golf course. If you stay here for a few days, you may find it hard to resist buying something in the gallery.
Rates: $–$$.
Contact: Mother Nature's Inn, 551 N. Lake Blvd., Tahoe City, CA 96145; 530/581-4278 or 800/558-4278, fax 530/581-4272.

Pepper Tree Inn

In the heart of Tahoe City, this seven-story, high-rise inn offers pleasant lake views, but its exterior aesthetics are nonexistent. The guest rooms include phones and televisions. Guests are within walking distance of beautiful Commons Beach, Tahoe City Marina, Tahoe City Golf Course, and the popular Truckee River walking and cycling trails. Also nearby are shops and restaurants.
Rooms: 50, on seven levels, with king beds, coffeemakers, hair dryers, ironing centers, cable TV, and on-demand video.
Amenities: Heated pool, indoor hot spa, laundry facilities, and covered parking.
Rates: $–$$$.
Contact: Pepper Tree Inn, 645 N. Lake Blvd./P.O. Box 29, Tahoe City, CA 96145; 530/583-3711 or 800/624-8590; website: www.peppertreetahoe.com.

Swiss Lakewood Lodge

These motel rooms and deluxe two-bedroom cabins include cable television, some full-sized fully equipped kitchens, and linen.
Amenities: A restaurant and a garden.
Rates: $$–$$$.
Contact: Swiss Lakewood Lodge, 5055 W. Lake Blvd./P.O. Box 205, Homewood, CA 96141; 530/525-5211.

Tahoe City Inn

Thirty-three guest rooms—some of which include water beds—offer phones, televisions, VCRs, free movies, some lake views, in-room coffee, some private in-room spas, and wheelchair access. All rooms are nonsmoking. The property is within walking distance to more than 15 restaurants and is less than a quarter of a block from the lake.
Rates: $$–$$$.
Contact: Tahoe City Inn, 790 N. Lake Blvd./P.O. Box 634, Tahoe City, CA 96145; 530/581-3333 or 800/800-8246; website: www.tahoecityinn.com.

Tahoe City Travelodge

The 47 nonsmoking guest rooms here, which were remodeled in 1992, provide phones, remote-control televisions (with free Showtime, Encore, and Disney channels), in-room coffee, and some lake views.

Amenities: A sauna, a lakeview spa, and a pool (during the summer only).

Rates: $$–$$$.

Contact: Tahoe City Travelodge, 455 N. Lake Blvd./P.O. Box 84, Tahoe City, CA 96145; 530/583-3766 or 800/578-7878.

Tahoe Lake Cottages

Almost everything you could ask for in a woodsy cabin is embodied in these recently refurbished bungalows, in Tahoma across from the lake, seven miles south of Tahoe City. Features include knotty-pine paneling on walls and ceilings; queen-sized beds with firm mattresses in one- and two-bedroom units; a living room with hideaway sofa bed and television; old-fashioned-style gas heater; handmade wooden furniture; a full-service kitchen with refrigerator, a gas stove, and utensils; a small dining/breakfast table; and a bathroom (most with showers only). The six-person cottage—with two bedrooms, a full kitchen, and a bathroom with a tub—is ideal for a large family. Owner Michael Lafferty has added many pleasant touches, and the facility is close to state parks, the lakeshore cycling path, ski areas, marinas, and hiking trails.

Rooms: Old Tahoe-style knotty-pine cottages with separate living rooms and bedrooms, televisions, and full-service kitchens, and motel-style units with beds and bathrooms only.

Amenities: A swimming pool, hot tub, barbecues, and play areas.

Policies: Some pets are allowed at the owner's discretion. If you book six nights, the seventh night is free.

Rates: $$$–$$$$. Midweek and off-season specials are available.

Contact: Tahoe Lake Cottages, 7030 W. Lake Blvd. (Hwy. 89)/P.O. Box 126, Tahoma, CA 96142; 530/525-4411 or 800/852-8246; email: mike@tahoelakecottages.com; website: www.tahoelakecottages.com.

Tahoma Lodge

Attractive from the outside and comfortable but not fancy on the inside, this property varies

Tahoe Lake Cottages

© KEN CASTLE

TAHOE ACCOMMODATIONS

from a main lodge unit next to the highway to individual cabins set back on a wooded, slightly hilly site. Cabins have mahogany paneling, full kitchens, and baths with showers. In Tahoma, the lodge is on the West Shore Bike Path, and close to state parks, beaches, and ski areas.

Rooms: 12 units, including cottages and two apartment units in the main lodge, with phones, televisions, kitchens, and woodstoves or fireplaces. There are one-bedroom, two-bedroom, and four-bedroom units.

Amenities: A hot tub and pool (during the summer only), with access to a private beach across the road.

Policies: Some pets are allowed.

Rates: $$–$$$.

Contact: Tahoma Lodge, 7018 Emerald Bay Rd., Tahoma, CA 96142; 530/525-7721, fax 530/525-7215; website: www.tahomalodge.com.

Tamarack Lodge Motel

Tamarack's 21 nonsmoking guest rooms and cottages include televisions, some kitchens, and some lake views.

Amenities: Four acres of pine forest, horseshoes, table tennis, barbecues, a picnic area, and outdoor fireplaces.

Rates: $–$$.

Contact: Tamarack Lodge Motel, 2311 N. Lake Blvd./P.O. Box 859, Tahoe City, CA 96145; 530/583-3350; website: www.TamarackAtTahoe.com.

KINGS BEACH/TAHOE VISTA/CARNELIAN BAY

Big 7 Motel

Rooms: Tahoe-style knotty-pine rooms with telephones and remote-control televisions.

Amenities: Dining, a heated pool, a picnic area, and beach access are also available.

Rates: $. Most major credit cards are accepted.

Contact: Big 7 Motel, 8141 N. Lake Blvd./P.O. Box 759, Kings Beach, CA 96143; 530/546-2541.

Cedar Glen Lodge

This family-run lodge—set in the tall trees across the highway from the lake—is meticu-

lously maintained and far superior to the average motel. On the lower section of the hill are attractive, woodsy cottages with log facades, hand-hewn furniture, and separate living rooms and bedrooms, as well as a few kitchens. In mid-2002, these 20 units were remodelled, with new flooring and kitchen cabinets installed. On the upper side of the hill is a two-story unit with a roomy upper deck overlooking the lodge and the lake. In the center of the property is a large heated swimming pool, a spa, a sauna, a children's playground, and a big grassy lawn that's a great place for relaxing in a hammock or having a barbecue. Across the road is a private beach for guests. Pleasant, homey touches include a newspaper at your front door each morning and free continental breakfast (with rolls, fruit, juice, and coffee) in the office. Owners Pat and Jodi Stone will gladly tell you about their favorite restaurants, secret beaches, and hiking trails. This is a wonderfully relaxing place for families.

Rooms: 31 units including cottages, suites and rooms with phones, televisions, some kitchens, fireplaces, lake views, and continental breakfast. Microwaves are available in many units, and rooms with refrigerators are available upon request.

Amenities: Indoor spa, sauna, pool, free newspaper, continental breakfast, and a private beach.

Policies: No pets are allowed.

Rates: $–$$$.

Contact: Cedar Glen Lodge, 6589 N. Lake Blvd./P.O. Box 188, Tahoe Vista, CA 96148; 530/546-4281 or 800/500-8246; website: www.cedarglenlodge.com.

Charmey Chalet Resort

Rooms: 28 standard and studio rooms with phones, televisions, some kitchens, fireplaces, in-room whirlpools, and lake views.

Amenities: A Jacuzzi, a pool, and a beach.

Rates: $–$$$.

Contact: Charmey Chalet, 6549 N. Lake Blvd./P.O. Box 316, Tahoe Vista, CA 96148; 530/546-2529 or 800/316-5253 (in California); website: www.charmeychalet.com.

Ferrari's Crown Resort

Owners are constantly upgrading their facilities here, and recently they acquired a lakefront building with six new rooms, five of them facing Tahoe. They offer 45 standard and family suites (two bedrooms) with phones, televisions, some kitchens, gas fireplaces, lakefronts, and lake views. All previously existing rooms have been remodelled and the swimming pool was recently refurbished as well.

Amenities: An indoor spa, a heated pool, and a beach.

Rates: $$–$$$.

Contact: Ferrari's Crown Motel, 8200 N. Lake Blvd./P.O. Box 845, Kings Beach, CA 96143; 530/546-3388 or 800/645-2260; website: www.tahoecrown.com.

Crystal Bay Motel

Rooms: 18 guest rooms with phones, televisions, and bath with shower, within walking distance of casinos and restaurants.

Rates: $–$$.

Contact: Crystal Bay Motel, 24 Hwy. 28, Crystal Bay, NV 89402; 775/831-0287.

Falcon Lodge and Suites

This lodge provides single rooms as well as two- and three-room suites with telephones, color televisions with HBO, some kitchens with refrigerators, some lakefronts, some lake views, continental breakfast, and in-room coffee. It boasts the largest outdoor heated pool in Kings Beach.

Amenities: A hot tub, swimming pool, laundry, and a private sandy beach.

Rates: $–$$$.

Contact: Falcon Lodge, 8258 N. Lake Blvd./P.O. Box 249, Kings Beach, CA 96143; 530/546-2583 or 800/682-4631; website: www.falconlodge.com.

Firelite Lodge

Rooms: 26 guest rooms with phones, televisions, and some lake views.

Amenities: A pool (during the summer only), a lounge with a television, and continental breakfast on weekends.

Rates: $–$$.

Contact: Firelite Lodge, 7035 N. Lake Blvd./P.O. Box 135, Tahoe Vista, CA 96148; 530/546-7222.

Franciscan Lakeside Lodge

Split between both sides of Highway 28, this property has lakefront cottages, suites and studios, as well as a private sandy beach and private pier. Across from the lake, nestled in pine forest, are studios and two-bedroom suites, some with fireplaces. Close to kayak and bicycle rentals, and one mile from North Tahoe Regional Park (snow-play, snowmobiling. and sledding in the winter).

Rooms: Studio to four-bedroom suites with phones, cable television, kitchens, some fireplaces, lakefronts, and lake views.

Amenities: Heated pool, gas barbecues, picnic tables, private beach, volleyball court, horseshoes, Ping-Pong, a pier, and buoys for mooring boats.

Rates: $$–$$$$.

Contact: Franciscan Lakeside Lodge, 6944 N. Lake Blvd./P.O. Box 280, Tahoe Vista, CA 96148; 530/546-6300 or 800/564-6754 (in California only); website: www.franciscanlodge.com.

Gold Crest Resort Motel

Rooms: This AAA-approved motel has lakefront and private beach, with a variety of accommodations, including one- and two-bedroom units and honeymoon suites, some with kitchens. Nice touches include in-room jet tubs, barbecues, and sun decks. Single rooms with phones, televisions, some kitchens, some lakefronts, some lake views, continental breakfast, and in-room coffee.

Amenities: A spa, a heated pool, phones, televisions, and continental breakfast.

Rates: $–$$$.

Contact: Gold Crest Resort Motel, 8149 N. Lake Blvd./P.O. Box 579, Kings Beach, CA 96143; 530/546-3301 or 800/852-5348; website: www.goldcresttahoe.com.

Holiday House

Accommodations include cottages and lakefront suites with televisions, kitchens, and stone hearth fireplaces. Some units have lake views, and there

is a private beach. Close to restaurants and casinos, and on the ski shuttle bus route.
Amenities: Lakefront outdoor hot tub.
Rates: $$.
Contact: Holiday House, 7276 N. Lake Blvd., Tahoe Vista, CA 96148; 530/546-2369 or 800/294-6378; website: www.tahoeguide.com/go/holidayhouse.

Mourelato's Lakeshore Resort

The first thing that catches your eye here is the big white Pontiac with the Texas steer horn on the hood, parked in front of the office. The car was used as a prop in several Hollywood movies, and Andreas and Mary Mourelato took a shine to it during an auction in Reno a few years back. Well, it certainly grabs your attention. And if it makes you stop and look close enough to see what a delightful place this is, then it has served its purpose. The Mourelatos, who have owned the property since 1978, have created a kind of beachfront miniparadise here. There are two wings of the resort, and they are separated by a 275-foot white-sand beach. One wing was recently rebuilt from the ground up, and now it matches the other wing that was also rebuilt a few years ago. Both sides have studio units, some with wet bars and some with a full kitchen. All rooms have elegant furnishings (including large armoires), white-washed walls, and bleached pine ceilings—offering a hint of the Greek Islands. (That's not accidental; Andreas, an architect, is from Greece.) These luxurious, oversized units have unusual shapes and a contemporary, cheerful feeling. The end units closest to the shoreline afford sparkling views of the lake. The beach is inviting, and guests can launch their own sailing dinghies or runabouts from here. Some of the North Shore's best restaurants—Le Petit Pier, The Old Steakhouse and Spindleshanks—are within walking distance. The resort is AAA Three Diamond-rated.
Rooms: 32 nonsmoking guest studios and one-room junior suites, including a honeymoon suite, with televisions, some kitchens, microwaves, refrigerators, and wet bars. Some units front the lake; some have lake views and balconies.

Amenities: A private beach with barbecues and picnic tables.
Rates: $$$–$$$$.
Contact: Mourelato's Lakeshore Resort, 6834 N. Lake Blvd./P.O. Box 77, Tahoe Vista, CA 96148; 530/546-9500 or 800/TAHOE-81 (800/824-6381); website: www.mourelatosresort.com.

North Lake Lodge

North Lake is a quaint, family-style lodge. Rooms have televisions, kitchens (with a refrigerator and microwave in all units), some fireplaces, and lake views.
Amenities: A hot tub.
Rates: $$.
Contact: North Lake Lodge, 8716 N. Lake Blvd./P.O. Box 955, Kings Beach, CA 96143; 530/546-2731.

Rustic Cottages

Janet and Marshall Tuttle have created a truly charming hideaway here, with 18 Old Tahoe-style cottages that were thoroughly remodelled when they bought the property a few years ago. All of the cabins are decorated with beautiful, custom-made wrought-iron furniture, which came from the Tuttles' own foundry and ironworks in the San Francisco Bay Area. The site has a rich history, serving as the sawmill and labor camp of the Brockway Lumber Company during the late 1800s and early 1900s. It was converted to vacation cottages in 1925, and the original brochure in those days touted the retreat has having a "homelike atmosphere" with "no rattle snakes, poison oak or poison ivy." Before the couple acquired it, the cottages had been dressed up as a Japanese-style *ryokan*, with guests sleeping on the floor on tatami mats. But that incarnation is long gone. Now the owners whimsically refer to them as "the not-so-funky little shacks." The historic main building has some marvellous touches and resembles a rustic fishing lodge with its collectibles and antiques. Here, the Tuttles serve a continental breakfast featuring homemade muffins and juices. Guests can drop by in the afternoon for fresh-baked chocolate chip cookies, and they can also borrow movie videos from a well-stocked film library.

© KEN CASTLE

Rustic Cottages

There are pleasant grassy areas both in front and in back of the cottages, on two acres of wooded land. Within walking distance are several excellent restaurants.

Amenities: All rooms have phones, TVs, VCRs, wrought-iron beds with beautiful linens, kitchenettes with microwave ovens, and decks with patio furniture. A sandy beach on the lake is just across the highway.

Policies: Some pets are allowed.

Rates: $–$$.

Contact: Rustic Cottages, 7449 N. Lake Blvd./P.O. Box 18, Tahoe Vista, CA 96148; 530/546-3523 or 888/7RUSTIC (888/778-7842); website: www.rusticcottages.com.

Stevenson's Holliday Inn

This recently refurbished inn offers spacious rooms—including king- and queen-sized beds—with phones, televisions, some kitchens (with refrigerators and microwaves), and fireplaces. It's close to restaurants and casinos.

Amenities: A heated pool, spas, and a recreation room.

Rates: $.

Contact: Stevenson's Holliday Inn, 8742 N. Lake Blvd./P.O. Box 235, Kings Beach, CA 96143; 530/546-2269.

Sun 'N Sand Lodge

Sun 'N Sand provides a fine beachfront location with a panoramic lake view. Recently remodeled rooms include telephones, televisions, some lakefront units, terrific lake views, and weekend continental breakfast.

Amenities: A private beach and a volleyball court.

Rates: $$–$$$.

Contact: Sun 'N Sand Lodge, 8308 N. Lake Blvd./P.O. Box 5, Kings Beach, CA 96143; 530/546-2515.

Tahoe Inn

Owned by Cal-Neva Resort, which is across the street, this large (100-room) property offers spacious units. Some of the rooms have filtered lake views. It's an easy walk to the lake, to casinos, and to one of North Shore's best restaurants, Soule Domaine.

Amenities: A heated pool and whirlpool, deluxe rooms with patios, cable television, in-room coffee, and meeting facilities.
Rates: $$–$$$.
Contact: Tahoe Inn, 9937 N. Lake Blvd., Brockway, CA/P.O. Box 295, Crystal Bay, NV 89402; 530/546-3341 or 800/648-2324.

Ta-Tel Lodge

Rooms: Nine guest rooms with phones, televisions, some kitchens, and in-room coffee.
Amenities: A swimming pool, during the summer only.
Rates: $–$$.
Contact: Ta-Tel Lodge, 8748 N. Lake Blvd./P.O. Box 1344, Kings Beach, CA 96143; 530/546-2411.

Woodvista Lodge

Woodvista's large guest rooms include phones, televisions, some kitchens, and some continental breakfasts.
Amenities: A spa, a pool, a children's play area, barbecues, and a large lawn area with pine trees.
Rates: $$–$$$.
Contact: Woodvista Lodge, 7699 N. Lake Blvd./P.O. Box 439, Tahoe Vista, CA 96148; 530/546-3839.

SOUTH LAKE TAHOE

A&A Tradewinds Resort and Spa

Garnering the South Lake Tahoe Chamber of Commerce's "Most Improved" award recently, this 68-room motel has completed a top-to-bottom renovation, including new siding, new lobby, new furniture, new gazebo with outdoor spa, picnic area in the rear, refurbished swimming pool, and a number of other improvements. This is one of the few motels in Tahoe with air conditioning (yep, sometimes it gets warm) and also one of the few with bathtubs (showers are the norm at most places). Facilities include telephones, microwave ovens, remote-control cable televisions, kitchens, in-room coffee, and some Heavenly Ski Resort views. There are four honeymoon suites with fireplaces and spas, and two two-bedroom suites with spas for families.

Amenities: A Jacuzzi and a pool (during the summer only).
Rates: $–$$$.
Contact: A&A Tradewinds Resort and Spa, 944 Friday Ave., South Lake Tahoe, CA 96150; 530/544-6459 or 800/AT-TAHOE; website: www.tahoeforyou.com.

Beachside Inn

This small AAA-approved motel offers family rooms, spa rooms, nonsmoking rooms, and honeymoon suites. It has access to a private lakeside beach and marina and is within a few blocks of the casinos at Stateline and within two miles of Heavenly resort. Rooms include double queens, single queens and suites, and some have fireplaces. All have TVs, microwaves, and refrigerators.
Amenities: The lobby offers beverages and an expanded Continental breakfast at no extra charge.
Policies: No pets allowed.
Rates: $$<\#208>$$$
Contact: Beachside Inn, 930 Park Ave., South Lake Tahoe, CA 96150; 530/542-3536 or 800/884-4920; website: www.beachsideinntahoe.com.

Best Western Station House Inn

This motor lodge offers comfortable, if not distinguished, accommodations and has earned the AAA Three-Diamond rating for both its rooms and the restaurant. It is centrally located, just over a block from the beach and 2.5 blocks from Stateline casinos.
Rooms: 100 units, including queen-sized beds, king-sized beds, double-doubles, suites, and a three-bedroom cabin. All accommodations have a 25-inch television, phones, in-room ski racks, outside entrance to rooms, and some in-room spas.
Amenities: A restaurant, a 24-hour hot tub, and free shuttles to casinos and local ski resorts.
Rates: $–$$.
Contact: Best Western Station House Inn, 901 Park Ave., South Lake Tahoe, CA 96150; 530/542-1101 or 800/822-5953; website: www.stationhouseinn.com.

Best Western Timber Cove Lodge Marina Resort

This 262-room Best Western property, the largest South Shore accommodation outside of the Stateline hotels, has a variety of rooms. Choices range from standard, undistinguished motel units to suites with lake views. All of the rooms are tastefully appointed, with air-conditioning and in-room movies. Common areas are the lodge's best assets, including a private beach and marina on the lake, a spacious heated swimming pool, and a hot tub. Timber Cove is centrally located to the Heavenly ski area and the casinos and is served by free shuttles. There's a family restaurant and a small wedding chapel on the property.

Rooms: 262 rooms and suites with telephones, color cable televisions, paid movie access, in-room coffee, some lakefronts, and some lake views.

Amenities: A heated pool, a Jacuzzi, a sauna (open year-round), a bar, a cocktail lounge, a restaurant, courtesy casino and ski shuttles, and wedding and banquet facilities.

Rates: $$–$$$$.

Contact: Timber Cove Lodge Marina Resort, 3411 U.S. 50, South Lake Tahoe, CA 96150; 530/541-6722 or 800/972-8558 (reservations only); website: www.timbercovetahoe.com.

Blue Jay Lodge

A half-block from the Stateline casinos, this motel has suites with fireplaces and Jacuzzi tubs, and some family-style two-room units. There's also access to a private beach.

Rooms: 65 guest rooms with phones, in-room hair dryers, televisions, some kitchens, and in-room coffee.

Amenities: A Jacuzzi and a pool (during the summer only),

Rates: $–$$$.

Contact: Blue Jay Lodge, 4133 Cedar Ave., South Lake Tahoe, CA 96150; 530/544-5232 or 800/258-3529.

Casino Area Travelodge

This franchise motor inn provides 66 guest rooms with telephones (offering free local calls), remote-control color televisions with HBO, AM/FM radio alarm clocks, air-conditioning, some non-smoking rooms, and in-room coffee.

Amenities: A seasonal heated outdoor pool, baby-sitting, and shuttle service to casinos, ski areas, and the airport.

Rates: $–$$.

Contact: Casino Area Travelodge, 4003 U.S. 50/P.O. Box 6500, South Lake Tahoe, CA 96157; 530/541-5000 or 800/578-7878.

The Cedar Lodge

This motor inn is conveniently located less than two blocks from casinos and one block from Heavenly Ski Resort's new gondola. Guest rooms have been newly renovated and some have fireplaces. There's a private beach nearby. Rated AAA.

Rooms: 56 with TV and HBO, coffeemakers and daily continental breakfast.

Amenities: Swimming pool and hot tub.

Rates: $$.

Contact: The Cedar Lodge, 4069 Cedar Ave., South Lake Tahoe, CA 96150; 530/544-6453 or 800/222-1177; website: www.cedarlodgetahoe.com.

Chamonix Inn

Rooms: 32 guest rooms with telephones, remote-control color televisions, and free HBO.

Amenities: A café, a spa, a pool, free casino shuttles, and ski shuttles to local resorts.

Rates: $–$$.

Contact: Chamonix Inn, 913 Friday Ave./P.O. Box 5274, South Lake Tahoe, CA 96157; 530/544-5274 or 800/447-5353.

Days Inn

Rooms: These 42 guest rooms—some of which offer water beds—provide televisions, some fireplaces, and continental breakfast. AAA-approved.

Amenities: A Jacuzzi and a pool (during the summer only).

Rates: $–$$$.

Contact: Days Inn, 3530 Lake Tahoe Blvd., South Lake Tahoe, CA 96150; 530/544-3445 or 800/350-3446; website: www.visitlaketahoe.com.

Econo Lodge

Rooms: 36 spacious rooms with hair dryers and electronic door locks, some fireplaces and suites. AAA-approved.
Amenities: Swimming pool, sauna and hot tub.
Rates: $–$$$.
Contact: Econo Lodge, 3536 Lake Tahoe Blvd., South Lake Tahoe, CA 96150; 530/544-2036; website: www.visitlaketahoe.com

Holiday Inn Express

Until 1995, this was a nondescript motel, but with a creative remodeling it has become the most elegant moderate-priced lodging in South Tahoe, with a wonderful rock and wood exterior that gives it the contemporary Tahoe look. The interiors are luxurious and beautifully styled, enough to earn AAA's Three-Diamond rating and accolades from numerous consumer surveys. Some special suites have fireplaces and private spas. There's a Carrows coffee shop next door, and the property is centrally located near Heavenly Ski Resort and all the action at the Stateline casinos.
Rooms: 89 guest rooms, including standards and suites, offering free deluxe continental breakfast each morning, 25-inch televisions with free movie channels, refrigerators, coffeemakers, hair dryers, telephones with free local calls, and data ports.
Amenities: A large indoor whirlpool and sauna, and casino and ski-area shuttles.
Rates: $$–$$$.
Contact: Holiday Inn Express, 3961 Lake Tahoe Blvd., South Lake Tahoe, CA 96150; 530/544-5900 or 800/544-5288; website: www.holidayinnexpresstahoe.com.

Holiday Lodge

Location is a big selling point here, especially for skiers, since this large, older motel is just steps away from Heavenly's gondola and the new Heavenly Village base area with restaurants and shops. It's also one block from the Stateline casinos and four blocks from the lake. Owners have completed a number of upgrades in the rooms and on the property, even though there is talk of tearing it down to make way for a con-

vention center. But, as of this writing, no such plans have materialized. So for now the lodge continues to operate with rooms, suites, and cabins on four acres of land.
Rooms: 165 with various configurations of kings, queens and doubles, with cable TV and air conditioning.
Amenities: Free continental breakfast, swimming pools, indoor hot tub and sauna, cooking and laundry facilities, and baby-sitting referrals.
Rates: $$.
Contact: Holiday Lodge, 4095 Laurel Ave., South Lake Tahoe, CA 96150; 530/544-4101 or 800/544-4095; website: www.holiday-lodge.com.

Lampliter Inn

Rooms: 28 guest rooms with phones, televisions, and in-room coffee. There's a view of Heavenly's Gunbarrel ski run, and it's one block to Stateline casinos.
Amenities: A Jacuzzi, a beach, and boat rentals.
Policies: Some pets are allowed.
Rates: $–$$.
Contact: Lampliter Inn, 4143 Cedar Ave., South Lake Tahoe, CA 96150; 530/544-2936; website: www.lampliterinn.com.

Lazy S Lodge

This classic, oh-so-clean knotty-pine lodge is on Highway 89 (Emerald Bay Road) next to bike trails and within easy driving distance of Emerald Bay. Owners Sung and Misook Park, who are sisters, bought the property in 2000 and have added a number of pleasing touches to an already charming place. There are 10 rustic cabins, each with wood-burning fireplace and kitchenette, and 11 one-room studios, all with wet bar, microwave, refrigerator, and coffeemaker. The lodge has a large heated swimming pool, an equally large green lawn, a picnic area, barbecues, and table tennis, all set in a woodsy area. Another bonus: Guests get discounts from Anderson's Bike Rentals next door. A paved bike trail leads to beaches and historic Camp Richardson Resort on the West Shore, or to various points of interest, including Tahoe Keys, on the South Shore.

Rooms: 21 units, including some suites, with TV, phones, kitchenettes or wet bar with microwave and refrigerator.

Amenities: Heated swimming pool, hot tub, picnic area, table tennis, and nearby bike rentals.

Policies: No smoking and no pets.

Rates: $–$$.

Contact: Lazy S Lodge, 609 Emerald Bay Rd., South Lake Tahoe, CA 96150; 530/541-0230 or 800/862-8881; website: www.lazyslodge.com.

The Lodge at Lake Tahoe

Situated on Pioneer Trail, which connects the gaming area with the California entrance of Heavenly Ski Resort, this family-oriented motel has easy access to South Shore attractions.

Rooms: 45 guest rooms, some with kitchens, that have TV/VCR and telephone.

Amenities: Pool, spa, playground, on-site laundry room, and video rentals.

Rates: $$.

Contact: The Lodge at Lake Tahoe, 3480 Pioneer Trail, South Lake Tahoe, CA 96157; 530/541-6226 or 800/540-4874; website: www.lodgeatlaketahoe.com.

Montgomery Inn and Suites

This is a rustic wooded lodge that is within easy walking distance of El Dorado and Regan beaches. It has two-bedroom cabins with in-room spa, full kitchen, full bathroom with tub, and wood-burning fireplace. And there are honeymoon suites with in-room spa, king-sized bed, bar, refrigerator, and wood-burning fireplace. Nonsmoking and family units also are available.

Rooms: 24 including budget and deluxe units, all equipped with direct dial phones and cable TV.

Amenities: Outdoor hot tub and spas. In-room VCRs, baby crib, refrigerator, and microwave are available at additional charge.

Rates: $–$$.

Contact: Montgomery Inn and Suites, 966 Modesto Ave., South Lake Tahoe, CA 96150; 530/541-5400 or 800/245-6343; email: lodging@sierra.net; website: www.tahoemontgomeryinn.com.

Motel 6

It's your basic Motel 6, but there are a lot of rooms here—140, to be exact. These comfortable but average units come with a television and a shower, as well as some of the lowest midweek prices in town.

Amenities: A swimming pool.

Rates: $.

Contact: Motel 6, 2375 Lake Tahoe Blvd., South Lake Tahoe, CA 96150; 530/542-1400.

Quality Inn and Suites

Rooms: 120 newly remodeled rooms that come with electronic locks and coffee machines.

Amenities: Free continental breakfast, on-premise restaurant, lounge, game room, and laundry.

Rates: $–$$.

Contact: Quality Inn and Suites, 3838 Lake Tahoe Blvd., South Lake Tahoe, CA 96150; 530/541-5400 or 800/245-6343, fax 530/541-7170; website: www.visitlaketahoe.com.

Roadside Inn

Rooms: 38 large rooms, some with microwave and refrigerator, as well as direct dial phones, air conditioning, and free coffee.

Amenities: Swimming pool, easy access to casinos (across from Harveys Casino).

Rates: $.

Contact: Roadside Inn, 952 Stateline Ave., South Lake Tahoe, CA 96150; 530/644-3369.

Royal Valhalla Lodge

Across from a private beach and marina and just a couple of blocks away from Stateline casinos and the Edgewood Tahoe Golf Course, the Royal Valhalla offers 80 guest units, some of which have balconies with partial views of the lake. This is an older property with average rooms. Continental breakfast is included in the room rate.

Amenities: Heated swimming pool, commercial-sized spa, telephones, carports, and free casino transportation.

Rates: $–$$.

Contact: Royal Valhalla Motor Lodge, 4104 Lakeshore Blvd., South Lake Tahoe, CA 96157;

530/544-2233 or 800/999-4104; email: RoyalVal
@aol.com.

Secret Honeymooner Inn

This inn provides 24 rooms—some of which
have water beds and heart-shaped spas—with
phones, televisions, in-room coffee, and some
fireplaces.
Amenities: A hot tub.
Rates: $$–$$$.
Contact: Secret Honeymooner Inn, 924 Park
Ave., South Lake Tahoe, CA 96150; 530/544-
6767 or 800/441-6610; website: www.stay-at-
tahoe.com/Secrets.html.

7 Seas Inn

Rooms: 17 rooms in a longtime family-owned
motel that is one block from casinos, shopping, and dining, and is close to a beach. Some
rooms have gas fireplaces; all have phones and
cable TV. Free continental breakfast of coffee,
doughnuts, and fruit is offered in the morning. AAA-approved.
Amenities: New whirlpool hot tub, off-street
parking.
Rates: $–$$.
Contact: 7 Seas Inn, 4145 Manzanita Ave., South
Lake Tahoe, CA 96150; 530/544-7031 or 800/
975-7653; website: www.sevenseastahoe.com.

South Tahoe Travelodge

The Travelodge South Tahoe has 59 guest
rooms with telephones (offering free local
calls), remote-control color televisions with
HBO, AM/FM radio alarm clocks, air-conditioning, some nonsmoking rooms, and in-
room coffee.
Amenities: A seasonal heated outdoor pool,
baby-sitting, and shuttle service to casinos, ski
areas, and the airport.
Rates: $–$$.
Contact: South Tahoe Travelodge, 3489 U.S.
50/P.O. Box 70512, South Lake Tahoe, CA
96156; 530/544-5266 or 800/578-7878.

Spruce Grove Cabins and Suites

Calling all dogs! This is where you can bring
your well-behaved humans. Just tell them not
to smoke. This Fido-friendly resort features
themed cabins, all decorated in vintage styles.
The Bears Den has a large river-rock fireplace, the
Prospector has a Gold Rush motif, the Washoe
Hut harkens back to Old Tahoe, El Snowshoe
has a rustic skiing look, Field and Stream is dedicated to the American angler, and the Steamer
Tahoe celebrates the days of nautical yore. One-
bedroom cabins and cottages sleep 2–4 people,
and two-bedroom cabins sleep 4–6 people. They
have fully equipped kitchens, gas fireplaces—
but no phones or daily maid service.
Amenities: Free beverages and appetizers for arriving guests on Friday nights, freshly ground
coffee and muffins in the morning, private hot
tub, and the Rockwell Room hospitality area has
a telephone for free local calls, TV with videos,
games, books, and music. The retreat is on a
fully fenced acre of land and next to an open
field of pine trees. Owners will provide directions to a dog-friendly beach at the lake. The
property is within walking distance of restaurants, shopping, and boating, and is only blocks
from Heavenly ski resort.
Policies: Pets, kids, and alternative lifestyles are
welcome.
Rates: $$$$.
Contact: Spruce Grove Cabins and Suites,
3601 Spruce Ave., South Lake Tahoe, CA
96150; 530/544-0549 or 800/777-0914; email:
info@sprucegrovetahoe.com; website: www
.sprucegrovetahoe.com.

Stateline Travelodge

The Travelodge Stateline encompasses 50 guest
rooms with phones (offering free local calls), remote-control color televisions with HBO,
AM/FM radio alarm clocks, air-conditioning,
some nonsmoking rooms, and in-room coffee.
Amenities: A heated outdoor pool (seasonal),
baby-sitting service, and shuttle service to casinos,
ski areas, and the airport.
Rates: $–$$.
Contact: Stateline Travelodge, 4011 U.S. 50/P.O.
Box 6600, South Lake Tahoe, CA 96157;
530/544-6000 or 800/578-7878.

Super 8 Motel

This large franchise motel—a favorite with budget-minded skiers from England—has a coffee shop, restaurant, full-service lounge, small conference center, swimming pool, and hot tub. Some units have kitchens, and suites are available. It is one mile to Heavenly ski resort and to Stateline and is within two blocks of the new Marina Village shopping and dining center, which is also home port for the *Tahoe Queen* paddlewheel excursion vessel. AAA-approved.

Rooms: 107 featuring king or double-double accommodations, cable TV with pay-per-view, in-room telephones, table and chairs, hair dryers, and air conditioning.

Amenities: Mulligan's Irish Pub, Restaurant, and Nightclub is on premises and offers frequent live entertainment and Irish drink specials. There's also an outdoor heated pool, outdoor year-round 12-person hot tub, 2,000-square foot meeting room, play area for children, shuffle board, free shuttle service to casinos, and four acres of landscaped grounds.

Rates: $–$$$.

Contact: Super 8 Motel, 3600 Lake Tahoe Blvd. (Hwy. 50), South Lake Tahoe, CA 96150; 530/544-3476 or 800/237-8882; website at: www.super8tahoe.com.

Tahoe Chalet Inn

Tahoe Chalet offers 67 rooms and cottages with phones, televisions, some kitchens, continental breakfast, and some fireplaces. There are luxury theme rooms such as the Cleopatra, King Arthur, and Marie Antoinette suites, which come with in-room hot tubs, fireplace, wet bar, refrigerator, microwave, and entertainment center. Newest in the luxury line is the Queen's Parlor, which has a heart-shaped bubble tub and a wood-burning fireplace. Accommodations vary from standard rooms with one or two beds to family-sized suites and chalets.

Amenities: A sauna, a Jacuzzi, a pool (open during the summer only), and a recreation room.

Rates: $–$$$.

Contact: Tahoe Chalet Inn, 3860 Lake Tahoe Blvd., South Lake Tahoe, CA 96150; 530/544-3311 or 800/821-2656; website: www.tahoechaletinn.com.

Tahoe Colony Inn

Centrally located and part of the Americana Inns group, this large motel with a plantation motif offers 104 rooms. The inn is one block from casinos and is across the street from the Crescent V Shopping Center, which has a Sizzler Steak House and a Raley's market. Free continental breakfast is served each morning.

Amenities: Year-round heated swimming pool, free shuttle to casinos and ski resorts.

Rates: $–$$.

Contact: Tahoe Colony Inn, 3794 Montreal Rd., South Lake Tahoe, CA 96150; 530/544-6481 or 800/338-5552; email: tahoecol@sierra.net; website:www.americana-inns.com/TahoeColony.html.

Tahoe Tropicana

You'll find a welcome bottle of champagne in each of the Tahoe Tropicana's 58 rooms—which consist of single, adjoining, and penthouse suites offering king-sized, queen-sized, and some water beds—as well as phones, color cable televisions, some kitchenettes, and air-conditioning.

Amenities: Dining, a Jacuzzi, a heated pool (during the summer only) in a gazebo, ice and vending machines, a cocktail lounge, outdoor parking, and free ski and casino shuttles.

Rates: $–$$.

Contact: Tahoe Tropicana, 4132 Cedar Ave./P.O. Box 4681, South Lake Tahoe, CA 96157; 530/541-3911 or 800/447-0246; website: www.tahoetropicana.com.

Tahoe Valley Lodge

These 21 recently remodelled rooms and suites, some of which are nonsmoking, provide gas fireplaces, air-conditioning, telephones, televisions, and in-room coffee. AAA Three-Diamond rating.

Amenities: A pool (during the summer only) and a year-round hot tub.

Policies: Some pets are allowed.

Rates: $–$$.

Contact: Tahoe Valley Lodge, 2241 Lake Tahoe Blvd., South Lake Tahoe, CA 96150;

530/541-0353 or 800/669-7544; website: www.TahoeValleyLodge.com.

Value Inn

With Jacuzzis and fireplaces in some units, this Value Inn's 62 guest rooms also include a phone and a television. Guests in certain units receive continental breakfast.

Rates: $–$$.
Contact: Value Inn, 2659 Lake Tahoe Blvd., South Lake Tahoe, CA 96150; 530/544-3959.

Viking Motor Lodge

These 58 guest rooms offer phones, remote-control color televisions, kitchenettes, continental breakfast, in-room coffee, and some fireplaces.

Amenities: A Jacuzzi, a pool (during the summer only), and a free ski shuttle.
Rates: $–$$.
Contact: Viking Motor Lodge, 4083 Cedar Ave., South Lake Tahoe, CA 96150; 530/541-5155 or 800/288-4083.

KIRKWOOD/HOPE VALLEY/MARKLEEVILLE

Alpine Inn

Set near the East Fork of the Carson River, which is famous for river rafting and fishing, the Alpine Inn is situated in historic Markleeville. It is also four miles from Grover Hot Springs.

Rates: $.
Contact: Alpine Inn, 14820 Hwy. 89/P.O. Box 367, Markleeville, CA 96120; 530/694-2591.

Woodfords Inn

A quarter mile south of Highway 88, Woodfords' guest rooms (including single queen-sized and some double twin-sized beds) offer large stall showers and color cable television. Snacks and sweet rolls are for sale.

Amenities: Free coffee, a Jacuzzi, a large yard, picnic tables, and barbecue pits.
Rates: $.
Contact: Woodfords Inn, 20960 Hwy. 89, Woodfords, CA 96120; 530/694-2410.

FEATHER RIVER COUNTRY/LAKES BASIN

Bassett's Station

Bassett's Station provides three guest rooms (each of which contains two double beds and a day couch) with fully equipped kitchens, baths, and dinettes.

Amenities: A café; a minimart with gasoline, groceries, auto supplies, fishing tackle, and camping goods; and phones in the common areas.
Rates: $$.
Contact: Bassett's Station, 100 Gold Lake Rd. (at Hwy. 49), Sierra City, CA 96125; 530/862-1297; website: www.sierracity.com/Stay/Bassetts.html.

The Buttes Resort

These one- and two-bedroom units run the gamut, from motel rooms to suites to honeymoon suites. Some have fully equipped kitchens, and some have decks overlooking the Yuba River. Cabins have recently been remodelled.

Amenities: Fishing boats for guests.
Policies: Book seven days and pay for only six days.
Rates: $–$$$.
Contact: Buttes Resort, Hwy. 49/P.O. Box 234, Sierra City, CA 96125; 530/862-1170 or 800/991-1170; website: www.sierracity.com.

River Pines Resort

River Pines provides cottages with fully equipped kitchens and 62 motel rooms, some with minikitchens, air-conditioning, and wheelchair access. The resort is on Highway 89, a quarter mile north of Graeagle.

Amenities: A restaurant, a cocktail lounge, a swimming pool, a Jacuzzi, a playground, a recreation room, a picnic, and a barbecue area.
Rates: $–$$.
Contact: River Pines Resort, 8296 Hwy. 89, Blairsden, CA/P.O. Box 249, Clio, CA 96106; 530/836-0313 or 800/696-2551.

Riverside Inn

These guest rooms—with king-sized, queen-sized, or double beds—include cable television, some kitchenettes, continental breakfast, and private decks overlooking the river.

Amenities: A patio, a barbecue area, and a beach.

Policies: A 24-hour cancellation notice is required.

Rates: $–$$.

Contact: Riverside Inn, 206 Commercial St./P.O. Box 176, Downieville, CA 95936; 530/289-1000.

Sierra Motel

The Sierra offers 23 guest rooms—each of which has a queen-sized bed—with telephones, color televisions with HBO, AM/FM radios, air-conditioning, some nonsmoking rooms, in-room coffee, and refrigerators.

Rates: $.

Contact: Sierra Motel, 380 E. Sierra St./P.O. Box 1265, Portola, CA 96122; 530/832-4223.

Sleepy Pines Motel

Rooms: 17 guest rooms with phones, color televisions, in-room coffee, continental breakfast on weekends, and some nonsmoking rooms.

Rates: $–$$.

Contact: Sleepy Pines Motel, 74631 Hwy. 70, Portola, CA 96122; 530/832-4291.

Hotels and Casinos

SQUAW VALLEY

The Resort at Squaw Creek

Bolstered by a new luxury spa, this elegant, full-service hotel is situated at the site of the 1960 Winter Olympics, and it has played a big part in transforming Squaw Valley into a year-round destination. Already known for its challenging ski slopes, the valley now has an equally gnarly golf course, an 18-holer that spreads out from the lower slopes of the mountain to a marshy meadow. The course was named one of the top five resort courses in the United States by *Golf Digest*. The Resort at Squaw Creek covers 626 acres and is chockablock with other sports amenities: tennis courts, an executive fitness center, a cross-country ski center, and an aquatic center with three swimming pools (including a 120-foot water slide). In winter, guests need only step outside their rooms to immediately board a chairlift that provides access to the mountain's more protected intermediate runs. Also, Squaw Creek is near a riding stable and several good hiking trails.

The resort complex is divided into two main buildings—one housing the lobby, meeting rooms, and restaurants, and the other with 403 rooms and suites. The suites are roomy and lavish, most with striking views. Standard rooms are considerably smaller. Recently, many of the rooms were refurbished with new carpeting, wall covering, and furniture. One inconvenience is that the two buildings are not interconnected, so guests must walk outside to get from their rooms to the lobby or to the restaurants.

The exterior layout is one of the resort's more attractive features; it includes meandering rock and stone terraces for outside dining, sunning, and sitting, and a commanding 250-foot cascading waterfall. The health and fitness center has 10,000 square feet of the latest in therapeutic treatments and exercise equipment, and the Spa at Squaw Creek has 10 massage/treatment rooms that include body wraps, body masks, hydrotherapy, and aloe vera skin treatments.

Resort employees are courteous and energetic, and management recently initiated a built-in service charge with room rates so that you don't have to be fishing into your pocket for tips every 10 minutes. Five restaurants serve everything from sandwiches to gourmet meals, and tend to be in Tahoe's higher price range. Although the resort caters to the executive conference trade, it has excellent supervised recreation programs for youngsters and teens, perhaps the best in Tahoe for upscale families.

Rooms: 403 guest rooms and suites with two speakerphones, televisions, and continental breakfast. Kitchens and fireplaces are available in some units.

KEY TO TAHOE RESORT RATES

$ = economy (less than $50 per room)
$$ = standard ($50–80 per room)
$$$ = deluxe ($81–110)
$$$$ = luxury (over $110)

Amenities: Five restaurants and lounges, including Glissandi, Cascades, Ristorante Montagna, Bullwhacker's Pub, and Sweet Potato Deli; retail shops offering clothing and ski rentals and accessories; an art gallery; laundry facilities; baby-sitting services; volleyball; soccer; in-line skating; three heated pools; a water slide; four spas; a salon; a complete fitness center; an eight-court tennis center; an 18-hole Robert Trent Jones Jr. golf course; an ice skating rink; ski-in/ski-out service via a triple chairlift to Squaw Valley USA; convention facilities covering 33,000 square feet; a program for kids ages 3–13; and special teen programs. Nearby activities include snowmobiling, horseback riding, fly-fishing, and rafting.
Rates: $$$–$$$$. Credit cards are accepted.
Contact: The Resort at Squaw Creek, 400 Squaw Creek Rd., Olympic Valley, CA 96146; 530/583-6300 or 800/403-4434; website: www.squawcreek.com.

INCLINE VILLAGE/CRYSTAL BAY
Cal-Neva Resort

If the walls here could talk, what stories they would tell about this grand hotel. Let's drop a few names: Marilyn Monroe, John F. Kennedy, and Frank Sinatra. The crooner bought the lodge in 1960, and it soon became a frequent hangout for his infamous "Rat Pack" and the Kennedy clan. One newsy tidbit circulating in those days was that a secret rendezvous between the president and the glamour queen allegedly took place here. Another piece of trivia is that Sinatra built an underground, brick-lined tunnel from the Celebrity Showroom to his private chalet so that he could avoid mingling with the crowds after his performances. The tunnel still exists, and guests can ask the concierge for a tour from the casino. But the outlet in Sinatra's chalet is sealed, although the chalet itself is still in use.

Certainly this stately lodge has a romantic ambience, with a lakefront view of turquoise Crystal Bay that is the envy of Tahoe. The lodge was built in 1926 by a wealthy San Francisco developer who coined the name "Cal-Neva" because the property straddles the California/Nevada state line. This has always been its most intriguing asset. In the California "wing," guests can marvel at the spacious Indian Room, which doubles as a museum of Washoe Indian culture and as a grand ballroom for conferences and weddings. Leave this room for the lobby and presto! you're in Nevada, with slot machines, gaming, and Sinatra's pride and joy—the Showroom. The lodge went through a succession of owners after the tenure of Ol' Blue Eyes, who lost it in 1963 during a legal tangle with the Nevada Gaming Control Board. It was acquired in 1985 by land developer Charles P. Bluth, who launched a major renovation that restored the "Lady of the Lake" to her original elegance.

Cal-Neva is consistently Tahoe-esque, with its rock and wood interior and cozy lodge feel. The views from the 200 lakefront rooms are breathtaking. In addition to the rooms, there are chalets and cabins (including the Marilyn Monroe cabin) for intimate tête-à-têtes. The swimming pools, decks, and wedding chapels (Cal-Neva is the wedding capital of the North Shore) are arrayed on bouldered terraces. Most of all, the environment is remarkably amiable and low-key. Bluth has wisely emphasized the "hotel" aspect of his property, rather than the "gaming," which is quite modest—this resort focuses on guest service. He still regards Cal-Neva as a work in progress and continually adds improvements and attractions. Recently, all of the guest rooms have been refurbished with more upscale and plush decor. Cal-Neva has strong repeat business, and the clientele includes upscale couples and families. This resort offers history, a whiff of scandal, and a splendid vista. What more could you ask for?
Rooms: 200 rooms, suites, cabins, and chalets with telephones, televisions, in-room coffee, and

some fireplaces. Some units are lakefront and some offer panoramic lake views.

Amenities: One restaurant (The Lakeview Dining Room), one bar (the famous Circle Bar); a casino; a full-service European health spa; a sauna; a steam room; a Jacuzzi; a pool (during the summer only); tennis courts; a video arcade; a wedding and honeymoon office; a photography studio; wedding gown and tuxedo rentals; and florist, banquet, and convention facilities for up to 400 people.

Policies: Children under 10 stay for free when accompanied by an adult.

Rates: $$–$$$.

Contact: Cal-Neva Resort, 2 Stateline Rd./P.O. Box 368, Crystal Bay, NV 89402; 775/832-4000 or 800/CAL-NEVA (800/225-6382); website: www.calnevaresort.com.

Hyatt Regency Lake Tahoe Resort and Casino

Recently completing a $27 million renovation, this hotel has reinvented itself with stunning interiors that include new common areas, such as the casino and restaurants, and invoke the 1920s' era of Tahoe's "Grand Lodges." When you step into the lobby, the warmth and rustic elegance of exposed wood beams, cathedral ceilings, rock floors, and open fireplace immediately give you a sense of a place. The improvements extend to all of the guest rooms, including the suites and 24 Lakeside Cottages, as well. Divided by a road into two sections—the main tower and a beachfront complex that includes the cottages and a lakeside restaurant—the Hyatt is in the beautiful, wooded environment of Incline Village. It has a 500-foot-long private white sand beach and a 270-foot-long floating pier that can accommodate the lake's largest vessels. Also, the Hyatt is close to Incline's Championship Golf Course and two ski areas, Diamond Peak and Mt. Rose. While the hotel has always excelled in service and cuisine, the aesthetics of the main tower, which was built in the 1960s, have changed very little. But as this was written, the Hyatt was forging ahead with another $30 million in exterior renovations, which will complete the transformation. In early 2002, the hotel began a reconstruction of the 150-room Aspen Terrace wing, which is behind the main tower. In its place: A new building with upscale rooms that overlook both the lake and some of the hotel's on-site recreation amenities. Everything in the rear of the property, in fact, is being upgraded. Among the additions: a multitiered swimming pool with a swim-out feature and a state-of-the-art, 15,000-square-foot spa and health club. The Hyatt, which hosted a major environmental summit with President Bill Clinton and Vice President Al Gore in 1997, features excellent gourmet restaurants and caters to upscale families with children. It is in Tahoe's wealthiest community and is surrounded by multimillion-dollar gated estates nestled in the pines. (You can get a look at these mountain palaces firsthand by jogging or cycling past them on paved trails.) Guests can reach the beachfront part of the property via an overhead pedestrian bridge, which spans the road. On this side are the Lone Eagle Grille, additional banquet rooms, the luxury cottages, and various types of waterfront recreational amenities, including an excursion boat and rental craft. Apart from the grill, the hotel has another excellent restaurant, Ciao Mein Trattoria, which combines Asian and Italian delicacies and is a memorable gourmet experience. A third restaurant, the Sierra Café, offers around-the-clock dining, with a menu that might be described as gourmet casual. The newest addition is Cutthroat's Saloon, an Old West-style bar that is named after the famous Lake Tahoe cutthroat trout. Here you can nosh on burgers, sandwiches, peel-and-eat shrimp, and quesadillas, while watching sports on any of nine TV monitors, including a big-screen. The hotel offers unique chaperoned programs for youngsters during the day and evening. And as the only large accommodation on the East Shore, the Hyatt and its environs are blissfully free of traffic congestion.

Rooms: 449 rooms, including suites and 24 lakeside cottages. Units consist of one- and two-bedroom configurations with king-sized and double beds, phones, cable TV with movie channels, stereo systems, some adjoining parlors with fireplaces and private sun decks facing the lake, some kitchens, an honor bar, a wet bar, wheelchair access, and nonsmoking rooms. Some units are lakefront and some offer panoramic lake views. One nice touch is the Regency Club, which consists of designated private floors with 48 rooms and eight executive king rooms, all with VIP service and amenities. The Club Lounge, on the 11th floor, provides a "Sierra Morning Continental Breakfast" 7 A.M.–10:30 A.M. and "Mountain Sunset Wine and Hors d'Oeuvres" 5 P.M.–8 P.M. daily.

Amenities: Four restaurants, VIP floors and lounge, room service, general store, 24-hour casino covering 18,900 square feet, sportsbook lounge, cocktail bar and lounge, periodic entertainment, spa and fitness club, outdoor pool, tennis courts, family arcade, laundry, private beach, private pier, volleyball net, boat rentals, boat excursions, parasailing, ski rentals, and ski shuttles. The Lakeside Lodge provides 5,817 square feet of meeting space and accommodates up to 690 people. For children there's Camp Hyatt, with arts and crafts, beach time, volleyball, swimming, tennis, bowling, miniature golf, supervised game room activities, and movies with popcorn and soda. Reservations are required for those activities.

Rates: $$–$$$$.

Contact: Hyatt Regency Lake Tahoe Resort and Casino, 111 Country Club Dr./P.O. Box 3239, Incline Village, NV 89450; 775/832-1234 or 888/899-7883; website: www.laketahoehyatt.com.

Tahoe Biltmore Lodge and Casino

The wave of renovations that swept the North Shore properties has also touched this vintage casino/hotel, which spruced up its interior and added a restaurant to the complex. The guest rooms are modest in decor, but the lodge is well situated on the main highway. The Tahoe Biltmore is popular with senior citizens and dyed-in-the-wool gamblers, as well as young skiers on a budget, and it offers cheap eats most times of the day.

Rooms: 92 with a choice between hotel and motor lodge accommodations, which feature phones, TVs, some lake views, wheelchair access, and nonsmoking rooms. All rooms include free breakfast daily.

Amenities: 24-hour dining, a 24-hour full-service casino, sportsbook, four bars, a lounge, free live entertainment, shows, beaches within walking distance, an outdoor pool (during the summer only), year-around hot tub, arcade, gift shop, free parking for cars and RVs, a wedding chapel, and a meeting room that accommodates up to 400 people.

Rates: $–$$$.

Contact: Tahoe Biltmore Lodge and Casino, 5 Hwy. 28/P.O. Box 115, Crystal Bay, NV 89402; 775/831-0660, 800/245-6267, or 800/245-8667; website: www.tahoebiltmore.com.

SOUTH SHORE/STATELINE
Caesars Tahoe

Among the moderately priced casino/hotels, Caesars has always gone after the younger crowds—and the young at heart. The 440 rooms were recently renovated, and all have whirlpool bathtubs. There are some fine restaurants here (including Primavera, a pasta place, and The Broiler Room, a steaks-and-seafood place), as well as the only full-time "big name" showroom at Stateline, a lively nightspot (Club Nero), and the always busy Planet Hollywood, christened in 1994 by co-owners Arnold Schwarzenegger, Sylvester Stallone, and Bruce Willis. The trendy café, which recently introduced a new menu, is not exactly the gourmet center of Tahoe, but it does have some eye-catching Hollywood props and memorabilia on the walls. Caesars recently replaced its Asian restaurant with Cuvee, a small, intimate place that features California cuisine.

There's a large indoor, lagoon-style swimming pool with waterfalls and, strangely enough, an elegant wedding chapel right next to it. Those who crave stellar entertainment, not risqué cabarets or low-budget Broadway shows, will find a selection that varies from country singer Wynonna to Chris Isaak, who perform in the recently remodelled Circus Maximus Showroom. If you can wrangle a tee time, you can golf at Edgewood Country Club (one of the nation's top 100 courses) across the street. Caesars offers a kid's day camp, with both day and evening sessions, and this supervised activity can include educational sessions and outdoor fun such as beach time. Regular shuttles from Reno and the ski resorts serve the hotel, and everything at Stateline (including the other casinos) is within walking distance.

Rooms: 440 deluxe guest rooms and suites (five theme suites: Bahamas, Hollywood, Oriental, Contemporary, and Roman) with telephones, televisions, whirlpools or oversized Roman tubs, and full-service bars. Some rooms have wheel chair access, some are nonsmoking, some have lake views, and some have dining areas.

Amenities: Six restaurants (Primavera, the Broiler Room, Cuvee, The Roman Feast (buffet), Planet Hollywood, and Subway sandwich deli), Club Nero nightclub, casino, showroom with 1,500 seats, retail shops and galleries, health spa, massage services, sauna, Jacuzzi, lagoon-style indoor pool, recreation room, wedding chapel and facilities, convention center that can accommodate up to 1,500 people, the *Odyssey* (a yacht for entertaining special guests), covered valet and self-parking, and the Tahoe Casino Express luxury Reno Airport shuttle (with 14 departures daily).

Rates: $$–$$$$.

Contact: Caesars Tahoe, 55 U.S. 50/P.O. Box 5800, Stateline, NV 89449; 775/588-3515 or 800/648-3353; website: www.caesars.com/tahoe.

Embassy Suites Resort

Don't want your kids hanging around slot machines? Embassy Suites Resort is the best large hotel for families on the South Shore. This AAA Four-Diamond resort, the largest luxury property on the California side of Stateline, is quiet and free of gaming. If you hunger for action, you need only walk next door, into Nevada, to spin the roulette wheel or crank the one-armed bandits at Harrah's. Embassy has its trademark atrium lobby—nine floors high—filled with the ambience of babbling brooks, indoor foliage, and a large historic flume and waterwheel reminiscent of the Gold Rush era. All rooms are two-room suites with two separate sleeping areas—a bedroom and a living room with sofa bed, so you can cordon off your kids and have some privacy. The hotel has won-

derful amenities, such as a respectable morning buffet breakfast (included in the price of the room), an afternoon happy hour with free drinks and snacks, and an indoor pool and exercise room (although the pool is a little too public—it's right next to the atrium lounge and breakfast area). In the summer of 2002, Echo Restaurant/Lounge was completely remodled, and the lunch and dinner menus now focus on "New American Cuisine" with a variety of ethnic influences. There's a ski and sports shop in the lobby, valet underground parking, and regular shuttles from the ski areas.

Rooms: 400 two-room suites with phones, cable televisions, VCRs, some lake views, kitchens, minibars, full breakfasts, two-hour free manager's cocktail reception, in-room coffee, wheelchair access, nonsmoking rooms, and room service.

Amenities: Echo Restaurant/Lounge serving lunch and dinner; cocktail lounge; Jacuzzi; indoor pool; outdoor sun deck; fitness club; family arcade; gift and sports shops offering rentals, sales, repairs, and accessories; convention, catering, and banquet facilities covering more than 6,200 square feet, with a single-room capacity of 450 people; covered valet parking; car rentals; and the Tahoe Casino Express luxury Reno Airport shuttle.

Rates: $$$–$$$$.

Contact: Embassy Suites Resort, 4130 Lake Tahoe Blvd., South Lake Tahoe, CA 96150; 530/544-5400, 800/EMBASSY (800/362-2779), or 800/924-9245; website: www.embassytahoe.com.

Embassy Vacation Resort Lake Tahoe

This impressive interval-ownership resort opened its doors in April 1997 at the busy intersection of U.S. 50 and Ski Run Boulevard. The six-story building with dormers, balconies, and a sloping green roof shares many of the Old Tahoe architectural qualities of its cousin down the street, but here the rooms are much larger. They consist of 141 condominiums, each with two bedrooms, two bathrooms, a full kitchen, and a living room with fireplace. Availability of rooms to the general public varies depending on time of year and use by owners.

As with Embassy Suites (see above), the Vacation Resort is well suited for families. There's a children's activities center with supervised games and crafts, an indoor/outdoor swimming pool, and excellent proximity to recreation. Heavenly Ski Resort is just up the street and the new Marina Village, with its shops, restaurants (including the Riva Grill), and sightseeing vessels and rental boats, is right next door. The revitalized marina is home port for the *Tahoe Queen* paddlewheel steamer.

Rooms: 141 condominium units, each of which can be divided into two one-bedroom hotel suites.

Amenities: Restaurant serving continental breakfast (free for guests), lunch, and dinner; exercise room with cardiovascular equipment; indoor/outdoor swimming pool with a sun deck and poolside food and beverage service; in-house bakery; children's playroom; indoor and outdoor saunas and whirlpool spas; VIP lounge for the manager's afternoon cocktail reception (free for guests); valet parking and bell service; concierge; outside parking lot; and access to shuttles that serve ski resorts, beaches, and casinos.

Policies: Children are welcome, but the kids' activities center is restricted to youngsters five and older.

Rates: $$–$$$$.

Contact: Embassy Vacation Resort Lake Tahoe, 901 Ski Run Blvd., South Lake Tahoe, CA 96150; 530/541-6122 or 800/465-3613; website: www.embassyvacationresort.com.

Harrah's Lake Tahoe

Built in 1973, this 18-story luxury hotel has plenty of spark and sophistication, thanks to constant improvements. The latest of these, a $26 million overhaul in 2000, consisted of an outside facelift with a more pleasing forest-green exterior and some Tahoe-esque trim, and a major renovation of the two 18th-floor restaurants (Friday's Station and The Forest Buffet) and The Summit restaurant on the 16th and 17th floors. Reflecting the Old Tahoe look, Harrah's lobby has attractive stonework, a spruced-up casino, new decor in its rooms and suites, and a woodsy-styled 24-hour gourmet restaurant, American River Cafe. High-quality food and entertainment define the experience of staying at Harrah's. The rooms are spacious and comfortable, and there are agreeable touches, such as small color TVs in the bathrooms. No establishment on the South Shore can beat the daily buffet breakfast in the top-floor Forest Room, with its panoramic, picture-window views of Tahoe and the snow-crested Sierra peaks. All of the restaurants on the upper floors, including The Summit—the hotel's signature dining room and one of the best in Tahoe—are popular and excellent. Harrah's has been experimenting with its entertainment lately, alternating between Broadway musicals, magic acts, acrobatics, and the occasional headline performer in its 800-seat showroom. For kids, there's a 12,000-square-foot Family Fun Center, which is filled with arcade games and the latest high-tech virtual reality mind-benders. Harrah's has been given a Four-Diamond rating by both AAA and *Mobil Travel Guide*.

Rooms: 517 recently remodeled deluxe rooms, suites, and all-new luxury suites with double sound-proofed walls, remote bedside controls for TV and lights, phones, TVs, VCRs, Nintendo, two bathrooms (with a television and a phone in each), and some lake views.

Amenities: Seven restaurants (The Summit, Friday's Station, Forest Buffet, American River Café, North Beach Deli, The Ice Creamery, and Club Cappuccino); several bars; Rendezvous Lounge with nightly live entertainment; casino; showroom; concierge; bell service; 24-hour room service; laundry service; in-room ski rentals and overnight ski tune-ups; retail shops; shoe shine service; men's and women's health spas; massage services; pet kennel; salons; tanning center; sauna; Jacuzzi; indoor glass-domed swimming pool; Family Fun Center; convention space (covering 18,000 square feet with 12 meeting rooms accommodating up to 1,000 people); uncovered valet and self-parking; rental cars; free ski shuttles; limousines; and the Tahoe Casino Express luxury Reno Airport shuttle.

Policies: No pets are allowed.

Rates: $$$–$$$$.

Contact: Harrah's Lake Tahoe, P.O. Box 8,

Stateline, NV 89449; 775/588-6611 or 800/ HARRAHS (800/427-7247); website: www .harrahstahoe.com.

Harveys Resort Casino

With 740 rooms and suites, Harveys is the largest hotel at Lake Tahoe and, as of 2001, it is joined at the hip with Harrahs, which is the hotel's new owner. Slick, modern, and very upscale, it is best described as a hotel first and a casino second. Being a good innkeeper was the philosophy of the late founder, Harvey Gross, a meat retailer from Sacramento who opened the place in 1944. Harveys celebrated its 50th anniversary in 1994, making it Tahoe's oldest operating casino. Service has always been top-notch, and the hotel has earned the coveted Mobil Four-Star and AAA Four-Diamond ratings. The 1986 opening of the $100 million Lake Tower created a rebirth for the property, with large rooms, firm and comfortable beds, contemporary furnishings, and splendid lake views. A full-service health club, the best at the Stateline casino properties, is available for guests. Other services include free continental breakfasts, an opulent VIP lounge for Harveys club members, and a recently remodeled and upgraded buffet. Among the eight restaurants, the old-timers are partial to the Sage Room, which has been a fixture since 1947 and prepares the finest steak dinners in town. A more refined restaurant on the top floor, Llewellyn's, serves excellent continental cuisine such as seafood and Viennese pastry and has deluxe views to match. The Hard Rock Café offers the usual American fare and nightly live entertainment. Harveys also has cabaret shows, some of them adult-oriented, and offers the occasional musical revue. During summer, the resort hosts outdoor concerts, with big-name entertainers, in an amphitheater next to the rear parking lot. As befitting its size and stature, Harveys has the largest casino at the lake.

Rooms: 740 luxury rooms and suites with phones, televisions, lake views, and in-room coffee.

Amenities: Eight restaurants (Llewellyn's, Hard Rock Café, Sage Room Steak House, Seafood Grotto, El Vaquero, Carriage House, Garden Buffet, and Emerald Bay Coffee Co.); several bars; lounges; casino; concierge; showroom; the Emerald Theater (a 285-seat lounge); retail shops; wedding chapel; sauna; Jacuzzi; outdoor lap swimming pool; health club and spa offering aromatherapy, massage, and a tanning salon; fitness club; barbershop; beauty salon; family arcade; the Kid's Day Camp for children ages 6–13, with daily activities promoting street smarts, safety, and outside play; convention center covering 15,000 square feet and accommodating up to 1,000 guests; valet and self-parking garage/lot; and the Tahoe Casino Express luxury Reno Airport shuttle.

Rates: $$$–$$$$.

Contact: Harveys Resort Casino, P.O. Box 128, Stateline, NV 89449; 775/588-2411 or 800/HARVEYS (800/427-8397); website: www.harveys-tahoe.com.

Horizon Casino Resort

Once a regular haunt of Elvis Presley, this casino/hotel is not as large or as lavish as its competitors, but it attracts guests with low prices, inexpensive buffet meals, and frequent goingson, such as country music and collectibles events outside of the front entrance. The famous Presley suite, where the King himself used to stay while he was performing here (back when the hotel was called Sahara Tahoe), is available for honeymoons and special functions. Horizon's entertainment includes cabaret shows of singers, magicians, comics, and dancers (some of them adult-themed), live bands and DJ music in a new nightspot called Club Z, free live music and dancing in The Aspen Lounge, and a multiscreen movie complex with all-digital Surround-Sound (Horizon Stadium Cinemas), which replaced the showroom where Presley performed. Also, the hotel has a large children's area for video and redemption games. The signature restaurant is Josh's, and there's a buffet room with average but inexpensive meals. A covered parking garage is adjacent to the hotel, and all ski and airport shuttles stop here. Horizon is closest major hotel to the elegant Edgewood Country Club golf course, just across the street.

Rooms: 539 deluxe guest rooms and suites with phones, televisions, some fireplaces, and some lake views.

Amenities: Three restaurants (Josh's, Four Seasons 24-hour restaurant, and Le Grande Buffet), Starbucks coffee nook, Baskin-Robbins 31 Flavors, bars, casino, Golden Cabaret Lounge, multiscreen cinema, nightclub, concierge, tour desk, Jacuzzi, outdoor heated pool (during the summer only), amusement center (with video and redemption games), recreation room, beauty salon, gift and flower shops, wedding chapel, convention facilities covering 25,000 square feet, covered and uncovered valet and self-parking, and the Tahoe Casino Express luxury Reno Airport shuttle.

Rates: $$–$$$.

Contact: Horizon Casino Resort, P.O. Box C, Stateline, NV 89449; 775/588-6211, 800/322-7723, or 800/684-3322; website: www.horizon-casino.com.

Lakeside Inn and Casino

For those who can't handle throngs of people and the beehive of high-rise casinos, this small, low-profile casino/inn just east of Horizon offers something of a haven. It's built like a motel, but rooms come with amenities such as chocolates and French-milled soap, and there are nice views of Edgewood Country Club from some of the rooms. Recently all of the rooms and many of the common areas have been remodelled, and the upgrades include a popular new Mexican restaurant, the second for the inn. It's on U.S. 50 at Kingsbury Grade.

Rooms: 124 guest rooms with phones, televisions, an in-room ski rack, in-room coffee, and some lake views.

Amenities: Timber House (specializing in prime rib) and Taberna Mexican Restaurants, three combination bar/lounges, free live entertainment, a casino, a clothing and gift shop, a family arcade, a pool, banquet and convention facilities, and uncovered self-parking.

Rates: $–$$.

Contact: Lakeside Inn and Casino, 168 U.S. 50/P.O. Box 5640, Stateline, NV 89449; 775/588-7777 or 800/624-7980; website: www.lakesideinn.com.

Marriott Grand Residence Club

Evoking a sense of Old Tahoe with its rustically elegant interiors and its early 1900s facades, this new condominium hotel, which consists of quarter-share ownerships, is the first of a new Marriott brand, one that is positioned between the company's luxury Ritz-Carlton and its well-established Vacation Club International. Originally it was intended to be American Skiing Company's Grand Summit Resort, but ASC sold the site to Marriott during a severe cash crunch. Since most owners never use more than a few weeks of their three-month intervals, they put their unused time into a rental pool. Therefore, the public has year-around access to some part of the room inventory, and the club is managed like an upscale hotel. Guests will find liberal use of stonework and beamed ceilings in the common areas, especially in the lobby. Each residence combines classic alpine themes with modern sophistication and amenities, including fireplace and private balcony in most units, granite countertops and ceramic tiled floors in the kitchen and bathrooms, custom wood cabinets, richly upholstered furniture, and tasteful artwork. The club's greatest asset is its location adjacent to Heavenly Ski Resort's new high-speed gondola and its proximity (one long block) to Stateline's casinos. Together with its sister property, Marriott's Timber Lodge, the Grand Residence Club forms the core of the Heavenly Village, which is the main California portal for the ski area. The village also offers several new restaurants, including Wolfgang Puck Express, a casual dining experience with pastas, pizzas, and soups; Quiznos Classic Subs, an upscale sandwhich shop; and Coldstone Creamery, a gourmet ice cream outlet. All are located on the ground floor of the Residence Club. New shops, an ice skating rink and a multiplex theater are included in the plans.

Rooms: 199 residences that range in size from 360 square feet to 2,496 square feet and include one, two, and three bedrooms, studios, and penthouses. Some units have sleeping accommodations for up to 12 guests.

Amenities: Underground valet parking, owner's private ski lockers, owner's club and library, health

TAHOE ACCOMMODATIONS

club with steam room and massage, year-round outdoor heated swimming pool, two outdoor spas, restaurants and shops, concierge services, daily maid service, and laundry service.

Rates: $$$–$$$$$.

Contact: Marriott Grand Residence Club, 1001 Park Ave. (at Hwy. 50), South Lake Tahoe, CA 96150; 866-20-GRAND (866-204-7263); website: www.vacationclub.com

Marriott's Timber Lodge

This new interval ownership resort, one of more than 50 Vacation Club International resorts worldwide, is the second pillar of the new Heavenly Village near Stateline, and is next to the ski resort's high-speed gondola. Using weeklong increments (as opposed to the three-month ownerships of the Grand Residence Club next door), Timber Lodge operates as a hotel for both its owners and nonowner guests. Availability to the public usually depends on the oc-cupancy of owners and exchange owners, who have priority, as well as the inventory of unsold intervals. Units are modest-sized condominiums, and each has features such as soaking tub in the master bath, fully equipped kitchen, dining area that can accommodate from four to eight people depending on size, living area, multiple televisions and a DVD player, washer and dryer, and private balcony. Borrowing from the rustic look of vintage national park lodges, the Timber Lodge is especially suited for families, since it has a number of features that are oriented to children. It also includes a restaurant, Fire & Ice, which has a pan-Asian display kitchen with teppan-style cooking (choose your ingredients and they chop and grill your meal). The lodge is within easy walking distance of the lake, the Stateline casinos, and a large shopping mall next door.

Rooms: 261 one-bedroom/one-bath and two-bedroom/two-bath villas (at buildout), rang-

TAHOE ACCOMMODATIONS

COURTESY OF MARRIOTT VACATION CLUB INTERNATIONAL

Marriott's Timber Lodge

ing from 835 square feet to 1,185 square feet of living space and accommodating from four to eight guests.

Amenities: Heated underground valet parking, self-service ski storage, Fire & Ice restaurant Children's Activity Center, center courtyard pool with children's pool and whirlpool spas, fitness center, restaurant, and The Marketplace convenience store and deli.

Rates: $$$–$$$$.

Contact: Marriott's Timber Lodge, 4100 Lake Tahoe Blvd. (Hwy. 50), South Lake Tahoe, CA 96150; 877/22-TAHOE (877/228-2163

Small Hotels and Condos

TRUCKEE/DONNER

Donner Lake Village Resort

Often overshadowed by Tahoe, Donner Lake is a delightful, self-contained community with homes, lodges, beaches, and virtually every type of water sport, yet it is just a couple of miles from historic Truckee's fine restaurants and eclectic boutiques. This lakefront resort is the largest at Donner, and it has a full marina where guests can berth their boats at no extra charge, or rent one on-site, lounge on the private beach, and cook steaks on one of several shoreline barbecues. Accommodations vary in type and quality, from modern, nondescript motel-style lodgettes and studios to rustically furnished two-story town houses. The lakeside one-bedroom suites offer the best views of Donner.

Free tea and coffee is available in each room, and a restaurant called High Sierra Coffee serves hot and cold beverages and snacks until 2 P.M. each day. A small conference room can accommodate up to 20 people. The lake itself offers fishing for trout (including Mackinaw), waterskiing, Jet Skiing, sailing, and swimming. On the lake's southeast side, there's a museum and a large beach at Donner Memorial State Park. For winter guests, the resort is minutes away from the Donner Summit ski areas of Sugar Bowl, Boreal, and Donner Ski Ranch, as well as Squaw Valley, Alpine Meadows, and Northstar.

Rooms: 66 modern lodgettes, studios, and one- and two-bedroom condominiums with telephones, color televisions, some kitchens, some fireplaces with wood-burning stoves, wheelchair access, nonsmoking rooms, daily maid service, and rollaways and cribs on request.

Amenities: Free coffee and tea; laundry facilities; guest saunas; a private beach; a private full-service marina with boats for water-skiing, cruising, and fishing, and personal watercraft; and a conference room.

Policies: No pets are allowed; bicycles and skateboards are not permitted in the courtyard or on the surrounding walkways.

Rates: $$–$$$$.

Contact: Donner Lake Village Resort, 15695 Donner Pass Rd., Ste. 101, Truckee, CA 96161; 530/587-6081 or 800/621-6664; website: www.donnerlakevillage.com.

Ice Lakes Lodge

This new lodge on Donner Summit has the look and feel of a Tyrolean Inn. It sits on the water's edge at Serene Lakes, two beautiful alpine jewels with forested shorelines. The lodge includes a deck overlooking the lakes, a lawn with shade trees, a full-service restaurant, a cocktail lounge, and a huge lobby with sitting area and fireplace. To reach the hotel, drive up Soda Springs Road (at the Norden exit of I-80) and pass the main entrance to Royal Gorge Cross Country Resort. Nearby are hiking and biking trails, along with both downhill and Nordic skiing. One of the lodge's most endearing qualities is the tranquil nature of its location, far away from traffic and crowds.

Rooms: 26, all accessible from indoor hallways on two floors. Nine sets of rooms adjoin, allowing for families. Each room has cable TV, phone with data port, and daily maid service. Some rooms have views of Serene Lakes.

Amenities: Restaurant, cocktail lounge, continental breakfast, large lobby with big-screen TV, private beach, boat and water toy rentals, and self-parking.

Rates: $$–$$$.

Contact: Ice Lakes Lodge, 1111 Soda Springs Rd., Soda Springs, CA 95728; 530/426-7660; website: www.icelakeslodge.com.

Northstar-at-Tahoe

As a moderately priced family destination, this giant four-seasons resort has it all: a challenging 18-hole golf course, one of the best intermediate ski areas in the state, the basin's most developed mountain biking park, a small "village" with three good restaurants, horseback riding stables, a cross-country ski center, and a wealth of other recreation options. The resort and its residential community encompass 2,560 forested acres, with many distinctive homes, especially near the golf course. The recommended Northstar experience is staying in one of the condominiums, each of which is decorated according to the preference of its owner. The ones closest to the ski hill offer ski-in, ski-out access. In the village, a motel-style lodge, which was recently upgraded, has the convenience of underground parking and proximity to the lifts.

If plans go as scheduled, Northstar was to have a much larger village, with upscale new condominiums, restaurants, and shops—all done in the rustic elegance of traditional national park mountain lodges. The project, expected to take several years, was being built by East West Partners of Colorado. Apart from its winter facilities, the resort also has considerable summer programs, including a lift-served mountain bike park, a ropes course, and an outdoor climbing wall. Northstar has its own internal shuttle system for guests and is six miles from either Truckee or Lake Tahoe's North Shore. Its location on an access road off Highway 267 gives this resort a great off-the-beaten-track feeling and mountain ambience. Just smell the pine needles!

Rooms: 252 units, varying from hotel-style rooms in the Village Lodge (with 51 rooms and village lofts with kitchens and living rooms) to four-bedroom condos and houses (some are daily and some are weekend rentals) with phones, cable television, fireplaces, linens, and some maid service.

Amenities: A ski hill; an 18-hole golf course; a summer golf camp; 10 hard-surface tennis courts and tennis lessons (during the summer only); a mountain bike park; a cross-country ski center; snowmobile tours; horseback riding stables; a sauna; a whirlpool spa; three pools, one of which is open year-round; a new full-service fitness center; a teen center with games and pool; three retail stores; four restaurants (Timbercreek, Village Food Company, Pedro's, and Golf Club House); sports equipment rentals; and some covered parking. Shuttles run between Northstar and Truckee hourly in both summer and winter. With notice, the resort will pick up guests at Truckee-Tahoe Airport and the Amtrak or Greyhound stations. Aero Trans and Budget Chauffeur, two private van services, operate from Reno-Tahoe International Airport.

Rates: $$–$$$$.

Contact: Northstar-at-Tahoe, Northstar Dr. and Hwy. 267/P.O. Box 2499, Truckee, CA 96160; 530/562-1113 or 800/GO-NORTH (800/466-6784); website: www.northstarattahoe.com.

Sugar Bowl Lodge

Probably no ski area in Lake Tahoe offers as European an environment as Sugar Bowl, one of the Sierra's first dedicated ski resorts. Built in 1939, the ski area and its 28-room guest lodge have seen a parade of celebrities over the decades, including Walt Disney, who was one of the original investors, and actors such as Errol Flynn, Charlie Chaplin, and James Stewart. There's a distinct Tyrolean flare in this rustic, three-story wood structure, which has a big parlor with a fireplace, the Belt Room lounge, and one of the region's best gourmet restaurants. Staying here might remind you of the Sun Valley Lodge or Yosemite's Ahwahnee Hotel—the lodge has Old-World charm and gives you the sense of experiencing a winter resort in its purest form. Once the skiers leave for the day, this is a cozy, uncrowded place to savor. It's nice to step outside in the morning and be one of the first skiers to cut tracks in fresh powder.

In recent years, many of the rooms have been remodelled. They feature new furnishings, cable television, down comforters, and cheerful pastel colors. The long, narrow hallways are lined with historic photographs, and guests must get accustomed to ascending and descending several sets of stairways. The best panoramas are had from the Mountain View rooms, which overlook the ski lifts and towering Mt. Lincoln (elevation 8,383 feet). There are several rooms for families, which sleep four to six people; these units have queen-sized beds in one room and twin beds in a loft. Mountain Family rooms have one queen-sized bed and a bunk bed in an adjacent room, with a private bathtub and shower. Rooms for couples and singles have queen-sized beds or twins, and there's a deluxe suite with a queen-sized bed, a living room with a queen-sized sofa sleeper, and a private bath with a tub and shower. All rooms have televisions. Guests park in a covered garage at the entrance and must take the gondola to reach the lodge. The lodge is open only in winter (except for weddings and private functions in summer), and popular holidays and weekends can be booked up to a year in advance. Sugar Bowl Lodge is on the Donner Summit, off I-80 at the Soda Springs/Norden exit on Old Highway 40.

Rooms: 28 rooms (in a variety of floorplans and sleeping configurations accommodating couples to families) with cable television and telephones.

Amenities: Dining service for three meals daily, a bar, a lounge with a fireplace, gondola access from an enclosed parking garage, a ski school, a rental shop, and lift-served ski slopes.

Rates: $$$–$$$$. Open mid-November–April only. Bed-and-breakfast packages include lodging, lift tickets, parking, and breakfast, and there are discounted prices for children who share a room with parents. Major credit cards are accepted.

Contact: Sugar Bowl Lodge, P.O. Box 5, Norden, CA 95724; 530/426-9000; website: www .skisugarbowl.com.

Tahoe Donner

Totally out of view from any major highway, this sprawling residential community is on a plateau north of Truckee. Despite its isolation, as you drive up the hill on Northwoods Boulevard, you will discover how much there is here: a challenging 18-hole golf course (with a second planned to open shortly), a downhill ski resort, a cross-country ski area, one of the best equestrian centers anywhere, a tennis complex, a recreation center with swimming pools, and more. Just about any type of accommodation you could want is available, from large homes and town houses to modest condominiums. Tahoe Donner is virtually a hidden city within the town of Truckee, yet it is close to I-80 and the historic district. Several agencies offer rentals here.

Rates: $$$–$$$$.

Contact: See the list of property management and rental agencies in the Lake Tahoe area; website: www.tahoedonner.com.

SQUAW VALLEY
The Olympic Village Inn

Constructed for the 1960 Winter Olympics and almost completely rebuilt in 1982, this 90-suite inn is rich in European elegance. The Olympic Village Inn is without a doubt one of Lake Tahoe's finest properties. It was refurbished in the late 1990s with new carpeting and interior designs, all in a French country style. Since the original main lodge building was sold to Squaw Valley Ski Corporation, the lobby/check-in area is now in the rear of the property. In summer, the grounds have a lush garden setting with a year-round heated swimming pool and five hot tubs. Skiers are so close to Squaw Valley that they could walk to the lifts, but a shuttle service whisks them to the base lodge.

Lots of small touches create a special ambience for guests, including free bicycles and sleds, guided hikes into Shirley Canyon, a videotape library, and a daily morning newspaper. Each suite is sumptuously furnished in a sort of country European style and offers modern conveniences such as a television, VCR, and stereo system. There are down comforters for the beds, terry cloth robes, and bathtubs with double shower heads. Each suite has a separate living room and bedroom, a small kitchenette, and (on the second and third floors) a private balcony. The deluxe suites also have wood-burning fireplaces. All units are part of a timeshare program, so the rental pool varies from day to day. Call ahead for availability.

Rates: $$–$$$$. Major credit cards are accepted.

Contact: The Olympic Village Inn, 1909 Chamonix Place/P.O. Box 2395, Olympic Valley, CA 96146; 530/581-6000 or 800/845-5243; website: www.vioa.com.

PlumpJack Squaw Valley Inn

This distinctive property, well-known for its gourmet restaurant and San Francisco pedigree, has an eclectic, Shakespearean interior that might best be described as a cross between art deco and Andy Warhol renaissance. I find the guest rooms imaginative and fun, though some people may consider them a bit weird. Pleasant touches include an amenity kit with a single-use camera, just in case you didn't bring one. The building itself has a woodsy, low-profile exterior, and the entrance is next to the tram station at Squaw Valley USA ski resort. In summer, there's an outdoor pool, an outdoor barbecue area, and a large patio for receptions and weddings. PlumpJack, an offspring of an award-winning San Francisco restaurant by the same name, is small, intimate, and quite simply one of the best gourmet dining experiences at the lake. There are also two large banquet rooms and ancillary meeting facilities that make this a great hotel for wedding parties, moderate-sized groups, and executive conferences.

Rooms: 60 guest rooms with phones and televisions.

Amenities: PlumpJack restaurant, English pub, Jacuzzi, swimming pool, banquet rooms, clothing and gift store, two hot spas, and a conference center for social functions and meetings.

Rates: $$$–$$$$.

Contact: PlumpJack Squaw Valley Inn, 1920 Squaw Valley Rd./P.O. Box 2407, Olympic Valley, CA 96146; 530/583-1576 or 800/323-ROOM (800/323-7666); website: www.plumpjack.com.

Squaw Tahoe Resort

The ski-in, ski-out condos here include phones, televisions, kitchens, and some fireplaces.

Amenities: Laundry facilities, a spa, and a sauna.

Rates: $$–$$$$.

Contact: Squaw Tahoe Resort, 2000 Squaw Loop Rd./P.O. Box 2612, Olympic Valley, CA 96146; 530/583-7226.

Squaw Valley Lodge

With spacious condominium accommodations, underground parking, and proximity to the ski slopes (just out the door), Squaw Valley Lodge offers guests a modicum of luxury and great convenience. Units are individually owned, so interiors vary considerably, but most have designer furnishings. Suites contain kitchenettes with a microwave oven, a dishwasher, and an electric range. There's a swimming pool in a central courtyard and an exercise room where aerobics classes and Nautilus machines are available. The lodge operates much like a hotel, with valet service and airport shuttles. In 2001, the lodge opened a new, 40-unit wing, where most of the two-bedroom suites are.

Rooms: 218 studio, one- and two-bedroom suites, all ski-in, ski-out, with telephones and cable television; kitchenettes including a microwave oven, a dishwasher, and an electric range; in-room coffee; and some continental breakfasts.

Amenities: A sauna, a steam bath, a Jacuzzi, a pool (during the summer only), on-site tennis courts, a complete Nautilus room, valet ski check, ski tuning, covered parking, a shuttle to Reno-Tahoe International Airport, and cable car access to the High Camp Bath and Tennis Club.

Rates: $$$–$$$$.

Contact: Squaw Valley Lodge, 201 Squaw Peak Rd./P.O. Box 2364, Olympic Valley, CA 96146; 530/583-5500 or 800/922-9970; website:www.squawvalleylodge.com.

The Village at Squaw Valley

Newly opened in 2002, the first condominiums in what will be an extensive slope-side village are available for rentals, depending on owner occupancy. Units in First Ascent and 22 Station, which vary from one to three bedrooms in size, are spacious and nicely appointed with rustic mountain furnishings. All have gas fireplaces with slate hearths, oversize bathrooms, and gourmet kitchens. From anywhere in the village, you can walk to ski lifts, including the Cable Car and the Funitel, and to a variety of restaurants in the base area. The village is being built by Intrawest of Canada, which owns Whistler and Blackcomb ski resorts.

Amenities: Heated underground parking, valet service, 24-hour front desk, outdoor hot tubs, exercise room, ski lockers and secured bike storage, concierge, grocery service, media room, billiards lounge, First Ascent Kid's Club, restaurant (Balboa's), plaza with stage for entertainment, Starbucks coffee, and sports shops.

Rates: $$$–$$$$$.

Contact: The Village at Squaw Valley, 1985 Squaw Valley Rd., P.O. Box 2025, Olympic Valley, CA 96146; 530/584-1000 or 888/805-5022; website: www.thevillageatsquaw.com.

TAHOE CITY/WEST SHORE

Chambers Landing

This upscale West Shore complex has 43 beautiful, prestigious town homes in a gated community with spectacular lake views, a premier restaurant, private docks, and a private sand beach. Properties are three and four bedrooms in size, and all are rented independently by their owners. Each property is oriented to the water and has a view of the lake. Custom tile, stained glass, Baldwin brass, river-rock fireplaces, decks, and interior spas are standard features. The 13.5-acre complex also has a freeform swimming pool, four tennis courts, and buoys. Chambers Landing is next to a popular bike trail and near Sugar Pine Point State Park.

Rates: $$$$.

Contact: Chambers Landing Homeowners Association, P.O. Box 537, Homewood, CA 96141; 530/525-7202.

Chinquapin

This is one of my favorites on the North Shore, largely because it has a whopping 95 acres of lush, forested terrain and an entire mile of shoreline. It is set below a high section of Highway 28, thus shielding it from traffic noise. Chinquapin has two private beaches, a series of biking and hiking trails, two floating swim docks, a heated swimming pool, and seven tennis courts. There are 172 town homes and condos in this development; many of them have beautiful lake views from outside decks and are elegantly furnished. This is a wonderful spot for children, and it's close to the restaurants of Tahoe City. Chinquapin also offers a rental agency and a service desk.

Rates: $$$$.

Contact: Chinquapin, 3600 N. Lake Blvd./P.O. Box 1923, Tahoe City, CA 96145; 530/583-6991 or 800/732-6721; website: www.chinquapin.com.

Granlibakken Resort

Tucked away in a forested valley two miles south of Tahoe City, this tranquil resort has developed a reputation as a wonderfully secluded conference center and family sports retreat. But Granlibakken also has an honored place in the history of American skiing, because the small but steep slope that it adjoins hosted the ski jumping tryouts for the 1932 Winter Olympics. The athletes who came here and went on to compete in the Games at Lake Placid, New York, were the elite skiers of their day, long before downhill and slalom events took over the limelight. The site, built by a resort called Tahoe Tavern (which later burned down), was the first developed skiing spot at the lake. The area wasn't called Granlibakken until 15 years later, however, when a Norwegian jumper named Kjell Rustad leased the land from the U.S. Forest Service and installed a 450-foot rope tow. The name means "a hillside sheltered by fir trees" and refers to a place in Norway where Rustad skied as a youngster. Today, the ski hill and rope tow are still operating, but the alpine jump is just a memory.

Current owners Bill and Norma Parson have developed a sizable conference center that can host up to 450 people. The conference center is surrounded by 159 units, including condominium units, suites, hotel-style rooms, and the Executive Lodge. The newest wing has additional condominiums with spacious first-floor living rooms, second-floor entertainment, family rooms with fireplaces, a meeting room, and a board room.

These facilities feature a gourmet kitchen and can accommodate groups of up to 72 people. Nearby you'll find a spacious lawn and gazebo ideally suited for weddings and special events.

The main building contains banquet and meeting rooms (accommodating up to 300 people), dining rooms, and a large outdoor terrace that hosts performing arts events in summer. The condos are well appointed, comfortable, and woodsy, and are shaded by forest. Summer recreation includes the annual Nike Tennis Camp for youngsters, an impressive ropes course for team-building, and a trailhead for mountain biking and hiking into Page Meadows, one of Tahoe's best wildflower areas. Granlibakken hosts major events of the annual Lake Tahoe Summer Music Festival on its large outdoor decks. Just down the road are three ski areas—Alpine Meadows, Squaw Valley, and Ski Homewood. Perhaps Granlibakken's most enduring asset is its proximity to the action at Tahoe City and the lake, in contrast to its distance from the traffic and noise of Highway 89.

Rooms: 159 rooms with phones, televisions, some kitchens, some fireplaces, a full hot buffet breakfast (included with all accommodations), and laundry facilities.

Amenities: Six tennis courts; an activities coordinator; a spa; a sauna; a pool (during the summer only); a ski hill; cross-country trails; a snow-play area; and facilities for conferences, weddings, and banquets.

Rates: $$$–$$$$. $85–90 per unit for a one- to two-bedroom lodge room, and $182–970 for one- to six-bedroom town houses (which sleep 12 people). Credit cards are accepted.

Contact: Granlibakken Resort, 625 Granlibakken Rd./P.O. Box 6329, Tahoe City, CA 96145; 530/583-4242 or 800/543-3221; website: www .granlibakken.com.

River Ranch Lodge

It's easy to see why this is one of the most popular small lodges in the region. River Ranch is perched on the edge of the Truckee River and, during years with normal snow levels, the overflow from Lake Tahoe creates frothy rapids along the "Big Bend," next to the spacious outdoor patio. Originally called Deer Park Inn, this property dates to 1888; passengers from a narrow-gauge train used to stop here on their journey between Truckee and Tahoe City. In 1950, the old timbers were torn down and replaced with a new building, which became a fashionable summertime fishing lodge. Ten years later, the Winter Olympics at Squaw Valley brought diplomats from around the world and helped to establish the 19-room lodge as a favorite of skiers.

Recently renovated, each room is decorated with Early American antiques. Across the river you'll see a condominium with three units. One accommodation is a suite with a queen-sized bed and two twins, and the others are both one-bed hotel rooms. The restaurant—which serves seafood, steaks, and lamb—has established a fine reputation, and the cocktail lounge is cantilevered over the rushing rapids. In summer, the lodge offers name jazz and other contemporary musical concerts on the patio. River Ranch is close to everything, and a paved bike trail (which follows the river and skirts the North and West Shores of Lake Tahoe) originates here. When the river is high enough, guests can rent small rafts in Tahoe City and float 4.5 miles downstream to the lodge. Great hiking is available just up the road (in the Five Lakes area of the Granite Chief Wilderness) as are the major ski areas of Alpine Meadows and Squaw Valley. The lodge is on Highway 89 at Alpine Meadows Road.

Policies: Children age six and under stay for free.

Rates: $$$–$$$$. Rates include daily continental breakfast. Major credit cards are accepted.

Contact: River Ranch Lodge, P.O. Box 197, Tahoe City, CA 96145; 530/583-4264 or 800/535-9900 (California only); website: www .riverranchlodge.com.

Three Buck Inn at River Run

Itching to take Fido along on your Tahoe vacation? Here's a unique lodging solution that lets you bring your furry friend. The "Inn" is actually a half-dozen condominium units that are within River Run, a complex that borders the Truckee River at Alpine Meadows Road, off Highway 89. But these aren't ordinary condos; they are luxury

pet amenity kit at Three Buck Inn

digs that even the most pampered pooch can appreciate. There are four "Riverfront" suites and two "Trailside" suites, and all are decorated in canine chic. Get this: A leopard-print dog bed, a squeaky toy, a ceramic food bowl, a "doggie" video collection, Good Dog towels, a Fido-friendly magazine, a bag of cookies, Le Bistro water feeder, a furniture sheet, vacation tags, and a full dog bath (after running in the woods, no doubt) that is in the new Riverfront Suites garage. There's a two-mile dirt hiking trail, just outside the condos, that borders the west side of the river and makes for an ideal doggie romp. In winter, you can strap on the snowshoes that are provided in each room and take your pet out on the snow.

Rooms: Six condominium units that consist of three one-bedroom units, one two-bedroom unit and two studios. Each Riverfront suite is accessible through a common foyer and has vaulted ceilings, full living room, robes, private deck, river-rock fireplace, separate bedroom with king bed, queen sleeper-sofa, two TVs with HBO and VCR, hair dryer and iron, and cordless phone

with digital answering machine. The two-bedroom unit, ideal for a family, has a full kitchen, dining room, outdoor barbecue and two full baths. Each Trailside studio (480 square feet) has king bed with down comforter, old hickory log furniture, electric pot-belly stove, in-room HEPA air filter, robes, executive desk with free local calls, efficiency kitchen, full bath with tub, 32-inch TV and VCR, and cordless phone with digital machine.

Policies: Dogs cannot be left unattended in the units (a list of dog sitters and day care is provided). Guests must pick up after their dogs and prevent incessant barking.

Rates: $$$–$$$$$.

Contact: Three Buck Inn, P.O. Box 2048, Olympic Valley, CA 96146; 530/550-8600 or 877/596-5200; website: www.threebuckinn.com.

Rocky Ridge

This interesting gated community of condominiums is situated on a high plateau overlooking Lake Tahoe, with some spectacular views of the lake. One of the older condo properties around, it has scattered tree cover and manzanita thickets. The quality of the units varies with the tastes of their owners. One three-bedroom lakeview unit that I saw was in dire need of a top-to-bottom overhaul in order to shed its ugly mid-1970s decor. Other units have more engaging appointments, so you'll need to shop around, which may be challenging over the phone. The complex includes two pools, four tennis courts, a spa, and access to a two-acre private beach. There are 123 units with two- to four-bedroom configurations. While this property has a real sense of seclusion, the access road is steep and may create driving challenges during the winter. The management company is O'Neal Brokers.

Rates: $$$$.

Contact: Rocky Ridge, 1877 N. Lake Blvd./P.O. Box 802, Tahoe City, CA 96145; 530/583-3723.

Sunnyside Lodge

Sunnyside is a luxurious small inn that embodies the Tahoe style of wood and rock in a contemporary setting. Built just a few years ago and blessed with one of the best locations on the lake, the lodge has two kinds of accommodations: lakefront suites and smaller rooms without views. The suites are by far the more impressive units and are worth the extra price; they are elegantly decorated in rich burgundy and dark green, and all have balconies overlooking the lake. The sunrises and sunsets here are magnificent—this is truly a place for romance to blossom. Regular rooms are smaller and face parking lots.

The lodge is full on most weekends, and its sumptuous cuisine probably contributes to this popularity. In the morning, a continental breakfast (included in the price of the room) is served upstairs in the library. It consists of fresh orange juice, cereal, and pastries baked at the lodge, including banana nut bread, muffins, scones, and fresh fruit. Lunch (during the summer only) and dinner are served downstairs in the restaurant, and they include a selection of pastas and fresh seafood.

Sunnyside also offers a cozy lobby with beamed ceilings and a big stone fireplace, a wonderful spot for an après-ski toddy. In summer, a sweeping outdoor deck with tables and chairs is a popular hangout. The deck fronts Sunnyside's own marina, where rental boats, Jet Skis, fishing charters, and sightseeing cruisers are available. Two miles south of Tahoe City on Highway 89, Sunnyside is on the West Shore Bike Path, and bike rentals are within walking distance. During winter, ski-area shuttles stop here and, in summer, the Tahoe City Trolley serves the area. Other amenities at the lodge include a concierge; meeting facilities that cater to large parties, weddings, banquets, and conferences; ski locker rooms; and bike racks. Traffic along Highway 89 can be severely congested on busy summer weekends, and there's a constant bustle of people in and out of the U.S. Forest Service campground across the road. A word of advice in booking Sunnyside: Call months in advance. The lodge is open year-round.

Policies: No pets are allowed. Discounts on fees for major ski resorts, ski rentals, sleigh rides, and snowmobiling are available to guests.

Rates: $$–$$$$. Midweek lodging discount packages are available. Major credit cards are accepted.

Contact: Sunnyside Lodge, 1850 W. Lake Blvd./P.O. Box 5969, Tahoe City, CA 96145; 530/583-7200 or 800/822-2SKI (800/ 822-2754; California only); website: www .sunnysideresort.com.

Tahoe Tavern

This is the shoreline sister property of Rocky Ridge, and it consists of the usual wood-frame condos built in the late 1960s and early 1970s. The complex replaced a historic and opulent resort called Tahoe Tavern, which defined much of the North Shore's history in the early 1900s. Today it offers pleasant tree-shaded grounds, a long pier stretching into the lake, and good beach access. The condos enjoy a great location in Tahoe City: set at the "Y" intersection of Highways 28 and 89, they put you near a paved and popular cycling trail; the Fanny Bridge, where trout can be seen; and the launch point for raft trips on the Truckee River.

Rates: $$$$.

Contact: Tahoe Tavern, 300 W. Lake Blvd./P.O. Box 82, Tahoe City, CA 96145; 530/583-3704.

KINGS BEACH/TAHOE VISTA/CARNELIAN BAY

Brockway Springs Resort

Below Highway 28 on the northernmost peninsula of Lake Tahoe, this lakeside condominium resort is nestled on a site that once housed a famous hot springs resort hotel that burned to the ground in the early 1900s. There is a series of wood-frame town houses and a seven-story condominium tower with great views of the lake. The exteriors of the buildings are not particularly attractive, but the grounds and view of the lake more than make up for any shortcomings. The property has its own rental office.

Rooms: Units are one to four bedrooms in size, and all have kitchens, a television, a VCR, and a patio.

Amenities: Two tennis courts right on the lake, a year-round swimming pool heated by the hot springs, a children's wading pool, a clubhouse, and a fishing and boating dock.

Rates: $$$$.
Contact: Brockway Springs Resort, 101 Chipmunk St./P.O. Box 276, Kings Beach, CA 96143; 530/546-4201; website: www .brockwaysprings.com.

Kingswood Village

Although it's an older property with the usual nondescript wood-frame architecture, this condominium complex is very popular with skiers, particularly for long-term winter leases, because it is strategically located on Highway 267 just up the hill from Highway 28. From here it's a relatively easy drive to Northstar, Diamond Peak, Squaw Valley, Alpine Meadows, and the Donner Summit ski resorts. It's also a short drive to North Shore beaches. Some units have a filtered lake view. Occupants have access to a beach club just a few blocks away, where they can enjoy a swimming pool and large whirlpool spa. The condos are usually well maintained, and the grounds of the complex are reasonably attractive. Several agencies rent units at Kingswood. See the list of property management and rental agencies in the Lake Tahoe area.
Rates: $$$.
Contact: Kingswood Village, 1001 Commonwealth Dr./P.O. Box 1646, Kings Beach, CA 96143; 530/546-2533 or 800/542-2533.

Sweetbriar

Strategically located near the intersection of Highways 267 and 28 at Kings Beach, this new and modern complex of luxury town houses has a lot going for it—including a private white sand beach, a nine-hole golf course (Old Brockway) across the street, and close proximity to Northstar and Diamond Peak ski resorts. These are immaculate accommodations, many with lake views, and are elegantly furnished. One of the units was featured on the cover of *Homes and Land,* a real estate magazine.
Rates: $$$$.
Contact: Sweetbriar, 8000 N. Lake Blvd., Kings Beach, CA 96143; 530/546-3340 or 800/979-3382; website: www.sweetbriar.com.

INCLINE VILLAGE/CRYSTAL BAY

Crystal Bay Cove

With a terraced, slopeside location, these condominiums offer truly breathtaking views of Lake Tahoe—arguably the best in the basin—and have luxuriously appointed interiors. Units are spacious and boast three bedrooms, each with a private bath, making them ideal for three couples. There's plenty of inspiration here for artists, writers, and romantics. These highly recommended accommodations are offered by several agencies. Crystal Bay Cove is on Highway 28 at Crystal Bay, Nevada.
Rates: $$$$.
Contact: See the list of property management and rental agencies in the Lake Tahoe area.

Forest Pines

This older condominium complex in Incline Village offers tastefully furnished one- to four-bedroom units that can accommodate up to eight people. Condos come with fully equipped kitchen, cable TV with VCR, washer/dryer, fireplace with free firewood, telephone, and linens. Close to golf courses, beaches, tennis, and ski resorts.
Amenities: Private pool, whirlpool and sauna, and large recreation center with Ping-Pong tables, video games, and a massive stone fireplace.
Rates: $$$$.
Contact: Forest Pines Vacation Rentals, 123 Juanita Dr., Incline Village, NV 89451; 775/831-1307 or 800/458-2463; website: www.forest-pines.com.

Inn at Incline and Condominiums

The Inn at Incline is a newly remodeled family resort in a secluded forest setting, featuring 38 spacious motel-style guest rooms and one-bedroom condominiums with phones, televisions with HBO, some kitchens, fireplaces, wheelchair access, and continental breakfast. Note: The condos are one mile from the inn. The inn is within walking distance of the lakeshore and the Hyatt Regency hotel and casino.
Amenities: Spa, sauna, indoor pool, lounge with

fireplace, laundry facilities, and privileges to private beaches and boat-launching facilities.
Policies: Some pets are allowed.
Rates: $$–$$$$.
Contact: Inn at Incline and Condominiums, 1003 Tahoe Blvd./P.O. Box 4545, Incline Village, NV 89450; 775/831-1052 or 800/824-6391; website: www.innatincline.com.

McCloud Condominiums

This is one of the newer condominium facilities in the area, and its grounds are beautifully landscaped with carefully manicured lawns and quaking aspens. McCloud is just two blocks from the beach in Incline Village. Each cluster of 32 units has a common hot tub and sauna, and all units are nicely designed; many have luxurious furnishings. There are one-, two-, and three-bedroom units available for rent. This complex is off Lakeshore Drive near Incline's millionaire's row, so you can't beat the neighborhood. McCloud's units are highly recommended and offered by several rental agencies.
Rates: $$$–$$$$.
Contact: See the list of property management and rental agencies in the Lake Tahoe area.

Mountain Shadows

Set just above the championship golf course and on the way to the Diamond Peak Ski Resort, these aging but reasonably well-maintained condos are in Incline Village. The two-story units have high, sloped ceilings, spacious living rooms, and wooden decks, and there are a few filtered views of Lake Tahoe. They offer three bedrooms or three bedrooms with a loft. This is a comfortable, middle-of-the-road complex that is off the main highway and has access to Incline Village's respectable restaurants, the casino action at the nearby Hyatt Regency, and Raley's (the best supermarket in Lake Tahoe). Several rental and property management agencies offer units here. Mountain Shadows is on Ski Run Boulevard off Highway 28.
Rates: $$$–$$$$.
Contact: See the list of property management and rental agencies in the Lake Tahoe area.

Stillwater Cove

At $350 or more per night, these rental units are the most expensive in Incline Village, but the high prices buy guests just about everything they could want: marvelous lake views of Crystal Bay from the shoreline location, luxurious furnishings, a private beach, a swimming pool, decks, and gated security.
Rates: $$$$.
Contact: See the list of property management and rental agencies in the Lake Tahoe area.

Third Creek Condominiums

You'll find wonderful design and aesthetics in this new complex, which has luxurious two- and three-bedroom units with wet bars, fireplaces, and inviting living rooms. Some of the owners have created very attractive interiors with expensive furnishings. Third Creek is in a mountain setting and has swimming, spa, and tennis facilities. Several agencies oversee these units.
Rates: $$$–$$$$.
Contact: See the list of property management and rental agencies in the Lake Tahoe area.

Tyrolian Village

This chalet-style complex on Ski Run Boulevard is next to the Diamond Peak Ski Resort, which makes it convenient for skiing. But it's a bit of a drive on a steep mountain road to and from the shoreline. Many of the accommodations are nicely furnished, however, including in-room hydro tubs. These units are offered by several agencies.
Rates: $$$–$$$$.
Contact: See the list of property management and rental agencies in the Lake Tahoe area.

The Villas at Incline

Just steps from the first hole of the Incline Championship Course, these three-bedroom, three-bath condos have fireplaces in the master bedroom and offer access to a small swimming pool. This is a perfect accommodation for golfers. The Villas at Incline are off Fairway Boulevard in Incline Village, and the units are offered by several agencies.
Rates: $$$$.

Contact: See the list of property management and rental agencies in the Lake Tahoe area.

SOUTH LAKE TAHOE/ STATELINE

Fantasy Inn

You can play Tarzan and Jane in the Rainforest Suite, share a bottle of bubbly in the Marie Antoinette Suite, soak in a sunken tub in the Roman Suite, or enjoy a hot summer night in the Sultan's Tent. This is South Lake Tahoe's most romantic small hotel, with a dozen ornate theme suites that are so creative, no one ever wants to leave them. Even the standard rooms are a cut above just about anything else at the lake, with circular beds, bathtubs built for two, ceiling-mounted swivel television sets, and double-tiled showers. This is a romantic, exotic, intimate retreat that is very popular for weddings, honeymoons, anniversaries, and other celebrations. Through its lavish appointments, this place redefines "overnight lodging." A Old English–style wedding chapel with a garden courtyard (open in the summer only), wine or champagne upon check-in, and excellent service from an attentive staff have given the Fantasy Inn strong repeat business. The theme rooms are extremely popular and need to be booked well in advance—six to 12 months ahead of time for weekends. In late 1996, a new Chevys Mexican-style restaurant opened on one side of the hotel, and there is an International House of Pancakes on the other side—so food is just a few steps away. When the blizzard of the century is ragin', this is the place to cuddle up.

Rooms: 53 guest rooms, including 13 one-of-a-kind theme rooms and 40 deluxe spa rooms that have a king-sized bed, cable television, a DMX music stereo system, an oversize whirlpool spa tub or a sunken, tiled bathing spa, gas fireplaces in eight rooms, and in-room coffee.

Amenities: A wedding chapel, an on-site minister, and a free casino and ski resort shuttle.

Policies: The Fantasy Inn is not suitable for children. Guests may reserve their favorite room up to one year in advance of arrival.

Rates: $$$–$$$$.

Contact: Fantasy Inn, 3696 Lake Tahoe Blvd., South Lake Tahoe, CA 96150; 530/541-4200, 800/367-7736, or 800/624-3837; website: www.fantasy-inn.com.

Forest Inn Suites

Situated on 5.5 acres of forested land, this is an upscale property with 124 elegantly appointed one- and two-bedroom units that include phones, televisions, and in-room coffee. Some rooms have kitchens. Forest Inn is just behind the new Heavenly Ski Resort gondola and is one block from the casinos.

Amenities: Free continental breakfast, heated outdoor swimming pools, hot tubs, fitness center, sauna and steam room, massage therapy studio, ski rental and repair shop, game room with billiard and ping-pong tables, wedding chapel, Al's Fireside Saloon, private beach access, and shuttle service to surrounding ski areas.

Rates: $$–$$$$.

Contact: Forest Inn Suites, 1 Lake Pkwy., South Lake Tahoe, CA 96150; 530/541-6655 or 800/822-5950; website: www.forestsuites.com.

Glenbrook

Tucked away in a secluded corner of the lake on the southeast shore, this gated, upscale residential community offers town houses, cottages, and custom homes, most nestled in a forested setting either on or near the shoreline. And there's another plus: the most attractive nine-hole golf course at the lake. Glenbrook is nine miles north of Stateline off U.S. 50. It's a piece of paradise and comes highly recommended.

Rates: $$$$.

Contact: Glenbrook Realty, 2070 Pray Meadow Rd./P.O. Box 300, Glenbrook, NV 89413; 775/749-5663.

Inn by the Lake

A deluxe, 100-room inn with large, beautifully furnished rooms, the Inn by the Lake provides comfortable beds and close proximity to beaches, cycling trails, and picnic areas. The units here are more spacious than most in South Tahoe, with king- or queen-sized beds, private balconies, and some refrigerators and wet bars. Tucked into a forested setting just two miles from the Stateline casinos, the inn has some nice touches, including a free continental breakfast with fresh-baked breads and bagels, a year-round heated swimming pool with spa and sauna, and free transportation to casinos and ski resorts. Across the street, there's a sandy beach with a selection of water sports. The view of the lake from the upstairs rooms is one of the best along U.S. 50. During off-season and midweek, the inn usually offers highly discounted rates, making it a great value and a wonderful alternative to the bustle of the casinos. In 1996, more than half of the rooms were remodeled, and heated decks have been added for the pool and spa area. There's a 24-hour coffee shop, Lyon's, next door.

Rooms: 100 guest rooms and suites (with one to three bedrooms, including king- and queen-sized beds) with phones, color cable televisions, AM/FM radios, some kitchens, in-room coffee, wet bars, continental breakfast, air-conditioning, lake views, private balconies, and hair dryers. There are 34 nonsmoking rooms and one room with wheelchair access.

Amenities: Ski and bicycle lockers; hot cider in the lobby during the winter; a concierge; a redwood sauna; a bilevel outdoor spa; a year-round heated pool; bicycles; free guest activities for children and adults; self-service laundry facilities; meeting facilities accommodating up to 50 people, with catering, equipment, and secretarial support; and free casino and ski shuttles.

Policies: Children under 12 stay free when they share their parents' room.

Rates: $$–$$$$.

Contact: Inn by the Lake, 3300 Lake Tahoe Blvd., South Lake Tahoe, CA 96157; 530/542-0330 or 800/877-1466; website: www.innbythelake.com.

Lakeland Village Resort

With its condominiums nudging right up to 1,000 feet of private beach, this 19-acre lakefront complex attracts families, corporate meetings, ski clubs, and other groups. Operated as a condo/hotel, the village units are nestled in pine forest on the north side of U.S. 50, just one mile from Heavenly Ski Resort and 1.5 miles from

the Stateline casinos. The condos are woodsy and spacious, each with large living rooms, color televisions with cable, fireplaces, and private decks. Walking to the water's edge on Tahoe, guests have their choice of a multitude of sports, including boating from the village's own dock. There's a terrific swimming pool with a spectacular view of the lake and its beaches. Restaurants and a major grocery store are just a few steps away from here.

Rooms: 212 units (including condos with lofts, studio condos, and four-bedroom town houses sleeping up to 10 people) with phones, color televisions, kitchens, fireplaces, in-room coffee, and daily maid service. Some units front the lake, and some have lake views and private decks.

Amenities: An underground parking garage, a ski shop, a 24-hour front desk, tennis courts (where lessons with a professional are available), a sauna, two whirlpool spas, two outdoor heated pools, a poolside snack bar, 1,000 feet of private beach, boat rentals, an on-site ski shop, two conference rooms accommodating up to 75 people, catering, free shuttles to casinos and local ski areas, underground lodge parking, and an outdoor parking lot.

Rates: $$–$$$$.

Contact: Lakeland Village Resort, 3535 Lake Tahoe Blvd. (U.S. 50)/P.O. Box 1356, South Lake Tahoe, CA 96150; 530/544-1685 or 800/822-5969; website: www.lakeland-village.com.

The Ridge Tahoe

Opened in 1982, this is South Tahoe's classiest condo/hotel, a luxurious resort of private suites. The Ridge, on a Nevada peak six miles above Stateline, is frequently used as a hideaway for celebrities performing at the casinos. Here, they can breathe the crisp mountain air, stay clear of the crowds, and indulge in their favorite pastimes. One of those is skiing; in fact, there's a private, 10-passenger gondola that runs guests between the resort and the Nevada side of Heavenly Ski Resort. Other amenities include an indoor/outdoor swimming pool, indoor and outdoor tennis, a state-of-the-art fitness center, sauna and spa, and indoor racquetball courts.

Each suite can sleep up to six people and is luxuriously appointed with a fireplace, a wet bar, a kitchen, and a living room entertainment center. Balconies have gas barbecues, as well as spectacular views of Carson Valley, Heavenly Ski Resort, or South Shore. The Ridge Club offers a restaurant and cocktail lounge with piano bar, and the meals are usually exceptional. Underground parking and hourly shuttles to the Stateline casinos complete the picture. Is this a great place for a honeymoon, or what?

Rooms: 302 suites and one- and two-bedroom units with phones, televisions, VCRs, some stereos, fireplaces, and kitchens.

Amenities: The Ridge Club Dining Room (for guests only); a concierge; maid service; gift and grocery stores; a cocktail lounge; a children's playground and arcade; tennis and racquetball courts; a sauna; a heated indoor/outdoor pool; a health spa; conference rooms accommodating up to 75 people, with equipment and catering; a shuttle to the casinos; and a private lift to Heavenly Ski Resort.

Policies: No pets are allowed.

Rates: $$$$.

Contact: The Ridge Tahoe, 400 Ridge Club Dr., Kingsbury, P.O. Box 5790, Stateline, NV 89449; 775/588-3131 or 800/334-1600; website: www.ridge-tahoe.com.

Tahoe Beach and Ski Club

Converted from an aging motel to an upscale, time-share condominium, Tahoe Beach and Ski Club now has excellent accommodations to go with a fine beach on the shores of Lake Tahoe. All of the condos are accessible from indoors, and some are two-story units. Beautiful polished fixtures, wood kitchen cabinets, and other deluxe touches (including a completely remodeled lobby) make the place attractive, even though the wood-frame, shingled exteriors still look much the same as they have for years. There's a large grassy area behind the beach for weddings and other functions.

Rooms: 125 units—including studio, deluxe, and standard one-bedroom condos and town houses—with telephones, color cable televisions, VCRs, some fully equipped kitchenettes and kitchens, and some four-person Jacuzzi tubs. Some units front the lake, and most have lake views and patios.

Amenities: Decks cocktail bar, a restaurant, an outdoor heated pool, a Jacuzzi and sauna (open year-round), a fitness club, a ski shop, and a free shuttle to the Heavenly ski area.

Rates: $$–$$$$.

Contact: Tahoe Beach and Ski Club, 3601 Lake Tahoe Blvd., South Lake Tahoe, CA 96150; 530/541-6220 or 800/822-5962; website: www.sunterra.com.

Tahoe Keys

Laced with 11 miles of artificial waterways, this is a 750-acre private community in the city of South Lake Tahoe. Condominiums here look pretty much the same from the outside, but there are big differences on the inside. I looked at several that are close to the lake, and they are very attractively decorated, with granite kitchen countertops, tiled bathrooms, and living rooms with sunken floors in front of fireplaces. Step outside the back door and there's usually a private dock, as well as a patio and small yard. For boating aficionados, this location is hard to beat, since the largest marina at South Shore is here. From many of the condos, you can watch power and sail yachts coming and going at the marina. There's a gourmet restaurant, tennis courts, a health club, a sauna, indoor and outdoor pools, a recreation room, and some covered parking. These units are offered by several agencies, and are at the end of Tahoe Keys Boulevard, north of U.S. 50.

Rates: $$$–$$$$.

Contact: See the list of property management and rental agencies in the Lake Tahoe area.

Tahoe Lakeshore Lodge and Spa

Longtime hotelier Pat Ronan recently acquired the Tahoe Marina Inn, a nondescript motel on the lakefront, and turned it into an attractive resort and health spa with a variety of condominium units. In late 1999, as part of the initial phase of what will be an Old Tahoe-style lodge, the interiors of all 46 rooms were completely remodeled and rooms were decorated with lodge pine furnishings, new carpet, and artwork by Tahoe artist Guy Joy. Each room boasts a private balcony or patio overlooking the property's private beach and across the lake. Many of the units feature kitchens, and some offer in-room fireplaces. The resort also manages 25 condominium units adjacent to the lodge. Added to the amenities was Elements, a full-service health spa, which features individually tailored treatments that include mud baths, herbal scrubs, facials, and hydrotherapy treatments. The property is just off Highway 50, one mile south of the Stateline casino corridor.

Rooms: 46 hotel rooms, many with kitchens, some with fireplaces, and 25 condominium rental units. Condos include one-bedroom loft, one-bedroom, and two-bedroom units, each with kitchen and fireplaces and beach frontage. There's also a romance condo with private indoor hot tub and canopy bed.

Amenities: Private beach, outdoor swimming pool, and full spa with therapy treatments.

Rates: $$$–$$$$.

Contact: Lakeshore Lodge and Spa, 930 Bal Bijou Rd., South Lake Tahoe, CA 96150; 530/541-2180 or 800/448-4577; website: www.tahoelakeshorelodge.com.

Tahoe Seasons Resort

The largest and most attractive lodging at the original California side of Heavenly Ski Resort, Tahoe Seasons has the unbeatable convenience of across-the-street proximity to the tram and ski lifts. Large chalet suites have separate living rooms, private spas, fireplaces, VCRs, refrigerators, and queen- or king-sized beds. The lobby is particularly creative and spacious and invites conversation with its big stone and brick fireplace, adjoining bar, and warm ambience. Down the hallway is a café that serves breakfasts. Outside, the heated swimming pool is a little cloistered by its surrounding walls, but there's plenty of open space on the rooftop where two tennis courts are. Removed from the traffic of U.S. 50 and the casinos, the resort is a quiet place much of the year, especially in summer. Its forested, residential hillside location, however, is within a brief shuttle ride of Stateline and the beaches. Also, one of the finer dinner

houses at the lake, Christiania Inn, is a short stroll down the road.

Rooms: 160 mountain chalet suites with phones, two to three televisions, VCRs, refrigerators, and microwaves; most have fireplaces, in-room coffee, and private spas, and some have maid service.

Amenities: A restaurant, a lounge, a general store, room service, guest security, a concierge, billiards, video arcade games, two tennis courts, a Jacuzzi, a heated pool, wedding and banquet facilities, and shuttle service to and from Harrah's.

Rates: $$$.

Contact: Tahoe Seasons Resort, 3901 Saddle Rd./P.O. Box 5656, South Lake Tahoe, CA 96157; 530/541-6700 or 800/540-4874; website: www.tahoeseasons.com.

Tahoe Summit Village

These spacious and reasonably priced condominiums are at the top of Kingsbury Grade next to the Heavenly Wells Fargo/Nevada entrance. Each of the 29 units has a wood-burning fireplace, whirlpool bathtub, fully equipped kitchen, microwave, refrigerator, telephone, TV and VCR, and washer/dryer. Two bedroom units sleep up to six people, and those with an added loft sleep up to eight people. You'll need your own vehicle to get here, since Stateline's casinos and South Lake Tahoe's restaurants are at least five miles down the hill. Access on the approach road can be tricky in winter when ice and snow may be on the pavement.

Amenities: Hot tub, sauna, gym, private community pool, barbecue grill, small library, indoor game room with Ping-Pong table and TV, and video rental.

Rates: $$–$$$.

Contact: Tahoe Summit Village, 750 Wells Fargo Ln., P.O. Box 4917, Stateline, NV 89449; 775/588-8571 (resort) or 800/540-4874 (reservations); website: www.tahoereservations.com/TahoeSummit.

KIRKWOOD
Kirkwood Ski and Summer Resort

In winter, Kirkwood bustles with thousands of skiers who enjoy the resort's high elevation, challenging slopes, and usually dry powder. In summer, the crowds are gone, the wildflowers are blooming, and the meadow is lush and green. There isn't much going on here—no golf course, no bands playing, no fashionable stores. And that's just fine with guests who are looking for a quiet place to enjoy the mountains. With lower rates in summer, Kirkwood serves as a base for exploring the hiking trails, high country lakes, and mountain bike routes of Eldorado National Forest. There's fishing down the road at Silver Lake or up the road at Caples Lake. At least a dozen day hikes are possible, and Kirkwood Stables offers a four-legged ticket into the high country. Several equestrian trails wind through the box canyon that cradles the resort, including part of the historic Mormon-Emigrant Trail.

Kirkwood unveiled its new Mountain Village in the winter of 1999, and this included several condominium complexes, restaurants, a spa, and a few shops. Among the first accommodations were the 40-unit Mountain Club, which includes a spa and full concierge services, The Lodge at Kirkwood with 19 units, and the Lost Cabin and Snowcrest condominiums. As of the 2002–03 winter season, three more projects have opened. They consist of Meadow Stone Lodge, an Old Tahoe-style building with 32 luxury condominium units, a fitness center and a spa; Timber Ridge, 28 three-bedroom, three-bath town homes, each with a private two-car garage and living areas that look out over Kirkwood Meadow; and The Sentinels, which has 10 town houses with three- and three-bedroom-plus-loft models and private garages. These new facilities are quite upscale; Meadow Stone has private balconies with log railings, Timber Ridge has quality finishes and high ceilings with vaulted beams, and The Sentinels have cabinlike settings and proximity to several lifts. Overall, Kirkwood's condominiums are well-appointed, with TVs, phones, and balconies overlooking the meadow, with some views of the mountain. Older but still quite comfortable units are in the Sun Meadows complex, and most condominiums have up to three bedrooms. Other units are at Edelweiss, Thimblewood, The Meadows, and Base Camp. The resort is involved in a 10-year, $250 million master development plan that envisions more chairlifts and another 500 acres of ski terrain. In addition to the Mountain Village, there are summer dining options at Kirkwood Inn (a great place for breakfast or a burger) and at nearby Kit Carson Lodge, Caples Lake Resort, Plasse's Resort, and Sorensen's Resort.

Rooms: More than 130 rental units, from hotel rooms to three-bedroom condominiums with kitchens, telephones, fireplaces, living rooms, televisions, and private baths.

Amenities: Timber Creek Lodge; Red Cliffs Lodge; Kirkwood Inn; Cornice Cantina Restaurant and Bar (in winter); Off the Wall Bar and Grill; Mountain Club Coffeehouse and Deli; Mountain Club spa and gym; shopping plaza; a general store; tennis courts; mountain bike park; horse stables; a downhill ski area; a cross-country ski center; group and conference facilities covering 11,000 square feet; underground parking, with one space per condo; winter day care for nonskiing children ages 3–6; and Kirkwood Explorer's Day Camp (during the summer only) for children ages 5–14, offering nature studies, sports, and arts and crafts Friday–Sunday.

Rates: $$–$$$$.

Contact: Kirkwood Ski and Summer Resort, P.O. Box 1, Kirkwood, CA 95646; 209/258-7000 or 800/967-7500; website: www.kirkwood.com.

FEATHER RIVER COUNTRY/LAKES BASIN

Spa Villas at Gold Mountain

This newly emerging resort had just four luxury villas for overnight lodging as this edition went to press, but more were on the way. An hour's drive north of Truckee in Plumas County, just west of the town of Portola, this brand-new lodge is part of a second-home community that includes a challenging golf course called The Dragon, which literally snakes its way along a rim high above the Feather River. What makes this area unique is an amazing lodge called Nakoma, which was originally designed in 1924 by famed American architect Frank Lloyd Wright but was not built until late 2000. The grand lodge with its peaked, tepee-style rooflines contains a spectacular restaurant, a spa, and the clubhouse. From the Villas—clearly designed as romantic getaways for couples— you have a view of the course and the Feather River Canyon. These cottages are just as unconventional as the main lodge. They are round, which makes for interesting rooms and sitting areas. Appointments include soft Frette bedding and king-sized beds, interiors accented with Oriental art and rich fabrics, and floors made of native stone and rustic wood. The Villas are being sold as interval ownerships of four weeks per year, so availability will vary depending on owner occupancy.

The gourmet restaurant, serving three meals a day, adjoins an elegant cocktail lounge. Want some pampering? Then head for the Ritual Day Spa for a massage or facial. Nakoma is a member of Small Luxury Hotels of the World.

Rooms: Four Spa Villas, ranging from 800 square feet to 1,600 square feet, with wood-burning fireplaces, Jacuzzis, outdoor showers, and hot tubs, private interior patios, and outdoor mountain view terraces.

Amenities: 18-hole golf course, putting course, restaurant, cocktail lounge, spa, indoor pool, wedding chapel, clubhouse, and pro shop.

Rates: $$$$–$$$$$.

Contact: Nakoma Resort and Spa, 348 Bear Run, Clio, CA; 530/832-6304 or 800/418-0880; website: www.nakomaresort.com.

CARSON VALLEY

David Walley's Resort, Hot Springs and Spa

This beautiful natural hot springs, originally built in 1862, was recently acquired by the Quintus group, the same company that owns The Ridge Tahoe. On the eastern base of Kingsbury Grade (Highway 207), just 30 minutes from Stateline, this born-again resort opened a 42-suite, interval-ownership condo-hotel in the summer of 1999, and planned to add 108 units more over the next few years. The resort is nestled against the mountains in a spectacular setting that offers vistas of snow-capped peaks on one side and a tranquil marsh teeming with ducks and other migratory birds on the other side. It is a short, 20-minute drive to the Nevada side base lodges of Heavenly ski resort, and just minutes from the stellar golf course of Genoa Lakes. As part of the ownership change, a long-dormant restaurant was reopened under the name of DW's, which offers gourmet dinners (expensive, starting at $19) and Sunday brunches in a rustic setting. The hot springs has six mineral pools ranging 98°–104°F, as well as a freshwater relaxation pool heated to 85°F. The spa and fitness center offers a new exercise room, remodeled locker rooms, massage treatments, and various body treatments including mud, seaweed, and hydrotherapy.

There are 42 rooms, including hotel rooms, each with king-sized bed and sofa sleeper; luxury suites, each with large bedroom, spacious full bath with Jacuzzi tub and shower, large living room with fireplace, queen-sized sofa sleeper, and a complete kitchen; and suites, each with two bedrooms and two baths along with full kitchen and fireplace.

Amenities: Hot springs mineral pools, freshwater pool, spa with therapy rooms, steam and dry sauna, weight room, two outdoor tennis courts, gift shop, deli-style café (Sierra Café), dinnerhouse (DW's Restaurant), banquet facilities, wedding gazebo, and grassy areas.

Policies: No pets allowed. Children are permitted, but youngsters under 12 may not use the freshwater pool without direct parental supervision.

Rates: $$$–$$$$. Overnight guests receive discounts on the day use rate of the hot springs.

Contact: David Walley's Resort, 2001 Foothill Rd. (south of the town of Genoa), P.O. Box 158, Genoa, NV 89411; 775/782-2103 or 800/628-7831, fax 775/782-2103; website: www.davidwalleys.com.

Bed-and-Breakfasts and Country Inns

In many ways, this is what a mountain vacation is all about: immersing yourself in the crispness of the air and the sweet aroma of pine needles; walking from your doorstep to the edge of a lake and watching hungry trout make ripples on the surface; sitting in front of a massive stone fireplace on chilly nights and sipping a glass of cabernet; and connecting with the ghosts of the past. Lake Tahoe is a place where you can revel in nature and history—it offers a treasure trove of unique inns, lodges, and vintage hotels that are vibrant with ambience and character. They vary from Victorian bed-and-breakfast inns to rough-and-tumble Gold Rush hotels and rustic lodges.

Tahoe has such a wealth of unique accommodations that even the most jaded traveler can find a fit. B&Bs often have amiable hosts, occasional ghosts, and century-old antiques. Venerable hotels that once catered to gamblers, railroad workers, miners, and prostitutes are now popular retreats for honeymooners and couples looking for a distinctive experience. Beyond the recommendations of a handful of devoted guests who return year after year, many of these places are never advertised, and a lot of them don't even produce brochures. It may take a year's advance reservation to squeeze inside the door during high season, but the effort is amply rewarded.

Some of the outstanding properties in the region have been in the same family for generations; others are born-again lodges that were recently restored by city-weary entrepreneurs. In recent years, in particular, Lake Tahoe's North and West Shores have experienced a boom in boutique accommodations. They include run-down motels that have been gentrified, cabins that have been rescued from near-certain oblivion, and classic rock-and-timber inns that have been lovingly restored. One caveat: A few properties that call themselves bed-and-breakfasts do not meet the criteria that I have for listing in this section. They more closely resemble motels, or they are private homes that occasionally offer rooms, or their owners are away from the premises so often that phone calls often go un-

KEY TO TAHOE BED-AND-BREAKFAST RATES

$ = Under $75
$$ = $75–100
$$$ = $101–150
$$$$ = Over $150

returned for days. Fortunately, help is on the way for traveling consumers. Some accreditation groups, such as The Select Registry (formerly the Independent Innkeepers Association) are setting high standards for membership, and these will provide credibility for the bona fide inns that truly operate as businesses. If you have any doubts, don't hesitate to ask innkeepers for a list of associations that they belong to. At Tahoe, there is one association, called Lake Tahoe Bed and Breakfast Association, that represents, at this writing, six inns and guesthouses on the north and west shores of the lake. For current listings, see the group's website at www.bedandbreakfasts.com.

If you're looking for historic hotels, it's hard to beat Truckee, where the mining, lumber, and railroad industries created lively traffic and sometimes extravagant wealth. Bed-and-breakfast inns are sprinkled liberally throughout the region. They include elegant Victorians that once served stagecoach routes, as well as modern chalets with rustic charm but plenty of modern comforts. And if you have an affinity for continental style, a handful of European inns in the area will conjure visions of Switzerland, the kind of place where the owner greets you at the door and serves fresh-baked croissants in the morning.

These unique inns and lodges have a wide range of policies and amenities. Some travelers like the intimacy and personal attention of a guesthouse or a B&B; others shy away from compulsory socializing (which always seems to be necessary at breakfast) or sharing a bathroom down the hall. If peace and quiet are preeminent in your plans, you may not be happy in an old hotel next to the railroad tracks or in a cottage close to a main highway. Then again, finding a location in proximity to your main points of interest may require a bit of compromise. Many of these distinctive inns do not offer television or private telephones, so if you're watching the daily stock quotes you may feel positively cut off from the world. The solution to contrived entertainment is usually the lost art of conversation or perhaps a good book pulled from a dusty shelf in the library.

The rejuvenation of many of Lake Tahoe's lodgings is a boon to the region: It finally reverses some of the more wretched excesses and insensitivities of the 1970s and 1980s, when it seemed that nobody cared much about tradition or history. The decor currently in vogue—widely referred to as Old Tahoe—consists of stonework and beams, knotty-pine paneling, Victorian wallpaper, and roaring fireplaces. Room rates generally range $75–225, and frequently the price includes a full or continental breakfast, as well as afternoon snacks and beverages. Of course, almost every inn offers a cozy parlor with a roaring fireplace and lots of opportunity to meet other guests in a relaxed setting.

TRUCKEE/DONNER

Bocks 10064 Southeast River Road

It looks like a private home, a modern replica of a Victorian, and it's one of several that line a residential street on the east side of the Truckee River. In fact, this place is the home of Kent and Monica Bocks, in addition to being a bed-and-breakfast inn, although you won't find a sign out front. Local ordinances are to blame for that omission, and the couple identify their inn simply by the address. The cozy, if obviously lived-in, abode offers a number of charming amenities, including antique furniture and fine views of the river, and provides two rooms: a large master unit with a spacious bathroom (with two pedestal sinks and an old-fashioned metal soaking tub); and a small basic room with a full-sized bed and full bath. The Bocks serve a complete breakfast that often includes pancakes, eggs Benedict, waffles, fruit, cereal, and beverages. In the afternoon, they offer wine or beer with cheese and crackers in the living room. The inn is a short distance from downtown Truckee and close to major ski resorts.

Policies: No smoking.

Rates: $–$$. Cash and checks are accepted.

Contact: 10064 Southeast River Rd./P.O. Box 1863, Truckee, CA 96160, tel./fax 530/582-1923.

Hania's Bed and Breakfast Inn

On a hillside within walking distance of historic Commercial Row in Truckee, this simple, vintage 1884 Victorian was completely renovated and modernized in 1997. Innkeeper Hania Jarmoc, who is originally from Poland, has created an intimate, attractive bed-and-breakfast with four guest rooms. All have Southwestern-style lodgepole furniture, queen beds, private bathrooms (three with showers and one with a tub), televisions and VCRs, and phones or modem outlets. Beds have down comforters and pillows, as well as flannel sheets for winter. The inn has an eclectic collection of art from various countries, and the overall impression is one of rustic elegance. Hania, who speaks English, Polish, German, and Russian, has an extensive background in the European hotel industry. She provides a full gourmet breakfast in the dining room, in your room, or outside on the deck, where you can enjoy views of the garden, the town, and the Sierra mountain range. Meals are served on European china and include Hania's homemade specials such as eggs Benedict, Polish-style potato or apple pancakes, omelets, crepes with cinnamon apples, pastries, fresh fruit, juices, and hot beverages. In the afternoon, she serves free wine from a rustic bar in front of a wood-burning stove. For a special occasion, you can have a bottle of champagne delivered to your room. The grounds contain a hot tub with a panoramic mountain view, and a terry cloth robe is provided for every guest. The garden is available for small weddings and family reunions. Below, in the Truckee historic district, guests can walk to several excellent restaurants and enjoy the boutiques and shops that comprise Tahoe's best shopping area.

Policies: No pets. Children sometimes permitted by arrangement.

Rates: $$$. Price includes full breakfast for two, afternoon wine, free local phone calls, and use of hot tub. Discounts available for full week stay. Some credit cards accepted.

Contact: Hania's Bed and Breakfast Inn, 10098 High St., Truckee, CA 96161; 530/582-5775; 888/600-3735; website: www.truckee.com/Hania.

Rainbow Lodge

The Rainbow Lodge was first a rustic stagecoach stop on the Mormon-Emigrant Trail, then a hangout for card sharks and con men from the late 1800s through the early 1920s. When you walk into the lodge, its character virtually envelops you; history reverberates within the granite rock and hand-hewn timber walls. The past is particularly well preserved in the bar off the lobby. On the wall here, there's a pair of wooden skis just like the ones Snowshoe Thompson wore, and at your feet there's an antique spittoon (reportedly one of only two originals left in California). Behind these walls is a genteel lodge with elegant rooms and Victorian furnishings. Rainbow Lodge also houses the regionally popular Engadine Cafe, which serves gourmet continental cuisine embellished with one of the finest wine lists in the region. You can also enjoy the historic Sierra Cocktail Lounge, a great place to drink hot toddies while perusing the collection of vintage black and white photos and Tahoe memorabilia on the walls. The lodge is a stone's throw from I-80, yet its isolation creates a splendid aura of seclusion.

Owner John Slouber, the founder of Royal Gorge Cross-Country Ski Resort, recently refurbished every one of the 32 rooms, and he's added his own unique collection of vintage ski posters from the United States and Europe. In winter, both alpine and Nordic skiers frequent the lodge and, in summer, it's a wonderful retreat for hikers and honeymooners. Rainbow is close to the Donner Summit ski areas, as well as some of the best hiking trails and alpine lakes in the region. Perched on the banks of the Yuba River, the lodge provides several rooms with river views and a bridal suite on the ground floor that overlooks the gardens. You'll also find the obligatory stone fireplace and a guest lounge with overstuffed chairs and shelves of books. The restaurant serves three meals a day, including a choice of six breakfast items that come with the price of the room.

And if the water tastes unusually good here, it's because it comes from an artesian well behind the property. In fact, Rainbow's water is commercially bottled. The rooms vary from doubles with complete baths to units with shared baths down the hall. There's a family suite with a queen-sized bed in one room and bunks in another. Room interiors are individually decorated in rich reds, greens, and blues, with floral bedspreads and matching drapes, antique furnishings, brass beds, and wood paneling.

Rates: $$-$$$, including full breakfast for two people. Major credit cards are accepted. Open year-round.

Contact: Rainbow Lodge, 50800 Hampshire Rocks Rd./P.O. Box 1100, Soda Springs, CA 95728; 530/426-3871 (reservations), 800/500-3871, and 530/426-3661 (lodge); website: www.royalgorge.com/Accommodation/rainbow.

Richardson House

The elegant Richardson House is perched on a hill above the historic district of Truckee and offers a commanding view of the surrounding Sierra as well as the home's English gardens. Centrally located to all that Truckee and Tahoe have to offer, the house is within easy access from the I-80 freeway. The inn was originally built by Warren Richardson, the owner of a Truckee lumber mill. Richardson occupies a page in the history books because he invented the "steam wagon" (sometimes called the "steam donkey"), a contraption that moved fallen trees along wooden rails to the mill. Completely restored and redecorated in 1996, this stately Victorian is one of the most elegant and luxurious inns of the region. It contains eight immaculately furnished rooms—six with private baths and two adjoining suites with a shared bath.

Antique furnishings are found in every room, and each unit features a unique period-style decor. Favorites include The Writer's Room and Bon Bon's Boudoir. The living room has a large picture window, and the dining room can comfortably seat every guest when there's a full house. Each morning the innkeeper prepares a sumptuous, full buffet breakfast, and entrées vary, sometimes including a holiday or special event theme. A refreshment center is accessible 24 hours a day, and a hilltop gazebo that's ideal for weddings is on a spacious lawn. The parlor has a television and a VCR. The inn is close to the boutiques and restaurants of historic Truckee, major golf courses, hiking and biking trails, and ski resorts. Richardson House is wheelchair-accessible.

Policies: Children 10 years of age and over are welcome. Pets and smoking are not allowed.
Rates: $$–$$$. Major credit cards are accepted.
Contact: Richardson House, 10154 High St./P.O. Box 2011, Truckee, CA 96160-2011; 530/587-5388 or 888/229-0365, fax 530/587-0927; website: www.richardsonhouse.com.

The River Street Inn

This 11-room executive-style inn overlooks the Truckee River and offers a range of luxuries generally not found in other B&Bs, including TV/VCR combos in every room. Spacious bathrooms with large clawfoot tubs, pedestal sinks, and slate floors are found in all but one room, which is wheelchair-accessible. The inn is an amalgam of three buildings: The first of these structures was constructed in 1885 by a Truckee sheriff. Actor Charlie Chaplin stayed in this building during the filming of the classic silent movie *The Gold Rush*. During the 1970s, it housed a restaurant that specialized in garlic dishes.

This B&B's three levels include a floor with a reception area and dining room, another with eight rooms, and a third with two rooms and the proprietors' living quarters. The premier room is on the top floor; its dormer windows provide a magnificent view of the river. The inn also offers an outside deck and an unusual tower with a spiral staircase. Every room has hand-carved armoires that hide the TV/VCR, queen beds (except for one room with two twins), and knotty-pine furniture.

Innkeepers Wendy Smith and Matt Brown have created an Italian country theme for the property, which also boasts a garden as well as decks on two levels.

Continental breakfasts include Truckee bagels and cream cheese, fresh fruit, cereals, blueberry muffins, and Truckee roast coffee. Guests will find themselves just a few steps away from the restaurants and shops of Truckee's historic district. Although the inn is alongside busy Highway 267 on the west—which sees traffic around the clock—and just south of the railroad station—which receives both freight and Amtrak trains—some noise is deadened by the thick rock walls and double-pane windows.

Policies: No pets or smoking.
Rates: $$–$$$. Major credit cards accepted.
Contact: The River Street Inn, 10009 E. River St., Truckee, CA 96161; 530/550-9290; website: www.riverstreetinntruckee.com.

The Sierra Club's Clair Tappaan Lodge

This weathered (some might say ramshackle) mountain lodge looks as if it were built by the Swiss Family Robinson. And that's not far from the truth. The lodge, on the Donner Summit off Old Highway 40, was constructed in 1934 entirely by volunteers, and it is owned and operated by the Sierra Club. While members have priority here and use the lodge heavily, nonmembers are welcome as long as they adhere to the co-op policies of the club, such as chipping in with daily chores; you should be handy with a broom, a Brillo pad, or a toilet plunger.

Sleeping accommodations are rustic, bordering on primitive. They consist of family bunk rooms, two-person cubicles, and large, single-gender dorms. All of these units require that you bring a sleeping bag or linens, towels, and a toilet kit. None of the doors has a lock, but you can store valuables in an office locker. The communal bathrooms are seedy-looking but adequate and clean. The assets of this lodge include a big sitting room with an enormous fireplace, a well-stocked library, a hot tub, and a large dining area, in which a professional cook provides family-style meals. Up to 140 people can be accommodated, so things tend to get hectic when there's a full house. In winter, you'll need to wear snow boots to reach the front door, which is 100 yards up a steep trail from the parking lot. Bring a flashlight in case you arrive after dark.

Facilities include the smaller Hutchinson Lodge, intended for groups of up to 25 people; a cross-country trail system with 12 kilometers of groomed track; a ski-rental and instruction program; and a network of four backwoods huts, each about a day's ski or hike apart. These accommodations are known as the Peter Grubb Hut, the Ludlow Hut, the Benson Hut, and Bradley Hut. Clair Tappaan is close to Royal Gorge Cross-Country Ski Resort, Sugar Bowl, Donner Ski Ranch, and Boreal. Take the Soda Springs/Norden exit from I-80 to get here.

Policies: Youngsters under the age of four are discouraged on winter weekends.

Rates: $. All rates are per person and include three meals a day. A two-night minimum stay is required to reserve all accommodations for winter weekends and holidays. Some credit cards are accepted, and proof of membership is required to receive the Sierra Club discount.

Contact: Clair Tappaan Lodge, 19940 Donner Pass Rd., Soda Springs, P.O. Box 36, Norden, CA 95724; 530/426-3632; website: www.sierraclub .org/outings/lodges/tappaan.html.

Truckee Hotel

In the boom years following the Gold Rush and the introduction of rail service over the crest of the Sierra Nevada, this historic four-story hotel at the end of Commercial Row, established in 1873, was originally a stagecoach stop for travelers on the Emigrant Trail. Now it is a haven for recreationists coming to Lake Tahoe. Amtrak passenger trains, as well as freight trains, still stop at the station across the street. If you stay in a south-facing room, you may hear the trains, but the north end is relatively quiet. (The management provides earplugs.) In 1990, the hotel underwent a major renovation—some might say gentrification. When you walk through the entrance you'll be transported to the Victorian era, with old-fashioned light fixtures, polished oak, and

raised, olive green wallpaper. The Victorian sitting parlor, to the left, has a marble fireplace and is furnished with antiques; in the adjoining dining area, guests enjoy a continental breakfast consisting of muffins, bagels, cold cereal, fresh fruit, yogurt, and a selection of teas and coffees. Snacks are served early evening on weekends. In mid-2002, a new restaurant—Moody's Bistro and Lounge—opened on the lower floor.

Of the hotel's 37 rooms, 24 are in the European style (with a washbasin and a shared bath down the hall), four are family rooms with a shared bath, and eight are in the American style with full baths featuring deep clawfoot tubs. All are furnished with antiques, quilts, and pillow shams and have radiated steam heat. The bridal suite has a canopied bed with white lace and satin. If you're a television addict, you'll have to compete with channel surfers in the Whitney Room, a meeting and television area on the second floor. There are convenient ski lockers on the ground floor, next to the registration desk. Happily, the hotel still has lots of character, exemplified by creaks and groans, funny little depressions in the floors beneath the carpeting, and long and steep stairways that narrow by the fourth floor. One of the advantages of staying at the Truckee Hotel is its proximity to North Tahoe resorts and the shops and restaurants of old Truckee.

Rates: $–$$$. Major credit cards are accepted.

Contact: Truckee Hotel, 10007 Bridge St., Truckee, CA 96161; 530/587-4444, fax 530/587-1599; website: www.thetruckeehotel.com.

SQUAW VALLEY
Christy Inn

Although not particularly ornate, Christy Inn, which is not a bed-and-breakfast, has a rich history and is marvelously close to the golf course and ski slopes of Squaw Valley. The inn was once the home of Wayne and Sandy Poulsen, Lake Tahoe's "First Family of Skiing," who founded the ski area in 1948 and raised a brood of eight children. Many of their offspring became ski champions and Olympians. Years ago, the Poulsens built a new family compound elsewhere in the valley and created this small inn, which has seven bedrooms, each with a private bath. The rooms have recently been completely refurbished and upgraded.

On the lower level, the Poulsens' former living and dining room is now Graham's, one of Tahoe's more celebrated gourmet dinner houses. There's a large outdoor deck and an adjacent lawn area.

Rates: $$–$$$. Rates are slightly higher during holiday periods. The entire building can be rented for $600 a night in summer or $800 a night in winter. Major credit cards are accepted.

Contact: Christy Inn, 1604 Christy Ln./P.O. Box 2008, Olympic Valley, CA 96146; 530/583-3451, fax 530/583-2040; website: www.tahoesbest.com and click on lodging.

TAHOE CITY/WEST SHORE

The Cottage Inn

Stepping into this woodsy and elegant property is like walking into an old hunting lodge. But you'll find a warmth that comes from the fresh-baked cookies and beverages that greet guests in the main lodge building every afternoon. Old Tahoe's trademark wood-and-stone decor receives some very contemporary touches in this lakeside haven, which consists of 17 units including five duplex cottages, two freestanding cabins, and a six-plex of studios. The inn is just south of Tahoe City on Highway 89.

In 1993, the inn was transformed from a collection of drab, aging cabins into upscale cottages with many charming touches, and in 1998 it was acquired by Susi Muhr, who moved to Lake Tahoe from Germany's Bavaria. Each unit has a rich brick, stone, or faux-stone facade and a theme-oriented interior. The Western-theme suite features knotty-pine walls, decorative boots next to a gas fireplace, a steer horn above the bed, and an entertainment credenza with its own library of Western videotapes (just in case you crave a John Wayne flick). Another cabin, The Bird's Nest, which is popular with honeymooners, has an open, two-story cathedral ceiling, with a queen-sized bed in a loft and a Jacuzzi bathtub below; the loft is accessible from a spiral staircase with branches for banisters. A sitting

area with a gas fireplace provides warmth for cozy couples. Just in case you don't know you're in the woods, a sound system pipes in the chirping of birds. The Romantic Hideaway, another honeymoon suite, offers lavish decor and something you don't find in your typical lakeside cabin: a giant stone bathtub big enough for a party, complemented by a cascading waterfall and Jacuzzi jets. This unit also provides a cathedral ceiling, a canopied bed, a sitting area, and a gas fireplace.

The inn serves a full breakfast in the main lodge. It also maintains its own library of videotapes to suit most any interest or mood. The Cottage Inn is a romantic place for couples, to be sure, and it has a feeling of intimacy that seems to suit Lake Tahoe. Also, it's on the quiet West Shore of Lake Tahoe, close to a wide array of golf and ski resorts, water sports, bicycle paths, and hiking trails.

Policies: Children under the age of 12 are not allowed.

Rates: $$$–$$$$. Some major credit cards are accepted.

Contact: The Cottage Inn, 1690 W. Lake Blvd./P.O. Box 66, Tahoe City, CA 96145; 530/581-4073 or 800/581-4073; website: www.thecottageinn.com.

Mayfield House

With its stone and wood facade, the Mayfield House bed-and-breakfast inn is a classic example of Old Tahoe-style architecture. It is also centrally located to shops, restaurants, and beachfront activities in Tahoe City. Built in 1932 by Norman Mayfield, a pioneer contractor in the area, the house was recently refurbished, with new furniture, floors, and bathrooms. It has six bedrooms, each appointed with a king- or queen-sized bed and down comforters. The atmosphere is cheery and, with its homemade log furniture, the property exudes a country-mountain decor. Among the more interesting units is the Mayfield Room (the master suite), with a large sitting area; and Julia's Room, which was once used by Julia Morgan, designer of Hearst Castle in San Simeon and a personal friend of Norman Mayfield. Five rooms in the main house and a cottage in the rear all have private baths. The common areas consist of a dining room and a large living room with a fireplace.

Innkeeper and owner Colleen McDevitt serves a full breakfast in the dining area, and that often consists of homemade breads, muffins, apple walnut pancakes, cinnamon and banana French toast, granola Belgian waffles, and fresh fruits and juices. Free cookies and other snacks are offered in the afternoon, along with wine, beer, and sodas. Mayfield House is in Tahoe City off Highway 28, just across the road from the lake.
Policies: No pets or smoking are allowed.
Rates: $$–$$$$. All rates are double occupancy with a full breakfast and afternoon refreshments. Some major credit cards are accepted.
Contact: Mayfield House, 236 Grove St./P.O. Box 8529, Tahoe City, CA 96145; 530/583-1001 or 888/518-8898; website: www.mayfieldhouse.com.

Chaney House

If you like mingling with outgoing innkeepers who are knowledgeable about Lake Tahoe and its attractions, you'll feel right at home in Gary and Lori Chaney's minicastle. This historic remnant of Old Tahoe is full of character, including that of the owners, who live on-site. Built in the 1920s by Italian stonemasons, it has 18-inch-thick walls, Gothic arches, and a massive stone fireplace that reaches to the top of a cathedral-like ceiling. The feeling is distinctly European, especially in the entryway and living room, and you almost expect to see a knight in armor clanking down the stairs.

The four rooms, upstairs and over the garage, convey a much livelier and more contemporary impression; each is richly appointed and has a private bathroom with a shower. The Chaneys named rooms after their now-grown children, Jeanine and Russell: One is calico feminine with a brass queen-sized bed covered by Wendy Moon quilts made in Lake Tahoe, and the other is masculine and pine-paneled, with a lake view. The Master Suite has a garden view and comes with a king-sized bed. The Honeymoon Hideaway, a one-bedroom apartment over the garage, is romantically inspired, with white lace and furniture,

a kitchen, an alcove with a sofa, a queen feather bed, fireplace, granite whirlpool tub/shower, TV and VCR, wet bar, and private bath. The house is set back from Highway 89, with a large driveway and plenty of parking. Across the road are a private beach and pier, as well as a fire pit for evening barbecues and stargazing.

Rates include a full breakfast served on the patio overlooking the lake on summer days or indoors in winter; refreshments are offered in the evenings around the fireplace. Breakfast is a buffet and consists of Lori's unique creations, dishes such as El Dorado eggs, a casserole with sausage, peppers, onions, and two types of cheese; Swahili pie, which is similar to Dutch pancakes but comes with honey and custard and covered with hot spiced apples; and crab puff, like a quiche with crab and eggs. There's a dog in residence, and smokers are relegated to the outdoors. Chaney House is five miles south of Tahoe City.
Rates: $$$–$$$$. All rooms are double occupancy. Credit cards are accepted.
Contact: Chaney House, 4725 W. Lake Blvd. (Hwy. 89), Homewood, CA/P.O. Box 7852, Tahoe City, CA 96145; 530/525-7333, website: www.chaneyhouse.com.

Norfolk Woods Inn

In 1993 Al and Patty Multon gave up their careers in Sydney, Australia (she's the Aussie, he's the Yank), and decided to put down roots as innkeepers at Lake Tahoe. They took over this seven-room European-style lodge in Tahoma—on the West Shore on Highway 89—and opened up five seldom-used cabins, redecorated the place to look less like the Tyrol and more like Tahoe, and hired top chefs. This is a place that makes a point of catering to families, as evidenced by the couple's own children. There is no extra charge for kids under the age of 12, and the Multons will even take dogs in the cabins. Four of the cabins are ideal for small fry (each will sleep a minimum of four people), and the fifth is a honeymooner's special. Elements of that cabin have existed since the turn of the century, when evangelist Aimee Semple MacPherson lived there. The cabin has been rebuilt and now has an elegant king-sized bed upstairs, a large sitting room with a fireplace, and a full kitchen.

When the Multons moved here from Down Under, they brought with them a huge collection of European tapestries and Australian paintings that adorn the restaurant. There's a small but cozy bar with stained glass panels and a selection of wines and brews. The restaurant has been winning local awards, and Thursday nights pull in diners for the prime rib special. Most of the rooms have been upgraded with antique or replica furnishings, wallpaper, and other homey touches. Some of the rooms closest to the highway are noisier in summer. Prices for the inn rooms include a full breakfast, with a choice of several entrées. The inn specializes in arranging weddings and small functions.

Rates: $$–$$$$. Major credit cards are accepted.
Contact: Norfolk Woods Inn, 6941 W. Lake Blvd./P.O. Box 262, Tahoma, CA 96142; 530/525-5000; website: www.norfolkwoods.com.

Rockwood Lodge

Here's a place for incurable romantics, wildlife aficionados, or those who love the style of Old Tahoe. Louis Reinkens and Connie Stevens, husband and wife, have operated this bed-and-breakfast since 1985. In a wooded area just off Highway 89 at Homewood, the house is a spacious mountain chalet. Rockwood was built in 1939 by Carlos Rookwood, a dairyman from Northern California who used it as a summer retreat. When Louis, a retired aerospace consultant, and Connie, an airline flight attendant, acquired it they changed an "o" to a "c" and it became Rockwood. Among various other projects, Connie runs a nonprofit organization called Wildlife Shelter, and operates a care facility for injured wildlife and birds next door.

The inn has knotty-pine walls, hand-hewn beams, a huge stone fireplace, and a cozy sitting room. The five guest rooms, all upstairs, have names such as Secret Harbor, Rubicon Bay, Zephyr Cove, and Emerald Bay, all famous sites at Lake Tahoe. Secret Harbor, the most elegant suite, features a four-posted, canopied, hand-painted Russian wedding bed, a private bath with a double shower and Roman tub, and a

partial view of the lake. All rooms have queen-sized feather beds, down comforters, pedestal sinks, and a sitting area for two. The interiors are richly appointed in Laura Ashley curtains and fabrics, Early American and European furniture, and brass and porcelain fixtures. Homey touches include a full supply of body lotions and shampoos, and a walk-in closet with terry cloth bathrobes.

A full breakfast—the specialty is Louis's Dutch Baby, a kind of fruit frittata—is served daily, on the patio when the weather permits. Other items might include fresh ground coffees, a selection of teas, fruit crepes, Belgian waffles, fresh fruit, cereals, and juices. Rockwood is seven miles south of Tahoe City, on a busy stretch of Highway 89—although it is set back from the road. About 100 feet from the lake, it has obstructed views.

Policies: No pets or smoking inside. Children by special arrangement only. The inn offers a no-shoes environment, with guests asked to wear slippers that are provided by the innkeepers. This is a formality that is quite common in Japan and Scandanavia but has occasionally made some guests feel uncomfortable.

Rates: $$$–$$$$. Cash, checks, and money orders are accepted; credit cards may only be used to hold reservations.
Contact: Rockwood Lodge, 5295 W. Lake Blvd. (Hwy. 89)/P.O. Box 226, Homewood, CA 96141; 530/525-5273 or 800/538-2463, fax 530/525-5949; website: www.rockwoodlodge.com.

Tahoma Meadows Bed-and-Breakfast

Recently acquired by Dick and Ulli White, this bucolic lodge of red duplex cabins on a forested site of the West Shore has been lovingly refurbished. It has 10 bed-and-breakfast rooms and four housekeeping cottages, each of which is brightened with country-style furnishings and cheerful colors. Some units are close to Highway 89, others are set back in the trees. Nine rooms have vintage clawfoot bathtubs, great for soaking in at the end of a day of hiking, cycling, or skiing. Seven cottages have gas-log fireplaces. Televisions are in all of the units.

Full breakfast, included in the rates, is served

in the main lodge, and might include fritattas, sweet potato pancakes, home fries, fresh juice, and fruit. The property also houses Stony Ridge Cafe, a gourmet restaurant that serves breakfast, lunch, and dinner on weekends. The inn is in Tahoma, 8.5 miles south of Tahoe City, near Sugar Pine Point State Park and its hiking trails, the famous Ehrman Mansion, an extensive paved bike trail, the Homewood ski area, and several lakefront marinas. During winter, the ski resort will send a free shuttle to pick up guests, upon request.

Policies: Accepts children and some pets.

Rates: $$–$$$$. Major credit cards are accepted.

Contact: Tahoma Meadows Bed-and-Breakfast, 6821 W. Lake Blvd. (Hwy. 89)/P.O. Box 810, Homewood, CA 96141; 530/525-1553 or 866/525-1553; website: www.tahomameadows.com.

KINGS BEACH/TAHOE VISTA/CARNELIAN BAY

The Shore House

Rustically elegant, this lakefront bed-and-breakfast on the North Shore of Lake Tahoe offers nine uniquely styled rooms, a small white-sand beach adjoining the property, a private pier, and a full gourmet hot breakfast each morning. Owners Barb and Marty Cohen, Tahoe residents for more than two decades, have created an intimate, romantic getaway with a main building and two cabins.

All rooms have king- and queen-sized beds and gas-log fireplaces. Each room has a private bath (five have whirlpool tubs), a private entrance, knotty-pine walls, custom-built log beds, and Scandia down feather beds and comforters. The Treehouse, on the upper floor, is decorated with a Native American motif and has a window overlooking the gardens and lake. Opa's Room features garden and lake views from its upper floor window, two double-sized log beds, and a private shower. The Pine Room, on the ground floor, is one of the largest rooms; it contains a king-sized log bed, a private pine bath with an oversize tub and shower, garden views, and a peek at the lake. The largest unit, the Moon Room, has a king-sized bed and a

ceiling painted with clouds and stars, and provides a large bathroom with double sinks and a raised Jacuzzi tub. The Honeymoon Cottage— a separate, elegant beachfront cabin—has a vaulted ceiling, panoramic view of the lake and a two-person whirlpool tub in the bedroom. A large lawn area, dotted with aspens and cottonwoods, extends to the lake, and the main building is surrounded with decking. There's also an outdoor hot tub with a panoramic view of the lake. Barb is an award-winning breakfast chef who prepares a hearty mountain breakfast, which may consist of her signature sweet and spicy Monte Cristo breakfast sandwich, stuffed French toast, sun-dried tomato quiche, homemade muffins and scones, fruit, juices, espressos, and lattes. This meal is served in the lakeside dining room or, in summer, on the lawn by the water's edge. In the afternoon, the couple serves wine and cheese and, at bedtime, they leave a fresh batch of homemade cookies in each room. Recent upgrades include new landscaping, a full parking lot, and the addition of a 36-foot cabin cruiser that is used to take guests on lake outings (Marty's the captain). There are no television sets and no phones. Small-group weddings (of up to 15 people) are a specialty here, and more than 500 have been held. Marty, an ordained minister, will even perform the ceremony. Seven gourmet restaurants are within walking distance of the property. Shore House is a member of the Select Registry and Unique Inns.

Policies: A two-night minimum stay is required on weekends. No pets or smoking are allowed.

Rates: $$$–$$$$. Major credit cards are accepted.

Contact: The Shore House, 7170 N. Lake Blvd., Tahoe Vista, CA 96148; 530/546-7270 or 800/207-5160; website: www.tahoeinn.com.

Shooting Star Bed and Breakfast

Rustic on the outside but contemporary on the inside, this new inn offers luxurious accommodations and modern conveniences. Built not as a home but as a B&B, the two-story building offers three rooms with outside access. It's in a quiet residential neighborhood at Carnelian Bay, just off Highway 28, and is close to restaurants and beaches. The spacious Aspen Suite upstairs has a king bed with down bedding in one room, two twin beds in another room, a custom-tiled bathroom with a dual-headed shower and two sinks, a walk-in closet, and an intimate seating area. The Bay Room, which has views of Lake Tahoe through large bay windows, offers down bedding and a Jacuzzi tub for two. The Carnelian Room has a queen bed and an oversized shower.

Interior appointments include paintings by local artist Randall Stauss, two fireplaces (one on each level), individual temperature controls and in-floor heating in each room, and a well-stocked library with comfortable chairs that are arranged around the downstairs fireplace. Outside, there's a natural garden with pine and fir trees, a front porch, and a horseshoe pit. **Rates:** $$$$. Major credit cards are accepted. The innkeeper prepares a hearty gourmet breakfast and afternoon hors d'ouevres each day, along with full concierge service.

Contact: Shooting Star Bed and Breakfast, 315 Olive St., P.O. Box 1573, Carnelian Bay, CA 96140; 530/546-8903 or 888/985-STAR (888/ 985-7827); website: www.shootingstarbandb.com.

SOUTH LAKE TAHOE/STATELINE
Black Bear Inn

Opened in 1999 by retired Texas attorney Jerry Birdwell and his partner, Kevin Chandler, this spectacular, all-new inn with its log porte cochere is halfway between the new Marina Village on Lake Tahoe and the California entrance to Heavenly ski resort. It is nestled between some nondescript motels, but don't let that bother you. The lodge and its one-acre grounds are so impressive and inviting that you'll feel like you're in the ultimate Tahoe Valhalla, more of a mountain executive retreat than a bed-and-breakfast inn. The most compelling feature is the magnificent lobby—something you would expect to see in a much larger lodge. It has a 34-foot-high cathedral ceiling, which is supported by massive cut logs and is graced by an equally stunning river-rock fireplace that rises from floor to ceiling. This Great

Room has intricate stone and lodgepole trim, giant picture windows, chandeliers, a grand piano, and rustic Western collectibles that Birdwell has scoured from the backroads of his native state. Adjoining this room is a large dining area with several tables and a wet bar, as well as a full commercial kitchen. Two guest rooms are downstairs, while the others are on the second floor and accessible from an open mezzanine that overlooks the parlor. All rooms are spacious and individually decorated, with design elements that vary from river-rock gas fireplaces to authentic barn-wood wall paneling. The Fallen Leaf Room has exposed log beams and French doors leading to a sitting balcony, the Seneca Room has a 10-foot ceiling and large bow window, and the Sequoia Room—really a suite—has a large sitting area, wet bar, and DVD player. All rooms come with a private bath, king bed, television, telephone with data port, daily maid service, a full hearty breakfast, and use of the lodge facilities, including an

the interior of the Black Bear Inn

outdoor hot tub. In addition to the lodge rooms, there are three cabins (including one duplex) in the large, wooded rear yard, all with rustic American decor. (If you remember the reality television series, *The Bachelor,* one segment was filmed in the honeymoon cabin, although our man on the prowl failed to make it to second base here with one of the eligible bachelorettes.) All units come with king beds, gas fireplaces, kitchenettes, TV/VCR/DVD (with a library of free movies), and telephones. Downstairs, next to the side entrance and parking lot, is a ski and boot storage room—a nice touch. In the main lodge, a chef serves a complete breakfast that might include omelets, frittatas, potatoes, bacon and sausage, fresh fruit, home-baked breads, juices, and coffee. The Black Bear Inn is so elegant, so inviting, and such a marvel of craftsmanship and design that you may find it difficult to leave. Without a doubt, this is the premier small inn of the region and one hopes it's the first of a new generation of upscale lodging properties that showcase the Old Tahoe style of architecture.

Policies: No pets or smoking indoors. The inn is not appropriate for children under 16. Two occupants per room or cabin. Two-night minimum on weekends.

Rates: $$$$. Some credit cards accepted.

Contact: Black Bear Inn, 1202 Ski Run Blvd., South Lake Tahoe, CA 96150; 530/544-4451 or 877/BEARINN (877/232-7466); website: www.TahoeBlackBear.com.

Christiania Inn

Here at one of Tahoe's most unabashedly European inns, everything about the place, from the quaint Bavarian exterior to the après-ski lounge with its Louis XIII cognac, brings the Alps to California. The inn is just 50 yards from the main chairlift of Heavenly Ski Resort, and it's a five-minute drive (down a steep hill that can be icy in winter) to the casinos of Stateline. The "Chris" also has what is acknowledged to be one of Tahoe's finest restaurants, with intimate lighting, a superb wine list, and meals prepared by graduates of the Culinary Institute of America. Upstairs are six suites and rooms, all meticu-

lously appointed with antiques, wood-burning fireplaces, and European decor. Each room has a private bath/shower, with furnishings such as brass and pedestal beds, lace curtains, sitting parlors, and dining nooks. Three suites have two floors, allowing for even more amenities, such as a living room, a wet bar, a dry sauna, and bathtubs with whirlpool jets. Room 1 and Suite 4 overlook the ski runs at Heavenly.

A continental breakfast is brought to your room every morning, and there's always a decanter of brandy to ward off the nighttime chill. In summer, the inn is blissfully quiet, surrounded by brilliant flowers and tall, fragrant pines. Across from the Heavenly California base lodge and parking lot, the inn has been in operation since 1965 and is owned by Jerry and Maggie Mershon.

Rates: $–$$$$. Some credit cards accepted.

Contact: Christiania Inn, 3819 Saddle Rd./P.O. Box 18298, South Lake Tahoe, CA 96151; 530/544-7337, fax 530/544-5342; website: www.christianiainn.com.

Echo Creek Mountain Ranch

It would be hard to find a more idyllic venue for a corporate retreat, a vacation for three or four families, or a wedding than this custom-built, 4,000-square-foot log estate, not far off U.S. 50 in South Lake Tahoe. To see this place is to immediately fall in love with it. The building is situated on 16 acres at the end of a quiet road, bordered by Eldorado National Forest and accessible to a half-mile section of Echo Creek, which has fishable trout and plunging rapids.

Recently constructed of timbers and knotty-pine paneling with vaulted ceilings, this luxurious ranch has five bedrooms: three with queen-sized beds, one with two bunk beds, and one with four bunks. A meandering deck partly encircles the building. There's also a bunkhouse with two bunks. The property sleeps up to 20 people but can provide banquet and conference services for up to 50 people. This is mountain luxury with a rustic, cozy touch that has all the comforts of home. Amenities include three river-rock fireplaces, handcrafted wood furniture, a full gourmet kitchen, a bar, a spacious living room with a big-screen television, three bathrooms, a multipurpose room, a ranch-style barbecue, and an outdoor hot tub. It's close to skiing, golf, hiking, and boating on Lake Tahoe, and is a 15-minute drive to Stateline.

Rates: $$$$. $900 to $1,500 per night, plus tax and cleaning. The cleaning fee is $250. Visa, MasterCard, and American Express are accepted. **Contact:** Echo Creek Mountain Ranch, c/o Tahoe Keys Resort, 599 Tahoe Keys Blvd., South Lake Tahoe, CA 96150. Reservations are available through Tahoe Keys Resort, at 530/544-5397 or 800/462-5397; website: www.tahoevacationguide.com.

Inn at Heavenly

Right away, it is important to know two things about this property: First, it is not connected in any way with Heavenly ski resort, which is up the road, and, second, it does not resemble what most people would consider to be a bed-and-breakfast inn. On the outside, it appears to be one of the plethora of aging motels that are scattered throughout the city of South Lake Tahoe. But on the inside, this place does have its charms, in what the owners describe as "country mountain" decor. Each of the 14 rooms has been gentrified with river-rock gas fireplaces, custom-crafted lodgepole furniture, and various country themes that include boating and fishing, ducks, birds and birdhouses, wildflowers, squirrels, and an enchanted forest. Some rooms are reasonably spacious, while others are small. Each has a private bath with shower; microwave, refrigerator, and coffeemaker; and cable television and VCR. Also available are kitchen units as well as private one- to four-bedroom cabins, on and off the property. Common areas include a small spa room with indoor hot tub and sauna, and a Gathering Room behind the office that offers tables and chairs for lounging in front of a large stone fireplace. A continental breakfast is served here, and this usually consists of homemade muffins, cereals, fruit, juices, and hot beverages such as coffee, tea, or hot chocolate. There is a lawn and large wooded area on the grounds, and this can accommodate groups such as weddings. The inn is one mile from the Heavenly resort

California entrance, and is within walking distance of the new Marina Village at the lake and of several good restaurants. Guests who stay here consider the place cozy and unpretentious, and it is certainly a rung or two up the ladder from the area's mostly nondescript motels.

Policies: Pets and children are welcome. **Rates:** $$$–$$$$. Rooms include continental breakfast daily. **Contact:** The Inn at Heavenly, 1261 Ski Run Blvd., South Lake Tahoe, CA 96150; 530/544-4244 or 800/MYCABIN (800/692-2246) (reservations); website: inn-at-heavenly.com.

HIGHWAY 50 (WEST OF SOUTH LAKE TAHOE)

Strawberry Lodge

Built in 1858 as a stagecoach stop, this spacious and rambling old wood building is virtually an institution on U.S. 50. One of the finest lodges of its type, Strawberry is comparable to the Rainbow Lodge, its northern neighbor on I-80. Apart from ornately furnished rooms with antiques and Victorian influences, the lodge has enormous common areas. There's a large, knotty-pine dining room, a huge lobby with a stone fireplace, a cocktail lounge, an outdoor gazebo and lawn, and a recreation room, featuring billiards and Ping-Pong, that doubles as a ballroom for banquets (with weddings among the more popular functions).

The property has two sections—the main lodge, which adjoins the South Fork of the American River, and an annex lodge with motel-style rooms across the highway. There are 43 rooms in total, including a riverside cabin and 12 brand new rooms, completed in 1998, that are in the main building above the ballroom. These have a modern Southwestern theme. The other upstairs wing, added two years earlier, has 12 rooms, each with private bath (tub or shower), a queen-sized bed, and windows that look out on the river and forest instead of the highway. Of the 16 rooms on the opposite wing, seven share bathrooms down the hall. Owner Richard Mitchell also has recently expanded the bar, and there's a wine cellar that can be used as a conference room. With

Strawberry's very visible location, the lodge gets plenty of motorists wandering in from the main highway, so employees challenge visitors to state their intentions. (There's a charge for those who ask to use the restrooms). Recreation options abound and include skiing at Sierra-at-Tahoe (with a free shuttle bus for weekenders), boating or fishing in Crystal Basin, or hiking in the Desolation Wilderness.

Policies: No pets and no smoking. Children are welcome.

Rates: $–$$$. Major credit cards are accepted.

Contact: Strawberry Lodge, 17510 U.S. 50, Kyburz, CA 95720; 530/659-7200; website: www.strawberry-lodge.com.

Camino Hotel Seven-Mile House Bed and Breakfast

Situated 45 minutes west of South Lake Tahoe off U.S. 50, this historic bed-and-breakfast inn is perhaps the most elegant lodging in the heart of a delightful growing region known as Apple Hill. Late August–mid-December, visitors, mostly from the Sacramento Valley, flock to the more than 60 apple growers, wineries, bakeries, and fruit stands scattered throughout the Gold Country foothills of the western Sierra. Numerous festivals and weekend events, centered around delicious local produce (including apple cider and homemade pies), make the Camino Hotel a great place to stay. And the property is within a 30-minute drive of major recreation areas—the Chili Bar rafting put-in on the South Fork of the American River and the west slope trails to the Desolation Wilderness and its pristine alpine lakes.

The hotel charms you the minute you walk through the door. On the ground floor, there's a spacious and elegant parlor, where a sit-down breakfast—homemade apple pancakes and rum-raisin French toast are among the specialties—is served each morning. Next to the parlor is The Jodar Wine Tasting Room, operated by a local winery by the same name. Of the nine upstairs guest rooms, three have private baths (one with an old-fashioned clawfoot tub, the others with showers) and six share two baths. All are decorated with antiques, and each is named after a fig-

ure of local history, such as Florence Nightingale, whose descendants are from Camino. The hotel was originally built in 1888 as a boarding house for the Camino Lumber Mill, which is still operating. Years later, it became a transition house for inmates leaving Folsom Prison.

Innkeeper Paula Nobert bought the place in 1990 and has created a warm, homey environment, a place for couples, families, weddings, and reunions. Dinners can be set up for groups and conferences, as well as for wedding parties. Camino Hotel is off the Camino/Carson exit of U.S. 50.

Policies: Children and some pets are accepted. No smoking in the hotel.

Rates: $$. Major credit cards are accepted.

Contact: Camino Hotel, 4103 Carson Rd./P.O. Box 1197, Camino, CA 95709; 530/644-7740 or 800/200-7740; website: www.caminohotel.com.

FEATHER RIVER COUNTRY/ LAKES BASIN

Coppin's Meadow Lodge

This two-story country inn, opened in January 1996 and recently acquired by Tom and Ella Dolly, is unique for several reasons. First, it is the only overnight lodging available in the Jackson Meadows Reservoir area. Second, at 7,000 feet in elevation, it is completely snowbound in winter, accessible only by snowmobile or cross-country skis. Third, it is amazingly luxurious for a fully self-contained inn; the power for the entire lodge is supplied by a generator. Coppin's Meadow offers four spacious bedrooms (each with a queen-sized bed and a private bath with a tub and a shower), a marvelous living room with high beamed ceilings, a big stone fireplace, and lots of Western memorabilia. All rooms have outside private entrances and small front porches, and most have queen-sized beds, but other configurations are available. In winter, snowmobile tours stop here for overnight stays, and the entire area is part of a vast network of 180 miles of groomed trails. Owners can also arrange snowcat access to the lodge. In summer, some of the best hiking (near the Pacific Crest Trail), mountain biking, fishing, and boating opportunities are just a few miles away.

All meals, including dinner and lunch (a bag lunch is available for excursions, with notice), come with the price of the room during winter. In summer, rooms are available without meals, and the home can be rented for weddings and special events. One of the big draws is the privately owned Webber Lake, which is teeming with large rainbow, brook, and brown trout. Boats are available to fish the lake. The lodge is creatively decorated with a rustic Western motif and exudes a quiet warmth that is certainly conducive to relaxation and reflection. Breakfast might include eggs and sausage, homemade muffins, potatoes, and fresh fruit. Dinner might include filet mignon with ruby port sauce, rack of lamb in mustard and garlic, or scampi, topped off with homemade apple pie or chocolate mousse. Recently, the garage was converted into a warming hut to serve snowmobilers and other midday guests. In the living room there's a television with satellite dish and VCR, and a cellular phone is available in the main lodge. Coppin's Meadow is eight miles west of Little Truckee Summit (on Highway 89) and 35 minutes north of Truckee.

Policies: Children are not recommended.

Rates: $$–$$$.

Contact: Coppin's Meadow Lodge, P.O. Box 272, Truckee, CA 96161; 916/837-3104 or 775/831-4125.

Sierra Hot Springs and Globe Hotel

This historic, vintage 1850s hotel and a nearby hot springs spa and resort are just a 30-minute drive north of Truckee. Recently acquired by the nonprofit New Age Church of Being, but not operated as a religious or cult retreat, the hotel has been substantially renovated and features nine guest rooms that are furnished in antiques, a large parlor with velvet couches, and a spacious rear deck. Though it is situated prominently at the intersection of Highways 89 and 49 in the heart of tiny Sierraville, guests must check in at the main lodge and hot springs, which are 1.5 miles east off Highway 49 and require you to drive over isolated dirt roads. At least one mem-

ber of the party must pay a membership fee ($5 per month as of this writing) to the New Age Church, but the reason for this, I am told, is to allow a "clothing optional" policy at the hot springs. The alternative lifestyle here also includes gourmet vegetarian dining, yoga exercise, massage, and holistic health workshops. While the Globe's rooms are semielegant, there are no private baths in them; guests must share two bathrooms and take their meals at the Main Lodge down the road. At this location is another vintage building with five additional private rooms, which are decorated European style, and one large room with five dorm-style beds, all sharing two bathrooms. Adjoining the Main Lodge are three natural hot mineral springs pools, which vary in temperature and which contain silica and small amounts of sulphur. The spa amenities include a heated swimming pool; an outdoor pool called the Medicine Bath, which has a sandy bottom and is surrounded by rock tile; and a Hot Pool, which is inside a large geodesic dome. In addition, there are private rooms in the Phoenix Baths, and these also use the warm springwater. On Saturday, Sunday, and holidays, the Main Lodge serves a gourmet brunch (extra) A.M.–11 A.M., and the menu might include a tofu scramble, egg soufflé, French toast, pancakes, roasted potatoes, hot or cold cereal, fresh baked muffins,fruit, juices, coffee, tea, and chai. During summer, a buffet-style dinner is served nightly by the retreat's award-winning chef, and there is a guest kitchen available to prepare your own meals. The Main Lodge and hot springs (formerly known as Campbell Hot Springs) have been in existence in some form for 150 years. They are part of 900 acres of meadows and forest that are owned by the New Age Church, which also operates Hardin Hot Springs north of Calistoga in Lake County, California.

Policies: No pets and no smoking. No nudity within view of the road. Well-behaved children are accepted, and there are specific times that youngsters may use the pools. No alcohol is allowed on the property. Membership in the New Age Church is required for one member of the party, at a token fee.

Rates: $–$$. Includes 24-hour use of all facilities. Some major credit cards are accepted.

Contact: Sierra Hot Springs, P.O. Box 366, Sierraville, CA 96126; 530/994-3773; website: www.sierrahotsprings.org.

High Country Inn Bed-and-Breakfast

This is a modern but woodsy bed-and-breakfast in Sierra City, about 45 miles northwest of Truckee on Highway 49. Nature surrounds this lovely home: on one side there's the Yuba River and a grove of aspens, to another side there's a private pond brimming with tame trout, and rising up beside another are the awesome Sierra Buttes, a magnificent series of rocky pinnacles.

There are five guest rooms, of which the Sierra Buttes Suite upstairs is the most impressive and most consistently romantic. It has cathedral windows that frame the Buttes and the pond, a private bath with antique tub and modern shower, a dressing room with a view of the river, a king-sized bed, and a fireplace. The Golden Pond Room has private access to a deck, a queen-sized bed, and a shared bath. The Howard Creek Suite also has views, as well as a private deck, Jacuzzi tub, gas fireplace, a king-sized bed, and a day bed. The spacious living room contains a telescope for viewing the buttes, and a large stone fireplace for cozy socializing; it adjoins the dining room and kitchen.

New owner Bob Latta offers a hearty country breakfast with various gourmet specialties. The inn is on Highway 49 in Sierra City, close to excellent hiking, mountain biking, fishing, and boating in the Lakes Basin area.

Policies: No pets are allowed, and smoking is restricted.

Rates: $$–$$$. Major credit cards are accepted.

Contact: High Country Inn Bed-and-Breakfast, 100 Greene Rd., HCR 2, Box 7, Sierra City, CA 96125; 530/862-1530 or 800/862-1530; website: www.hicountryinn.com.

Holly House Bed and Breakfast Inn

Named after holly trees that one of the owners planted years ago, the Holly House is an Italianate Victorian that was opened to guests in 1997. It was built in 1886 by H. Watt Hughes, who was a partner in the Young America Mine, and served as a boarding house, an annex to the Sierra Buttes Inn, and a home to several families. In 1974 it was acquired by current innkeepers Rich and Mary Nourse, who renovated it and lived there as their family residence. This stately, two-story mansion has five guest rooms, each with queen bed. Three rooms have private bath (two have a double-width spa tubs) and two have shared bath and shower. Two rooms, the Olivia and Adeline, can be rented as a suite and closed off from the rest of the house. All are tastefully furnished with classic antiques. A full breakfast is served 8 A.M.–9 A.M., with coffee available at 7:30 A.M. Guests can take their meals in the country kitchen, or as brunch in the formal parlor. Free wine and hors d'oeuvres are offered 5 P.M.–6 P.M. each evening. Open Memorial Day weekend–Labor Day, the inn is on Highway 49 in Sierra City, close to hiking, mountain biking, fishing, and boating in the Lakes Basin area.

Policies: Smoking and pets are not permitted.

Rates: $$–$$$. Major credit cards are accepted.

Contact: Holly House Bed and Breakfast Inn, 119 Main St. (Hwy. 49), P.O. Box 350, Sierra City, CA 96125; 530/862-1123; website: www.hollyhouse.com.

Molly's Bed and Breakfast

North of Truckee and four miles south of Graeagle, this recently opened inn is part of a restored, late 1800s-era building that was converted from a general store into a house. It is tucked into the former milltown of Clio (population: 76) and is within a short walk of the scenic Feather River. The inn has four comfortable and cozy bedrooms, each with private bath, and all rooms have views of the mountains and forest. Innkeeper Carolyn Van Stralen prepares a full breakfast, which guests can take either in the dining area or outside in the garden. She also accommodates requests for low-fat, restricted, or vegetarian meals and also serves afternoon wine and cheese. The inn is proximate to four major 18-hole golf courses and the Lakes Basin recreation area. Note: Owner may be difficult to reach.

© KEN CASTLE

main sitting room of Molly's Bed & Breakfast in Clio

Policies: Pets are permitted (innkeeper has two dogs). Smoking is prohibited. There is a minimum stay of two nights required on weekends and holiday periods.

Rates: $$–$$$ including breakfast.

Contact: Molly's Bed and Breakfast, Main St., Clio, CA; 530/836-4436, fax 530/836-4432; website: www.mollysb-n-b.com.

Pullman House

If you're a train buff, this comfortable railroad-themed bed-and-breakfast in downtown Portola (50 miles northeast of Truckee) will put you on the right track for a little history. Just a stone's throw from the famous Portola Railroad Museum—with its working diesel locomotives, some of which you can drive—the Pullman was recently refurbished by owners George and Jan Breitwieser, who acquired it in 1993. The building, originally constructed in 1910 and operat-

ed as a hotel and boardinghouse (and, according to some, a bordello), offers six rooms—two downstairs and four upstairs—all with private bath, television, and telephones. Three of the units have queen-sized beds, one has a king, one has twins, and the sixth has a queen-sized and a king-sized. Each room is named after a different rail company, and all have a welcome blackboard slate on the door inscribed with the name of the guest.

From the upstairs windows and a large deck, you can see the museum as well as the Middle Fork of the Feather River and the Union Pacific Railroad switching yard. Railroad memorabilia, including old lanterns, Pullman hats, and paintings, are cleverly arranged among the period-style furnishings. There's a parlor with a television, a VCR, music, board games, and puzzles, as well as an upstairs sitting room with a TV/VCR. Breakfast is served family-style in a small dining room, where the walls have been outfitted with a model train that circles while you eat. The hot meal might include meat, eggs, waffles, pancakes, biscuits, toast, fresh fruit, and juice. The town of Portola encompasses a few shops and restaurants, and it is close to good fishing at Lake Davis and golf in Graeagle.

Policies: No pets or smoking are allowed. Children are accepted.

Rates: $–$$. Major credit cards are accepted.

Contact: Pullman House, 256 Commercial St., Portola, CA 96122; 530/832-0107; website: www.psln.com/pullman.

Sierra Shangri-La

One minute you're driving along winding Highway 49 west of Sierra City and the next minute you're slamming on your brakes to see what that was all about. It's the place you glimpsed briefly—an incredibly high perch above the rollicking Yuba River. It takes a while to find the small access road that crosses the river, but wow! When you stand on the balcony of the main lodge, you have a breathtaking view of the river gushing rapidly over giant boulders just below you. The lodge and its nearby cabins are nestled into verdant riparian forest, and this indeed is a Shangri-la of natural beauty.

Innkeepers Fran and Frank Carter operate a truly unique property. It includes a bed-and-breakfast with three rooms, private baths, and a common balcony, and seven housekeeping cottages with kitchens, four of them ensconced on the banks of the Yuba. One, the very private "honeymoon" cottage, has a deck that overlooks the river and Jim Crow Creek. The other cottages are of varying sizes, accommodating from two to eight people; each has a full kitchen, a private bath, a shower, a spacious deck, an individual patio with a barbecue, and potbellied or Franklin stove. B&B rooms come with a deluxe continental breakfast served in your room. And there's a Great Room for meetings, seminars, reunions, weddings, and retreats. The inn is close to the magnificent Sierra Buttes (hiking to the top of them is a popular outing), the Lakes Basin region, and quaint Gold Country towns, and is about a 75-minute drive northwest of Truckee on Highway 49.

Policies: No pets or smoking. Children accepted.

Rates: $–$$$. Major credit cards accepted. Weekly rates available. Open April 1–Jan. 1.

Contact: Sierra Shangri-La, P.O. Box 285, Downieville, CA 95936; 530/289-3455; website: www.sierrashangrila.com.

Sierra Valley Lodge

Just 33 miles north of Truckee is the sleepy town of Calpine, which is easy to miss since it's sequestered in the trees off Highway 89. If you stop to explore, or to have a bite to eat, you find the Sierra Valley Lodge, a delightful discovery. The locals know that the lodge has one of the best steak houses in the region, as well as occasional entertainment that may run the gamut from a small band in the lounge to a cowboy poetry reading in a 2,000-square-foot music hall. This multipurpose room features a stone fireplace, a hardwood dance floor, and its own stage.

Beyond that impressive facility, surprising for a town so small, is a cozy overnight lodge with 12 guest rooms. The rooms themselves are nothing fancy, just motel-style units with comfortable beds, varying from one or two queens to kings. But the hallway is a work of art. Previous owners created a series of three-dimensional facades along the walls, and these include a cave, a caboose, a jail, a field, and a forest. Each room is named after a tree. Once a year, on the last weekend in July, the lodge is the site of the Calpine Kit 'n Caboodle, a gathering that includes a chili cookoff, entertainment, an arts and crafts fair, and other merriment. No doubt about it, the kids will love this place. And it goes easy on the pocketbook. New owner Joe Canavero acquired the property in late 1999.

Rates: $. Major credit cards are accepted.

Contact: Sierra Valley Lodge, P.O. Box 115, Calpine, CA 96124; 530/994-3367 or 800/858-0322.

Twenty Mile House

Once a stagecoach stop, this attractive red-brick inn (built in 1854) is the ultimate haven for fly fishers who can virtually cast to the Middle Fork of the Feather River from the backyard. The building is in an idyllic setting, with a lovely yard, a covered porch, and a wonderful time machine called the General Store. Inside this large, detached structure, built in 1923, is a potbellied stove, counters, wood floors, shelves lined with collectibles, and rich memories of an unhurried, bygone era. The store is a favorite haunt for anglers returning from a day on the river, a place where they can sip coffee and tell whoppers.

The inn has been carefully restored, and it is richly appointed with decorative fretwork, hand-crafted beams, and carved Victorian furnishings. There are four rooms in the main house and three cabins on the creek. The Parlor Room, off the main porch, has an aristocratic ambience with a library of vintage books, a fireplace, and a double brass bed. It's a comfortable unit, including a full bath with tub and shower, with subdued natural lighting. The Trading Post Room is cheery and bright and is dressed up in a Western theme. It has a queen bed and a single, a seating area, a private bath with shower, and an

outside entrance from the porch. Upstairs are two large adjacent attic rooms with full bath, one with king bed, the other with two twins. The Creekside Cottage has a delightful king bed, surrounded by windows, and is cantilevered over the creek. It also has a double room, a living room, dining area and well-stocked kitchen. The Northfield Cabin sleeps six in three bedrooms that include a king, double, and two twins. It has a large deck, living room with fireplace, and two bathrooms.

Proprietor Barbara Gage, who lives on-site, serves a full breakfast on a large wooden table with benches; meals might include German pancakes with lingonberries, eggs Benedict, breakfast burritos, hot muffins, and scones. The inn has a mile of private river access, and Gage frequently offers fly-fishing seminars. One shortcoming is that trains pass frequently on the Union Pacific Railroad tracks just behind the house. Twenty Mile House is about an hour's drive north of Truckee.

Policies: Children are okay, but pets and smoking are prohibited.

Rates: $$$.

Contact: Twenty Mile House, Old Cromberg Rd., Cromberg, CA 96103; 530/836-0375; website: www.graeagle.com/marketplace/twentymilehouse.

Yuba River Inn

Imagine a handful of rustic cabins scattered across 20 acres of forest, with a short walk to the North Fork of the Yuba River or to the historic community of Sierra City—this is the essence of a mountain getaway. The inn recently came under new ownership, and it offers 10 cabins, seven with full kitchens, bedding, a private bath with a shower, and built-in barbecue. Two of the cabins, Ponderosa and Aspen, are brand new and are closest to the river's edge; these have two bedrooms each, a front room/kitchen combination, a private patio, and extra large showers. These units are great for families, since they sleep four to six people. The other cabins, situated on a hill above the river, can sleep two to four people. Pets are permitted as long as they are leashed.

© KEN CASTLE

Twenty Mile House

The inn is situated near great fishing (on one-third of a mile of river frontage) and great hiking (near the Sierra Buttes). The Yuba River Inn is on Highway 49 in Sierra City, and is open year-round.

Rates: $–$$$. Cash and checks are welcome, but credit cards are not accepted.
Contact: Yuba River Inn, 510 Main St., P.O. Box 236, Sierra City, CA 96125; 530/862-1122; website: www.yubariverinn.com.

Property Management and Rental Agencies

A recent development at Lake Tahoe is the arrival of a new breed of professional property management companies. In times past, it seemed that everything in the rental market was provided by mom-and-pop realtors who were never in their offices when you had a problem. The old system (and it's still practiced!) is to throw you the keys and a pile of towels. The new system is to have a plethora of guest services, including 24-hour emergency repair service, a staffed central check-in facility, a computerized reservation system, a maintenance department that clears snow from parking lots and walkways, a concierge service, and a bottle of wine in the refrigerator. With so many of the accoutrements of a fine hotel (everything but room service), how can you lose?

There are a few things to know when renting a condominium or home. If possible, try to obtain a spec sheet with photographs of the interior and a description of amenities. Be sure to ask about cleaning charges: Are they extra or included in the price of the rentals? If damage deposits are collected, how soon is your money returned? If you're looking for a ski rental, ask about access to the property: Is it on a steep hill with potentially icy roads? Is the snow cleared expeditiously after a storm? How quickly are repairs made if the water pipes freeze or the stove stops working? Also, be aware of the liberal descriptions of sleeping quarters. When a brochure says "Sleeps eight," this may mean a queen-sized bed (for two), an open loft with four bunks (that's another four), and a miserable sofa bed in the living room (that's two more). If you're a family with two adults and four kids, that may be fine. But if your group consists of three couples, that's not so fine. The other im-

portant caveat relates to the words "lake view." Everybody wants one, of course, but there's been some big-time disappointment when people discover that their so-called view is mostly obscured by trees or other buildings.

LAKE TAHOE (ALL AREAS)
Lake Tahoe Accommodations
This is the largest vacation rental operation at the lake, with offices in four locations (South Lake Tahoe, Kingsbury, Tahoe City, and Incline Village), a central reservations system, more than 400 properties including 200 homes, and around-the-clock service. Owner Jim Morris has established a truly professional company with high standards of quality, location, and cleanliness. Virtually every type of property imaginable is in his inventory: small cottages and cabins nestled in the trees, elegant homes on the lake, rustic and spacious chalets next to ski areas, and immaculate and lavishly furnished condominiums. The rental properties can sleep from two to 20, and many of them have unique features such as designer furnishings, private piers, hot tubs, game rooms with billiard or Ping-Pong tables, big-screen home theaters, rumpus rooms for kids, garages or carports, or large decks with sweeping views of the lake. Some units are approved for pets. I've personally inspected more than 25 of these properties and have come away amazed at the variety and quality. Morris has a rating system, color fliers for each property, and a large staff of reservationists. What is most impressive about his rentals is their immaculate condition. All linens and towels are provided, cleaning is included in the rental price, all units have full kitchens, and check-in/check-out is always handled

TAHOE'S FAMOUS RENT-A-MANSION

Have you ever dreamed of staying in a luxurious mountain chalet that is normally reserved for celebrities? You can do so at Lake Tahoe.

Throughout the region, there are hundreds of homes for rent, from palatial lakeside estates to cozy mountain cabins. If you're planning a family reunion, a gathering of friends, an executive work retreat, or even a wedding, there are places that will meet your needs.

Most homes are available through property management companies or local realtors, though some can be rented directly from their owners, who may or may not be occupants. You can find properties that will sleep 20 or more people, even small ranches that can accommodate up to 50!

Perhaps the most famous rental property at the lake is "Bob's at the Beach," a three-story, 7,000-square-foot nautical-styled fantasy that is in an exclusive, gated section of the Tahoe Keys residential area of South Lake Tahoe. Sharing a peninsula with a dozen other multimillion-dollar homes, this particular abode, which was built in the 1980s by a local diamond merchant, the late Bob Lindner, has seen its share of high-profile occupants.

Guests have included Charlie Sheen, Diana Ross, Pat Benatar, Kenny Rogers, Natalie Cole, Boys II Men, The Judds, Robert Culp, Barry Manilow, Martin Lawrence, Roseanne Barr, Patrick Stewart, and even the prince of Malaysia. Often, the entertainers were in town performing at one of the Stateline casino showrooms.

Lindner made his connection with Hollywood by being known as the "jeweler to the stars." He and his two sons, who now manage the property, crafted beautiful, custom bracelets and pendants for Sammy Davis Jr., pianist Liberace, singer Engelbert Humperdinck, comedian Rich Little, and even former President Gerald Ford. So, as you might expect, "Bob's at the Beach" is definitely geared to the party set; in fact, it has been featured on television's *Lifestyles of the Rich and Famous.*

The list of amenities includes an indoor swimming pool and waterfall on the lower level; a bar that is fashioned from the hull of a 1949 Chris Craft "woody"; a "Habitat" that drenches your body in simulated sun, steam, or rain; a baby grand Yamaha player piano with an endless supply of music diskettes; a home theater with a 10-foot screen that descends from the ceiling; a commercial-grade kitchen with a pizza oven and every cooking appliance known to man; and a master bedroom suite that features a large round bed, a whirlpool tub for two, his and hers bathrooms, and a cheerful solarium that overlooks the lake. In fact, three of the four bedrooms are minisuites with gas fireplaces, wet bars, TVs, microwaves, and other features that make them self-contained.

The walls are festooned with photographs of the guest celebrities, and Lindner left one signature item of his craft—a trash bin in the kitchen that has the word "Trash" written on the door in diamond studs. The interior of the home is lavish, with extensive use of glass, mirror, tile, marble, copper, brass, and mahogany. One of the downstairs commodes has a submarine hatch as a doorway, and the front door handles are shaped like a ship's wheel.

There's more. The outdoor features include a private sandy beach, a hot tub, a large patio with barbecue and food preparation facilities, and a boat dock. Every room has a deck overlooking the lake or Tahoe Keys Marina. Not surprisingly, the people who rent this place usually find it difficult to leave for such seemingly mundane pursuits as boating, skiing, golfing, or dining.

So how much is it to splurge on this kind of decadence? Prices range $1,200–,800 a night (2001 rates), plus cleaning fees, with lower rates during the winter season. If four couples split the costs (the home sleeps eight adults), the expense is about equal to four luxury hotel rooms—but with many more features and, of course, the exclusivity of a private estate. (Among the policies, weddings and outside parties are not allowed, and minimal rental periods are required.)

Information: Bob's at the Beach, P.O. Box 8096, South Lake Tahoe, CA 96158; 530/541-3731; website: www.bobsatthebeach.com.

nearby, at one of four offices around the lake. In 2002, the company acquired a major Incline Village property management company, BRAT Resort Properties, and incorporated much of that inventory into its overall offerings. All properties are described on the company's website, and all can be booked online.

Rates: $$–$$$$.

Contact: Lake Tahoe Accommodations, 2048 Dunlap Dr., Stes. 3 and 4, South Lake Tahoe, CA 96150; 530/544-3234 or 800/544-3234; email: lta@TahoeAccommodations.com; website: www.tahoeres.com.

TRUCKEE/DONNER

Martis Valley Associates

Rents 25 to 30 homes and condominiums, mostly at Northstar-at-Tahoe resort.

Rates: $$–$$$$.

Contact: Martis Valley Associates, 10880 Hwy. 267, Truckee, CA 96161; 530/587-1515 or 800/587-2070; website: www.martisvalley.com.

Martis Valley Vacation Rentals

Owned by Dick and Sharon Hadsell, who are both licensed real estate brokers, this company has more than 10 years of experience renting and managing vacation homes and condominiums. Inventory runs at 120 to 130 units, with both short-term and long-term rentals available. One 5,000-square-foot house on the Northstar Golf Course can sleep 23 people. Cleaning/damage deposits are required on all properties, and no pets or smoking are allowed in units. Maintains a 24-hour answering service.

Rates: $$–$$$$.

Contact: Martis Valley Vacation Rentals, 10015 Palisades Dr., Truckee, CA 96161; 530/587-4500 or 800/287-7685; website: www.mvvr.com.

SQUAW VALLEY/ ALPINE MEADOWS

Squaw Valley Accommodations

Owned by the Poulsen family, the founders of Squaw Valley USA, this company has about 60 properties, including homes, condos, and the Christy Inn (the original Poulsen family compound). The agency provides several upscale properties with fine mountain views, all within a short drive or walk of the Squaw Valley resort. Both short-term and ski leases are available. Linens and towels are included, the cleaning deposit is separate, and there is 24-hour emergency service. The agency office is open 9 A.M.–5 P.M. daily, and after-hours arrangements can be made for key pickup.

Rates: $$–$$$$.

Contact: Squaw Valley Accommodations, 1604 Christy Ln./P.O. Box 2008, Olympic Valley, CA 96146; 530/583-3451 or 800/330-3451; email: svrealty@ltol.com.

Alpine Rental Group

Owners Linda Morris and Geoff Feige offer about 45 short- and long-term rentals, mostly houses, in Alpine Meadows, Squaw Valley, Tahoe City, and the West Shore. Some larger houses can sleep more than 20, and some unadvertised estates are available for special functions such as weddings. No smoking is permitted in any of the properties, but some allow well-behaved pets. Damage deposits range $300–500.

Contact: Alpine Rental Group, 150 Alpine Meadows Rd., Alpine Meadows, CA 96146; 530/583-3550; email: info@alpinerentalgroup.com; website: www.alpinerentalgroup.com.

TAHOE CITY/TAHOE VISTA/ CARNELIAN BAY

Hauserman Rental Group

This locally owned company has been in business since the mid-1960s, and it offers more than 120 short-term house and condo rentals, as well as 60 long-term (four- to five-month) ski leases in the winter. The area covered ranges from Tahoma on the West Shore to Kings Beach on the North Shore, and more than half the properties are homes. The rental group offers variety and luxury, from beachfront rentals to budget condominiums. Some properties are approved for pets. On a rating system from 1 to 10, the lowest-scored offering is 6.5. Linens and towels are provided, property description leaflets are available, and 24-hour emergency service is available. The office is open 9 A.M.–5 P.M. daily; after-hours arrangements are made for key pickup. The minimum rental period, during nonholidays, is two days.

Rates: $$–$$$$.

Contact: Hauserman Rental Group, 475 N. Lake Blvd./P.O. Box 1901, Tahoe City, CA 96145; 530/583-3793 or 800/208-2463; website: www.enjoytahoe.com.

INCLINE VILLAGE/CRYSTAL BAY

Coldwell Banker Realty

Offering more than 75 homes and condos in the Incline Village area, this agency's units can include private beaches, piers, tennis courts, saunas, pools, recreation rooms, and covered parking.

Rates: $$–$$$$.

Contact: Incline Village Coldwell Banker Realty, 120 Country Club Dr., Ste. 3/P.O. Box 3549, Incline Village, NV 89450; 775/831-4800 or 800/572-5009; website: www.cbvillagerealty.com.

Sierra Vacation Rentals

This agency offers more than 60 condos, houses, and studio units with phones, televisions, kitchens, fireplaces, some lake views, linen, and maid service. Other conveniences include tennis courts, saunas, spas, swimming pools, and rec rooms.

Rates: $$–$$$$.

Contact: Sierra Vacation Rentals, 7252 N. Lake Blvd., Ste. 101/P.O. Box 37, Carnelian Bay, CA 96140; 530/546-8222 or 800/521-6656; website: www.sierravacations.com.

Vacation Station

This property management company, operating since 1981, offers rental condos and houses exclusively in Incline Village/Crystal Bay, an upscale and highly desirable community on the northeast shore of the lake. Incline is full of multimillion-dollar beachfront estates, but you can forget about renting those because the owners don't need the money. Still, it's comforting to know that you can rent something in the neighborhood, as well as having access to the immaculate private beaches, tennis courts, golf courses,

the ski area, and the recreation center of Incline. Vacation Station offers more than 115 individually owned condos and homes, varying from budget units to deluxe lakefront affairs, some with hot tubs and lake or mountain views. Apart from the rental, the company charges a cleaning fee and holds a credit card number as a damage deposit. Daily maid service or trash and towel takeout is optional. The rental office is open only during daytime hours, seven days a week, but guests checking in during the evening will receive instructions for key pickup.

Rates: $$–$$$$.

Contact: Vacation Station, 110 Country Club Dr./P.O. Box 7180, Incline Village, NV 89452; 775/831-3664 or 800/841-7443; website: www.vacationstation.com.

SOUTH LAKE TAHOE/STATELINE

Accommodation Station Rentals

Selection of more than 75 rental homes and condos in the South Shore area.

Rates: $$–$$$$.

Contact: Accommodation Station Rentals, 2516 Lake Tahoe Blvd., South Lake Tahoe, CA 96150; 530/542-5850 or 800/344-9364; email: astation @aol.com; website: www.tahoelodging.com.

Almost Home Retreats

Small, family-run business rents three large properties in South Lake Tahoe, including a one-acre lodge with cabins that will sleep up to 95 people. Business is oriented to church groups, family reunions, weddings, anniversaries, and special events.

Rates: $$$–$$$$.

Contact: Almost Home Retreats, 532 Emerald Bay Rd., South Lake Tahoe, CA 96150; 800/ 700-2022; website: www.groupretreats.com.

Coldwell Banker McKinney and Associates

This well-known local real estate agency offers more than 140 homes, condos, and cabins in the South Shore area. You can call for a free video or view properties on the Internet.

Rates: $$–$$$$.

Contact: Coldwell Banker McKinney and Associates, 2196 Lake Tahoe Blvd., South Lake Tahoe, CA 96150; 530/542-0557 or 800/748-6857; website: www.stayintahoe.com.

Lake Tahoe Lodging

Lake Tahoe Lodging offers more than 70 units, including condos, homes, cabins, lakefront and lakeview homes, and celebrity and corporate retreats. One unique feature is a concierge service that arranges ski rentals, discount car rentals, show reservations, lake excursions, and adventure tours.
Rates: $$$–$$$$.
Contact: Lake Tahoe Lodging, 212 Elks Point Dr., Zephyr Cove, NV 89448; 775/588-5253 or 800/654-5253; website: www.laketahoelodging.com.

Tahoe Keys Resort

This well-established business specializes in rentals of condominiums, homes, and villas in the Tahoe Keys, a large South Lake Tahoe residential community designed so that every property has frontage on water, either on an artificial channel that snakes through the area or on the lake itself. The company offers around 240 properties; 150 of them are in the keys and the rest are found in other areas of South Shore. Rentals vary from inexpensive, modestly furnished condominiums to million-dollar luxury homes behind locked gates. There are several moderately priced homes with unusual architecture and interior layouts. Plus, there's the convenience of a full-service marina and gourmet restaurant, along with parks, tennis courts, and other recreational amenities. Outside of the keys, the company rents a large, elegantly furnished rustic lodge called Echo Creek Mountain Ranch, suitable for groups of up to 24 people. This is a quality operation run by longtime businessman and civic leader Tom Davis. The check-in office is near Tahoe Keys Marina.
Rates: $$–$$$$.
Contact: Tahoe Keys Resort/Lake Tahoe Vacation Rentals, 599 Tahoe Keys Blvd., Ste. B2/P.O. Box 20088, South Lake Tahoe, CA 96151;

530/544-5397 or 800/698-2463; website: www.tahoevacationguide.com or www.calltahoe.com.

Selective Accommodations

Selective Accommodations specializes in more than 100 ski condominiums, cabins, homes, and executive residences near Heavenly. Amenities include fully equipped kitchens, fireplaces, private whirlpool spas, lakefront or liftside locations, lake and mountain views, televisions, VCRs, and stereos.
Rates: $$–$$$$.
Contact: Selective Accommodations, 188 U.S. 50/P.O. Box 6090, Lake Tahoe, NV 89449; 775/588-8258 or 800/242-5387; email: rentals@tahoe-estates.com; website: www.tahoe-estates.com.

Tahoe Management Company

Operating since 1982, this company offers close to 150 one- to eight-bedroom condos, cabins, and homes, from modest to luxurious. Has ski-in/ski-out lodgings and lakeviews. Many units have fireplaces, hot tubs, kitchens, and pools.
Rates: $$–$$$$.
Contact: Tahoe Management Company, 601 Hwy. 50, Zephyr Cove, NV 89448; 775/588-4504 or 800/624-3887; email: tahoemgt@aol.com; website: ww.tahoevacations.com.

Tahoe Rental Connection

In excess of 100 properties are in inventory with this agency, including houses, cabins, town houses, and honeymoon retreats. Tahoe Rental Connection has been in business since 1981. Properties come with linens and towels, and cleaning is included in the price.
Rates: $$–$$$$.
Contact: Tahoe Rental Connection, 2241 James St., Ste. 3, South Lake Tahoe, CA 96150; 530/542-2777 or 800/542-2100; website: www.tahoerentalconnection.com.

Tamarack Rentals

Offers more than 75 properties including condos, chalets. and cabins throughout the South Shore. Moderate accommodations for 2–14 people have fireplaces, color TVs, and full kitchens.

TAHOE ACCOMMODATIONS

Rates: $$–$$$.
Contact: Tamarack Rentals,3816 Pioneer Trail, P.O. Box 5747, South Lake Tahoe, CA 96157; 530/541-2595 or 866/251-2827; website: www.tamarackrentals.com.

FEATHER RIVER COUNTRY/ LAKES BASIN

Graeagle Meadows Vacation Rentals

Offers more than 65 condominium units around Graeagle Meadows Golf Course.
Rates: $$$–$$$$.
Contact: Graeagle Meadows Vacation Rentals, Hwy. 89, Graeagle, CA 96103; 530/836-1100 or 800/800-6282; website: www.graeagle.com/meadows.

Graeagle Vacation Rentals

A rental inventory of more than 40 cabins, homes, and town homes in the Graeagle Meadows, Plumas Pines, and Whitehawk Ranch resort areas is controlled by this agency. Packages that include golf and tee-time reservations are also available.
Rates: $$$–$$$$.

Contact: Graeagle Properties, 26 Poplar Valley Rd./P.O. Box 100, Graeagle, CA 96103; 530/836-2525 or 800/836-0269.

Plumas Pines Realty

This agency rents nearly 60 homes and town houses at Plumas Pines and Whitehawk golf courses. Plumas Pines rentals include access to tennis courts and a swimming pool on the resort property.
Rates: $$$–$$$$.
Contact: Plumas Pines Realty, 307 Poplar Valley Rd./P.O. Box 879, Blairsden, CA 96103; 530/836-0444 or 800/655-4440.

River Pines Realty

Offering about 30 rental properties, River Pines Realty's holdings include condominiums at Plumas Pines and Whitehawk and private homes in Graeagle. Some packages come with golf and tee-time reservations. The agency is at River Pines Resort.
Rates: $$$$.
Contact: River Pines Realty, 8296 Hwy. 89, Blairsden, CA/P.O. Box 249, Clio, CA 96106; 530/836-0313.

Mountain Resorts and Lodges

If you're looking for a rustic mountain cabin with a wood-burning stove and a front porch from which to watch the sunset—and no television or telephone within sight or sound—you'll find it in the Lake Tahoe region. If your style runs more to the contemporary, with a modern suite overlooking an 18-hole golf course or a vibrant ski area, you'll find that here, too. If you're seeking atmosphere, such as having a great lakefor fishing or boating practically at your front door, several resorts will fill that bill.

Although at first glance the Lake Tahoe area appears to contain little more than a few high-rise casino hotels and a multitude of lakefront motels, there is more here than meets the eye. Some of the best resorts are not even on the lake; they are tucked away in mountain valleys and at the end of narrow dirt roads. On Lake Tahoe itself, there are two trends: the first combines modern conveniences with a woodsy but gentrified environment, while the other celebrates rustic simplicity and an emphasis on

Ice Lakes Lodge

old-fashioned family togetherness. Each approach has its following.

One way to choose a resort is to determine which activities appeal to you most. If golf is your passion, you probably won't be happy in an isolated mountain cabin. If hiking, fishing, and mountain biking are your main pursuits, you may want to be away from the crowds and the main roads. Check the brochures and descriptions carefully; a lot of places that call themselves resorts may be just motels with fancy names and very few on-site amenities. While the definition of a resort may be somewhat nebulous, those listed here include lakefront and riverfront lodges or major properties with a multitude of activities such as on-site golf, skiing, fishing, or cycling.

There are four major resort regions in the area: Lake Tahoe, with its proximity to boating, cycling trails, and beaches; Carson Pass, with its emphasis on history, nature, and hiking; the Lakes Basin area, with its unique string of 1920s-style small lodges and magnificent hiking trails; and the Feather River Country, with its golf courses, historic towns, and scenic river frontage. Moreover, Lake Tahoe encompasses several subregions, including Donner Lake, Echo Lakes, Fallen Leaf Lake, and Angora Lakes. Although not as crowded as Tahoe during the summer, all of these places do brisk business, and accommodations can be difficult to secure during peak seasons.

Some truly unique lodges exist in the Carson Pass and Lakes Basin areas, both within an hour's drive of Tahoe. Along Highway 88 (south of Lake Tahoe) some of the lodges have their roots in the pioneering days of the mid-1800s, when Kit Carson forged a route—later known as the Mormon-Emigrant Trail—that brought thousands of settlers across the Sierra to California. Some of the small trading posts that sprang up to serve these westward-bound im-

There are four major resort regions in the area: Lake Tahoe, with its proximity to boating, cycling trails, and beaches; Carson Pass, with its emphasis on history, nature, and hiking; the Lakes Basin area, with its unique string of 1920s-style small lodges and magnificent hiking trails; and the Feather River Country, with its golf courses, historic towns, and scenic river frontage.

migrants later became resorts. In the Lakes Basin country north of Tahoe, the miners, loggers, and railroad workers who established camps in the area opened the door for the resorts that materialized in the early 1900s.

It can be difficult to book rooms and cabins in Tahoe's outlying areas. A short summer season and limited accommodations put these places in high demand; typically, they have long waiting lists, often a year or two in advance. The seven rustic lodges along the Gold Lake Road from Bassett's Station to Graeagle, for instance, have fewer than 80 cabins among them. Most of these lodges are leased from the U.S. Forest Service and are restricted in their ability to expand or improve their properties, so demand always outstrips supply. Some families have been coming to these places for decades, and repeat business runs 80 percent or higher.

The best chance of getting a spot is to book in the early or late season (May–June or September–October) or engage in the lottery system for new arrivals. These months can be delightful, or they can be rainy, snowy, and cold; you can never predict weather patterns in the Sierra. Another thing to know about these lodges is that they are mostly family-run businesses, often handed down through the generations. Thus, attitudes toward guests can range from folksy to frosty, and you should not expect the kind of management efficiencies you'd find at a major resort. You may encounter the occasional cantankerous soul who ought to find some other line of work. However, most of the owners are laid-back and accommodating. These individuals run their lodges out of a sense of tradition or obligation, or just because they like living in the mountains.

Note: Many of these lodges require a minimum one-week stay during the peak summer months.

TRUCKEE/DONNER

Royal Gorge Wilderness Lodge

Situated in the heart of America's largest cross-country ski resort, the Wilderness Lodge is a rustic overnight retreat with a reputation for serving gourmet French country-style cuisine. At its doorstep is a trail system that extends for 203 miles over 9,172 acres, so vast that most skiers can hope to see only a small part of it during a week's stay. The 35 private rooms on the first and second levels of this knotty-pine lodge are small and spartan, and all share adequate but not deluxe bathrooms down the hall. Showers (along with a hot tub and sauna) are in a separate building outside; it's best to time your visit there for the middle of the day, so you don't have to run out in the cold to shower.

Making up for those inconveniences, however, are the spacious and posh common areas, including a huge parlor with overstuffed couches, a fireplace, books, games, videos, and views of a frozen lake. Breakfast and lunch are served buffet-style and dinner is served at your table by candlelight in a large dining room. The youthful employees, representing various nationalities, are exceptionally courteous and helpful. All guests arriving at night transfer to the lodge in a motorized sleigh from the Summit Day Lodge, and many ski out while luggage is taken separately. In addition to the lodge, two cabins with full bath were recently added to the compound. The lodge is open only in winter and is on the Donner Summit, off I-80 at the Soda Springs/Norden exit and one mile east of Old Highway 40.

Rooms: 35 private rooms, some with doubles, doubles and bunks, and bunks only; a sauna and hot tub; shared toilets and wash basins and a separate building for shared showers.

Amenities: The Lake Lounge, with games, books, a fireplace, and a self-service bar; a full dining room with buffets and table service (dinner only); a ski school; and a trail network with 90 trails and 330 kilometers of machine-set track.

Policies: Toddlers are not recommended.

Rates: $$$–$$$$. Rates are quoted per person and include all meals, skiing passes, lessons, and accommodations. Rates for children are generally less. Major credit cards are accepted.

Contact: Royal Gorge Wilderness Lodge, P.O. Box 1100, Soda Springs, CA 95728; 530/426-3871 or 800/500-3871 or 800/666-3871; website: www.royalgorge.com.

TAHOE CITY/WEST SHORE

Meeks Bay Resort

With an attractive beach, a protected cove, and reasonably priced boat launching, this is a great spot on Lake Tahoe for a summer family vacation. Ten miles south of Tahoe City on Highway 89, the site was once used by the Washoe Indians as a camp for fishing and foraging, and recently it was acquired by the Washoe Tribe of Nevada and California, which began major renovations of lodging units, the campground, and the marina. In the 1920s, the resort was established by Oswald Kehlet, who built a large home bordered by the lake on three sides. The residence was later owned by William Hewlett, co-founder of the Hewlett-Packard Corporation, and then by San Francisco billionaire Gordon Getty, who used it as a summer home. Today, the Kehlet Mansion is a popular rental for groups—it includes seven bedrooms, three baths, and an observation deck over the water. But there are 20 additional units at the resort, including one- and two-story cabins and condominiums, most of which have lake views. In recent years, management has been systematically upgrading the rooms.

Kids love the beach, where they can find a roped-off swimming lagoon and a variety of water toys for rent. The resort also operates a campground right next to busy Highway 89. A boutique and notions store and snack stand serve the beach crowd. Meeks Bay is close to major hiking and cycling trails, and to the boating mecca of Emerald Bay. You'll find a trailhead for several alpine lakes in Desolation Wilderness just across the street. Meeks Bay Resort is open June–September.

Rooms: 21 one- and two-story cabins, lakefront condominiums, and the Kehlet Mansion. Larger condos include big living rooms and fireplaces, separate bedrooms, full kitchens, and bathrooms with tubs/showers. Two-story cabins have open beams with upstairs sleeping lofts and downstairs bedrooms, and all cabins have kitchens. Other features include some fireplaces, eating utensils, rollaways, cribs, and special linen services.

Amenities: 28 campsites, 110-slip marina, snack bar, visitor center, picnic grounds, large sand beach, showers, laundry facilities, nonpowerboat rentals, and launching facilities.

Policies: No pets are allowed. One-week minimum stay required in high season. Maximum stay is two weeks. All lodging facilities are non-smoking.

Rates: $$–$$$$. Credit cards are accepted.

Contact: Meeks Bay Resort, 7941 Emerald Bay Rd. (Hwy. 89), Meeks Bay, CA; P.O. Box 787, Tahoma, CA 96142; 530/525-6946 or 877/326-3357; website: www.meeksbayresort.com.

SOUTH SHORE/STATELINE

Angora Lakes Resort

Here's one of those off-the-beaten-path resorts that never advertises. Although it's a bit difficult to find—just above Fallen Leaf Lake on a dirt road—the resort is a little piece of paradise that constantly has a waiting list. The lakes are twin alpine jewels that are popular with local cyclists, hikers, and swimmers, and there is considerable day use, especially at Upper Angora Lake, where the resort operates a beach, a rowboat rental concession, and a snack stand, which is famous for its homemade lemonade.

The upper lake is in a granite-rimmed bowl flanked by Echo and Angora Peaks and was named after a herd of Angora goats that were pastured here by homesteader Nathan Gilmore in the 1870s. Lower Angora Lake offers several privately leased cabins.

The resort was opened in 1921 by the Hildinger family, and today it is operated by Jim and Gloria Hildinger, who offer eight rustic cabins, each with electricity, hot showers, and chemical toilets. Every cabin has a different layout, varying from studios to two-bedroom configurations. The lake, about one-third of a mile

across, provides swimming from a beach of decomposed granite, which is OK for bare feet. A snack shed, with tables and chairs on a porch, sells cold drinks, sandwiches, ice cream, and candy. The resort is in such demand for overnight stays that the Hildingers say they are backlogged with demand. The best advice is to book a year or two in advance.

To reach the resort, take Highway 89 north from the South Shore, turn left on Fallen Leaf Road, then take the first left up the hill and watch for a poorly marked dirt road on the summit (Forest Service Road 1214). Follow this road along the ridge to the unused Angora Fire Lookout, and park in the lot—there's room here for about 100 cars, but it fills fast on weekends. From this point, you can walk one-half mile on a hiking trail to Upper Angora Lake. Or arriving guests and their luggage can be picked up by a truck using a private road parallel to the trail.

Rooms: Eight cabins, each accommodating 4–6 people. These are housekeeping units, and guests must bring their own linens and towels; there is no maid service or washing machine available. No meals are included with overnight stays. The season is mid-June–mid-September.

Amenities: A swimming beach, 10 rowboats for rent, nearby hiking and cycling trails, and a snack stand that operates daily.

Policies: The minimum rental is one week.

Rates: $$$. Credit cards are not accepted.

Contact: Angora Lakes Resort, Angora Ridge Rd., South Lake Tahoe, CA 96158; 530/541-2092 (summer) or 530/577-3593 (winter).

Camp Richardson Resort

If a resort can be measured by its energy output, this place would score number one in wattage. This is the hangout for the younger crowd on the South Shore. One reason may be the constant beat of live music from the outdoor deck of the Beacon Restaurant, which is right on the beach. Another reason may be the ebb and flow of watercraft, which vary from rafts to ski boats and from parasailing runabouts to sightseeing cruisers. The large pier at the marina is constantly busy and seems to be a magnet for the sun worshippers who line the sparkling, white-sand beaches north and south of here.

Location is everything, and Richardson's—a vintage family-oriented resort established in the 1920s—is at the center of Tahoe's recreational universe. Its leeward site offers protection from winds as well as having the closest full-service marina to Emerald Bay. The resort is also on a popular paved bike trail, is within a short stroll of the famous Tallac Historic Site and its resident artists' colony, has a riding stable across the street, and is within four miles of the major hiking routes into Desolation Wilderness, including trailheads at Glen Alpine, Bayview, and Eagle Falls. Shopping, golf, and casinos are minutes away, and guests can hop on the inexpensive South Tahoe Trolley to reach most points of interest.

Accommodations at Richardson's include small rooms in a large, rustic lodge with bed and bath, a motel-type complex next to the beach with spacious rooms and baths, a lakeside condominium, nearly 40 cabins, and campgrounds for tents and RVs. The cabins, named after vintage automobiles, have the requisite knotty-pine ceilings and most amenities except televisions and telephones. They are tucked into a pleasant pine forest well off the main highway yet close to the beach. Recently, the resort has been renovating its cabins and has added a spa with a hot tub. It also overhauled the Great Room in the main lodge. Richardson's, a private concession on U.S. Forest Service land, is open year-round. In winter, a small cross-country ski center with trails along the beach and through the woods is available. In summer, there's a sports center with bike rentals and a climbing wall. Next door, the Tallac estates hold major events including musical presentations and art exhibitions.

Rooms: Lakefront cabins and condos, rustic ski cabins, hotel and inn rooms, and tent and RV campsites. Crib rentals and rollaways are available.

Amenities: The Beacon Restaurant, which offers lunch, dinner, Sunday brunch, private-party and banquet facilities, outdoor dining, and entertainment (during the summer only); ice cream parlor; deli, which serves breakfast and lunch; meeting/reception facility; children's playground;

RV and tent campground country store; gas station; casino shuttle bus; hiking and biking trails; bike-rental shops and tours; climbing wall; spa; tennis court; volleyball courts; cross-country skiing; charter and boat rentals; personal watercraft rentals; kayak and canoe rentals; water-ski school; inflatable raft tours; catamaran sailing cruises; personal watercraft rentals; launch ramp; and sandy beach. Horseback riding can be arranged through a nearby stable.

Policies: No pets are allowed.

Rates: $–$$$$. Credit cards are accepted.

Contact: Camp Richardson Resort, P.O. Box 9028, South Lake Tahoe, CA 96158; 530/541-1801 or 800/544-1801; website: www.camprichardson.com.

Echo Chalet

Echo Lake is close to South Lake Tahoe, but, like Angora Lakes, it's off the beaten path. Everyone who comes to the region should make an effort to visit this place. Nestled between high granite peaks, it is a truly magnificent body of water with a wealth of natural and recreational attractions. Take U.S. 50 west of South Lake Tahoe, then look for Echo Lake Road (a poorly marked right turn from the highway just west of Echo Summit) and drive through a residential area for two miles before reaching the lodge and marina.

One of the important trailheads into Desolation Wilderness begins at Upper Echo Lake, on the Pacific Crest Trail, and hikers can reach it via a boat taxi from Lower Echo Lake. Even if you don't trek into the backcountry, there's a marvelous three-mile, mostly level trail that follows the east rim of the lakes. Several attractive summer homes and cabins are sprinkled around the shoreline. Lower Echo Lake is a happening place; it has a launch ramp, a dock, sightseeing and rental boats, a store, a post office, and several housekeeping cabins. The cabins, called "Chaletlees," are weathered and basic, with knotty-pine interiors, and are on a shaded hillside overlooking the main lodge. Some have kitchenettes, small living rooms, and equally small bedrooms. The furniture and appliances in these units are old, although a few units have recently been remodelled. The biggest advantage of staying in the cabins is your proximity to the lake. The best accommodations at the lake are the few—and highly prized—summer homes that are occasionally available for rent, mostly by word of mouth.

Rooms: Nine housekeeping cabins (dishes and cooking utensils supplied) with beds, kitchenettes, living rooms, and balconies. There are no telephones or televisions. All units have electricity, hot and cold running water, and a bathroom with shower. Bedding and linens are provided, and a midweek cleaning is conducted for week-long stays. Most Chaletless are double units that share a common front deck. They require a short hike on an unlit footpath, so guests are advised to bring flashlights. Units 1 and 2 are next to the lodge, and face Lake Tahoe. Chaletlee 11 has been converted to a suite with a large front deck, full kitchen, and king-sized bed.

Amenities: A chalet store with groceries, fishing tackle, boat equipment, and ice cream fountain service; a picnic area with barbecues; a service station with fuel, boat and motor sales, and boat and motor service; sightseeing trips around both Echo Lakes; daily summer water taxi service to the Desolation Trailhead fishing boat rentals; a launch ramp; and overnight slips.

Rates: $$$. Usually rented on a weekly basis. Credit cards are accepted.

Contact: Echo Chalet, 9900 Echo Lakes Rd., Echo Lake, CA 95721; 530/659-7207; website: www.echochalet.com.

Hansen's Resort

Just a snowball's throw from the California entrance to Heavenly Ski Resort, this small, quaint lodge's assets include a tube and saucer hill, a big attraction for families with children. Owner "Little John" Foggitt, who hails from South Africa, offers six cabins and two motel rooms, all set among the pines on a rise south of U.S. 50. The cabins sleep from two to eight people, and all have kitchens, a private bath with a shower, and telephones. Two cabins are connected and can be used as one family unit; another cabin has two bedrooms and a sofa bed in the living room. Some units have fireplaces. There are no kitchens or telephones in the motel units. One caveat:

The hill leading to the resort is quite steep and can be icy in the winter, especially at night. In the summer, the peaceful, wooded surroundings offer an escape from the crowds and traffic, though the property is just a couple of minutes' drive to the lakeshore and five minutes' drive to the bustling Stateline casinos.

Rooms: Six cabins that sleep two to eight people, with kitchens, private bath and shower, and telephones. Two motel rooms are available.

Amenities: A hot tub (at extra cost); the saucer hill, which features banked and maintained runs and its own sliding equipment (no outside gear is allowed); and a snack shop selling hot and cold drinks and food.

Policies: A refundable kitchen deposit is required for all cabin rentals.

Rates: $–$$$$. Most credit cards are accepted.

Contact: Hansen's Resort, 1360 Ski Run Blvd./P.O. Box 316, South Lake Tahoe, CA 96156; 530/544-3361; website: www.hansensresort.com.

Zephyr Cove Resort

Mark Twain wrote about the "Washoe Zephyrs," the western winds that kick up many afternoons on the east side of the lake, especially in spring and fall. But this cove, a few miles north of Stateline, does have tranquil moments during which it is arguably the most picturesque cove on the lake, second in beauty only to Emerald Bay. Zephyr Cove Resort, which offers rustic cabins and campsites, is the East Shore counterpart of Richardson's Resort. This resort is home to two of Tahoe's most famous cruiseboats, the *M.S. Dixie II* and the *Woodwind* sailing yacht. It also has a lively beach scene, with water-skiing, parasailing, fishing, Jet Skiing, and volleyball. Zephyr also offers a big, rambling lodge next to U.S. 50 with a restaurant, a grocery store, and guest rooms. The rustic cabins are between the lodge and the beach, and a campground for tents and RVs is across the highway.

As might be expected, crowds are a fact of life here in summer. There's a constant stream of traffic on the road, as well as buses arriving with hundreds of passengers for the *M.S. Dixie II* cruises. Other attractions include horseback riding stables across the street and snowmobile tours of Spooner Summit in the winter. Public transportation is available between Zephyr and the casinos, and the resort is also near trailheads for the Tahoe Rim Trail, the famous Flume Trail for mountain bikes, and one of the area's best catch-and-release fishing lakes at Spooner Lake in Lake Tahoe-Nevada State Park. In 2000, the resort began a major renovation of its campground and planned similar improvements with its lodge and other buildings.

Rooms: 32 units. Lodge rooms sleep two to six; cabins (some housekeeping units with dishes and cooking utensils) sleep two to eight, and have twins, doubles, rollaways, televisions, some kitchens, some fireplaces, and limited linen and towel service.

Amenities: A restaurant; a beachside bar and grill; a campground; an RV park with a dump station and showers; tent sites; coin-operated laundry facilities; a general store; a gift shop; one mile of sandy beach; a marina; boat charters, including the *M.S. Dixie II, Woodwind II,* and

fishing boats; boat rentals; parasailing rides; horse stables; and a snowmobile center.

Policies: Pets are allowed in the RV park, campground, and cabins; there is a daily fee per pet.

Rates: $–$$$$. Major credit cards are accepted.

Contact: Zephyr Cove Resort, 760 U.S. 50/P.O. Box 830, Zephyr Cove, NV 89448; 775/588-6644; website: www.tahoedixie2.com.

KIRKWOOD/HOPE VALLEY/ MARKLEEVILLE

Caples Lake Resort

An inspiring view greets new arrivals at Caples Lake Resort. In front of you stretches an indigo lake a mile long and filled with six species of trout. Beyond is a backdrop of dramatic volcanic peaks dominated by 10,380-foot Round Top Mountain. It doesn't matter whether you take all of this in at sunset, with the alpenglow on the mountains, or at sunrise, with Sierra reflections in the water—you will be captivated by this 7,800-foot alpine oasis. John Voss has created

Kirkwood Ski and Summer Resort

a miniparadise here for fishing, boating, cycling, hiking, and horseback riding.

There's nothing pretentious about the accommodations. Small rooms on the second floor of the main lodge (which have recently been remodelled) have queen beds and semiprivate bathrooms that are directly across the hall. Nine housekeeping cabins have varying floor plans that can sleep four to six people. While there's nothing fancy about the lodging, everything else is truly exceptional. The restaurant, with its Nouveau California cuisine, draws aficionados from miles around and is clearly within the upper echelon of Tahoe's fine dining establishments. You could spend hours on the lake (where, fortunately, water-skiing is prohibited), but there are other attractions as well: hiking the four-mile loop from Woods Lake to Round Top Lake, mountain biking on one of several trails (bike rentals are available at the resort), horseback riding at Kirkwood Stables, and in winter, skiing at Kirkwood's downhill or cross-country ski areas. Caples Lake Resort is particularly cozy at night, when guests can play games, read books, practice the lost art of conversation, or enjoy the warmth of a roaring blaze in the big stone fireplace. The resort is open year-round.

Rooms: Six lodge guest rooms (with separate men's and women's restrooms and showers across the hall), sleeping two per room; seven housekeeping cabins (with kitchens, bathrooms, wall heaters, and bedding), sleeping up to six per unit.

Amenities: A lounge with a fireplace; a restaurant serving breakfast, lunch, and dinner; a dry sauna; a retail shop; snowshoe, aluminum boat, and mountain bike rentals; fishing; and a marina with a boat launch. Hiking trails are nearby.

Policies: No smoking is allowed in the lodge or the cabins.

Rates: $–$$$$. In summer, cabins usually book by the week. Major credit cards are accepted.

Contact: Caples Lake Resort, 1111 Hwy. 88, P.O. Box 88, Kirkwood, CA 95646; 209/258-8888; website: www.capleslake.com.

Kay's Silver Lake Resort

A rest stop has existed here since 1860, long before Highway 88 was built. Today, this place is a bit more than a stop—it offers nine housekeeping cabins on a hill overlooking Silver Lake. These are rustic accommodations, with no televisions or telephones, and reaching them requires a 100- to 200-yard hike (and maybe a bit of slogging on snowshoes in the winter), since there is no maintained trail. Summer is the main season, and the resort operates a small concrete launch ramp, rents 13-foot aluminum boats with 7.5-horsepower motors, and sells fuel, gas, tackle, and some groceries at its store, which is right on the highway. All parking is in front of the store. This unpretentious place provides proximity to excellent hiking trails, horseback riding, skiing, and cycling. The resort is open year-round.

Rooms: Nine housekeeping cabins (including studios and one- and two-bedroom units), with gas heat, stoves, refrigerators, dishes, cooking utensils, linens, and towels. No maid service is available.

Amenities: A grocery store, boat rentals, a launch ramp, and a beach. Fishing, swimming, water-skiing, hiking, horseback riding, Nordic skiing, and alpine skiing are available nearby.

Policies: No pets, tents, RVs, or visitors from local campgrounds are allowed. A deposit of a minimum night's stay (usually two nights' rental) is required and is fully refundable with 14 days' notice.

Rates: $$–$$$$. Often rents by the week in summer.

Contact: Kay's Silver Lake Resort, 48400 Kay's Rd., Pioneer, CA 95666; 209/258-8598.

Kit Carson Lodge

Perched on the eastern shores of Silver Lake between boulders and pine trees, this rustic wood-frame lodge feels like a 1950s kind of place, where your father or grandfather might have taken you when you were a child. You could sit on the deck overlooking the lake and talk about trivial things as you watched fishing boats trolling for trout. Actually, the history of the lodge goes back to 1926, so it's more than three-quarters of a century old. The richness of knotty pine envelops the place, imparting a sense of timeless antiquity to the rooms and common areas. Two types of accommodations are available: the lakeshore hotel rooms, each with a bedroom, a bath, and a private sun deck; and the housekeeping cottages, which are furnished with kitchens, fireplaces, barbecues, and baths with stall showers.

The main lodge houses a gourmet restaurant, an art gallery, and a reception desk, and next door is a general store that sells groceries, drinks, and fishing tackle. The lodge is on its own access road well off Highway 88, so traffic noise is never a problem. It's clear that many of the guests are repeat visitors and do not mind the resort's lengthy list of policies. Kit Carson has its own dock with boat rentals and a swimming area. It's open June–mid-October, with one cabin open in winter.

Rooms: Eight rooms and 18 cottages. Lakeshore motel rooms sleep one to three people; housekeeping cottages sleep two to six people and include refrigerators, gas ranges, decks, fireplaces, private baths, gas furnaces, and barbecues. Cooking utensils and bedding are supplied for the cabins, but guests must bring their own kitchen linens, dish soap, bath towels, and toiletries.

Amenities: A gourmet restaurant, an art gallery, a private beach, boat rentals, hiking trails (with free tour guides and slide shows available), a retail store, a gift shop, and laundry facilities.

Policies: No pets are allowed. No smoking is allowed in any of the units. Children of all ages are permitted in the cottages, but only those 12 and older are allowed in the rooms. A two-night minimum rental is required for motel rooms on weekends.

Rates: $$–$$$$. Off-season midweek discounts are available on daily rates.

Contact: Kit Carson Lodge, P.O. Box 1, Kit Carson, CA 95644; 209/258-8500 (summer) or 530/676-1370 (winter); website: www .kitcarsonlodge.com.

Sorensen's Resort

It is only 20 minutes from South Lake Tahoe, and yet Sorensen's might as well be a world away. This historic, 165-acre complex of cabins, owned by John and Patty Brissenden, is a kind of back-to-nature retreat that emphasizes low-impact recreation: cross-country skiing, hiking, fly-fishing, birding, photography, history tours, and wildflower walks. The resort, built next to the West Fork of the Carson River, was developed by Danish sheepherders in the 1920s. Situated in verdant Hope Valley—a region of meadows crisscrossed by mountain streams—Sorensen's caters to a clientele that appreciates the uniqueness of the resort, its easygoing staff, and its hearty, home-cooked meals. The Brissendens, who are political and environmental advocates, have made a point of creating a learning environment, especially for children, and families find this particularly stimulating.

There is nothing humdrum about the accommodations; virtually every cabin is unique and attractive. The Chapel, with its circular staircase and loft bedroom, is a reconstructed log cabin from a theme park in Santa Cruz, California, known as Santa's Village. The Norway House is a replica of a 13th-century Norwegian building, with its hand-carved facade and sod roof; it has dormitory-style accommodations, and guests must bring their own sleeping bags. The Snowshoe, Creekside, and Sheepherder log cabins—which have wood-burning stoves, kitchenettes, separate bathrooms and showers, queen-sized beds, and sleeping lofts with twin futons—are great for small families or honeymooners. The café in the main lodge serves three meals a day and is known for its beef burgundy stew, robust soups, and seafood. In winter, Sorensen's is headquarters for the Hope Valley Cross-Country Ski Center; in summer, the Horse Feathers Fly-Fishing School holds forth. In 1996, the resort added to its holdings with the acquisition of nearby Hope Valley Resort, which has a private campground and general store. Sorensen's is close to magnificent hiking trails and lakes in the Mokelumne Wilderness, the Kirkwood downhill and cross-country ski areas, and the soothing waters of Grover Hot Springs State Park.

Rooms: 30 units with some kitchens, some fireplaces with wood-burning stoves, limited maid service, and free drinks: Cocoa, coffee, tea, and wine are served daily until 5 P.M. Cabins sleep one to eight, homes sleep six, and bed-and-breakfast accommodations sleep two.

Amenities: Sorensen's Country Cafe, serving breakfast, lunch, and dinner; a campground for RVs and tents; a gift shop; a wood-fired sauna; Hope Valley Cross-Country Ski Center, offering rentals, lessons, wildlife and full-moon tours, backcountry seminars, and learn-to-ski weekends; and the Horse Feathers Fly-Fishing School. Programs include historic Mormon-Emigrant Trail walking tours, from May to October; stargazing programs in November; Bach and banjo performances in December; Sierra watercolor workshops in October; holiday wreath-making in November; fly-fishing and tying classes; and hiking, fishing, and bicycling. Mineral hot springs, Kirkwood skiing, horseback riding, river rafting, and Lake Tahoe are nearby.

Policies: Children under eight stay for free. Pets are limited to log and wagon-wheel cabins. A two-night minimum stay is required on weekends; a minimum stay of up to four nights is required during holidays and special events.

Rates: $$–$$$$. Group rates are available. Reservations are recommended.

Contact: Sorensen's Resort, 14255 Hwy. 88, Hope Valley, CA 96120; 530/694-2203 or 800/423-9949; website: www.sorensensresort.com.

LAKES BASIN/ FEATHER RIVER COUNTRY

Elwell Lakes Lodge

Built in 1920, this small lodge one-half mile off the Gold Lake Road is operated by Sugie and John Barker, grandchildren of the original owners. Nestled in pine and fir forest, the 10 housekeeping cabins offer rustic simplicity with modern conveniences. A separate recreation building has two rooms for bed-and-breakfast stays (with a full hot breakfast), a large fireplace with books, games, and a telephone. Another building, which used to be the dining hall, is used as a lounge. Except for the bed-and-breakfast rooms, no meals are included, but there's usually a potluck among guests once a week.

Anglers are in seventh heaven here because they can reach as many as 23 lakes within a three-mile radius of the lodge. On Long Lake, three-quarters of a mile away, the lodge provides boats and motors for guests to use for fishing or cruising. One of the requisite activities for those staying a week or so is the three-mile hike to the top of Mt. Elwell, at 7,812 feet, which has a panoramic view of the basin. Youngsters and adults alike can cool off in a creek-fed swimming pool, or at Bear and Grassy Lakes, less than a quarter mile away. The lodge is open June–September, and the best availability is usually after Labor Day.

Rooms: 10 cabins and two bed-and-breakfast rooms, which are on the second floor of the recreation building, sharing a bath down the hall. Cabins have double and twin beds; fully equipped kitchenettes with an electric or gas stove, refrigerators, and sinks; bathrooms with showers; linens; and electric heaters. The largest cabin sleeps up to six people. There are also several tent cabins for two people.

Amenities: A recreation room with a fireplace, Ping-Pong tables, books, and games; a lounge building with views of the forest; barbecues; boating at Long Lake, with three boats for guest use (free); swimming early in the season in a pool created by Bear Creek; and seminar facilities. Good fishing and hiking opportunities are available nearby.

Policies: No pets are allowed.

Rates: $–$$$.

Contact: Elwell Lakes Lodge, P.O. Box 68, Blairsden, CA 96103; 530/836-2347; website: www.elwellodge.com.

Feather River Inn

With its Tudor-style facade, stone foundation, and massive timbered entryway, the 100-acre Feather River Inn is one of the grand old lodges of the West. It was built in 1911 by the First Interstate Company of Chicago, a venture capital firm that also constructed the Tovar Lodge at the Grand Canyon. Originally designed as a resort, the property once rivaled Yosemite's famous Ahwahnee Hotel in elegance. In the 1960s, it was acquired by the University of the Pacific and operated as a prep school for 17 years. In 1988, the UOP Alumni Association took it over and converted it to a conference center, but it makes an ideal family retreat as well.

In Blairsden, an hour's drive north of Truckee, the inn is open to the public April 1–November 1. The lodge building itself is ornately appointed, with cheerful meeting rooms. In 2000, new management took over the inn and reopened 26 rooms on the second floor as part of a $1.2 million restoration. Each room has a private bath with tub or shower, Mission-style furniture, queen bed or two extra-long double beds, and phones with data ports.

Overnight guests also have the option of staying in alpine "chalets" and rustic log cabins, which are scattered throughout a forested hillside and connected with wooden boardwalks. These accommodations are basic and far removed from the style of the main lodge. Each room has two twin beds, simple furnishings, and front porches. Most units have private baths. During conferences, meals are offered three times a day. Mid-May–early September, an elegant Sunday brunch is served in the massive dining room and outside on the veranda.

Rooms: 26 hotel rooms, each with private bath, and 17 cabins and chalets offering 50 units, with two twin beds and most with private baths (showers or tubs). Many cabins overlook the

ninth green of the golf course. Hotel rooms have two suites, with bedroom and separate living room, and two rooms for those with impaired mobility. Open March–December.

Amenities: A nine-hole golf course (par 34) open for public play; a heated swimming pool; a gymnasium; basketball, tennis, and volleyball courts; horseshoes; a catch-and-release fishing pond; a dance hall; and two conference rooms accommodating up to 150 people. Note: Golfing is not included in the room price.

Policies: Children are allowed, but pets are not.

Rates: $$–$$$.

Contact: Feather River Inn, P.O. Box 67, Blairsden, CA 96103; 530/836-2623; website: www.featherriverinn.com.

Feather River Park Resort

Situated in the community of Graeagle, this is a grand, old-fashioned resort with bigger-than-average log cabins, a fine nine-hole golf course, and many recreation facilities scattered among 160 pine-studded acres. Amid a truly serene environment, there's still plenty to do on a family vacation. The resort has two swimming pools surrounded by manicured lawns; two tennis courts; and a large recreation building with Ping-Pong and billiards tables, games, and a snack bar. Kids can prowl the shores of the Middle Fork of the Feather River, which borders the resort, or try fishing for trout in its waters.

Built in 1923, the resort is owned by a corporation that acquired it in the 1970s. Its goal was to prevent the resort from being torn down and the land developed, and so this large area of open space remains a crowning attraction in the heart of Graeagle. The management is constantly adding new things to the cabins and grounds, and the quality shows. About 90 percent of the business is repeat traffic, so it's necessary to book well in advance, except for the shoulder seasons, early May–mid-June and early September–mid-October. On Highway 89, the Feather River Park Resort is close to the Plumas Pines and Graeagle Meadows golf courses, Plumas Eureka State Park, the hiking and equestrian trails of the Lakes Basin, and great fishing lakes from Davis to Sardine.

Feather River Inn

Rooms: 35 housekeeping cabins (with cooking facilities), varying from one- to three-bedroom units. All have comfortable beds, kitchens, private baths, heaters, living rooms with river-stone fireplaces, and porches or decks. All linens and bedding are provided. There are no televisions or telephones. Many cabins are along the golf course.

Amenities: A nine-hole golf course on flat terrain with few bunkers or other hazards, which is available to guests at reduced rates. Other facilities include two tennis courts, bike rentals, firewood (supplied to each cabin), a snack bar and refreshments, a small retail counter, river access, and a game room with Ping-Pong and billiards. The resort is open May 1–October 15.

Policies: Outside play is allowed on the golf course. Minimum one-week stays are required June 15–September; two-day stays are required May 1–June 15 and September 1–October 15.

Rates: $$–$$$$.

Contact: Feather River Park Resort, P.O. Box 37, Blairsden, CA 96103; 530/836-2328, fax 530/836-2707.

Gold Lake Beach Resort

On the isolated southwestern shore of Gold Lake, the largest lake in the Lakes Basin, this is a rustic lodge where people go to escape the world. Other than four-wheeling a rough road, the only way you can get there is by 10-minute ride on a shuttle boat. The resort is the essence of mountain simplicity, with accommodations in two houses, two small wood-frame cabins, and eight tent cabins nestled in the forest. The houses have indoor bathrooms, while the other facilities share a central bath and a central dining area where breakfast and dinner are served, family-style, at tables and benches. Sometimes the resort offers an evening meal service for nonguests, with boat pickup and return. Gourmet California cuisine is emphasized, and the resort can cater to special dietary needs or preferences.

Gold Lake Beach Resort has a small marina and offers a variety of water sports including fishing, canoeing, and boating, and there's a gravel beach for swimming. Proximity to the Pacific Crest Trail provides a wealth of hiking opportu-

nities to other lakes. In the resort compound, other activities include volleyball, Ping-Pong, and horseshoes, and there's a pack station nearby. Most stays include a meal plan (covering breakfast, lunch, and dinner), and box lunches can be prepared for guests to take with them during the day. A large deck overlooking the lake next to the dining room is used for relaxing. Owner/operator Jim Reid specializes in groups (the resort can handle up to 30 guests), but welcomes families with children (and pets!) as well as couples. The resort enjoys a strong repeat business, so book far in advance. The resort is open July–September.

Rooms: 10 tent and wood cabins with twin, queen-sized, and optional rollaways and electricity. There are two bathhouses with showers and toilets; there are no televisions or telephones. Two additional buildings, a new house and a cabin, may be available on a limited basis; check with the management.

Amenities: Complete meal service and pickup at the dock. Swimming, fishing, hiking, and horseback riding opportunities are nearby.

Policies: Pets are allowed. There is a three-night minimum stay, but weekly stays are preferred. Groups of at least 20 may rent the entire premises.

Rates: $$$. Lower rates are available for children. Special family rates are also available.

Contact: Gold Lake Beach Resort, P.O. Box 906, Graeagle, CA 96103; 530/836-2491.

Gold Lake Lodge

A onetime fishing retreat, Gold Lake Lodge was built in 1912 by Mac and Mava McCormick, who also built the White Sulphur Springs Ranch in Clio. The lodge is not actually on the lake but rather a quarter mile north of it. It is, however, at the trailhead of the most popular one-day hiking route in the Lakes Basin (the Round Lake Loop) and next to the Gold Lake Road, making it convenient for coming and going. Owner Jeremy Barker has has achieved some repute with the lodge dining room, which is open to the public as well as to guests.

Accommodations here are of two types: rustic and standard cabins. The former use a central bath and shower facility, while the latter have their own bathrooms. Most are one-room buildings, and there are no kitchenettes, as all guests are on a meal plan. The cabins are furnished, include linens, and have electricity and heaters. Daily maid service is available.

Guests can walk easily to any of several lakes for fishing, and the lodge offers a rowboat on Bear Lake for its guests. Recreation also includes volleyball on the premises, and there is a packhorse station nearby. Both guests and locals rave about the meals in the woodsy, knotty-pine dining room. Breakfasts include home-baked breads and cinnamon rolls, and dinners offer four to five entrées, including fresh pasta, seafood, chicken, and steaks, with desserts of homemade pies and cheesecakes. The kitchen will cook your fresh-caught trout, if you wish, and will also make an optional sack lunch. Gold Lake Lodge works well for guests who like the easy highway access for exploring the sights of the area, yet who want to remain close to the Lakes Basin. The lodge, which is listed on the National Register of Historic Places, is open June–September.

Rooms: 11 rustic and standard cabins, some with private baths, some with shared outdoor baths. New queen-sized, double, and twin beds are available, and two cabins have two bedrooms. Rustic furnishings, electric heaters, linens, daily maid service, and the Modified American Plan (breakfast and dinner) are included.

Amenities: A central dining room open to the lodge and outside guests for breakfast and dinner. Fishing, hiking, volleyball, and swimming are available, with golf, horseback riding, and tennis in nearby Graeagle.

Policies: No pets are allowed.

Rates: $$–$$$$. Special rates for children, and family discounts are available.

Contact: Gold Lake Lodge, P.O. Box 25, Graeagle, CA 96103; 530/836-2350 or 530/836-2751; website: www.lakesbasin.com/gold.

Gray Eagle Lodge

Opened in 1923, Gray Eagle is the most upscale and expensive lodge on the Gold Lake Road. The main building is a new log structure with bleached wood, arched and beamed ceilings, and an impressive rock fireplace, all of which impart a quiet elegance to the dining room, bar, and salon. The restaurant, known for its gourmet cuisine (including roast duck, sautéed sea bass, leg of lamb, grilled swordfish, and other delicacies) is one of the most popular dinner houses in Plumas County. This giant lodge, which has a large adjoining game room with billiards, Ping-Pong, and other table games, is clearly the centerpiece of the resort. However, the cabins have their own special ambience; they are the best appointed in the region, with comfortable furnishings, firm beds, and well-maintained interiors with knotty-pine walls. They are situated in an idyllic, protected forest along meandering Gray Eagle Creek, and guests can wade in the stream or swim in the 10-foot-deep natural pond at the base of Gray Eagle Falls, just a short hike away.

On an access road off the Gold Lake Road, just five miles south of Graeagle, the lodge does not have a lake in its front yard. But short hiking trails will take guests to Smith Lake, a rock-rimmed beauty about one mile north, or to nearby Hidden, Lily, and Long Lakes. Every cabin contains a detailed hiking guide written by the owners. All accommodations include breakfast, dinner, and daily maid service. Owner Bret Smith clearly enjoys mingling with guests and offering his personal recommendations. Gray Eagle Lodge is open late May–mid-October.

Rooms: 18 cabins, sleeping from one to four people (although some can accommodate more) with baths, comfortable beds, and heaters. There are no televisions or telephones.

Amenities: A restaurant, a cocktail lounge, a lodge, and a game room. Nearby activities include hiking, fishing, horseback riding, golf, tennis, and swimming.

Policies: Up to two pets per cabin are allowed at extra charge and must be kept on a leash. A three-night minimum stay is required.

Rates: $$$$. Rates include breakfast and dinner for two people and daily maid service. There are lower rates for children and an extra charge for each additional adult. Personal checks and some major credit cards are accepted.

Contact: Gray Eagle Lodge, Gold Lake Rd./P.O. Box 38, Blairsden, CA 96103; 530/836-2511 or 800/635-8778 (in Northern California only); website: www.grayeaglelodge.com.

Layman Resort

On a pine-studded site just 100 yards uphill from the Middle Fork of the Feather River, this rustic retreat offers tranquillity and access to the river, one of California's most scenic waterways. The site originally was known as Camp Layman, and it was used in the late 1800s during the construction of the railroad to the Feather River Country. The 13 cabins were built in the late 1920s and early 1930s and have kitchenettes and bathrooms with showers. Clean linens are provided weekly. The resort, off Highway 70/89 northwest of Graeagle, is close to the golf resorts, hiking trails, horseback riding, and the many fishing waters of the Lakes Basin. There's a beach nearby on the Feather River. Because it is at a relatively low elevation, 4,200 feet, the resort opens in April, earlier than most other lodges.

Rooms: 13 rustic cabins, including nine with one bedroom and four with two or more bedrooms. The largest is the Pine Cabin, a two-story building with two upstairs bedrooms and two hide-a-beds in the living room. All units have kitchenettes, bathrooms, and showers. There are no televisions or telephones.

Amenities: Swimming and fishing opportunities on the Middle Fork of the Feather River, 100 yards away; evening campfires; barbecues; horseshoes; and shuffleboard.

Policies: A seven-day minimum stay is required for long-term reservations.

Rates: $$–$$$. Major credit cards are accepted.

Contact: Layman Resort, Hwy. 70, P.O. Box 8, Blairsden, CA 96103; 530/836-2356.

The Lodge at Whitehawk Ranch

This new and elegant 14-acre retreat, opened in 2000, offers a grand main lodge and 12 rustically elegant cabins, each with a covered porch that overlooks the spectacular 18-hole golf course at Whitehawk and the bucolic Mohawk Valley. Every cabin has vaulted pine ceilings, a wood floor with area rugs, and Adirondack chairs on the porch. Two cabins have two bedrooms, and the second bedroom is furnished with two twin beds. Owners Eric and Sheila Hickman clearly intend to cater to golfers, and this is the first overnight lodging that is available at Whitehawk, which is a planned resort community with many full-time residents. The main lodge, a classy, ranch-style building with lots of river-rock trim, has a large stone fireplace, exposed beams, and a great room with a full bar that offers cocktails and beer. A well-regarded restaurant serves gourmet dinners. The lodge is close to five other golf courses, shops in Graeagle, and other restaurants in Blairsden and Johnsville. Many hiking trails exist in nearby Plumas-Eureka State Park and the Lakes Basin area.

Rooms: 12 cabins, each with private bath, air conditioning and heating, queen or king bed, writing desk, armoire, Jacuzzi bathtub, phone with data port, television, and VCR.

Amenities: Restaurant, cocktail lounge, access to swimming pool, tennis court, spa, fly-fishing pond, and weekly barbecue wagon rides.

Rates: $$$$.

Contact: The Lodge at Whitehawk Ranch, 985 Whitehawk Dr., P.O. Box 175, Clio, CA 96106; 530/836-4985 or 877/945-6343; website: www.lodgeatwhitehawk.com.

Packer Lake Lodge

Packer Lake is a four- to five-acre lake set 3.5 miles off the Gold Lake Road on a road that is mostly paved. Its greatest assets are an esteemed restaurant and its proximity to much more scenic lakes (notably Sardine and Tamarack) and to the road that leads to the summit of the Sierra Buttes. Packer Lake is somewhat nondescript, though it's a pleasant enough lake for fishing; trout are stocked every week or so. The lodge, built in 1926, has a main building and 14 cabins—six of which are the original one-room lakefront log cabins, with no cooking facilities or private baths. These units share three central bath/shower facilities. Eight cabins (three with two rooms and three with three rooms) have private baths and kitchens, including electric stoves and refrigerators. All cabins have electricity and linoleum floors, and linen is provided, with one exchange midweek.

The main lodge offers dinner nightly except Tuesday and is open to the general public with two seatings, one starting at 6 P.M., the other at 8 P.M. The chef will cook your catch, or you can

© KEN CASTLE

Lodge at Whitehawk Ranch near Graeagle

sample one of six entrées such as baby-back spareribs, prime rib (available on Saturday nights only), seafood, pasta, and chicken. Meals are not included with accommodations.

The lodge has a big stone fireplace and a full bar, along with a small retail area for fishing tackle and miscellaneous items. There's a rowboat for each cabin, as well as some rental boats, including a canoe; motors are not permitted on the lake. The lodge is near the Pacific Crest Trail, along with hiking trails to Tamarack and Deer Lakes and the Sierra Buttes; the scenic Sardine Lakes are on the other side of the ridge, along with Sand Pond, the best swimming hole in the region. The lodge, 17 miles south of Graeagle and close to Bassett's Station, has heavy advance bookings each year. The best openings are before June 10 or after the first week of September. The season runs May–October.

Rooms: 14 cabins (one-, two-, and three-bedroom units) with some kitchens, some bathrooms, and some lakefronts.

Amenities: Free rowboats for guests, additional boat rentals, a dock, limited swimming, fishing, hiking, a retail area, a restaurant, and a full bar.

Policies: Pets are allowed.

Rates: $$–$$$$. Major credit cards are accepted. Meals are extra.

Contact: Bill Macquattie, Packer Lake Lodge, 3901 Packer Lake Rd./P.O. Box 237, Sierra City, CA 96125; 530/862-1221 or 415/921-5943 (off-season).

Salmon Lake Lodge

Gorgeous, granite-rimmed Salmon Lake has immediate visual appeal, and the lodge is accessible only by boat from the main access road, which gives it an isolated quality that lures guests back year after year. At an elevation of 6,500 feet, the lodge is framed by rocky peaks and mixed fir and pine forest, and there's a small island where guests can take the barge to a twice-weekly barbecue. Of the 14 cabins, 10 are tent cabins with wooden floors and canvas roofs, over a hill just out of sight from the main building. These have a double bed, two bunks, and a simple kitchen with an electric cooktop stove and a small refrigerator; guests share a central shower house, which has dish- and clothes-washing facilities. You must bring your own sleeping bags, towels, and cooking and eating utensils. The Hill Cabin sleeps five people, two in a double bed downstairs and three in a loft. It has a fully equipped kitchen with a sink, a refrigerator, and a toaster oven, but you'll need to bring sleeping bags and towels here, as well. The Tank House Cabin, Lakeshore Cabin, and Ridge Cabin sleep 6–8 people, and each has a private bath with a tub or a shower. The most deluxe unit is the Ridge, with all bedding provided (but not towels), three bedrooms, a living room, and a full kitchen.

The lake is great for swimming and boating. Motorboats are allowed, though they can run up to only five miles per hour. Guests have free use of all rowboats, kayaks, canoes, and sailboats. Built in 1929, the lodge is owned by the Christian family, and various siblings take turns running things. It is usually sold out a year in advance, with openings only in late spring and fall, if then.

Rooms: 14 cabins, including 10 tent cabins with shared exterior bath facilities and electricity and wood-burning stoves, and four regular cabins, three with private baths. All cabins are housekeeping units and include cooking facilities. Guests must bring bedding or sleeping bags (unless they're staying in the Ridge Cabin) and towels. Tent cabins are open only mid-June–mid-September.

Amenities: A central utility house with showers, a refrigerator, and washing machines; a barbecue; a retail shop with charcoal, maps, stamps, and postcards; and nonpowered boats for guests. Guests may bring small boat motors and waterskiing equipment. Swimming (July–September) and boating are allowed in nearby Gold Lake. Groceries, fishing licenses, and equipment are available in Sierra City.

Note: A phone at the parking lot and dock can be used to call the resort for barge pickup.

Policies: Camping is not permitted. Guests in excess of the listed capacity will be charged extra.

Rates: $$–$$$$. Rented by the week.

Contact: Salmon Lake Lodge, P.O. Box 121, Sierra City, CA 96125; 530/757-1825.

Sardine Lake Resort

Without a doubt, this is the most extraordinary site for a lodge in the Lakes Basin. When you stroll through the forest to the shoreline and peer up at the sweeping Sierra Buttes framing the lake, you'll be convinced that you've been transported to the Swiss Alps. But it will take an act of Congress to get a booking at this small resort, which probably has the region's most extensive backlog of requests. Owners Dorothy and Chandler Hunt have just nine cabins, and they have such strong repeat business that it's difficult for newcomers to get a booking. However, you might have a chance at squeezing into their restaurant, known as one of the finer local gourmet dinner houses, if you reserve a few weeks in advance. Also, the resort operates a small marina where anyone can rent rowboats or boats with electric motors.

The lodge was built in 1941 by Mrs. Hunt's parents, George and Audrey Browning, who first came to the area in 1936. Several generations of the family have worked here and continue to do so. Reportedly the lake was originally known as Emerald Lake, but it was renamed in the late 1800s when a miner's mule named Sardine fell into the water. There is little doubt that this is the premier spot to be in the Lakes Basin; there are hiking trails to Upper Sardine Lake, Tamarack Lakes, and the Sierra Buttes fire lookout. The cabins are rustic but comfortable and are scattered on a forested hillside above the main building. The season runs June–early October.

Rooms: Nine cabins, including simple one-room cabins with kitchens and baths; a two-bedroom cabin with a living room, kitchen, and bath; and deluxe two-bedroom cabins. Some units have bunk beds.

Amenities: A small dock with trolling-motor fishing boats and rowboats available for rent. There are extensive hiking trails nearby, including one to the summit of Sierra Buttes. Sand Pond, a Forest Service impoundment managed for swimming, is just down the access road from the Gold Lake Road. The resort is close to Bassett's Station and Sierra City.

Policies: A deposit is required for weekly reservations.

Rates: $$–$$$$. Weekly rentals are preferred. Rates do not include meals.

Contact: Sardine Lake Resort, Gold Lake Rd., Lakes Basin, CA 96125; 530/862-1196; website: www.sierracity.com/Stay/SardineLkeResrt.html

Reno/ Carson Valley Accommodations

Engaged in frantic expansion during the last decade, hotels in Reno and Carson Valley have now completed a number of multimillion-dollar projects and are concentrating on the task of filling rooms. And with an oversupply much of the year, particularly during midweek, rates for luxurious accommodations are among the cheapest in the country. Along North Virginia Street ("The Strip"), visitors are flocking to Silver Legacy, Eldorado, Harrah's, and Circus Circus, all of which have benefited from an ongoing campaign to rehabilitate the downtown area. Outdone by their newer and more lavish competitors, some of the older casino-hotels have been closed, sold, or demolished. In late 2001, the 23-year-old Flamingo Hilton Reno on Sierra Street changed

hands and was reopened the following year as the Golden Phoenix. A few blocks away, next to the Truckee River, new owners of the old Holiday Hotel finally ended several years of remodeling and millions of dollars of investment with the unveiling of the posh, Tuscan-styled Siena Hotel Spa Casino, which opened in the summer of 2001. But several other aging landmarks have not fared as well. Despite outcries from historians and preservationists, the famous old Mapes Casino Hotel—where much of "The Rat Pack" hung out during the 1960s—was torn down. So was the Pioneer. The Riverboat was converted to a convention-only facility, and the Comstock has become a long-term live-in apartment building. The bottom line is that when the top properties

Peppermill Resort and Casino

are offering rooms as cheap as $40 a night, it's difficult for the tired, worn-out hotels to generate much business. What may have sealed their fate was the 1995 linkup of the new Silver Legacy with its two neighbors, Eldorado and Circus Circus. This fully interconnected triumvirate offers a safe, indoor mecca of shopping, dining, gaming, and entertainment that sprawls across six square blocks. Joined by skyways, the three hotels call themselves Reno's Center of Entertainment and together offer more than 4,000 rooms, 20 restaurants, an indoor shopping mall, and diverse nightlife that varies from a rowdy brew pub to circus acts. Not to be outdone, Harrah's Reno, John Ascuaga's Nugget and Boomtown Hotel Casino, the latter on the western outskirts of town, have been engaged recently in major expansions of their own. And in the south part of Reno, near the newly enlarged convention center, both Atlantis Casino Resort and Peppermill Hotel Casino have traded bragging rights by unveiling new restaurants, attractions, and towers. Such improvements have drawn more families, couples, and upscale conferences, and have made Reno a lively destination in its own right. But the city core is still blighted by cheesy, rundown motels, some of which have little future except as havens for drifters and down-and-outers. As with many tourist towns, the quality of service varies. During conventions, major events, and warm-weather weekends, expect longer lines for hotel registration, restaurants, and shows.

With so many rooms available, Reno is a good place for bargain-hunters, especially in winter, when it becomes the fly-in gateway to Lake Tahoe's ski slopes. Midweek specials can

> *In 1995, the new Silver Legacy linked up with its two neighbors, Eldorado and Circus Circus. This fully interconnected triumvirate offers a safe, indoor mecca of shopping, dining, gaming, and entertainment that sprawls across six square blocks.*

bring first-rate hotel rooms down to a paltry $40–50 a night, unheard of at any other major ski destination. You are an hour away from Squaw Valley, Alpine Meadows, Northstar-at-Tahoe, Heavenly, Sugar Bowl, and Diamond Peak, and within 45 minutes of Reno's own ski hill, Mt. Rose. Throughout the other seasons, you're within an hour's drive of nearly 40 golf courses, a third of them relatively new. Keep in mind that room rates go up during high-profile events such as Hot August Nights and the National Championship Air Races, when the city is often sold out. In general, visitors can save substantially by buying all-inclusive air/land packages from tour operators that include recreation activities, shows, meals, and other perks.

The Reno/Sparks area has four hotel districts: downtown Reno along North Virginia Street, which is the location of Eldorado, Circus Circus, Harrah's, and Silver Legacy; near the convention center on South Virginia Street, containing Atlantis and Peppermill; near the airport, where you'll find the Reno Hilton; and in the adjoining community of Sparks, home to the Nugget. South of Reno, the Best Western Pinon Plaza Resort in Carson City provides a good location from which to explore the historic silver mining town of Virginia City and Lake Tahoe. For general information on Reno, contact the Reno-Sparks Convention and Visitors Authority, P.O. Box 837, Reno, NV 89504-0837; 800/FOR-RENO (800/367-7366); website: www.renotahoe.com. Another good website, operated by the *Reno Gazette-Journal*, the city's daily newspaper, is www.renotahoefun.com.

Hotels

RENO/SPARKS

Airport Plaza Hotel

Although convenient to the airport, this deluxe hotel is not close to anything else unless you have wheels. In that case, it's a short drive downtown or to the convention center. This is an above-average hotel, and the rooms here are attractive and well appointed. Furthermore, the Plaza Court Restaurant is a favorite among locals with its creative offerings of salads, seafood and steaks.

Rooms: 270 guest rooms and parlor suites with phones, satellite televisions, AM/FM radios, some fireplaces, wheelchair access, and some non-smoking units.

Amenities: The Plaza Court Restaurant; the Library Lounge; a casino; room service; a business center; safe-deposit boxes; an outdoor pool and spa; a health club with fitness machines, a spa, and a sauna; meeting and banquet facilities accommodating up to 500 people; self-parking; and an airport shuttle.

Rates: $$.

Contact: Airport Plaza Hotel, 1981 Terminal Way, Reno, NV 89502; 775/348-6370 or 800/648-3525; website: www.bestwestern.com/airportplazahotel.

Atlantis Casino Resort

This hotel, one of the best in the city, just keeps getting bigger and better. Apart from its colorful façade, the hotel has a huge Sky Terrace that extends over South Virginia Street. Recently, the resort introduced its Grand Penthouse suites on the 26th and 27th floors of the hotel's Concierge Tower, and a luxurious VIP lounge and check-in area on the main level. The Tower comprises the 21st–27th floors and houses luxury suites that have their own concierge, a private lounge, personal butler service, slippers and robes, continental breakfast, and afternoon hors d'oeuvres. Atlantis is directly across the street from the Reno-Sparks Convention Center, making it popular

$ = economy (less than $40 per room)
$$ = standard ($40–60 per room)
$$$ = deluxe (over $60)

RENO ACCOMMODATIONS

with conference-goers. The hotel's standard rooms are spacious and well appointed, with large comfortable beds, marble entryways and fixtures in all bathrooms, and tropical decor. Rooms have views of the Sierra Nevada range and the Reno cityscape and offer deluxe amenities such as cable television with premium channels and two DID phone lines. For nonsmokers, there are entire smoke-free floors. The casino has a unique air filtration system that creates a nearly smoke-free environment. The Health Spa contains a state-of-the-art workout facility, massage and facial therapies, indoor and outdoor pools, Jacuzzi, steam room, sauna, cold lunge, refreshments, and beauty products. Several of the eight restaurants have received a number of accolades, including the exotically themed Atlantis Seafood Steakhouse, known for its elaborate tableside service, and Toucan Charlie's, which consistently wins local polls as Reno's "best buffet." The Oyster Bar on the Sky Terrace has been called "A Tropical Oasis in the Sky" by editors of *Reno Gazette-Journal* and MonteVigna Italian Ristorante recently won the "Nevada's Choice" award for best Italian cuisine. Other dining choices include Café Alfresco, Purple Parrot (open 24 hours), Java Coast, and the Fun Center Snack Bar and Deli. Atlantis has a nightclub for disco dancing into the wee morning hours, and the Center Stage Cabaret showcases various musical acts.

Rooms: 1,000 guest rooms and suites with king-sized beds, direct-dial phones, a message alert, wake-up service, remote control color televisions with movie channels, 24-hour room service, wheelchair access, nonsmoking units, some units with in-room Jacuzzis, living rooms with wet bars, and in-room keno.

Amenities: Eight restaurants and several lounges; live entertainment and dancing; a casino with sportsbook; the Entertainment Fun Center with video and redemption games, pool tables, air hockey, and a snack bar; Health Spa with massage services; indoor and outdoor swimming pools; a sun deck; workout facility with sauna, steamroom, Jacuzzi, and personal training; free 24-hour valet parking and self-parking lot; a 32,000-square-foot convention facility; and airport/downtown shuttle services.

Rates: $–$$$.

Contact: Atlantis Casino Resort, 3800 S. Virginia St., Reno, NV 89502; 775/825-4700 or 800/723-6500; website: www.AtlantisCasino.com.

McCarran House

This nine-story hotel is in Sparks next to Victorian Square. It houses the Garden Café and the intimate Firelite Lounge, which has weekend live music and dancing. Conference facilities include two meeting rooms and an 8,000-square-foot ballroom. The hotel is four miles from downtown Reno.

Rooms: 220 guest rooms and suites (some nonsmoking) with phones and televisions.

Amenities: One restaurant, one lounge, an outdoor pool, Tiffany Ballroom, and an airport shuttle.

Rates: $$.

Contact: McCarran House Inn, 55 E. Nugget Ave., Reno, NV 89431; 775/358-6900 or 800/548-5798.

Boomtown Hotel Casino

Best described as a combination theme park, Middle America destination, and gaming salon dressed up in an Old West facade, Boomtown is a thriving business on I-80. It used to pull in the crowds largely because of an indoor game arcade and an interactive movie experience for the kids. Now there is much more. Recently, Boomtown unveiled a completely new hotel, with new rooms and suites, and there are plans to continue expanding. Latest amenities include a TVi television system, which offers free cable, In-

ternet, and email access, account review, express check-out and multimedia display of hotel information in each guest room. Other additions include a completely revamped all-you-can-eat restaurant, the Silver Screen Buffet, which is one of the best in the city, as well as a new Bean Counter Coffee Bar and Deli and a newly renovated Mexican-themed coffee shop called Sundance Cantina. Boomtown is off I-80 at the Boomtown exit (#4).

Rooms: 318 guest rooms and suites with phones, televisions (some closed-captioned), cribs and rollaways, hair dryer, iron and ironing board, coffee, assortment of teas, some wheelchair access, and some nonsmoking units.

Amenities: Five restaurants, four bars, a cabaret lounge, a casino, shows, recently renovated indoor swimming pool, a family arcade with more than 200 games, a prize redemption center, 3D Dynamic Motion Theater, an antique carousel, an indoor 18-hole miniature golf course, a party room, a minimart, and an award-winning Chevron gas station. RV park amenities include

Boomtown Hotel Casino

203 paved and lighted spaces; full hookups, including cable television; a message and mail center; video rentals; an outdoor swimming pool; two spas; coin-operated laundry facilities; a free casino shuttle; and 24-hour security.

Policies: Children under 12 stay free.

Rates: $$–$$$. Major credit cards are accepted.

Contact: Boomtown Hotel Casino, I-80 W and Garson Rd./P.O. Box 399, Verdi, NV 89439; 775/345-6000 or 800/648-3790; website: www.boomtownreno.com.

Circus Circus Hotel Casino Reno

As one of the three interconnected downtown hotels, Circus Circus aims for budget-minded families but offers many upscale amenities. Among them are an attractive lobby with marble floors, a cheery casino, and elegantly appointed guest rooms with European circus themes from the early 1900s. On the Midway—the focal point of the hotel—is a stage with ongoing free circus acts, including stars from Cirque Du Soleil, Imperial Acrobats of China, and Ringling Brothers and Barnum and Bailey Circus. There are also live carnival games and arcade games for the kids. The hotel is linked via skyway with the Silver Legacy and Eldorado hotels, so guests need never step outside. Worth visiting are Art Gecko's Southwest Grill, an eclectic place with Hispanic and Southwestern cuisine, and Kokopelli's Sushi Bar. There's also a 1,850-car parking structure (the second on-site), which is connected to the north tower by a skybridge.

Rooms: 1,572 guest rooms with phones, data ports, televisions, Nintendo, and wheelchair access. Nonsmoking units are available.

Amenities: Six restaurants including The Steakhouse at Circus, Art Gecko's Southwest Grill, Kokopelli's Sushi, Courtyard Buffet, Three Ring Coffee Shop, and Main Street Deli and Ice Creame Shoppe; more than 22,000 square feet of meeting and convention space; a casino; midway featuring live circus acts; carnival and redemption games; a family arcade; five retail stores; free valet and self-parking; and free airport shuttle.

Rates: $–$$$.

Contact: Circus Circus Hotel Casino Reno, 500 N. Sierra St., Reno, NV 89503; 775/329-0711 or 800/648-5010; website: www.circusreno.com.

Club Cal Neva (formerly the Virginian and the Riverboat)

Originally opened in 1962, this property has undergone a number of renovations and management changes over the years. What was once two jointly operated hotels has been downsized to one hotel, and it occupies a city block between Center and Virginia and 2nd and 1st Streets. In 2000, a new San Francisco-style lobby was unveiled on the first floor casino, which was formerly known as the Wells Fargo Building. This 6,400-foot area has marbled walls, floor-to-ceiling windows, and a 1933 Franklin car that is on loan from the National Automobile Museum. Other improvements include the addition of the Cabaret, an expanded Hof Brau restaurant, and the remodeling of 120 hotel rooms and suites, some of which are now appointed in Asian and safari motifs.

Rooms: 222 deluxe rooms and suites with phones, cable television, and wheelchair access. Nonsmoking units are available.

Amenities: Four restaurants, two snack bars, nine bars, casino, cabaret, airport shuttle; 1,400 free parking spaces in two garages, and free valet parking.

Rates: $–$$$.

Contact: Club Cal Neva, 140 N. Virginia St., Reno, NV 89501; 775/954-4540 or 877/777-7303; email: yourfriends@calneva.net; website: www.clubcalneva.com.

Eldorado Hotel Casino

Without question, this is downtown Reno's most stylish and elegant property, with a beautiful marble lobby, excellent restaurants, and well-appointed rooms with firm, comfortable beds. Eldorado is connected via skyway with Circus Circus Hotel Casino and the Silver Legacy Casino Resort, and the arcade from the latter property leads into the spectacular Grand Plaza on the mezzanine level. The centerpiece of the plaza is the baroque-style Fountain of Fortune, which gushes 50 feet high and has 20 mythological figures sculpted in marble and bronze.

COURTESY OF ELDORADO HOTEL CASINO

the Eldorado Showroom

The mezzanine itself was designed to look like a grand European avenue, with boutiques, a cappuccino bar, a game arcade, and the Brew Brothers microbrewery, where visitors can enjoy nightly live entertainment. In early 1997 the hotel opened a 175-seat restaurant and bar called Roxy's, created by famed San Francisco restaurant designer Pat Kuleto (of Postrio, Kuleto's, and Boulevard fame). Roxy's has seven exterior and interior architecture styles, reflecting various themes of a European village, and is one of the most popular restaurants in town. Chefs' Pavilion, a buffet restaurant, has several stations where meals are made to order, and featured cuisines are American, Italian, Chinese, Mongolian grill, and Mexican, with seafood on Friday. The Brew Brothers, with its eight custom microbrews, gourmet pizzas, and nightly live entertainment, is popular and always crowded. The hotel has an impressive 580-seat showroom with tiered, theater-style seating (including balconies) and lavish Broadway musicals. For more entertainment, there's the Bubinga Lounge, a luxurious and eclectic place that is trimmed in West African Bubinga wood and hosts live musical acts and DJ club dancing. At Eldorado, guests consistently rave about the high quality of service, the excellent restaurants, and the European sophistication of the hotel.

Rooms: 817 guest rooms with phones, televisions, and wheelchair access. Nonsmoking units are available.

Amenities: Ten restaurants, a bar, a lounge, a casino, a nightclub, showroom, cabaret, an outdoor pool, and an airport shuttle.

Rates: $$–$$$.

Contact: Eldorado Hotel Casino, 345 N. Virginia St., Reno, NV 89501; 775/786-5700 or 800/648-5966; website: www.eldoradoreno.com.

Fitzgerald's Casino/Hotel

Right at the Reno Arch at the foot of the Strip on North Virginia Street, "The Fitz" is one of the city's older downtown hotels. It carries an Irish theme through just about everything, from its country-style suites to its Limericks Pub and Grille restaurant, a dinner house that offers lamb shank, scampi, potato dumplings, and five flavors of prime rib. The hotel also has a buffet room called Lord Fitzgeralds Feast and Merriment, and Molly's Garden, a casual dining spot that specializes in potato leek soup, burgers, corned beef and cabbage, and other Irish and American favorites. Whether you'll have the luck of the Irish in the casino is anyone's guess, but at least the dealers won't snap at you. The staff is friendly and accommodating, and that's no blarney.

Rooms: 351 Irish-themed rooms and suites with phones, televisions, and wheelchair access.

Amenities: Three restaurants, a bar, a lounge, two floors of casino games, covered valet parking, and shows.

Rates: $–$$.

Contact: Fitzgerald's Casino Hotel, 255 N. Virginia St., Reno, NV 89501; 775/785-3300 or 800/648-5022; email: reno@fitzgeraldsreno.com; website: www.fitzgeraldsreno.com.

Golden Phoenix Hotel Casino and Resort (formerly Flamingo Hilton Reno)

In late 2001, Park Place Entertainment Corp., which also operates the Reno Hilton, closed the venerable Flamingo Hilton. But the hotel was reopened in early 2002 under Vista Hospitality Co., and the new owner launched an overhaul that included new carpeting, wall coverings, and a remodelled casino. Left in place were the coffee shop and Benihana Japanese Steak House. The signature restaurant on the highest floor was renamed The Vista Room. Reno's only rooftop dinner house offers sweeping views of the city and the Sierra Nevada. The 1,000-seat showroom, which hosted celebrity impersonations and other acts, was converted to meeting space and a weekend nightclub called Club Aftermath, although live entertainment (watch for occasional headliners) holds forth on a regular basis. One new convenience is self-parking in the underground garage, formerly limited to valet parking. Since the guest rooms were refurbished in 2000 under a previous owner, the interior is like new, even if the exterior looks weathered and tired. Standard rooms are spacious, with two queen-sized beds, but without bathtubs. Can the Phoenix rise from the ashes of the old Flamingo? Given its location on Sierra Street, a secondary artery in the downtown area that has been plagued with hotel closures in recent years, only time will tell.

Rooms: 604 rooms (including 66 suites) with phones, televisions with optional pay-per-view movies, in-room coffeemaker, and some wheelchair access. Some nonsmoking units and Jacuzzi suites are available.

Amenities: Three restaurants (at this writing), several lounges, a nightclub, a casino, live entertainment, a 12,000-square-foot banquet facility serving 400 people, 24-hour room service, and free airport shuttles.

Rates: $$.

Contact: Golden Phoenix Hotel Casino and Resort, 255 N. Sierra St., Reno, NV 89501; 775/785-7100; email: reno@vistahotels.com; website: www.vistahotels.com/hotels_reno.htm.

Harrah's Reno

A dependable heavyweight on the gaming scene, Harrah's Reno has been on a roll lately with lots of upgrades and expansions. Originally founded in 1937 by casino magnate William F. Harrah, this luxurious hotel has undergone a major transformation in its more than six decades of operation. Among the latest improvements are a $10 million remake of Sammy's Casino (the main gaming area), a $5 million renovation of all hotel rooms and hallways, a consolidated check-in desk for both towers, refurbishing of the old hotel lobby in the West Tower to include a new restaurant, the addition of a summer outdoor entertainment venue called The Plaza (which converts to an ice-skating rink in winter), and the creation of a posh gaming area for high-rollers known as High Limit Salon, where steamed towels are available 24 hours a day. (And if you don't win at baccarat, you might get plenty steamed without them!) There's also an exclusive VIP check-in area and lounge, the Diamond Club. Are we talking classy digs, or what? Yeah, we are. And what could be more fitting than to carry on in the style of Hollywood's famous "Rat Pack"? Indeed, legendary entertainer Sammy Davis Jr., who had enough star wattage to light up several casinos from coast to coast, was once a featured performer here, making more than 40 appearances in 22 years. The 400-seat theater still bears his name—Sammy's Showroom—and it still holds forth with occasional headliners, though The Plaza and its adjoining city streets have hosted more than 5,000 spectators for musical events, boxing matches, car shows, circus acts, and the nightly laser light show. The Plaza is on what used to be the site of two casinos—Nevada Club and Harolds Club—until Harrah's bought and demolished them in 1999. Apart from its central downtown location and its myriad of spiffs, another reason to stay at Harrah's is the pampering of your palate. The restaurants vary from good to exceptional. Harrah's Steak House, perhaps the finest dinner house in the city with its tuxedoed waiters and tableside flambés, deserves a visit for important occasions. Fresh Market Square Buffet is a feast for anyone who is hungry enough to indulge, maybe after all of that handle-pulling on the slot machines. Its themes reflect the ethnic diversity of San Francisco, including Fisherman's Wharf, Farmer's Market, Chinatown, and Little Italy. Café Napa is a 24-hour attraction that combines the ambience of California's Napa Valley wine region (with a wine bar that offers more than 30 selections) with fresh Asian, seafood, and California cuisine. And Café Andreotti is the requisite Italian bistro with plenty of pastas and other favorites. Another popular amenity is The Spa at Harrah's, which offers aromatherapy and deep-tissue massages. Repeat clientele at Harrah's swear by the overall service and the quality of its restaurants, and the property has been honored with the Mobil Four-Star Award.

Rooms: 958 guest rooms with phones and data ports, cable TV, Nintendo entertainment system, Saf-Lok electronic room key system, blow dryer, coffeemaker, cribs and rollaways by request, and wheelchair access. Over half of the rooms are designated as nonsmoking units. New ultraluxurious skyline suites feature Jacuzzi bathtubs.

Amenities: Six restaurants (including a deli), several lounges, a casino, showroom, an outdoor pool, complete spa and fitness club, Sun Center with tanning beds, barber shop, beauty parlor, 26,000 square feet of banquet space, Atlantic City Ballroom, The Plaza with nightly choreographed laser light show and strolling entertainers (in summer), VIP check-in and lounge, free valet/garage parking, and an airport shuttle.

Policies: Pets are not allowed, but an on-site kennel is available on the fifth floor of the West Tower.

Rates: $$–$$$.

Contact: Harrah's Reno, 219 N. Center St., Reno, NV 89501; 775/786-3232 or 800/HARRAHS (800/427-7247); website: www.harrahsreno.com.

Holiday Inn and Diamonds Casino

This 13-story hotel is close to downtown and is one of the older properties, but it offers well-appointed rooms, a large banquet/conference facility, and a restaurant.

Rooms: 283 units—consisting of guest rooms, deluxe double accommodations, and suites—provide phones, cable TV, and wheelchair access. Nonsmoking units are available.

Amenities: One restaurant; a bar; a casino with entertainment; health club; an outdoor pool; an 8,700-square-foot banquet and convention facility, which seats up to 400, with audiovisual equipment and catering services available; parking; and an airport shuttle.

Policies: Pets are allowed.

Rates: $$.

Contact: Holiday Inn and Diamonds Casino, 1000 E. 6th St., Reno, NV 89512; 775/786-5151 or 800/648-4877.

John Ascuaga's Nugget

Practically a self-contained resort, this large hotel/casino in Sparks includes attractive features such as a large indoor pool; the 900-seat Celebrity Showroom, which showcases stellar acts such as Tony Bennett, Al Jarreau, and Jay Leno; several restaurants; and proximity to Victorian Square, a turn-of-the-century-style shopping district across the street. In late 1996 the hotel opened its West Tower with 802 rooms, making the Nugget the third-largest property in the Reno area, after the Reno Hilton and Silver Legacy. The expansion, coming on the heels of a new enclosed parking structure, added the

Restaurante Orozko, a Spanish/Mediterranean-style restaurant, along with 28,000 feet of additional convention space. Doubling the accommodations at Nugget has triggered new development at adjacent Victorian Square, including the addition of a 14-theater movie complex. Although the square is clearly starting to blossom, the view from many of the Nugget's spacious rooms provides a less-than-appealing vista of railroad tracks and heavy industry. Also, some restaurants are mediocre and overall service can be spotty. Among the impressive features of this cavernous place are the Olympic-sized indoor swimming pool and spa facilities, which are brightly illuminated from skylights that can be opened, and the rustic, creative decor of Restaurante Orozko. The Nugget is the best venue in Reno for big-name entertainment, one of the reasons it gets such strong repeat business.

Rooms: 1,600 standard rooms and luxurious suites with phones, televisions, and wheelchair access. Nonsmoking units are available.

Amenities: Eight restaurants; five lounges; an aquarium; a casino; a lower level pavilion with sportsbook, a pub and pantry, a gift shop, and a bingo parlor; a showroom; a Jacuzzi; a sun deck; indoor and outdoor pools with poolside service; a health club; a beauty salon; a barbershop; shoe-shine service; an 110,000-square-foot convention center; a wedding chapel; the 30,000-square-foot Rose Ballroom, which seats 2,500 people; concierge service; free 24-hour covered and uncovered valet parking; and self-parking with 1,252 spaces in a five-story parking garage with security lighting, a sound system, and a skyway.

Rates: $$–$$$.

Contact: John Ascuaga's Nugget, 1100 Nugget Ave., Sparks, NV 89431; 775/356-3300 or 800/648-1177; website: www.janugget.com.

Peppermill Hotel Casino

A dazzling, streamlined building with three wings and modernistic neon lights, the Peppermill consistently wins awards for the quality of its rooms, cuisine, and casino. Its south Reno location, on South Virginia Street near the convention center, is far removed from the hustle and bustle of downtown. With 1,070 rooms, it is the city's fifth-largest casino property, and it has plenty of unique features, including 185 suites (the most in northern Nevada), elaborately themed restaurants, and a year-around outdoor swimming pool with its own waterfall. The pool, by the way, has a miniversion of a mountain, along with a computer-driven wildlife show. Who likes the Peppermill? Just about everyone, it seems, although women and families with children seem to find it especially attractive because it is truly a self-contained resort. And the entertainment is not just on stage. Dining is clearly an adventure in its own right. The Island Buffet, for example, features four 22-foot-high waterfalls and tropical squalls that have rain, mist, thunder, and lightning. And Romanza Ristorante Italiano has its own Hollywood-style special effects, including a high domed ceiling that changes from sunrise to sunset, a 17-foot-high statue of a Roman hero with two maidens set on a rotating platform, pyrotechnic torches, and Corinthian columns that surround the dining area. Other standouts in the food chain include Reno's Premier Steak House and White Orchid, a gourmet restaurant of American cuisine that is rated Four Diamond by AAA and has won *Wine Spectator*'s Award of Excellence. The International Food Court serves Italian, Chinese, Mexican, and American dishes, complemented by a vast salad bar, and the popular Peppermill Coffee Shop, a staple with conventioneers, offers heaping portions from Eggs Benedict to prime rib. And you can do an indoor pub crawl, visiting 11 different bars and lounges, each of which has a unique theme and offers specialty drinks, cocktails, wines, microbrews, and imported beers. Entertainment runs the gamut, from second-tier celebrity shows (Don Ho, Don McLean, Jefferson Starship, and The Marshall Tucker Band) to comedy and sports events. Also, the cabaret stage offers free nightly musical acts, which you can choose to watch on closed-circuit TV in your room if you don't want to brave the crowds. And if all of these things aren't enough to keep you inside for a weekend, then the quality of the guest rooms will probably tip the balance. Interiors are spacious, pleasing and elegantly sophisticated, with no casino gaudiness. Beds have custom-made mattresses, triple sheeting, and goosedown and nonallergenic foam pillows. The 44 Spa Suites are a cut above the standard rooms in appointments and include a Jacuzzi and sitting area. Imperial Suites are 595 square feet and have a Jacuzzi, sofa, dining area for four, and two television sets. At the top of the suite chain are the two Super Suites, each with 4,000 square feet and extravagant furnishings. One has a Safari Adventure theme ("Me Tarzan, you Jane"), while the other mirrors the opulence of ancient Rome, fit for an emperor and his empress. Clearly, this hotel aims to attract special-occasion guests for honeymoons, birthdays, anniversaries, and other occasions. And if all of that eating, drinking, gambling, etc., wears you out, you can always relax at the Salon and Spa with a massage, facial, new "do," or a manicure.

Rooms: 1,070 rooms (including 185 "five-star" suites in eight different designs and two "Super Suites") with phones and data,ports, TV with pay-per-view movies, hair dryers, iron, minibar, and wheelchair access. Some nonsmoking units. Safes and fax machines are available in suites.

Amenities: Seven restaurants, 11 themed bars, 24-hour casino, free nightly entertainment, year-around waterfall pool, free full-service health club and spa, gift shop, shoe shine, hair salon, business center, VIP check-in lounge, banquet and catering facilities, free 24-hour valet parking, spacious self-parking, free airport shuttle service, and on-site Hertz Rent-a-Car.

Rates: $$–$$$.

Contact: Peppermill Hotel Casino, 2707 S. Virginia St., Reno, NV 89502; 775/826-2121 or 800/648-6992; website: www.peppermillreno.com.

Plaza Resort Club

What's this? A luxury downtown hotel with no gaming at all? Not even a few weathered slot machines? That's correct. This boutique hotel with large and luxurious rooms is on a quiet, secondary street overlooking the Truckee River. Yet it's within easy walking distance of all the action on The Strip. Clearly, the hotel is aimed at upscale leisure travellers and business guests. VIP touches that you'd expect at the large casino hotels are

here: an indoor heated swimming pool, a fitness center, and a rooftop sun deck and whirlpool spa. The sun deck and many of the rooms have sweeping views of the Reno skyline and Sierra Nevada. The lobby and common areas have an Old World decor reminiscent of San Francisco's elegant small hotels.

Rooms: 103, each with data port telephone, cable TV, and VCR, microwave and refrigerator, hair dryer, in-room coffee, in-room safe, and electronic key card lock system. The upgraded Regal Rooms have large console TVs, whirlpool tubs, and full kitchens. Nonsmoking and wheelchair-access rooms are available.

Amenities: Fitness center, indoor heated pool, rooftop sun deck, billiards room, bell desk and concierge, indoor valet parking, lounge, guest laundry facilities, video library, and fax and copy service.

Rates: $$–$$$.

Contact: Plaza Resort Club, 121 West St., Reno, NV 89501; 775/786-2200 or 800/648-5990; website: www.plazaresortclub.com.

Ramada Inn/Speakeasy Casino

With a Roaring '20s motif that recalls the era of gangsters and gun molls, this recently remodeled hotel has been spiffed up with Tiffany chandeliers and stained glass throughout the casino and guest areas and has a a 24-hour restaurant/café.

Rooms: 234 deluxe tower rooms and suites with phones, televisions, and wheelchair access.

Amenities: Restaurant, casino, bar, nightclub with entertainment, sauna and fitness room, free continental breakfast, nonsmoking rooms, free parking (including an area for trucks and RVs), and airport shuttle.

Rates: $$.

Contact: Ramada Inn/Speakeasy Casino, 200 E. 6th St., Reno, NV 89501; 775/329-7400 or 888/298-2054; website: www.renoramada.com.

Reno Hilton

Close to the airport, the largest hotel in Reno (with 2,003 rooms) is practically a city within a city, a 27-story monolith sitting on 148 acres. Management could lock the doors and you wouldn't get bored for days. You can browse among the 20 shops in the downstairs mall; dine in nine restaurants; knock down pins in the 50-lane bowling center; watch a first-run movie at the cinema; see a dazzling live show in the 1,600-seat Hilton Theater; hang out at the Pylon Bar, which features full-sized racing airplanes commemorating the National Championship Air Races; boogie in the Garage nightclub with its celebration of the automobile; and lose yourself to virtual reality games at the Fun Quest Family Amusement Center. Did we forget the tennis courts, the golf driving range, and the swimming pool? Sorry. The Hilton continues to renovate hotel rooms and convention space to offer the most updated facility. Dining is diverse with Andiamo, which has an Italian neoclassic ambience, and the Grand Canyon Buffet, which has a cheery Southwestern interior and excellent variety of dishes. For elegant tableside service with steaks and seafood, The Steak House is always a favorite. Asiana offers California infused dining with noodle dishes, Cantonese favorites, and a full sushi bar. Lindy's 24-hour coffee shop specializes in down-home favorites and, for retro freaks, there's Johnny Rockets diner on the casino floor, where 1940s-style food (heavy on the meat, potatoes, and gravy) is served by a costumed staff of singing and dancing waiters. Another option is the Tex-Mex restaurant chain, Chevys. The Hilton Theater hosts some big-name celebrity acts as well as full-scale productions on the world's largest stage. Reno Hilton is well away from the Strip and provides a relatively safe haven for those who don't want to contend with some of the downtown hassles.

Rooms: 2,003 guest rooms (including 418 suites) with phones, televisions, and wheelchair access. Nonsmoking units are available.

Amenities: Nine restaurants; 5,200 spaces for valet or self-parking; 115,000 square feet of casino space; 200,000 square feet of convention and meeting space; a health club; a swimming pool; outdoor tennis; the Fun Quest Family Amusement Center; a 20-store shopping mall; a 50-lane bowling center; the Hilton Theater; Outdoor Hilton Amphitheater; The Garage nightclub;

the SuperBook race and sportsbooks; the Pylon Bar; and a free airport shuttle.

Rates: $$$.

Contact: Reno Hilton, 2500 E. 2nd St., Reno, NV 89595; 775/789-2000 or 800/648-5080; website: www.renohilton.net.

Sands Regency Hotel Casino

A quirky marriage of old and new, the Sands Regency combines its old casino and lobby with three towers of rooms. The additions were made without a grand redesign, so there are several logistical problems: a small and hopelessly overworked check-in desk; a rabbit warren of corridors and confusing pathways to tower elevators; and a patchwork of parking, either on the street, in a garage, or next to a motel annex. The main building is, as they say in the hotel trade, "tired." Still, the Sands is popular with people looking for inexpensive digs, and the rooms (especially in the Dynasty Tower) are clean, modern, and spacious—in fact, they are the city's largest standard rooms. All have been recently renovated. There are five restaurants, including Reno's only Tony Roma's (specializing in ribs) and The Original Mel's Diner (specializing in burgers and shakes), so you can dine in relative style or nosh on fast food. There is nightly, cabaret-style entertainment in the Tequila Bar lounge and at the Just for Laughs Comedy Club. Also, the Sands has the largest outdoor pool in downtown Reno, and it throws Friday evening pool parties for guests and locals. The clientele (mostly senior citizens and budget-minded Gen-X types) tends to describe the Sands as average and comfortable, with some of the best room values in town. While on a side street (North Arlington Avenue), the hotel is just a few blocks west of The Strip.

Rooms: 836 deluxe rooms (including executive Jacuzzi and penthouse suites) with telephones, cable TV with pay-per-view movies, and wheelchair access and assistance. On request, you can get a rollaway, crib, refrigerator, hair dryer, iron and ironing board. More than 500 rooms are nonsmoking units.

Amenities: Five restaurants, 24-hour room service, new and improved Penthouse Health Club with sauna and massage services, cabaret lounge, three bars, 24-hour casino, heated outdoor swimming pool, hair salon, video arcade, laundry and dry-cleaning services, gift shop, 12,000 square feet of meeting and convention space, fax and copying services, safe-deposit boxes, catering, car rentals, RV parking, 500-car parking garage, and free airport shuttle.

Rates: $$.

Contact: Sands Regency Hotel Casino, 345 N. Arlington Ave., Reno, NV 89501; 775/348-2200 or 800/648-3553; website: www.sandsregency.com.

Siena Hotel Spa Casino

A short walk from the hubbub of The Strip, and right across the street from the National Automobile Museum, is this new, European-style hotel on the banks of the Truckee River. Compared to its flashy high-rise neighbors, Siena is smaller (214 rooms) and decidedly low-key, with subdued color schemes and an understated elegance that combines Old World and con-

temporary stylings. By Reno standards, this is something of a boutique hotel, with a terraced restaurant along the river, a clock tower in front of the entryway, and a distinct lack of gaudy neon lights. Actually, Siena is not really new. It's an elaborate and expensive ($70 million) remake of an older hotel, but it was done so well that when it opened in the summer of 2001 guests could see few traces of its previous incarnation. Both the exterior and interior aesthetics borrow heavily from the Tuscany region of Italy, and the property has the trappings of an upscale business hotel, which is not exactly Reno's forte. Rooms have high-speed Internet access and Web TV, and the hotel meeting spaces are wired for video-conferencing. Developer Barney Ng has infused his creation with designer furnishings, such as beds with down comforters, feather (and nonallergenic) pillows, and custom Egyptian cotton linens. Other highlights include an ornately themed, 18,000-bottle wine cellar and bar called Enoteca; Lexie's, an Italian

Siena Hotel Spa Casino

restaurant that overlooks the river and is quiet enough to actually engage in conversation; and a full-service day spa with 11 therapy rooms. If Reno were a popular site for Fortune 500 corporate meetings (it's not), Siena would be everyone's first choice. But for now it will have to settle for sophisticated leisure travelers. One peculiar feature of the hotel is a small, rooftop swimming pool that is enclosed by walls on two sides and seems like a design aberration. The casino, couched in a theme of ancient Roman ruins outside the city of Siena, is modest (23,000 square feet) compared to the vast gaming halls of other casino-hotels. While lacking a showroom or cabaret, the hotel is close enough to the high-powered entertainment along The Strip, though it's a foreboding stroll at night—one you probably shouldn't make without company. Also, there is no covered or underground parking, an amenity you'd normally expect from a property of this quality.

Rooms: 214 rooms and suites, many with river or mountain views, with color television and Web TV, two-line speakerphones with data ports, in-room coffeemakers, minibar, and refrigerator, and iron with ironing board. Wheelchair-accessible and nonsmoking rooms are available.

Amenities: Two restaurants consist of Lexie's, serving morning breakfast pastries and dinner, and Contrada Café, a 24-hour coffee shop. Enoteca is a wine bar/lounge with a huge wine cellar and a special appetizer menu that includes more than 100 European cheeses. Other guest services include a day spa with rooms for massage, facial and body treatments, and "serenity"; a 23,000-square-foot casino; 13,000 square feet of meeting space with a ballroom, five meeting rooms and a hospitality suite; high-tech conferencing facilities including integrated audio and video systems and high-speed Internet access; 24-hour room service; free continental breakfast; valet parking (on an open lot); free on-site fitness center; outdoor swimming pool; Jacuzzi spa; gift and sundry shop; retail wine center; fully staffed business center; and free on-demand shuttle to/from the airport.

Rates: $$–$$$.

Contact: Siena Hotel Spa Casino, 1 S. Lake St., Reno, NV 89501; 877/743-6233; website: www.sienareno.com.

Silver Club Hotel Casino

Cose to Victorian Square in Sparks (four miles from downtown Reno), the Silver Club Hotel Casino has 206 fully appointed rooms (including eight suites) that were recently renovated and now sport a AAA rating. Each standard room has two queen beds, color TV, and telephone, and nonsmoking rooms are available. Guests can choose from three restaurants including Port of Subs (submarine sandwiches), the 24-hour Town Square Restaurant, and Anna Maria's Italian Ristorante. There is a large casino, entertainment nightly in the Gazebo Lounge, and free parking for guests along with space for motor homes. Guests consider the hotel to be clean, comfortable, and friendly, and room rate promotions often fall below $30 a night, making it one of the better budget values in the area.

Rooms: 206 rooms, including eight suites, with phones, televisions, and wheelchair access.

Amenities: Three restaurants, bar, lounge, shows, and an airport shuttle.

Rates: $.

Contact: Silver Club Hotel Casino, 1040 Victorian Ave., Sparks, NV 89431; 775/358-4771 or 800/905-7774; website: www.silverclub.com.

Silver Legacy Casino Resort

Dominating the Reno skyline, this 37-floor, 1,720-room Victorian-themed hotel is the tallest in northern Nevada. And it features a giant dome, 180 feet in diameter, that encloses a 120-foot-high replica of a silver mine and ore crusher. The exterior, ground-level facade re-creates storefront views of Reno in the 1890s and early 1900s. Inside, a Victorian lobby is luxuriously appointed in dark woods, marble floors, rich carpeting, gold and crystal chandeliers, and various collections of art. Guest rooms are well decorated and carry the theme with turn-of-the-century replicas. The Resort Casino features the Catch-a-Rising-Star Comedy Club, six restaurants and eateries, Rum

Bullions Island Bar (Reno's only rum bar), a showroom with top-name entertainment, elegant boutiques, and a highly rated health club and spa. The composite dome features laser, light, and sound shows, which occur regularly above the casino floor and attract spectators along the shopping and dining mezzanine. Silver Legacy is the middle property in the trio of interconnected casino properties that includes Eldorado and Circus Circus. Of the dining options, The Victorian Buffet is average in quality but ample in choices. Sterling's Seafood Steakhouse, the only gourmet option at the hotel, gets favorable reviews for its menu and woodsy nautical decor, and it is known for its Sunday champagne brunch. Covered parking is convenient to the lobby.

Rooms: 1,720 guest rooms, including 149 Spa Suites and eight executive suites featuring telephones with data ports, hair dryers, irons/ironing boards, cable television with pay-per-view, daily room service, and bell desk/concierge service.

Amenities: Six restaurants and eateries, four bars, 85,000-square-foot casino, 1,600-seat amphitheater, outdoor pool and sun deck, beauty and barber salon, boutique shops, arcade, 2,000 self-parking and valet spaces, and 150,000 additional square feet for special events, meetings and conventions.

Rates: $$–$$$.

Contact: Silver Legacy Casino Resort, 407 N. Virginia St., Reno, NV 89501; 775/325-7401 or 800/687-7733; website: www.silverlegacy.com.

Sundowner Hotel Casino

This older downtown hotel has a range of accommodations and about 9,000 square feet of convention space. It also has two floors of gaming along with three restaurants, including GK's Steakhouse and Bar, Garden Gazebo Buffet, and a 24-hour coffee shop. Budget travelers rate the Sundowner highly for its courteous staff and large and clean (but not luxurious) rooms.

Rooms: 586 (including 10 two-room suites complete with in-room hot tubs), phones and televisions, and nonsmoking rooms available.

Amenities: Three restaurants, bar, cabaret lounge with live weekend entertainment, 24-hour casino on two floors, outdoor pool, hot tub, and four floors of free, covered parking.

Rates: $–$$$.

Contact: Sundowner Hotel Casino, 450 N. Arlington Ave., Reno, NV 89503; 775/786-7050 or 800/648-5490; website: www.sundowner-casino.com.

Motels

RENO/SPARKS

Ace Motor Lodge

Rooms: 48 guest rooms with phones, televisions, and wheelchair access.

Amenities: Dining, a bar, a lounge, and a casino.

Rates: $.

Contact: Ace Motor Lodge, 222 N. Sierra St., Reno, NV 89501; 775/322-2178.

Adventure Inn

All 45 of the elaborately themed guest suites at the Adventure Inn—varying from interplanetary to tropical motifs—have private spas and custom furniture with imaginative appointments. Some of the units also include 18-foot pools.

Rooms: Accommodations include a television, phones, and many extras.

Amenities: Champagne and stretch limousines are included with all suites. There's a wedding chapel on-site.

Rates: $$–$$$.

Contact: Adventure Inn, 3575 S. Virginia St., Reno, NV 89502; 775/828-9000 or 800/937-1436; website: www.adventureinn.com.

Best Inn and Suites

Rooms: 103 guest rooms with telephones and color televisions; some nonsmoking units are available. Formerly the Continental. Recently remodeled.

Amenities: A restaurant, a bar/lounge, and a swimming pool.
Rates: $.
Contact: Best Inn and Suites, 1885 S. Virginia St., Reno, NV 89502; 775/329-1001 or 800/626-1900.

Colonial Motor Inn

This is a no-frills, older motel in downtown Reno within walking distance of casinos and restaurants.
Rooms: 100 standard and deluxe guest rooms with telephones and color televisions.
Amenities: Outdoor swimming pool.
Rates: $.
Contact: Colonial Motor Inn, 232 West St., Reno, NV 89501; 775/786-5038 or 800/255-7366.

Courtyard by Marriott–Reno

This newer property is in the south section of the city, close to shopping malls and the convention center. The four-story motor inn features spacious guest rooms with conveniences that are clearly intended for the business traveller.
Rooms: 117, with comfortable sitting area, large work desk, two phones with data ports, cable TV, and in-room coffee. Cribs are available.
Amenities: On-site restaurant (The Courtyard Café) open for breakfast, two meeting rooms, free parking, and self-service laundry facilities.
Policies: Service animals for people with disabilities only.
Rates: $$.
Contact: Courtyard by Marriott, 6855 S. Virginia St., Reno, NV 89511; 775/851-8300 or 800/321-2211; website: www.courtyardbymarriott.com.

Days Inn Reno

Older budget hotel that is next to the Highway 395 freeway (with attendant traffic noise) and near the Reno Livestock Event Center. It is six blocks from downtown Reno.
Rooms: 137, some designated nonsmoking.
Amenities: Outdoor pool, free parking.
Policies: Pets are allowed.
Rates: $.

Contact: Days Inn Reno, 701 E. 7th St., Reno, NV 89512; 775/786-4070 or 800/448-4555.

Econo Lodge

Rooms: 93, including some nonsmoking.
Amenities: One restaurant, wheelchair access.
Rates: $–$$.
Contact: Econo Lodge, 666 N. Wells Ave., Reno, NV 89512; 775/329-3125 or 800/553-2666.

Executive Inn

Rooms: 85 guest rooms with phones, televisions, and wheelchair access. Nonsmoking units are available.
Amenities: An outdoor pool.
Rates: $$.
Contact: Executive Inn, 205 S. Sierra St., Reno, NV 89501; 775/786-4050

Fairfield Inn and Suites Reno/Sparks

Near the commercial and industrial area of Sparks and six miles east of downtown Reno, this new, three-story motor inn has lots of extra features, including Marriott's newest designer rooms and suites, Jacuzzi spas, an indoor swimming pool, an exercise room, and 1,200 square feet of meeting space. It's close to the new golf course at D'Andrea (three miles away) and the two courses at Red Hawk (10 miles away). For kids, the Wild Islands Water Park, great for the midsummer heat, is just one mile away.
Rooms: 88, with cable TV and in-room movies, work desk with lamp, two phones with data ports and voice mail, free weekday newspaper, iron and ironing board, hair dryer, and in-room coffee. Suites feature 32-inch TV and CD stereo entertainment systems. Cribs are available.
Amenities: Expanded free continental breakfast, full business center, self-service laundry facilities, and dinner delivery service from local restaurants.
Policies: Service animals for people with disabilities only.
Rates: $$–$$$.
Contact: Fairfield Inn and Suites, 2085 Brierly Way, Sparks, NV 89434; 775/355-7700 or 800/228-2800; website: www.marriott.com.

Gatekeeper Inn

Rooms: 28 guest rooms with phones, televisions, and wheelchair access. Nonsmoking units are available. This is a fairly standard, two-story motel with outside entrances, but with clean and well-appointed rooms. Operated by Certified Quality Motels.
Rates: $$$.
Contact: Gatekeeper Inn, 221 W. 5th St., Reno, NV 89503; 775/786-3500 or 800/324-2499.

Gold Dust West Motor Lodge

Four blocks west of downtown next to a busy casino that is popular with locals, this motel was recently renovated, and new interiors provide a pleasant overall appearance, though rooms are small. Both the inside and outside of the adjoining casino also were overhauled. Newly opened is the Wildwood Restaurant and Cigar Bar, which serves breakfast, lunch, and dinner. Guests consider the motel comfortable and affordable.
Rooms: 103.
Amenities: Casino, one restaurant, bar/lounge, and wheelchair access.
Rates: $.
Contact: Gold Dust West Casino and Motor Lodge, 444 Vine St., Reno, NV 89503; 775/323-2211 or 800/438-9378.

La Quinta Inn

This two-story motel is close to Reno-Tahoe International Airport, freeways, and the convention center. Rooms have contemporary decor, oversized desks, and spacious, bright bathrooms with Corian vanities and tiled floors.
Rooms: 130 guest rooms with phones and data ports, voice mail, free local calls, cable TV, Nintendo video games, and coffeemaker. Wheelchair access and nonsmoking units are available.
Amenities: One restaurant, free continental breakfast, an outdoor pool, health club, and an airport shuttle.
Policies: Pets are allowed. Children under 18 are free.
Rates: $$.
Contact: La Quinta Inn, 4001 Market St., Reno, NV 89502; 775/348-6100 or 800/531-5900; website: www.laquinta.com.

Mardi Gras Motor Lodge

Rooms: 30 guest rooms with phones and televisions. Nonsmoking units are available.
Rates: $.
Contact: Mardi Gras Motor Lodge, 200 W. 4th St., Reno, NV 89501; 775/329-7470 or 800/228-2800.

Motel 6

This national chain has four properties scattered throughout Reno and Sparks—near the airport, downtown, south near the convention center, and near the Reno Events Center.
Rooms: Motel 6 Airport, 95; Motel 6 Reno Events Center, 142; Motel 6 Reno West (downtown), 123; and Motel 6 Reno South, 115. Some nonsmoking rooms are available.
Amenities: All have outdoor pools. Reno South has a restaurant.
Policies: All permit pets.
Rates: $.
Contact: Motel 6 Airport, 2405 Victorian Ave., Sparks, NV 89431, 775/358-1080; Motel 6 Reno Events Center, 866 N. Wells Ave., Reno, NV 89512, 775/786-9852; Motel 6 Reno West, 1400 Stardust St., Reno, NV 89503, 775/747-7390; and Motel 6 Reno South, 1901 S. Virginia St., Reno, NV 89502, 775/827-0255. Toll-free reservations can be made by calling the national Motel 6 line at 800/4-MOTEL-6 (800/466-8356); website: www.motel6.com.

National Nine Inn

Rooms: The National Nine Inn offers 32 guest rooms with phones, televisions, and wheelchair access.
Rates: $.
Contact: National Nine Inn, 645 S. Virginia St., Reno, NV 89501; 775/323-5411 or 800/FOR-RENO (800/367-7366).

Nevada Inn

Rooms: You'll find 43 guest rooms with phones and televisions.
Amenities: An outdoor pool.
Rates: $.
Contact: Nevada Inn, 330 E. 2nd St., Reno, NV 89501; 775/323-1005 or 800/999-9686.

Oxford Motel

Rooms: Phones and televisions are in each of the 28 guest rooms.
Policies: Pets are allowed.
Rates: $.
Contact: Oxford Motel, 111 Lake St., Reno, NV 89501; 775/786-3170 or 800/648-3044.

Residence Inn by Marriott

This relatively new, long-stay property, which is oriented to business travellers, is in the south part of Reno near shopping malls and restaurants, and offers deluxe accommodations and an outdoor swimming pool. It has three floors,
Rooms: 120 suites, including studios, one- and two-bedroom units with separate living areas, with work desk and lamp, phones with data ports and voice mail, cable TV with in-room movies, full kitchen with refrigerator and microwave oven, coffeemaker, iron and ironing board, hair dryer. Fireplaces are in some rooms. Cribs are available. Nonsmoking and wheelchair-accessible rooms are available.
Amenities: Swimming pool, heated spa, Sport Court, 750 square feet of meeting space, free parking, room service, free continental breakfast in the Gatehouse, weekly barbecue, laundry valet, exercise room, and copying/printer services.
Policies: Pets are permitted, but charges may apply (call for details).
Rates: $$$.
Contact: Residence Inn by Marriott, 9845 Gateway Dr., Reno, NV 89511; 775/853-8800 or 800/331-3131 (national Marriott reservations); website: www.residenceinn.com/rnori.

Reno Downtown Travelodge

Rooms: 98 deluxe rooms and suites with king or double bed configurations, direct-dial phones, cable TV, electronic security locks, and in-room coffee. Nonsmoking and designated pet units are available.
Amenities: Seasonal outdoor pool, free daily newspaper, free limited guest parking, and free airport shuttle.
Policies: Pets are permitted in some rooms.
Rates: $–$$.
Contact: Reno Downtown Travelodge, 655 W. 4th St., Reno, NV 89503; 775/329-3451 or 800/578-7878; website: www.renotravelodge.com.

Rodeway Inn Reno (formerly Travelodge Reno)

Rooms: The 210 guest rooms and suites provide wheelchair access. Other features are direct-dial phones, cable TV, in-room coffee, and some kitchens. Nonsmoking units are available. Units include some suites and executive suites.
Amenities: A sauna, a hot tub, laundry facilities (for guests only), free parking, a heated pool, and an airport shuttle.
Rates: $–$$$.
Contact: Rodeway Inn Reno, 2050 Market St., Reno, NV 89502; 775/786-2500 or 800/648-3800; website: www.rodewayinnreno.com.

Season's Inn

Rooms: 56 guest rooms with phones, free local calls, cable TV, free coffee, free covered parking, and wheelchair access. Nonsmoking units are available.
Rates: $–$$$.
Policies: Pets are welcome.
Contact: Season's Inn, 495 West St., Reno, NV 89503; 775/322-6000 or 800/322-8588; website: www.seasonsinn.com.

Showboat Inn

Right off I-80 and across from the Circus Circus, this older motel considers itself "a comfortable oasis in the hustle and bustle of downtown Reno." The four-story motel has a variety of accommodations, varying from singles with queen beds to luxury Jacuzzi units, but all are reasonably priced. The inn is within walking distance of the other major casino hotels on The Strip.
Rooms: 99 rooms and suites with phones, expanded cable TV, and wheelchair access. Nonsmoking units are available.
Amenities: Self-parking, some covered parking, and access to Downtown Casino Shuttle to/from the airport (at extra cost).
Rates: $–$$$.
Policies: Pets are welcome upon approval.
Contact: Showboat Inn, 660 N. Virginia St.,

Reno, NV 89501; 775/786-4032 or 800/648-3960; website: www.showboatinn.com.

Star Dust Lodge

Rooms: The Star Dust offers 59 guest rooms with telephones, televisions, and wheelchair access. Nonsmoking units are available. Part of the Quality Certified Motels group.
Amenities: An outdoor pool.
Rates: $–$$$.
Contact: Star Dust Lodge, 455 N. Arlington Ave., Reno, NV 89503; 775/322-5641.

Super 8 Motel at Meadow Wood Courtyard

This well-appointed motor inn with modern rooms is across from Northern Nevada's largest shopping mall. It features Hart's Café and Lounge and a 24-hour desk, along with its own conference center.
Rooms: 153 rooms, some nonsmoking, some with wheelchair access, with cable TV, coffeemaker, and phones with data ports. Refrigerators are available.
Amenities: One restaurant, casino, bar/lounge, Jacuzzi, outdoor swimming pool, convention center, free continental breakfast.
Policies: Small pets are allowed at extra charge.
Rates: $–$$.
Contact: Super 8 Motel, 5851 S. Virginia St., Reno, NV 89502; 775/825-2940 or 800/797-RENO (800/797-7366); website: www.meadowwoodcourtyard.com.

Super 8 Motel Reno (formerly Miner's Inn)

This motel, an older property, is close to the University of Nevada at Reno and its planetarium.
Rooms: 70, some wheelchair-accessible, with cable TV.
Amenities: Free parking and outdoor swimming pool.
Policies: Pets are allowed with a refundable deposit.
Rates: $$.
Contact: Super 8 Motel Reno, 1651 N. Virginia St., Reno, NV 89503; 775/329-3464 or 800/800-8000; website: www.super8.com.

Super 8 Motel Sparks

Rooms: 71, some nonsmoking, some wheelchair-accessible, with cable TV, king beds, phones with data ports and free local calls, and free coffee.
Amenities: One restaurant, casino, lounge, entertainment, free parking, and outdoor swimming pool. Close to Victorian Square shops and restaurants.
Policies: Pets are allowed with permission. Children 12 and under are free.
Rates: $$.
Contact: Super 8 Motel Sparks, 1900 E. Greg St., Sparks, NV 89431; 775/358-8884 or 800/800-8000; website: www.super8.com.

Town House Motor Lodge

Rooms: You'll find 79 guest rooms with phones and televisions. Nonsmoking units are available.
Amenities: An outdoor pool.
Rates: $–$$.
Contact: Town House Motor Lodge, 303 W. 2nd St., Reno, NV 89503; 775/323-1821 or 800/438-5660.

Truckee River Lodge

Reno's only 100 percent nonsmoking hotel is at a quiet location next to the Truckee River and within walking distance of casinos. It does not have any gaming, and it emphasizes clean and healthy living. There is a whole earth-type restaurant, called Pneumatic Diner (food served in a "nitrogen/oxygen-based atmosphere," whatever that means), as well as extras such as 24-hour bicycle rentals and a free cardiovascular workout center.
Rooms: The Truckee River Lodge encompasses 214 guest rooms and one- or two-bedroom suites with kitchens, air-conditioning, phones, in-room coffee, voice mail, and cable televison. All units provide wheelchair access.
Amenities: A restaurant, 24-hour minimart, bicycle rentals, free popcorn each night, free parking, coin-operated laundry, and a health club.
Policies: Pets are allowed.

Rates: $–$$$.
Contact: Truckee River Lodge, 501 W. 1st St., Reno, NV 89503; 775/786-8888 or 800/635-8950; website: www.truckeeriverlodge.com.

University Inn

Rooms: Nonsmoking units are available at the University Inn, which provides 170 guest rooms with phones, televisions, and wheelchair access. Part of the Quality Certified Motels group. Close to the University of Nevada–Reno campus.
Amenities: A buffet-style café and a bar.
Rates: $$.
Contact: University Inn, 1001 N. Virginia St., Reno, NV 89557; 775/323-0321 or 800/FOR-RENO (800/367-7366); website: www.unr.edu/unr/uinn.

Vagabond Inn

Rooms: The Vagabond Inn consists of 129 guest rooms with phones and televisions. Nonsmoking units are available.
Amenities: Two restaurants, a lounge, an outdoor pool, and an airport shuttle.
Policies: Pets are allowed.
Rates: $$.
Contact: Vagabond Inn, 3131 S. Virginia St., Reno, NV 89502; 775/825-7134 or 800/522-1555; website: www.vagabondinns.com.

Victorian Inn

Rooms: Nonsmoking units are available at the Victorian Inn, where you'll find 22 guest rooms with phones and televisions.
Rates: $.
Contact: Victorian Inn, 1555 Victorian Ave., Sparks, NV 89431; 775/331-3203 or 800/FOR-RENO (800/367-7366).

Western Village Inn and Casino

Rooms: 280 guest rooms with phones, televisions, and wheelchair access.
Amenities: Three restaurants, a bar, a lounge, a casino, shows, an outdoor pool, and an airport shuttle.
Policies: Pets are allowed.
Rates: $–$$.
Contact: Western Village Inn Casino, 815 E. Nichols Blvd., Sparks, NV 89431; 775/331-1069 or 800/648-1170; website: www.westernvillagecasino.com.

Wonder Lodge

Rooms: Next to the National Bowling Stadium, Wonder Lodge consists of 63 guest rooms with phones, televisions, and air-conditioning. Part of the Quality Certified Motels group.
Amenities: An outdoor pool.
Rates: $$.
Contact: Wonder Lodge, 430 Lake St., Reno, NV 89501; 775/786-6840 or 800/454-0303.

CARSON CITY/DAYTON
Best Western Carson Station

Across the street from a good restaurant (the Station Grill and Rotisserie, which it owns), the Carson Station is an aging but well-managed and above-average small hotel.
Rooms: 92 guest rooms and suites with phones, televisions, private balconies, and some nonsmoking units.
Amenities: Two restaurants (one in the hotel, Station Restaurant, and one across the street), casino, cabaret/bar lounge with live entertainment, sports bar, sportsbook lounge, two small conference rooms, and RV parking.
Rates: $$.
Contact: Carson Station Hotel Casino, 900 S. Carson St., Carson City, NV 89701; 775/883-0900 or 800/501-2929; website: www.carson-station.com

Best Western Pinon Plaza Resort

This new Best Western hotel has become the lodging beehive of Carson City and a favorite for golfers who come to town to play "The Divine Nine"—courses here and in nearby Carson Valley. Jointly managed with the Carson Station Inn and originally opened in 1995, Pinon Plaza is on Highway 50 east of the city's central business district. With a Southwestern theme throughout, the resort is noted for its state-of-the-art, 32-lane bowling center, which has quickly made it popular with the younger crowd. After a series of expansions, the property now has a fine restaurant

(The Steak House), a coffee shop (Branding Iron Café), and a snack bar and lounge in its bowling center. Other features include a casino, spacious outdoor swimming pool and spa, and a 70-space RV park. The hotel is clean, modern, and serviced by friendly employees.

Rooms: 148, including double queens, deluxe kings, and 49 Jacuzzi king suites (with minikitchens and living rooms). The oversized rooms (each more than 500 square feet) each have a conversation area, wet bar, Jacuzzi, and data port telephone.

Amenities: Casino, two restaurants, bowling center with pro shop and snack bar, Margarita Saloon with live music and dancing, Pizza Hut Express, sports bar, sportsbook, swimming pool, spa, exercise room, video arcade, Good Sam RV park, three high-tech conference rooms with 4,000 square feet of space, and children's play room.

Policies: Hotel guests are welcome to bowl in the center.

Rates: $$–$$$.

Contact: Pinon Plaza Resort, 2171 Hwy. 50 E, Carson City, NV 89701; 775/885-9000 or 877/519-5567; website: www.pinonplaza.com.

City Center Motel

Rooms: Owned by the Carson Nugget Casino, City Center Motel provides 81 modern guest rooms with phones and televisions.

Amenities: A coffee shop; a restaurant; an oyster bar; a buffet; a 24-hour casino; a theater lounge; a gold display; a free, supervised kid's arcade lounge; convention facilities; and RV parking in a free parking lot.

Rates: $$.

Contact: City Center Motel, 800 N. Carson St., Carson City, NV 89701; 775/882-5535.

Days Inn

Rooms: Some nonsmoking and wheelchair-accessible facilities are available at this Days Inn, which consists of 61 guest rooms with phones, cable television with free movies, air-conditioning, and kitchens.

Amenities: An adjacent restaurant, a fax machine, and RV parking.

Policies: Children age 12 and under stay for free.

Rates: $$.

Contact: Days Inn, 3103 N. Carson Hwy., Carson City, NV 89701; 775/883-3343 or 800/325-2525.

Ormsby House Hotel and Casino

With frequent ownership changes in recent years, the once-fabled Ormsby House, Carson City's largest hotel and casino, seems to be a continuing work in progress. As of this writing, yet another ownership change has occurred and the hotel was involved in a major remodelling, with the property closed until construction is completed (reopening was planned for 2003). Given the unpredictability of this property, it's best to call ahead before planning a visit. In its heyday, this was a lavish casino-hotel—the largest in town—complete with live music and a 24-hour casino. Can it return to its former glory? Only time will tell. In the original Ormsby House, writer Mark Twain was inspired to create some of his earliest characters.

Rooms: Likely to be less than the original 230 rooms and suites.

Amenities: May include three restaurants, casino, outdoor swimming pool, spa, and entertainment venue.

Rates: Call for details.

Contact: Ormsby House Hotel Casino, 600 S. Carson St., Carson City, NV 89701; 775/882-1890.

Park Inn
(formerly The Hardman House)

Above-average motel with nice decor and well-appointed rooms.

Rooms: 62 rooms and suites, including 50 nonsmoking units and nine suites. All units provide a phone and a television, and some units contain refrigerators and microwave ovens.

Amenities: Continental breakfast, afternoon wine, meeting space, and a parking garage.

Rates: $–$$.

Contact: Park Inn, 917 N. Carson St., Carson City, NV 89701; 775/882-7744.

Plaza Hotel

With new and remodeled rooms (the latter from acquiring an older motel), this relatively new (1998) property is in downtown Carson City, within walking distance of the State Capital Complex, casinos, restaurants, and museums.

Rooms: 148 rooms and suites with refrigerators, microwave ovens, and phones with data ports. 93 rooms are nonsmoking units and 16 are suites. Wheelchair-accessible rooms are available.

Amenities: 24-hour office equipped with fax and copy machines, banquet and meeting space, and free parking.

Rates: $$$.

Contact: Plaza Hotel, 801 S. Carson St., Carson City, NV 89701; 775/883-9500 or 888/227-1499; website: www.carsoncityplaza.com.

CARSON VALLEY

Carson Valley Inn

With its woodsy decor and extensive landholdings along U.S. 395, this deluxe property is a pleasant, out-of-the-way retreat and is arguably the most popular lodging in Carson Valley. The large complex consists of a 152-room hotel, a 76-room motor lodge, and a 60-space RV park. In the quiet community of Minden, south of Carson City, it has a repeat clientele of families and retirees. In early 2000, the inn completed a modest renovation of its rooms, hallways, casino, and restaurant areas, replacing garish casino red with more pleasant green for carpets and walls. Management also added Job's Perk coffee bar, the fourth food service. The hotel is well known for its restaurants (most popular are Michael's and Fiona's Bar and Grill) and for its frequent live entertainment. One significant new feature is a long-awaited pool/spa/fitness center on the second floor. The pool is shaped like the state of Nevada and offers year-around access, while the workout area has aerobics and weight-lifting equipment. In December 2001, a fire started by a welding accident destroyed much of the adjoining motor lodge, which had been closed for renovation at the time. Fortunately, the flames did not touch the main hotel/casino, nor the historic Wennhold House, a red brick building that dates from the 1920s and is used for registration. By mid-2002, the front building of the motor lodge was reconstructed and reopened for use. The inn is situated near great Basque restaurants, quaint Victorian homes, a hot springs (outside of Markleeville), and the alpine beauty of Highway 88 and Carson Pass.

Rooms: In the inn, 153 rooms (including seven suites) with king, double queen, king deluxe, or standard deluxe units, and spa suites. All hotel rooms have hair dryers, iron and ironing board, cable TV with pay-per-view movies, and telephones with data ports. In the motor lodge (detached), 76 rooms (of which 38 are newly rebuilt) have phones, cable TV, air-conditioning, and wheelchair access. More than half the units are designated nonsmoking.

Amenities: Three restaurants; one coffee bar; four cocktail lounges; nightly live entertainment and dancing in the cabaret lounge; 24-hour casino; two whirlpool indoor spas; fitness center; indoor swimming pool; supervised fun center for children ages 4–12; video arcade; 60-site RV resort offering full hookups, laundry, showers, dump station, pet area, and convenience store with fuel; convention center suitable for meetings, banquets, and receptions; wedding chapel; full wedding services; and free valet parking. Limousine transportation is available.

Rates: $–$$$.

Contact: Carson Valley Inn, 1627 U.S. Hwy. 395, Minden, NV 89423; 775/782-9711 or 800/321-6983; website: www.cvinn.com.

Historian Inn

As the newest (2000) motor inn in Gardnerville, this 35-room inn has several upscale touches, most of them centering on the history of the area. The Historian is downtown and is within walking distance of famous Basque restaurants and the recently restored central business district with its antique shops and boutiques. While the lobby and common areas (including a gift shop) borrow from the architectural style of the late 1800s, the rooms are thoroughly modern and all are designated nonsmoking.

Rooms: 35 with outdoor access, air conditioning, cable TV, phones with data ports and high-speed

Internet access, iron and ironing board, hair dryer, and in-room coffeemaker.

Amenities: Free continental breakfast in the parlor, free outdoor parking, and a gift shop.

Rates: $$–$$$.

Contact: Historian Inn, 1427 U.S. Hwy. 395 N, P.O. Box 1848, Gardnerville, NV 89410; 775/783-1175 or 877/783-9910; email: rooms @historianinn.com; website:www.historianinn.com.

Bed-and-Breakfasts and Country Inns

The inns that lie scattered throughout the Washoe and Carson Valleys south of Reno are diverse and interesting—some might even say eclectic. They vary from mining-era houses and Victorian replicas tucked away in historic districts to modern ranch-style buildings. Many are close to the eastern slopes of the Sierra and are situated among lush, green pastures or wetlands that teem with waterfowl. The two valleys represent a geologic west-to-east transition from alpine forest to rocky, semiarid high desert. This change is so abrupt you can actually see both types of terrain within a quarter mile.

There are several compelling reasons to select one of these properties over those nearer to Lake Tahoe. If you're passionate about history, you can be close to some of Nevada's best museums and oldest towns, places such as Virginia City, Carson City, and Genoa. Golfers will be within chipping distance of more than 20 courses that stretch along a 45-mile corridor from Reno to Gardnerville. Nearly half of these courses were built within the last five years. And because of their lower elevations, they are able to operate year-round, except for when the rare dusting of snow during a severe winter causes closures.

If you like to ski and golf you can do both in the same day by staying below the snow zone and driving a mere 30 to 45 minutes to some of Tahoe's best ski slopes. The spring months of March and April are great times to ski in the morning and golf in the afternoon. Of course, if you like to be near the nightlife and shopping of downtown Reno but prefer to sleep far from the neon lights and jangling slot machines, these places may fill the bill.

RENO/SPARKS
Bed-and-Breakfast South Reno

On the outskirts of town-in a bucolic place called Steamboat Valley, which is 12 miles south of The Strip—retired schoolteacher Caroline Walters operates her two-room inn in an Early American setting. She and her late husband spent years adding on to their two-story 1950 farmhouse, claiming wood beams from an abandoned bridge to build ceilings in the living room, collecting old books, and furnishing the interior with antiques. The property is surrounded by open space, though it's not far from Reno's spreading suburbia. There are three acres of well-manicured lawns, gardens, and decks, with a heated swimming pool as the centerpiece.

There are several compelling reasons to select one of these properties over those nearer to Lake Tahoe. If you're passionate about history, you can be close to some of Nevada's best museums and oldest towns. Golfers will be within chipping distance of more than 20 courses that stretch along a 45-mile corridor from Reno to Gardnerville.

The rooms, one of which has its own entrance off the porch, afford views of adjacent ranch-lands and of Mt. Rose and Slide Mountain, two popular ski hills. Both guest rooms are spacious and appointed with poster beds and modern private bathrooms; one unit comes with a shower, the other with a tub and shower.

There's a sitting room with a television, and the living room has a large brick fireplace. In a separate dining room, Mrs. Walters serves a continental breakfast. The home is full of placards bearing such homilies as "Live Well, Laugh Often, Love Much" with original paintings by her husband. Guests regard the inn as homey and comfortable. The property is near Washoe Lake, a popular windsurfing spot; the road to historic Virginia City; and the Mt. Rose Highway, which is the shortest route to Lake Tahoe from Reno.

Rates: $$, including breakfast.

Contact: Bed-and-Breakfast South Reno, 136 Andrew Ln., Reno, NV 89511; 775/849-0772.

CARSON CITY/DAYTON

Bliss Mansion Bed-and-Breakfast

Forget the budget and leave the kids at home for this dream Victorian mansion, which long was in need of tender loving care until Theresa Sandrini put a fortune into it and opened the region's premier B&B in early 1995. Now, as of late 2001, it is being operated by new proprietors Joyce Harrington and Ron Smith, formerly of Santa Cruz, California. Not only is this B&B in the best neighborhood of Carson City—right across from the Governor's Mansion—but it consumes an entire residential block. Cinderella would be lost here, but she'd probably find a Prince Charming in one of the corridors. Consider four of the five guest rooms of this truly dramatic three-story estate. Each averages more than 400 square feet and has high ceilings and a gas-fed Honduran mahogany fireplace. Three rooms offer full baths, with large tubs and separate showers. Four rooms are decorated with a combination of antiques and expensive, custom-made hardwood replicas. The fifth room, formerly used by the Sandrini family, is now available as a more contemporary double suite.

This house, in the historic section of Nevada's state capital, was built in 1879 by timber and railroad baron Duane L. Bliss, who left behind estates throughout the Carson Valley and Lake Tahoe areas. When it was constructed, it was the largest home in Carson Valley, but over the years it had a checkered pattern of ownership, several times facing the prospect of

demolition. Mrs. Sandrini gutted the interior and built a truly glorious bed-and-breakfast inn. Just stepping inside the front door takes your breath away. A 35-foot-long foyer, with its original wallpapered ceiling and Italian Carrara marble floor, continues into a cavernous dining room decorated with porcelain chandeliers. On one side is a large stairway. To the left of the foyer is a parlor and billiards room, although the latter is now a "media room," complete with large-screen television and ample reading materials.

All of the rooms are light and airy, which suited the Bliss family just fine. The acre-sized property has sprawling lawns, roomy verandas, and beautiful old trees and roses. In the morning, a full breakfast is served, including eggs du jour, pastries and breads, fresh fruit, coffee, and fresh-squeezed juices. Throughout the day and night there are snacks, drinks, ice cream, and goodies available to guests at their whim. Four guest rooms are on the second floor and the fifth is on the third floor. The innkeepers describe this place as "Victorian with modern comforts," and those include pillow-top mattresses, down comforters, plush towels and robes, instant-on hot water, and individual room heat and A/C controls.

Rates: $$$–$$$$. Major credit cards are accepted.

Contact: Bliss Mansion Bed-and-Breakfast, 710 W. Robinson St., Carson City, NV 89703; 775/887-8988 or 800/887-3501; email: innkeeper@blissmansion.com; website: www.blissmansion.com.

Deer Run Ranch Bed-and-Breakfast

Decorated with Western and Native American artifacts, this modern, two-room bed-and-breakfast north of Carson City is on land that is used as a working alfalfa ranch in summer. It is splendidly isolated, surrounded by sagebrush and baying coyotes, and stands across from Washoe Lake State Park off U.S. 395. Owner David Vhay, an architect and builder, and his wife, Muffy, a potter, have added some unique touches to the inn, including a passive solar heating/cooling system.

The ranch is nestled against an earthen berm on the north and east and has sweeping views of the high desert and the Sierra Nevada range on the south and west. Each of the two guest rooms has a queen-sized bed with handmade quilt and a window seat filled with pillows. Private baths are across the hall. A spacious sitting area, shared by both rooms, has a fireplace, a television with a VCR, a telephone, books, games, a guest refrigerator, and free beverages. Navajo rugs, ranch photographs, and paintings adorn the floors and walls.

A full breakfast, served on a handmade table in the sitting room, includes specialties such as omelets Florentine or provençal, Dutch babies, and home-baked breads and muffins. The meal is served on plates made on the premises by Muffy. Guests receive a basket of fruit, wine, and snacks upon arrival. Apart from the main house, the ranch includes a pottery studio (where you can watch Muffy at work), a horseshoe pit, a workshop, an aboveground swimming pool, a pond that freezes over for ice skating in winter, and a garden. Washoe Lake is a favorite spot for windsurfing and sailing, and McClellan Peak (above the ranch) is used for hang gliding and mountain biking. The ranch, 22 miles south of Reno and eight miles north of Carson City (off Exit 42), is 3.9 miles east of U.S. 395 on East Lake Boulevard.

Policies: A two-night minimum stay is required for holidays and special-events weekends.

Rates: $$. Visa, MasterCard, and American Express are accepted.

Contact: Deer Run Ranch Bed-and-Breakfast, 5440 E. Lake Blvd., Carson City, NV 89704; 775/882-3643; website: www.virtualcities.com/nv/deerrun.htm.

VIRGINIA CITY

Tyson's Canyon Ranch

Reno television personality John Tyson and his wife, Carol, have been entertaining visitors since 1995 with their Western ranch-style barbecues, equestrian events, country music (he's an accomplished singer and guitar player), and cowboy poetry. Now, with five luxurious guest cottages, their spread combines the comforts of a bed-

Tyson's Canyon Ranch

and-breakfast inn with the romantic ambience of a working cattle ranch. In the dramatic, high-desert hills south of Reno and 10 minutes north of Virginia City, the ranch has a herd of Texas longhorn cattle, a novelty in itself. During the warm weather, the Tysons offer daytime and full-moon horseback rides and excursions to see wild mustangs. In winter, they have cross-country skiing and snowshoeing. Groups and guests can partake in a barbecue lunch or a sit-down dinner, usually accompanied by musicians, singers, and poets performing on an outdoor stage. In a nearby arena, cowboys demonstrate team penning and roping. Three cabins have king-sized lodgepole beds, suitable for couples, and two are two-bedroom units suitable for families. Each cabin has a bathroom, gas fireplace, satellite television, and telephone. Two have full kitchens and the others have kitchenettes. All are lovingly and creatively decorated with cowhides and Western artwork. Hearty ranch breakfasts, delivered to your door, might include omelets, bacon and eggs, waffles and juices. In summer, guests can enjoy gourmet dining in the Canyon Ranch Room restaurant on Friday and Saturday nights. The outdoor dinner shows (extra but at reduced rates for guests) serve beef tri-tip, baked potatoes, ranch beans, corn, salad, fresh fruit Mexican cornbread, dessert, coffee, and iced tea. During their stay, guests are encouraged to ride into neighboring Long Valley, one of the last retreats for free-roaming wild mustangs. The property also has a gift shop, large yard, gazebo with adjoining garden area, and big commercial kitchen that can serve up to 300 people. The ranch is popular with groups that arrive by tour bus and with wedding parties.

Policies: Children are permitted, dogs are not (there are plenty of ranch dogs around).

Rates: $$$. Some major credit cards accepted.

Contact: Tyson's Canyon Ranch, 7 Mile Canyon, P.O. Box 425, Virginia City, NV 89440; 775/847-7223; email: tyson@alpine.net; website: www.nevadaduderanch.com.

Chollar Mansion

Built in 1861, this historic building was originally the home of Billy Chollar, who discovered the adjacent Chollar Silver Lode and started what became the nation's fifth-largest silver mine. A special feature of the bed-and-breakfast inn, owned by Ken and Kay Benton, is a 164-square-foot arched vault that once stored millions of dollars worth of gold and silver bullion. Another feature is the Pay Master's booth, where each month the miners would draw their pay. As an inn, the Chollar Mansion sits on a hill and affords picturesque views of the rugged Six Mile Canyon and Forty Mile Desert. Listed on the National Register of Historic Places, the building has 12-foot-high ceilings, 14-inch-thick floors, and entrances from two streets. The owners have a bookstore on the premises with many tomes on Virginia City and the West. Three rooms in the mansion and an adjoining cottage comprise the offerings for guests. All are ornately decorated in antiques and Victorian stylings. The ground-floor suite, Bedroom No. 1, is where the first mine superintendent and his wife used to hold their daughters' cotillions. This suite comes with a private bath. The two upstairs bedrooms have a shared bath. The cottage, next to the gardens, is popular as a honeymoon retreat and has its own bath. Each morning, the Bentons serve a large continental breakfast with fruit, breads and muffins, egg dishes, coffee, tea, and juices. The inn is within easy walking distance of many other historic buildings and attractions in town.

Policies: No pets. No smoking inside the buildings. Children, preferably seven and older, are permitted only in the cottage.

Rates: $$–$$$. No credit cards are accepted. Payment is by cash or traveler's checks only.

Contact: Chollar Mansion, 565 S. D St., P.O. Box 889, Virginia City, NV 89440; 775/847-9777.

Gold Hill Hotel

Nevada's oldest hotel—perched on the slopes of the rugged high desert east of Carson City, the state capital—is just down the road from one of the most important gold strikes in history. Built in 1859 as Vesey's Hotel, the 19-room inn (which includes four nearby guesthouses and a duplex apartment unit) were mainstays of Gold Hill and Virginia City, boomtowns that sprang up with the discovery of the Comstock Lode. The original stone structure and a luxurious addition (built in 1987) allow guests to experience some of the opulence that characterized what was once the largest population center west of the Mississippi. Proprietors Carol and Bill Fain decorated all of the rooms in period furnishings, using antiques or reproductions. The four rooms in the original structure are small but quaint; two share a bathroom found down the hallway, with an antique clawfoot tub, and two have showers. One caveat for insomniacs is that noise tends to filter up from the restaurant and Great Room below. Eight rooms in the new addition are spacious, quiet, luxurious, and still maintain the historic ambience. Amenities include king-sized beds, fireplaces, air-conditioning, televisions, telephones, and full bathrooms with modern tubs.

Three of the guesthouses (the duplex, the Brewery Lodge, and the Gray House) are across the street and two others (the Little House and the Honeymoon House) are a half-mile up the road toward Virginia City. Of these the most luxurious is the Honeymoon House, which has a spacious bedroom with a king bed upstairs, two baths (one with clawfoot tub), a living room with a cathedral ceiling, and a kitchen. A sixth detached building, called Miner's Lodge, is behind the hotel and has two adjoining units which can be rented separately or together (through a connecting door). Large families can find the most space in the Brewery Lodge, which dates to 1862 and has a master bedroom with king bed, two small bedrooms, a large living room, kitchen, fireplace, and 1.5 baths. It also has an outdoor gazebo, which can be used for parties, weddings, and picnics. A continental breakfast of juice, coffee, and muffins is provided daily in the Great Room. The Crown Point Restaurant serves dinners Wednesday–Sunday and offers an eclectic menu that varies from wild game to continental favorites such as beef Wellington and chateaubriand. Lecturers hold forth on Tuesday night, when there is a special dinner menu, and a newly initiated After Dinner Theater offers plays on Wednesday and Thursday evenings. The Gold Hill Saloon stocks a vast selection of beers, cognacs, liqueurs, and single malt scotches. Another asset is the hotel's excellent bookstore, which showcases Virginia City and Nevada history. Gold Hill Hotel is one mile south of Virginia City on Highway 342.

Rates: $–$$$$. Rooms include daily continental breakfast. Major credit cards are accepted.

Contact: Gold Hill Hotel, P.O. Box 740, Virginia City, NV 89440; 775/847-0111; email: GLDHILHOTL@aol.com; website: www.goldhillhotel.net.

CARSON VALLEY

Genoa House Inn

Genoa is Nevada's oldest settlement, and it's well situated for golfers, skiers, history buffs, and hot springs aficionados. With lush green pastures and rolling hills, the town snuggles against the eastern slopes of the Sierra and is within a 20-minute drive of South Lake Tahoe, the Nevada entrance of Heavenly Ski Resort, and Carson City. This quaint, two-story Victorian bed-and-breakfast, operated by Linda and Bob Sanfilippo,

was originally built in 1872 by A. C. Pratt, a newspaper publisher who printed the valley's first newspaper. Although it's been restored, the home is still listed in the National Register of Historic Places.

There are three quite elegant guest rooms. Upstairs is the Rose Room, which is accented in mallard green and burgundy and features a handmade barn-wood queen-sized bed, Victorian antiques, stained glass windows, a private bath with a tiled shower, and a private balcony. Off the same hall is the Blue Room, decorated in soft gray-blues and featuring mahogany antiques, a queen-sized bed, and a lavish bathroom with a Jacuzzi tub and an overhead shower. Downstairs is the Garden Room, with its private entrance off the ground floor, accents of green marbling, antique furnishings, a faux fireplace, and a full bathroom with a clawfoot tub and a shower above.

Coffee is delivered to your door early in the morning and is followed by a full breakfast either in your room or in the sunlit dining room. On the menu are items such as homemade cinnamon rolls, fresh fruit topped with yogurt, baked or coddled egg dishes, and a variety of juices. The inn is 1.5 miles down the road from one of the region's newest and best 18-hole golf courses, Genoa Lakes, and is two miles from David Walley's Hot Springs Resort, the finest natural hot springs spa in the region. Genoa House Inn is on Nixon Street in Genoa, next to the Genoa Community Church.

Policies: Smoking is not permitted inside. No children or pets are allowed.

Rates: $$ for double occupancy. Includes daily breakfast, refreshments on arrival, and discounted admission to the hot springs resort. Major credit cards accepted.

Contact: Genoa House Inn, P.O. Box 141, Genoa, NV 89411; 775/782-7075; email: genoahouseinn@pyramid.net; website: www.genoahouseinn.com.

The Wild Rose Inn

Outside the historic Nevada town of Genoa, Wild Rose Inn was built in 1989 as a replica of a Queen Anne-style Victorian. This is a country inn surrounded by lawns and natural stone walls. The exterior charm and beautifully appointed rooms offer a romantic getaway with views over the eastern Sierra and the lush, green Carson Valley. Innkeeper Sue Knight acquired the three-story home in 1998. The five guest rooms come with queen-sized iron or brass beds and private bathrooms accented with brass. The Gables, on the third floor, is a large suite with two queen beds and a daybed, a wet bar, an eating area, a sitting area, and a large bathroom. The Cameo Rose Room, decorated in Wedgwood blue wallpaper, is elegant and features a bath and separate dressing room with a built-in wardrobe and vanity. The Garden Gate Room, which is on the second floor in the cupola, has five windows with panoramic views of the Carson Valley and the Sierra, and it is decorated with an iron bed and antique oak furnishings. The Cottage Corners is a cozy room with northern views of the peaks and valley. The Stage Stop room, on the ground floor, is appointed with equestrian brass pieces and farm accents. A full buffet breakfast is served daily, along with afternoon tea. Evening refreshments are always available. The Wild Rose Inn is close to the Golf Club at Genoa Lakes and David Walley's Hot Springs Resort and is within a 25-minute drive of Lake Tahoe. It's on Main Street (Jacks Valley Road), about 10 miles southwest of Carson City. Pickup is offered from the Douglas/Minden airport (which serves generation aviation aircraft).

Policies: No smoking is allowed inside. Pets are not permitted. Children over 12 years are welcome. Two-night minimum during holiday and special event weekends.

Rates: $$–$$$. Major credit cards accepted.

Contact: Wild Rose Inn, 2332 Main St./P.O. Box 605, Genoa, NV 89411; 775/782-5697 or toll-free at 877/819-4225; email: wildrose@ wildrose-inn.com; website: www.wildrose-inn.com.

RENO ACCOMMODATIONS

Campgrounds

Every year our extended family (15 and counting) embarks on a midsummer camping expedition. With so many logistical challenges, we might as well be packing for Mt. Everest. Everyone has a favorite pastime and, happily, some of them coincide with others. But the prerequisites are substantial. For example, my wife and I have a Coleman Scanoe (a combination skiff and canoe) with a small outboard motor, so we like to be near a lake for cruising and fishing. But we prefer the leeward side, so the Sierra's almost predictable afternoon winds won't blow us off the

water, or worse, swamp our little vessel. And we like being in a tent.

By contrast, my sister-in-law and her husband, after camping for years in a tent, finally succumbed to a 22-foot RV, breaking the tradition of our clan. So now we need side-by-side campsites that are large enough to accommodate an RV and a half-dozen tents. And everyone's fussy. We have infants and mothers who want a beach or a shoreline for sunning. We have older youngsters who want a cove or shallow lagoon for swimming. Mountain bikes are high on the activity list for the older boys, so we need to be near paved or graded trails to accommodate them. You want more? The boys and fathers

Boomtown RV Park

are fishing fanatics, so the lake had better be well supplied with trout. My wife's favorite activity, above all others, is hiking. She wants to be near trails that lead to out-of-the-way alpine lakes, and she prefers long, strenuous forced marches of 8–10 miles that equal the "pump" of her high-impact aerobics classes.

Somehow, we always manage to find a place around Lake Tahoe that fills our demanding and diverse requirements. For the multiuse, multidimensional camper, Lake Tahoe is a paradise in the summer and early fall, and it's easy to see why sites fill up rapidly—especially in the more desirable campgrounds, close to the water's edge. You can find perfect seclusion, with your tent or small RV nestled deep in a ponderosa pine forest. Or you can be close to the action, near town centers with access to public transportation and within cycling or walking distance of restaurants, nightspots, and other points of interest.

More than 125 public and private campgrounds exist around Lake Tahoe, Reno, Carson Valley, and the surrounding areas. They are operated by the U.S. Forest Service, the California Department of Parks and Recreation, the Nevada Department of Parks and Recreation, the Bureau of Land Management, PG&E, the U.S. Army Corps of Engineers, and various city, county, and regional agencies. The facilities vary in quality, but in general, the state and local agency campgrounds and most of the private campgrounds, such as KOA, have more amenities—especially showers and flush toilets. In recent years some large and very luxurious RV resorts have opened in Nevada, around the Reno/Sparks area and along Carson Valley, and some of these provide spas, pools, playgrounds, cable TV, and clubhouses. The Forest Service sites are primitive, generally with vault toilets (the exception is in Tahoe, where all of them have flush toilets) and no showers, but they are inexpensive and tend to be in more pristine or remote locations.

> *Lake Tahoe is a paradise in the summer and early fall, and it's easy to see why campsites fill up rapidly—especially in the more desirable campgrounds, close to the water's edge.*

Of course, if you're in a self-contained RV, you'll have all the comforts of home. Personally, I'm not keen on high-tech camping. More than once, I've set up my humble little North Face dome tent next to the Mother of All RVs, complete with portable satellite dish, color TV, and gas generator. What we'd endure most of the evening was enough accessory lighting to illuminate a Broadway stage show, reruns of *Charlie's Angels* or some godawful slasher video playing on a blaring TV set, and the consistent drone of a generator to run all this stuff. That scenario doesn't fit my definition of camping.

The key to securing a great campsite in this region is planning. Because the majority of public sites can be booked only through a reservation service during the high season, you may have to choose a date months ahead of time and then be poised to work your phone and the redial function for an hour or longer to get through. However, most campgrounds that offer reservations usually hold out a few sites for first-come, first-served arrivals. Some of the more remote public campgrounds accept no reservations and are rarely full. For those on the shore of Lake Tahoe, though, you'd better make reservations. Many of the public sites can be reserved as far as eight months in advance, and for the popular areas you are advised to call on the first day reservations become available. The Great Land Rush of the mid-1800s is nothing compared to the Great Camping Rush of modern times.

The fastest way to book a public site is through the Internet, which allows you to avoid the telephone hassles. As of 2002, campsites operated by the U.S. Forest Service and U.S. Army Corps of Engineers are available through the National Recreation Reservation Service (website: www.ReserveUSA.com), and campsites owned by the California Department of Parks and Recreation are available through ReserveAmerica (website: www.ReserveAmerica.com). You may book individual campsites up to 240 days in advance and get instant confirmation by using a major credit card. You will need to pay the campsite fees for your entire stay, as well as a reservation fee, in one transaction. If you change or cancel your reservation, if you do not arrive on your first day, or if you leave early, you will be charged extra service fees. The online service asks for your name, address, and phone number, as well as the type of site required and the campground or state that you wish to camp in. Sometimes we've had difficulty logging in because of high traffic volume. As alternative, there's always the telephone, though that, too, can be fraught with busy signals during peak booking hours and days.

Even if you choose not to book online, you can still get information from the various government agencies by checking out their respective websites. Here are Web addresses for most public agencies mentioned in this chapter:

• California Department of Parks and Recreation (Sierra District): www.cal-parks.ca.gov
• Nevada State Parks: www.state.nv.us/stparks
• Eldorado National Forest: www.r5.fs.fed.us/eldorado/html/recreate.htm
• Tahoe National Forest: www.r5.fs.fed.us/tahoe
• Lake Tahoe Basin Management Unit: www.r5.fs.fed.us/ltbmu
• Plumas National Forest: www.r5.fs.fed.us/plumas/recr/camping/camppnf2.htm
• Toiyabe National Forest (Carson Ranger District): www.fs.fed.us/htnf/carcamp.htm
• Bureau of Land Management (Carson City office): www.nv.blm.gov/carson
• Pacific Gas and Electric Company: www.pge.com/recreation
• Washoe County (Nevada) Regional Parks: www.co.washoe.nv.us/parks/group.htm
• U.S. Army Corps of Engineers (Martis Creek Lake): www.usace.army.mil

A Word about Pets

Virtually all public and most private campgrounds accept them; however, policies require that they be leashed at all times. Most public campgrounds charge $1 per animal extra; private campgrounds charge as much as $3.50, though a few charge nothing. There's an honor system for cleaning up after your pet. Some private facilities even have special dog-walking or -running areas. In addition to pets, the campground may charge an "extra vehicle" fee, usually around $5 per vehicle per day.

Camping Regions

There are six major camping regions in the Lake Tahoe/Reno area.

The 72-mile shoreline of **Lake Tahoe** itself is studded with a variety of campgrounds, most of which are on the more wooded West Shore stretching from Tahoe City to South Lake Tahoe. By far the best public campgrounds, and generally the best locations, are in the California state parks. Emerald Bay and D. L. Bliss have wonderful shoreline access, while Sugar Pine Point is a great spot for cyclists and hikers. Several federal and private campgrounds along Highway 89, from Truckee to South Lake Tahoe, are so close to the road that the constant intrusion from traffic makes them much less desirable. For members of the RV crowd who like to be near casinos and restaurants, the city of South Lake Tahoe has a large and well-situated campground off U.S. 50, and there's a similar but smaller campground in Tahoe City.

The **Truckee/Donner** region stretches along I-80 from Truckee to Grass Valley—all within the Tahoe National Forest—with campgrounds along the Yuba River and along a series of PG&E reservoirs, including Lake Spaulding. The best campsites are those off the main highway, particularly along the less-traveled Highway 20. A large region of hiking trails to pristine backcountry lakes in the Grouse Lake area is near here, though many of the trailheads require a four-wheel-drive or high-clearance vehicle to reach them. Donner Memorial State Park is right next to Donner Lake and close to the town of Truckee, though it gets noise from busy I-80 on one side and the Southern Pacific Railroad on the other. On a section of Highway 89 from Truckee to Tahoe City, several Forest Service campgrounds parallel the road and the Truckee River. When the Truckee is flowing and fishing is good, that's a great location. But it's not quiet.

Lakes Basin/Feather River Country is another area not widely known to nonresidents; it's along Highways 89 and 49 north of Truckee.

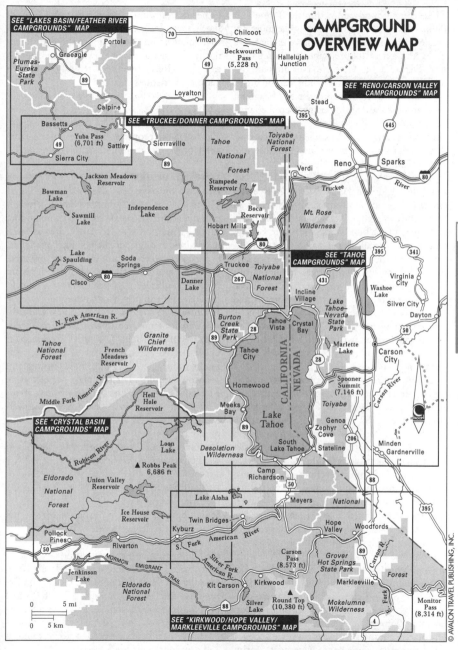

These campgrounds are within the Tahoe and Plumas National Forests. Probably the most desirable locations are in what is known as the Lakes Basin area, a network of hikable lakes stretching from Sierra City to Graeagle. Not only are the hikes here spectacular, but fishing can be great, especially in the nearby Feather River. The crown jewel and the most visible element on the landscape is the Sierra Buttes, a series of jagged peaks reminiscent of the Swiss Alps, which makes a great destination for a vigorous but not impossible hike with rewarding vistas along the way.

About 40 minutes south of South Lake Tahoe, a 40-mile **Kirkwood/Hope Valley/Markleeville** stretch of scenic Highway 88 affords access to wonderful campgrounds at secluded alpine lakes, with some of the best hiking, mountain biking, and equestrian trails in the region. The area traverses two national forests—Eldorado in California and Toiyabe in both states. It ranges from Bear River Reservoir on the west to Indian Creek Reservoir on the east. Some tremendous small campgrounds, such as those around the Blue Lakes region operated by PG&E, can be reached on well-marked but twisty dirt roads. One of the jewels of the Tahoe Sierra, this area is well worth exploring.

Crystal Basin's labyrinth of reservoirs for boating, water-skiing, and fishing, along with some pristine alpine lakes reserved for float fishing and nonmotorized boats, offer the single largest camping area in this part of Northern California. And yet none of it is visible from U.S. 50. The entire complex of lakes is accessible from only two paved roads, both of which climb a steep mountain flank and are easy to miss when you're driving along the highway. Great swimming holes, fishing for trophy trout, and a plethora of less well known backcountry trails to the west side of Desolation Wilderness make this area a winner for multiuse campers.

The **Reno/Carson Valley** offers a handful of public and private campgrounds along the eastern slopes of the Sierra, all within Nevada, suitable if you like low-alpine or high-desert camping. Some of these are in windswept, desolate places, but there is always a wetlands area, a lake, a river, or some other waterway nearby.

Other campgrounds hug the eastern slopes of the Sierra and Carson ranges and offer trailheads to high-elevation vistas. A lot of them, unfortunately, are next to busy highways. Some are just east of Mt. Rose, the site of a recently designated national wilderness area.

TRUCKEE/DONNER

The following properties are keyed to the Truckee/Donner Campgrounds map.

Lake Spaulding
(see map on page 493, site 1)
The main boat ramp at the sprawling reservoir is near this attractive, heavily forested campground. Although sites are close together, they are well maintained and include the luxury of brick barbecues. Recently new vault toilets were installed. The campground is far enough from the main highway to offer a sense of seclusion. Boat launching is free for campers, $5 for others.
Essentials: 25 sites (some are walk-ins and suitable only for tents), tent spaces, five picnic areas, picnic tables, benches, fire grills, refuse containers, piped water, vault toilets, parking, fishing, swimming, a boat ramp, water-skiing, and overflow camping. Leashed pets are permitted. The fee is $13. In Tahoe National Forest about a 40-minute drive west of Truckee. Follow I-80 to Highway 20 and watch for the turnoff on the right.
Contact: PG&E Land Project; 916/386-5164; website: www.pge.com/recreation.

Indian Springs
(see map on page 493, site 2)
Indian Springs is next to the South Fork of the Yuba River on the north side of I-80. Most sites are sheltered in heavy pine forest, but noise from the freeway can be intrusive.
Essentials: 35 sites (some accommodating RVs), piped water, vault toilets, picnic tables, and fire rings. Leashed pets are permitted. The fee is $13 plus $6 for an extra vehicle, and sites are first-come, first-served. Take the Eagle Lakes exit off I-80, about 30 minutes west of Truckee; turn north and drive one-half mile.

Contact: Tahoe National Forest, Nevada City Ranger District; 530/265-4538.

Lodgepole (see map on page 493, site 3)
Recently enlarged and upgraded, Lodgepole Campground now accommodates RVs as well as tent campers. Some new features include storage lockers, an additional double toilet, and wheelchair-accessible campsites.

Essentials: 35 sites for RVs and tents, tables, benches, fire grills, refuse containers, water, restrooms, parking, fishing, swimming, boating, overflow camping, and a nearby boat ramp. The fee is $15, extra vehicles are $3, and pets are $1. The campground is in Tahoe National Forest. From I-80, take the Yuba Gap exit to Lake Valley Reservoir.

Contact: PG&E Land Project; 916/386-5164; website: www.pge.com/recreation.

Woodchuck (see map on page 493, site 4)
Set at an elevation of 6,300 feet, this small, rela-

tively remote campground is adjacent to Rattlesnake Creek.

Essentials: Eight tent sites, some barbecues, picnic tables, vault toilets, and limited parking. There is no water. Pack in and pack out—there are no garbage containers. Leashed pets are permitted. Sites are free on a first-come, first-served basis. Take the Cisco Grove exit off I-80 and turn north. Turn left onto the frontage road after crossing over the freeway. Turn right, just before Thousand Trails, onto Rattlesnake Road. Proceed three miles to the campground.

Contact: Tahoe National Forest, Nevada City Ranger District; 530/265-4538.

Lake Sterling
(see map on page 493, site 5)
Hiking trails are in the vicinity of this campground adjacent to Lake Sterling in a remote setting.

Essentials: Six sites, vault toilets, and fire rings. There is no water. Pack in and pack out—there

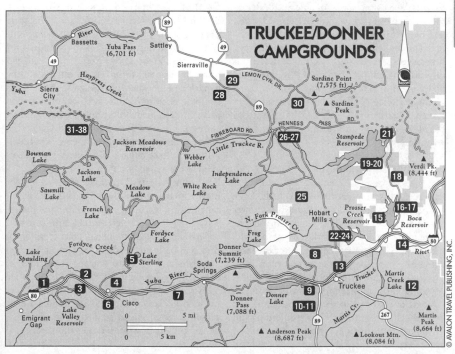

TRUCKEE/DONNER CAMPGROUNDS

© AVALON TRAVEL PUBLISHING, INC.

are no garbage containers. Sites are free on a first-come, first-served basis. Follow the directions to Woodchuck Campground (see campground number 60) and proceed 3.5 miles past Woodchuck to Lake Sterling. Campers must hike in about one-quarter mile, as the access road was closed because of site damage caused by vehicles. The elevation is 7,000 feet.

Contact: Tahoe National Forest, Nevada City Ranger District; 530/265-4538.

Hampshire Rocks
(see map on page 493, site 6)

This may be a lovely campground with heavily wooded sites, but noise from the freeway is intrusive. On the plus side, it's close to the Loch Leven Lakes Trailhead, a highly recommended route to beautiful backcountry lakes, and to Rainbow Lodge, which has an excellent restaurant should you tire of barbecued weenies. The campsites are adjacent to the South Fork of the Yuba River.

Essentials: 31 sites (some suitable for RVs), picnic tables, barbecues, vault toilets, piped water, and limited parking. Leashed pets are permitted. The fee is $12. Sites are on a first-come, first-served basis. Take the Rainbow Road exit off I-80. The campground is off a frontage road on the south side of the freeway.

Contact: Tahoe National Forest, Nevada City Ranger District; 530/265-4538, reservations 877/444-6777, or on the Internet at website: www.ReserveUSA.com.

Kidd Lake Campground
(see map on page 493, site 7)

An excellent group campground, Kidd Lake has paved roads and spurs and enough tree cover for shade. Groups of 2–100 people can rent the entire campground. If you want to camp in the lakeside area, you must rent all five of the lakeside units, because they have common food preparation areas. Weeklong stays can be reserved as early as February 1, while weekend stays are open for reservation from March 1. If you cancel, payment, which is required within 14 days of confirmation, is nonrefundable. The attractiveness of this campground depends on the water level at Kidd Lake, which can be drawn down substantially in mid- to late summer. There's a good hiking trail nearby. The access road can be bumpy for big rigs, and it is somewhat difficult to find.

Essentials: Group sites for up to 100 people, tent and RV spaces, tables, benches, fire grills, refuse containers, water, restrooms, parking, fishing, swimming, and boating. The fee is $18 for sites 6–10 and $23 for sites 1–5 (lakeside). There is a two-site, two-night minimum for regular sites and all five lakeside campsites must be booked at one time to one group. Take the Soda Springs exit on I-80. Turn right on Soda Springs Road and head .8 mile to Pohatsi Road, then turn west and continue to the end of the pavement. Follow signs for another 2.8 miles to the campground. The elevation is 6,750 feet.

Contact: PG&E Land Project; 916/386-5164; website: www.pge.com/recreation.

Alder Creek Campground at Tahoe Donner (see map on page 493, site 8)

Well off the beaten path in Truckee's upscale Tahoe Donner resort and residential community, this campground is nestled in a wooded area on a high plateau above the historic railroad town. In summer, the recreation amenities nearby include a top-rated 18-hole golf course, tennis complex, recreation center with swimming pool, private beach at nearby Donner Lake, and an equestrian center with lessons and trail rides. Tahoe Donner members and their guests usually get first choice of dates and sites; the rest are offered to the general public.

Essentials: 42 sites for tents and RVs (40-foot maximum length), hot showers, laundry, electrical hookups, RV sewer dump, horseshoes, sandbox, Ping-Pong table, and badminton and volleyball courts. Each site has a picnic table, fire ring, and barbecue. Fees are $18 for individual campsites and $100 for a group campsite that can accommodate up to 50. Electrical hookups are $5 extra, an extra vehicle is $5, and dogs are $1 per night. Wood is available at $4 per bundle. Registration is required and stays are limited to two weeks. Closed in winter. Reservations accepted beginning May 20. At 13813 Alder Creek Rd.

(off Northwoods Drive from Donner Lake Boulevard), with access from I-80.

Contact: Tahoe Donner, Alder Creek Campground, 530/587-9462, website: www.tahoedonner.com.

Donner Memorial State Park
(see map on page 493, site 9)

One of the most popular public campgrounds in the Tahoe region, and deservedly so, this is nestled in pine trees and meanders through hills. It offers a wide range of recreational opportunities, including an excellent museum at the park entrance. There's a warm, shallow lagoon where small fry can swim, raft, and canoe, as well as an extensive beach for hanging out. The lake itself accommodates fishing, windsurfing, Jet Skiing, and water-skiing, and there's a concession that rents watercraft. Rangers conduct summer campfire programs at an amphitheater and host nature walks, and there's a self-guided nature trail. One disadvantage is noise at night from I-80 and the Southern Pacific Railroad tracks, which flank the park. Also, the proximity to the highway makes it essential to take higher security measures for your belongings.

Tip: The best sites are in the Split Rock loop, closest to the lake and the attendant water sports concessions. Site selection is on a first-come, first-served basis, and while rangers try to accommodate specific requests, it's wise to arrive early and at least a day in advance of weekends to begin the haggling ritual.

Essentials: 154 sites, including 83 RV sites (28-foot maximum length), piped water, pay showers, chemical toilets, stoves, fire rings, picnic tables, and swimming in the lake and a lagoon. Leashed pets are permitted. The fee is $12, plus $1 per pet per night. Closed in winter. Off I-80 on Donner Pass Road, three miles west of Truckee.

Contact: Donner Memorial State Park; 530/582-7892, reservations 800/444-PARK (800/444-7275), or on the Internet at website: www.ReserveAmerica.com.

Granite Flat
(see map on page 493, site 10)

With a noisy highway and lack of seclusion, this campground is similar to neighboring Goose Meadows. But it's next to the scenic Truckee River and close to town and golf/ski resorts such as Squaw Valley, Tahoe Donner, and Northstar. Because of its centralized location, it's best for RVs.

Essentials: 72 sites, all accommodating RVs up to 40 feet long, 17 wheelchair-accessible sites, vault toilets, piped water from an artesian well, and a wheelchair-accessible river trail. Leashed pets are permitted. The fee is $12. Closed in winter. On Highway 89, three-quarters mile southwest of Truckee.

Contact: Tahoe National Forest, Truckee Ranger District; 530/587-3558, reservations 877/444-6777, or on the Internet at www.ReserveUSA.com.

Goose Meadows
(see map on page 493, site 11)

Situated amid scattered pine trees alongside a busy and noisy highway, with almost no seclusion, Goose Meadows does offer one benefit: proximity to the Truckee River. When fishing is strong in late spring and early summer, chances are the noise will become less of an issue.

Essentials: 27 sites for tents and RVs, hand-pumped well water, and older vault toilets. Leashed pets are permitted. The fee is $8. Closed in winter. On Highway 89, five miles southwest of Truckee.

Contact: Tahoe National Forest, Truckee Ranger District; 530/587-3558, reservations 877/444-6777, or on the Internet at website: www.ReserveUSA.com.

Martis Creek Lake
(see map on page 493, site 12)

This is a beautiful, largely undiscovered, and frequently underused campground and a great place for catch-and-release fly-fishing. The well-dispersed sites are generally under trees, and the area is close to Truckee, the Northstar-at-Tahoe ski resort, and the North Shore of Lake Tahoe. The entire campground is meticulously maintained, with freshly painted tables and clean sites. Lantern hangers are a welcome touch. Also, larger RVs can negotiate the pull-through sites much more easily than the back-in sites at other campgrounds. Hiking and mountain biking trails are nearby. One drawback: The campground is next to the Truckee-Tahoe Airport. However, it is well removed from Highway 267 (via a quarter-mile access road), so evenings are blissfully free of the traffic noise that bedevils many campgrounds in the region.

Essentials: 25 sites (all suitable for RVs up to 30 feet), piped water, flush and chemical toilets, an amphitheater with weekend interpretive programs, a telephone, barbecues, fire rings, lantern hangers, wheelchair-accessible facilities, and picnic tables. Leashed pets are permitted. The fee is $10. All camping is on a first-come, first-served basis. A campground host collects fees and assigns sites. The season is May 1–September 30; closed in winter. Off Highway 267, five miles southeast of Truckee.

Contact: U.S. Army Corps of Engineers; 530/639-2342.

Coachland RV Park
(see map on page 493, site 13)

This park, which is right off the freeway, is close to Prosser Creek Reservoir and Donner Lake, although there are no recreational amenities per se in the campground itself. Sites are nestled in the trees but are subject to noise from both highways. This is a good spot for overnighters heading for other points in the region, or for boaters, skiers, golfers, and anglers who want to be near the major resort areas. The campground is within walking distance of downtown Truckee, if you don't mind negotiating a hill. An advantage is that this is one of the few campgrounds in the area to remain open year-round.

Essentials: 131 sites on 55 acres, full hookups, water, toilets, showers, sewage disposal, a spa, picnic tables, laundry facilities, cable TV, and some telephone connections. Pets are allowed on leash only. The fee is $31 a night, $187 a week, with about 25 sites reserved for short stays. At 10500 Hwy. 89 N at I-80 in Truckee.

Contact: Coachland; 530/587-3071.

United Trails
(see map on page 493, site 14)

Conveniently near Truckee and Reno, this full-service campground is near the highway and the Truckee River and is geared to RVers.

Essentials: 56 sites, full hookups, water, restrooms, showers, sewage disposal, fishing, a spa, a general store, and laundry facilities. Fees range $25–36, plus $3 a day for children and $2 a day for a pet. On I-80 at the Hirschdale exit, east of Truckee.

Contact: United Trails; 530/587-8282.

Boca (see map on page 493, site 15)

Nestled among some pine trees, these campsites are on a ridge top overlooking Boca Reservoir.

Essentials: 30 primitive and dry sites (some accommodating RVs), vault toilets (one wheelchair-accessible), picnic tables, and fire pits. There is no piped water. Leashed pets are permitted. The fee is $10 per vehicle. Closed in winter. On the west shore of Boca Reservoir off I-80 at the Hirschdale exit, seven miles east of Truckee.

Contact: Tahoe National Forest, Truckee Ranger District; 530/587-3558.

Boca Rest (see map on page 493, site 16)

On the east shore of the lake, this campground is at its best in late spring and early summer before the reservoir is drawn down. After that it becomes hot and dusty.

Essentials: 29 sites (all accommodating RVs), piped water, older vault toilets, barbecues, fire rings, and picnic tables. Leashed pets are permitted. The fee is $8 per vehicle. Closed in winter. Off I-80, 9.5 miles east of Truckee.

Contact: Tahoe National Forest, Truckee Ranger District; 530/587-3558.

Boca Springs
(see map on page 493, site 17)

A rustic setting and some tree cover are offered at this off-the-beaten-path campground near Boca Reservoir, a good fishing lake.

Essentials: 16 sites (all accommodating RVs, but there is a rough access road), a small group campground oriented to equestrian use, piped water, chemical toilets, and fire rings. Leashed pets are permitted. The fee is $10 per vehicle. In a canyon two miles east of Boca Reservoir off Boca Springs Road, directly across from Boca Rest Campground.

Contact: Tahoe National Forest, Truckee Ranger District; 530/587-3558.

Boyington Mill
(see map on page 493, site 18)

This is an open, flat area in Little Truckee River Canyon on the Little Truckee River, with good fishing access and a somewhat cooler location than on Boca Reservoir. If the lake level is down, this is a prettier place to camp.

Essentials: 12 sites (all accommodating RVs), older vault toilets, barbecues, fire rings, and picnic tables. There is no piped water. Leashed pets are permitted. The fee is $10 per vehicle. Closed in winter. Off I-80, 10 miles northeast of Truckee and two miles north of Boca Reservoir, on Boca-Stampede Road, midway between Stampede and Boca Reservoirs.

Contact: Tahoe National Forest, Truckee Ranger District; 530/587-3558.

Logger (see map on page 493, site 19)

Logger is nestled in a tree-shaded area on a rise overlooking Stampede Reservoir, which offers excellent fishing for kokanee salmon, as well as rainbow and brown trout. It is the most highly developed of the local Forest Service campgrounds, with paved roads and spurs. A launch ramp for Stampede is two miles west of here.

Tip: The best sites are at the Iron Ox and Crosscut loops, which are closest to the lake. Because of the campground's size, it rarely fills, making it an excellent choice for camping on holiday weekends.

Essentials: 252 sites (all suitable for RVs up to 40 feet), piped water, chemical recirculating toilets, barbecues, fire rings, picnic tables, a dump station, and some wheelchair-accessible sites and toilets. Leashed pets are permitted. The fee is $13. Closed in winter. Exit I-80 at Hirschdale, seven miles east of Truckee, then drive eight miles north on Boca-Stampede Road.

Contact: Tahoe National Forest, Truckee Ranger District; 530/587-3558; reservations 877/444-6777, or on the Internet at website: www .ReserveUSA.com.

Emigrant Group Campground
(see map on page 493, site 20)

One of the most popular group campgrounds in the region, Emigrant has paved roads and spurs and plenty of shade trees. Some groups return year after year, with fishing in Stampede for kokanee salmon the prime attraction. Book early, and try for a midweek date.

Essentials: Two 25-person group sites and two 50-person sites offer wheelchair-accessible camping as well as piped water, chemical recirculating toilets, picnic tables, fire rings, barbecues, and a dump station. The fee is $55 for 25 people and $110 for 50 people. Off I-80, northeast of Truckee and east of Logger Campground, near the south shore of Stampede Reservoir off Boca-Stampede Road.

Contact: Tahoe National Forest, Truckee Ranger District; 530/587-3558, reservations 877/444-6777, or on the Internet at website: www.ReserveUSA.com.

Davies Creek
(see map on page 493, site 21)

This small campground is in an open meadow between trees, but it has some shaded campsites. It's on the north shore of Stampede Reservoir, about a half mile from the water, and there are good horseback riding opportunities north of the campground on a primitive dirt road.

Essentials: 10 sites. There are no toilets, campfire rings, tables, or water—in other words, this is basic dry camping. But it's free and is recommended for equestrian users. Leashed pets are permitted. Drive to the end of Boca-Stampede Road, then head west for approximately one mile. Warning: This is a rough road and is not advised for large RVs.

Contact: Tahoe National Forest, Truckee Ranger District; 530/587-3558.

Prosser (see map on page 493, site 22)

In a desolate area with sparse tree cover, this camp sits on a windy knoll overlooking the reservoir. When the lake is down, there is little to recommend the place. Geese and white pelicans are frequently seen on this side of the lake.

Essentials: 29 sites (14 suitable for RVs), piped water, older vault toilets, barbecues, fire rings, and picnic tables. Leashed pets are permitted. The fee is $10. Closed in winter. Off Highway 89 on Prosser Recreation Access Road, two miles north of Truckee.

Contact: Tahoe National Forest, Truckee Ranger District; 530/587-3558.

Prosser Group Campground
(see map on page 493, site 23)

This campground has some tree cover, but its best asset is proximity to the boat launch, which is just across the day-use parking lot.

Essentials: A group site accommodating up to 50 people (RVs are OK), piped water, older vault toilets, a large barbecue, and picnic tables. Leashed pets are permitted. The fee is $75. Closed in winter. Off Highway 89 on Prosser Recreation Access Road, north of Truckee.

Contact: Tahoe National Forest, Truckee Ranger District; 530/587-3558.

Lakeside (see map on page 493, site 24)

Aside from a few trees, this place is fairly unremarkable and is worthwhile only when Prosser Creek Reservoir is full. When the water is drawn down, the area becomes hot, dusty, and windy—not at all attractive.

Essentials: 30 undesignated spaces for RVs, older vault toilets, some picnic tables, some barbecues, and piped water (at the campground entrance). Leashed pets are permitted. The fee is $8 per vehicle. Closed in winter. On the west shore of Prosser Creek Reservoir off Highway 89 on Prosser Recreation Access Road, north of Truckee.

Contact: Tahoe National Forest, Truckee Ranger District; 530/587-3558.

Sagehen (see map on page 493, site 25)

This campground is well off the beaten path, though many people do venture out here for the good wildlife viewing. The tree-shrouded campsites are next to a large meadow, and Sagehen Creek, which harbors brook and brown trout,

is nearby. There's not a lot of heavy use in the summer, but fall brings hunters.

Essentials: 15 sites, older vault toilets, fire rings, and nearby fishing spots. There is no piped water. Garbage containers are not provided, so pack it in and pack it out. The rough dirt access road is not recommended for large RVs. Leashed pets are permitted. Sites are free. Closed in winter. Off Highway 89, 11 miles north of Truckee; take the turnoff and follow signs six miles west to the campground.

Contact: Tahoe National Forest, Truckee Ranger District; 530/587-3558.

Lower Little Truckee
(see map on page 493, site 26)

This campground is next to a busy highway, but it's nestled in trees adjacent to the Little Truckee River, which offers fishing and swimming opportunities. Cattle graze upstream and may pollute the river.

Essentials: 15 sites (suitable for RVs up to 40 feet), piped water, vault toilets, picnic tables, and fire rings. Leashed pets are permitted. The fee is $11. It's 12 miles north of Truckee on Highway 89.

Contact: Tahoe National Forest, Sierraville Ranger District; 530/994-3401, reservations 877/444-6777, or on the Internet at website: www.ReserveUSA.com.

Upper Little Truckee
(see map on page 493, site 27)

This campground is spread out along a busy highway, but most sites are in the trees and adjoin the Little Truckee River, offering trout fishing and swimming. Cattle graze upstream and may pollute the river.

Essentials: 26 campsites (15 suitable for RVs up to 40 feet), piped water, vault toilets, picnic tables, and fire rings. Leashed pets are permitted. The fee is $11. It's 12.5 miles north of Truckee on Highway 89.

Contact: Tahoe National Forest, Sierraville Ranger District; 530/994-3401, reservations 877/444-6777, or on the Internet at website: www.ReserveUSA.com.

Cold Creek (see map on page 493, site 28)

This campground is next to Cold Stream, which provides some fishing for trout. It's also next to a busy highway, with little seclusion.

Essentials: 13 sites (some suitable for RVs up to 35 feet), piped water, vault toilets, picnic tables, and fire rings. Leashed pets are permitted. The fee is $11 per night. It's on Highway 89 approximately 19 miles north of Truckee.

Contact: Tahoe National Forest, Sierraville Ranger District; 530/994-3401, reservations 877/444-6777, or on the Internet at website: www.ReserveUSA.com.

Cottonwood (see map on page 493, site 29)

Of all the campgrounds along Highway 89 North, this is the best. It is nestled in trees next to Cottonwood Creek, set back somewhat from the highway, and it has an angler's trail which follows along the stream and an overlook trail with beautiful views of the surrounding area. The campsites are well dispersed, so there is no crowding. This campground is not as heavily used as it once was.

Essentials: 49 sites (28 accommodating RVs up to 35 feet), piped water, vault toilets, picnic tables, and fire rings. The upper half of the campground is used as a group camp with a 125-person capacity. Leashed pets are permitted. The fee is $11 per night for individual sites, plus $5 for extra vehicle. It's 19.5 miles north of Truckee and 4.5 miles south of Sierraville adjacent to Highway 89, at elevation 5,800 feet.

Contact: Tahoe National Forest, Sierraville Ranger District; 530/994-3401, reservations 877/444-6777, or on the Internet at website: www.ReserveUSA.com.

Bear Valley (see map on page 493, site 30)

A major forest fire burned this area in 1994, and although the campground has been rebuilt, there are no trees left. The Bear Valley Loop Trail, an 18-mile, four-wheel-drive trail, is adjacent to the campground.

Essentials: 10 sites for tents and car campers, piped water, picnic tables, and fire rings. Leashed pets are permitted. There is no fee. Six miles east

of Little Truckee Summit on Cottonwood Creek Road at elevation 6,700 feet.

Contact: Tahoe National Forest, Sierraville Ranger District; 530/994-3401.

JACKSON MEADOWS RESERVOIR CAMPS

The following Forest Service campgrounds (numbers 32–39, keyed to the Truckee/Donner Campgrounds map) are in the Jackson Meadows area, 17 miles north of Truckee on Highway 89 and 16 miles west on Forest Service Road 07. The highlight is a large, attractive lake with forested shoreline, and activities include boating, fishing, swimming, picnicking, and hiking. There's a self-guided nature trail on the southwest side of the lake and an RV dump station across from the information turnout. The Pacific Crest Trail runs through the area; hikers can access the trail near East Meadow Campground. The elevation is 6,100 feet. Leashed pets are permitted.

Aspen Group Camp
(see map on page 493, site 31)

This camp offers tree-shaded sites well off the road, near a swimming beach and a boat ramp. The adjacent parking areas are suitable for RVs, while tent camping is possible within the campground. A trail leads to the lake.

Essentials: Two 25-person group camps, one 50-person group camp, picnic tables, piped water, vault toilets, and central parking. The fee is $55 for the smaller sites, $110 for the large site. Reservations are necessary. Next to the Aspen picnic site on the northeast shore of Jackson Meadows Reservoir.

Contact: Tahoe National Forest, Sierraville Ranger District; 530/994-3401, reservations 877/444-6777, or on the Internet at website: www.ReserveUSA.com.

East Meadow
(see map on page 493, site 32)

East Meadow, with its larger-than-normal sites, some lake views, and flush toilets, is the most desirable campground on the east shore of the lake. It's on a rise above the water offering some lake views. Extras include firewood for sale.

Tip: The best sites are 20, 23, and 24, which offer partial lake views, and 28 and 29, which combine to make a great two-family camping spot.

Essentials: 46 sites (26 suitable for RVs), piped water, flush toilets, picnic tables, and fire rings. The fee is $13. On the northeast shore of Jackson Meadows Reservoir, one mile off Forest Service Road 07 on a paved access road.

Contact: Tahoe National Forest, Sierraville Ranger District; 530/994-3401, reservations 877/444-6777, or on the Internet at website: www.ReserveUSA.com.

Findley (see map on page 493, site 33)

Findley, on the reservoir's less-frequented west shore, is worth making the effort to get to for the dispersed, tree-shaded sites that are near the water.

Essentials: 12 single-family sites, three two-family sites (some suitable for small RVs), piped water, flush toilets, picnic tables, and fire rings. The fee is $13. On the west side of Jackson Meadows Reservoir, 2.5 miles across the dam on a well-graded hard-pack gravel road.

Contact: Tahoe National Forest, Sierraville Ranger District; 530/994-3401, reservations, 877/444-6777, or on the Internet at website: www.ReserveUSA.com.

Fir Top (see map on page 493, site 34)

Fir Top offers the same advantages as Findley Campground.

Essentials: 11 single-family sites and one two-family site, piped water, flush toilets, picnic tables, and fire rings. The fee is $13. On the west side of Jackson Meadows Reservoir, across the dam.

Contact: Tahoe National Forest, Sierraville Ranger District; 530/994-3401, reservations 877/444-6777, or on the Internet at website: www.ReserveUSA.com.

Jackson Point
(see map on page 493, site 35)

Jackson Point, on a peninsula that juts into the lake, is a secluded and very scenic camping spot

for tents. It's more exposed to afternoon winds than other campgrounds.

Essentials: 10 boat-in sites, vault toilets, picnic tables, and fire rings. No piped water is provided. Sites are free. On the forested shore of the reservoir one-half mile southwest of the Pass Creek boat ramp. Sites are first-come, first-served.

Contact: Tahoe National Forest, Sierraville Ranger District; 530/994-3401.

Pass Creek (see map on page 493, site 36)

Pass Creek, because of the proximity of the launch ramp, is well suited for campers with boats. But sites are small, close together, and in dark, heavy forest on sloping hillsides. There's an overflow campground just below the main campground on the road to the boat ramp, which has six sites with picnic tables and fire rings; the camping fee is $13.

Essentials: 30 sites (15 suitable for RVs), piped water, flush toilets, picnic tables, fire rings with grills, a concrete boat ramp, and a swimming beach at the nearby Aspen picnic site. The fee is $13. On the northeastern shore of Jackson Meadows Reservoir.

Contact: Tahoe National Forest, Sierraville Ranger District; 530/994-3401, reservations 877/444-6777, or on the Internet at website: www.ReserveUSA.com.

Silver Tip Group
(see map on page 493, site 37)

Silver Tip Group is, of the two group camps here (the other is Aspen), the better choice, because of its greater isolation on the scenic west shore, its spaciousness, and its proximity to boat launching, beaches, picnic sites, and hiking trails.

Essentials: Two 25-person walk-in sites (tent), adjacent parking suitable for autos and RVs, picnic tables, barbecues, a fire ring, piped water, vault toilets, central parking, and access to a swimming beach at the nearby Woodcamp picnic site. The fee is $60. Reservations are necessary. Next to Woodcamp Campground on the southwest shore of Jackson Meadows Reservoir.

Contact: Tahoe National Forest, Sierraville Ranger District; 530/994-3401, reservations 877/444-6777, or on the Internet at webste:www .ReserveUSA.com.

Woodcamp (see map on page 493, site 38)

Woodcamp is arguably the best campground at the lake, largely because of its location to so many lakeside facilities. It is next to both the day-use site, which has the best swimming beach, and the Woodcamp Creek Interpretive Trail, a half-mile, self-guided trail. Brochures available at the trailhead explain some of the natural features of the area.

Essentials: 20 sites (10 suitable for RVs), piped water, flush toilets, picnic tables, fire rings with grills, a concrete boat launch, and a swimming beach at the nearby Woodcamp picnic site. The fee is $13. On the southwest shore of Jackson Meadows Reservoir, across the dam at the end of a well-graded gravel road. Reservations are necessary.

Contact: Tahoe National Forest, Sierraville Ranger District; 530/994-3401, reservations 877/444-6777, or on the Internet at website: www.ReserveUSA.com.

LAKE TAHOE

The following properties are keyed to the Lake Tahoe Campgrounds map.

Silver Creek
(see map on page 502, site 39)

This campground has the same conditions as nearby Granite Flat (11) and Goose Meadows (12): beside a noisy highway but also next to the scenic Truckee River.

Essentials: 31 sites (19 suitable for RVs), hand-pumped well water, older vault toilets, stoves, fire rings, and tables. Leashed pets are permitted. The fee is $8. Closed in winter. On Highway 89, eight miles south of Truckee.

Contact: Tahoe National Forest, Truckee Ranger District; 530/587-3558, reservations 877/ 444-6777, or on the Internet at website: www .ReserveUSA.com.

Sandy Beach Campground
(see map on page 502, site 40)

This campground is centrally located on the North Shore with access to beaches, restaurants, golf courses, and water sports.

Essentials: 44 sites, including 20 RV sites (35-foot maximum length), full hookups, piped water, flush toilets, showers, stoves, fire rings, picnic tables, and swimming. Pets are allowed with restrictions. Fees are $20–25. Closed in winter. At 6873 N. Lake Tahoe Boulevard (Highway 28) in Tahoe Vista, just one mile west of Kings Beach.

Contact: Sandy Beach Campground; 530/546-7682.

Tahoe State Recreation Area
(see map on page 502, site 41)

Though this campground has frontage on Lake Tahoe, it's next to a busy highway. On the positive side, it is within walking distance of restaurants, shops, and water excursions and next to a paved bicycle path. This is a good venue for RVs, but not necessarily for tent campers.

Essentials: 31 sites, including 23 RV sites (24-foot maximum length), piped water, flush toilets, showers, fire rings, picnic tables, fishing, and swimming. Pets are allowed with restrictions, at $1 per day. The fee is $12. Closed in winter. On Highway 28, a quarter mile northeast of Tahoe City.

Contact: Seasonal park office; 530/583-3074, reservations 800/444-PARK (800/444-7275), or on the Internet at website: www .ReserveAmerica.com.

Lake Forest (see map on page 502, site 42)

Lake Forest, a campground off Highway 28, is a good place for people who have a boat in tow, since it's next to the only public launch ramp on the North Shore. A public beach is within walking distance, and restaurants and shops are nearby.

Essentials: 20 sites for tents and RVs (20-foot maximum length), piped water, flush toilets, freestanding barbecue pits, picnic tables, proximity to a boat ramp, and swimming in the lake. Leashed pets are permitted. Sites are first-come,

TAHOE CAMPGROUNDS

To Graeagle

80

89

80

Donner
Lake

Donner
Memorial
State Park

Truckee

Martis
Creek
Lake

Tahoe

National

Forest

Mt. Rose
Wilderness

48

Washoe
City

395

Martis Creek

267

Tahoe
Vista

Kings
Beach

Rose Knob
Peak
(9,696 ft)

431

Mt. Rose
Summit

Toiyabe

Washoe
Lake

Tahoe

National

Forest

89

Lookout Mtn.
(8,084 ft)

Mt. Watson
(8,424 ft)

Carnelian
Bay

Agate
Bay

40

Crystal
Bay

Incline
Village

National

Forest

39

Burton
Creek
State
Park

28

41-42

Tahoe
City

Truckee River

Sand
Harbor

Lake
Tahoe–
Nevada
State Park

Marlette
Lake

63-64

CALIFORNIA
NEVADA

Five Lakes Creek

Alpine
Peaks

Granite
Chief
Wilderness

Ward Creek
State Park

43-44

Tahoe
Pines

Lake

28

Spooner
Lake

50

Homewood
Ellis Peak
(8,740 ft)

Tahoma

45

46-47

Glenbrook

Tahoe

Spooner
Summit

Duane Bliss
Peak
(8,658 ft)

Barker Cr.

Sugar Pine
Point State
Park

Meeks Bay

Toiyabe

Genoa Peak
(9,150 ft)

Rubicon R.

89

National

206

Loon
Lake

49

D.L. Bliss
State Park

51

Emerald
Bay

Emerald Bay
State Park

50

61

62

Zephyr
Cove

Kingsbury Grade

Genoa

Desolation

52

Camp
Richardson

54

South
Lake
Tahoe

Stateline

60

Daggett
Pass

207

Forest

Eldorado

Wilderness

Cascade
Lake

53

Mt. Tallac
(9,735 ft)

Fallen
Leaf
Lake

Tahoe
Valley

59

55

56

Eldorado

Eldorado

National

Fallen
Leaf

50

National

Forest

Creek

Silver

Lake
Aloha

Wrights
Lake

Echo
Lake

Meyers

57-58

89

0   5 mi

0   5 km

MOON

© AVALON TRAVEL PUBLISHING, INC.

first-served, with no reservations. The fee is $15 per night, with a drop box. There is a 10-day maximum stay. Closed in winter. Off Highway 28 on Lake Forest Road near the Coast Guard station, two miles northeast of Tahoe City.

Contact: Tahoe City Public Utility District; 530/583-3796, ext. 29.

William Kent
(see map on page 502, site 43)
Kent's proximity to the elegant Sunnyside Lodge and William Kent Beach (a Forest Service facility) are the biggest advantages. Water excursions, boating, fishing, and other activities are just a stroll across the highway. And there's an inexpensive bus system (Tahoe Area Regional Transit) that stops here and can take you to points throughout the North and West Shores of the lake. The campground also connects to an extensive network of paved bike trails. Sites are tucked into heavy forest and are fairly close together; the best ones are farthest from the road. Sunnyside is a beehive of activity in summer, when there is considerable traffic congestion along the highway.

Essentials: 95 sites, including 40 suitable for RVs, piped water, flush toilets, fire rings, barbecues, picnic tables, and swimming in the lake. Leashed pets are permitted. The fee is $15. Closed in winter. On Highway 89, two miles south of Tahoe City.

Contact: Lake Tahoe Visitor Center; 530/583-3642, reservations 877/444-6777, or on the Internet at website: www.ReserveUSA.com.

Kaspian (see map on page 502, site 44)
Close to the lake and near Homewood, this small campground is great for water sports, but it's often pounded by noise from the busy highway.

Essentials: 10 walk-in sites for tents, piped water, flush toilets, stoves, fire rings, tables, and swimming in the lake. Leashed pets are permitted. The fee is $12. Closed in winter. On Highway 89, five miles south of Tahoe City.

Contact: Lake Tahoe Visitor Center; 530/583-3642, reservations 877/444-6777, or on the Internet at website: www.ReserveUSA.com.

Sugar Pine Point State Park/General Creek (see map on page 502, site 45)
A fairly flat campground with moderate tree cover on the west side of Highway 89, General Creek is nonetheless well situated for many recreational activities. The best section of the park is on the east side of the highway and contains the posh Ehrman Mansion with its manicured lawns, tall trees, and scenic lake frontage—though there are no campsites here. The long, paved West Shore Bike Path originates from this point, and at General Creek there are trailheads to several alpine lakes. For those who enjoy winter camping (without the showers), this is one of the few public campgrounds open then. In summer, it gets heavy use and the common facilities (including the showers) frequently seem overburdened.

Essentials: 175 sites (all suitable for RVs up to 30 feet), piped water, flush toilets, a sanitary dump station, pay showers, barbecues, fire rings, picnic tables, swimming, hiking, and cycling. Leashed pets are permitted. The fee is $12. Open year-round. Reservations are strongly advised for May–September. One mile south of Tahoma on Highway 89.

Contact: Sugar Pine Point State Park; 530/525-7982, reservations 800/444-PARK (800/444-7275), or on the Internet at website: www .ReserveAmerica.com.

Meeks Bay Resort
(see map on page 502, site 46)
This historic resort, operated by the Washoe Tribe of California and Nevada, is wonderful for families with children, even though the campground is unremarkable and close to the highway. RVers will enjoy the place more than tent campers, since the resort is crowded in peak summer months. A large, white sand beach with a myriad of rentable water toys for children is the major asset. There's also a general store and a snack bar.

Essentials: 28 sites (10 suitable for RVs), piped water, flush toilets, showers, stoves, fire rings, tables, swimming, boating, fishing, a store, and an ice cream parlor. No pets are allowed. The fee is $18–26. No reservations are accepted. Closed in winter. On Highway 89, 10 miles south of Tahoe City.

Contact: Meeks Bay Resort; 530/525-6946 or 877/326-3357; website: www.meeksbayresort.com.

Meeks Bay Campground
(see map on page 502, site 47)

The only things going for this unappealing campground are immediate access to Lake Tahoe and a protected white sand beach with shallow water for wading, swimming, and paddling. The crescent-shaped beach is backed by pine trees, and there is a private boat ramp nearby. Unfortunately, the campground is rather exposed and much too close to the highway to afford any privacy or scenic beauty.

Essentials: 40 sites (some suitable for RVs up to 20 feet), piped water, flush toilets, stoves, fire rings, tables, and swimming in the lake. Leashed pets are permitted. The fee is $15, with additional car fee of $5. Closed in winter. On Highway 89, 10 miles south of Tahoe City.

Contact: Lake Tahoe Visitor Center; 530/583-3357, reservations 877/444-6777, or on the Internet at website: www.ReserveUSA.com.

Mt. Rose (see map on page 502, site 48)

This campground, the only one on Mt. Rose Highway, is in Toiyabe National Forest—close to good hiking on the Mt. Rose Wilderness Trail, the Ophir Creek Trail, and a future extension of the Tahoe Rim Trail. Also, it's a stone's throw from the popular and beautiful Tahoe Meadows, which is ablaze with wildflowers in early summer. Hikes can be made to the top of Slide Mountain for dramatic views of Reno, Tahoe, and the Carson Valley, when the wind isn't blowing. The elevation is much higher than Lake Tahoe—8,900 feet—and nights can get cold.

Tip: The best sites are 13 and 14, which are at the end of a loop next to an attractive meadow.

Essentials: 24 sites, including nine RV/trailer sites (16-foot maximum length), piped water, flush toilets, fire rings with grills, and picnic tables. Leashed pets are permitted. The fee is $10. Sites 2–6 are on the reservation system; the rest are on a first-come, first-served basis. Golden Age and Golden Access Passports are honored. Closed in winter. Nine miles northeast of In-

cline Village on the south side of Highway 431, near the Mt. Rose summit.

Contact: Toiyabe National Forest, Carson Ranger District; 775/882-2766, reservations 877/444-6777, or on the Internet at website: www .ReserveUSA.com.

D. L. Bliss State Park
(see map on page 502, site 49)

Bliss is Tahoe's most spectacular and diverse campground as well as one of the best in all of California. All sites are in wooded surroundings well off the highway, and many are on a hill above the lake. The state park has one of Tahoe's largest and most picturesque white sand beaches and some ruggedly beautiful, wind-protected rocky coves, where swimming is delightful in warm, shallow water. The five-mile-long Emerald Bay Trail originates at the south end of the park, providing a scenic but not too intimidating day hike along the high granite shelf of the West Shore to Emerald Bay. Just north of the park on Highway 89 is the lake's longest and most scenic paved bicycle trail, starting at Sugar Pine Point State Park and continuing to Tahoe City. One drawback: Sites nearest to the beach are close together and always crowded.

Tip: If you can assemble 10 people or several families, rent the group campsite, which is totally isolated from other sites and has an almost luxurious assortment of near-private amenities: tiled and spotlessly clean shower rooms, flush toilets, and an outdoor sink. One drawback is that a dumpster nearby attracts bears. Also, the group site accommodates tents or small RVs only.

Essentials: 168 sites, including 21 suitable for RVs (15-foot maximum length), piped water, flush toilets, barbecues, fire rings, picnic tables, pay showers, swimming, fishing, hiking, and access to Vikingsholm Castle. Leashed pets are permitted, at $1 per night. The fee is $12 for individual sites, $35 for group sites. Closed in winter. Off Highway 89 south of Homewood.

Contact: Seasonal park office; 530/525-7277, reservations 800/444-PARK (800/444-7275), or on the Internet at website: www .ReserveAmerica.com.

Emerald Bay State Park/Eagle Point
(see map on page 502, site 50)

Situated on a high, rocky promontory on the southern flanks of Emerald Bay, this large campground—one of the most popular camping spots in the region—is well off the highway and offers bird's-eye views of Lake Tahoe and the bay. Sites, however, are small and clustered closely together, occasionally separated by mounds of boulders, and it's a quarter-mile hike down to the beach at Emerald Bay from the nearest access point (although considering the seclusion, many campers feel the trek is worth it). The best sites are closest to the lake and have some tree cover, but they are subject to potentially strong afternoon winds.

Essentials: 100 units (suitable for RVs up to 21 feet), pay showers, water, picnic tables, barbecues, flush toilets, and swimming in the lake. Leashed pets are permitted. The fee is $12. At Emerald Bay State Park about six miles north of South Lake Tahoe.

Contact: Emerald Bay State Park; 530/525-7277, reservations 800/444-PARK (800/444-7275), or on the Internet at website: www.ReserveAmerica.com.

Emerald Bay Boat-In Camp
(see map on page 502, site 51)

Other than a backpack site in the high country, this is the most secluded and scenic organized camping spot at Tahoe. The lake's only boat-in campground is tucked away in protected pine forest just west of the Emerald Bay inlet and has a large pier and plenty of beach shoreline to accommodate everything from dinghies to opulent pleasure yachts. Views of the Sierra peaks from here are splendid, and it's an easy walk (or cruise) to Vikingsholm Castle and the scenic beach there, or to the Emerald Bay Trail, which leads to D. L. Bliss State Park. The campground is very popular, and the bay can fill with hundreds of watercraft on a warm summer day. Evenings and mornings, however, are much more peaceful and devoid of traffic.

Essentials: 20 sites for tents only, piped water, chemical toilets, barbecues, fire rings, picnic tables, beaches, and swimming in the lake. Leashed pets are permitted. The fee is $10. Sites are first-come, first-served. Closed in winter. On the north shore of Emerald Bay.

Contact: Emerald Bay State Park; 530/525-7277.

Bayview (see map on page 502, site 52)

Although sites are undeveloped, they are fairly spacious. The campground is near a heavily traveled section of the highway, but it's a great location for hiking and fishing. The reason: One trailhead leads into Desolation Wilderness at the east end and another leads to Cascade Lake. The former goes to Granite Lake (an excellent fishing spot) and beyond to the Velma Lakes, which are among the more spectacular in the wilderness, while the latter is a short but scenic hike to Cascade Lake and Cascade Falls (about one mile away).

Essentials: 10 campsites (some are suitable for large RVs), vault toilets, and fire rings. Camping is available in summer only, and is limited to 48-hour stays. Sites are on a first-come, first-served basis, and the fee is $8. On Highway 89 across from the Emerald Bay overlook, about seven miles north of South Lake Tahoe.

Contact: Lake Tahoe Visitor Center; 530/544-5994.

Fallen Leaf (see map on page 502, site 53)

This flat campground with moderate tree cover from scattered pines is level and has good proximity to hiking trails. But it's a fair walk to the Tahoe shoreline, and it can get crowded, hot, and dusty in midsummer. It is, however, on the road to Fallen Leaf Lake, an attractive place with fair fishing and boating for small craft, and is close to trailheads for hiking and horseback riding into Desolation Wilderness. Access to cycling trails is another plus. Unlike nearby Camp Richardson, most sites are well off Highway 89 and are quieter.

Essentials: 205 sites (130 suitable for RVs up to 40 feet), piped water, flush toilets, barbecues, fire rings, and picnic tables. Leashed pets are permitted. The fee is $16. Closed in winter. On Highway 89, one-quarter mile south of Camp Richardson and two miles north of South Lake Tahoe.

Contact: Lake Tahoe Visitor Center; 530/544-0426, reservations 877/444-6777, or on the Internet at website: www.ReserveUSA.com.

CAMPGROUNDS

Historic Camp Richardson Resort
(see map on page 502, site 54)

Camp Richardson is popular, crowded, and arguably Tahoe's largest and most diverse family resort. The privately operated campground is on flat terrain in scattered pine forest next to busy Highway 89, with little seclusion and minimal scenic appeal. But the extraordinary beaches and other recreational amenities make this a highly desirable location. Equipment for every conceivable type of water sport is available for rent at the marina, including kayaking, water-skiing, Jet Skiing, parasailing, sailing, and windsurfing. Charter fishing and sightseeing cruises are also possible. There's a roped-off swimming lagoon and a myriad of water toys for kids, along with four of Tahoe's most spectacular white sand beaches—Jameson, Baldwin, Kiva, and Pope. A paved bike trail, an equestrian center, beach volleyball sites, and the estates at Tallac Historic Site are next door. The Glen Alpine Trailhead into Desolation Wilderness is just up the road at Fallen Leaf Lake and offers one of Tahoe's best day hikes. The Beacon Restaurant on the beach has excellent food and, with live music day and night, the best "vibes" on the lake. Camp Richardson is the closest marina to Emerald Bay; in fact, it's within easy kayaking distance.

Essentials: 333 sites, group sites, showers, a boat ramp, piped water, flush toilets, barbecues, fire rings, picnic tables, swimming in the lake, horseback riding, bicycling, and hiking. The campground is close to Fallen Leaf Lake, Valhalla Estate, the U.S. Forest Service Lake Tahoe Visitor Center, and Emerald Bay. No pets are allowed. Fees range $22–25. Closed in winter. On Highway 89, two miles north of South Lake Tahoe.

Contact: Historic Camp Richardson Resort; 530/541-1801 or 800/544-1801.

Tahoe Valley
(see map on page 502, site 55)

The largest and most deluxe private campground in the Tahoe basin, Tahoe Valley has just about everything a camper (or even a non-camper) could want. This is a wonderful spot for families with small children. It's a block off the main highway, on flat ground among tall pines, but it feels remarkably secluded. Sites are shaded, clean, and spacious, and tenters are as welcome as RVers. The recreation facilities are as complete as you'll find anywhere, and are well patrolled. The Upper Truckee River is in back of the park, and the Factory Stores at the Y, South Shore's largest outlet center, is just next door. The park is close to two 18-hole golf courses and trails for horseback riding and bicycling. It's five miles from Stateline but is regularly served by free casino shuttles and public buses.

Essentials: 413 sites (301 accommodating RVers), full hookups, piped water, cable TV, flush toilets, barbecues, fire rings, showers, a swimming pool, picnic tables, tennis courts, sport courts, a 3,000-square-foot rec hall, a convenience store, a dump station, a storage yard, a visitor center with concierge service, and a bus stop for casino and city shuttles. Leashed pets are permitted, at no extra charge. The fee is $35–38. Open year-round, with about 25 sites available in the winter. Tahoe Valley is on U.S. 50 and C Street, at 1175 Melba Dr. in South Lake Tahoe.

Contact: Tahoe Valley; 530/541-2222; website: www.Rvonthego.com.

Chris Haven
(see map on page 502, site 56)

This older mobile home and RV park, family-owned and operated since 1960, accepts overnight and long-term stays. It's at Highway 50 and E Street, one-half mile south of the "Y" near the city limits of South Lake Tahoe. Sites lie among tall pines and are shaded.

Essentials: 30 sites with full connections, cable TV, telephone, hot showers, and laundry. City bus service is available (Stateline casinos are five miles away), and the park is near restaurants and shopping areas, including the Factory Outlet Stores. Pets are permitted on leash. Fees are $30 per night, $180 per week. Open year-around.

Contact: Chris Haven Mobilehome and RV Community, 2030 E St., South Lake Tahoe, CA; 530/541-1895; website: www.chrishaven.com.

Tahoe Pines
(see map on page 502, site 57)
There is nothing fancy about this place. The campground is considerably more rustic (and can be dusty from unpaved roads) than the KOA campground next door. Situated on the Upper Truckee River, it offers some swimming holes (with a private beach) when the river is flowing, and most sites are under tall pines. Noise from the busy highway can be intrusive.

Essentials: 80 sites (50 suitable for RVs), piped water, flush toilets, showers, barbecues, a playground, fire rings, picnic tables, and swimming in the lake. Leashed pets are permitted, at $3.50 per day. Fees are $22–40. Closed in winter. At 860 U.S. 50 in Tahoe Paradise, at the foot of Echo Summit.

Contact: Tahoe Pines; 530/577-1653.

KOA of South Lake Tahoe
(see map on page 502, site 58)
The campground is well maintained, but it is subject to noise from busy U.S. 50. Quieter and more secluded campsites (such as numbers 45–47) are off the road in the upper loop, which meanders through trees and is snuggled against a rocky hillside. This KOA is near the Upper Truckee River.

Essentials: 60 sites (52 suitable for RVs up to 40 feet), full hookups, piped water, flush toilets, cable TV at some sites, picnic tables, showers, a laundry room, a rec room, a general store, a dump station, and a swimming pool. Leashed pets are permitted, at an extra charge of $3.50. Fees are $28–36, with extra people and extra vehicles, $3.50 apiece. Open April–October, closed in winter. On U.S. 50 at the bottom of Echo Pass in South Lake Tahoe.

Contact: KOA of South Lake Tahoe; 530/577-3693 or 800/KOA-3477.

Campground by the Lake
(see map on page 502, site 59)
This is a wooded and very pleasant municipal campground ideally situated for RVs, although tent campers abound. It's close to the Stateline casinos and next to bike trails, shoreline access, and public bus/shuttle systems that travel throughout South Shore. Unlike the state parks, there is no extra charge for using showers. The 35-acre campground is next to a large and beautifully maintained recreation complex with a heated pool, a fitness center, and a senior center; there are additional fees for using these facilities. Most sites are in the trees. Be forewarned: There is heavy traffic day and night on busy U.S. 50, so if this bothers you, ask for a site farther from the highway. Casinos, just 2.3 miles away, regularly service the campground with free shuttles.

Essentials: 160 sites (all suitable for RVs), piped water, free showers, flush toilets, elevated barbecues, fire rings, picnic tables, a boat ramp, and swimming at the lake. Leashed pets are permitted, at $1 per day. High-season fee is $18, plus $7 for hookups (electricity and water) and $2 for an extra vehicle. Spring and fall rates, $11 per vehicle for up to four people. Closed in winter. On U.S. 50 in South Lake Tahoe, at South Lake Tahoe Recreation Area. The entrance is at 1150 Rufus Allen Boulevard.

Contact: South Lake Tahoe Parks and Recreation Department; 530/542-6096.

Lakeside Mobile Home and RV Park
(see map on page 502, site 60)
The only RV park near Stateline, Lakeside is situated in a quieter motel area among mature pines two blocks off the main highway and 2.5 blocks from the lake. The park is convenient to casinos, restaurants, golf courses, and shopping. Guests receive passes to a private beach at Lakeside Marina, with an array of water sports.

Essentials: 43 sites (10 accommodating RVs up to 37 feet), full hookups, piped water, flush toilets, showers, cable TV, a laundry room, picnic tables, daily continental breakfast, and pass for swimming at a nearby private beach. Leashed pets are permitted. The fee is $30. Open year-round. At 3987 Cedar Ave., on the north side of U.S. 50 in South Lake Tahoe (California side), three blocks from Stateline casinos, and across from Crescent V Shopping Center and Raley's Supermarket.

Contact: Lakeside Mobile Home and RV Park; 530/544-4704; website: www.tahoerv.com.

CAMPGROUNDS

Zephyr Cove
(see map on page 502, site 61)
Here is a good place for families with children, if you don't mind the lack of seclusion. Sites are next to a noisy highway, but most are in the trees. A 10-month, $4 million renovation completed in 2001 upgraded the campground and adjacent resort. In summer, the campground is packed and there's a constant influx of people for lake cruises. Major recreation amenities include the *M.S. Dixie II* paddle wheel cruiser, horseback riding at Zephyr Cove Stables, snowmobile tours in the winter, fishing charters, water-skiing and Jet Skiing, powerboat rentals, parasailing, beach volleyball, and the *Woodwind* catamaran cruise boat. The large, attractive beach is subject to afternoon winds. Shuttles are available to Stateline casinos.

Essentials: 93 newly redesigned RV sites, 47 "walk-in" sites and 10 "drive-in" sites, full hookups, telephone with an extra jack for Internet connection, cable TV, piped water, flush toilets, showers, stoves, fire rings, picnic tables, access to a sandy beach, lake cruises, fishing, swimming, boating, restaurants, horseback riding, outdoor patio at the new "Four Seasons" recreation center, a convenience store, free shuttle service to casinos, and snow-clearing in winter. Tent sites have bear-proof lockers. Leashed pets are permitted. Fees range $20–44, with $4 extra per person per day for more than four people. Open year-round. On U.S. 50, four miles north of Stateline in Zephyr Cove, Nevada.

Contact: Zephyr Cove Resort; 775/588-6644; email: zcr-campground@aramark.com; website: www.tahoedixie2.com.

Nevada Beach
(see map on page 502, site 62)
One of the two best Forest Service campgrounds at the lake (the other is William Kent), this spot sees heavy use from daytime visitors as well as from campers. Location is everything; it's on a wide, sandy beach (though not as scenic as the West Shore beaches), it's close to Stateline casinos, and it's well away from the traffic of U.S. 50. The flat site has some tree cover, although not the heavy forest typical of the West Shore. Boat-ing at the south end (at a boat-in picnic area) and swimming opportunities abound, along with picnicking on the beach. The area, however, usually gets strong afternoon winds.

Essentials: 54 sites (30 suitable for RVs up to 24 feet), piped water, flush toilets, barbecues, fire rings, a picnic area, picnic tables, a beach, boating, swimming in the lake, fishing, and volleyball. Leashed pets are permitted. The fee is $18 for standard sites and $20 for premium lakefront sites. Closed in winter. On Elks Point Road, one mile northeast of Stateline in Nevada.

Contact: 775/588-5562, reservations 877/444-6777, or on the Internet at website: www.ReserveUSA.com.

Marlette/Hobart Backcountry Area
(see map on page 502, site 63)
Here, at one of two hike-in sites along the eastern section of the Tahoe Rim Trail, campers can enjoy great vistas of Lake Tahoe, Spooner Lake, and the Carson Valley from high points nearby. The campground is also close to equestrian and mountain biking trails.

Essentials: 18 hike-in (backpack) campsites just off the Tahoe Rim Trail. Pit toilets are available. Leashed pets are permitted. There is no fee. The trailhead is at the Tahoe Rim Trail access on U.S. 50 at Spooner Summit, east of Stateline, and the campground is about six miles farther north.

Contact: Nevada State Parks; 775/831-0494.

Marlette Peak Campground
(see map on page 502, site 64)
Hikers can climb to the top of Marlette Peak for spectacular vistas of Lake Tahoe and the Carson Valley, then stay at this campground, one of two hike-in sites along the eastern section of the Tahoe Rim Trail.

Essentials: Six hike-in (backpack) campsites next to the Tahoe Rim Trail, picnic tables, fire rings, and a pit toilet. Leashed pets are permitted. There is no fee. It's about eight miles north of the Spooner Summit Trailhead on U.S. 50.

Contact: Nevada State Parks; 775/831-0494.

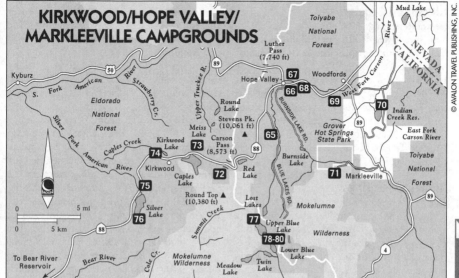

KIRKWOOD/HOPE VALLEY/ MARKLEEVILLE CAMPGROUNDS

© AVALON TRAVEL PUBLISHING, INC.

CAMPGROUNDS

KIRKWOOD/HOPE VALLEY/ MARKLEEVILLE

The following properties are keyed to the Kirkwood/Hope Valley/Markleeville Campgrounds map.

Hope Valley
(see map on page 509, site 65)

The pleasant, wooded campground in scenic Hope Valley is near the region's spectacular meadow and close to the West Fork of the Carson River, a good fishery in early summer. Historic Sorensen's Resort, with a restaurant and small store, is nearby, and the popular boating and fishing mecca of Blue Lakes provides plenty of recreation options just 11 miles south of the campground.

Essentials: 20 sites for tents and RVs, drinking water, vault toilets, picnic tables, fire pits, limited wheelchair access, and proximity to a store and a restaurant. Leashed pets are permitted. The fee is $10. For Hope Valley Group Campground, the fee is $18. Open June–September. On Blue Lakes Road in Toiyabe National Forest, near the Highway 88/89 junction in Hope Valley, 14 miles south of South Lake Tahoe.

Contact: Toiyabe National Forest, Carson Ranger District; 775/882-2766, reservations 877/444-6777, or on the Internet at website: www.ReserveUSA.com.

Hope Valley RV Park
(see map on page 509, site 66)

Operated by nearby Sorensen's Resort, this campground is on a moderately busy highway, but it's in a spectacular canyon next to the West Fork of the Carson River. It's a good location for hiking, fishing, and visiting Grover Hot Springs State Park. Campers have full access to a variety of special excursions, lectures, and other recreational amenities offered by the resort. This is a "no-smoking" campground.

Essentials: 25 sites, some for RVs and some for walk-in tent campers, full hookups, showers, flush toilets, and water. Pets are permitted, at $3 per night. The fee is $15 for tent sites, and $20–30 for RV sites, some with full hookups. Reservations are accepted. On Highway 88, about two miles east of the junction with Highway 89, in Hope Valley.

Contact: Hope Valley RV Park; 530/694-2203 or 800/423-9949; website: www.sorensensresort.com.

Kit Carson Campground

(see map on page 509, site 67)

This small, wooded campground is next to a busy road, but it's also close to fishing in the West Fork of the Carson River.

Essentials: 12 units offer vault toilets, picnic tables, water, and fire pits. Leashed pets are permitted. The fee is $10. Camping is on a first-come, first-served basis. Closed in winter. On Highway 88 east of the Highway 89 junction.

Contact: Toiyabe National Forest, Carson Ranger District; 775/882-2766.

Snowshoe Springs

(see map on page 509, site 68)

Snowshoe Springs is a small campground next to a busy highway and the West Fork of the Carson River, in a spectacular canyon setting. It's close to Sorensen's Resort, Indian Valley Reservoir, Markleeville, and Grover Hot Springs State Park.

Essentials: 13 units offer water, picnic tables, and fire pits. Leashed pets are permitted. The fee is $10. Camping is on a first-come, first-served basis. Golden Age and Golden Access Passports are honored. On Highway 88, two miles east of the junction with Highway 89.

Contact: Toiyabe National Forest, Carson Ranger District; 775/882-2766.

Crystal Springs

(see map on page 509, site 69)

A busy highway runs beside this campground, which is adjacent to the West Fork of the Carson River. Nearby is Indian Valley Reservoir, a great fly-fishing lake, and Grover Hot Springs State Park with its relaxing mineral pools.

Essentials: 22 sites, picnic tables, water, vault toilets, and fire pits. Leashed pets are permitted. The fee is $10. Camping is on a first-come, first-served basis. Golden Age and Golden Access Passports are honored. Closed in winter. On Highway 88, four miles east of the Highway 89 junction.

Contact: Toiyabe National Forest, Carson Ranger District; 775/882-2766.

Indian Creek Campground

(see map on page 509, site 70)

This clean, pleasant campground offers lots of conveniences and is set in moderate tree cover next to Indian Creek Reservoir. For fly-fishing and float-tubing, this is an excellent trout fishery. Trout are stocked in the reservoir, and the nearby Carson River is managed as a trophy fishery (catch-and-release). The campground is close to historic Markleeville and Grover Hot Springs State Park.

Essentials: 29 sites, including 10 tent pads and 19 RV sites (30-foot maximum length), group sites, a dump station, free hot showers, water, flush toilets, a boat ramp, and swimming. Leashed pets are permitted. The fee is $8 for walk-in tent sites, $12 for RV sites, and $35 for group sites (all tents, accommodating 15–40 people). There is an extra vehicle charge of $5 in the main campground, and there is a dump station charge of $5. The maximum stay is 14 days. With recent water shortages in the area, RV campers are encouraged to fill their water tanks before arriving. The season is May–October; closed in winter. Camping is on a first-come, first-served basis except for the group site, for which reservations are required. Group sites may not be reserved on holidays or during special events, when they are used for overflow campers. Four miles off Highway 4, just south of the Highway 88 turnoff at Woodfords.

Contact: Bureau of Land Management, Carson City District; 775/885-6000.

Grover Hot Springs State Park

(see map on page 509, site 71)

One of the finest state-run campgrounds in the region is made more attractive by its proximity to natural hot springs pools, just 0.3 miles away. The well-dispersed sites—most of which are under pine trees—are set off paved access roads and close to attractive meadows and a hiking trail to Burnside Lake. Sparkling clear night skies make for excellent stargazing. The hot springs offer 102°–104°F soaks. Visits cost $4 for adults, $2 for children, and are a great tonic for sore hiking muscles. There is excellent trout fishing at nearby Indian Valley Reservoir, as well as early season river rafting on the East Fork of the Carson River.

Essentials: 76 sites (many suitable for RVs), showers, water, flush toilets, picnic tables, barbecues, fire pits, a telephone, swimming, natural hot springs, a fishing pond, and self-guided nature trails. The fee is $12. There are added charges of $5 for an extra vehicle and $1 for pets. Reservations are accepted. Open year-round except a two-week closure in September for maintenance. It's on Hot Springs Road, six miles west of Markleeville.

Contact: Grover Hot Springs State Park; 530/694-2248, reservations 800/444-PARK (800/444-7275), or on the Internet at website: www.ReserveAmerica.com.

Woods Lake
(see map on page 509, site 72)

Woods Lake is the highest and, some might argue, the prettiest of the Carson Pass public campgrounds. It is well off the road in a secluded, beautifully forested valley next to a picturesque jewel of a lake that offers paddling and swimming. Campsites are well dispersed, meander around hills and depressions, and are mostly in shade. Trailheads here lead to Round, Winnemucca, and Fourth of July Lakes, and a spectacular though strenuous hike can be made to the summit of Round Top Peak (elevation 10,380 feet). There's a large picnic area with shallow, sandy lake access for wading. The location is very popular with day users, including picnickers and hikers. The small parking lot fills quickly on weekends.

Essentials: 25 sites (a few suitable for RVs, but most for tents), hand-pumped water, vault toilets, picnic tables, eight picnic sites adjacent to the lake, barbecues, and fire pits. Leashed pets are permitted. The fee is $11 ($22 double), $5 for each additional vehicle. Camping is on a first-come, first-served basis. Two miles south of Highway 88 near Carson Pass. No motorboats are allowed. The elevation is 8,200 feet.

Contact: Eldorado National Forest, Amador Ranger District; 209/295-4251.

Caples Lake
(see map on page 509, site 73)

This is a great camping location on the Carson Pass for many activities, including hiking, fishing, boating, and mountain biking. Sites are generally small, mostly set among the trees and nestled against a hillside. Some are beside a busy highway.

Caples Lake and its namesake resort are directly across the road, offering supplies and fishing boat rentals. The lake has good fishing for trout and spectacular vistas of magnificent Round Top (elevation 10,380 feet) and Thimble (9,827 feet) Peaks. If you're tired of camp food, Caples Lake Resort has an excellent gourmet restaurant. The area is near good hiking trails to Emigrant, Round Top, and Winnemucca Lakes, and a mountain bike route over Schneider Cow Camp to U.S. 50 at Echo Pass.

Essentials: 35 units (many suitable for RVs), piped water, vault toilets, picnic tables, barbecues, fire pits, and access to a boat ramp, boat rentals, mountain bike rentals, a convenience store, and a restaurant. Leashed pets are permitted. The fee is $11 ($5 for each additional vehicle). Camping is on a first-come, first-served basis. It's 26 miles south of South Lake Tahoe on Highway 88. The elevation is 7,800 feet.

Tip: The best sites are 25 and 26, at the end of a cul-de-sac against a granite rock wall.

Contact: Eldorado National Forest, Amador Ranger District; 209/295-4251.

Kirkwood Lake
(see map on page 509, site 74)

This is a beautiful, small campground on an equally beautiful, small lake, one-half mile off the highway down a steep, paved road. Sites are in a "rock garden," spaced close together among moderate pine cover. The bouldered lake offers fishing and canoeing, and many recreation amenities are nearby, including Kirkwood, riding stables, and hiking and cycling trails. For tent campers this a wonderful, idyllic retreat.

Essentials: 12 sites (best for tents), piped water, vault toilets, picnic tables, barbecues, a fire pit, and a pay telephone. The fee is $10, plus $5 for each additional vehicle. Camping is on a first-come, first-served basis. It's 28 miles southwest of South Lake Tahoe on Highway 88 and one-half mile west of the turnoff to the Kirkwood ski resort. Trailers are not advisable because of a narrow access road. No motorboats and no swimming or washing are allowed in the lake. The elevation is 7,600 feet.

Contact: Eldorado National Forest, Amador Ranger District; 209/295-4251.

Silver Lake, East/Silver Lake, West
(see map on page 509, site 75)

Of the two campgrounds across the highway from each other, the east side, which is run by the U.S. Forest Service, has the more spacious and centrally located sites. There's a trail from here to Kit Carson Lodge (with a store, a restaurant, and boat rentals) and to the east end of Silver Lake, which has some pretty coves, beaches, and a small island. Nearby options include horseback riding, hiking, and fishing, though afternoon winds can be strong. Both campgrounds are well situated in thick forest. The West Campground, operated by the Eldorado Irrigation District, has access to the American River. A nearby hiking trail goes to Shealor Lakes, a short jaunt with good swimming-hole possibilities.

Tip: The best sites in the East Campground are 46, 55, and 57. The best sites in the West Campground are 75 and 76.

Essentials: The East Campground has 62 units, and the West has 35 units (most suitable for RVs). They offer piped water, vault toilets, picnic tables, barbecues, fire pits, overflow vehicle parking, boat rentals, and a store nearby. Leashed pets are permitted. The fee for West Campground is $13, plus $5 for each additional vehicle, $1 per pet, and $6.50 for disabled senior citizens. East Campground sites are $13 ($5 for each additional vehicle) and are on a first-come, first-served basis. At Silver Lake, 32 miles southwest of South Lake Tahoe on Highway 88. The elevation is 7,200 feet.

Contact: East Campground-Eldorado National Forest, Amador Ranger District; 209/295-4251. West Campground-Eldorado Irrigation District; 530/644-1960.

Plasse's Resort
(see map on page 509, site 76)

Dusty but scenic campsites are close to the lake and to historic Plasse's Resort, where you'll find a store, a restaurant, a bar, and a post office. The resort has been run by the same family for more than 150 years. Equestrian routes from here follow the spectacular Mormon-Emigrant Trail to the back side of the Kirkwood ski resort, with many striking vistas. A good restaurant serving dinner on the weekends and a lively bar (often full of buckaroos) make this an interesting place to camp. Most sites are in moderate tree cover and meander on rough roads over rocky terrain. Kids love this place, and there are many repeat campers. It is ideal for people with horses. Though most sites are taken by summerlong campers, a few are available for daily rental.

Essentials: 60 sites, showers, piped water, flush and pit toilets, phones, an equestrian camping area, riding stables for backcountry trips, a store, a bar, and a restaurant. Pets are permitted. Fees are $25 per night, $150 per week. Two-night minimum required on weekends and three-night minimum on holiday weekends. Group rates are available. Horse-camping is $35 per night for one or two horses in designated areas. Reservations are accepted. Day-use parking, $5. Boat launch fee, $10. Open June–October. On Highway 88, on the west end of Silver Lake at Plasse's turnoff.

Contact: Plasse's Resort; 209/258-8814 (seasonal); website: www.plasses-resort.com.

Upper Blue Lake
(see map on page 509, site 77)

Offering recently upgraded facilities, this is the best of the campgrounds in the Blue Lakes area, though access roads are unpaved and dusty. There is moderate tree cover, and the campground is close to the Lost Lakes, which are accessible via four-wheel-drive vehicle or a short hike. Upper Blue Lake is the largest of the Blue Lakes and quite popular, so expect crowds during the warm summer months.

Tip: The best sites are 8 and 12, which are large and well shaded.

Essentials: 32 units (most suitable for RVs) in a clean campground with paved roads and spurs, piped water, vault toilets, picnic tables, barbecues, fire pits, and a boat-launch area. The fee is $15, plus $3 for each additional vehicle and $1 for pets. Camping is on a first-come, first-served basis. It's 1.3 miles past Upper Blue Lake Dam Campground. The elevation is 8,200 feet.

Contact: PG&E Land Projects; 916/386-5164, website: www.PGE.com/recreation.

Upper Blue Lake Dam
(see map on page 509, site 78)

There are some nice campsites here in a moderately shaded area. The campground is near the trailhead to Grouse and Granite Lakes, as well as four-wheel-drive roads to other nearby fishing spots, including Tamarack, upper and lower Sunset, Summit, Twin, and Meadow Lakes. By late summer, however, these lakes may be drawn down substantially.

Essentials: 25 units, piped water, vault toilets, picnic tables, barbecues, fire pits, fishing, and boating. The fee is $15, plus $3 for each additional vehicle and $1 for pets. Camping is on a first-come, first-served basis. At Blue Lakes, one-quarter mile beyond Middle Creek Campground. The elevation is 8,200 feet.

Contact: PG&E Land Projects; 916/386-5164, website: www.PGE.com/recreation.

Middle Creek/ Blue Lakes
(see map on page 509, site 79)

This is a small campground sandwiched between the larger campgrounds at popular Blue Lakes, a favorite boating and fishing destination.

Essentials: Five campsites (some suitable for RVs), vault toilets, piped water, picnic tables, barbecues, and fire pits. The fee is $15 per night, plus $3 for each additional vehicle and $1 for pets. Camping is on a first-come, first-served basis. The elevation is 8,200 feet.

Contact: PG&E Land Projects; 916/386-5164; website: www.PGE.com/recreation.

Lower Blue Lake
(see map on page 509, site 80)

The best time to camp here is early to midsummer when the Blue Lakes are at their fullest. Sites are in moderate forest cover, and most are fairly close to the shoreline. There's a long and dusty dirt/gravel access road from Highway 88. Good fishing opportunities abound in this popular and crowded area.

Essentials: 16 sites (most suitable for RVs), piped water, vault toilets, picnic tables, barbecues, fire pits, fishing, and boating. The fee is $15, plus $3 for each additional vehicle and $1 for pets. Camping is on a first-come, first-served basis. Take Blue Lakes Road 6.6 miles east of Carson Pass or 2.5 miles west of the Highway 89/88 junction for 12 miles. The elevation is 8,100 feet.

Contact: PG&E Land Projects; 916/386-5164, website: www.PGE.com/recreation.

CRYSTAL BASIN/HIGHWAY 50

The following properties are keyed to the Crystal Basin Campgrounds map.

Loon Lake (see map on page 514, site 81)

The spectacular Rockbound Valley, a range of huge granite massifs, flanks this excellent campground on the east. Campers at Loon Lake are well positioned for long day hikes or overnight pack trips into the less-crowded part of Desolation Wilderness via the Loon Lake Trailhead. Tree cover is more sparse here than at lower lakes in the Crystal Basin, sites are rockier and closer together, and the area is subject to strong afternoon winds. The sprawling reservoir with an irregular, rocky shoreline occasionally has good fishing for trout, but it's often crowded with water-skiers and pleasure boaters. A good picnic area with tables overlooks the water near the boat ramp. Spectacular sunsets bathe Rockbound Valley, especially McConnell (elevation 9,099 feet) and Silver (8,930 feet) Peaks.

Tip: The best sites, 32 and 33, are on a high embankment with gorgeous lake views.

Essentials: 53 designated sites (many suitable for RVs), two wheelchair-accessible units, a large parking lot for overflow campers, piped water, picnic tables, fire rings, barbecues, vault toilets, a boat ramp, and 18 picnic units. The fee is $15 for a single site, $30 for a double, and $5 for each additional vehicle. On the south shore of Loon Lake Reservoir, 29 miles north of U.S. 50 via the Ice House and Loon Lake Roads. The elevation is 6,500 feet, the highest among Crystal Basin campgrounds.

Contact: Eldorado National Forest, Camino Information Center; 530/644-6048, reservations 877/444-6777, or on the Internet at website: www.ReserveUSA.com.

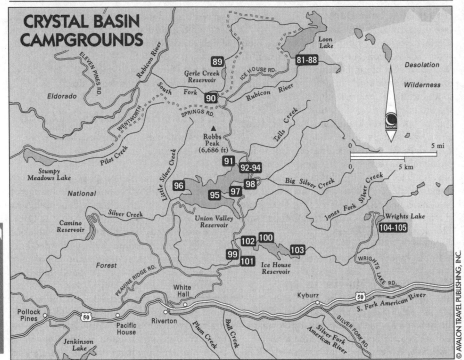

CRYSTAL BASIN CAMPGROUNDS

© AVALON TRAVEL PUBLISHING, INC.

Loon Lake Boat Ramp
(see map on page 514, site 82)

This is basically an overflow camping area for Loon Lake, and not a bad one at that. The parking lot is often lined shoulder to shoulder with rigs.
Essentials: 10 sites for self-contained RVs, vault toilets, and wheelchair-accessible units. There is no water. No campfires are allowed. The fee is $15. At Loon Lake, next to the boat ramp.
Contact: Eldorado National Forest, Camino Information Center; 530/644-6048.

Loon Lake Group Campground No. 1
(see map on page 514, site 83)

The attractions here are similar to those at Loon Lake Campground.
Essentials: 10 sites for walk-in group tent camping (up to 50 people), vault toilets, piped water, fire pits, barbecues, and picnic tables. The fee is $85. Reservations are required. On the south shore of Loon Lake Reservoir, 29 miles north of

U.S. 50 via the Ice House and Loon Lake Roads. The elevation is 6,500 feet.
Contact: Eldorado National Forest, Camino Information Center; 530/644-6048, reservations 877/444-6777, or on the Internet at website: www.ReserveUSA.com.

Loon Lake Group Campground No. 2
(see map on page 514, site 84)

This better-than-average group campground is very close to the lake, though it doesn't offer the lake views enjoyed by other campsites.
Essentials: A group site for up to 25 people and six vehicles, vault toilets, piped water, picnic tables, fire pits, and barbecues. The fee is $60. Reservations are required. At Loon Lake Dam, 29 miles north of U.S. 50 via the Ice House and Loon Lake Roads.
Contact: Eldorado National Forest, Camino Information Center; 530/644-6048, reservations 877/444-6777, or on the Internet at website: www.ReserveUSA.com.

Loon Lake Equestrian
(see map on page 514, site 85)
Independent campers bringing their horses with them for trips into Desolation Wilderness will find this campground a good staging area.
Essentials: Nine sites, piped water, vault toilets, and picnic tables. The fee is $15, plus $5 for each additional vehicle. On the south shore of Loon Lake Reservoir, 29 miles north of U.S. 50 via the Ice House and Loon Lake Roads at an elevation of 6,500 feet.
Contact: Eldorado National Forest, Camino Information Center; 530/644-6048, reservations 877/444-6777, or on the Internet at website: www.ReserveUSA.com.

Loon Lake Equestrian Group Camp
(see map on page 514, site 86)
The large group camping area for equestrians here is not too far from other facilities, though it is set back from the lake itself.
Essentials: Sites for up to 25 people, piped water, vault toilets, and picnic tables. The fee is $60. Reservations are required. The elevation is 6,500 feet.
Contact: Eldorado National Forest, Camino Information Center; 530/644-6048, reservations 877/444-6777, or on the Internet at website: www.ReserveUSA.com.

Northshore/Loon Lake
(see map on page 514, site 87)
With a commanding, lofty view of Loon Lake and the spectacular Rockbound Valley in Desolation Wilderness, this is the best free RV campground in the region. It is set in an open area on a high ridge with few trees and is subject to afternoon winds. Still, Northshore is a picturesque spot for watching sunsets and sunrises and, as might be expected, it's popular. There are paved access roads and spurs. Note: Some tent campers find undesignated sites nearby in small stands of pine.
Essentials: 15 sites for self-contained vehicles, vault toilets, wheelchair-accessible units, and five picnic sites. Tents are allowed. There is no water. On the north shore of Loon Lake, across from the main campground. Sites are $5 and are first-

come, first-served, plus $5 for each additional vehicle. The elevation is 6,500 feet.
Contact: Eldorado National Forest, Camino Information Center; 530/644-6048.

Pleasant/Loon Lake
(see map on page 514, site 88)
The attractions here are similar to those at Loon Lake Campground.
Essentials: 10 tent sites offer access by boat or trail only, with vault toilets, stream water (purify before drinking), and fire pits. Sites are free and first-come, first-served. On the northeast shore of Loon Lake. The distance from the boat ramp is about three miles. The elevation is 6,500 feet.
Contact: Eldorado National Forest, Camino Information Center; 530/644-6048.

Gerle Creek (see map on page 514, site 89)
Although the campground is unspectacular, with closely spaced sites, the reservoir is a wondrous playground for swimmers, paddlers, and float-tube fly-fishers. It has a spectacular mountain setting, a large rocky island within swimming distance, and a self-sustaining population of brown trout. The area is popular with day users who enjoy access to warm, shallow water. It has a fishing pier and several strategic picnic spots with rocky outcrops that invite sunbathers. This is an excellent family venue for lazing in a raft or canoe, since the lake isn't too large. It has interesting coves and a sloping, forested shoreline.
Essentials: 50 sites (some suitable for RVs), piped water, vault toilets, fire pits, barbecues, tables, four picnic sites, a self-guided nature trail along the creek, and a paved, wheelchair-accessible trail. The fee is $15, plus $5 for each additional vehicle. No motorboats are allowed. On Gerle Creek Reservoir, 27 miles north of U.S. 50 via Ice House Road, at 5,300 feet.
Contact: Eldorado National Forest, Camino Information Center; 530/644-6048, reservations 877/444-6777, or on the Internet at website: www.ReserveUSA.com.

South Fork Group
(see map on page 514, site 90)
Campers will find some decent sites here, but

there is only limited tree cover and for the most part the area is dusty and dry. On the plus side, South Fork Campground is not far from its namesake, the South Fork of the Rubicon River. Access is via a dirt road.

Essentials: Group site, with some RV access, accommodates up to 125 people, with vault toilets, picnic tables, barbecues, fire pits, and stream water (purify before drinking). Fee is $100 per night. It's 23 miles north of U.S. 50 via Ice House Road at an elevation of 5,200 feet.

Contact: Eldorado National Forest, Camino Information Center; 530/644-6048.

Yellowjacket

(see map on page 514, site 91)

A few sites at this heavily wooded campground, which is similar to Sunset, afford glimpses of Union Valley Reservoir. The best site is 20, with a lake view.

Essentials: 40 sites (most suitable for RVs), a boat ramp, piped water, vault and flush toilets, picnic tables, barbecues, and fire pits. The fee is $15, plus $5 for each additional vehicle. On the north shore of Union Valley Reservoir, two miles off Ice House Road and 19.5 miles north of U.S. 50. The elevation is 4,900 feet.

Contact: Eldorado National Forest, Camino Information Center; 530/644-6048, reservations 877/444-6777, or on the Internet at website: www.ReserveUSA.com.

Wench Creek (see map on page 514, site 92)

Wench Creek Campground has sparse to moderate tree cover, with lots of forest debris. If you haven't got a reservation elsewhere in Crystal Basin during a popular weekend, this is the place to try.

Tip: The best sites are 70 and 71, which have lake views, and 79, 80, and 81.

Essentials: 100 sites (many suitable for RVs), piped water, flush and vault toilets, picnic tables, barbecues, and fire pits. The fee is $15 per night plus $5 for each additional vehicle. No reservations are accepted. It's on the east shore of Union Valley Reservoir, about 15 miles north of U.S. 50 via Ice House Road. The elevation is 4,900 feet.

Contact: Eldorado National Forest, Camino Information Center; 530/644-6048.

Wench Creek Group Camp

(see map on page 514, site 93)

When the water level is up at Union Valley Reservoir, this is a decent location for several families or two large groups. There's a new paved four-mile bicycle trail from here to Fashoda Campground.

Essentials: Two group sites suitable for RVs (up to 50 people each), piped water, flush and vault toilets, picnic tables, barbecues, and fire pits. The fee is $80. May be reserved May 27–October 1. It's on the east shore of Union Valley Reservoir at an elevation of 4,900 feet.

Contact: Eldorado National Forest, Camino Information Center; 530/644-6048, reservations 877/444-6777, or on the Internet at website: www.ReserveUSA.com.

Fashoda Tent (see map on page 514, site 94)

Sites here are in pine forest, and several are situated right on the beach. There's a good put-in spot for canoes and other small boats, and a new four-mile bicycle trail goes to Wench Creek Campground. Campers share the area with day users.

Essentials: 30 walk-in sites (one is wheelchair-accessible), piped water, vault toilets, fire pits, a large parking area, and five picnic units. The fee is $13. Camping is on a first-come, first-served basis. On the peninsula at Union Valley Reservoir, 14 miles north of U.S. 50 via Ice House Road. The elevation is 4,900 feet.

Contact: Eldorado National Forest, Camino Information Center; 530/644-6048.

Sunset (see map on page 514, site 95)

Most of the sites at this campground, which is the largest in Crystal Basin, are set in heavy forest and offer a sense of seclusion. Some campsites offer lake views. A café and store are within five miles of here.

Tip: The best sites are 51, a double unit on a wooded hill with a view of the lake; 74, which is ideal for a large family and also has a view; and most of sites 81–111. Sites 112–131 are closer together and less desirable. Sites 1–36 are spacious but have no lake views.

Essentials: 131 sites (many suitable for RVs), piped water, vault toilets, picnic tables, fire pits, barbecues, a picnic area, a swimming beach, a boat ramp, and a dump station. The fee is $15, $30 for double sites and $5 for each additional vehicle. It's on the peninsula at Union Valley Reservoir, 14 miles north of U.S. 50 via Ice House Road. The elevation is 4,900 feet.

Contact: Eldorado National Forest, Camino Information Center; 530/644-6048, reservations 877/444-6777, or on the Internet at website: www.ReserveUSA.com.

Camino Cove (see map on page 514, site 96)

This new campground, which opened in the summer of 1999, is on the northwest shore of Union Valley Reservoir.

Essentials: 32 sites, vault toilets, fire rings, grills, picnic tables, but no water. There is no fee. From Highway 50 go seven miles north on Ice House Road, turn left on Peavine Ridge Road, go three miles west to Bryant Springs Road, turn right, go five miles north past West Point boat ramp, then continue 1.5 miles east to the campground turnoff on the right. No reservations.

Contact: Eldorado National Forest, Camino Information Center; 530/644-6048.

Lone Rock (see map on page 514, site 97)

You can reach this small, new campground on the east shore of Union Valley Reservoir either by bicycle from the new Union Valley Bike Trail or by boat from the Sunset Boat Ramp or Jones Fork parking area. It makes a pleasant escape for bike or boat campers.

Essentials: Five sites, vault toilets, picnic tables, fire rings, bike rack, with no water and no garbage service. There is no fee. You must pack out all refuse. To reach the site, go 12 miles from Highway 50 on Ice House Road (Primary Forest Road 3). No reservations.

Contact: Eldorado National Forest, Camino Information Center; 530/644-6048.

Big Silver Group Campground
(see map on page 514, site 98)

Along the new Union Valley Bike Trail on the east shore of Union Valley Reservoir, this brand new group campground (1999) is ideal for cycling campers.

Essentials: One group unit for 50 people, vault toilet, picnic tables, fire rings, grills, no water. Fee is $45. To reach the campground, go 14 miles from Highway 50 along Ice House Road (Primary Forest Route 3). There is parking for the bike trail. Reservations are available from May 26–October 16.

Contact: Eldorado National Forest, Camino Information Center; 530/644-6048, reservations 877/444-6777, or on the Internet at website: www.ReserveUSA.com.

Silver Creek
(see map on page 514, site 99)

There is moderate tree cover here, but the access is on a rough dirt road and the sites are not close to the creek.

Essentials: 11 tent sites, vault toilets, fire rings, and stream water (purify before drinking). Fee is $7, plus $5 for each additional vehicle. Next to Silver Creek, seven miles north of U.S. 50 via Ice House Road, near Ice House Resort. The elevation is 5,200 feet.

Contact: Eldorado National Forest, Camino Information Center; 530/644-6048.

Northwind (see map on page 514, site 100)

Although Northwind is in an attractive, wooded area on a high point overlooking the reservoir, there isn't much in the way of seclusion. In fact, sites are close together and crowded.

Essentials: 10 sites for self-contained vehicles, vault toilets, wheelchair access, picnic tables, and barbecues. Tents are allowed. There is no water. Fee is $5, plus $5 for each additional vehicle. On the north shore of Ice House Reservoir at an elevation of 5,500 feet.

Contact: Eldorado National Forest, Camino Information Center; 530/644-6048.

Ice House Resort
(see map on page 514, site 101)

Built in 1954, this privately operated campground and small motel is literally the most popular place in the Crystal Basin area, largely because it is the supply depot for everyone. It has a grocery store, tackle supply, ice machine, restaurant serving three meals daily, bar with television, gas station, and propane refills. After a week of tent camping, when you have that craving for ice cream, this is a welcome stop. The resort also has a large campground with the only full hookup sites (nine) in the vicinity, and these go quickly. During winter, the resort is just in the snowline and the campground is available for special functions. Cross-country trails are close by at Loon Lake and other areas of the forest, and the road is regularly plowed all winter by the Sacramento Municipal Utility District (SMUD).

> *For those who enjoy hiking, fishing, and nonmotorized boating, Wrights Lake is the finest campground in Eldorado National Forest and one of the finest in the Sierra.*

Essentials: 35 dry family sites for tents and self-contained RVs; nine RV sites with full hookups of water, electricity (from the resort's own generator) and sewer; and one group campground that can accommodate up to 100 people, with picnic tables, large fire ring, and access to water. Other facilities at the resort include shower house, flush toilets, and five-unit motel. Fees: $14 for dry campsites, $25 for full hookup sites, and $75 for the group site for up to 25 people, $2 per person extra for more than that. At 9000 Ice House Rd., nine miles off Highway 50.
Contact: Ice House Resort; 530/293-3321.

Ice House (see map on page 514, site 102)
Among the most attractive and popular campgrounds in Crystal Basin, Ice House has spacious, shaded sites nestled among towering old-growth pines. Several are close to the lake, where there's a shallow cove ideal for hand-launching small boats or for swimming. Some sites offer relative seclusion for tent campers. The campground is close to Ice House Resort, where there's gas, a large general store, a restaurant, ice, and showers.
Essentials: 83 sites (most suitable for medium to large RVs), some double units, three wheelchair-accessible units, piped water, vault toilets, picnic tables, fire rings, elevated barbecues, a picnic area, a boat ramp, and a dump station. The fee is $15, $30 for a double unit, plus $5 for each additional vehicle. At Ice House Reservoir, three

miles from Union Valley Reservoir and 1.5 miles north of U.S. 50 via Ice House Road. The elevation is 5,500 feet.
Contact: Eldorado National Forest, Camino Information Center; 530/644-6048, reservations 877/444-6777, or on the Internet at website: www.ReserveUSA.com.

Strawberry Point
(see map on page 514, site 103)
The narrow, paved access road to this windy, high campground is usually crowded with large RVs. Other than a view of the lake, the place isn't aesthetically pleasing, though it is close to a small boat-launching area.
Essentials: 10 sites for self-contained vehicles, vault toilets. Tents are allowed. There is no water. Fee is $5 on a first-come, first-served basis, plus $5 for each additional vehicle. On the north shore of Ice House Reservoir at an elevation of 5,200 feet.
Contact: Eldorado National Forest, Camino Information Center; 530/644-6048.

Wrights Lake
(see map on page 514, site 104)
For those who enjoy hiking, fishing, and non-motorized boating, this is the finest campground in Eldorado National Forest and one of the finest in the Sierra. Its many features include excellent, tree-shaded sites; separate loops that give tent campers their own area, if they wish; a stunningly beautiful natural lake dotted with rocky islets; warm shallow areas for swimming; a green freshwater marsh with a creek channel that is wonderful for canoeing; an adjoining lake, Dark Lake, which is a kind of Golden Pond for float-tube fly-fishers; and a half dozen high-country trails to some of the most spectacular lakes in Desolation Wilderness, most reachable on day hikes. A large wooded picnic area has magnificent vistas of the lake and Sierra peaks. There are a number of cabins available at both Wrights and Dark Lakes. This is the closest lake in Crystal Basin to Lake Tahoe, yet it is the most off the beaten path. Still, the campground is extremely popular and books up well in advance.

Tip: The best tent sites are 17 and 18, which are more spacious than the others; the best RV sites are 25 and 26, which are on a corner of a loop, are extra large and are nearest to the lake.

Essentials: 70 sites (20 for tents only, a half dozen for walk-ins, the rest for RVs), piped water, vault toilets, picnic tables, barbecues, fire pits, 10 picnic units, trails to Desolation Wilderness, and a free horse camp nearby. The fee is $13, $26 for a double, plus $5 for each additional vehicle. Reservations are required July–early September. No motorboats are allowed. It's 34 miles east of Placerville and eight miles north of U.S. 50 at Wrights Lake Road. The elevation is 7,000 feet.

Contact: Eldorado National Forest, Camino Information Center; 530/644-6048, reservations 877/444-6777, or on the Internet at website: www.ReserveUSA.com.

Wrights Lake Equestrian
(see map on page 514, site 105)
This wooded area has parking and access to the trailheads of Desolation Wilderness, but all riders who intend to stay overnight in the wilderness area must get a permit in advance. These are available at the Camino Forest Service Information Center 5.5 miles east of Placerville on Highway 50. Self-issue same-day permits are available at the lake.

Essentials: 15 sites with piped water, vault toilets, and fire rings. Picnic area, fishing, and the family campground are nearby. Some units are reservable through the National Recreation Reservation Service July–early September. Weather permitting, the campground is available on a first-come, first-served basis before and after those dates. Fee is $13, plus $5 for each additional vehicle.

Contact: Eldorado National Forest, Camino Information Center; 530/644-6048, reservations 877/444-6777, or on the Internet at website: www.ReserveUSA.com.

LAKES BASIN/ FEATHER RIVER COUNTRY
The following properties are keyed to the Lakes Basin/Feather River Campgrounds map.

Little Bear RV Park
(see map on page 520, site 106)
This destination camping park managed by owners Don and Sue Frisk is adjacent to the Middle Fork of the Feather River and within a five-minute drive of the area's four golf courses. In fact, just across the street is the nine-hole Feather River Inn Golf Course. Although quiet time begins at 10 P.M., no one mentioned that to the trains, which roar through the Feather River canyon tooting their horns at all hours of the night. Most sites are shaded, and there are two common lawn areas.

Essentials: 95 RV sites, 80 with full hookups, 10 with water and electric only, and five that are dry. Also, there are 10 camping cabins. No tents are allowed. Facilities include picnic tables, satellite TV, fire rings, laundry, a shower room, toilets, a club room, horseshoes, shuffleboard, Ping-Pong, swings, and a small market. Open April 1–November 1, weather permitting. Reservations are accepted up to one year in advance. The fees are $22–24 a night, or $147 weekly. Fees for camping cabins are $28 without electricity, $38 with electricity. At 102 Little Bear Rd. in Blairsden.

Contact: Little Bear RV Park; 530/836-2774.

Feather River RV Park
(see map on page 520, site 107)
This Good Sam park, a former KOA with impressive recreation facilities, is the only private campground in the region where tent campers are welcome and can make reservations (most local public campgrounds are on a first-come, first-served basis). While other Mohawk Valley private RV parks cater to retirees, this one is geared toward families with children. Most sites are situated in the trees. Contrary to the name, the park is not close to the Feather River, but it is within easy driving distance (10 minutes).

Essentials: 71 spaces, 35 with full hookups (for rigs up to 45 feet) and 36 with no hookups (for tents and self-contained RVs), and four camping cabins. Facilities include flush toilets, hot showers, laundry, public phones, a grocery store, ice, picnic tables, fire rings, firewood, a rec room, a video game room, pool tables, a heated swimming pool,

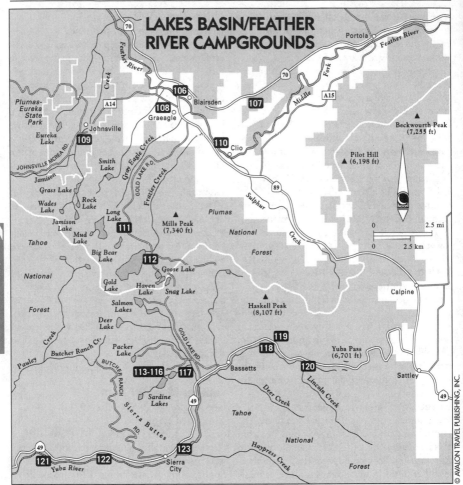

LAKES BASIN/FEATHER RIVER CAMPGROUNDS

a "tot lot" playground, and areas for horseshoes, volleyball, and badminton. There are tables at each site and a large common picnic area. The fee is $20 for RVs, $20–27 for small cabins. Open year-round. At 71326 Hwy. 70, six miles east of Blairsden.

Contact: Feather River RV Park; 530/836-2183 or 888/836-2183.

Movin' West Trailer Camp
(see map on page 520, site 108)

Tucked away among tall pine trees, this is the only campground right in the center of Graeagle. It is next to the nine-hole Feather River Park Golf Course and within a brief walk of shops and restaurants. A short drive will take you to Lakes Basin hiking trails and the historic Plumas Eureka State Park. The park is enormously popular and is often booked months in advance. It is owned and operated by Ron Madden.

Essentials: 51 sites for RVs up to 40 feet, full hookups, showers, cable TV, picnic tables, fire pits, a bathhouse, a grassy picnic area, a dump station, and a horseshoe area. A group area with a large barbecue pit is available. The fee is $24.50 for full hookups, $21.50 for tent sites, and $29 for two tent cabins. Open May 1–October. Reservations are strongly advised. At 305 Johnsville Rd. in Graeagle.

Contact: Movin' West Trailer Camp; 530/836-2614.

Plumas Eureka State Park
(see map on page 520, site 109)

Inviting and secluded, this campground is well off the main highway, nestled in a heavily wooded area. It has impressive views of high, surrounding peaks, four hiking trails to high- and low-elevation lakes and to lofty Eureka Peak, and an excellent museum on mining history at the park entrance. The park is close to the Middle Fork of the Feather River and four golf courses, as well as the spectacular Lakes Basin region. The only unfortunate aspect is that this is the only one of the Sierra region parks not on the reservation system, making it difficult for campers to try "potluck" after a long drive. Although weekends are usually busy, most times it's easy to get a campsite in the middle of the week.

Essentials: 67 sites (many suitable for RVs), free hot showers, picnic tables, barbecues, food lockers, piped drinking water, restrooms, laundry tubs, hiking trails, lakes, and a mining history museum. The fee is $12, an extra vehicle is $5, dogs are $1, and there are discounts for seniors. Camping is on a first-come, first-served basis. Dogs must be on leashes and are not permitted on hiking trails, except the U.S. Forest Service trail to Grass Lake. It's five miles west of Graeagle in Johnsville.

Contact: Plumas Eureka State Park; 530/836-2380.

Clio's River Edge Trailer Resort
(see map on page 520, site 110)

Set beside the Middle Fork of the Feather River, this park is the largest campground in eastern Plumas County and a favorite with retirees who stay for a month or longer. Only RVs are permitted; tents are forbidden. The park is close to golf courses and hiking trails. Sixty percent of the spaces are among the trees, and

all sites are paved. Twenty overnight sites have picnic tables.

Essentials: 220 sites for RVs only (40-foot maximum length), full hookups, some telephones, some picnic tables, a bathhouse with tiled hot showers, restrooms with flush toilets, cable TV, patios, fire rings, firewood, and laundry facilities. Recreation on the grounds includes badminton, horseshoes, and volleyball. The season is May 1–October 31. The fee is $24 a night for two, $155 a week. It's 3.5 miles south of Graeagle at 3754 Hwy. 89 in Clio.

Contact: Clio's River Edge Trailer Resort, P.O. Box 111, Clio, CA 96106; 530/836-2375; website: www.riversedgervpark.net.

Lakes Basin
(see map on page 520, site 110)

Recently refurbished, this campground is a pleasant, forested venue well off the highway. The Grassy Lake Trailhead originates here, but the road to the Long Lake Trailhead now bypasses the campground, thus assuring more privacy. The renovation included some redesign of the loop system, and now sites are closer together. The campground is two miles northwest of the Gold Lake boat ramp.

Essentials: 24 sites (some suitable for RVs), picnic tables, barbecues, fire pits, vault toilets, piped water, four wheelchair-accessible sites, and a group campground that can accommodate up to 40 people. Leashed pets are permitted. The fee is $13 for a family site, $26 for a double, and $50 for the group camp. Open Memorial Day–October 15, weather permitting. Off Highway 89, eight miles south of Graeagle on the Gold Lake Road; the elevation is 6,400 feet.

Contact: Plumas National Forest, Mohawk Ranger Station; 530/836-2575, reservations 877/444-6777, or on the Internet at website: www.ReserveUSA.com.

Snag Lake (see map on page 520, site 112)

Yes, this is an attractive, small lake and the campsites are surrounded by pine trees, but, unfortunately, they are right on the highway and the area is subjected to strong afternoon winds. Fishing is fair to good, and small boats,

CAMPGROUNDS

such as canoes and rowboats, can be launched from the shoreline. Boat rentals are available at Salmon Lake Lodge.

Essentials: 16 undesignated sites (some suitable for small trailers), vault toilets, and fire rings. There is no water. Leashed pets are permitted. Sites are free on a first-come, first-served basis. Five miles north of Bassett's Station on the Gold Lake Road next to Snag Lake, at elevation 6,600 feet.

Contact: Tahoe National Forest, North Yuba Ranger Station; 530/288-3231.

Berger (see map on page 520, site 113)

Most of the campsites are in shaded areas, and the campground has a creek flowing through it.

Essentials: 10 undesignated sites (some suitable for small trailers), vault toilets, primitive fire pits, and some picnic tables. There is no water. Sites are $6 and are on a first-come, first-served basis. Two miles west of the Gold Lake Road on the Packer Lake Road, at elevation 5,900 feet.

Contact: Tahoe National Forest, North Yuba Ranger Station; 530/288-3231.

Packsaddle Camping Area
(see map on page 520, site 114)

There's plenty of room for horse trailers, since Packsaddle was designed for equestrian use. There's a multiuse trail to Deer Lake (about 3.5 miles from here), and the campground is close to the Tamarack Lakes Trailhead to the Sierra Buttes, as well as to Packer and Sardine Lakes. The site was recently upgraded.

Essentials: 14 undeveloped sites (some suitable for RVs), new vault toilets, picnic tables, fire rings, a corral, and ample parking for pack and saddle stock. There is no piped water (although it is close to a stream). Leashed pets are permitted. The fee is $13, with $3 for an extra vehicle. Camping is on a first-come, first-served basis. It's 2.5 miles west of the Gold Lake Road on Packer Lake Road, at elevation 6,000 feet.

Contact: Tahoe National Forest, North Yuba Ranger Station; 530/288-3231.

Diablo Camping Area
(see map on page 520, site 115)

In this rustic yet not unattractive camping area, most sites are set among the trees. It is close to Packer and Sardine Lakes and also offers proximity to several popular trailheads in the shadow of the Sierra Buttes. There's a short but rough dirt entryway from the road.

Essentials: About 20 undesignated sites, one vault toilet, picnic tables, and fire pits. There is no piped water. Leashed pets are permitted. Sites are $6 and are on a first-come, first-served basis. It's 1.5 miles west of the Gold Lake Road on Packer Lake Road, at elevation 5,800 feet.

Contact: Tahoe National Forest, North Yuba Ranger Station; 530/288-3231.

Salmon Creek
(see map on page 520, site 116)

Sites at this excellent venue are placed among scattered evergreens and aspens. The campground is on an open, elongated site next to a creek and a meadow, and a short trail leads to Sand Pond and other hiking trails. It also offers proximity to Sardine Lake and to high-country trailheads, including those to the Sierra Buttes.

Tip: The most desirable sites are on the west side of the paved road and along the creek: numbers 16–29. The most secluded site is 33.

Essentials: 32 sites (seven suitable for RVs), piped water, vault toilets, picnic tables, stone fire pits, and metal barbecues. There is room for RVs off the paved access road. Leashed pets are permitted. The fee is $13, plus $3 for an extra vehicle. Camping is on a first-come, first-served basis. Two miles north of Bassett's Station on the Gold Lake Road near Salmon Creek.

Contact: Tahoe National Forest, North Yuba Ranger Station; 530/288-3231.

Sardine Lake
(see map on page 520, site 117)

Of the available Forest Service campgrounds near the Lakes Basin, this is the best and offers proximity to the spectacular Sardine Lakes, among the jewels of the Sierra. Campsites were recently upgraded with the latest conveniences, and most of them are under pine trees. Nearby is a delightful swimming hole, Sand Pond, which is warm and shallow (about seven feet deep), but there is no lifeguard on duty. The campground is

3

CAMPGROUNDS

close to good hiking trails, including one to the Sierra Buttes, the most prominent peak in the region. Boat rentals and fishing are available at Sardine Lake Resort, which also has one of the area's top restaurants and the most magnificent view of any lodge in the area.

Tip: The best site is 13.

Essentials: 23 sites (18 suitable for RVs up to 30 feet), piped water, barbecues, picnic tables, fire pits, new vault toilets, washbasins, a fish-cleaning station, a swimming pond with a beach, wheelchair-accessible sites, and a self-guided nature trail. Leashed pets are permitted. Fees range $13–26, plus $3 for an extra vehicle. Camping is on a first-come, first-served basis. It's 1.5 miles north of Bassett's Station on the Gold Lake Road and one-half mile southwest on Sardine Lake Road. The elevation is 5,800 feet.

Contact: Tahoe National Forest, North Yuba Ranger Station; 530/288-3231.

Sierra (see map on page 520, site 118)

The North Fork of the Yuba River runs alongside this campground, but some sites also are next to the highway. Most sites are small and wooded, and those that adjoin the river are the most popular.

Tip: The largest and most secluded sites are 7 (with two picnic tables), 14, and 16.

Essentials: 16 sites (seven suitable for RVs), vault toilets, picnic tables, and fire rings. There is no water. Leashed pets are permitted. Fee is $10, plus $3 for an extra vehicle. Seven miles northeast of Sierra City on Highway 49 on the North Fork of the Yuba River.

Contact: Tahoe National Forest, North Yuba Ranger Station; 530/288-3231.

Chapman Creek
(see map on page 520, site 119)

Here at what is perhaps the nicest campground in the Yuba Pass area, sites are set among trees with a large meadow in the middle. There's a good hiking trail along Chapman Creek, and a trail to Haskell Peak is nearby. This is not a heavily used campground, and sites are frequently available on weekends and holidays.

Tip: The best sites are 5 and 9, both near the creek, and 11, which is spacious but away from the shore.

Essentials: 27 sites (most suitable for RVs), metal fire rings, piped water, vault toilets, picnic tables, and barbecues. Leashed pets are permitted. The fee is $13, plus $3 for an extra vehicle. Camping is on a first-come, first-served basis. It's eight miles northeast of Sierra City across Highway 49 from the North Fork of the Yuba River.

Contact: Tahoe National Forest, North Yuba Ranger Station; 530/288-3231.

Yuba Pass (see map on page 520, site 120)

At this scenic campground, sites are situated in a stand of old-growth red fir trees bordering the headwaters of the North Fork of the Yuba River. A large meadow next to the campground attracts deer in the mornings and evenings.

Tip: The best, most spacious sites are 8 and 11.

Essentials: 20 sites (nine suitable for RVs to 30 feet), piped water (purify before drinking), vault toilets, picnic tables, and metal fire rings. Leashed pets are permitted. The fee is $13 per night plus $3 for an extra vehicle. The campground is now on the national reservation system. On Highway 49, 11 miles west of Sierraville at Yuba Pass Summit.

Contact: Tahoe National Forest, North Yuba Ranger Station; 530/288-3231, reservations 877/444-6777, or on the Internet at website: www.ReserveUSA.com.

Union Flat (see map on page 520, site 121)

Gold panning and dredging are the main attractions at this campground beside the North Fork of the Yuba River.

Essentials: 13 sites (six suitable for RVs), piped water, vault toilets (one wheelchair-accessible), fire rings, and barbecues. Leashed pets are permitted. Fees are $13, $26 for a double, and $3 for extra vehicles. Camping is on a first-come, first-served basis. Six miles east of Downieville on the North Fork of the Yuba River on Highway 49, at elevation 3,400 feet.

Contact: Tahoe National Forest, North Yuba Ranger Station; 530/288-3231.

Loganville (see map on page 520, site 122)

Mighty oaks and young pine trees surround the sites at this little-used campground near Sierra County Historic Park and the Kentucky Mine Museum. RVers should stick to the lower loop; the upper sites are not advisable for large vehicles. Fishing is possible in the river.

Essentials: 18 sites (four suitable for RVs), picnic tables, fire rings, and vault toilets. Water is not available. Leashed pets are permitted. The fee is $13, plus $3 for an extra vehicle. Camping is on a first-come, first-served basis. Two miles west of Sierra City on the North Fork of the Yuba River on Highway 49, at elevation 4,200 feet.

Contact: Tahoe National Forest, North Yuba Ranger Station; 530/288-3231.

Wild Plum (see map on page 520, site 123)

Campsites here are under large, mature trees next to Haypress Creek. There is good proximity to the Wild Plum Trail, the Pacific Crest Trail, the Kentucky Mine Museum, and Sierra City's restaurants and shops. Swimming, fishing, and gold panning are available in the creek. This is a popular campground, with a spectacular view of the Sierra Buttes and within easy range of the popular Lakes Basin area.

Tip: The best sites in the three loops are next to the creek.

Essentials: 47 sites (21 suitable for RVs up to 30 feet), piped water, vault toilets, barbecues, and fire rings. Leashed pets are permitted. Fees are $13, $26 for a double, and $3 for extra vehicles. Camping is on a first-come, first-served basis. One mile east of Sierra City on the Wild Plum Road along Haypress Creek, off Highway 49, at elevation 4,400 feet.

Contact: Tahoe National Forest, North Yuba Ranger Station; 530/288-3231.

RENO/CARSON VALLEY

The following properties are keyed to the Reno/Carson Valley Campgrounds map.

Boomtown RV Park
(see map on page 525, site 124)

This wide-open campground is sequestered in rolling hills, just a few minutes west of downtown Reno off I-80. It's part of an elaborate minitheme park that includes a casino, family fun center, several restaurants, and a new 318-room hotel. Both kids and senior citizens love this place. The main casino/hotel building has an Old West facade, indoor miniature golf, antique carousel, Dynamic Motion Theater, indoor ferris wheel, 50 video arcade games, and more than 200 redemption games. Boomtown has been booming in recent years with the addition of its new hotel wing and refurbished restaurants and gaming areas.

Essentials: 203 sites, full hookups, indoor and outdoor swimming pools, two spas, private showers, 24-hour security, cable TV, video rentals, fuel, a 24-hour minimart, a casino, free shuttle service, and a children's arcade. The fee is $27.15–29.17 weekdays, and $31.18–33.20 on weekends, with a 10 percent discount for Good Sam and AARP members. On I-80, seven miles west of Reno at the Boomtown exit.

Contact: Boomtown Hotel Casino; 775/345-8650 or 877/626-6686, with online reservations at www.boomtowncasinos.com.

Gold Ranch Casino RV Resort
(see map on page 525, site 125)

What was once mainly a truck stop and café for motorists heading west on I-80 from Reno to Truckee has now become a beautifully landscaped RV park set into the foothills of the eastern Sierra range, though the casino and restaurant are still there. Among the attributes are the wide RV spaces (both pull-through and back-ins), which have grassy areas on each side so that rigs aren't crowded together. Each site has a picnic table, but there is also a central picnic area with barbecues. Opened in 2001, the park has some shade trees, but it can warm up in the summer. It's close to Boomtown Casino, downtown Reno, and the town of Truckee near Lake Tahoe. And here's a quirk: Since the property straddles the California/Nevada border, you play the slot machines on the Nevada side and buy lottery tickets on the California side.

Essentials: 105 sites, all with full hookups including phone and cable TV, swimming pool, spa, Sierra Café (open 6 A.M.–10 P.M. daily),

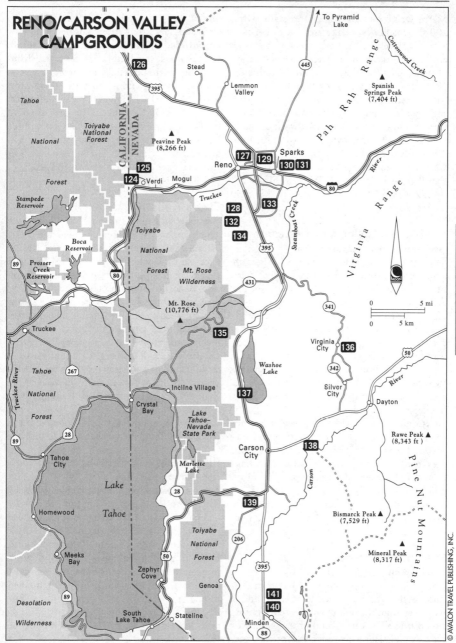

RENO/CARSON VALLEY CAMPGROUNDS

CAMPGROUNDS

© AVALON TRAVEL PUBLISHING, INC.

nearby Jack in the Box restaurant, casino with 200 slot machines, sitting area (in the office) with fireplace and TV, bathrooms with showers, laundry room, minimart, and gas station. Fees are $29 a night, $157.50 weekly, plus $1 per night for dogs, $2 for a 50-amp hookup, $1 for extra people (more than four), and slightly higher rates ($34) for holidays. Good Sam discounts are available. Open year-around. It's on Gold Ranch Road at westbound Exit 2 at Verdi and I-80.

Contact: Gold Ranch Casino-RV Resort, Verdi Exit 2 from I-80, Verdi, NV; 775/345-6789 or 877/728-6789; website: http://goldranch .casinocity.com.

Bordertown Casino and RV Resort
(see map on page 525, site 126)
This campground, which opened in 1999, is on a hill near the Nevada/California border. It has beautiful landscaped grounds and views of the Sierra Nevada and is in a quiet, unpopulated high-desert area just off Highway 395. There are large and easy pull-through spaces for RVs, and a grassy, tree-shaded area for tents. Campers can walk to the nearby casino and restaurant that are part of the Bordertown complex. There are two drawbacks: It's 17 miles to downtown Reno and the campground does not have sewer hookups (dump station only).

Essentials: 50 sites, electricity, water, phone, cable TV, picnic table, dump station, gas station, and nearby casino, restaurant, and gift shop. Fees are $11.20 for tent and $24 for RVs, with no extra charge for pets or children. At 19575 Hwy. 395 N near Reno, NV.

Contact: Bordertown Casino and RV Resort; 775/972-1309 or 800/218-9339; website: bordertowncasinorvresort.com.

Shamrock RV Park
(see map on page 525, site 127)
This park is in the open desert on blacktop a bit north of the Strip (2.5 miles, to be exact) and is well away from the hubbub of the central business district. The campground has a large picnic area, and management strictly controls access (no rigs older than 1978) and noise (no loud

music). A highly rated facility, Shamrock is very clean and does strong repeat business.

Essentials: 165 sites (about 40 for dailies), full hookups, some cable TV, a heated swimming pool, laundry facilities, showers, a store, a dump station, and a shuttle to downtown Reno. No tents are allowed. Pets are permitted. The fee is $25.76, with a 10 percent discount for Good Sam members. At 260 Parr Ave., Reno, NV; at the intersection with North Virginia Street.

Contact: Shamrock RV Park; 775/329-5222 or 800/322-8248.

Chism Trailer Park
(see map on page 525, site 128)
This campground, originally opened in 1928, has a scenic location, bordered by the Truckee River and Idlewild Park. Yet it's just one mile west of the glitzy neon signs and casinos of downtown Reno. Overnight campers share the facilities with resident mobile homes that are on 124 permanent spaces. Most of the sites are situated under tall trees, a pleasant haven from the hot, high-desert sun.

Essentials: 28 RV sites, full hookups, basic cable, laundry, and showers. Fees are $18.50 per day, $111 per week. At 1300 W. 2nd St., Reno, NV; just south of I-80 (take the Keystone Avenue exit).

Contact: Chism Trailer Park; 775/322-2281 or 800/638-2281; website: www.chismtrailerpark.com

River's Edge RV Park
(see map on page 525, site 129)
True to its name, this park is next to the Truckee River. It's also close to cycling and hiking trails and golf courses. The campground is AAA-approved and a Good Sam park.

Essentials: 164 sites (about 70 for dailies), full hookups, a swimming pool, laundry, showers, propane, a dump station, and shuttle service to downtown Reno/Sparks casinos. Pets are permitted. The fee is $25.53 (less for Good Sam members, more for those paying with a credit card). At 1405 S. Rock Blvd., Sparks, NV; off Exit 17 from I-80.

Contact: River's Edge RV Park; 775/358-8533.

Victorian RV Park

(see map on page 525, site 130)

This new campground in Sparks offers paved, landscaped sites in a suburban area that is one mile from Victorian Square (and John Ascuaga's Nugget) in downtown Sparks and is three miles from downtown Reno.

Essentials: 92 sites, full hookups and pull-throughs, lawn and gazebo areas for picnicking, bicycle rentals, shuttle service, 24-hour security, new RV slips, cable access, in-RV telephone service, convenience store, mobile RV washing service, laundry services, private showers, sanitary disposal station, and free shuttle to local casinos. Fees are $20 (10 percent less with Good Sam or AAA membership), plus $1 each for phone service and cable TV. Pets are free. At 205 Nichols Blvd., Sparks, NV.

Contact: Victorian RV Park; 775/356-6400 or 800/955-6405.

Sparks Marina RV Park

(see map on page 525, site 131)

Although it was not yet complete, this luxurious new RV resort is on the shores of Sparks Marina Park, a large lake that was accidentally created when an extremely wet winter caused a gravel pit to overflow in the late 1990s. Now the "accident"—one billion gallons worth—has been turned into a developed city park, with opportunities for boating and other water sports from two newly created beaches. With depths ranging 60–120 feet, the lake is suitable for anglers (rainbow and German browns are stocked and catch-and-release fishing is encouraged) and even scuba divers. With the myriad of recreation amenities, including a lighted trail system (two miles around the lake), two sand volleyball courts, and numerous picnic tables and gazebos, the park is literally a vast, high-desert playground. And you can launch any boat that you can carry to the water, from a sailing dinghy to a small outboard motor pram. The RV park, the largest in Reno and Carson Valley, features a spa, swimming pool, Jacuzzis, and a convenience store. The park is proximate to downtown Sparks and its casinos, as well as to some of the area's new golf courses. It's at the end of Lincoln off McCarran Boulevard in Sparks.

Essentials: 338 wide paved sites, with more than 200 that are pull-through, full hookups, laundry, showers, restrooms, store and deli, swimming pool, spa, Jacuzzis, propane gas, dump stations, and 50-amp service.

Contact: Sparks Marina RV Park; 775/851-8888.

Keystone RV Park

(see map on page 525, site 132)

This facility is one mile west of downtown Reno, and all spaces are landscaped. It accepts rigs of up 55 feet, but there is no pull-through. You can walk or hitch a cab to the casinos.

Essentials: 104 sites with 30/50-amp service, phone, cable TV. Fee is $23.52, and Good Sam discounts are available. At 1455 W. 4th St., Reno, NV.

Contact: Keystone RV Park; 775/324-5000 or 800/686-8559; website: www.keystonervpark.com.

Reno Hilton KOA

(see map on page 525, site 133)

Don't expect any great aesthetics here; this campground is pretty much in the open. But with its proximity to the Reno Hilton, it's like being next to a resort minicity. You have access to several restaurants, a big showroom and other live entertainment, a kids' fun center, a shopping mall, a bowling center, and a movie theater. Among the big attractions are a huge outdoor swimming pool, popular with families, and a golf driving range where you hit balls into a lagoon. Campers can bring their pets, and there's a dog-walking area where Fido can hang out while his owner is pulling on a one-armed bandit. KOA management took over in 2001.

Essentials: 265 RV sites, full hookups, a swimming pool, spas, laundry, restrooms, showers, shows, a store, and a dump station. No tents are allowed. Pets are permitted. Summer rates range $28–35, less for winter. At 2500 E. 2nd St., Reno, NV.

Contact: Reno Hilton Camperland; 888/562-5698; website: www.koa.com/where/nv/28136.htm.

CAMPGROUNDS

Silver Sage RV Park

(see map on page 525, site 134)

This is one of Reno's newest and best-appointed recreation vehicle parks. It is directly across from the posh Peppermill Hotel in the south end of the city, near shopping malls, restaurants, and the convention center.

Essentials: 43 sites for rigs up to 50 feet, full hookups, phones, cable, security system, grassy area with gazebo and barbecues, use of Peppermill pool and exercise room, and on-site managers. Fees range $24.65–28.45, less with Good Sam or AAA membership. At 2760 S. Virginia St., Reno, NV.

Contact: Silver Sage RV Park; 775/829-1919 or 888/823-2002; website: www.cris.com/~rvparks.

Davis Creek County Park

(see map on page 525, site 135)

Beautiful facilities, with campsites under sparse pine trees in a high-desert setting, are featured at this large camping area. The campground is next to the Ophir Creek Trailhead, which offers a six-mile, one-way hike to Tahoe Meadows on the Mt. Rose Summit. There is easy access to and from the freeway. Campfires are not allowed within the park.

Essentials: 63 tent and trailer sites, two group camping sites (maximum of 100 people; tents only), restrooms, showers, fishing, drinking water, a picnic/barbecue area, volleyball, a winter ice skating area, a three-acre pond, a dump station, hiking trails, and nature displays. It's open year-round. The fee is $13 for nonresidents, plus $5 for an extra car and $1 per pet. No reservations are taken, except for group camps. Off U.S. 395 against Slide Mountain on the eastern slope of the Sierra, south of Reno.

Contact: Washoe County Parks and Recreation Department; 775/849-0684.

Virginia City RV Park

(see map on page 525, site 136)

A Good Sam park as well as a AAA-approved facility, this is the only RV campground in the historic mining town of Virginia City. It is within walking distance of shops, museums, and restaurants.

Essentials: 50 paved sites (all suitable for RVs), full hookups, piped water, flush toilets, showers, laundry, a market/gift shop, and picnic tables. Leashed pets are permitted. The fee is $23. Open year-round. In Virginia City, Nevada, three blocks north of the central business district.

Contact: Virginia City RV Park; 775/847-0999; website: www.vcrvpark.com

Washoe Lake State Park

(see map on page 525, site 137)

After a long drought, Washoe Lake is full again and this campground is now highly desirable. There's a pleasant wildness to the place, with high-desert sage, occasional elm trees, and frequent animal and bird sightings, including deer and coyotes. The area is a favorite for hanggliding pilots and mountain bikers. Although most campsites are in open sage country (and quite hot in summer), the first loop has cabanas over the picnic tables—a welcome touch. The day-use area has huge shade trees and a well-manicured lawn with picnic facilities. Washoe is close to the museums and restaurants of Carson City and not far from the silver mining district of Virginia City.

Essentials: 49 sites (all suitable for RVs), piped water, flush toilets, showers, barbecues, fire rings, picnic tables, telephones, hiking trails, a boat launch, group picnic grounds, a dump station, a grassy shaded picnic area, and an equestrian area. Leashed pets are permitted. The fee is $11, and sites are on a first-come, first-served basis. Open year-round. Off U.S. 395 north of Carson City on Highway 428.

Contact: Washoe Lake State Park; 775/687-4319.

Pinon Plaza RV Park

(see map on page 525, site 138)

This new campground east of downtown Carson City is part of a large new hotel/casino complex, the Best Western Pinon Plaza Casino Resort. Within walking distance of the campground is a state-of-the-art, 32-lane bowling center, a 148-room hotel, a steak house, a coffee shop, a lounge with live entertainment, and a casino. The RV park is centrally located to several golf courses along Highway 50 and to the museums and other attractions of Nevada's state capital.

Essentials: 70 sites (pull-through and perimeter) with full hookups, picnic tables, convenience store, coin-operated laundromat, 24-hour security, restrooms and showers, and a grassy common area. Campers may use all hotel facilities including an outdoor pool, indoor spa, and exercise area. The summer RV rate is $16 ($10 off-season), with all major credit cards accepted and discounts provided for Good Sam, AAA, and AARP members. Open year-round. It's 1.5 miles east of Highway 395, at 2171 Hwy. 50 E, Carson City, NV.

Contact: Pinon Plaza Resort; 775/885-9000 or 800/501-2929; website: www.pinonplaza.com.

Comstock Country RV Resort
(see map on page 525, site 139)

Not only is this campground, at the south end of Nevada's state capital, clean and well managed, but there's also a popular restaurant (Bodine's) within a short walk. Lake Tahoe is just 20 minutes over the hill, and a unique railroad museum is just a mile north of here.

Essentials: 156 full hookups, piped water, cable TV, flush toilets, showers, laundry, a store, a dump station, tennis courts, horseshoe pits, picnic tables, a swimming pool, a basketball court, a volleyball court, and spas. Pets are allowed with some restrictions. The fee is $28, plus $2 for pets. Open year-round. At 5400 S. Carson St. (U.S. 395), Carson City, NV.

Contact: Comstock Country RV Resort; 775/882-2445 or 800/NEVADA-1 (800/638-2321).

Carson Valley RV Resort
(see map on page 525, site 140)

Carson Valley RV Resort is in an open, grassy area within easy walking distance of the Carson Valley Inn casino complex. The park has paved access roads and pads, as well as a lawn area for each site. Bonuses: The main hotel has a day-care center for young children, and campers have complete access to the hotel's spa deck with its two hot tubs.

Essentials: 70 sites, full hookups, spas, cable TV, laundry, showers, a dump station, a general store, and gas and diesel fuel. It's adjacent to the Carson Valley Inn, which has two restaurants, three lounges, a casino, free nightly entertainment, a children's fun center, banquet rooms,

© KEN CASTLE

Pinon Plaza RV Park, Carson City

and a wedding chapel. The fee is $21.78. Downtown at 1639 U.S. 395, Minden, NV.

Contact: Carson Valley RV Resort; 775/782-9711 or 800/321-6983; website: www.cvinn.com.

Silver City RV Resort
(see map on page 525, site 140)

Without a doubt, this new campground is one of the cleanest and most deluxe in the entire region. It's right on Highway 395 on the northern outskirts of Minden, making it centrally located to Lake Tahoe (24 miles away), the Basque restaurants of Gardnerville (four miles), Carson City (15 miles), and historic Virginia City (30 miles). Among the terrific amenities are the well-stocked market, a spa, and a spacious recreation room in the clubhouse, which has a big-screen TV and a selection of videos. It's a convenient in-and-out spot if you have a separate vehicle for day trips, not as much so with a motor home. Since the resort is on a busy highway, traffic noise intrudes somewhat. If this bothers you, request a site at the rear of the property.

Essentials: 206 sites, all with full hookups and 35-foot-wide pull-through spaces, telephone, cable TV, swimming pool, spa, convenience store, playground, clubhouse and arcade, fitness area, laundry facilities, paved roads, gas station (including diesel and propane). Fees are $23 a day, plus $3 extra for 50-amp service, $2 for cable TV, $2.50 for instant phone service, $2 each for more than two people, and $2.50 per week for pets (two maximum). Good Sam and Gulf Streamers discounts are available. At 3165 Hwy. 395, Minden, NV.

Contact: Silver City RV Resort; 775/267-3359 or 800/997-6393; website: www.silvercityrvresort.com.

SNOW AND WINTER CAMPING

It may sound like a cold, uncomfortable activity, but snow camping has its adherents. Cross-country ski centers, especially Kirkwood, offer overnight snow camping trips on an occasional basis, usually in early spring when the threat of winter storms has abated. If you've a mind to try snow camping on your own, consider the various Forest Service campgrounds that can provide uncrowded venues. These are not open with full services during the winter, but some of the areas can still be used. Here are two popular locations:

Highway 89/Little Truckee Summit

From the parking lot here, overnight camping is permitted November–April for five days or fewer. This is also a popular parking area for cross-country skiers and snowmobilers. Nearby Prosser Campground is also open in winter, but it requires a 1.5-mile ski or hike to get there. Visitors must pack out their trash and provide their own toilet paper and drinking water. Please be sure to leave a clean camp.

Fees: No fees are charged.

Contact: Tahoe National Forest, 631 Coyote St./P.O. Box 6003, Nevada City, CA 95959-6003; 530/265-4531.

Highway 49 North of Truckee

Chapman Creek, Sierra, and Yuba Pass Campgrounds, operated by Tahoe National Forest, are good locations for snow camping. Parking is limited at both Chapman Creek and Sierra. Yuba Pass is quite popular as a day-use area, and parking is available. In the Lakes Basin area off Gold Lake Road (which is closed because of snow in winter), you can ski-hike or snowshoe with a backpack to Sardine Lake, Salmon Lake, Berger Creek, and Snag Lake Campgrounds. Visitors must pack out their trash and provide their own toilet paper and drinking water. Please be sure to leave a clean camp.

Fees: No fees are charged.

Contact: Tahoe National Forest, 631 Coyote St./P.O. Box 6003, Nevada City, CA 95959-6003; 530/265-4531.

Dining and Nightlife

Tahoe Dining and Nightlife

Food and Drink

After a hard day of mountain biking, hiking, boating, or skiing, nothing is more attractive than a good dinner, unless it's good company—and the two are best when they go together. One of the delights of visiting Lake Tahoe, Reno, and the Carson Valley is visiting the area's top-quality dinner houses. Award-winning chefs, many of whom have de-cided that life in the mountains is better than in the city, have made their homes in this region, and consumers reap the rewards. Almost every type of American and ethnic cuisine is represented, from Tex-Mex to Nouveau California to French to Swiss to Asian. There is constant turnover in restaurants, and recently some of Tahoe's more enduring bistros have closed. Among them were Captain Jon's and the Crystal Bay Club's Steakhouse on the North Shore, Café Meridian in Truckee, and Midnight Mine, Greenstone Bar and Grill, and Frank's on the South Shore. Challenges in running a restaurant at Tahoe are

Lakeside Beach Grill at South Lake Tahoe

substantial, and finding qualified staff and creative chefs is usually the most difficult task. Close behind is the need to keep tables full during the slow periods of spring and fall, when tourism is at its lowest ebb. Typically, the casinos and large hotels offer the most consistent, high-quality dining, at times more so than the small restaurants whose business tends to fluctuate with the seasons. We've had varying experiences, from mediocre to superb, during repeat visits to the same places. (You can see comments and reviews of some restaurants online, as well as post your own, at www.tahoesbest.com/restaurants.) While consistency year-around is hard for many places to achieve, we've found that during the peak months of summer and winter, the Tahoe dining scene is at its best. You'll find splendid diversity, as well as an emphasis on fresh, regional ingredients. While there's never been a lack of beef and poultry in the mountains, more and more chefs are flying in fresh seafood to meet the growing demand for lighter, heart-healthy meals. Of course, if you've skied or hiked all day and have a craving for a pizza, there are more than a few places where you can indulge.

Award-winning chefs, many of whom have decided that life in the mountains is better than in the city, have made their homes in this region, and consumers reap the rewards. Almost every type of American and ethnic cuisine is represented, from Tex-Mex to Nouveau California to French to Swiss to Asian.

TRUCKEE/DONNER/ SODA SPRINGS
Andy's Truckee Diner
Everything about this place beckons you to come inside, from its strategic location next to the railroad tracks in the historic district of Truckee, to the charming, refurbished diner car (built in 1948) that is the centerpiece of the building, to the attractive interior with the just-perfect retro look. Since opening in 1995, the diner has undergone a number of management changes in an attempt to find its groove. Its forte is stick-to-your-ribs food that won't empty your pocketbook. The mainstays are meat loaf and mashed potatoes, hot turkey sandwiches with cranberries, and breakfast items such as

corned beef hash made fresh daily, chicken-fried steak with eggs, and poached salmon omelets. Be prepared for long waits on weekends. Andy's is next to the railroad station in downtown Truckee, on Highway 267.

Hours: Open 7 A.M.–9 P.M. Sun.–Thurs. and 7 A.M.–11 P.M. Fri. and Saturday.
Prices: $.
Contact: Andy's Truckee Diner, 10144 W. River St., Truckee, CA; 530/582-6925.

Clubhouse Bar and Grill (formerly Northwoods Restaurant)
Tucked inside the Tahoe Donner Recreation Center, in the sprawling mountainside subdivision above downtown Truckee, this restaurant has seen several incarnations over the years, largely because of its out-of-the-way location. The latest effort offers a pub-style dinner menu with all entrées priced at under $10. Among them: burritos, beef ribs (a house specialty), pizza, Philly cheese steak sandwich, fish-and-chips, chicken strips, coconut prawns, French dip, barbecued beef, quesadilla, and a house special, the Teri-Ahi Steak Sandwich (ahi tuna steak served with pineapple-jalapeno salsa and wasabi aioli). Offering three televisions, including a big-screen, the grill aims to be a sports bar and hangout for skiers in winter and golfers in summer. On Saturday night, the menu adds a prime rib special for around $20. Adjoining the restaurant is a large and spacious lounge as well as a sizeable banquet area. Dinner reservations are accepted.

TAHOE DINING

Hours: Open Thurs.–Mon. 4 P.M.–9 P.M., closed Tues. and Wednesday.

Prices: $–$$. Some credit cards are accepted.

Contact: Clubhouse Bar and Grill, 11509 Northwoods Blvd., Truckee, CA; 530/587-9435. Menus at this website: www.tahoedonner.com.

Cottonwood

The exterior does not hint that Cottonwood may be one of the best restaurants in Truckee. Ah, but looks can be deceiving. You drive to the top of a hill, past dilapidated seasonal housing, and arrive in front of a squat, weathered building that looks as if it might blow down in the next storm. But inside is a picture of warmth and coziness and a menu that will delight the palate. There's also a fine view of Commercial Row in Truckee below. The menu changes daily and can include sautéed prawns with garlic, roasted pork tenderloin with maple and black pepper demiglace, baby-back ribs, jerk-spiced rock prawns, seafood stew with shellfish and *boudin* sausage, and starters such as a large Caesar salad, grilled homemade sausage with pears and Gorgonzola cheese over mixed baby greens, and roasted yellow corn polenta with wild mushrooms and garlic. Children can enjoy a cheeseburger with shoestring fries. Amenities include a funky bar, live jazz entertainment on weekends, a patio, and a banquet section. Cottonwood is at Hilltop Lodge, off Highway 267.

Hours: Happy hour from 4:30 P.M., dinner from 5:30 P.M. daily.

Policies: Reservations are accepted.

Prices: $$–$$$. Some credit cards are accepted.

Contact: Cottonwood Restaurant and Bar, 1042 Rue Hilltop, Truckee, CA; 530/587-5711.

Dragonfly

This new Truckee restaurant, in the second-floor space formerly occupied by Café Meridian, was launched in early 2002 by local chef Billy McCullough, who was previously with Wolfdale's in Tahoe City. Think of the eclectic menu as "California Cuisine Meets Asia" and you'll get the idea. Dishes are creative, piquant, and full of fresh ingredients. They are matched by an international wine list and a selection of West Coast

microbrews. Prices are on the high side (appetizers alone start at $8), but you're not likely to find such unique combinations anywhere else in Tahoe. How about this for a "starter": Thai-style fish cakes with mahimahi, snapper, cucumber *sunomono*, and guava sweet-and-sour sauce? Or maybe you'd care to go right to the Kobacha squash sweet-and-sour soup with caramelized pumpkin seeds? For your main course, consider the alderwood-roasted, sake-soaked wild salmon with baby carrots, avocado-wasabi cream, jasmine rice, and spicy roasted tomato sauce. Or the grilled Asian marinated tri-tip steak with Chinese long beans, wasabi mashed potatoes, pineapple salsa. and teriyaki sauce. Come here prepared for an adventure in dining. Dragonfly is in the Porter-Simon Building on historic Commercial Row, with seating upstairs and on an outside deck for warm weather dining. With all new decor, the restaurant was completely renovated before it became Dragonfly. Reservations are highly recommended.

Hours: Lunch is 11 A.M.–2:30 P.M. and dinner is from 5:30 P.M.–9:30 P.M. Wed.–Mon., closed Tuesday.

Prices: $$–$$$. Major credit cards are accepted.

Contact: Dragonfly, 10118 Donner Pass Rd., Truckee, CA; 530/587-0557; website: www.dragonflycuisine.com.

Earthly Delights

What began as a tiny bakery in Truckee has blossomed into one of the lake's finest food purveyors, offering everything from drop-in lattes at a large coffee bar (with tables and chairs), to deli counter sandwiches and salads, to three-course take-out dinners. All of the food is creatively prepared and features many gourmet touches. When we're in Truckee, this is our standard morning munchies stop (especially if we're on the go for skiing or golf). We load up on homemade scones, coffee cake, muffins, fresh-baked loaves of bread, and cookies. But we're just as likely to grab some luncheon wraps, couscous salad, or other slightly exotic fare. For condo and rental home dwellers, this place is the solution to the otherwise cumbersome chore of cooking for yourself. Homemade soups and stews (including jambalaya, clam chowder, and white chicken chili) are on the take-out menu, along with vegetable salads, appetizers, and main dishes such as lasagna and stuffed chicken breasts. This is a quintessentially Truckee kind of place—offbeat, full of surprises, and clearly a one-of-a-kind institution. While it's not on Commercial Row, the historic district that is frequented by most tourists, it's on the other side of the railroad tracks on West River Road, still within walking distance from downtown. Parking at Earthly Delights itself is limited to a few diagonal spots.

Hours: Open Mon.–Thurs. 7:30 A.M.–6 P.M., 7:30 A.M.–7 P.M. Fri. and Sat., and 8 A.M.–6 P.M. Sunday.

Prices: $–$$. Major credit cards are accepted.

Contact: Earthly Delights, 10087 W. River Rd., Truckee, CA; 530/587-7793; email: earthlydelights@mail.telis.org.

El Toro Bravo

Hailing from the beaches of Capitola (south of Santa Cruz, California), this favorite Mexican restaurant, in a vintage Truckee house on the west end of Commercial Row, will spice up your palate on those cold winter evenings. Entrées include chicken and steak fajitas, chimichangas, *chiles rellenos,* grilled prawns, and red snapper Santa Cruz.

Hours: Daily from 11:30 A.M.–9 P.M.

Prices: $–$$. Major credit cards are accepted.

Contact: El Toro Bravo, 10186 Donner Pass Rd., Truckee, CA; 530/587-3557.

Engadine Cafe

Simply one of the finest and most elegant restaurants in the Tahoe area, Engadine Cafe is worth driving a few minutes west of Truckee on I-80. John Slouber—the creator of Royal Gorge Cross-Country Ski Resort—owns the delightful Victorian-style Rainbow Lodge bed-and-breakfast and has created an exceptional dinner house to match. The menu, with French influences, includes one of the largest and most interesting wine lists in the region. Among the entrées are medallions of roasted zucchini, apple-glazed chicken, raspberry lamb, and fettuccine *arrabiata* (a vegetarian dish with mushrooms and sweet peppers in a spicy tomato sauce). Specials on the blackboard might include sole amandine with amaretto sauce and rice pilaf, as well as other seasonal seafood. Healthy-heart menu items are available. Rainbow Lodge is on Hampshire Rocks Road, off I-80.

Hours: Daily for lunch 11 A.M.–2 P.M. and dinner from 5:30 P.M.–9:30 P.M.

Prices: $$. Some credit cards are accepted. No personal checks are accepted.

Contact: Engadine Cafe, 50800 Hampshire Rocks Rd., Soda Springs, CA; 530/426-3661.

Ice Lakes Lodge

This new, European-style lodge—reminiscent of a three-star pension in the Alps—is on one of the most attractive sites in the region. It is perched on the shores of Serene Lakes, two lovely but fairly shallow impoundments that are at the end of Soda Springs Road, southwest of the main entrance to Royal Gorge Cross-Country Resort on Donner Summit. In the summer, canoes and small sailing dinghies scoot across the lakes, and the restaurant's large picture windows look out over the water, the tree-covered shoreline, and distant Castle Peak. In winter, the lodge is within a short drive of Sugar Bowl, Donner Ski Ranch, Soda Springs, and Boreal ski areas, and the lakes are frozen and snowbound. The restaurant menu changes daily and seasonally, but it usually offers a combination of surf and turf, varying from salmon to steaks. Homemade cobblers and other desserts are a specialty, and you can have wine, beer, or cocktails with your meal. The dining room is adjacent to a bar and a spacious lobby, with a large fireplace and other rustic touches. There are separate menus for breakfast, lunch, and dinner, but usually full operation is on weekends only. Often, outside diners mingle with guests who are staying overnight. The lodge is named after an icehouse operation that existed here during the late 19th century.

Hours: Dinner from 5:30 P.M. Thurs.–Sun.; breakfast from 8 A.M. and lunch from 11:30 A.M. on weekends only. Closed Mon.–Wednesday.

Prices: $–$$. Major credit cards accepted.

Contact: Ice Lakes Lodge, 111 Soda Springs

Rd., Soda Springs, CA; 530/426-7660; website: www.icelakeslodge.com.

Moody's Bistro and Lounge

This completely remodelled restaurant is the latest tenant in the historic Truckee Hotel, which has seen three dinner houses in as many years, the last one known as Coburn's Station. But the third try, launched in the summer of 2002, may be the charm, since it has one of Tahoe's most talented young chefs in the kitchen. With impeccable credentials, Mark Estee has paid his dues as executive chef of Hyatt's Long Eagle Grill in Incline Village and as chef at the posh Lahontan Golf Club nearby. Originally from New England, Estee has devised an outstanding menu. And his partner, J J Morgan, a music impresario and former owner of the Up and Down Club in San Francisco, has fashioned an art deco interior that is reminiscent of a 1930s speakeasy. Knock twice, tell 'em Charlie sent you, and kick back with some live jazz. So what have Moody's investors created? While the menu changes daily, the East/West theme includes appetizers such as *cippolini* onion tart with Skyhill Farms goat cheese and wilted spinach, tempura ahi sashimi with sesame roasted cucumbers, and wood oven-roasted asparagus and morel mushroom tortellini with truffle broth. Among the entrées you may find black pepper and herb-crusted flank steak with truffled potato purée, Bordelaise sauce, and buttered bacon Brussel sprouts; pan-roasted monkfish with fennel gratin, orange jus and Nutty Butter gnocchi; and rack of pork with apples, Tuscan kale, and a smoky ham stock sauce. Vegetarians will always find something to their liking as well. Among the bold strategies of Moody's are early lunches and late-night dinners, along with service during those in-between times when most restaurants are closed. Throughout the seasons, the lounge serves up hot sounds from vibrant jazz to gritty urban DJ cuts. In summer, the convivial atmosphere spills out onto a large patio in the rear, which can seat up to 50 people.

Hours: Lunch served from 10 A.M., dinner from mid-afternoon until late evening.

Prices: $–$$$.

Contact: Moody's Bistro and Lounge, 10007 Bridge St., Truckee (inside the Truckee Hotel), CA; 530/587-8688; website: www.moodysbistro.com.

Pianeta Cucina Italiana

This rustic restaurant on Truckee's Commercial Row has established itself as a favorite among locals and visitors alike, largely because of its house-made pastas, reasonable prices, and intimate atmosphere. Seating is on two levels, with the first floor downstairs and below the sidewalk, and the second floor upstairs on a mezzanine. Among the standouts on the creative Italian menu are these: *cavatappi* (corkscrew pasta with artichokes, peas, spring garlic, cream, and prosciutto topped with pecorino romano and hazelnuts), *pappardelle con anatra e panna* (braised duck with house-made ribbon noodles, roasted peppers, shaved garlic, sun-dried tomato, and sweet onions, served with crème fraiche and grana cheese), and lasagne bolognese (beef and veal ragu layered with fresh pasta, bechamel sauce, herbs, parmesan, mozzarella, and ricotta). Other entrées include *bistecca alla modenese* (grilled and marinated rib-eye steak topped with Gorgonzola and grilled onions) and fungi portabella (grilled and marinated portabella mushrooms over porcini polenta, served over artichoke, tomato, pearl onion, and snap pea ragu with fresh mozzarella and herbs). There are also antipastos, salads, desserts, and specials of the week. Pianeta has a full bar and wine list. Be sure to make reservations, even on weeknights.

Hours: Open daily for dinner from 5:30 P.M. Be sure to make reservations on weekends.

Prices: $$–$$$. Major credit cards accepted.

Contact: Pianeta Cucina Italiana, 10096 Donner Pass Rd., Truckee, CA; 530/587-4694.

O'B's Pub and Restaurant

As close to the quintessential Truckee eating establishment as you can get, O'B's Pub and Restaurant has been a fixture in town for more than 20 years. The place is woodsy, rustic, and full of antiques, and has intimately arranged seating. The menu includes a quiche of the day, grilled Cajun chicken, fresh pastas, and prime rib. A children's menu and fun book are available, and for adults there's a full bar.

Hours: Daily for lunch from 11:30 A.M.–3:30 P.M. and dinner from 5:30 P.M.–10 P.M. There's also a brunch on Sunday.

Prices: $–$$. Major credit cards are accepted.

Contact: O'B's Pub and Restaurant, 10046 Commercial Row, Truckee, CA; 530/587-4164.

Pacific Crest

This gourmet restaurant, which is in Truckee's historic district and has a rustic bistro atmosphere, offers a menu that is influenced by Mediterranean and Asian cuisine. Antipasto includes roasted portabella mushrooms and fresh Washington state oysters; wood-fired pizzas come with toppings such as lamb sausage and Thai chicken; and pastas vary from Japanese *soba* noodles with ginger-sesame vegetable stir fry to a risotto with wild mushrooms and water chestnuts. Entrées include treats such as fresh seafood bouillabaisse cassoulet and grilled sea bass. Pacific Crest is a favorite hangout for lunch as well, with an excellent selection of salads and gourmet sandwiches.

Hours: Daily for lunch from 11:30 A.M.–3 P.M. and nightly for dinner from 5:30 P.M.–9:30 P.M.

Prices: $–$$. Some credit cards are accepted.

Contact: Pacific Crest, 10042 Donner Pass Rd., Truckee, CA; 530/587-2626.

Sizzler Steak House

A predictable, inexpensive chain restaurant, Sizzler offers steaks, chicken, and seafood, plus the popular all-you-can-eat salad bar. The building is attractive, with accents of brass and etched glass. This Sizzler serves breakfast, with dishes such as eggs Benedict and chicken-fried steak.

Hours: Daily 7 A.M.–9 P.M., Sun. brunch 8 A.M.–1 P.M.

Prices: $. Major credit cards are accepted.

Contact: Sizzler, Gateway Center, 11262 Donner Pass Rd., Truckee, CA; 530/587-1824.

Soul Sushi and BBQ

Now here's a combination that you don't find everywhere—California-style sushi on one hand and barbecued ribs and chicken on the other.

You can have the rawest sashimi, or meat that is well-done, or poultry that is smoked, or a little of everything. The motto is, "The only place in Truckee you can eat ribs with chopsticks." And you can order just about anything in advance online. The menu is extensive and specializes in organic produce for its sushi and original "contemporary" *maki* rolls. Some of the sushi dishes can also be smoked, grilled, baked, and fried tempura-style. Among the whimsically named specials are the Handgrenades (two large prawns stuffed with shrimp and topped with a spicy Japanese pepper sauce); My First Love (house-smoked *hamachi,* mango, cucumber, and chives wrapped in soybean paper); and Tuna Yaki Maki (grilled ahi marinated in basil, ginger, orange and soy sauce, rolled with cucumber and garnished with *aoi* nori). The barbecue side of the menu includes ribs, rib-eye steak, pork shoulder, beef briscuit, smoked Cornish game hen, smoked turkey, grilled sea bass, and grilled salmon. There's also a large selection of salads, including Chinese tofu, *soba* noodles (in winter), Korean kimchi, and seaweed marinated in sesame oil. You can order sushi in one or two pieces, or select complete dinners with a choice of salads. Desserts include mango, deep-fried coconut, and green tea ice creams. There's a deli that offers up to 21 organic salads ready to go, along with whole or sliced smoked meats.

Hours: 11:30 A.M.–10 P.M. Mon.–Fri., 5 P.M.–10 P.M. Sat. and 2 P.M.–10 P.M. Sunday. To-go orders accepted weekdays 11:30 A.M.–10 P.M. and Sat. and Sun. 2 P.M.–10 P.M.

Prices: $–$$. Major credit cards are accepted.

Contact: Soul Sushi and BBQ, 11429 Donner Pass Rd. (Westgate Shopping Center), Truckee, CA; 530/587-2680 or to go at 530/587-1281; website: www.ssabbq.com.

Squeeze In

Literally a closet of a restaurant, Squeeze In cooks a staggering variety of delicious omelets, and it is arguably the best breakfast house in downtown Truckee. You'll find American-style healthy cuisine featuring 57 omelets (try the Racy Tracy), Ecuadorian soup, and veggie sandwiches. It's on Commercial Row.

Hours: Daily 7 A.M.–2 P.M.
Prices: $.
Contact: Squeeze In, 10060 Donner Pass Rd., Truckee, CA; 530/587-9814.

Taco Station

This informal restaurant has fast become a hit with Amtrak train passengers and locals alike, who stop in to savor a variety of burritos and tacos. Service during peak periods, however, can be slow. Taco Station is next to the railroad station in downtown Truckee.
Hours: Open Mon.–Thurs. from 10:30 A.M. until 8 P.M., Fri. and Sat. from 10:30 A.M.–9 P.M., and Sun. 11 A.M.–7:30 P.M.
Prices: $.
Contact: Taco Station, 10100 W. River St., Truckee, CA; 530/587-8226.

Timbercreek

Northstar's year-round dinner house constantly experiments with new entrées, most of them winners. The ambience re-creates the logging days of Tahoe and Truckee, and the atmosphere is woodsy but airy. The menu includes California cabernet fillet, served with caramelized shallots and a cabernet sauce; pan-seared mountain trout; grilled Mohawk shrimp; nut- and herb-crusted pork tenderloin; wild mushroom ravioli; and penne pasta with smoked salmon, sun-dried tomatoes, artichoke hearts, and capers in an olive oil lemon sauce. Salads are a speciality and include the Black and Blue Caesar. During ski season, there's a daily breakfast buffet, and a children's menu is available.
Hours: Breakfast and dinner daily (during the winter season only); dinner only in summer and fall.
Prices: $$.
Contact: Timbercreek, 50 Trimont Ln., Truckee, CA; 530/562-2250.

Truckee Trattoria

This small but attractive restaurant serves contemporary California-style Italian cuisine that includes *frutti di mare* (shrimp, scallops, and clams in a white wine garlic sauce), chicken fettuccine with garlic cheese sauce, pesto-filled ravioli with Gorgonzola cream sauce and sun-dried tomatoes. All desserts are made fresh daily and include favorites such as tiramisu, chocolate soufflé torte, and strawberry Napolean. An espresso bar, wine, and beer are available. The indoor dining capacity is 26, and the outdoor patio opens when weather permits. Don't be in a hurry here, since the service can be slow. But the restaurant, at the Gateway Shopping Center (Truckee's largest), has clearly established a local following.
Hours: Open Wed.–Sun. 5 P.M.–9 P.M.
Prices: $–$$. Some credit cards are accepted.
Contact: Truckee Trattoria, 11310-1 Donner Pass Rd., Truckee, CA; 530/582-1266.

Wong's Garden

A locals' favorite, this restaurant serves a large variety of Sichuan and Cantonese Chinese dishes, in a setting that includes a 16-foot aquarium filled with colorful fish and a cherry blossom tree hanging from the ceiling. The menu includes Cantonese *chow fun,* sesame chicken, crispy shrimp, and a seafood basket, and there is a full bar with wine, beer, and cocktails.
Hours: Daily (except Mon.) 11 A.M.–9 P.M.
Policies: Reservations are accepted.
Prices: $. Major credit cards are accepted.
Contact: Wong's Garden, 11430 Deerfield Dr., Truckee (in Deerfield Plaza), CA; 530/587-1831.

SQUAW VALLEY
Alexander's at High Camp

Yes, there's a mind-boggling view of granite cliffs plunging to the valley. And yes, it snows here a lot in the wintertime. Beyond that, you may see a bungee jumper swinging past your window. Alexander's is the signature restaurant of Alexander Cushing, the owner of the Squaw Valley ski area, and is at the top of High Camp, where the tram ride terminates. The menu features salads, hamburgers, and nightly dinner specials. Entrées include sea scallops with bell peppers, grilled lemon chicken with green chile purée, steak Diane, baby-back pork ribs, and linguine provençale.

Hours: Open Nov.–April, daily 4 P.M.–8:30 P.M., weekends 11 A.M.–9 P.M., weather permitting.
Policies: Reservations are accepted for evening dining only.
Prices: $–$$$. Major credit cards are accepted.
Contact: Alexander's, 1960 Squaw Valley Rd., Olympic Valley, CA; 530/583-1742 or 530/583-2555.

Balboa Cafe

Destined to become a landmark of the newly emerging Village at Squaw Valley, this latest addition to the local dining scene offers ski-in or bike-in access, since it's right on the plaza within view of the Olympic resort's famous KT-22 lift. Operated by the same company that owns PlumpJack Squaw Valley Inn next door, the restaurant has quite a pedigree. Its roots are in San Francisco, where the first Balboa Café and the first PlumpJack Café have been delighting diners and food critics for years.

© CHRIS BECK/FLASH PHOTOGRAPHY

Balboa Cafe

The Nouvelle California cuisine matches the trendy, hip atmosphere of the interior, which wraps, in horseshoe fashion, around one corner of a building that houses luxury condominiums in its upper floors. There's a labyrinth of dining areas, from an eclectic bar to a cozy dining room to a meandering, outside patio, which is warmed by heat lamps. The restaurant looks like something from San Francisco's Financial District, but the atmosphere is decidedly more casual. Still, this is a place for people-watching, romantic encounters (one-night stands?), and fast-track deal-making. With Joe Lakavage, who moved here from PlumpJack Squaw Valley Inn, overseeing the kitchen as executive chef, the menu has plenty of imagination and an emphasis on fresh, regional ingredients. You can nosh from the bar menu, which includes appetizers and lunch-sized meals. Among these selections are crispy duck confit and goat cheese spring roll, Prince Edward Island mussels, Caesar and Cobb salads, burger on a baguette, pork and chorizo panini, smoked brisket sandwich, and pulled chicken and roasted chile quesadilla. The dinner menu has starters such as watercress and red cabbage salad, warm marinated calamari, and soup du jour. Main courses might include pork porterhouse au poivre, grilled New York strip steak, *Istrozzapretti* pasta, pan-roasted Pacific snapper, Alaskan halibut with *edamame,* lemongrass skewered shrimp with *mizuna* salad and lime-chile sauce, and Muscovy duck breast. The menu changes seasonally and there are usually daily specials. Given the upscale ambience of this place, everything is pricey. Expect a full-course dinner to hover around $50 a head, more with wine. Still, no one leaves disappointed.

Hours: 11:30 A.M. until late evening daily. The dinner menu is usually curtailed to weekends only during the spring and fall months, 6 P.M.–9 P.M.
Prices: $$–$$$. Major credit cards are accepted.
Contact: PlumpJack Balboa Café, 1995 Squaw Valley Rd., Ste. 14, Olympic Valley, CA; 530/583-5850; website: www.plumpjack.com/balboasv.

Bullwhacker's Pub

This Old West-style pub serves lunch, dinner, and microbrewed beers. It includes a sports bar with a big-screen television, pool tables, shuffleboard, and drink specials. Bullwhacker's is at the Resort at Squaw Creek.

Hours: Daily for lunch 11 A.M.–3:30 P.M. and dinner 5 P.M.–11 P.M.

Prices: $–$$$. Major credit cards are accepted.

Contact: Bullwhacker's Pub, 400 Squaw Creek Rd., Olympic Valley, CA; 530/583-6300.

Cascades

In the Resort at Squaw Creek, this recently remodelled restaurant specializes in buffets for breakfast and dinner. You can choose from the cold buffet, which includes dessert, or the complete buffet. The dinner menu features pesto-flavored carved turkey with toasted pita bread, home-smoked Pacific sturgeon, and blackened rib-eye steak with Cajun relish. A children's menu is available.

Hours: Breakfast daily from 6:30 A.M.–11 A.M. and dinner on Fri. and Sat. 6 P.M.–9:30 P.M.

Policies: Reservations are suggested.

Prices: $$–$$$. Major credit cards are accepted.

Contact: Cascades, 400 Squaw Creek Rd., Olympic Valley, CA; 530/583-6300.

Glissandi

Expensive, elegant, and ample, this is the premier restaurant at the Resort at Squaw Creek, and one of the best on the North Shore. The menu changes seasonally but might include New Zealand venison with plum and ginger *coulis,* fresh guinea hen with corn crepe and black truffle, roast wild boar with peppercorns and chipotle chiles, and a nightly selection of fresh fish. Starters, soups, and salads also are creative—and pricey. They include salmon ravioli, paté of California rabbit, goat cheese soufflé tartlet, purée of roasted yellow tomato with leeks and rouille, and consommé of pheasant with wild rice. If you have to look at your bill when you get it, you can't afford to eat here.

Hours: Open Tues.–Sat. 6 P.M.–10 P.M.

Prices: $$$. Major credit cards are accepted.

Contact: Glissandi, 400 Squaw Creek Rd., Olympic Valley, CA; 530/581-6621.

Graham's at Squaw Valley

This property was the original home of Wayne and Sandy Poulsen, the founders of Squaw Valley USA, and it still operates as a small inn. But the ground floor belongs to Graham Rock, one of Tahoe's most respected restaurateurs and the operator of Chambers Landing restaurant in the summer. Here he serves his signature entrées, known for their Mediterranean influences. The menu changes frequently and might include Greek leg of lamb, seafood paella, grilled Mediterranean pork loin, lamb ragout, and *fusilli con bucco*—corkscrew-shaped pasta with fresh artichokes, morel mushrooms, and prosciutto *di parma* in a light cream sauce. Appetizers include *melanzane ripiene*—grilled eggplant stuffed with zucchini, sun-dried tomato, basil, and fresh buffalo mozzarella—and desserts include daily specials as well as regulars such as tiramisu and fruit strudel.

Hours: During the summer 6 P.M.–10 P.M. Wed.–Sun., and during the winter 6 P.M.–10 P.M. Tues.–Sunday. During the winter the wine bar opens at 4:30 P.M.

Prices: $$. Some credit cards are accepted.

Contact: Graham's at Squaw Valley, 1650 Squaw Valley Rd., Olympic Valley, CA; 530/581-0454.

PlumpJack Cafe

Unusual and pleasantly surprising, this highly recommended and intimate restaurant brings a touch of San Francisco style to the high country. The menu changes every two weeks and offers a handful of entrées, but everything is exquisitely prepared and the service is impeccable. Dishes might include grilled quail, cider-cured pork loin chop, grilled filet mignon, roasted duck breast, Canadian halibut, risotto with sweet corn, and seared ahi tuna. All dishes are garnished with flavorful sauces. The desserts are among the best in Tahoe—try the hazelnut semi-Freddo with chocolate sauce and crème anglaise or the Amor di Polenta, with strawberries and crème chantilly.

One nice touch is that you can select from 20 wines by the glass, and most bottles of wine are just a few dollars over retail. The Tahoe sis-

© KEN CASTLE

PlumpJack Cafe

ter of a popular San Francisco dinner house, the restaurant is part of the highly eclectic PlumpJack Squaw Valley Inn. The decor mingles Shakespeare with pop art, and the result is visually dramatic. There's a cozy lounge with a fireplace adjacent to the dining room. Breakfast often includes a choice of buffet or menu items. PlumpJack is next to the tram building of the Squaw Valley ski resort. A sister restaurant, Balboa Café, is a short walk away in the new Village at Squaw Valley.

Hours: Breakfast 7 A.M.–11 A.M. daily, lunch 11 A.M.–2 P.M., dinner from 5:30 P.M. Reservations suggested.

Prices: $$–$$$. Major credit cards are accepted.

Contact: PlumpJack Cafe, 1920 Squaw Valley Rd., Olympic Valley, CA; 530/583-1576.

Ristorante Montagna

At the Resort at Squaw Creek, Ristorante Montagna serves California Italian cuisine with rotisserie cooking, homemade soups, salads, pastas, and a wood-burning oven-baked pizza, complemented by an extensive wine list.

Hours: Lunch and dinner daily 11 A.M.–10 P.M.

Prices: $–$$$. Major credit cards are accepted.

Contact: Ristorante Montagna, 400 Squaw Creek Rd., Olympic Valley, CA; 530/581-6618.

TAHOE CITY/WEST SHORE
Angela's Pizzaria

If you're staying on the West Shore, this is great place for a casual dinner or a take-out, and it's clearly a favorite joint for locals. The menu offers good, hearty food with crisp, thin pizza crusts, fresh ingredients and a few unique combinations. For example, there's a pizza called Nutbelly, which has sun-dried tomato pesto sauce, mozzarella, zucchini, artichoke hearts, sunflower seeds, red onion, and parmesan cheese. Other selections include calzones (stuffed pizza), spaghetti and meatballs, antipasta and Caesar salads, foccacia, house-made garlic bread, and a half-dozen sandwiches. Beverages include beer, wine, and soft drinks. The restaurant, in a tiny strip mall, is rustic but intimate, with a handful of tables and booths. The staff can be a bit brusque at times, especially during the busy evening hours when take-out orders roll in. You may also have to step around a couple of dogs to get through the front door.

TAHOE DINING

Hours: Open Tues.–Sat. 11:30 A.M.–9 P.M., 1 P.M.–9 P.M. Sun., and closed Monday.
Prices: $–$$. No credit cards accepted.
Contact: Angela's Pizzaria, 7000 W. Lake Blvd., Tahoma, CA; 530/525-4771.

Bacchi's Inn

Talk about longevity—this popular place has been operated by the same family since 1932 and the menu has stayed consistent. The restaurant serves robust dishes with a rich, and sometimes overwhelming, tomato sauce and a winning homemade minestrone soup. Don't look for any calorie-savers. There are more than 40 dinner entrées featured on the menu, and a banquet room is available. Bacchi's Inn is off Highway 28 near Dollar Point, two miles northeast of Tahoe City.
Hours: Dinner daily from 5:30 P.M.–9 P.M.; the bar is open 4 P.M.–9 P.M.
Policies: Reservations are suggested.
Prices: $$–$$$. Major credit cards are accepted.
Contact: Bacchi's Inn, 2905 Lake Forest Rd., Tahoe City, CA; 530/583-3324.

Black Bear Tavern

Taste Old Tahoe in this 1933 building of peeled logs, vaulted ceilings, river-rock fireplaces, and antique oil lamps. Its charm is genuine, and the minute you walk inside there's a feeling of antiquity and warmth. And keep an eye out for old Bruin, because bears have been known to come down from the woods and check out the menu. And why shouldn't they? Dinner includes nightly specials such as charbroiled ribeye steak, pan-seared duck breast, grilled Chilean sea bass, stuffed pork chop, and local favorites such as meat loaf, salmon, stuffed eggplant, crab cakes, fish tacos, and pasta. The killer dessert—if you can handle it—is the strawberry shortcake, which is almost certainly unlike anything you've had before in the way of that dish. When we visited, the service was slow, and the kitchen ran out of the most popular specials early in the evening. The restaurant has a bar, convenient parking, and close proximity to the West Shore Bike Path, a fact that is not lost on the cycling crowd.

Hours: Lunch noon–3 P.M. weekdays, dinner from 6 P.M. daily.
Policies: Reservations are accepted.
Prices: $$. Some credit cards are accepted.
Contact: Black Bear Tavern, 2255 W. Lake Blvd., Tahoe City, CA; 530/583-8626.

The Blue Agave (formerly Mi Casa Too)

Originally built in 1868, the historic Tahoe Inn now houses a large and popular Mexican restaurant, which is gaily decorated with piñatas and bright interior colors. The menu offers fajitas of beef, shrimp, and chicken; pork *carnitas;* seven types of quesadillas; *albondigas* (Mexican meatball) soup; and combination plates with enchiladas, tacos, and *chile relleno,* all prepared with fresh and healthy ingredients. Desserts include flan, sopaipillas, raspberry *churros,* and deep-fried ice cream. There are 16 draft beers, 16 different margaritas, and more than 200 brands of tequila. A separate bar with TV is a hangout for sports junkies, and summer brings outdoor dining options on the patio and on a recently opened veranda. The building has a rich and storied past, since it was first owned by Robert Watson, a local pioneer, gold-seeker, and conservationist. A number of area landmarks, including Mt. Watson and Watson Lake, are named after him. The inn served as a speakeasy during Prohibition and reportedly was a hangout for gangster "Baby-Face" Nelson. Fire destroyed the building in 1934, but it was rebuilt and was reopened in its present configuration. Over the years it became a kind of unofficial town hall, housing service organizations such as the Tahoe City Rotary. Walls of the restaurant are festooned with photographs and murals depicting life in Tahoe between the 1890s and 1930s. The Blue Agave is in the heart of the shopping district in Tahoe City, across from Commons Beach.
Hours: Lunch and dinner daily from 11:30 A.M.–11 P.M. Happy hour is 4 P.M.–6 P.M. Sun.–Fri., and daily lunch specials are served until 4 P.M.
Prices: $–$$. Major credit cards are accepted.
Contact: The Blue Agave, 425 N. Lake Blvd., Tahoe City, CA; 530/583-8113.

The Bridge Tender Tavern and Grill

One of the oldest watering holes and burger joints on the North Shore has a new home. The original building, which was constructed in the 1930s as Tahoe's first souvenir store, was demolished in the summer of 2002 by the California Department of Parks and Recreation. The state, which owns the land, wanted to create more lakeside walkways and interpretive displays next to the outlet of the Truckee River, where people gather at "Fanny Bridge" to watch migrating trout. Furthermore, the Bridge Tender was a ramshackle structure that failed to meet modern building codes. Still, many tales were told around the bar and many burgers were happily digested. Fortunately, the new "BT," directly across the street, continues in the rustic vein, with siding made of cedar logs and recycled snow fencing from Wyoming. As in the old tavern, there's a bar, wooden seats for diners, and stained glass signs, which were brought over from the previous building. The new patio has seating along the Truckee River and comes complete with its own bar and kitchen. Although some locals are nostalgic about the loss of the original BT, the new location is more scenic and convenient. What's on the menu? A dozen types of burgers, as well as fries, onion rings, fish tacos, chili cheesedogs, barbecued chicken sandwiches, soups, salads, and other pub food. Among the burger specials: the Sour Cream Burger, with mushrooms, black olives, jack cheese, and sour cream. Does BT serve the ultimate Tahoe burger? The answer is yes, in the view of many residents and repeat visitors. Another asset: The Bridge Tender is right next to the paved bike trails at the Tahoe City "Y."

Hours: Daily, 11 A.M.–11 P.M., midnight on Thurs., Fri. and Saturday.
Prices: $.
Contact: The Bridge Tender Tavern and Grill, 65 W. Lake Blvd., Tahoe City, CA; 530/583-3342.

Café Cobblestone

A fixture in the main business district at the Cobblestone Shopping Center, this casual eatery offers substantial menus for breakfast and lunch. In the morning, you can enjoy ample portions with dishes such as Huevos Cobblestone (flour tortilla topped with black beans, salsa, two eggs, melted cheese, sour cream, and guacamole), biscuits and gravy, chicken fried steak, poached eggs Florentine, nearly a dozen varieties of omelets, and pancakes. Lunch brings an assortment of salads and sandwiches including chicken Parmesan, the S. S. Tahoe (an open-faced sandwich with broiled Angus ground chuck), the Hattie Belle (sliced turkey, tomato, cream cheese, and Indian chutney on wheat bread), Rueben, crab melt, several types of burgers, French dip, and turkey dip. Homemade soups and scones are among the specialities. A children's menu is available, and the restaurant also serves a variety of beverages including espressos.

Hours: Daily 7 A.M.–4 P.M.
Prices: $.
Contact: Café Cobblestone, 475 N. Lake Blvd., Tahoe City, CA; 530/583-2111.

Christy Hill

This delightful lakeside dinner house serves some of the best gourmet food in the basin. You can make a meal of the appetizers alone, choosing from Maryland soft-shell crab sautéed with toasted hazelnuts, garlic, and brown butter; tiger prawns sautéed with sun-dried tomatos in a lemon, garlic, and butter cream sauce; and three-cheese ravioli with a fresh sage, roasted garlic, and sun-dried tomato demi-cream sauce. Hungry yet? Now move on to the main course, if you can. The menu features Alaskan halibut, Australian lamb loin marinated with a house-made chutney, beef tenderloin sautéed with garlic mushrooms, and Hawaiian albacore tournedos. Sauces are the kitchen's true forte: Test your taste buds on a Bourbon demi-glace; sorrel demi cream; or a sauce that blends garlic, ginger, sesame, soy, scallions, and cilantro. Christy Hill is at Lakehouse Mall.

Hours: Dinner daily (except Mon.) from 5:30 P.M.–9 P.M.
Policies: Reservations are suggested.
Prices: $$$. Some credit cards are accepted.
Contact: Christy Hill, 115 Grove St., Tahoe City, CA; 530/583-8551.

TAHOE DINING

Chambers Landing

Chef Graham Rock has earned a strong local following, and deservedly so, with his creative sauces and cuisine from the Mediterranean, southern Spain, southern France, Italy, Greece, and Northern Africa. This summer-only restaurant features Catalan *romesco* (fish stew), veal saltimbocca, and grilled duck breast. Chambers Landing is seven miles south of Tahoe City.

Hours: Lunch daily (except Tues.) from 11:30 A.M.–2:30 P.M., and dinner daily (except Mon.) 6 P.M.–10 P.M. The bar is open daily noon–midnight, with happy hour 5 P.M.–7 P.M. Open in summer only.

Policies: Reservations are accepted.

Prices: $$. Some credit cards are accepted.

Contact: Chambers Landing, 6300 Chambers Lodge Rd., Homewood, CA; 530/525-7262.

Coyote's Mexican Grill

What was once primarily a casual fast-food and take-out place has been recently expanded into a more complete, dine-in restaurant. The tasty Mexican food is prepared without lard or preservatives. Fresh menu items include fajitas, homemade salsa, vegetarian dishes, and microbrewed beers. A children's menu is available, and phone orders are welcome.

Hours: Daily 10 A.M.–10 P.M.

Prices: $.

Contact: Coyote's Mexican Grill, 521 N. Lake Blvd., Tahoe City, CA; 530/583-6653.

Fast Eddie's Texas Bar-B-Que

You'll find family-style barbecue here, as well as vegetarian cuisine and a salad bar. Takeout and a children's menu are available.

Hours: Daily 11 A.M.–10 P.M.

Prices: $–$$. Major credit cards are accepted.

Contact: Fast Eddie's Texas Bar-B-Que, 690 N. Lake Blvd., Tahoe City, CA; 530/583-0950.

Fiamma

Offering pizza, pasta, and creative Italian-style dinner entrées, Fiamma is a locals' favorite. Try the antipasto special of a roasted *poblano* chile stuffed with Sonoma jack, chevre, and pine nuts served with avocado, cilantro cream, and smoked tomato *coulis*. Of the various pizzas, one unique topping combination consists of roasted eggplant, zucchini, red bell peppers, scallions, basil, smoked mozzarella, and tomato sauce. Pastas include veal and mushroom ravioli, *capellini*, fettuccine, and linguine; other entrées include roasted chicken breast with polenta cakes, roasted duck breast over crisp *capellini* with a blackberry port sauce, veal scallopini pan-seared with sautéed onion and spinach, and a wild mushroom sauce served with risotto.

Hours: 5:30 P.M.–9:30 P.M. daily.

Prices: $$. Major credit cards are accepted.

Contact: Fiamma, 521 N. Lake Blvd., Tahoe City, CA; 530/581-1416.

Fire Sign Cafe

This unassuming restaurant is a locals' hangout, prized particularly for breakfast, for which it has garnered numerous accolades. Menu items include huevos rancheros, dill and artichoke omelets, Cape Cod Benedict, kielbasa and eggs, nut and seed waffles, and buckwheat pancakes. The menu also features teriyaki steak, turkey club and chicken salad sandwiches, and veggie potatoes. The café also offers wine, beer, espresso, and fresh-squeezed juices. There is outside dining during warm weather. It's two miles south of Tahoe City on Highway 89.

Hours: Daily 7 A.M.–3 P.M.

Prices: $. Some credit cards are accepted.

Contact: Fire Sign Cafe, 1785 W. Lake Blvd., Tahoe City, CA; 530/583-0871.

Hacienda del Lago

Reasonably priced Mexican entrées and picturesque views of Lake Tahoe are the strong points of this casual, attractive restaurant. The menu features salmon, shrimp, beef, turkey, and vegetable fajitas; chimichangas; burritos; and a dozen or so combination dinners, including the El Grande. The full bar blends up just about every flavor of frozen margarita you can imagine, and the place is well known for its happy hour. It's in the Boatworks Mall.

Hours: Daily 4 P.M.–10 P.M. Happy hour lasts 4 P.M.–6 P.M.

Prices: $. Some credit cards are accepted.

TAHOE DINING

Contact: Hacienda del Lago, 760 N. Lake Blvd., Tahoe City, CA; 530/583-0358.

Jake's on the Lake

The formulaic and fairly predictable Jake's on the Lake provides a mixture of steaks, seafood, and chicken. But with its reasonable prices and delightful lake views, its popularity has endured. The menu includes prosciutto basil prawns, Hawaiian swordfish, ginger chicken, scampi, and a dessert called Kimo's Original Hula Pie. Seafood specials change frequently. Jake's is at the Boatworks Mall.

Hours: Breakfast, lunch, and Sun. brunch 10 A.M.–2:30 P.M., and dinner nightly from 5:30 P.M.–10:30 P.M.

Prices: $–$$$. Major credit cards are accepted.

Contact: Jake's on the Lake, 780 N. Lake Blvd., Tahoe City, CA; 530/583-0188.

Lakehouse

Two restaurants—The Eggschange and Lakehouse—have been combined on the lower level of this waterfront mainstay, which has undergone extensive remodeling. This place has one of the best views on the North Shore, right above the lake. Breakfast features home-style cooking with a few interesting twists: eggplant omelets; huevos rancheros; homemade corned-beef hash; mountain mush, consisting of oats, walnuts, raisins, brown sugar, and fresh fruit; fresh-baked muffins in a basket; an espresso bar; and fresh-squeezed specialty juices, including honeydew, pineapple, orange, and grapefruit. Lunch and dinner items include Chinese chicken salad, pizza pies, burgers, Philly cheese steak, and club sandwiches. If you just want to hang out on the deck and sip something, try the microbrews, lattes, and fruit smoothies.

Hours: Daily 7 A.M.–10 P.M.

Prices: $–$$. Major credit cards are accepted.

Contact: Lakehouse, 120 Grove St., Tahoe City, CA; 530/583-2222.

Mandarin Villa

Offering average Chinese food, this second-floor, shoreline restaurant has wonderful views of Tahoe that complement a dazzling array of menu items. These entrées include walnut prawns, scallops with gingerroot and scallions, beef with asparagus, chicken with garlic sauce, Peking shredded pork, and Chinese cabbage with dry shrimp. À la carte menus and combination family dinners are both available. The chefs use no MSG, and they employ low-fat cooking techniques. It's upstairs at Lakehouse Mall.

Hours: Lunch and dinner Tues.–Sun. from 11:30 A.M.–9:30 P.M.

Prices: $–$$. Major credit cards are accepted.

Contact: Mandarin Villa, 120 Grove St. at Lakehouse Mall, Tahoe City, CA; 530/583-1188.

Naughty Dawg Saloon and Grill

This lively après-ski and après-beach hangout is popular with 20-somethings. Naughty Dawg is decorated in a dalmatian theme, and its walls are plastered with snapshots of the owners' dogs. Matching the decor, the menu features some unique items: Start out with one of the mixed drinks served in a dog bowl. Then sample the quesadilla El Naughto Dawgo, the French poodle Brie sandwich, fish tacos, the snow crab pita, the Cajun catfish sandwich, the Pit Bull bacon burger, or the "dirt" dessert, which consists of crushed Oreos, Kahlua cake, whipped cream, and chocolate pudding. That "dirt" alone will have you howling at the moon all night.

Hours: Daily from 11:30 A.M.–11 P.M. The bar is open until 2 A.M.

Prices: $–$$. Major credit cards are accepted.

Contact: Naughty Dawg Saloon and Grill, 255 N. Lake Blvd., Tahoe City, CA; 530/581-DAWG (530/581-3294).

Norfolk Woods Inn

This cozy, award-winning restaurant inside a charming, 1940s-era country inn on the West Shore serves breakfast, lunch, and dinner. Dinner highlights include filet mignon with cracked peppercorn demi-glace, stuffed marinated chicken breast, lamb loin with garlic and herbs, and various pasta dishes, including the longtime favorite, pasta pillows. Breakfast includes corned-beef hash, crepes, and egg dishes. A children's menu, wine, and microbrewed beers are available.

Hours: Breakfast and lunch daily, A.M.–3 P.M. and dinner Thurs.–Sun. from 5:30 P.M.
Policies: Reservations are accepted.
Prices: $–$$. Major credit cards are accepted.
Contact: Norfolk Woods Inn, 6941 W. Lake Blvd., Tahoma, CA; 530/525-5000.

Old Tahoe Cafe

This restaurant offers home-style cooking, with a large breakfast and lunch menu.
Hours: 7 A.M.–2:30 P.M. daily.
Prices: $.
Contact: Old Tahoe Cafe, 5335 W. Lake Blvd., Homewood, CA; 530/525-5437.

Pfeifer House

Remember the 1982 movie *Forbidden Love,* with Yvette Mimieux and Andrew Stevens? No? Anyway, scenes from that film were shot here. But that's not the reason to dine at one of Tahoe's oldest restaurants, which was established in 1939. The real draw is the excellent touch that gold-medal winner Franz Fassbender, who moved here from Germany in the 1960s, brings to every course he serves. This is a low-light kind of place, with lots of old European ambience. The menu includes pepper steak, leg of lamb with garlic butter, duckling with orange sauce, and veal *piccata.* All dinners are served with soup and salad. Pfeifer House is a quarter mile north of Tahoe City on Highway 89.
Hours: Cocktails from 5 P.M., dinner from 5:30 P.M.–10 P.M. Wed.–Sunday.
Policies: Reservations are advised.
Prices: $$–$$$. Major credit cards are accepted.
Contact: Pfeifer House, 760 River Rd., Tahoe City, CA; 530/583-3102.

Pisano's

This small restaurant, which replaced West Side Pizza in 1999, is across from Obexer's Marina. It specializes in gourmet pizzas, pastas, soups, and sandwiches. Among the pizza specials is The Sinatra with pesto, fresh tomatoes, and mozzarella cheese, and The Carnivore, with homemade meatballs, bacon, sausage, and other meats.

Hours: Lunch and diinner served noon–10 P.M.in summer; with dinner only 5 P.M.–10 P.M. the rest of the year. Closed Wed. during ski season.
Prices: $–$$.
Contact: Pisano's, 5335 W. Lake Blvd., Homewood, CA; 530/525-6464.

River Grill

One of Tahoe City's newest and most delightful restaurants is a bit difficult to find, even though it's at the "Y" and just downstream from Fanny Bridge. But it's worth the effort. The grill has imaginative and well-prepared dishes, served by a professional and attentive wait staff. It also has a terraced outdoor deck with tables that face the lush, tree-lined river. This is an intimate and enchanting spot during summer evenings, one that is enhanced by candlelight and propane heat towers. In the indoor dining area, there are large picture windows through which you can watch waterfowl swimming along the river. For a gourmet restaurant, the grill's prices are among the most reasonable at North Shore. The menu includes excellent starters such as stuffed seafood strudel (with salmon, halibut, shrimp, green onions, and cream cheese), Brie *en croute,* spinach salad with goat cheese, and New England clam chowder. Entrées include cornmeal-crusted Alaskan halibut, braised lamb shank, St. Louis spare ribs, duck and mushroom ravioli, and our favorite—Tahoe City Mixed Grill (with chicken apple sausage, grilled tri-tip, and ribs with a sweet and spicy mustard dipping sauce). Desserts also are excellent and vary on a daily basis. The restaurant is set back from Highway 89, and the parking lot is to the side and rear of the building. You might drive by a couple of times before you find it, but the search is well worth the effort.
Hours: Open daily, with lunch from 11:30 A.M. and dinner from 5:30 P.M.
Policies: Reservations are recommended.
Prices: $$. Major credit cards are accepted.
Contact: River Grill, 55 W. Lake Blvd. (Hwy. 89), Tahoe City, CA; 530/581-2644.

River Ranch Lodge

When water is released from Lake Tahoe in late spring and early summer, it comes kicking down

Food and Drink 547

the Truckee River like a herd of mustangs. This restaurant, part of an attractive country inn and one of the North Shore's most popular hangouts, is a warm, inviting place to enjoy dinner and view the river. There's a pleasant touch with the bar—it protrudes over the stream, allowing you to check out the trout. An excellent gourmet menu includes fresh fish and game, with mountain rainbow trout, filet mignon, New York pepper steak, roasted fresh Montana elk loin, rack of lamb, and smoked free-range chicken. Desserts are made fresh each day. The riverside patio, open during the summer, often features jazz groups and other entertainment, and it is also available for private parties. River Ranch is at the end of a popular cycling and skating trail, on Highway 89 and Alpine Meadows Road.

Hours: Lunch daily in midsummer on the patio 11 A.M.–6 P.M., and dinner daily from 5:30 P.M.–9:30 P.M. (5–10 P.M. on weekends). The bar is open and appetizers are served from 4 P.M.

Prices: $$–$$$. Major credit cards are accepted.

Contact: River Ranch Lodge, 2285 River Rd., Tahoe City, CA; 530/583-4264.

Rosie's Cafe

A funky, purely Tahoe kind of place that oozes history and character from every corner, Rosie's Cafe is a locals' favorite. It serves a darned good meal, especially breakfast. Vintage 1950s bicycles hang from the ceiling, and old wood skis and big-game trophies are mounted on the walls. Some of the memorabilia came from Tahoe Tavern Resort, a palatial hotel that was torn down in the late 1960s. Rosie's had several previous incarnations but it was always an eating or drinking place and could always be found next to Tahoe City's most famous landmark—the Big Tree. This stately pine straddled Highway 28 and was the center of many festivities until it died from a prolonged drought and was cut down in 1994. Still, a piece of the trunk resides in Rosie's, like a talisman for good karma. Certainly, it must inspire the staff, because everyone has a smile.

TAHOE DINING

© KEN CASTLE

Rosie's Cafe, Tahoe City

Morning offers some of the most creative fare, although Rosie's also serves lunch and dinner. Try the Cajun eggs—which are mixed with red and green bell peppers, red onions, and Jack and cheddar cheese—or the Swedish oatmeal pancakes topped with applesauce, sour cream, and imported lingonberries. The menu has lots of influences (including Hispanic, Asian, and European) mixed with good ol' down-home American cooking. Rosie's offers a wonderful, casual atmosphere.

Hours: Daily from 6:30 A.M.–10 P.M. Happy hour is 4 P.M.–6 P.M., and the bar is open until 2 A.M.

Prices: $–$$. Major credit cards are accepted.

Contact: Rosie's Cafe, 571 N. Lake Blvd., Tahoe City, CA; 530/583-8504.

Sierra Vista Lakefront Dining

In a century-old building next to the Tahoe City Marina Mall, this shoreside restaurant is a great place to watch boats coming and going. Restauranteur Wayne Smith has added some creative touches to his cuisine, including a special International Menu that varies from week to week. You might see Japanese sesame sea bass, Hungarian goulash, German veal schnitzel, Kenyan beef banana, Thai peanut chicken, and Australian Outback barbecue. The main dinner menu offers starters such as baked goat cheese and Caesar salads, and entrées such as broiled Hawaiian mahimahi, San Francisco-style cioppino, chicken parmigiana, lasagna, cheese tortellini, filet mignon, homemade potato gnocchi, pork tenderloin, and rack of lamb. There is an extensive list of wines and beers, which can be matched to any particular international cuisine. Desserts include tiramisu, chocolate truffle cake, Grand Marnier cheesecake, and a special "berry surprise." This latter dish consists of lemon and raspberry sorbet served in a dark chocolate shell with fresh strawberries and topped with a blueberry sauce. Smith has created an interior that he calls "mountain rustic," with wall displays from local artists and photographers. The building has a woodsy feel to it; dining alcoves are scattered throughout the ground floor and there's a large heated outdoor deck overlooking the lake. The full bar has a cozy fireplace and a variety of house cocktails and beers, and it often hosts live music. Lunches include salads and sandwiches.

Hours: Lunch, 11:30 A.M.–3 P.M.; happy hour, 3 P.M.–6 P.M. daily (and until 9 P.M. Tues. and Thurs.); and dinner, 5 P.M. until closing.

Prices: $$. Major credit cards accepted.

Contact: Sierra Vista Lakefront Dining, 700 N. Lake Blvd., Tahoe City, CA; 530/583-0233; website: www.sierravistatahoe.com.

Stony Ridge Cafe

This small restaurant, at the Tahoma Meadows Bed and Breakfast Inn on the West Shore of the lake, is a popular locals' hangout. While some passersby might be deterred by its diminutive size and rustic exterior, the insiders know that this is one of Tahoe's gourmet jewels. Owners/chefs Doug and Dawn Baehr have combined whole-earth freshness with Asian influences to serve some of the tastiest fare in the region. Breakfast includes a variety of egg dishes, pancakes, and omelets, and lunch includes sandwiches with whole-grain breads and other nutritious ingredients. The dinner menu, which changes weekly (check the website for updates), might offer chicken vindaloo, an Indian curry dish with apple-mango chutney; Chinese pepper steak, stir-fried with onions, ginger, garlic, and sherry-oyster sauce; sesame-crusted salmon, accompanied by Thai green curry/coconut sauce; and house-made gnocchis, a potato pasta served with a sauté of wild mushrooms, greens, Marsala wine, and red bell pepper sauce. Seating is limited to two small rooms, one in front and one in back, and the wait (outside only) can be lengthy, especially for weekend breakfast. Also, service is typically slow (partly because of a tiny kitchen), so allow for an extended and leisurely meal.

Hours: Breakfast and lunch, offered only in summer, is served daily 6:30 A.M.–2 P.M. June–Sept.; dinner, offered year-around, is served 6 P.M.–9 P.M. Thurs.–Saturday.

Prices: $–$$. No credit cards are accepted.

Contact: Stony Ridge Café, 6821 W. Lake Blvd. (Hwy. 89), Tahoma, CA; 530/525-0905; website: www.stonyridgecafe.com.

Sunnyside Lodge Restaurant

An elegant and romantic lakeside lodge, Sunnyside features the Old Tahoe-style architecture of stone and wood-beamed ceilings. Its handful of guest rooms are always full, and its restaurant is always crowded, so forget about dropping in. Service is usually above average and the menu is simple and fairly straightforward. It includes entrées such as New York steak, Pacific king salmon, Hawaiian mahimahi, fettuccine with seafood, and ginger chicken. There's always a special dessert of the day. The restaurant is at Sunnyside Marina, and the lake vistas coupled with the rustic Old Tahoe look of the Lodge tend to generate repeat business.

Hours: Daily from 5:30 P.M.–9:30 P.M. (the bar is open until midnight).

Policies: Don't even think about coming here without reservations.

Prices: $$. Major credit cards are accepted.

Contact: Sunnyside Lodge Restaurant, 1850 W. Lake Blvd., Tahoe City, CA; 530/583-7200.

Swiss Lakewood

This is an institution on the West Shore, and it's garnered a bushel of culinary awards. With its European stylings, wine cellar dining nook (a special corner of the house that seats 12), and cozy environs, this restaurant has a lot to recommend it. You almost expect the waiters to yodel. The menu includes roast duck with orange sauce, pepper steak flambé, beef Wellington, and escallops *de chevreuil*—grilled escallops of venison with glazed chestnuts and balsamic vinegar-lingonberry sauce. Desserts include cherries jubilee flambé and Grand Marnier soufflé.

Hours: Daily (except Mon.) from 5:30 P.M.– 10 P.M.; weekends only in winter. Open on holidays.

Prices: $$. Some credit cards are accepted.

Contact: Swiss Lakewood Lodge, 5055 W. Lake Blvd., Homewood, CA; 530/525-5211.

Tahoe House Bakery and Gourmet

Family-owned and -operated since 1977, this former dinner house has been converted to a

© KEN CASTLE

Swiss Lakewood

TAHOE DINING

large bakery and deli, and it has become a regular morning stop for cyclists, hikers, skiers, and boaters who want upscale food to go. You can order a variety of sandwiches along with deli items that include casseroles, salads, pastas, meat loaf, and enchiladas. There's a gourmet food store within the complex, and you'll find the European breads, pastries, and chocolates irresistible. Tahoe House is a half mile south of the "Y" on Highway 89.

Hours: Open 6 A.M.–6 P.M. daily.
Contact: Tahoe House Bakery and Gourmet, 625 W. Lake Blvd., Tahoe City, CA; 530/583-1377; website: www.tahoe-house.com.

Wolfdale's

The structure that houses this restaurant is nearly a century old; it was built at Glenbrook and barged to the present location beside the lake in 1901. Douglas Dale, the owner and chef, calls his menu "cuisine unique," because it has touches of Asian cooking and California cuisine. The menu includes light and creative fare such as Thai barbecued chicken over kale and jasmine rice, alderwood-roasted Columbia River sturgeon, fresh and wild mushroom pasta with broccoflower, and marinated and grilled venison loin with demi-glace and a purée of fennel and Jerusalem artichokes. Try the spicy red pepper soup with a grilled tomatillo onion relish, or a starter of Dungeness crab cakes with a wasabi and sour cream sauce. Yum!

Hours: Dinner daily from 5:30 P.M. The bar opens at 5 P.M.
Policies: Reservations are accepted.
Prices: $$. Major credit cards are accepted.
Contact: Wolfdale's, 640 N. Lake Blvd., Tahoe City, CA; 530/583-5700.

Yama Sushi and Robata Grill

At Lighthouse Shopping Center on Highway 28, this small Japanese restaurant serves a variety of sushi, sashimi, and grilled meats. Dinner entrées include shrimp and vegetable tempura; steak, chicken, and salmon teriyaki; chicken *katsu;* and *yaki soba.* House sushi specials include the Punk Rock Roll (salmon, cream cheese, sun-dried tomatoes, and green onion

tempura-fried), the Avalanche Roll (shrimp tempura, avocado, and cucumber), and the Maeflower Roll (California roll with *hamachi,* a sweet spicy sauce, and macadamia nuts). During the middle of the week, there are all-you-can-eat sushi specials.

Hours: Dinner daily starting at 5 P.M.
Policies: Reservations are accepted.
Prices: $–$$. Major credit cards are accepted.
Contact: Yama Sushi and Robata Grill, 950 N. Lake Blvd., Tahoe City, CA; 530/583-YAMA (530/583-9262).

KINGS BEACH/TAHOE VISTA/ CARNELIAN BAY

Boulevard Cafe

Traditional and creative Northern Italian cuisine is the order of the day at this small, intimate restaurant, which is highly regarded by locals. Restaurant critics from major newspapers and magazines have been effusive in their praise of each carefully prepared dish and of the European sophistication that permeates the place. Entrées include rack of lamb, osso buco, cioppino (assorted shellfish and fresh seafood in a tomato sauce), and chicken stuffed with goat cheese and roasted garlic. A half dozen pasta dishes include angel-hair pasta; cheese ravioli with porcini mushroom sauce; linguine with fresh Manila clams; and cannelloni stuffed with veal, ricotta, and pecorino cheese. Desserts include tiramisu and *panna cotta.*

Hours: Daily from 6 P.M.
Policies: Reservations are accepted.
Prices: $–$$. Some credit cards are accepted.
Contact: Boulevard Cafe, 6731 N. Lake Blvd., Tahoe Vista, CA; 530/546-7213.

CB's Pizza and Grill

Pizza, calzone, lasagna, meatball subs, and chicken parmesan—CB's serves all the usual favorites.

Hours: Weekdays 11 A.M.–9:30 P.M. and weekends 11 A.M.–10 P.M.
Prices: $–$$. Major credit cards are accepted.
Contact: CB's Pizza and Grill, 5075 N. Lake Blvd., Carnelian Bay, CA; 530/546-4738.

The Char-Pit

The Char-Pit offers espresso drinks and croissants in the morning, and salads, barbecued sandwiches, hamburgers, and hot dogs in the afternoon. Happy hour takes place nightly.
Hours: Weekdays from 8:30 A.M.–7 P.M. and weekends from 8:30 A.M.–9 P.M.
Prices: $.
Contact: The Char-Pit, 8732 N. Lake Blvd., Kings Beach, CA; 530/546-3171.

Gar Woods Grill and Pier

Boasting one of the longest deepwater guest piers on the lake, this well-patronized restaurant is named after Garfield Wood, the famous boat designer and builder whose elegant mahogany powerboats became a fixture on the Tahoe yachting scene from the 1920s through the 1940s. The restaurant, with its vaulted ceilings, multiple dining levels, huge picture windows, and outdoor deck, is usually crowded and rarely disappoints. Featured menu items include beer-battered coconut prawns, New York steak, white chocolate Snickers cheesecake, and the Wet Woody tropical drink, a house specialty. The big event here is the Sunday buffet brunch, which offers a dozen entrées. A children's menu is available, and children under four are welcome for brunch for free. This restaurant offers wheelchair access to the restaurant and pier. Live music holds forth on Friday and Saturday, 7 P.M.–11 P.M., and banquet facilities are available. Valet boat parking is provided.
Hours: Lunch and dinner Mon.–Fri. during summer from 11:30 A.M.–10 P.M., Sat. from 10:30 A.M.–10 P.M., and Sun. noon–10 P.M. Sun. brunch from 9:30 A.M.–2 P.M.
Policies: Reservations are suggested.
Prices: $–$$. Major credit cards are accepted.
Contact: Gar Woods Grill and Pier, 5000 N. Lake Blvd., Carnelian Bay, CA; 530/546-3366; website: www.garwoods.com.

Hiro Sushi

A local favorite, Hiro Sushi serves Japanese cuisine and features all-you-can-eat sushi dinners.
Hours: Open Tues.–Sun. 5 P.M.–10 P.M.
Prices: $–$$.
Contact: Hiro Sushi, 8159 N. Lake Blvd., Kings Beach, CA; 530/546-4476.

Jason's Beachside Grille

Perched on the lake at Kings Beach State Recreation Area, this popular and informal haunt features American classics and regional favorites, such as slow-roasted prime rib, smoked chicken pasta, barbecued baby-back ribs, Cajun-seasoned salmon, and a 12-foot-long salad bar. There are also half-pound gourmet burgers, pastas, and desserts such as homemade cobblers and tiramisu. The food is good, not extraordinary, and the salad bar has perhaps the most creative touches. A full bar offers wine, microbrews, and cocktails. This is a funky, woodsy place with sweeping lake views from the deck and validated parking.
Hours: Daily from 11 A.M.
Prices: $–$$. Major credit cards are accepted.
Contact: Jason's Beachside Grille, 8338 N. Lake Blvd., Kings Beach, CA; 530/546-3315.

Lanza's

If you've got the whole family, a hearty appetite, a limited budget, and no desire to dress up, this longtime Tahoe favorite should satisfy. The traditional Italian menu includes stuffed *lumaconi*, filled with beef, cheese, and spinach; calamari; lasagna; chicken Milanese; Italian and California wines; and homemade spumoni. Full bar service is available, and during happy hour, which begins at 4:30 P.M., patrons receive free pizza slices.
Hours: Dinner daily 5 P.M.–10 P.M.
Prices: $–$$. Some credit cards are accepted.
Contact: Lanza's, 7739 N. Lake Blvd., Kings Beach, CA; 530/546-2434.

Las Panchitas

Two North Shore locations—one in Kings Beach on the California side and another in Incline Village on the Nevada side—keep locals and visitors satisfied with an extensive variety of Mexican food. There is an emphasis on fajitas, tostadas, chimichangas, and *machaca* (shredded beef with scrambled eggs), but the menu also has seafood specials such as snapper and prawns. A special menu for children under 12 is available.

Hours: Daily from 11:30 A.M.–10 P.M.
Prices: $–$$. Major credit cards are accepted.
Contact: Las Panchitas, 8345 N. Lake Blvd., Kings Beach, CA; 530/546-4539; or 930 Tahoe Blvd., Incline Village, NV; 775/831-4048.

Le Petit Pier

With a flair for creative dishes, this small restaurant has become one of North Shore's signature dinner houses. Le Petit Pier has an insistently French ambience, with an elegant view of the lake and an award-winning wine list to complement the excellent cuisine. The appetizers alone could carry a meal here, but you can also get the works, with entrées such as medallions of veal with wild mushrooms, New Zealand venison medallions, filet mignon, and live Maine lobster. Appetizers include grilled prawns and lobster ravioli. Homemade French desserts top off the meal.
Hours: Daily (except Tues.) 6 P.M.–10 P.M.
Policies: Reservations are accepted.
Prices: $$$. Major credit cards are accepted.
Contact: Le Petit Pier, 7252 N. Lake Blvd., Tahoe Vista, CA; 530/546-4464 or 775/833-0338.

Log Cabin Cafe

This small breakfast house, always crowded, gets my vote for the best breakfast in Tahoe, and apparently the locals agree, as it frequently wins surveys on the North Shore. There are usually lots of people waiting outside the tiny building, which has just a few tables, sometimes for an hour. But the meals tend to be so memorable they're worth the wait. Waffles are a specialty—try the lemon poppy seed or cranberry orange waffles. To spice up your morning, sample the Cajun eggs Benedict or the chicken fajita egg scramble. Pancakes can be served with fruit and nut toppings. Go ahead, splurge with a fruit smoothie, fresh-squeezed OJ, or one of the special espresso drinks. Can breakfast get any better? We think not. The kitchen is small but turns out an amazing number of quality meals. The dishes are wonderfully creative, all made with fresh ingredients and served by a cheerful staff.
Hours: Daily 7 A.M.–2 P.M.

Prices: $.
Contact: Log Cabin Cafe, 8692 N. Lake Blvd., Kings Beach, CA; 530/546-7109.

Old Post Office Coffee Shop

In a rustic, wood-frame building that used to house the U.S. Mail, this locals' favorite makes a first-class breakfast based on your imagination. Choosing from the large selection of ingredients listed on the menu, you can have the kitchen create your ideal omelet, scramble, or potato dish, all served with fresh-ground coffee and espresso. Lunch includes a Mexican tuna melt, Philly beef, and lemon chicken, along with homemade chili.
Hours: Breakfast and lunch daily from 6:30 A.M.–3 P.M.
Prices: $.
Contact: Old Post Office, 5245 N. Lake Blvd., Carnelian Bay, CA; 530/546-3205.

Old Range Steakhouse

This recent arrival has become a local favorite. It has a Chicago influence, meaning big portions of Midwestern aged and corn-fed beef and plenty of potatoes. The menu is the antithesis of the lighter California cuisine, making no bones about its obsession with meat. Come with a hearty appetite for dishes such as salt-roasted prime rib (the house specialty), Texas pork chops, and garlic steak. If just the thought of so much flesh makes your arteries contract, you can find solace in the house-made pastas, entrée salads, and half-portions of steak. Every table has a lake view and is set with pewter tableware and checkered napkins. The restaurant has a woodsy interior, in keeping with the Old Tahoe style. Casual dress is the norm.
Policies: No reservations are taken.
Hours: Dinner 5 P.M.–10 P.M.
Prices: $$.
Contact: Old Range Steakhouse, 7081 N. Lake Blvd., Tahoe Vista, CA; 530/546-4800.

Soule Domain

A wonderfully romantic log cabin restaurant, Soule Domain specializes in piquant ethnic sauces, yet many entrées are low in fat and calories. Try the baby bitter greens with bacon and walnut oil dressing, Gorgonzola cheese, sliced pears, candied pecans, and balsamic vinegar. Nouveau California cuisine is the mainstay, and the menu includes seven fresh pastas a day. Other gourmet dishes are grilled Hawaiian ahi tuna; Oriental ginger beef; filet mignon sautéed with shiitake mushrooms and pepper sauce; sea scallops poached in champagne with kiwi and papaya cream sauce; and fresh vegetables baked in a pastry shell with Swiss cheese, herbs, roasted garlic, and tomato cream sauce. Soule Domain is across from the Tahoe Biltmore Lodge and Casino.

Hours: Daily 6 P.M.–10 P.M.

Policies: Reservations are requested.

Prices: $$–$$$. Major credit cards are accepted.

Contact: Soule Domain, 9983 Cove Ave., Kings Beach, CA; 530/546-7529; website: www.soule-domain.com.

Spindleshanks

This relatively new American bistro in Tahoe Vista has become a standout on the North Shore, and it has a strong repeat clientele from residents and visitors alike. It offers a variety of innovative dishes, with entrées that might include blackened rib-eye steak, live Maine lobster, house-made butternut raviolis with toasted pecans and a brown butter sage sauce, grilled New York steak with griddled onions and mushrooms, and chipotle lime marinated brick chicken with *chile relleno*.

steak dinner at Spindleshanks

Starters might include cream of asparagus soup, house-made onion soup, spinach and raspberry salad, and a soft Gorgonzola cheese plate. There are daily seafood specials, fresh pastas, and a wine bar. Seating is in several intimate rooms inside, which have woodsy, inviting decor, or along the veranda outside, where tables are warmed by propane heat towers.

Hours: Daily from 5:30 P.M.–9:30 P.M. The wine bar opens at 5 P.M., and happy hour (appetizers at half price) runs 5:30 P.M.–6:30 P.M. daily and all night long Wednesday.

Prices: $$–$$$. Some major credit cards are accepted.

Contact: Spindleshanks, 6873 N. Lake Blvd., Tahoe Vista, CA; 530/546-2191.

Steamer's Beachside Bar and Oven

Borrowing from the Old Tahoe ambience, when elegant passenger steamships plied the lake with ladies and gents, this casual shoreside eatery specializes in hand-tossed pizzas, calzone, oven-baked Louisiana hot sausage, and turnover sandwiches stuffed with a blend of cheeses, meats, tomatoes, and red onions. The restaurant features upper deck dining, an outdoor heated bar, and take-out service for those sultry days on the beach.

Hours: Daily 11 A.M.–11 P.M.

Prices: $–$$. Some credit cards are accepted.

Contact: Steamer's Beachside Bar and Oven, 8290 N. Lake Blvd., Kings Beach, CA; 530/546-2218.

Sunsets on the Lake

Completing a major renovation in 2002, this lakeside restaurant serves a blend of California and classic American cuisine and has a loyal base of repeat customers. Entrées include wood-fired Alaskan halibut, pan-blackened ahi tuna, homemade ravioli, spit-roasted chicken, wood-fired pork chops, braised beef shortribs, and Angus rib-eye steak. Starters and appetizers include seared ahi tuna sashimi, fried calamari, wood-grilled polenta, house-smoked salmon, Thai chicken pizza, chilled prawns and asparagus, white bean vegetable soup, and Caesar salad. An extensive wine list featuring California vintages and a well-stocked bar provide just about every libation known to man. Offering a traditional Tahoe atmosphere, the restaurant has a stone fireplace inside, a glass-enclosed heated deck outside, and heated driveways and walkways to keep the snow clear in winter. There is valet parking for both cars and boats in the summer, and every table has a stunning view of the lake. Come prepared to spend substantial lucre, since most entrées are priced well over $20. At North Tahoe Marina, one mile west of Highway 267.

Hours: Dinner daily 5 P.M.–9 P.M. Happy hour 4 P.M.–6 P.M.

Policies: Reservations are accepted.

Prices: $$–$$$. Major credit cards are accepted.

Contact: Sunsets on the Lake, 7320 N. Lake Blvd., Tahoe Vista, CA; 530/546-3640; website: www.sunsetslaketahoe.com.

INCLINE VILLAGE/CRYSTAL BAY

Austin's

A local favorite, Austin's serves home-cooked American lunch and dinner favorites including chicken-fried steak and hand-mashed potatoes with country gravy, rib-eye steak, buttermilk French fries (possibly the most popular house specialty), beef stew, Texas chili, and homemade pies and ice cream.

Hours: Daily from 11:30 A.M.–3 P.M. and 5:30 P.M.–9:30 P.M.

Prices: $–$$. Major credit cards are accepted.

Contact: Austin's, 120 Country Club Dr., Ste. 61, Incline Village, NV; 775/832-7778.

Azzara's

This popular and reasonably priced restaurant features Italian dinners such as steak Toscano, osso buco, risotto, roasted chicken, paella, pizza, and fresh seafood. Azzara's is near Raley's in Incline Village.

Hours: Daily (except Mon.) 5 P.M.–9:30 P.M.

Prices: $–$$. Major credit cards are accepted.

Contact: Azzara's, 930 Tahoe Blvd., Incline Village, NV; 775/831-0346.

Big Water Grille

Perhaps no new restaurant has had such an impact on the Tahoe dining scene in recent years as

this outstanding mountaintop dinner house. Perched on the best high-elevation site on the North Shore, the Big Water Grille is well off the beaten path, in a building that has seen considerable turnover in restaurant proprietors. But the word of mouth has assured a steady stream of visitors driving up Ski Way, the road that leads from Incline Village to Diamond Peak ski area. First, let it be said that the owners of the grill have long experience running resort-area restaurants. They own and manage the Sea Watch Restaurant in Wailea, Maui, the Plantation House Restaurant in Kapulua, Maui, and the Beach House at Koloa, Kauai. The setting they have chosen for their Tahoe operation has an insistently romantic quality, with stunning views of the lake and forest through large picture windows. Happily, there's an inspiring menu to match the panorama. Entrées are colorful, flavorful, and simple, mingling elements of American contemporary cuisine with those of the Mediterranean and Pacific Rim. Try these for appetizers: Hawaiian ahi *poke* with fried wonton chips, grilled prawns with creamy polenta in red pepper *coulis*, or macadamia nut-crusted Brie with Asian pear relish. Starters include wild rice, leek and potato soup, and hearts of romaine salad with parmesan chips and Caesar dressing. Entrées include at least one Hawaiian seafood special, as well as maple-smoked pork chop with sweet potato-apple hash, mustard greens, and dried fruit port sauce; spiced crusted salmon in coriander broth; grilled venison flank with wild rice and Sichuan pepper whiskey sauce; and five-spice roasted duck breast with shredded duck and scallion crepe in Hoisin sauce. Whatever you do, save room for dessert, because the presentation alone is worth the price. These masterpieces might include macadamia nut and coconut cake, Maui rum-soaked pineapple and coconut ice cream, and pistachio cheesecake with Kiwi Coulie. While food preparation is impressive, the atmosphere at Big Water Grille is drenched in romance, especially if you time your visit before sunset. Interiors reflect Old Tahoe influences, with Native American petroglyph designs, wine displays, etched glass, local artworks, and a fireplace of indigenous stone. Also, there's a deck for outdoor summer evenings.

Hours: Dinner from 5:30 P.M.–10 P.M. daily. The bar opens at 4:30 P.M.

Policies: Reservations are recommended.

Prices: $$–$$$. Major credit cards are accepted.

Contact: Big Water Grille, 341 Ski Way (across from the Diamond Peak ski area parking lot), Incline Village, NV; 775/833-0606.

Cafe 333

With its country French theme and eclectic menu of what the owners call "Nou-vada" cuisine combined with Southwestern, Tuscan, and Pacific Rim specials, this small but successful restaurant first developed its reputation as a breakfast house. Muffins and breads are baked fresh daily, and the menu includes something called "breakfast strata," a bread pudding baked with prosciutto, spinach, tomato, basil, mascarpone, parmesan cheese, and cream. Dinners include portabello mushrooms stuffed with house-made chicken and pork sausage, grilled shrimp with sun-dried tomato pesto on bruschetta, parmesan herb-roasted rack of lamb, and grilled fillet of beef with Gorgonzola butter. Most menu items are available for takeout. This is a nonsmoking establishment.

Hours: Daily for breakfast and lunch 7 A.M.–3 P.M. and dinner from 5:30 P.M.–9 P.M. nightly.

Policies: Reservations are accepted.

Prices: $–$$. Some credit cards are accepted.

Contact: Cafe 333, 333 Village Blvd., Incline Village, NV; 775/832-7333.

Ciao Mein Trattoria

Relocated to a new area within the main floor of the Hyatt Regency, as part of the hotel's ongoing renovation, this elegant restaurant provides one of Lake Tahoe's finest dining experiences, combining Pacific Rim and Italian influences in a single meal. The menu features tempura prawns, Sichuan-style salmon (in a ginger butter sauce), garlic-rubbed lamb chops, Kung Pao shrimp or chicken, fried or steamed whole striped bass, *pollo ripieno* (chicken breast stuffed with prosciutto, ricotta, spinach, and pine nuts), crab-seared

swordfish, veal piccata, and Mongolian beef. Some of the delicious appetizers include Dungeness crab fritters (with pineapple dipping sauce), Kung Pao calamari, wonton soup, Caesar salad, and the Mein Platter, which consists of spare ribs, pot stickers, Kung Pao calamari, and grilled asparagus. You can also select from several pasta and noodle dishes, including ravioli, shrimp *pad thai* noodles, *fettuccine al pescatore,* or lo mein noodles with stir-fried meat or vegetables. There's also an outstanding wine list.

Hours: Dinner Wed.–Sun. from 5:30 P.M.–9:30 P.M.

Policies: Reservations are accepted. No cigar or pipe smoking is allowed.

Prices: $$–$$$. Major credit cards are accepted.

Contact: Ciao Mein Trattoria, 111 Country Club Dr., Incline Village, NV; 775/832-1234.

Fredrick's Bistro and Bar (formerly Jack Rabbit Moon)

Owners of this new restaurant have created what they call a French-Asian menu, complemented by a sushi bar. Among the main courses are filet mignon and grilled baby lobster tails (with braised bok choy, lobster-ginger butter, and a Shioxiang wine/green peppercorn sauce), sesame dry-rubbed halibut steak (grilled with shiitake mushroom and roasted garlic couscous), lentil-stuffed zucchini topped with Asiago cheese and polenta cake, lamb sirloin braised in green curry with Thai pineapple fried rice, and pork chop stuffed with toasted walnuts and smoked Gouda cheese. House-made sushi specials include the Tuna Colada (hand roll with *maguro,* pineapple, toasted coconut, and cucumber), Feeling Crabby (graham cracker-breaded soft-shell crab, lump snow crab, *tobiko,* roasted garlic, cucumber, avocado, and house rooster sauce), and Striped Dragon (tempura shrimp and cucumber rolled up and topped with *tombo* tuna, *unagi, hamachi,* avocado, *tobiko* and *unagi* sauce). Starters include marinated tempura prawns, crispy calamari curried slaw salad, roasted red pepper gazpacho soup topped with avocado ice cream, and parmesan gnocchi with oyster mushrooms, baby spinach, and applewood bacon folded in a sherry cream reduction. It's across the highway from Raley's.

Hours: Dinner 5:30 P.M.–10:30 P.M. Closed Monday.
Prices: $$. Major credit cards are accepted.
Contact: Fredrick's, 907 Tahoe Blvd., Incline Village, NV; 775/832-3007.

Hacienda de la Sierra

Bring your appetite and dine in a tropical setting on ample portions of traditional Mexican food, featuring grilled shrimp fajitas, seafood chimichangas, and deep-fried ice cream. A full bar (the happy hour here is popular with locals because it includes free appetizers), takeout, a children's menu, live music, an outside deck, and banquet facilities are available. Hacienda de la Sierra is across the street from Raley's in Incline Village.
Hours: Dinner daily from 4:30 P.M., Happy Hour from 4 P.M. Mon.–Fri., lunch from 11:30 A.M. June–September.
Prices: $–$$. Major credit cards are accepted.
Contact: Hacienda de la Sierra, 931 Tahoe Blvd., Incline Village, NV; 775/831-8300.

La Fondue

Swiss-style European charm envelopes this restaurant, which is a longtime locals' favorite. The menu includes baked Brie, Holstein schnitzel, and 12 Swiss fondues, including bourguignonne, Alpine cheese, chocolate, and ice cream. Meats for dipping include meatballs, turkey, scallops, chicken breast, and top sirloin. For dessert, fresh fruit, berries, and marshmallows can be dipped in rich chocolate. All entrées are served with soup and salad. La Fondue is across from the Hyatt Regency.
Hours: Dinner daily (except Tues.) 6 P.M.–9 P.M.
Prices: $$$. Major credit cards are accepted.
Contact: La Fondue, 120 Country Club Dr., Ste. 66, Incline Village, NV; 775/831-6104.

Lake Tahoe Brewing Company

As North Tahoe's lone brew pub, this casual place offers fresh ales on tap along with pub food that includes fish-and-chips, pizza, "brats and mash," shepherd's pie, fresh fish, steaks, and pasta. Thursday is Cajun night, with spicy dishes. Happy hour specials are offered seven days a week, 4 P.M.–6 P.M. The pub is in a historic building—reportedly a former bordello—next to the North Shore casinos. The beer is so popular that it is served at more than 150 locations around the lake.
Hours: Weekdays 4 P.M. until 10 P.M., weekends 11:30 A.M. until closing.
Prices: $.
Contact: Lake Tahoe Brewing Company, 24 Stateline Rd., Crystal Bay, NV; 775/831-5822.

Lakeview Dining Room

Try for a window table and the fabulous elevated view of Tahoe at one of the lake's most romantic and historic casino hotels, the Cal-Neva. Dinner features linguine primavera, veal and crab dijonnaise, salmon béarnaise, and New York steak au poivre. Frank Sinatra used to own this place, and many are the rich and famous who have cavorted here. For small fry, there's a children's menu.
Hours: Breakfast 7 A.M.–11:30 A.M., lunch from 11:30 A.M.–closing, and dinner from 5:30 P.M.–closing.
Prices: $–$$. Major credit cards are accepted.
Contact: Cal-Neva Resort, 2 Stateline Rd., Crystal Bay, NV; 775/832-4000.

Le Bistro Restaurant and Bar

Operated by Jean-Pierre and Sylvia Doignon, this cozy French restaurant in a woodsy setting usually offers four à la carte entrées a night, including fresh grilled Pacific halibut, *chausson* of duck with broiled sweetbreads, tournedos of Black Angus, and noisette of domestic lamb. There is a five-course prix fixe menu as well. This is an intimate, elegant place, with a full bar, a substantial wine menu, and sinful desserts (try the warm chocolate torte or the crème brûlée). Dedicated to hopeless romantics, Le Bistro is across from the Hyatt Regency.
Hours: Open Tues.–Sat. 6 P.M.–9:30 P.M.
Prices: $$–$$$. Major credit cards are accepted.
Contact: Le Bistro Restaurant and Bar, 120 Country Club Dr., Ste. 29, Incline Village, NV; 775/831-0800.

Lone Eagle Grille

If you had just one night to spend at Tahoe, this would be the place to go for dinner. On the most scenic corner of the North Shore, among the megamansions of Incline Village, the Lone Eagle Grille is the flagship restaurant of the Hyatt Regency Lake Tahoe, though it is physically detached from the hotel/casino. Fronted by a private beach, this architectural jewel reminiscent of a grand old mountain lodge enjoys a stunning view of the lake and offers a diverse menu. The lounge, with its two-story rock fireplace and Ivy League decor, is constantly abuzz with wheeling and dealing from the well-connected business types who hang out here, especially in summer after a round of golf at Incline Championship Course.

From the entrance, you descend one flight of stairs to the lounge and dining area, then are shown to a table in either a cozy alcove, the main dining room with its vaulted ceilings, or the outdoor patio (where heat lamps ward off the evening chill). The menu tends toward hearty entrées such as prime rib, sautéed veal medallions, pork loin, and stuffed Sonoma chicken breast (with shiitake mushrooms, spinach, peppers, Jack cheese, grilled vegetables, and spicy rice). But there are some seafood selections such as scampi, seared ahi tuna, and sea bass. Starters include spicy crab cakes and tortilla soup. There are nightly specialties as well. For dessert, try the strawberry cream puff or the crème brûlée. The service is excellent and the total experience is quite satisfying. The Lone Eagle Grille is across from the Hyatt Regency, on Country Club Drive at Lakeshore Drive.

Hours: Daily for lunch and dinner from 11:30 A.M.–9:15 P.M. (last seating), and for Sun. brunch from 10:30 A.M.

Policies: Reservations are required.

Prices: $$–$$$. Major credit cards are accepted.

Contact: Lone Eagle Grille, 111 Country Club Dr., Incline Village, NV; 775/832-3250.

Mayflower (formerly China Chef)

A mainstay of Incline Village, this place is one of the better Chinese restaurants at the lake. It fea-

© KEN CASTLE

Lone Eagle Grille at Hyatt Regency Lake Tahoe

tures typical but piquant Cantonese and Sichuan cuisine—minus the MSG—prepared by long-time owner and chef Kwong Chiong. Menu items include sizzling *wor bar* (a combination of pork, chicken, shrimp, and scallops with vegetables), *mu shu* pork, sizzling rice soup, and Cantonese shrimp chow mein. A full bar—the site of nightly karaoke performances—and takeout and delivery are available. Mayflower is at the Christmas Tree Shopping Center.

Hours: Daily 11 A.M.–10 P.M.

Prices: $–$$$. Major credit cards are accepted.

Contact: Mayflower, 874 Tahoe Blvd., Incline Village, NV; 775/831-9090.

Mofo's Pizza and Pasta

Mofo's serves New York-style pizza, calzone, eggplant parmesan, and a variety of pasta dishes. For veggie lovers, there's also a large salad bar. It's at Christmas Tree Village.

Hours: Lunch from 11:30 A.M.–2 P.M. Mon.–Fri., dinner from 4:30 P.M.–8:30 P.M. (9 P.M. Fri. and Sat.) seven days a week.

TAHOE DINING

Prices: $–$$. Major credit cards and checks are accepted.
Contact: Mofo's Pizza and Pasta, 868 Tahoe Blvd., Ste. 23, Incline Village, NV; 775/831-4999.

Rookies Sports Bar and Grill

The best burger joint in Incline, Rookie's Sports Bar features gourmet, half-pound heavyweight burgers with names such as Heisman, End Zone, and Matador. It's at Raley's in Incline Village.
Hours: Open 24 hours daily.
Prices: $. Some credit cards are accepted.
Contact: Rookie's Sports Bar and Grill, 930 Tahoe Blvd. (at Raley's Center), Incline Village, NV; 775/831-9008.

Sierra Cafe

The Sierra Cafe serves a breakfast buffet; a salad bar, chili, and soup for lunch; and prime rib, a seafood buffet, and a salad bar on Friday and Saturday. It's in the Hyatt Regency, on Country Club Drive at Lakeshore Drive.
Hours: Open 24 hours.
Policies: Reservations are accepted.
Prices: $–$$. Major credit cards are accepted.
Contact: Sierra Cafe, 111 Country Club Dr., Incline Village, NV; 775/832-1234.

T's Mesquite Rotisserie

T's Mesquite Rotisserie serves mesquite-roasted chicken with Yucatán or soy lime marinades. Sandwiches and burritos are also featured.
Hours: Open Mon.–Sat. 11 A.M.–8 P.M. and Sun. noon–8 P.M.
Prices: $–$$. No credit cards are accepted.
Contact: T's Mesquite Rotisserie, 901 Tahoe Blvd., Incline Village, NV; 775/831-2832.

Wildflower Cafe

There are few breakfast houses at Incline Village, and this one is popular with golfers, skiers, and locals. It serves a good, if not great, breakfast, and there's always more than you can eat. The small indoor dining area is supplemented in summer with patio seating, both for breakfast and lunch. I recommend sticking to the house specials such as Wildflower Potatoes, home-fried potatoes with tomatoes, onions, mushrooms, and melted Swiss cheese with options for salsa, sour cream, bacon, ham, or sausage. Or try the breakfast burrito, a hearty helping of your choice of four omelet ingredients combined with scrambled eggs and wrapped in a flour tortilla. Pancakes are served in huge proportions (some optional fruit toppings are too sweet or too gooey), so stick with an unadorned short stack if you're a lighter eater. Homemade muffins and cinnamon rolls are also available, and there is fresh-squeezed orange juice to wash them down. Lunch provides burgers, cold sandwiches, salads, and homemade chili.
Hours: Open Mon.–Sat. 7 A.M.–2:30 P.M. and Sun. 8 A.M.–2 P.M.
Prices: $.
Contact: Wildflower Cafe, 869 Tahoe Blvd. (Hwy. 28), Incline Village, NV; 775/831-8072.

STATELINE/KINGSBURY/ ZEPHYR COVE (NEVADA)

American River Cafe

On the lower level of Harrah's Lake Tahoe, this casual restaurant operates around the clock. The design of the 200-seat café incorporates a stream and two waterfalls amid bold river-rock formations and groves of quaking aspen trees. Menu items include a hearty Hangtown Fry oyster omelet for breakfast and maple-glazed barbecued baby-back ribs for dinner. The American River Picnic Basket is filled with ribs, a grilled chicken breast, and homemade broccoli slaw. Desserts include a fudge brownie chocolate cheesecake and a towering lemon meringue pie.
Hours: Open 24 hours daily for breakfast, lunch, dinner, and late-night dining.
Prices: $. Major credit cards are accepted.
Contact: American River Cafe, U.S. 50, Stateline, NV; 775/588-6611; website: www .harrahstahoe.com.

Black Olive Bistro and Bar

Round Hill Square shopping center at Zephyr Cove, on the Nevada side of South Shore, has seen a constant turnover of restaurants. Although it's not that far from Stateline, visitors seem reluctant to explore this recently renovated mall unless they're shopping at Safeway for groceries. However, this new (2001) Mediterranean-style restaurant is worth a try. With polished wood floors and white tablecloth-covered tables, the atmosphere is definitely upscale, even if there are no views of the lake. Greek-influenced cuisine is in short supply at Tahoe, and Black Olive does a good job filling the void, although there are Italian dishes as well. The menu includes fresh seafood, lamb, and pasta, and there's an extensive wine list to complement your choice. Among the sterling entrées are calamari stuffed with fresh herbs, spinach, feta cheese, and bread crumbs; swordfish piccata in lemon-caper butter, herb-encrusted ahi with ginger-Dijon vinaigrette, and pork chop in a sun-dried cherry port glaze. Starters include a house special, raviolis in sherry cream sauce with tomato and spinach. Lunch here is popular with locals, who graze on meatball and calamari sandwiches and Caesar salads. The restaurant has a bar and a full array of cocktails.

Hours: Lunch daily 11 A.M.–2:30 P.M., dinner daily 6 P.M.–10 P.M., breakfast on weekend mornings.

Prices: $–$$. Major credit cards accepted.

Contact: Black Olive, Round Hill Square, Zephyr Cove, NV; 775/588-9030.

The Broiler Room

Here's a traditional steak house, with formal waiters, leather chairs, and intimate, subdued lighting, that is next to the casino floor in Caesars Tahoe. It features grilled New York steak, Jack Daniel's barbecued shrimp, Louisiana seafood gumbo, and Cajun desserts. The wine list frequently has been honored by *Wine Spectator* magazine.

Hours: Daily 6 P.M.–11 P.M.

Policies: Reservations are accepted.

Prices: $–$$$. Major credit cards are accepted.

Contact: Caesars Tahoe, 55 U.S. 50, Stateline, NV; 775/586-2044; website: www.caesars.com.

Chart House

With more than 40 locations across mainland United States and Hawaii, the Chart House has established a successful and usually predictable formula that revolves around a mammoth salad bar, grilled surf and turf, and ample desserts. Recently, the franchise revised its menu to include more seafood and other lighter fare, which diners often prefer in this high-altitude environment. You'll have to drive up Kingsbury Grade to get here, but the bird's-eye views of the lake and of the Stateline casinos are worth the effort, particularly if you time your visit around sunset. While the Chart House is pricey compared to, say, the Sizzler Steak House in town, the overall dining experience has much more atmosphere. And the latest menu flirts with gourmet touches. Appetizers include grilled chicken satay, coconut crunchy shrimp, seared peppered ahi tuna, calamari, and lobster tails tempura. Starters (apart from the salad bar) include New England clam chowder, lobster bisque, and the restaurant's signature Caesar salad. The steaks are all there, of course, including filet mignon, prime rib, New York strip, and teriyaki beef medallions. But the fresh fish selections have been increased, with entrées such as sesame-crusted salmon, scampi, steamed Maine lobster, Alaskan king crab legs, macadamia-crusted mahimahi, herb-crusted sea bass, gazpacho grouper, spiced yellowfin ahi, and bronzed halibut. There are usually eight fresh fish selections each day. Sides include coconut-ginger rice, garlic mashed potatoes, sizzling mushrooms, and fresh asparagus with mustard sauce. And for dessert, if you still have room, you can select from Key lime pie, hot chocolate lava cake (with Godiva chocolate liqueur topped with vanilla ice cream and Heath Bar Crunch, served warm at your table), raspberry crème brûlée, and the ever-popular Original Mud Pie (coffee ice cream, chocolate sauce, and whipped cream on a chocolate wafer crust, topped with toasted almonds). Chart House is for those with hearty appetites.

Hours: The restaurant is open from 5:30 P.M.–10 P.M. Sun.–Fri., and 5 P.M.–10:30 P.M. Saturday. The lounge is open 5 P.M.–10 P.M. Sun.–Fri., and 4:30 P.M.–10:30 P.M. Saturday.

Policies: Reservations are accepted.

Prices: $$–$$$. Major credit cards are accepted.

Contact: Chart House, 392 Kingsbury Grade, Stateline, NV; 775/588-6276; website: www.chart-house.com.

TAHOE DINING

Coyote Grill

This relative newcomer at Round Hill Square, next to Safeway, has become a local institution. Remodelled extensively in 2002, the restaurant has a full bar, more seating, and a new menu. Known to the lunch crowd for its fresh ahi and halibut tacos, Coyote's offers nightly fish and pasta specials along with beer and wine.

Hours: Daily for lunch and dinner, 11 A.M.–9 P.M. Sun.–Thurs., 11 A.M.–10 P.M. Fri. and Saturday.

Prices: $.

Contact: Coyote Grill, 212 Elks Point Rd. (Round Hill Square off Hwy. 50), Zephyr Cove, NV; 775/586-1822.

Cuvee

Located inside Caesars Tahoe, this restaurant replaced Empress Court, a Chinese dinner house, in the summer of 2002. There are still some Asian-influenced dishes on the menu, which emphasizes California cuisine. Among the entrees: Kasu marinated Atlantic salmon with oven-roasted Chinese long beans and miso broth; tea-smoked duck with green onion pancakes, spicy orange scented hoisin and shaved scallions; and lemon-grilled lobster enchilada, with chili mole, guacamole and black bean salad. Desserts include Thai banana fritters with coconut-kefir lime ice cream, and Grand Marnier crème brûlée. In this small, very intimate dining room, you can ask your server to pair a glass of wine with your meal.

Hours: Dinner nightly from 6 P.M.

Policies: Reservations are accepted.

Prices: $$-$$$. Major credit cards are accepted.

Contact: Caesars Tahoe, 55 U.S. 50, Stateline, Nevada, 775/586-2044; website: www.caesars.com.

Edgewood Restaurant

Lake Tahoe's premier golf resort has an elegant clubhouse and restaurant with vaulted, beamed ceilings and sweeping views of the lake and the course. Service and food are usually excellent, making this one of Tahoe's finest restaurants. The menu includes seared ahi tuna with creamy wasabi sauce (one of my favorites), swordfish broiled with passion fruit habanero sauce, roast loin of elk with sun-dried cherry relish on a bed of spinach spaetzle, and tournedos of scallops drizzled with curry vinaigrette. A full bar and a nonsmoking dining room are available.

Hours: Lunch from 11:30 A.M.–2 P.M., dinner 6 P.M.–9 P.M., and Sun. brunch during the summer only 10 A.M.–2 P.M. In the winter, dinner is served 6 P.M.–9 P.M. Wed.–Sunday.

Policies: Reservations are recommended.

Prices: $$–$$$. Visa, MasterCard, and American Express are accepted.

Contact: Edgewood Restaurant, 100 Lake Pkwy., Stateline, NV; 775/588-2787; website: www.edgewood-tahoe.com.

El Vaquero

On the lower level of Harveys, this nicely appointed Mexican restaurant gets strong ratings from locals. Albóndigas and black bean soups, avocado ceviche (marinated sea scallops), and seafood quesadilla are among the appetizers. A large cocktail lounge adjoins the dining room.

Hours: Nightly for dinner and Wed.–Sun. for lunch.

Policies: Reservations are suggested.

Prices: $–$$$. Major credit cards are accepted.

Contact: Harveys Resort Casino, U.S. 50, Stateline, NV; 775/588-2411; website: www.harveys-tahoe.com.

Echo Restaurant and Lounge

When it was acquired in 2001 by the Japan-based Ken Corporation, the Embassy Suites Hotel near Stateline also took over ownership of its food and beverage operations. Among the changes was the arrival of a new executive chef, Roy Choi, from San Diego, who is an advocate of flying in fresh seafood, beef and vegetables from the country's best food distributors. The restaurant (originally known as Zachary's) was completely remodeled in the summer of 2002, to provide a more casual, Tahoe-esque décor, and Choi has introduced a new menu. All of his dishes have unique variations and sauces that make them anything but conventional. For example, his grilled mushroom quesadilla, served as an appetizer, is a thick, multi-layered dish that bears little resemblance to the classic flat tortilla and cheese. Dinner entrees include pan-roasted pork chop with homemade red onion marmalade; poached salmon with roasted corn relish; marinated London broil with a garlic Zinfandel sauce; Chinese five-spice crusted duck, miso-glazed Hawaiian ono with fruit-coconut milk relish, and Echo's signature pan-seared filet mignon, which is served over a grilled polenta crouton with a roasted garlic-thyme jus and a grape tomato-citrus relish. Starters include broiled French onion soup, apple-fennel salad, and warm herb crusted goat cheese salad. The new dining room is cheerier, contemporary in appointments and more casual than its predecessor, and the walls are festooned with old photographs of Tahoe. There are separate menus for children and for the lounge.

Hours: Lunch daily from 11:30 A.M. to 2 P.M.; dinner from 6 P.M. to 9 P.M. Sunday through Thursday, and from 6 P.M. to 10 P.M. Friday and Saturday. The lounge is open from 11 A.M. to 11 P.M. daily.

Policies: Reservations are accepted.

Prices: $$-$$$. Major credit cards are accepted.

Contact: Embassy Suites Hotel, 4130 Lake Tahoe Blvd. (U.S. 50), South Lake Tahoe, California, 530/544-5400; website: www.embassytahoe.com.

Forest Room Buffet

Completely renovated and enlarged during spring of 2000—part of a major remodeling at Harrah's Lake Tahoe—this buffet restaurant has established its reputation as one of the best at South Shore. The menu features 17 cold salads, roast turkey, ham, roast beef, and 35 varieties of special desserts, baked fresh daily by award-winning chefs. Of special note is the Friday night seafood buffet, Saturday night steak buffet, and a bountiful Sunday champagne brunch buffet. Breakfast has incomparable high-rise views, with huge plate glass windows overlooking the mountains, the lake, and Sierra scenery. The new restaurant has new floor, ceiling, wall, and column treatments, and the cooking and serving stations have been redesigned to offer more dining options.

Hours: Breakfast 8 A.M.–11 A.M. daily, lunch from 11:30 A.M.–2 P.M., dinner 5 P.M.–9 P.M. on weekdays, dinner 5 P.M.–10 P.M. on weekends, and Sun. brunch from 8:30 A.M.–2 P.M.

Prices: $–$$. Visa, MasterCard, American Express, Diners Club, and Carte Blanche are accepted.

Contact: Harrah's Casino Hotel, U.S. 50, Stateline, NV; 775/588-6611; website: www.harrahstahoe.com.

Friday's Station Steak and Seafood Grill

On the top floor of Harrah's, this high-rise casino restaurant puts enough beef on your plate to feed an army. So forget the calorie counters and be sure to bring a big appetite. The house specialties include prime rib, aged for 28 days and roasted very slowly; Wenatchee salmon rubbed with Seattle barbecue spices and baked on a plank of cured alderwood; Alaskan king crab legs; grilled teriyaki tiger prawns; and chicken grilled with teriyaki, Dijon garlic, or barbecue sauce. All entrées are served with a choice of smoked shrimp and scallop chowder or the house Caesar salad. Save room for a dessert of chilled grasshopper mint soufflé or turtle sundae. The restaurant was remodeled in early 2000, with all new furnishings and fixtures, improved views from every table, a glassed-in wine cellar, and an impressive new entrance.

Hours: Open Sun. and Mon. from 5:30 P.M.–10 P.M. and Fri. and Sat. from 5:30 P.M.–11 P.M.

Policies: Reservations are accepted.

Prices: $$-$$$. Major credit cards are accepted.

Contact: Harrah's Casino Hotel, U.S. 50, Stateline, NV; 775/588-6606 or 775/588-6611, ext. 2158; website: www.harrahstahoe.com.

Garden Buffet

This large buffet room in Harveys Resort has a pleasant, outdoorsy feel and seating areas that are separate from the food service stations. It offers above-average fare for breakfast, lunch, and dinner, with many dishes cooked to order. The dessert bar is one of the best around, giving diners some upscale dishes such as bananas Foster and cherries jubilee. Dinner changes nightly with

TAHOE DINING

different themes, the most popular being the Friday seafood buffet, a feast of Maine lobster tails, shrimp, crab, and other delights.
Hours: Breakfast 9 A.M.–11 A.M., lunch from 11:30 A.M.–2:30 P.M., and dinner 5 P.M.–9 P.M. on weekdays; 4 P.M.–10 P.M. on weekends.
Policies: Reservations are accepted.
Prices: $–$$. Major credit cards are accepted.
Contact: Harveys Resort Casino, U.S. 50, Stateline, NV; 775/588-2411; website: www.harveys-tahoe.com.

Hard Rock Café

Inside Harveys Resort Hotel/Casino at Stateline, this is where rock 'n roll meets rock 'n timber. Incorporating the trendy Old Tahoe look, this version of the international franchise has two massive stone fireplaces, exposed logs, tipi lamps, glass with etched mountain scenery, and a fully functional stage. Some of the 300 pieces of rock memorabilia include a white bustier from Madonna's wardrobe, a shirt from Elvis Presley, and a maroon bass guitar played by Paul McCartney. Other than the atmosphere, the food is the usual assortment of "classic" American coffee shop cuisine—burgers, fries, steaks, and salads. There's a merchandise store inside.
Hours: Lunch and dinner from 11 A.M.
Prices: $–$$.
Contact: Hard Rock Café at Harveys, Stateline Ave., Stateline, NV; 775/588-6200; website: www.harveys-tahoe.com.

Josh's

An award-winning casino restaurant with a strong Italian flavor, Josh's offers fisherman's fettuccine Bodega Bay, cannelloni Romano, and veal scaloppine marsala among its main courses. It's in the Horizon Casino Resort on U.S. 50.
Hours: Daily from 5:30 P.M.–10:30 P.M.
Prices: $$. Major credit cards are accepted.
Contact: Horizon Casino Resort, U.S. 50, Stateline, NV; 775/588-6211.

Le Grande Buffet

Three times a day, Le Grande Buffet in the Horizon Casino provides a very inexpensive, although generally undistinguished, buffet.

Hours: Dinner on Mon., Thurs., and Fri. from 5:30 P.M.–9:30 P.M. and Sat. and Sun. 5 P.M.–9 P.M. Brunch on Sat. and Sun. 9 A.M.–2 P.M.
Prices: $–$$. Major credit cards are accepted.
Contact: Horizon Casino Resort, U.S. 50, Stateline, NV; 775/588-6211.

Llewellyn's

High-rise views of Lake Tahoe and an elegant dining environment make this restaurant one of the standouts of the South Shore. Appetizers include Thai red curry frog legs, escargot in phyllo dough, and lobster bisque en croûte. Dinner entrées feature lamb rack Gilroy with caramelized garlic, tournedos fromage, and salmon involtini. Llewellyn's is on the 19th floor of Harveys Resort Casino.
Hours: Lunch from 11:30 A.M.–2:30 P.M. Wed.–Sat.; dinner from 6 P.M. on Tues., Wed., Thurs., Fri., and Sun.; dinner from 5 P.M. on Mon. and Sat.; and Sun. brunch 10 A.M.–2 P.M.
Prices: $$–$$$. Major credit cards are accepted.
Contact: Harveys Resort Casino, U.S. 50, Stateline, NV; 775/588-2411; website: www.harveys-tahoe.com.

Mirabelle French Cuisine

Chef Camille Schwartz hails from the Alsace-Lorraine region of France, and she has brought the first and only French dinner house to the South Shore, which seems to have an overabundance of Italian and Asian food. Although it's tucked away in a nondescript strip mall on Kingsbury Grade, just up the hill from the intersection with Highway 50, the restaurant comes highly recommended from locals. But it's not for the price-conscious. Since most entrées are over $25, a meal with a starter, wine, and dessert will set you back at least $50 per person, more with an after-dinner drink. The dining room is small and intimate, appointed in French country decor, and is an ideal place to celebrate a honeymoon, an anniversary, or an engagement. Savor the appetizers such as onion soup gratinée, *tarte* niçoise with small prawns, escargots Maison, sautéed *gigolettes* of frogs on wilted spinach, or lobster bisque. For entrées, select from pasta du jour (the least expensive dinner), baked butterflied prawns provençale, sautéed fillet of beef (coated with crushed black peppercorns, Cognac-roasted shallot *demie,* and a touch of cream), grilled veal chop, and grilled lamb chops and prawns. There's usually a fresh catch of the day, as well. For dessert, you know what's coming: crème brûlée *au citron,* Marquise du Lac (chocolate hazelnut Frangelico mousse wrapped with white chocolate mocha sauce), meringue mimosa, warm dark rum chocolate cake, and a chef's selection of tarts. Bon appetit!

Hours: Dinner is served Tues.–Sun., from 5:30 P.M.

Prices: $$–$$$. Major credit cards are accepted.

Contact: Mirabelle French Cuisine, 290 Kingsbury Grade, Stateline, NV; 775/586-1007.

Mott Canyon Tavern and Grill

Just up from Highway 50 on Kingsbury Grade, on the Nevada side, is this nondescript locals' hangout, which is a great place to grab a quick but creative meal that is well above the average coffee shop fare and is reasonably priced. There are plenty of appetizers for noshing with one of 13 beers on tap, including jalapeño poppers, chicken wings, quesadillas, mozzarella sticks, and pot stickers. For lunch or dinner, there are six salads, including the popular Cobb and crispy chicken salads; a dozen sandwiches, of which the house special is the Mott Melt (turkey, bacon, cheddar, tomato, and avocado on sourdough); and the stir-fry basket (highly recommended for large appetites) with choice of Asian beef, grilled chicken, or crispy chicken, which is mixed with vegetables and served with a tangy sauce over steamed white rice. The bar is a popular place for happy hour, or for watching sports events on any of several TVs, and there's a large rock fireplace.

Hours: Daily 11 A.M.–4 A.M., with full menu offered until 3 A.M. There are two happy hour periods—4 P.M.–6 P.M. and midnight to 4 A.M.

Prices: $. Major credit cards accepted.

Contact: Mott Canyon Tavern and Grill, 259 Kingsbury Grade, Lake Tahoe, NV; 775/588-8989.

Planet Hollywood

Opened in 1994 by Arnold Schwarzenegger and Bruce Willis, two of the chain's owners, this place is festooned with Hollywood props and memorabilia, which act as the main attractions. Once you get past the decorations, however, Planet Hollywood is not exactly out of this world. It's a glorified coffee shop, with basic burgers, pizzas, salads, and sandwiches, although a new menu has added a few upgrades. You might pop in for a drink or, the house forte, a dessert. Planet Hollywood is at Caesars Tahoe.

Hours: Daily 11 A.M.–2 A.M.

Prices: $–$$. Major credit cards are accepted.

Contact: Caesars Tahoe, 55 U.S. 50, Stateline, NV; 775/588-7828; website: www.caesars.com.

Primavera

Next to the main casino floor, this restaurant has a relaxing environment and wonderful service. The food is well above average, with authentic Italian specialties such as chicken piccata, tortellini *baronessa,* veal-filled pasta with prosciutto, mushrooms, peas, and Alfredo sauce; *rollatini di pollo,* a breast of chicken filled with prosciutto and mozzarella; and *fileti con tre pepi,* made of beef tenderloin with peppercorns, garlic, white wine, and veal stock.

Hours: Open Thurs.–Mon. 6 P.M.–11 P.M.

Policies: Reservations are accepted.

Prices: $$. Major credit cards are accepted.

Contact: Caesars Tahoe, 55 U.S. 50, Stateline, NV; 775/586-2044; website: www.caesars.com.

Rockwater Bar and Grill

Over the years, there's been a substantial turnover in restaurants on Highway 89 north of the "Y" intersection, but South Shore restauranteur Keith Simpson, whose Dory's Oar and Tudor English Pub has become a local and international favorite, recently acquired this dinner house and reinvigorated it with new energy and a new menu. Evening entrées, known as "Big Plates," include home-style grilled New York strip steak with tobacco onions and herb butter; the house recipe of fish and chips (an import from Dory's Oar); Baja-style fish tacos; fettuccine Carbonara with light Gorgonzola cream sauce and artichoke hearts; and blackened prime rib of beef. All dinner plates have hearty portions with choice of potato and chef's vegetable. Lunch entrées center on "Mile High Sandwiches" that include a Reuben, a half-pound burger, blackened prime rib and something called "Mr. Toad's Wild Fried Ahi Sandwich," which is named after a hairball mountain bike trail. Starters consist of three salads, including Caesar and spinach, a housemade clam chowder, and appetizers such as chicken wings, beer-battered onion rings and Southwestern egg rolls with red pepper sauce. The atmosphere is rustic, lively, and casual, and there's an outdoor deck and bar for warm weather. Come here with an appetite, and leave the calorie counter behind.

Hours: Lunch and dinner daily, from 11 A.M. to 11 P.M. (but appetizers only after 10 P.M.).
Policies: Reservations are accepted.
Prices: $$-$$$. Major credit cards are accepted.
Contact: Rockwater Bar and Grill, 787 Emerald Bay Road, South Lake Tahoe, California, 530/544-8004; website: www.rockwaterbarandgrill.com.

Sage Room

One of the finest steak houses anywhere—and a fixture on the local dining scene since 1947—this restaurant is virtually an institution, and it's a favorite among frequent guests at Harveys Resort Casino. It's expensive, but it has intimate lighting, a romantic ambience, and exquisite service. Decor includes the original bar, original Native American lamps given to Harveys by the Washoe tribe, and hand-hewn beams that were part of Harveys log cabin in 1944. The menu includes inch-thick Black Angus rib-eye steak; Southwestern lobster enchiladas; Sage Room Steak Gilroy, garnished with garlic purée and topped with a potato crust; an appetizer of crisp raclette potatoes with *pancetta* and scallions; honey rabbit sausage lasagna; venison *grand veneur;* and such desserts as bananas Foster and cherries jubilee prepared tableside for two.

Hours: Open Mon.–Fri. 6 P.M.–10 P.M. and Sat. and Sun. from 5:30 P.M.–10 P.M.
Policies: Reservations are suggested.
Prices: $$$. Major credit cards are accepted.

Contact: Harveys Resort Casino, U.S. 50, Stateline, NV; 775/588-2411; website: www. harveys-tahoe.com.

Sam's Place

This longtime locals' joint on Highway 50 at Zephyr Cove has become rejuvenated lately. With two happy hours (one at 4 P.M.–6 P.M., the other at 10 P.M.–2 A.M.), a beer garden, pool tables, pub fare, and an outdoor barbecue, Sam's has most of the bases covered. Goodies include pizza and chicken wings. There are seven TVs for sports fans, a large fireplace, and video poker, along with Wednesday open mike nights.

Hours: 11 A.M. until 2 A.M. daily.
Prices: $.
Contact: Sam's Place, 611 Hwy. 50, Zephyr Cove, NV; 775/588-2844.

Seafood Grotto

This popular small restaurant off the main casino floor of Harveys serves inexpensive seafood dishes that are above average. Entrées include calamari amandine, San Francisco-style cioppino, live Maine lobster, Australian lobster tails, scampi, sautéed red Thai curry shrimp, a Pacific clambake for two, and bouillabaisse Marseilles style. For turf eaters, there are filet mignon and New York steak, all complemented by an extensive wine list. Starters include crab or shrimp Louies, oysters Rockefeller, steamed clams, crab cakes, and both New England- and Manhattan-style clam chowder. Desserts include Key lime pie, mud pie, and New York—style cheesecake.

Hours: Nightly from 5:30 P.M. for dinner, except Wed. and Thursday.
Policies: Reservations are accepted.
Prices: $$. Major credit cards are accepted.
Contact: Harveys Resort Casino, U.S. 50, Stateline, NV; 775/588-2411; website: www.harveys-tahoe.com.

The Summit

Benefiting from a $2 million renovation in 2001, South Shore's most prestigious hotel restaurant is arguably one of the best dinner houses anywhere, as demonstrated by a bushel of national culinary awards. There's an intimate and elegant dining environment (with a pianist playing nightly), along with great views of the mountains from the Summit's lofty location on the 16th floor of Harrah's. Before 1991, those floors were suites reserved for celebrities such as Sammy Davis Jr., Frank Sinatra, and Wayne Newton, who stayed here during their stints at the casino showroom. Dress up in your finest to dine at this restaurant. The menu changes weekly and offers a chef's recommendation. Entrées might include roulade of veal Oscar, roast rack of lamb with anise crust, grilled venison, and salmon with lemon couscous. For starters, select from dishes such as seared Hudson Valley foie gras and a warm spinach and Muscovy duck salad (prepared tableside). And be sure to have the house special dessert, Grand Marnier soufflé. Everything is outstanding, creatively prepared, and masterfully presented. All entrées are served à la carte.

Hours: Open Sun.–Thurs. from 5:30 P.M.–10 P.M. and Fri. and Sat. from 5:30 P.M.–11 P.M. Closed Tuesday.

Policies: Reservations are suggested.

Prices: $$$. Major credit cards are accepted.

Contact: Harrah's Casino Hotel, U.S. 50, Stateline, NV; 775/588-6611, ext. 2394 or 2196; website: www.harrahstahoe.com.

Taberna Mexican Food

Newest of the two restaurants at Lakeside Inn and Casino, this place serves three meals a day, including super-cheap breakfasts for broke and bleary-eyed gamblers. There are some creative dishes, though, for dinners. Among them are the crab-stuffed fillet of sole Mazatlan-style (with homemade potato salad, beets, rice, and chipotle dressing), goat Birria (braised goat meat in a tomato sauce with dried chiles and spices), and pork *chile verde.* Lunch specialties include an Oaxacan-style quesadilla, which is open-faced with your choice of meat, black beans, melted cheese, tomato, onion, avocado, and cilantro.

Hours: 8 A.M.–10 P.M. daily for breakfast, lunch and dinner.

Prices: $. Major credit cards are accepted.

Contact: Lakeside Inn and Casino, U.S. 50, Stateline, NV; 775/588-7777 or 800/624-7980; website: www.lakesideinn.com.

Timber House

Open around the clock, this popular restaurant at the Lakeside Inn and Casino serves aged Monfort prime rib, Alaskan king salmon, barbecued baby-back ribs, chicken piccata, turkey, and blackened halibut on its dinner menu at incredibly reasonable prices (under $10 for some entrées). Meals come with choice of soup or salad, plus twice-baked potato and vegetable of the day. Breakfast, which includes huevos rancheros and eggs Benedict, and lunch, which includes Philly cheese steak and French dip sandwiches, are also available, and there are daily specials.

Hours: Open 24 hours daily except Tues., when breakfast is served 7 A.M.–11 A.M.

Policies: Reservations are accepted.

Prices: $. Major credit cards are accepted.

Contact: Lakeside Inn and Casino, U.S. 50, Stateline, NV; 775/588-7777 or 800/624-7980; website: www.lakesideinn.com.

Water Wheel

This is a decent Chinese restaurant on the South Shore, and recently it added a large, all-you-can-eat sushi bar, giving diners a pan-Asian experience. The Chinese menu includes the usual chow mein, *chow fun,* egg foo yung, fried rice, and various chef's seafood, beef, and poultry specials. The Japanese menu includes shrimp and vegetable tempura, teriyaki beef and chicken, spicy crab roll, California roll, and various lunch and dinner combinations. No MSG is used.

Hours: Daily from 11:30 A.M.–10 P.M.

Policies: Reservations are accepted.

Prices: $–$$$. Major credit cards are accepted.

Contact: Water Wheel, 195 U.S. Hwy. 50, Stateline, NV; 775/588-0555.

Zephyr Cove Restaurant

Unpretentious and very casual, this restaurant serves home-style meals, including steak and shrimp, fettuccine Alfredo, and basil chicken. It's at Zephyr Cove Resort, four miles north of Stateline.

Hours: Daily from 7:30 A.M.–3 P.M. in winter and 7:30 A.M.–10 P.M. in summer.

Prices: $–$$.

Contact: Zephyr Cove Resort, U.S. 50, Zephyr Cove, NV; 775/588-6644.

SOUTH LAKE TAHOE/CAMP RICHARDSON (CALIFORNIA)

Alpen Sierra Coffee Co.

This popular locals' hangout is a great place to get caffeine-fortified for the day, as well as to grab a fresh muffin, croissant, or sandwich. Specialty coffees and teas (also sold from a retail store) and a large assortment of lattes and espressos keep people hooked. At the junction of Pioneer Trail and Highway 50 near Stateline.

Hours: 6 A.M.–8 P.M.

Prices: $.

Contact: Alpen Sierra Coffee Co., 3940 Lake Tahoe Blvd. (Hwy. 50) at Pioneer Trail, South Lake Tahoe, CA; 530/544-7740.

Alpina Cafe

What was once the original location of Alpen Sierra Coffee is now under new ownership, but it still pours Alpen's signature java. In a historic building on Emerald Bay Road near the "Y" intersection, the café also offers a variety of scones, European pastries, teas, soups, and sandwiches.

Hours: From 6 A.M. daily.

Prices: $.

Contact: Alpina Café, 822 Emerald Bay Rd., South Lake Tahoe, CA; 530/541-7449.

The Beacon Restaurant

Good vibes are always felt here, especially when a jazz, blues, or folk band is playing on the outside deck. Recently under new ownership, this beachfront restaurant at Camp Richardson Resort offers a captivating view of Tahoe as well as an intimate dining room that serves lunch, dinner, and brunch (the latter on Saturday and Sunday only). The dinner menu offers Black Angus prime rib, macadamia-crusted salmon, pasta carbonara, salad suzette, and a hearty clam chowder. Desserts are varied and delightful. There's a bar and a large deck—both favored by the beach crowd—with an enormous selection of appetizers and exotic drinks, such as the Rum Runner, to choose from.

Hours: Lunch 11 A.M.–3 P.M. on weekdays and 10 A.M.–3 P.M. on weekends; dinner daily 5 P.M.–9:30 P.M.

Prices: $–$$$. Some credit cards are accepted, but no personal checks are allowed.

Contact: The Beacon Restaurant, 1900 Jameson Beach Rd., South Lake Tahoe, CA; 530/541-0630; website: www.camprichardson.com.

Boathouse Bar and Grill

Among the few lakefront restaurants at South Shore, this one emphasizes casual fare, alcoholic libations, and people-watching. It's also a wonderful vantage point to see the sunset. The fairly simple pub-type menu offers soups, sandwiches, tacos, salads, wraps, and various noshing goodies. The grill throws various midweek specials (one promotion was for all you can eat and drink on Thursday night for $10) and has disco and hip-hop DJ music Thursday–Saturday evenings. The Boathouse is actually built on a pier over the water and is behind the Best Western Timber Cove Lodge. Its motto is "Work is the curse of the drinking classes," so party on, dude.

Hours: Lunch daily from 11:30 A.M. daily; the bar is open from 11:30 A.M.–sunset Sun.–Wed. and 11:30 A.M.–late evening Sun.–Wednesday. Buffet is featured Thurs. 6 P.M.–9 P.M.

Policies: No reservations needed.

Prices: $–$$$. Major credit cards are accepted.

Contact: The Boathouse Bar and Grill, 3411 Lake Tahoe Blvd., South Lake Tahoe, CA; 530/541-0113.

Bountiful

Granola-eaters, rejoice! This new breakfast and lunch place on Emerald Bay Road (north of the "Y" intersection) is another entry in the health food dining scene at South Shore. The breakfast menu includes organic oatmeal with warm berry compote, vanilla French toast, pumpkin and buckwheat pancakes, meatless omelets, and tofu/brown rice burritos served in whole wheat tortillas. For lunch, there are a half dozen tofu and rice bowls with various sauces, homemade vegetable soups, a selection of salads, and sandwiches that include grilled eggplant, buffalo mozzarella, tuna, turkey, and grilled rib eye.

Hours: Open Tues.–Sat. 8 A.M.–3 P.M., 8 A.M.–2 P.M. on Sun. (breakfast only).
Prices: $. Cash only.
Contact: Bountiful, 717 Emerald Bay Rd., South Lake Tahoe, CA; 530/542-4060.

Breakwater Cafe

Providing a view of the Tahoe Queen paddle-wheel excursion boat and miscellaneous water traffic at Ski Run Marina, this small café with indoor and outdoor seating serves three meals a day. Breakfast includes scrambled egg burrito, French toast, made-to-order omelets, and a scramble with eggs, swiss cheese, diced ham, onions, and peppers. Lunch offers salads, home-made soup of the day served in a bread bowl, burgers, and the usual assortment of sandwiches. Dinner, relatively inexpensive, includes tenderloin medallions in a portabella cream sauce, peppered New York steak, Southwestern chicken fillet, teriyaki stir-fried pasta, and a vegetable sauté in white wine sauce. There's a full espresso bar, along with a children's menu.
Hours: Breakfast 8 A.M.–noon, lunch 11:30 A.M.–4:30 P.M., and dinner from 4:30 P.M.–9 P.M. daily.
Prices: $–$$. Major credit cards accepted.
Contact: Breakwater Café, 900 Ski Run Blvd., South Lake Tahoe, CA; 530/543-0116.

The Brewery at Lake Tahoe

The South Shore's only microbrewery serves veg-gie fare and sandwiches. The best spots to eat are on the outside deck, a great people-watch-ing spot, though the traffic on busy U.S. 50 may drown you out.
Hours: Daily noon–11 P.M.
Prices: $.
Contact: The Brewery at Lake Tahoe, 3542 U.S. 50, South Lake Tahoe, CA; 530/544-BREW (530/544-2739).

Cafe Fiore

Cafe Fiore is a tiny and intimate Italian restaurant with atmosphere and great cuisine—perhaps the favorite date and honeymoon restaurant at South Shore. A menu sampling of the more popular dishes includes *bistecca alla Veneziana,* a tender-loin of beef with a sauce of green peppercorns,

mustard, cream, and cognac; linguine *alla di-avolo,* consisting of pasta with seafood such as scallops, shrimp, calamari, and salmon cooked with extra virgin olive oil, garlic, and a spicy red sauce; and veal saltimbocca, comprising scallops of veal and mozzarella cheese rolled inside pro-sciutto ham and cooked with butter, shallots, mushrooms, and a Madeira wine glaze. Because of the size of the restaurant—seven tables seating just 28 people, with five more tables outside in summer—reservations are a must.
Hours: Daily from 5:30 P.M.–10 P.M.
Prices: $$–$$$. Major credit cards are accepted.
Contact: Cafe Fiore, 1169 Ski Run Blvd. #5, South Lake Tahoe, CA; 530/541-2908; website: www.cafefiore.com.

The Cantina

The owners of Evan's, a popular gourmet restau-rant in South Shore, also own The Cantina, and the menu offers their trademark creativity. This place emphasizes trendy Southwestern spe-cialties such as blue corn sautéed salmon, cala-mari *relleno,* Texas crab cakes, smoked chicken polenta, and barbecued baby-back ribs. A few Mexican favorites are represented, including burritos, enchiladas, tacos, fajitas, and *chile verde.* Also, you can select from 16 draft beers and a dazzling array of margaritas. There is def-initely an upscale ambience to the place, with waiters taking great pains to describe the daily specials. The food is an eclectic mix, more like California cuisine taking a slight detour through Santa Fe by way of Europe. Still, the restaurant has found quick acceptance among locals. Don't expect authentic Mexican food; if you want something smothered in *picante* sauce, there are other places in town.
Hours: Lunch and dinner daily from 11:30 A.M.–9:30 P.M., later on weekends.
Prices: $–$$. Major credit cards are accepted.
Contact: The Cantina, 765 Emerald Bay Rd., South Lake Tahoe, CA; 530/544-1233; website: www.cantinatahoe.com.

Chase's Bar and Grill

Well-regarded local restauranteur Mike Weber, who ran The Beacon and Fresh Ketch for many years, has tapped into his Louisiana roots to come up with Lake Tahoe's first full-on New Orleans–style restaurant. In the terminal of the South Lake Tahoe Airport, in a remodelled upstairs dining area that overlooks the runways and scenic Monument Peak, this new restaurant has plenty of classic New Orleans dishes, some of them made from mom's recipes. To achieve authenticity, Weber has kicked up everything a notch with spices and ingredients brought from the South. Your taste buds will tingle from menu items such as these: homemade gumbo with chicken and andouille sausage, jambalaya (served once a week as a lunch special), crab cakes with roasted red pepper tartar sauce, New Orleans Shrimp Boil with a house-made cocktail sauce, Caesar salad with blackened shrimp or chicken breast, red beans and rice with blackened or grilled pork chops, blackened or pan-fried catfish, Creole mustard chicken breast, and—as another daily special—Mother Dears Meatloaf with debris gravy or tomato basil garlic sauce. For dessert, who can resist the house-made banana pudding, Bananas Foster, bread pudding with bourbon sauce, or the requisite pralines and cream? Serving both lunch and dinner, Chase's also has a variety of "po'boy" and New Orleans sandwiches (with house-made breads), such as fried oyster po'boy with bacon and spicy slaw, hot house roast beef po'boy, barbecued andouille sausage po'boy, and a half-pound blackened or charbroiled burger. Everything is reasonably priced, with most lunch items and some entrées under $10. In addition to the indoor dining area and full cocktail lounge (where live entertainment often holds forth on Tuesday night), there's a spacious outdoor deck where you can ogle at arriving private jets and their high rollers, or just appreciate the mountain vistas. Will Weber become the Paul Prudhomme of Lake Tahoe? Will the airport become the French Quarter of South Shore? Stay tuned. And speaking of tunes, spin Jimmy Buffet's "I Will Play For Gumbo" to get yourself in the mood for Chase's.

Hours: Lunch and dinner from 11:30 A.M.–9 P.M.; cocktail lounge open from 11 A.M. until closing.
Policies: Reservations are accepted.
Prices: $–$$. Major credit cards are accepted.

Contact: Chase's Bar and Grill, 1901 Airport Rd. (South Lake Tahoe Airport), South Lake Tahoe, CA; 530/544-9080.

Chevys

When Chevys opened in 1996 in the site of the former Carlos Murphy's, the theme didn't change much. But Chevys is at least a peg up in quality and service, and it offers dishes such as homemade tamales, daily fresh fish, chicken fajitas, chicken enchiladas, and combination meals. Salsa is blended fresh hourly, the chips are warm, and the tortillas are homemade. Also, there's an array of fresh fruit margaritas.
Hours: Daily for lunch and dinner.
Prices: $–$$. Major credit cards are accepted.
Contact: Chevys, 3678 Lake Tahoe Blvd., South Lake Tahoe, CA; 530/542-1741.

Christiania Inn

A fixture on the local dining scene for more than 35 years, this European country inn is across the street from Heavenly Resort's California lodge. It serves elegant gourmet meals in a romantic, candlelit setting. The menu varies seasonally and features grilled pork chops, filet mignon, New Zealand rack of lamb, New York strip loin, pan-roasted chicken breast (served with spicy tomato mole), marinated breast of duck and scampi. Specials of the day usually include seafood, pasta, and wild game. Starters include bruschetta, escargot, crab and artichoke dip, smoked salmon, French onion soup, and Caesar salad. Desserts include some elaborate dishes such as bananas flambé and cherries jubilee, along with rum-drenched bread pudding (from a family recipe), Key lime pie, and chocolate mousse. The staff and kitchen seem to be at their best in winter. Like other restaurants around the basin, the Christiania lacks consistency, and the off-season might find the restaurant missing some of its wines and menu entrées. There's a large and terrific après-ski bar, the Fireside Lounge, with a big fireplace and weekend live music, typically jazz or blues. Banquet facilities are available.
Hours: Dinner from 5:30 P.M.–10 P.M. daily, Happy Hour (with a bistro menu) from 2 P.M. daily.

Policies: Reservations are suggested.
Prices: $$–$$$. Major credit cards are accepted.
Contact: Christiania Inn, 3819 Saddle Rd., South Lake Tahoe, CA; 530/544-7337; website: www.christianiainn.com.

Dixon's Restaurant and Brewery

At Dixon's, contemporary American cuisine is combined with fresh Italian pastas and South-western/Mexican dishes. It's as unusual as it sounds, with a menu that features salmon dill linguine, half chicken Santa Fe, angel hair pasta, turkey burritos, and scampi. Several microbrews are on tap at the bar, along with a couple that are made on premises, and there is live weekend entertainment.
Hours: Lunch 11 A.M.–3 P.M. and dinner 5 P.M.–9:30 P.M.
Prices: $–$$.
Contact: Dixon's Restaurant and Brewery, 675 Emerald Bay Rd., South Lake Tahoe, CA; 530/542-3389.

The Dory's Oar and The Tudor Pub

Set in an authentic Cape Cod cottage with cheery white interiors, elegant tablecloth settings, fine china, and starched napkins, the Dory's Oar gets you in the mood for almost anything nautical. You can select seafood from two oceans, including ahi and mahimahi from Hawaii, king salmon from the Northwest, live Maine lobster, char-broiled swordfish, and deep-fried soft-shell crabs from Chesapeake Bay. One unique feature is that you can choose from a menu of sauces, including pineapple Dijon, mango salsa, spicy lime remoulade, and Nantua cream (house-made shellfish stock with garlic, cream, and white wine reduced). There are also steaks, pastas, chicken dishes, and European house specials. Proprietors Keith and Jeannette Simpson, originally from Surrey, England, once catered for the royal family, and they treat their clientele like royalty, as well. With so many English skiers in town, the upstairs bar has become a lively spot to indulge in British draft ales and pub food, and to ask visitors how the pound is doing.
Hours: Daily from 5 P.M.
Prices: $–$$$. Major credit cards are accepted.

Contact: The Dory's Oar, 1041 Fremont Ave., South Lake Tahoe, CA; 530/541-6603; website: www.dorysoar.com.

Emerald Palace

This restaurant offers decent, if uninspiring, Chinese food.
Hours: Daily for lunch from 11:30 A.M.–3 P.M. and dinner 5 P.M.–9 P.M.
Policies: Reservations are suggested.
Prices: $–$$. Credit cards are accepted.
Contact: Emerald Palace, 871 Emerald Bay Rd., South Lake Tahoe, CA; 530/544-2421.

Ernie's Coffee Shop

A locals' favorite, Ernie's underscores the tendency of wonderful breakfast houses to be well away from South Shore's major tourist areas. If you want to mingle with residents and hear the latest gossip (which Little League team won, who's getting married, and who's fighting the local government), just sit here for a spell and enjoy the 1960s retro ambience. And don't forget to eat something. Savor the calories, cholesterol, and nostalgia with all kinds of eggs, home-fry potatoes, biscuits, and country gravy.

Ernie's excels in sauces and salsas, just the ticket to warm up frosty winter mornings. Try the tostada omelet, which consists of spiced shredded beef in a special sauce with avocado, cheese, and sour cream; or the Tahoe Scram, three eggs scrambled with sausage, mushrooms, onions, and your choice of melted cheese. Lunch includes burgers, grilled sandwiches, and hot turkey and barbecued beef sandwiches. Finish everything on your plate, so that grandma will be proud of you.
Hours: Daily 6 A.M.–2 P.M.
Prices: $.
Contact: Ernie's Coffee Shop, 1146 Emerald Bay Rd., South Lake Tahoe, CA; 530/541-2161.

Evans American Gourmet Cafe

One of Lake Tahoe's outstanding dining options, Evan's is a small, 35-seat restaurant that is housed in an old-fashioned cottage. There is no waiting lobby, so bring a jacket during cool evenings, because you will likely spend some time outside.

Indoors, the dining room has charm and intimacy, and nothing from the kitchen disappoints. For their tremendously popular restaurant, Evan and Candice Williams prepare sterling dishes with entrées such as port-glazed fillet of beef with porcini mushroom and green peppercorn sauce, venison with balsamic roast cherries and fresh tarragon, peppered tenderloin of pork with apple-smoked bacon, and roast loin of veal with garlic mashed potatoes. Don't miss out on the appetizers, such as the scallop quenelles with sherry-lobster cream or the wild mushroom and chevre phyllo pastry with baby greens, preserved lemon vinaigrette, and truffle honey. Daily specials depend on availability of produce, seafood, and meats. The award-winning wine list features about 200 wines, many from California. Both *Bon Appetit* magazine and *The Robb Report* have rated the restaurant very highly.

Hours: Dinner nightly 6 P.M.–9:30 P.M.
Policies: Reservations are advised.
Prices: $$–$$$. Some credit cards are accepted.
Contact: Evans American Gourmet Cafe, 536 Emerald Bay Rd., South Lake Tahoe, CA; 530/542-1990; website: www.evanstahoe.com.

Freshies Restaurant and Bar

Natural foods meet gourmet cooking in this new casual, health-conscious restaurant, which has quickly established its popularity with locals. Soups, salads, and sandwiches are the mainstay for the lunch crowd, and all are prepared with a eye toward freshness. The chicken sandwich, for instance, is make from free-range chicken, and the grilled vegetable sandwich has seasonal veggies grilled and mixed with melted Havarti cheese and pesto mayonnaise, and served on multigrain bread. Other menu items include chicken and shrimp satay salad, hearts of palm salad, fish tacos, a low-cal plate lunch of grilled fillet of snapper with cottage cheese and organic house rice, and a California Club with avocado, lettuce, tomatoes, and Swiss cheese with tofu and tempeh. Dinner offers dishes such as spicy Jamaican jerk chicken breast, Nilman Ranch organic filet mignon (topped with dried cherry and pinot noir sauce), tempeh and golden fried tofu stir-fry, blackened tofu, organic

house-made pasta with condiments of your choice, and salmon Florentine. Also, there's a rarity on Tahoe menus: paella. This Spanish-style seafood stew contains shrimp, fish, scallops, grilled chicken, calamari, and mussels, all simmered in saffron broth, rice, and vegetables. You can stop in for appetizers as well (there's a late-night menu 10 P.M.–11 P.M.), and these include sun-dried tomato hummus with goat cheese, tempura vegetables, potato skins, and sautéed calamari. Everything is reasonably priced, with most dinner entrées under $17 and lunch items under $8. The restaurant is in Lakeview Plaza, a small strip mall about 2.5 miles southwest of Stateline on Highway 50.

Hours: Lunch and dinner 11 A.M.–11 P.M. daily.
Policies: Reservations aren't necessary.
Prices: $–$$.
Contact: Freshies, 3330 Lake Tahoe Blvd., #3, South Lake Tahoe, CA; 530/542-3630.

Fresh Ketch

Recently under new ownership, this lakeside restaurant overlooking Tahoe Keys Marina offers casual dining downstairs and on an outside deck, and formal dining upstairs in an elegant dining room. The menu varies seasonally, but dinner might include halibut, lamb chops, grilled salmon, pork porterhouse steak, mixed grill, sea bass, bouillabaisse, Alaskan king crab, and Australian lobster tail. The "Big Plates" downstairs include fish tacos, marinated chicken breast, fish-and-chips, grilled steak sandwich, a half-dozen salads, and a half-pound burger. Desserts offer hula pie, chocolate expresso mousse cake, New York cheesecake, and Key lime pie. There's also an extensive wine list, a full bar with nearly 50 beers, and a fireside lounge. On a summer day, the deck is a great place to hang out and watch boats arriving and departing.

Hours: Lunch is daily from 11:30 A.M. and dinner is daily from 5:30 P.M.
Policies: Dinner reservations are highly recommended.
Prices: $$–$$$. Major credit cards are accepted.
Contact: Fresh Ketch, 2435 Venice Dr., South Lake Tahoe, CA; 530/541-5683.

TAHOE DINING

Grand Central Pizza and Pasta

Off Highway 50 in Kings Center, this place serves a variety of New York—style pizzas and pastas, among them lasagna, calzone, linguine, manicotti, and fettuccine. There's also a salad bar.
Hours: Daily 11 A.M.–11 P.M.
Prices: $–$$. Some credit cards are accepted.
Contact: Grand Central Pizza, 2229 U.S. 50, South Lake Tahoe, CA; 530/541-7665.

Greenhouse Restaurant and Bar

A popular South Shore restaurant, this place offers American continental gourmet dining in an atmosphere of green plants and European antique stained glass. Entrées include chicken *cordon bleu,* roast duckling *à l'orange, langouste et veau* (sautéed medallions of veal and lobster), and prawns à la cognac. There's an extensive wine list along with nightly chef's specials. The restaurant also offers banquet and wedding facilities.
Hours: Daily from 5:30 P.M.–10 P.M., with a full bar 4 P.M.–10 P.M.
Policies: Reservations are recommended.
Prices: $–$$$. Visa, MasterCard, and American Express are accepted.
Contact: Greenhouse Restaurant and Bar, 4140 Cedar Ave., South Lake Tahoe, CA; 530/541-5800.

Heidi's Pancake House

With a quaint, Bavarian-style setting, this is one of the older and more crowded breakfast houses in South Shore. Typically the service is slow, and the food quality ranges from average to good. The menu features a myriad of omelets, crepes, German pancakes, old-fashioned hamburgers, and heart-healthy items. The restaurant serves both breakfast and lunch.
Hours: Daily from 6:30 A.M.–2 P.M.
Prices: $. Some credit cards are accepted.
Contact: Heidi's Pancake House, 3485 Lake Tahoe Blvd., South Lake Tahoe, CA; 530/544-8113.

Hoss Hoggs

This is a longtime fixture for ribs, steak, chicken, and Mexican cuisine.
Hours: Daily from 11:30 A.M.–2 A.M.
Prices: $–$$.
Contact: Hoss Hoggs, 2543 Lake Tahoe Blvd., South Lake Tahoe, CA; 530/541-8328.

Hunan Garden

Lunch and dinner buffets are the main attraction of this Chinese restaurant, which prepares all dishes without MSG. You can also order off the menu, with the best deals being the gourmet and special dinners for two to four people. House specials include walnut prawns, New Zealand mussels sautéed in black bean sauce, spicy crispy sesame beef, spicy pineapple chicken, spicy garlic fish fillet, and crispy duck.
Hours: Daily from 11:30 A.M.–9:30 P.M.
Prices: $–$$. Some credit cards are accepted.
Contact: Hunan Garden, 900 Emerald Bay Rd., South Lake Tahoe, CA; 530/544-5868 or 530/544-7268.

International House of Pancakes

The standard IHOP menu—with chocolate chip pancakes, waffles, and omelets—is available here. This is a particularly well-managed restaurant with fast and attentive service.
Hours: Daily 7 A.M.–2 P.M.
Prices: $. Major credit cards are accepted.
Contact: International House of Pancakes, 3730 Lake Tahoe Blvd., South Lake Tahoe, CA; 530/544-4880.

Lake Tahoe Pizza Company

No question about it; this is the pizza place on the South Shore and a great treat for families with kids. The large, woodsy restaurant serves fresh pizzas with house specialty or whole-wheat doughs that are made fresh daily per order, not prerolled. All meats are ground and sliced daily. You can create your own pizza or choose from gourmet treats such as Mogul Masher, Gut Buster, and a spinach-garlic-shrimp combo. Hot meatball sandwiches are made from homemade wheat or white bread and are served with a pasta salad and a pickle. The full bar features local microbrewery beer on tap. Lake Tahoe Pizza Company is south of the "Y" and north of the South Lake Tahoe Airport.

TAHOE DINING

Hours: Daily 4 P.M.–10 P.M.
Policies: Smoking is allowed in the bar and lounge only.
Prices: $–$$. Some credit cards are accepted.
Contact: Lake Tahoe Pizza Company, 1168 Emerald Bay Rd.; South Lake Tahoe, CA; 530/544-1919.

Lew Mar Nel's Restaurant

Next to the Best Western Station House Inn is this AAA Three Diamond-rated restaurant, which has a rustic Western decor with original artwork and a number of Remington bronze statues. The white tablecloth service and subdued lighting should put you in the mood for one of the house specialties, which emphasize American and continental cuisine. Among the entrées are scampi, poached salmon, roast duckling, steak Diane, peppercorn steak, Cornish game hen, and steak and lobster. All beef, certified Angus, is mesquite-grilled. The wine list, which won the *Wine Spectator* Grand Award, offers more than 400 wines to complement your dinner. Entrées are moderately priced and dress is casual.
Hours: Breakfast from 7:30 A.M.–10:30 A.M. (ski season, 7 A.M.–10 A.M.), dinner from 5:30 P.M.–10 P.M. weekdays and 5:30 P.M.–10:30 P.M. on weekends. Closed Wednesday.
Policies: Reservations are suggested.
Prices: $$. Some credit cards accepted.
Contact: Lew Mar Nel's, 901 Park Ave. (two blocks from Stateline), South Lake Tahoe, CA: 530/542-1072; website: www.stationhouseinn.com/lewmarnels.html.

Mama's Red Tomato

Tucked inside the Best Western Timber Cove Lodge, this charming, cheerfully appointed Italian bistro has plenty of atmosphere and loads of pasta. Designed with Tuscan elements, including Italian tile on the floors and smooth wood-beamed ceilings, the Red Tomato features decorative murals by local artist John Holland, stained glass chandeliers, and old-fashioned posters. It also has a small, intimate feeling, and you almost expect to see a rotund and smiling "Mama" appear from the kitchen, her apron stained with tomato sauce. House specialities include ricotta-

and spinach-stuffed ravioli, *capellini* scallops, pizzas, steaks, chicken, and charbroiled fresh fish. There is often live (and mellow) jazz on weekend evenings. It's behind the Bijou Center and Safeway Plaza, south of Stateline.
Hours: Breakfast 7 A.M.–11 A.M., dinner 5 P.M.–10 P.M. daily.
Prices: $–$$. Major credit cards are accepted.
Contact: Mama's Red Tomato, 3411 Lake Tahoe Blvd. (Timber Cove Lodge), South Lake Tahoe, CA; 530/541-7239.

Mandarin Garden

Near the intersection of Highway 50 and Highway 89 (known as the "Y"), this Chinese restaurant serves typical dishes such as lemon chicken, sweet and sour pork, broccoli beef and shrimp with snow peas, along with chef's specials such as tea-smoked duckling, triple mushroom beef, shrimp and scallops in a spicy Sichuan sauce, and bird's-nest chicken. Family dinners for two are the best price. The restaurant offers low-fat meals with no MSG.
Hours: From 11 A.M. for lunch and dinner daily.
Prices: $–$$.
Contact: Mandarin Garden, 2502 Lake Tahoe Blvd., South Lake Tahoe, CA; 530/544-8885.

McP's Irish Pub and Grill

Close to the Stateline casinos, this place offers corned beef, mulligan stew, fish-and-chips, burgers, and steaks. With plenty of beer on tap, the pub is a favorite hangout of British visitors who come for the live nightly music. Free parking is available.
Hours: Daily for lunch and dinner.
Prices: $–$$. Major credit cards are accepted.
Contact: McP's Irish Pub and Grill, 4090 Lake Tahoe Blvd., South Lake Tahoe, CA; 530/542-4435.

Marie Callender's Restaurant and Bakery

When you've got a craving for cherry or Key lime pie, this is the place to go. This franchise restaurant also has a diverse menu of burgers, sandwiches, pastas, salads, and dinner plates. Signature evening dishes include baked French onion soup, Cobb salad, chicken pot pie, home-style pot roast, fish-and-chips, and baked meatloaf. What gets your attention, though, is the huge selection (usually around 20) of freshly made pies, which you can order by the slice or take home the entire thing.

Hours: Daily for breakfast, lunch and dinner, A.M.–9:30 P.M.

Prices: $–$$. Major credit cards are accepted.

Contact: Marie Callender's Restaurant and Bakery, 3601 Lake Tahoe Blvd., South Lake Tahoe, CA; 530/544-5535.

Meyers Downtown Cafe

This locals' favorite is a popular spot for hikers and skiers heading up Echo Summit on U.S. 50 from South Lake Tahoe. Breakfast consists of eggs Benedict, breakfast burritos, Dave's huevos rancheros, Godfather eggs (with Italian sausage), macadamia nut pancakes, and waffles. Lunch includes a variety of salads and sandwiches. In summer, the patio will accommodate additional patrons.

Hours: Daily 6 A.M.–2 P.M.

Prices: $.

Contact: Meyers Downtown Cafe, 3200 U.S. 50, South Lake Tahoe, CA; 530/573-0228.

Mulligan's Irish Pub and Restaurant

An increase in skiers and summer visitors from the United Kingdom has made Mulligan's the pub hangout of choice for anything Irish. There's as much blarney served in the bar as there is corned beef and cabbage served in the dining room. And the late-night hours (until midnight weekdays and 2 A.M. weekends) allow for plenty of beer-drinking and conviviality. With a rustic Irish charm, a large fireplace, and white tablecloth-covered tables, dinners clearly have an Old World ambience, giving U.K. travellers a touch of home. Hearty appetites are rewarded with a 14-ounce aged rib-eye steak (served with garlic mashed potatoes), lamb shanks braised in red wine, and herb-crusted Chilean sea bass (breaded with Japanese bread crumbs, Dijon mustard, horseradish, and a cilantro pesto). The pub menu has just the right accompaniment for ale: homemade cottage pie (with ground beef, onions, carrots, and spices) and homemade Irish stew (lamb with potatoes, onions, celery, carrots, and various spices). In summer, lunch and dinner are served on a patio. It's at the Super 8 Motel, one mile west of the Stateline casinos.

Hours: Dinner from 5 P.M. daily, lunch from 11 A.M. Sat. and Sun., pub 4 P.M.–midnight weekdays, 11 A.M.–2 A.M. weekends. Limited menu served from 10 P.M. until 1 A.M.

Prices: $–$$. Major credit cards accepted.

Contact: Mulligan's Irish Pub and Restaurant, 3600 Lake Tahoe Blvd., South Lake Tahoe, CA; 530/542-1095 or toll-free at 866/4-TAHOE-1; email: eiretahoe@aol.com, website: www.mulligansirishpub.com.

The Naked Fish

This outstanding sushi house—one of the best in the mountains—has made a major impact on Japanese cuisine on the South Shore and has rapidly become a popular locals' hangout. It has a casual, nautical décor, with counter seating where you can watch each dish being assembled, as well as separate tables in two dining areas. The menu includes fresh-made sushi and sashimi, much of it California-style and very ornate, as well as teriyaki and tempura dishes, complimented by your choice of sake, beer or wine. Among some of the delectable dishes are these: an appetizer called Adam's Leaf (yellowtail with Dynamite sauce sandwiched between shiso leaves, deep fried and served with Ponzu sauce); the spider roll (tempura soft shell crab, cucumber and avocado); the Aloha roll (asparagus, cucumber, avocado and papaya topped with tuna and macadamia nuts); and the House Roll (tempura shrimp, cucumber and avocado topped with tuna, hamachi and tobiko). The restaurant is located in a small retail and restaurant complex at the intersection of Pioneer Trail and Highway 50, a couple of blocks west of the Stateline casinos. Come early or late, since there is often a wait even for weeknights.

Hours: Dinner and noshing from 5 P.M. daily.

Prices: $.

Contact: The Naked Fish, 3940 Lake Tahoe

TAHOE DINING

Blvd., Unit 3, South Lake Tahoe, CA; 530/541-FISH (530/541-3474).

Needles Restaurant

Situated inside the Tahoe Four Seasons, a condominium-hotel that is across the street from the California entrance to Heavenly ski resort, this restaurant is well off the beaten path but still near Stateline. With rustically elegant decor and subdued lighting, Needles serves dinner favorites such as grilled filet mignon (topped with port wine demi-glace and snow crab béarnaise sauce) and Penne Pacifica (ahi and shrimp served in a roasted sweet red pepper vermouth cream sauce with artichokes and toasted pine nuts). Starters include shrimp bisque, California salad (spinach and arugula tossed with oranges, toasted almonds, and feta cheese), Newfoundland steamed mussels, and pan-seared Maine crab cakes.

Hours: For breakfast, 7 A.M.–noon daily; for dinner, 5 P.M.–9 P.M. Wed.–Sunday.
Prices: $–$$$. Major credit cards are accepted.
Contact: Needles Restaurant (Tahoe Four Seasons), 3901 Saddle Rd., South Lake Tahoe, CA; 530/541-6700.

Nephele's

This rustic place has been around since 1977, and its forte is fresh, creative California cuisine, with daily fish, vegetable, and game specials. Patrons have an informal dining experience here, especially when seated in a small back room that can be a bit claustrophobic. Tahitian-style stuffed prawns, roasted lamb tenderloin, pecan-encrusted free-range chicken breast, eggplant parmesan, and New Zealand baby clams are among the regular entrées. Fresh fish and fresh game entrées might include ahi tuna, baked halibut, broiled swordfish, venison, broiled elk, and wild boar chops.

Hours: Nightly 5 P.M.–10 P.M. The cocktail lounge is open 2 P.M.–2 A.M.
Prices: $$. Major credit cards are accepted.
Contact: Nephele's, 1169 Ski Run Blvd., South Lake Tahoe, CA; 530/544-8130; website: www.nepheles.com.

Passaretti's

This family-style Italian restaurant, which has a loyal following among residents, serves a variety of traditional dishes such as lasagna, manicotti, tortellini, veal parmesan, homemade ravioli, and cannelloni. It has a 22-item soup and salad bar, and if you're not careful you might overindulge before the main course. Specialties include the Giovanni (prawns and chicken-breast strips sautéed with onion, garlic, and bell peppers and tossed with fettuccini in a spicy red sauce) and the Sophia (oil and garlic sauce tossed with fresh tomato, mushrooms, artichoke hearts, feta cheese, and cappellini with choice of grilled chicken or prawns). This is not gourmet dining, and the execution sometimes lapses on the more complicated entrées. But you'll never leave hungry, and the reasonable prices go easy on your pocketbook. The restaurant also has a large wine list, a selection of domestic and imported beers, a homemade dessert selection, low-cal menus, and a children's menu. Passaretti's is a quarter mile south of the "Y" on U.S. 50.

Hours: Breakfast from 8:30 A.M. on Sat. and Sun., lunch from 11 A.M. and dinner 4 P.M.–9:30 P.M. daily.
Policies: Reservations are recommended.
Prices: $–$$. Major credit cards are accepted.
Contact: Passaretti's, 1181 Emerald Bay Rd., South Lake Tahoe, CA; 530/541-3433.

Red Hut

Want to know where the locals eat breakfast? If so, go to the Red Hut on Kingsbury Grade, on the Nevada side, where tourists seldom venture. Ironically, the locals seem to shun the more visible location, the Red Hut Waffle Shop, on Highway 50, which is always packed with out-of-towners. It doesn't matter. At either place, you'll have a feast. Breakfast and lunch menus feature strawberry-banana waffles and pancakes; spinach and cheese omelets; and Bad Burgers, with avocado, bacon, and cheese.

Hours: Daily 6 A.M.–2 P.M.
Prices: $.
Contact: Red Hut, 2723 Lake Tahoe Blvd., South Lake Tahoe, CA; 530/541-9024. Or

229 Kingsbury Grade, Kingsbury, NV; 775/588-7488.

Riva Grill

The location is stellar—in the new Marina Village shopping complex at the end of Ski Run, with a waterfront view of the lake, the paddlewheel steamer *Tahoe Queen,* and the surrounding mountains. This is the twin brother of Gar Woods Grill and Pier on the North Shore, with the same ownership, the same type of menu, and the same lively atmosphere. It's a large, two-story building, with a spacious bar and a nautical, woodsy motif throughout the interior. Seating is on two levels, though private banquets often consume the second floor. Entrées include daily specials and fresh seafood, along with filet mignon, lamb loin, shellfish such as scampi, roasted or blackened prime rib, and rosemary chicken. Starters include crab cakes, peel-and-eat prawns, Caesar salad, and shrimp and lobster bisque. House-made desserts are often Gar Woods favorites, such as the Godiva silk torte with a pistachio crust and lemon drop cheese-cake. Most residents give Riva Grill a thumbs-up, though they note inconsistencies in quality and service, as well as higher-than-average prices for what is a middle-of-the-road casual dining experience. Helping to generate the crowds are the restaurant's prime vantage point at the marina and its proximity to Heavenly ski resort just up the road.

Hours: From 11 A.M., with lunch and dinner Mon.–Sat., and brunch and dinner on Sunday.
Prices: $–$$. Major credit cards are accepted.
Contact: Riva Grill, 900 Ski Run Blvd., South Lake Tahoe, CA; 530/542-2600; website: www.rivagrill.com.

Rojo's

Boasting a rustic, Old Tahoe atmosphere, this restaurant is known for its friendly service and reasonably priced entrées, as well as regular live entertainment. The menu features fettuccine Mediterranean, baby-back pork ribs, steak Sicilian, and Alaskan king crab. A full bar, appetizers, and a children's menu are available. Live music and dancing are held most nights in the downstairs cabaret. Rojo's is at U.S. 50 and San Francisco Avenue.

Hours: Lunch and dinner daily from 11:30 A.M.–10 P.M.
Prices: $–$$. Major credit cards are accepted.
Contact: Rojo's, 3091 Harrison Ave., South Lake Tahoe, CA; 530/541-4960.

Samurai Japanese Restaurant

Kimono-clad servers present authentic Japanese cuisine to diners seated at tables or on tatami mats. Don't expect the kind of fresh sushi and sashimi that you can get in San Francisco, though; after all, you are in the mountains. Another drawback is that service can be slow. The menu includes sushi, teriyaki chicken, sukiyaki, yakitori, and tempura. Sake, beer, and wine are available. For traditional Japanese dining, ask for the tatami room.

Hours: Daily 5 P.M.–10 P.M.
Policies: Reservations are suggested.
Prices: $–$$. Major credit cards are accepted.
Contact: Samurai Japanese Restaurant, 2588

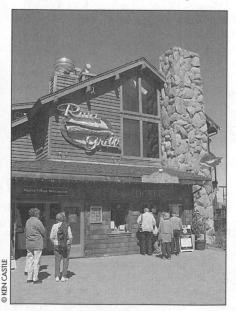

© KEN CASTLE

Riva Grill, South Shore

U.S. 50, South Lake Tahoe, CA; 530/542-0300; website: www.sushitahoe.com.

Sato Japanese Restaurant

Sato Japanese Restaurant serves decent, if not inspiring, sushi, shrimp Katsu, beef teriyaki, and seafood tempura. You'll get the best sushi by sitting at the counter, bantering with the owner over what's just arrived, and letting him make the selections for you.

Hours: Daily for lunch from 11:30 A.M.–2:30 P.M. and dinner 5 P.M.–10 P.M.
Policies: Reservations are accepted.
Prices: $–$$. Major credit cards are accepted.
Contact: Sato Japanese Restaurant, 3436 U.S. 50, South Lake Tahoe, CA; 530/541-3769.

Scusa!

One of the South Shore's best-loved Italian restaurants is Scusa!, where the house specialty is fresh pasta. The atmosphere is casual, the decor is simple, and the service is usually good. Among the menu items are smoked chicken and ravioli, oven-roasted eggplant parmesan, seafood fettuccini, seared sea scallops Mediterranean (with artichoke hearts, button mushrooms, sun-dried tomatoes, and capers), veal Scusa (scallopini of veal with capers, mushrooms, and marsala wine sauce), Greek salad, cream of roasted garlic soup, and garlic bread with melted mozzarella.

Hours: Daily 5 P.M.–10 P.M.
Policies: Reservations are recommended.
Prices: $–$$. Some credit cards are accepted, but no checks are allowed.
Contact: Scusa!, 1142 Ski Run Blvd., South Lake Tahoe, CA; 530/542-0100.

Siam Restaurant

This is the only Thai restaurant at Lake Tahoe, and it has the obligatory long menu with dishes indicated by number. Thai food is spicy and flavorful, with liberal use of curry, chili paste, peanut sauce, lemon, garlic, ginger, coconut milk, and peppers. Among Siam's house specials are Mongolian beef served over crispy noodles, ginger chicken, curried duck, and New Zealand green mussels in a chili basil sauce. Starters include chicken or beef saté, *nam sood* (ground pork or

chicken mixed with ginger, onion, chile, and peanuts in a spicy lime juice), *yum nua* (beef salad with a hot spicy lemon juice), and *tom yum koong* (hot and sour shrimp soup with mushrooms, lemon grass, and lime juice). Here is a sampling of the 50-odd à la carte entrées: *phad kaproa* (hot and spicy meat or shrimp stir-fried with green chiles, garlic, onions, and sweet basil leaves), *phad thai* noodles (a house special with a mixture of shrimp, chicken, eggs, bean sprouts, and peanuts), *mussamun* (tender beef in coconut milk and mild red curry with potatoes and onions), and Gulf of Siam (a stew of shrimp, fish, crab, scallops, squid, and mussels sautéed with ginger, cashews, and a spicy sauce). Apart from ordering à la carte, you can also get combination plates that serve two people, and most dishes can be made vegetarian. Beverages include Thai iced coffee and Thai tea, and desserts consist of fried banana, coconut ice cream, and Thai coconut custard. It's on Highway 50 between the "Y" and Tahoe Keys Boulevard.

Hours: Open Mon.–Fri. 11 A.M.–9 P.M., noon–9 P.M. Sat. and Sunday.
Prices: $–$$. Major credit cards are accepted.
Contact: Siam Restaurant, 2180 Lake Tahoe Blvd., South Lake Tahoe, CA; 530/544-0370.

Sizzler

The all-you-can-eat salad bar is the main attraction at this popular chain restaurant, along with inexpensive entrées of steak, chicken, and seafood. Sizzler serves three meals a day, including breakfast.

Hours: Daily for lunch 11 A.M.–4 P.M., and dinner 4 P.M.–9 P.M., Sun. brunch 10 A.M.–2 P.M.
Prices: $. Major credit cards and traveler's checks are accepted.
Contact: Sizzler, 4022 Lake Tahoe Blvd., South Lake Tahoe, CA; 530/541-8039.

Sprouts Natural Foods Café

This is one of the busiest places in South Shore, where local athletes—skiers, mountain bikers, climbers, and runners—find inspiration and sustenance. They come for fresh-squeezed fruit and vegetable juices, fruit smoothies, homemade fat-free soups, large sandwiches on crunchy rolls, big burritos, homemade lasagna, tempeh burgers, nachos, salads, and the house specialty, the Tahoe Turkey sandwich. Breakfasts include plenty of muffins, juices, and other healthy selections. If you're heading out for a hike or a picnic, this is one of the best stops in the area.

Hours: 8 A.M.–10 P.M. daily.
Prices: $.
Contact: Sprouts Natural Foods Café, Hwy. 50 and Alameda Ave., South Lake Tahoe, CA; 530/541-6969.

Swiss Chalet

You'll think that you've stepped into Europe when you enter Kurt and Ruth Baumann's ornately appointed restaurant, which oozes Old-World charm and has been a fixture of Tahoe since 1957. Don't be surprised to hear plenty of German voices, because this is where the German-speaking tourists hang out. The requisite Swiss clocks, cowbells, alpenhorns, and other decorations festoon the walls. As is typical of Swiss cooking, everything is heavily salted, including soups and sauces. Veal dishes feature the house special, a *cordon bleu,* which is both crusty and tender, and other menu items include cheese fondue, curry stroganoff, German sauerbraten, Wiener schnitzel, a giant T-bone steak, fillet of sole, Columbia River salmon, and other fresh seafood of the day. The house-made pastries are spectacular and heavily loaded with chocolate. Try the chocolate cheesecake for a jolt to your system. Swiss Chalet is four miles west of Stateline on U.S. 50.

Hours: Daily (except Mon.) from 5 P.M. The bar is open from 4 P.M.
Policies: Smoking is not allowed.
Prices: $$–$$$. Major credit cards are accepted.
Contact: Swiss Chalet, 2544 Lake Tahoe Blvd., South Lake Tahoe, CA; 530/544-3304.

Tep's Villa Roma

Tep's is a moderately priced Italian and seafood restaurant with an extensive menu that includes veal saltimbocca, scampi, calamari, fettuccine Alfredo, veal scallopini, chicken cacciatore, seafood marinara, and lobster tails. All entrées

come with trips to the all-you-can-eat antipasto bar, including soup and salad. Daily blackboard specials are available, as is full cocktail service.
Hours: Daily 5 P.M.–10:30 P.M.
Policies: No smoking is allowed in the dining room.
Prices: $–$$. Major credit cards are accepted.
Contact: Tep's Villa Roma, 3450 U.S. 50, South Lake Tahoe, CA; 530/541-8227; website: www.tepsvillaroma.com.

KIRKWOOD/HOPE VALLEY/ MARKLEEVILLE

Alpine Restaurant and Cutthroat Saloon

Near Grover Hot Springs on Main and Montgomery in Markleeville, this rustic place with a rowdy bar in front and the dining room in back serves breakfast, lunch, and dinner, with specials that can be quite good.
Hours: Daily 8 A.M.–11 P.M. weekdays, with the bar open until 2 A.M. on weekends.
Prices: $–$$.
Contact: Alpine Restaurant and Cutthroat Saloon, Hwy. 89 and Montgomery St., Markleeville, CA; 530/694-2150.

Caples Lake Resort

One of the best places to eat in the Tahoe region, this restaurant is in a rustic, weathered lodge overlooking Caples Lake, and it has fabulous views, a fitting complement to the creative gourmet meals. Breakfast is served daily and dinner is served nightly except Tuesday. Featured menu items include New York steak, charbroiled chicken, scampi, fettuccine Alfredo, the fresh catch of the day from Caples Lake, and vegetable casserole. Be sure to check out weekend specials such as grilled salmon, pan-seared halibut with raspberry dill vinaigrette, and grilled lamb chops. Starters include tomato bisque soup and Caesar salad, and the desserts (made fresh each day) include creative fruit pastries. Children's menu items are available.
Hours: Daily for breakfast from 7:30 A.M., and dinner (except Tues.) from 5 P.M. Caples Lake is a 35-minute drive from South Lake Tahoe and

is on Highway 88 one mile east of the Kirkwood ski resort.
Prices: $$–$$$.
Contact: Caples Lakes Resort, Hwy. 88, Kirkwood, CA; 209/258-8888.

Kirkwood Inn

This historic building offers plenty of character, as well as food that sticks to your ribs. The menu features barbecued beef ribs, Zack's fries (named after Zackary Kirkwood), chicken quesadilla, barbecued chicken sandwiches, and prime rib. Among the favorites for drinkers and nibblers are the nachos, a huge plate of blue and yellow chips smothered with beans, cheese, tomato, sour cream, and guacamole. Breakfast includes cinnamon French toast with apple butter; a skillet scramble with eggs, sausage, onions, peppers, tomatoes, and Jack cheese; and a house special omelet that comes with spicy chicken, mild green chili, and cheddar cheese. Nightly dinner specials and a full bar are available. In summer, there is seating on the patio. Come prepared for a leisurely meal, since service is typically slow. Kirkwood Inn is on Highway 88, a quarter mile east of the Kirkwood ski resort exit.
Hours: Open Mon.–Thurs. from 6:30 A.M.–9 P.M. and Sat. and Sun. from 6:30 A.M.–10 P.M. The bar is open until 11 P.M.
Policies: No smoking is allowed.
Prices: $. Major credit cards are accepted.
Contact: Kirkwood Inn, Hwy. 88, Kirkwood, CA; 209/258-7304; website: www.skikirkwood.com.

Kit Carson Lodge Restaurant

You'll find peekaboo views of Silver Lake at this rustic lodge in a woodsy setting. The menu features Nouveau California and French cuisine, such as rack of lamb, scampi, steaks, and fresh seafood. The lodge offers a continental breakfast buffet daily, a Sunday champagne brunch, and children's portions (children 12 and under eat for half price). Kit Carson Lodge Restaurant is on Highway 88 at Silver Lake, west of Kirkwood.
Hours: Breakfast buffet daily 8 A.M.–10 A.M., dinner 6 P.M.–9 P.M. Tues.–Sat., and Sun. brunch

from 10:30 A.M.–1:30 P.M. The restaurant is open mid-June–late September.
Policies: Reservations are recommended.
Prices: $$.
Contact: Kit Carson Lodge Restaurant, Hwy. 88 on Silver Lake; Kit Carson, CA; 209/258-8500 (summer) or 209/245-4760 (winter); website: www.kitcarsonlodge.com.

"Off the Wall" Bar and Grill

In the new village at Kirkwood Mountain Resort, this dinner house is open Friday and Saturday nights only, but the menu is quite varied and has a gourmet flair. Among the entrées are tournedos of beef (served on a pool of blackberry béarnaise sauce with a light mushroom demi-glace), peppered apricot lamb, duck empanadas (puff pastry squares stuffed with minced duck, wild mushrooms, golden raisins, and kalamata olives), and sesame-encrusted ahi tuna (served over rice noodles with mixed Asian vegatables). Starters include chipotle shrimp with corncakes, grilled calamari, artichoke and spinach dip, gazpacho soup, and Caesar salad. There's a cocktail lounge with full selection of drinks in the restaurant.
Hours: Dinner Fri. and Sat. only, from 5 P.M. Usually closed in May.
Policies: Reservations are recommended.
Prices: $$–$$$.
Contact: "Off the Wall" Bar and Grill, Hwy. 88 at Kirkwood, CA; 209/258-7365; website: www.skikirkwood.com.

Plasse's Thunder Mountain Restaurant

Under new ownership after decades of operation by the pioneering Plasse family, this summer-only restaurant has a new look as well, with more upscale interior decor and tablecloths. For campers who are ready for someone else to cook, or for those staying in the rustic cabins and inns along Highway 88, this is a good respite. Gone is the signature chicken-fried steak with two kinds of gravies (yeah, a throwback to less cholesterol-worrisome times). Now on the dinner menu are entrées such as Café D'Paris Steak, charbroiled New York steak with roasted garlic zinfandel sauce, grilled pork chops, grilled calamari steak, and grilled salmon. Weekday evenings usually have special themes, with a Mexican buffet on Monday, pizza on Tuesday, and an Italian buffet on Wednesday.

Breakfast and lunch are served Friday and Saturday, with brunch on Sunday. Omelets, Cobb and Caesar salads, burgers, and club sandwiches are on the daytime menus. One thing that's a holdover from the previous ownership is an old saddle on the wall, one that is reputed to have belonged to famous Western scout Kit Carson. The adjacent bar, rustic enough to look like a cowboy hangout (and often it is), is open from 4 P.M. weekdays and from 10 A.M. Friday–Sunday. The restaurant is at Plasse's Resort, at Silver Lake off Highway 88.

Hours: Open in summer only. Breakfast from 7 A.M. until 10:30 A.M. on Fri. and Sat., champagne brunch on Sun. 9 A.M.–1 P.M., dinner Mon.–Sat. from 5 P.M., and a barbecue Sun. 1 P.M.–8 P.M.

Prices: $–$$. Some credit cards are accepted.

Contact: Plasse's Thunder Mountain Restaurant, 30001 Plasse Rd., Silver Lake, CA; 209/258-8814; website: www.plasses-resort.com.

Sorensen's Resort

This vintage resort in Hope Valley serves hearty and creative western California cuisine, such as Caribbean stew, grilled salmon with caper sauce, New York steak, barbecued chicken, and pasta pesto linguine with clam sauce. Beer and wine are available.

Hours: Breakfast and lunch daily from 7:30 A.M.– 4 P.M. and dinner from 5:30 P.M.–8:30 P.M.

Policies: Reservations are advised.

Prices: $–$$. Personal checks and some credit cards are accepted.

Contact: Sorensen's Resort, 14255 Hwy. 88, Hope Valley, CA; 530/694-2203 or 800/423-9949.

Villa Gigli

What may be the most sought-after Italian restaurant in the region is also the hardest to get into, thanks to articles in *Gourmet* magazine and major metropolitan newspapers. That's because chef Ruggero Gigli and his wife, Gina, have no desire

to expand their small restaurant operation beyond three nights days a week—on Friday, Saturday, and Sunday. Nearly as many people get turned away as can be seated at this eclectic dinner house, which showcases Gina's many artworks with Ruggero's artistry in the kitchen. In remote and sleepy Markleeville, on the road to Grover Hot Springs State Park, the Gigli compound consists of the restaurant/gallery, the couple's home, and a guest cottage. Villa Gigli has far surpassed its status as an underground discovery in the countryside; it is a flat-out sensation. High-rollers from Tahoe arrive in stretch limousines. San Francisco Bay Area gourmands plan their trips to Tahoe around an evening at the Villa Gigli. Visitors flying into Reno from around the country have heard the buzz and they, too, make the pilgrimage to Markleeville. So what's all the fuss about? Just this: Ruggero, who is from Florence in the heart of Italy's Tuscany region, produces homemade pastas and home-baked bread that may be the food of the gods. He scours the countryside for the freshest vegetables, making trips to Monterey to pick up items here and there, and choosing from local gardens. He frequently tinkers with the menu, which never has more than four entrées, and he spends most of his day preparing everything from scratch, including the pasta and sauces. Behold his cannelloni with cream sauce, which is hardly a simple dish. Ruggero's version has five cheeses and five vegetables rolled into his trademark pasta. Then there's the *pastasciutta*, which consists of thin slices of marinated and grilled New York steak on top of a bed of pasta that is smothered in a sauce derived from 10 vegetables. Typically, the menu includes two vegetarian and two meat, poultry, or seafood dishes. All of them are oven-baked, largely out of necessity from the constraints of a small kitchen and the need to do advance preparation. Meals can be accompanied (everything is à la carte) by soup in the winter, or by mixed salad in the spring and summer. You can embellish your meal with the house red or white wine, or one of a dozen mostly California wines priced $20–70. Desserts also reflect the Gigli talents and can include homemade spumoni ice cream, pecan tarts, or special cakes. The restaurant seats just 24 guests inside, and there is only one sitting. But in summer a spacious outdoor deck can easily double that number. Unique touches include red bandana napkins and leather placemats. On Sunday, the meal is a set menu and is served family-style, on long tables, and sometimes is accompanied by live music. To be assured of a table, try the fall or winter months, and always make reservations.

Hours: From 6:30 P.M. until closing on Sat. and Sun. only. Open year-round except for Nov. and December.

Prices: $$. A bottle of wine can raise the tab significantly.

Contact: Villa Gigli, 145 Hot Springs Rd., Markleeville, CA; 530/694-2253.

FEATHER RIVER COUNTRY/ LAKES BASIN

Café Mohawk

Formerly the Mohawk Deli, this place is now a full-scale restaurant that serves breakfast and lunch, a welcome addition to the tiny hamlet of Blairsden. Morning entrées feature six different omelets, including the Fowl Play (with smoked turkey, fresh spinach, and portabella, topped with hollandaise and chives), eggs Benedict, breakfast scramble, French toast, and pancakes. Lunch includes the Signature Sandwich (Cajun or grilled chicken breast with lettuce, tomato, red onion, bacon, Swiss cheese, and cucumber dill dressing on a kaiser roll), tuna melt, Reuben, BLT, patty melt, knockwurst and sauerkraut, smoked ribs, and three types of pizza.

Hours: From 7:30 A.M.–11:30 A.M. for breakfast, and from 11:30 A.M.–3 P.M. for lunch, daily except Tuesday.

Prices: $.

Contact: Café Mohawk,1228 Johnsville Rd., Blairsden, CA; 530/836-0901.

Coyote Bar and Grill (at River Pines Resort)

This is a popular place for residents and visitors alike. It offers Southwestern-flavored cuisine in a kind of Tex-Mex environment with old saddles, branding irons, lariats and, of course, plenty of coyote statues. There are 30 different tequilas, and fresh-fruit margaritas are available during the season. The hungry-man entrée is a whopping 26-ounce porterhouse steak, which you can have traditionally grilled or topped with fire-roasted garlic or Spanish sherry sauce (made from 25-year-old dry sherry). That dish comes with a shot of tequila to help you finish. For lighter appetites, there are large salads, prawns, fresh blackened salmon, calamari steak, tequila lime chicken, and chicken Santa Fe (skinless chicken breast served with avocado, salsa, and cheese). Pork dishes include baby-back ribs with special seasoning and barbecue sauce, and something called Mexican Milanesa (pork steaks taken from the shoulder that are breaded and topped with fresh mushroom sauce). You can also order enchiladas, tacos, and tostadas, with your choice of seafood, chicken, or beef fillings. All meals come with soup or salad, homemade tortilla chips, salsa, Cowboy Caviar (a house special bean dip), rice, and beans. The dessert menu includes coconut ice cream with shaved Mexican chocolate, topped with crème de cacao. If tequila isn't your thing, there's a respectable wine list, along with beer and cocktails. This is a small place, with only 48 seats in the dining room, and reservations are strongly advised for the peak summer season.

Hours: 5 P.M.–9 P.M. for dinner. Full bar opens at 3 P.M. seven days a week. The restaurant is closed Mon. and Jan.–February.

Prices: $$–$$$.

Contact: Coyote Bar and Grill, 8296 Hwy. 89, Blairsden, CA; 530/836-2002.

Feather River Inn

This elegant and historic lodge—comparable to the Ahwahnee Hotel in Yosemite—is worth visiting for the Wednesday and Friday night dinners, which, as this edition went to press, involved buffets. Sunday brunch, once a major happening, is now limited only to holidays and special occasions. With brunch, guests can sit inside in the dining room or outside on big verandas. The menu usually features omelets, a waffle bar, a California fresh fruit station, quiche, juice and dessert bars, champagne, coffee, and tea. Otherwise, the Wednesday dinner is all-you-can-eat fried chicken, and Friday is all-you-can eat prime rib. Policies and operations change frequently, so call ahead first before visiting. The inn is managed by the alumni association of the University of the Pacific (UOP).

Hours: Dinners on Wed. and Fri. 5:30 P.M.–8:30 P.M., April–December.
Policies: Reservations are recommended.
Prices: $–$$.
Contact: Feather River Inn, 65899 Hwy. 70, Blairsden, CA; 530/836-2623.

Gold Lake Lodge

Situated in the heart of the Lakes Basin, the rustic but popular Gold Lake Lodge serves American cuisine, including prime rib, seafood, and pasta.
Hours: Daily for breakfast from 8:30 A.M.–10 A.M. and dinner from 5:30 P.M.–7:30 P.M. The lodge is closed Oct.–mid-June.
Policies: Reservations are required. Smoking is not allowed.
Prices: $–$$.
Contact: Gold Lake Lodge, 7 Gold Lake Rd., Graeagle, CA; 530/836-2350.

Graeagle Meadows Clubhouse

You'll find above-average breakfasts here, geared to get the engines running for early morning duffers. Menu items include American and Mexican selections, such as the Greenskeeper omelet, chicken nachos supreme, and grilled turkey sandwiches. A full bar features mild or wild Bloody Marys. The restaurant is closed December–March.
Hours: Daily breakfast and lunch 7 A.M.–3 P.M. April–November.
Prices: $.
Contact: Graeagle Meadows Clubhouse, Hwy. 89, Graeagle, CA; 530/836-2348.

Firewoods Restaurant at Gray Eagle Lodge

With a large local following and strong repeat business, this woodsy but modern retreat is known for its gourmet meals and intimate dining experience. The interior of this log building is quite impressive, with its spacious gathering room, big rock fireplace, full-service bar, and recreation area. The restaurant features innovative

cuisine for both breakfast and dinner, and the evening menu usually includes rainbow trout, broiled tri-tip with roasted red pepper butter, barbecued baby-back pork ribs, marinated half chicken, and pasta of the day. One featured special each night might add grilled salmon with tropical salsa, grilled rib-eye steak with shallot sauce, braised lamb shanks, pan-roasted duck breast, and Cornish game hen. Breakfast offers a chef's daily special, as well as eggs, fruit, cereals, and homemade breads and pastries. A children's menu is also available, and there's an extensive wine list along with gourmet coffees. Early-bird specials are available 5 P.M.–6 P.M.
Hours: From 7:30 A.M.–9 A.M. for breakfast, and 5 P.M.–8:15 P.M. for dinner. The lodge is open May–October. Reservations are required.
Prices: $$.
Contact: Gray Eagle Lodge, 5000 Gold Lake Rd., Graeagle, CA; 530/836-2511 or 800/635-8778.

Grizzly Grill

From locals to visitors, almost everybody agrees that this is one of the best gourmet restaurants in Plumas County. In the hamlet of Blairsden, among several golf courses, this dinner house has a delectable and creative menu that includes grilled Norwegian salmon, shrimp provençal, boneless breast of chicken (with prosciutto, mushrooms, artichoke hearts, and Asiago cheese), braised lamb shank, Tuscan-style pork ribs, fettuccine with smoked chicken, and a daily fresh seafood entrée. With salads and pastas, both small and large portions are offered, and there are nightly specials and desserts. A full bar is available, with a large list of fine wines.
Hours: Daily from 5:30 P.M.–9 P.M. year-around.
Policies: Reservations are highly recommended.
Prices: $$. Some credit cards are accepted.
Contact: Grizzly Grill, 250 Bonta St., Blairsden, CA; 530/836-1300.

Iron Door

The rustic and delightful interior—almost resembling a museum—is a warm place to enjoy one of the best meals in the Sierra. The building once housed a general store and post office for the town of Johnsville, which was founded in 1876 during the development of the Plumas Eureka gold mine. This restaurant has been around since 1961 and is the only business in what is now Plumas Eureka State Park. The place is rich in antiquity, including the bar with its old tintype photographs of the mining days. There are big, open-beamed ceilings in the main dining room and an adjoining greenhouse-style room next to the road. Among the menu entrées are New York steak, pepper steak Diablo (steak with crushed black peppercorns and mushrooms, topped with a brandy cream sauce), prime rib, chicken Bangalore (chicken breasts in a spicy curry sauce), Thai shrimp, fresh halibut and salmon fillets, pastas that include Cajun Jambalaya (pasta tossed with shrimp, chicken, and chorizo in a spicy Cajun sauce), and German dishes such as Wiener schnitzel and Jaeger schnitzel. There's a museum, of sorts, upstairs.

Hours: Nightly from 5 P.M. April–October. Closed on Tuesday.

Policies: Reservations are suggested; make them several days in advance for a weekend meal during the summer. Smoking is only allowed at the bar.

Prices: $$–$$$. Some credit cards are accepted.

Contact: Iron Door, 5417 Main St., Johnsville, CA; 530/836-2376.

The Lodge at Whitehawk Ranch

This delightful and upscale bed-and-breakfast inn, next to a scenic 18-hole golf course, has one of the area's newest restaurants. Inside a grand lodge building, with a rustically elegant mountain motif, the dinner house features a half-dozen entrées, either grilled or sautéed. They include New York sirloin steak, charbroiled Scottish salmon and blue fin tuna flown in fresh, filet mignon, pecan-crusted chicken, bourbon-braised game hen, linguini and prawns, and mixed vegetable penne pasta. When they are available, the chef uses locally grown organic vegetables. Dinners come with a petite salad or bowl of soup. Also, you can supplement your meal with appetizers such as antipasto with baked Brie, blackened chicken salad, fried calamari, marinated and grilled artichokes, crispy polenta cakes and

prawns, and baby spinach salad. There's a small but well-selected wine list, with most bottles reasonably priced and a half-dozen vintages available by the glass.

Hours: Lunch from 11:30 A.M., dinner 5 P.M.–9 P.M. daily except Tues., when the restaurant is closed. The cocktail lounge opens at 11:30 A.M.

Policies: Reservations are suggested.

Prices: $$–$$$. Credit cards are accepted.

Contact: The Lodge at Whitehawk Ranch, 985 Whitehawk Dr., Clio, CA; 530/836-4985.

The Log Cabin

This is quite possibly the most popular dinner house in Portola (well, there aren't many!), and it's a favorite with anglers and golfers who look forward to a hearty meal at the end of the day. This locals' favorite is presided over by owner/chef Wolfgang Heuser, who serves a variety of American and German dishes. The menu offers six different steaks (try pepper steak Napoleon, a New York cut with ground peppercorn and mushroom sauce), prime rib (on weekends), fried chicken, Wiener schnitzel, Jaeger schnitzel, German-style sauerbraten, and veal *cordon bleu*. All meals come with homemade soup in a crock, salad, potato du jour, bread, and coffee or tea. There's also a full bar, and live entertainment is booked occasionally.

Hours: 5 P.M.–9:30 P.M. for dinner. Closed Tuesday.

Prices: $$.

Contact: The Log Cabin, 64 E. Sierra Ave. (Hwy. 70), Portola, CA; 530/832-5243.

Longboards Bar and Grill

Named after miners-turned-skiers of the late 1800s, this recently renovated dinner house at Plumas Pines Golf Resort has a warm, intimate environment with its polished wood floors, linen-covered tables, and inlaid stone walls. Large picture windows overlook the course, which unfolds below the clubhouse, as well as the surrounding mountains, and the interior is festooned with historic photographs of longboard races. Upscale in every way, this place is a true epicurean experience, with an emphasis on presentation and creative sauces. While the menu changes seasonally, it might include grilled elk T-bone steak, roast beef tenderloin with Gorgonzola mashed potatoes, seared rare ahi tuna, grilled marinated rack of lamb with balsamic demi-glace, salmon with leek risotto and grilled shiitake mushrooms, and whole chicken marinated in lemon, garlic, and rosemary and grilled under a brick. Pasta selections include penne *alla bolognese* (veal, pork, and beef sauce), house-made ravioli, linguini and prawns, and house-made Italian sausage. The cocktail lounge is elegant and attractive and serves just about anything you can order.

Hours: Daily for lunch from 11:30 A.M. and dinner 5 P.M.–9 P.M. weekdays and 5 P.M.–10 P.M. weekends.

Policies: Reservations are suggested.

Prices: $$–$$$. Credit cards are accepted.

Contact: Longboards Bar and Grill at Plumas Pines Golf Resort, 402 Poplar Valley Rd., Blairsden, CA; 530/836-1111 or the bar at 530/836-1305.

Mount Tomba Inn Dinner House

A restaurant with plenty of character—mostly in the form of memorabilia related to John Wayne, whose image adorns the walls of the interior along with keepsakes from other Western figures—this inn is named after a mountain in Sicily and has been in operation since the late 1930s. Music from the 1940s plays in the two dining rooms, lending the inn a sense of nostalgia. The house specialty is prawns, served deep-fried in light beer batter, broiled with drawn butter, or sautéed scampi-style in garlic butter, olive oil, lemon, and white wine. There's also a variety of steaks, from top sirloin to filet mignon, and chicken, from marsala to teriyaki. Accompaniments include homemade soup, salad, bread, potato or rice, coffee, and dessert. These are hearty meals for large appetites.

Hours: Dinner Tues.–Sat. 5 P.M.–at least 9 P.M. and from 4 P.M. on Sunday. Closed Monday. Winter hours may vary.

Prices: $$. Some credit cards are accepted.

Contact: Mount Tomba Inn Dinner House, Hwy. 70, Cromberg, CA; 530/836-2359.

Nakoma Resort and Spa at Gold Mountain

Enclosed by a truly inspirational building—one that was designed by famed architect Frank Lloyd Wright to resemble a giant Native American wigwam—this is arguably the most visually stunning restaurant in the entire region. While it doesn't have Lake Tahoe as a backdrop, it does have views of a challenging golf course (The Dragon) and the grandeur of the Feather River Canyon from its perch on a high knoll. Meals are superb in their own right, but it's worth the hour's drive from Tahoe just to be captivated by the architecture: the soaring, tepeelike ceilings, the skylights, and the exposed wood beams and liberal use of rock. Then marvel at the fact that Wright created this design in 1923 but never lived to see it built. Opened in 2001, the Nakoma complex includes the golf pro shop, a spa, four luxury villas, a wedding chapel, separate banquet rooms, and an elegantly appointed cocktail lounge, with an interplay of light and color that is visually arresting. Breakfast, lunch, and

© KEN CASTLE

dining room at Nakoma

TAHOE DINING

dinner each have signature dishes and unique presentations. You can start your day with Pennsylvania Dutch baked apple and buttermilk pancakes, brioche French toast, a variety of omelets, or eggs Benedict. You can accompany these with fresh juices, teas, or organic blend Guatemalan coffee. For lunch, select from dishes such as Cajun popcorn crispy fried crawfish and okra, crab Louis, smoked chicken Waldorf with dried cranberries, pan-seared Sierra trout, or a hefty burger with Vermont cheddar and apple-smoked bacon on a house-made kaiser roll. For dinner, the kitchen pulls out all the stops. Entrées include baked stuffed prawns (with crab and scallops), roast pheasant breast stuffed with wild rice, sesame-encrusted seared ahi tuna, and roast pork chop with apple shallot butter. Note to the ambitious diner: You couldn't possibly eat three meals a day here, even if you survive a round of golf on this extremely challenging course. But the idea is certainly tempting.

Hours: Breakfast 6 A.M.–1 P.M. daily, lunch from 11:30 P.M.–3 P.M. daily, and dinner from 5:30 P.M.–10 P.M. daily.
Policies: Dinner reservations are recommended.
Prices: $–$$$. Credit cards are accepted.
Contact: Nakoma Resort at Gold Mountain, five miles east of Graeagle on County Rd. A-15, Portola, CA; 530/832-4889 or toll-free at 877/416-0880; website: www.nakomaresort.com.

Olsen's Cabin

Set in the trees off the Johnsville Road, this attractive restaurant has an inviting interior and an excellent menu. Complete dinners are served with soup, salad, baked potato or seasoned rice, fresh vegetables, homemade muffins with honey butter, dessert, and coffee or tea. Wine and beer are available. Featured menu items include the Lucky Logger (broiled chopped sirloin, stuffed with green chili and a blend of cheeses), the Captain's Combo (prawns, scallops, and Alaskan king crab), and the Gourmet Special (your choice of any two items such as steak, chicken, pork chop, lamb chop, trout, scallops, or prawns). Other entrées include steaks, chicken teriyaki, pork chops, lamb chops, Eastern scallops, and mountain trout. A child's plate is available on selected

half orders, for children under 12. Olsen's Cabin is on County Road A-14, at Johnsville and Mohawk Roads.
Hours: Open Tues.–Sat. 6 P.M.–10 P.M.
Policies: Reservations are advised.
Prices: $$. Some credit cards are accepted.
Contact: Olsen's Cabin, 589 Johnsville Rd., Graeagle, CA; 530/836-2801.

Packer Lake Lodge

This small restaurant is set in a rustic cabin next to an equally small lake. Nightly specials include New York steak, baby-back pork ribs, and a pasta of the day. The chef will happily cook to order your catch of the day. Sunday brunch includes eggs Benedict, stuffed French toast, buttermilk fruit pancakes, huevos rancheros, champagne, and fresh juices. Packer Lake Lodge is 20 miles southwest of Graeagle, off Gold Lake Road in Sierra City. The lodge is closed in winter.
Hours: Breakfast 8 A.M.–10 A.M., lunch noon–2 P.M., dinner 6 P.M.–8:30 P.M. Wed.–Mon., and brunch 9 A.M.–1 P.M. on Sunday. The lodge is open in summer only.
Policies: Reservations are appreciated.
Prices: $$. Some credit cards are accepted.
Contact: Packer Lake Lodge, Packer Lake Rd. (off Gold Lake Rd.), Sierra City, CA; 530/862-1221.

Sardine Lake Resort

Set on what is surely the most spectacular lake in the Lakes Basin—with a view of the majestic Sierra Buttes to match—this delightful but rustic lodge offers a tiny, woodsy restaurant that serves prime rib, chicken, seafood, New York steak, and lamb chops. All menus include soup, salad, vegetable, a potato, and sourdough bread. A children's plate is available for youngsters under 12. There is also a full bar and a gazebo. Sardine Lake Resort is one mile south of Gold Lake Road.
Hours: There are two dinner seatings daily (except Thurs.), at 6 P.M. and 8 P.M. Closed in winter.
Policies: Reservations are required.
Prices: $$.
Contact: Sardine Lake Resort, 990 Sardine Lake Rd., Graeagle, CA; 530/862-1196 or 530/645-8882.

Nightlife

Throughout every season of the year, Lake Tahoe pulses with the sights and sounds of nightly entertainment, from headline acts at casino showrooms to gritty country-and-western bars in Truckee. The area is a magnet for major performing artists, who play clubs and restaurants as well as several outdoor pavilions, parks, and amphitheaters that come alive in the summertime.

Musicals, magic shows, and Broadway-style productions tend to dominate the main stages at the gaming resorts, simply because they are less expensive to produce and can stay in residence for several weeks or months. Harrah's and Harveys offer these types of shows for the majority of the year. Caesars Tahoe, occasionally joined by Harrah's, is the leader in providing short runs and one-night stands of pop, jazz, and country headliners, although Harveys also books the occasional star performer. For guests of the casino/hotels, a show sometimes is offered as part of an incentive package with the room, especially during off-season midweek stays. In addition to the showrooms, most casinos have more intimate cabarets where small groups play, and these range from awful to very good, depending on how many drinks you've had or how many hands of blackjack you've lost.

One of the delights of vacationing in Tahoe is the opportunity to play all day and party all night. A day in the outdoors combined with a fine dinner and a lively show is a fairly compelling escape. Artists who've appeared in Tahoe recently have included Chris Isaak, Boz Scaggs, Pat Benatar, the Moody Blues, Diana Ross, James Brown, Lou Rawls, Natalie Cole, Ray Charles, Bill Cosby, Tony Bennett, Chicago, Blood, Sweat, and Tears, Santana, Tricia Yearwood, Vince Gill, and Wynonna Judd. The important thing is to reserve or buy tickets in advance, for popular artists are frequently sold out well before show time.

Apart from the headliners, entertainment around the lake is varied and frequent during the summer, varying from lilting jazz concerts on the patio of the River Ranch Lodge to full presentations by symphonies at the Topol Pavilion, both on the North Shore. The Tallac Historic Site on the South Shore stages regular open-air concerts throughout the summer, featuring jazz, folk, classical, and New Age music. Other concert venues include ski areas (both Heavenly and Squaw Valley have hosted big-name entertainment), Granlibakken Resort, Truckee Regional Park's Gebhardt Amphitheater, and Lake Tahoe-Nevada State Park. The annual Shakespeare at Sand Harbor Festival is held in August and September at Sand Harbor State Park, as are occasional jazz and New Age music concerts. Also, several bars and nightclubs are venues for regular live music. Weekly entertainment publications, available locally for free at hotels and restaurants, provide up-to-date schedules.

> *In addition to the showrooms, most casinos have more intimate cabarets where small groups play, and these range from awful to very good, depending on how many drinks you've had or how many hands of blackjack you've lost.*

NORTH SHORE

Balboa Café

Large restaurant and bar in the new Village at Squaw Valley has an outdoor stage next to a plaza and offers live music in summer.

Contact: PlumpJack Balboa Café, 1995 Squaw Valley Rd., Ste. 14, Olympic Valley, CA; 530/583-5850; website: www.plumpjack.com/balboasv.

Bar of America

The Bar of America provides live bands and dancing on Friday and Saturday nights.

Contact: Bar of America, 10040 Commercial Row, Truckee, CA; 530/587-3110.

Bar One

Occasional live music, especially during ski season.

Contact: Bar One, base of Squaw Valley Ski Resort, Squaw Valley, CA; 530/583-1588.

Best Western Tahoe Truckee Inn

This large motor inn holds acoustic open mike night every Tuesday 6 P.M.–9 P.M. in the Pizza Hut.
Contact: 11331 Hwy. 267, Truckee, CA; 530/587-4525.

Cal-Neva Resort

This major casino/resort has an excellent show venue, the Frank Sinatra Room, where Ol' Blue Eyes himself held sway years ago during his ownership. Most of the time the stage is dark, though there are occasional local productions and touring shows. Music presentations range from blues to symphonies. The resort also offers lounge entertainment and dancing.
Contact: Cal-Neva Resort, 2 Stateline Rd., Crystal Bay, NV; 775/832-4000 or 800/CAL-NEVA (800/225-6382).

Cottonwood

Music and dancing fill Cottonwood on Friday and Saturday nights, with jazz offered occasionally. It's off Highway 267 at Hilltop, overlooking Commercial Row.
Contact: Cottonwood, 10142 Rue Hilltop, Truckee, CA; 530/587-5711.

Gar Woods Grill and Pier

Gar Woods provides music on Friday and Saturday nights.
Contact: Gar Woods Grill and Pier, 5000 N. Lake Blvd., Carnelian Bay, CA; 530/546-3366.

Granlibakken

This resort in Tahoe City offers outdoor concerts during the summer.
Contact: Granlibakken, 725 Granlibakken Rd., Tahoe City, CA; 530/583-4242.

Hacienda de la Sierra

This Mexican restaurant in Incline Village features various bands on the weekends, usually on Friday night.
Contact: Hacienda de la Sierra, 931 Tahoe Blvd., Incline Village, NV; 775/831-8300.

Hacienda del Lago

At Boatworks Mall in Tahoe City, this lakeside Mexican restaurant occasionally features live music.
Contact: Hacienda del Lago, 760 N. Lake Blvd., Tahoe City, CA; 530/583-0358.

Hyatt Regency Lake Tahoe

In Incline Village on the North Shore, this major resort/casino offers occasional concerts such as jazz festivals in the Lakeside Lodge Ballroom. Live entertainment is frequently featured in the new Cutthroat's Saloon.
Contact: Hyatt Regency Lake Tahoe, 111 Country Club Dr., Incline Village, NV; 775/832-1234 or 800/233-1234.

Jim Kelley's Nugget

At Crystal Bay on the North Shore, this small casino sometimes offers concerts during the summer in its outdoor amphitheater. In years past, groups that have performed have included Foghat, country crooner Merle Haggard, blues performer Charlie Musselwhite, and renowned jazz combo Russ Freeman and the Rippingtons.
Contact: Jim Kelley's Nugget, Hwy. 28, Crystal Bay, NV; 775/831-0455.

Moody's Bistro and Lounge

This new restaurant and blues/jazz-style lounge, with a cosmopolitan art deco interior, offers both DJ and live music.
Contact: Moody's Bistro and Lounge, 10007 Bridge St., Truckee (inside The Truckee Hotel), CA; 530/587-8688; website: www.moodys-bistro.com.

O'B's Pub and Restaurant

O'B's is often the site of live music shows on weekends.
Contact: O'B's Pub and Restaurant, 10046 Commercial Row, Truckee, CA; 530/587-4164.

Pastime Club

You'll find various live bands and "open mike" jams here three or four nights a week. The Pastime Club is on Commercial Row in Truckee. **Contact:** Pastime Club, 10096 Donner Pass Rd., Truckee, CA; 530/582-9219.

The Resort at Squaw Creek

Bullwhacker's Pub provides live music one or more nights a week, depending on the season. **Contact:** The Resort at Squaw Creek, 400 Squaw Creek Rd., Olympic Valley, CA; 530/583-6300.

River Ranch Lodge

Big-name jazz groups and other musical entertainers hold forth occasionally in the summer on the grand patio overlooking the Truckee River. River Ranch Lodge is on Highway 89 and Alpine Meadows Road. **Contact:** River Ranch Lodge, 2285 River Rd., Tahoe City, CA; 530/583-4264.

Sierra Vista

This large lakeside restaurant in the Tahoe City Marina Mall often features live music. **Contact:** Sierra Vista, 700 N. Lake Blvd., Tahoe City, CA; 530/583-0233.

Sunnyside Lodge

The Sunnyside Lodge occasionally books musical acts. **Contact:** Sunnyside Lodge, 1850 W. Lake Blvd., Tahoe City, CA; 530/583-7200.

Tahoe Biltmore Lodge and Casino

This venue furnishes live music and dancing in the Aspen Lounge. **Contact:** Tahoe Biltmore Lodge and Casino, 5 Hwy. 28, Crystal Bay, NV; 775/831-0660.

Tahoe Taps

This tavern in Truckee presents live bands Friday and Saturday nights. **Contact:** Tahoe Taps, 10015 Palisades Dr. (off Hwy. 267 behind 7-Eleven and next to Martis Village Theater), Truckee, CA; 530/587-7777.

Tradewinds Bar

This tavern that is part of a Kings Beach motel offers live bands on Friday and Saturday nights. **Contact:** Tradewinds Bar, 8545 N. Lake Blvd., Kings Beach, CA; 530/546-2497.

SOUTH SHORE

The Beacon Restaurant

At Camp Richardson's Resort, the Beacon offers live music and other entertainment on the beach on Wednesday, Saturday, and Sunday. **Contact:** Camp Richardson's Resort, 1900 Jameson Beach Rd., South Lake Tahoe, CA; 530/541-0630.

The Boathouse Bar and Grill

On a pier above the water, this casual hangout at Best Western Timber Cove Lodge offers DJ music Thursday–Saturday nights. **Contact:** The Boathouse Bar and Grill, 3411 Lake Tahoe Blvd., South Lake Tahoe, CA; 530/541-0113.

Caesars Tahoe

The Circus Maximus Showroom offers regular big-name entertainment as well as occasional magic shows. Nero's, a major nightclub with lavish DJ setups, books funk, Motown, and reggae dance bands once or twice a week, with disco dancing available on other nights from 9 P.M. until the wee hours of the morning. There's a cover charge that usually ranges $4–8 per person. Call Nero's 24-hour hot line for entertainment details: 775/586-2000. **Contact:** Caesars Tahoe, 55 U.S. 50, Stateline, NV; 775/588-3515 or 800/648-3353.

The Cantina Bar and Grill

Highly popular (and upscale) Mexican restaurant occasionally offers live music. **Contact:** The Cantina Bar and Grill, 765 Emerald Bay Rd., South Lake Tahoe, CA; 530/544-1233.

Chase's Bar and Grill

This New Orleans–style restaurant, in the terminal

of the South Lake Tahoe Airport, offers music during its "Fat Tuesday Mardi Gras Party."
Contact: Chase's Bar and Grill, 1901 Airport Rd. (off Hwy. 50), South Lake Tahoe, CA; 530/544-9080.

Chevys

This franchise Mexican restaurant offers occasional live music, especially in May during the Cinco de Mayo celebration.
Contact: Chevys, 3678 Lake Tahoe Blvd., South Lake Tahoe, CA; 530/542-1742.

Christiania Inn

Live music, usually jazz, is presented on Friday and Saturday in the lounge. Christiania Inn is across from Heavenly Ski Resort.
Contact: Christiania Inn, 3819 Saddle Rd., South Lake Tahoe, CA; 530/544-7337.

Fresh Ketch

Jazz combos are presented on Friday night at this restaurant, which is at Tahoe Keys Marina.
Contact: Fresh Ketch, 2435 Venice Dr., South Lake Tahoe, CA; 530/541-5683.

Harrah's Casino Hotel

Broadway and Hollywood shows are offered in the South Shore Room, with the occasional name entertainer. There is live music at the Casino Center Stage most nights of the week.
Contact: Harrah's Casino Hotel, U.S. 50, Stateline, NV; 775/588-6606 or 800/HARRAHS (800/427-7247).

Harveys Resort Casino

The Improv at Harveys presents comics Tuesday–Saturday nights. In summer, big-name summer entertainers are presented in an outdoor amphitheater that is set up on the rear parking lot. Hard Rock Café offers live rock bands on weekends. El Vaquero restaurant has open comedy night on Friday and karaoke singing on Saturday night. Harveys is on U.S. 50 at Stateline.
Contact: Harveys Resort Casino, U.S. 50, Stateline, NV; 775/588-2411 or 800/648-3361 (show reservations).

Horizon Casino Resort

Club Z brings in various rock, Latin, funk, and R&B bands several nights a week. The Golden Cabaret Lounge presents variety stage shows with dancing, acrobatics, and adult revues nightly except Monday. Singers hold forth nightly in the Aspen Lounge. In early 2000, this hotel replaced its major showroom with a multiscreen movie theater. Horizon is on U.S. 50 at Stateline.
Contact: Horizon Casino Resort, U.S. 50, Stateline, NV; 775/588-6211.

Hoss Hoggs

Hoss Hoggs supplies live music and entertainment several nights a week during high season. It's on U.S. 50 and Sierra Boulevard.
Contact: Hoss Hoggs, 2543 Lake Tahoe Blvd., South Lake Tahoe, CA; 530/541-8328.

Mama's Red Tomato

This intimate Italian bistro in the Best Western Timber Cove Lodge offers live, mellow jazz Friday and Saturday nights.
Contact: Mama's Red Tomato, 3411 Lake Tahoe Blvd., South Lake Tahoe, CA; 530/541-7239.

The Pub Tahoe (formerly The Island)

This party place, which is one block west of the casinos at Stateline, offers bands on weekends and acoustic nights or solo musicians on weekdays. It's operated by the owners of McP's Irish Pub.
Contact: The Pub Tahoe, 4093 Lake Tahoe Blvd., South Lake Tahoe, CA; 530/542-4435.

Riva Grill

This large, lakeside restaurant with a huge deck overlooking Ski Run Marina offers occasional live music on weekends.
Contact: Riva Grill, 900 Ski Run Blvd., South Lake Tahoe, CA; 530/542-2600; website: www.rivagrill.com.

Rojo's Tavern

Live bands and dancing hold forth in the Downstairs Cabaret on Thursday–Saturday nights. Rojo's is on U.S. 50.

Contact: Rojo's Tavern, 3091 Harrison St., South Lake Tahoe, CA; 530/541-4960.

Strange Brew Cyber Lounge

Live music Thursday–Saturday nights, with open mike on Tuesday.

Contact: Strange Brew Cyber Lounge, 2660 Lake Tahoe Blvd., South Lake Tahoe, CA; 530/542-4169.

The Tudor Pub and Dory's Oar Restaurant

The pub, which is upstairs above this British-style restaurant, features live music on weekends.

Contact: The Tudor Pub, 1041 Fremont Ave. (off Hwy. 50 one mile west of Stateline), South Lake Tahoe, CA; 530/541-6603; website: www.dorysoar.com.

Reno Area Dining and Nightlife

It's difficult to find a bad meal in "The Biggest Little City in the World," where restaurants are an important attraction along with gaming, big-name entertainment, and history. Almost every large casino/hotel boasts at least one top-rated restaurant, and the robust expansion of these properties in recent years has yielded a new crop of dinner houses. Many of these feature elaborate and expensive interiors, with themes varying from intergalactic to European to San Franciscan. It's interesting to note that Reno is getting attention from notable San Francisco restaurateurs and chefs, who are among the consultants and designers of several new dining establishments.

Apart from the casinos, there's a burgeoning group of independently owned restaurants, as well as some ever-popular landmarks. Steak houses and Italian restaurants are more frequent than

Harrah's Plaza, site of outdoor concerts

© KEN CASTLE

tumbleweeds, and you practically can't go wrong choosing any of them. Thankfully, the Reno dining scene is remarkably consistent, whereas even the best Tahoe restaurants sometimes go into a tailspin during the low seasons.

Of course, the presence of a year-round gaming market, frequent conventions, and a booming local population keeps the restaurant business highly competitive in Reno, to the delight of visiting diners.

Food and Drink

RENO/SPARKS

Adele's at the Plaza
Long considered one of Reno's best restaurants, Adele's offers a continental-style menu with fresh, creative ingredients that are used for the weekly specials and gourmet appetizers, as well as regular dishes. Typical of what you might find are filet mignon with Sherriea *cremini* mushrooms and a syrah demi-glace, rack of lamb with a port and sun-dried cherry reduction, Canadian halibut with chardonnay *beurre blanc* sauce accented with grapes and sun-dried cherries, and Australian lobster tails stuffed with prosciutto. The restaurant features a new bistro menu in the lounge, with items such as barbecued prawns, escargot, steamed clams, Cobb salad, crab melt, chicken primavera, and seafood crepe. A selection of creative, homemade desserts tops off any meal here. Other amenities include covered, validated parking, banquet facilities, and lunch and dinner specials. It's in the Bank of America Plaza.
Hours: Lunch and dinner daily; bistro menu served 4 P.M.–midnight.
Policies: Reservations are recommended.
Prices: $$–$$$. Major credit cards are accepted.
Contact: Adele's at the Plaza, 425 S. Virginia St., Reno, NV; 775/333-6503.

Art Gecko's Southwest Grill
With an eclectic decor, large portions, and a piquant, casual menu of burritos, Tex-Mex ribs, and other Southwestern specialties, this recent addition to the Circus Circus Hotel Casino draws its share of patrons from the crowds that browse through the shops and bistros along the skywalks connecting the Silver Legacy and Eldorado Hotels. The menu is clearly a hybrid: from the Cabo Labo lobster quesadilla appetizer to specialties

KEY TO RENO DINING PRICES

$ = under $10
$$ = $10–19
$$$ = $20 and up

such as Baja shrimp and Laughing Coyote fettuccine sauté. There is a seven-salsa sampler that you can use to spice up anything from appetizers to the main course. Desserts are seductive-sounding things such as margarita cheesecake and jalapeño apple pie. This is a big, airy restaurant with lots of ambient noise, plenty of unusual wall and ceiling murals, giant gecko lizards, and sculptures of Kokopelli, the mischievous Native American deity. Art Gecko's works well for a group that's in a festive mood.
Hours: Lunch and dinner daily 11 A.M.–10 P.M.
Prices: $–$$. Major credit cards are accepted.
Contact: Circus Circus Hotel Casino, 500 N. Sierra St., Reno, NV; 775/329-0711; website: www.circusreno.com.

Atlantis Seafood Steakhouse
One of Nevada's great dining establishments, the Atlantis has redefined the concept of tableside preparation, elevating it to an art form. Moreover, the 1,100-gallon aquarium and subdued lighting create an aquatic ambience for an incredible repast. Start with appetizers (everyone does) and don't miss the flaming coconut prawns, presented at your table with a flaming pineapple crown, spiced marmalade, and honey mustard. Another must is the bouquet of onion soup, a creamy soup with five kinds of onions baked in a colossal onion and crowned with Valio Swiss cheese gratiné. The entrées include

fish specialties such as seafood fettuccine, Alaskan halibut fillet, swordfish Mediterranean, and seafood pan roast (Gulf prawns, scallops, clams, and king crab simmered in a creamy wine sauce). Should you not be in the mood for fish, you'll also find beef kabob, New York steak, pepper steak, and double French-cut lamb chops. Maître d' Jan Sanders, a former chef and a restaurateur in his own right, has the magic touch in preparing dishes such as hot spinach salad, dessert crepes, and a host of unannounced specials. One after-dinner liqueur whose creation is worth witnessing is something called Fire in Paradise. Oh, and the service is exceptional. Free 24-hour valet and self-parking is available.

Hours: Nightly 5 P.M.–10 P.M.

Policies: Reservations are recommended.

Prices: $$–$$$. Major credit cards are accepted.

Contact: Atlantis Casino Resort, 3800 S. Virginia St., Reno, NV; 775/825-4700 or 800/723-6500; website: www.atlantiscasino.com.

Baldini's Triple Crown Restaurant

For inexpensive eats, this place has achieved a big reputation with locals. Just ask any cab driver. Includes all-you-can-eat buffet.

Hours: Breakfast 7 A.M.–10 A.M. Mon.–Fri., brunch 7 A.M.–8:30 A.M. Sat. and Sun., lunch 11 A.M.–3 P.M. Mon.–Fri., dinner 4 P.M.–10 P.M. Mon.–Fri. and 3 P.M.–10 P.M. Sat. and Sun., and Sun. champagne brunch 9 A.M.–3 P.M.

Prices: $.

Contact: Baldini's Casino, 865 S. Rock Blvd., Sparks, NV; 775/358-0116.

Benihana Japanese Steakhouse

Part of the chain built by flamboyant entrepreneur Rocky Aoki, this Japanese steak house is in the Golden Phoenix Hotel Casino and Resort (formerly Flamingo Hilton Reno). With counter seats surrounding the grills, the dining experience comes from watching the cooking gymnastics and dexterity of the chefs, who

Atlantis Seafood Steakhouse, winner of *Wine Spectator's* "Award of Excellence"

chop and flip everything from steak to shrimp. It helps if you're part of a group or if you're gregarious enough to sit next to strangers. The mainstays are combination dinners variously mixing hibachi steak, shrimp, chicken, and lobster tails, along with veggies such as mushrooms, onions, and zucchini. Full dinners include Japanese onion soup, a salad with ginger dressing, steamed rice, and green tea. For dessert, try Mandarin cheesecake, the house specialty. Wines, sake, and tropical cocktails are also available. Benihana is on the second floor of the Flamingo Hilton Reno.

Hours: Nightly 5 P.M.–11 P.M.; closed Monday.
Prices: $$–$$$.
Contact: Benihana Japanese Steakhouse, 255 N. Sierra St., Reno, NV; 775/785-7373.

Steak houses and Italian restaurants are more frequent than tumbleweeds, and you practically can't go wrong choosing any of them. Thankfully, the Reno dining scene is remarkably consistent, whereas even the best Tahoe restaurants sometimes go into a tailspin during the low seasons.

Big Top Buffet

One of the best low-cost buffets in town features 15 hot items, carved ham and roast beef, a wide variety of salads, fresh fruits, and desserts including an ice cream bar. Special menus are offered during Friday night's seafood buffet and Saturday night's sirloin and scampi buffet. Oriental, Italian, German, and Mexican specials are featured on various evenings. Validated covered parking is available.

Hours: Breakfast 6 A.M.–11 A.M., lunch 11 A.M.–4 P.M., dinner 4 P.M.–11 P.M., and weekend brunch 6 A.M.–4 P.M.
Prices: $. No credit cards are accepted.
Contact: Circus Circus Hotel Casino, 500 N. Sierra St., Reno, NV; 775/329-0711 or 800/648-5010; website: www.circusreno.com.

The Brew Brothers

The first microbrewery to open in a hotel/casino, the Brew Brothers is part of the shopping arcade that connects the Eldorado and the Silver Legacy. Average but ample menu items include gourmet wood-fired pizzas, burgers, barbecued ribs, sandwiches, homemade soups, and salads. Check out the Thai chicken wings, New York steak sandwich, house-made fries, and, for dessert, a macadamia chocolate tart. Seven microbrews are made on-site, and you can order a sampler to try all of them. The place has the atmosphere of a funky turn-of-the-last-century warehouse with its copper brewing tanks, exposed steel trusses, a 1930 Model A pickup truck that appears to be delivering kegs of beer, music videos and sports on 18 monitors, and live dueling pianists who perform Sunday–Thursday nights. Weekend crowds can cause long waits, because reservations are not accepted. The Brew Brothers is at 4th and Virginia Streets.

Hours: From 11 A.M. daily. Happy hour 3 P.M.–6 P.M. daily. Live music begins at 9:30 P.M. nightly.
Prices: $–$$. Major credit cards are accepted.
Contact: Eldorado Hotel Casino, 345 N. Virginia St., Reno, NV; 775/786-5700; website: www.eldoradoreno.com.

Cafe Andreotti

Excellent Italian cuisine is offered here in an informal dining atmosphere. Entrées include veal Andreotti, prepared marsala-, piccata-, or parmigiana-style; cioppino; scampi; chicken cacciatore; tortellini Andreotti, which consists of pasta stuffed with Gorgonzola; and seafood fettuccine. The creative and delicious desserts include ricotta cheesecake, Italian rum cake, mint cannoli, tiramisu, and peppermint and espresso bombe—made of layers of coffee and mint ice cream covered with chocolate and whipped cream.

Hours: 5 P.M.–10 P.M. nightly.
Policies: Reservations are recommended.
Prices: $–$$. Major credit cards are accepted.
Contact: Harrah's Reno, 219 N. Center St., Reno, NV; 775/786-3232; website: www.harrahs.com.

RENO AREA DINING

Cafe de Thai

With its popularity assured, this restaurant moved in 2001 from a nondescript strip mall to a larger and more prominent location in the burgeoning south side of town. But it still has the same great menu and is headed by Chef Sakul, who is a graduate of the acclaimed Culinary Institute of America in New York. He offers delicious, freshly prepared Thai dishes, along with the renowned sweet and rich coffees and several desserts. You can order a combination plate and sample several foods, or order à la carte. There's also an extensive wine and beer list. The new location has a full bar, patio seating, and banquet room, all housed within a contemporary setting.

Hours: Open Tues.–Sat., 11:30 A.M.–10 P.M.
Prices: $–$$. Some credit cards are accepted.
Contact: Cafe de Thai, 7499 Longley Ln. at Patriot (off S. Virginia St.), Reno, NV; 775/829-8424.

Café Napa

Harrah's casual restaurant puts life into a 24-hour menu by borrowing liberally from California's Napa Valley and its nouvelle cuisine. Opened in 2000, the restaurant is on the second floor of the skyway of the hotel's west tower, and it has rich decorations including stone pillars and wood trim, along with a specially commissioned water fountain. It adjoins Vintage Court, a wine bar with more than 30 red, white, and sparkling wines. Menu items include the Bodega Bay Benedict (crab cakes with pesto hollandaise sauce and fresh herbs) for breakfast; Seafood Golden Gate (a bread bowl filled with smoked salmon, crabmeat, bay shrimp, avocado, and tomatoes) for lunch, and Thai Grilled Pork Chops (served with Thai marinade and fresh fruit chutney and accompanied by rice pilaf or potatoes) for dinner. There are also various other Asian dishes such as noodle specials and steamed whole fish—just the ticket if you lose your whole enchilada on the blackjack table.

Hours: 24 hours daily.
Prices: $.
Contact: Harrah's Reno, 219 N. Center St., Reno, NV; 775/327-6981; website: www.harrahs.com.

Cassidy's

Inside Boomtown, this fine dinner house specializes in four different cuts of prime rib, which is carved right at your tableside from a silver cart. The restaurant also serves steaks, seafood, chicken, and pasta dishes.

Hours: From 5 P.M. daily.
Prices: $$.
Contact: Boomtown Hotel Casino, I-80 at the Boomtown exit, Reno, NV; 775/345-6000; website: www.boomtownreno.com.

Chefs' Pavilion

With a seating capacity of nearly 600, this lavish buffet provides a continental setting with a sky-painted ceiling, murals of lush European gardens, limestone and bronze columns, and a bronze trellis entwined with creeping ivy and miniature roses. Various international courses are available from different food preparation areas, including American, Italian, Chinese, and Hispanic dishes. There are two six-foot rotisseries and a nine-foot glass case displaying spit-roasted beef, lamb, chicken, and game. One of the more popular stations is the Mongolian barbecue, from which you select vegetables and meats to be flash-cooked on one of two L-shaped grills. There are separate salad, dessert, and ice cream bars, so hungry diners can gorge themselves from wall to wall. The Chefs' Pavilion is in the Eldorado Hotel Casino, at 4th and Virginia Streets.

Hours: Open 7:45 A.M.–2 P.M., and 4 P.M.–10 P.M. daily.
Policies: No reservations are accepted.
Prices: $–$$. Major credit cards are accepted.
Contact: Eldorado Hotel Casino, 345 N. Virginia St., Reno, NV; 775/786-5700; website: www.eldoradoreno.com.

Christmas Tree

High above Reno on the Mt. Rose Highway, this famous dinner house is a longtime favorite with locals, though service and quality can vary. The menu features the restaurant's trademark mountain mahogany-broiled steaks, grilled chicken breast, scampi, New Zealand rack of lamb, salmon, Alaskan king crab pasta, and lobster.

Desserts are house-made. Weekly chef specials, a full bar, and great views of Reno and the Washoe Valley are also available. Live music, usually jazz, sometimes holds forth on weekend nights.

Hours: Dinner 5 P.M.–9 P.M. on weekdays and until 10 P.M. on weekends. The lounge opens at 3:30 P.M.

Policies: Reservations are recommended.

Prices: $$–$$$. Major credit cards are accepted.

Contact: Christmas Tree, 20007 Mt. Rose Hwy., Reno, NV; 775/849-0127.

Freddie's Roost Grille and Sports Bar

You don't have to play golf to enjoy a meal at this nicely appointed restaurant, which combines sports memorabilia with the ambience and service of a fine country club. On the Springs Course of Red Hawk Golf Club at Wingfield Springs, in the northernmost corner of Sparks, the grill serves three meals a day and caters to the golf crowd, but casually dressed nongolfers are always welcome. There's an inspiring view of the course and its adjoining wetlands, along with a large deck for outdoor dining. Freddie's specializes in fresh-baked pizzas, burgers, pastas, salads, and soups (including a rich clam chowder with smoked bacon), along with full-on dinners. Evening entrées, served with a choice of house or Caesar salad, include the Tahoe Steak Topper (with sautéed mushrooms, garlic, onions, blue cheese, and sherry), smoked baby-back pork ribs, filet mignon, steak au poivre (pan-seared black pepper-crusted New York steak with mushroom brandy sauce), portabella chicken, tequila-marinated steak or chicken fajitas, herb- and potato-crusted halibut, broiled Atlantic salmon, and linguine with clam sauce. Desserts include specialties such as the Grand Marnier cake, which is filled with toasted macadamia nut mousse and white chocolate. Most of the entrées and side dishes work, and the place has developed a local following. The main drawback is that it's a 20-minute drive northeast of downtown Reno.

Hours: Serving breakfast, lunch and dinner 6 A.M.–10 P.M. Sun.–Thurs., and until midnight Fri.–Saturday.

Policies: Reservations are accepted.

Prices: $–$$$. Major credit cards are accepted.

Contact: Freddie's Roost Grille and Sports Bar, 7755 Spanish Springs Rd., Sparks, NV; 775/626-6000; website: www.wingfieldsprings.com.

Fresh Market Square Buffet

Harrah's lavish buffet reflects the current trend toward independent food preparation stations, which reduces lines and offers fresher dishes. The restaurant can seat more than 400 people but disperses them in a colorful urban market atmosphere that invokes memories of San Francisco's ethnic enclaves. Stroll through Fisherman's Wharf for seafood, Little Italy for fresh focaccia and pizza, or Chinatown for a whiff of garlic sizzling in a wok. If you don't gorge yourself on main courses, you might sample the Sweet Dreams pastry shop, where you can order bananas Foster or almost anything else that tickles your sweet tooth. Then top it all off with a cappuccino from the coffee bar. Harrah's claims that this is Reno's only nonsmoking buffet.

Hours: Brunch 8 A.M.–3 P.M. and dinner from 5 P.M. daily.

Prices: $–$$ (weekend meals are more expensive). Major credit cards are accepted.

Contact: Fresh Market Square Buffet, 219 N. Center St., Reno, NV; 775/327-6981; website: www.harrahs.com.

Galena Forest Restaurant and Bar

Situated at the foot of Mt. Rose Highway, this romantic yet casual restaurant is far from the madding crowds of downtown Reno and within a short drive of the Mt. Rose Ski Area. For years it was known for German/Swiss food, but recently it changed ownership and now offers an eclectic menu that might best be described as California cuisine. Locals are effusive in their praise, and for these reasons: entrées such as salmon en papillote with garlic, spinach, tomato, and shallots; linguini with prawns, scallops and saffron; penne pasta with goat cheese; and lamb shank with Moroccan spices. Desserts include crème brûlée, warm apple turnover with vanilla sauce, and lemon cheesecake.

Hours: Dinner from 5 P.M. Tues.–Sunday. Bar opens at 3 P.M.

Policies: Reservations are preferred.

Prices: $$. Major credit cards are accepted.
Contact: Galena Forest Restaurant and Bar, 17025 Mt. Rose Hwy., Reno, NV; 775/849-2100.

G.K.'s Steakhouse

Sundowner Hotel Casino's dinner house in downtown Reno offers entrées such as porterhouse steak, prime rib, New York strip steak, filet mignon (topped with crab leg and béarnaise sauce), lamb chops, medallions of veal, scampi, swordfish steak, and broiled lobster. Appetizers include Bay shrimp and avocado, marinated herring, and escargots. Specially priced prime rib dinners are offered Sunday–Friday, and steak and scampi Saturday night.
Hours: Dinner 5 P.M.–10 P.M. daily.
Policies: Reservations are accepted.
Prices: $$. Major credit cards are accepted.
Contact: Sundowner Hotel Casino, 450 N. Arlington,Reno, NV; 775/786-7050.

Golden Palace (formerly Emperor's Garden)

In the Golden Phoenix Hotel Casino and Resort, in the skyway between the Virginia and Sierra Street casinos, this Chinese restaurant provides an elegant setting for food that varies from fair to good. Specialties include prawns with honey-glazed walnuts, baked black cod fillet, eggplant with garlic sauce, Kung Pao chicken, Mongolian beef, and Sichuan-style tofu.
Hours: Lunch 11 A.M.–2:30 P.M.; and dinner from 5 P.M. daily.
Prices: $–$$. Major credit cards are accepted.
Contact: Golden Palace, 240 N. Sierra St., Reno, NV; 775/785-7128.

Grand Canyon Buffet

This cheery buffet restaurant at the Reno Hilton offers pasta and wok stations, carved items rotating daily—including roast turkey, ham, prime rib, and roast top round, crab legs, peeled shrimp, salads, and an ice cream bar and dessert station.
Hours: Breakfast 7 A.M.–10:30 A.M. Mon.–Sat.; lunch from 11:30 A.M.–2 P.M. Mon.–Sat.; dinner 5 P.M.–9 P.M. nightly; and Sun. brunch from 8:30 A.M.–2 P.M.

Prices: $–$$. Major credit cards are accepted.
Contact: Reno Hilton, 2500 E. 2nd St., Reno, NV; 775/789-2000.

Great Basin Brewing Company

Situated on Victorian Square in Sparks, this microbrewery and restaurant features fresh homemade beer, ale-battered fish-and-chips, salmon tacos with fresh mango salsa, beer-cheese soup, shepherd's pie, and a selection of sandwiches, including bratwurst and burgers. In general the food is standard and undistinguished pub grub. The most popular appetizer is the garlic french fries, made from hand-cut potatoes. There's a children's menu and designated drivers get free soft drinks, but beer is the main attraction—the restaurant won gold and bronze medals in recent years at Denver's prestigious Great American Beer Festival. Local musicians perform in the evening, and special group arrangements and tours are available.
Hours: Lunch and dinner from 11:30 A.M. daily.
Prices: $. Major credit cards are accepted.
Contact: Great Basin Brewing Company, 846 Victorian Ave., Sparks, NV; 775/355-7711; website: www.greatbasinbrewing.com.

Hardy House

This elegant restaurant, which opened in late 2001, is in a vintage mansion in Reno's historic residential area, about two miles west of downtown. Listed on the National Register of Historic Places, the home was built in 1911 by a prominent sheepherder, and over the years it was reportedly occupied by a range of unsavory characters, from bank robbers to bootleggers. Now the goings-on here are more savory, with a posh restaurant serving New American-style cuisine. For lunch, Hardy House offers sandwiches such as cabernet braised beef short rib and a gourmet hamburger grilled on toasted focaccia bread. Starters include sweet onion soup, chicken salad with applewood smoked bacon and pickled onions, Dungeness crab and potato fritters, warm wild mushroom and leek tart, and fried calamari. The dinner offers dishes such as grilled lamb chops with ginger glazed eggplant and herb salsa, roasted sea bass, pumpkin ravioli, linguine, and grilled pork chop.

Hours: Lunch from 11 to 2:30 A.M. Tues.–Fri., dinner 5 P.M.–9 P.M. weeknights, 5 P.M.–10 P.M. Fri. and Sat., and 4 P.M.–8 P.M. Sunday.
Policies: Reservations are recommended.
Prices: $$–$$$. Major credit cards are accepted.
Contact: Hardy House, 442 Flint St., Reno, NV; 775/322-4555.

Harrah's Steak House

When you're ready to pull out the stops for the best steak dinner in Reno—with accommodating waiters, flambés, and rich desserts in a traditional setting—this is the place to go. Some creative touches add adventure and delight to the main fare, which includes New York pepper steak, chateaubriand, steak Diane, rack of lamb, filet mignon, buffalo Wellington (buffalo tenderloin in a puff pastry), prime rib, and calamari Oscar. Try starters such as Northwest Dungeness crab cakes, grilled portabella mushroom crowned with smoked cheddar, and the grilled radicchio and Belgian endive salad. The creamy five-onion soup, baked in a Carruso onion with a Gruyère cheese crust, is highly recommended. The ambience is low-light and intimate, and the service is impeccable. Dinner just doesn't get any better than this, and a slew of national awards attest to the restaurant's excellence. This is where the high-rollers dine, and it's the only Reno restaurant to receive a Four-Diamond rating by the American Automobile Association.
Hours: Lunch 11 A.M.–3 P.M. Mon.–Fri., and dinner 6 P.M.–10 P.M. nightly.
Policies: Reservations are required.
Prices: $$$. Major credit cards are accepted.
Contact: Harrah's Reno, 219 N. Center St., Reno, NV; 775/327-6981; website: www.harrahs.com.

Ichiban Japanese Steak House and Sushi Bar

Full of fountains and small bridges in a serene Japanese garden setting, this restaurant has some of the same dynamics—entertaining chefs and food prepared *teppanyaki*-style at your table—as nearby Benihana's, but with a more intimate style and, say some patrons, with better food. Knife-wielding chefs (not as dangerous as it sounds) carve filet mignon, shrimp, lobster, scal-

lops, and chicken. Dinners include appetizer, soup, salad, dessert, and green tea. Apart from the Teppanyaki Room, you can also dine in the Traditional Steak House, or the casual atmosphere of the Sushi Bar, where you'll find popular Japanese fare such as teriyaki steak and chicken, shrimp and vegetable tempura, *udon* and *soba* noodles. The Sushi Bar, purportedly the largest in Reno, features an "all you can eat" deal, a raw fish lover's delight.
Hours: Dinner served daily from 4:30 P.M.
Prices: $–$$$. Major credit cards accepted.
Contact: Ichiban, 210 N. Sierra St., 2nd Floor (next to the Reno Live nightclub), Reno, NV; 775/323-5550.

La Strada

In the Eldorado Hotel Casino, this award-winning Northern Italian restaurant features specialties such as porcini mushroom ravioli, which is perhaps the hotel's signature dish, chicken and veal entrées, Gulf snapper, and a dozen homemade pastas. La Strada has won the *Wine Spectator* Award of Excellence for several years running, and it's easy to see why with a selection of more than 300 wines. There are three dining environments to choose from: an outdoor café, a living room, and a brick wine cellar. A full bar is available.
Hours: Dinner from 5 P.M. nightly.
Policies: Reservations are suggested.
Prices: $$–$$$. Major credit cards are accepted.
Contact: Eldorado Hotel Casino, 345 N. Virginia St., Reno, NV; 775/786-5700; website: www.eldoradoreno.com.

La Vecchia Italian Restaurant

One of the local favorites, this small and friendly restaurant close to the Strip consistently wins raves for its service, cheerful ambience, and excellent Italian dishes. The place is not dedicated to a heavy, sauce-laden style of Italian dining, since many of the menu items are labeled as low-fat. You can order baked fish or boneless chicken breast, which are flavorful without breaking the calorie counter. Appetizers such as *carpaccio*, salads with house-made dressing, and sourdough bread are delicious and well presented. Entrées also include spaghetti alla carbonara and something called involtini *di parma,* which consists of beef wrapped around prosciutto, spinach, and mozzarella and topped with a wine/mushroom sauce. Desserts include spumoni, tiramisu, and other house specials.

Hours: 11:30 A.M.–2 P.M. Mon.–Fri. for lunch; 5:30 P.M.–9:30 P.M. daily for dinner.

Prices: $–$$.

Contact: La Vecchia Italian Restaurant, 130 West St., Reno, NV; 775/322-7486.

Lexie's Ristorante

This elegant dining room in the new Siena Hotel Spa Casino overlooks the Truckee River and is clearly aimed at an upscale clientele. Menu items, a mixture of West Coast and Tuscan cuisine, are creative and well presented, as they should be for the high prices. Seafood is weighted toward shellfish, with dishes such as Lobster Bella Vista, Cioppino Livernese, mussels and clams sautéed with garlic and white wine, and a huge Caribbean seafood stew that is cooked in coconut sauce and contains just about everything the chef can put into it. You can also order grilled Hawaiian ahi, roasted sea bass, and halibut, most with various wine sauce derivatives. Meat entrées include grilled New York steak, pan-roasted rib eye (finished with Chianti wine, pearl onions, and black truffle sauce), venison chops, pan-roasted rack of lamb, and a layered chicken breast with eggplant, Parma prosciutto, and melted provolone cheese. The meat dishes are served with garlic mashed potatoes or torte potatoes and roasted vegetables, and you can order sides such as grilled asparagus and sautéed wild mushrooms in Madeira sauce. Of course, there are the obligatory pastas, varying from seafood risotto to walnut spinach ravioli. For starters, take your pick from polenta soft-shell crab, Sevruga caviar and fresh oysters, crab cakes with a lobster whiskey sauce, Tuscany salad, or a Tuscan tomato soup simmered with *ciabatta* bread, garlic, onions, and basil. There is what could well be Reno's largest selection of wines, from Siena's own Wine Cave downstairs from the restaurant.

Hours: 11 A.M.–2 P.M. daily except Sat. and Sun., dinner 5 P.M.–10 P.M. weekdays and 5 P.M.–11 P.M. Fri. and Sat., Sun. brunch 10 A.M.–2 P.M.

Policies: Reservations are accepted.

Prices: $$–$$$. Major credit cards are accepted.

Contact: Siena Hotel Spa Casino, 1 S. Lake St., Reno, NV; 775/337-6260; website: www .SienaReno.com.

Liberty Belle Restaurant

A favorite with locals and families, this steak house has an enjoyable, lively atmosphere and is near the Reno-Sparks Convention Center. It is full of Nevada antiques, including a huge collection of vintage slot machines, many of which aren't even displayed. The restaurant is known for its prime rib and spinach salad, both served in huge portions. But you can also order ribs, chicken, and seafood.

Hours: Lunch 11 A.M.–2:30 P.M. Mon.–Fri. and dinner 5 P.M.–10 P.M. nightly.

Prices: $–$$. Major credit cards are accepted.

Contact: Liberty Belle Saloon, 4250 S. Virginia St., Reno, NV; 775/825-1776; website: www .LibertyBelleReno.com.

Louis' Basque Corner

Even if it's not in the better part of town, this is a Reno institution. Louis and Lorraine Erreguible make food that is heavy, spicy, and full of character, and their place draws visitors from throughout the world. Louis, who is from the French Pyrenees, served his apprenticeship in Bordeaux. The walls in the restaurant are adorned with pictures of France, pottery from the Ciboure, and famous Basque sayings. The cuisine includes paella, shrimp, and tongue à la Basquaise, lamb stew, chicken with Spanish rice, rabbit in wine sauce, and calamari. The menu changes daily, but family-style dinners come with soup du jour, a tossed green salad, French bread, Basque beans, potatoes, ice cream, and choice of wine, coffee, milk, or tea. You may not want to eat anything else for the rest of the day. The waitresses dress in authentic Basque garb. A full bar and two private banquet dining rooms are available.

Hours: Lunch 11 A.M.–2:30 P.M. Mon.–Sat. and dinner 5 P.M.–9:30 P.M. nightly.

Policies: Reservations are accepted.
Rates: $–$$. Major credit cards are accepted.
Contact: Louis' Basque Corner, 301 E. 4th St., Reno, NV; 775/323-7203.

Luciano's

You won't see this place advertised in the tourist dining guides, but Reno residents and lucky visitors quite often rate Luciano's as the best Italian restaurant in the city. It's small, with about a dozen tables (be sure to make reservations), and it's a few blocks south of the downtown casinos on Virginia Street. Stellar service, a European ambience, careful attention to every dish, and a large assortment of daily specials keep clients coming back for more. Restauranteur Luciano Pilisi, who hails from Bologna, Italy, provides creative cuisine that includes fresh-baked bread; antipasto with marinated mushrooms, sliced meats, and cheeses, garlic-flavored eggplant and bruschetta; ravioli filled with veal or porcini mushrooms; penne pasta with sausage; cioppino; gnocchi with tomato sauce; and fresh meat, poultry, and seafood dishes. Minestrone soup, salad with Gorgonzola dressing, and other starters will please your palate. If you can get through an entire meal and you still have room for dessert, try the *pannacotta* or tiramisu.
Hours: Lunch from 11:30 A.M.–2 P.M. Tues.–Fri., and dinner 5 P.M.–9 P.M. Tues.–Sunday. Closed Monday.
Policies: Accepts reservations and credit cards.
Rates: $–$$.
Contact: Luciano's, 719 S. Virginia St., Reno, NV; 775/322-7373.

Market Place Buffet

The buffet house at Eldorado Hotel Casino includes prime rib, homemade mushroom ravioli, salads, and desserts. A full bar and free valet and self-parking are available.
Hours: Breakfast from 7:45 A.M.–11 A.M. daily, dinner 11 A.M.–2 P.M., and weekend brunch from 7:45 A.M.–2 P.M.
Prices: $–$$. Major credit cards are accepted.
Contact: Eldorado Hotel Casino, 345 N. Virginia St., Reno, NV; 775/786-5700; website: www.eldoradoreno.com.

Montevigna Italian Ristorante

This new restaurant, part of a major expansion of Atlantis Casino Resort, is already getting accolades from locals. It offers authentic Tuscan cuisine with what it calls "a contemporary flair." You'll find regional pastas, steaks, seafood, and a wine cellar stocked with 4,000 bottles. This is a casual fine-dining establishment, so you don't need to dress up.
Hours: Open nightly from 5 P.M.
Prices: $–$$.
Policies: Reservations are accepted.
Contact: Atlantis Casino Resort, 3800 S. Virginia St., Reno, NV; 775/825-4700 or 800/723-6500; website: www.atlantiscasino.com.

Orozko

This 300-seat restaurant—part of the West Tower at John Ascuaga's Nugget—has a highly themed ambience that borrows from the Mediterranean and northern Spain. Ascuaga, whose family originated in the Pyrenees, has made this the signature dinner house of his growing hotel/casino. Antique-finished Botticino marble with black mosaic inserts covers the floor, and vaulted brick ceilings give way to rock arches and columns. Photographs of northern Spanish people and landscapes adorn the walls, and Basque artifacts poke out of alcoves. While the decor is quite elegant, the atmosphere is casual and cozy, with columns arranged to divide the large dining room into more intimate sections. The menu includes French, Italian, and Spanish cuisine, including paella (the tasty Spanish casserole of rice, meat, and seafood), pasta, mesquite-broiled steaks, pizza, and seafood specialties.
Hours: Open for dinner daily and brunch on weekends.
Prices: $$. Major credit cards are accepted.
Contact: John Ascuaga's Nugget, 1100 Nugget Ave., Sparks, NV; 775/356-3300 or 800/843-2427; website: www.janugget.com.

Peppermill Island Buffet

This restaurant is full of Hollywood-style special effects that play on an exotic rainforest theme. It has four 26-foot-high, 20-foot-wide waterfalls, a special effects tropical thunder and lightning storm complete with tsunami waves and vibrating booths, a surround sound system that is recessed into each booth and—oh, yeah—food, if you are not too distracted. The "action" buffet has daily seafood, an Asian wok station, a Southwestern station, a steak and carving station, a fresh garden market station, an omelet and frittatas station, and a dessert station with flaming bananas Foster, flaming cherries jubilee, ice cream sundaes, and seasonal fruit. A full bar and free 24-hour valet parking are available.

Hours: Breakfast and lunch daily from 7:30 A.M.–3 P.M.; dinner from 4:30 P.M.–10 P.M. Sun.–Thurs. or from 4:30 P.M.–11 P.M. Fri. and Saturday.
Prices: $–$$. Major credit cards are accepted.
Contact: Peppermill Hotel Casino, 2707 S. Virginia St., Reno, NV; 775/826-2121 or 800/648-6992; website: www.PeppermillReno.com.

Peppermill Steak House
Since 1996 this restaurant has been offering an ambitious menu with eight types of beef steak (including aged steak Diane and New York steak) and house specialties such as pan-seared venison chop; roast rack of lamb; and steak and shrimp étouffée, a delightful concoction of filet mignon and shrimp sautéed in a Cajun cream. There are also pastas such as lobster thermidor and fettuccine, and fresh fish such as swordfish, salmon, and mountain trout. If you're indecisive, you can order any of five land-and-sea combinations. For starters, try to decide between steamed clams, lobster strudel, sautéed button mushrooms, Caesar salad, or five-onion soup. The dessert menu has a unique almond taco shell with white chocolate mousse and fresh fruit, along with fresh strawberry shortcake Foster, cherries jubilee, and crème brûlée. The interior is rather strange—dark with purple and blue neon lights, something like the intergalactic bar in the first *Star Wars* movie.
Hours: From 5:30 P.M.–10 P.M. Sun.–Thurs., and from 5:30 P.M.–10:30 P.M. Fri. and Saturday.
Policies: Reservations are recommended.
Prices: $$–$$$.
Contact: Peppermill Hotel Casino, 2707 S. Virginia St., Reno, NV; 775/826-2121 or 800/648-6992; website: www.PeppermillReno.com.

Planet Hollywood
This celebrity-rich environment has the film props, big-screen TVs showing movie clips, photographs, costumes, and other memorabilia that serve as the trademarks for the restaurant group. The food varies from poor to passable, and menu items include a turkey burger, a Cajun chicken breast sandwich, spicy chicken and tomato pasta, Thai shrimp pasta, St. Louis ribs, a roasted vegetable pizza, and white-chocolate bread pudding. Come for the atmosphere, not the meal. Planet Hollywood is in Harrah's at Virginia and 2nd Streets.
Hours: Lunch and dinner (same menu) daily 11 A.M.–11 P.M.
Prices: $–$$. Major credit cards are accepted.
Contact: Harrah's Reno, 206 N. Virginia St., Reno, NV; 775/323-7837.

Rapscallion Seafood House and Bar
Considered one of Reno's best seafood restaurants and a favorite with locals, this place always has 10–20 varieties of fresh seafood and 140 wine selections. Starters include the Cajun coconut prawns. Among the main courses are breaded calamari steak; Rapscallion stew, made of scallops, shrimp, clams, fish fillets sautéed with orange and lemon rind, leeks, tomatoes, and garlic; and specials such as halibut, sea bass, snapper, king salmon, swordfish, and thresher shark.
Hours: Lunch 11 A.M.–2 P.M. weekdays; dinner 5 P.M.–10 P.M. weekdays, 5 P.M.–10:30 P.M. Sat., and 5 P.M.–10 P.M. Sun.; and Sun. brunch 10 A.M.–2 P.M.
Prices: $$–$$$. Major credit cards are accepted.
Contact: Rapscallion Seafood House and Bar, 1555 S. Wells St., Reno, NV; 775/323-1211.

Reno Hilton Steakhouse
The steak house menu features roast prime rib of beef, surf and turf, and cedar-plank salmon.
Hours: From 5:30 P.M.–10:30 P.M. Sun.–Thurs., and from 5:30 P.M.–11 P.M. Fri. and Saturday.
Policies: Reservations are suggested.
Prices: $$–$$$. Major credit cards are accepted.

Contact: Reno Hilton, 2500 E. 2nd St., Reno, NV; 775/789-2000.

Rotisserie Restaurant and Buffet at John Ascuaga's Nugget

This popular casino restaurant features various food stations that might offer peel-and-eat shrimp, chicken, pasta, prime rib, a salad bar, and desserts. Specialty nights include fresh fish on Monday, chocolate on Tuesday, ribs on Wednesday, prime rib on Thursday, and seafood on Friday.

Hours: From 4:30 P.M.–10 P.M. nightly; Sun. brunch from 8:30 A.M.–2 P.M.

Policies: Reservations are suggested.

Prices: $–$$. Major credit cards are accepted.

Contact: John Ascuaga's Nugget, 1100 Nugget Ave., Sparks, NV; 775/356-3300 or 800/843-2427; website: www.janugget.com.

Roxy

In the Eldorado Hotel Casino overlooking the hotel's opulent Fountain of Fortune, this innovative and outstanding restaurant was developed in collaboration with San Francisco restaurant designer Pat Kuleto, whose signature dinner houses—Kuleto's, Postrio, and Boulevard—have achieved wide acclaim. The interior represents a European village atmosphere, with settings including a "centuries-old" wine cellar connected to a wine warehouse, a turret to an old city wall, an authentic Parisian-style bistro, an old-fashioned exhibition bakery, a European sidewalk café, and an atrium bar reminiscent of Toulouse-Lautrec's vision of Paris. Each room is intimate and has subdued lighting. The menu changes frequently, but entrées consist of unpretentious food prepared with basic ingredients "bistro style." Offerings include shellfish paella, wood oven-roasted Pacific snapper, fresh Gulf prawns, maple-glazed quail, grilled lamb chops, grilled dry-aged New York steak, and spit-roasted chicken. Starters might include seared ahi tuna sashimi, Dungeness crab and sweet corn gratin, butterleaf lettuce with creamy niçoise olive dressing, and roasted butternut squash soup. The staff offers a fresh bread basket throughout your dinner. Meals are prepared in front of guests in an ex-

hibition kitchen and bakery, and the presentation for every dish is impressive, as is the service and the extensive list of 350 wines. A café menu with breakfast and lunch items includes fresh-baked beignets, croissants, salads, sandwiches, and gourmet coffees. Roxy is in the Eldorado Hotel Casino at 4th and Virginia Streets.

Hours: Dinner from 5 P.M. daily.

Policies: Reservations strongly recommended.

Prices: $$–$$$. Major credit cards are accepted.

Contact: Eldorado Hotel Casino, 345 N. Virginia St., Reno, NV; 775/786-5700; website: www.eldoradoreno.com.

Silver Peak Restaurant and Brewery

Not quite a mile south of downtown is this lively brew pub and restaurant, which is in an historic building with a large sun deck. Crafting its own beers, Silver Peak has an extensive menu of American cuisine. You can sample the various ales and graze on appetizers such as crab cakes, New Zealand green lip mussels, sun-dried tomato polenta, steamed shrimp in Cajun spices, black bean nachos, or seared pepper-crusted ahi. For more substantial fare, you can order from a half-dozen pizzas, an assortment of soups and salads, sandwiches such as lamb burger and beer-steamed bratwurst, and pub fare such as baby-back ribs, salmon fish-and-chips, and spinach and goat cheese raviolis. Dinner entrées include herbed chicken breast, Monterey cioppino (crab legs, prawns, mussels, and fish in a spicy tomato and fennel broth), charbroiled New York steak, sesame-crusted salmon, grilled lamb sirloin, and penne pasta. On a warm day or evening, the spacious rooftop deck adds to the experience. If you're a midnight nibbler, this is an ideal spot. The restaurant has its own parking lot.

Hours: Lunch, dinner and snacking daily from 11 A.M. until late evening, Happy Hour 4 P.M.–6:30 P.M. Mon.–Friday.

Policies: Reservations are accepted.

Prices: $–$$. Major credit cards are accepted.

Contact: Silver Peak Restaurant and Brewery, 124 Wonder St. (at Holcomb), Reno, NV; 775/324-1864; website: www.themenupage.com/silverpeak.html.

Silver Screen Buffet

Boomtown, the giant resort/hotel/casino complex west of town off I-80, has been adding attractions at a rapid clip, and it gets phenomenal business. One reason might be the quality of its restaurants, which can certainly hold their own against any of the much larger casino hotels on Virginia Street. While there is major competition among the buffet rooms in town, this one, in our opinion, ranks at the top. Management here has elevated the all-you-can-eat genre into a new dimension, much above the production-line taste and appearance that you find elsewhere. Every dish, from salads to hot entrées to desserts, is creatively and carefully prepared, which is truly amazing considering that the kitchen serves more than 200 items daily. Specials rotate each day but usually include a selection of American, Asian, Italian, and seafood dishes. On Friday, Saturday, and Sunday, there's a whole Maine lobster buffet, and a special mimosa brunch on weekends. Desserts, which are extensive, even include flaming bananas Foster.

Hours: 9 A.M.–10 P.M. daily for breakfast, lunch and dinner, with Sat. and Sun. brunch 9 A.M.–2:30 P.M. and late lunch and dinner from 3:30 P.M.–10 P.M.

Prices: $–$$$. Children 3–10 eat half-price on the regular buffets. Major credit cards are accepted.

Contact: Boomtown Hotel Casino, I-80 at the Boomtown exit, Reno, NV; 775/345-6000; website: www.boomtownreno.com.

The Steakhouse Grill at John Ascuaga's Nugget

The menu at this signature casino/hotel restaurant features prime rib, New York steak, veal piccata, seafood specials, poultry, and pastas. An intimate setting with subdued lighting, this dinner house also offers starters such as cream of potato soup, oysters on the half shell, and spinach salad. Among the nightly specials are dishes such as filet mignon on a grilled portabella mushroom, topped with crumbled blue cheese and a port wine sauce. Desserts come with a flourish, and include classics such as cherries jubilee, baked Alaska, bananas Foster, and crepes suzette. Tableside preparations include flambés, which make any meal an entertaining experience.

Hours: Dinner 5 P.M.–11 P.M. nightly.

Policies: Reservations are recommended.

Prices: $$–$$$. Major credit cards are accepted.

Contact: John Ascuaga's Nugget, 1100 Nugget Ave., Sparks, NV; 775/356-3300 or 800/843-2427; website: www.janugget.com.

Sterling's Seafood Steakhouse

In the Silver Legacy Casino Resort, this elegant dinner house provides gourmet dining with seafood specials served daily, as well as steaks, chicken, pastas, and veal. Many of the entrées are prepared Mediterranean-style.

Hours: From 5 P.M. nightly.

Prices: $$. Major credit cards are accepted.

Contact: Silver Legacy Casino Resort, 407 N. Virginia St., Reno, NV; 775/329-4777 or 800/687-8733; website: www.silverlegacy.com.

Toucan Charlie's Buffet and Grille

The award-winning buffet at the Atlantis Casino Resort features food stations offering hand-carved prime rib, specialty salads made to order, Mongolian barbecue, and custom-cooked omelets. Sunday brunch is an especially large affair, with crab legs, peel-and-eat shrimp, blintzes, miniwaffles, bread pudding, and cobbler. The dessert counter is several notches above the local buffets, displaying an array of rich pies, cheesecakes, layer cakes, cookies, and other goodies. Each night there's a different theme: Monday is Southwestern, Tuesday is Asian, Wednesday is international, Thursday is Italian, and Friday is seafood. A tropical setting adds to the dining experience. Free 24-hour valet and self-parking is available.

Hours: From 7:30 A.M.–10 P.M. daily.

Prices: $–$$. Major credit cards are accepted.

Contact: Atlantis Casino Resort, 3800 S. Virginia St., Reno, NV; 775/825-4700 or 800/723-6500; website: www.atlantiscasino.com.

Trader Dick's Restaurant Aquarium

Does the name remind you of something? Oh, well, never mind. If you like aquariums, this place has a 6,000-gallon, 30-ton saltwater tank, which at 45 feet long is one of the largest private aquariums in the West. Three pillars supporting I-80 above the restaurant have been integrated into the lush tropical appointments. A new menu with more contemporary Asian dishes was recently introduced, and it includes Polynesian coconut shrimp, Siam crab cakes, Lomi Lomi salmon, Mongolian lamb chops, Thai-style spicy scampi, Indian-flavored vegetables with curry, and asparagus in black bean sauce. Sunday brunch, called The Island Way, features a rotisserie and various food preparation stations, made-to-order omelets, crepes, and desserts.

Hours: Nightly 5 P.M.–11 P.M.
Policies: Reservations are recommended.
Prices: $$–$$$. Major credit cards are accepted.
Contact: John Ascuaga's Nugget, 1100 Nugget Ave., Sparks, NV; 775/356-3300 or 800/648-1177; website: www.janugget.com.

Viaggio Italian Cuisine

One of Reno's newest Italian restaurants—they seem to be popping up everywhere—has already earned a passionate following with its huge selection of 500 wines (there's a large retail wine shop inside), its elegant interiors, its freshly made pastas, and its innovative menu. House specialties include Pesce Stufato (clams, mussels, sea bass, shrimp, and scallops served over fresh *pappardelle* pasta), crab ravioli, osso bucco (braised veal shank roasted in veal stock with fresh vegetables), rack of lamb, pork tenderloin, and seafood risotto.

Hours: Lunch Mon.–Sat. from 11 A.M. and dinner nightly from 5 P.M.
Prices: $$.
Contact: Viaggio, Franktown Corners Shopping Center, 2309 Kietzke Ln., Reno, NV; 775/828-2708; website: www.viaggio.net.

The Victorian Buffet

Silver Legacy's all-you-can-eat restaurant serves prime rib and a variety of other American favorites, and it has ample but standard club buffet fare. On Saturday, the menu includes Italian and Asian dishes as well, and on Friday it combines seafood and prime rib.

Hours: Breakfast from 7:30 A.M., lunch from 11 A.M., and dinner from 4:30 P.M.

Prices: $–$$. Major credit cards are accepted.
Contact: Silver Legacy Casino Resort, 407 N. Virginia St., Reno, NV; 775/329-4777; website: www.silverlegacy.com.

Virginian Steak House

This is a recently opened fine dinner house on the third floor of the born-again Club Cal Neva, which has undergone extensive remodelling and upgrading. The menu includes prime rib, New York, and filet mignon steak as well as a variety of Asian entrées.

Hours: Open Tues.–Sun., 5 P.M.–10 P.M.
Prices: $–$$. Major credit cards are accepted.
Contact: Club Cal Neva, 2nd and Virginia Sts., Reno, NV; 775/323-1046 or 877/777-7303; website: www.clubcalneva.com.

Western Village Steakhouse

For serious carnivores, this restaurant inside the Western Village Inn and Casino in Sparks serves prime beef that is aged 21 days or longer. The kitchen employs a special cooking process that double broils at 1,800° to lock in the juices, and all steaks are present on 400° hot plates to keep your steak warm through your dinner. Other entrées, with nightly specials, include lighter fare such as Sicilian chicken with shrimp and angel hair pasta. There's a good selection of reasonably priced, mostly California wines. The interior is quite eclectic, some might say sophisticated, with a ceiling of mirrors, glass globes, and tiny lights.

Hours: Dinner from 4:30 P.M.–10 P.M. nightly.
Policies: Reservations are recommended.
Prices: $$–$$$. Major credit cards are accepted.
Contact: Western Village Steak House, 815 Nichols Blvd., Sparks, NV; 775/331-1069.

White Orchid

Ongoing expansions of the Peppermill Hotel Casino have yielded this delightful dinner house. Elegantly appointed in the Mediterranean style with plush high-back chairs and subdued lighting, the interior has an unusual centerpiece—a white orchid "tree" that rises and blooms. Fresh orchids grace each table, and the restaurant is graced with accents of fine art, floral arrangements, and decorative glass. Although the menu changes every week, a representative sampling includes a tower of ahi tuna tartar with avocado and sweet yellow peppers, California quail stuffed with Maine lobster and shiitake mushrooms and served with couscous, sautéed halibut with black pepper and Japanese bread crumbs, and roasted lamb loin with fresh mint demi-glace. Starters might include Normandy Brie soup, French escargot in mushroom caps with Brie cheese, and California romaine salad served in a parmesan blossom with shaved Reggiano cheese and Caesar dressing. Among the possible desserts are chocolate raspberry truffle torte, coconut-orange mousse, and frozen pistachio Bavarian with Grand Marnier crème anglaise. Entrées include soup or salad, or you can order a four-course, prix fixe meal that includes dessert, or one that adds wine.

Hours: From 5:30 P.M. daily.
Policies: Reservations are suggested.
Prices: $$–$$$. Major credit cards are accepted.
Contact: Peppermill Hotel Casino, 2707 S. Virginia St., Reno, NV; 775/689-7300 or 800/648-6992, ext. 7300; website: www. PeppermillReno.com.

CARSON CITY/DAYTON
Adele's Restaurant

Set in a Victorian house with period furnishings, this favorite continental restaurant features local lamb dishes; filet mignon stuffed with lobster, crab, shrimp, and cognac sauce and topped with poached oysters; chicken breast stuffed with goat cheese; and a mixed grill of prawns, scallops, and fish fillets served on a bed of steamed spinach. All entrées come with a salad, which is substantial. Daily specials can be quite extensive, and everything is prepared from scratch. Heart-healthy menu items, an extensive and prize-winning wine list, and a full bar are available. A consistent favorite among locals.

Hours: Lunch 11 A.M.–3 P.M. Mon.–Fri., and dinner from 5:30 P.M.–9 P.M. Mon.–Thurs. and from 5:30 P.M.–10:30 P.M. Fri. and Saturday.
Policies: Reservations are recommended.
Prices: $$–$$$. Major credit cards are accepted.
Contact: Adele's, 1112 N. Carson St., Carson City, NV; 775/882-3353.

Applebee's Neighborhood Grill

Can't decide where to eat? It's hard to go wrong at Applebee's, the well-known casual lunch and dinner place that has more than 1,400 locations in the United States and the world. With a large and diverse menu, cheerful service, and pleasant surroundings, Applebee's has the formula to make almost anyone happy. That's because the food is consistently good, and there are always new specials to keep people returning. You can eat a light salad, nosh on appetizers, or indulge in a substantial meal. Among the favorites: chicken fingers platter, riblets basted with Applebee's own barbecue sauces, grilled beef or chipotle chicken fajitas, house sirloin steak with country potatoes, Chinese stir-fry with choice of beef or chicken, honey-grilled Atlantic salmon, and chicken and broccoli pasta Alfredo. While desserts vary by location, the hands-down favorite is the cinnamon-apple crisp à la mode—baked apples, cinnamon, and spices topped with a cinnamon-brown sugar streusel, vanilla ice cream, and caramel sauce. Delectable!

Hours: Lunch and dinner 11 A.M.–10 P.M. daily.
Prices: $–$$. Major credit cards are accepted.
Contact: Applebee's, 3300 S. Carson (Hwy. 395), Carson City, NV; 775/882-0222.

Carson Nugget Steak House

For more than two decades, this casino dinner house has turned out top-notch cuisine, served in an elegant setting. Entrées focus on beef, and include a 10-ounce filet mignon topped with chanterelle mushroom butter, a 20-ounce porterhouse steak, and prime rib. Other specialties include rack of lamb marinated with honey-Dijon mustard, steak and lobster, jumbo prawns, chicken sauté sec, chicken Oscar, shrimp fettuccini, and smoked salmon over angel hair pasta. Starters include grilled crab cakes, coconut prawns, lobster bisque, and spinach salad. If you can get through the entire meal, then sample a dessert such as tiramisu, amaretto cheesecake, or chocolate truffle cake. This is not a loss-leader casino deal, so come prepared to pay for a full gourmet meal.

Hours: Dinner 5 P.M.–9 P.M. Sun.–Thurs., until 10 P.M. Fri. and Saturday.

Prices: $$–$$$.
Contact: Carson Nugget Steak House, 507 N. Carson St., Carson City, NV; 775/882-1626; website: www.ccnugget.com.

Cattlemen's Restaurant and Saloon

Rarely a disappointment for meat-eating buckaroos and other devotees of the Western lifestyle, this lively restaurant a few miles north of Carson City on a sparsely populated stretch of Highway 395 has giant steaks, all-you-can-eat salad, hot sourdough bread, ranch-style beans, and baked potato. Come with a big appetite, because you can order a two-pound porterhouse steak or prime rib that is "sizzled" at your table. For lighter appetites, there are poultry and more-than-passable seafood dishes. If you're not from these parts, you can marvel at all of those folks wearing Stetsons and snakeskin boots. Some of them might even be real cowboys, but don't bet on it.
Hours: Dinner only, 5 P.M.–10 P.M. weekdays, and 4 P.M.–10 P.M. on weekends.
Prices: $–$$.
Contact: Cattlemen's Restaurant and Saloon, 555 Hwy. 395 N, Washoe Valley, NV (halfway between Carson City and Reno), 775/849-1500.

The East Ocean Restaurant

Serves Chinese cuisine.
Hours: Open Mon.–Sat. 11 A.M.–9 P.M.
Prices: $. Some credit cards are accepted.
Contact: The East Ocean Restaurant, 1214 N. Carson St., Carson City, NV; 775/883-6668.

Garibaldi's

With large picture windows, vaulted ceilings, intimate seating, and a solid walnut antique bar, this European-style restaurant offers northern Italian cuisine. Entrées include chicken *della casa,* which consists of chicken breast sautéed with artichoke hearts and mushrooms; rigatoni *botticelli,* made of chicken and vegetables sautéed in parmesan cream with rigatoni; linguine tossed with seafood; and veal saltimbocca, a veal scaloppine stuffed with prosciutto and mozzarella. Nonsmoking dining, a full bar, and an extensive wine list are available.

Hours: Lunch on weekdays from 11:30 A.M.–1:30 P.M., and dinner 5 P.M.–10 P.M. daily.
Policies: Reservations are suggested.
Prices: $–$$. Major credit cards are accepted.
Contact: Garibaldi's, 301 N. Carson St., Carson City, NV; 775/884-4574.

Glen Eagles

Housed in a Western ranch-style building on the northern outskirts of Carson City, this popular restaurant has changed hands several times in recent years, and its latest incarnation continues a long tradition of mixing various ethnic foods including Italian, Asian, and Mexican dishes. Overlooking the new Silver Oak Golf Course, Glen Eagles offers an eclectic menu that emphasizes made-to-order meals with no deep-frying or microwave cooking. Entrées include Caesar salad topped with a meat of your choice, fresh seafood of the day, a variety of pastas, steaks, chicken, ribs, and lamb chops. For starters, try the fire-roasted jalapeño raviolis to wake up your taste buds. Desserts have a distinctly French touch, but with occasional Caribbean flavors, such as the *pastel de leche.* There's a small but diverse wine list of California, European, and Australian wines.
Hours: Lunch and dinner daily 11 A.M.–11 P.M.
Prices: $–$$.
Contact: Glen Eagles, 3700 N. Carson St., Carson City, NV; 775/884-4414.

Heiss' Steak and Seafood House

Early-bird and dinner-for-two menus are available.
Hours: Open Tues.–Sun. from 4:30 P.M.–9 P.M., until 10 P.M. on Fri. and Saturday.
Prices: $–$$. Major credit cards are accepted.
Contact: Heiss' Steak and Seafood House, 107 E. Telegraph St., Carson City, NV; 775/882-9012.

Mi Casa Too

This locals' favorite serves good Mexican dishes.
Hours: Daily 11 A.M.–11 P.M.
Policies: Reservations are accepted on weekdays.
Prices: $. Major credit cards are accepted.
Contact: Mi Casa Too, 3809 N. Carson St., Carson City, NV; 775/882-4080.

Mia's Swiss Restaurant

In historic Odeon Hall, Mia's was used in 1960 as a location during the filming of *The Misfits*, starring Clark Gable, Marilyn Monroe, and Montgomery Clift. A beautiful ballroom and theater are upstairs. Continental cuisine features buffalo steaks, grilled halibut, beef stroganoff, veal Oscar, and Wiener schnitzel. There's a full bar in an adjoining room, and nightly specials are available.
Hours: Lunch weekdays from 11:30 A.M.–2:30 P.M., and dinner 5 P.M.–9 P.M. nightly.
Policies: Reservations are accepted.
Prices: $–$$$. Major credit cards are accepted.
Contact: Mia's Swiss Restaurant, 65 Pike St., Dayton, NV; 775/246-3993.

Panda Kitchen

In a shopping mall, Panda's serves average Chinese cuisine in a clean but somewhat undistinguished setting.
Hours: Open Mon.–Sat. 11 A.M.–9:30 P.M. and Sun. noon–9 P.M.
Prices: $. Major credit cards accepted.
Contact: Panda Kitchen, 2416 U.S. 50 E, Carson City, NV; 775/882-8128.

Silvana's Italian Cuisine

Intimate and friendly Old-World charm envelops this restaurant, which features authentic Venetian dishes. The menu includes 25 homemade pastas, chicken marsala, pasta primavera, and New York rib-eye steak. Complete dinners are served with soup or salad and garlic bread.
Hours: Open Tues.–Sat. 5 P.M.–10 P.M.
Policies: Reservations are suggested.
Prices: $$. Major credit cards are accepted.
Contact: Silvana's Italian Cuisine, 1301 N. Carson St., Carson City, NV; 775/883-5100.

Station Grill and Rotisserie

Modern decor, friendly service, and creative presentations complement a menu that includes diverse entrées such as grilled pizza, smoked pepper tenderloin, stuffed jumbo shells, spit-roasted leg of lamb and baby-back ribs, seafood crepes, and turkey enchiladas. For starters, try the chicken and corn tortilla soup or the crab cakes. A locals' favorite and uniformly satisfying.

Hours: From 11:30 A.M.–2 P.M. Mon., from 11:30 A.M.–10 P.M. Tues.–Fri., and 5 P.M.–10 P.M. Saturday.
Policies: Reservations are suggested.
Prices: $–$$. Major credit cards are accepted.
Contact: Station Grill and Rotisserie, 1105 S. Carson St., Carson City, NV; 775/883-8400.

Water Wheel Restaurant

Under the same ownership as the popular Stateline Water Wheel at Lake Tahoe, this new restaurant, in premises formerly occupied by Stanley's, offers a variety of above-average Chinese dishes and has an all-you-can-eat sushi bar. Lunch also includes Japanese favorites such as shrimp and vegetable tempura, teriyaki chicken, and California rolls.
Hours: Lunch from 11:30 A.M.–3 P.M., dinner 3 P.M.–10 P.M. daily.
Policies: Reservations are suggested for dinner.
Prices: $–$$. Major credit cards are accepted.
Contact: Water Wheel Restaurant, 4239 N. Carson St., Carson City, NV; 775/883-7826.

VIRGINIA CITY

Crown Point

In Nevada's oldest hotel, this restaurant boasts atmosphere and a sure hand in the kitchen. The menu features New York steak, linguine with clams, daily fresh fish dishes, and homemade desserts. A full bar and an extensive wine list are available.
Hours: Open Wed.–Sun. 5:30 P.M.–9 P.M.
Policies: Reservations are recommended on weekends.
Prices: $$–$$$. Some credit cards are accepted.
Contact: Gold Hill Hotel, 1540 S. Main St., Gold Hill, NV; 775/847-0111.

CARSON VALLEY/MINDEN/ GARDNERVILLE

Carson Valley Country Club Bar and Restaurant

Basque cuisine, with the usual parade of hearty soup, salad, bread, French fries, wine, and various meat selections, preside at this country club sct-ting, next to the Carson Valley Golf Course in Gardnerville. Main course options include steak, shrimp, salmon, and lamb chops. A bit off the beaten path, this restaurant has been a favorite of locals for more than 25 years.

Hours: Lunch daily (except Tues. and Sun.) from 11:30 A.M.–2:30 P.M.; dinner nightly 6 P.M.–9 P.M. (5 P.M.–8 P.M. on Sun.), except Tues., when the restaurant is closed.

Policies: Reservations are suggested for parties of 10 or more.

Prices: $$.

Contact: Carson Valley Country Club, 1029 Riverview Dr., Gardnerville, NV; 775/265-3715.

Fiona's

With plants and plenty of sunlight, this tropical restaurant's menu offers a soup and salad bar, sandwiches, top sirloin steak, grilled scallops, scampi, Polynesian prawns, ribs, broiled halibut, and nightly pasta specials. Dinners include an unlimited soup and salad bar; fresh-baked bread; a fresh vegetable of the day; and your choice of potato, rice, or pasta. Sunday brunch features a fruit and pastry bar, crepes, omelets, and bacon. A full bar is available. This is a nonsmoking restaurant.

Hours: Lunch from 11:30 A.M.–2 P.M. Tues.–Fri., dinner 5 P.M.–9 P.M. Tues.–Sun., and Sun. brunch 9 A.M.–2 P.M. Closed Monday.

Policies: Reservations are suggested.

Prices: $–$$. Major credit cards are accepted.

Contact: Carson Valley Inn, 1623 U.S. 395 N, Minden, NV; 775/782-9711, ext. 650.

J&T Basque Bar and Dining Room

This restaurant dates back to 1896, making it the granddaddy of Carson Valley Basque bistros. Recently both the bar and the dining room underwent extensive restoration, and now they exude more of the style and atmosphere of the Victorian age. Big appetites are in order, because you'll be offered plenty of soup, salad, red wine, bread, and beverages. Stews are a specialty, and you might have oxtail, lamb, beef, chicken and rice, or beef tongue. There are also entrées of beef steak, lamb chops and steaks, chicken, sweetbreads, shrimp, and roasted rabbit. Dessert is usually ice cream, perhaps the only thing you'll have room for at the end of this orgy of eating.

Hours: From 11:30 A.M.–2 P.M. for lunch daily except Sun., and from 5:30 P.M.–9 P.M. for dinner (Sat. starting at 5 P.M.) except Sunday.

Policies: Reservations are accepted.

Prices: $–$$. Some credit cards are accepted.

Contact: J&T Bar and Dining Room, 1426 Hwy. 395, Gardnerville, NV; 775/782-2074.

Michael's

This casino/dinner house provides chandeliers, intimate booth seating, and white tablecloths for meals that include tournedos Sierra piñon, crab and angel hair pasta, blackened prime rib, and rack of lamb. The Cajun strawberries, served sautéed with cracked black pepper in a Florentine cup, is an unusual dessert. A nonsmoking section and a full bar are available.

Hours: Open Wed.–Mon. 5 P.M.–9 P.M. Closed Tuesday.

Policies: Reservations are recommended.

Prices: $$. Major credit cards are accepted.

Contact: Carson Valley Inn, 1627 U.S. 395 N, Minden, NV; 775/782-9711, ext. 745.

Overland Hotel

The Overland has one of the most popular Basque family-style restaurants in the area. Hearty red wine, soup, daily stew, sirloin steaks, fried chicken, deep-fried shrimp, French fries, salads, and ice cream for dessert provide a filling repast. Come hungry, and be prepared to wait on weekends. The bar and dining room have recently been remodeled, though the exterior still looks its age, more than 100 years old. In contrast with other Basque restaurants in the area, this one has individual tables rather than family-style seating.

Hours: lunch, 11:45 A.M.–2 P.M.; dinner, 4:45 P.M.–9:30 P.M. (10 P.M. in summer). Closed Monday.

Policies: Reservations are accepted.

Prices: $–$$. Some credit cards are accepted.

Contact: Overland Hotel, 691 Main St. (U.S. 395 S), Gardnerville, NV; 775/782-2138.

RENO AREA DINING

GENOA

Antoci's Supper Club at Genoa Lakes

With a stunning new clubhouse and a recent change of ownership, the Golf Club at Genoa Lakes now has an equally impressive dinner house with original Italian dishes. Chef Valter Montanari, a native of Bologna, Italy, and his wife, Teresa, use fresh ingredients, carve their own cuts of meat, prepare pasta and sauces from scratch, and import various cheeses and oils from Italy. Among their dishes are Risotto al Scampi con Salsa Champagne (Italian rice with scampi in a champagne cream), Filetto alla Vodka (fillet in a creamy vodka sauce with black olives and garlic), and Spiedini alla Sebastiano (beef on a skewer, marinated in garlic and olive oil and coated with a mixture of bread crumbs and Romano cheese). California and Italian wines, antipasto, and a variety of desserts complement the main course.

Hours: Hours and days vary seasonally.
Policies: Reservations are suggested.
Prices: $$–$$$. Credit cards are accepted.
Contact: Golf Club at Genoa Lakes, 1 Genoa Lakes Dr., Genoa, NV; 775/782-6645; website: www.genoalakes.com.

La Ferme

This quaint, country French restaurant in the equally quaint hamlet of Genoa, which happens to be Nevada's oldest settlement, offers gourmet cuisine and is not for those on a budget. Chef Yves Gigot and owner Gilles La Gourgue offer some classic French dishes along with wild game. Entrées include chicken coq au vin, rabbit with mustard sauce, grilled Angus beef rib-eye with béarnaise sauce, shank of lamb provençal style, saddle of venison, roasted duck breast with apple honey sauce, tenderloin of beef in a shallot beer sauce, and fresh fish and pasta of the day. For starters, you can choose from country-style pâté, cabbage stuffed with vegetables, escargots in garlic butter, salad with duck confit, house-smoked salmon, and lamb tongue salad vinaigrette. There's an ample selection of homemade and seasonal desserts. The small, intimate dining area is full of antiques and imparts a Victorian ambience to the meal.

Hours: From 5 P.M. Tues.–Sunday. Closed Monday.
Policies: Reservations are suggested.
Prices: $$–$$$. Some credit cards are accepted.
Contact: La Ferme, 2291 Main St., Genoa, NV; 775/783-1004.

Nightlife

RENO/SPARKS

As you'd expect, one of the principal places to go for a wide variety of entertainment in Reno/Sparks is casinos.

HOTELS/CASINOS

Atlantis Casino Resort

The Grand Ballroom hosts major stars and music productions, while the Center Stage Cabaret offers live bands and disco dancing nightly except Monday. Piano bar with jazz stylings holds forth in the MonteVigna Italian Ristorante Wednesday–Sunday. The Atlantis Nightclub, transformed from the resort's elegant steak house, has a nautical theme, with an animated, octopus-shaped light fixture and laser shooting sharks. DJ dancing is offered Thursday–Saturday 10 P.M.–3 A.M.
Contact: Atlantis Casino Resort, 3800 S. Virginia St., Reno, NV; 775/825-4700; website: www.atlantiscasino.com.

Bonanza Casino

The lounge at this small club usually hosts two different musical groups a week, and shows are held nightly.
Contact: Bonanza Casino, 4720 N. Virginia St., Reno, NV; 775/323-2724.

Boomtown Hotel Casino

In Verdi on I-80, seven miles west of Reno, the Boomtown Hotel Casino hosts live music nightly except Monday. The Dynamic Motion Theater offers four virtual reality-type films.

Contact: Boomtown Hotel Casino, I-80 W and Garson Rd., Verdi, NV; 775/345-6000.

Circus Circus Hotel Casino

World-class circus acts from different countries are offered on the Midway Stage under the Big Top twice an hour daily 11 A.M.–midnight.

Contact: Circus Circus Hotel Casino, 590 N. Sierra St., Reno, NV; 775/329-0711 or 800/648-5010.

Eldorado Hotel Casino

The 580-seat Eldorado Showroom is one of the most comfortable in Reno, offering theater-style rocking chair seats with drink holders in the armrests. You order drinks in the lobby, so there are no waiters to obstruct your view of the stage. The sound system is great, the room offers a sense of intimacy (with balconies, even), and you don't get kinks in your neck trying to look sideways, as you do at other showrooms. Broadway musicals and variety shows are the staples, and you can usually get a dinner/show package for just a few dollars more than the price of the show alone. Also at the Eldorado, various musical groups play in the Cabaret, Brew Brothers Microbrewery, and the posh BuBinga Lounge nightclub. Also, there's a piano bar at Roxy's restaurant. Among the frequent performers at Eldorado is Rob Hanna, who impersonates rocker Rod Stewart and bears a striking physical resemblance to him.

Contact: Eldorado Hotel Casino, 345 N. Virginia St., Reno, NV; 775/786-5700 or 800/648-4597.

Fitzgerald's

The Fitz Showbar offers daily live lounge entertainment 2 P.M.–2 A.M. Monday–Wednesday and noon–4 A.M. Thursday–Sunday. With its Irish legacy, Fitzgerald's is the place to be on St. Patrick's Day (late March), when it kicks things up a notch with marching bands, free live entertainment, and a crafts fair on Virginia Street, along with Irish bands inside at Limericks Pub and Grille.

Contact: Fitzgerald's, 255 N. Virginia St., Reno, NV; 775/786-3300.

Harrah's Reno

Headliners, musical variety shows, and adult (i.e., T&A) revues are presented nightly except Thursday in Sammy's Showroom (named after Sammy Davis Jr.). Also, the Plaza at Harrah's hosts outdoor concerts with name entertainers during warm weather months.

Contact: Harrah's Reno, 219 N. Center St., Reno, NV; Sammy's Showroom: 775/788-2900 or 800/427-7247 (for tickets and information).

John Ascuaga's Nugget

The Celebrity Showroom and the Rose Ballroom are the most frequent venues in Reno for star-studded shows such as those by Las Vegas regulars Paul Anka, Al Jarreau, Tony Bennett, Jay Leno, Rich Little, and Wayne Newton, along with various headline country artists. Nightclub acts are booked in the Casino Cabaret. Both Trader Dick's and Orozko restaurants host live entertainment.

Contact: John Ascuaga's Nugget, 1100 Nugget Ave., Sparks, NV; 775/356-3300, 775/356-3300, or 800/648-1177.

Peppermill Hotel Casino

Three venues are in the Peppermill—the Tahoe Room, which occasionally books name acts, the Casino Cabaret, and the Steak House Lounge.

Contact: Peppermill Hotel Casino, 2707 S. Virginia St., Reno, NV; 775/826-2121 or 800/648-6992.

Rail City Casino

In Sparks, about four miles east of downtown Reno, this small casino in the heart of Victorian Square hosts lounge acts Thursday–Saturday nights and karaoke on Tuesday night.

Contact: Rail City Casino, 2121 Victorian Ave., Sparks, NV; 775/359-9440.

Reno Hilton

Big, lavish, and high-energy, Broadway-style productions in the Hilton Theater are among the most impressive variety shows in Reno.

Occasionally, name artists such as Bob Dylan also perform here. An annual summer concert series in the Outdoor Amphitheater features name rock, jazz, and country artists. Also, a nightclub, The Garage, offers country, bluegrass, jazz, Cajun, ska, and rock bands on various nights of the week.
Contact: Reno Hilton, 2500 E. 2nd St., Reno, NV; 775/789-2285 or 800/648-3568. The Garage hot line is 775/789-2565.

Siena Hotel Spa Casino
This new and elegant hotel near downtown Reno offers live music Thursday–Saturday nights, varying from DJ music to smooth jazz in its wine cellar.
Contact: Siena Hotel Spa Casino, 1 S. Lake St., Reno, NV; 775/337-6260.

Silver Club
This recently expanded but modest-sized hotel/casino in Sparks, a few miles east of downtown Reno, hosts live music and dancing nightly except Monday.
Contact: Silver Club, 1040 Victorian Ave., Sparks, NV; 775/358-4771.

Silver Legacy Casino Resort
Big-name performers such as Engelbert Humperdinck and Julio Iglesias appear intermittently in the Grande Exposition Hall. Local bands play in the Silver Baron Lounge Tuesday–Saturday, and DJ music or dueling pianos hold forth nightly at Rum Bullions Island Bar.
Contact: Silver Legacy Casino Resort, 407 N. Virginia St., Reno, NV; 775/329-4777 or 800/687-7733.

Sundowner
This downtown hotel offers small-group music Thursday–Sunday.
Contact: Sundowner, 450 N. Arlington Ave., Reno, NV; 775/786-7050.

Something positively remarkable is going on in Carson City, the capital of Nevada. The Brewery Arts Center, the city's community arts venue, is well on its way to creating an arts campus covering two square blocks.

CARSON CITY/DAYTON
Carson Nugget
This downtown Carson City casino stages live music nightly except Monday.
Contact: Carson Nugget, 800 N. Carson, Carson City, NV; 775/882-5535.

Carson Station
Duos, trios, and small acts take the stage in the lounge here.
Contact: Carson Station, 900 S. Carson St., Carson City, NV; 775/883-0900.

Pinon Plaza
This Best Western hotel and casino in Carson City offers live entertainment Tuesday–Saturday.
Contact: Pinon Plaza, 2171 Hwy. 50 E, Carson City, NV; 775/885-9000.

CARSON VALLEY/MINDEN
Carson Valley Inn
The Cabaret Lounge books various musical and dance bands.
Contact: Carson Valley Inn, 1627 U.S. 395, Minden, NV; 775/782-9711.

EVENTS CENTERS
The high visibility and easy accessiblity of the casinos should not tempt you to overlook the varied and interesting options offered by the other major entertainment venues in the area.

Brewery Arts Center
Something positively remarkable is going on in Carson City, the capital of Nevada. The Brewery Arts Center, the city's community arts venue, is well on its way to creating an arts campus covering two square blocks. Founded in 1976 in an historic brewery building, the center has been pursuing a master plan that entails the acquisition of other historic places, construction of an

outdoor amphitheater with a covered stage, and remodeling of the Donald W. Reynolds black box theater. In late 2001 the organization bought the vintage Saint Teresa of Avila Catholic Church, converting it to a first-rate, 350-seat performance hall. The church has brilliant acoustics, and already it has played host to several name entertainers, including jazz and classical artists. If you're in the area, don't miss the chance to catch a performance here. Check the website for the calendar.

Contact: Brewery Arts Center, 444 W. King St., Carson City, NV; 775/883-1976; website: www.breweryarts.org.

Lawlor Events Center

At the University of Nevada, Reno, this large facility offers big-name shows with rock and country music stars.

Contact: Lawlor Events Center, UNR, Reno, NV; 775/793-1098.

Pioneer Center for the Performing Arts

Diverse productions are offered here, from ballet and Broadway plays to folk and rock music with major recording artists.

Contact: Pioneer Center for the Performing Arts, 100 S. Virginia St., Reno, NV; 775/686-6600.

Reno Livestock Events Center

The site of rodeos, flea markets, and other events offers summer country-western concerts, usually with well-known recording artists.

Contact: Reno Livestock Events Center, 1350 N. Wells Ave., Reno, NV; 775/688-5750 or 775/688-5751.

COMEDY CLUBS

Want a laugh (or maybe just a chuckle)? Reno's new genre of comedy clubs—all of them in casino hotels—may be the answer. Performers and performances are usually ribald—sometimes at the expense of audience members—but are generally very entertaining, a good antidote for stakes you may have lost at the tables.

Catch a Rising Star (Silver Legacy)

This is a small, intimate, cabaret-sized club adjacent to the ground-floor casino that usually has one warm-up act (a lounge singer) and a stand-up comic. There are two shows nightly Tuesday–Saturday.

Contact: Silver Legacy Casino Resort, 407 N. Virginia St., Reno, NV; 775/325-7454.

Just for Laughs (Sands Regency)

This new club inside the Sands Regency often presents themed comedy, such as "down-home" country-western humor, on weekends, and contemporary comedy on weekdays. Showtimes are 8:30 P.M. Wednesday–Sunday, with a second show added on Friday and Saturday nights at 10:30 P.M.

Contact: Sands Regency, 4th at Arlington, Reno, NV; 775/348-1346.

NIGHTCLUBS, BARS, AND RESTAURANTS

Adele's at the Plaza

This popular and upscale restaurant in the south part of the city offers live jazz Friday and Saturday nights starting at 9 P.M.

Contact: Adele's at the Plaza, 425 S. Virginia St., Reno, NV; 775/333-6503.

Alturas Bar and Nightclub

Blues hold forth at this downstairs joint, with bands scheduled on Friday and Saturday nights.

Contact: Alturas, 1044 E. 4th St., Reno, NV; 775/324-5050.

Art Gecko's Southwest Grill

Various blues, rock, dance, and humor acts appear at this restaurant/nightclub, in Circus Circus on the skywalk between the hotel and the Silver Legacy, 10 A.M.–2 A.M., mostly on weekends.

Contact: Art Gecko's Southwest Grill, 500 N. Sierra St., Reno, NV; 775/329-0711.

Baron Lounge

Live music on Friday and Saturday nights, usually with a cover charge.

Contact: Baron Lounge, 1483 E. 4th St., Reno, NV; 775/323-1956.

Cantina Los Tres Hombres
The two cantinas, one in Reno and one in Sparks, offer live music Friday–Sunday.
Contact: Cantina Los Tres Hombres, 7111 S. Virginia St., Reno, NV, 775/852-0202; and on 926 Victorian Ave., Sparks, NV, 775/356-6262.

Club Voodoo
From punk rock to country to comedy, this place offers weekend entertainment.
Contact: Club Voodoo, 1126 E. 4th St., Reno, NV; 775/333-6942.

Flowing Tide Pub
Live music is usually held on Thursday, with karaoke on Tuesday.
Contact: Flowing Tide Pub, 10580 N. McCarran, Ste. 109, Reno, NV; 775/747-7707.

Great Basin Brewing Company
Blues, folk, reggae, classic rock, and jazz groups and solo musicians play on an outdoor stage during summer evenings. On Sunday night, there are free, one-act plays performed by the Great Basin Players.
Contact: Great Basin Brewing Company, 846 Victorian Ave., Sparks, NV; 775/355-7711.

Hacienda Restaurant and Bar
This Mexican restaurant offers entertainment four nights a week, with live jazz on Thursday, rock bands on Friday, DJ dancing on Saturday, and salsa dancing on Wednesday. Program start times range 8 P.M.–10 P.M.
Contact: Hacienda Restaurant and Bar, 10580 N. McCarran Blvd., Reno, NV; 775/746-2228; website: www.renodining.com.

Haywire Waikiki Country Night Club
For all you buckaroos and cowgirls, this is the place for line dancin' on Reno's largest hardwood dance floor, with free boot scootin' lessons Thursday–Friday. Country DJ music holds forth Thursday–Saturday, and karaoke is on Friday and Saturday starting at 9 P.M.

Contact: Haywire Country Night Club, 701 S. Virginia (at St. Lawrence), Reno, NV; 775/337-2345.

Joe Bob's Roadhouse
At Carson Hot Springs in Carson City, this funky bar presents bands on Friday and Saturday nights and karaoke Thursday nights.
Contact: Joe Bob's Roadhouse, 1500 Hot Springs Rd., Carson City, NV; 775/883-7799.

Little Waldorf Saloon
Wednesday–Saturday nights, Little Waldorf provides live music and entertainment, and there's a large sports bar with a dozen TV sets. Close to the University of Nevada, and definitely a college kids' hangout.
Contact: Little Waldorf, 1661 N. Virginia St., Reno, NV; 775/323-3682.

Paul Revere's Kicks
Inside the National Bowling Stadium, this club, founded by the aging but still-rockin' Paul Revere (of the Raiders), features plenty of memorabilia of 1960s-era rock and 1970s disco, which should give you an idea of the age group that it aims for. The crowd consists mostly of tourists, not hip locals. The club is open from 9 P.M. Wednesday–Saturday, and there is ample free parking in the massive adjoining garage.
Contact: Kicks Nightclub, 300 N. Center St., Reno, NV; 775/322-4860.

Reno Live
This multiclub complex, close to downtown Reno, has several different dance floors and DJ music programs, varying from techno to hip-hop to '80s dance hits. Usually open Thursday–Saturday nights, with the biggest blowout on Saturday.
Contact: Reno Live, 45 W. 2nd St., Reno, NV; 775/329-1952.

Rocky's
Bands play Thursday–Sunday nights. No cover charge for some groups.
Contact: Rocky's, 2nd and Virginia Sts., Reno, NV; 775/322-7620.

West 2nd Street Bar and Night Club

Reno's only full-time karaoke nightclub offers singing options seven nights a week, using a state-of-the-art sound and video system and more than 4,000 selections. You can dance if you want.
Contact: West 2nd Street Bar and Night Club, 118 W. 2nd St., Reno, NV; 775/348-7976.

Zephyr Lounge

You'll find nightly live entertainment that varies among jazz, rock, swing, and blues music, and might also include comedy and improvisational theater.
Contact: Zephyr Bar and Grill, 1074 S. Virginia St., Reno, NV; 775/324-9853.

Basics

Transportation

AIRPORTS

Reno-Tahoe International Airport: This is the main point of arrival for most air passengers coming to the Lake Tahoe/Reno area. The airport provides more than 100 daily flights by Alaska Air, America West, American, Continental, Delta, Northwest, Skywest, Southwest, Trans World Airlines, and United. Driving time to the North Shore is approximately 45 minutes, and to the South Shore, 75–90 minutes. Off U.S. 395 at 2001 Plumb Ln., Reno, NV. Contact: 775/328-6400 or general information recording at 888/766-4685; website: www.renoairport.com.

Lake Tahoe Airport: Close to South Lake Tahoe and the Stateline casinos, this airport has experienced a constant turnover of commercial air carriers. As this edition went to press, discussions were under way with two airlines that may serve the airport from various West Coast cities. Otherwise, the airport is used mainly by private aircraft and charter companies. It's two miles south of the "Y" intersection on U.S. 50 at 1901 Airport Rd., South Lake Tahoe, CA. For latest information on commercial flights call 530/542-6180 or check the website for posted schedules, at www.laketahoeairport.com.

Carson City Airport: General aviation airport serving the Carson City area. At 2640 E. Graves Ln., Carson City, NV. Contact: 775/884-1163.

Minden-Tahoe Airport (formerly Douglas County Airport): General aviation airport

view of Harrah's and Lake Tahoe

serving the Gardnerville-Minden and Carson Valley areas. At 1146 Airport Rd., Gardnerville, NV. Contact: 775/782-9871.

Truckee-Tahoe Airport: General aviation airport serving the North Lake Tahoe and Truckee-Donner areas. On Highway 267, 10 miles north of Lake Tahoe, at 10356 Truckee Airport Rd., Truckee, CA. Contact: 530/587-4119.

RAILWAY

Amtrak: Daily passenger trains serve Reno and Truckee from points west and east. The station is at East Commercial Row and Lake Street in Reno, Nevada. Contact: 800/USA-RAIL (800/872-7245); website: www.amtrak.com.

AIRPORT BUS AND VAN SHUTTLES

Greyhound Bus Lines: You can arrange transportation to and from various points at Lake Tahoe and Reno, though this is more of a long-haul than a short-haul option. Stations at Stateline and the city of South Lake Tahoe are open daily 8 A.M.–5 P.M. Contact: 775/588-4645 (Stateline), 530/543-1050 (South Lake Tahoe), 775/322-2970 (Reno), 775/882-3375 (Carson City), or 800/231-2222 (reservations/general information); website: www.greyhound.com. Greyhound stops in Truckee but there is no local agent. For information on that schedule contact the Reno office.

No Stress Express: There are several departures daily from Reno-Tahoe International Airport. Route 1 includes the Hyatt Regency Lake Tahoe at Incline Village, Northstar-at-Tahoe, Cal-Neva Resort, the Biltmore Hotel, and the Kings Beach/Carnelian Bay area. Route 3 includes Truckee, Squaw Valley, and Tahoe City. Route 4 serves South Shore at Stateline and South Lake Tahoe. No Stress uses 11- and 14-passenger vans. Prices are around $40 one way. Contact: 775/885-7550 or 888/474-8885 or 800/426-5644; website: www.nostressexpress.com.

Royal Limousine Service: Minibuses, seven- and 12-passenger vans, and luxury eight-passenger limousines are available for airport shuttles or charters throughout the Lake Tahoe basin, Truckee, and Reno areas. Contact: 530/582-1300 (Truckee) or 800/660-4546; email: limolink @aol.com.

Tahoe Casino Express: This is the easiest and least expensive transportation option to South Lake Tahoe. Luxury motorcoaches operate 14 times a day in summer and 18 times a day in winter each way between Reno-Tahoe International Airport and hotels in South Lake Tahoe (Caesars, Harrah's, Harveys, Horizon, Embassy Suites and Lakeside Inn). The Casino Express has its own waiting lounge near the baggage claim area of the airport. The trip takes 75–90 minutes and costs $19 one way or $34 round-trip; two children under 12 years old per adult ride free. Buy tickets through travel agents, at the airport, and at casinos. Reservations are recommended for weekend trips. Contact: 775/785-2424 or 800/446-6128; email: info@tahoecasinoexpress .com. To see detailed schedules, check out the website: www.tahoecasinoexpress.com.

Truckee Tahoe Limousine and Tours: Vans and six- to eight-passenger limousines offer airport shuttle, custom tours, and wedding transportation in the Reno, Truckee, Squaw Valley, and Lake Tahoe areas. Contact: 530/587-2160 or 800/255-2160.

PUBLIC TRANSPORTATION LAKE TAHOE AREA

Bus Plus: Using six- to eight-passenger mini-vans to serve South Lake Tahoe, this is an on-demand ride-share program whose major benefit is 24-hour daily operation. Door-to-door pickup is just $3 per person each way within the city of South Lake Tahoe or Stateline areas, or $5 to Lake Tahoe Airport and points in Eldorado County. You must make reservations at least an hour in advance, two hours during inclement weather. Parents must bring safety seats for youngsters. Contact: 530/542-6077.

Nifty "50" Trolley: A San Francisco-style open-air, rubber-tire trolley serves the South Shore from July to Labor Day, operating 10 A.M.–11 P.M. daily. Major stops are at beaches, campgrounds, casinos, the Heavenly Tram, shopping centers, recreation sites, restaurants, and paddlewheel excursion boats. Though routes and times may change from year to year, there are usually two routes. Route A runs between Stateline on U.S. 50 and Historic Camp Richardson Resort on Highway 89. Route B runs between Stateline and Zephyr Cove. Along the routes are about 40 stops, each served once an hour. Drivers are dressed in period costume and provide live narration. The cost for a full day of riding is $3 for adults, $1 for children 3–7, free for under three. Contact: 530/542-6077.

South Tahoe Area Ground Express (STAGE): This South Shore bus service goes from the transportation center at the "Y" intersection of Highways 50 and 89 to the Stateline casinos, stopping in select neighborhoods in between. The cost is $1.25 each way or $2 for an unlimited day pass; children under seven ride free. Hours of operation are 6 A.M.–1 A.M. daily. Contact: 530/542-6077.

Tahoe Area Regional Transit (TART): This is a regular bus service that operates along 30 miles of shoreline on the west and north shores of Lake Tahoe between Meeks Bay, Tahoe City, and Incline Village. There's also a shuttle that runs several times daily between Truckee and Tahoe City. One very big plus: The bus will accommodate bicycles in summer and skis in winter. Also, most lodging properties are near the bus stops. TART connects with the Truckee Trolley, Tahoe City Trolley, Greyhound bus lines, and Amtrak. The bus stops hourly in each direction. Special schedules are available when certain events are under way. The cost for a one-way ride is $1.25 for adults, free for children under five. An all-day unlimited pass is $3 for adults and children. TART operates from 6:30 A.M.–6:30 P.M. daily, year-round. Contact: 530/581-6365 or 800/736-6365.

Tahoe City Trolley: This rubber-tire trolley serves Tahoe City, Squaw Valley, Stateline, Tahoma, and other points on the north and west shores of the lake late June–early September. By day (10:30 A.M.–6 P.M.), there are two routes: Meeks Bay on the West Shore to Stateline, Nevada, and back, and Stateline to Carnelian Bay and back. By night (6 P.M.–midnight), the trolley runs from Squaw Valley to Stateline and back,

and Tahoe City to Tahoma and back, thus serving restaurants, bars, and casinos. The cost is $3 per person (including children) for an all-day (and night) pass. Stops are made at most designated TART bus stops, and you may need to use a combination of TART buses and the trolley to reach your destination. Contact: 800/736-6365; website: www.laketahoetransit.com.

Truckee Trolley: Service runs between Donner Lake (West End Beach), Tahoe Donner, Commercial Row, and other points in Truckee, from 9:15 A.M.–5:15 P.M. spring–fall. In winter, there is service from the downtown Truckee transportation depot to Northstar-at-Tahoe ski resort. The one-way cost is $1.25 for adults ($2 for an all-day pass); seniors (60 and over) and children (12 and under) pay half price. At night, from 6 P.M. on, all rides are free. For current schedule, call 800/736-6365; website: www.laketahoetransit.com.

PUBLIC TRANSPORTATION RENO AREA

Citifare: This public bus service runs through Reno and Sparks, providing wheelchair access on all routes. Airport transportation is available. The cost is $1.25 for adults, $.90 for ages 7–18, $.60 for seniors and disabled passengers; children six and under ride free. Free transfers may be used between routes. Daily, weekly, and monthly commuter books and passes are available. Discount identification cards are available for seniors and disabled people. Daily regular service is provided, with 24-hour service on some routes. Contact: Regional Transportation Commission; 775/348-7433 (24-hour info) or 775/348-7450 (hearing-impaired callers); website: www.rtcwashoe.com.

SKI SHUTTLES

Alpine Meadows: During the winter ski season, an extensive free shuttle service operates along three routes. The North Shore Route, which is daily, has one departure in the morning beginning at 8 A.M. at the Hyatt Regency Lake Tahoe in Incline Village and extending through the North

Shore communities through Tahoe City, arriving at Alpine Meadows at 8:50 A.M. The West Shore Route, also daily, has two morning departures that leave from Sunnyside Resort, Granlibakken Resort, the Tahoe City Bank of America, River Ranch, and Mineral Springs Estate. There is one departure in the morning from The Resort at Squaw Creek, and on weekends there's a third route, to the Sherwood Chair (no beginners recommended), from most of the West Shore stops. Contact: 530/581-8341 or check the schedule on the resort's website: www.skialpine.com.

Diamond Peak Ski Resort: This free shuttle service runs throughout Incline Village and Crystal Bay in Nevada, daily 8 A.M.–5 P.M. Contact: 775/832-1177; website: www.diamondpeak.com.

Heavenly Ski Resort: The free shuttle service at Heavenly stops near or at most lodging properties throughout South Lake Tahoe and Stateline every 20–30 minutes (8 A.M.–5:30 P.M. daily). Buses serve both the California and Nevada entrances to the resort, as well as the new transportation center in front of the gondola at Heavenly Village. Contact: 775/586-7000 or check out the resort website at www.skiheavenly.com. Also, Sierra Nevada Stage Lines offers daily bus service from seven hotels in Reno and three hotels at Incline Village (including the Hyatt Regency Lake Tahoe and Cal-Neva Resort). The package price includes round-trip transportation and lift ticket, and varies from year to year. Information: 775/331-1147 or 800/822-6009, or check out the website: www.frontiertours.com/heavenly.html.

Kirkwood: In winter, the ski resort is served daily by shuttles from various South Shore properties, but only with reservations. Limited service may be available in summer. There is a round-trip fare charged. Contact: 800/446-2928 or 209/258-6000 or check out the resort website at www.skikirkwood.com.

Mt. Rose: Sierra Nevada Stage Line operates two daily ski shuttles from Reno to Mt. Rose, one in the morning and one in the afternoon, December–April. The package includes skiing and round-trip transportation from major Reno hotels, including Eldorado, Harrah's, John Ascuaga's Nugget, the Reno Hilton, Atlantis, and the Peppermill. Cost of the shuttle includes the price of a discounted lift ticket, which varies from year to year. Contact: 775/331-1147 or 800/822-6009 (outside Nevada); website: www.frontiertours.com.

Northstar-at-Tahoe: December–March, this free ski shuttle offers daily service between Tahoe Vista, Kings Beach, Incline Village, Truckee, and Northstar. Northstar's ski shuttle connects to TART public transit buses for skiers from the West Shore and Tahoe City. Year-round there's a free shuttle from the Truckee Tahoe Airport and the Amtrak and Greyhound depots in Truckee, but you must make reservations at least 24 hours in advance. Contact: 530/562-2257 or 800/-GO-NORTH (800/466-6874); website: www.northstarattahoe.com.

Royal Gorge Cross-Country Ski Resort: A free shuttle bus runs daily between Rainbow Lodge and Summit Station for guests of Rainbow and skiers on the Interconnect Trail. Contact: 530/426-3871; website: www.royalgorge.com.

Sierra-at-Tahoe: The free ski shuttle bus stops at regular intervals at more than 30 locations in South Shore. Contact: 530/541-7548 or check out the resort's website: www.sierratahoe.com.

Homewood Mountain Resort: A free ski shuttle runs between North and South Lodge and downtown Homewood. Contact: 530/525-2992. North Shore and West Shore access is provided by Tahoe Area Regional Transit (TART) with connections to Reno-Tahoe International Airport. Use TART ($1.25 per person one way) and apply the full bus fare toward a lift ticket. Contact: 530/581-6365.

Squaw Creek Transportation: For guests staying at The Resort at Squaw Creek, shuttles are available to/from the Reno-Tahoe International Airport, with reservations required. To Tahoe City, there are free shuttles for shopping and dining. There are also free shuttles to the ski slopes at Squaw Valley USA. Contact: 530/581-6628 or 800/327-3353, ext. 8; website: www.squawcreek.com.

Squaw Valley USA: You can reach Squaw Valley on public transit from virtually any point at Lake Tahoe or Reno. From North Lake Tahoe, the resort operates a free daily ski shuttle (one bus per morning only) from the Hyatt at Incline Village to the Bank of America at Tahoe City. Another bus serves the West Shore from Sunnyside Resort to River Ranch. Reservations are required no later than 12 hours in advance. The shuttle operates mid-December–mid-April. Contact: 530/581-7181 or check out the resort website: www.squaw.com. From South Lake Tahoe and Stateline, Sierra Nevada Stage Lines operates one morning departure daily from 10 stops, arriving at 9 A.M. From Reno, the same bus line picks up from 12 hotels (three by reservation only) along two routes, including Eldorado, Flamingo Hilton, Sands Regency, John Ascuaga's Nugget, Reno Hilton, Atlantis, Peppermill, and Harrah's, arriving at 9 A.M. Fares include an all-day discounted lift ticket and transportation, and vary from year to year. Contact: 775/331-1147 or 800/822-6009 or check out the website: www.frontiertours.com./skisquaw.html. Also, the South Shore-based Lake Tahoe Cruises runs weekday morning ski shuttle voyages on the *Meteor,* a high-speed, canopy-covered power boat, from Marina Village at the end of Ski Run Boulevard, in the city of South Lake Tahoe, to Tahoe City on the North Shore, where a ski bus meets arriving passengers for the short drive to the mountain. For passengers originating at South Lake Tahoe, the return trip is made aboard the much slower-moving *Tahoe Queen* paddlewheel excursion vessel. Contact: Hornblower Cruises; 530/541-3364, or check the website at www.laketahoecruises.com.

Sugar Bowl: This free ski shuttle operates from several points in Truckee and the Tahoe Donner, Donner Lake, and Donner Summit areas. Hours are 6:50 A.M.–5:50 P.M. Contact: 530/426-3651, or the resort website at www.sugarbowl.com.

LIMOUSINES AND TOUR SERVICES

Abracadabra Airport Limousine Service: Contact: 530/544-2200 or 800/334-1826.

Airport Mini Bus: Charters and airport shuttles serve the Reno area. At 100 Sunshine Ln. in Reno. Contact: 775/786-3700.

All Seasons Tahoe Limousine Service: Stretch limousines are available for airport transfers (Reno and Tahoe), weddings, birthdays, anniversaries, and tours of the Tahoe area. In South Lake Tahoe, California. Contact: 530/577-2727 or 800/334-1826.

Bell Limo: Scenic tours of northern Nevada and airport shuttle service is provided by Bell, which features Cadillac and Lincoln stretch limousines. Corporate Town Cars are available. At 100 Sunshine Ln. in Reno. Contact: 775/786-3700 or 800/BEL-LIMO (800/235-5466).

Executive Limousine and Shuttle Service: This Reno-based service operates 24 hours a day. In addition to airport pickup, it also offers tours of Carson City and Virginia City. Contact: 775/333-3300 or 775/882-5536 or 800/323-3958; website: www.executive-limousine.com.

Frontier Tours: This charter bus company serves the Carson City, Reno, and Sparks areas. Contact: 775/331-8687 or 800/831-2877; website: www.frontiertours.com.

Gray Line Tours: This company serves the Lake Tahoe area, Reno, Carson City, and Virginia City. Contact: 775/331-2877 or 800/454-2487.

North Shore Limousine: Luxury transportation service and tours available. Contact: 530/832-0100 or 800/832-8213.

Royal Limousine Service: Minibuses, 14-passenger vans, and stretch limousines are available for airport shuttles or charters in the Lake Tahoe basin, Truckee, and Reno areas. Contact: 530/582-1300 or 800/660-4546.

Sierra West Limousine: Serving Tahoe, Reno, and the surrounding areas 24 hours a day, seven days a week, with a fleet of presidential and stretch limousines. Sierra West offers airport transfers, wedding rides, tours, and lodging packages. Contact: Reno Airport; 775/329-4310, or Lake Tahoe; 775/588-1079.

Truckee Tahoe Limousine and Tours: Stretch limos and a classic 1957 Cadillac limousine can be arranged year-round for airport transportation, weddings, tours, and special charters. Contact: 530/587-2160 or 800/255-2160; website: www.tahoeguide.com/go/transportation.

RENTAL CARS

A&A Perkins Auto Rental: Serving the Truckee area, this company has a fleet that includes four-wheel-drives. At 10689 E. River St. in Truckee. Contact: 530/587-7823.

Airport Auto Rental: The company offers four-wheel-drives, vans, station wagons, and moving trucks. On Highway 267 and Airport Road near the Truckee-Tahoe Airport. Contact: 530/587-2688 or 800/200-2688.

Alamo Rent-a-Car: At the Reno-Tahoe Airport. Contact: 775/323-5843 or 800/327-9633 (nationwide reservations).

Alpine Car Rental: In Incline Village at 1056 Tahoe Boulevard. Contact: 775/833-4424.

Avis Rent-a-Car: At Caesars Tahoe in Stateline, Nevada, and at the Reno-Tahoe Airport. Contact: 775/588-4450 (Caesars) or 800/831-2847 (nationwide reservations).

Budget Rent-a-Car: At the Reno-Tahoe Airport and at Center Street in Reno. Contact: 775/785-2545 or 800/527-0700 (nationwide reservations).

Dollar Rent-a-Car: At the Reno-Tahoe Airport. Contact: 775/348-2800 or 800/800-4000 (nationwide reservations).

Enterprise Rent-a-Car: In Reno, South Lake Tahoe, Truckee, Carson City, and Gardnerville. Contact: 775/329-3773 (Reno), 775/586-1077 (Stateline), 530/550-1550 (Truckee), or 800/736-8222 (nationwide reservations).

Hertz Rent-a-Car: At Stateline and Reno-Tahoe airports. Contact: 775/785-2554 (Reno), 530/586-0041 (Stateline), or 800/654-3131 (nationwide reservations).

Lakeside Towing: Minivans and four-wheel-drives may be rented from this company, which serves the Truckee/North Shore areas. At 10745 W. River St. in Truckee. Contact: 530/587-6000 (Truckee) or 530/581-3015 (Tahoe City).

National Car Rental: South Lake Tahoe; 530/541-7994 and the Reno-Tahoe Airport; 775/785-2756. For nationwide reservations, call 800/227-7368.

Resort Rent-a-Car: In the Reno-Tahoe International Airport. Contact: 775/348-1535 or 800/289-5343 (nationwide reservations).

Tahoe Valley Auto: At 1190 Bonanza Ave., South Lake Tahoe, CA. Contact: 530/541-7830.

Thrifty Car Rental: At the Reno-Tahoe Airport. Contact: 775/329-0096 or 800/367-2277 (nationwide reservations).

Truckee Rent-a-Car: At 11036 W. River St. in Truckee, this company serves the Truckee/Tahoe area. Contact: 530/587-2841.

TAXIS

Bus Plus: This taxi service is in South Lake Tahoe, California. Contact: 530/542-6077.

Capitol Cab: This Carson City company offers 24-hour service throughout the entire Carson area. Wheelchair-accessible vans are available. Contact: 775/885-0300.

De Luxe Taxi: Taxicab, courier, and delivery service to the Reno/Sparks area. Wake-up calls are available. Visa, American Express, and MasterCard are accepted. Contact: 775/355-5555.

Paradise Taxi: In South Lake Tahoe, California, Paradise provides sightseeing tours, airport service from the South Shore, and local delivery service 24 hours a day. Contact: 530/577-4708.

Reno Sparks Cab: Serving Reno and Sparks 24 hours a day. Wheelchair-accessible vans are available. Contact: 775/333-3333.

Star Taxi: This company serves Reno and Sparks. Contact: 775/355-5555.

Sunshine Taxi: Serving Lake Tahoe areas. Contact: 530/544-5555 or 530/542-1234.

Tahoe Truckee Taxi: Serving the North and West Shores of Lake Tahoe. Contact: 530/583-8294, 530/582-8294 (Truckee), 775/832-8294 (Incline Village), or 888/881-8294.

Whittlesea Checker Taxi: This company serves the Reno area. Contact: 775/322-2222.

Yellow Cab: Operating 24 hours daily, this taxi service covers all the major communities in Lake Tahoe, Reno, and Sparks. Contact: 530/544-5555 (South Lake Tahoe), 775/588-8294 (Stateline), 530/546-9090 (Kings Beach, Truckee, Donner, and Tahoe City), 775/831-8294 (Incline Village), or 775/331-2500 (Reno and Sparks).

Information and Services

ROAD CONDITIONS

CalTrans Department of Transportation: 916/445-1534, 530/587-3563, or 800/427-7623.

Nevada State Road Condition Report: 775/793-1313.

Tahoe Hot Line (for road conditions, weather, dining, and entertainment): South Lake Tahoe, California; 530/542-INFO (530/542-4636); North Lake Tahoe and Truckee, California; 530/546-LAKE (530/546-5253); Reno, Sparks, and Carson City, Nevada; 775/831-6677.

WEATHER CONDITIONS

Lake Tahoe, North Shore: 530/546-7251 and enter category number 5050.

Casino Floor at Harrah's

Lake Tahoe, South Shore: 530/541-0200 and enter category number 5050.

National Weather Service, Reno: 775/673-8100.

TRANSPORTATION AGENCIES

Coast Guard

Lake Tahoe Coast Guard Station: 2500 Lake Forest Rd., Lake Forest, CA 96145; 530/583-4433.

Federal Aviation Administration

Air Traffic Control Tower: 1701 Airport Blvd., Lake Tahoe Airport, South Lake Tahoe, CA 96150; 530/541-3302.

Flight Service Station, Pilot Weather Briefing: 601 Rock Blvd., Reno, NV 89502; 775/858-1300 or 800/992-7433.

BUREAUS AND CHAMBERS OF COMMERCE

Alpine County Chamber of Commerce: P.O. Box 265, Markleeville, CA 96120; 530/694-2475; email: alpinecounty@alpinecounty.com; website: www.alpinecounty.com.

Carson City Convention and Visitors Bureau: 1900 S. Carson St., Ste. 200, Carson City, NV 89701; 775/687-7410 or 800/NEVADA-1 (800/638-2321); website: www.carson-city.org.

Carson City Chamber of Commerce: 1900 S. Carson St., Carson City, NV 89701; 775/882-1565; website: www.carsoncitychamber.com.

Carson Valley Chamber of Commerce and Visitors Authority: 1513 U.S. 395 N, Ste. 1, Gardnerville, NV 89410; 775/782-8144 or 800/727-7677; website: www.carsonvalleynv.org.

Dayton Area Chamber of Commerce: 15 Main St., P.O. Box 2408, Dayton, NV 89403; 775/246-7909.

Eastern Plumas Chamber of Commerce: 424 E. Sierra Ave. (Hwy. 70), P.O. Box 1379, Portola, CA 96122; 530/832-5444 or 800/995-6057.

Incline Village-Crystal Bay Chamber of Commerce: 969 Tahoe Blvd., Incline Village, NV 89451; 775/831-4440.

Lake Tahoe, Incline Village/Crystal Bay Visitors and Convention Bureau: 969 Tahoe Blvd., Incline Village, NV 89451; 775/832-1606 or 800/GO-TAHOE (800/468-2463); website: www.gotahoe.com.

Lake Tahoe Visitors Authority: 1156 Ski Run Blvd./P.O. Box 16299, South Lake Tahoe, CA 96151; 530/544-5050 or 800/AT-TAHOE (800/288-2463); website: www.virtualtahoe.com.

North Lake Tahoe Chamber of Commerce: 245 N. Lake Blvd., Tahoe City, CA 96145; 530/581-6900.

North Lake Tahoe Resort Association: P.O. Box 1757, Tahoe City, CA 96145; 530/583-3494 or 800/TAHOE-4U (800/824-6348); website: www.tahoefun.org.

Plumas County Visitors Bureau: 550 Crescent St., P.O. Box 4120, Quincy, CA 95971; 530/283-6345 or 800/326-2247; website: www.plumas.ca.us.

Greater Reno-Sparks Chamber of Commerce: 405 Marsh Ave., Reno, NV 89505; 775/686-3030; website: www.reno-sparkschamber.org.

ADDITIONAL INFORMATION SOURCES

Alpine County Chamber of Commerce: Call for the latest in fishing and tips or pick up a complete fishing packet; P.O. Box 265, Markleeville, CA 96120; 530/694-2475; website: www.alpinecounty.com.

California Department of Fish and Game (Headquarters): 3211 S St., Sacramento, CA 95816; 916/227-2244; website: www.dfg.ca.gov.

California Department of Fish and Game (Region 2 Office): 1701 Nimbus Rd., Rancho Cordova, CA 95670; 916/355-0978.

Nevada Division of Wildlife: P.O. Box 10678, Reno, NV 89520; 775/688-1500; website: www.state.nv.us/cnr/nvwildlife.

Plumas County Visitors Bureau: Knowledgeable about the Feather River, Lake Davis, and Lakes Basin areas; 91 Church St., Quincy, CA 95971; 530/283-6345 or 800/326-2247; website: www.plumas.ca.us.

Reno-Sparks Convention and Visitors Authority: 4590 S. Virginia St./P.O. Box 837, Reno, NV 89504; 775/827-7600; 800/752-1177, or 800/FOR-RENO (800/367-7366); websites: www.renolaketahoe.com or www.playreno.com.

Reno-Sparks Indian Colony Tribal Council: 98 Colony Rd., Reno, NV 89502; 775/329-2936.

Sierra County Chamber of Commerce: P.O. Box 222, Downieville, CA 95936; 530/862-0308.

Sparks Community Chamber of Commerce: 831 Victorian Ave., Sparks, NV 89431; 775/358-1976; website: www.sparkschamber.org.

South Lake Tahoe Chamber of Commerce: 3066 Lake Tahoe Blvd., South Lake Tahoe, CA 96150; 530/541-5255; website: www.tahoe.com.

Tahoe Douglas Chamber of Commerce and Visitor Center: 195 U.S. 50/P.O. Box 7139, Stateline, NV 89449; 775/588-4591; website: www.tahoechamber.org.

Truckee-Donner Chamber of Commerce: 10065 Commercial Row/P.O. Box 2757, Truckee, CA 96160; 530/587-2757 or 800/548-8388; website: www.truckee.com.

Virginia City Chamber of Commerce: Virginia and Truckee Railroad Car, 131 S. C St., P.O. Box 464, Virginia City, NV 89440; 775/847-0311; website: www.vcnevada.com.

Virginia City Visitors Bureau: 38 S. C St., Virginia City, NV 89440; 775/847-0311; website: www.virginiacity-nv.org.

CITY AND MUNICIPAL PARKS AND RECREATION AGENCIES

California State Department of Parks and Recreation: P.O. Box D, Tahoma, CA 96142; 530/525-7232, 530/653-6995, or 530/653-8380.

Carson City Parks and Recreation Department: 2621 Northgate Ln., Ste. 57, Carson City, NV 89706; 775/887-2262.

Douglas County Parks and Recreation: P.O. Box 218, Minden, NV 89423; 775/782-9828.

Incline Village General Improvement District: 900 Incline Way, Incline Village, NV 89451; 775/832-1310.

North Tahoe Public Utility District: 8318 N. Lake Blvd., Kings Beach, CA 96143; 530/546-7248.

South Lake Tahoe Parks and Recreation Department: 1180 Rufus Allen Blvd., South Lake Tahoe, CA 96150; 530/542-6055.

Tahoe City Public Utility District: 850 N. Lake Blvd., Tahoe City, CA 96145; 530/583-3796.

Washoe County Parks and Recreation Department: 2610 Plumas St., Reno, NV 89509; 775/828-6642.

STATE PARKS
Regional Offices
California Department of Parks and Recreation, Sierra District: P.O. Drawer D, Tahoma, CA 96142; 530/525-7232; website: www.ceres.ca.gov/sierradsp.

Nevada State Parks (Carson/Tahoe Region): 1060 Mallory Way, Carson City, NV 89701; 775/687-4379; website: www.state.nv.us/stparks.

Specific Parks
Burton Creek State Park: P.O. Box 266, Tahoe City, CA 96142; 530/525-7982.

D. L. Bliss State Park: P.O. Box 266, Tahoma, CA 96142; 530/525-7277.

Dayton State Park: P.O. Box 1478, Carson City, NV 89403; 775/687-5678.

Donner Memorial State Park: 12593 Donner Pass Rd., Donner, CA 96161; 530/582-7892.

Emerald Bay State Park: P.O. Box 266, Tahoma, CA 96142; 530/525-7277.

Grover Hot Springs State Park: P.O. Box 188, Markleeville, CA 96120; 530/694-2248.

Lake Tahoe-Nevada State Park: 2005 Hwy. 28, Incline Village, NV 89451; 775/831-0494.

Sugar Pine Point State Park: P.O. Box 266, Tahoma, CA 96142; 530/525-7982.

Washoe Lake State Park: P.O. Box 1478, Carson City, NV 89403; 775/687-4319.

INFO & SERVICES

BUREAU OF LAND MANAGEMENT

California State Office: 2800 Cottage Way, Sacramento, CA 95825; 916/978-4746.

Nevada State Office: 850 Harvard Way, Reno, NV 89520; 775/785-6628 or 775/785-6483.

Carson City District Office: 1535 Hot Springs Rd., Carson City, NV 89706; 775/885-6000.

PG&E RECREATIONAL FACILITIES

PG&E Campgrounds and Recreational Facilities: 925 L St., Ste. 890, Sacramento, CA 94010; 916/446-6616 or 916/386-5164 (group reservations); website: www.pge.com/recreation/p3.html.

FISH AND GAME/ WILDLIFE AGENCIES

California Department of Fish and Game: 1701 Nimbus Rd., Rancho Cordova, CA 95670; 916/358-2900; website: www.dfg.ca.gov.

Nevada Division of Wildlife: 1100 Valley Rd., Reno, NV 89520; 775/688-1500; website: www.state.nv.us./cnr/nvwildlife/.

U.S. Fish and Wildlife Service: 1340 Financial Blvd., NV 89520; 775/861-6300.

U.S. FOREST SERVICE

National Recreation Reservation Service (campground reservations): 877/444-6777; website: www.reserveusa.com.

U.S. Forest Service Visitors Center: 870 Emerald Bay Rd., South Lake Tahoe, CA 96150; 530/573-2600 or 530/573-2674 (tour information).

Eldorado National Forest

Headquarters: 100 Forni Rd., Placerville, CA 95667; 530/622-5061.
Amador Ranger District; 209/295-4251.
Placerville Ranger District; 530/644-2324.

Pollack Pines Ranger District; 530/644-2349.
Lake Tahoe Basin Management Unit: 870 Emerald Bay Rd., South Lake Tahoe, CA 96150; 530/573-2600; website: www.r5.fs.fed.us/ltbmu.

Plumas National Forest

Headquarters: P.O. Box 11500, Quincy, CA 95971; 530/283-2050.
Blairsden Ranger District; 530/836-2575.
Downieville Ranger District; 530/288-3231.
Foresthill Ranger District; 530/367-2224.
Nevada City Ranger District; 530/265-4531.
Sierraville Ranger District; 530/994-3401.
Truckee Ranger District; 530/587-3558.

Tahoe National Forest

Headquarters: P.O. Box 6003, Nevada City, CA 95959; 530/265-4531.
Downieville Ranger District; 530/288-3231.
Foresthill Ranger District; 530/367-2224.
Nevada City Ranger District; 530/265-4531.
Sierraville Ranger District; 530/994-3401.
Truckee Ranger District; 530/587-3558.

Toiyabe National Forest

Headquarters: 1200 Franklin Way, Sparks, NV 89431; 775/331-6444.
Carson Ranger District; 775/882-2766.

FOREIGN LANGUAGE ASSISTANCE

The Northern Nevada Language Bank (free volunteer switchboard available 24 hours a day): 4100 Canyon Rd., Reno, NV 89509; 775/323-0500.

HISTORICAL SOCIETIES

Carson Valley Historical Society: P.O. Box 957, Minden, NV 89423; 775/265-2889.

Lake Tahoe Historical Society: 3058 U.S. 50, South Lake Tahoe, CA 96156; 530/541-5458.

Nevada Historical Society: 650 N. Virginia St., Reno, NV 89503; 775/688-1190.

North Tahoe Historical Society: P.O. Box 6141, Tahoe City, CA 96145; 530/583-1762.
Truckee-Donner Historical Society: P.O. Box 893, Truckee, CA 96160; 530/582-0893.

Tahoe Rim Trail Fund: 297 Kingsbury Grade/P.O. Box 4647, Stateline, NV 89449; 775/588-0686 or 775/588-8799 (hot line).
Wildlife Care: 1485 Cherry Hills Circle, South Lake Tahoe, CA 96150; 530/577-2273.

NATIVE AMERICAN ORGANIZATIONS

Bureau of Indian Affairs: 1677 Hot Springs Rd., Carson City, NV 89706; 775/887-3500.
Pyramid Lake Tribal Council (Paiute Indians): P.O. Box 256, Nixon, NV 89424; 775/574-1000.
Stewart Community Council: 5352 Dat-So-La-Lee Way, Carson City, NV 89701; 775/883-7767.
Washoe Community Council: 400 Shoshone St., Carson City, NV 89701; 775/883-6431.

ENVIRONMENTAL AGENCIES AND ORGANIZATIONS

League to Save Lake Tahoe: 955 Emerald Bay Rd., South Lake Tahoe, CA 96150; 530/541-5388.
California Tahoe Conservancy: This is a California state agency involved in land and wetlands preservation and recreational facilities throughout the Lake Tahoe basin; 2161 Lake Tahoe Blvd., Ste. 2, South Lake Tahoe, CA 96150; 530/542-5580.
Tahoe Regional Planning Agency (TRPA): 301 Doria Court, Zephyr Cove, NV 89449; 775/588-4547.

NEWSPAPERS

North Tahoe Truckee This Week: Free weekly tabloid, available throughout the North Lake Tahoe area, that features news, dining, event information, art, nightlife, and other topics; website: www.tahoethisweek.com.
Tahoe Daily Tribune, Tahoe World, North Lake Tahoe Bonanza, Sierra Sun, and *Nevada Appeal:* All of these newspapers are owned by the same company. A great source of news and travel/recreation information is available from the publishing company's website, which is the oldest regionwide website on Lake Tahoe. Go to: www.tahoe.com.
Reno Gazette Journal: Major daily newspaper with extensive website. Go to: www.rgj.com for news and www.RenoTahoeFun.com for visitor information, dining, lodging, and nightlife.
Reno News and Review: Weekly free tabloid guide to news and entertainment in the Reno and Lake Tahoe area. Available throughout the region.
Squaw Valley Times: Squaw Valley's own local newspaper; website: www.squawvalleytimes.com.
Tahoe Mountain News: Alternative free monthly newspaper serving South Lake Tahoe. Available throughout the South Lake Tahoe area.

Resources

Suggested Reading

Human History

Frohlich, Robert, *Mountain Dreamers - Visionaries of Sierra Nevada Skiing,* Coldstream Press, Truckee, Calif., 1997. Writer Frohlich is a resident of Tahoe City, an avid skier and an award-winning freelance journalist. In this exemplary work, in which he teamed up with photographers Carolyn Caddes and Tom Lippert, Frohlich weaves wonderful portraits of Lake Tahoe's ski pioneers, from Squaw Valley founder Alexander Cushing to Olympians Jimmie Heuga and Tamara McKinney. Several of Tahoe's ski resort founders passed away shortly after the publication of this book. A must for skiers.

James, George Wharton, *Lake of the Sky,* Nevada Publications, Las Vegas, 1915, reprinted 1992 by Stanley W. Paher. This oversized paperback is a classic early history of the lake, with a mix of lifestyle, history and folklore. Includes geology, flora and fauna, and is extensively illustrated with photography. James celebrates the heydays of Tahoe's early 1900s lifestyle with its posh resorts and excursion steamboats.

Land, Barbara and Myrick, *A Short History of Reno,* University of Nevada Press, Reno, 1995. This small paperback filled the void that had long existed on "The Biggest Little City in the World." It describes the rise of the casinos, from the early card sharks to the gaming moguls of the twentieth century such as Bill Harrah. It also discusses the parade of big-name entertainers, including Sammy Davis, Jr. and Frank Sinatra, that formed a constant parade of Hollywood glitterati in the casino showrooms. Well-researched with interviews and newspaper archives.

Landauer, Lyndall Baker, *The Mountain Sea, A History of Lake Tahoe,* Flying Cloud Press, Honolulu, 1996. Wonderful short history of Tahoe, with a number of black and white photographs, in this paperback written by a local professor and long-time member of the Lake Tahoe Historical Society. You can find the book at the Society's Museum in South Lake Tahoe and in other Tahoe-area bookstores.

Lekisch, Barbara, *Tahoe Place Names,* Great West Books, Lafayette, Calif., 1988. Indispensable paperback to have when exploring any part of Tahoe. Provides the origin and history of names in the Lake Tahoe Basin. One of my favorite true stories is the naming of Floating Island Lake.

Mullen Jr., Frank, *The Donner Party Chronicles,* Nevada Humanities Committee, Reno, 1997. Mullen and photographer Marilyn Newton, both staff members of the Reno Gazette-Journal, have assembled perhaps the most exhaustive work in print on the fate of the doomed wagon train that became bogged down by early blizzards in the winter of 1846-47 on its way to California. This hard-cover book is generously illustrated by drawings and by Newton's photography. The work commemorated the 150th anniversary of the ill-fated trek.

Scott, E.B., *The Saga of Lake Tahoe,* Pebble Beach (Volumes I and II), Sierra-Tahoe Publishing Co., first published in 1957 (P.O. Box 1083, Pebble Beach, CA 93953). This hardbound, two-volume set is most important "must-have" collection for Tahoe aficionados. Colorfully described history of the area is lavishly illustrated by hundreds of black-and-white photographs. The books follow the development of Tahoe from the mining and railroad days of the 1860s to the arrival of the first ski resorts in the 1950s.

Stollery Jr., David J., *Tales of Tahoe and More Tales of Tahoe*, Stollery Books, Grass Valley, Calif., 1969. These two paperbacks, written by the late author, assemble a treasure-trove of history, legend and folklore, with short vignettes such as "The Plug in the Bottom of the Lake" and "The Legend of Cave Rock." Wonderful anecdotes and stories for the campfire or fireplace.

Van Etten, Carol, *Tahoe City Yesterdays*, Sierra Maritime Publications, Tahoe City, 1987. Large paperback chronicles the history of Tahoe City, with black-and-white photographs and old newspaper clippings.

Wheeler, Sessions S., *Nevada's Black Rock Desert*, The Caxton Printers, Ltd., Caldwell, Idaho, 1985. Delightful historical retrospective of the place that is now internationally famous as the site of the annual "Burning Man" festival in September. Covers the wagon trains, Native American tribes, the Indian War of the 1860s, and the arrival of the ranchers. Includes geology, prehistory and natural history of this most fascinating region 100 miles northeast of Reno.

Natural History and Pictorials

Storer, Tracy L. and Usinger, Robert L., *Sierra Nevada Natural History*, University of California Press, Berkeley, 1963. Want to know what a sugarpine cone looks like? This paperback is a handy field guide to all of the flora and fauna in the Sierra Nevada, including the Lake Tahoe region. Black-and-white illustrations, along with a profusion of color plates, are great for identifying wildflowers, mushrooms, trees, birds, animals, amphibians and insects.

Ravize, Linde Christiana and John Thomas, *Hearts of Light-Impressions of Lake Tahoe*, Hearts of Light Publishing, Lake Tahoe, Nevada, 2000. This large, coffee-table book offers spectacular, full-color photography of Tahoe's many moods, all shot without filters or special effects. This husband-and-wife team owns and operates A Frame of Mind Gallery inside Harvey's Resort at Stateline (South Shore). Keep this volume at home, to remind you why you should visit Lake Tahoe often.

Maps

"Bathymetry and Selected Perspective Views of Lake Tahoe, California and Nevada," U.S. Geological Survey, 1999. A series of incredible maps, using satellite and computer digital imaging techniques, show, in color, the underwater topography of Lake Tahoe, including peaks, mounts, glacier-scoured canyons, and drop-offs. For anyone who wants to know "what's underneath the surface," these maps give vivid impressions. Order from the USGS Branch of Information Services, Box 25286, Denver, CO 80225-0286.

Videos

"The Best of John Tyson's Journal," KOLO-TV, Channel 8, Reno, 1995-2000. Tyson, a veteran reporter for Reno's ABC-affiliate television station, is the quintessential Western man, and this series of videos explores some of the most fascinating aspects of life and history in Nevada's high desert. The videos, compilations of his TV features, cover topics such as railroads, mining camps, cowboys, wild mustangs, and forest fire fighters. Tyson and his wife, Carol, own and operate Tyson's Canyon Ranch near Virginia City. He also sings professionally.

"Sunken Treasures of Lake Tahoe," Skyfire, Reno, 1993. This 60-minute video, sold around the Tahoe basin, describes some of the underwater mysteries of the lake, in an occasionally over-the-top but nonetheless interesting fashion. Learn about the underwater forest and unusual lake "mounts" and pinnacles, along with the final resting place of the 190-foot Steamer Tahoe, which was scuttled in the 1940s. Fascinating footage shot by remotely-operated underwater video cameras.

Suggested Reading

Internet Resources

There are numerous sites on Lake Tahoe and Reno, some with general information and some with specific agendas, such as promoting lodging and various activities.

News, Weather, and General Information

Lake Tahoe newspapers
www.tahoe.com
Daily headlines, articles, weather, events and real estate are culled from six commonly owned newspapers of Lake Tahoe and Nevada: *Tahoe Daily Tribune, Tahoe World, North Lake Tahoe Bonanza, Sierra Sun* and *Nevada Appeal*. Comprehensive and topical.

Reno Gazette Journal
www.rgj.com and www.RenoTahoeFun.com
Both sites are produced by the largest daily newspaper in northern Nevada. The first has local news and sports, the second emphasizes dining and entertainment.

Weather Underground
www.wunderground.com/US/CA/ Lake_Tahoe.html
Check on storms and forecasts here.

Lake Tahoe Cam
www.laketahoecam.com
Scenic Lake Tahoe videos; requires Real Player.

Resort Sports Network
www.rsn.com/cams/tahoe/
Live cam shots of Tahoe, especially useful for weather and snow conditions.

California Division of Tourism
www.visitCalifornia.com
State-sponsored site offers some general information and events at Tahoe.

Nevada Commission on Tourism
www.travelnevada.com
State-sponsored site offers in-depth information on events, activities, lodging and dining in northern Nevada, including Lake Tahoe.

Visitors Bureaus and Chambers of Commerce

These sites contain extensive listings of accommodations, restaurants, wedding services, points of interest and upcoming events. Most sites are directed to a specific region of the area.

North Lake Tahoe Resort Association
www.tahoefun.org
Emphasizes the North Shore but contains a booking engine and central reservation service for lodging throughout the Lake Tahoe basin.

Lake Tahoe Visitors Authority
www.virtualtahoe.com
Covers only the South Shore, including Stateline, but has thorough list of visitor-related services, dining, lodging and activities, including numerous links to other sites.

Lake Tahoe/Incline Village/Crystal Bay Visitors and Convention Bureau
www.gotahoe.com
Covers the northeast shore of the lake, and has booking engine for activities such as tours of the Thunderbird Lodge at Incline Village.

Plumas County Visitors Bureau
www.plumascounty.org
A good resource for Plumas County area north of Lake Tahoe.

South Lake Tahoe Chamber of Commerce
www.tahoeinfo.com
Provides general information and links to local businesses, as well as facts for new residents.

Tahoe Douglas Chamber of Commerce
and Visitor Center
www.tahoechamber.org

Covers the southeast, i.e. Nevada section of Tahoe, with an emphasis on the Douglas County areas of Stateline, Kingsbury and Glenbrook.

Truckee-Donner Chamber of Commerce
www.truckee.com

Good information on dining, lodging and historic sites in the Truckee, Tahoe Donner and Donner Lake areas.

Alpine County Chamber of Commerce
www.alpinecounty.com

General information on areas south of Lake Tahoe in California, including Kirkwood, Caples Lake and Markleeville.

Reno-Sparks Convention and
Visitors Authority
www.renolaketahoe.com

A broad-based site on the Reno area, with some references to Tahoe. Large listing of hotels, casinos and restaurants.

Carson City Convention and Visitors Bureau
www.carson-city.org

Covers Nevada's state capital with information on lodging, dining, golf, historic sites and events.

Carson Valley Chamber of Commerce and
Visitors Authority
www.carsonvalleynv.org

A small site covering Minden, Gardnerville, and Genoa areas south of Carson City.

Virginia City Chamber of Commerce
www.vcnevada.com.

Offers information on the many historic points of interest, dining, events and lodging of this quaint silver mining town.

General Commercial Sites

Tahoe Made
www.tahoemade.com

New Web site, launched in late 2002, carries a diversity of products ranging from boutique soaps and cooking sauces to lavish posters and photography, all produced in the Tahoe region.

Tahoe Online
www.tahoeonline.com.

This site is a third-party booking engine for Tahoe area accommodations, including condominiums and houses.

High Sierra
www.highsierra.com

Includes visitor information on lodging, recreation, real estate and businesses.

Tahoe Guide
www.tahoeguide.com

A resource guide for lodging, activities and dining.

Tahoe Country
www.tahoecountry.com

A good site to visit for information on history, arts and crafts, photography and books on Lake Tahoe. Links to pages for local clubs and historical societies.

Tahoe's Best
www.tahoesbest.com

A general guide with youth orientation (nude beaches, cool hangouts).

Forest Service and Other Government Agencies

U.S. Forest Service, Lake Tahoe Basin
Management Unit
www.r5.fs.fed.us/ltbmu/

Provides overall information on forest conditions and activities around the lake.

Internet Resources

California Department of Parks and Recreation, Sierra District
www.ceres.ca.gov/sierradsp/
Information on California state parks, tours, camping and sights at Tahoe, Truckee, Markleeville and Graeagle.

Nevada State Parks
www.state.nv.us/stparks/
Information on state parks on the east shore of Tahoe and Reno/Carson City areas.

California Department of Fish and Game
www.dfg.ca.gov
Information on fishing and hunting licenses in Tahoe and neighboring waters.

Nevada Division of Wildlife
www.state.nv.us/cnr/nvwildlife
Information on fishing and hunting licenses in northern Nevada.

U.S. Geological Survey
http://tahoe.usgs.gov/
Contains interesting maps and other geologic information on the Tahoe basin.

Reno/Tahoe International Airport
www.renoairport.com/
It's not a very large airport, but you can check here to see where your flight will arrive, and who flies here.

Conservation and Nonprofit Organizations

League to Save Lake Tahoe
www.keeptahoeblue.com/
This is the lake's most active environmental organization.

Tahoe Research Group
www.trg.ucdavis.edu
The most extensive ongoing research of Lake Tahoe's water clarity and resource issues in

the surrounding area is available here, at this site operated by the Division of Environmental Studies, University of California at Davis.

Tahoe Rim Trail Fund
www.tahoerimtrail.org
This organization encompasses private and public efforts on behalf of the recently completed Tahoe Rim Trail. Go here for information on events, trail maintenance days and fund-raisers.

Skiing, Boating, and Outdoor Recreation

Ski Lake Tahoe
www.skilaketahoe.com
Contains ongoing information on the six largest ski resorts of Lake Tahoe: Squaw Valley, Heavenly, Kirkwood, Northstar, Sierra-at-Tahoe and Alpine Meadows. Links to those resorts' sites.

Golf the High Sierra
www.golfthehighsierra.com
Very thorough site on the dozens of public and private golf courses in the region, in both California and Nevada. Links to each course.

Boating Guide
www.boattahoe.com/
Elaborate and well-researched site on boating facilities, rentals, marinas, excursions and nautical history of Tahoe, with many links.

Lake Tahoe Ski Resorts
www.laketahoeskiing.com
Guide to ski and snowboard areas.

Snow Web
www.snoweb.com
Guide to Tahoe-area alpine, cross-country and snowboarding areas.

Accommodations Index

A

A&A Tradewinds Resort and Spa: 389
Accommodation Station Rentals: 442
Ace Motor Lodge: 474
Adventure Inn: 474
Airport Plaza Hotel: 463
Alder Creek Campground at Tahoe Donner: 494–495
Almost Home Retreats: 442
Alpine Inn: 395
Alpine Rental Group: 441
Angora Lakes Resort: 448
Aspen Group Camp: 499
Atlantis Casino Resort: 463–464

B

Bassett's Station: 395
Bayview: 505
Beachside Inn: 389
Bear Valley: 499
Bed-and-Breakfast South Reno: 482–483
Berger: 522
Best Inn and Suites: 474–475
Best Western Carson Station: 479
Best Western Pinon Plaza Resort: 479–480
Best Western Station House Inn: 389
Best Western Timber Cove Lodge Marina Resort: 390
Best Western Truckee Tahoe Inn: 381
Big 7 Motel: 385
Big Silver Group Campground: 517
Black Bear Inn: 430–431
Bliss Mansion Bed-and-Breakfast: 483
Blue Jay Lodge: 390
Boca Rest: 496
Boca Springs: 496–497
Boca: 496
Bocks 10064 Southeast River Road: 422
Boomtown Hotel Casino: 464–465
Boomtown RV Park: 524
Bordertown Casino and RV Resort: 526
Boreal Inn: 381
Boyington Mill: 497
Brockway Springs Resort: 412–413
Buttes Resort: 395

C

Caesars Tahoe: 399–400
Cal-Neva Resort: 397–398
Camino Cove: 517
Camino Hotel Seven-Mile House Bed and Breakfast: 433
Camp Richardson Resort: 448–449
Campground by the Lake: 507
Caples Lake Resort: : 451–452
Caples Lake: 511
Carson Valley Inn: 481
Carson Valley RV Resort: 529–530
Casino Area Travelodge: 390
Cedar Glen Lodge: 385
Chambers Landing: 409
Chamonix Inn: 390
Chaney House: 427
Chapman Creek: 523
Charmey Chalet Resort: 385
Chinquapin: 409
Chism Trailer Park: 526
Chollar Mansion: 485
Chris Haven: 506
Christiania Inn: 431
Christy Inn: 425–426
Circus Circus Hotel Casino Reno: 465
City Center Motel: 480
Clio's River Edge Trailer Resort: 521
Club Cal Neva (formerly the Virginian and the Riverboat): 465
Coachland RV Park: 496
Cold Creek: 499
Coldwell Banker McKinney and Associates: 442–443
Coldwell Banker Realty: 442
Colonial Motor Inn: 475
Comstock Country RV Resort: 529
Coppin's Meadow Lodge: 433–434
Cottage Inn: 426
Cottonwood: 499
Courtyard by Marriott–Reno: 475
Crystal Bay Cove: 413
Crystal Bay Motel: 386
Crystal Springs: 510

D

D. L. Bliss State Park: 504
David Walley's Resort, Hot Springs and Spa: 420
Davies Creek: 497
Davis Creek County Park: 528
Days Inn Reno: 475
Days Inn: 390, 480
Deer Run Ranch Bed-and-Breakfast: 483–484
Diablo Camping Area: 522
Donner Lake Village Resort: 405
Donner Memorial State Park: 495

E

East Meadow: 499–500
Echo Chalet: 449–450
Echo Creek Mountain Ranch: 431–432
Econo Lodge: 391, 475
Eldorado Hotel Casino: 465–466
Elwell Lakes Lodge: 454
Embassy Suites Resort: 400
Embassy Vacation Resort Lake Tahoe: 400–401
Emerald Bay Boat-In Camp: 505
Emerald Bay State Park/Eagle Point: 505
Emigrant Group Campground: 497
Executive Inn: 475

F

Fairfield Inn and Suites Reno/Sparks: 475
Falcon Lodge and Suites: 386
Fallen Leaf: 505
Fantasy Inn: 415
Fashoda Tent: 516
Feather River Inn: 454–455
Feather River Park Resort: 455–456
Feather River RV Park: 519–520
Ferrari's Crown Resort: 386
Findley: 500
Fir Top: 500
Firelite Lodge: 386
Fitzgerald's Casino/Hotel: 466–467
Forest Inn Suites: 415
Forest Pines: 413
Franciscan Lakeside Lodge: 386

G

Gatekeeper Inn: 476
Genoa House Inn: 486
Gerle Creek: 515

Glenbrook: 415
Gold Crest Resort Motel: 386
Gold Dust West Motor Lodge: 476
Gold Hill Hotel: 485–486
Gold Lake Beach Resort: 456
Gold Lake Lodge: 456–457
Gold Ranch Casino RV Resort: 524, 526
Golden Phoenix Hotel Casino and Resort (formerly Flamingo Hilton Reno): 467
Goose Meadows: 495
Graeagle Meadows Vacation Rentals: 444
Graeagle Vacation Rentals: 444
Granite Flat: 495
Granlibakken Resort: 409–410
Gray Eagle Lodge: 457
Grover Hot Springs State Park: 510–511
Grubstake Lodge: 382

H

Hampshire Rocks: 494
Hania's Bed and Breakfast Inn: 422–423
Hansen's Resort: 450
Harrah's Lake Tahoe: 401–402
Harrah's Reno: 467–468
Harveys Resort Casino: 402
Hauserman Rental Group: 441–442
High Country Inn Bed-and-Breakfast: 435
Highway 49 North of Truckee: 530
Highway 89/Little Truckee Summit: 530
Historian Inn: 481–482
Historic Camp Richardson Resort: 506
Holiday House: 386–387
Holiday Inn Express: 381–382, 391
Holiday Inn and Diamonds Casino: 468
Holiday Lodge: 391
Holly House Bed and Breakfast Inn: 435
Homewood Marina Lodge: 382–383
Hope Valley RV Park: 509
Hope Valley: 509
Horizon Casino Resort: 402–403
Hyatt Regency Lake Tahoe Resort and Casino: 398–399

IJK

Ice House Resort: 517–518
Ice House: 518
Ice Lakes Lodge: 405–406
Indian Creek Campground: 510
Indian Springs: 492–493
Inn at Heavenly: 432

Inn at Incline and Condominiums: 413–414
Inn by the Lake: 415–416
Inn at Truckee: 382
Jackson Point: 500
John Ascuaga's Nugget: 468–469
KOA of South Lake Tahoe: 507
Kaspian: 503
Kay's Silver Lake Resort: 452
Keystone RV Park: 527
Kidd Lake Campground: 494
Kingswood Village: 413
Kirkwood Lake: 511–512
Kirkwood Ski and Summer Resort: 418–419
Kit Carson Campground: 510
Kit Carson Lodge: 452–453

L
La Quinta Inn: 476
Lake Forest: 501, 503
Lake Spaulding: 492
Lake Sterling: 493–494
Lake Tahoe Accommodations: 439, 441
Lake Tahoe Lodging: 443
Lake of the Sky Motor Inn: 383
Lakeland Village Resort: 416
Lakes Basin: 521
Lakeside Inn and Casino: 403
Lakeside Mobile Home and RV Park: 507
Lakeside: 498
Lampliter Inn: 391
Layman Resort: 458
Lazy S Lodge: 391–392
Little Bear RV Park: 519
Loch Leven Lodge: 382
Lodge at Lake Tahoe: 392
Lodge at Whitehawk Ranch: 458
Lodgepole: 493
Loganville: 524
Logger: 497
Lone Rock: 517
Loon Lake Boat Ramp: 514
Loon Lake Equestrian Group Camp: 515
Loon Lake Equestrian: 515
Loon Lake Group Campground No. 1: 514
Loon Lake Group Campground No. 2: 514
Loon Lake: 513
Lower Blue Lake: 513
Lower Little Truckee: 498

M
Mardi Gras Motor Lodge: 476
Marlette Peak Campground: 508
Marlette/Hobart Backcountry Area: 508
Marriott Grand Residence Club: 403–404
Marriott's Timber Lodge: 404–405
Martis Creek Lake: 495–496
Martis Valley Associates: 441
Mayfield House: 426–427
McCarran House: 464
McCloud Condominiums: 414
Meeks Bay Campground: 504
Meeks Bay Resort: 447, 503-504
Middle Creek/ Blue Lakes: 513
Molly's Bed and Breakfast: 435–436
Montgomery Inn and Suites: 392
Motel 6: 392, 476
Mother Nature's Inn: 383
Mountain Shadows: 414
Mourelato's Lakeshore Resort: 387
Movin' West Trailer Camp: 520–521
Mt. Rose: 504

NO
National Nine Inn: 476
Nevada Beach: 508
Nevada Inn: 476
Norfolk Woods Inn: 427–428
North Lake Lodge: 387
Northshore/Loon Lake: 515
Northstar-at-Tahoe: 406
Northwind: 517
Olympic Village Inn: 407–408
Ormsby House Hotel and Casino: 480
Oxford Motel: 477

PQ
Packer Lake Lodge: 458–459
Packsaddle Camping Area: 522
Park Inn (formerly The Hardman House): 480
Pass Creek: 500
Pepper Tree Inn: 383
Peppermill Hotel Casino: 469–470
Pinon Plaza RV Park: 528–529
Plasse's Resort: 512
Plaza Hotel: 481
Plaza Resort Club: 470
Pleasant/Loon Lake: 515
Plumas Eureka State Park: 521

Plumas Pines Realty: 444
PlumpJack Squaw Valley Inn: 408
Prosser Group Campground: 498
Prosser: 497–498
Pullman House: 436–437
Quality Inn and Suites: 392

R
Rainbow Lodge: 423
Ramada Inn/Speakeasy Casino: 470
Reno Downtown Travelodge: 477
Reno Hilton KOA: 527
Reno Hilton: 470–471
Residence Inn by Marriott: 477
Resort at Squaw Creek: 396–397
Richardson House: 423–424
Ridge Tahoe: 416–417
River Pines Realty: 444
River Pines Resort: 395
River Ranch Lodge: 410
River's Edge RV Park: 526
Riverside Inn: 395–396
River Street Inn: 424
Roadside Inn: 392
Rockwood Lodge: 428
Rocky Ridge: 411
Rodeway Inn Reno (formerly Travelodge Reno): 477
Royal Gorge Wilderness Lodge: 447
Royal Valhalla Lodge: 392–393
Rustic Cottages: 387–388

S
Sagehen: 498
Salmon Creek: 522
Salmon Lake Lodge: 459–460
Sands Regency Hotel Casino: 471–472
Sandy Beach Campground: 501
Sardine Lake Resort: 460
Sardine Lake: 522–523
Season's Inn: 477
Secret Honeymooner Inn: 393
Selective Accommodations: 443
7 Seas Inn: 393
Shamrock RV Park: 526
Shooting Star Bed and Breakfast: 429–430
Shore House: 429
Showboat Inn: 477–478
Siena Hotel Spa Casino: 472–473
Sierra Club's Clair Tappaan Lodge: 424–425

Sierra Hot Springs and Globe Hotel: 434–435
Sierra Motel: 396
Sierra Shangri-La: 437
Sierra Vacation Rentals: 442
Sierra Valley Lodge: 437
Sierra: 523
Silver City RV Resort: 530
Silver Club Hotel Casino: 473
Silver Creek: 501, 517
Silver Lake, East/Silver Lake, West: 512
Silver Legacy Casino Resort: 473–474
Silver Sage RV Park: 528
Silver Tip Group: 500–501
Sleepy Pines Motel: 396
Snag Lake: 521–522
Snowshoe Springs: 510
Sorensen's Resort: 453–454
South Fork Group: 515–516
South Tahoe Travelodge: 393
Spa Villas at Gold Mountain: 419–420
Sparks Marina RV Park: 527
Spruce Grove Cabins and Suites: 393
Squaw Tahoe Resort: 408
Squaw Valley Accommodations: 441
Squaw Valley Lodge: 408
Star Dust Lodge: 478
Stateline Travelodge: 393
Stevenson's Holliday Inn: 388
Stillwater Cove: 414
Strawberry Lodge: 432–433
Strawberry Point: 518
Sugar Bowl Lodge: 406–407
Sugar Pine Point State Park/General Creek: 503
Sun 'N Sand Lodge: 388
Sundowner Hotel Casino: 474
Sunnyside Lodge: 411–412
Sunset: 516–517
Super 8 Motel Reno (formerly Miner's Inn): 478
Super 8 Motel Sparks: 478
Super 8 Motel at Meadow Wood Courtyard: 478
Super 8 Motel: 394
Sweetbriar: 413
Swiss Lakewood Lodge: 383

T
Ta-Tel Lodge389
Tahoe Beach and Ski Club: 417
Tahoe Biltmore Lodge and Casino: 399

Tahoe Chalet Inn: 394
Tahoe City Inn: 383
Tahoe City Travelodge: 383–384
Tahoe Colony Inn: 394
Tahoe Donner: 407
Tahoe Inn: 388–389
Tahoe Keys Resort: 443
Tahoe Keys: 417
Tahoe Lake Cottages: 384
Tahoe Lakeshore Lodge and Spa: 417–418
Tahoe Management Company: 443
Tahoe Pines: 507
Tahoe Rental Connection: 443
Tahoe Seasons Resort: 418
Tahoe State Recreation Area: 501
Tahoe Summit Village: 418
Tahoe Tavern: 412
Tahoe Tropicana: 394
Tahoe Valley Lodge: 394–395
Tahoe Valley: 506
Tahoma Lodge: 384–385
Tahoma Meadows Bed-and-Breakfast: 428–429
Tamarack Lodge Motel: 385
Tamarack Rentals: 443–444
Third Creek Condominiums: 414
Three Buck Inn at River Run: 410–411
Town House Motor Lodge: 478
Truckee Hotel: 425
Truckee River Lodge: 478–479
Twenty Mile House: 437–438
Tyrolian Village: 414
Tyson's Canyon Ranch: 484–485

UV
Union Flat: 523
United Trails: 496

University Inn: 479
Upper Blue Lake Dam: 513
Upper Blue Lake: 512
Upper Little Truckee: 498
Vacation Station: 442
Vagabond Inn: 479
Value Inn: 395
Victorian Inn: 479
Victorian RV Park: 527
Viking Motor Lodge: 395
Village at Squaw Valley: 408–409
Villas at Incline: 414–415
Virginia City RV Park: 528

W
Washoe Lake State Park: 528
Wench Creek Group Camp: 516
Wench Creek: 516
Western Village Inn and Casino: 479
Wild Plum: 524
Wild Rose Inn: 486–487
William Kent: 503
Wonder Lodge: 479
Woodcamp: 501
Woodchuck: 493
Woodfords Inn: 395
Woods Lake: 511
Woodvista Lodge: 389
Wrights Lake Equestrian: 519
Wrights Lake: 518–519

YZ
Yellowjacket: 516
Yuba Pass: 523
Yuba River Inn: 438–439
Zephyr Cove: 508
Zephyr Cove Resort: 450–451

Accommodations Index

Restaurant Index

A

Adele's Restaurant: 604
Adele's at the Plaza: 591, 611
Alexander's at High Camp: 538–539
Alpen Sierra Coffee Co.: 566
Alpina Café: 566
Alpine Restaurant and Cutthroat Saloon: 577
Alturas Bar and Nightclub: 611
American River Café: 558
Andy's Truckee Diner: 533
Angela's Pizzaria: 541–542
Antoci's Supper Club at Genoa Lakes: 608
Applebee's Neighborhood Grill: 604
Art Gecko's Southwest Grill: 591, 611
Atlantis Casino Resort: 608
Atlantis Seafood Steakhouse: 591–592
Austin's: 554
Azzara's: 554

B

Bacchi's Inn: 542
Balboa Café: 585, 539
Baldini's Triple Crown Restaurant: 592
Bar One: 586
Bar of America: 585
Baron Lounge: 611–612
Benihana Japanese Steakhouse: 592–593
Beacon Restaurant: 566, 587
Best Western Tahoe Truckee Inn: 586
Big Top Buffet: 593
Big Water Grille: 554–555
Black Bear Tavern: 542
Black Olive Bistro and Bar: 558–559
Blue Agave (formerly Mi Casa Too): 542
Boathouse Bar and Grill: 566
Bonanza Casino: 608
Boomtown Hotel Casino: 608–609
Boulevard Café: 550
Bountiful: 566–567
Breakwater Café: 567
Brewery Arts Center: 610–611
Brew Brothers: 593
Brewery at Lake Tahoe: 567
Bridge Tender Tavern and Grill: 543
Broiler Room: 559
Bullwhacker's Pub: 540

C

CB's Pizza and Grill: 550
Caesars Tahoe: 587
Café Cobblestone: 543
Café Mohawk: 580
Café Napa: 594
Cafe 333: 555
Cafe Andreotti: 593
Cafe Fiore: 567
Cafe de Thai: 594
Cal-Neva Resort: 586
Cantina: 567
Cantina Bar and Grill: 587
Cantina Los Tres Hombres: 612
Caples Lake Resort: 577–578
Carson Nugget Steak House: 604–605
Carson Nugget: 610
Carson Station: 610
Carson Valley Country Club Bar and
　　Restaurant: 606–607
Carson Valley Inn: 610
Cascades: 540
Cassidy's: 594
Catch a Rising Star (Silver Legacy): 611
Cattlemen's Restaurant and Saloon: 605
Chambers Landing: 544
Char-Pit: 551
Chart House: 559
Chase's Bar and Grill: 567–568, 587–588
Chefs' Pavilion: 594
Chevys: 568, 588
Christiania Inn: 568–569, 588
Christmas Tree: 594–595
Christy Hill: 543
Ciao Mein Trattoria: 555
Circus Circus Hotel Casino: 609
Club Voodoo: 612
Clubhouse Bar and Grill (formerly North-
　　woods Restaurant): 533–534
Cottonwood: 534
Cottonwood: 586
Coyote Bar and Grill (at River Pines Resort):
　　580
Coyote Grill: 560
Coyote's Mexican Grill: 544

Crown Point: 606
Cuvee: 560

DE
Dixon's Restaurant and Brewery: 569
Dory's Oar and The Tudor Pub: 569
Dragonfly: 534
Earthly Delights: 534–535
East Ocean Restaurant: 605
Echo Restaurant and Lounge: 560–561
Edgewood Restaurant: 560
El Toro Bravo: 535
El Vaquero: 560
Eldorado Hotel Casino: 609
Emerald Palace: 569
Engadine Café: 535
Ernie's Coffee Shop: 569
Evans American Gourmet Café: 569–570
Fast Eddie's Texas Bar-B-Que: 544

F
Feather River Inn: 580–581
Fiamma: 544
Fiona's: 607
Fire Sign Café: 544
Firewoods Restaurant at Gray Eagle Lodge:
    581
Fitzgerald's: 609
Flowing Tide Pub: 612
Forest Room Buffet: 561
Freddie's Roost Grille and Sports Bar: 595
Fredrick's Bistro and Bar (formerly Jack Rabbit
    Moon): 555–556
Fresh Ketch: 570
Fresh Ketch: 588
Fresh Market Square Buffet: 595
Freshies Restaurant and Bar: 570
Friday's Station Steak and Seafood Grill: 561

G
G.K.'s Steakhouse: 596
Galena Forest Restaurant and Bar: 595–596
Gar Woods Grill and Pier: 551, 586
Garden Buffet: 561
Garibaldi's: 605
Glen Eagles: 605
Glissandi: 540
Gold Lake Lodge: 581
Golden Palace (formerly Emperor's Garden):
    596

Graeagle Meadows Clubhouse: 581
Graham's at Squaw Valley: 540
Grand Canyon Buffet: 596
Grand Central Pizza and Pasta: 571
Granlibakken: 586
Great Basin Brewing Company: 596, 612
Greenhouse Restaurant and Bar: 571
Grizzly Grill: 581

H
Hacienda Restaurant and Bar: 612
Hacienda de la Sierra: 556, 586
Hacienda del Lago: 544–545, 586
Hard Rock Café: 562
Hardy House: 596–597
Harrah's Casino Hotel: 588
Harrah's Reno: 609
Harrah's Steak House: 597
Harveys Resort Casino: 588
Haywire Waikiki Country Night Club: 612
Heidi's Pancake House: 571
Heiss' Steak and Seafood House: 605
Hiro Sushi: 551
Horizon Casino Resort: 588
Hoss Hoggs: 571, 588
Hunan Garden: 571
Hyatt Regency Lake Tahoe: 586

IJK
Ice Lakes Lodge: 535–536
Ichiban Japanese Steak House and
    Sushi Bar: 597
International House of Pancakes: 571
Iron Door: 581–582
J&T Basque Bar and Dining Room: 607
Jake's on the Lake: 545
Jason's Beachside Grille: 551
Jim Kelley's Nugget: 586
Joe Bob's Roadhouse: 612
John Ascuaga's Nugget: 609
Josh's: 562
Just for Laughs (Sands Regency): 611
Kirkwood Inn: 578
Kit Carson Lodge Restaurant: 578

L
La Ferme: 608
La Fondue: 556
La Strada: 597
La Vecchia Italian Restaurant: 597–598

Lake Tahoe Brewing Company: 556
Lake Tahoe Pizza Company: 571–572
Lakehouse: 545
Lakeview Dining Room: 556
Lanza's: 551
Las Panchitas: 551–552
Lawlor Events Center: 611
Le Bistro Restaurant and Bar: 556
Le Grande Buffet: 562
Le Petit Pier: 552
Lew Mar Nel's Restaurant: 572
Lexie's Ristorante: 598
Liberty Belle Restaurant: 598
Little Waldorf Saloon: 612
Llewellyn's: 562
Lodge at Whitehawk Ranch: 582
Log Cabin: 582
Log Cabin Café: 552
Lone Eagle Grille: 557
Longboards Bar and Grill: 582–583
Louis' Basque Corner: 598–599
Luciano's: 599

M
Mama's Red Tomato: 572, 588
Mandarin Garden: 572
Mandarin Villa: 545
Marie Callender's Restaurant and Bakery:
    572–573
Market Place Buffet: 599
Mayflower (formerly China Chef): 557
McP's Irish Pub and Grill: 572
Meyers Downtown Café: 573
Mi Casa Too: 605
Mia's Swiss Restaurant: 606
Michael's: 607
Mirabelle French Cuisine: 562–563
Mofo's Pizza and Pasta: 557–558
Montevigna Italian Ristorante: 599
Moody's Bistro and Lounge: 536, 586
Mott Canyon Tavern and Grill: 563
Mount Tomba Inn Dinner House: 583
Mulligan's Irish Pub and Restaurant: 573

NO
Naked Fish: 573–574
Nakoma Resort and Spa at Gold Mountain:
    583–584
Naughty Dawg Saloon and Grill: 545
Needles Restaurant: 574

Nephele's: 574
Norfolk Woods Inn: 545–546
O'B's Pub and Restaurant: 536–537, 586
Off the Wall Bar and Grill: 578
Old Post Office Coffee Shop: 552
Old Range Steakhouse: 552
Old Tahoe Café: 546
Olsen's Cabin: 584
Orozko: 599
Overland Hotel: 607

P
Pacific Crest: 537
Packer Lake Lodge: 584
Panda Kitchen: 606
Passaretti's: 574
Pastime Club: 587
Paul Revere's Kicks: 612
Peppermill Hotel Casino: 609
Peppermill Island Buffet: 599–600
Peppermill Steak House: 600
Pfeifer House: 546
Pianeta Cucina Italiana: 536
Pinon Plaza: 610
Pioneer Center for the Performing Arts: 611
Pisano's: 546
Planet Hollywood: 563, 600
Plasse's Thunder Mountain Restaurant:
    578–579
PlumpJack Café: 540–541
Primavera: 563
Pub Tahoe (formerly The Island): 588

R
Rail City Casino: 609
Rapscallion Seafood House and Bar: 600
Red Hut: 574–575
Reno Hilton Steakhouse: 600–601
Reno Hilton: 609–610
Reno Live: 612
Reno Livestock Events Center: 611
Resort at Squaw Creek: 587
Ristorante Montagna: 541
Riva Grill: 575, 588
River Grill: 546
River Ranch Lodge: 546–547, 587
Rockwater Bar and Grill: 563–564
Rocky's: 612
Rojo's Tavern: 588–589
Rojo's: 575

Rookies Sports Bar and Grill: 558
Rosie's Café: 547–548
Rotisserie Restaurant and Buffet at
  John Ascuaga's Nugget: 601
Roxy: 601

S

Sage Room: 564
Sam's Place: 564
Samurai Japanese Restaurant: 575–576
Sardine Lake Resort: 584
Sato Japanese Restaurant: 576
Scusa!: 576
Seafood Grotto: 564
Siam Restaurant: 576
Siena Hotel Spa Casino: 610
Sierra Café: 558
Sierra Vista Lakefront Dining: 548
Sierra Vista: 587
Silvana's Italian Cuisine: 606
Silver Club: 610
Silver Legacy Casino Resort: 610
Silver Peak Restaurant and Brewery: 601
Silver Screen Buffet: 602
Sizzler Steak House: 537
Sizzler: 576
Sorensen's Resort: 579
Soul Sushi and BBQ: 537
Soule Domain: 552–553
Spindleshanks: 553
Sprouts Natural Foods Café: 576–577
Squeeze In: 537–538
Station Grill and Rotisserie: 606
Steakhouse Grill at John Ascuaga's Nugget: 602
Steamer's Beachside Bar and Oven: 553
Sterling's Seafood Steakhouse: 602
Stony Ridge Café: 548
Strange Brew Cyber Lounge: 589
Sundowner: 610
Sunnyside Lodge Restaurant: 549

Sunnyside Lodge: 587
Sunsets on the Lake: 553–554
Summit: 564–565
Swiss Chalet: 577
Swiss Lakewood: 549

T

T's Mesquite Rotisserie: 558
Taberna Mexican Food: 565
Taco Station: 538
Tahoe Biltmore Lodge and Casino: 587
Tahoe House Bakery and Gourmet: 549–550
Tahoe Taps: 587
Tep's Villa Roma: 577
Timber House: 565
Timbercreek: 538
Toucan Charlie's Buffet and Grille: 602
Trader Dick's Restaurant Aquarium: 602–603
Tradewinds Bar: 587
Truckee Trattoria: 538
Tudor Pub and Dory's Oar Restaurant: 589

VW

Viaggio Italian Cuisine: 603
Victorian Buffet: 603
Villa Gigli: 579–580
Virginian Steak House: 603
Water Wheel Restaurant: 606
Water Wheel: 565
West 2nd Street Bar and Night Club: 613
Western Village Steakhouse: 603
White Orchid: 603–604
Wildflower Café: 558
Wolfdale's: 550
Wong's Garden: 538

YZ

Yama Sushi and Robata Grill: 550
Zephyr Cove Restaurant: 565–566
Zephyr Lounge: 613

General Index

A

aerial sports: 287–293
Agatam Beach: 143
airplane rides: 288, 291–292
airports: 616–617; shuttles 617
air travel: 616–617
Alpine County Museum: 36
Alpine Meadow Wedding Chapel: 103
Alpine Meadows Ski Area: 322–324
Alpine Meadows Stables: 234
Alpine skiing: 310–334; *see also specific place*
American Century Celebrity Golf
    Championship: 60
America's Most Beautiful Bike Ride: 58–59
amusement centers: 76–78
Angora Lakes and Lookout: 34
Angora Lakes Trail: 227
Angora Ridge: 258
Angora Road ski trail: 354
Animal Ark: 74–75
animals: 6
Antique Fair: 64
Autumn Food and Wine Festival: 65
Avalanche: 114

B

bait: *see specific site*
Baldwin Beach: 146
Baldwin Estate: 33
balloons, hot-air: 288–289
Bassett's Station: 363
beaches: 138–148; *see also specific beach*
Best in the West Nugget Rib Cook-Off, The: 64
bicycling: *see biking, mountain biking*
Big Bend Lakes: 175
Big Bend ski trail: 351–352
Big Meadows Trail: 209–210
Bijou Community Park: 227, 300, 349
Bijou Golf Course: 269
Bijou Skate Park: 79
biking: 240–261; mountain biking 250–261;
    paved trails 245–249; rentals/shops 242–244;
    tours 244–245; *see also mountain biking,
    specific trails*
Blackwood Canyon: 21; ski trail 353–354
Blue Lakes: 173–174, 260

Boarding for Breast Cancer: 57
boating: 110–138; charters 177–184; marinas
    122–125; public ramps 121–122; regulations
    112; rentals 125–128; safety 112
Boca Reservoir: 163
Boca-Stampede Reservoir: 364
Boomtown Fun Center: 77
Boreal Mountain Playground and Ski Area: 359
Boreal Ski Resort: 317–318
Bowers Mansion/Franktown bike trail: 249
Bowers Mansion Regional Park: 46, 301
Brewery Arts Center: 52–54
Brockway Summit: 256
Brookside Reno Municipal Golf Course: 278–279
Buck's Beach (Speedboat Beach): 142
Bureau of Land Management (BLM): 625
bureaus, visitors': 623–624
Burnside Lake Trail: 212
Burnt Cedar Beach: 144
Burton Creek State Park: 21

C

Cabin Creek Trail ski trail: 353
California Trail Days: 60
Cal-Neva Resort: 24–25
Camp Hyatt: 70
Camp Richardson: 34
Camp Richardson Corral and Pack Station:
    235, 365
Camp Richardson Cross-Country and
    Snowshoe Center: 344–345
camps: day 68–72; summer 68–72
Cannibal Cruise Car Show and Fair: 60
canoeing: 129–130
Caples Lake: 174–175, 260–261
car travel: 621, 622; road conditions 312
Carnelian Bay Lake Access/Patton Landing:
    143–144
Carson and Mills Park Narrow Gauge
    Railroad: 54
Carson City: 52
Carson City Airport: 616
Carson City Garden Tour: 60
Carson City Rendezvous: 59
Carson Hot Springs Resort: 302–303
Carson Pass: 35, 365

Carson River: East Fork 171–172; West Fork 170–171
Carson Valley Golf Course: 283
Carson Valley Museum and Cultural Center: 56
Cascade Creek Falls Trail: 207
Cascade Lake: 29
Cascade Stables: 235
Castle Mansion: 47
Cathedral Lake: 156–157
Cave Rock, Lake Tahoe-Nevada State Park: beach 148; boat ramp 122
Celtic New Year Celebration: 65
Chambers Beach: 141–142
chambers of commerce: 623–624
Championship Course at Incline Village, The: 268
Chapel at Lake Tahoe, A: 103
Chapel of the Bells: 103
Chapel of the Pines: 103–104
Children's Museum of Northern Nevada: 54
children, travel with: 80; see also specific activity, specific site
Chili Cook-Off and Parade, Cinco de Mayo: 58
Chimney Beach: 144–145
Chollar Mine: 47–49
Christmas Eve Torchlight Parade: 66
Christmas on the Comstock: 66
Cinco de Mayo: 58
Circus Circus Hotel Casino: 77
Clair Tappaan Lodge: 340–341
climate: 5
climbing: 69–70, 72–73, 293–296
Cloud 9 Chapel and Suites: 104
Coast Guard: 623
Coldstream Canyon Trail: 253–254
Commemorative Emigrant Trail: 201
Commons Beach: 140
Comstock Firemen's Museum: 49
Comstock Historic Preservation Week: 58
Concours d'Elegance Wooden Boat Show: 63
conditions: road 622; weather 622–623
Connolly Beach: 147
Coon Street Picnic Area: 142–143
Corley Ranch, The: 96
Cottonwood Creek Botanical Trail: 225
Cove East Beach: 147
Coyote Moon Golf Course: 265–266
cross-country skiing: 335–357; resorts 338–347; wilderness trails 351–357; see also specific resort, trail

cruises: 113–120; see also specific vessel

D
D'Andrea Golf Club: 275–276
D. L. Bliss State Park: 27–28, 226
Dark Lake: 169
David Walley's Resort, Hot Springs and Spa: 303–304
Davis Creek County Park: 301
day camps: 68–72
Dayton State Park: 52
Dayton Valley Country Club: 281
Death Ride: 60
Desolation Wilderness: 191–192; lakes 155–158
Diamond Peak Ski Resort: 326–327
diving: 136–138
dogsled rides: 366
Dollar Point: 21; trail 246–247
Donner Lake: 165–166
Donner Lake Marina: 124
Donner Lake Swim: 63
Donner Memorial State Park: 14–15, 140, 225, 299–300, 348, 359, 364–365
Donner Party Hike: 65
Donner Pass, Old Highway 40 Scenic Overlook: 14
Donner Ski Ranch: 315–316
Dragon at Gold Mountain, The: 272–273
Dream-Maker Wedding Chapel: 103
driving: 621, 622; road conditions 312

E
Eagle Falls Trail: 205–207
Eagle Rock: 21
Eagle Valley Golf Courses: 280
Eagle Valley Muzzle Loaders Spring Rendezvous: 58
East Peak Lake: 176
Echo Chalet Marina: 124
Echo Lakes: 170; ski trail 355
Echo Lakes Trail: 210–211
Echo Summit: 362
Echo Summit to Kirkwood Cross-Country Race: 57
Edgewood Tahoe Golf Course: 268–269
Ehrman Mansion, Sugar Pine Point State Park: 22–23, 94
El Dorado Beach: 147; boat ramp 122
Ellis Lake: 255

General Index

Ellis Peak: 220, 255
Ellis Peak Trail: 203
Emerald Bay Beach: 146
Emerald Bay State Park: 28–29, 226
Emigrant Lake Trail: 214
Emigrant Trail Museum and Pioneer
    Monument: 15
Empire Ranch Golf Course: 280–281
environment: information 626; issues: 6–7,
    9–10
Eureka Peak: 221
events: 56–66; *see also specific event*

F
Fallen Leaf Dam Trail: 226–227
Fallen Leaf Lake: 29, 170, 248; marina 124
Fanny Bridge: 20–21
farmers' markets: 59
Father's Day Pow Wow: 60
fauna: 6
Feather River Inn Golf Course: 271
Feather River, Middle Fork: 158–159
Feather River Park Resort: 271
Federal Aviation Administration: 623
Ferguson Point: 300
Ferrari Club of America Hill Climb: 64
films: 18
fish/fishing: 149–189; charter boats 177–184;
    fly-fishing 185–189; guides 177–189; in-
    formation 152, 625; licenses 150; ponds
    73–74; schools 185–189; tackle 151–153;
    waters 73–74, 153–176; *see also specific site*
fitness centers: 304–308; *see also specific place*
Five Lakes Trail: 202
Fleischmann Planetarium: 42
Fleur du Lac (Kaiser Estate): 21
flight-seeing: 287–293
flora: 6
fly-fishing: guides and schools 185–189; *see also
    specific place;* fish/fishing
foreign languages: 625
forests, national: 625
Forest Tree Trail: 227
Fourth of July: 61
Fourth of July Lake: 175
Fourth Ward School: 49
Frazier Falls Trail: 229
Freel Peak: 35
Fuller Lake: 166, 300

G
Galena Creek County Park Campfire Pro-
    grams: 72
Galena Creek Park: 361
Gatekeeper's Cabin and Marion Steinbach In-
    dian Basket Museum: 20
Genoa: 55
Genoa Candy Dance: 65
Genoa Community Church: 107
Genoa Courthouse Museum: 55–56
Genoa Peak: 220, 260
geography: 5
geology: 5, 9–10
Gerle Creek Reservoir: 167–168
Gilmore Lake: 157
Glen Alpine Springs Resort: 29–31
Glen Alpine Trail: 208–209
Glenshire: 256
gliding: 287, 290
Gold Hill Hotel: 52
Gold Lake: 159
Gold Lake Pack Station and Stables: 237–238
Gold Lake Road ski trail: 356–357
golf: 60, 262–283; *see also specific course*
Golf Club at Genoa Lakes, The: 282
golf, miniature: 79
Governor's Mansion: 54
Graeagle Fall Festival: 63
Graeagle Meadows Golf Course: 271
Graeagle Stables: 237
Granite Chief Wilderness: 192
Granite Lake: 157
Granite Lake Trail: 207
Granlibakken Ski Resort: 324–325, 344, 361
Grass Lake ski trail: 355
Great Eldorado BBQ, Brews and Blues Festival: 62
Great Gatsby Festival: 63
Great Italian Festival: 65
Great Reno Balloon Race, The: 64
Great Ski Race: 57
Grouse Lake: 175
Grover Hot Springs State Park: 35–36, 228, 300,
    302, 350
guides: climbing 293–296; cross-country skiing
    337–338; fishing 177–189; hiking 222–223;
    snowmobiling 366–372

H
hang gliding: 292
Harrah's Family Fun Center: 76–77

Harveys Virtual Forest Arcade: 77
Haskell Peak: 221
health, backcountry: 193
Heather Lake: 157
Heavenly Ski Resort: 329–331; gondola
34–35; gondola trails 209
Heenan Lake: 172–173
helicopter rides: 291–292
Heller Estate: 33
High Sierra Stables: 238–239
Highway 50 Wagon Train: 58
hiking: 190–223; guides 222–223; see also spe-
cific mountain, trail, wilderness area
Hilton Bay Aquarange: 278
historical societies: 625–626
Historic Camp Richardson Marina: 123
Historic Longboard Skiing Revival Series: 57
Historic Skiing Revival: 56–57
history: 3–10
Hole in the Ground Trail: 199–201
Holiday Faire Victorian Style: 66
Hometowne Christmas: 66
Homewood High and Dry Marina: 122
Homewood Mountain Resort: 325–326
Hope Valley Cross-Country Ski Center: 346;
ski trail 355–356
horses/horseback riding: 230–239; sleigh rides
365–366; see also specific outfitter
Horsetail Falls Trail: 215–216
Hot August Nights: 63
hot-air ballooning: 288–289
hot springs: 301–304; see also specific site
100-Mile Endurance Race: 65

IJ
Ice House Reservoir: 168
ice skating: 70, 363–364
Idlewild Bike Trail: 249
Idlewild Playland: 77–78
Incline Beach: 144
Incline Village: 361; Lakeshore Drive Bike
Path 248
Independence Lake: 162–163
Indian Creek Reservoir: 171
information: 622–626; fishing 152, 625; road
conditions 312; ski conditions 312; weather
312
Island Lake: 217
Jackson Meadows Reservoir: 161
Jameson Beach: 146–147

Jenkinson Lake: 169
Jet Skis: 125–128
Julia C. Bullette Red Light Museum: 50

K
Kaspian Recreation Area: 141
kayaking: lake 129–130; river 130–136
Kentucky Mine Museum: 37
Kids Camp: 70–71
Kilner Park beach: 141
Kingfish: 114
Kings Beach State Recreation Area: 143; boat
ramp 121
Kingvale lakes: 175
Kirkwood Cross-Country Center: 346–347
Kirkwood Mountain Bike Park: 252
Kirkwood Ski Resort: 73, 252, 236–237,
333–334, 365–366, 346–347
Kirkwood Stables and Lazy K Pack Station:
236–237
Kit Carson Trail "Ghost Walk": 66
Kit Carson Trail—Wild West Tour: 58
Kiva Beach: 146
Kokanee Salmon Festival: 65

L
Lahontan National Fish Hatchery: 75
Lake Davis: 158
Lake Forest Beach: 141; boat ramp 121
LakeFront Wedding Chapel: 104
Lake Margaret Trail: 214–215
Lake of the Sky Trail: 227
Lakeridge Golf Course: 279
Lakeside Marina: 124
Lake Spaulding: 166
Lake Tahoe Airfest: 63
Lake Tahoe Airport: 616
Lake Tahoe Center for Environmental
Research: 10
Lake Tahoe Chautauqua Festival: 60
Lake Tahoe, fishing on: 153–155
Lake Tahoe Golf Course: 269–270, 371
Lake Tahoe Historical Society Museum: 34
Lake Tahoe Marathon Week: 65
Lake Tahoe-Nevada State Park: 25–26
Lake Tahoe Pioneering in Film Festival: 57–58
Lake Tahoe Shakespeare Festival: 60–62
Lake Tahoe Summer Music Festival: 62
Lake Tahoe Visitor Center: 31, 74, 226–227
languages, foreign: 625

Lester Beach, D. L. Bliss State Park: 145–146
Liberty Belle Slot Machine Collection: 42
licenses: fishing 150; marriage 82
limousine services: 620
Little Round Top: 221
Little Truckee River: 161–162
Living History Day: 59, 62
Loch Leven Lakes Trail: 199
Loon Lake: 167
Loon Lake Winter Recreation Area: 349–350
Lover's Leap Trail: 216
Love's Lake Tahoe Wedding Services: 104
Lower Lola Montez Trail: 253
Lunch Creek/Yuba Pass Ski Trail: 357

M
Mackay Mansion: 49, 97
Mackay School of Mines: 42
mackinaw, how to catch: 156–157
marinas: 122–125
Marlette Lake Trail: 212; Flume Trail: 257–258
marriage licenses: 82
marriages: *see weddings*
Marshall Mint Gold Shop and Museum: 49
Martis Creek Lake Recreation Area: 17, 164, 300
Martis Lookout Trail ski trail: 353
Martis Peak: 256
massages: 304–308; *see also specific place*
McKinney-Rubicon Springs Road ski trail: 354
McKinney-Rubicon Trail: 256
media: 626
Meeks Bay Beach: 142
Meeks Bay Marina: 123
Meeks Bay Trail: 203
Meeks Creek ski trail: 354
Meiss Lake Trail: 212–213
Meiss Trail: 259
Memorial Point: 25
Middle Velma Lake: 157–158
Mills Peak Lookout Ride: 261
Milton Reservoirs: 161
Minden-Tahoe Airport: 616–617
miniature golf: 79
Minors' Camp at Northstar: 68
Mohawk Valley Spring Arts and Crafts Fair: 58
Mokelumne Wilderness: 192–194
Moondunes Beach: 143
Moraine Trail: 227
Mormon-Emigrant Trail: 194–196
Mormon Station Historic State Monument: 56

mountain biking: 250–261; parks 250–252; safety 254; trails 253–261; *see also specific trail*
Mountain Buddy's Club: 68
Mountain Course at Incline Village, The: 268
mountain hiking: 219–221; *see also specific mountain, trail, wilderness area*
Mountain Lake Weddings and A Country Chapel: 105
movies: 18
Mr. Toad's Wild Ride: 258–259
M.S. Dixie II: 99, 118–119
Mt. Elwell: 221
Mt. Judah: 219
Mt. Lola: 219
Mt. Rose: 25, 220, 362
Mt. Rose ski resort: 327–329
Mt. Rose Trail: 203–204
Mt. Rose Wilderness: 194
Mt. Tallac: 29, 220
Mt. Tallac Trail: 207–208
museums: *see specific museum;* Sights and Events

N
Natalie Lake: 175
National Automobile Museum: 42–43
National Bowling Stadium: 43
National Championship Air Races: 65
national forests: 190–191, 625
Native Americans: 626
nature centers: 74–75
nature trails: 223–229; *see also specific trail, site*
Nevada Beach: 147–148
Nevada Day Celebration: 66
Nevada Gambling Museum: 50
Nevada Historical Society Museum: 43–44
Nevada Museum of Art: 44
Nevada State Capitol: 55
Nevada State Fair: 63
Nevada State Library and Archives: 54
Nevada State Museum: 54
Nevada State Railroad Museum: 55; Steam Up: 65
newspapers: 626
Nike Lake Tahoe Tennis Camp: 69
North Shore Jazz Festival: 66
North Tahoe Beach Center: 143
North Tahoe Marina: 123
North Tahoe Regional Park: 226, 252, 348, 361, 370
Northgate Golf Club: 277

Northstar Adventure Park: 72
Northstar Stables: 233–234
Northstar-at-Tahoe: 250–251, 266, 318–320, 342, 359–360, 369
Northstar-at-Tahoe Cross-Country, Telemark and Snowshoe Center: 342
Northstar-at-Tahoe Golf Course: 266

OP

Obexer's: 122–123
off-highway vehicles (OHVs): 297–298
Old Brockway Golf Course: 267–268
Old Truckee Jail Museum: 16
Olympic Ice Pavilion: 363
Ophir Creek Trail: 204
Pacific Crest National Scenic Trail: 194, 202
Packer Lake Trail: 356
Page Meadows: 225; ski trail 353
paintball: 296
Paradise: 115
paragliding: 292
parasailing: 292–293
parks: city 624
parks, state: Burton Creek State Park 21; D. L. Bliss State Park 27–28, 145–146, 226; Dayton State Park 52; Donner Memorial State Park 14–15, 140, 225, 299–300, 348, 359, 364–365; Emerald Bay State Park 28–29, 96, 226; Grover Hot Springs State Park 35–36, 228, 300, 302, 350; information 624; Lake Tahoe-Nevada State Park 25–26, 95, 144, 148; Plumas Eureka State Park 36–37, 228–229, 350–351; Sugar Pine Point State Park 23, 94, 142, 225, 348–349; Washoe Lake State Park 46, 229, 301; weddings 94–97; William B. Layton State Park 20
parks, theme: 76–78
Party Boat, The: 99, 117
permits, backcountry: *see specific trail, wilderness area*
permits, Sno-Parks: 361
Peter Grubb Hut/Castle Peak/Donner Summit ski trail: 352
PG&E lands: 625
picnicking: 299–301; *see also specific site*
Piper's Opera House: 50
plants: 6
Pleasant Valley Creek: 173
Plumas Eureka State Park: 36–37, 228–229, 350–351

Plumas Pines Country Club: 270–271
Pole Creek: 255
Pole Creek Trail System ski trail: 353
pollution: 6–7
Ponderosa Golf Course: 266
Ponderosa Mine Tour and Saloon: 49
Ponderosa Ranch: 25, 76
Ponderosa Ranch Chapel: 105
Pope-Baldwin Bike Path: 248–249
Pope Beach: 147
Pope Estate: 33; boathouse 33–34
Portola Railroad Days: 63
Portola Railroad Museum: 37
preservation: 6–10
Prey Meadows/Skunk Harbor Trail: 228
Prosser Creek Reservoir: 163
public boat ramps: 121–122
public cross-country ski areas: 348–351; *see also specific area, park*
public transportation: Lake Tahoe 617–618; Reno 618
Pyramid Lake: 38, 159–160; marina 124

QR

Queen of the Snows Catholic Church: 105
rafting, white-water: 131–136
Rage'n @ the Ranch Mountain Bike Race: 62
rail travel: 617
Rainbow Trail: 227
Ralston Peak: 220
ramps, public: 121–122
Red Hawk Golf Club: 275
Red Lake: 173, 260
Regan Beach: 147
regulations: boating 112; fishing150, 155; hiking 191; horseback riding 230–232; Sno-Parks 361; *see also specific trail, wilderness area*
Reno: 40–41; bike trails 249
Reno Basque Festival: 62
Reno Hilton Fun Quest Center: 78
Reno International Jazz Festival: 58
Reno Rodeo: 59
Reno-Tahoe International Airport: 616
Reno-Tahoe Open: 63–64
rentals: bikes 242–244; boats 125–128; cars 621; Jet Skis 125–128
Resort at Squaw Creek, The: 266–267, 343–343, 363–364
Resort at Squaw Creek Cross-Country Ski Center, The: 342–343

General Index

resorts, ski: Alpine 314–334; cross-country 338–347; *see also specific resort*
rides: airplane 288, 291–292; balloon 288–289; dogsled 366; glider 287, 290; hang glider 292; helicopter 291–292; paraglider 292; parasail 292–293; sleigh: 365–366
River Holiday and Festival of the Trees (Reno): 66
road conditions: 312, 622
Roberts House Park and Museum: 55
rock climbing: 293–296
Roller Kingdom: 79–80
roller skating: 79–80
Rolling on the River Concert Series: 59
rope climbing: 69–70, 72–73, 293–296
Rosewood Lakes Golf Course: 277–278
Round Lake Loop Trail: 218–219
Round Top Lake: 213–214
Round Top Peak: 220–221
Royal Gorge Cross-Country Ski Resort: 338–340
Rubicon Trail: 205

S
safety: backcountry 193; boating 112; horseback riding 230–232; mountain biking 254
Sagehen Creek: 163
Sagehen Summit ski trail: 352
Sailing Ventures: 119
Salmon Lake: 175
salons: 304–308; *see also specific place*
Sand Harbor, Lake Tahoe-Nevada State Park: 26, 95; beach 144; boat ramp 121–122
Sand Mountain: 298
Sand Pond Interpretive Loop Trail: 229
Sand Springs: 298
Sawmill Flat Loop: 251
Sawmill Lake: 176
Saw Mill Pond: 73
schools, cross-country skiing: 337–338
scuba diving: 136–138
Secline Beach: 143
Secret Harbor/ Paradise Beach: 145
services: 622–626
Shaffer's High Sierra Camp: 71
Shealor Lakes Trail: 215
Shoreline-Nevada Beach Trail: 259–260
shuttles: airport 617; ski 618–620
Sierra Boat Company: 123
Sierra Buttes: 221; lookout 218
Sierra Cloud: 114

Sierra Discovery Trail: 223–225
Sierra Hot Springs: 301
Sierra Nevada Children's Museum: 15
Sierra Nevada Golf Ranch: 282–283
Sierra Safari Zoo: 75
Sierra Sage Golf Course: 274–275
Sierra-at-Tahoe: 331–333, 362–363
sights: 11–56; Carnelian Bay 23–24; Crystal Bay 24–27; Feather River Country 36–37; Hope Valley 35–36; Incline Village 24–27; Kings Beach 23–24; Kirkwood 35–36; Lakes Basin 36–37; Lake Tahoe and vicinity 11 37; Markleeville 35–36; Reno/Carson Valley 38–56; South Lake Tahoe 27–35; Squaw Valley 17–19; Stateline 35; Tahoe City 19–23; Tahoe Vista 23–24; Truckee 11–17; West Shore 19–23; Zephyr Cove 35
Silver and Snowflake Festival of Lights: 66
Silver Dollar Car Classic: 62
Silver Lake: 174
Silver Lake Chapel: 107
Silver Oak Golf Course: 280
Skate Trak: 80
skating, ice: 70, 363–364
skating, roller/skateboarding: 79–80
ski areas, public cross-country: 348–351; *see also specific area, park*
Ski Run Marina Village: 123
ski schools: 337–338
skiing: Alpine 310–334; cross-country 335–357; jet 125–128; water- 125–128
ski shuttles: 618–620
sledding: 359–363
sleigh rides: 365–366
Smith Lake: 216–217
Smokey's Trail: 227
Sno-Parks: 351, 360, 361, 373
Snowfest Winter Carnival: 57
snowmobiling: 366–374
snow play areas: 359–363
snowshoeing: 364–365
Snowshoe Thompson Festival: 60
soaring: 287, 290
Soda Springs ski resort: 316–317
South Lake Tahoe Bike Path: 249
South Lake Tahoe Ice Arena and Recreation Complex: 70
South Lake Tahoe's Labor Day Celebration: 64
Sparks Heritage Foundation Museum: 44–45
Sparks Hometowne Farmer's Market: 59

Sparks Marina Park: 45–46, 73–74
spas: 304–308; *see also specific place*
Spooner Lake: 167, 300; cross-country ski area 345
Spooner Lake Trail: 227–228
Sports Exchange, The: 72–73
sports, winter: 309–374
Spring Arts and Crafts Festival (Minden): 58
Spring Awakening Pow Wow: 57
springs, hot: 301–304; *see also specific site*
Squaw Valley Art and Wine Festival: 62
Squaw Valley Stables: 234
Squaw Valley USA: 17–19, 73, 234, 320–322, 360–361
stables: 230–239
St. John's in the Wilderness Episcopal Church: 105–107
St. Patrick's Day Celebration: 57
Stampede Reservoir: 162
Stanford Rock: 255–256
stargazing: 75
Star Lake: 175
Star Safaris: 75
state parks: Burton Creek State Park 21; D. L. Bliss State Park 27–28, 145–146, 226; Dayton State Park 52; Donner Memorial State Park 14–15, 140, 225, 299–300, 348, 359, 364–365; Emerald Bay State Park 28–29, 96, 226; Grover Hot Springs State Park 35–36, 228, 300, 302, 350; information 624; Lake Tahoe-Nevada State Park 25–26, 95, 144, 148; Plumas Eureka State Park 36–37, 228–229, 350–351; Sugar Pine Point State Park 23, 94, 142, 225, 348–349; Washoe Lake State Park 46, 229, 301; weddings 94–97; William B. Layton State Park 20
Stateline Fire Lookout: 24
Stateline Lookout Trail: 226
statistics, lake: 5
Steamboat Villa Hot Springs Spa: 302
"Steam Up" Weekends: 62
Stewart Indian Museum: 55
Strawberry: 260–261
Street Vibrations: 65
Sugar Bowl: 314–315
Sugar Pine Point State Park: 23, 142, 225, 348–349
summer camps: 68–72
Summit Lake Trail: 199
Sunnyside Marina: 122
Sunridge Golf Course: 281–282

T
tackle, fishing: 151–153; *see also specific site*
Tahoe Amusement Park: 77
Tahoe City Farmer's Market: 59
Tahoe City Golf Course: 267
Tahoe City Marina: 122
Tahoe City Parks and Recreation Day Camps: 70
Tahoe Community Church: 107
Tahoe Cross-Country Ski Area: 343–344
Tahoe Donner: 68, 232–233, 318, 341–342, 360
Tahoe Donner Cross-Country: 341–342
Tahoe Donner Equestrian Center: 68, 232–233
Tahoe Donner Golf Course: 265
Tahoe Extreme Soccer Camp: 68–69
Tahoe Extreme Sports Camp: 69
Tahoe Gal: 99, 113–114
Tahoe International Film Festival: 64
Tahoe Keys Marina: 123–124
Tahoe Keys Resort: 34
Tahoe Maritime Museum: 21–22
Tahoe Meadows: 365; ski trail: 354
Tahoe Para-Dice II: 99–100
Tahoe Princess: 115–116
Tahoe Queen: 100, 116
Tahoe Rim Trail: 196–198, 211, 259
Tahoe Star: 116–117
Tahoe State Recreation Area: 140
Tahoe Tessie's Lake Tahoe Monster Museum: 23–24
Tahoe, The: 120
Tahoe Thunder: 117
Tahoe Trout Farm: 73, 176
Tahoe Vista Recreation Area: 143
Tallac Historic Site: 30–34
Tallac Historic Site Living History for Kids: 71
Tallac Historic Site Trail: 227, 349
Tamarack Lakes Trail: 218
taxi services: 621
Taylor Creek: 363; ski trail: 354–355
tennis: 69, 284–285
Territorial Enterprise: 50
Tevis Cup Western States Trail Ride: 62
theme parks: 76–78
Thunderbird Lodge (George Whittell Estate): 26–27, 94–95
Timber Cove Marina: 124
Tin Cup Adventures: 239
Tinkers Knob: 219–220
Topaz Lake: 175–176

Topaz Landing Marina: 124
tours, bike: 244–245
trails: guides 222–223; hiking 190–219; mountain 219–221; nature 223–229; off-highway vehicles (OHVs) 298; snowmobiling 372–374; snowshoeing 364–365; wilderness cross-country skiing 351–357; *see also specific trail, wilderness area*
train travel: 617
transportation: 616–621
travel: air 616–617; car 621; rail 617; shuttle 617
Trout Creek/Fountain Place ski trail: 355
Truckee: 15–16
Truckee Championship Rodeo: 63
Truckee Railroad Days: 64
Truckee River Bike Trail: 249
Truckee River Recreation Trail: 245–246
Truckee River: Lower Section 165; Middle Section 164; Upper Section 166–167
Truckee-Tahoe Airport: 617
Truckee Tahoe Airport AirAffair: 59
tubing: 359–363
Twin Peaks: 220, 255–256, 258

UV
Union Valley Reservoir: 168
Upper Loch Leven: 175
Upper Sardine Lake ski trail: 356
Uptown Downtown Artown: 62
Valhalla Arts and Music Festival: 60
Valhalla Boathouse Theatre: 33
Valhalla Grand Hall: 95–96
Valhalla Renaissance Festival: 59
Verdi Peak Trail: 254–255
Verdi Trails West: 238
Victorian Home Christmas Tour: 66
Victorian Square: 45
Vikingsholm Castle, Emerald Bay State Park: 96
Virginia and Truckee Railroad Company: 50–51
Virginia City: 46–47
Virginia City International Camel Races: 65
Virginia City Radio Museum: 51
Virginia Lake bike trail: 249
visitors' bureaus: 623–624

WXYZ
walls, climbing: 72–73, 293–296
Walton's Grizzly Lodge: 71–72

Ward Canyon: 255–256
Washoe Golf Course: 278
Washoe Lake State Park: 229, 301, 46
watercraft, personal: 125–128
water-skiing: 125–128
water sports: 110–148
Watson Cabin Museum: 19
Watson Lake Loop: 250–251
Way It Was Museum, The: 51–52
Way It Was Rodeo, The: 62
weather: conditions 622–623; reports: 312
weddings: 81–107; information 106; prices 83; services 83; sites 84–107; *see also specific site*
wedding sites: chapels 103–105; churches 105–107; country clubs 97–99; golf courses 97–99; historic sites 94–97; hotels/motels 84–87; resorts/inns/retreats 88–93; restaurants 101–102; state parks 94–97; vessels 99–100; *see also specific site*
West End Beach: 138–140
Western SkiSport Museum: 11–14
Western States 100-Mile Endurance Run: 59
West Shore Bike Path: 247–248
Wheeler Loop ski trail: 352
Whitehawk Ranch Golf Course: 273–274
white-water rafting: 131–136
Wilbur D. May Center, The: 44
Wildcreek Golf Course: 276–277
wilderness areas: 191–194; cross-country skiing trails 351–357; *see also specific area, trail*
Wild Island: 78
wildlife: 6; information 625
William B. Layton State Park: 20
William Kent Campground beach: 141
Windsong: 117
Winnemucca Lake Loop: 356
winter sports: 309–374
Wolf Run Golf Club: 279
Woodcamp Creek Interpretive Trail: 229
Woods Lake: 300–301
Woods Lake to Round Top Loop Trail: 213–214
Woodwind I: 117–118
Woodwind II: 120
Woodwind Sailing Cruises: 100
World Championship Outhouse Races: 66
Wrights Lake: 169
Wrights Lake to Island Lake Trail: 217
Wrights Lake to Smith Lake Trail: 216–217
Yuba Pass: 363
Yuba Pass Sno-Park: 351

Yuba River, North Fork: 160–161
Zephyr Cove: 35
Zephyr Cove Beach: 148

Zephyr Cove Marina: 124
Zephyr Cove Resort Stables: 236
zoos: 74–75

General Index

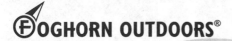

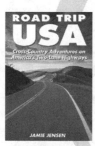

U.S. ~ Metric Conversion

1 inch	= 2.54 centimeters (cm)
1 foot	= .304 meters (m)
1 yard	= 0.914 meters
1 mile	= 1.6093 kilometers (km)
1 km	= .6214 miles
1 fathom	= 1.8288 m
1 chain	= 20.1168 m
1 furlong	= 201.168 m
1 acre	= .4047 hectares
1 sq km	= 100 hectares
1 sq mile	= 2.59 square km
1 ounce	= 28.35 grams
1 pound	= .4536 kilograms
1 short ton	= .90718 metric ton
1 short ton	= 2000 pounds
1 long ton	= 1.016 metric tons
1 long ton	= 2240 pounds
1 metric ton	= 1000 kilograms
1 quart	= .94635 liters
1 US gallon	= 3.7854 liters
1 Imperial gallon	= 4.5459 liters
1 nautical mile	= 1.852 km

To compute celsius temperatures, subtract 32 from Fahrenheit and divide by 1.8. To go the other way, multiply celsius by 1.8 and add 32.

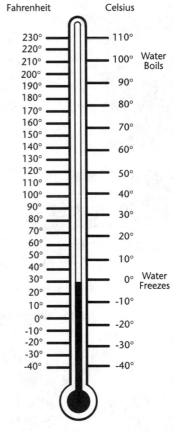

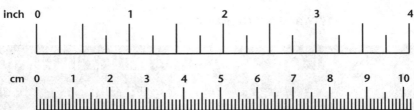